Handy Road Atlas

A-Z GREAT BRITAIN

KU-168-964

CONTENTS

Reference and Tourist Information...................... 2-3

Road Maps at approx. 5 miles to 1" (1:307,865).... 4-169

Outer Hebrides at 9.72 miles to 1" (1:615,730)..... 170-171

Northern Isles at 9.72 miles to 1" (1:615,730)..... 172-173

Index to Towns, Villages & Hamlets..............180-256

Route Planning Maps.......................... 176-179

Channel Tunnel Map....................... 174

Mileage Chart....................... 175

Geographers' A-Z Map Company Ltd.

Fairfield Road, Borough Green, Sevenoaks, Kent TN15 8PP
Telephone : 01732 781000 (Enquiries & Trade Sales)
01732 783422 (Retail Sales)

Edition 15 2007 Copyright © Geographers' A-Z Map Company Ltd. 2006
No reproduction by any method whatsoever of any part of this publication is
permitted without the prior consent of the copyright owners.

An AtoZ publication

English	Français	Deutsch
MOTORWAY — M1	Autoroute — M1	Autobahn — M1
MOTORWAY UNDER CONSTRUCTION	Autoroute en construction	Autobahn im Bau
MOTORWAY PROPOSED	Autoroute prévue	Geplante Autobahn
MOTORWAY JUNCTIONS WITH NUMBERS / Unlimited interchange 4 / Limited interchange 5	Echangeur numéroté / Echangeur non limité 4 / Echangeur limité 5	Autobahnanschlußstelle mit Nummer / Unbeschränkter Fahrtrichtungswechsel 4 / Beschränkter Fahrtrichtungswechsel 5
MOTORWAY SERVICE AREA — HESTON (S) / with access from one carriageway only (S)	Aire de services d'autoroute — HESTON (S) / à sens unique (S)	Rastplatz oder Raststätte — HESTON (S) / Einbahn (S)
MAJOR ROAD SERVICE AREAS / with 24 hour Facilities Primary Route — LEEMING (S) / Class A Road — OLDBURY (S)	Aire de services de route prioriataire / Ouverte 24h sur 24 Route à grande circulation — LEEMING (S) / Route de type A — OLDBURY (S)	Raststätte / Durchgehend geöffnet Hauptverkehrsstraße — LEEMING (S) / A-Straße — OLDBURY (S)
PRIMARY ROUTE — A41	Route à grande circulation — A41	Hauptverkehrsstraße — A41
PRIMARY ROUTE JUNCTION WITH NUMBER — 5	Echangeur numéroté — 5	Hauptverkehrsstraßenkreuzung mit Nummer — 5
PRIMARY ROUTE DESTINATION — **DOVER**	Route prioritaire, direction — **DOVER**	Hauptverkehrsstraße Richtung — **DOVER**
DUAL CARRIAGEWAYS (A & B Roads)	Route à deux chaussées séparées (route A & B)	Zweispurige Schnellstraße (A- und B-Straßen)
CLASS A ROAD — A129	Route de type A — A129	A-Straße — A129
CLASS B ROAD — B177	Route de type B — B177	B-Straße — B177
NARROW MAJOR ROAD (Passing Places)	Route prioritaire étroite (possibilité de dépassement)	Schmale Hauptverkehrsstaße (mit Überholmöglichkeit)
MAJOR ROADS UNDER CONSTRUCTION	Route prioritaire en construction	Hauptverkehrsstaße im Bau
MAJOR ROADS PROPOSED	Route prioritaire prévue	Geplante Hauptverkehrsstaße
GRADIENT 1:5(20%) & STEEPER (Ascent in direction of arrow)	Pente égale et supérieure à 20% (dans le sens de la montée)	20% Steigung und steiler (in Pfeilrichtung)
TOLL	Péage	Gebührenpflichtig
MILEAGE BETWEEN MARKERS — 8	Distance en milles entre les flèches — 8	Strecke zwischen Markierungen in Meilen — 8
RAILWAY AND STATION	Voie ferrée et gare	Eisenbahnlinie und Bahnhof
LEVEL CROSSING AND TUNNEL	Passage à niveau et tunnel	Bahnübergang und Tunnel
RIVER OR CANAL	Rivière ou canal	Fluß oder Kanal
COUNTY OR UNITARY AUTHORITY BOUNDARY	Limite des comté ou de division administrative	Grafschafts- oder Verwaltungsbezirksgrenze
NATIONAL BOUNDARY	Frontière nationale	Landesgrenze
BUILT-UP AREA	Agglomération	Geschlossene Ortschaft
VILLAGE OR HAMLET	Village ou hameau	Dorf oder Weiler
WOODED AREA	Zone boisée	Waldgebiet
SPOT HEIGHT IN FEET — · 813	Altitude (en pieds) — · 813	Höhe in Fuß — · 813
HEIGHT ABOVE SEA LEVEL / 400' - 1,000' 122m - 305m / 1,000' - 1,400' 305m - 427m / 1,400' - 2,000' 427m - 610m / 2,000' + 610m +	Altitude par rapport au niveau de la mer / 400' - 1,000' 122m - 305m / 1,000' - 1,400' 305m - 427m / 1,400' - 2,000' 427m - 610m / 2,000' + 610m +	Höhe über Meeresspiegel / 400' - 1,000' 122m - 305m / 1,000' - 1,400' 305m - 427m / 1,400' - 2,000' 427m - 610m / 2,000' + 610m +
NATIONAL GRID REFERENCE (Kilometres) — $^{1}00$	Coordonnées géographiques nationales (Kilometres) — $^{1}00$	Nationale geographische Koordinaten (Kilometer) — $^{1}00$
PAGE CONTINUATION — 48	Suite à la page indiquée — 48	Seitenfortsetzung — 48

0 1 2 3 4 5   10   15   20 Miles

0 1 2 3 4 5   10   15   20   25   30 Kilometres

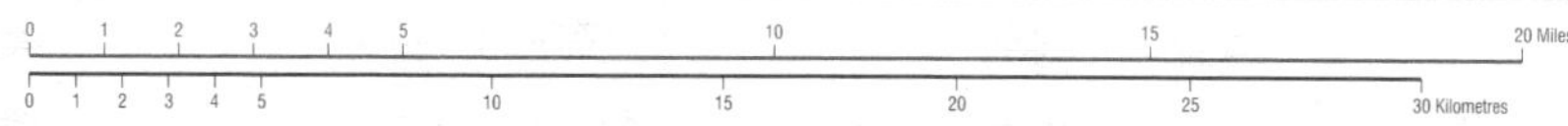

Tourist Information		Information		Touristeninformationen	
AIRPORT	✈	Aéroport	✈	Flughafen	✈
AIRFIELD	✛	Terrain d' aviation	✛	Flugplatz	✛
HELIPORT	✈	Héliport	✈	Hubschrauberlandeplatz	✈
BATTLE SITE AND DATE	⚔ 1066	Champ de bataille avec date	⚔ 1066	Schlachtfeld mit Datum	⚔ 1066
CASTLE (Open to Public)	🏰	Château (ouvert au public)	🏰	Schloss / Burg (für die Öffentlichkeit zugänglich)	🏰
CASTLE WITH GARDEN (Open to Public)	⛫	Château et parc (ouvert au public)	⛫	Schloß mit Garten (für die Öffentlichkeit zugänglich)	⛫
CATHEDRAL, ABBEY, CHURCH, FRIARY, PRIORY	✠	Cathédrale, abbaye, église, monastère, prieuré	✠	Kathedrale, Abtei, Kirche, Mönchskloster, Kloster	✠
COUNTRY PARK	⚘	Parc régional	⚘	Landschaftspark	⚘
FERRY (Vehicular, sea)	⛴	Bac (véhicules, mer)	⛴	Fähre (Autos, meer)	⛴
(Vehicular, river)	⛴	(véhicules, rivière)	⛴	(Autos, fluß)	⛴
(Foot only)	⛴	(Piétons)	⛴	(nur für Personen)	⛴
GARDEN (Open to Public)	✿	Jardin ouvert au public	✿	Garten (für die Öffentlichkeit zugänglich)	✿
GOLF COURSE (9 Hole)	⛳	Terrain de golf (9 trous)	⛳	Golfplatz (9 Löcher)	⛳
(18 Hole)	⛳	(18 trous)	⛳	(18 Löcher)	⛳
HISTORIC BUILDING (Open to Public)	🏛	Monument historique (ouvert au public)	🏛	Historisches Gebäude (für die Öffentlichkeit zugänglich)	🏛
HISTORIC BUILDING WITH GARDEN (Open to Public)	🏛	Monument historique avec jardin (ouvert au public)	🏛	Historisches Gebäude mit Garten (für die Öffentlichkeit zugänglich)	🏛
HORSE RACECOURSE	🐎	Hippodrome	🐎	Pferderennbahn	🐎
INFORMATION CENTRE	🛈	Syndicat d'initiative	🛈	Information	🛈
LIGHTHOUSE	⛯	Phare	⛯	Leuchtturm	⛯
MOTOR RACING CIRCUIT	🏁	Circuit automobile	🏁	Automobilrennbahn	🏁
MUSEUM, ART GALLERY	🖼	Musée	🖼	Museum, Galerie	🖼
NATIONAL PARK OR FOREST PARK	▨	Parc national ou forêt domaniale	▨	National- oder Waldpark	▨
NATIONAL TRUST PROPERTY (Open)	NT	National Trust Property (ouvert)	NT	National Trust-Eigentum (geöffnet)	NT
(Restricted Opening)	NT	(heures d'ouverture)	NT	(beschränkte Öffnungszeit)	NT
(National Trust of Scotland)	NTS NTS	(National Trust of Scotland)	NTS NTS	(National Trust of Scotland)	NTS NTS
NATURE RESERVE OR BIRD SANCTUARY	⚘	Réserve naturelle botanique ou ornithologique	⚘	Natur- oder Vogelschutzgebiet	⚘
NATURE TRAIL OR FOREST WALK	♣	Chemin forestier, piste verte	♣	Naturpfad oder Waldweg	♣
PLACE OF INTEREST	Monument •	Site, curiosité	Monument •	Sehenswürdigkeit	Monument •
PICNIC SITE	⛱	Lieu pour pique-nique	⛱	Picknickplatz	⛱
RAILWAY, STEAM OR NARROW GAUGE	🚂	Chemin de fer, à vapeur ou à voie étroite	🚂	Eisenbahn, Dampf- oder Schmalspurbahn	🚂
THEME PARK	🎡	Centre de loisir	🎡	Vergnügungspark	🎡
VIEWPOINT (360 degrees)	☀	Vue panoramique (360 degré)	☀	Aussichtspunkt (360 grade)	☀
(180 degrees)	☀	(180 degré)	☀	(180 grade)	☀
WILDLIFE PARK	♈	Réserve de faune	♈	Wildpark	♈
WINDMILL	🏚	Moulin à vent	🏚	Windmühle	🏚
ZOO OR SAFARI PARK	🐘	Parc ou réserve zoologique	🐘	Zoo oder Safari-Park	🐘

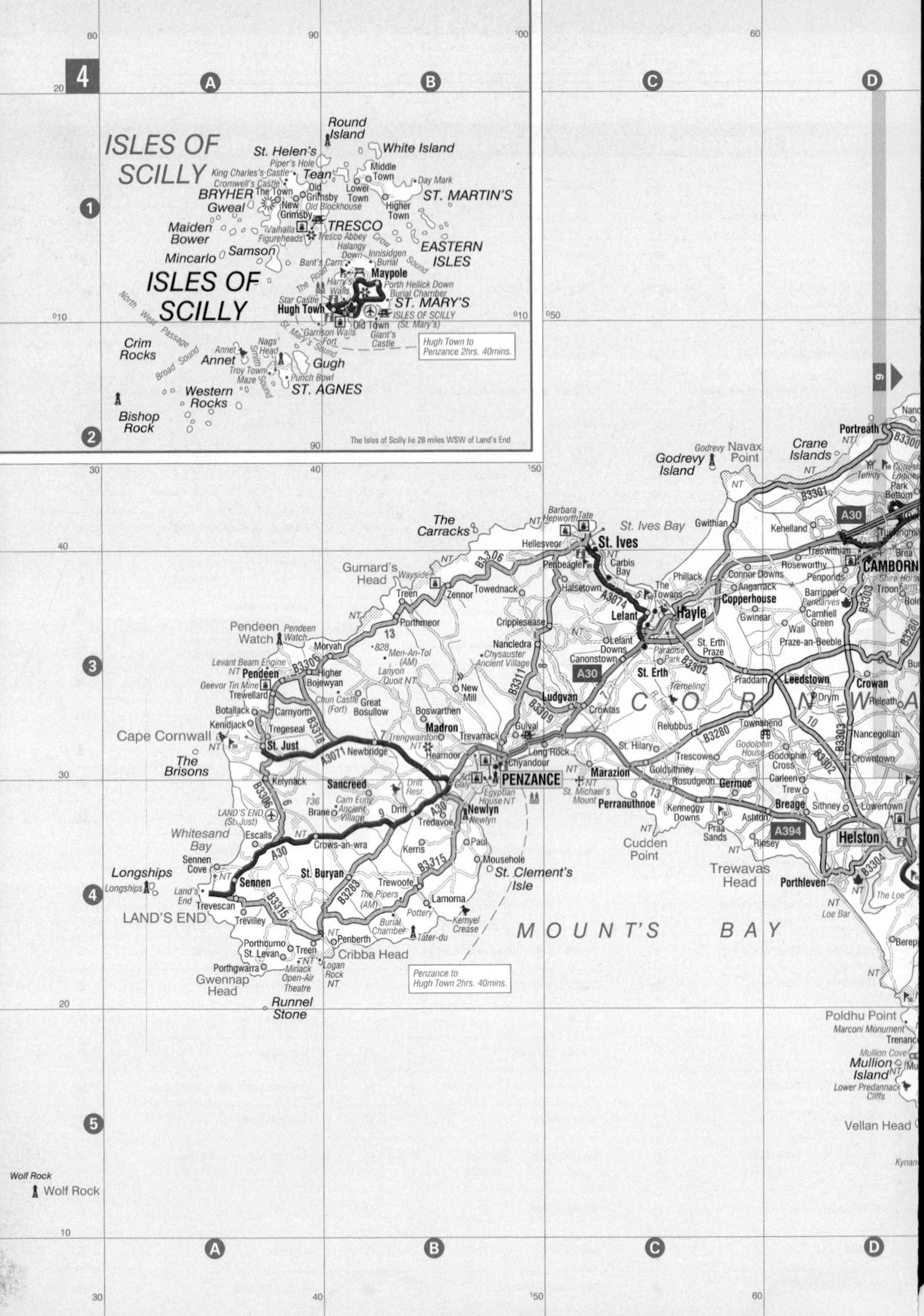
4
ISLES OF SCILLY
Round Island
White Island
St. Helen's
Tean
Middle Town
BRYHER
Gweal
Lower Town
Higher Town
ST. MARTIN'S
Day Mark
Maiden Bower
TRESCO
Tresco Abbey
Samson
Mincarlo
EASTERN ISLES
Maypole
Hugh Town
ST. MARY'S
Old Town
Crim Rocks
Annet
Gugh
ST. AGNES
Western Rocks
Bishop Rock
Hugh Town to Penzance 2hrs. 40mins.
The Isles of Scilly lie 28 miles WSW of Land's End
Godrevy Island
Navax Point
Crane Islands
Portreath
The Carracks
St. Ives Bay
St. Ives
Gwithian
Gurnard's Head
Zennor
Hayle
Copperhouse
CAMBORNE
Pendeen Watch
Pendeen
Lelant
St. Erth
Cape Cornwall
St. Just
The Brisons
Madron
Ludgvan
PENZANCE
Marazion
Newlyn
Sancreed
Whitesand Bay
Sennen
St. Buryan
Mousehole
St. Clement's Isle
LAND'S END
Longships
MOUNT'S BAY
Cribba Head
Gwennap Head
Runnel Stone
Penzance to Hugh Town 2hrs. 40mins.
Perranuthnoe
Cudden Point
Trewavas Head
Porthleven
Helston
Leedstown
Crowan
Breage
Germoe
Poldhu Point
Mullion Island
Vellan Head
Wolf Rock
C O R N W A

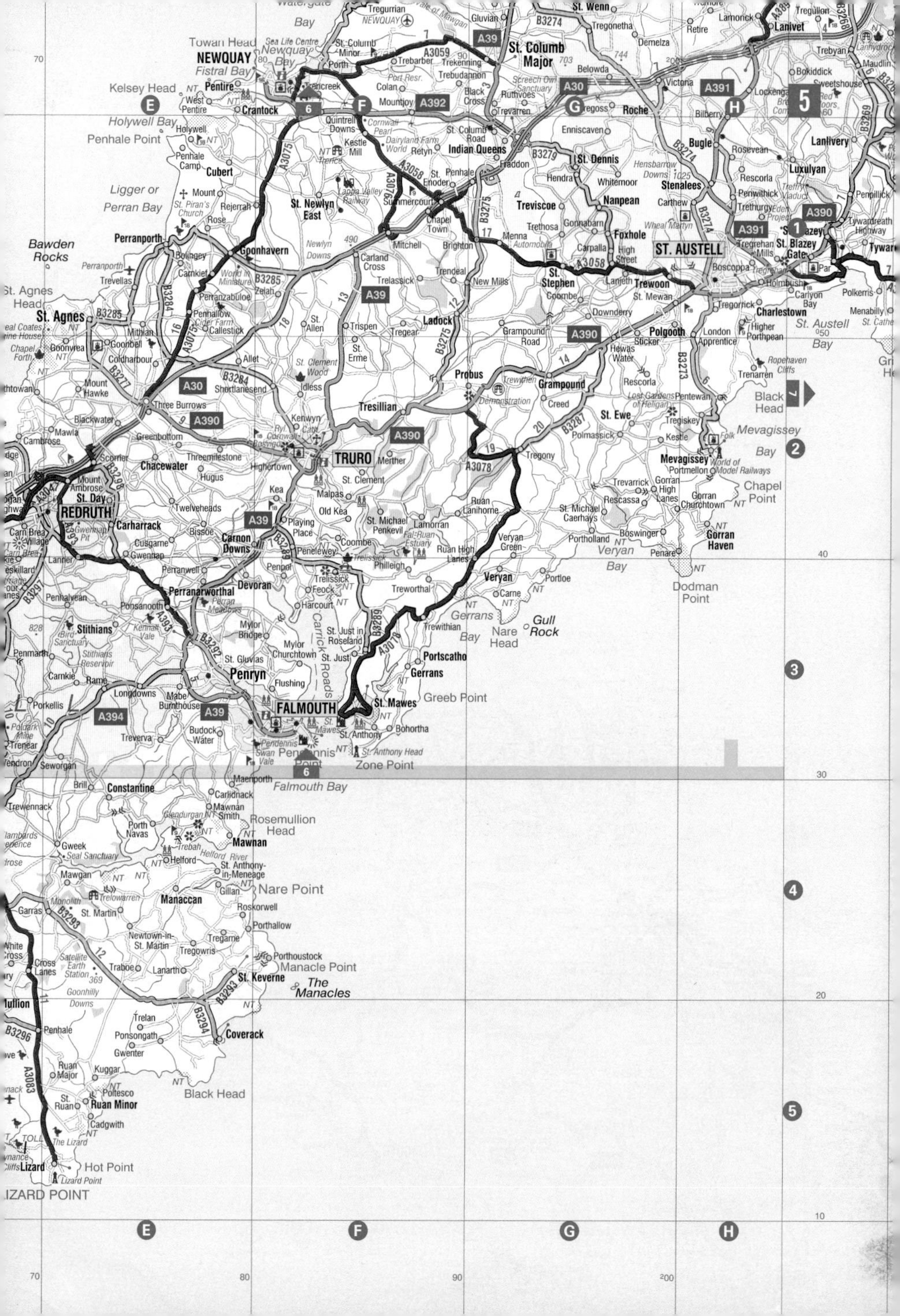
Watergate Bay
Tregurrian
NEWQUAY
Vale of Mawgan
Gluvian
St. Wenn
Tregonetha
Retire
Lamorick
Lanivet
Tregullon
Towan Head
Sea Life Centre
Newquay Bay
St. Columb Minor
A3059
St. Columb Major
A39
Trekenning
Trebarber
Porth
Trebudannon
Demelza
Belowda
Victoria
Lanhydrock
Trebyan
Maudlin
Bokiddick
Sweetshouse
NEWQUAY
Fistral Bay
Kelsey Head
NT
Pentire
West Pentire
Crantock
Trencreek
Colan
Port Resr.
Black Cross
Screech Owl Sanctuary
Ruthvoes
Trevarren
A30
A391
Lockengate
5
Mountjoy
A392
Goss Moor
Roche
Bilberry
Holywell Bay
Penhale Point
Holywell
Quintrell Downs
Cornwall Pearl
Dairyland Farm World
St. Columb Road
Indian Queens
Enniscaven
Bugle
Rosevean
Lanlivery
Penhale Camp
Cubert
Kestle Mill
Trerice
Retyn
Fraddon
B3279
St. Dennis
Hensbarrow Downs
B3274
Luxulyan
Ligger or Perran Bay
Mount
St. Piran's Church
Rejerrah
A3075
St. Newlyn East
Lappa Valley Railway
A3058
A3076
St. Enoder
Summercourt
Penhale
Hendra
Whitemoor
Stenalees
Rescorla
Penwithick
Treffry Viaduct
Penpillick
Rose
Chapel Town
B3275
Treviscoe
Nanpean
Carthew
Trethurgy
Eden Project
A390
Tywardreath Highway
Perranporth
Bawden Rocks
Goonhavern
Newlyn Downs
Mitchell
Brighton
Menna
Automobilia
Trethosa
Gonnabarn
Foxhole
Wheal Martyn
A391
St. Blazey
Bolingey
Carland Cross
Carpalla
High Street
ST. AUSTELL
Tregrehan Mills
St. Blazey Gate
Par
Tywardreath
Trevellas
Carnkief
World in Miniature
B3285
Trelassick
Trendeal
New Mills
St. Stephen
Lanjeth
Trewoon
Boscoppa
Holmbush
Polkerris
St. Agnes Head
Perranzabuloe
Zelah
A39
Coombe
St. Mewan
Carlyon Bay
St. Agnes
Penhallow
Cider Farm
Callestick
St. Allen
Trispen
Ladock
Downderry
Tregorrick
Charlestown
Menabilly
Seal Coates
Goonvrea
Goonbell
Mithian
Tregear
Grampound Road
Polgooth
London Apprentice
Higher Porthpean
St. Austell Bay
Chapel Porth
Coldharbour
St. Erme
A390
Sticker
Hewas Water
B3273
Ropehaven Cliffs
Allet
St. Clement Wood
Probus
Trewithen
Grampound
Rescorla
Trenarren
Mount Hawke
B3277
A30
B3284
Shortlanesend
Idless
Demonstration
Lost Gardens of Heligan
Pentewan
Black Head
Three Burrows
Tresillian
Creed
St. Ewe
Tregiskey
Blackwater
A390
Kenwyn
Mawla
Cambrose
Greenbottom
Threemilestone
Royal Cornwall Museum
A390
B3287
Polmassick
Kestle
Mevagissey
Mevagissey Bay
Scorrier
Chacewater
Hugus
Highertown
TRURO
Merther
Tregony
A3078
World of Model Railways
Portmellon
Mount Ambrose
St. Day
A3047
B3298
St. Clement
Trevarrick
Gorran High Lanes
Chapel Point
REDRUTH
Twelveheads
Kea
Malpas
Ruan Lanihorne
Rescassa
Gorran Churchtown
Carharrack
Bissoe
A39
Old Kea
St. Michael Penkevil
Lamorran
St. Michael Caerhays
Carn Brea Village
Gwennap Pit
Cusgarne
Gwennap
Carnon Downs
Playing Place
B3289
Coombe
Fal-Ruan Estuary
Ruan High Lanes
Veryan Green
Portholland
Boswinger
Gorran Haven
Lanner
Perranwell
Penelewey
Trelissick
Philleigh
Veryan Bay
Penare
Veryan
Portloe
Dodman Point
Perranarworthal
Devoran
Penpol
Feock
Treworthal
Carne
Penhalvean
Ponsanooth
Perran Meadows
Harcourt
Carrick Roads
Gerrans Bay
Gull Rock
Stithians
Kennall Vale
Mylor Bridge
B3289
Trewithian
Nare Head
Bird Sanctuary
Stithians Reservoir
B3292
Mylor Churchtown
St. Just in Roseland
A3078
Penmarth
St. Gluvias
St. Just
Portscatho
Carnkie
Rame
Penryn
Gerrans
Longdowns
Flushing
Greeb Point
Porkellis
A394
Mabe Burnthouse
A39
FALMOUTH
St. Mawes
Treverva
Budock Water
Pendennis
Bohortha
St. Anthony
Trenear
Swan Vale
Pendennis Point
St. Anthony Head
Zone Point
Seworgan
6
Maenporth
Falmouth Bay
Brill
Constantine
Carlidnack
Trewennack
Mawnan Smith
Rosemullion Head
Glendurgan
Porth Navas
Trebah
Mawnan
Gweek
Seal Sanctuary
Helford River
Helford
St. Anthony-in-Meneage
Mawgan
Trelowarren
Nare Point
Gillan
Monolith
Manaccan
Garras
B3293
St. Martin
Roskorwell
Porthallow
Newtown-in-St. Martin
Tregarne
White Cross
Tregowris
Porthoustock
Cross Lanes
Satellite Earth Station
Traboe
Lanarth
Manacle Point
St. Keverne
The Manacles
Goonhilly Downs
B3293
Mullion
Trelan
B3294
B3296
Penhale
Ponsongath
Coverack
Gwenter
A3083
Ruan Major
Kuggar
Black Head
St. Ruan
Poltesco
Ruan Minor
Cadgwith
The Lizard
Lizard
Hot Point
Lizard Point
LIZARD POINT
E
F
G
H
1
2
3
4
5
7
70
80
90
200
40
30
20
10

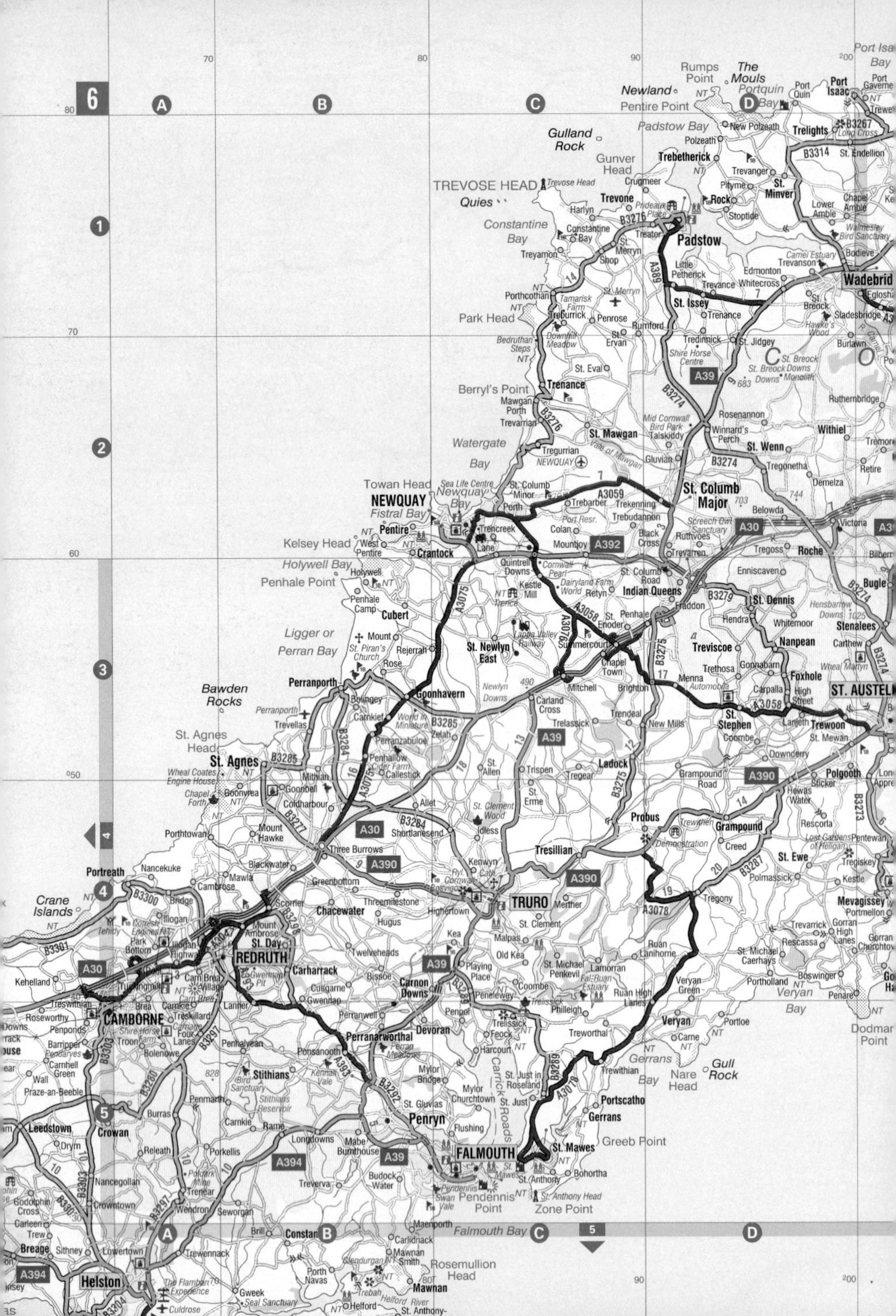

6
70
80
90
200
A
B
C
D
Port Isaac Bay
Rumps Point
The Mouls
Newland
Pentire Point
Portquin Bay
Port Quin
Port Isaac
Port Gaverne
Padstow Bay
New Polzeath
Polzeath
Trelights
Long Cross
B3267
B3314
St. Endellion
Gulland Rock
Gunver Head
Trebetherick
Trevanger
Pityme
Rock
St. Minver
Stoptide
Crugmeer
TREVOSE HEAD
Trevose Head
Quies
Trevone
Harlyn
Prideaux Place
B3276
Constantine Bay
Treator
Padstow
Lower Amble
Chapel Amble
Walmsley Bird Sanctuary
St. Merryn
Shop
Treyarnon
Little Petherick
A389
Edmonton
Camel Estuary
Trevanson
Bodieve
Wadebridge
Egloshayle
Trevance
Whitecross
Porthcothan
Tamarisk Farm
St. Merryn
St. Issey
Trenance
St. Breock
Sladesbridge
Park Head
Treburrick
Penrose
Rumford
Hawke's Wood
Downhill Meadow
St. Ervan
Tredinnick
St. Jidgey
Burlawn
Bedruthan Steps
Shire Horse Centre
St. Breock
St. Breock Downs
Downs Monolith
St. Eval
A39
683
Berryl's Point
Trenance
Mawgan Porth
Ruthernbridge
Trevarrian
B3274
Rosenannon
Mid Cornwall Bird Park
Talskiddy
Winnard's Perch
Withiel
B3276
St. Mawgan
Watergate Bay
Tregurrian
Vale of Mawgan
NEWQUAY
Gluvian
B3274
St. Wenn
Tregonetha
Retire
Demelza
Towan Head
Sea Life Centre
Newquay Bay
St. Columb Minor
A3059
St. Columb Major
NEWQUAY
Fistral Bay
Porth
Trebarber
Trekenning
703
744
Belowda
Pentire
Trencreek
Lane
Port Resr.
Trebudannon
Screech Owl Sanctuary
A30
Victoria
Colan
Black Cross
Ruthvoes
Kelsey Head
West Pentire
Crantock
Mountjoy
A392
Trevarren
Tregoss
Roche
Bilberry
Holywell Bay
Quintrell Downs
Cornwall Pearl
St. Columb Road
Enniscaven
Penhale Point
Holywell
Dairyland Farm World
Kestle Mill
Retyn
Indian Queens
Bugle
Penhale Camp
Trerice
B3279
St. Dennis
Cubert
A3075
A3058
St. Enoder
Penhale
Fraddon
Hensbarrow Downs
1025
Stenalees
Ligger or Perran Bay
Mount
St. Piran's Church
Rejerrah
Lappa Valley Railway
Summercourt
Hendra
Whitemoor
St. Newlyn East
B3275
Treviscoe
Nanpean
Carthew
Rose
Chapel Town
Trethosa
Gonnabarn
Wheal Martyn
Perranporth
Bolingey
Goonhavern
Mitchell
Brighton
Menna
Automobilia
Foxhole
Carpalla
High Street
ST. AUSTELL
Bawden Rocks
Perranporth
Newlyn Downs
490
Carland Cross
Trendeal
A3058
Trevellas
Carnkief
World in Miniature
B3285
Zelah
Trelassick
New Mills
St. Stephen
Lanjeth
Trewoon
St. Mewan
St. Agnes Head
B3284
Perranzabuloe
A39
Coombe
Downderry
St. Agnes
B3285
Penhallow
Cider Farm
Callestick
St. Allen
Trispen
Tregear
Ladock
Grampound Road
A390
Polgooth
Wheal Coates Engine House
Boonvrea
Goonbell
Mithian
St. Erme
Sticker
Chapel Porth
Coldharbour
Allet
St. Clement Wood
Probus
Trewithen
Hewas Water
Grampound
Rescorla
A3075
B3277
B3284
Demonstration
Lost Gardens of Heligan
Pentewan
Porthtowan
Mount Hawke
A30
Shortlanesend
Idless
Three Burrows
Tresillian
Creed
St. Ewe
Portreath
Nancekuke
Blackwater
A390
Kenwyn
Royal Cornwall Museum
A390
B3287
Tregiskey
Crane Islands
Mawla
Cambrose
Greenbottom
Polmassick
Kestle
B3300
Bridge
Scorrier
TRURO
Merther
Tregony
Mevagissey
Portmellon
Illogan
Threemilestone
Chacewater
Highertown
A3078
Tehidy
Cornish Engines
Mount Ambrose
Hugus
St. Clement
Trevarrick
Gorran High Lanes
B3301
Park Bottom
Illogan Highway
St. Day
Malpas
Kea
Twelveheads
Old Kea
Ruan Lanihorne
Rescassa
St. Michael Caerhays
Gorran Churchtown
A30
REDRUTH
Carharrack
A39
Playing Place
St. Michael Penkevil
Lamorran
Kehelland
Pool
Tuckingmill
Carn Brea Village
Gwennap Pit
Cusgarne
Bissoe
Carnon Downs
Fal-Ruan Estuary
Veryan Green
Portholland
Boswinger
Treswithian
Carn Brea
Gwennap
Coombe
Ruan High Lanes
Veryan Bay
Penare
Roseworthy
CAMBORNE
Treskillard
Lanner
Perranwell
Penelewey
Trelissick
Philleigh
Penponds
Shire Horse Farm
Four Lanes
Penpol
Veryan
Portloe
Dodman Point
Barripper
Troon
Devoran
Trelissick
Feock
Carne
Carnhell Green
Bolenowe
Penhalvean
Perranarworthal
Perran Meadows
Harcourt
Treworthal
Gerrans Bay
Gull Rock
Wall
Ponsanooth
Carrick Roads
Trewithian
Nare Head
Praze-an-Beeble
Stithians
828
Bird Sanctuary
Kennall Vale
Mylor Bridge
St. Just in Roseland
A3078
B3289
Penmarth
Stithians Reservoir
Mylor Churchtown
St. Just
Portscatho
Leedstown
Crowan
Burras
St. Gluvias
Penryn
Gerrans
Drym
Carnkie
Rame
Flushing
Greeb Point
Releath
Porkellis
Longdowns
Mabe Burnthouse
A39
FALMOUTH
St. Mawes
A394
Nancegollan
Polgrain Mine
Trenear
Budock Water
Pendennis
St. Anthony
Bohortha
Godolphin Cross
Crowntown
Treverva
Swan Vale
Pendennis Point
St. Anthony Head
Zone Point
Wendron
Seworgan
Carleen
Trew
Brill
Constantine
Maenporth
Falmouth Bay
5
Breage
Sithney
Lowertown
Trewennack
Carlidnack
Mawnan Smith
Rosemullion Head
A394
Helston
The Flambards Experience
Porth Navas
Glendurgan
Mawnan
Gweek
Seal Sanctuary
Trebah
Helford River
B3304
Culdrose
Helford
St. Anthony-

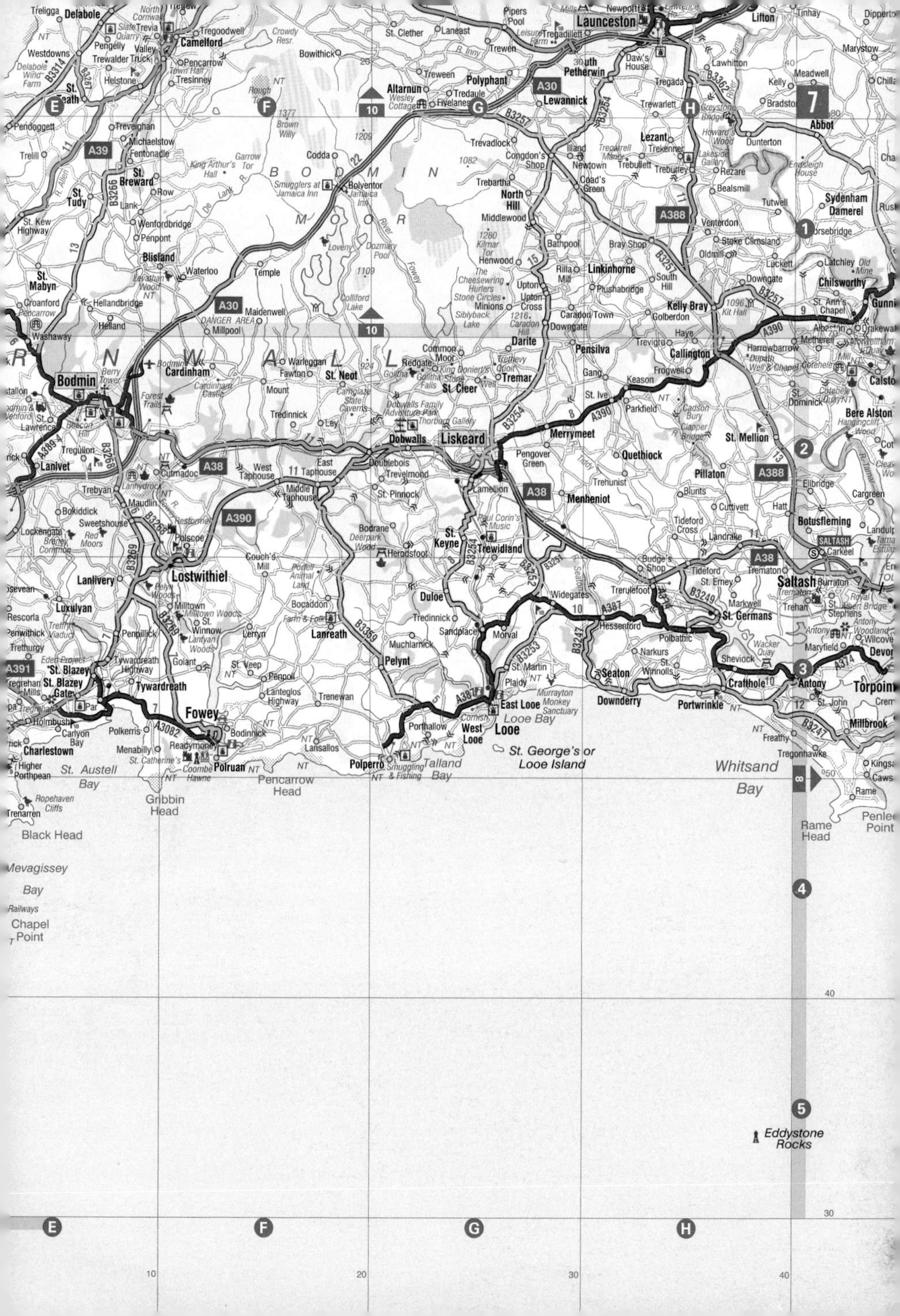

Treligga
Delabole
Slate Quarry
Trevia
Camelford
Tregoodwell
Crowdy Resr.
Pengelly
Westdowns
Trewalder
Delabole Wind Farm
Helstone
Pencarrow
Tresinney
Rough Tor
St. Teath
Pendoggett
Treveighan
Michaelstow
Fentonadle
Trelill
St. Breward
King Arthur's Hall
Garrow Tor
St. Tudy
Row
Lank
Wenfordbridge
Penpont
St. Kew Highway
Blisland
Waterloo
St. Mabyn
Croanford
Pencarrow
Hellandbridge
Helland
Washaway
Bodmin
Berry Tower
Cardinham
Cardinham Castle
Forest Trails
Lanivet
Tregullon
Cutmadoc
Lanhydrock
Trebyan
Maudlin
Bokiddick
Sweetshouse
Lockengate
Red Moors
Restormel
Polscoe
Lostwithiel
Lanlivery
Luxulyan
Treffry Viaduct
Rescorla
Penwithick
Trethurgy
Eden Project
St. Blazey
St. Blazey Gate
Tregrehan Mills
Par
Holmbush
Carlyon Bay
Charlestown
Higher Porthpean
St. Austell Bay
Ropehaven Cliffs
Trenarren
Black Head
Mevagissey Bay
Chapel Point
Penpillick
Milltown
St. Winnow
Lantyan Woods
Golant
Tywardreath Highway
Tywardreath
Polkerris
Menabilly
St. Catherine's
Readymoney
Fowey
Bodinnick
Polruan
Coombe Hawne
Gribbin Head
Pencarrow Head
Lerryn
St. Veep
Penpoll
Lanteglos Highway
Trenewan
Lansallos
Polperro
Talland Bay
Couch's Mill
Boconnoc
Bocaddon
Lanreath
Pelynt
Muchlarnick
Trenewan
Porthallow
West Looe
East Looe
Looe
Looe Bay
St. George's or Looe Island
Plaidy
St. Martin
Murrayton Monkey Sanctuary
Morval
Sandplace
Tredinnick
Duloe
St. Keyne
Trewidland
Herodsfoot
Deerpark Wood
Bodrane
St. Pinnock
Trevelmond
Doublebois
Dobwalls
Middle Taphouse
East Taphouse
West Taphouse
Tredinnick
Ley
Mount
Warleggan
Fawton
St. Neot
Carnglaze Slate Caverns
Redgate
Golitha Falls
Common Moor
St. Cleer
Tremar
Darite
Liskeard
Lamellion
Menheniot
Pengover Green
Merrymeet
Quethiock
Trehunist
Blunts
St. Ive
Parkfield
Keason
Pensilva
Gang
Callington
Frogwell
Kelly Bray
Golberdon
Haye
Trevigro
Caradon Town
Downgate
Minions
Upton Cross
Siblyback Lake
Maidenwell
Millpool
Temple
Colliford Lake
Dozmary Pool
Bolventor
Jamaica Inn
Codda
Altarnun
Tredaule
Fivelanes
Polyphant
Treween
Bowithick
St. Clether
Laneast
Trewen
Pipers Pool
Tregadillett
Launceston
Newport
South Petherwin
Daw's House
Lewannick
Trevadlock
Congdon's Shop
Trebartha
North Hill
Middlewood
Henwood
Bathpool
Rilla Mill
Linkinhorne
Plushabridge
South Hill
Bray Shop
Illand
Newtown
Coad's Green
Trebullett
Treburley
Lezant
Trekenner
Trewarlett
Tregada
Lawhitton
Lifton
Tinhay
Marystow
Kelly
Bradstone
Meadwell
Greystone Bridge
Dunterton
Rezare
Bealsmill
Endsleigh House
Tutwell
Sydenham Damerel
Venterdon
Stoke Climsland
Oldmill
Luckett
Latchley
Chilsworthy
St. Ann's Chapel
Gunnislake
Albaston
Drakewalls
Metherell
Harrowbarrow
Cotehele
Calstock
St. Dominick
Bere Alston
St. Mellion
Pillaton
Cargreen
Ellbridge
Botusfleming
Landulph
Hatt
Cuttivett
Tideford Cross
Landrake
Tideford
St. Erney
Trematon
Saltash
Carkeel
Burraton
Trehan
St. Stephens
Markwell
St. Germans
Budge's Shop
Trerulefoot
Widegates
Hessenford
Polbathic
Sheviock
Wacker Quay
Narkurs
Seaton
Downderry
Portwrinkle
Crafthole
Antony
Torpoint
St. John
Millbrook
Freathy
Tregonhawke
Whitsand Bay
Rame Head
Rame
Penlee Point
Kingsand
Cawsand
Eddystone Rocks
A30
A38
A39
A388
A390
A387
A374
A3082
A391
B3266
B3268
B3269
B3254
B3257
B3252
B3247
B3253
B3249
B3359
B3362
B3251
E
F
G
H
1
2
3
4
5
7
8
10
20
30
40

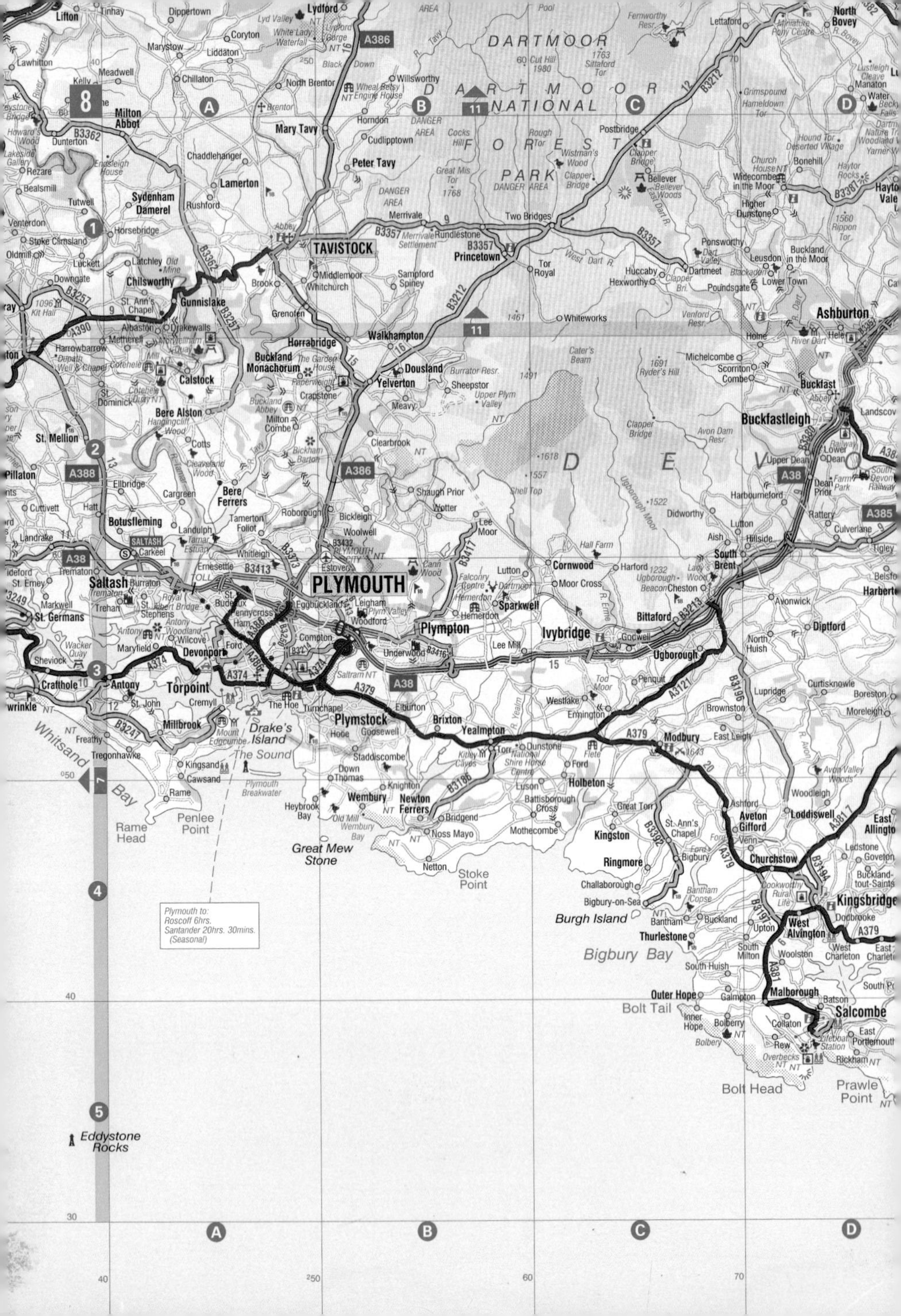

8
A
B
C
D
1
2
3
4
5
7
11
DARTMOOR
DARTMOOR NATIONAL FOREST PARK
DEVON
TAVISTOCK
PLYMOUTH
SALTASH
A386
A388
A38
A374
A379
A3121
A385
A381
A384
B3362
B3257
B3357
B3212
B3213
B3196
B3186
B3392
B3247
B3413
B3373
B3417
B3432
B3249
B3387
B3380
A390
Lifton
Lydford
Dippertown
Coryton
Marystow
Liddaton
Lawhitton
Meadwell
Chillaton
North Brentor
Willsworthy
Milton Abbot
Mary Tavy
Horndon
Dunterton
Cudlipptown
Peter Tavy
Chaddlehanger
Lamerton
Sydenham Damerel
Rushford
Tutwell
Horsebridge
Venterdon
Stoke Climsland
Luckett
Latchley
Chilsworthy
Gunnislake
St. Ann's Chapel
Albaston
Drakewalls
Metherell
Harrowbarrow
Calstock
Brook
Grenofen
Whitchurch
Middlemoor
Sampford Spiney
Merrivale
Rundlestone
Princetown
Two Bridges
Tor Royal
Postbridge
Bellever
Whiteworks
Walkhampton
Horrabridge
Buckland Monachorum
Yelverton
Dousland
Sheepstor
Meavy
Crapstone
Milton Combe
Bere Alston
Bere Ferrers
Clearbrook
Shaugh Prior
Wotter
Lee Moor
Bickleigh
Roborough
Woolwell
Tamerton Foliot
Landulph
Whitleigh
Estover
Ernesettle
St. Budeaux
Pennycross
Ham
Eggbuckland
Leigham
Woodford
Plympton
Compton
Devonport
Ford
Underwood
Saltram NT
Torpoint
Cremyll
Millbrook
The Hoe
Turnchapel
Plymstock
Hooe
Goosewell
Staddiscombe
Drake's Island
The Sound
Kingsand
Cawsand
Rame
Rame Head
Penlee Point
Whitsand Bay
Plymouth Breakwater
Heybrook Bay
Wembury
Down Thomas
Knighton
Newton Ferrers
Noss Mayo
Bridgend
Netton
Stoke Point
Great Mew Stone
Elburton
Brixton
Yealmpton
Dunstone
Torr
Holbeton
Battisborough Cross
Mothecombe
Luson
Lee Mill
Ivybridge
Sparkwell
Hemerdon
Lutton
Cornwood
Moor Cross
Harford
Bittaford
Ugborough
Godwell
Ermington
Westlake
Penquit
Modbury
Flete
Kingston
Great Torr
Ringmore
Challaborough
Bigbury-on-Sea
Bigbury
Burgh Island
Bigbury Bay
Bantham
Buckland
Thurlestone
South Milton
South Huish
Outer Hope
Inner Hope
Galmpton
Bolt Tail
Bolberry
Malborough
Salcombe
Collaton
Batson
Bolt Head
Prawle Point
East Portlemouth
Rickham
West Alvington
Kingsbridge
Dodbrooke
Churchstow
Aveton Gifford
Loddiswell
Woodleigh
Ashford
Venn
Woolston
West Charleton
Ledstone
Goveton
Buckland-tout-Saints
East Allington
Diptford
North Huish
Avonwick
Curtisknowle
Lupridge
Brownston
East Leigh
Moreleigh
Boreston
Harberton
South Brent
Aish
Lutton
Hillside
Didworthy
Harbourneford
Dean Prior
Rattery
Culverlane
Tigley
Buckfastleigh
Buckfast
Ashburton
Holne
Hele
Scorriton
Michelcombe
Combe
Poundsgate
Lower Town
Leusdon
Buckland in the Moor
Ponsworthy
Dartmeet
Huccaby
Hexworthy
Widecombe in the Moor
Higher Dunstone
Bonehill
Manaton
North Bovey
Lettaford
Saltash
Burraton
Trematon
Carkeel
Botusfleming
Hatt
Cargreen
Landrake
St. Erney
Markwell
St. Germans
Trehan
Maryfield
Wilcove
Antony
Sheviock
Crafthole
St. John
Freathy
Tregonhawke
Pillaton
St. Mellion
St. Dominick
Cuttivett
Ellbridge
Plymouth to:
Roscoff 6hrs.
Santander 20hrs. 30mins.
(Seasonal)
Eddystone Rocks
40
250
60
70
050
30

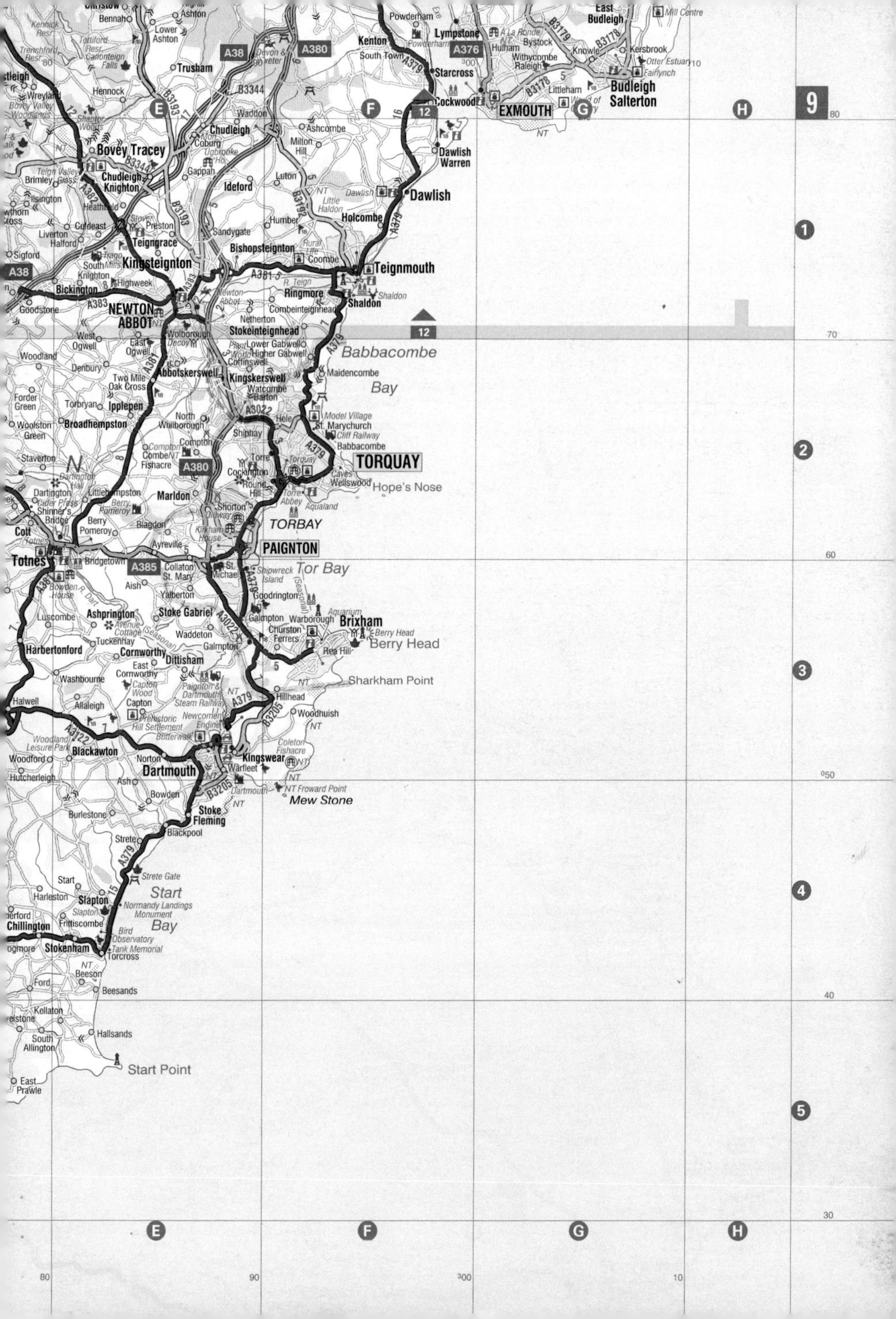
9
Powderham
Lympstone
East Budleigh
Mill Centre
Kenton
South Town
Starcross
Cockwood
EXMOUTH
Littleham
Budleigh Salterton
Knowle
Kersbrook
Otter Estuary
Fairlynch
Withycombe Raleigh
Bystock
A La Ronde
Hulham
Dawlish Warren
Dawlish
Holcombe
Teignmouth
Shaldon
Ringmore
Combeinteignhead
Stokeinteignhead
Netherton
Bishopsteignton
Coombe
Humber
Little Haldon
Luton
Ashcombe
Milton Hill
Ideford
Chudleigh
Chudleigh Knighton
Bovey Tracey
Trusham
Lower Ashton
Ashton
Bennah
Hennock
Wreyland
Waddon
Mon Coburg
Ugbrooke Ho
Gappah
Sandygate
Preston
Teigngrace
Coldeast
Liverton
Halford
Heathfield
Brimley
Sigford
Kingsteignton
South Knighton
Highweek
Bickington
Goodstone
NEWTON ABBOT
Wolborough
Decoy
West Ogwell
East Ogwell
Woodland
Denbury
Two Mile Oak Cross
Forder Green
Torbryan
Ipplepen
Woolston Green
Broadhempston
Abbotskerswell
Kingskerswell
Lower Gabwell
Higher Gabwell
Coffinswell
Watcombe
Barton
North Whilborough
Compton
Combe Fishacre
Babbacombe Bay
Maidencombe
Model Village
St. Marychurch
Cliff Railway
Babbacombe
Hele
Shiphay
Torre
Torquay
TORQUAY
Cockington
Round Hill
Caves
Wellswood
Hope's Nose
Torre Abbey
Aqualand
TORBAY
Shorton
Oldway
Kirkham House
PAIGNTON
Tor Bay
Staverton
Dartington
Dartington Hall
Cider Press
Shinner's Bridge
Littlehempston
Berry Pomeroy
Marldon
Blagdon
Ayreville
Totnes
Cott
Bridgetown
Collaton St. Mary
St. Michaels
Shipwreck Island
Goodrington
Aish
Yalberton
Bowden House
Luscombe
Ashprington
Avenue Cottage
Stoke Gabriel
Waddeton
Tuckenhay
Galmpton
Churston Ferrers
Warborough
Brixham
Aquarium
Berry Head
Rea Hill
Harbertonford
Cornworthy
Dittisham
East Cornworthy
Capton Wood
Capton
Paignton & Dartmouth Steam Railway
Washbourne
Allaleigh
Prehistoric Hill Settlement
Newcomen Engine
Butterwalk
Sharkham Point
Hillhead
Woodhuish
Coleton Fishacre
Kingswear
Warfleet
Halwell
Woodland Leisure Park
Blackawton
Woodford
Norton
Dartmouth
Hutcherleigh
Ash
Bowden
Froward Point
Mew Stone
Burlestone
Stoke Fleming
Blackpool
Strete
Strete Gate
Start Bay
Start
Harleston
Slapton
Normandy Landings Monument
Frittiscombe
Bird Observatory
Tank Memorial
Chillington
Stokenham
Torcross
Beeson
Beesands
Ford
Kellaton
Hallsands
South Allington
Start Point
East Prawle
A38
A380
A376
A379
A381
A382
A383
A385
A3022
A3122
B3193
B3344
B3192
B3179
B3178
B3205
12
E
F
G
H
1
2
3
4
5
80
70
60
50
40
30
90
300
10

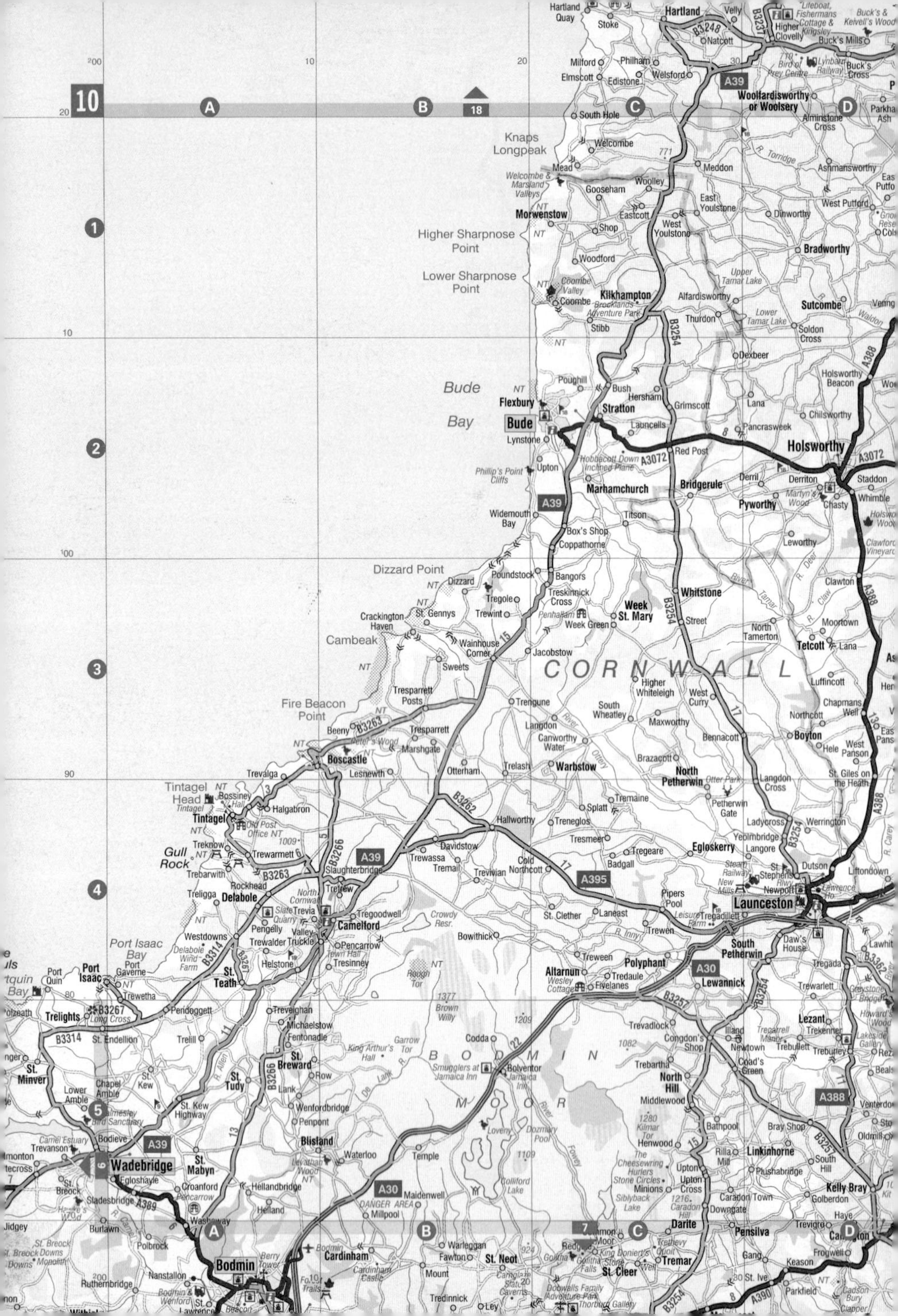
10
A
B
18
C
D
1
2
3
4
5
Hartland Quay
Stoke
Hartland
Velly
B3248
Natcott
B3237
Higher Clovelly
Lifeboat, Fishermans Cottage & Kingsley
Buck's & Keivell's Wood
Buck's Mills
Bird of Prey Centre
Lynbarn Railway
Buck's Cross
Milford
Elmscott
Philham
Edistone
Welsford
A39
Woolfardisworthy or Woolsery
Almstone Cross
Parkham Ash
South Hole
Knaps Longpeak
Welcombe
Mead
Welcombe & Marsland Valleys
R. Torridge
Meddon
Ashmansworthy
Gooseham
Woolley
East Youlstone
West Putford
Morwenstow
Eastcott
West Youlstone
Dinworthy
Higher Sharpnose Point
Shop
Bradworthy
Woodford
Lower Sharpnose Point
Upper Tamar Lake
Coombe Valley
Coombe
Kilkhampton
Brocklands Adventure Park
Alfardisworthy
Sutcombe
Stibb
Thurdon
Lower Tamar Lake
Soldon Cross
B3254
Dexbeer
A388
Bude Bay
Poughill
Bush
Hersham
Holsworthy Beacon
Flexbury
Bude
Stratton
Launcells
Grimscott
Lana
Pancrasweek
Chilsworthy
Lynstone
A3072
Red Post
Holsworthy
Hobbacott Down Inclined Plane
Phillip's Point Cliffs
Upton
Marhamchurch
Bridgerule
Derril
Derriton
Pyworthy
Martyn's Wood
Chasty
Staddon
Whimble
Holsworthy Wood
Widemouth Bay
Titson
Box's Shop
Coppathorne
Leworthy
Clawford Vineyard
Dizzard Point
Dizzard
Poundstock
Bangors
Clawton
Tregole
Treskinnick Cross
Whitstone
Crackington Haven
St. Gennys
Trewint
Penhallam
Week St. Mary
Week Green
Street
Moortown
Cambeak
Wainhouse Corner
Jacobstow
North Tamerton
Tetcott
Lana
Sweets
CORNWALL
Higher Whiteleigh
Luffincott
Tresparrett Posts
Fire Beacon Point
Trengune
South Wheatley
West Curry
Chapmans Well
Langdon
Maxworthy
Northcott
Beeny
B3263
Tresparrett
Canworthy Water
Bennacott
Boyton
Peter's Wood
Marshgate
Hele
West Panson
Boscastle
Lesnewth
Otterham
Trelash
Warbstow
Brazacott
Trevalga
North Petherwin
Otter Park
St. Giles on the Heath
Langdon Cross
Tintagel Head
Bossiney
Halgabron
Tremaine
Petherwin Gate
B3262
Tintagel
Old Post Office NT
Hallworthy
Splatt
Treneglos
Ladycross
Werrington
Tresmeer
Yeolmbridge
Langore
Treknow
Trewarmett
B3266
A39
Davidstow
Tregeare
Egloskerry
Gull Rock
Trewassa
Tremail
Cold Northcott
Badgall
Dutson
Liftondown
Trebarwith
Slaughterbridge
Trevivian
A395
Steam Railway
St. Stephens
Treligga
Rockhead
Trefrew
North Cornwall
New Mills
Newport
Delabole
Trevia
Pipers Pool
Launceston
Slate Quarry
Tregoodwell
Crowdy Resr.
St. Clether
Laneast
Leisure Farm
Tregadillett
Pengelly
Camelford
Westdowns
Valley Truckle
Bowithick
R. Inny
Trewen
Port Isaac Bay
Trewalder
Pencarrow
Daw's House
Delabole Wind Farm
Helstone
Tresinney
Treween
South Petherwin
Lawhitton
Port Gaverne
St. Teath
Rough Tor
Altarnun
Wesley Cottage
Polyphant
Tredaule
Fivelanes
A30
Lewannick
Tregada
B3362
Port Quin
Port Isaac
Trewetha
B3314
B3267
Trewarlett
Trelights
Long Cross
Pendoggett
Treveighan
1377 Brown Willy
B3257
Trevadlock
Lezant
Trekenner
Michaelstow
Fentonadle
Tregarrell Manor
Trebullett
Treburley
Howard's Wood
B3314
St. Endellion
Trelill
King Arthur's Hall
Garrow Tor
Codda
Congdon's Shop
Illand
Newtown
Lakeside Gallery
St. Minver
St. Breward
BODMIN MOOR
Smugglers at Jamaica Inn
Bolventor
Trebartha
Coad's Green
Chapel Amble
St. Kew
Row
St. Tudy
B3266
Lank
North Hill
Lower Amble
Walmsley Bird Sanctuary
St. Kew Highway
Wenfordbridge
De Lank
Middlewood
Penpont
A388
Camel Estuary
Bodieve
Blisland
Dozmary Pool
1280 Kilmar Tor
Bathpool
Bray Shop
Trevanson
A39
Wadebridge
St. Mabyn
Waterloo
Temple
Henwood
Linkinhorne
South Hill
Oldmill
Egloshayle
Croanford
Hellandbridge
Colliford Lake
The Cheesewring Hurlers Stone Circles
Minions
Rilla Mill
Upton
Upton Cross
Plushabridge
St. Breock
Slade's Bridge
Pencarrow
A389
Helland
A30
Maidenwell
DANGER AREA
Millpool
Siblyback Lake
Caradon Town
Kelly Bray
Golberdon
Hawke's Wood
Burlawn
Washaway
Downgate
Haye
Polbrock
Warleggan
Darite
Pensilva
Trevigro
Callington
St. Breock Downs Monolith
Bodmin
Berry Tower
Cardinham
Fawton
St. Neot
King Doniert's Stone
Golitha Falls
St. Cleer
Trethevy Quoit
Tremar
Gang
Frogwell
Keason
Ruthernbridge
Cardinham Castle
Mount
Carnglaze Slate Caverns
Dobwalls Family Adventure Park
Thorburn Gallery
St. Ive
Parkfield
A390
Cadson Bury
Clapper
Nanstallon
Bodmin & Wenford Railway
Lawrence
Tredinnick
Ley
B3254

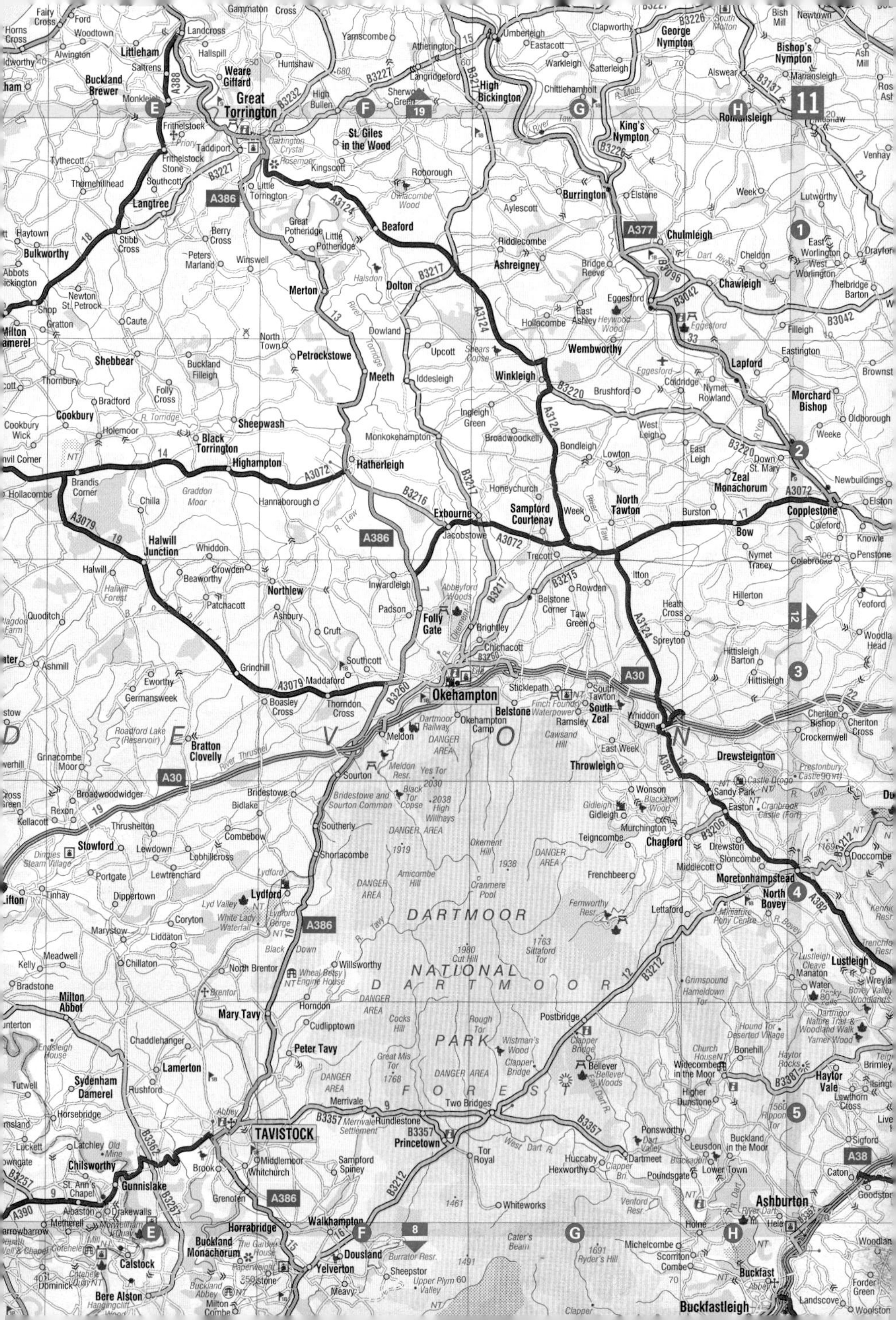

11
Great Torrington
Littleham
Weare Giffard
Buckland Brewer
Landcross
Alwington
Woodtown
Monkleigh
Frithelstock
Frithelstock Stone
Taddiport
Dartington Crystal
Rosemoor
St. Giles in the Wood
Kingscott
Roborough
High Bickington
Atherington
Umberleigh
Eastacott
Warkleigh
Satterleigh
Chittlehamholt
Clapworthy
George Nympton
South Molton
King's Nympton
Bish Mill
Newtown
Bishop's Nympton
Alswear
Mariansleigh
Romansleigh
Meshaw
Burrington
Elstone
Chulmleigh
Cheldon
East Worlington
West Worlington
Thelbridge Barton
Chawleigh
Eggesford
Heywood Wood
Wembworthy
Lapford
Nymet Rowland
Coldridge
Morchard Bishop
Down St. Mary
Zeal Monachorum
Copplestone
Bow
North Tawton
Sampford Courtenay
Winkleigh
Bondleigh
Brushford
Ashreigney
Riddlecombe
Aylescott
Beaford
Dolton
Merton
Petrockstowe
Meeth
Iddesleigh
Hatherleigh
Highampton
Black Torrington
Sheepwash
Shebbear
Cookbury
Bradford
Holsworthy
Langtree
Stibb Cross
Bulkworthy
Milton Damerel
Brandis Corner
Halwill Junction
Halwill Forest
Beaworthy
Northlew
Inwardleigh
Exbourne
Jacobstowe
Folly Gate
Okehampton
Sticklepath
Finch Foundry
South Tawton
South Zeal
Belstone
Whiddon Down
Spreyton
Hittisleigh
Cheriton Bishop
Crockernwell
Drewsteignton
Castle Drogo
Sandy Park
Chagford
Gidleigh
Throwleigh
Moretonhampstead
North Bovey
Lustleigh
Manaton
Dartmoor Railway
Meldon
Okehampton Camp
Sourton
Bridestowe
Lydford
Mary Tavy
Peter Tavy
Tavistock
Princetown
Two Bridges
Postbridge
Bellever
Widecombe in the Moor
Haytor Vale
Ashburton
Buckfast
Buckfastleigh
Dartmeet
Poundsgate
Holne
Yelverton
Dousland
Walkhampton
Horrabridge
Buckland Monachorum
Buckland Abbey
Bere Alston
Calstock
Gunnislake
Chilsworthy
Lamerton
Sydenham Damerel
Milton Abbot
Stowford
Lifton
Bratton Clovelly
Roadford Lake (Reservoir)
DARTMOOR
DARTMOOR NATIONAL PARK
FOREST
DEVON
DANGER AREA
Yes Tor 2030
High Willhays 2038
Cranmere Pool
A30
A38
A386
A3072
A3079
A3124
A382
A377
A388
A390
B3212
B3357
B3220
B3227
B3217
B3216
B3260
B3215
B3232
B3042
B3226
B3137
B3206
B3387
B3257
B3362

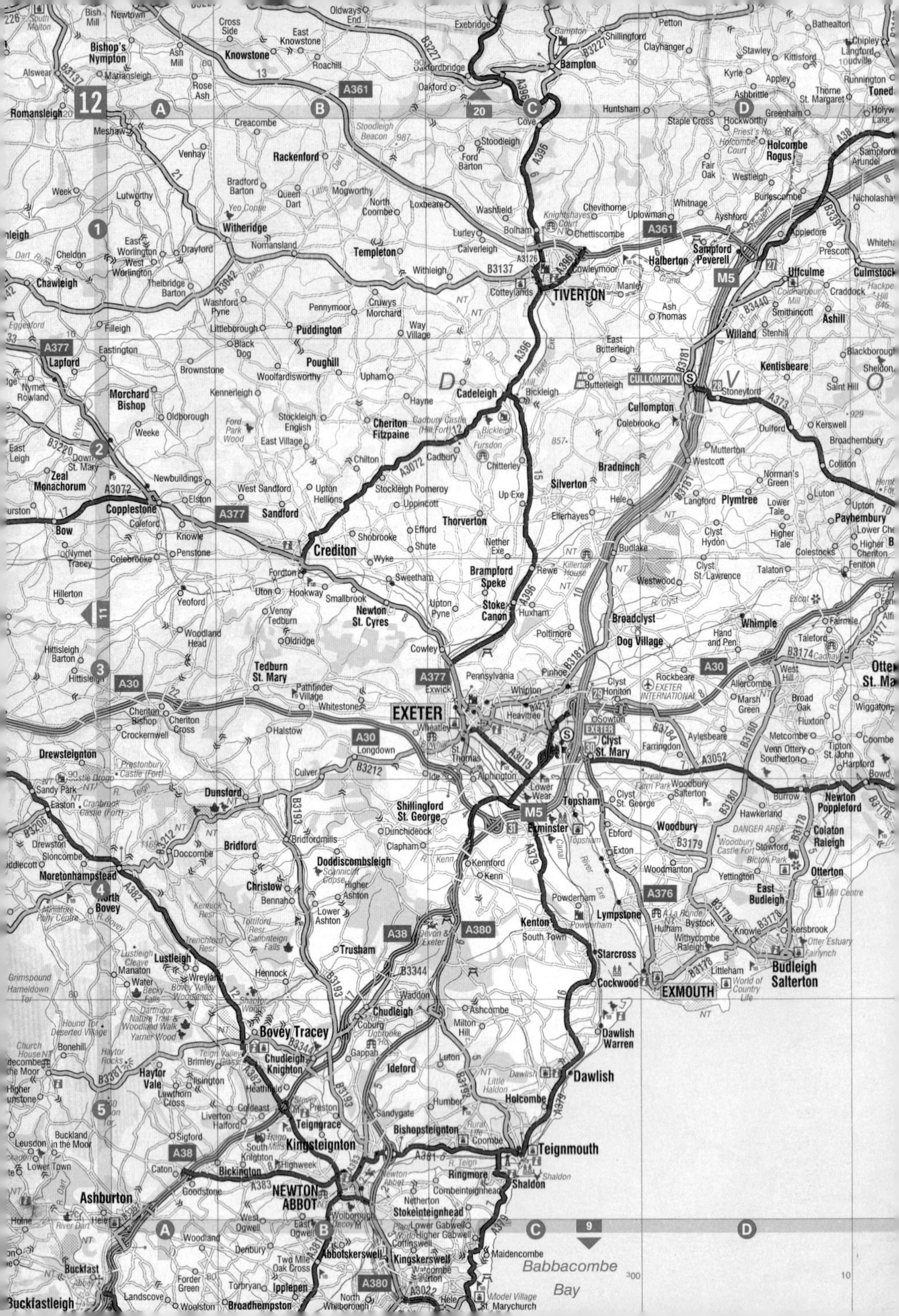12
A
B
C
D
1
2
3
4
5
20
9
Bish Mill
Newtown
Oldways End
Exebridge
Petton
Bathealton
South Molton
Bishop's Nympton
Cross Side
East Knowstone
Bampton
Shillingford
Clayhanger
Stawley
Kittisford
Chipley
Langford Budville
Ash Mill
Knowstone
Roachill
Oakfordbridge
Kyrle
Appley
Runnington
Alswear
Mariansleigh
Rose Ash
Oakford
Ashbrittle
Thorne St. Margaret
Toned
Romansleigh
Huntsham
Greenham
Holywell Lake
Meshaw
Creacombe
Cove
Staple Cross
Hockworthy
Stoodleigh Beacon
Stoodleigh
Priest's Hill
Holcombe Court
Holcombe Rogus
Sampford Arundel
Venhay
Rackenford
Ford Barton
Fair Oak
Westleigh
Bradford Barton
Queen Dart
Mogworthy
Week
Lutworthy
North Coombe
Loxbeare
Washfield
Chevithorne
Whitnage
Burlescombe
Nicholashayne
Yeo Copse
Knightshayes Court
Uplowman
Ayshford
Witheridge
Bolham
Chettiscombe
Appledore
East Worlington
Nomansland
Lurley
Calverleigh
Sampford Peverell
Prescott
Cheldon
Drayford
Templeton
Cowleymoor
Halberton
Whitehall
West Worlington
Withleigh
Chawleigh
Thelbridge Barton
Cotteylands
TIVERTON
Manley
Uffculme
Culmstock
Washford Pyne
Cruwys Morchard
Pennymoor
Coldharbour Mill
Craddock
Hackpen Hill
Eggesford
Filleigh
Littleborough
Puddington
Way Village
Ash Thomas
Smithincott
Ashill
Willand
Stenhill
Lapford
Eastington
Black Dog
Poughill
East Butterleigh
Blackborough
Nymet Rowland
Brownstone
Woolfardisworthy
Upham
CULLOMPTON
Stoneyford
Kentisbeare
Sheldon
Morchard Bishop
Kennerleigh
Cadeleigh
Bickleigh
Butterleigh
Saint Hill
Oldborough
Hayne
Cullompton
Ford Park Wood
Stockleigh English
Cheriton Fitzpaine
Cadbury Castle (Hill Fort)
Colebrook
Dulford
Kerswell
Weeke
East Village
Broadhembury
East Leigh
Down St. Mary
Chilton
Cadbury
Fursdon
Mutterton
Westcott
Norman's Green
Colliton
Zeal Monachorum
Chitterley
Bradninch
Newbuildings
West Sandford
Upton Hellions
Stockleigh Pomeroy
Silverton
Luton
Upton
Copplestone
Elston
Uppincott
Up Exe
Hele
Langford
Plymtree
Lower Tale
Payhembury
Bow
Coleford
Knowle
Sandford
Thorverton
Ellerhayes
Higher Tale
Lower Cheriton
Nymet Tracey
Penstone
Shobrooke
Efford
Clyst Hydon
Higher Cheriton
Colebrooke
Crediton
Shute
Nether Exe
Budlake
Colestocks
Wyke
Killerton House
Clyst St. Lawrence
Talaton
Fenton
Fordton
Sweetham
Brampford Speke
Rewe
Westwood
Hillerton
Yeoford
Uton
Hookway
Smallbrook
Newton St. Cyres
Upton Pyne
Stoke Canon
Huxham
R. Clyst
Escot
Venny Tedburn
Poltimore
Broadclyst
Whimple
Fairmile
Woodland Head
Oldridge
Hand and Pen
Taleford
Hittisleigh Barton
Cowley
Dog Village
Cadhay
Hittisleigh
Tedburn St. Mary
Pennsylvania
Pinhoe
Clyst Honiton
Rockbeare
EXETER INTERNATIONAL
West Hill
Ottery St. Mary
Pathfinder Village
Exwick
Whipton
Allercombe
Cheriton Bishop
Cheriton Cross
Whitestone
EXETER
Heavitree
Sowton
Marsh Green
Broad Oak
Wiggaton
Crockernwell
Halstow
Wheatley
Fluxton
Drewsteignton
Longdown
St. Thomas
Clyst St. Mary
Faringdon
Aylesbeare
Metcombe
Coombe
Prestonbury Castle (Fort)
Culver
Ide
Alphington
Venn Ottery
Southerton
Tipton St. John
Castle Drogo
Sandy Park
Crealy Farm Park
Harpford
Bowd
Easton
Cranbrook Castle (Fort)
Dunsford
Shillingford St. George
Lower Wear
Topsham
Clyst St. George
Woodbury Salterton
Burrow
Newton Poppleford
Drewston
Bridfordmills
Dunchideock
Exminster
Ebford
Woodbury
Hawkerland
Colaton Raleigh
Sloncombe
Bridford
Doccombe
Clapham
Exton
DANGER AREA
Woodbury Castle Fort
Stowford
Moretonhampstead
Doddiscombsleigh
Kennford
Kenn
Woodmanton
Bicton Park
Otterton
Scanniclift Copse
Christow
Higher Ashton
Yettington
East Budleigh
North Bovey
Bennah
Powderham
Lympstone
Mill Centre
Miniature Pony Centre
R. Bovey
Kennick Resr
Tottiford Resr
Canonteign Falls
Lower Ashton
A La Ronde
Bystock
Knowle
Kersbrook
Trenchford Resr
Devon & Exeter
Kenton
South Town
Hulham
Withycombe Raleigh
Otter Estuary
Fairlynch
Lustleigh Cleave
Lustleigh
Trusham
Starcross
Manaton
Wreyland
Hennock
Cockwood
Littleham
Budleigh Salterton
Grimspound
Hameldown Tor
Water
Becky Falls
Bovey Valley Woodlands
Waddon
EXMOUTH
World of Country Life
Shaptor Woods
Chudleigh
Ashcombe
Hound Tor Deserted Village
Dartmoor Nature Trail & Woodland Walk
Yarner Wood
Coburg
Milton Hill
Dawlish Warren
Bovey Tracey
Ugbrooke
Church House Inn
Bonehill
Haytor Rocks
Brimley
Teign Valley Glass
Chudleigh Knighton
Gappah
Luton
Widecombe in the Moor
Little Haldon
Haytor Vale
Ilsington
Ideford
Dawlish
Lewthorn Cross
Heathfield
Higher Dunstone
Liverton
Halford
Goldeast
Stover
Preston
Humber
Holcombe
Sandygate
Teigngrace
Rural Life
Leusdon
Buckland in the Moor
Sigford
South Knighton
Kingsteignton
Bishopsteignton
Coombe
Teignmouth
Lower Town
Caton
Bickington
Highweek
Ringmore
Shaldon
Newton Abbot
Ashburton
Goodstone
NEWTON ABBOT
Combeinteignhead
Netherton
Stokeinteignhead
Holne
Hele
West Ogwell
East Ogwell
Wolborough
River Dart
Lower Gabwell
Higher Gabwell
Coffinswell
Woodland
Denbury
Maidencombe
Abbotskerswell
Kingskerswell
Twd Mile Oak Cross
Babbacombe Bay
Buckfast
Watcombe
Forder Green
Torbryan
Ipplepen
Landscove
North Whilborough
Model Village
Buckfastleigh
Woolston
Broadhempston
St. Marychurch
DEVON
A361
A396
A3126
B3137
B3042
A377
B3220
A3072
A30
B3212
A3015
M5
A379
B3193
A38
A380
B3344
A382
B3387
A383
A381
A3022
B3227
B3181
B3440
A373
B3391
B3174
B3177
B3184
A3052
B3180
B3178
B3179
A376
B3206
NT
300
10

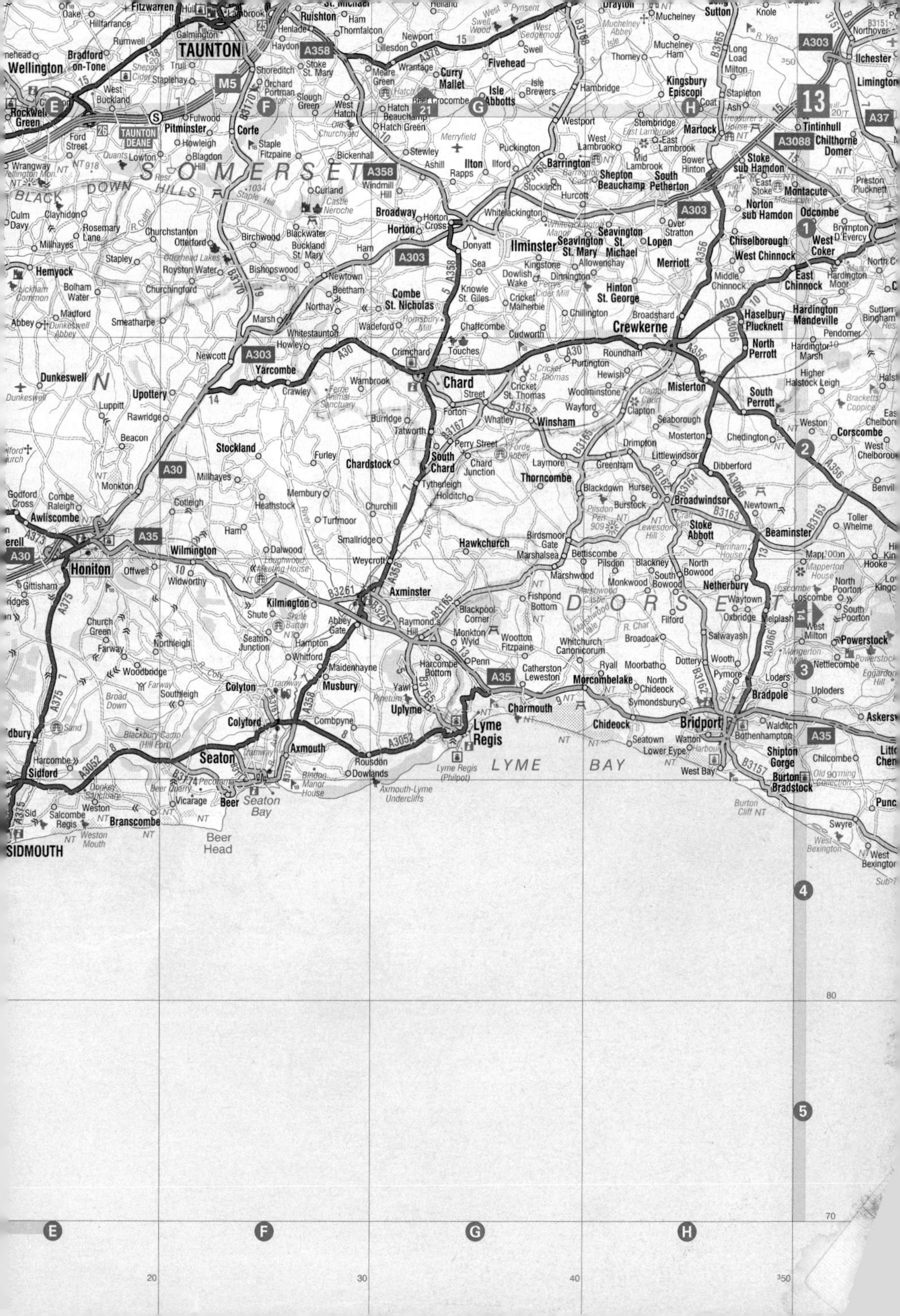

Fitzwarren
Oake
Hillfarrance
Ruishton
Henlade
Ham
Thornfalcon
Drayton
Muchelney
Sutton
Knole
Galmington
TAUNTON
Rumwell
Haydon
A358
Lillesdon
Newport
Swell Wood
West Sedgemoor
Swell
Muchelney Abbey
Thorney
Muchelney Ham
Long Load
Milton
Northover
Ilchester
Wellington
Bradford on-Tone
Trull
Shoreditch
Stoke St. Mary
Meare Green
Wrantage
Curry Mallet
Fivehead
Limington
West Buckland
Staplehay
M5
Orchard Portman
Slough Green
Hatch Court
Beer Crocombe
Isle Abbotts
Isle Brewers
Hambridge
Kingsbury Episcopi
Stapleton
Coat
Ash
13
Rockwell Green
Pitminster
Fulwood
Corfe
West Hatch
Hatch Beauchamp
21
Westport
Stembridge
East Lambrook
Martock
Treasurer's House
Tintinhull
A37
TAUNTON DEANE
Ford Street
Howleigh
Staple Fitzpaine
Old Churchyard
Hatch Green
Merryfield
West Lambrook
Mid Lambrook
East Lambrook
A3088
Chilthorne Domer
Wrangway
Quants
Lowton
Blagdon Hill
Bickenhall
Stewley
Ashill
Puckington
Ilton
Ilford
Barrington
Barrington Court
Shepton Beauchamp
South Petherton
Bower Hinton
Stoke sub Hamdon
Wellington Mon.
NT 918
SOMERSET
A358
Windmill Hill
Rapps
Stocklinch
Hurcott
Priory
East Stoke
Montacute
Preston Plucknett
BLACK DOWN HILLS
1034 Staple Hill
Curland
Castle Neroche
Broadway
Horton Cross
Horton
Whitelackington
Whitelackington Manor
A303
Norton sub Hamdon
Odcombe
Culm Davy
Clayhidon
Rosemary Lane
Churchstanton
Otterford
Birchwood
Blackwater
Buckland St. Mary
Donyatt
Ilminster
Seavington St. Mary
Seavington St. Michael
Lopen
Over Stratton
Chiselborough
West Coker
Brympton D'Evercy
Millhayes
Stapley
Otterhead Lakes
Royston Water
Ham
Bishopswood
A303
A358
Sea
Kingstone
Allowenshay
Merriott
West Chinnock
North Coker
Hemyock
Culmstock Common
Bolham Water
Churchingford
Newtown
Beetham
Combe St. Nicholas
Dowlish Wake
Perry's Cider Mill
Dinnington
Hinton St. George
Middle Chinnock
East Chinnock
Hardington Moor
Madford
Dunkeswell Abbey
Abbey
Smeatharpe
Marsh
Northay
Wadeford
Hornsbury Mill
Knowle St. Giles
Cricket Malherbie
Chillington
Broadshard
Crewkerne
Haselbury Plucknett
Hardington Mandeville
Sutton Bingham
Whitestaunton
Howley
Chaffcombe
Cudworth
Pendomer
Newcott
A303
Yarcombe
A30
Crimchard
Touches
Chard
Purtington
Roundham
North Perrott
Hardington Marsh
Dunkeswell
Upottery
Crawley
Ferne Animal Sanctuary
Wambrook
Cricket St. Thomas
Hewish
Misterton
Higher Halstock Leigh
Luppitt
Rawridge
Street
Forton
Whatley
Winsham
Woolminstone
Wayford
Clapton Court
Clapton
South Perrott
Brackett's Coppice
Beacon
Stockland
Burridge
Tatworth
Perry Street
Forde Abbey
Seaborough
Mosterton
Chedington
Weston
Corscombe
East Chelborough
West Chelborough
Furley
Chardstock
South Chard
Chard Junction
Laymore
Drimpton
Littlewindsor
Dibberford
A30
Monkton
Millhayes
Membury
Tytherleigh
Holditch
Thorncombe
Greenham
Blackdown
Hursey
Broadwindsor
Newtown
Benville
Godford Cross
Combe Raleigh
Awliscombe
Cotleigh
Heathstock
Churchill
Turfmoor
Burstock
Pilsdon Pen 909
Lewesdon Hill
Stoke Abbott
Beaminster
Toller Whelme
Honiton
A35
A373
A30
Wilmington
Ham
Dalwood
Loughwood Meeting House
Smallridge
Weycroft
Hawkchurch
Birdsmoor Gate
Marshalsea
Bettiscombe
Pilsdon
Blackney
North Bowood
South Bowood
Parnham House
Mapperton
Mapperton House
Hooke
Gittisham
Offwell
Widworthy
Kilmington
Axminster
B3261
Marshwood
Monkwood
Netherbury
North Poorton
Loscombe
Shute
Shute Barton
Abbey Gate
Blackpool Corner
Fishpond Bottom
DORSET
Marshwood Castle
Marshwood Vale
Waytown
Oxbridge
Melplash
South Poorton
Church Green
Farway
Northleigh
Seaton Junction
Hampton
Raymond's Hill
Monkton Wyld
Wootton Fitzpaine
Whitchurch Canonicorum
R. Char
Filford
Broadoak
Salwayash
West Milton
Powerstock
Woodbridge
Whitford
Maidenhayne
Harcombe Bottom
Penn
Catherston Leweston
Ryall
Moorbath
Dottery
Wooth
Mangerton Mill
Nettlecombe
Eggardon Hill
Farway
Southleigh
Broad Down
Colyton
Tramway
Musbury
Yawl
Pinetum
Uplyme
A35
Charmouth
Morcombelake
North Chideock
Symondsbury
Pymore
Loders
Bradpole
Uploders
Sand
Colyford
Combpyne
Lyme Regis
Chideock
Bridport
Walditch
Bothenhampton
Askerswell
Blackbury Camp (Hill Fort)
Seaton
Axmouth
A3052
Rousdon
Dowlands
Seatown
Watton
Lower Eype
West Bay
Harbour
Shipton Gorge
A35
Chilcombe
Litton Cheney
Sidford
Harcombe
Donkey Sanctuary
Beer Quarry
Pecorama
Bindon Manor House
Axmouth-Lyme Undercliffs
Lyme Regis (Philpot)
LYME BAY
Old Timing Collection
Burton Bradstock
Weston
Vicarage
Beer
Seaton Bay
Burton Cliff NT
Punc
Sid
Salcombe Regis
Weston Mouth
Branscombe
Swyre
SIDMOUTH
Beer Head
West Bexington
1
2
3
4
5
E
F
G
H
20
30
40
350
70
80

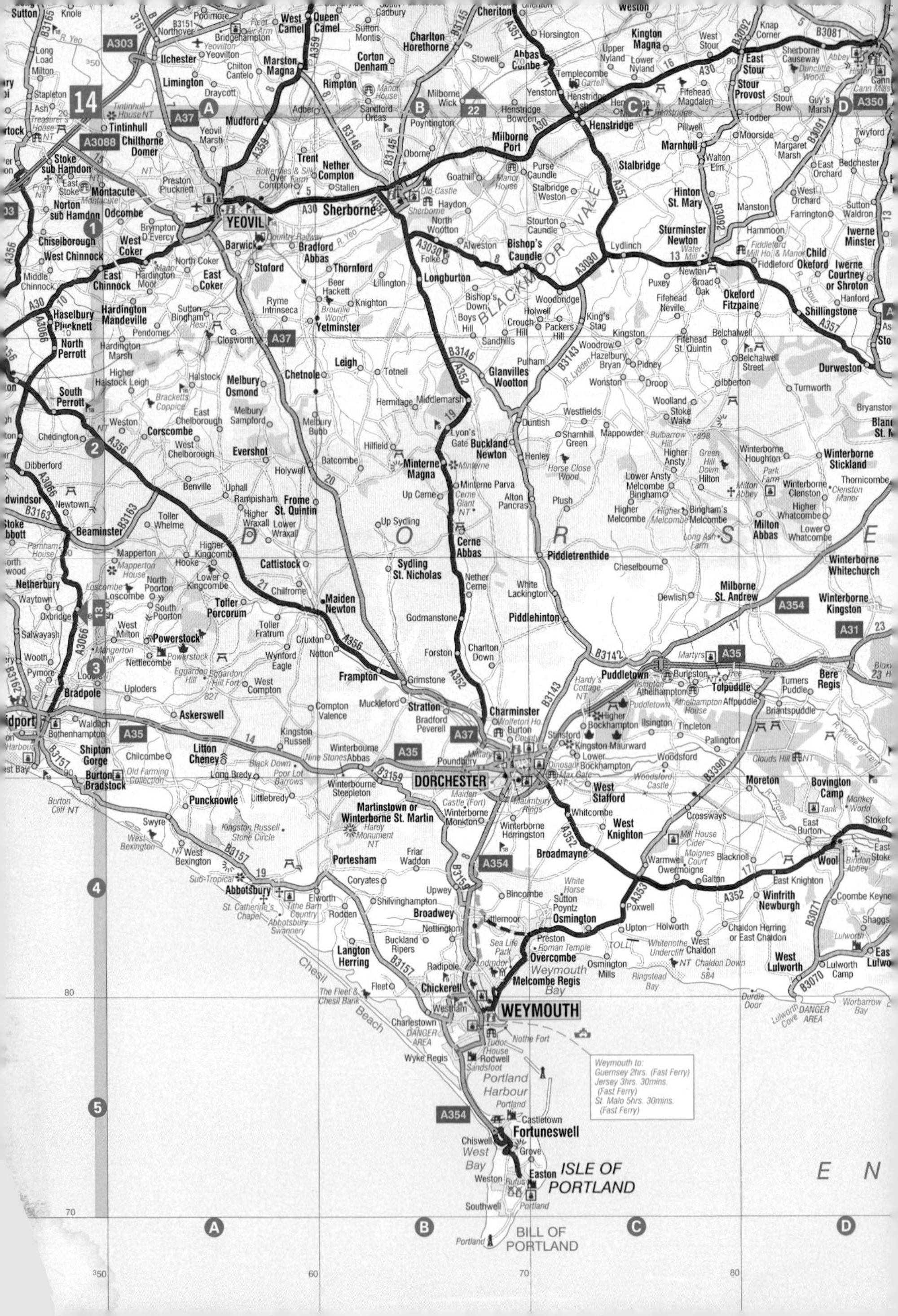
14
Ilchester
Yeovilton
Limington
Marston Magna
Queen Camel
West Camel
Sutton Montis
Charlton Horethorne
Corton Denham
Rimpton
Cheriton
Abbas Combe
Horsington
Templecombe
Kington Magna
Upper Nyland
Lower Nyland
West Stour
East Stour
Stour Provost
Knap Corner
Sherborne Causeway
Henstridge
Henstridge Ash
Henstridge Bowden
Milborne Wick
Milborne Port
Stowell
Yenston
Fifehead Magdalen
Todber
Marnhull
Stalbridge
Hinton St. Mary
Sturminster Newton
Manston
Iwerne Minster
Child Okeford
Iwerne Courtney or Shroton
Shillingstone
Okeford Fitzpaine
Durweston
Tintinhull
Chilthorne Domer
Mudford
Yeovil Marsh
Stoke sub Hamdon
Montacute
Norton sub Hamdon
Odcombe
Preston Plucknett
YEOVIL
Brympton D'Evercy
West Coker
East Coker
Chiselborough
West Chinnock
East Chinnock
Barwick
Stoford
Bradford Abbas
Thornford
Sherborne
Nether Compton
Over Compton
Trent
Poyntington
Oborne
Sandford Orcas
Haydon
North Wootton
Alweston
Folke
Bishop's Caundle
Stourton Caundle
Purse Caundle
Stalbridge Weston
BLACKMOOR VALE
Lydlinch
Longburton
Lillington
Beer Hackett
Knighton
Yetminster
Ryme Intrinseca
Haselbury Plucknett
North Perrott
Hardington Mandeville
Hardington Marsh
Pendomer
Sutton Bingham
Closworth
Halstock
Melbury Osmond
Melbury Sampford
Chetnole
Leigh
Totnell
Hermitage
Middlemarsh
Glanvilles Wootton
Holwell
Crouch Hill
Packers Hill
King's Stag
Woodbridge
Kingston
Hazelbury Bryan
Pidney
Droop
Woolland
Ibberton
Belchalwell
Turnworth
South Perrott
Corscombe
Chedington
East Chelborough
West Chelborough
Evershot
Batcombe
Hilfield
Minterne Magna
Minterne Parva
Buckland Newton
Dunthsh
Henley
Mappowder
Plush
Higher Ansty
Lower Ansty
Melcombe Bingham
Hilton
Winterborne Houghton
Winterborne Stickland
Milton Abbas
Winterborne Clenston
Holywell
Benville
Uphall
Rampisham
Frome St. Quintin
Higher Wraxall
Lower Wraxall
Up Cerne
Cerne Abbas
Alton Pancras
Up Sydling
Sydling St. Nicholas
Piddletrenthide
Cheselbourne
Beaminster
Mapperton
Hooke
Toller Whelme
Cattistock
Chilfrome
Maiden Newton
Nether Cerne
White Lackington
Piddlehinton
Dewlish
Milborne St. Andrew
Winterborne Whitechurch
Winterborne Kingston
Netherbury
Loscombe
North Poorton
South Poorton
Toller Porcorum
Toller Fratrum
Powerstock
West Milton
Nettlecombe
Wynford Eagle
Cruxton
Notton
Frampton
Grimstone
Godmanstone
Forston
Charlton Down
Puddletown
Tolpuddle
Athelhampton
Bere Regis
Bradpole
Uploders
Askerswell
West Compton
Compton Valence
Muckleford
Stratton
Bradford Peverell
Charminster
Stinsford
Higher Bockhampton
Lower Bockhampton
Kingston Maurward
Tincleton
Pallington
Affpuddle
Briantspuddle
Turners Puddle
Bothenhampton
Shipton Gorge
Burton Bradstock
Chilcombe
Litton Cheney
Long Bredy
Kingston Russell
Winterbourne Abbas
Winterbourne Steepleton
Poundbury
DORCHESTER
West Stafford
Woodsford
Moreton
Bovington Camp
Puncknowle
Littlebredy
Martinstown or Winterborne St. Martin
Winterborne Monkton
Winterborne Herringston
Whitcombe
West Knighton
Crossways
East Burton
Wool
Swyre
West Bexington
Abbotsbury
Portesham
Friar Waddon
Coryates
Upwey
Broadmayne
Warmwell
Owermoigne
Galton
East Knighton
Winfrith Newburgh
Coombe Keynes
Elworth
Rodden
Shilvinghampton
Broadway
Bincombe
Sutton Poyntz
Osmington
Poxwell
Upton
Holworth
Chaldon Herring or East Chaldon
West Chaldon
West Lulworth
Lulworth Camp
Langton Herring
Buckland Ripers
Nottington
Littlemoor
Preston
Overcombe
Osmington Mills
Radipole
Chickerell
Fleet
Melcombe Regis
Weymouth Bay
WEYMOUTH
Westham
Charlestown
Wyke Regis
Rodwell
Portland Harbour
Castletown
Fortuneswell
Chiswell
West Bay
Grove
Easton
Weston
Southwell
ISLE OF PORTLAND
BILL OF PORTLAND
Chesil Beach
Weymouth to:
Guernsey 2hrs. (Fast Ferry)
Jersey 3hrs. 30mins. (Fast Ferry)
St. Malo 5hrs. 30mins. (Fast Ferry)
D O R S E
E N
A303
A37
A30
A3088
A359
A357
A3030
A352
A356
A3066
A35
A354
A353
A31
B3157
B3159
B3143
B3146
B3142
B3390
B3070
B3071
B3081
B3092
B3091
B3145
B3148
B3163
B3162
A
B
C
D
1
2
3
4
5
350
60
70
80

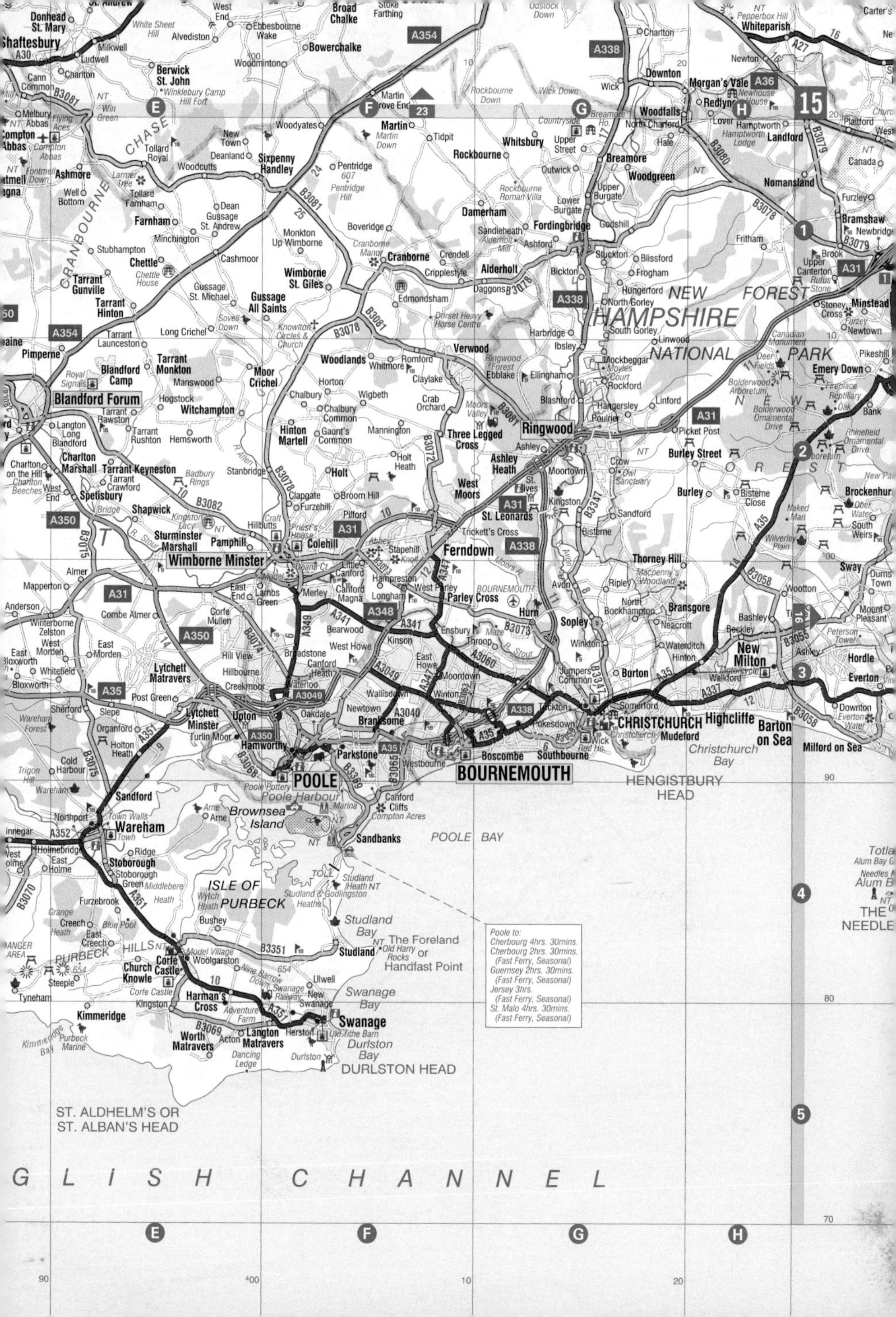
Donhead St. Mary
Shaftesbury
A30
Ludwell
Cann Common
Charlton
Berwick St. John
Winklebury Camp Hill Fort
Alvediston
West End
White Sheet Hill
Ebbesbourne Wake
Broad Chalke
Bowerchalke
Stoke Farthing
A354
Woodminton
Melbury Abbas
Compton Abbas
Win Green
CRANBORNE CHASE
Tollard Royal
New Town
Deanland
Woodcutts
Sixpenny Handley
Woodyates
Martin
Martin Down
Tidpit
Pentridge
Pentridge Hill
Ashmore
Larmer Tree
Tollard Farnham
Farnham
Dean
Gussage St. Andrew
Minchington
Stubhampton
Chettle
Chettle House
Cashmoor
Tarrant Gunville
Tarrant Hinton
Gussage St. Michael
Gussage All Saints
Monkton Up Wimborne
Boveridge
Cranborne
Cranborne Manor
Wimborne St. Giles
Edmondsham
Crendell
Cripplestyle
Alderholt
Daggons
A354
Pimperne
Tarrant Launceston
Long Crichel
Sovell Down
Knowlton Circles & Church
Dorset Heavy Horse Centre
Blandford Camp
Royal Signals
Blandford Forum
Tarrant Monkton
Manswood
Moor Crichel
Woodlands
Whitmore
Romford
Verwood
Ringwood Forest
Ebblake
Hogstock
Witchampton
Horton
Chalbury
Chalbury Common
Wigbeth
Crab Orchard
Claylake
Tarrant Rawston
Tarrant Rushton
Hemsworth
Langton Long Blandford
Hinton Martell
Gaunt's Common
Mannington
Moors Valley
Three Legged Cross
Charlton Marshall
Tarrant Keyneston
Badbury Rings
Stanbridge
Holt
Holt Heath
Ashley Heath
West Moors
Charlton on the Hill
Spetisbury
Tarrant Crawford
Shapwick
Kingston Lacy
Clapgate
Furzehill
Broom Hill
Pilford
A350
Sturminster Marshall
Pamphill
Hillbutts
Colehill
A31
Ferndown
Trickett's Cross
St. Leonards
St. Ives
Wimborne Minster
Stapehill
Little Canford
Almer
Mapperton
Anderson
Winterborne Zelston
East End
Lambs Green
Merley
Canford Magna
Hampreston
Longham
West Parley
Parley Cross
Bournemouth
Hurn
Combe Almer
Corfe Mullen
Bearwood
A348
A341
A349
Ensbury
Throop
East Bloxworth
West Morden
East Morden
Whitefield
Bloxworth
Lytchett Matravers
Hill View
Broadstone
West Howe
Canford Heath
Kinson
East Howe
A3060
Hillbourne
Creekmoor
Waterloo
A3049
Moordown
Winton
Wallisdown
A35
Post Green
Slepe
Sherford
Wareham Forest
Lytchett Minster
Upton
Oakdale
Newtown
A3040
Branksome
Organford
Turlin Moor
Hamworthy
A350
Holton Heath
Cold Harbour
Parkstone
Westbourne
Boscombe
Southbourne
Pokesdown
Tuckton
BOURNEMOUTH
POOLE
Poole Pottery
Poole Harbour
Marina
Canford Cliffs
Compton Acres
Sandford
Arne
Brownsea Island
Northport
Wareham
Town Walls
Sandbanks
POOLE BAY
Holmebridge
Ridge
Stoborough
Stoborough Green
Middlebere Heath
East Holme
West Holme
ISLE OF PURBECK
Studland Heath
Studland & Godlingston Heaths
Wytch Heath
Furzebrook
Grange Heath
Creech
East Creech
Blue Pool
Bushey
Studland Bay
The Foreland or Handfast Point
Old Harry Rocks
Studland
PURBECK HILLS
Model Village
Woolgarston
Nine Barrow Down
Corfe Castle
Church Knowle
Steeple
Tyneham
Ulwell
Swanage Railway
Harman's Cross
Adventure Farm
Swanage
Swanage Bay
Kingston
Kimmeridge
Kimmeridge Bay
Purbeck Marine
Worth Matravers
Acton
Langton Matravers
Herston
Old Tithe Barn
Durlston Bay
Durlston
DURLSTON HEAD
Dancing Ledge
ST. ALDHELM'S OR ST. ALBAN'S HEAD
GLISH CHANNEL
Poole to:
Cherbourg 4hrs. 30mins.
Cherbourg 2hrs. 30mins. (Fast Ferry, Seasonal)
Guernsey 2hrs. 30mins. (Fast Ferry, Seasonal)
Jersey 3hrs. (Fast Ferry, Seasonal)
St. Malo 4hrs. 30mins. (Fast Ferry, Seasonal)
Rockbourne Down
Wick Down
Rockbourne
Whitsbury
Upper Street
Breamore
Woodgreen
Outwick
Rockbourne Roman Villa
Damerham
Lower Burgate
Upper Burgate
Fordingbridge
Sandleheath
Alderholt Mill
Ashford
Godshill
Charlton
Downton
Wick
Woodfalls
North Charford
Hale
A338
Morgan's Vale
Redlynch
Newhouse
Lover
Hamptworth
Hamptworth Lodge
Landford
Whiteparish
Pepperbox Hill
Newton
A36
A27
Plaitford
Canada
Nomansland
Furzley
Bramshaw
Newbridge
Fritham
Brook
Upper Canterton
Rufus Stone
A31
Stuckton
Blissford
Frogham
Bickton
Hungerford
North Gorley
South Gorley
NEW FOREST
HAMPSHIRE
NATIONAL PARK
Harbridge
Ibsley
Linwood
Mockbeggar
Moyles Court
Rockford
Ellingham
Blashford
Hangersley
Poulner
Linford
Canadian Monument
Deer Fields
Bolderwood Arboretum
Bolderwood Ornamental Drive
Stoney Cross
Minstead
Furzey
Newtown
Pikeshill
Emery Down
Fireplace Reptiliary
Bank
Ringwood
Ashley
Picket Post
Burley Street
Crow
Owl Sanctuary
Moortown
Rhinefield Ornamental Drive
Kingston
Burley
Bisterne Close
Brockenhurst
Sandford
Bisterne
Naked Man
Ober Water
Wilverley Plain
South Weirs
Thorney Hill
Macpenny's Woodland
Sway
Ripley
Avon
Bransgore
North Bockhampton
Sopley
Neacroft
Wootton
Bashley
Beckley
Peterson Tower
Mount Pleasant
Winkton
Waterditch
Hinton
Burton
Jumpers Common
New Milton
Walkford
Ashley
Hordle
Everton
Somerford
CHRISTCHURCH
Highcliffe
Mudeford
Christchurch Bay
Barton on Sea
Downton
Everton Water
Milford on Sea
HENGISTBURY HEAD
Totland
Alum Bay
Needles
THE NEEDLES
15
16
E
F
G
H
1
2
3
4
5
90
80
70
90
400
10
20

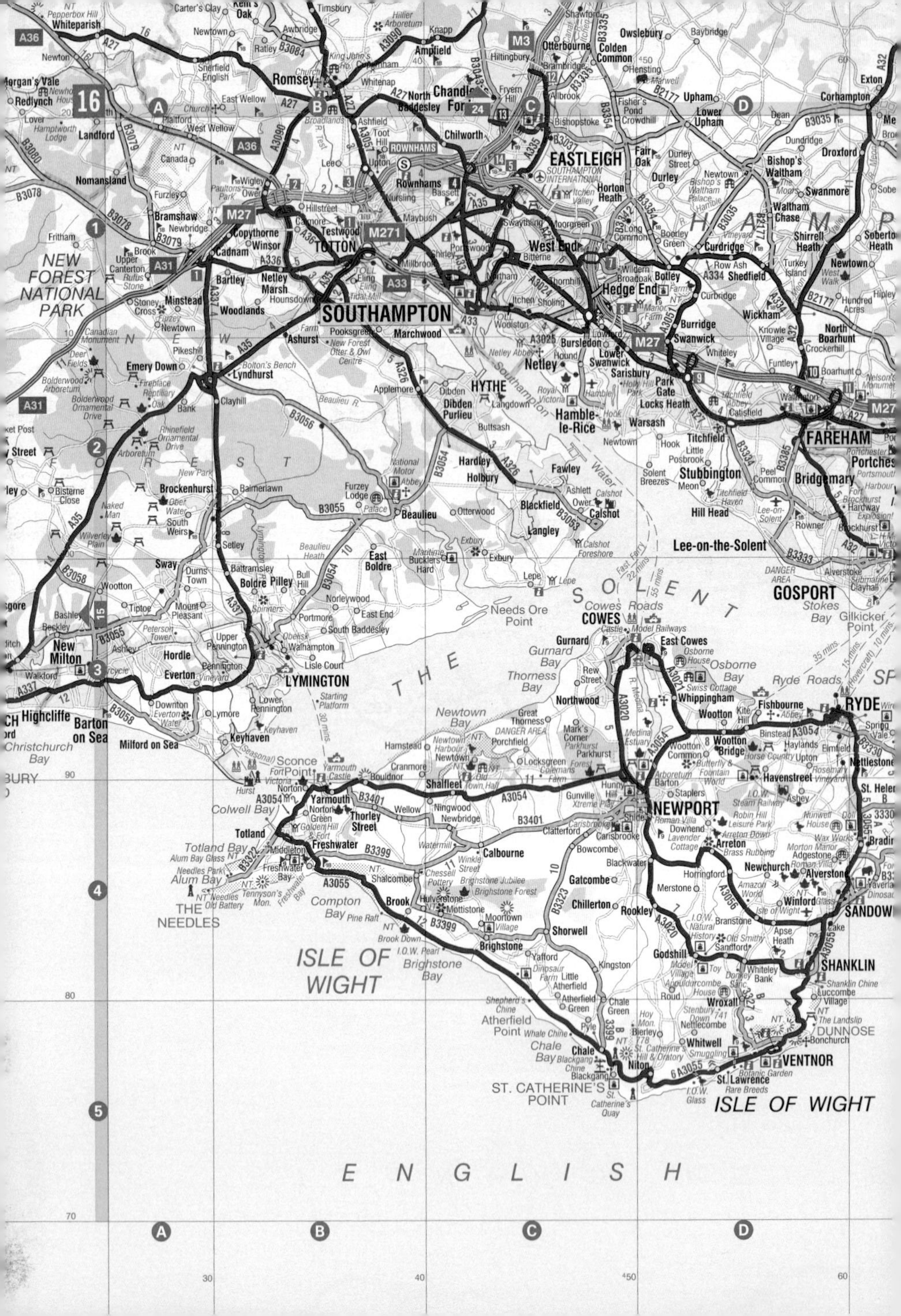

16
Whiteparish
Romsey
Chandler's Ford
Eastleigh
Southampton
Totton
Rownhams
Otterbourne
Colden Common
Owslebury
Upham
Lower Upham
Bishop's Waltham
Droxford
Corhampton
Exton
Landford
Nomansland
Bramshaw
Cadnam
Copythorne
Netley Marsh
Minstead
Woodlands
Ashurst
Marchwood
New Forest National Park
Lyndhurst
Emery Down
Brockenhurst
Sway
Boldre
Pilley
Lymington
New Milton
Highcliffe
Barton on Sea
Milford on Sea
Keyhaven
Hordle
Everton
Beaulieu
East Boldre
Hythe
Dibden Purlieu
Fawley
Holbury
Hardley
Blackfield
Calshot
Langley
Netley
Hamble-le-Rice
Bursledon
Hedge End
West End
Botley
Shedfield
Wickham
Swanwick
Park Gate
Locks Heath
Sarisbury
Warsash
Titchfield
Stubbington
Fareham
Portchester
Bridgemary
Gosport
Lee-on-the-Solent
Hill Head
The Solent
Cowes
East Cowes
Gurnard
Northwood
Newport
Ryde
Fishbourne
Wootton
Wootton Bridge
Havenstreet
Nettlestone
St. Helens
Brading
Sandown
Shanklin
Ventnor
Bonchurch
Wroxall
Whitwell
Niton
St. Lawrence
St. Catherine's Point
Chale
Godshill
Rookley
Arreton
Newchurch
Alverstone
Shorwell
Brighstone
Calbourne
Shalfleet
Yarmouth
Freshwater
Totland
Alum Bay
The Needles
Brook
Compton Bay
Atherfield Point
Chale Bay
Carisbrooke
Chillerton
Gatcombe
Isle of Wight
English
A
B
C
D
1
2
3
4
5
M27
M271
M3
A31
A35
A36
A337
A326
A3054
A3020
A3055

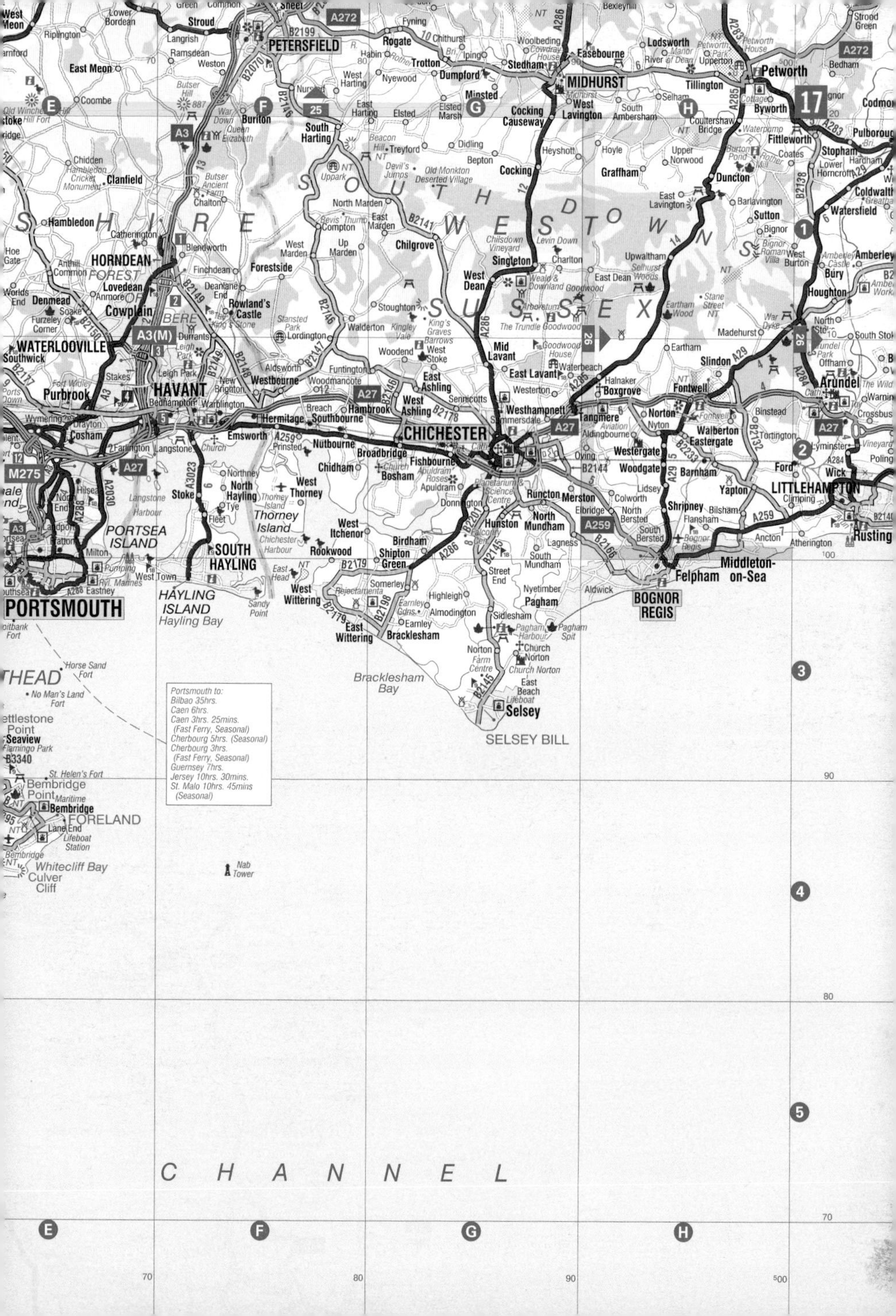

Portsmouth to:
Bilbao 35hrs.
Caen 6hrs.
Caen 3hrs. 25mins. (Fast Ferry, Seasonal)
Cherbourg 5hrs. (Seasonal)
Cherbourg 3hrs. (Fast Ferry, Seasonal)
Guernsey 7hrs.
Jersey 10hrs. 30mins.
St. Malo 10hrs. 45mins (Seasonal)

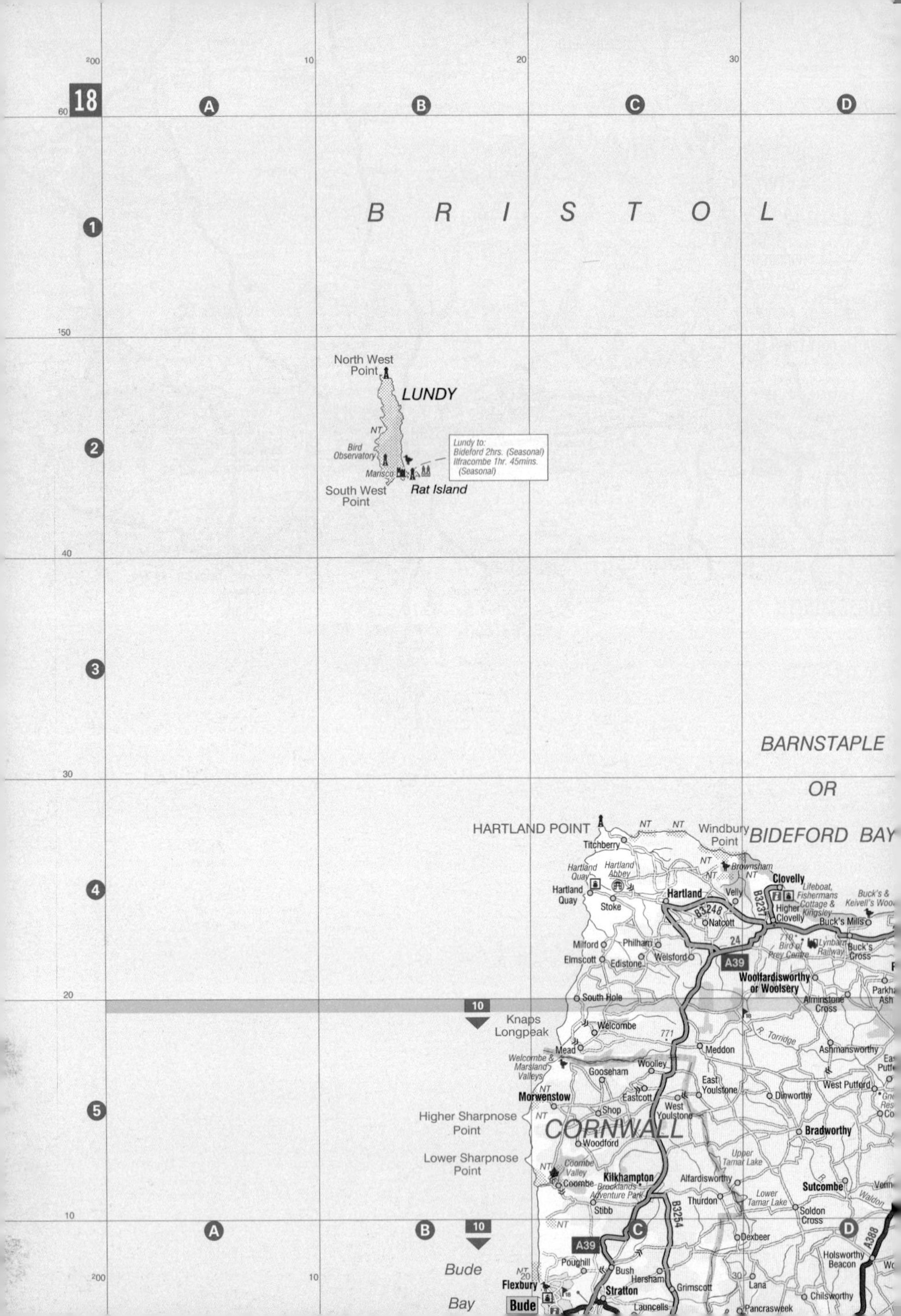

BRISTOL
North West Point
LUNDY
NT
Bird Observatory
Marisco
South West Point
Rat Island
Lundy to:
Bideford 2hrs. (Seasonal)
Ilfracombe 1hr. 45mins. (Seasonal)
BARNSTAPLE OR BIDEFORD BAY
HARTLAND POINT
Titchberry
Windbury Point
Brownsham
Hartland Quay
Hartland Abbey
Stoke
Hartland
Clovelly
Lifeboat, Fishermans Cottage & Kingsley
Higher Clovelly
Buck's Mills
Buck's & Keivell's Woods
Velly
B3248
B3237
Natcott
Milford
Philham
Welsford
Elmscott
Edistone
Bird of Prey Centre
Lynbarn Railway
Buck's Cross
A39
Woolfardisworthy or Woolsery
South Hole
Almsworthy Cross
Parkham Ash
10
Knaps Longpeak
Welcombe
R. Torridge
Meddon
Mead
Welcombe & Marsland Valleys
Gooseham
Woolley
Ashmansworthy
East Youlstone
Eastcott
West Putford
Morwenstow
Shop
West Youlstone
Dinworthy
Higher Sharpnose Point
CORNWALL
Bradworthy
Woodford
Lower Sharpnose Point
Coombe Valley
Coombe
Kilkhampton
Brocklands Adventure Park
Upper Tamar Lake
Alfardisworthy
Sutcombe
Thurdon
Lower Tamar Lake
Soldon Cross
Stibb
B3254
Dexbeer
Holsworthy Beacon
A388
Poughill
Bush
Bude Bay
Flexbury
Hersham
Grimscott
Lana
Chilsworthy
Bude
Stratton
Launcells
Pancrasweek

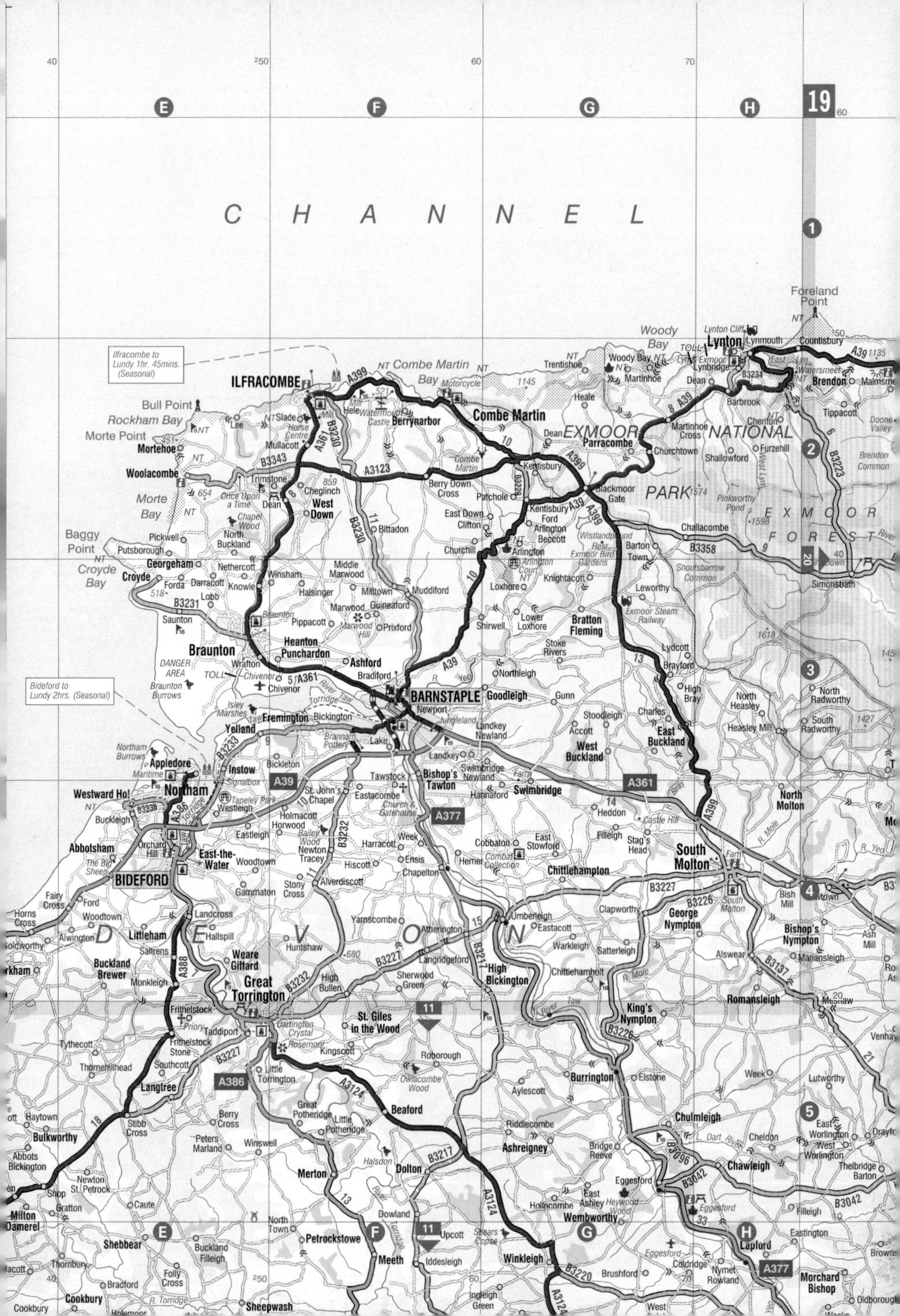

C H A N N E L
Foreland Point
Woody Bay
Lynton Cliff
Lynton
Lynmouth
Countisbury
Ilfracombe to Lundy 1hr. 45mins. (Seasonal)
ILFRACOMBE
Combe Martin Bay
Combe Martin
Berrynarbor
Bull Point
Rockham Bay
Morte Point
Mortehoe
Woolacombe
Morte Bay
Baggy Point
Croyde Bay
Croyde
Georgeham
Braunton
Saunton
Braunton Burrows
Bideford to Lundy 2hrs. (Seasonal)
EXMOOR NATIONAL PARK
EXMOOR FOREST
Parracombe
Blackmoor Gate
Brendon
Simonsbath
Challacombe
West Down
Muddiford
Heanton Punchardon
Ashford
BARNSTAPLE
Goodleigh
Bratton Fleming
Fremington
Yelland
Instow
Appledore
Northam
Westward Ho!
BIDEFORD
Abbotsham
East-the-Water
Bishop's Tawton
Swimbridge
West Buckland
East Buckland
North Molton
South Molton
Chittlehampton
Umberleigh
High Bickington
George Nympton
Bishop's Nympton
Great Torrington
Weare Giffard
St. Giles in the Wood
King's Nympton
Burrington
Chulmleigh
Beaford
Langtree
Bulkworthy
Merton
Dolton
Ashreigney
Chawleigh
Wembworthy
Petrockstowe
Meeth
Winkleigh
Lapford
Morchard Bishop
Shebbear
Milton Damerel
Cookbury
Sheepwash
Littleham
Buckland Brewer
D E V O N
A39
A361
A377
A386
A399
A3123
A3124
B3227
B3226
B3217
B3232
11

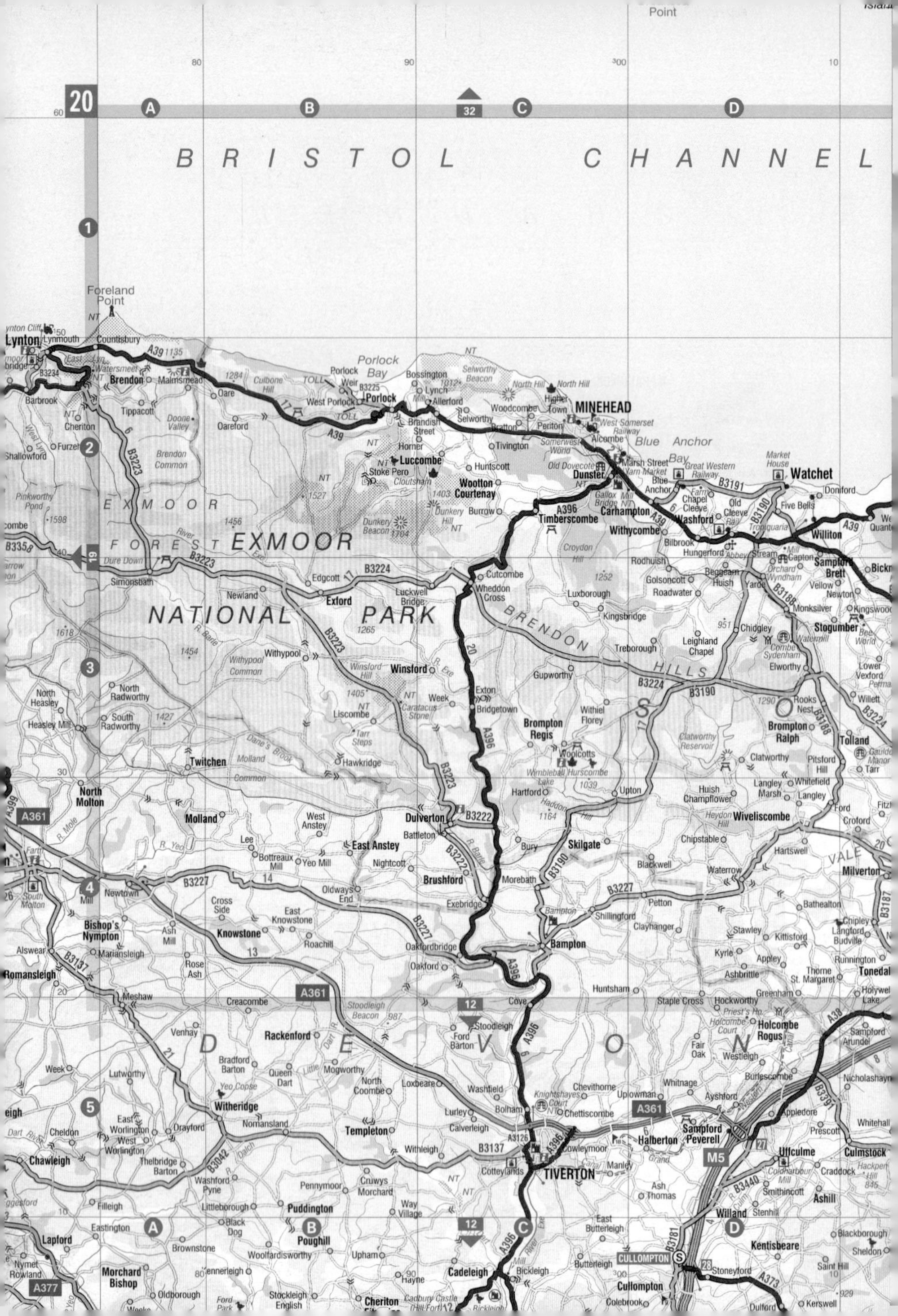

20
A
B
C
D
32
19
12
1
2
3
4
5
80
90
300
10
60
40
30
20
BRISTOL CHANNEL
Foreland Point
Lynton
Lynmouth
Countisbury
Watersmeet
Brendon
Malmsmead
Barbrook
Cheriton
Tippacott
Oare
Oareford
Culbone Hill
Doone Valley
Brendon Common
Furzehill
Shallowford
West Lyn
Pinkworthy Pond
EXMOOR
EXMOOR
FOREST
NATIONAL PARK
Porlock
Porlock Bay
Porlock Weir
West Porlock
Bossington
Lynch
Allerford
Selworthy Beacon
Selworthy
North Hill
Higher Town
MINEHEAD
Alcombe
Woodcombe
Bratton
Periton
Brandish Street
Horner
Luccombe
Stoke Pero
Cloutsham
Tivington
Huntscott
Wootton Courtenay
Dunkery Hill
Dunkery Beacon
Burrow
Dunster
Somerwest World
West Somerset Railway
Blue Anchor Bay
Marsh Street
Yarn Market
Old Dovecote
Gallox Bridge
Carhampton
Timberscombe
Withycombe
Blue Anchor
Chapel Cleeve
Old Cleeve
Washford
Great Western Railway
Market House
Watchet
Doniford
Five Bells
Williton
Bilbrook
Hungerford
Tropiquaria
Rodhuish
Golsoncott
Roadwater
Beggearn Huish
Yarde
Capton
Orchard Wyndham
Sampford Brett
Vellow
Newton
Monksilver
Kingswood
Stogumber
Chidgley
Leighland Chapel
Combe Sydenham
Elworthy
Lower Vexford
Willett
Simonsbath
Dure Down
Edgcott
Exford
Luckwell Bridge
Newland
Cutcombe
Wheddon Cross
Croydon Hill
Luxborough
Kingsbridge
BRENDON HILLS
Treborough
Gupworthy
Withypool
Withypool Common
Winsford
Winsford Hill
Caratacus Stone
Tarr Steps
Liscombe
Week
Exton
Bridgetown
Brompton Regis
Withiel Florey
Woolcotts
Wimbleball Lake
Hurscombe
Hartford
Haddon Hill
Upton
Clatworthy Reservoir
Clatworthy
Brompton Ralph
Rooks Nest
Tolland
Pitsford Hill
Tarr
North Heasley
Heasley Mill
North Radworthy
South Radworthy
Twitchen
Molland Common
Dane's Brook
Hawkridge
North Molton
Molland
West Anstey
East Anstey
Dulverton
Battleton
Bury
Skilgate
Huish Champflower
Heydon Hill
Wiveliscombe
Langley Marsh
Whitefield
Langley
Ford
Croford
Chipstable
Hartswell
Milverton
Lee
Bottreaux Mill
Yeo Mill
Nightcott
Brushford
Morebath
Blackwell
Waterrow
South Molton
Mill
Newtown
Cross Side
East Knowstone
Knowstone
Oldways End
Exebridge
Petton
Shillingford
Bampton
Clayhanger
Bathealton
Stawley
Kittisford
Chipley
Langford Budville
Bishop's Nympton
Ash Mill
Mariansleigh
Alswear
Romansleigh
Rose Ash
Roachill
Oakfordbridge
Oakford
Kyrle
Appley
Ashbrittle
Thorne St. Margaret
Runnington
Tonedale
Meshaw
Creacombe
Stoodleigh Beacon
Cove
Huntsham
Staple Cross
Hockworthy
Greenham
Holywell Lake
Venhay
Rackenford
Stoodleigh
Ford Barton
Priest's Ho.
Holcombe Court
Holcombe Rogus
Sampford Arundel
DEVON
Bradford Barton
Queen Dart
Mogworthy
North Coombe
Loxbeare
Washfield
Chevithorne
Whitnage
Fair Oak
Westleigh
Burlescombe
Nicholashayne
Week
Lutworthy
Yeo Copse
Witheridge
Nomansland
Templeton
Lurley
Calverleigh
Bolham
Knightshayes Court
Chettiscombe
Uplowman
Ayshford
Appledore
Whitehall
Cheldon
East Worlington
West Worlington
Drayford
Thelbridge Barton
Chawleigh
Withleigh
Cotteylands
Cowleymoor
Halberton
Sampford Peverell
Prescott
Uffculme
Culmstock
Washford Pyne
Pennymoor
Cruwys Morchard
TIVERTON
Manley
Grand Western Canal
Ash Thomas
Craddock
Coldharbour Mill
Smithincott
Hackpen Hill
Ashill
Filleigh
Littleborough
Puddington
Way Village
Willand
Stenhill
Lapford
Eastington
Black Dog
Poughill
East Butterleigh
Kentisbeare
Blackborough
Sheldon
Brownstone
Woolfardisworthy
Upham
Nymet Rowland
Morchard Bishop
Hayne
Cadeleigh
Bickleigh
Butterleigh
CULLOMPTON
Cullompton
Stoneyford
Saint Hill
Oldborough
Stockleigh English
Cheriton
Cadbury Castle
Colebrook
Dulford
Kerswell
A39
A396
A361
A377
A399
A3126
A38
A373
M5
B3234
B3223
B3225
B3358
B3224
B3222
B3190
B3191
B3188
B3227
B3137
B3042
B3391
B3440
B3181
B3187

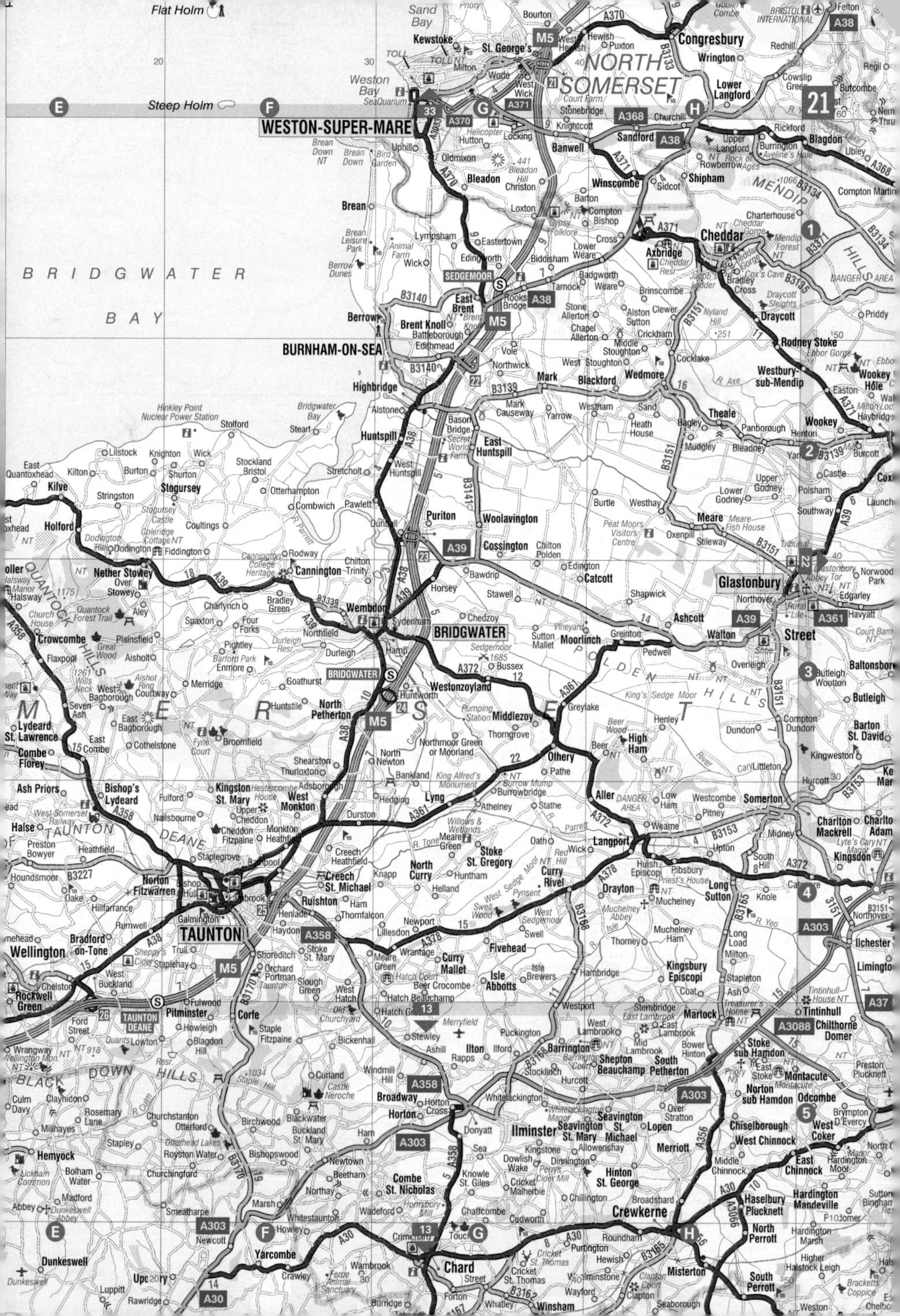

Flat Holm
Sand Bay
Kewstoke
St. George's
Bourton
A370
M5
Hewish
Puxton
Congresbury
BRISTOL INTERNATIONAL
Felton
A38
NORTH SOMERSET
Wrington
Redhill
Regil
Weston Bay
Milton
Worle
West Wick
Lower Langford
Cowslip Green
Butcombe
21
Steep Holm
WESTON-SUPER-MARE
SeaQuarium
33
A370
A371
Court Farm
Stonebridge
A368
Churchill
Rickford
Blagdon
Ubley
Locking
Knightcott
Sandford
Upper Langford
Burrington
Aveline's Hole
Brean Down NT
Uphill
Hutton
Banwell
Rowberrow
Oldmixon
Bleadon Hill
Winscombe
Sidcot
Shipham
MENDIP
Bleadon
Christon
Compton Martin
Brean
Loxton
Barton
Compton Bishop
Charterhouse
Gypsy Folklore
Cheddar
Cheddar Gorge
Mendip Forest
Brean Leisure Park
Animal Farm
Lympsham
Eastertown
Cross
Axbridge
Lower Weare
Cheddar Resr
B3371
B3134
HILLS
Wick
Edingworth
Biddisham
Tarnock
Badgworth
Weare
Brinscombe
Jacob's Ladder
Cox's Cave
Bradley Cross
B3135
DANGER AREA
BRIDGWATER BAY
Berrow Dunes
SEDGEMOOR
Rooks Bridge
A38
East Brent
Stone Allerton
Alston Sutton
Clewer
Nyland Hill
Draycott Sleights
Draycott
Priddy
B3140
Berrow
Brent Knoll
Battleborough
Edithmead
Chapel Allerton
Crickham
Middle Stoughton
Rodney Stoke
Ebbor Gorge
BURNHAM-ON-SEA
Vole
West Stoughton
Wedmore
Cocklake
Westbury-sub-Mendip
Wookey Hole
Northwick
Mark
Blackford
R. Axe
Easton
Highbridge
B3139
Mark Causeway
Yarrow
Westham
Sand
Theale
Wookey
Haybridge
Hinkley Point Nuclear Power Station
Bridgwater Bay
Alstone
Bason Bridge
Heath House
Bagley
Panborough
Henton
Stolford
Steart
Huntspill
Secret World Farm
East Huntspill
Mudgley
Bleadney
Yarley
Burcott
Lilstock
Knighton
Wick
Stockland Bristol
B3151
Castle
East Quantoxhead
Kilton
Burton
Shurton
Stretcholt
West Huntspill
Upper Godney
Kilve
Stringston
Stogursey
Otterhampton
Lower Godney
Polsham
Combwich
Pawlett
B3141
Burtle
Westhay
Southway
Holford
Stogursey Castle
Coultings
R. Parrett
Puriton
Woolavington
Meare
Meare Fish House
Launcher
Dodington Hall
Dodington
Coleridge Cottage NT
Fiddington
Dunball
Peat Moors Visitors Centre
Oxenpill
Stileway
A39
Rodway
Cossington
Chilton Polden
QUANTOCK
Nether Stowey
Cannington College Heritage
Cannington
Chilton Trinity
Bawdrip
Edington
Catcott
Glastonbury
Glastonbury Abbey
Tor
Norwood Park
Halsway Manor
Halsway
Over Stowey
1175
Charlynch
Bradley Green
B3339
Wembdon
Horsey
Stawell
Shapwick
Northover
Edgarley
Church House
Quantock Forest Trail
Aley
Spaxton
Four Forks
Northfield
Sydenham
Chedzoy
Ashcott
A361
Havyatt
A358
Crowcombe
HILLS
Great Wood
Plainsfield
Pightley
Durleigh Resr
BRIDGWATER
Sutton Mallet
Vineyard
Moorlinch
Greinton
Walton
Street
Court Barn
Flaxpool
Aisholt
Barford Park
Enmore
Durleigh
Hamp
Sedgemoor 1685
Pedwell
Shoe
Overleigh
1261 Wills Neck
Aishot Wood
Merridge
Goathurst
Bussex
POLDEN
Baltonsborough
West Bagborough
Courtway
Huntstile
Huntworth
Westonzoyland
A372
King's Sedge Moor
Butleigh Wootton
Seven Ash
North Petherton
Pumping Station
Greylake
Butleigh
Lydeard St. Lawrence
East Bagborough
Broomfield
Middlezoy
Beer Wood
Henley
Compton Dundon
Barton St. David
East Combe
Fyne Court
Cothelstone
Thorngrove
High Ham
Dundon
Combe Florey
Shearston
Northmoor Green or Moorland
Beer
Kingweston
Thurloxton
North Newton
Othery
Pathe
Littleton
Ash Priors
Bishop's Lydeard
Kingston St. Mary
Hestercombe House
Bankland
King Alfred's Monument
Burrow Mump
Burrowbridge
Hurcott
Adsborough
West Monkton
Lyng
Aller
Low Ham
Westcombe
Somerton
Fulford
Upper Cheddon
Hedging
Athelney
Stathe
DANGER AREA
Pitney
West Somerset Railway
Nailsbourne
Cheddon Fitzpaine
Durston
Willows & Wetlands
Wearne
Charlton Mackrell
Halse
TAUNTON
DEANE
Monkton Heathfield
Meare Green
Oath
Langport
B3153
Midney
Preston Bowyer
Heathfield
Staplegrove
R. Tone
Stoke St. Gregory
Red Hill
Wick
Upton
Lyte's Cary
Kingsdon
Bathpool
Creech Heathfield
Curry Rivel
A378
Huish Episcopi
Pibsbury
South Hill
Houndsmoor
B3227
Norton Fitzwarren
Creech St. Michael
Knapp
North Curry
Huntham
Priest's House
Long Sutton
Oake
Bishop's Hull
Helland
Drayton
Muchelney
Knole
Ruishton
Ham
Pynsent
Muchelney Abbey
B3165
R. Yeo
Hillfarrance
Rumwell
Galmington
Henlade
Thornfalcon
Newport
West Sedgemoor
Northover
TAUNTON
Haydon
Lillesdon
Swell Wood
Swell
Isle
Thorney
Muchelney Ham
Long Load
A303
Ilchester
Bradford on-Tone
Wellington
Trull
Sheppy's Cider
Staplehay
Shoreditch
Stoke St. Mary
A358
Wrantage
Meare Green
Curry Mallet
Fivehead
Milton
Limington
Orchard Portman
Hatch Court
Beer Crocombe
Isle Abbotts
Isle Brewers
Hambridge
Kingsbury Episcopi
Chelston
West Buckland
Slough Green
West Hatch
Hatch Beauchamp
Stapleton
Rockwell Green
Fulwood
Pitminster
Corfe
Old Churchyard
Hatch Green
Westport
Coat
Ash
Tintinhull House NT
Tintinhull
A37
Ford Street
TAUNTON DEANE
Howleigh
Staple Fitzpaine
Merryfield
Stembridge
East Lambrook
Treasurer's House
Martock
A3088
Chilthorne Domer
Wrangway
Wellington Mon.
Lowton
Blagdon Hill
Bickenhall
Stewley
Ashill
Ilton
Ilford
Puckington
West Lambrook
Mid Lambrook
Bower Hinton
Stoke sub Hamdon
BLACK DOWN HILLS
Staple Hill
Rapps
Barrington
Barrington Court
Shepton Beauchamp
South Petherton
Preston Plucknett
Windmill Hill
Stocklinch
Hurcott
Priory Hill
East Stoke
Montacute
Culm Davy
Clayhidon
Curland
Castle Neroche
A358
Broadway
Whitelackington
Norton sub Hamdon
Odcombe
Rosemary Lane
Churchstanton
Otterford
Blackwater
Horton
Horton Cross
Whitelackington Manor
Over Stratton
Brympton D'Evercy
Millhayes
Birchwood
Buckland St. Mary
Donyatt
Ilminster
Seavington St. Mary
Seavington St. Michael
Lopen
Chiselborough
West Coker
Stapley
Otterhead Lakes
Harn
A303
Sea
Kingstone
Allowenshay
Merriott
West Chinnock
Hemyock
Royston Water
Bishopswood
Newtown
Dowlish Wake
Dinnington
A356
Middle Chinnock
East Chinnock
Hardington Moor
Bolham Water
Churchingford
Beetham
Combe St. Nicholas
Knowle St. Giles
Perry's Cider Mill
Hinton St. George
Culmstock Common
Northay
Cricket Malherbie
Haselbury Plucknett
Hardington Mandeville
Madford
Dunkeswell Abbey
Marsh
Wadeford
Hornsbury Mill
Chillington
Broadshard
Crewkerne
Abbey
Smeatharpe
Whitestaunton
Chaffcombe
Cudworth
A3066
Bingham
Newcott
Howley
Crimchard
Touch
Roundham
North Perrott
Hardington Marsh
A30
Yarcombe
Chard
Purtington
Cricket St. Thomas
Hewish
Higher Halstock Leigh
Dunkeswell
Wambrook
Street
Cricket St. Thomas
Misterton
Crawley
Ferne Animal Sanctuary
Whitminstone
Clapton Court
Clapton
South Perrott
Bracketts Coppice
Upottery
Luppitt
Rawridge
Burridge
Forton
Whatley
B3162
Winsham
Wayford
Seaborough
Weston

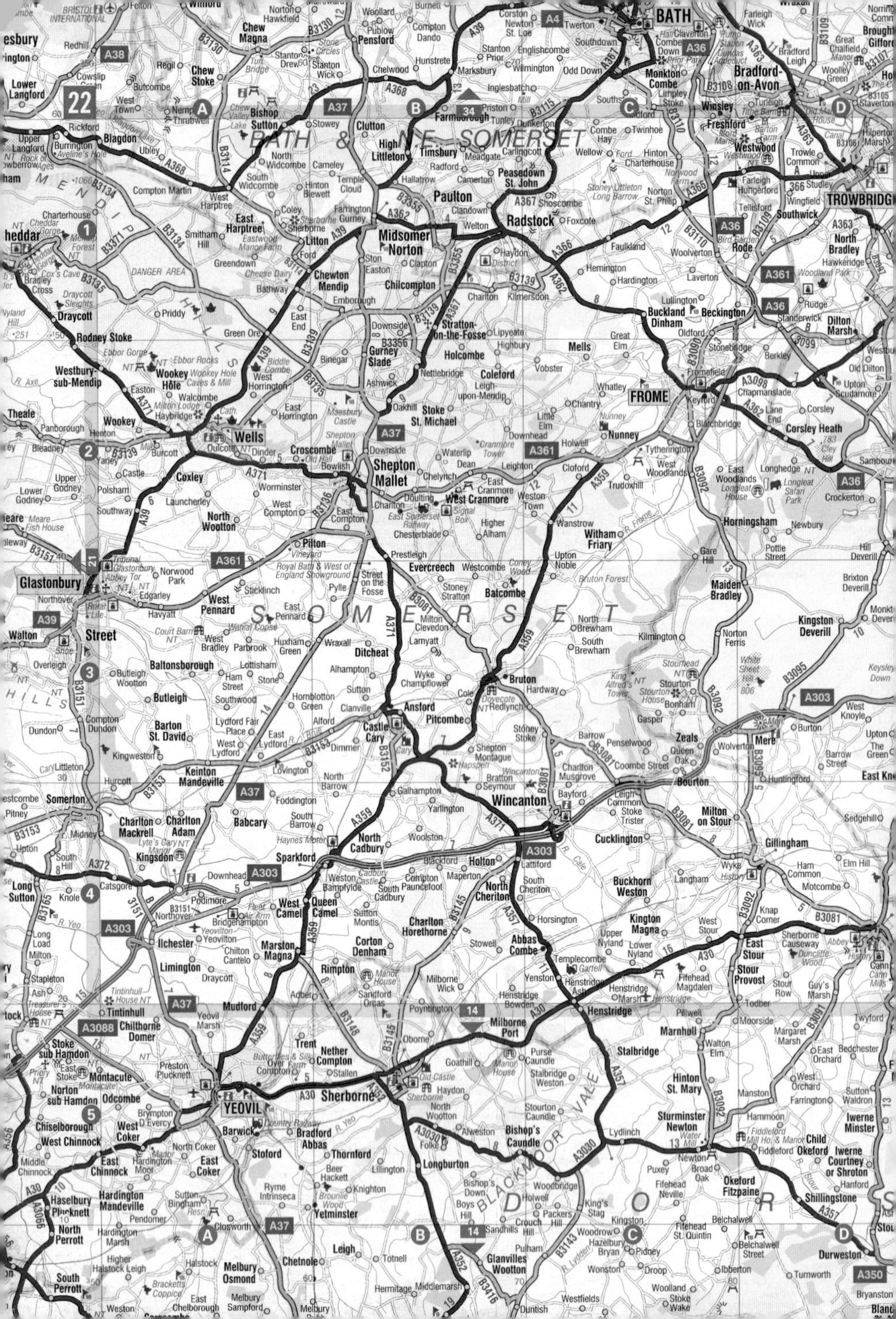

22
34
21
14
BATH & N.E. SOMERSET
SOMERSET
MENDIP HILLS
BLACKMOOR VALE
BATH
Bradford-on-Avon
TROWBRIDGE
FROME
Wells
Shepton Mallet
Glastonbury
Street
YEOVIL
Sherborne
Wincanton
Bruton
Castle Cary
Midsomer Norton
Radstock
Paulton
Cheddar
Somerton
Ilchester
Gillingham
Mere
Warminster
Chew Magna
Pensford
Chew Stoke
Bishop Sutton
Blagdon
Clutton
Timsbury
Peasedown St. John
Farmborough
Marksbury
Chelwood
Compton Dando
Stanton Drew
Englishcombe
Twerton
Southdown
Odd Down
Combe Down
Monkton Combe
Claverton
Winsley
Freshford
Westwood
Farleigh Hungerford
Norton St. Philip
Southwick
Rode
North Bradley
Beckington
Buckland Dinham
Mells
Nunney
Whatley
Coleford
Holcombe
Stratton-on-the-Fosse
Chilcompton
Chewton Mendip
Litton
East Harptree
West Harptree
Compton Martin
Priddy
Draycott
Rodney Stoke
Westbury-sub-Mendip
Wookey Hole
Wookey
Theale
Croscombe
Dinder
Coxley
Pilton
Doulting
West Cranmore
Evercreech
Batcombe
Witham Friary
Upton Noble
Ditcheat
Baltonsborough
Butleigh
West Pennard
North Wootton
Ansford
Pitcombe
Keinton Mandeville
Charlton Mackrell
Charlton Adam
Babcary
Sparkford
North Cadbury
Queen Camel
West Camel
Marston Magna
Rimpton
Mudford
Charlton Horethorne
Milborne Port
Henstridge
Templecombe
Abbas Combe
Holton
North Cheriton
Stalbridge
Marnhull
Hinton St. Mary
Sturminster Newton
Child Okeford
Shillingstone
Okeford Fitzpaine
Durweston
Bishop's Caundle
Longburton
Yetminster
Thornford
Bradford Abbas
Barwick
East Coker
West Coker
Montacute
Odcombe
Stoke sub Hamdon
Norton sub Hamdon
Tintinhull
Chilthorne Domer
Limington
Chiselborough
West Chinnock
East Chinnock
Hardington Mandeville
Haselbury Plucknett
North Perrott
South Perrott
Melbury Osmond
Leigh
Glanvilles Wootton
Stour Provost
East Stour
Kington Magna
Buckhorn Weston
Cucklington
Milton on Stour
Zeals
Stourton
Kilmington
Maiden Bradley
Horningsham
Kingston Deverill
Corsley Heath
Dilton Marsh
Long Sutton
Kingsdon
Cheddar Gorge
Longleat House
Stourhead
A4
A36
A37
A38
A39
A303
A30
A350
A357
A359
A361
A362
A363
A366
A367
A368
A371
A372
A3030
A3088
A352
B3139
B3151
B3153
B3081
B3092

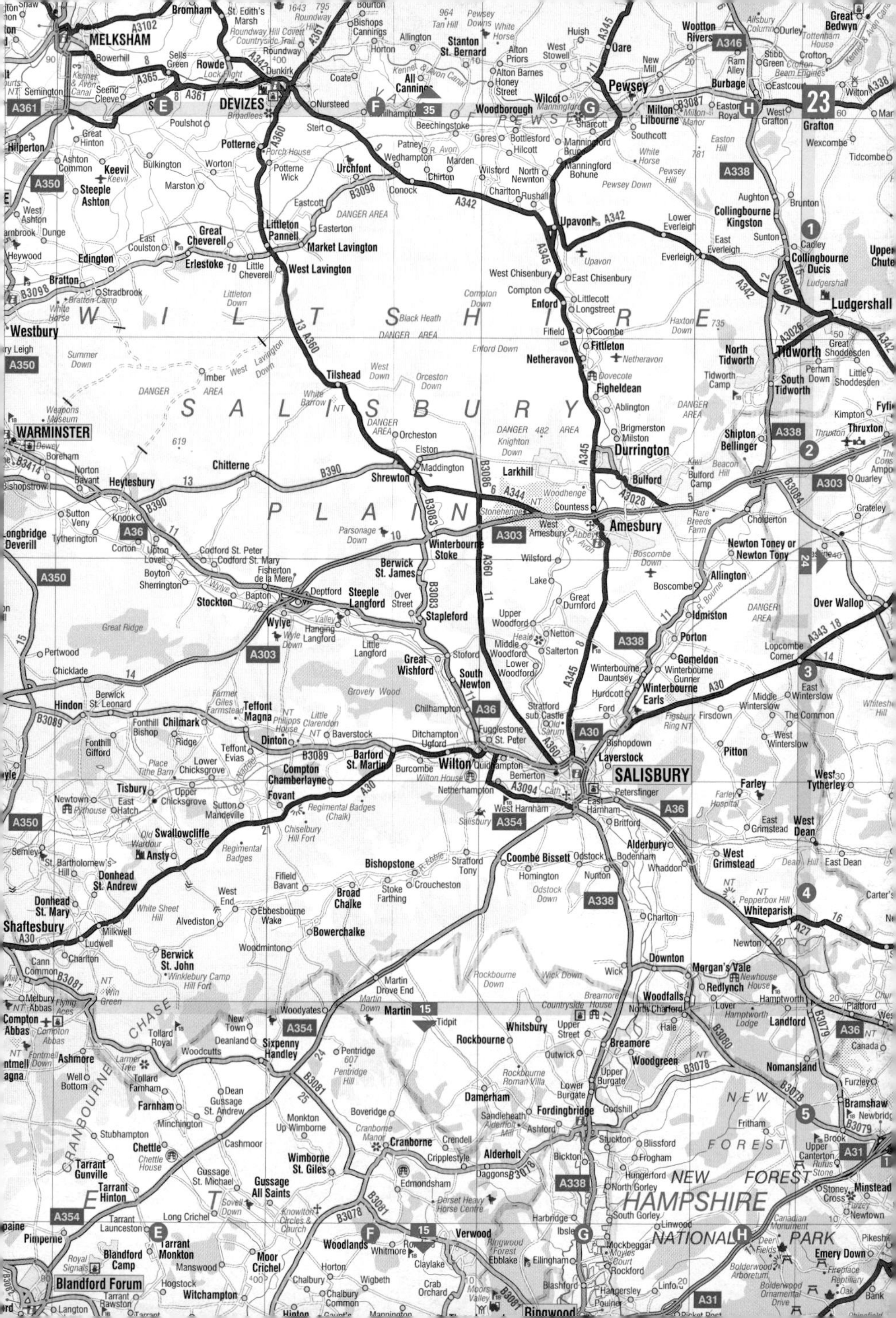

23
MELKSHAM
Bromham
St. Edith's Marsh
Roundway Hill Covert Countryside Trail
Roundway
Bourton
Bishops Cannings
Allington
Horton
Stanton St. Bernard
Pewsey Downs
White Horse
Huish
Oare
Wootton Rivers
Great Bedwyn
Durley
Tottenham House
Sells Green
Rowde
Bowerhill
Dunkirk
Coate
All Cannings
Alton Priors
Alton Barnes
Honey Street
West Stowell
New Mill
Ram Alley
Stibb Green
Crofton
Crofton Beam Engines
Semington
Seend Cleeve
DEVIZES
Nursteed
Etchilhampton
VALE OF PEWSEY
Woodborough
Wilcot
Manningford
Pewsey
Milton Lilbourne
Burbage
Eastcourt
Easton Royal
West Grafton
Grafton
Wilton
Poulshot
Stert
Beechingstoke
Gores
Bottlesford
Sharcott
Southcott
Hilperton
Great Hinton
Potterne
Porch House
Patney
Wedhampton
Hilcott
Manningford Bruce
White Horse
Easton Hill
Wexcombe
Tidcombe
Ashton Common
Keevil
Bulkington
Worton
Potterne Wick
Urchfont
Marden
Chirton
Wilsford
North Newnton
Manningford Bohune
Pewsey Hill
Steeple Ashton
Marston
Conock
Charlton
Rushall
Pewsey Down
West Ashton
Eastcott
Easterton
DANGER AREA
Upavon
Lower Everleigh
Aughton
Collingbourne Kingston
Brunton
Dunge
Littleton Pannell
Market Lavington
East Coulston
Great Cheverell
East Everleigh
Everleigh
Sunton
Cadley
Collingbourne Ducis
Upper Chute
Heywood
Edington
Erlestoke
Little Cheverell
West Lavington
West Chisenbury
East Chisenbury
Ludgershall
Bratton
Stradbrook
Bratton Camp
White Horse
Littleton Down
Compton Down
Compton
Enford
Littlecott
Longstreet
WILTSHIRE
Black Heath
DANGER AREA
Fifield
Coombe
Haxton Down
Westbury
Fittleton
Netheravon
North Tidworth
Tidworth
Great Shoddesden
Summer Down
Imber
West Lavington Down
Enford Down
Dovecote
Tilshead
West Down
Orcheston Down
Figheldean
Tidworth Camp
South Tidworth
Perham Down
Little Shoddesden
SALISBURY PLAIN
White Barrow
DANGER AREA
Weapons Museum
WARMINSTER
Dewey
Boreham
Orcheston
Ablington
Brigmerston
Milston
Knighton Down
Durrington
Shipton Bellinger
Thruxton
Kimpton
Norton Bavant
Chitterne
Elston
Maddington
Shrewton
Larkhill
Bulford
Bulford Camp
Beacon Hill
Bishopstrow
Heytesbury
Woodhenge
Countess
Quarley
Sutton Veny
Knook
Stonehenge
West Amesbury
Amesbury
Rare Breeds Farm
Cholderton
Grateley
Longbridge Deverill
Tytherington
Parsonage Down
Winterbourne Stoke
Abbey
Newton Toney or Newton Tony
Corton
Upton Lovell
Codford St. Peter
Codford St. Mary
Fisherton de la Mere
Berwick St. James
Wilsford
Boscombe Down
Boyton
Sherrington
Lake
Great Durnford
Boscombe
Allington
Over Wallop
Stockton
Bapton
Deptford
Steeple Langford
Over Street
Stapleford
Upper Woodford
Idmiston
Great Ridge
Wylye
Hanging Langford
Heale
Netton
Porton
Lopcombe Corner
Pertwood
Wylye Down
Little Langford
Middle Woodford
Salterton
Lower Woodford
Gomeldon
Winterbourne Gunner
Winterbourne Dauntsey
Chicklade
Great Wishford
Stoford
South Newton
Hurdcott
Winterbourne Earls
East Winterslow
Middle Winterslow
The Common
Hindon
Berwick St. Leonard
Farmer Giles Farmstead
Teffont Magna
Grovely Wood
Chilhampton
Stratford sub Castle
Old Sarum
Ford
Figsbury Ring
Firsdown
West Winterslow
Fonthill Bishop
Chilmark
Ridge
Little Clarendon
Philipps House
Dinton
Baverstock
Ditchampton
Ugford
Fugglestone St. Peter
Bishopdown
Laverstock
Pitton
Fonthill Gifford
Teffont Evias
Barford St. Martin
Wilton
Quidhampton
Bemerton
SALISBURY
Lower Chicksgrove
Place Tithe Barn
Compton Chamberlayne
Burcombe
Wilton House
Cath.
Petersfinger
Farley
West Tytherley
Tisbury
Upper Chicksgrove
Fovant
Netherhampton
West Harnham
East Harnham
Farley Hospital
Newtown
Pythouse
East Hatch
Sutton Mandeville
Regimental Badges (Chalk)
Salisbury
Britford
East Grimstead
West Dean
Old Wardour
Swallowcliffe
Chiselbury Hill Fort
Alderbury
Bodenham
Whaddon
West Grimstead
Dean Hill
East Dean
Semley
St. Bartholomew's Hill
Ansty
Regimental Badges
Bishopstone
Stratford Tony
Coombe Bissett
Odstock
Nunton
Homington
Donhead St. Andrew
Fifield Bavant
Broad Chalke
Stoke Farthing
Croucheston
Odstock Down
Pepperbox Hill
Carter's
Donhead St. Mary
White Sheet Hill
West End
Alvediston
Ebbesbourne Wake
Charlton
Whiteparish
Shaftesbury
Milkwell
Ludwell
Bowerchalke
Newton
Cann Common
Charlton
Berwick St. John
Woodminton
Winklebury Camp Hill Fort
Rockbourne Down
Wick Down
Wick
Downton
Morgan's Vale
Redlynch
Newhouse
Melbury Abbas
Flying Aces
Win Green
Martin Drove End
Martin Down
Martin
Breamore House
Countryside Museum
Woodfalls
North Charford
Lover
Hamptworth
Hamptworth Lodge
Plaitford
Compton Abbas
Compton Abbas
CHASE
New Town
Woodyates
Tidpit
Tollard Royal
Deanland
Whitsbury
Upper Street
Hale
Landford
Fontmell Magna
Ashmore
Larmer Tree
Woodcutts
Sixpenny Handley
Pentridge
Rockbourne
Outwick
Breamore
Canada
Well Bottom
Tollard Farnham
Pentridge Hill
Woodgreen
Nomansland
CRANBOURNE
Dean
Upper Burgate
Lower Burgate
Furzley
Farnham
Gussage St. Andrew
Monkton Up Wimborne
Boveridge
Damerham
Rockbourne Roman Villa
NEW FOREST
Bramshaw
Newbridge
Minchington
Sandleheath
Alderholt Mill
Ashford
Fordingbridge
Godshill
Fritham
Stubhampton
Chettle
Chettle House
Cashmoor
Cranborne Manor
Cranborne
Crendell
Cripplestyle
Stuckton
Blissford
Brook
Upper Canterton
Rufus Stone
Tarrant Gunville
Gussage St. Michael
Wimborne St. Giles
Alderholt
Daggons
Bickton
Frogham
Hungerford
Tarrant Hinton
Gussage All Saints
Edmondsham
North Gorley
NEW FOREST
HAMPSHIRE
Minstead
Stoney Cross
Furzey
Newtown
Long Crichel
Sovell Down
Knowlton Circles & Church
Dorset Heavy Horse Centre
South Gorley
Linwood
Canadian Monument
Tarrant Launceston
Pimperne
Tarrant Monkton
Woodlands
Whitmore
Verwood
Ringwood Forest
Harbridge
Ibsley
Mockbeggar
Moyles Court
NATIONAL PARK
Deer Fields
Pikeshill
Emery Down
Royal Signals
Blandford Camp
Manswood
Moor Crichel
Claylake
Ebblake
Ellingham
Rockford
Bolderwood Arboretum
Fireplace Reptiliary
Blandford Forum
Hogstock
Witchampton
Horton
Chalbury
Wigbeth
Chalbury Common
Crab Orchard
Moors Valley
Blashford
Hangersley
Linford
Bolderwood Ornamental Drive
Oak
Bank
Tarrant Rawston
Langton
Hinton
Mannington
Ringwood
Poulner
A361
A3102
A342
A365
A350
A360
A3098
B3098
A346
A338
A345
A342
A3026
A303
B3084
A343
A30
A36
A344
A3028
B3086
B3083
B390
B3414
A303
B3089
A3094
A354
A27
B3081
B3079
B3080
B3078
A31
A338

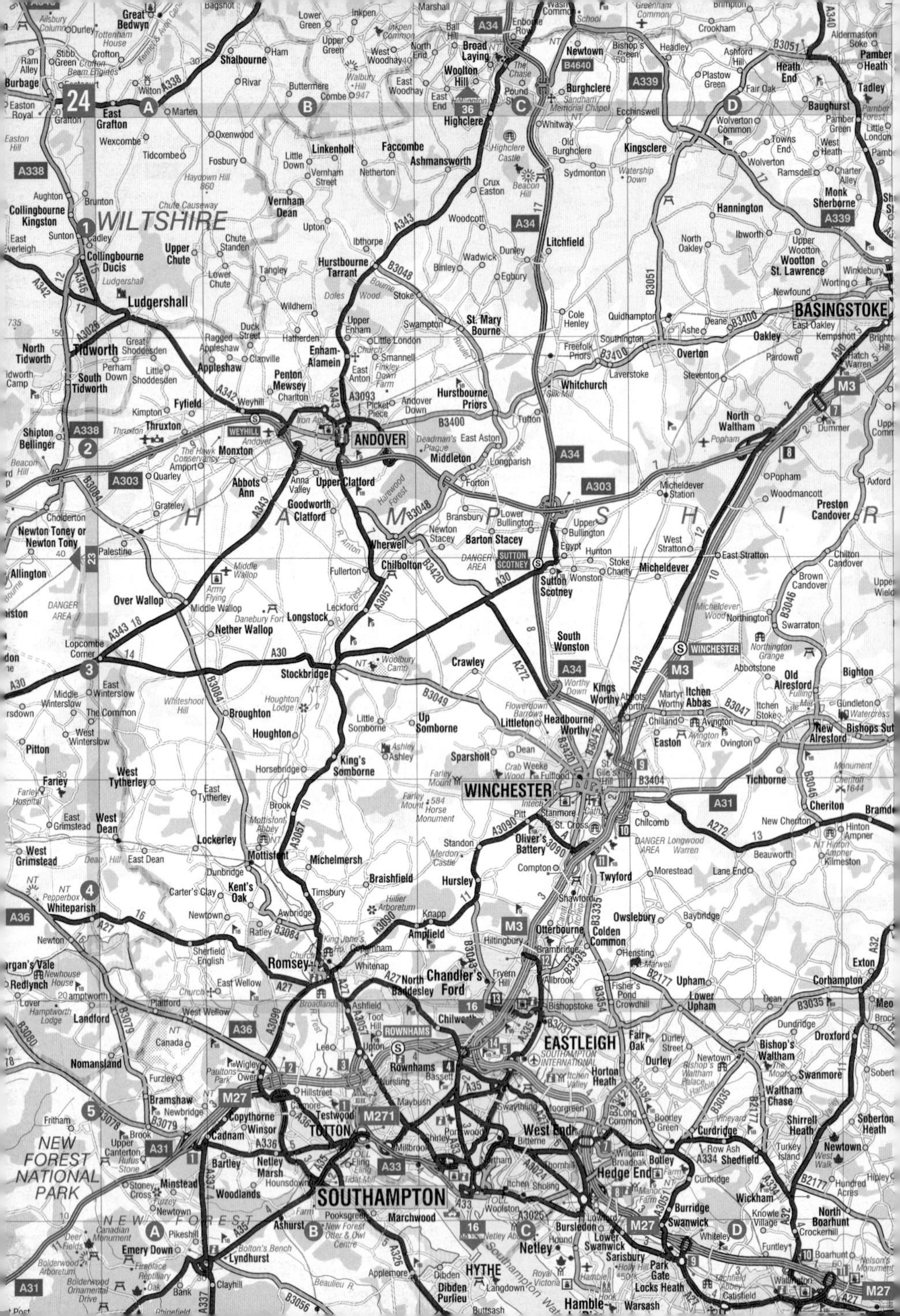
24
WILTSHIRE
HAMPSHIRE
NEW FOREST NATIONAL PARK
NEW FOREST
Great Bedwyn
Bagshot
Lower Green
Inkpen
Marshall
Ball Hill
A34
Enborne Row
Greenham Common
Crookham
A340
Aldermaston Soke
Durley
Tottenham House
Upper Green
Inkpen Common
Broad Laying
Newtown
Bishop's Green
Headley
B3051
Pamber Heath
Ram Alley
Stibb Green
Crofton
Shalbourne
Ham
West Woodhay
North End
Woolton Hill
The Chase
B4640
Plastow Green
Ashford Hill
Heath End
Tadley
Burbage
Wilton
A338
Rivar
Buttermere
East Woodhay
Pound St
Burghclere
Sandham Memorial Chapel
A339
Fair Oak
Easton Royal
Grafton
East Grafton
Marten
Combe
East End
36
Highclere
Ecchinswell
Baughurst
Pamber Green
Wexcombe
Oxenwood
Whitway
Wolverton Common
Little London
Tidcombe
Linkenholt
Faccombe
Highclere Castle
Old Burghclere
Kingsclere
Towns End
West Heath
Fosbury
Little Down
Vernham Street
Netherton
Ashmansworth
Beacon Hill
Sydmonton
Watership Down
Wolverton
Ramsdell
Charter Alley
Haydown Hill 860
Crux Easton
Monk Sherborne
Aughton
Brunton
Vernham Dean
Collingbourne Kingston
Chute Causeway
A339
Hannington
Sunton
Cadley
Upton
Woodcott
A34
East Everleigh
Upper Chute
Chute Standen
Ibthorpe
Litchfield
Ibworth
Upper Wootton
Collingbourne Ducis
A343
Dunley
North Oakley
Wootton St. Lawrence
Ludgershall
Tangley
Hurstbourne Tarrant
Binley
Wadwick
Egbury
Winklebury
Lower Chute
B3048
Worting
Ludgershall
Doles Wood
Stoke
B3051
Newfound
A342
A3026
Wildhern
Cole Henley
BASINGSTOKE
Duck Street
Upper Enham
Swampton
St. Mary Bourne
Quidhampton
Deane
B3400
East Oakley
Kempshott
North Tidworth
Great Shoddesden
Ragged Appleshaw
Hatherden
Little London
Ashe
Tidworth
Enham-Alamein
Freefolk Priors
Southington
Oakley
Perham Down
Clanville
Smannell
B3400
Overton
Pardown
Tidworth Camp
South Tidworth
Little Shoddesden
Appleshaw
Penton Mewsey
East Anton
Finkley Down Farm
Laverstoke
Steventon
Hatch Warren
A3093
Hurstbourne Priors
Whitchurch
M3
Kimpton
Fyfield
Charlton
Picket Piece
Andover Down
Silk Mill
Weyhill
A343
B3400
North Waltham
Thruxton
Iron Age
Tufton
Shipton Bellinger
A338
WEYHILL
ANDOVER
Deadman's Plague
East Aston
Popham
Dummer
Monxton
The Hawk Conservancy
Middleton
Longparish
A34
Amport
Beacon Hill
Quarley
Anna Valley
Upper Clatford
Harewood Forest
Forton
Popham
A303
B3084
A303
Abbots Ann
Micheldever Station
Woodmancott
Axford
Grateley
Goodworth Clatford
B3048
Bransbury
Lower Bullington
Preston Candover
Cholderton
Upper Bullington
Newton Toney or Newton Tony
A343
Wherwell
Newton Stacey
Barton Stacey
Egypt
Hunton
West Stratton
R. Anton
DANGER AREA
SUTTON SCOTNEY
Stoke Charity
Chilton Candover
23
Palestine
Fullerton
Chilbolton
B3420
East Stratton
Micheldever
Allington
Wonston
Brown Candover
Middle Wallop
A30
Sutton Scotney
Army Flying
Over Wallop
Middle Wallop
Danebury Fort
Leckford
A3057
Micheldever Wood
Northington
B3046
DANGER AREA
Longstock
Swarraton
Nether Wallop
South Wonston
Lopcombe Corner
A343
Northington Grange
WINCHESTER
A30
A33
A272
Abbotstone
Bighton
Stockbridge
Woolbury Camp
Crawley
A34
M3
East Winterslow
Middle Winterslow
Worthy Down
Kings Worthy
Abbots Worthy
Martyr Worthy
Itchen Abbas
Old Alresford
Whiteshoot Hill
B3049
Flowerdown Barrows
Headbourne Worthy
Chilland
Itchen Stoke
Gundleton
B3047
Avington
The Common
B3084
Houghton Lodge
Little Somborne
Up Somborne
Littleton
Fulling Mill
Watercress
West Winterslow
Broughton
Houghton
Ashley
Avington Park
Ovington
New Alresford
Bishops Sutton
Pitton
Easton
Sparsholt
Dean
King's Somborne
Crab Wood
Weeke
Fulflood
St. Giles's Hill
Tichborne
Farley
Horsebridge
Farley Mount
WINCHESTER
B3404
Monument
Cheriton 1644
West Tytherley
East Tytherley
Farley Mount
584
Horse Monument
Intech
A31
B3046
Farley Hospital
Brook
A3057
Pitt
Stanmore
Cath.
Cheriton
East Grimstead
West Dean
Mottisfont Abbey
A3090
St. Cross
Chilcomb
New Cheriton
A272
Hinton Ampner
Lockerley
Standon
Oliver's Battery
DANGER AREA
Longwood Warren
Beauworth
West Grimstead
Dean Hill
East Dean
Mottisfont
Michelmersh
Merdon Castle
Compton
Morestead
Lane End
Kilmeston
Dunbridge
Braishfield
Hursley
Twyford
Pepperbox Hill
Carter's Clay
Kent's Oak
Timsbury
Hillier Arboretum
Shawford
B3335
Whiteparish
A36
A27
Newtown
Awbridge
Knapp
Otterbourne
Colden Common
Owslebury
Baybridge
Ratley
B3084
A3090
Ampfield
M3
Newton
Sherfield English
King John's
Cupernham
Hiltingbury
Brambridge
Hensting
Marwell
A32
Exton
Redlynch
Newhouse
Romsey
Whitenap
North Baddesley
Chandler's Ford
Fryern Hill
Allbrook
B2177
Upham
Corhampton
East Wellow
A27
Fisher's Pond
Lower Upham
Lover
Hamptworth Lodge
Landford
Plaitford
West Wellow
Broadlands
Ashfield
16
Chilworth
Bishopstoke
Crowdhill
B3354
B3035
Meonstoke
A36
A3090
A3057
Toot Hill
ROWNHAMS
B3037
Dundridge
Droxford
B3080
B3079
Canada
Lee
EASTLEIGH
Fair Oak
Durley Street
Bishop's Waltham
SOUTHAMPTON INTERNATIONAL
Nomansland
Wigley
Upton
Horton Heath
Durley
Newtown
Swanmore
Soberton
Furzley
Paultons Park
Ower
Rownhams
Bassett
Itchen Valley
Bishop's Waltham Palace
Bramshaw
Newbridge
M27
Hillstreet
Bursling
Maybush
B3354
Waltham Chase
Shirrell Heath
Soberton Heath
Fritham
B3078
Copythorne
Calmore
Testwood
M271
Swaythling
Moorgreen
Long Common
Boorley Green
Curdridge
Brook
B3079
Cadnam
Winsor
TOTTON
Shirley
Portswood
West End
Bitterne
Row Ash
Shedfield
Newtown
Upper Canterton
A31
A336
Millbrook
Wildern
Botley
A334
Turkey Island
West Walk
Rufus Stone
Bartley
Netley Marsh
A33
Northam
A3024
Thornhill
Hedge End
Curbridge
B2177
Hundred Acres
Stoneycross
Minstead
Woodlands
Eling
Hounsdown
Itchen
Sholing
Manor Farm
Wickham
Burridge
North Boarhunt
Furzey Gardens
Newtown
SOUTHAMPTON
Woolston
A3025
Lowford
A3051
Knowle Village
Canadian Monument
Ashurst
Pooksgreen
Marchwood
16
Bursledon
M27
Swanwick
D
Crockerhill
Deer Fields
Pikeshill
A35
New Forest Otter & Owl Centre
Netley Abbey
Hound
Lower Swanwick
Whiteley
Funtley
Bolderwood Arboretum
Emery Down
Bolton's Bench
Lyndhurst
A326
HYTHE
Netley
Royal Victoria
Sarisbury
Holly Hill
Park Gate
Boarhunt
Nelson's Monument
Fireplace
Reptiliary
Applemore
Dibden
Langdown
Southampton Water
Hamble
Locks Heath
Titchfield
Wallington
Bolderwood Ornamental Drive
A31
Bank
Clayhill
A337
Beaulieu R.
Dibden Purlieu
B3056
Buttsash
Hamble
Warsash
A27
M27

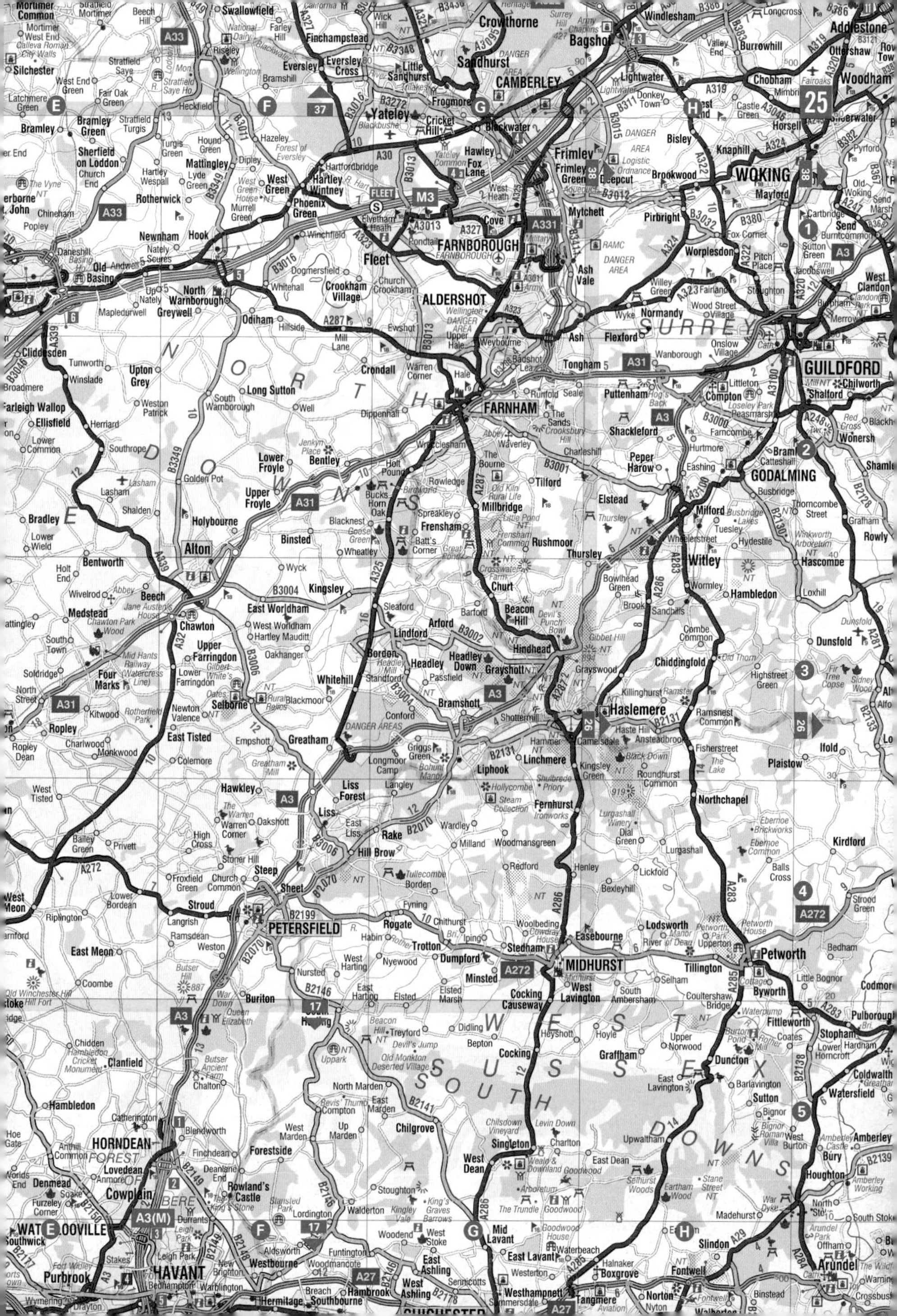

25
Crowthorne
Bagshot
Windlesham
Addlestone
Sandhurst
CAMBERLEY
Yateley
Blackwater
Frimley
Fleet
FARNBOROUGH
ALDERSHOT
WOKING
GUILDFORD
FARNHAM
Godalming
Haslemere
Alton
PETERSFIELD
MIDHURST
Petworth
HAVANT
HORNDEAN
WATERLOOVILLE
Cowplain
Arundel
Liphook
Liss
Selborne
Chawton
Bentley
Hindhead
Grayshott
Milford
Witley
Chiddingfold
Hook
Odiham
Old Basing
Silchester
Eversley
Hartley Wintney
Crondall
Tongham
Ash
Pirbright
Worplesdon
Chobham
Compton
Shalford
Elstead
Frensham
Tilford
Thursley
Churt
Kingsley
Medstead
Four Marks
Ropley
East Meon
Buriton
Clanfield
Hambledon
Rowland's Castle
Emsworth
Westbourne
Singleton
Cocking
West Dean
Fernhurst
Northchapel
Kirdford
Fittleworth
Duncton
Graffham
Sutton
Bury
Amberley
Slindon
Fontwell
Tangmere
Westhampnett
Boxgrove
Petersfield
A3
A31
A33
A272
A27
A3(M)
M3
S U R R E Y
N O R T H D O W N S
W E S T S U S S E X
S O U T H D O W N S
FOREST OF BERE
26
37
38
17

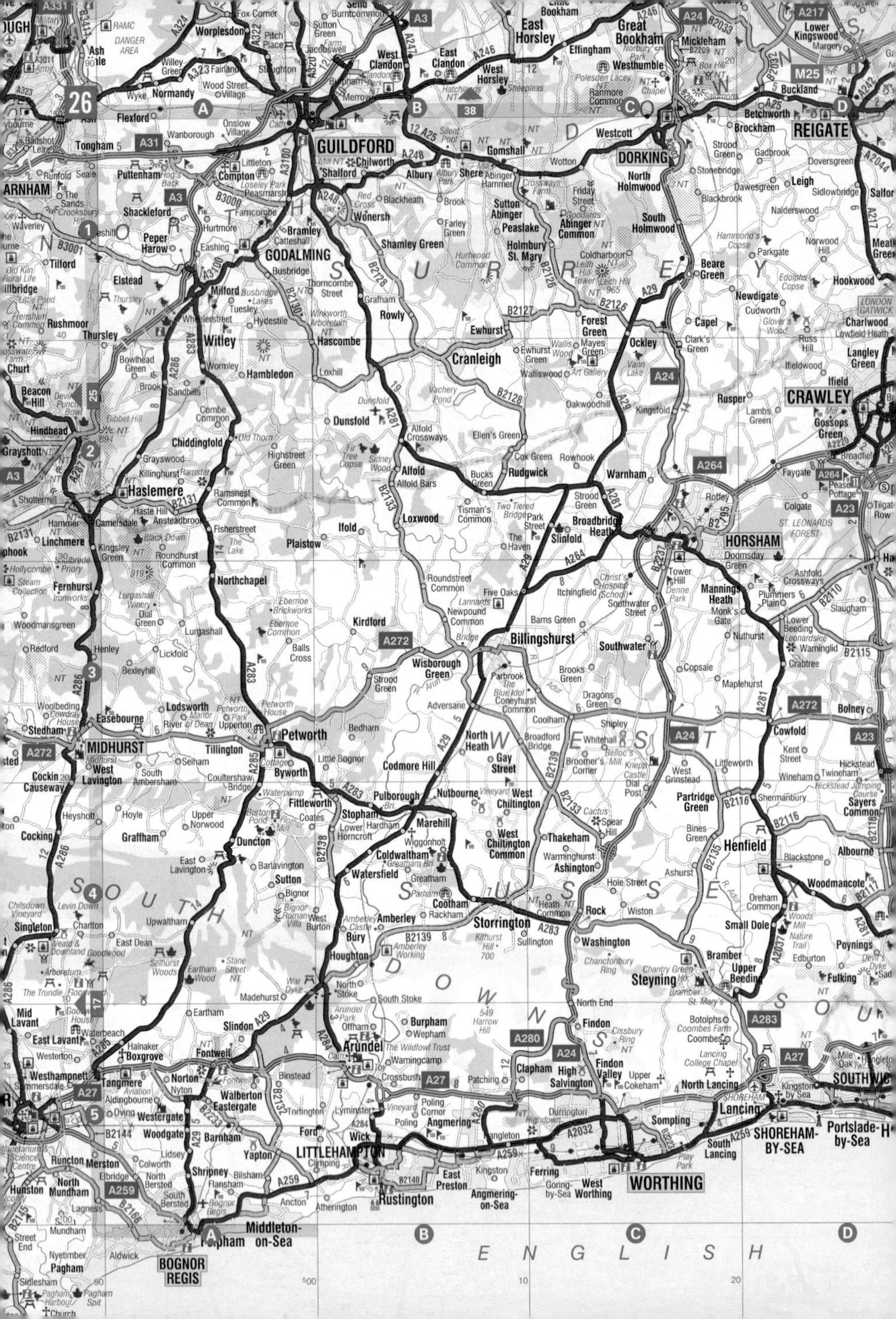

26
A
B
C
D
GUILDFORD
DORKING
REIGATE
CRAWLEY
HORSHAM
GODALMING
MIDHURST
WORTHING
BOGNOR REGIS
SHOREHAM-BY-SEA
LITTLEHAMPTON
Worplesdon
Fox Corner
Pitch Place
Sutton Green
Burntcommon
Jacobswell
Stoughton
Ash
Normandy
Wyke
Flexford
Wood Street Village
Onslow Village
Wanborough
Tongham
Seale
Runfold
Puttenham
Compton
Littleton
Shalford
Chilworth
Albury
Shere
Gomshall
Abinger Hammer
Wotton
Westcott
East Horsley
West Horsley
Effingham
Great Bookham
Mickleham
Westhumble
Ranmore Common
West Clandon
East Clandon
Merrow
Burpham
Lower Kingswood
Buckland
Betchworth
Brockham
Strood Green
Gadbrook
Leigh
Doversgreen
Dawesgreen
Sidlowbridge
North Holmwood
South Holmwood
Beare Green
Newdigate
Capel
Clark's Green
Ockley
Forest Green
Mayes Green
Ewhurst
Ewhurst Green
Walliswood
Cranleigh
Peaslake
Holmbury St. Mary
Sutton Abinger
Abinger Common
Friday Street
Coldharbour
Leith Hill 965
Wonersh
Bramley
Blackheath
Farley Green
Shamley Green
Peasmarsh
Farncombe
Hurtmore
Shackleford
Peper Harow
Eashing
Elstead
Tilford
Milford
Witley
Wormley
Thursley
Rushmoor
Churt
Beacon Hill
Hindhead
Grayshott
Busbridge
Hydestile
Tuesley
Hambledon
Thorncombe Street
Grafham
Rowly
Hascombe
Loxhill
Dunsfold
Alfold Crossways
Alfold
Alfold Bars
Loxwood
Ifold
Plaistow
Chiddingfold
Grayswood
Killinghurst
Haslemere
Haste Hill
Camelsdale
Ramsnest Common
Fisherstreet
Kingsley Green
Roundhurst Common
Northchapel
Linchmere
Fernhurst
Lurgashall
Dial Green
Lickfold
Henley
Bexleyhill
Woolbeding
Easebourne
Lodsworth
Stedham
Tillington
Petworth
Byworth
Cocking Causeway
West Lavington
South Ambersham
Selham
Coultershaw Bridge
Heyshott
Cocking
Graffham
Duncton
Upper Norwood
East Lavington
Barlavington
Sutton
Bignor
West Burton
Singleton
Charlton
East Dean
Upwaltham
Mid Lavant
East Lavant
Westerton
Westhampnett
Halnaker
Boxgrove
Tangmere
Slindon
Fontwell
Eartham
Madehurst
Arundel
Norton
Walberton
Eastergate
Westergate
Woodgate
Barnham
Yapton
Ford
Wick
Lyminster
Climping
Shripney
Bilsham
Flansham
North Bersted
South Bersted
Colworth
Merston
Runcton
North Mundham
Hunston
Middleton-on-Sea
Felpham
Aldwick
Pagham
Sidlesham
Nyetimber
Rustington
Atherington
Ancton
East Preston
Angmering
Angmering-on-Sea
Poling
Kingston
Ferring
Goring-by-Sea
West Worthing
High Salvington
Findon Valley
Findon
Clapham
Patching
Durrington
Upper Cokeham
Sompting
Lancing
North Lancing
South Lancing
Portslade-by-Sea
Southwick
Kingston by Sea
Coombes
Botolphs
Bramber
Upper Beeding
Steyning
Small Dole
Edburton
Fulking
Poynings
Woodmancote
Henfield
Blackstone
Albourne
Sayers Common
Shermanbury
Partridge Green
West Grinstead
Littleworth
Cowfold
Bolney
Wineham
Twineham
Hickstead
Warnham
Rowhook
Rudgwick
Bucks Green
Slinfold
Broadbridge Heath
Strood Green
Itchingfield
Christ's Hospital
Southwater
Southwater Street
Barns Green
Billingshurst
Five Oaks
Newpound Common
Roundstreet Common
Kirdford
Wisborough Green
Strood Green
Balls Cross
Adversane
Coneyhurst Common
Coolham
Shipley
North Heath
Gay Street
Codmore Hill
Pulborough
Nutbourne
West Chiltington
West Chiltington Common
Thakeham
Ashington
Warminghurst
Storrington
Sullington
Washington
Heath Common
Rock
Wiston
Cootham
Amberley
Bury
Houghton
Greatham
Coldwaltham
Watersfield
Marehill
Stopham
Fittleworth
Mannings Heath
Nuthurst
Maplehurst
Copsale
Monk's Gate
Lower Beeding
Crabtree
Slaugham
Faygate
Colgate
Pease Pottage
Roffey
Rusper
Kingsfold
Ifield
Gossops Green
Charlwood
Hookwood
Norwood Hill
Parkgate
ST. LEONARDS FOREST
LONDON GATWICK
M25
A3
A24
A25
A27
A29
A31
A217
A259
A264
A272
A280
A283
A286
ENGLISH
SOUTH DOWNS
SURREY
WEST SUSSEX

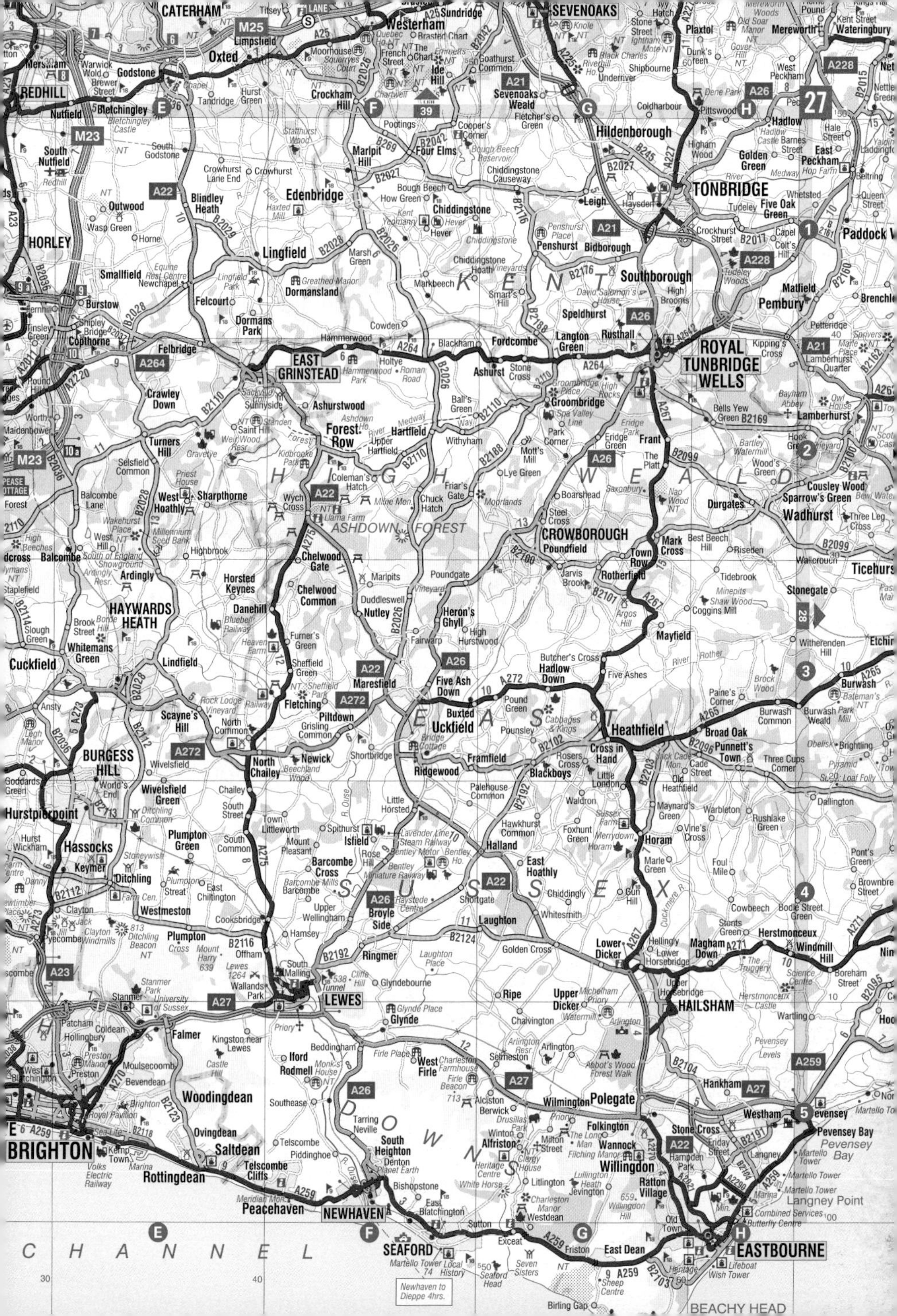

27
CATERHAM
SEVENOAKS
Westerham
Oxted
Limpsfield
Godstone
REDHILL
Bletchingley
Nutfield
South Nutfield
Crockham Hill
Ide Hill
Sevenoaks Weald
Hildenborough
TONBRIDGE
Hadlow
East Peckham
Golden Green
Five Oak Green
Paddock Wood
HORLEY
Outwood
Smallfield
Lingfield
Edenbridge
Chiddingstone
Hever
Penshurst
Bidborough
Leigh
Southborough
Pembury
Matfield
Dormansland
Felcourt
Dormans Park
Copthorne
Burstow
Felbridge
Crawley Down
EAST GRINSTEAD
Hammerwood
Holtye
Blackham
Fordcombe
Ashurst
Langton Green
Rusthall
Speldhurst
ROYAL TUNBRIDGE WELLS
Groombridge
Withyham
Hartfield
Forest Row
Ashurstwood
Turners Hill
West Hoathly
Sharpthorne
Frant
Lamberhurst
Wadhurst
Durgates
Cousley Wood
Sparrow's Green
CROWBOROUGH
Poundfield
Mark Cross
Rotherfield
Town Row
Mayfield
Ticehurst
Stonegate
ASHDOWN FOREST
HIGH WEALD
KENT
Chelwood Gate
Chelwood Common
Nutley
Duddleswell
Danehill
Horsted Keynes
Ardingly
Balcombe
HAYWARDS HEATH
Cuckfield
Whitemans Green
Lindfield
Scayne's Hill
Fletching
Sheffield Green
Maresfield
Piltdown
Heron's Ghyll
Fairwarp
Five Ash Down
Buxted
Uckfield
Hadlow Down
Heathfield
Cross in Hand
Burwash
Burwash Common
Broad Oak
Punnett's Town
Framfield
Blackboys
Ridgewood
North Chailey
Newick
BURGESS HILL
Wivelsfield Green
Hurstpierpoint
Hassocks
Keymer
Ditchling
Plumpton Green
Plumpton
Westmeston
Isfield
Barcombe Cross
Little Horsted
Halland
East Hoathly
Horam
Chiddingly
Laughton
Ringmer
Broyle Side
Golden Cross
Lower Dicker
Upper Dicker
Hellingly
HAILSHAM
Magham Down
Herstmonceux
Windmill Hill
LEWES
Glynde
Falmer
Ripe
Chalvington
Arlington
Selmeston
Iford
Rodmell
West Firle
Woodingdean
Ovingdean
Saltdean
Rottingdean
BRIGHTON
Telscombe Cliffs
Peacehaven
NEWHAVEN
SEAFORD
South Heighton
Alfriston
Polegate
Wilmington
Folkington
Wannock
Willingdon
Ratton Village
Westham
Pevensey
Pevensey Bay
Stone Cross
Langney Point
EASTBOURNE
East Dean
Friston
Exceat
BEACHY HEAD
EAST SUSSEX
SOUTH DOWNS
CHANNEL
Newhaven to Dieppe 4hrs.
M25
M23
A22
A21
A26
A27
A259
A264
A272
A275

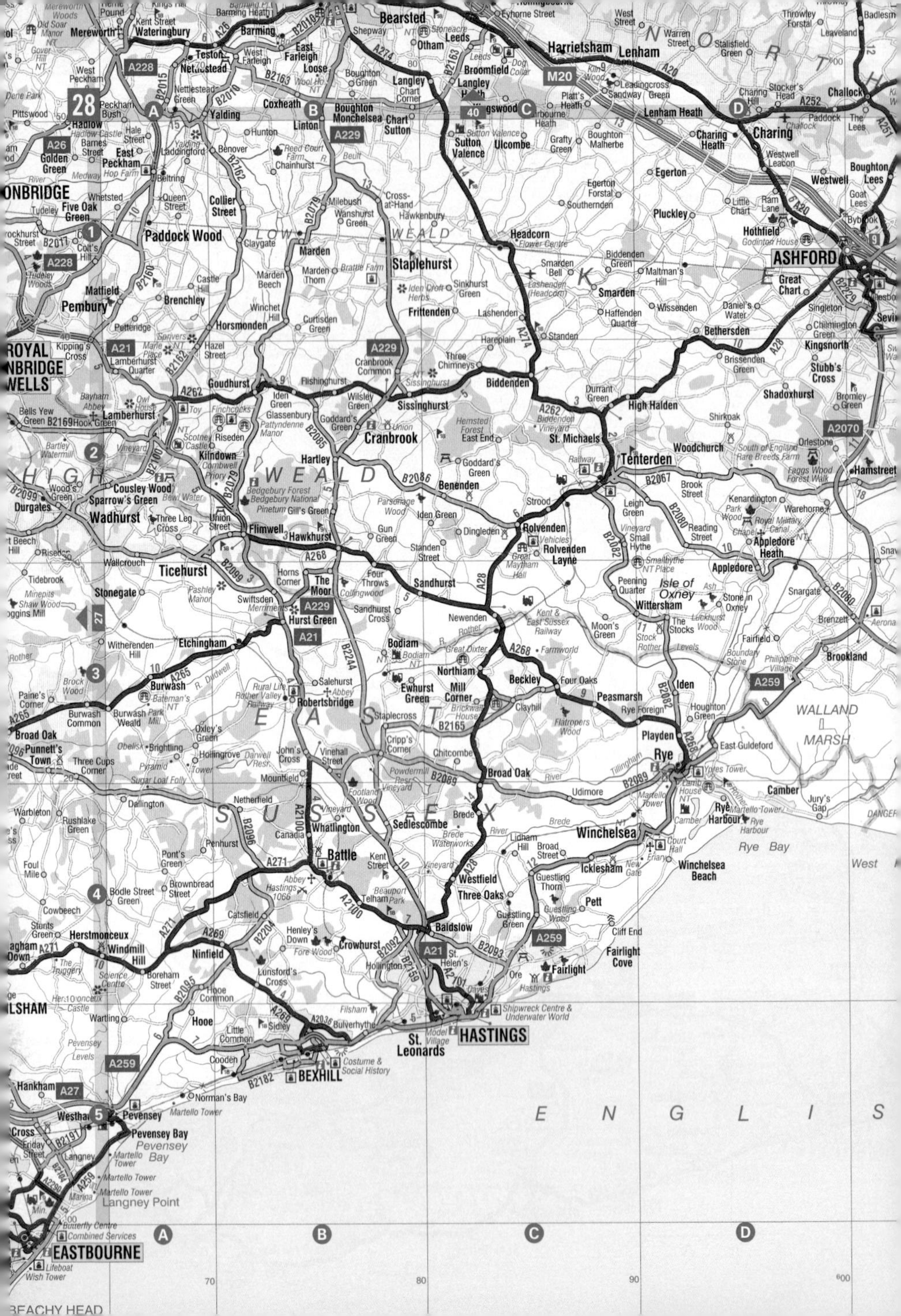

28
Mereworth
Wateringbury
Barming
Bearsted
Otham
Leeds
Harrietsham
Lenham
Teston
Nettlestead
East Farleigh
Loose
Broomfield
M20
A228
A20
Coxheath
Boughton Monchelsea
Chart Sutton
Langley
Kingswood
Lenham Heath
Challock
Charing
Hadlow
Yalding
Linton
A229
Sutton Valence
Ulcombe
Charing Heath
Egerton
Westwell
Boughton Lees
Golden Green
East Peckham
TONBRIDGE
Collier Street
Pluckley
Paddock Wood
Marden
Staplehurst
Headcorn
LOW WEALD
Hothfield
ASHFORD
Great Chart
Matfield
Pembury
Brenchley
Frittenden
Smarden
Horsmonden
Bethersden
Kingsnorth
ROYAL TUNBRIDGE WELLS
A21
A262
A274
A28
Goudhurst
Sissinghurst
Biddenden
High Halden
Shadoxhurst
Lamberhurst
Cranbrook
St. Michaels
Tenterden
Woodchurch
A2070
Hamstreet
HIGH WEALD
Cousley Wood
Durgates
Wadhurst
Benenden
Rolvenden
Rolvenden Layne
Appledore
Flimwell
Hawkhurst
Ticehurst
Stonegate
Sandhurst
Isle of Oxney
Wittersham
Snargate
Newenden
Hurst Green
Etchingham
Bodiam
Northiam
Beckley
Four Oaks
Peasmarsh
Brookland
Burwash
Robertsbridge
Ewhurst Green
Iden
A259
WALLAND MARSH
Broad Oak
Playden
Rye
Camber
EAST SUSSEX
Udimore
Rye Harbour
Rye Bay
Winchelsea
Sedlescombe
Battle
Westfield
Icklesham
Winchelsea Beach
Three Oaks
Pett
Herstmonceux
Windmill Hill
Ninfield
Crowhurst
Baldslow
Fairlight Cove
Fairlight
Hooe
HASTINGS
St. Leonards
BEXHILL
Pevensey
Pevensey Bay
ENGLISH
Langney Point
EASTBOURNE
BEACHY HEAD
A
B
C
D
70
80
90
600

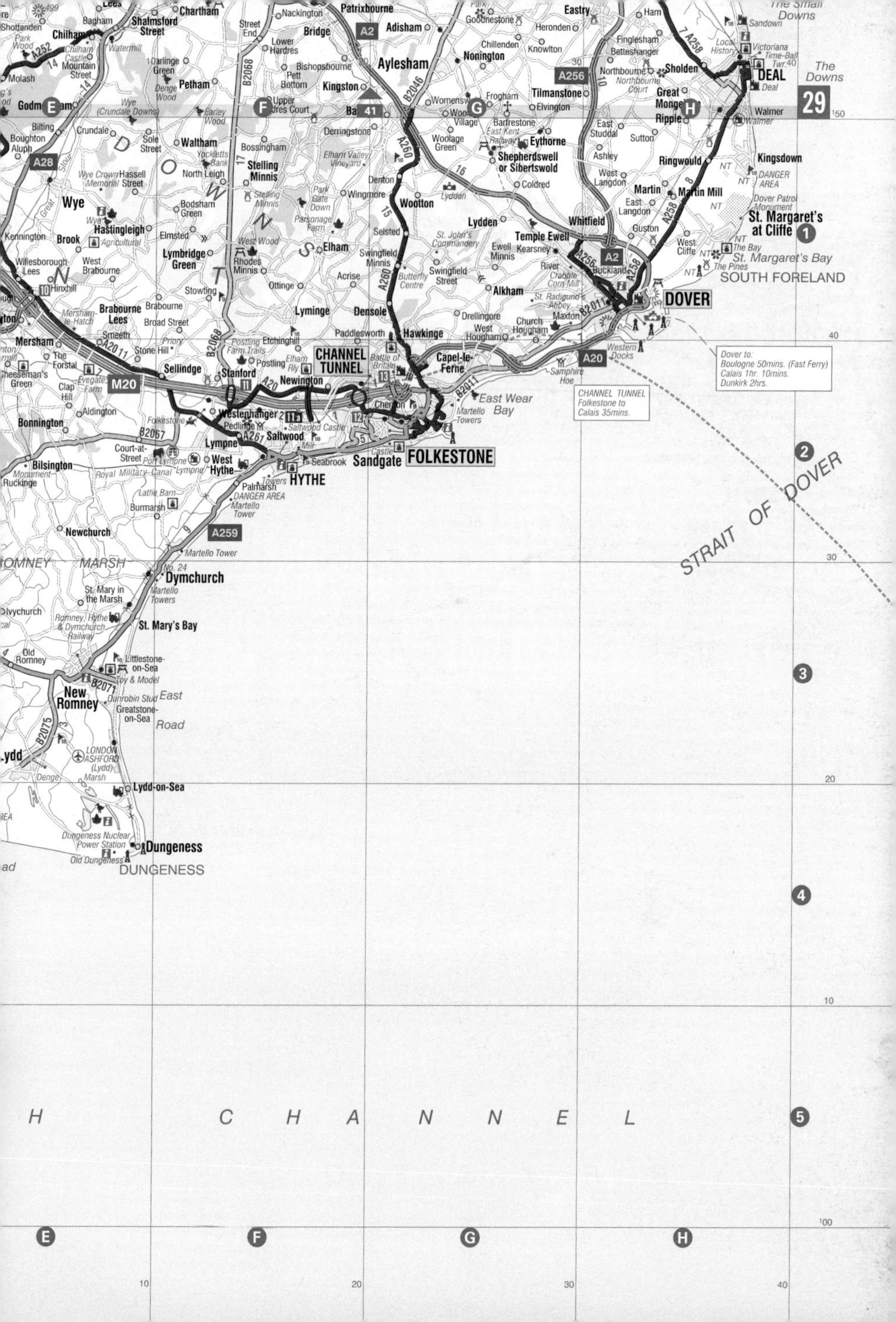

29
Chartham
Patrixbourne
Nackington
Goodnestone
Eastry
Ham
The Small Downs
Sandown
Shottenden
Bagham
Shalmsford Street
Street End
Bridge
A2
Adisham
Heronden
Finglesham
Betteshanger
Local History
Victoriana Time-Ball Twr.
Chilham
Chilham Castle
Mountain Street
Watermill
Lower Hardres
Chillenden
Knowlton
Nonington
Northbourne
Northbourne Court
Sholden
DEAL
The Downs
Deal
Molash
Garlinge Green
Bishopsbourne
Pett Bottom
Aylesham
A256
Tilmanstone
Great Mongeham
Godmersham
Petham
Denge Wood
Kingston
Upper Hardres Court
Frogham
Womenswold
Elvington
Wye (Crundale Downs)
Earley Wood
41
Woolage Village
Barfrestone
East Kent Railway
Ripple
Walmer
East Studdal
Sutton
Bilting
Crundale
Sole Street
Waltham
Bossingham
Derringstone
Elham Valley Vineyard
Woolage Green
Eythorne
Shepherdswell or Sibertswold
Boughton Aluph
Yocketts Bank
Ashley
Kingsdown
A28
Wye Crown Memorial
Hassell Street
North Leigh
Stelling Minnis
Denton
Ringwould
West Langdon
Coldred
Martin
Martin Mill
DANGER AREA
Wye
Stelling Minnis
Wingmore
Park Gate Down
Wootton
Lydden
East Langdon
Dover Patrol Monument
Bodsham Green
Parsonage Farm
Lydden
Whitfield
St. Margaret's at Cliffe
Hastingleigh
Kennington
Brook
Agricultural
Elmsted
West Wood
Selsted
St. John's Commandery
Temple Ewell
Guston
West Cliffe
The Bay
St. Margaret's Bay
Willesborough Lees
West Brabourne
Lymbridge Green
Rhodes Minnis
Elham
Swingfield Minnis
Ewell Minnis
Kearsney
A2
River
Crabble Corn Mill
Buckland
The Pines
SOUTH FORELAND
Hinxhill
Ottinge
Acrise
Butterfly Centre
Swingfield Street
Alkham
St. Radigund's Abbey
DOVER
Stowting
Mersham-le-Hatch
Brabourne Lees
Brabourne
Lyminge
Densole
Drellingore
Maxton
B2011
Smeeth
Broad Street
Paddlesworth
Hawkinge
West Hougham
Church Hougham
Mersham
Stone Hill
Priory Farm Trails
Etchinghill
Postling
Elham Rly.
CHANNEL TUNNEL
Battle of Britain
Capel-le-Ferne
Western Docks
A20
Dover to: Boulogne 50mins. (Fast Ferry) Calais 1hr. 10mins. Dunkirk 2hrs.
The Forstal
Cheeseman's Green
Clap Hill
Evegate Farm
Sellindge
Stanford
Newington
Samphire Hoe
M20
Aldington
Westenhanger
Pedlinge
Saltwood Castle
Cheriton
East Wear Bay
Martello Towers
CHANNEL TUNNEL Folkestone to Calais 35mins.
Bonnington
Folkestone
B2067
Lympne
A261
Saltwood
Court-at-Street
Port Lympne
Lympne
West Hythe
Seabrook
Sandgate
FOLKESTONE
Castle
Bilsington
Monument
Ruckinge
Royal Military Canal
HYTHE
Palmarsh
Towers
DANGER AREA
Martello Tower
Lathe Barn
Burmarsh
STRAIT OF DOVER
Newchurch
A259
Martello Tower
ROMNEY MARSH
No. 24
Dymchurch
Martello Towers
St. Mary in the Marsh
Ivychurch
Romney, Hythe & Dymchurch Railway
St. Mary's Bay
Old Romney
Littlestone-on-Sea
Toy & Model
B2071
New Romney
Dunrobin Stud
East Road
Greatstone-on-Sea
B2075
Lydd
LONDON ASHFORD (Lydd)
Denge Marsh
Lydd-on-Sea
Dungeness Nuclear Power Station
Old Dungeness
Dungeness
DUNGENESS
H C H A N N E L
E
F
G
H
1
2
3
4
5
150
40
30
20
10
100
10
20
30
40

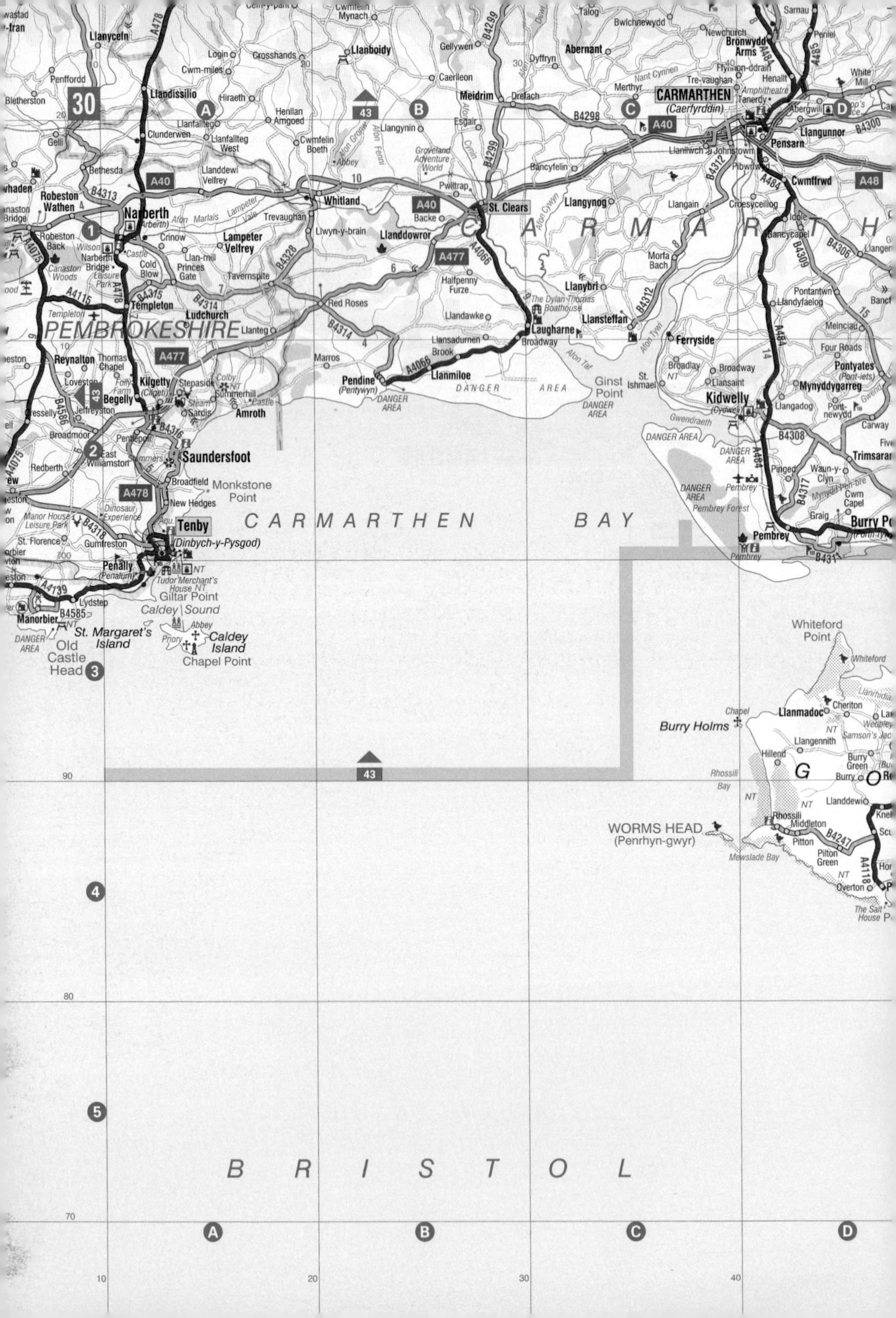
30
43
CARMARTHEN
(Caerfyrddin)
CARMARTH
PEMBROKESHIRE
CARMARTHEN BAY
BRISTOL
G O
Llanycefn
Login
Crosshands
Llanboidy
Gellywen
Talog
Bwlchnewydd
Abernant
Dyffryn
Newchurch
Bronwydd Arms
Samau
Cwm-miles
Hiraeth
Caerlleon
Meidrim
Drefach
Merthyr
Nant Cynnen
Tre-vaughan
Henallt
White Mill
Penffordd
Bletherston
Llandissilio
Llanfallteg
Llanfallteg West
Henllan Amgoed
Cwmfelin Boeth
Llangynin
Esgair
Abergwili
Llangunnor
Pensarn
Johnstown
Llanllwch
Gelli
Clunderwen
Bethesda
Llanddewi Velfrey
Groveland Adventure World
Abbey
Bancyfelin
Pibwrlwyd
Cwmffrwd
Robeston Wathen
Narberth
(Arberth)
Whitland
Pwlltrap
St. Clears
Llangynog
Llangain
Croesyceiliog
Idole
Bancycapel
Robeston Back
Canaston Woods
Narberth Bridge
Crinow
Lampeter Velfrey
Trevaughan
Llwyn-y-brain
Llanddowror
Backe
Cold Blow
Llan-mill
Princes Gate
Taverspite
Halfpenny Furze
Morfa Bach
Llanybri
The Dylan Thomas Boathouse
Templeton
Ludchurch
Red Roses
Llandawke
Laugharne
Llansteffan
Ferryside
Pontantwn
Llandyfaelog
Meinciau
Four Roads
Pontyates
(Pont-iets)
Llanteg
Llansadurnen
Broadway
Brook
Reynalton
Thomas Chapel
Marros
Llanmiloe
Pendine
(Pentywyn)
DANGER AREA
Ginst Point
St. Ishmael
Broadlay
Llansaint
Kidwelly
(Cydweli)
Mynyddygarreg
Llangadog
Pont-newydd
Carway
Kilgetty
(Cilgeti)
Stepaside
Colby
Summerhill
Amroth
Begelly
Jeffreyston
Cresselly
Broadmoor
Pentlepoir
East Williamston
Saundersfoot
Redberth
Gwendraeth
Trimsaran
Pinged
Waun-y-Clyn
Pembrey
Pembrey Forest
Cwm Capel
Graig
Burry Port
Broadfield
Monkstone Point
New Hedges
Tenby
(Dinbych-y-Pysgod)
Manor House Leisure Park
Dinosaur Experience
St. Florence
Gumfreston
Penally
(Penalum)
Tudor Merchant's House NT
Giltar Point
Caldey Sound
Lydstep
Manorbier
St. Margaret's Island
Caldey Island
Priory
Abbey
Chapel Point
Old Castle Head
Whiteford Point
Whiteford
Llanmadoc
Cheriton
Burry Holms
Chapel
Llangennith
Hillend
Burry Green
Burry
Rhossili Bay
Rhossili
Middleton
Llanddewi
Worms Head
(Penrhyn-gwyr)
Pitton
Pilton Green
Mewslade Bay
Overton
The Salt House
NT
A40
A477
A478
A4066
A484
A485
A48
B4313
B4314
B4315
B4316
B4318
B4328
B4299
B4298
B4312
B4308
B4309
B4306
B4317
B4311
B4586
B4585
A4075
A4115
A4139
B4247
A4118
B4300
A B C D
1 2 3 4 5
10 20 30 40
90 80 70

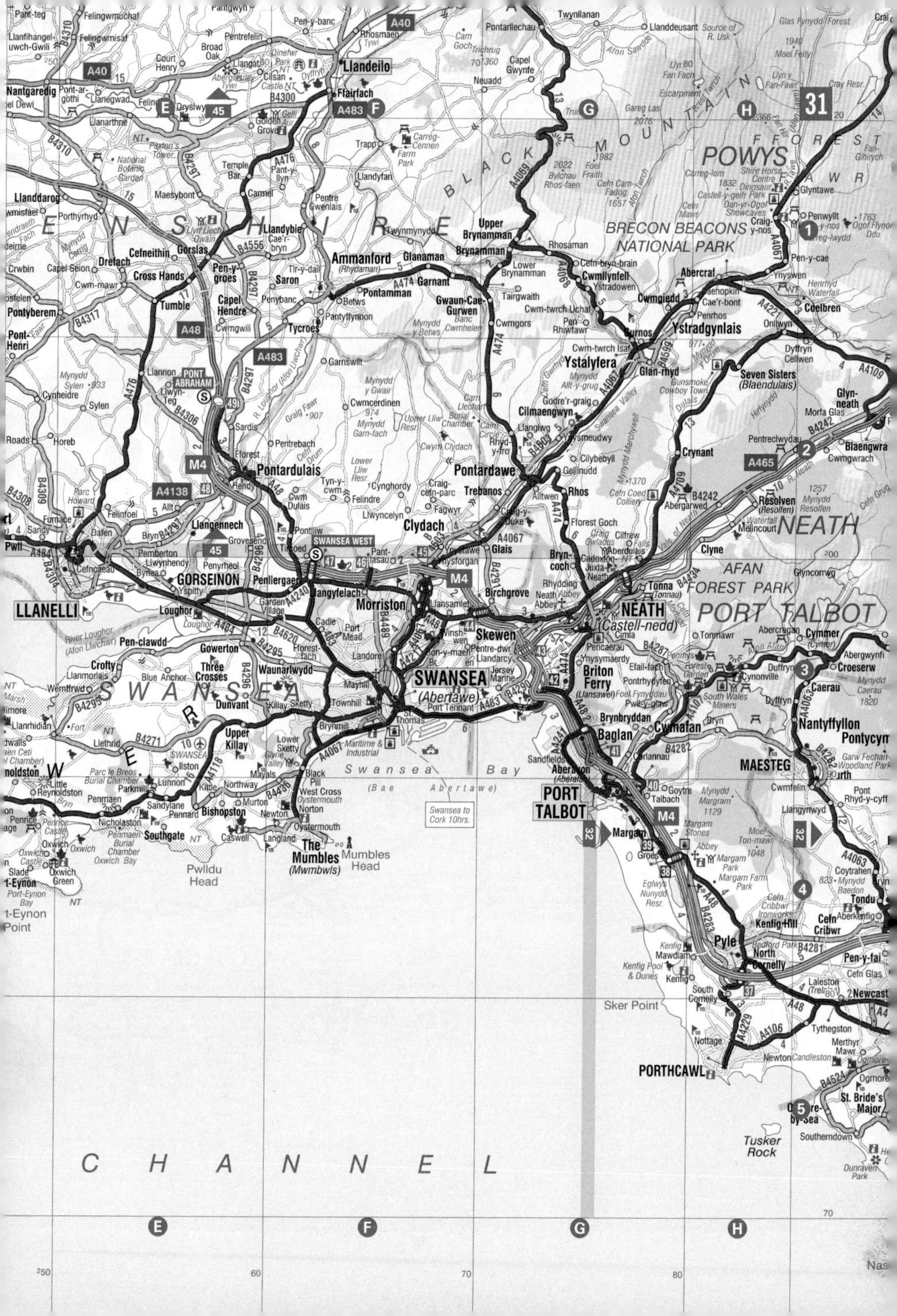
31
Llandeilo
Ffairfach
A40
A483
A48
A474
A4067
A4069
A4068
A476
A465
A4109
A484
A4138
A4240
A4118
A4063
A4229
A4106
M4
45
BLACK MOUNTAIN
BRECON BEACONS
NATIONAL PARK
POWYS
FFOREST FAWR
CARMARTHENSHIRE
Llanddarog
Cross Hands
Drefach
Tumble
Gorslas
Cefneithin
Llandybie
Penygroes
Capel Hendre
Saron
Tycroes
Ammanford
(Rhydaman)
Glanaman
Garnant
Pontamman
Betws
Pantyffynnon
Gwaun-Cae-Gurwen
Upper Brynamman
Brynamman
Lower Brynamman
Rhosaman
Cwmllynfell
Ystradowen
Cefn-bryn-brain
Tairgwaith
Cwmgors
Cwm-twrch Uchaf
Cwm-twrch Isaf
Gurnos
Ystalyfera
Ystradgynlais
Abercraf
Cwmgiedd
Coelbren
Onllwyn
Seven Sisters
(Blaendulais)
Glyn-neath
Crynant
Resolven
(Resolfen)
Melincourt
Cilmaengwyn
Pontardawe
Trebanos
Clydach
Rhos
Alltwen
Gellinudd
Cilybebyll
Glais
Craig-cefn-parc
Felindre
Garnswllt
Pontardulais
Hendy
Fforest
Llangennech
Pontlliw
Tircoed
Penllergaer
Gorseinon
Loughor
Pontyberem
Llannon
Pont Abraham
Llwyn-Teg
Sylen
Cynheidre
Horeb
Furnace
Felinfoel
Dafen
Pwll
Cefncaeau
LLANELLI
Bynea
Pemberton
Llwynhendy
Penyrheol
Gowerton
Three Crosses
Waunarlwydd
Dunvant
Crofty
Pen-clawdd
Llanrhidian
Llanmorlais
Blue Anchor
SWANSEA
(Abertawe)
SWANSEA WEST
Llangyfelach
Morriston
Landore
Cadle
Fforest-fach
Port Mead
Mayhill
Townhill
Sketty
Killay
Upper Killay
Brynmill
St. Thomas
Port Tennant
Llansamlet
Birchgrove
Skewen
Jersey Marine
Llandarcy
Swansea Bay
(Bae Abertawe)
Swansea to Cork 10hrs.
Black Pill
West Cross
Norton
Oystermouth
The Mumbles
(Mwmbwls)
Mumbles Head
Langland
Caswell
Newton
Murton
Bishopston
Pennard
Kittle
Mayals
Parkmill
Ilston
Southgate
Pwlldu Head
Nicholaston
Penmaen
Oxwich
Oxwich Green
Oxwich Bay
Penrice
Port-Eynon Point
NEATH
(Castell-nedd)
Neath Abbey
Tonna
(Tonnau)
Cadoxton-Juxta-Neath
Aberdulais
Bryn-coch
Cimla
Briton Ferry
(Llansawel)
Baglan
Cwmafan
Aberavon
(Aberafan)
PORT TALBOT
Taibach
Margam
Goytre
Groes
AFAN FOREST PARK
NEATH PORT TALBOT
Cymmer
Croeserw
Abergwynfi
Caerau
Nantyffyllon
MAESTEG
Pontycymer
Llangynwyd
Coytrahen
Tondu
Cefn Cribwr
Kenfig Hill
Pyle
North Cornelly
South Cornelly
Kenfig
Mawdlam
Sker Point
Nottage
PORTHCAWL
Newton
Tythegston
Laleston
Ogmore-by-Sea
St. Bride's Major
Southerndown
Tusker Rock
Dunraven Park
CHANNEL
E
F
G
H
250
60
70
80

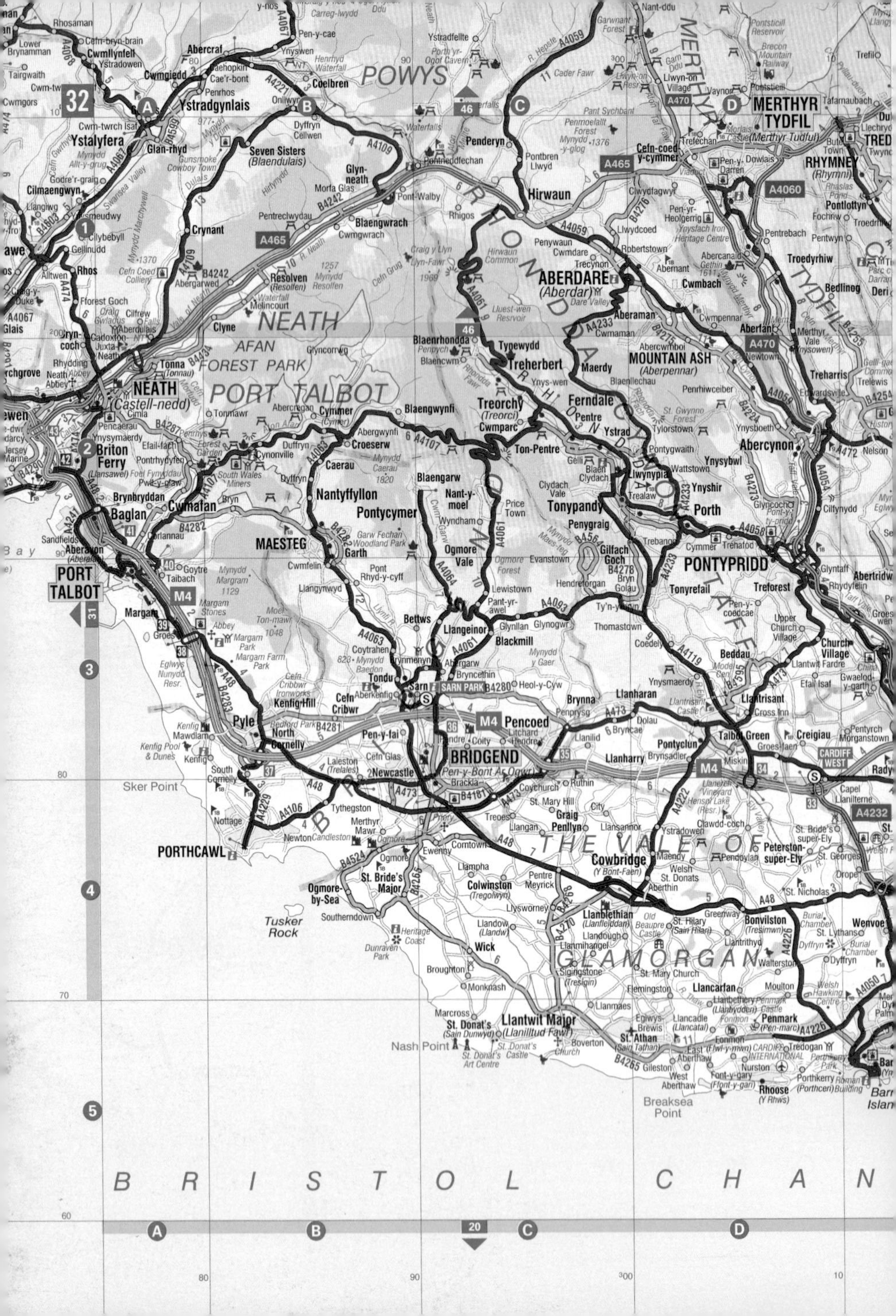

32
46
20
POWYS
MERTHYR TYDFIL
NEATH
PORT TALBOT
AFAN FOREST PARK
RHONDDA
BRIDGEND
THE VALE OF GLAMORGAN
BRISTOL CHAN
Rhosaman
Lower Brynamman
Cefn-bryn-brain
Cwmllynfell
Ystradowen
Tairgwaith
Cwm-twrch
Cwmgors
Abercraf
Caehopkin
Cae'r-bont
Penrhos
Cwmgiedd
Ystradgynlais
Onllwyn
Coelbren
Ystradfellte
Henrhyd Waterfall
Pen-y-cae
Ynyswen
Porth yr Ogof Cavern
Cader Fawr
Cwm-twrch Isaf
Ystalyfera
Glan-rhyd
Dyffryn Cellwen
Seven Sisters (Blaendulais)
Gunsmoke Cowboy Town
Godre'r-graig
Cilmaengwyn
Ynysmeudwy
Llangiwg
Swansea Valley
Mynydd Marchywel
Crynant
Clydach
Cilybebyll
Gellinudd
Rhos
Alltwen
Fforest Goch
Cefn Coed Colliery
Abergarwed
Resolven (Resolfen)
Mynydd Resolfen
Melincourt
Blaengwrach
Cwmgwrach
Glyn-neath
Morfa Glas
Pont-Walby
Pentreclwydau
Rhigos
Pontneddfechan
Penderyn
Pontbren Llwyd
Hirwaun
Waterfalls
Penmoelallt Forest
Mynydd-y-glog
Pant Sychbant
Garwnant Forest
Nant-ddu
Llwyn-on Resr.
Llwyn-on Village
Pontsticill Reservoir
Brecon Mountain Railway
Vaynor
Pontsticill
Trefil
Tafarnaubach
Cefn-coed-y-cymmer
Trefechan
Morlais Castle
(Merthyr Tudful)
Pen-y-Darren
Dowlais
Rhymney (Rhymni)
Pontlottyn
Fochriw
Troedrhiw
Pentrebach
Pentwyn
Troedyrhiw
Bedlinog
Deri
Abercanaid
Gethin
Ynysfach Iron Heritage Centre
Abernant
Cwmbach
Cwmpennar
Aberfan
Merthyr Vale (Ynysowen)
Heolgerrig
Llwydcoed
Robbertstown
Clwydfagwyr
Hirwaun Common
Penywaun
Cwmdare
Trecynon
ABERDARE (Aberdar)
Dare Valley
Aberaman
Cwmaman
Abercwmboi
MOUNTAIN ASH (Aberpennar)
Blaenllechau
Maerdy
Ferndale
Penrhiwceiber
Treharris
Edwardsville
Trelewis
Nelson
Craig y Llyn
Llyn-Fawr
Cefn Grug
Lluest-wen Resrvoir
Blaenrhondda
Penpych
Blaencwm
Tynewydd
Treherbert
Ynys-wen
Treorchy (Treorci)
Cwmparc
Ton-Pentre
Pentre
Ystrad
Gelli
Blaen Clydach
Llwynypia
Clydach Vale
Tonypandy
Trealaw
Penygraig
Ynyshir
Porth
Pontygwaith
Wattstown
Ynysybwl
Abercynon
Tylorstown
St. Gwynno Forest
Ynysboeth
Cilfynydd
Glyncoch
Pont-y-ty-pridd
Trehafod
Cymmer
Trebanog
PONTYPRIDD
Glyntaff
Treforest
Rhydyfelin
Abertridwr
Tonyrefail
Pen-y-coedcae
Upper Church Village
Church Village
Llantwit Fardre
Efail Isaf
Gwaelod-y-garth
Beddau
Llantrisant
Cross Inn
Talbot Green
Creigiau
Pentyrch
Morganstown
Groes-faen
Miskin
CARDIFF WEST
Radyr
Capel Llanilterne
Gilfach Goch
Evanstown
Hendreforgan
Bryn Golau
Ty'n-y-ywen
Thomastown
Coedely
Ynysmaerdy
Llanharan
Brynna
Penprysg
Dolau
Bryncae
Llanilid
Llanharry
Pontyclun
Brynsadler
Glyncorrwg
Tonna (Tonnau)
Cefn Mawr
Aberdulais
Cilfrew
Cadoxton Juxta-Neath
Bryn-coch
Glais
Rhydding
Neath Abbey
Llandarcy
Jersey Marine
Skewen
Briton Ferry (Llansawel)
Ynysymaerdy
Pencaerau
Cimla
Efail-fach
Pontrhydyfen
Foel Fynyddau
Pwll-y-glaw
Tonmawr
Abercregan
Cymmer (Cymer)
Abergwynfi
Blaengwynfi
Croeserw
Dyffryn
Caerau
Mynydd Caerau
South Wales Miners
Cynonville
Forest Garden
Brynbryddan
Cwmafan
Bryn
Baglan
Sandfields
Aberavon (Aberafan)
Oriannau
PORT TALBOT
Goytre
Taibach
Mynydd Margam
Margam
Margam Stones
Abbey
Margam Park
Margam Farm Park
Groes
Eglwys Nunydd Resr.
Moel Ton-mawr
Nantyffyllon
MAESTEG
Garth
Cwmfelin
Llangynwyd
Garw Fechan Woodland Park
Blaengarw
Pontycymer
Nant-y-moel
Wyndham
Price Town
Ogmore Vale
Ogmore Forest
Lewistown
Pont Rhyd-y-cyff
Pant-yr-awel
Glynllan
Glynogwr
Llangeinor
Blackmill
Bettws
Coytrahen
Brynmenyn
Abergarw
Bryncethin
Heol-y-Cyw
Mynydd y Gaer
Mynydd Baedon
Cefn Cribbwr Ironworks
Cefn Cribwr
Aberkenfig
Tondu
Sarn
SARN PARK
Kenfig Hill
Bedford Park
Pyle
North Cornelly
Kenfig
Mawdlam
Kenfig Pool & Dunes
South Cornelly
Sker Point
Nottage
PORTHCAWL
Pen-y-fai
Laleston (Trelales)
Cefn Glas
Newcastle
Pendre
Coity
Litchard
Pencoed
Hendre
BRIDGEND (Pen-y-Bont Ar Ogwr)
Brackla
Coychurch
Ruthin
St. Mary Hill
City
Treoes
Llangan
Graig Penllyn
Llansannor
Tythegston
Merthyr Mawr
Newton
Candleston
Ogmore
Ewenny
Priory
Corntown
Ogmore-by-Sea
St. Bride's Major
Southerndown
Tusker Rock
Heritage Coast
Dunraven Park
Llampha
Colwinston (Tregolwyn)
Pentre Meyrick
Llysworney
Llandow (Llandŵ)
Wick
Broughton
Monknash
Marcross
St. Donat's (Sain Dunwyd)
Nash Point
St. Donat's Castle
St. Donat's Art Centre
Llantwit Major (Llanilltud Fawr)
Church
Boverton
Cowbridge (Y Bont-Faen)
Aberthin
Maendy
Welsh St. Donats
Ystradowen
Clawdd-coch
Llanerch Vineyard
Hensol Lake (Resr.)
Pendoylan
Peterston-super-Ely
St. Bride's super-Ely
St. Georges
Drope
St. Nicholas
Llanblethian (Llanfleiddan)
Llandough
Llanmihangel
Old Beaupre Castle
St. Hilary (Sain Hilari)
Llantrithyd
Greenway
Bonvilston (Tresimwn)
Burial Chamber
Dyffryn
Wenvoe
St. Lythans
Sigingstone (Tresigin)
St. Mary Church
Walterston
Flemingston
Llancarfan
Moulton
Llanmaes
Llanbethery
Penmark Castle
Penmark (Pen-marc)
Welsh Hawking Centre
Eglwys-Brewis
Llancadle (Llancatal)
Fonmon
Fonmon Castle
St. Athan (Sain Tathan)
East Aberthaw
Aberthaw
Gileston
West Aberthaw
Font-y-gary (Ffont-y-gari)
Rhoose (Y Rhws)
Cardiff International
Tredogan
Nurston
Porthkerry
Porthkerry Park
Roman Building
Breaksea Point
Barry Island
M4
A465
A470
A4060
A4059
A4061
A4233
A4107
A4063
A4058
A473
A48
A4232
A4050
A4226
A4222
A4119
A4093
A4064
A4229
A4106
A4241
A4067
A474
A4109
A4221
A4068
B4242
B4287
B4282
B4283
B4281
B4280
B4181
B4524
B4265
B4268
B4270
B4275
B4276
B4564
B4278
B4595
B4224
B4273
B4255
B4254
B4290
B4434
B4599
B4603
A4054
A4472
1
2
3
4
5
A
B
C
D
80
90
300
10
70
60

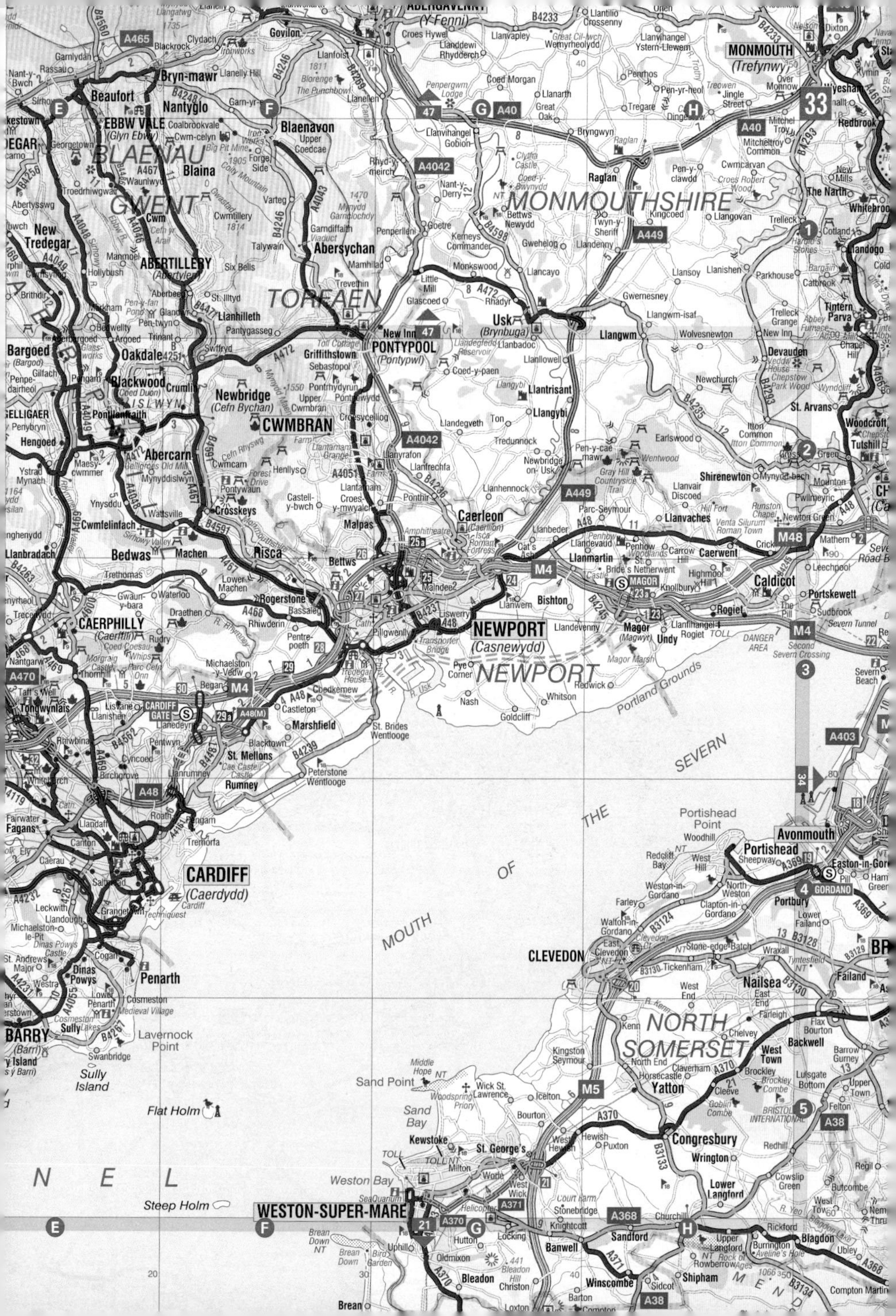

33
ABERGAVENNY
(Y-Fenni)
Govilon
Blackrock
Clydach
Llanfoist
Garnlydan
Brynmawr
Llanelly Hill
Beaufort
Nantyglo
EBBW VALE
(Glyn Ebwy)
Coalbrookvale
Cwm-celyn
Blaenavon
Upper Coedcae
Forge Side
BLAENAU
GWENT
Blaina
Georgetown
Waunlwyd
Troedrhiwgwair
Cwm
Varteg
Cwmtillery
Abersychan
Talywain
ABERTILLERY
(Abertyleri)
Six Bells
New Tredegar
Hollybush
Manmoel
Aberbeeg
St. Illtyd
Llanhilleth
Pentwyn
Trinant
Pantygasseg
Markham
Bedwellty
Argoed
Oakdale
Bargoed
Gilfach
Pengam
Blackwood
(Coed Duon)
Crumlin
Newbridge
(Cefn Bychan)
CWMBRAN
Pontllanfraith
ISLWYN
Hengoed
Penybryn
GELLIGAER
Abercarn
Maesycwmmer
Ystrad Mynach
Ynysddu
Cwmcarn
Pontywaun
Crosskeys
Wattsville
Cwmfelinfach
Llanbradach
Bedwas
Machen
Risca
Trethomas
Lower Machen
Rogerstone
Bassaleg
Rhiwderin
Draethen
Waterloo
Gwaun-y-bara
CAERPHILLY
(Caerffili)
Rudry
Nantgarw
Thornhill
Taff's Well
Tongwynlais
Lisvane
Llanishen
CARDIFF GATE
Llanedeyrn
Pentwyn
Cyncoed
Rhiwbina
Birchgrove
Whitchurch
Llanrumney
Rumney
St. Mellons
Marshfield
Castleton
Michaelston-y-Vedw
Began
Coedkernew
Peterstone Wentlooge
St. Brides Wentlooge
Fairwater
Fagans
Llandaff
Canton
Roath
Pengam
Tremorfa
CARDIFF
(Caerdydd)
Caerau
Ely
Leckwith
Llandough
Michaelston-le-Pit
Dinas Powys
St. Andrews Major
Cogan
Penarth
Lower Penarth
Cosmeston
Sully
Swanbridge
Lavernock Point
BARRY
(Barri)
Sully Island
Flat Holm
Steep Holm
TORFAEN
Griffithstown
Sebastopol
PONTYPOOL
(Pontypwl)
New Inn
Pontnewydd
Croesyceiliog
Llanyrafon
Upper Cwmbran
Henllys
Castell-y-bwch
Croes-y-mwyalch
Llantarnam
Malpas
Bettws
Ponthir
Caerleon
(Caerllion)
Llanfrechfa
Llandegveth
Tredunnock
Newbridge on-Usk
Llanhennock
Llangybi
Llantrisant
Llanllowell
Llanbadoc
Usk
(Brynbuga)
Coed-y-paen
Glascoed
Little Mill
Monkswood
Rhadyr
Llancayo
Kemeys Commander
Goetre
Penperlleni
Mamhilad
Trevethin
Garndiffaith
Nant-y-Derry
Llanvihangel Gobion
Rhyd-y-meirch
Llanellen
Llanddewi Rhydderch
Croes Hywel
Llanvapley
Coed Morgan
Llanarth
Great Oak
Bryngwyn
Clytha
Raglan
Bettws Newydd
Gwehelog
Llandenny
Twyn-y-Sheriff
Kingcoed
Llangovan
MONMOUTHSHIRE
MONMOUTH
(Trefynwy)
Llantilio Crossenny
Llanvihangel Ystern-Llewern
Penrhos
Pen-yr-heol
Tregare
Dingestow
Jingle Street
Mitchel Troy
Mitcheltroy Common
Cwmcarvan
Pen-y-clawdd
Trelleck
Llanishen
Llansoy
Parkhouse
Gwernesney
Llangwm-isaf
Llangwm
Wolvesnewton
Devauden
Newchurch
St. Arvans
Itton Common
Earlswood
Shirenewton
Mynydd-bach
Mounton
Pwllmeyric
Llanvair Discoed
Llanvaches
Parc-Seymour
Penhow
Carrow Hill
Caerwent
Crick
Mathern
Caldicot
Portskewett
Sudbrook
Rogiet
Llanfihangel Rogiet
Undy
Magor
(Magwyr)
MAGOR
Knollbury
Llanmartin
Llandevaud
Llanbeder
Cat's Ash
Bishton
Llanwern
Llandevenny
Liswerry
Maindee
Pillgwenlly
NEWPORT
(Casnewydd)
Pye Corner
Nash
Whitson
Goldcliff
Redwick
Portland Grounds
Tintern Parva
Llandogo
Whitebrook
Redbrook
Wyesham
Woodcroft
Tutshill
Chapel Hill
Dixton
Second Severn Crossing
Severn Beach
SEVERN
THE
MOUTH
OF
Portishead Point
Woodhill
Portishead
Avonmouth
Redcliff Bay
West Hill
Sheepway
Easton-in-Gordano
Pill
Weston-in-Gordano
North Weston
Portbury
Farley
Clapton-in-Gordano
Walton-in-Gordano
East Clevedon
CLEVEDON
Stone-edge Batch
Wraxall
Tickenham
Nailsea
Failand
Lower Failand
West End
East End
Farleigh
Kenn
NORTH
SOMERSET
Chelvey
Backwell
Flax Bourton
Barrow Gurney
Kingston Seymour
North End
Horsecastle
Claverham
Yatton
West Town
Brockley
Cleeve
Lulsgate Bottom
Felton
BRISTOL INTERNATIONAL
Sand Point
Middle Hope
Sand Bay
Wick St. Lawrence
Icelton
Bourton
Kewstoke
St. George's
Hewish
West Hewish
Puxton
Congresbury
Wrington
Redhill
Milton
Worle
West Wick
Weston Bay
WESTON-SUPER-MARE
Locking
Banwell
Sandford
Churchill
Lower Langford
Cowslip Green
Butcombe
Regil
Knightcott
Stonebridge
Hutton
Uphill
Brean Down
Oldmixon
Bleadon
Christon
Winscombe
Sidcot
Shipham
Upper Langford
Rowberrow
Rickford
Burrington
Blagdon
Ubley
Compton Martin
Barton
Loxton
Brean
N E L
M4
M5
M48
A40
A48
A449
A4042
A370
A371
A368
A38
A403
A465

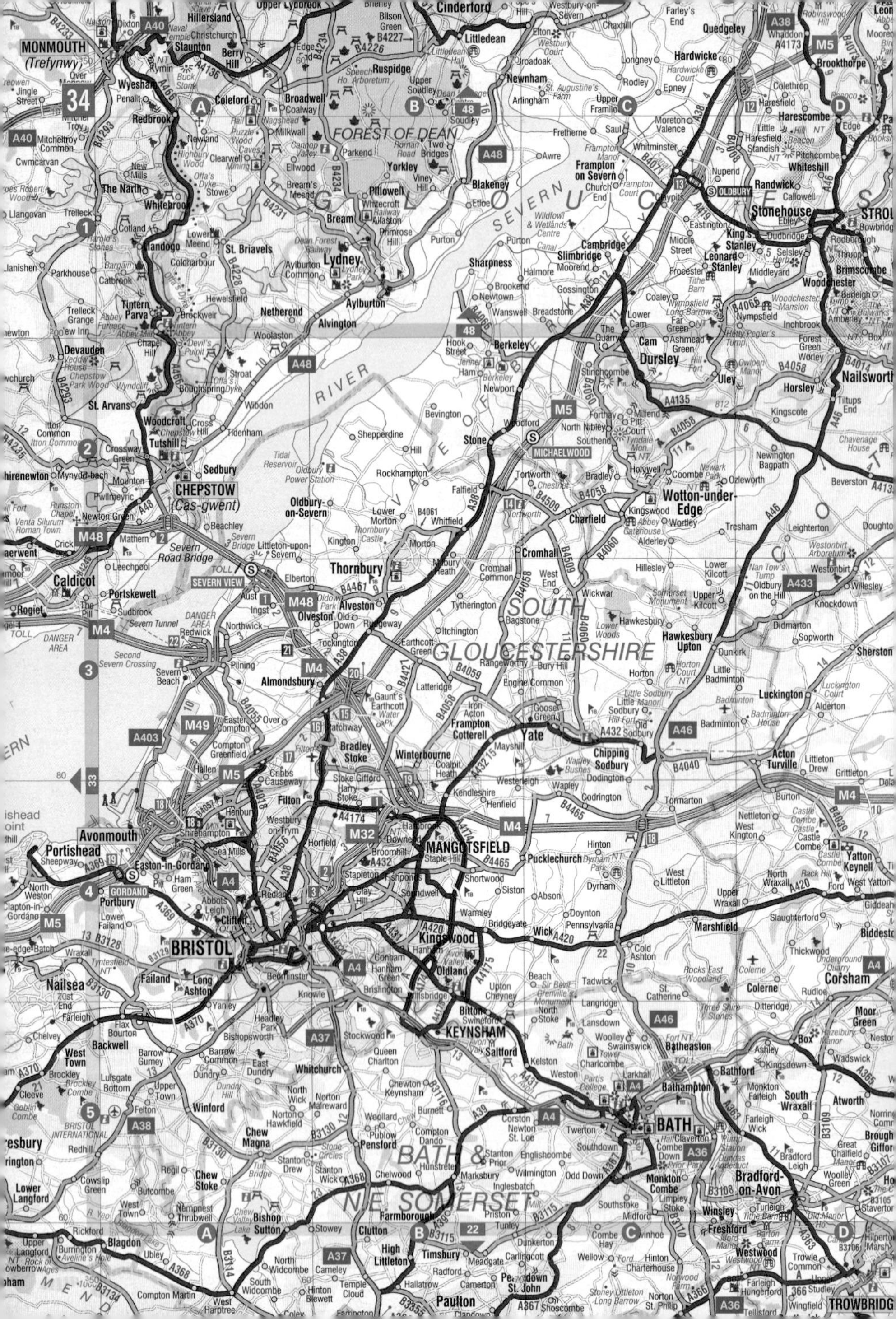
34
MONMOUTH
(Trefynwy)
Dixton
Hillersland
Staunton
Berry Hill
Upper Lydbrook
Cinderford
Littledean
Westbury-on-Severn
Chaxhill
Farley's End
Quedgeley
Hardwicke
Whaddon
Brookthorpe
Wyesham
Penallt
Redbrook
Newland
Coleford
Broadwell
Coalway
Ruspidge
Upper Soudley
Soudley
Newnham
Arlingham
Longney
Rodley
Epney
Upper Framilode
Saul
Moreton Valence
Harescombe
Haresfield
FOREST OF DEAN
Milkwall
Parkend
Yorkley
Two Bridges
Viney Hill
Clearwell
Ellwood
Blakeney
Awre
Fretherne
Whitminster
Frampton on Severn
Nupend
Standish
Pitchcombe
Whiteshill
Randwick
Cwmcarvan
Mitcheltroy Common
The Narth
Whitebrook
Bream's Meend
Pillowell
Whitecroft
Bream
Etloe
Church End
Claypits
OLDBURY
Callowell
Stonehouse
Ebley
STROUD
Trelleck
Llangovan
Cotland
Llandogo
Lower Meend
St. Briavels
Lydney
Primrose Hill
Purton
SEVERN
Cambridge
Slimbridge
Moorend
Middle Street
Eastington
King's Stanley
Leonard Stanley
Dudbridge
Rodborough
Bowbridge
Thrupp
Brimscombe
Llanishen
Parkhouse
Catbrook
Coldharbour
Hewelsfield
Aylburton Common
Aylburton
Sharpness
Halmore
Gossington
Frocester
Middleyard
Woodchester
Trelleck Grange
Tintern Parva
Brockweir
Netherend
Alvington
Brookend
Newtown
Wanswell
Breadstone
Lower Cam
Coaley
Nympsfield
Inchbrook
Amberley
Devauden
Chapel Hill
Woolaston
Hook Street
Berkeley
The Quarry
Cam
Dursley
Ashmead Green
Uley
Forest Green
Nailsworth
Horsley
St. Arvans
Stroat
Boughspring
Wibdon
RIVER
Bevington
Newport
Stinchcombe
North Nibley
Kingscote
Tiltups End
Woodcroft
Tutshill
Itton Common
Crossway Green
Cross Hill
Tidenham
Shepperdine
Hill
Stone
Woodford
Southend
MICHAELWOOD
Chavenage House
Newington Bagpath
Mynydd-bach
Shirenewton
Mounton
Pwllmeyric
Sedbury
CHEPSTOW
(Cas-gwent)
Oldbury Power Station
Rockhampton
Tortworth
Bradley
Holywell
Coombe
Ozleworth
Beverston
Falfield
Oldbury-on-Severn
Lower Morton
Whitfield
Charfield
Kingswood
Wotton-under-Edge
Wortley
Alderley
Tresham
Leighterton
Doughton
Newton Green
Beachley
Mathern
M48
Crick
Caerwent
Severn Road Bridge
Littleton-upon-Severn
Kington
Morton
Thornbury
Milbury Heath
Cromhall
Cromhall Common
West End
Hillesley
Lower Kilcott
Westonbirt
Caldicot
Leechpool
Portskewett
SEVERN VIEW
Elberton
Aust
Ingst
Alveston
Olveston
Tytherington
SOUTH
Wickwar
Upper Kilcott
Oldbury on the Hill
Knockdown
Rogiet
The Pill
Sudbrook
Severn Tunnel
Redwick
Northwick
Old Down
Rudgeway
Itchington
Bagstone
Hawkesbury
Hawkesbury Upton
Didmarton
Sopworth
M4
DANGER AREA
Second Severn Crossing
Severn Beach
Pilning
Tockington
Earthcott Green
GLOUCESTERSHIRE
Rangeworthy
Bury Hill
Dunkirk
Little Badminton
Sherston
Almondsbury
Latteridge
Engine Common
Horton
Luckington
Alderton
Easter Compton
Over
Gaunt's Earthcott
Iron Acton
Frampton Cotterell
Goose Green
Yate
Little Sodbury
Old Sodbury
Badminton
M49
A403
Compton Greenfield
Patchway
Bradley Stoke
Winterbourne
Mayshill
Chipping Sodbury
Acton Turville
Littleton Drew
Hallen
Cribbs Causeway
Stoke Gifford
Harry Stoke
Coalpit Heath
Westerleigh
Wapley
Dodington
Codrington
Grittleton
Filton
Kendleshire
Henfield
Tormarton
Burton
Avonmouth
Shirehampton
Henbury
Westbury on Trym
Horfield
M32
Downend
MANGOTSFIELD
Staple Hill
Pucklechurch
Hinton
Dyrham
Nettleton
West Kington
Castle Combe
Yatton Keynell
Portishead
Sheepway
Easton-in-Gordano
Sea Mills
Broomhill
Stapleton
Fishponds
Shortwood
Siston
West Littleton
North Wraxall
Upper Wraxall
Ford
West Yatton
North Weston
GORDANO
Portbury
Pill
Ham Green
Redland
Clay Hill
Soundwell
Abson
Clapton-in-Gordano
Abbots Leigh
Clifton
Warmley
Bridgeyate
Doynton
Pennsylvania
Marshfield
Slaughterford
Biddestone
Lower Failand
Wick
Kingswood
BRISTOL
Hanham
Cold Ashton
Thickwood
Wraxall
Tyntesfield
Failand
Long Ashton
Bedminster
Conham
Hanham Green
Oldland
Beach
Tadwick
Colerne
Corsham
Nailsea
Brislington
Knowle
Willsbridge
Upton Cheyney
Langridge
St. Catherine
Rudloe
Farleigh
Yanley
Headley Park
Bitton
Swineford
North Stoke
Lansdown
Ditteridge
Moor Green
Flax Bourton
Chelvey
Backwell
Bishopsworth
Stockwood
KEYNSHAM
Saltford
Woolley
Swainswick
Batheaston
Ashley
Box
West Town
Barrow Gurney
Barrow Common
East Dundry
Dundry
Whitchurch
Queen Charlton
Kelston
Weston
Charlcombe
Larkhall
Bathampton
Bathford
Kingsdown
Wadswick
Brockley
Lulsgate Bottom
Upper Town
Chewton Keynsham
Monkton Farleigh
South Wraxall
Atworth
Cleeve
Felton
Winford
North Wick
Norton Malreward
Norton Hawkfield
Burnett
Corston
Newton St. Loe
Twerton
BATH
Claverton
Farleigh Wick
BRISTOL INTERNATIONAL
Redhill
Chew Magna
Woollard
Publow
Pensford
Compton Dando
Southdown
Combe Down
Great Chalfield
Wrington
Stanton Drew
Stanton Wick
Stanton Prior
Englishcombe
Hunstrete
Marksbury
Wilmington
Odd Down
Bradford Leigh
Woolley Green
Regil
Chew Stoke
Chelwood
BATH &
N.E. SOMERSET
Monkton Combe
Limpley Stoke
Bradford-on-Avon
Lower Langford
Cowslip Green
Butcombe
Inglesbatch
Priston
Tunley
Southstoke
Midford
Winsley
Turleigh
Staverton
West Town
Nempnett Thrubwell
Bishop Sutton
Stowey
Clutton
Farmborough
Dunkerton
Combe Hay
Freshford
Wingfield
Upper Langford
Rickford
Blagdon
Burrington
Ubley
High Littleton
Timsbury
Meadgate
Carlingcott
Wellow
Hinton Charterhouse
Westwood
Trowle Common
Hilperton
North Widcombe
Cameley
Radford
Camerton
Peasedown St. John
Farleigh Hungerford
Compton Martin
West Harptree
South Widcombe
Hinton Blewett
Temple Cloud
Hallatrow
Paulton
Shoscombe
Norton St. Philip
TROWBRIDGE

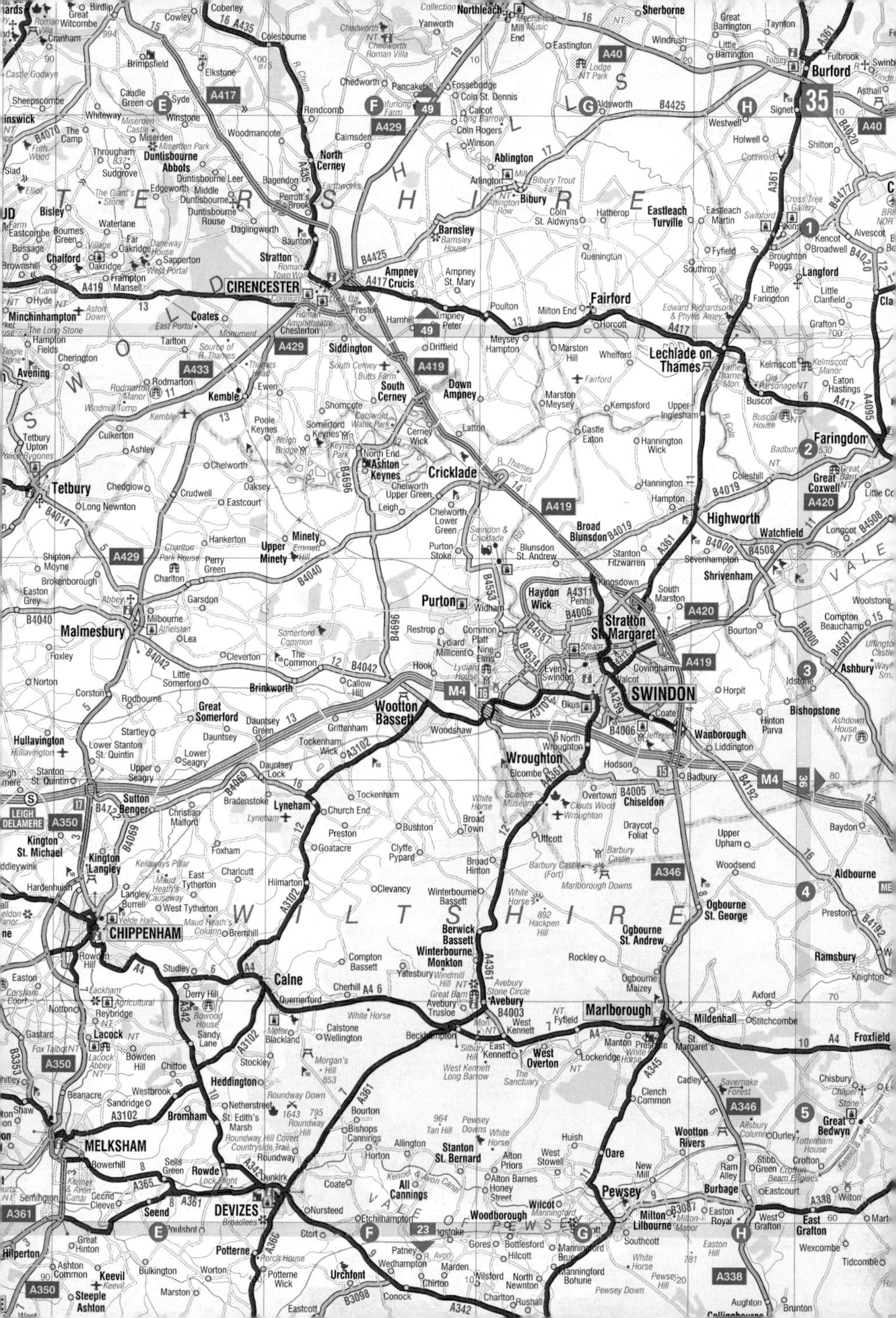

35
Birdlip
Great Witcombe
Cranham
Coberley
Cowley
Colesbourne
Brimpsfield
Elkstone
Castle Godwyn
Caudle Green
Syde
Sheepscombe
Whiteway
Winstone
Miserden
Painswick
The Camp
Througham
Duntisbourne Abbots
Woodmancote
Rendcomb
Sudgrove
Duntisbourne Leer
Edgeworth
Middle Duntisbourne
Duntisbourne Rouse
Daglingworth
Bisley
Waterlane
Eastcombe
Bournes Green
Far Oakridge
Bussage
Brownshill
Chalford
Oakridge
Sapperton
Frampton Mansell
Stratton
Baunton
Bagendon
Perrott's Brook
North Cerney
Calmsden
Chedworth
Yanworth
Northleach
Mill End
Pancakehill
Fossebridge
Coln St. Dennis
Calcot
Coln Rogers
Winson
Ablington
Arlington
Bibury
Coln St. Aldwyns
Barnsley
Sherborne
Great Barrington
Taynton
Windrush
Little Barrington
Eastington
Burford
Fulbrook
Aldsworth
Westwell
Signet
Holwell
Shilton
Hatherop
Eastleach Turville
Eastleach Martin
Kencot
Broadwell
Alvescot
Fyfield
Quenington
Southrop
Broughton Poggs
Langford
Little Faringdon
Little Clanfield
Filkins
CIRENCESTER
Ampney Crucis
Ampney St. Mary
Ampney St. Peter
Preston
Harnhill
Poulton
Milton End
Fairford
Horcott
Grafton
Minchinhampton
Hyde
Coates
Tarlton
Chesterton
Siddington
Driffield
Meysey Hampton
Marston Hill
Whelford
Lechlade on Thames
Kelmscott
Eaton Hastings
Buscot
Hampton Fields
Cherington
Avening
Rodmarton
Kemble
Ewen
South Cerney
Down Ampney
Marston Meysey
Kempsford
Upper Inglesham
Faringdon
Tetbury Upton
Culkerton
Ashley
Poole Keynes
Shorncote
Somerford Keynes
Cerney Wick
Latton
Castle Eaton
Hannington Wick
Chelworth
North End
Ashton Keynes
Cricklade
Tetbury
Chedglow
Crudwell
Oaksey
Eastcourt
Long Newnton
Chelworth Upper Green
Leigh
Chelworth Lower Green
Hannington
Coleshill
Great Coxwell
Little Coxwell
Hampton
Highworth
Broad Blunsdon
Watchfield
Longcot
Shipton Moyne
Hankerton
Minety
Upper Minety
Purton Stoke
Blunsdon St. Andrew
Stanton Fitzwarren
Sevenhampton
Shrivenham
Brokenborough
Charlton
Perry Green
Easton Grey
Garsdon
Kingsdown
Haydon Wick
Penhill
South Marston
Purton
Widham
Malmesbury
Milbourne
Restrop
Common Platt
Stratton St. Margaret
Bourton
Compton Beauchamp
Woolstone
Foxley
Lea
Lydiard Millicent
Nine Elms
Cleverton
The Common
Somerford Common
Even Swindon
Covingham
Walcot
Ashbury
Idstone
Norton
Little Somerford
Brinkworth
Callow Hill
Hook
SWINDON
Horpit
Corston
Rodbourne
Great Somerford
Dauntsey Green
Grittenham
Wootton Bassett
Woodshaw
Okus
Coate
Wanborough
Bishopstone
Liddington
Hinton Parva
Startley
Dauntsey
Hullavington
Lower Stanton St. Quintin
Lower Seagry
Upper Seagry
Tockenham Wick
North Wroughton
Wroughton
Elcombe
Hodson
Badbury
Stanton St. Quintin
Sutton Benger
Dauntsey Lock
Bradenstoke
Tockenham
Lyneham
Church End
Overtown
Chiseldon
Christian Malford
Kington St. Michael
Kington Langley
Foxham
Preston
Bushton
Broad Town
Uffcott
Draycot Foliat
Upper Upham
Baydon
Goatacre
Clyffe Pypard
Broad Hinton
Hardenhuish
East Tytherton
Charlcutt
Langley Burrell
West Tytherton
Hilmarton
Clevancy
Winterbourne Bassett
Woodsend
Aldbourne
CHIPPENHAM
Bremhill
Berwick Bassett
Winterbourne Monkton
Ogbourne St. George
Ogbourne St. Andrew
Preston
Rowden Hill
Compton Bassett
Yatesbury
Rockley
Ramsbury
Easton
Studley
Calne
Cherhill
Avebury
Avebury Trusloe
Ogbourne Maizey
Knighton
Derry Hill
Quemerford
Marlborough
Mildenhall
Axford
Stitchcombe
Notton
Reybridge
Sandy Lane
Blackland
Calstone Wellington
Beckhampton
West Kennett
Fyfield
Manton
Preshute
St. Margaret's
Froxfield
Lacock
Bowden Hill
Chittoe
Stockley
East Kennett
West Overton
Lockeridge
Gastard
Cadley
Chisbury
Beanacre
Westbrook
Heddington
Clench Common
Sandridge
Netherstreet
St. Edith's Marsh
Bourton
Bishops Cannings
Great Bedwyn
Shaw
Bromham
Huish
Wootton Rivers
Durley
MELKSHAM
Bowerhill
Sells Green
Rowde
Allington
Horton
Roundway
Stanton St. Bernard
Alton Priors
West Stowell
Oare
Alton Barnes
Honey Street
Stibb Green
Crofton
Ram Alley
New Mill
Pewsey
Burbage
Eastcourt
Wilton
Semington
Seend Cleeve
Seend
DEVIZES
Dunkirk
Coate
Nursteed
All Cannings
Woodborough
Wilcot
Milton Lilbourne
Easton Royal
West Grafton
East Grafton
Poulshot
Etchilhampton
Southcott
Hilperton
Great Hinton
Potterne
Urchfont
Patney
Wedhampton
Gores
Bottlesford
Hilcott
Manningford Bruce
Wexcombe
Tidcombe
Ashton Common
Keevil
Bulkington
Worton
Potterne Wick
Marden
Chirton
Wilsford
North Newnton
Manningford Bohune
Steeple Ashton
Marston
Eastcott
Conock
Charlton
Rushall
Aughton
Brunton
Collingbourne
A417
A419
A429
A433
A435
A40
A361
A4095
A420
A4311
A4312
A4259
A3102
A350
A4
A342
A345
A346
A338
A365
A360
A4361
B4425
B4040
B4042
B4014
B4019
B4000
B4508
B4507
B4005
B4006
B4192
B4069
B4696
B4553
B4534
B4587
B4003
B3087
B3098
B3353
B4070
B4477
B4020
M4
LEIGH DELAMERE
W I L T S H I R E
V A L E O F P E W S E Y

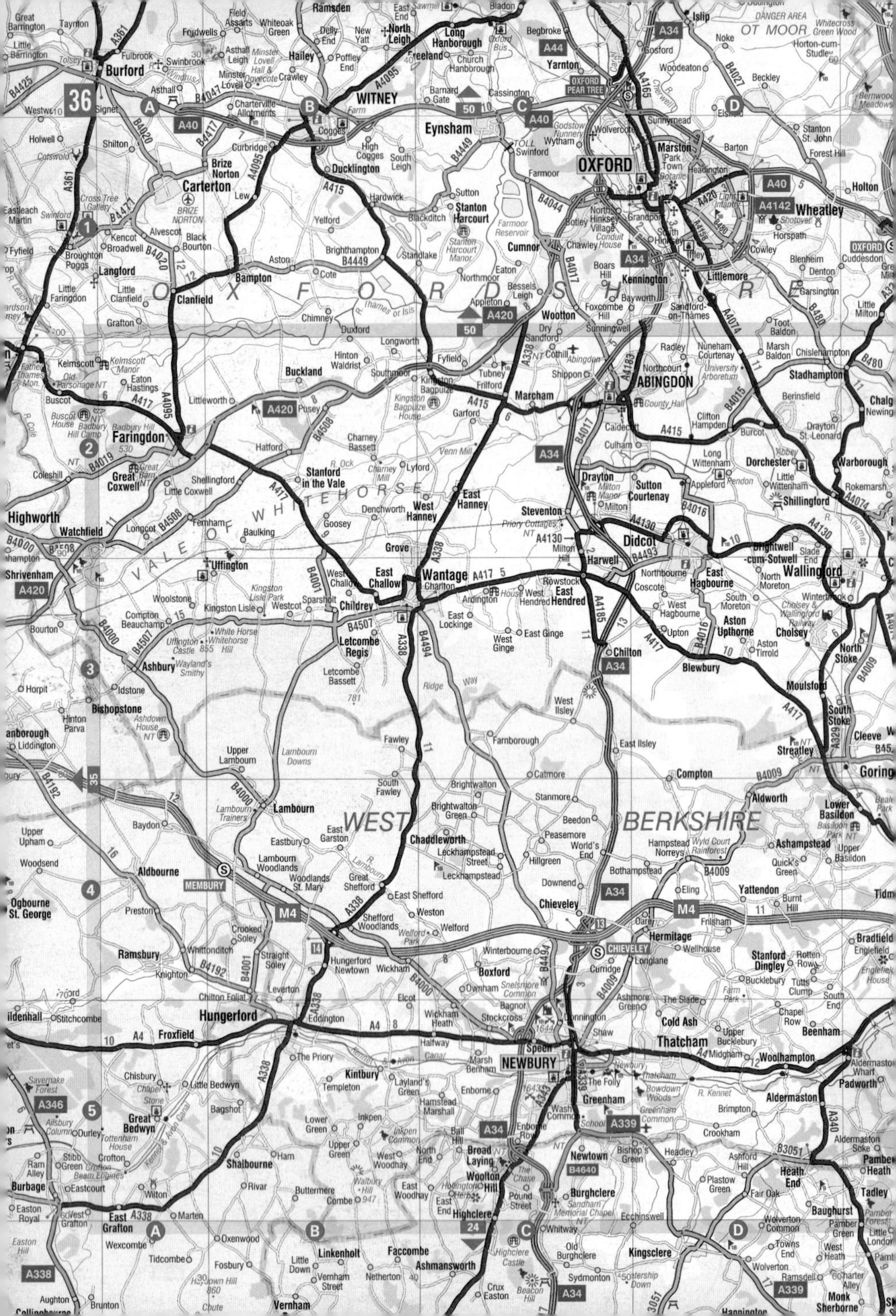
36
Great Barrington
Taynton
Little Barrington
Burford
Fulbrook
Swinbrook
Asthall
Asthall Leigh
Minster Lovell
Fordwells
Field Assarts
Whiteoak Green
Ramsden
Delly End
Hailey
Poffley End
Crawley
New Yatt
North Leigh
East End
Long Hanborough
Freeland
Church Hanborough
Bladon
Begbroke
Yarnton
Oxford Bus
Barnard Gate
Cassington
Eynsham
WITNEY
Cogges
High Cogges
South Leigh
Ducklington
Signet
Westwell
Holwell
Shilton
Charterville Allotments
Curbridge
Brize Norton
Carterton
Lew
Cross Tree Gallery
Swinford
Eastleach Martin
Kencot
Broadwell
Alvescot
Black Bourton
Fyfield
Broughton Poggs
Langford
Little Faringdon
Little Clanfield
Clanfield
Bampton
Aston
Cote
Grafton
Chimney
Duxford
Hardwick
Yelford
Brighthampton
Standlake
Stanton Harcourt
Sutton
Blackditch
Northmoor
Eaton
Appleton
Bessels Leigh
Cumnor
Farmoor
Farmoor Reservoir
Swinford
Wytham
Godstow Nunnery
Wolvercote
OXFORD
OXFORD PEAR TREE
Marston
Park Town
Headington
Botley
North Hinksey Village
Conduit House
Grandpont
South Hinksey
Chawley
Boars Hill
Kennington
Iffley
Littlemore
Bayworth
Foxcombe Hill
Wootton
Sunningwell
Sandford-on-Thames
Dry Sandford
Cothill
Shippon
Abingdon
ABINGDON
Radley
Nuneham Courtenay
University Arboretum
Northcourt
County Hall
Islip
Noke
OT MOOR
DANGER AREA
Whitecross Green Wood
Horton-cum-Studley
Beckley
Gosford
Woodeaton
Elsfield
Sunnymead
Stanton St. John
Barton
Forest Hill
Holton
Wheatley
Shotover
Horspath
Cowley
OXFORD
Cuddesdon
Blenheim
Denton
Garsington
Little Milton
Toot Baldon
Marsh Baldon
Chislehampton
Stadhampton
Berinsfield
Drayton St. Leonard
Clifton Hampden
Burcot
Warborough
Dorchester
Little Wittenham
Long Wittenham
Shillingford
Rokemarsh
Kelmscott
Kelmscott Manor
Eaton Hastings
Buscot
Old Parsonage
Buscot House
Badbury Hill Camp
Faringdon
Littleworth
Buckland
Hinton Waldrist
Longworth
Southmoor
Kingston Bagpuize
Kingston Bagpuize House
Fyfield
Tubney
Frilford
Marcham
Garford
Pusey
Hatford
Charney Bassett
Venn Mill
Lyford
Stanford in the Vale
Coleshill
Great Coxwell
Great Barn
Little Coxwell
Shellingford
Highworth
Watchfield
Shrivenham
Longcot
Fernham
Baulking
Goosey
Denchworth
West Hanney
East Hanney
Caldecott
Culham
Drayton
Milton Manor
Milton
Sutton Courtenay
Appleford
Steventon
Priory Cottages
Didcot
Milton Hill
Harwell
Rowstock
Grove
Wantage
Charlton
East Challow
West Challow
Childrey
Ardington
West Hendred
East Hendred
Uffington
Woolstone
Kingston Lisle
Kingston Lisle Park
Sparsholt
Westcot
Compton Beauchamp
Bourton
White Horse
Whitehorse Hill
Uffington Castle
Ashbury
Wayland's Smithy
Letcombe Regis
Letcombe Bassett
East Lockinge
West Ginge
East Ginge
Chilton
Northbourne
Coscote
West Hagbourne
East Hagbourne
Upton
South Moreton
Aston Upthorne
Aston Tirrold
Blewbury
Brightwell-cum-Sotwell
Slade End
North Moreton
Wallingford
Winterbrook
Cholsey
Cholsey & Wallingford Railway
North Stoke
Moulsford
South Stoke
Streatley
Cleeve
Goring
Horpit
Idstone
Bishopstone
Hinton Parva
Ashdown House
Liddington
Ridge Way
West Ilsley
East Ilsley
Fawley
Farnborough
Catmore
Compton
Aldworth
Lower Basildon
Basildon Park
Upper Basildon
Ashampstead
Quick's Green
Upper Lambourn
Lambourn Downs
Lambourn
Lambourn Trainers
South Fawley
Brightwalton
Brightwalton Green
Stanmore
Beedon
Peasemore
World's End
WEST BERKSHIRE
Hampstead Norreys
Wyld Court Rainforest
Baydon
Upper Upham
Woodsend
Aldbourne
MEMBURY
Eastbury
East Garston
Lambourn Woodlands
Woodlands St. Mary
Chaddleworth
Leckhampstead Street
Leckhampstead
Hillgreen
Bothampstead
Downend
Chieveley
Eling
Yattendon
Burnt Hill
Ogbourne St. George
Preston
Great Shefford
East Shefford
Weston
Welford
Shefford Woodlands
Welford Park
Crooked Soley
Whittonditch
Straight Soley
Ramsbury
Knighton
Hungerford Newtown
Wickham
Winterbourne
CHIEVELEY
Curridge
Hermitage
Wellhouse
Frilsham
Oare
Stanford Dingley
Rotten Row
Bradfield
Englefield
Englefield House
Bucklebury
Tutts Clump
South End
Boxford
Ownham
Snelsmore Common
Longlane
Ashmore Green
The Slade
Farm Park
Chapel Row
Beenham
Chilton Foliat
Leverton
Elcot
Bagnor
Donnington
Cold Ash
Stitchcombe
Hungerford
Froxfield
Eddington
Wickham Heath
Stockcross
Shaw
Speen
Halfway
Thatcham
Upper Bucklebury
Midgham
Woolhampton
Aldermaston Wharf
Padworth
The Priory
Kennet & Avon Canal
Marsh Benham
NEWBURY
The Folly
Bowdown Woods
R. Kennet
Savernake Forest
Chisbury
Chapel
Little Bedwyn
Kintbury
Templeton
Layland's Green
Enborne
Hamstead Marshall
Greenham
Greenham Common
Brimpton
Aldermaston
Crookham
Aldermaston Soke
Stone
Great Bedwyn
Bagshot
Ailsbury Column
Durley
Tottenham House
Lower Green
Inkpen
Inkpen Common
Upper Green
Ball Hill
Wash Common
Enborne Row
School
Newtown
Bishop's Green
Headley
Ashford Hill
Pamber Heath
Heath End
Tadley
Stibb Green
Ram Alley
Crofton
Crofton Beam Engines
Ham
Shalbourne
West Woodhay
North End
Broad Laying
Woolton Hill
The Chase
Burghclere
Sandham Memorial Chapel
Plastow Green
Fair Oak
Baughurst
Burbage
Eastcourt
Wilton
Rivar
Buttermere
Walbury Hill
Combe
East Woodhay
Highclere
Pound Street
East End
Ecchinswell
Wolverton Common
Pamber Forest
Pamber Green
Little London
Easton Royal
Vest Grafton
East Grafton
Marten
Oxenwood
Whitway
Old Burghclere
Kingsclere
Towns End
West Heath
Easton Hill
Wexcombe
Tidcombe
Fosbury
Linkenholt
Little Down
Faccombe
Ashmansworth
Highclere Castle
Beacon Hill
Sydmonton
Watership Down
Wolverton
Ramsdell
Charter Alley
Monk Sherborne
Netherton
Vernham Street
Vernham
Crux Easton
Haydown Hill
Chute
Aughton
Brunton
Collingbourne
OXFORDSHIRE
VALE OF WHITEHORSE
R. Thames or Isis
R. Ock
R. Cole
R. Lambourn
A40
A44
A34
A4095
A4165
A4142
A420
A415
A417
A338
A4130
A4185
A4074
A4183
A4017
A329
A361
A4
A346
A339
A343
A340
B4425
B4020
B4047
B4477
B4449
B4044
B4017
B4027
B4015
B480
B4019
B4508
B4000
B4507
B4001
B4494
B4493
B4016
B4009
B4192
B4640
B3051
M4
50
35
24
A
B
C
D
1
2
3
4
5

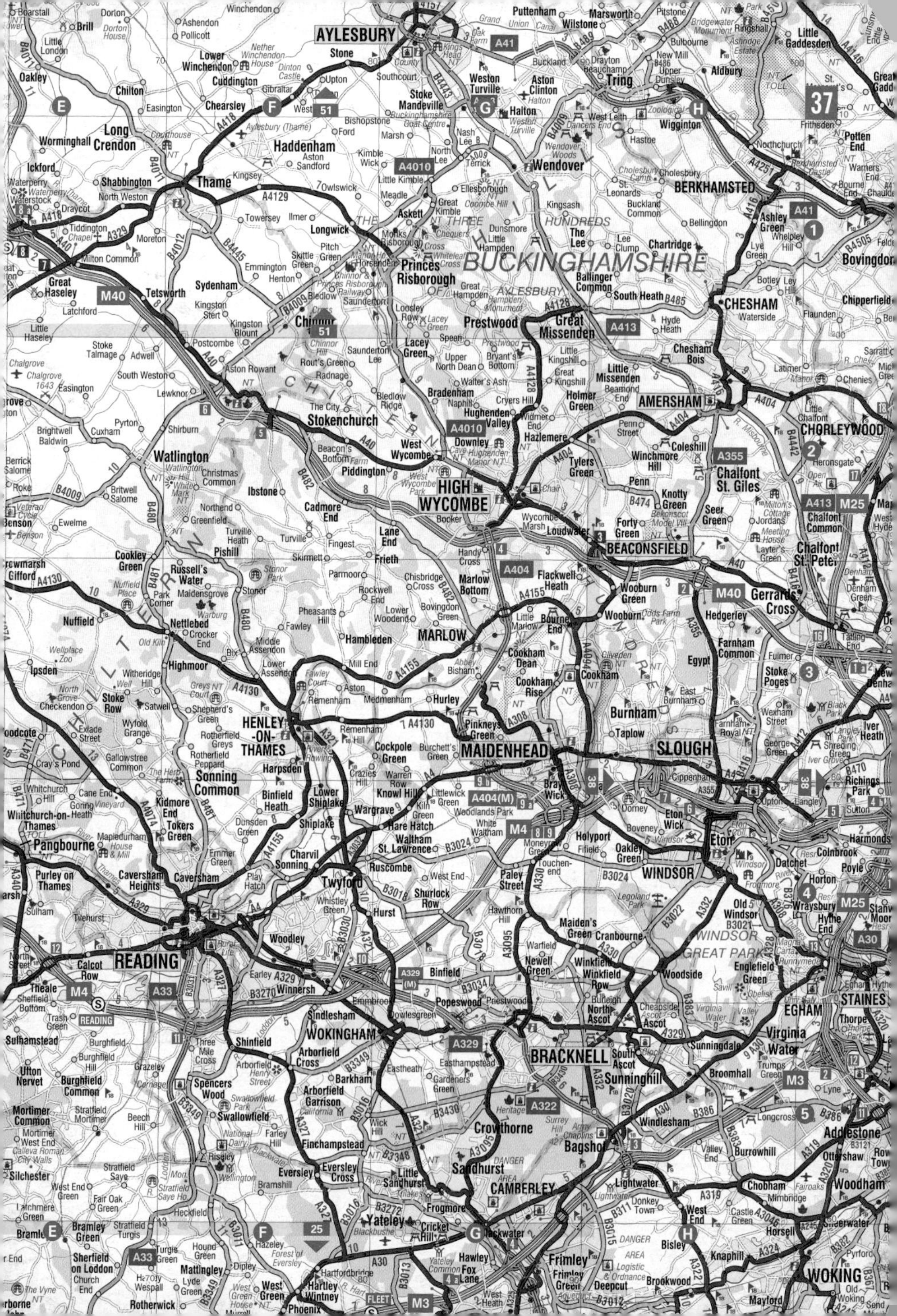
Boarstall
Brill
Dorton
Dorton House
Winchendon
Ashendon
Pollicott
AYLESBURY
Puttenham
Wilstone
Marsworth
Pitstone
Ringshall
Little Gaddesden
Little London
Oakley
Lower Winchendon
Nether Winchendon House
Stone
Grand Union Canal
Buckland
Drayton Beauchamp
Bulbourne
Bridgewater Monument
Ashridge Estate
New Mill
Upper Dunsley
Aldbury
Chilton
Cuddington
Gibraltar
Dinton Castle
Upton
Southcourt
Stoke Mandeville
Weston Turville
Aston Clinton
Halton
Tring
Wigginton
Frithsden
Potten End
Chearsley
Easington
West
Bishopstone
Buckinghamshire Goat Centre
Weston Turville
West Leith
Hastoe
Northchurch
Berkhamsted Castle
Long Crendon
Worminghall
Aylesbury (Thame)
Courthouse
Haddenham
Aston Sandford
Ford
Marsh
Kimble Wick
Nash Lee
North Lee
Terrick
Wendover
Wendover Woods
Dancers End
Cholesbury Camp
Cholesbury
BERKHAMSTED
Warners End
Bourne End
Ickford
Shabbington
Thame
Kingsey
Owlswick
Little Kimble
Ellesborough
Coombe Hill
St. Leonards
Buckland Common
Waterperry
Waterstock
North Weston
Draycot
A4129
Meadle
Great Kimble
Kingsash
HUNDREDS
Askett
THE
THREE
Chequers
Dunsmore
The Lee
Bellingdon
Ashley Green
Whelpley Hill
Tiddington
Chapel
Towersey
Ilmer
Longwick
Monks Risborough
Little Hampden
Lee Clump
Chartridge
Lye Green
Feldon
Bovingdon
Moreton
Milton Common
Pitch Green
Skittle Green
Horsenden
Princes Risborough
Whiteleaf Cross
BUCKINGHAMSHIRE
Ballinger Common
Great Haseley
Emmington
Henton
Chinnor & Princes Risborough Railway
OF
AYLESBURY
South Heath
Botley
Ley Hill
Tetsworth
Sydenham
Bledlow
Saunderton
Great Hampden
Hampden Monument
CHESHAM
Waterside
Chipperfield
Latchford
Kingston Stert
Kingston Blount
Chinnor
Chinnor Hill
Loosley Row
Lacey Green
Prestwood
Great Missenden
Hyde Heath
Flaunden
Little Haseley
Stoke Talmage
Adwell
Postcombe
Rout's Green
Saunderton Lee
Lacey Green
Speen
Upper North Dean
Bryant's Bottom
Little Kingshill
Great Kingshill
Chesham Bois
Sarratt
Chalgrove
Chalgrove 1643
South Weston
Aston Rowant
CHILTERN
Radnage
Walter's Ash
Little Missenden
Beamond End
Latimer
Chenies
Easington
Lewknor
Bledlow Ridge
Bradenham
Naphill
Cryers Hill
Holmer Green
AMERSHAM
Little Chalfont
CHORLEYWOOD
Pyrton
Cuxham
Shirburn
The City
Stokenchurch
Hughenden Valley
Widmer End
Hazlemere
Penn Street
Coleshill
Brightwell Baldwin
Downley
Hughenden Manor
West Wycombe
Tylers Green
Winchmore Hill
Chalfont St. Giles
Heronsgate
Berrick Salome
Watlington
Watlington Hill
White Mark
Christmas Common
Beacon's Bottom
Piddington
West Wycombe Park
Penn
Knotty Green
Open Air
Roke
Britwell Salome
Ibstone
Cadmore End
HIGH WYCOMBE
Booker
Forty Green
Seer Green
Jordans
Milton's Cottage
Bekonscot Model Vill
Chalfont Common
Benson
Ewelme
Northend
Greenfield
Turville Heath
Turville
Fingest
Lane End
Wycombe Marsh
Loudwater
Meeting House
Chalfont St. Peter
Layter's Green
BEACONSFIELD
Handy Cross
Crowmarsh Gifford
Cookley Green
Russell's Water
Pishill
Stonor Park
Skirmett
Frieth
Parmoor
Chisbridge Cross
Marlow Bottom
Flackwell Heath
Wooburn Green
Gerrards Cross
Denham
Denham Green
Nuffield Place
Park Corner
Maidensgrove
Warburg
Stonor
Rockwell End
Pheasants Hill
Lower Woodend
Bovingdon Green
Little Marlow
Bourne End
Wooburn
Odds Farm Park
Hedgerley
Nuffield
Nettlebed
Crocker End
Old Kiln
Fawley
Hambleden
MARLOW
Farnham Common
Tatling End
Wellplace Zoo
Highmoor
Bix
Middle Assendon
Lower Assendon
Mill End
Abbey
Bisham
Cookham Dean
Cliveden
Egypt
Fulmer
Ipsden
Witheridge Hill
Greys Court
Fawley Court
Aston
Medmenham
Hurley
Cookham
Cookham Rise
East Burnham
Stoke Poges
North Grove
Checkendon
Stoke Row
Satwell
Shepherd's Green
HENLEY-ON-THAMES
Remenham
Pinkneys Green
Burnham
Wexham Street
Black Park
Iver Heath
Woodcote
Exlade Street
Wyfold Grange
Rotherfield Greys
Remenham Hill
River & Rowing
Cockpole Green
Burchett's Green
MAIDENHEAD
Taplow
SLOUGH
Farnham Royal
George Green
Shredding Green
Iver Grove
Gallowstree Common
Rotherfield Peppard
Harpsden
Crazies Hill
Warren Row
Knowl Hill
Cippenham
Langley
Richings Park
Crays Pond
The Herb Farm
Sonning Common
Lower Shiplake
Littlewick Green
Bray Wick
Dorney
Upton
Sutton
Whitchurch Hill
Cane End
Goring Heath
Vineyard
Kidmore End
Binfield Heath
Wargrave
Kiln Green
Woodlands Park
Eton Wick
Boveney
Windsor
Whitchurch-on-Thames
Toll
Tokers Green
Dunsden Green
Shiplake
Hare Hatch
White Waltham
Holyport
Eton
Harmondsworth
Pangbourne
Mapledurham House & Mill
Emmer Green
Charvil
Sonning
Waltham St. Lawrence
Moneyrow Green
Fifield
Oakley Green
Colnbrook
Datchet
Poyle
Purley on Thames
Caversham Heights
Caversham
Play Hatch
Twyford
Ruscombe
West End
Paley Street
Touchen-end
WINDSOR
Frogmore
Horton
Sulham
Tilehurst
Whistley Green
Hurst
Shurlock Row
Legoland Park
Old Windsor
Wraysbury
Stanwell Moor
Hythe End
Woodley
Hawthorn Hill
Maiden's Green
Cranbourne
WINDSOR
GREAT PARK
Magna Carta
Runnymede
North Street
Calcot Row
READING
Rural Life
Warfield
Newell Green
Winkfield
Winkfield Row
Woodside
Englefield Green
Egham Hythe
Theale
Sheffield Bottom
Earley
Winnersh
Binfield
Popeswood
Priestwood
Bullbrook
Cheapside
Ascot
North Ascot
Savill
Obelisk
Virginia Water
Valley
EGHAM
STAINES
Thorpe
Trash Green
READING
Sindlesham
Emmbrook
Dowlesgreen
WOKINGHAM
Sulhamstead
Burghfield
Three Mile Cross
Shinfield
Arborfield Cross
Arborfield
Henry Street
Barkham
Easthampstead
Eastheath
Gardeners Green
BRACKNELL
South Ascot
Sunninghill
Sunningdale
Broomhall
Trumps Green
Virginia Water
Lyne
Ufton Nervet
Burghfield Common
Grazeley
Spencers Wood
Arborfield Garrison
California
Heritage
Crowthorne
Surrey Hill
Windlesham
Longcross
Addlestone
Mortimer Common
Stratfield Mortimer
Beech Hill
Swallowfield Park
Swallowfield
National Dairy
Farley Hill
Wick Hill
Finchampstead
Army Chaplains
Bagshot
Valley End
Burrowhill
Ottershaw
Row Town
Mortimer West End
Calleva Roman City Walls
Silchester
Risley
Stratfield Saye
Wellington
Stratfield Saye Ho
Eversley
Eversley Cross
Bramshill
Little Sandhurst
Sandhurst
CAMBERLEY
DANGER
Lightwater
Chobham
Mimbridge
Fairoaks
Woodham
West End Green
Fair Oak Green
Heckfield
Yateley
Blackbushe
Cricket Hill
Frogmore
Blackwater
Donkey Town
West End
Castle Green
Horsell
Sheerwater
Latchmere Green
Bramley
Bramley Green
Stratfield Turgis
Turgis Green
Hazeley
Forest of Eversley
Hawley
Fox Lane
Yateley Common
Frimley
DANGER AREA
Bisley
Knaphill
Pyrford
Sherfield on Loddon
Hound Green
Mattingley
Dipley
Hartfordbridge
Frimley Green
Logistic & Ordnance
Deepcut
Brookwood
WOKING
Church End
Heckfield
Hartley Wintney
Lyde Green
Herons Wespall
Rotherwick
West Green
West Green House
Phoenix
West Heath
Mayford
Old Woking
The Vyne
Sherborne
FLEET
NT
TOLL

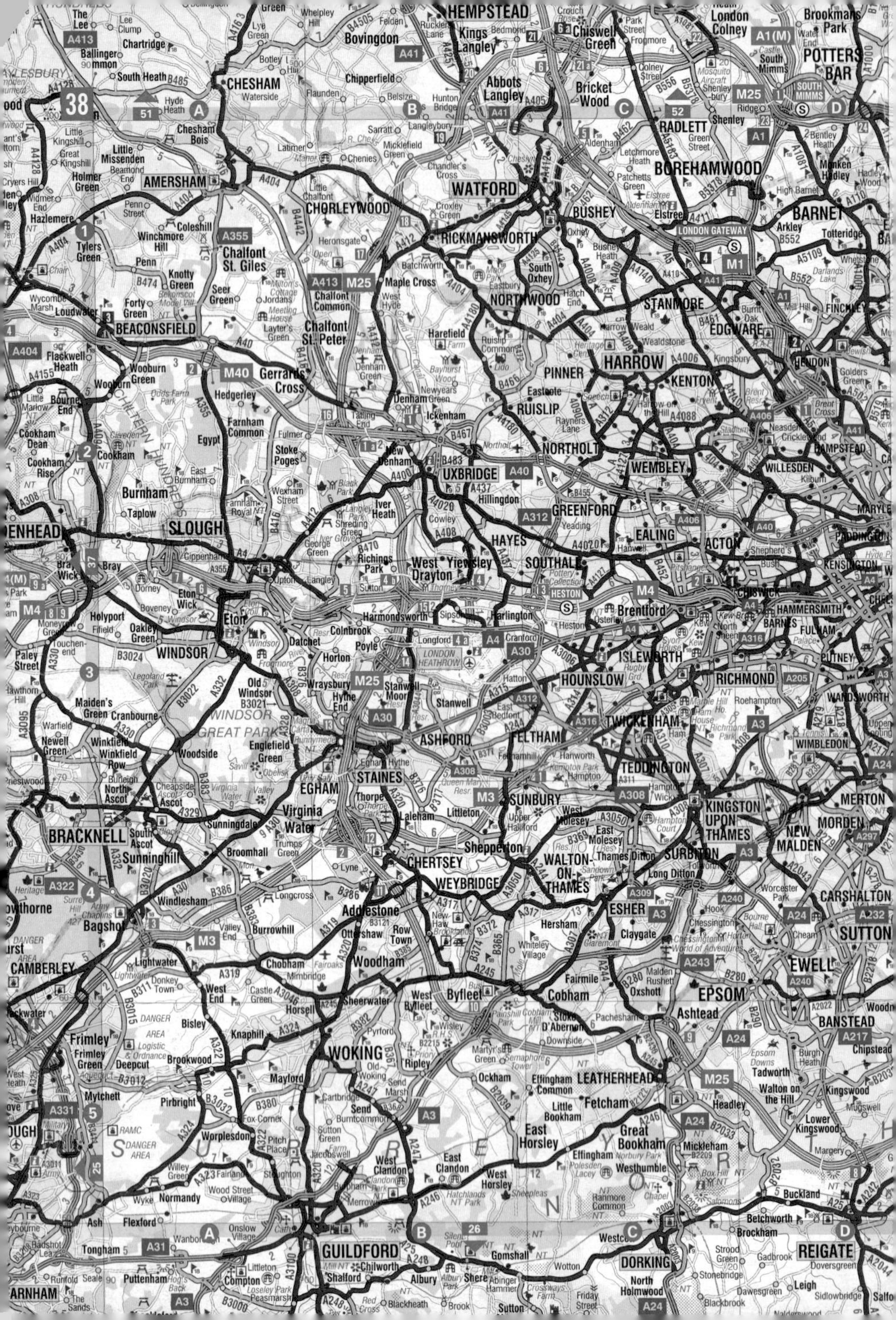

38
HEMPSTEAD
Bovingdon
Kings Langley
Chiswell Green
London Colney
Brookmans Park
A1(M)
POTTERS BAR
South Mimms
SOUTH MIMMS
CHESHAM
Chesham Bois
Abbots Langley
Bricket Wood
RADLETT
Shenley
M25
The Lee
Lee Clump
Chartridge
Ballinger Common
South Heath
Hyde Heath
A413
A41
52
51
Chipperfield
Belsize
Sarratt
Latimer
Chenies
Little Kingshill
Great Kingshill
Little Missenden
Holmer Green
AMERSHAM
WATFORD
BOREHAMWOOD
BUSHEY
Elstree
BARNET
Arkley
Totteridge
CHORLEYWOOD
RICKMANSWORTH
LONDON GATEWAY
M1
Hazlemere
Tylers Green
Penn
Knotty Green
Coleshill
Winchmore Hill
Chalfont St. Giles
A355
Seer Green
Jordans
A413
Chalfont Common
Chalfont St. Peter
Maple Cross
Batchworth
South Oxhey
NORTHWOOD
STANMORE
EDGWARE
FINCHLEY
Wycombe Marsh
Loudwater
BEACONSFIELD
Forty Green
Harefield
HARROW
PINNER
KENTON
HENDON
Golders Green
A404
Flackwell Heath
Wooburn Green
Gerrards Cross
M40
Hedgerley
Denham
Ruislip Common
Eastcote
RUISLIP
Ickenham
Bourne End
Little Marlow
Cookham Dean
Cookham
Cookham Rise
Farnham Common
Egypt
Stoke Poges
Fulmer
NORTHOLT
WEMBLEY
Neasden
WILLESDEN
HAMPSTEAD
Burnham
East Burnham
Taplow
SLOUGH
UXBRIDGE
Hillingdon
GREENFORD
Iver Heath
Farnham Royal
Wexham Street
DENHEAD
Bray Wick
Bray
HAYES
EALING
ACTON
MARYLEBONE
PADDINGTON
Yeading
West Drayton
Yiewsley
SOUTHALL
Langley
Richings Park
Dorney
Eton Wick
Eton
Holyport
Oakley Green
WINDSOR
Datchet
Colnbrook
Harmondsworth
Sipson
Harlington
HESTON
Brentford
CHISWICK
KENSINGTON
HAMMERSMITH
BARNES
FULHAM
Paley Street
Poyle
Longford
LONDON HEATHROW
Cranford
ISLEWORTH
RICHMOND
PUTNEY
Old Windsor
Horton
Wraysbury
Stanwell Moor
Stanwell
HOUNSLOW
Roehampton
WANDSWORTH
Maiden's Green
Cranbourne
WINDSOR GREAT PARK
Warfield
Newell Green
Winkfield
Winkfield Row
Englefield Green
Hythe End
ASHFORD
FELTHAM
TWICKENHAM
WIMBLEDON
Woodside
EGHAM
STAINES
Hanworth
TEDDINGTON
North Ascot
Ascot
Sunningdale
Virginia Water
Thorpe
Laleham
Littleton
SUNBURY
West Molesey
East Molesey
KINGSTON UPON THAMES
MERTON
MORDEN
NEW MALDEN
BRACKNELL
South Ascot
Sunninghill
Broomhall
CHERTSEY
Shepperton
WALTON-ON-THAMES
SURBITON
Long Ditton
Lyne
WEYBRIDGE
ESHER
Worcester Park
CARSHALTON
Windlesham
Longcross
Addlestone
Hersham
Claygate
Chessington
SUTTON
Bagshot
Burrowhill
Ottershaw
Row Town
New Haw
Cheam
EWELL
CAMBERLEY
Lightwater
Chobham
Woodham
Whiteley Village
Fairmile
EPSOM
Cobham
Oxshott
Ashtead
BANSTEAD
Frimley
West End
Bisley
Knaphill
Horsell
Sheerwater
West Byfleet
Byfleet
Stoke D'Abernon
Frimley Green
Deepcut
Brookwood
WOKING
Pyrford
Ripley
Ockham
Downside
Effingham Common
LEATHERHEAD
Tadworth
Burgh Heath
Chipstead
Mytchett
Pirbright
Mayford
Old Woking
Send Marsh
Send
Fetcham
Little Bookham
Walton on the Hill
Kingswood
Headley
Worplesdon
Fox Corner
Pitch Place
Sutton Green
Burntcommon
East Horsley
Great Bookham
Mickleham
Lower Kingswood
Stoughton
Jacobswell
West Clandon
East Clandon
West Horsley
Effingham
Westhumble
Box Hill
Normandy
Wood Street Village
Wyke
Merrow
Ranmore Common
Buckland
Ash
Flexford
Onslow Village
Betchworth
Brockham
Tongham
Puttenham
Compton
GUILDFORD
Chilworth
Shalford
Albury
Shere
Gomshall
Abinger Hammer
Wotton
DORKING
Westcott
North Holmwood
Strood Green
Gadbrook
REIGATE
Leigh
Doversgreen
Sidlowbridge
Dawesgreen
Blackbrook
FARNHAM
Runfold
Seale
The Sands
Peasmarsh
Blackheath
Brook
Sutton
Friday Street
A3
A24
A25
A31
A246
A247
A320
A322
A324

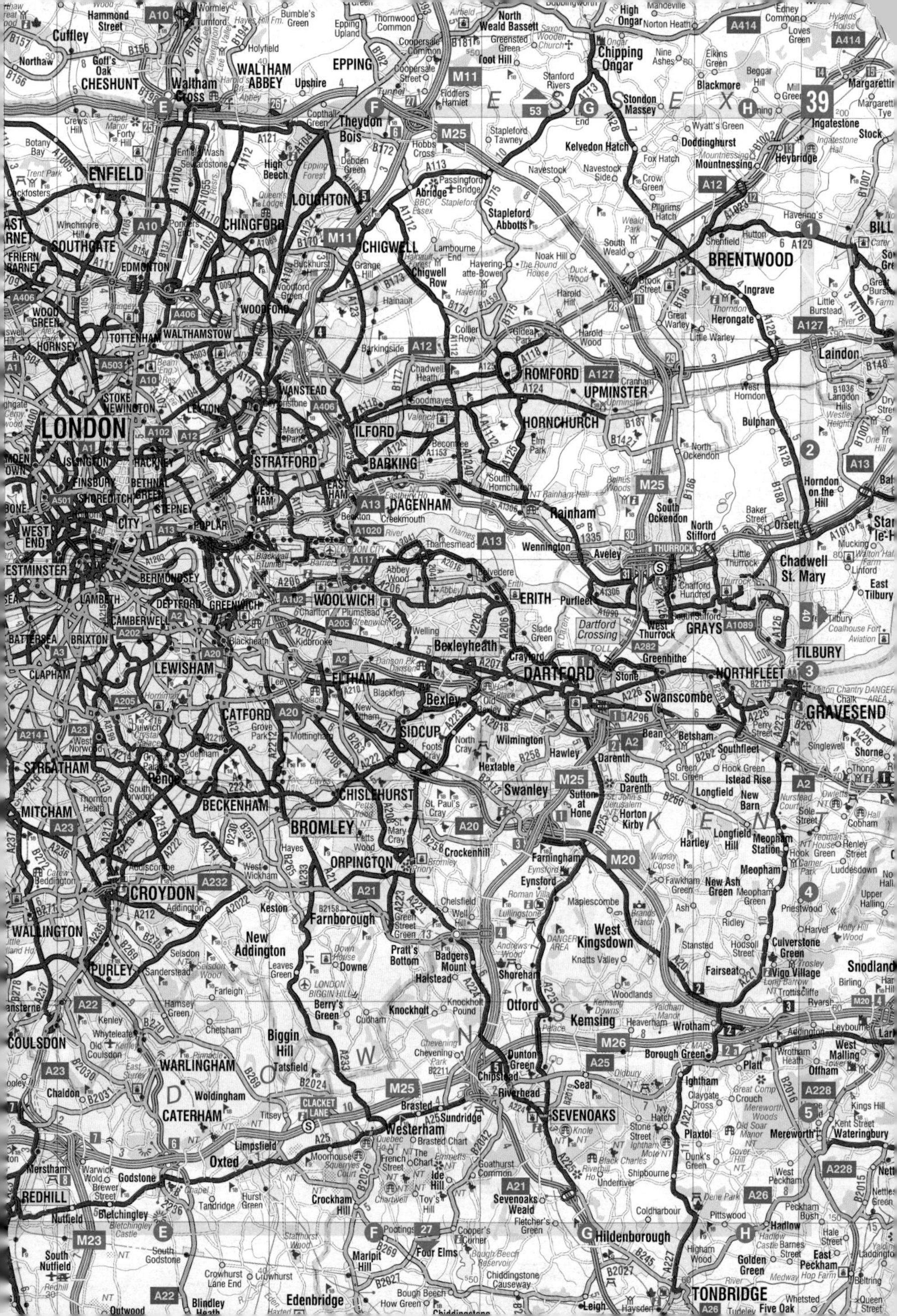
39
E
F
G
H
E S S E X
K E N T
LONDON
ENFIELD
CHESHUNT
Waltham Cross
WALTHAM ABBEY
EPPING
Theydon Bois
LOUGHTON
CHINGFORD
CHIGWELL
Chipping Ongar
BRENTWOOD
SOUTHGATE
EDMONTON
WOODFORD
WALTHAMSTOW
TOTTENHAM
ROMFORD
UPMINSTER
HORNCHURCH
ILFORD
BARKING
DAGENHAM
STRATFORD
Rainham
THURROCK
GRAYS
TILBURY
Chadwell St. Mary
Laindon
WOOLWICH
ERITH
Bexleyheath
DARTFORD
Dartford Crossing
NORTHFLEET
Swanscombe
GRAVESEND
ELTHAM
Bexley
SIDCUP
CATFORD
LEWISHAM
CHISLEHURST
BROMLEY
BECKENHAM
ORPINGTON
Swanley
CROYDON
STREATHAM
MITCHAM
WALLINGTON
PURLEY
COULSDON
WARLINGHAM
CATERHAM
Oxted
Westerham
SEVENOAKS
Hildenborough
TONBRIDGE
REDHILL
Edenbridge
M25
M11
M20
M26
M23
A13
A2
A20
A21
A22
A23
A12
A127
A406

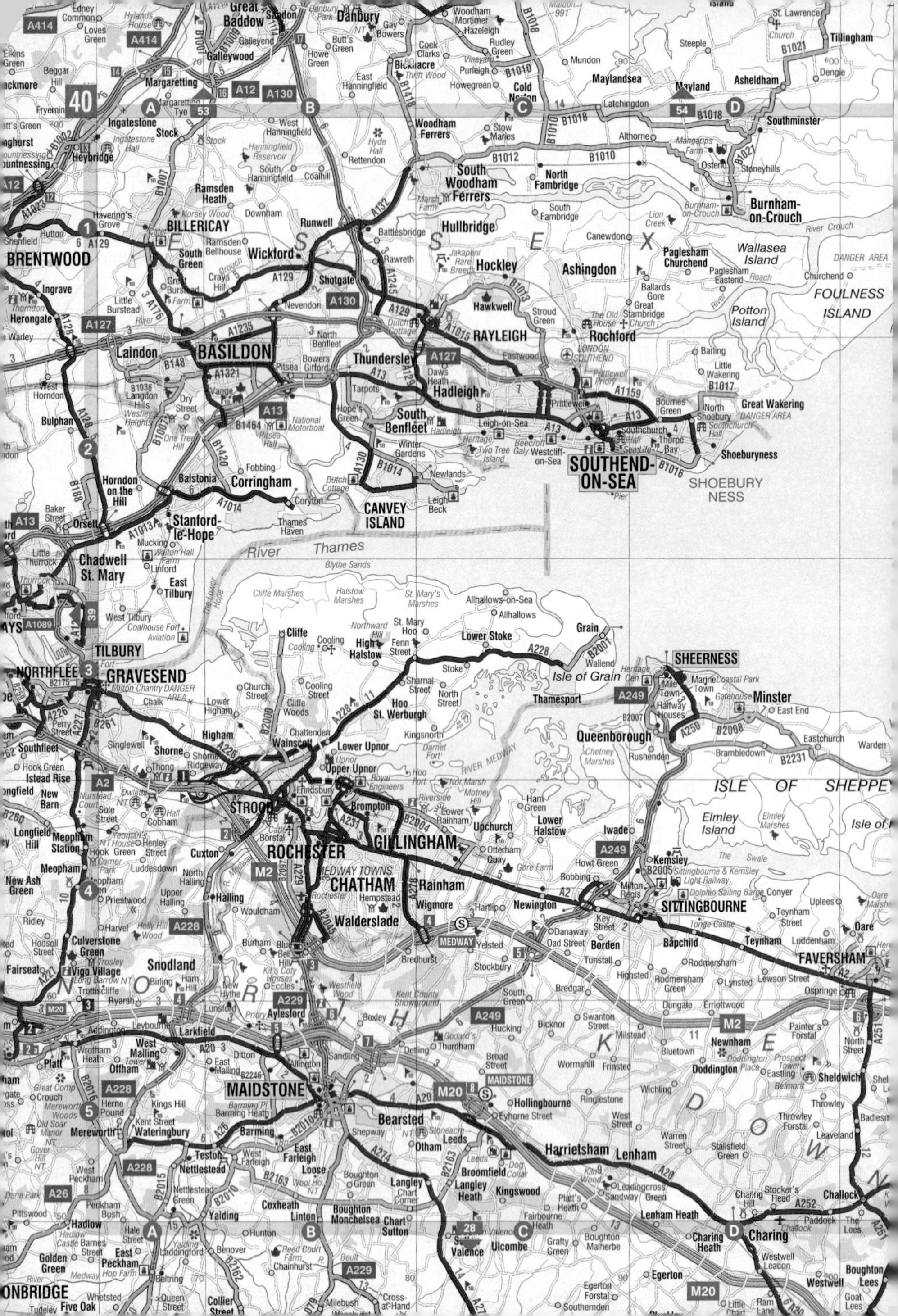
40
Edney Common
Loves Green
Hylands House
Great Baddow
Sandon
Danbury Park
Danbury
Gay Bowers
Woodham Mortimer
Hazeleigh
Rudley Green
Maldon
Steeple
St. Lawrence
Tillingham
Galleyend
Galleywood
Butt's Green
Howe Green
Cock Clarks
Purleigh
Mundon
Maylandsea
Mayland
Asheldham
Dengie
Elkins Green
Beggar Hill
Margaretting
Margaretting Tye
Bicknacre
Thrift Wood
East Hanningfield
Howegreen
Cold Norton
Latchingdon
Southminster
Fryerning
Ingatestone
Stock
West Hanningfield
Woodham Ferrers
Stow Maries
Althorne
Mangapps Farm
Heybridge
Ingatestone Hall
Hanningfield Reservoir
Hyde Hall
Rettendon
Ostend
Stoneyhills
Mountnessing
South Hanningfield
Coalhill
South Woodham Ferrers
North Fambridge
Marsh Farm
Burnham-on-Crouch
Ramsden Heath
Norsey Wood
Downham
Runwell
South Fambridge
Lion Creek
Hutton
Havering's Grove
BILLERICAY
Battlesbridge
Hullbridge
River Crouch
Shenfield
BRENTWOOD
Ramsden Bellhouse
South Green
Wickford
Rawreth
Canewdon
Paglesham Churchend
Wallasea Island
Jakapeni Rare Breeds
Hockley
Ashingdon
Paglesham Eastend
Roach
DANGER AREA
Churchend
Crays Hill
Great Burstead
Shotgate
Ballards Gore
FOULNESS ISLAND
Ingrave
Little Burstead
Nevendon
Hawkwell
Great Stambridge
Church
Potton Island
Herongate
Thorndon
Stroud Green
The Old House
Warley
Dutch Cottage
RAYLEIGH
Rochford
Laindon
BASILDON
North Benfleet
Eastwood
LONDON SOUTHEND
Barling
Bowers Gifford
Thundersley
Daws Heath
Prittlewell Priory
Little Wakering
West Horndon
Pitsea
Langdon Hills
Vange
Tarpots
Hadleigh
Westley Heights
Dry Street
Hope's Green
Prittlewell
Bournes Green
North Shoebury
Great Wakering
Bulphan
One Tree Hill
Pitsea Hall
National Motorboat
South Benfleet
Leigh-on-Sea
Southchurch
Southchurch Hall
Thorpe Bay
Winter Gardens
Two Tree Island
Beecroft Galy.
Westcliff-on-Sea
Sea Life
Shoeburyness
SOUTHEND-ON-SEA
Fobbing
Newlands
SHOEBURY NESS
Horndon on the Hill
Balstonia
Corringham
Dutch Cottage
Leigh Beck
Pier
Coryton
CANVEY ISLAND
Baker Street
Orsett
Stanford-le-Hope
Thames Haven
Mucking
Walton Hall Farm
River Thames
Little Thurrock
Chadwell St. Mary
Linford
Blythe Sands
Thurrock
East Tilbury
The Lower Hope
Cliffe Marshes
Halstow Marshes
St. Mary's Marshes
Allhallows-on-Sea
Allhallows
West Tilbury
Coalhouse Fort
Aviation
Northward Hill
St. Mary Hoo
Lower Stoke
Grain
TILBURY
Cliffe
Cooling
High Halstow
Fenn Street
Wallend
Isle of Grain
SHEERNESS
NORTHFLEET
GRAVESEND
Milton Chantry DANGER AREA
Fort
Church Street
Cooling Street
Stoke
Sharnal Street
Heritage Cen.
Marine Town
Coastal Park
Mile Town
Chalk
Lower Higham
Cliffe Woods
North Street
Thamesport
Gatehouse
Minster
East End
Halfway Houses
Perry Street
Higham
Chattenden
Hoo St. Werburgh
Southfleet
Singlewell
Shorne
Wainscott
Lower Upnor
Kingsnorth
Queenborough
Eastchurch
Warden
Shorne Ridgeway
Upnor
Rushenden
Chetney Marshes
Brambledown
Hook Green
Istead Rise
Thong
Upper Upnor
Darnet Fort
RIVER MEDWAY
Hoo Fort
Nor Marsh
Royal Engineers
Motney Hill
ISLE OF SHEPPEY
Dwelts NT
Frindsbury
New Barn
Nurstead Court
Sole Street
Cobham Hall
STROOD
Brompton
Riverside
Lower Rainham
Ham Green
Lower Halstow
Upchurch
Elmley Island
Elmley Marshes
Isle of
Longfield
Longfield Hill
Meopham Station
Yeoman's House
Henley Street
Camer Park
Cuxton
Borstal
ROCHESTER
GILLINGHAM
Otterham Quay
Gore Farm
Iwade
Kemsley
Howt Green
The Swale
Hook Green
Luddesdown
MEDWAY TOWNS
CHATHAM
Rainham
Bobbing
Sittingbourne & Kemsley Light Railway
Dolphin Sailing Barge
Milton Regis
SITTINGBOURNE
Conyer
Meopham
New Ash Green
North Halling
Upper Halling
Halling
Wouldham
Rochester
Hempstead
Wigmore
Walderslade
Hartlip
Newington
Key Street
Uplees
Teynham Street
Oare
Ridley
Priestwood
Harvel
Holly Hill Wood
Tonge Castle
Danaway
Oad Street
Borden
Bapchild
Teynham
Luddenham
Hodsoll Street
Culverstone Green
Burham
Blue Bell Hill
Bredhurst
Yelsted
Stockbury
Tunstall
FAVERSHAM
Rodmersham
Fairseat
Vigo Village
Trosley
Snodland
Long Barrow NT
Trottiscliffe
Birling
Ham Hill
Kit's Coty House
Eccles
Westfield Wood
Highsted
Rodmersham Green
Lynsted
Lewson Street
Ospringe
Kent County Showground
South Green
Bredgar
Dungate
Erriottwood
New Hythe
Lunsford
Priory
Aylesford
Boxley
Ryarsh
Addington
Leybourne
Larkfield
Swanton Street
Bicknor
Milstead
Painter's Forstal
Platt
Wrotham Heath
West Malling
Ditton
Sandling
Detling
Godard's
Thurnham
Hucking
Newnham
North Street
Offham
East Malling
Allington
Broad Street
Wormshill
Frinsted
Bluetown
Doddington Place
Prospect Tower
Doddington
Eastling
Belmont
Sheldwich
Great Comp
Crouch
Kings Hill
MAIDSTONE
Barming Pl.
Wichling
Ringlestone
Hollingbourne
Eyhorne Street
Throwley
Mereworth Woods
Herne Pound
Kent Street
Barming Heath
Bearsted
Stoneacre NT
West Street
Throwley Forstal
Badlesmere
Old Soar Manor NT
Mereworth
Wateringbury
Barming
Shepway
Otham
Leeds
Warren Street
Stalisfield Green
Leaveland
Gover Hill NT
Teston
West Farleigh
East Farleigh
Loose
Leeds Castle
Harrietsham
Lenham
West Peckham
Nettlestead
Nettlestead Green
Boughton Green
Langley
Broomfield
Dog Collar
Kingswood
Kiln Wood
Leadingcross Green
Sandway
Dene Park
Wool Ho. NT
Chart Corner
Langley Heath
Platt's Heath
Peckham Bush
Coxheath
Yalding
Linton
Boughton Monchelsea
Chart Sutton
Fairbourne Heath
Lenham Heath
Charing Hill
Stocker's Head
Challock
Pittswood
Hadlow
Hadlow Castle
Barnes Street
Hale Street
Hunton
Valence
Ulcombe
Grafty Green
Boughton Malherbe
Charing Heath
Charing
Paddock
The Lees
Golden Green
East Peckham
Hop Farm
Laddingford
Yalding
Benover
Reed Court Farm
Chainhurst
Beult
Westwell
Westwell Leacon
Medway
Beltring
Egerton
Egerton Forstal
Boughton Lees
ONBRIDGE
Whetsted
Queen Street
Collier Street
Milebush
Cross-at-Hand
Southernden
Little Chart
Ram Lane
Goat Lees
Five Oak
Tudeley
A414
A12
A130
A132
A1245
A129
A127
A13
A176
A1235
A1321
A128
A1159
A1015
A130
A1014
A1013
A1089
A126
A228
A249
A226
A227
A2
A250
A229
A278
A2045
A20
A26
A274
A229
A252
A251
A28
B1002
B1007
B1008
B1009
B1418
B1018
B1010
B1012
B1021
B1013
B1036
B1464
B1420
B1007
B1014
B1016
B1017
B148
B188
B2175
B261
B260
B2000
B2001
B2007
B2008
B2231
B2004
B2005
B2097
B2016
B2015
B2246
B2010
B2163
B2162
M2
M20
M25
A B C D
1 2 3 4 5
NT
S
MEDWAY
MAIDSTONE
14 15 16 17 53 54 39 28
E S S E X
N O R T H K E N T D O W N S

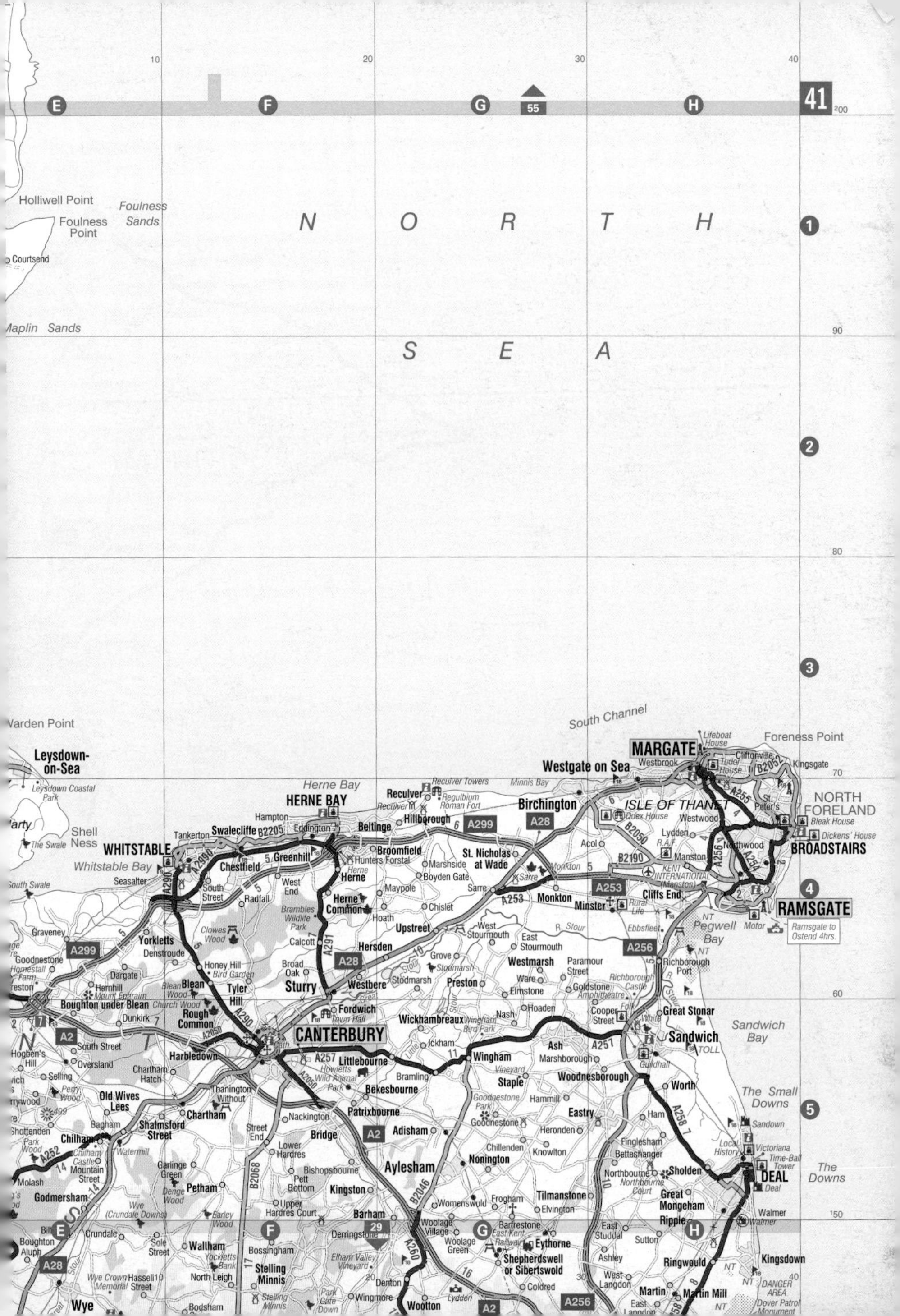

41
NORTH SEA
Holliwell Point
Foulness Point
Foulness Sands
Courtsend
Maplin Sands
Warden Point
Leysdown-on-Sea
South Channel
MARGATE
Foreness Point
Westgate on Sea
Westbrook
Cliftonville
Kingsgate
Herne Bay
HERNE BAY
Reculver
Birchington
ISLE OF THANET
NORTH FORELAND
BROADSTAIRS
Bleak House
Dickens' House
WHITSTABLE
Whitstable Bay
Shell Ness
Swalecliffe
Tankerton
Chestfield
Greenhill
Broomfield
Herne
Herne Common
St. Nicholas at Wade
Monkton
Minster
Manston
Cliffs End
RAMSGATE
Ramsgate to Ostend 4hrs.
Pegwell Bay
Richborough Port
Sandwich Bay
Sandwich
Sturry
Fordwich
CANTERBURY
Harbledown
Boughton under Blean
Wickhambreaux
Littlebourne
Wingham
Ash
Woodnesborough
Worth
The Small Downs
Bekesbourne
Patrixbourne
Bridge
Adisham
Aylesham
Nonington
Eastry
Sholden
DEAL
The Downs
Walmer
Kingsdown
Chartham
Chilham
Godmersham
Petham
Barham
Kingston
Eythorne
Shepherdswell or Sibertswold
Ringwould
Martin Mill
Wye
Wootton
A2
A28
A299
A253
A256
A257
A258
A290
A291
A2050
A252
A260
A255
A254
B2205
B2050
B2190
B2046
B2068

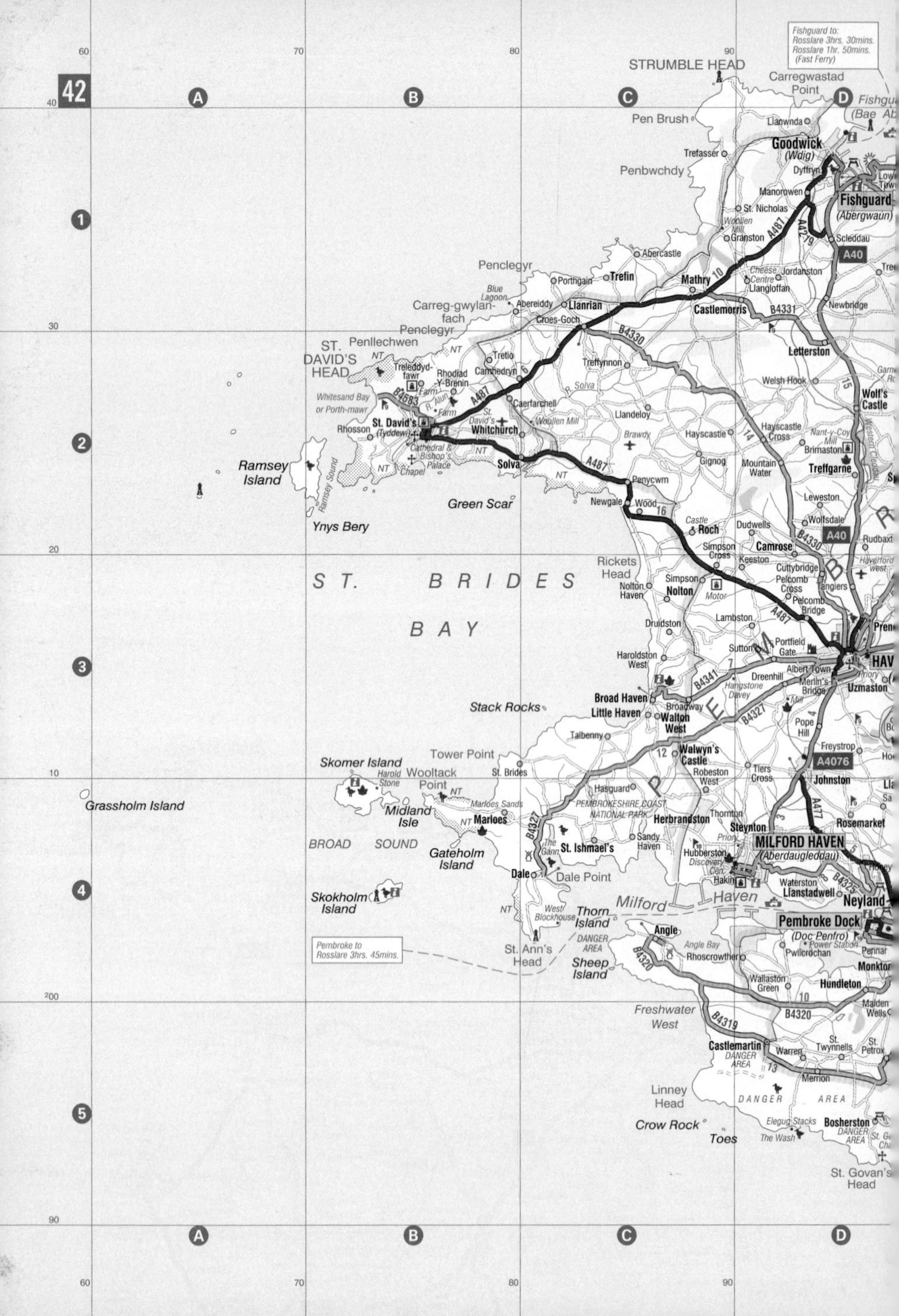
60
70
80
90
A
B
C
D
40
30
20
10
200
90
1
2
3
4
5
Fishguard to:
Rosslare 3hrs. 30mins.
Rosslare 1hr. 50mins.
(Fast Ferry)
STRUMBLE HEAD
Carregwastad Point
Pen Brush
Llanwnda
Goodwick
(Wdig)
Trefasser
Penbwchdy
Dyffryn
Manorowen
Fishguard
(Abergwaun)
St. Nicholas
Woollen Mill
Granston
A487
A40
A4219
Scleddau
Abercastle
Penclegyr
Porthgain
Trefin
Mathry
Cheese Centre
Jordanston
Llangloffan
Blue Lagoon
Abereiddy
Llanrian
Castlemorris
B4331
Newbridge
Carreg-gwylan-fach
Croes-Goch
Penclegyr
ST. DAVID'S HEAD
Penllechwen
NT
Tretio
B4330
Treffynnon
Letterston
Treleddyd-fawr
Rhodiad Y-Brenin
Carnhedryn
Farm
R. Alun
R. Solva
Welsh Hook
Wolf's Castle
Whitesand Bay or Porth-mawr
B4583
Caerfarchell
Llandeloy
St. David's
(Tyddewi)
St. David's
Whitchurch
Woollen Mill
Brawdy
Hayscastle
Hayscastle Cross
Rhosson
Cathedral & Bishop's Palace
Chapel
Solva
Gignog
Mountain Water
Brimaston
Treffgarne
Ramsey Island
Ramsey Sound
Western Cleddau
Penycwm
Green Scar
Newgale
Wood
16
Leweston
Wolfsdale
Ynys Bery
Castle
Roch
Dudwells
Camrose
B4330
A40
Rudbaxton
Simpston Cross
Keeston
Cuttybridge
Rickets Head
ST. BRIDES
Nolton Haven
Simpson
Nolton
Motor
Pelcomb Cross
Pelcomb Bridge
Tangiers
Haverfordwest
BAY
Druidston
Lambston
Haroldston West
Sutton
Portfield Gate
Albert Town
Merlin's Bridge
Uzmaston
Broad Haven
B4341
Dreenhill
Hangstone Davey
Stack Rocks
Little Haven
Broadway
Walton West
B4327
Mill
Pope Hill
Talbenny
Freystrop
Tower Point
Walwyn's Castle
A4076
Skomer Island
Harold Stone
Wooltack Point
St. Brides
Robeston West
Tiers Cross
Johnston
Grassholm Island
Hasguard
PEMBROKESHIRE COAST NATIONAL PARK
Marloes Sands
Midland Isle
Marloes
Herbrandston
Thornton
A477
Rosemarket
Steynton
Priory
MILFORD HAVEN
(Aberdaugleddau)
BROAD SOUND
The Gann
St. Ishmael's
Sandy Haven
Gateholm Island
Hubberston
Discovery Cen.
Dale
Dale Point
Hakin
Waterston
Llanstadwell
Neyland
Skokholm Island
Milford Haven
West Blockhouse
Thorn Island
Pembroke Dock
(Doc Penfro)
Power Station
Angle
Angle Bay
Pembroke to Rosslare 3hrs. 45mins.
St. Ann's Head
DANGER AREA
Sheep Island
Rhoscrowther
Pwllcrochan
B4320
Monkton
Wallaston Green
Hundleton
Freshwater West
B4320
B4319
Maiden Wells
Castlemartin
DANGER AREA
Warren
St. Twynnells
St. Petrox
Merrion
Linney Head
DANGER AREA
Crow Rock
Toes
Elegug Stacks
The Wash
Bosherston
St. Govan's Head

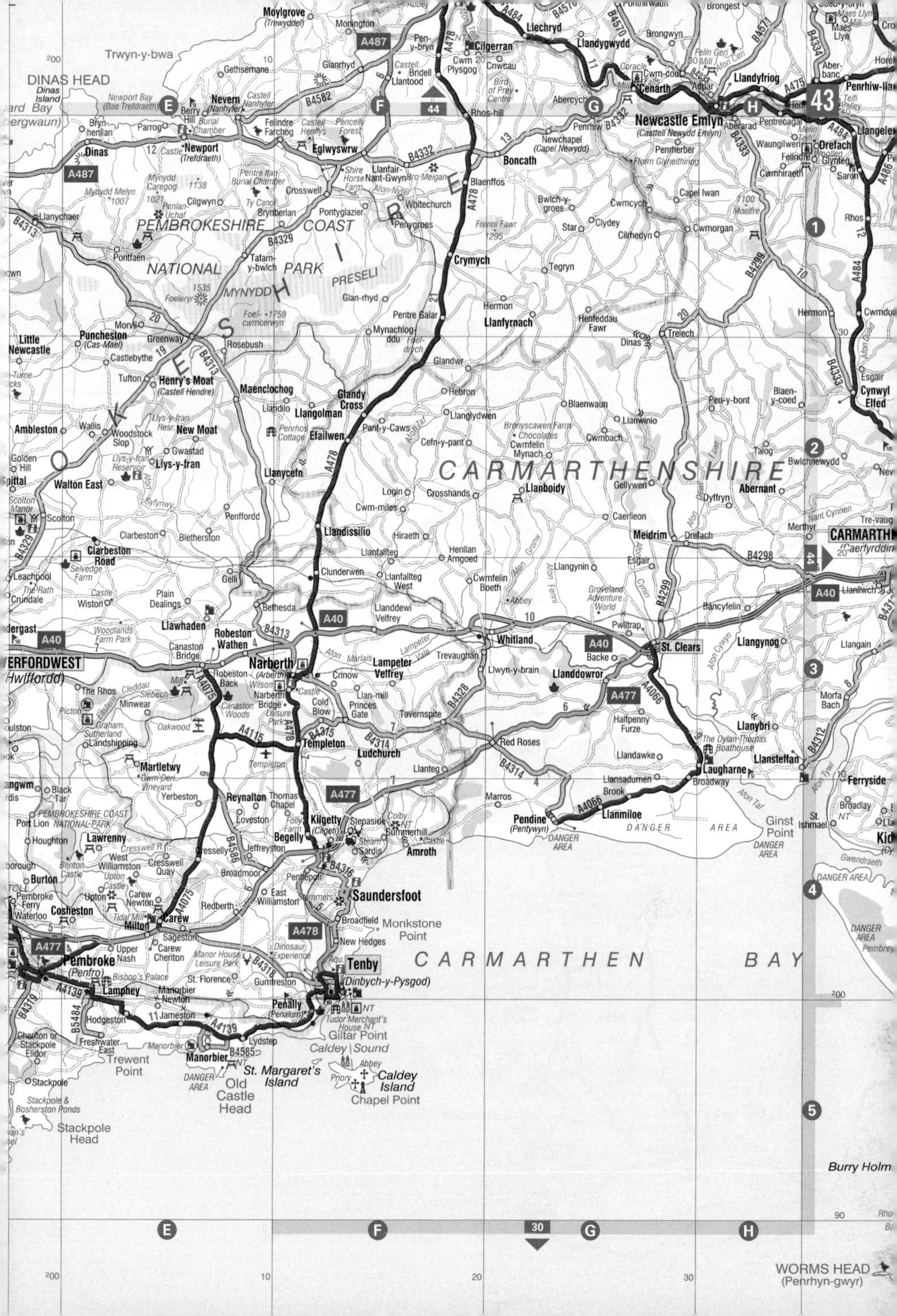
Moylgrove
(Trewyddel)
Monington
A487
Pen-y-bryn
Cilgerran
A484
Llechryd
Llandygwydd
Brongest
Brongwyn
Trwyn-y-bwa
Glanrhyd
Castell
Bridell
Llantood
Cwm
Plysgog
Cnwcau
Bird of Prey Centre
Felin Geri
Coracle
Cwm-cou
Llandyfriog
Aber-banc
Penrhiw-llan
DINAS HEAD
Dinas Island
Gethsemane
Castell Nanhyfer
Nevern
(Nanhyfer)
Newport Bay
(Bae Trefdraeth)
Berry Hill
Burial Chamber
B4582
44
Rhos-hill
Abercych
Cenarth
Adpar
Newcastle Emlyn
(Castell Newydd Emlyn)
Aberarad
Pentrecagal
Teifi Valley
43
Llangeler
Bryn-henllan
Parrog
Newport
(Trefdraeth)
Felindre Farchog
Castell Henllys
Pencelly Forest
Eglwyswrw
B4332
Boncath
Penrhiw
Newchapel
(Capel Newydd)
Penmerber
Waungilwen
Drefach
Felindre
Glynteg
Dinas
Castle
A487
Mynydd Carregog
1138
Pentre Ifan Burial Chamber
Shire Horse Farm
Llanfair-Nant-Gwyn
Bro Meigan
Blaenffos
Ffynnon Glyneithinog
Cwmhiraeth
Saron
Mynydd Melyn
1007
1021
Penlan-Uchaf
Cilgwyn
Ty Canol
Crosswell
Afon Nyfer
Whitechurch
Bwlch-y-groes
Cwmcych
Capel Iwan
Moelfre
Llanychaer
Brynberian
Pontyglazier
Penygroes
Star
Clydey
Cilrhedyn
Cwmorgan
Rhos
PEMBROKESHIRE
COAST
Frenni Fawr
1295
Pontfaen
B4329
Tafarn-y-bwlch
NATIONAL
PARK
PRESELI
Crymych
Tegryn
B4299
A484
MYNYDD
Foelcwmcerwyn
1535
Glan-rhyd
Hermon
Llanfyrnach
Henfeddau Fawr
Hermon
Cwmduad
Foel-cwmcerwyn
1759
Pentre Galar
Morvil
Puncheston
(Cas-Mael)
Greenway
Rosebush
Mynachlog-ddu
Foel drych
Dinas
Trelech
Little Newcastle
Castlebythe
Glandwr
Afon Duad
B4333
Esgair
Tufton
Henry's Moat
(Castell Hendre)
Maenclochog
Glandy Cross
Hebron
Blaenwaun
Pen-y-bont
Blaen-y-coed
Cynwyl Elfed
Llandilo
Llangolman
Ambleston
Wallis
Llys-y-fran Resr.
Woodstock Slop
New Moat
Penrhos Cottage
Efailwen
Pant-y-Caws
Llanglydwen
Bronyscawen Farm
Chocolates
Cwmfelin Mynach
Llanwinio
Cwmbach
Talog
Bwlchnewydd
Golden Hill
Llys-y-fran Reservoir
Gwastad
Llys-y-fran
Llanycefn
A478
Cefn-y-pant
CARMARTHENSHIRE
Gellywen
Spittal
Walton East
Scolton Manor
Scolton
Sylfynwy
Penffordd
Login
Cwm-miles
Crosshands
Llanboidy
Caerlleon
Dyffryn
Abernant
Nant Cynnen
Merthyr
Tre-vaughan
CARMARTHEN
(Caerfyrddin)
Clarbeston
Bletherston
Llandissilio
Hiraeth
Meidrim
Drefach
Clarbeston Road
Selvedge Farm
Gelli
Clunderwen
Llanfallteg
Henllan Amgoed
Llangynin
Esgair
B4298
Llanfallteg West
Cwmfelin Boeth
Afon Gronw
Afon Fenni
Groveland Adventure World
Bancyfelin
Leachpool
The Rath
Crundale
Castle
Wiston
Plain Dealings
Bethesda
Llanddewi Velfrey
Abbey
A40
Llanllwch
Haverfordwest
(Hwlffordd)
Woodlands Farm Park
Llawhaden
Robeston Wathen
Canaston Bridge
Narberth
(Arberth)
B4313
Lampeter Velfrey
Afon Marlais
Lampeter Vale
Trevaughan
Whitland
Pwlltrap
St. Clears
Backe
Llangynog
Llangain
The Rhos
Picton
Cleddau
Slebech
Minwear
Robeston Back
Wilson
Narberth Bridge
Leisure Park
Castle
Crinow
Lan-mill
Cold Blow
Princes Gate
Llwyn-y-brain
Llanddowror
A477
A4066
Afon Cywyn
Morfa Bach
Graham Sutherland
Landshipping
Oakwood
Canaston Woods
A4075
A4115
Templeton
B4315
B4314
Tavernspite
B4328
Red Roses
Halfpenny Furze
The Dylan Thomas Boathouse
Llanybri
Martletwy
Cwm Deri Vineyard
Ludchurch
Llanteg
Llandawke
Laugharne
Llansteffan
B4312
Ferryside
Black Tar
Yerbeston
Reynalton
Thomas Chapel
Marros
Llansadurnen
Brook
Broadway
Afon Tar
Afon Tywi
Broadlay
PEMBROKESHIRE COAST NATIONAL PARK
Loveston
Folly Farm
Kilgetty
(Cilgeti)
Stepaside
Colby
Summerhill
Pendine
(Pentywyn)
A4066
Llanmiloe
DANGER AREA
Ginst Point
St. Ishmael
Port Lion
Houghton
Lawrenny
Cresswell R.
West Williamston
Jeffreyston
Begelly
Steam
Sardis
Amroth
Castle
Kidwelly
Benton Castle
Cresswell Quay
Cresselly
B4586
Broadmoor
B4316
Gwendraeth
Burton
Upton Castle
Pembroke Ferry
Waterloo
Upton
Carew Newton
Carew
A4075
Redberth
East Williamston
Pentlepoir
Saundersfoot
Cosheston
Tidal Mill
Milton
Sageston
Broadfield
Monkstone Point
A478
A477
Upper Nash
Carew Cheriton
Pembroke
(Penfro)
Bishop's Palace
Manor House Leisure Park
B4318
Dinosaur Experience
New Hedges
Tenby
(Dinbych-y-Pysgod)
CARMARTHEN
BAY
Pembrey
St. Florence
Gumfreston
Lamphey
Manorbier Newton
A4139
B4319
B5484
Hodgeston
Jameston
Penally
(Penalun)
Tudor Merchant's House
Giltar Point
Cheriton or Stackpole Elidor
Freshwater East
Manorbier
B4585
Lydstep
Caldey Sound
Trewent Point
Abbey
Priory
Caldey Island
St. Margaret's Island
Stackpole
DANGER AREA
Old Castle Head
Chapel Point
Stackpole & Bosherston Ponds
Stackpole Head
Burry Holm
E
F
30
G
H
WORMS HEAD
(Penrhyn-gwyr)

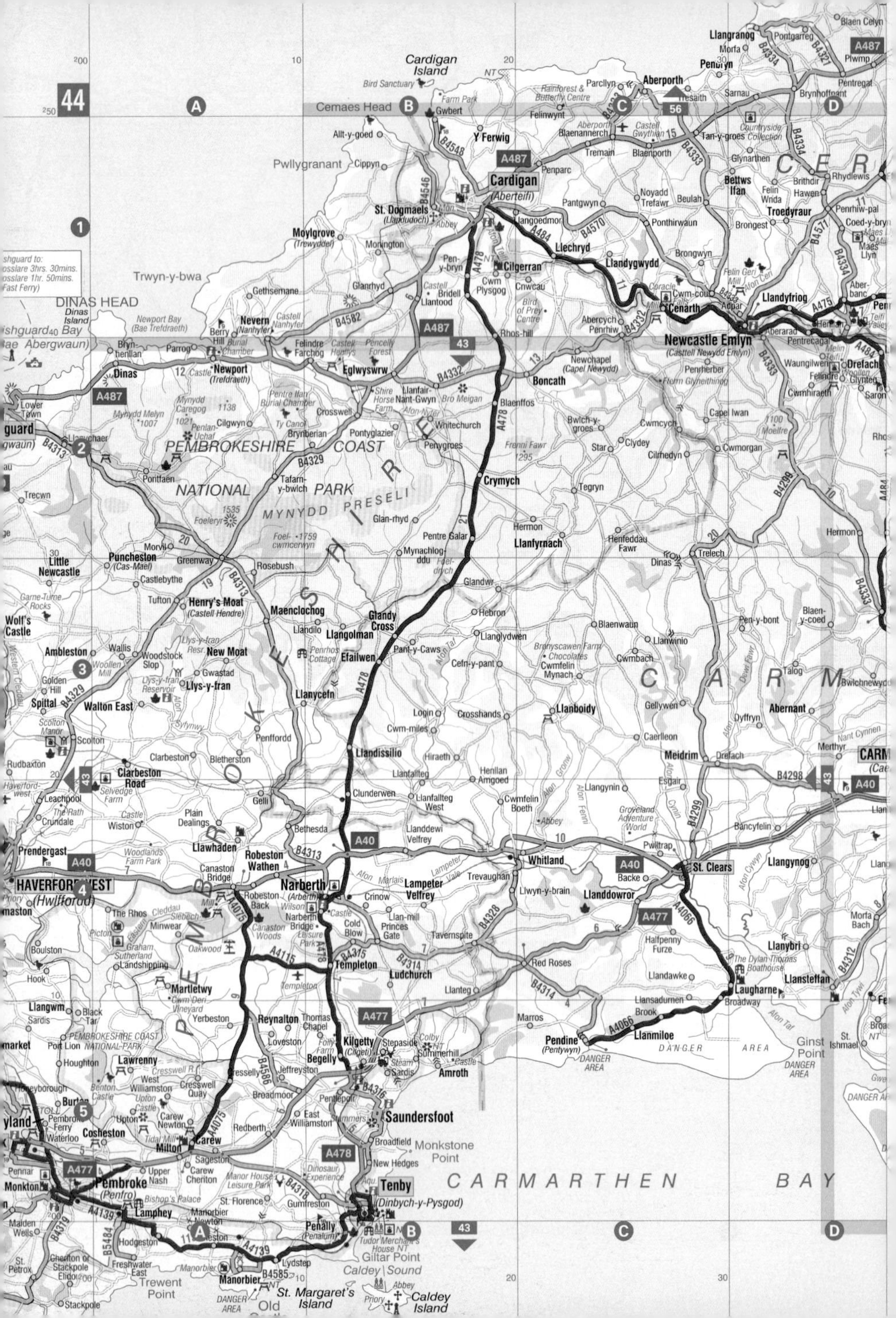
44
Cardigan Island
Bird Sanctuary
Cemaes Head
Gwbert
Farm Park
Y Ferwig
Allt-y-goed
Pwllygranant
Cippyn
Cardigan
(Aberteifi)
St. Dogmaels
(Llandudoch)
Abbey
Moylgrove
(Trewyddel)
Monington
Trwyn-y-bwa
Glanrhyd
Gethsemane
DINAS HEAD
Dinas Island
Fishguard to:
Rosslare 3hrs. 30mins.
Rosslare 1hr. 50mins.
(Fast Ferry)
Newport Bay
(Bae Trefdraeth)
Fishguard Bay
(Bae Abergwaun)
Berry Hill
Nevern
(Nanhyfer)
Castell Nanhyfer
Bryn-henllan
Parrog
Newport
(Trefdraeth)
Burial Chamber
Dinas
Lower Town
Felindre Farchog
Castell Henllys
Pencelly Forest
Eglwyswrw
Castell
Bridell
Llantood
Pen-y-bryn
Cilgerran
Cwm Plysgog
Cnwcau
Bird of Prey Centre
Rhos-hill
Llangoedmor
Llechryd
Llandygwydd
Llangranog
Morfa
Penbryn
Pontgarreg
Blaen Celyn
Plwmp
Pentregat
Parcllyn
Aberporth
Tresaith
Rainforest & Butterfly Centre
Felinwynt
Sarnau
Brynhoffnant
Blaenannerch
Aberporth
Castell Gwythian
Tan-y-groes
Countryside Collection
Tremain
Blaenporth
Glynarthen
Penparc
CER
Bettws Ifan
Felin Wrida
Brithdir
Rhydlewis
Hawen
Penrhiw-pal
Troedyraur
Coed-y-bryn
Maes Llyn
Pantgwyn
Noyadd Trefawr
Ponthirwaun
Beulah
Brongest
Brongwyn
Felin Geri Mill
Afon Ceri
Aber-banc
Llandyfriog
Coracle
Cwm-cou
Cenarth
Adpar
Abercych
Penrhiw
Newcastle Emlyn
(Castell Newydd Emlyn)
Aberarad
Pentrecagal
Henllan
Teifi Valley
Drefach
Felindre
Woollen
Glynteg
Saron
Waungilwen
Cwmhiraeth
Newchapel
(Capel Newydd)
Boncath
Penrherber
Fferm Glyneithinog
Shire Horse Farm
Llanfair-Nant-Gwyn
Bro Meigan
Afon Nyfer
Crosswell
Pentre Ifan Burial Chamber
Mynydd Carregog
Mynydd Melyn
Penlan-Uchaf
Cilgwyn
Ty Canol
Brynberian
Pontyglazier
Whitechurch
Penygroes
Blaenffos
Bwlch-y-groes
Capel Iwan
Cwmcych
Moelfre
Star
Clydey
Cilrhedyn
Cwmorgan
Frenni Fawr
Goodwick
Llanychaer
PEMBROKESHIRE COAST
NATIONAL PARK
Pontfaen
Tafarn-y-bwlch
MYNYDD PRESELI
Crymych
Tegryn
Trecwn
Foeleryr
Foel-cwmcerwyn
Glan-rhyd
Hermon
Pentre Galar
Llanfyrnach
Henfeddau Fawr
Trelech
Dinas
Hermon
Little Newcastle
Puncheston
(Cas-Mael)
Morvil
Greenway
Rosebush
Mynachlog-ddu
Foel-drych
Castlebythe
Garne Turne Rocks
Tufton
Henry's Moat
(Castell Hendre)
Glandwr
Hebron
Wolf's Castle
Maenclochog
Llandilo
Llangolman
Glandy Cross
Blaenwaun
Pen-y-bont
Blaen-y-coed
Ambleston
Wallis
Woodstock Slop
Llys-y-fran Resr.
New Moat
Penrhos Cottage
Efailwen
Pant-y-Caws
Llanglydwen
Bronyscawen Farm Chocolates
Cwmfelin Mynach
Llanwinio
Cwmbach
Talog
Bwlchnewydd
Woollen Mill
Golden Hill
Gwastad
Llys-y-fran Reservoir
Llys-y-fran
Cefn-y-pant
CARM
Spittal
Walton East
Llanycefn
Gellywen
Abernant
Scolton Manor
Scolton
Login
Crosshands
Llanboidy
Dyffryn
Cwm-miles
Caerlleon
Nant Cynnen
Merthyr
Rudbaxton
Clarbeston
Bletherston
Penffordd
Llandissilio
Hiraeth
Meidrim
Drefach
Clarbeston Road
Selvedge Farm
Llanfallteg
Henllan Amgoed
Llangynin
Esgair
Haverfordwest
Leachpool
The Rath
Crundale
Gelli
Clunderwen
Llanfallteg West
Cwmfelin Boeth
Abbey
Groveland Adventure World
Bancyfelin
Plain Dealings
Castle
Wiston
Bethesda
Llanddewi Velfrey
Pwlltrap
Llawhaden
Robeston Wathen
Narberth
(Arberth)
Whitland
St. Clears
Llangynog
Prendergast
Woodlands Farm Park
Canaston Bridge
Lampeter Vale
Trevaughan
Backe
HAVERFORDWEST
(Hwlffordd)
Robeston Back
Wilson Museum
Crinow
Lampeter Velfrey
Llwyn-y-brain
Llanddowror
Priory
Haroldston
The Rhos
Cleddau
Slebech
Narberth Bridge
Castle
Cold Blow
Lan-mill
Princes Gate
Tavernspite
Halfpenny Furze
Morfa Bach
Picton
Minwear
Canaston Woods
Leisure Park
Eastern Cleddau
Graham Sutherland
Oakwood
Templeton
Boulston
Landshipping
Ludchurch
Red Roses
Llanybri
Dylan Thomas Boathouse
Llandawke
Llansteffan
Hook
Martletwy
Cwm Deri Vineyard
Llanteg
Laugharne
Llansadurnen
Brook
Broadway
Llangwm
Black Tar
Sardis
Yerbeston
Reynalton
Thomas Chapel
Loveston
Folly Farm
Marros
Pendine
(Pentywyn)
Llanmiloe
DANGER AREA
Ginst Point
St. Ishmael
Neyland
PEMBROKESHIRE COAST NATIONAL PARK
Port Lion
Houghton
Lawrenny
Kilgetty
(Cilgeti)
Begelly
Stepaside
Colby
Summerhill
Steam
Sardis
Amroth
Castle
West Williamston
Cresswell Quay
Cresselly
Jeffreyston
Honeyborough
Burton
Benton Castle
Upton Castle
Broadmoor
Pentlepoir
Saundersfoot
Pembroke Ferry
Waterloo
Cosheston
Upton
Carew Newton
Redberth
East Williamston
Tidal Mill
Milton
Carew
Broadfield
Monkstone Point
Sageston
Upper Nash
Carew Cheriton
New Hedges
Pennar
Monkton
Pembroke
(Penfro)
Bishop's Palace
Manor House Leisure Park
Dinosaur Experience
Tenby
(Dinbych-y-Pysgod)
CARMARTHEN BAY
St. Florence
Gumfreston
Lamphey
Manorbier Newton
Penally
(Penalun)
Tudor Merchant's House
Maiden Wells
Hodgeston
Jameston
Gilltar Point
Caldey Sound
Cheriton or Stackpole Elidor
Freshwater East
Manorbier
Lydstep
St. Petrox
Trewent Point
St. Margaret's Island
Caldey Island
Abbey
Priory
Stackpole
DANGER AREA

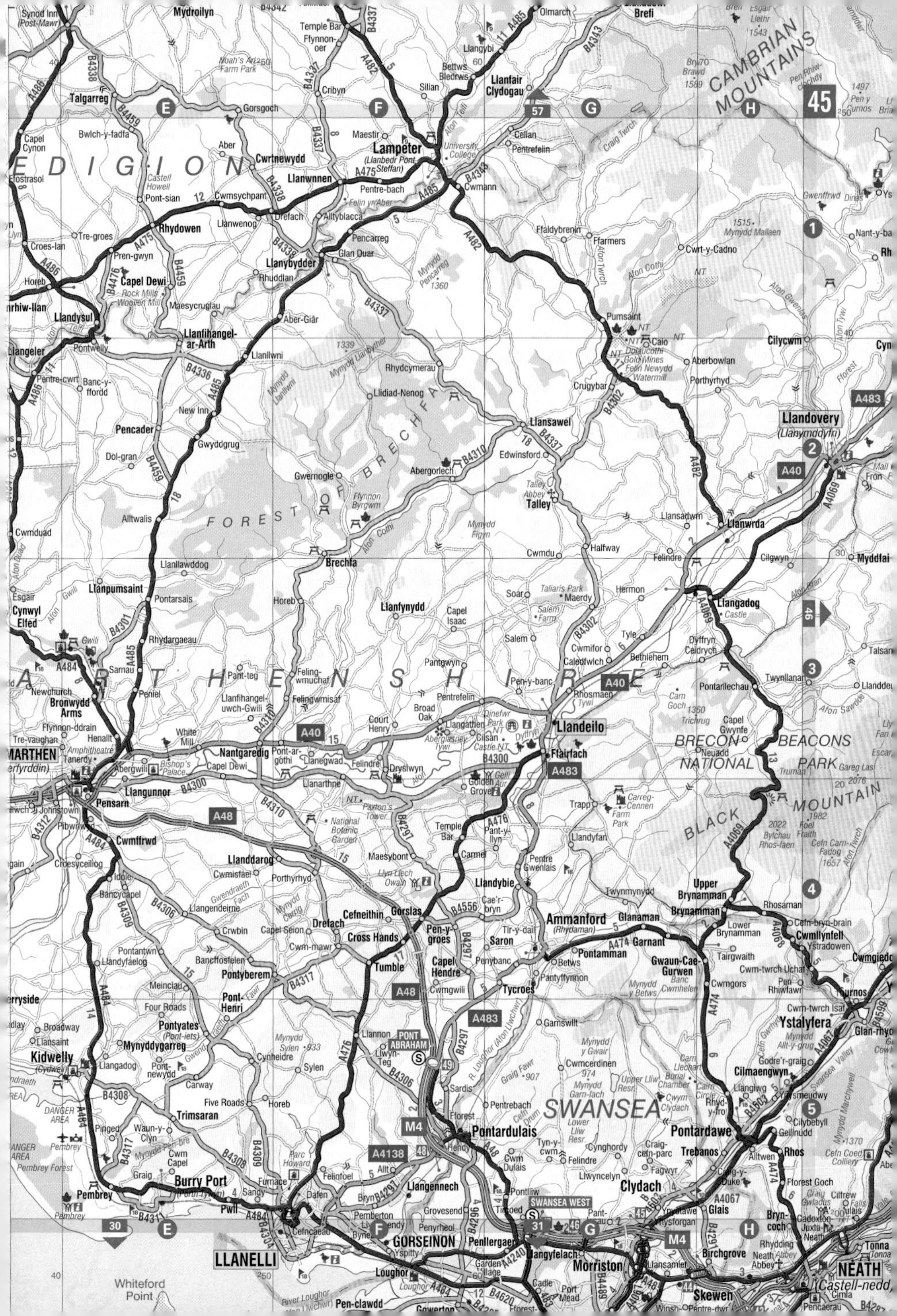

45
CAMBRIAN MOUNTAINS
E
F
G
H
57
30
46
1
2
3
4
5
Synod Inn
(Post-Mawr)
Mydroilyn
Temple Bar
Ffynnon-oer
Olmarch
Brefi
Llangybi
Bettws Bledrws
Llanfair Clydogau
Noah's Ark Farm Park
Talgarreg
Gorsgoch
Cribyn
Silian
Maestir
Lampeter
(Llanbedr Pont Steffan)
University College
Cellan
Pentrefelin
Craig Twrch
Bryn Brawd
1589
Pen Rhiw-wchdy
1497
Pen y Gurnos
Bwlch-y-fadfa
Capel Cynon
Aber
Cwrtnewydd
EDIGION
Ffostrasol
Castell Howell
Pont-sian
Llanwnnen
Pentre-bach
Cwmann
Cwmsychpant
Drefach
Felin yr Aber
Alltyblacca
Rhydowen
Llanwenog
Tre-groes
Pencarreg
Glan Duar
Llanybydder
Croes-lan
Pren-gwyn
Capel Dewi
Rock Mills Woollen Mill
Horeb
Rhuddlan
Mynydd Pencarreg
1360
Gwenffrwd
Dinas
1515
Mynydd Mallaen
Nant-y-bai
Ffaldybrenin
Ffarmers
Afon Twrch
Cwrt-y-Cadno
Afon Cothi
NT
Llandysul
Maesycrugiau
Aber-Giâr
Pumsaint
Caio
Dolaucothi Gold Mines
Felin Newydd Watermill
Cilycwm
Afon Gwenlas
Afon Tywi
Llangeler
Pontwelly
Llanfihangel-ar-Arth
Llanllwni
1339
Mynydd Llanybyther
Rhydcymerau
Aberbowlan
Porthyrhyd
Ffforest
Pentre-cwrt
Banc-y-ffordd
Mynydd Llanllwni
Lllidiad-Nenog
Crugybar
Llansawel
Edwinsford
Llandovery
(Llanymddyfri)
Pencader
New Inn
Gwyddgrug
FOREST OF BRECHFA
Abergorlech
Dol-gran
Gwernogle
Ffynnon Byrgwm
Talley Abbey
Talley
Mail
Fron
Cwmduad
Alltwalis
Mynydd Figyn
Llansadwrn
Llanwrda
Llanllawddog
Brechfa
Cwmdu
Halfway
Felindre
Cilgwyn
Myddfai
Esgair
Afon Gwili
Llanpumsaint
Pontarsais
Horeb
Soar
Taliaris Park
Maerdy
Hermon
Llangadog
Castle
Cynwyl Elfed
Llanfynydd
Capel Isaac
Salem Farm
Salem
Tyle
Dyffryn Ceidrych
Rhydargaeau
Cwmifor
Caledfwlch
Bethlehem
Sarnau
Pantgwyn
Pen-y-banc
Twynllanan
Talsarn
Llanddeusant
Afon Sawdde
Newchurch
Pant-teg
Feling-wmuchaf
Felingwmisaf
Bronwydd Arms
Penlel
Pentrefelin
Rhosmaen
Pontarllechau
Carn Goch
Llanfihangel-uwch-Gwili
Broad Oak
1360
Trichrug
Capel Gwynfe
Ffynnon-ddrain
White Mill
Court Henry
Llangathen
Dinefwr Park
Llandeilo
BRECON NATIONAL BEACONS PARK
Tre-vaughan
Henallt
Aberglasney
Cilsan
Dryslwyn
Castle NT
Escar
Amphitheatre
Nantgaredig
Pont-ar-gothi
Neuadd
Ffairfach
Tanerdy
Abergwili
Bishop's Palace
Capel Dewi
Llanegwad
Felindre
Dryslwyn
Trumian
Gareg Las
2076
Pensarn
Llangunnor
Llanarthne
Golden Grove
Gelli Aur
Trapp
Carreg Cennen
Farm Park
Johnstown
Paxton's Tower
National Botanic Garden
BLACK MOUNTAIN
Pibwrlwyd
Cwmffrwd
Temple Bar
Pant-y-llyn
Llandyfan
2022
Bylchau Rhos-faen
1982
Foel Fraith
Cefn Cam-Fadog
1657
Afon Twrch
Croesyceiliog
Llanddarog
Maesybont
Carmel
Pentre Gwenlais
Cwmisfael
Porthyrhyd
Llyn Llech Owain
Llandybie
Twynmynydd
Upper Brynamman
Idole
Gwendraeth Fach
Rhosaman
Bancycapel
Llangendeirne
Mynydd Cerrig
Cefneithin
Gorslas
Cae'r-bryn
Ammanford
(Rhydaman)
Glanaman
Brynamman
Cefn-bryn-brain
Crwbin
Capel Seion
Drefach
Cross Hands
Pen-y-groes
Tir-y-dail
Saron
Garnant
Lower Brynamman
Cwmllynfell
Ystradowen
Cwmgiedd
Pontantwn
Cwm-mawr
Tumble
Pontamman
Betws
Gwaun-Cae-Gurwen
Tairgwaith
Cwm-twrch Uchaf
Llandyfaelog
Bancffosfelen
Capel Hendre
Penybanc
Pantyffynnon
Cwmgors
Pen Rhiwfawr
Gurnos
Ferryside
Meinciau
Pontyberem
Cwmgwili
Tycroes
Mynydd y Betws
Banc Cwmhelen
Cwm-twrch Isaf
Ystalyfera
Glan-rhyd
Broadway
Four Roads
Pont-Henri
Pontyates
(Pont-iets)
Garnswllt
Llansaint
Mynyddygarreg
Llannon
PONT ABRAHAM
Mynydd Sylen
933
Mynydd Allt-y-grug
Kidwelly
(Cydweli)
Llangadog
Gwendraeth
Pont-newydd
Cynheidre
Llwyn-Teg
Sylen
Cwmcerdinen
974
Mynydd Garn-fach
Upper Lliw Resr.
Carn Llechart
Burial Chamber
Cairn Circle
Godre'r-graig
Cilmaengwyn
DANGER AREA
Carway
B4306
Sardis
Graig Fawr
907
Cwym Clydach
Llangiwg
Ynysmeudwy
Swansea Valley
Five Roads
Horeb
Trimsaran
Pentrebach
Cefn Drum
SWANSEA
Lower Lliw Resr.
Rhyd-y-fro
Cilybebyll
Gellinudd
1370
Pinged
Waun-y-Clyn
Mynydd Pen-bre
Forest
Pontardulais
Tyn-y-cwm
Pontardawe
Alltwen
Rhos
Cefn Coed Colliery
Pembrey
Cwm Capel
Parc Howard
Hendy
Cynghordy
Craig-cefn-parc
Trebanos
Pembrey Forest
Graig
Burry Port
(Porth Tywyn)
Furnace
Felinfoel
Allt
Llangennech
Cwm Dulais
Felindre
Fagwyr
Craig-y-Duke
Fforest Goch
Cilfrew
Pembrey
Sandy
Pwll
Dafen
Bryn
Pemberton
Llwynhendy
Pontlliw
Llwyncelyn
Clydach
Ysnystawe
Glais
Cwm Gwladus
Aberdulais
Cadoxton Juxta-Neath
Bryn-coch
SWANSEA WEST
Pant-lasau
Ynysforgan
Tonna
Cefncaeau
Bynea
Penyrheol
Tircoed
Birchgrove
Rhyddings
Neath Abbey
LLANELLI
GORSEINON
Penllergaer
Llangyfelach
Morriston
Llansamlet
NEATH
(Castell-nedd)
Ysbytty
Loughor
Garden Village
Cadle
Port Mead
Skewen
Pencaerau
Cimla
Whiteford Point
River Loughor
(Afon Llwchwr)
Pen-clawdd
Gowerton
Winsh-wen
Pentre-dwr
40
250
M4
A40
A48
A483
A4138
A4069
A482
A485
A486
A484
A476
A474
A475
A4067
A4240
B4336
B4337
B4338
B4459
B4302
B4310
B4300
B4297
B4306
B4309
B4317
B4308
B4301
B4312
B4556
B4343
B4342
B4476
B4304
B4296
B4620
B4489
B4603
B4291
B4599
49
48
47
46
45
44
31

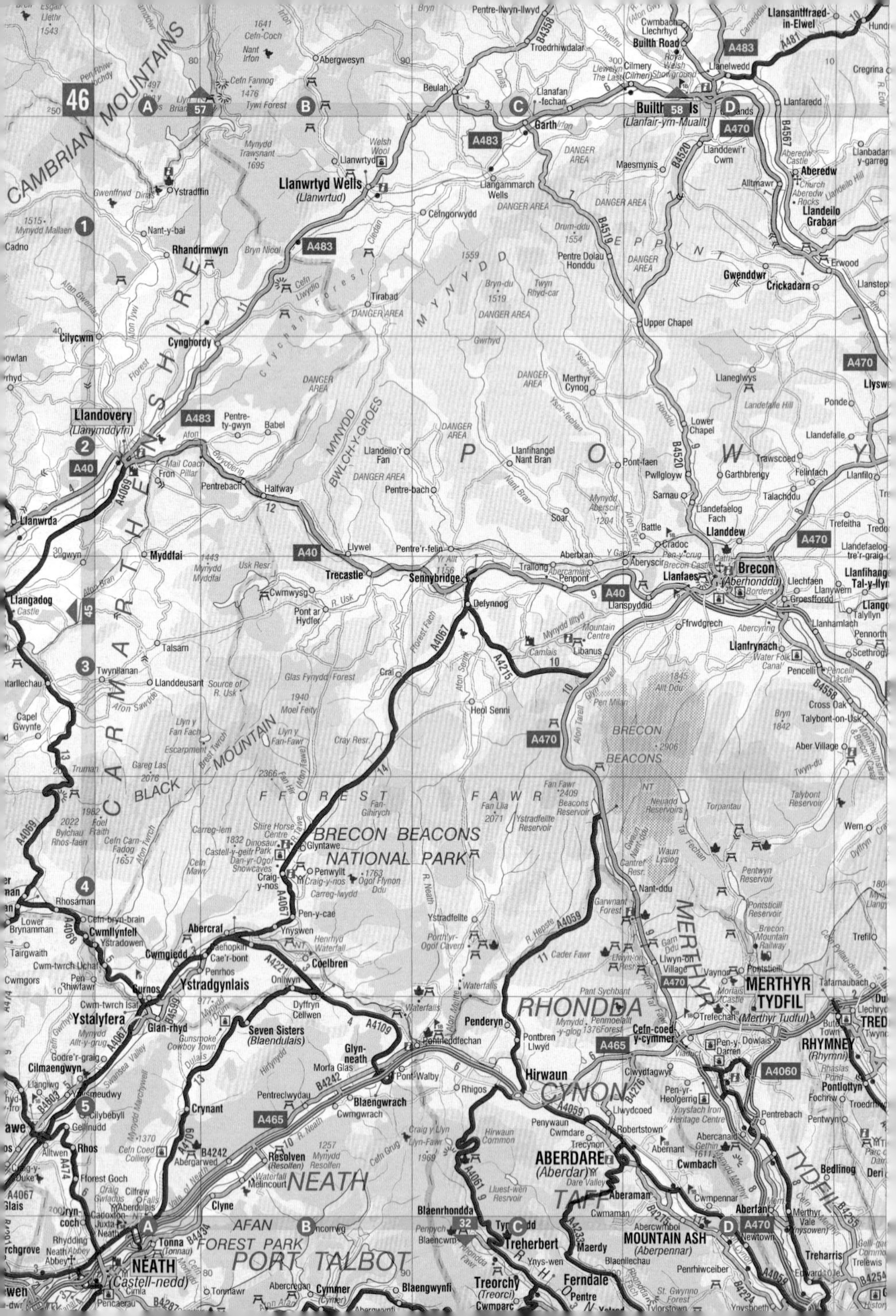

46
57
58
45
32
CAMBRIAN MOUNTAINS
CARMARTHENSHIRE
POWYS
MYNYDD EPPYNT
MYNYDD BWLCH-Y-GROES
BLACK MOUNTAIN
FFOREST FAWR
BRECON BEACONS
BRECON BEACONS NATIONAL PARK
MERTHYR TYDFIL
RHONDDA CYNON TAFF
NEATH PORT TALBOT
AFAN FOREST PARK
Llansantffraed-in-Elwel
Pentre-llwyn-llwyd
Cwmbach Llechrhyd
Builth Road
Abergwesyn
Troedrhiwdalar
Cilmery (Cilmeri)
Llewelyn The Last
Royal Welsh Showground
Llanelwedd
Cregrina
Beulah
Llanafan-fechan
Builth Wells (Llanfair-ym-Muallt)
Garth
Llanfaredd
Tywi Forest
Cefn Fannog
Nant Irfon
Cefn-Coch
Welsh Wool
Llanwrtyd
Llanwrtyd Wells (Llanwrtud)
Mynydd Trawsnant 1695
Llangammarch Wells
Maesmynis
Llanddewi'r Cwm
Aberedw
Aberedw Castle
Aberedw Rocks
Alltmawr
Llanbadarn-y-garreg
Llandeilo Graban
Ystradffin
Gwenffrwd
Dinas
Mynydd Mallaen 1515
Nant-y-bai
Cadno
Rhandirmwyn
Bryn Nicol
Cefngorwydd
DANGER AREA
Drum-ddu 1554
Pentre Dolau Honddu
Erwood
Gwenddwr
Crickadarn
Llanstephan
Cefn Llwydlo
Tirabad
Crychan Forest
Bryn-du 1519
Twyn Rhyd-car
Upper Chapel
Cilycwm
Cynghordy
Afon Tywi
Afon Gwenlas
Gwrhyd
Merthyr Cynog
Llandovery (Llanymddyfri)
Pentre-ty-gwyn
Babel
Llaneglwys
Landefalle Hill
Ponde
Llandefalle
Lower Chapel
Mail Coach Pillar
Fron
Pentrebach
Halfway
Llandeilo'r Fan
Pentre-bach
Llanfihangel Nant Bran
Pont-faen
Pwllgloyw
Trawscoed
Garthbrengy
Felinfach
Llanfilo
Llanwrda
Sarnau
Llandefaelog Fach
Talachddu
Mynydd Myddfai 1443
Myddfai
Usk Resr.
Llywel
Pentre'r-felin
Soar
Mynydd Aberscir 1204
Battle
Cradoc
Llanddew
Trefeitha
Tredomen
Cilgwyn
Trecastle
Sennybridge
Yr Allt 1156
Trallong
Aberbran
Abercamlais
Penpont
Y Gaer
Aberyscir
Pen-y-crug
Brecon Castle
Brecon (Aberhonddu)
Borders
Llanfaes
Llechfaen
Llanfihangel Tal-y-llyn
Llandefaelog-tre'r-graig
Llangadog
Castle
Cwmwysg
Pont ar Hydfer
R. Usk
Defynnog
Llanspyddid
Groesffordd
Llanywern
Llangors
Talyllyn
Talsarn
Mynydd Illtyd
Mountain Centre
Libanus
Camlais
Ffrwdgrech
Abercynrig
Llanhamlach
Pennorth
Scethrog
Llanfrynach
Water Folk Canal
Pencelli
Pencelli Castle
Twynllanan
Llanddeusant
Source of R. Usk
Glas Fynydd Forest
Crai
Afon Senni
Heol Senni
Glyn Tarell
Allt Ddu 1845
Pen Milan
Afon Sawdde
Capel Gwynfe
Moel Feity 1940
Llyn y Fan Fach
Llyn y Fan-Fawr
Cray Resr.
Escarpment
Brest Twrch
Gareg Las 2076
Truman
Fan Hir 2366
Afon Tawe
Fan-Gihirych
Fan Fawr 2409
Fan Llia 2071
Beacons Reservoir
Ystradfellte Reservoir
2906
Neuadd Reservoirs
Torpantau
Talybont Reservoir
Cross Oak
Talybont-on-Usk
Bryn 1842
Aber Village
Monmouthshire & Brecon Canal
Twyn-du
Wern
Foel Fraith 1982
Bylchau Rhos-faen 2022
Cefn Carn-Fadog 1657
Afon Twrch
Carreg-lem 1832
Shire Horse Centre
Dinosaur Park
Castell-y-geifr
Dan-yr-Ogof Showcaves
Glyntawe
Penwyllt
Craig-y-nos
Ogof Ffynon Ddu 1763
Carreg-lwydd
Cefn Mawr
Cantref Resr.
Waun Lysiog
Taf Fechan
Pentwyn Reservoir
Pontsticill Reservoir
Brecon Mountain Railway
Nant-ddu
Garwnant Forest
Gwaun Nant-ddu
Rhosaman
Lower Brynamman
Cefn-bryn-brain
Cwmllynfell
Ystradowen
Pen-y-cae
Abercraf
Ynyswen
Henrhyd Waterfall
Ystradfellte
Porth'yr-Ogof Cavern
R. Hepste
Cader Fawr
Garn Ddu
Llwyn-on Resr
Llwyn-on Village
Vaynor
Pontsticill
Morlais Castle
Trefil
Tafarnaubach
Dukestown
Llechryd
Tredegar
Rhymney (Rhymni)
Tairgwaith
Cwm-twrch Uchaf
Cwmgiedd
Caehopkin
Cae'r-bont
Penrhos
Coelbren
Onllwyn
Cwmgors
Pen Rhiwfawr
Gurnos
Ystradgynlais
Cwm-twrch Isaf
Ystalyfera
Glan-rhyd
Dyffryn Cellwen
Seven Sisters (Blaendulais)
Gunsmoke Cowboy Town
Waterfalls
Afon Mellte
Penderyn
Pontneddfechan
Pant Sychbant
Mynydd-y-glog
Penmoelallt Forest 1376
Pontbren Llwyd
Cefn-coed-y-cymmer
Trefechan (Merthyr Tudful)
Pen-y-Darren
Dowlais
Viaduct
Butetown
Rhaslas Pond
Pontlottyn
Fochriw
Troedrhiwfuwch
Mynydd Allt-y-grug
Godre'r-graig
Cilmaengwyn
Llangiwg
Ynysmeudwy
Swansea Valley
Dulais
Hirfynydd
Glyn-neath
Morfa Glas
Pont Walby
Rhigos
Hirwaun
Clwydfagwyr
Pen-yr-Heolgerrig
Ynysfach Iron Heritage Centre
Pentrebach
Pentwyn
Cilybebyll
Gellinudd
Crynant
Pentreclwydau
Blaengwrach
Cwmgwrach
Craig y Llyn
Llyn-Fawr 1969
Hirwaun Common
Penywaun
Cwmdare
Llwydcoed
Robertstown
Trecynon
Abernant
Gethin 1611
Mynydd Merthyr
Abercanaid
Rhos
Alltwen
Cefn Coed Colliery
Abergarwed
Resolven (Resolfen)
Mynydd Resolfen 1257
Cefn Grug
ABERDARE (Aberdar)
Dare Valley
Cwmbach
Cwmpennar
Bedlinog
Craig-y-Duke
Fforest Goch
Craig Gwladus
Cilfrew
Aberdulais
Falls
Melincourt
Vale of Neath
Lluest-wen Resrvoir
Aberaman
Cwmaman
Aberfan
Merthyr Vale (Ynysowen)
Glais
Clyne
Blaenrhondda
Tynewydd
Abercwmboi
Newtown
Treharris
Trelewis
Cadoxton-Juxta-Neath
Rhydding
Neath Abbey
Tonna (Tonnau)
Penpych
Blaencwm
Treherbert
Maerdy
MOUNTAIN ASH (Aberpennar)
Blaenllechau
Penrhiwceiber
Rhondda Fawr
Ynys-wen
NEATH (Castell-nedd)
Cimla
Pencaerau
Tonmawr
Abercregan
Cymmer (Cymer)
Blaengwynfi
Treorchy (Treorci)
Cwmparc
Ferndale
Pentre
St. Gwynno Forest
Ynysboeth
Edwardsville
A483
A40
A4069
A470
A481
A4067
A4215
A4221
A4109
B4242
A465
A4059
B4276
A4060
A4061
A4233
B4275
A474
B4603
A4068
B4599
B4434
B4358
B4520
B4519
B4567
B4558
A4224
B4255
B4254
B4287

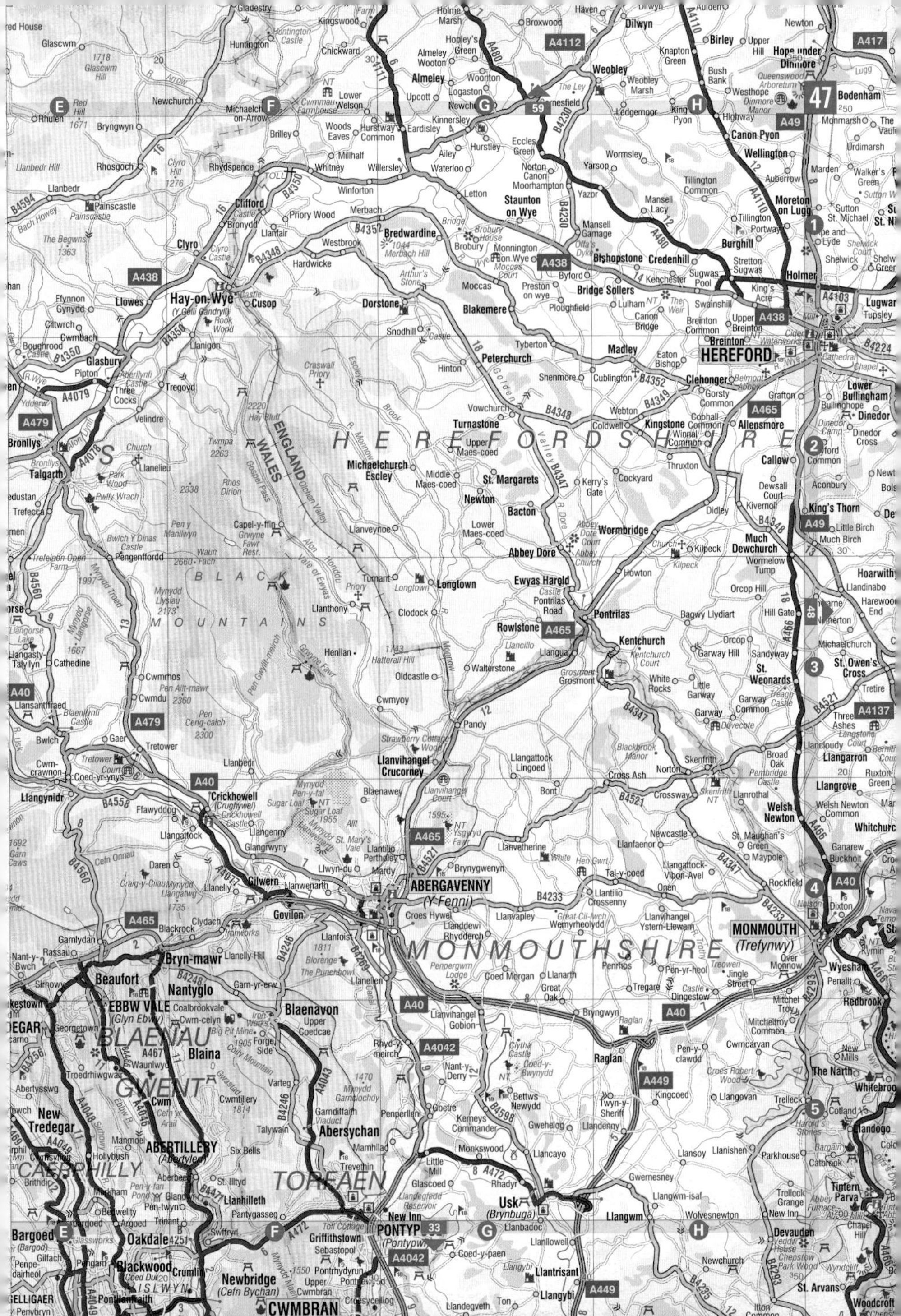

47
Gladestry
Kingswood
Holme Marsh
Broxwood
Dilwyn
A4112
Huntington
Huntington Castle
Chickward
Almeley Wooton
Hopley's Green
Weobley
Weobley Marsh
Knapton Green
Birley
Upper Hill
Hope under Dinmore
Queenswood Arboretum
A417
Glascwm
Glascwm Hill
Almeley
Woonton
Logaston
Bush Bank
Westhope
Dinmore Manor
Bodenham
Newchurch
Michaelchurch-on-Arrow
Lower Welson
Cwmmau Farmhouse
Upcott
Newchurch
59
Sarnesfield
Ledgemoor
King Pyon
Highway
A49
Red Hill
Rhulen
Bryngwyn
Woods Eaves
Hurstway Common
Eardisley
Kinnersley
Canon Pyon
Brilley
Millhalf
Ailey
Hurstley
Eccles Green
Wormsley
Wellington
Urdimarsh
Llanbedr Hill
Rhosgoch
Clyro Hill
Rhydspence
Whitney
Willersley
Waterloo
Norton Canon
Yarsop
Marden
Moorhampton
Tillington Common
Llanbedr
Painscastle
Winforton
Letton
Auberrow
B4594
Clifford
Clifford Castle
Bronydd
Priory Wood
Merbach
Staunton on Wye
Yazor
Mansell Lacy
Moreton on Lugg
Sutton St. Michael
B4350
Bach Howey
Bredwardine
Brobury House
Brobury
Merbach Hill
Llanfair
Westbrook
B4352
Mansell Gamage
Offa's Dyke
Tillington
Portway
Burghill
The Begwns
Clyro
Clyro Castle
Hardwicke
Monnington on Wye
Moccas Court
A438
Bishopstone
Credenhill
Stretton Sugwas
Holmer
Shelwick
B4348
Arthur's Stone
Moccas
Preston on wye
Byford
Kenchester
Sugwas Pool
King's Acre
Llowes
Hay-on-Wye
(Y Gelli Gandryll)
Cusop
Dorstone
Blakemere
Bridge Sollers
Lulham
The Weir
Swainshill
A4103
Efynnon Gynydd
Rook Wood
Canon Bridge
Breinton Common
Upper Breinton
A438
Cwmbach
Snodhill
Snodhill Castle
Llanigon
Tyberton
Breinton
Cider Museum
Boughrood
B4350
Glasbury
Craswall Priory
Hinton
Peterchurch
Madley
Eaton Bishop
HEREFORD
Cathedral
B4224
Pipton
Aberllynfi Castle
Three Cocks
Tregoyd
Shenmore
Cublington
B4352
Clehonger
Belmont Abbey
A4079
R. Wye
Golden Valley
Gorsty Common
Grafton
Lower Bullingham
Bullinghope
A479
Velindre
Hay Bluff
Vowchurch
B4348
Webton
B4349
Cobhall Common
A465
Dinedor
Dinedor Camp
ENGLAND
WALES
Turnastone
Coldwell
Kingstone
Allensmore
Dinedor Cross
Bronllys
H E R E F O R D S H I R E
Twmpa
Upper Maes-coed
Winnal Common
Callow
A4078
Church
Llanelieu
Gospel Pass
Olchon Valley
Michaelchurch Escley
Middle Maes-coed
St. Margarets
Thruxton
Talgarth
Park Wood
Rhos Dirion
Kerry's Gate
Cockyard
Dewsall Court
Aconbury
Pwlly Wrach
Newton
B4347
R. Dore
Kivernoll
King's Thorn
Trefecca
Bacton
Didley
B4348
Pen y Manllwyn
Capel-y-ffin
Grwyne Fawr Resr.
Lower Maes-coed
Llanveynoe
Abbey Dore Court
Wormbridge
Much Dewchurch
Little Birch
Bwlch Y Dinas Castle
Pengenffordd
Waun Fach
Abbey Dore
Abbey Church
Church
Kilpeck
Much Birch
Trefeinon Open Farm
B L A C K
Vale of Ewyas
Afon Honddu
Wormelow Tump
Hoarwithy
B4560
Mynydd Troed
Mynydd Llysiau
Priory
Longtown
Ewyas Harold
Castle
Howton
Orcop Hill
Llandinabo
M O U N T A I N S
Llanthony
Clodock
Pontrilas Road
Pontrilas
Bagwy Llydiart
Hill Gate
48
Harewood End
Llangorse Lake
Mynydd Llangorse
Rowlstone
A465
Kentchurch
Orcop
Llangasty-Talyllyn
Cathedine
Henllan
Hatterall Hill
Llancillo
Llangua
Kentchurch Court
Garway Hill
Sandyway
Michaelchurch
Grwyne Fawr
Walterstone
Grosmont
St. Weonards
St. Owen's Cross
Pen Gwyllt-meirch
Oldcastle
White Rocks
Little Garway
Cwmrhos
Pen Allt-mawr
Cwmdu
Cwmyoy
Tretire
A40
Llansantffraed
Blaenllynfi Castle
Pen Cerrig-calch
Garway
Garway Common
Treago Castle
A4137
A479
Pandy
B4347
Dovecote
Three Ashes
Bwlch
Gaer
Tretower
Strawberry Cottage Wood
Blackbrook Manor
Skenfrith
Llancloudy
Langstone Court
Tretower Court
Llanbedr
Llanvihangel Crucorney
Llangattock Lingoed
Norton
Broad Oak
Llangarron
Cwm-crawnon
Coed-yr-ynys
Cross Ash
Pembridge Castle
Ruxton Green
Llangynidr
A40
Crickhowell
(Crughywel)
Blaenawey
Mynydd Pen-y-fal
Sugar Loaf
Llanvihangel Court
Bont
B4521
Crossway
Skenfrith
Llanrothal
Llangrove
B4558
Ffawyddog
Crickhowell Castle
Sugar Loaf
Welsh Newton
Welsh Newton Common
Llangattock
Llangenny
Allt
Ysgyryd Fawr
Newcastle
Whitchurch
Glangrwyney
St. Mary's Vale
A465
Llantilio Pertholey
Llanvetherine
Hen Gwrt
Llanfaenor
St. Maughan's Green
Maypole
Ganarew
Buckholt
Cefn Onnau
B4560
Daren
Llwyn-du
Mardy
B4521
Brynygwenyn
White
Llangattock-Vibon-Avel
B4347
Craig-y-Cilau
Mynydd Llangatwg
Llanelly
A4077
Gilwern
Llanwenarth
ABERGAVENNY
(Y-Fenni)
Tal-y-coed
Onen
Rockfield
A40
Llantilio Crossenny
B4233
Dixton
Clydach
Govilon
Croes Hywel
Llanvapley
Great Cil-lwch
Llanvihangel Ystern-Llewern
Nelson Museum
A465
Garnlydan
Blackrock
Ironworks
Llanfoist
Llanddewi Rhydderch
Wernyrheolydd
MONMOUTH
(Trefynwy)
Rassau
Bryn-mawr
Llanelly Hill
Blorenge
B4246
B4269
M O N M O U T H S H I R E
Nant-y-Bwch
Sirhowy
Beaufort
B4248
The Punchbowl
Penpergwm Lodge
Coed Morgan
Llanarth
Penrhos
Pen-yr-heol
Treowen
Jingle Street
Over Monnow
Wyesham
Penallt
Redbrook
Garn-yr-erw
Llanellen
Great Oak
Tregare
Castle
Dingestow
Mitchel Troy
EBBW VALE
(Glyn Ebwy)
Nantyglo
Coalbrookvale
Cwm-celyn
Blaenavon
A40
Llanvihangel Gobion
Bryngwyn
Raglan
A40
Mitcheltroy Common
Georgetown
BLAENAU
Blaina
Big Pit Mine
Iron Works
Upper Coedcae
Forge Side
A4042
Rhyd-y-meirch
Raglan
Cwmcarvan
New Mills
Coity Mountain
B4246
A4043
Pen-y-clawdd
Nant-y-Derry
Clytha Castle
Coed-y-Bwynydd
A449
Croes Robert Wood
The Narth
Whitebrook
Troedrhiwgwair
Abertysswg
GWENT
A4046
Cwm
Cwmtillery
Varteg
Mynydd Garnclochdy
Garndiffaith
Goetre
Bettws Newydd
Twyn-y-Sheriff
Kingcoed
Llangovan
Trelleck
Cotland
New Tredegar
A4048
Cefn yr Arail
Talywain
Abersychan
Penperlleni
Kemeys Commander
B4598
Gwehelog
Llandenny
Harold's Stones
Llandogo
Manmoel
ABERTILLERY
(Abertyleri)
Mamhilad
Monkswood
Llancayo
Llansoy
Llanishen
Parkhouse
Catbrook
Hollybush
Six Bells
Little Mill
A472
CAERPHILLY
Trevethin
Rhadyr
Brithdir
St. Illtyd
TORFAEN
Glascoed
Gwernesney
Trellech Grange
Tintern Parva
Aberbeeg
Pen-y-fan Pond
Llanhilleth
Llandegfedd Reservoir
Usk
(Brynbuga)
Llangwm-isaf
Abbey Furnace
Markham
Glandwr
B4471
Pen-twyn
Pantygasseg
New Inn
Llangwm
Wolvesnewton
New Inn
Chapel Hill
Bargoed
(Bargod)
Glassworks
Bedwellty
Argoed
Trinant
Swffryd
A472
PONTYPOOL
(Pontypwl)
33
Llanbadoc
Devauden
Gilfach
Oakdale
B4251
Toll Cottage
Griffithstown
Sebastopol
Coed-y-paen
Llanllowell
Yeddw House
Chepstow Park Wood
Wyndcliff
Penpedairheol
Pengam
Blackwood
(Coed Duon)
Crumlin
Newbridge
(Cefn Bychan)
Pontrhydyrun
Mynydd Maen
A4042
Llangybi
Llantrisant
Newchurch
ISLWYN
Upper Pontnewydd
B4235
B4293
St. Arvans
GELLIGAER
Penybryn
Pontllanfraith
A4049
CWMBRAN
Croesyceiliog
Llandegveth
Ton
Llangybi
A449
Itton
Woodcroft

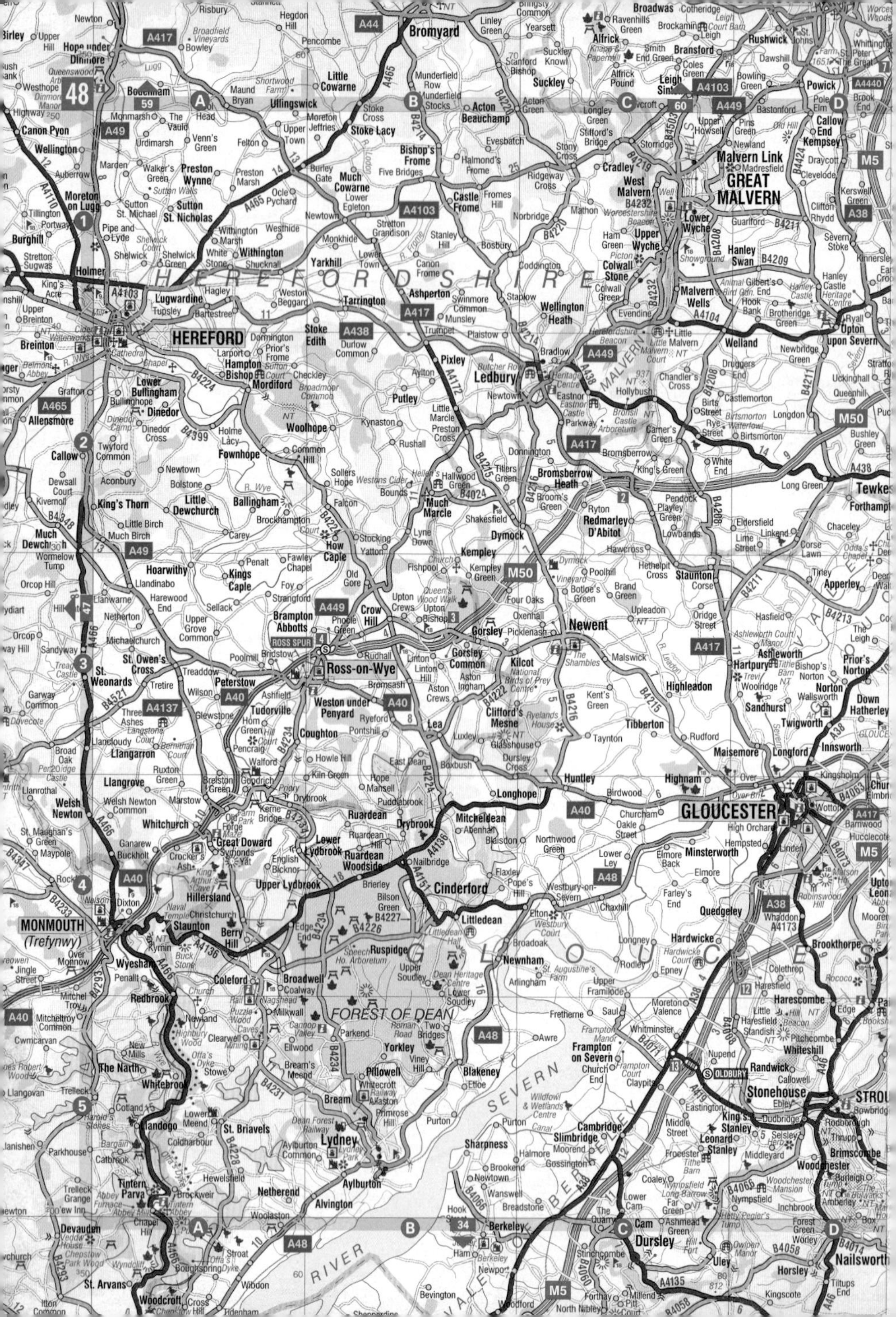
48
59
60
34
A
B
C
D
1
2
3
4
5
HEREFORDSHIRE
HEREFORD
Ross-on-Wye
ROSS SPUR
Ledbury
Bromyard
Newent
GLOUCESTER
GREAT MALVERN
Malvern Link
MONMOUTH
(Trefynwy)
Cinderford
Lydney
Coleford
FOREST OF DEAN
Stonehouse
Dursley
Berkeley
Nailsworth
Tewkes
STROU
MALVERN HILLS
RIVER SEVERN
OLDBURY
A44
A417
A49
A465
A4103
A438
A449
A4172
A40
A4137
A48
A466
A4136
A38
A4173
A4104
A4440
A46
M5
M50
Hope under Dinmore
Bodenham
Ullingswick
Little Cowarne
Stoke Lacy
Acton Beauchamp
Canon Pyon
Wellington
Moreton on Lugg
Preston Wynne
Sutton St. Nicholas
Withington
Holmer
Burghill
Lugwardine
Tarrington
Ashperton
Stoke Edith
Mordiford
Hampton Bishop
Fownhope
Woolhope
Much Marcle
Dymock
Kempley
Redmarley D'Abitot
Bromsberrow Heath
Upton upon Severn
Welland
Hanley Swan
Malvern Wells
Colwall Stone
Cradley
West Malvern
Powick
Callow End
Kempsey
Allensmore
Callow
King's Thorn
Much Dewchurch
Little Dewchurch
Ballingham
How Caple
Hoarwithy
Kings Caple
Brampton Abbotts
Crow Hill
Gorsley
Kilcot
Clifford's Mesne
Upton Bishop
Peterstow
Tudorville
Weston under Penyard
Lea
Huntley
Longhope
Mitcheldean
Drybrook
Ruardean
Lydbrook
Upper Lydbrook
Ruardean Woodside
Llangarron
Llangrove
Welsh Newton
Whitchurch
Great Doward
Hillersland
Staunton
Berry Hill
Broadwell
Ruspidge
Littledean
Newnham
Blakeney
Yorkley
Pillowell
Bream
St. Briavels
Llandogo
Tintern Parva
Devauden
St. Arvans
Woodcroft
Aylburton
Alvington
Netherend
Sharpness
Slimbridge
Cambridge
Frampton on Severn
Cam
Uley
Horsley
King's Stanley
Leonard Stanley
Woodchester
Brimscombe
Randwick
Whiteshill
Harescombe
Brookthorpe
Quedgeley
Hardwicke
Minsterworth
Highnam
Maisemore
Longford
Innsworth
Twigworth
Sandhurst
Norton
Hartpury
Ashleworth
Highleadon
Tibberton
Staunton
Apperley
Tewkes
Forthampt
Prior's Norton
Down Hatherley
Hucclecote
Upton
Westbury-on-Severn
Flaxley
St. Weonards
St. Owen's Cross
Wormelow Tump
Garway Common
Broad Oak
The North
Whitebrook
Redbrook
Wyesham
Penallt
Trelleck
Trellech Grange

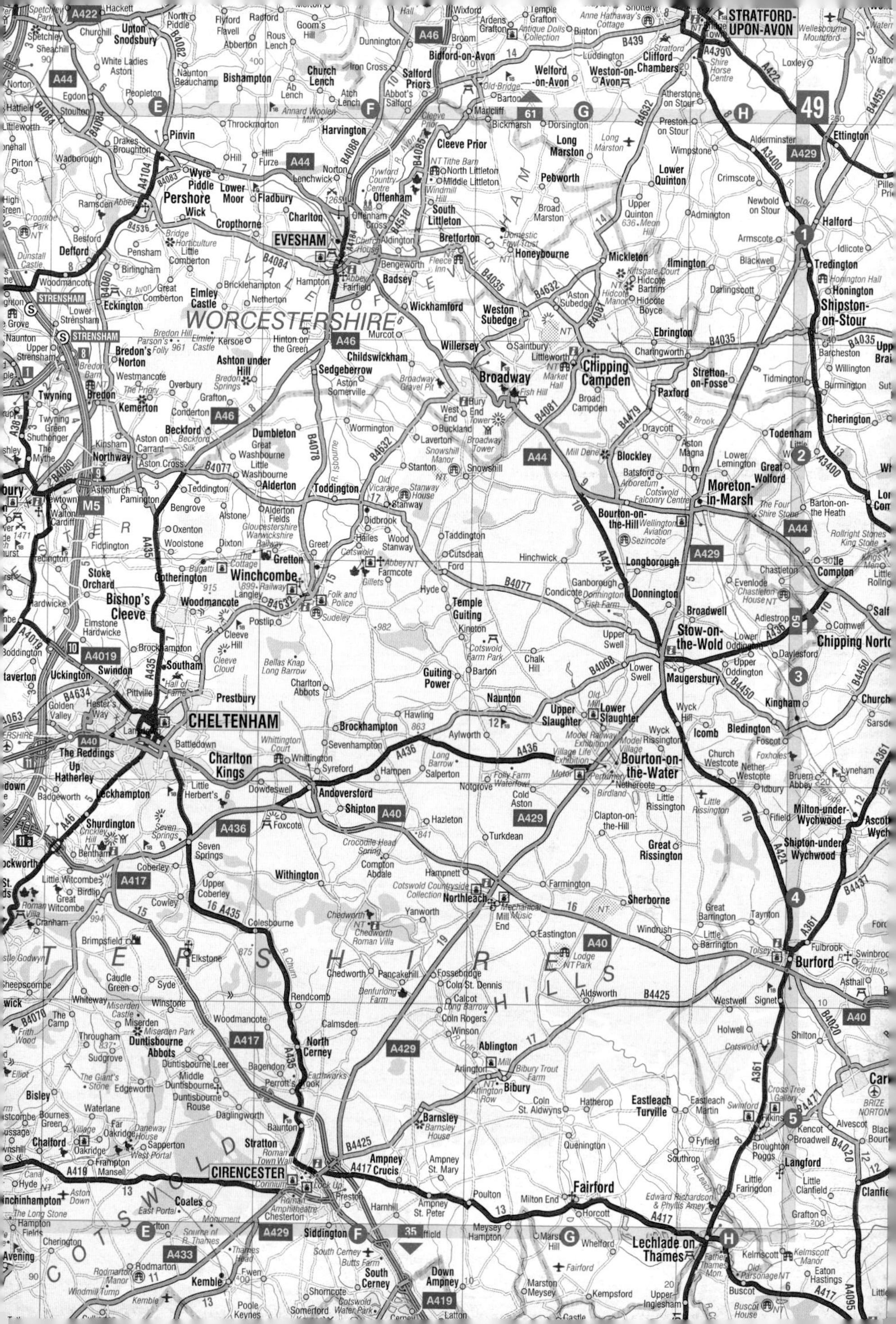

STRATFORD-UPON-AVON
49
Spetchley
Upton Snodsbury
North Piddle
Flyford Flavell
Radford
Rous Lench
Abberton
Goom's Hill
Dunnington
Wixford
A46
Broom
Bidford-on-Avon
Ardens Grafton
Temple Grafton
Binton
Anne Hathaway's Cottage
Shottery
Wellesbourne Mountford
Churchill
Sheachill
White Ladies Aston
Naunton Beauchamp
Bishampton
Iron Cross
Church Lench
Ab Lench
Atch Lench
Salford Priors
Abbot's Salford
Welford -on-Avon
Weston-on-Avon
Clifford Chambers
Luddington
Shire Horse Centre
Loxley
A44
Norton
Egdon
Peopleton
Stoulton
Hatfield
Littleworth
Throckmorton
Harvington
Cleeve Prior
Marlcliff
Bickmarsh
Barton
Dorsington
Atherstone on Stour
Preston on Stour
Alderminster
Ettington
Pinvin
Drakes Broughton
Wadborough
Pirton
Hill
Hill Furze
Norton
Lenchwick
North Littleton
Middle Littleton
Long Marston
Pebworth
Wimpstone
Lower Quinton
Crimscote
A429
Wyre Piddle
Lower Moor
Fladbury
Pershore
Ramsden
Wick
Cropthorne
Charlton
Offenham
South Littleton
Upper Quinton
Admington
Newbold on Stour
Halford
EVESHAM
Bretforton
Broad Marston
Honeybourne
Mickleton
Ilmington
Armscote
Idlicote
Tredington
Defford
Besford
Pensham
Little Comberton
Birlingham
Great Comberton
Bengeworth
Aldington
Badsey
Hampton
Wickhamford
Blackwell
Honington Hall
Honington
Shipston-on-Stour
Darlingscott
Hidcote Bartrim
Hidcote Boyce
Aston Subedge
Weston Subedge
Woodmancote
STRENSHAM
Eckington
Bricklehampton
Elmley Castle
Netherton
WORCESTERSHIRE
VALE OF EVESHAM
Murcot
Ebrington
Charingworth
Lower Strensham
Upper Strensham
Naunton
Bredon's Norton
Bredon Hill
Kersoe
Hinton on the Green
Childswickham
Willersey
Saintbury
Broadway
Chipping Campden
Stretton-on-Fosse
Paxford
Barcheston
Willington
Tidmington
Burmington
Cherington
Twyning
Bredon
Kemerton
Westmancote
Overbury
Ashton under Hill
Sedgeberrow
Aston Somerville
Grafton
Conderton
Beckford
Dumbleton
Wormington
Laverton
Buckland
West End
Broad Campden
Blockley
Draycott
Aston Magna
Todenham
Great Wolford
Lower Lemington
Dorn
Batsford
Moreton-in-Marsh
Barton-on-the Heath
Northway
Kinsham
Aston on Carrant
Aston Cross
Great Washbourne
Little Washbourne
Alderton
Toddington
Stanton
Snowshill
Stanway
Bourton-on-the-Hill
Sezincote
Ashchurch
Pamington
Teddington
Bengrove
Oxenton
Woolstone
Dixton
Alstone
Alderton Fields
Didbrook
Hailes
Wood Stanway
Taddington
Cutsdean
Ford
Hinchwick
Longborough
Chastleton
Little Compton
Evenlode
M5
Tewkesbury
Walton Cardiff
Fiddington
Stoke Orchard
Bishop's Cleeve
Gotherington
Woodmancote
Winchcombe
Gretton
Greet
Langley
Farmcote
Hyde
Temple Guiting
Condicote
Ganborough
Donnington
Broadwell
Adlestrop
Cornwell
Chipping Norton
Elmstone Hardwicke
Postlip
Cleeve Hill
Sudeley
Kineton
Upper Swell
Lower Swell
Stow-on-the-Wold
Maugersbury
Lower Oddington
Upper Oddington
Daylesford
Kingham
Boddington
Staverton
Uckington
Swindon
Brockhampton
Southam
Prestbury
Charlton Abbots
Guiting Power
Barton
Chalk Hill
Naunton
Upper Slaughter
Lower Slaughter
Icomb
Bledington
Wyck Rissington
Golden Valley
Hester's Way
Pittville
CHELTENHAM
Brockhampton
Sevenhampton
Hawling
Aylworth
The Reddings
Up Hatherley
Battledown
Charlton Kings
Whittington
Syreford
Hampen
Salperton
Bourton-on-the-Water
Church Westcote
Nether Westcote
Foscot
Lyneham
Bruern Abbey
Idbury
Badgeworth
Leckhampton
Dowdeswell
Andoversford
Shipton
Notgrove
Cold Aston
Little Rissington
Fifield
Milton-under-Wychwood
Shurdington
Bentham
Seven Springs
Foxcote
A40
A436
Hazleton
Turkdean
Clapton-on-the-Hill
Great Rissington
Shipton-under-Wychwood
Little Witcombe
Great Witcombe
Birdlip
Coberley
Upper Coberley
Cowley
Withington
Compton Abdale
Hampnett
Northleach
Farmington
Sherborne
Great Barrington
Taynton
Cranham
A417
Colesbourne
Yanworth
Mill End
Eastington
Windrush
Little Barrington
Burford
Fulbrook
Swinbrook
Brimpsfield
Elkstone
Chedworth
Pancakehill
Fossebridge
Coln St. Dennis
Lodge Park
Aldsworth
Caudle Green
Syde
Sheepscombe
Rendcomb
Calcot
Coln Rogers
Winson
Westwell
Signet
Asthall
Whiteway
Winstone
Woodmancote
Calmsden
Ablington
Holwell
Shilton
The Camp
Throughham
Miserden
Duntisbourne Abbots
North Cerney
Duntisbourne Leer
Middle Duntisbourne
Duntisbourne Rouse
Bagendon
Perrott's Brook
Arlington
Bibury
Coln St. Aldwyns
Hatherop
Eastleach Turville
Eastleach Martin
Bisley
Sudgrove
Edgeworth
Waterlane
Daglingworth
Baunton
Barnsley
Barnsley House
Quenington
Fyfield
Kencot
Broadwell
Alvescot
Bournes Green
Far Oakridge
Sapperton
Chalford
Frampton Mansell
Stratton
Ampney Crucis
Ampney St. Mary
Southrop
Broughton Poggs
Langford
CIRENCESTER
Preston
Poulton
Fairford
Milton End
Horcott
Little Faringdon
Little Clanfield
Coates
Hampton Fields
Harnhill
Ampney St. Peter
Meysey Hampton
Whelford
Grafton
Cherington
Siddington
Lechlade on Thames
Kelmscott
Avening
Rodmarton
South Cerney
Down Ampney
Kemble
Marston Meysey
Kempsford
Buscot
Eaton Hastings
Poole Keynes
Somerford
Upper Inglesham
COTSWOLD HILLS
GLOUCESTERSHIRE
35
50

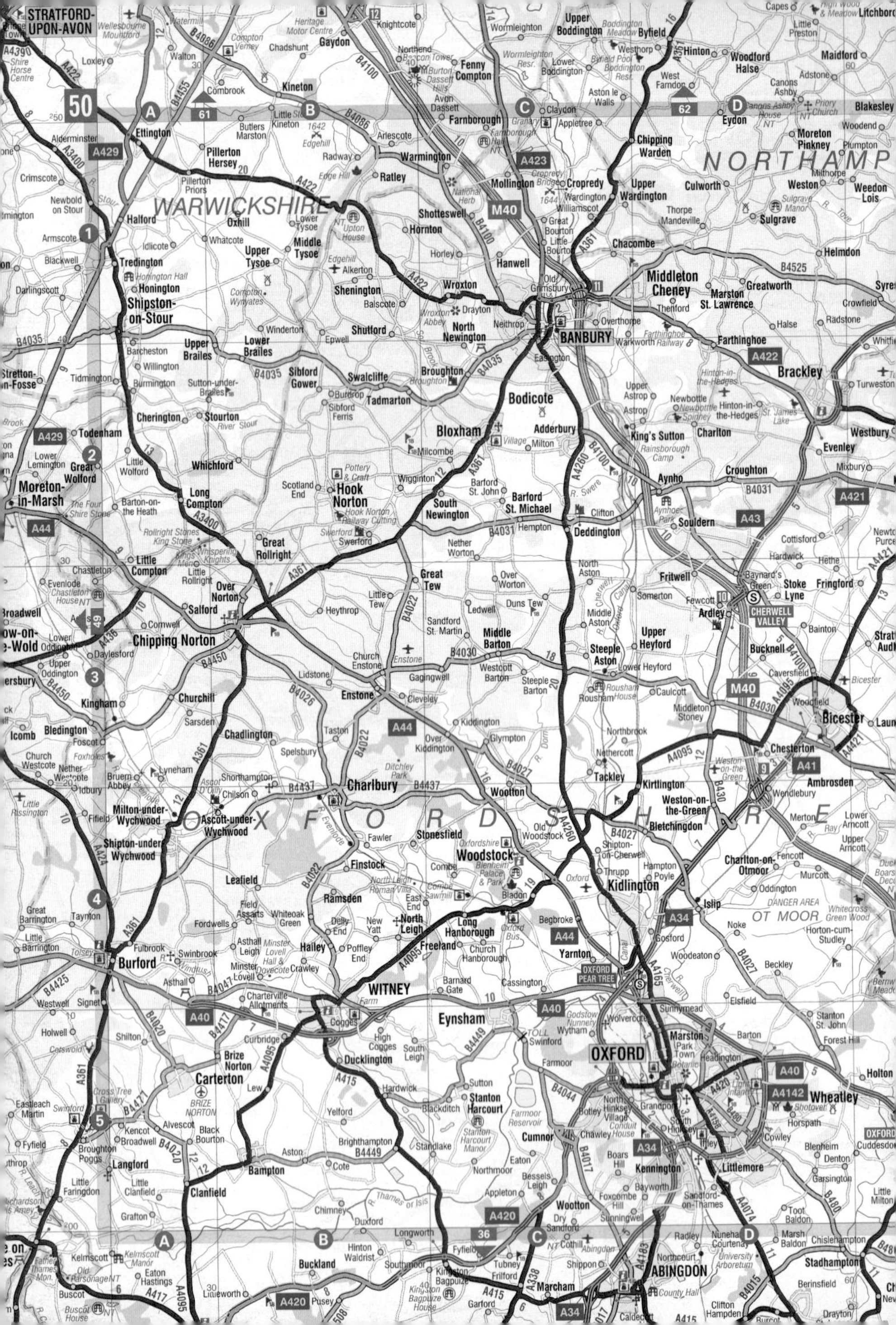

50
STRATFORD-UPON-AVON
Wellesbourne Mountford
Heritage Motor Centre
Knightcote
Gaydon
Wormleighton
Upper Boddington
Byfield
Hinton
Woodford Halse
Maidford
Litchborough
Capes
Little Preston
Loxley
Walton
Compton Verney
Chadshunt
Northend
Fenny Compton
Burton Dassett Hills
Lower Boddington
Westhorp
West Farndon
Adstone
Canons Ashby
Combrook
Kineton
Avon Dassett
Aston le Walls
Claydon
Eydon
Blakesley
Priory Church
Ettington
Butlers Marston
Little Kineton
Edgehill
Arlescote
Farnborough
Appletree
Chipping Warden
Moreton Pinkney
Woodend
Plumpton
Alderminster
Pillerton Hersey
Radway
Warmington
NORTHAMP
Crimscote
Pillerton Priors
Edge Hill
Ratley
Mollington
Cropredy
Upper Wardington
Culworth
Weston
Weedon Lois
Newbold on Stour
WARWICKSHIRE
Oxhill
Lower Tysoe
Upton House
Shotteswell
Wardington
Williamscot
Thorpe Mandeville
Sulgrave
Sulgrave Manor
Halford
Armscote
Whatcote
Idlicote
Upper Tysoe
Middle Tysoe
Hornton
Great Bourton
Little Bourton
Chacombe
Helmdon
Blackwell
Tredington
Honington Hall
Honington
Alkerton
Horley
Hanwell
B4525
Darlingscott
Shipston-on-Stour
Compton Wynyates
Shenington
Wroxton
Old Grimsbury
Middleton Cheney
Marston St. Lawrence
Greatworth
Crowfield
Balscote
Wroxton Abbey
Drayton
Thenford
Overthorpe
Halse
Radstone
Barcheston
Winderton
Epwell
Shutford
North Newington
Neithrop
BANBURY
Warkworth
Farthinghoe
Willington
Upper Brailes
Lower Brailes
Sibford Gower
Swalcliffe
Broughton
Easington
A422
Brackley
Tidmington
Stretton-on-Fosse
Burmington
Sutton-under-Brailes
Burdrop
Tadmarton
Bodicote
Upper Astrop
Astrop
Newbottle
Hinton-in-the-Hedges
Turweston
Cherington
Stourton
Sibford Ferris
Bloxham
Adderbury
Milton
King's Sutton
Charlton
St. James Lake
Todenham
Village
Milcombe
Rainsborough Camp
Westbury
Evenley
Lower Lemington
Great Wolford
Little Wolford
Whichford
Pottery & Craft
Wigginton
Barford St. John
Aynho
Croughton
Mixbury
Moreton-in-Marsh
Long Compton
Scotland End
Hook Norton
South Newington
Barford St. Michael
B4031
The Four Shire Stone
Barton-on-the-Heath
Hook Norton Railway Cutting
Clifton
Aynhoe Park
Souldern
A421
Rollright Stones King Stone
Great Rollright
Swerford
Hempton
Deddington
Nether Worton
Cottisford
Hardwick
Hethe
Chastleton
Little Compton
Little Rollright
Great Tew
Over Worton
North Aston
Fritwell
Baynard's Green
Evenlode
Chastleton House
Over Norton
Little Tew
Heythrop
Ledwell
Duns Tew
Somerton
Fewcott
Stoke Lyne
Fringford
Broadwell
Salford
Middle Aston
Ardley
CHERWELL VALLEY
Cornwell
Chipping Norton
Sandford St. Martin
Middle Barton
Steeple Aston
Upper Heyford
Bucknell
Bainton
Lower Oddington
Daylesford
Church Enstone
B4030
Westcott Barton
Lower Heyford
Caversfield
Upper Oddington
Lidstone
Gagingwell
Steeple Barton
Rousham
Rousham House
Caulcott
Bicester
Kingham
Churchill
Enstone
Cleveley
Middleton Stoney
Woodfield
Icomb
Bledington
Sarsden
Chadlington
Taston
Kiddington
Northbrook
Foscot
Spelsbury
Over Kiddington
Glympton
Nethercott
Chesterton
Church Westcote
Nether Westcote
Lyneham
Shorthampton
Ditchley Park
Tackley
Kirtlington
Weston-on-the-Green
Ambrosden
Bruern Abbey
Idbury
Chilson
Charlbury
Wootton
Wendlebury
Little Rissington
Fifield
Milton-under-Wychwood
Ascott-under-Wychwood
OXFORDSHIRE
Old Woodstock
Bletchingdon
Merton
Lower Arncott
Upper Arncott
Shipton-under-Wychwood
Fawler
Stonesfield
Oxfordshire
Woodstock
Shipton-on-Cherwell
Hampton Poyle
Fencott
Charlton-on-Otmoor
Murcott
Leafield
Finstock
Combe
Blenheim Palace & Park
Thrupp
Kidlington
Oddington
North Leigh Roman Villa
Ramsden
East End
Bladon
Islip
DANGER AREA
OT MOOR
Great Barrington
Taynton
Field Assarts
Whiteoak Green
North Leigh
Long Hanborough
Begbroke
Gosford
Noke
Horton-cum-Studley
Little Barrington
Fordwells
Delly End
New Yatt
Oxford Bus
Fulbrook
Asthall Leigh
Minster Lovell Hall & Dovecote
Hailey
Poffley End
Freeland
Church Hanborough
Yarnton
Woodeaton
Beckley
Burford
Swinbrook
Minster Lovell
Crawley
OXFORD PEAR TREE
Barnard Gate
Cassington
Westwell
Signet
Asthall
Charterville Allotments
WITNEY
Elsfield
Holwell
Cogges
Eynsham
Sunnymead
Stanton St. John
Shilton
Curbridge
High Cogges
South Leigh
Godstow Nunnery
Wytham
Wolvercote
Swinford
Marston
Barton
Forest Hill
Brize Norton
Ducklington
Farmoor
OXFORD
Park Town
Headington
Holton
Carterton
Lew
Hardwick
Sutton
Stanton Harcourt
Eastleach Martin
Cross Tree Gallery
BRIZE NORTON
Yelford
Blackditch
North Hinksey Village
Botley
Grandpont
Wheatley
Shotover
Horspath
Kencot
Alvescot
Black Bourton
Stanton Harcourt Manor
Farmoor Reservoir
Cumnor
Chawley
Conduit House
South Hinksey
Iffley
Cowley
Fyfield
Broadwell
Broughton Poggs
Brighthampton
B4449
Standlake
Cuddesdon
Langford
Aston
Cote
Eaton
Boars Hill
Kennington
Littlemore
Blenheim
Denton
Bampton
Northmoor
Bessels Leigh
Bayworth
Garsington
Little Faringdon
Little Clanfield
Clanfield
Appleton
Foxcombe Hill
Sandford-on-Thames
Little Milton
Grafton
Chimney
R. Thames or Isis
Wootton
Toot Baldon
Duxford
Dry Sandford
Sunningwell
Marsh Baldon
Longworth
Hinton Waldrist
Fyfield
Cothill
Radley
Nuneham Courtenay
Chislehampton
Kelmscott
Kelmscott Manor
Buckland
Southmoor
Tubney
Shippon
Northcourt
University Arboretum
Stadhampton
Eaton Hastings
Kingston Bagpuize
Frilford
ABINGDON
Berinsfield
Buscot
Littleworth
Pusey
Kingston Bagpuize House
Garford
Marcham
County Hall
Clifton Hampden
Drayton
Buscot Park
A420
A34
A415
Caldecott
Burcot

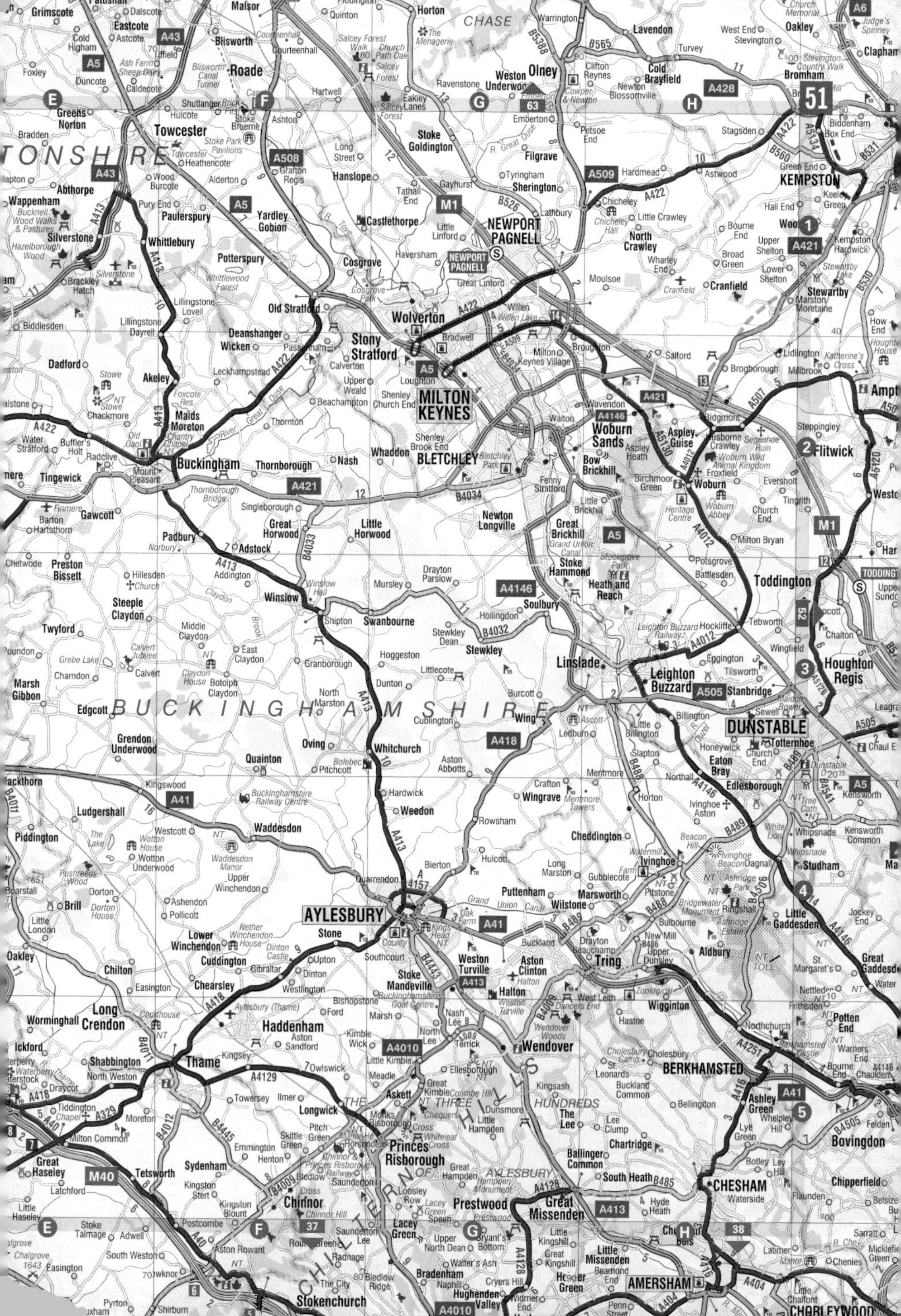
Grimscote
Dalscote
Eastcote
Astcote
Cold Higham
Malsor
Blisworth
Roade
Quinton
Horton
The Menagerie
CHASE
Warrington
Lavendon
West End
Stevington
Oakley
Clapham
Judge's Spinney
Church Memorial
Foxley
Duncote
Caldecote
Tiffield
Courteenhall
Salcey Forest Walk
Church Path Oak
Salcey Forest
Olney
Weston Underwood
Ravenstone
Clifton Reynes
Cold Brayfield
Turvey
Bromham
Stevington Country Walk
Newton Blossomville
Greens Norton
Towcester
Shutlanger
Hulcote
Stoke Bruerne
Stoke Park Pavilions
Hartwell
Ashton
Eakley Lanes
Emberton
Petsoe End
Stagsden
Biddenham
Box End
Bradden
TONSHIRE
Towcester Heathencote
Alderton
Grafton Regis
Long Street
Stoke Goldington
Filgrave
Hardmead
Astwood
Green End
KEMPSTON
Abthorpe
Wood Burcote
Pury End
Paulerspury
Hanslope
Tathall End
Gayhurst
Tyringham
Sherington
Chicheley
Little Crawley
North Crawley
Keeley Green
Hall End
Wappenham
Bucknell Wood Walks & Pastures
Silverstone
Hazelborough Wood
Whittlebury
Yardley Gobion
Castlethorpe
Little Linford
NEWPORT PAGNELL
Lathbury
Chicheley Hall
Bourne End
Upper Shelton
Kempston Hardwick
Potterspury
Whittlewood Forest
Cosgrove
Haversham
Great Linford
Moulsoe
Broad Green
Wharley End
Cranfield
Lower Shelton
Stewartby Lake
Stewartby
Marston Moretaine
Brackley Hatch
Lillingstone Lovell
Old Stratford
Wolverton
Willen
Willen Lake
Biddlesden
Lillingstone Dayrell
Deanshanger
Wicken
Passenham
Stony Stratford
Bradwell
Milton Keynes Village
Broughton
Salford
Lidlington
Katherine's Cross
Houghton House
How End
Dadford
Stowe
Leckhampstead
Calverton
Loughton
Upper Weald
Shenley Church End
MILTON KEYNES
Brogborough
Millbrook
Akeley
Chackmore
Foxcote Res.
Maids Moreton
Beachampton
Wavendon
Walton
Woburn Sands
Aspley Heath
Aspley Guise
Husborne Crawley
Ridgmont
Segenhoe Ruin
Woburn Wild Animal Kingdom
Steppingley
Flitwick
Water Stratford
Buffler's Holt
Radclive
Old Gaol
Chantry Chapel
Thornton
Shenley Brook End
Bletchley Park
BLETCHLEY
Whaddon
Nash
Bow Brickhill
Birchmoor Green
Froxfield
Woburn
Woburn Abbey
Heritage Centre
Eversholt
Tingrith
Church End
Tingewick
Mount Pleasant
Buckingham
Thornborough
Thornborough Bridge
Fenny Stratford
Little Brickhill
Finmere
Barton Hartshorn
Gawcott
Singleborough
Great Horwood
Little Horwood
Newton Longville
Great Brickhill
Grand Union Canal
Milton Bryan
Padbury
Norbury
Adstock
Chetwode
Preston Bissett
Hillesden
Addington
Drayton Parslow
Mursley
Stoke Hammond
Stockgrove Park
Heath and Reach
Potsgrove
Battlesden
Toddington
Steeple Claydon
Winslow
Winslow Hall
Shipton
Swanbourne
Hollingdon
Soulbury
Hockliffe
Tebworth
Chalton
Twyford
Middle Claydon
East Claydon
Stewkley Dean
Stewkley
Leighton Buzzard Railway
Linslade
Eggington
Wingfield
Houghton Regis
Poundon
Grebe Lake
Calvert Jubilee
Calvert
Hoggeston
Granborough
Littlecote
Dunton
Leighton Buzzard
Tilsworth
Stanbridge
Marsh Gibbon
Charndon
Claydon House
Botolph Claydon
North Marston
Burcott
Edgcott
BUCKINGHAMSHIRE
Cublington
Wing
Ascott
Ledburn
Little Billington
Billington
Sewell
Maiden Bower
DUNSTABLE
Totternhoe
Leagrave
Grendon Underwood
Oving
Whitchurch
Bolebec
Pitchcott
Quainton
Aston Abbotts
Slapton
Honeywick
Eaton Bray
Church End
Dunstable Downs
Kensworth
Kingswood
Ludgershall
Buckinghamshire Railway Centre
Hardwick
Weedon
Crafton
Wingrave
Mentmore
Mentmore Towers
Horton
Northall
Edlesborough
Ivinghoe Aston
Tree Cath.
Piddington
The Lake
Westcott
Wotton House
Wotton Underwood
Waddesdon
Waddesdon Manor
Rowsham
Cheddington
Whipsnade
Kensworth Common
Brill
Boarstall
Dorton
Dorton House
Pusheeds Wood
Upper Winchendon
Quarrendon
Bierton
Hulcott
Long Marston
Gubblecote
Ivinghoe
Ivinghoe Beacon
Beacon Hill
Dagnall
Studham
Ashendon
Pollicott
Little London
AYLESBURY
Grand Union Canal
Oak Farm
Puttenham
Marsworth
Wilstone
Pitstone
Bridgewater Monument
Ashridge Park
Ringshall
Ashridge Estate
Little Gaddesden
Jockey End
Lower Winchendon
Nether Winchendon House
Stone
Kings Head
Buckland
Drayton Beauchamp
New Mill
Bulbourne
Aldbury
Oakley
Cuddington
Dinton Castle
Gibraltar
Upton
Dinton
Southcourt
Stoke Mandeville
Weston Turville
Aston Clinton
Halton
Tring
Upper Dunsley
Zoological
St. Margaret's
Great Gaddesden
Chilton
Easington
Chearsley
Westlington
Bishopstone
Buckinghamshire Goat Centre
West Leith
Dancers End
Wigginton
Nettleden
Frithsden
Worminghall
Long Crendon
Courthouse
Aylesbury (Thame)
Haddenham
Ford
Marsh
Nash Lee
Wendover
Wendover Woods
Hastoe
Northchurch
Potten End
Ickford
Aston Sandford
Kimble Wick
North Lee
Terrick
Cholesbury Camp
Cholesbury
Berkhamsted Castle
Warners End
Shabbington
Thame
Kingsey
Owlswick
Little Kimble
Ellesborough
St. Leonards
BERKHAMSTED
Bourne End
Chaulden
North Weston
Draycot
Waterstock
Towersey
Meadle
Great Kimble
Coombe Hill
Kingsash
Buckland Common
Ashley Green
Whelpley Hill
Felden
Tiddington
Ilmer
Longwick
Askett
Monks Risborough
Chequers
Dunsmore
HUNDREDS
The Lee
Bellingdon
Moreton
Milton Common
Pitch Green
Skittle Green
Horsenden
Whiteleaf Cross
Little Hampden
Lee Clump
Lye Green
Bovingdon
Great Haseley
Emmington
Henton
Chinnor & Princes Risborough Railway
Princes Risborough
Chartridge
Botley
Ley Hill
Latchford
Sydenham
Tetsworth
Bledlow
Saunderton
Great Hampden
Hampden Monument
AYLESBURY
Ballinger Common
South Heath
Chesham
Chipperfield
Little Haseley
Kingston Stert
Kingston Blount
Bledlow Cross
Chinnor
Loosley Row
Lacey Green
Speen
Prestwood
Great Missenden
Hyde Heath
Waterside
Flaunden
Belsize
Stoke Talmage
Adwell
Postcombe
Chinnor Hill
Saunderton Lee
Lacey Green
Bryant's Bottom
Kingshill
Little Kingshill
Great Kingshill
Chesham Bois
Sarratt
Chalgrove 1643
South Weston
Aston Rowant
Radnage
Upper North Dean
Walter's Ash
Little Missenden
Beamond End
Latimer
Chenies
Mickelfield Green
Easington
The City
Bledlow Ridge
Bradenham
Naphill
Cryers Hill
Hughenden Valley
Widmer End
Holmer Green
AMERSHAM
Little Chalfont
CHORLEYWOOD
Pyrton
Shirburn
Stokenchurch
Penn Street
CHILTERN HILLS
A5
A43
A508
A413
A422
A421
A428
A509
A6
A5134
B531
B560
B526
B565
B5388
M1
A4146
A5130
A4012
A507
A5120
B530
B4034
B4033
B4032
A505
A418
A41
A4157
B4443
A4010
A4011
B4011
A4129
A329
A40
M40
B4012
B4445
B4009
A4128
B485
A413
A416
A4251
A404
B489
B488
B4506
B4541
B4505
B4009
A4146
63
37
38
52
14
13
12
8
7
6
5
1
2
3
4
E
F
G
H
NEWPORT PAGNELL
TODDINGTON

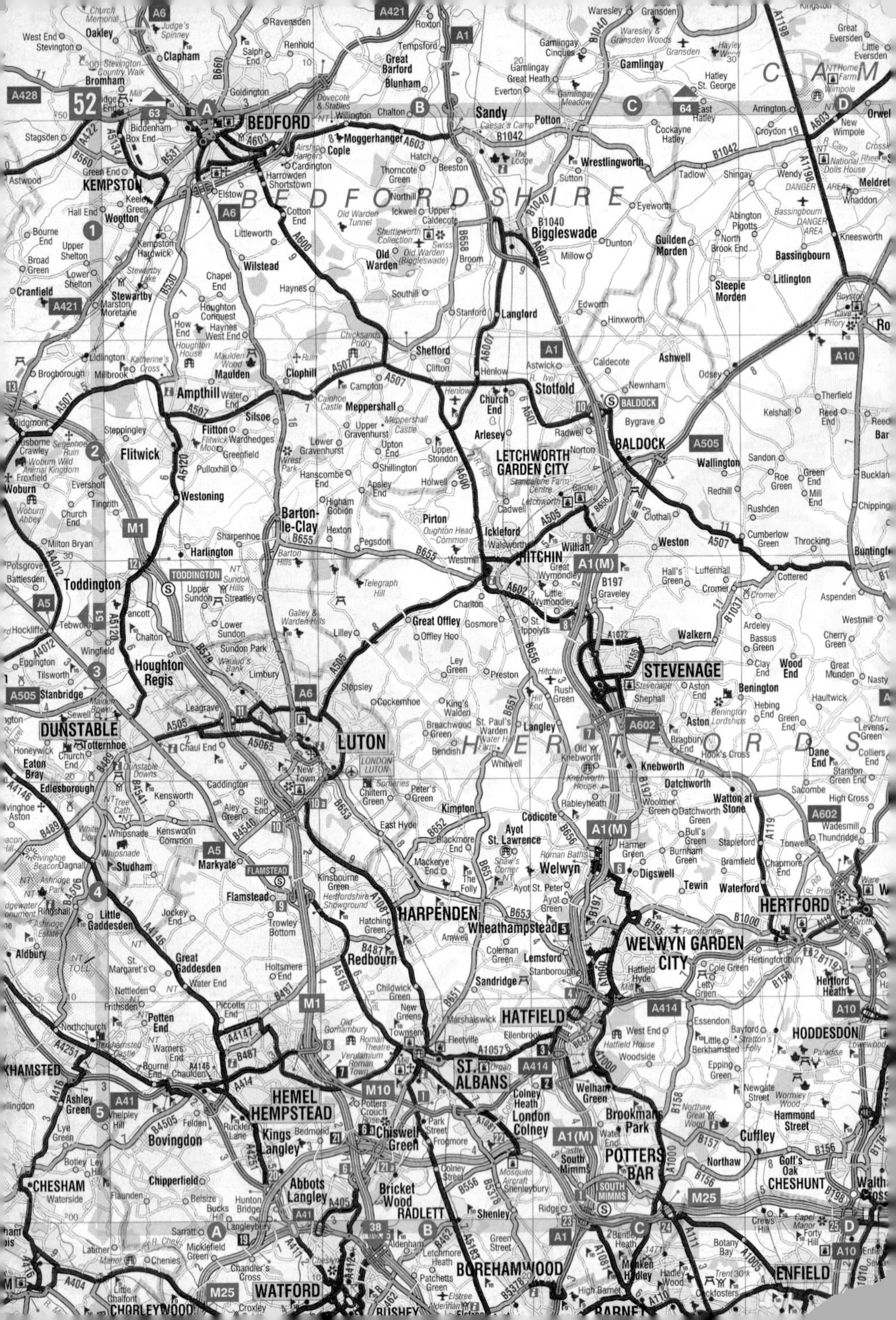
52
BEDFORDSHIRE
HERTFORDS
CAM
A
B
C
D
1
2
3
4
5
63
64
BEDFORD
KEMPSTON
Oakley
Clapham
Bromham
Biddenham
Stagsden
Astwood
Elstow
Wootton
Kempston Hardwick
Stewartby
Cranfield
Marston Moretaine
Wilstead
Houghton Conquest
Haynes
Cople
Cardington
Moggerhanger
Willington
Great Barford
Blunham
Tempsford
Roxton
Ravensden
Renhold
Sandy
Potton
Gamlingay
Everton
Northill
Old Warden
Ickwell
Upper Caldecote
Biggleswade
Dunton
Southill
Langford
Shefford
Clifton
Henlow
Stotfold
Arlesey
Clophill
Maulden
Ampthill
Flitton
Silsoe
Meppershall
Flitwick
Westoning
Barton-le-Clay
Harlington
Toddington
Houghton Regis
DUNSTABLE
LUTON
LONDON LUTON
Stopsley
Leagrave
Caddington
Kensworth
Markyate
Flamstead
Studham
Whipsnade
Totternhoe
Eaton Bray
Edlesborough
Woburn
Woburn Abbey
Ridgmont
Lidlington
Tingrith
Pirton
Hexton
Pegsdon
Higham Gobion
Shillington
LETCHWORTH GARDEN CITY
BALDOCK
HITCHIN
Ickleford
Great Wymondley
Little Wymondley
Graveley
St. Ippolyts
Great Offley
Lilley
Preston
STEVENAGE
Knebworth
Codicote
Welwyn
Kimpton
HARPENDEN
Wheathampstead
Redbourn
ST. ALBANS
HATFIELD
WELWYN GARDEN CITY
HERTFORD
Ware
HODDESDON
CHESHUNT
Cuffley
Hammond Street
POTTERS BAR
Brookmans Park
London Colney
Colney Heath
HEMEL HEMPSTEAD
Kings Langley
Abbots Langley
Bovingdon
CHESHAM
KHAMSTED
Little Gaddesden
Great Gaddesden
Aldbury
Northchurch
Potten End
WATFORD
BUSHEY
CHORLEYWOOD
BOREHAMWOOD
RADLETT
Shenley
Bricket Wood
Chiswell Green
ENFIELD
BARNET
High Barnet
Monken Hadley
Ashwell
Royston
Guilden Morden
Steeple Morden
Bassingbourn
Litlington
Kneesworth
Wrestlingworth
Sandon
Therfield
Kelshall
Reed
Buntingford
Cottered
Walkern
Benington
Aston
Watton at Stone
Datchworth
Tewin
Waterford
Stapleford
Wadesmill
Thundridge
Northaw
Goff's Oak
Essendon
Welham Green
South Mimms
SOUTH MIMMS
TODDINGTON
FLAMSTEAD
BALDOCK
M1
M10
M25
A1
A1(M)
A6
A5
A10
A41
A414
A421
A428
A505
A507
A600
A602
A603
A6001
A4146
A1057

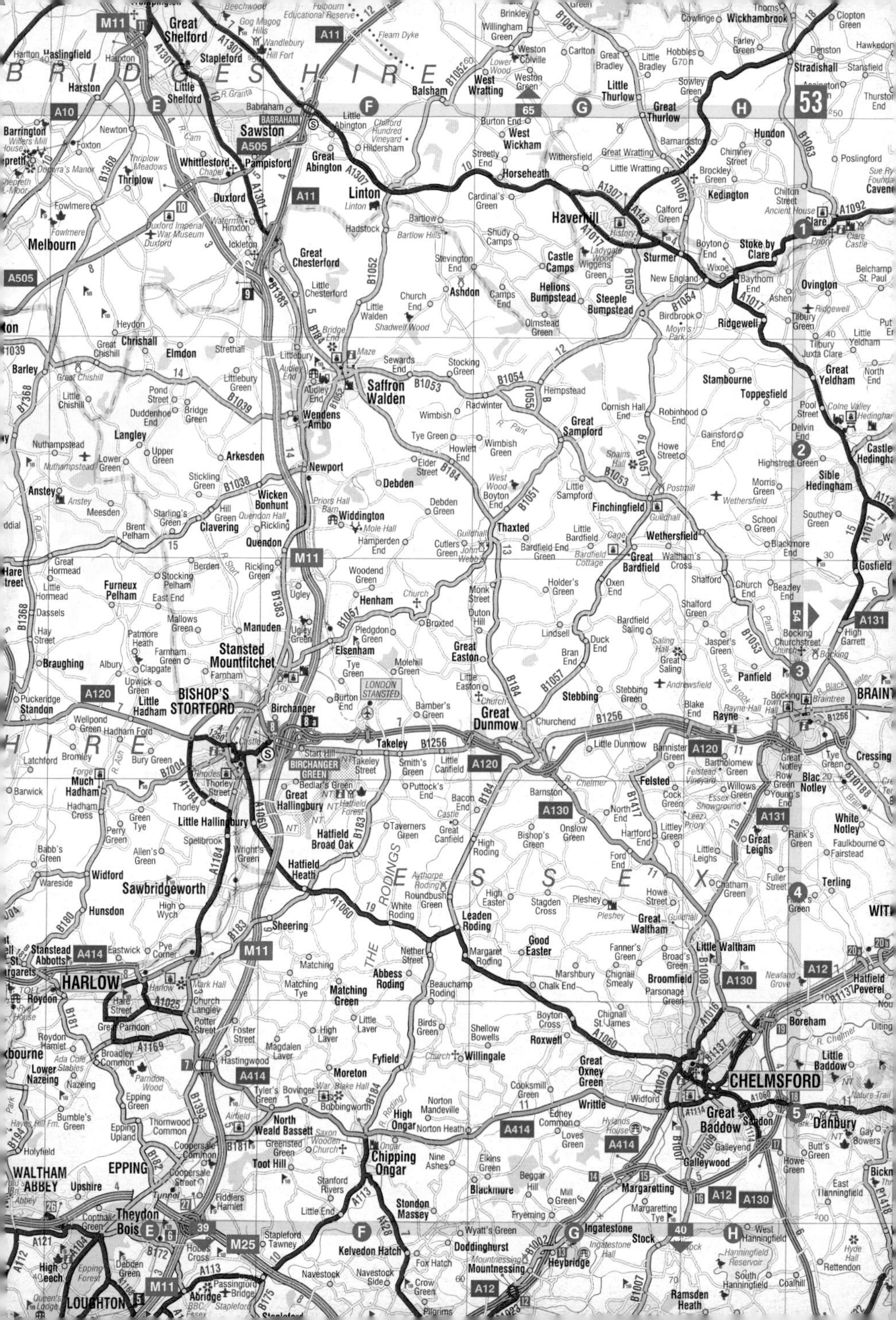

53
M11
Great Shelford
Stapleford
Gog Magog Hills
Wandlebury
Hill Fort
Beechwood
Fulbourn Educational Reserve
A11
Fleam Dyke
Brinkley
Willingham Green
Weston Colville
Carlton
Great Bradley
Little Bradley
Hobbles Green
Cowlinge
Wickhambrook
Clopton Green
Farley Green
Hawkedon
Denston
Stradishall
Stansfield
Harlton
Haslingfield
Hauxton
B R I D G E S H I R E
Little Shelford
R. Granta
Balsham
Lower Wood
West Wratting
Weston Green
Little Thurlow
Sowley Green
Harston
A10
E
F
G
H
65
Babraham
BABRAHAM
Little Abington
Chilford Hundred Vineyard
Hildersham
Burton End
West Wickham
Great Thurlow
Barnardiston
Hundon
Thurston End
Barrington
Willers Mill
Foxton
Newton
Sawston
A505
Cam
Whittlesford
Pampisford
Great Abington
Streetly End
Horseheath
Withersfield
Great Wratting
Little Wratting
Chimney Street
Poslingford
Brockley Green
Kedington
Dogora's Manor
Thriplow Meadows
Thriplow
Duxford
A11
Linton
A1307
Cardinal's Green
Haverhill
A143
A1017
Calford Green
Chilton Street
Ancient House
Clare
A1092
Clare Castle
Fowlmere
Melbourn
Duxford Imperial War Museum
Hinxton
Hadstock
Bartlow
Bartlow Hills
Shudy Camps
Castle Camps
Ladygate Wood
Wiggens Green
Sturmer
Boyton End
Stoke by Clare
Wixoe
Ickleton
Great Chesterford
Stevington End
A505
Little Chesterford
Church End
Ashdon
Camps End
Helions Bumpstead
Steeple Bumpstead
New England
Baythorn End
Ovington
Belchamp St. Paul
Little Walden
Shadwell Wood
Olmstead Green
Birdbrook
Moyn's Park
Ashen
Ridgewell
Tilbury Green
Heydon
Chrishall
Great Chishill
Elmdon
Strethall
Littlebury
Bridge End
Maze
Audley End
Sewards End
Stocking Green
Hempstead
Tilbury Juxta Clare
Little Yeldham
Great Yeldham
North End
Barley
Littlebury Green
Saffron Walden
B1053
Radwinter
B1054
Stambourne
Toppesfield
Little Chishill
Pond Street
Duddenhoe End
Bridge Green
B1039
Wendens Ambo
Wimbish
Cornish Hall End
Robinhood End
Pool Street
Colne Valley
Hedingham
Delvin End
Langley
Upper Green
Lower Green
Nuthampstead
Arkesden
Tye Green
Howlett End
Wimbish Green
Great Sampford
Gainsford End
Howe Street
Spains Hall
Castle Hedingham
Highstreet Green
Newport
Elder Street
Debden
West Wood
Boyton End
Little Sampford
Postmill
Morris Green
Sible Hedingham
Wethersfield
Anstey
Stickling Green
Wicken Bonhunt
Priors Hall Barn
Widdington
Mole Hall
Debden Green
Thaxted
Finchingfield
Guildhall
School Green
Southey Green
Meesden
Starling's Green
Hill Green
Quendon Hall
Clavering
Rickling
Brent Pelham
Quendon
Hamperden End
Cutlers Green
John Webb's
Little Bardfield
Bardfield End Green
Cage
Bardfield Cottage
Great Bardfield
Wethersfield
Waltham's Cross
Blackmore End
Gosfield
Great Hormead
Berden
Rickling Green
Woodend Green
Holder's Green
Oxen End
Shalford
Church End
Beazley End
Little Hormead
Furneux Pelham
Stocking Pelham
East End
Ugley
Henham
Monk Street
Dassels
Mallows Green
Manuden
Ugley Green
Pledgdon Green
Broxted
Duton Hill
Lindsell
Bardfield Saling
Shalford Green
A131
Hay Street
Patmore Heath
Farnham Green
Stansted Mountfitchet
Elsenham
Great Easton
Bran End
Duck End
Saling Hall
Great Saling
Jasper's Green
Bocking Churchstreet
High Garrett
Braughing
Albury
Clapgate
Farnham
Tye Green
Molehill Green
Little Easton
Panfield
Puckeridge
Standon
Upwick Green
Little Hadham
BISHOP'S STORTFORD
Birchanger
Burton End
LONDON STANSTED
Bamber's Green
Great Dunmow
Stebbing
Stebbing Green
Andrewsfield
Blake End
Rayne
Rayne Hall
Bocking
Town Hall
Braintree
A120
Wellpond Green
Hadham Ford
Takeley
Churchend
B1256
Little Dunmow
Bannister Green
Bartholomew Green
Great Notley
Cressing
H I R E
Latchford
Bromley
Bury Green
Start Hill
Takeley Street
Smith's Green
Little Canfield
Felsted
Felstead Vineyard
Tye Green
Much Hadham
Forge
Thorley Street
BIRCHANGER GREEN
Bedlar's Green
Great Hallingbury
Hatfield Forest
Puttock's End
Bacon End
Barnston
R. Chelmer
Cock Green
Willows Green
Essex Showground
Black Notley
Barwick
Hadham Cross
Thorley
Little Hallingbury
Castle
Great Canfield
A130
North End
Leez Priory
Littley Green
A131
White Notley
Perry Green
Green Tye
Spellbrook
Hatfield Broad Oak
Taverners Green
High Roding
Bishop's Green
Onslow Green
Hartford End
Great Leighs
Rank's Green
Faulkbourne
Fairstead
Babb's Green
Allen's Green
Wright's Green
Hatfield Heath
Aythorpe Roding
Ford End
Little Leighs
Terling
Widford
Sawbridgeworth
E S S E X
THE RODINGS
High Easter
Stagden Cross
Chatham Green
Fuller Street
Wareside
High Wych
Roundbush Green
White Roding
Pleshey
Howe Street
Hunsdon
Sheering
Leaden Roding
Great Waltham
Good Easter
Stanstead Abbotts
Eastwick
Pye Corner
Nether Street
Margaret Roding
Fanner's Green
Broad's Green
Little Waltham
A414
HARLOW
Mark Hall
Matching
Abbess Roding
Chignall Smealy
Marshbury
Broomfield
A130
A12
Newland Grove
Hatfield Peverel
Roydon
Hare Street
Church Langley
Matching Tye
Matching Green
Beauchamp Roding
Chalk End
Parsonage Green
Boreham
Great Parndon
Potter Street
Foster Street
Little Laver
Birds Green
Shellow Bowells
Boyton Cross
Chignall St. James
Roydon Hamlet
A1169
High Laver
Magdalen Laver
Roxwell
Ulting
R. Chelmer
Little Baddow
Broadley Common
Ada Cole Stables
Lower Nazeing
Hastingwood
Fyfield
Willingale
Great Oxney Green
CHELMSFORD
Nature Trail
Parndon Wood
A414
Moreton
Blake Hall
Bovinger
Tyler's Green
Bobbingworth
Norton Mandeville
Cooksmill Green
Writtle
Widford
Great Baddow
Sandon
Danbury
Epping Green
Airfield
North Weald Bassett
High Ongar
Norton Heath
Edney Common
Hylands House
Loves Green
Gay Bowers
Bumble's Green
Epping Upland
Thornwood Common
Greensted Green
Saxon Wooden Church
Chipping Ongar
Ongar
Galleywood
Butt's Green
Howe Green
Coopersale Common
Toot Hill
Nine Ashes
Elkins Green
Holyfield
WALTHAM ABBEY
EPPING
Upshire
Coopersale Street
Tunnel
Fiddlers Hamlet
Stanford Rivers
Little End
Blackmore
Beggar Hill
Mill Green
Margaretting
Margaretting Tye
A12
A130
East Hanningfield
Theydon Bois
Copthall Green
Stondon Massey
Fryerning
Ingatestone
Stock
West Hanningfield
M25
Stapleford Tawney
Kelvedon Hatch
Wyatt's Green
Doddinghurst
Ingatestone Hall
Heybridge
Hanningfield Reservoir
Hyde Hall
Rettendon
High Beech
Epping Forest
Debden Green
Hobbs Cross
A113
Navestock
Navestock Side
Fox Hatch
Mountnessing
A12
South Hanningfield
Coalhill
Passingford Bridge
Abridge
Crow Green
Pilgrims
Ramsden Heath
LOUGHTON
Stapleford

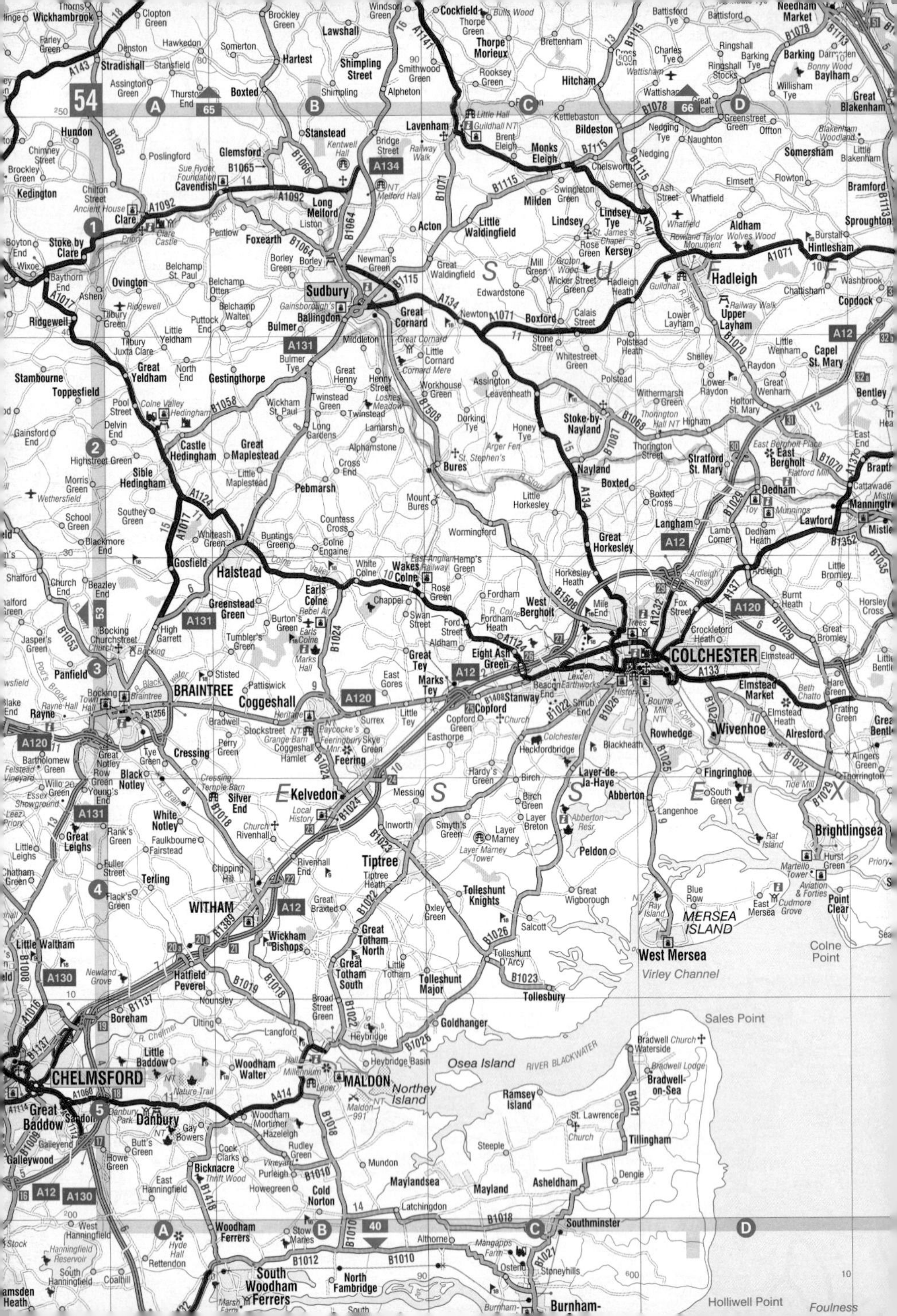

54
Wickhambrook
Clopton Green
Farley Green
Denston
Hawkedon
Somerton
Brockley Green
Lawshall
Windsor Green
Cockfield
Bulls Wood
Thorpe Green
Thorpe Morieux
Brettenham
Battisford Tye
Battisford
Needham Market
Stradishall
Stansfield
Hartest
Shimpling Street
Smithwood Green
Rooksey Green
Hitcham
Charles Tye
Ringshall
Ringshall Stocks
Barking Tye
Barking
Darmsden
Bonny Wood
Baylham
Assington Green
Thurston End
Boxted
Shimpling
Alpheton
Wattisham
Willisham Tye
Great Blakenham
A
B
C
D
65
66
Hundon
Stanstead
Lavenham
Little Hall
Guildhall NT
Kettlebaston
Bildeston
Nedging Tye
Naughton
Greenstreet Green
Offton
Blakenham Woodland
Chimney Street
Poslingford
Glemsford
Kentwell Hall
Bridge Street
Railway Walk
Brent Eleigh
Monks Eleigh
Nedging
Somersham
Little Blakenham
Brockley Green
Sue Ryder Foundation
Cavendish
A134
Chelsworth
Elmsett
Flowton
Bramford
Kedington
Chilton Street
Ancient House
Clare
A1092
Long Melford
NT Melford Hall
Swingleton Green
Milden
Semer
Ash Street
Whatfield
Sproughton
Stoke by Clare
Clare Castle
Priory
Pentlow
Foxearth
Liston
Acton
Little Waldingfield
Lindsey
Lindsey Tye
St. James's Chapel
Rose Green
Kersey
Rowland Taylor Monument
Aldham
Wolves Wood
Burstall
Hintlesham
Boyton End
Wixoe
Baythorn End
Ovington
Belchamp St. Paul
Belchamp Otten
Borley Green
Borley
Newman's Green
Great Waldingfield
Mill Green
Groton Wood
Wicker Street Green
Hadleigh Heath
Guildhall
Hadleigh
Chattisham
Washbrook
Ashen
Ridgewell
Tilbury Green
Belchamp Walter
Puttock End
Sudbury
Gainsborough's
Ballingdon
Bulmer
Great Cornard
Newton
Edwardstone
Boxford
Calais Street
Lower Layham
Railway Walk
Upper Layham
Copdock
Little Yeldham
Tilbury Juxta Clare
Middleton
Great Cornard
Little Cornard
Cornard Mere
Stone Street
Whitestreet Green
Polstead Heath
A12
Little Wenham
Capel St. Mary
Great Yeldham
North End
Gestingthorpe
A131
Bulmer Tye
Great Henny
Henny Street
Workhouse Green
Assington
Leavenheath
Polstead
Shelley
Raydon
Lower Raydon
Great Wenham
Bentley
Stambourne
Toppesfield
Pool Street
Colne Valley
Hedingham
B1058
Wickham St. Paul
Twinstead Green
Twinstead
Loshes Meadow
Withermarsh Green
Thorington Hall NT
Holton St. Mary
Higham
Stoke-by-Nayland
Delvin End
Gainsford End
Castle Hedingham
Great Maplestead
Long Gardens
Lamarsh
Dorking Tye
Honey Tye
Arger Fen
East Bergholt Place
East Bergholt
Highstreet Green
Alphamstone
St. Stephen's
Thorington Street
Stratford St. Mary
Flatford Mill
Sible Hedingham
Little Maplestead
Cross End
Bures
Nayland
Boxted
Dedham
Morris Green
Wethersfield
Pebmarsh
Mount Bures
Little Horkesley
Boxted Cross
Toy
Munnings
Cattawade
Manningtree
Lawford
Mistley
School Green
Southey Green
Countess Cross
Wormingford
Langham
Lamb Corner
Dedham Heath
Blackmore End
Whiteash Green
Buntings Green
Colne Engaine
East Anglian Railway
Hemp's Green
Great Horkesley
Gosfield
Halstead
White Colne
Wakes Colne
Horkesley Heath
Ardleigh Resr
Ardleigh
Little Bromley
Shalford
Church End
Beazley End
Earls Colne
Chappel
Rose Green
Fordham
West Bergholt
Mile End
Fox Street
A120
Burnt Heath
Horsley Cross
Greenstead Green
Rebel Air
Burton's Green
Swan Street
Ford Street
Fordham Heath
R. Colne
Crockleford Heath
Great Bromley
Jasper's Green
Bocking Churchstreet
Bocking
High Garrett
Tumbler's Green
Marks Hall
Aldham
Great Tey
Eight Ash Green
Trees
COLCHESTER
Elmstead
Panfield
Stisted
Pattiswick
East Gores
Marks Tey
Lexden Earthworks
History
A133
Elmstead Market
Beth Chatto
Hare Green
Bocking Town Hall
Braintree
BRAINTREE
Coggeshall
Heritage
Little Tey
Stanway
Beacon End
Copford
Church
Shrub End
Bourne Mill NT
Frating Green
Rayne
Rayne Hall
B1256
Bradwell
Stockstreet
Grange Barn
Paycocke's
Feeringbury Mnr.
Surrex
Skye Green
Copford Green
Easthorpe
Colchester
Rowhedge
Wivenhoe
Elmstead Heath
Alresford
Great Notley
Tye Green
Cressing
Perry Green
Coggeshall Hamlet
Feering
Heckfordbridge
Blackheath
Aingers Green
Thorrington
Bartholomew Green
Felstead Vineyard
Black Notley
Cressing Temple Barn
Hardy's Green
Birch
Layer-de-la-Haye
Fingringhoe
Willows Green
Young's End
Essex Showground
Silver End
Kelvedon
Messing
Birch Green
Layer Breton
Abberton
Langenhoe
South Green
Tide Mill
Leez Priory
White Notley
Local History
Abberton Resr
Great Leighs
Rank's Green
Faulkbourne
Fairstead
Church
Rivenhall
Inworth
Smyth's Green
Layer Marney
Layer Marney Tower
Rat Island
Brightlingsea
Little Leighs
Fuller Street
Terling
Chipping Hill
Rivenhall End
Tiptree
Tiptree Heath
Peldon
Hurst Green
Martello Tower
Aviation & Forties
Priory
Chatham Green
Flack's Green
WITHAM
Great Braxted
Oxley Green
Tolleshunt Knights
Great Wigborough
Blue Row
Ray Island
East Mersea
Cudmore Grove
Point Clear
MERSEA ISLAND
Little Waltham
Wickham Bishops
Great Totham North
Great Totham South
Little Totham
Salcott
Tolleshunt D'Arcy
West Mersea
Colne Point
Newland Grove
Hatfield Peverel
Tolleshunt Major
Tollesbury
Virley Channel
Nounsley
Broad Street Green
Boreham
Ulting
Langford
Goldhanger
Heybridge
Sales Point
Little Baddow
Woodham Walter
Heybridge Basin
Millennium
Osea Island
RIVER BLACKWATER
Bradwell Church
Bradwell Waterside
Bradwell Lodge
Bradwell-on-Sea
CHELMSFORD
Nature Trail
MALDON
Leper
Northey Island
Maldon 991
Ramsey Island
Great Baddow
Sandon
Danbury Park
Danbury
Gay Bowers
Woodham Mortimer
Hazeleigh
St. Lawrence
Church
Galleyend
Galleywood
Butt's Green
Howe Green
Cock Clarks
Bicknacre
Thrift Wood
Rudley Green
Vineyard
Purleigh
Mundon
Steeple
Tillingham
East Hanningfield
Howegreen
Cold Norton
Maylandsea
Mayland
Asheldham
Dengie
Latchingdon
A130
West Hanningfield
Woodham Ferrers
Stow Maries
40
Althorne
Southminster
Stock
Hanningfield Reservoir
Hyde Hall
Rettendon
Mangapps Farm
Ostend
Stoneyhills
South Hanningfield
Coalhill
South Woodham Ferrers
North Fambridge
Burnham-
Holliwell Point
Foulness
Ramsden Heath

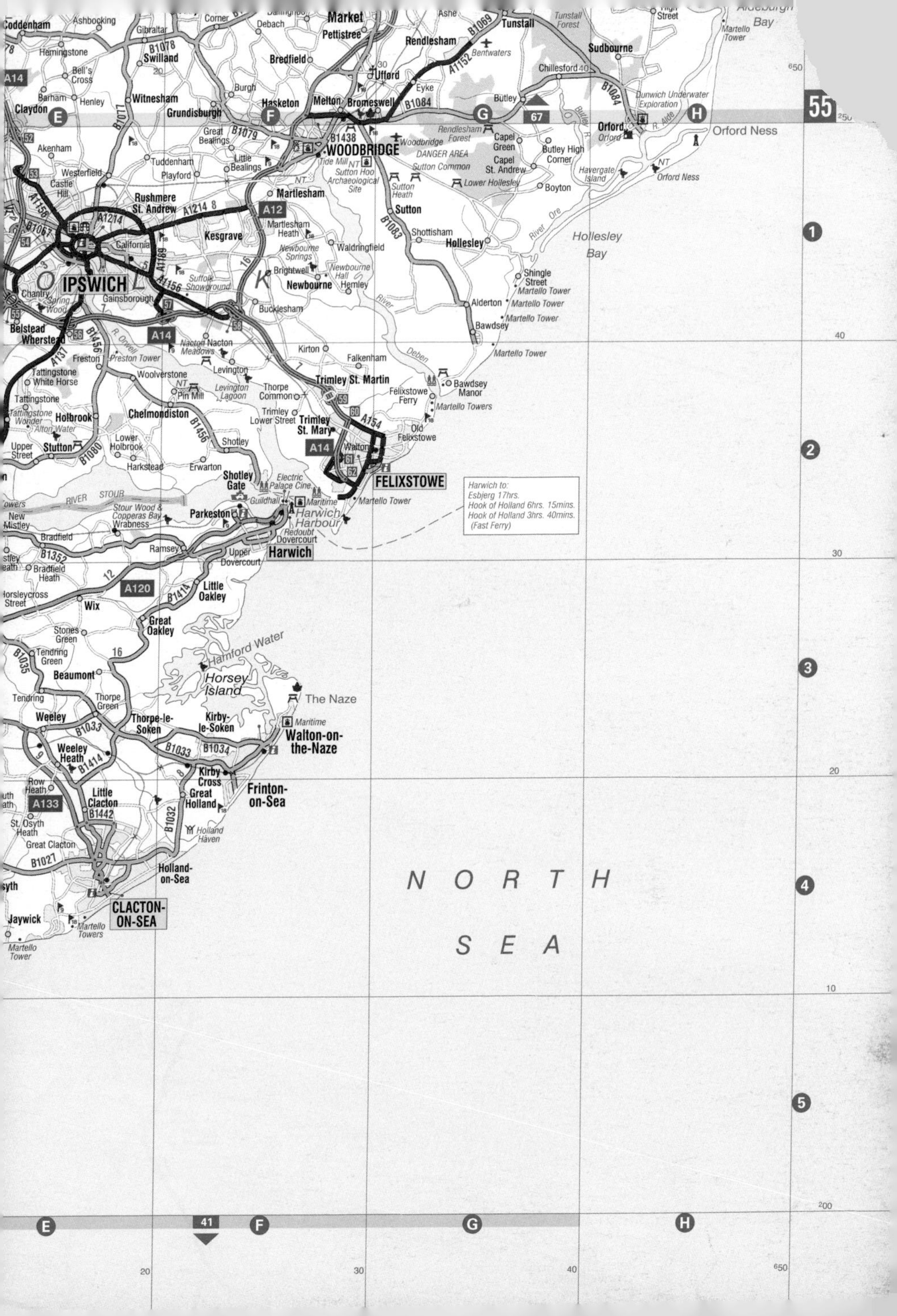

55
Coddenham
Ashbocking
Gibraltar
Corner
Debach
Market
Pettistree
Ashe
B1069
Tunstall
Tunstall Forest
Street
Aldeburgh Bay
Martello Tower
Hemingstone
B1078
Swilland
Bredfield
Rendlesham
Bentwaters
A1152
Sudbourne
Bell's Cross
Ufford
Eyke
Chillesford
650
A14
Barham
Henley
Witnesham
Burgh
Hasketon
Melton
Bromeswell
B1084
Butley
Dunwich Underwater Exploration
Claydon
Grundisburgh
Great Bealings
B1079
B1438
Rendlesham Forest
Capel Green
Orford
Orford Ness
Akenham
Tuddenham
Little Bealings
WOODBRIDGE
Woodbridge
DANGER AREA
Butley High Corner
Westerfield
Castle Hill
Playford
Tide Mill
Sutton Hoo Archaeological Site
Sutton Common
Capel St. Andrew
Havergate Island
NT
Lower Hollesley
Boyton
Martlesham
Sutton Heath
Rushmere St. Andrew
A1214
A12
Sutton
A1156
Martlesham Heath
B1083
Shottisham
Hollesley
River Ore
Hollesley Bay
B1067
California
Kesgrave
Newbourne Springs
Waldringfield
A1189
Brightwell
Newbourne Hall
Hemley
Shingle Street
Martello Tower
IPSWICH
Suffolk Showground
Newbourne
Chantry
Spring Wood
Gainsborough
Bucklesham
River
Alderton
Martello Tower
Bawdsey
Belstead
Wherstead
B1456
A14
Nacton
Nacton Meadows
R. Orwell
Kirton
Falkenham
Martello Tower
A137
Freston
Preston Tower
Levington
Deben
Tattingstone White Horse
Woolverstone
Thorpe Common
Trimley St. Martin
Bawdsey Manor
Pin Mill
Levington Lagoon
Felixstowe Ferry
Tattingstone
Tattingstone Wonder
Alton Water
Holbrook
Chelmondiston
Trimley Lower Street
Trimley St. Mary
A154
Martello Towers
Old Felixstowe
Upper Street
Stutton
B1080
Lower Holbrook
Shotley
A14
Walton
Harkstead
Erwarton
Shotley Gate
Electric Palace Cine.
FELIXSTOWE
Harwich to:
Esbjerg 17hrs.
Hook of Holland 6hrs. 15mins.
Hook of Holland 3hrs. 40mins.
(Fast Ferry)
RIVER STOUR
Guildhall
Maritime
Martello Tower
Harwich Harbour
Stour Wood & Copperas Bay
New Mistley
Parkeston
Wrabness
Redoubt
Dovercourt
Bradfield
Ramsey
Upper Dovercourt
Harwich
30
B1352
Bradfield Heath
A120
B1414
Little Oakley
Horsleycross Street
Wix
Great Oakley
Stones Green
Hamford Water
Tendring Green
Beaumont
Horsey Island
The Naze
Tendring
Thorpe Green
Weeley
B1033
Thorpe-le-Soken
Kirby-le-Soken
Maritime
Walton-on-the-Naze
Weeley Heath
B1414
B1033
B1034
Kirby Cross
Row Heath
Little Clacton
Great Holland
Frinton-on-Sea
A133
B1442
B1032
St. Osyth Heath
Holland Haven
Great Clacton
B1027
Holland-on-Sea
NORTH SEA
CLACTON-ON-SEA
Jaywick
Martello Towers
Martello Tower
41
E
F
G
H
1
2
3
4
5
20
30
40
650
250
200
10

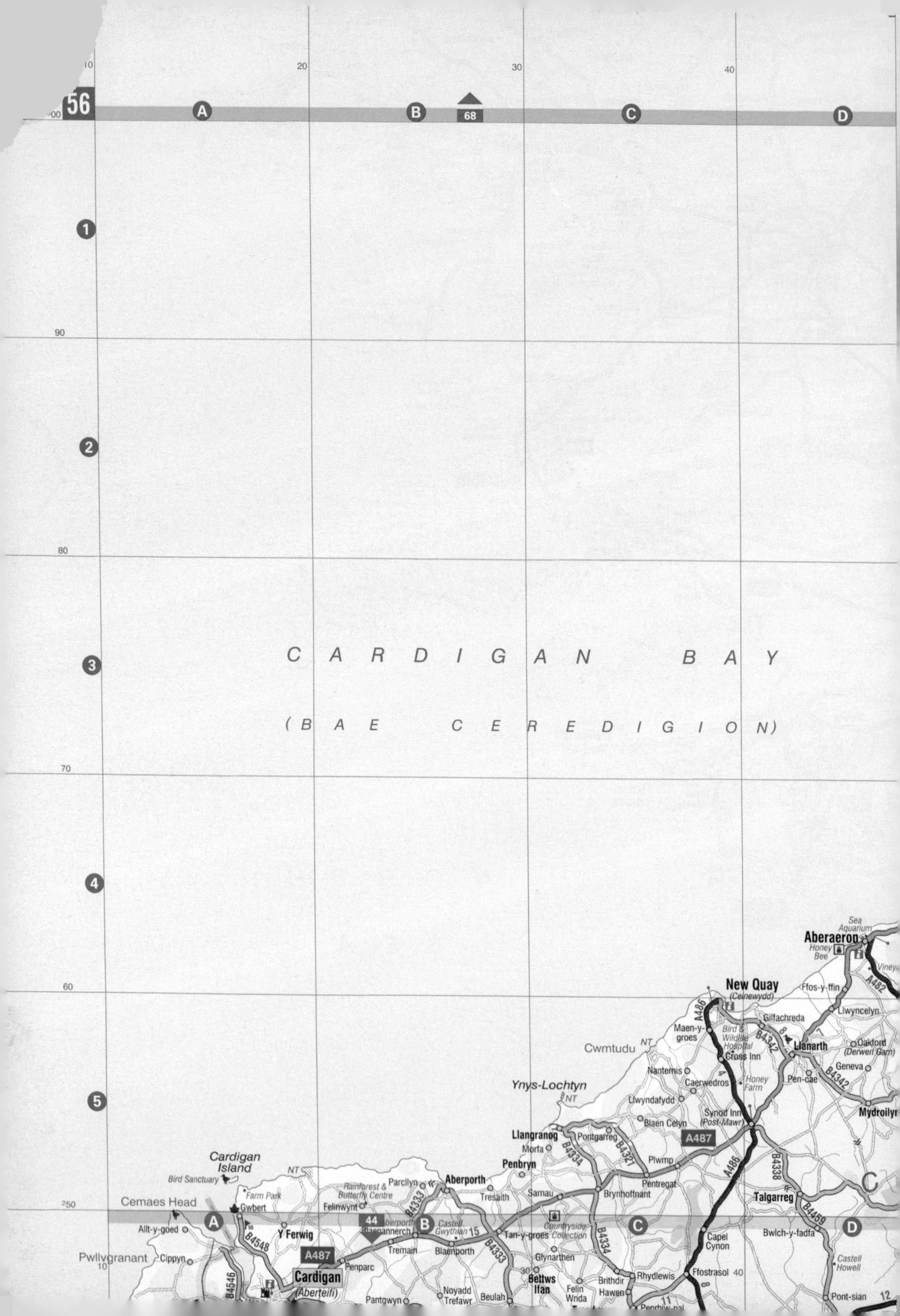
56
68
A
B
C
D
1
2
3
4
5
10
20
30
40
300
90
80
70
60
250
C A R D I G A N B A Y
(B A E C E R E D I G I O N)
Sea Aquarium
Aberaeron
Honey Bee
Ffos-y-ffin
A482
New Quay
(Ceinewydd)
A486
Gilfachreda
Llwyncelyn
Maen-y-groes
Bird & Wildlife Hospital
B4342
Llanarth
Oakford
(Derwen Gam)
Cwmtudu
NT
Cross Inn
Geneva
Nanternis
Pen-cae
B4342
Caerwedros
Honey Farm
Ynys-Lochtyn
NT
Llwyndafydd
Mydroilyn
Synod Inn
(Post-Mawr)
Blaen Celyn
Llangranog
Pontgarreg
A487
Morfa
B4334
B4321
Plwmp
Cardigan Island
Penbryn
A486
B4338
Bird Sanctuary
NT
Rainforest & Butterfly Centre
Parcllyn
Aberporth
Pentregat
Farm Park
Talgarreg
Cemaes Head
Gwbert
Felinwynt
B4333
Tresaith
Sarnau
Brynhoffnant
B4459
44
Castell Gwythian
Countryside Collection
Allt-y-goed
B4548
Y Ferwig
B4334
Bwlch-y-fadfa
Blaenannerch
15
Tan-y-groes
Capel Cynon
A487
Tremain
Blaenporth
Pwllygranant
Cippyn
B4333
Glynarthen
Castell Howell
Penparc
Ffostrasol
40
B4546
Cardigan
(Aberteifi)
30
Bettws Ifan
Brithdir
Rhydlewis
Felin Wnda
Hawen
Noyadd Trefawr
Beulah
Pantgwyn
Pont-sian
12

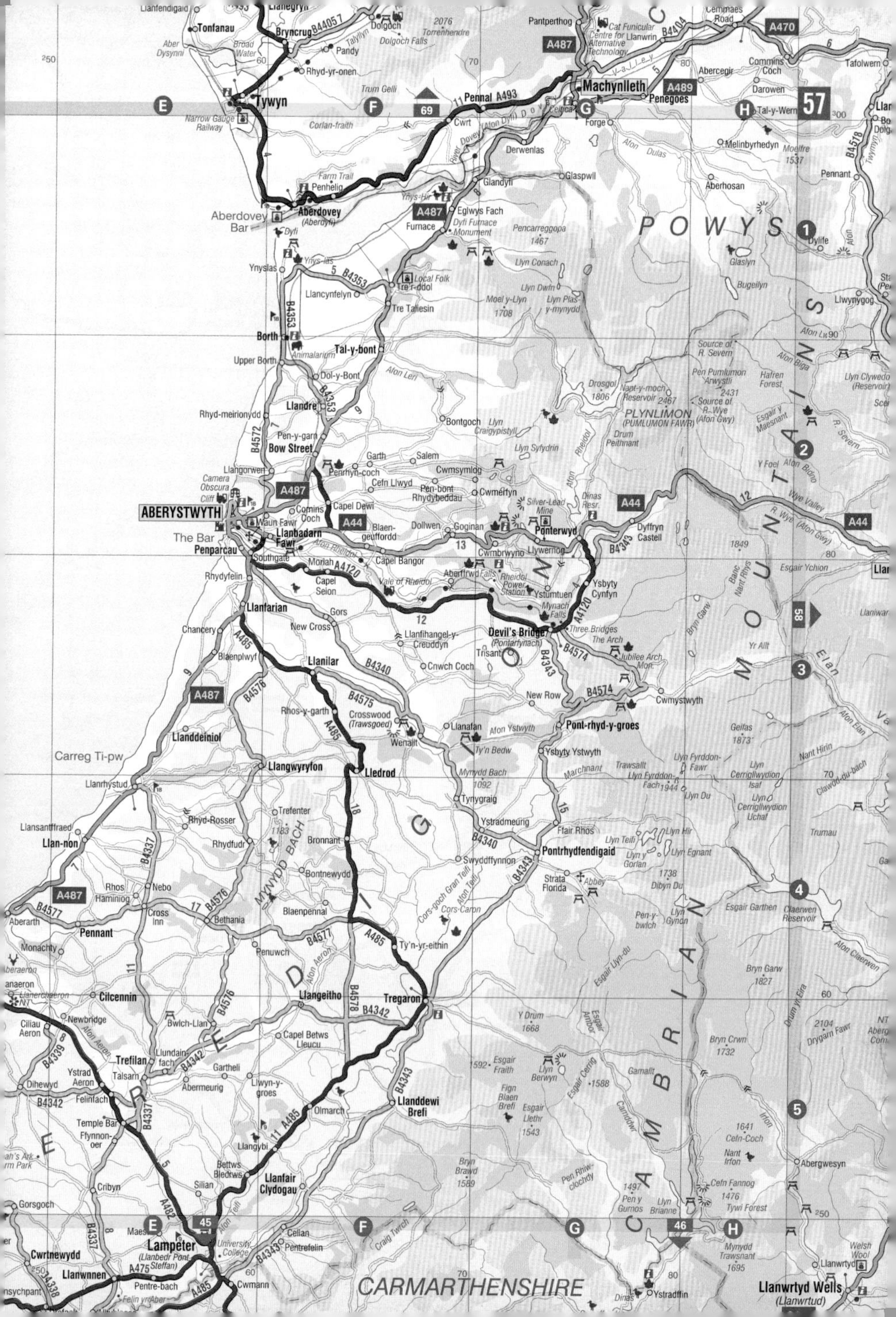

57
Llanfendigaid
Llanegryn
Tonfanau
Bryncrug
B4405
Dolgoch
Dolgoch Falls
2076
Torrenhendre
Pantperthog
Cat Funicular
Centre for Alternative Technology
Llanwrin
B4404
Cemmaes Road
A470
A487
Aber Dysynni
Broad Water
Pandy
Talyllyn
Rhyd-yr-onen
Tafolwern
Commins Coch
Abercegir
Machynlleth
A489
Penegoes
Darowen
Tywyn
Narrow Gauge Railway
Trum Gelli
69
Pennal
A493
Forge
Tal-y-Wern
Corlan-fraith
Cwrt
River Dovey
Derwenlas
Afon Dulas
Melinbyrhedyn
Moelfre 1537
B4518
Farm Trail
Penhelig
Glandyfi
Glaspwll
Aberhosan
Pennant
Aberdovey Bar
Aberdovey (Aberdyfi)
Ynys-Hir
Eglwys Fach
Dyfi Furnace Monument
Furnace
Dyfi
Pencarreggopa 1467
POWYS
Dylife
Glaslyn
Ynyslas
Ynys-las
Llyn Conach
B4353
Local Folk
Tre'r-ddol
Llancynfelyn
Llyn Dwfn
Moel y-Llyn 1708
Llyn Plas-y-mynydd
Bugeilyn
Llwynygog
Tre Taliesin
Borth
Animalarium
Tal-y-bont
Upper Borth
Dol-y-Bont
Afon Leri
Source of R. Severn
Pen Pumlumon Arwystli 2431
Hafren Forest
Afon Biga
Llyn Clywedog (Reservoir)
Drosgol 1806
Nant-y-moch Reservoir
2467
PLYNLIMON (PUMLUMON FAWR)
Source of R. Wye (Afon Gwy)
Esgair y Maesnant
R. Severn
Rhyd-meirionydd
Llandre
Bontgoch
Llyn Craigypistyll
Drum Peithnant
B4572
Pen-y-garn
Bow Street
Garth
Salem
Llyn Syfydrin
Afon Rheidol
Y Foel
Afon Bidno
Llangorwen
Penrhyn-coch
Cwmsymlog
Camera Obscura
Cliff
A487
Cefn Llwyd
Pen-bont Rhydybeddau
Cwmerfyn
ABERYSTWYTH
Capel Dewi
Comins Coch
Waun Fawr
Silver-Lead Mine
Dinas Resr.
A44
Wye Valley
R. Wye (Afon Gwy)
The Bar
Llanbadarn Fawr
Blaen-geuffordd
Dollwen
Goginan
Ponterwyd
Dyffryn Castell
B4343
Penparcau
Southgate
Afon Rheidol
Moriah
Capel Bangor
Cwmbrwyno
Llywernog
1849
Esgair Ychion
Rhydyfelin
A4120
Capel Seion
Vale of Rheidol
Aberffrwd
Falls
Rheidol Power Station
Ystumtuen
Ysbyty Cynfyn
Banc Nant Rhys
Llanfarian
Gors
Mynach Falls
58
Chancery
New Cross
Llanfihangel-y-Creuddyn
Devil's Bridge (Pontarfynach)
Three Bridges
The Arch
Bryn Garw
Yr Allt
A485
Blaenplwyf
Llanilar
Trisant
Cnwch Coch
Jubilee Arch Mon.
B4574
Elan
B4340
B4576
B4575
New Row
Cwmystwyth
Rhos-y-garth
Crosswood (Trawsgoed)
Wenallt
Llanafan
Afon Ystwyth
Pont-rhyd-y-groes
Afon Elan
Llanddeiniol
Ty'n Bedw
Ysbyty Ystwyth
Gelfas 1873
Nant Hirin
Carreg Ti-pw
Llangwyryfon
Lledrod
Mynydd Bach 1092
Marchnant
Trawsallt
Llyn Fyrddon-Fawr
Llyn Fyrddon-Fach
1944
Llyn Cerrigllwydion Isaf
Llyn Cerrigllwydion Uchaf
Clawdd-du-bach
Llanrhystud
Llyn Du
Trefenter
Tynygraig
Llansantffraed
Rhyd-Rosser
1183
MYNYDD BACH
Ystradmeurig
Ffair Rhos
Llyn Teifi
Llyn Hir
Trumau
Llan-non
Rhydfudr
Bronnant
Pontrhydfendigaid
Llyn y Gorlan
Llyn Egnant
Swyddffynnon
1738
Dibyn Du
Bontnewydd
Strata Florida
Abbey
Rhos
Haminiog
Nebo
Cors-goch Glan Teifi
Afon Teifi
Cors-Caron
Pen-y-bwlch
Llyn Gynon
Esgair Garthen
Claerwen Reservoir
A487
B4577
Aberarth
Pennant
Cross Inn
Bethania
Blaenpennal
Ty'n-yr-eithin
Monachty
Penuwch
Afon Aeron
Afon Claerwen
Esgair Llyn-du
Aberaeron
Llanerchaeron
NT
Cilcennin
Llangeitho
Tregaron
Bryn Garw 1827
Drum yr Eira
Ciliau Aeron
Newbridge
B4576
B4578
B4342
Bwlch-Llan
Y Drum 1668
Esgair Ambor
2104
Drygarn Fawr
Capel Betws Lleucu
B4339
Trefilan
Llundain-fach
Bryn Crwn 1732
Ystrad Aeron
Talsarn
Gartheli
Esgair Fraith
1592
Llyn Berwyn
Esgair Cerrig
1588
Gamallt
Dihewyd
Abermeurig
Llwyn-y-groes
Fign Blaen Brefi
Esgair Llethr 1543
B4342
Felinfach
Olmarch
Llanddewi Brefi
Camddwr
Irfon
Temple Bar
Ffynnon-oer
B4337
Llangybi
1641
Cefn-Coch
Nant Irfon
Bettws Bledrws
Llanfair Clydogau
Bryn Brawd 1589
Pen Rhiw-clochdy
Abergwesyn
Silian
Cribyn
1497
Pen y Gurnos
Llyn Brianne
Cefn Fannog 1476
Tywi Forest
Gorsgoch
A482
45
46
250
Maesy
Lampeter (Llanbedr Pont Steffan)
University College
Cellan
Pentrefelin
Craig Twrch
Mynydd Trawsnant 1695
Welsh Wool
Cwrtnewydd
Llanwnnen
A475
Pentre-bach
Cwmann
CARMARTHENSHIRE
Ystradffin
Dinas
Llanwrtyd
Llanwrtyd Wells (Llanwrtud)
B4338
CAMBRIAN MOUNTAINS
CEREDIGION

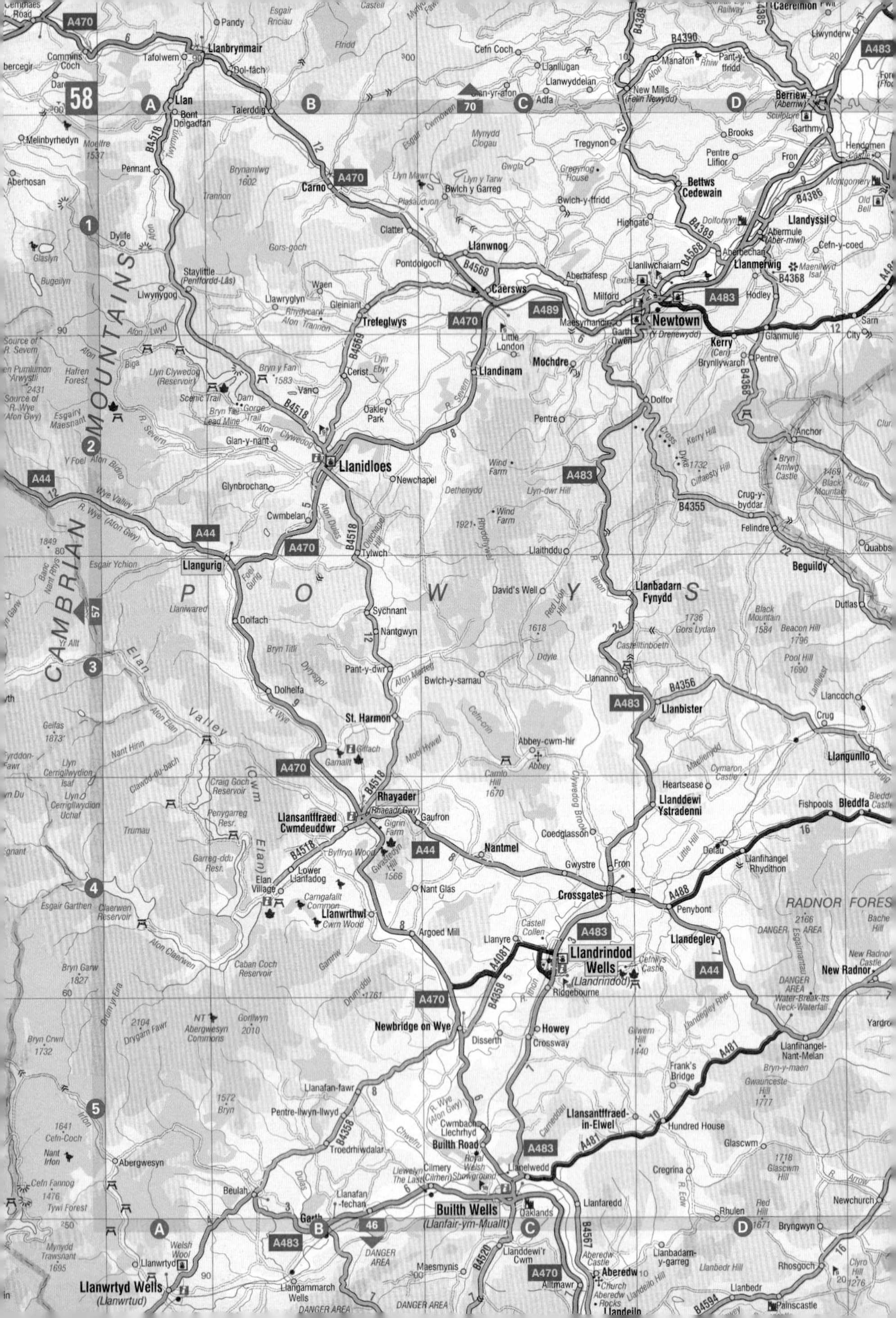

58
A470
Pandy
Llanbrynmair
Tafolwern
Dol-fâch
Commins Coch
Esgair Rhiciau
Ffridd
Cefn Coch
Llanllugan
Llanwyddelan
Glan-yr-afon
Adfa
70
B4389
B4390
Manafon
Pant-y-ffridd
New Mills
(Felin Newydd)
Llwynderw
A483
Berriew
(Aberriw)
Sculpture
Garthmyl
Brooks
Pentre Llifior
Fron
Hendomen Castle
Montgomery
Old Bell
A
B
C
D
Llan
Bont Dolgadfan
Talerddig
Melinbyrhedyn
Moelfre
1537
B4518
Twymyn
Pennant
Aberhosan
Brynamlwg
1602
Trannon
Carno
Esgair Cwmowen
Mynydd Clogau
Llyn Mawr
Bwlch y Garreg
Llyn y Tarw
Gwgia
Tregynon
Gregynog House
Bwlch-y-ffridd
Plasauduon
Bettws Cedewain
Highgate
B4386
Dolforwyn
Llandyssil
Abermule
(Aber-miwl)
Cefn-y-coed
1
Dylife
Afon
Clatter
Gors-goch
Llanwnog
Pontdolgoch
B4568
Caersws
Aberhafesp
Llanllwchaiarn
Textile
Aberbechan
Llanmerwig
Maenllwyd Isaf
B4368
Hodley
Glaslyn
Bugeilyn
Staylittle
(Penffordd-Lâs)
Llwynygog
Waen
Llawryglyn
Gleiniant
Rhydycarw
Afon Trannon
Trefeglwys
A470
A489
Milford
Maesyrhandir
Newtown
(Y Drenewydd)
Garth Owen
Kerry
(Ceri)
Glanmule
Sarn
City
Afon Lwyd
Source of R. Severn
Afon
Pen Pumlumon Arwystli
2431
Hafren Forest
Source of R. Wye
(Afon Gwy)
Biga
Llyn Clywedog
(Reservoir)
Bryn y Fan
1583
Van
Scenic Trail
Dam
Gorge Trail
Bryn Tail Lead Mine
Esgairy Maesnant
MOUNTAINS
Cerist
Llyn Ebyr
Little London
Llandinam
Mochdre
Brynllywarch
Pentre
Oakley Park
R. Severn
Dolfor
Pentre
Cross Dyke
Kerry Hill
1732
Ciffaesty Hill
Anchor
Bryn Amlwg Castle
1469
Black Mountain
R. Clun
2
Y Foel
Afon Biga
R. Severn
Afon Clywedog
Glan-y-nant
Llanidloes
Newchapel
Wind Farm
Dethenydd
Llyn-dwr Hill
A483
A44
12
Wye Valley
Glynbrochan
Crug-y-byddar
B4355
Felindre
R. Wye (Afon Gwy)
Cwmbelan
Afon Dulas
B4518
Olchapel Hill
1921
Wind Farm
Rhydothwel
1849
80
A44
A470
Tylwch
Llaithddu
22
Quabbs
Banc Nant Rhys
Esgair Ychion
Llangurig
Foel Gurig
Beguildy
P
O
W
Y
S
David's Well
Red Lion Hill
Llanbadarn Fynydd
CAMBRIAN
57
Llaniwared
Dolfach
Sychnant
Nantgwyn
12
1618
24
1736
Gors Lydan
Black Mountain
1584
Beacon Hill
1796
Dutlas
Yr Allt
Bryn Titli
Dyrysgol
Ddyle
Castelltinboeth
3
Elan
Pant-y-dwr
Afon Marteg
Bwlch-y-sarnau
Llananno
Pool Hill
1690
Dolhelfa
Cefn-crin
B4356
Llanbister
Llancoch
Crug
Afon Elan
R. Wye
Valley
St. Harmon
Geifas
1873
Nant Hirin
Gilfach
Garnallt
Moel Hywel
Abbey-cwm-hir
Abbey
Llangunllo
Llyn Cerrigllwydion Isaf
Clawdd-du-bach
(Cwm
Craig Goch Reservoir
A470
B4518
Camlo Hill
1670
Clywedog Brook
Cymaron Castle
Heartsease
R. Lugg
Llyn Cerrigllwydion Uchaf
Rhayader
(Rhaeadr Gwy)
Llansantffraed Cwmdeuddwr
Gigrin Farm
Gaufron
Llanddewi Ystradenni
Fishpools
Bleddfa
Penygarreg Resr.
Trumau
Coedglasson
Little Hill
Dolau
16
Llanfihangel Rhydithon
Elan)
Garreg-ddu Resr.
B4518
Byffryn Wood
Gwastedyn Hill
1566
A44
Nantmel
Gwystre
Fron
Elan Village
Lower Llanfadog
Carngafallt Common
Llanwrthwl
Cwm Wood
Nant Glas
Crossgates
A488
Penybont
RADNOR FOREST
2166
DANGER AREA
4
Esgair Garthen
Claerwen Reservoir
Argoed Mill
Castell Collen
Llanyre
A483
Llandrindod Wells
(Llandrindod)
Cefnllys Castle
Llandegley
A44
New Radnor
Bache Hill
New Radnor Castle
Afon Claerwen
Caban Coch Reservoir
Gamrw
A4081
B4358
5
Ridgebourne
Esgairnantau
DANGER AREA
Water-Break-Its Neck-Waterfall
Bryn Garw
1827
60
Drum-ddu
1761
A470
Llandegley Rhos
Drum yr Eira
NT
Abergwesyn Commons
2104
Drygarn Fawr
Gorllwyn
2010
Newbridge on Wye
Howey
Crossway
Disserth
Gilwern Hill
1440
Llanfihangel-Nant-Melan
Yardro
Bryn Crwn
1732
A481
Bryn-y-maen
Frank's Bridge
Gwaunceste Hill
1777
1572
Bryn
Llanafan-fawr
8
Pentre-llwyn-llwyd
R. Wye
(Afon Gwy)
Cwmbach Llechrhyd
Carneddau
Llansantffraed-in-Elwel
10
Hundred House
5
Irfon
1641
Cefn-Coch
Nant Irfon
B4358
Troedrhiwdalar
Chwefru
Builth Road
Royal Welsh Showground
A483
Glascwm
1718
Glascwm Hill
Abergwesyn
Cefn Fannog
1476
Tywi Forest
Dulas
Llewelyn The Last
Cilmery
(Cilmeri)
Llanelwedd
Cregrina
R. Arrow
Beulah
Llanafan-fechan
6
Builth Wells
(Llanfair-ym-Muallt)
Oaklands
Llanfaredd
R. Edw
Red Hill
1671
Rhulen
Newchurch
Bryngwyn
A
B
C
D
Garth
A483
46
DANGER AREA
B4520
B4567
Welsh Wool
Mynydd Trawsnant
1695
Llanwrtyd
Maesmynis
Llanddewi'r Cwm
Aberedw Castle
Aberedw
Llanbadarn-y-garreg
Llanbedr Hill
Rhosgoch
Clyro Hill
1276
Llanwrtyd Wells
(Llanwrtud)
90
Llangammarch Wells
300
DANGER AREA
A470
Alltmawr
Church
Aberedw Rocks
Llandeilo Hill
Llanbedr
B4594
Painscastle

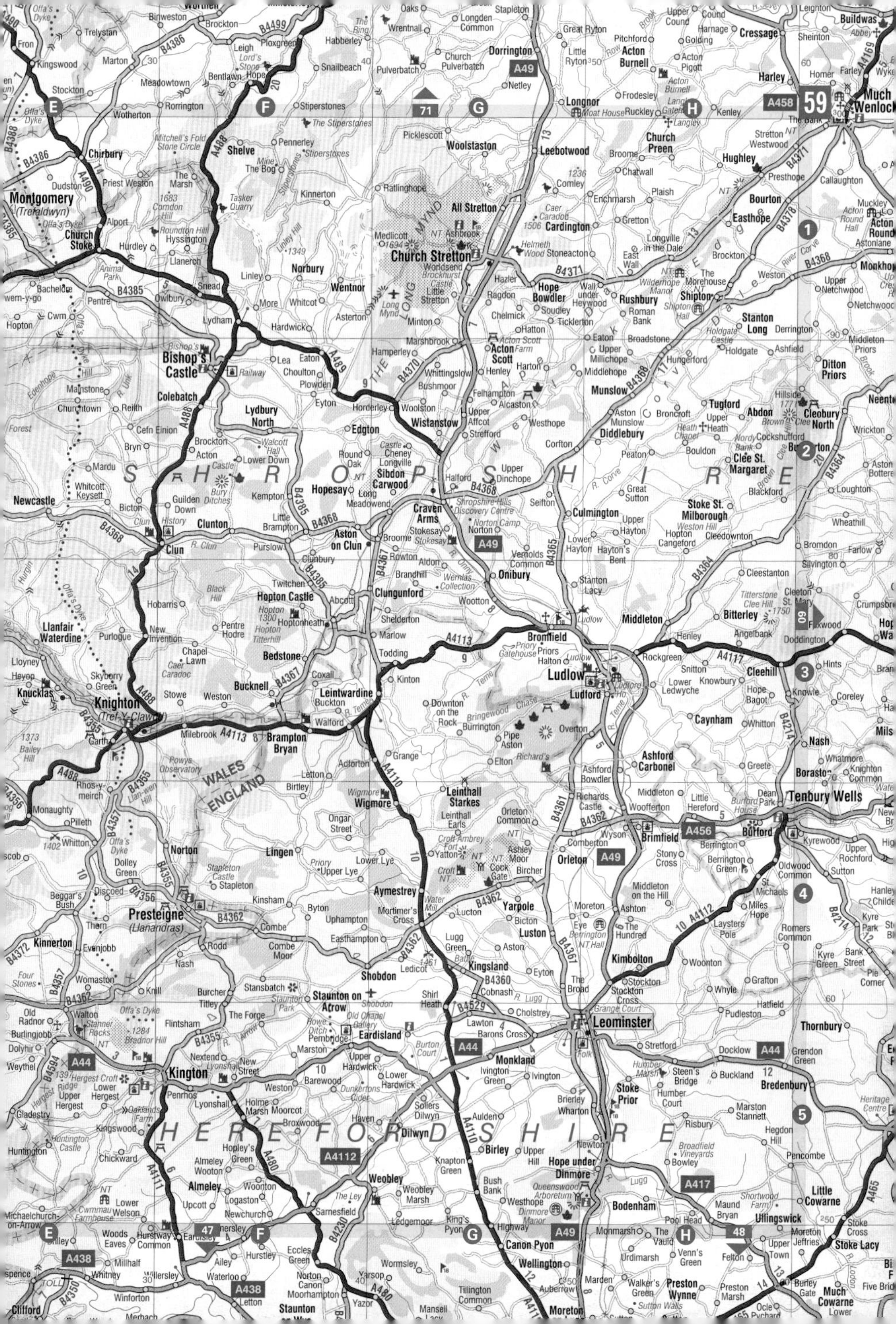

59
71
47
48
60
SHROPSHIRE
HEREFORDSHIRE
WALES
ENGLAND
Montgomery
(Trefaldwyn)
Church Stoke
Chirbury
Kingswood
Trelystan
Binweston
Brockton
Leigh
Ploxgreen
Hope
Snailbeach
Habberley
Pulverbatch
Church Pulverbatch
Wrentnall
Longden Common
Stapleton
Dorrington
Great Ryton
Little Ryton
Acton Burnell
Pitchford
Golding
Acton Pigott
Cressage
Harnage
Sheinton
Buildwas
Harley
Homer
Farley
Wyke
Much Wenlock
Longnor
Moat House
Frodesley
Ruckley
Langley
Kenley
Netley
Stiperstones
The Stiperstones
Shelve
Pennerley
The Bog
Mitchell's Fold Stone Circle
Priest Weston
The Marsh
Corndon Hill
Tasker Quarry
Roundton Hill
Hyssington
Hurdley
Alport
Dudston
Offa's Dyke
Ratlinghope
Picklescott
Woolstaston
Leebotwood
Comley
Church Preen
Broome
Chatwall
Hughley
Stretton Westwood
Presthope
Callaughton
Kinnerton
All Stretton
Long Mynd
Medlicott
Ashbrook
Church Stretton
Caer Caradoc
Cardington
Enchmarsh
Gretton
Plaish
Longville in the Dale
East Wall
Bourton
Easthope
Muckley
Acton Round
Stoneacton
Helmeth Wood
Astonlane
Brockton
Weston
Monkhopton
Upper Netchwood
Netchwood
Llanerch
Linley
Norbury
Wentnor
Minton
Little Stretton
Hazler
Ragdon
Hope Bowdler
Soudley
Wall under Heywood
Rushbury
Roman Bank
Wilderhope Manor
The Morehouse
Shipton
Shipton Hall
Stanton Long
Derrington
Middleton Priors
Snead
Owlbury
Bachelldre
Pentre
Cwm
Hopton
Lydham
Hardwick
Asterton
More
Whitcot
Chelmick
Ticklerton
Hatton
Eaton
Upper Millichope
Broadstone
Holdgate
Ashfield
Ditton Priors
Bishop's Castle
Lea
Eaton
Choulton
Plowden
Hamperley
Marshbrook
Acton Scott
Henley
Harton
Whittingslow
Middlehope
Hungerford
Bushmoor
Munslow
Mainstone
Churchtown
Reilth
Colebatch
Eyton
Horderley
Woolston
Felhampton
Alcaston
Upper Affcot
Aston Munslow
Broncroft
Tugford
Abdon
Cleobury North
Neenton
Lydbury North
Edgton
Wistanstow
Strefford
Westhope
Diddlebury
Upper Heath
Heath Chapel
Cockshutford
Burwarton
Wrickton
Cefn Einion
Bryn
Brockton
Walcott Hall
Acton
Lower Down
Round Oak
Castle
Cheney Longville
Mardu
Sibdon Carwood
Corfton
Peaton
Bouldon
Clee St. Margaret
Aston Botterell
Whitcott Keysett
Newcastle
Bicton
Bury Ditches
Hopesay
Long Meadowend
Halford
Upper Dinchope
Great Sutton
Blackford
Loughton
Guilden Down
Kempton
Craven Arms
Shropshire Hills Discovery Centre
Norton Camp
Seifton
Culmington
Stoke St. Milborough
Weston Hill
Wheathill
Clun
Clunton
Little Brampton
Aston on Clun
Broome
Stokesay
Norton
Upper Hayton
Hopton Cangeford
Cleedownton
Bromdon
Farlow
Purslow
Clunbury
Rowton
Vernolds Common
Lower Hayton
Hayton's Bent
Silvington
Aldon
Brandhill
Wernlas Collection
Onibury
Stanton Lacy
Cleestanton
Black Hill
Twitchen
Hopton Castle
Abcott
Clungunford
Wootton
Cleeton St. Mary
Crumpsbrook
Titterstone Clee Hill
Llanfair Waterdine
Hobarris
Pentre Hodre
New Invention
Hoptonheath
Shelderton
Marlow
Middleton
Bitterley
Henley
Angelbank
Doddington
Foxwood
Purlogue
Bromfield
Priors Halton
Ludlow
Lloyney
Heyop
Knucklas
Chapel Lawn
Caer Caradoc
Skyborry Green
Bedstone
Todding
Priory Gatehouse
Rockgreen
Snitton
Cleehill
Hints
Knighton
(Tref-Y-Clawdd)
Stowe
Weston
Bucknell
Coxall
Kinton
Leintwardine
Buckton
Lower Ledwyche
Knowbury
Hope Bagot
Knowle
Coreley
Garth
Bailey Hill
Milebrook
Brampton Bryan
Walford
Downton on the Rock
Burrington
Bringewood Chase
Ludford
Caynham
Whitton
Powys Observatory
Grange
Pipe Aston
Overton
Nash
Rhos-y-meirch
Letton
Adforton
Elton
Richard's Castle
Ashford Carbonel
Ashford Bowdler
Greete
Whatmore
Knighton Common
Boraston
Monaughty
Pilleth
Birtley
Wigmore
Leinthall Starkes
Middleton
Little Hereford
Dean Park
Tenbury Wells
Whitton
Llan-wen Hill
Ongar Street
Leinthall Earls
Orleton Common
Richards Castle
Woofferton
Burford House
Burford
Kyrewood
Norton
Lingen
Lower Lye
Upper Lye
Croft Ambrey
Yatton
Ashley Moor
Comberton
Wyson
Brimfield
Berrington
Upper Rochford
Dolley Green
Stapleton Castle
Stapleton
Croft
Cock Gate
Bircher
Orleton
Stony Cross
Berrington Green
Oldwood Common
Sutton
Discoed
Presteigne
(Llanandras)
Kinsham
Byton
Aymestrey
Water Mill
Mortimer's Cross
Lucton
Yarpole
Moreton
Middleton on the Hill
St. Michaels
Hanley Childe
Beggar's Bush
Thorn
Combe
Uphampton
Easthampton
Bicton
Eye
Ashton
The Hundred
Miles Hope
Laysters Pole
Romers Common
Kyre Park
Kinnerton
Evenjobb
Rodd
Combe Moor
Shobdon
Ledicot
Lugg Green
Luston
Aston
Berrington NT Hall
Kimbolton
Woonton
Kyre Green
Bank Street
Nash
Knill
Stansbatch
Staunton on Arrow
Kingsland
Eyton
The Broad
Stockton
Stockton Cross
Whyle
Grafton
Pie Corner
Four Stones
Womaston
Burcher
Titley
Shirl Heath
Cobnash
Hatfield
Old Radnor
Walton
Burlingjobb
Stanner Rocks
Bradnor Hill
The Forge
Flintsham
Staunton Park
Old Chapel Gallery
Eardisland
Pembridge
Lawton
Barons Cross
Cholstrey
Leominster
Grange Court
Pudleston
Thornbury
Dolyhir
Weythel
Kington
Hergest Croft
Lower Hergest
Upper Hergest
Hergest Ridge
Oaklands Farm
Nextend
Lyonshall
New Street
Marston
Upper Hardwick
Burton Court
Monkland
Stretford
Docklow
Grendon Green
Bredenbury
Gladestry
Penrhos
Weston
Barewood
Lower Hardwick
Ivington Green
Ivington
Humber Marsh
Steen's Bridge
Buckland
Kingswood
Holme Marsh
Moorcot
Dunkertons Cider
Sollers Dilwyn
Brierley
Wharton
Stoke Prior
Humber Court
Marston Stannett
Heritage Centre
Huntington
Huntington Castle
Broxwood
Haven
Dilwyn
Aulden
Birley
Upper Hill
Risbury
Hegdon Hill
Chickward
Hopley's Green
Almeley Wooton
Newton
Hope under Dinmore
Broadfield Vineyards
Bowley
Pencombe
Almeley
Woonton
Knapton Green
Bush Bank
Queenswood Arboretum
Dinmore Manor
Westhope
Bodenham
Little Cowarne
Upcott
Logaston
Newchurch
Sarnesfield
The Ley
Weobley
Weobley Marsh
Ledgemoor
Shortwood Farm
Maund Bryan
Ullingswick
Lower Welson
Cwmmau Farmhouse
Michaelchurch-on-Arrow
Hurstway Common
Woods Eaves
Eardisley
King's Pyon
Highway
Canon Pyon
Monmarsh
The Vauld
Pool Head
Moreton Jeffries
Stoke Cross
Stoke Lacy
Millhalf
Hurstley
Ailey
Eccles Green
Wormsley
Urdimarsh
Venn's Green
Felton
Upper Town
Whitney
Willersley
Waterloo
Norton Canon
Moorhampton
Yarsop
Wellington
Tillington Common
Marden
Walker's Green
Sutton Walls
Preston Wynne
Preston Marsh
Burley Gate
Much Cowarne
Five Bridges
Clifford
Winforton
Letton
Staunton on Wye
Yazor
Mansell Lacy
Auberrow
Moreton
Ocle Pychard
Merbach
TOLL
A49
A458
A488
A489
A490
A4113
A4117
A4110
A456
A44
A4112
A417
A480
A438
A4111
A465
A4169
B4386
B4499
B4385
B4370
B4368
B4371
B4378
B4364
B4365
B4367
B4361
B4362
B4355
B4356
B4357
B4360
B4372
B4529
B4230
B4350
B4214
B4594

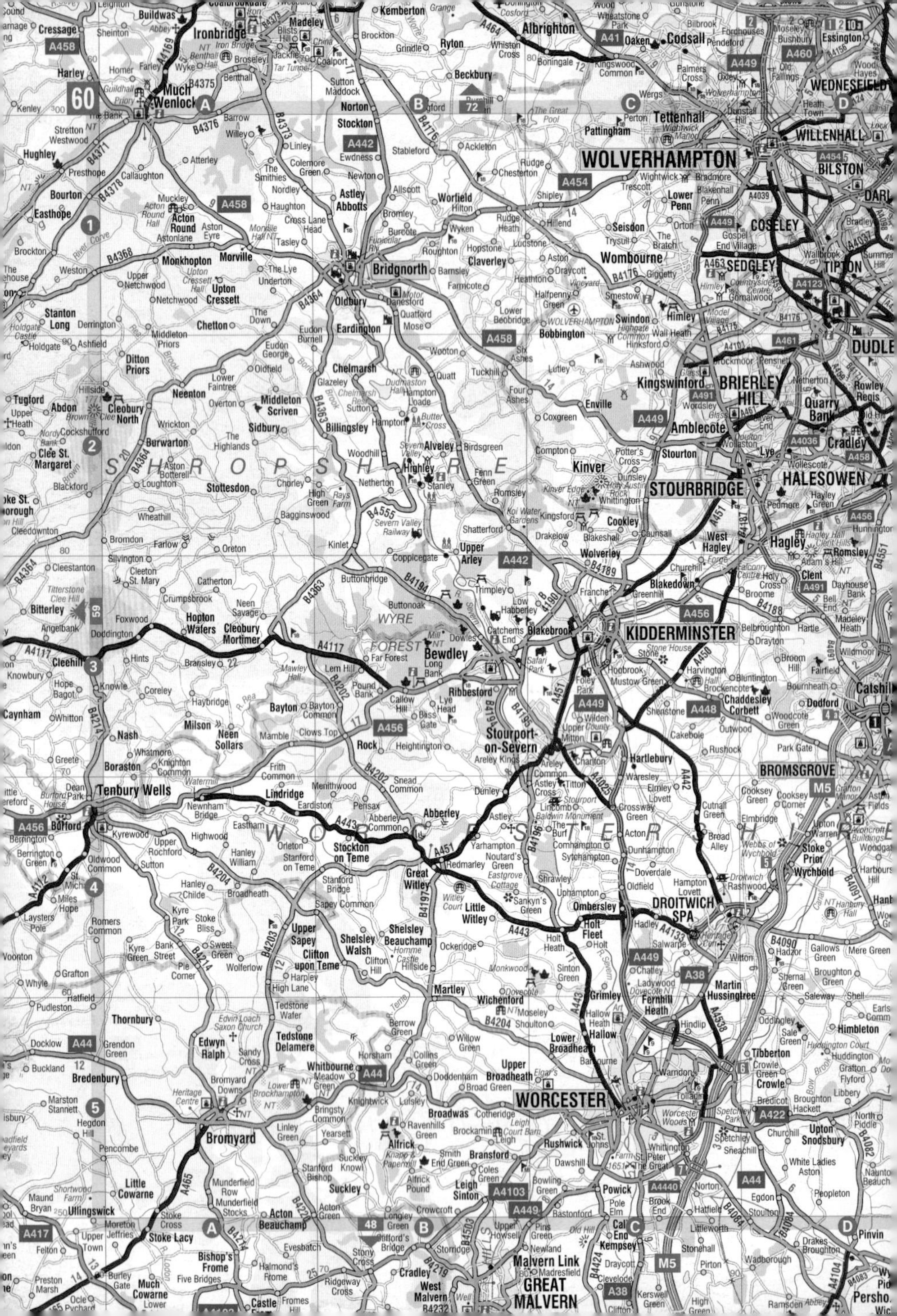

60
Buildwas
Ironbridge
Madeley
Kemberton
Albrighton
Codsall
Oaken
Essington
Cressage
Sheinton
Iron Bridge
Blists Hill
Jackfield
Coalport
Tar Tunnel
Broseley
Benthall
Brockton
Grindle
Ryton
Beckbury
Whiston Cross
Boningale
Kingswood Common
Pendeford
Bilbrook
Fordhouses
Moseley
Bushbury
Harley
Homer
Farley
Wyke
Much Wenlock
Sutton Maddock
Norton
Stockton
Badger
Burnhill Green
The Great Pool
Pattingham
Perton
Wergs
Tettenhall
Wolverhampton
Oxley
Palmers Cross
Old Fallings
Wednesfield
Heath Town
Willenhall
Kenley
The Bank
Barrow
Willey
Stretton Westwood
Hughley
Presthope
Callaughton
Atterley
Linley
The Smithies
Colemore Green
Ewdness
Newton
Stableford
Ackleton
Chesterton
Rudge
Wightwick Manor
WOLVERHAMPTON
Wightwick
Bradmore
Trescott
Blakenhall
Penn
Bilston
Bourton
Easthope
Muckley
Acton Round
Acton Round Hall
Aston Eyre
Astonlane
Morville Hall
Nordley
Haughton
Cross Lane Head
Astley Abbotts
Allscott
Worfield
Hilton
Bromley
Burcote
Wyken
Roughton
Rudge Heath
Shipley
Hillend
Lower Penn
Orton
Seisdon
Trysull
The Bratch
Wombourne
Coseley
Gospel End Village
Sedgley
Tipton
Darlaston
Brockton
Weston
Monkhopton
Morville
The Lye
Tasley
Bridgnorth
Underton
Upper Netchwood
Netchwood
Upton Cressett
Oldbury
Danesford
Motor Museum
Quatford
Mose
Eardington
Hopstone
Claverley
Barnsley
Farmcote
Ludstone
Aston
Draycott
Heathton
Halfpenny Green
Smestow
Swindon
Himley
Wall Heath
Gornalwood
Stanton Long
Holdgate Castle
Holdgate
Derrington
Ashfield
Chetton
The Down
Middleton Priors
Eudon Burnell
Eudon George
Lower Beobridge
Bobbington
WOLVERHAMPTON
Hinksford
Dudley
Ditton Priors
Oldfield
Chelmarsh
Wooton
Six Ashes
Tuckhill
Ashwood
Kingswinford
Brockmoor
Brierley Hill
Tugford
Abdon
Hillside
Cleobury North
Brown Clee
Neenton
Lower Faintree
Middleton Scriven
Glazeley
Chelmarsh Reservoir
Sutton
Dudmaston Hall
Hampton Loade
Quatt
Four Ashes
Lutley
Enville
Wordsley
Netherton
Rowley Regis
Quarry Bank
Upper Heath
Nordy Bank
Cockshutford
Wrickton
Overton
Sidbury
Billingsley
Hampton
Butter Cross
Coxgreen
Amblecote
Clee St. Margaret
Burwarton
The Highlands
Woodhill
Severn Valley
Alveley
Birdsgreen
Compton
Potter's Cross
Stourton
Wollaston
Lye
Cradley
Halesowen
SHROPSHIRE
Blackford
Aston Botterell
Loughton
Stottesdon
Chorley
High Green
Rays Farm
Highley
Stanley
Fenn Green
Kinver
Kinver Edge
Holy Austin Rock
Dunsley
Stourbridge
Pedmore
Hayley Green
Stoke St. Milborough
Wheathill
Bagginswood
B4555
Severn Valley Railway
Romsley
Kingsford
Whittington
Cookley
Kinver Edge
Koi Water Gardens
Cleedownton
Bromdon
Farlow
Oreton
Kinlet
Shatterford
Drakelow
Blakeshall
Caunsall
West Hagley
Hagley
Hagley Hall
Clent Hills
Romsley
Hunnington
Cleestanton
Silvington
Cleeton St. Mary
Coppicegate
Upper Arley
Wolverley
Churchill
Falconry Centre
Holy Cross
Adam's Hill
Clent
Dayhouse Bank
Titterstone Clee Hill
Catherton
Crumpsbrook
Buttonbridge
Buttonoak
Trimpley
Franche
Blakedown
Greenhill
Broome
Bell End
Madeley Heath
Bitterley
Foxwood
Neen Savage
Hopton Wafers
Cleobury Mortimer
WYRE FOREST
Low Habberley
Catchems End
Blakebrook
Kidderminster
Belbroughton
Hartle
Angelbank
Doddington
Dowles
Bewdley
Drayton
Wildmoor
Cleehill
Hints
Bransley
Mawley Hall
Far Forest
Long Bank
Lem Hill
Safari Park
Stone House
Stone
Broom Hill
Knowbury
Hope Bagot
Knowle
Coreley
Haybridge
Pound Bank
Callow Hill
Ribbesford
Hoobrook
Mustow Green
Harvington
Bluntington
Brockencote
Fairfield
Bournheath
Catshill
Caynham
Whitton
Bayton
Bayton Common
Lye Head
Bliss Gate
Foley Park
Wilden
Shenstone
Chaddesley Corbett
Dodford
Woodcote Green
Nash
Milson
Neen Sollars
Mamble
Clows Top
Rock
Heightington
Stourport-on-Severn
Areley Kings
Upper Mitton
Charlton
Cakebole
Outwood
Rushock
Park Gate
Greete
Whatmore
Knighton Common
Boraston
Frith Common
Snead Common
Menithwood
Hartlebury
Waresley
Elmley Lovett
Bromsgrove
Tenbury Wells
Burford House
Dean Park
Newnham Bridge
Lindridge
Eardiston
Pensax
Abberley
Dunley
Areley Common
Astley Cross
Titton
Lincomb
Crossway Green
Cooksey Green
Cooksey Corner
Burford
Kyrewood
Eastham
Highwood
Upper Rochford
Hanley William
Orleton
Abberley Common
Stockton on Teme
Stanford on Teme
Astley
Yarhampton
Noutard's Green
Baldwin Monument
The Burf
Acton
Cutnall Green
Elmbridge
Upton Warren
Avoncroft Buildings
Berrington
Berrington Green
Oldwood Common
Sutton
Great Witley
Redmarley
Eastgrove Cottage
Comhampton
Sytchampton
Dunhampton
Broad Alley
Webbs of Wychbold
Stoke Prior
Wychbold
WORCESTERSHIRE
St. Michaels
Miles Hope
Hanley Childe
Broadheath
Stanford Bridge
Sapey Common
Witley Court
Little Witley
Sankyn's Green
Shrawley
Uphampton
Ombersley
Doverdale
Oldfield
Hampton Lovett
Droitwich
Rashwood
Droitwich Spa
Laysters Pole
Romers Common
Kyre Park
Stoke Bliss
Upper Sapey
Clifton upon Teme
Shelsley Walsh
Shelsley Beauchamp
Homme Castle
Ockeridge
Holt Fleet
Holt Heath
Holt
Hadley
Salwarpe
Heritage Centre
Witton
Hanbury Hall
Hanbury
Kyre Green
Bank Street
Sweet Green
Wolferlow
Pie Corner
Clifton Hill
Hillside
Harpley
Monkwood
Sinton Green
Chatley
Ladywood
Dovecote
Martin Hussingtree
Hadzor
Gallows Green
Mere Green
Broughton Green
Shernal Green
Saleway
Shell
Woonton
Grafton
Whyle
Hatfield
High Lane
Martley
Wichenford
Moseley
Grimley
Fernhill Heath
Hindlip
Oddingley
Sale Green
Himbleton
Pudleston
Thornbury
Edwin Loach
Saxon Church
Tedstone Wafer
Berrow Green
Shoulton
Hallow Heath
Hallow
Lower Broadheath
Huddington Court
Huddington
Docklow
Grendon Green
Edwyn Ralph
Sandy Cross
Tedstone Delamere
Horsham
Willow Green
Collins Green
Upper Broadheath
Elgar's Birthplace
Barbourne
Tibberton
Crowle Green
Crowle
Grafton Flyford
Buckland
Bredenbury
Whitbourne
Meadow Green
Doddenham
Broad Green
Warndon
Tolladine
Libbery
Marston Stannett
Hegdon Hill
Bromyard Downs
Lower Brockhampton
Knightwick
Lulsley
Broadwas
Cotheridge
WORCESTER
Worcester Woods
Spetchley Park
Bredicot
Broughton Hackett
North Piddle
Bringsty Common
Linley Green
Ravenhills Green
Brockamin
Leigh Court Barn
Leigh
Spetchley
Churchill
Upton Snodsbury
Bromyard
Pencombe
Yearsett
Alfrick
Knapp & Papermill
Smith End Green
Bransford
Rushwick
St. Johns
Dawshill
Whittington
St. Peter The Great
Sneachill
White Ladies Aston
Naunton Beauchamp
Shortwood Farm
Munderfield Row
Munderfield Stocks
Little Cowarne
Suckley Knowl
Stanford Bishop
Suckley
Alfrick Pound
Leigh Sinton
Coles Green
Bowling Green
Powick
Pole Elm
Brook End
Norton
Egdon
Peopleton
Maund Bryan
Ullingswick
Moreton Jeffries
Stoke Cross
Acton Beauchamp
Acton Green
Longley Green
Crowcroft
Upper Howsell
Pins Green
Bastonford
Old Hills
Callow End
Hatfield
Littleworth
Stoulton
Pinvin
Felton
Upper Town
Stoke Lacy
Evesbatch
Stifford's Bridge
Storridge
Newland
Kempsey
Stonehall
Drakes Broughton
Bishop's Frome
Halmond's Frome
Stony Cross
Cradley
Malvern Link
Madresfield
Draycott
Pirton
Wadborough
Preston Marsh
Burley Gate
Much Cowarne
Five Bridges
Ridgeway Cross
West Malvern
GREAT MALVERN
Clevelode
Kerswell Green
Ramsden
High Green
Pershore
Ocle Pychard
Castle Frome
Fromes Hill
MALVERN HILLS
A458
A41
A460
A449
A4169
B4375
B4376
B4373
B4176
A442
A454
A464
A4039
A463
A4123
B4371
B4378
B4368
B4364
B4363
B4176
B4175
A4101
A461
A491
A4036
A458
A4187
A451
A456
B4189
B4190
B4194
A4117
A456
B4202
B4188
A448
A450
B4195
B4196
A4025
A442
A4133
M5
A443
A451
B4197
B4203
B4204
A4214
A4112
A44
A4538
B4090
B4091
A38
A4103
A4440
A422
B4082
B4084
A465
A417
B4220
B4214
B4503
B4424
B4219
B4232
B4083
A4104
72
48
59

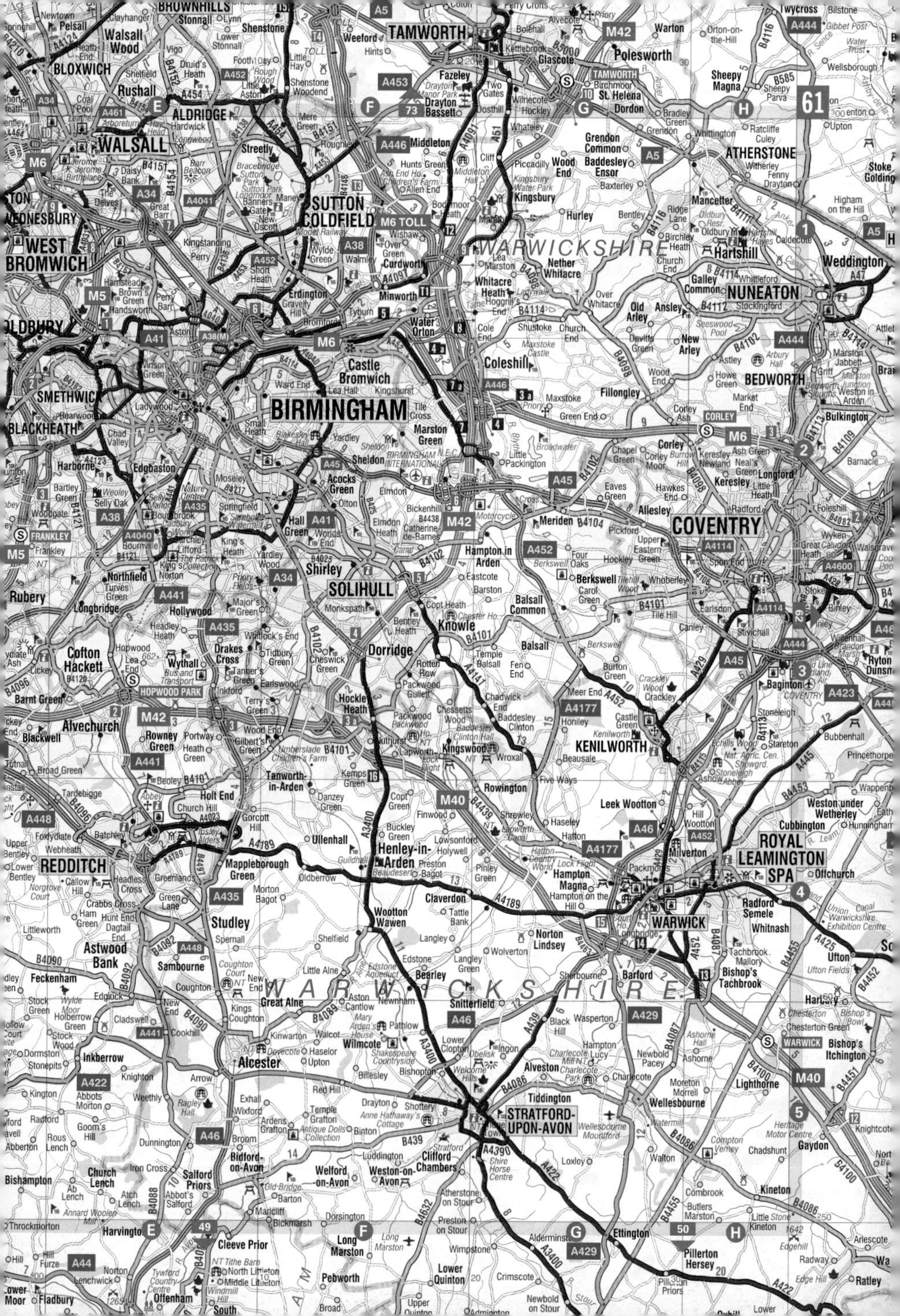

61
BROWNHILLS
TAMWORTH
Polesworth
Warton
Twycross
Bilstone
A444
A5
M42
Pelsall
Walsall Wood
BLOXWICH
Shenstone
Weeford
Fazeley
Drayton Bassett
Glascote
Dordon
St. Helena
Sheepy Magna
Rushall
ALDRIDGE
WALSALL
Streetly
Middleton
Grendon Common
Baddesley Ensor
Wood End
ATHERSTONE
Mancetter
Hartshill
Kingsbury
Hurley
SUTTON COLDFIELD
M6 TOLL
WEDNESBURY
WEST BROMWICH
WARWICKSHIRE
Nether Whitacre
Weddington
NUNEATON
Erdington
Minworth
Curdworth
Water Orton
Coleshill
OLDBURY
Ansley
Old Arley
New Arley
M6
M5
Castle Bromwich
BEDWORTH
SMETHWICK
BIRMINGHAM
BLACKHEATH
Maxstoke
Fillongley
Bulkington
Corley
Marston Green
Sheldon
Harborne
Edgbaston
Acocks Green
Meriden
Allesley
Keresley
Longford
COVENTRY
Hall Green
Shirley
SOLIHULL
Hampton in Arden
Berkswell
Balsall Common
Northfield
Rubery
Longbridge
Hollywood
Knowle
Dorridge
Cofton Hackett
Wythall
Drakes Cross
Hockley Heath
Kenilworth
Baginton
Ryton Dunsmore
Barnt Green
Alvechurch
M42
Honiley
Kingswood
Lapworth
Rowington
Tanworth-in-Arden
M40
Leek Wootton
Weston under Wetherley
Cubbington
ROYAL LEAMINGTON SPA
REDDITCH
Henley-in-Arden
Ullenhall
Mappleborough Green
Claverdon
Hatton
Hampton Magna
WARWICK
Offchurch
Radford Semele
Whitnash
Studley
Wootton Wawen
Norton Lindsey
Barford
Bishop's Tachbrook
Ufton
Astwood Bank
Feckenham
Sambourne
Coughton
Great Alne
Snitterfield
WARWICKSHIRE
Harbury
Inkberrow
Alcester
Wilmcote
Wellesbourne
Bishop's Itchington
Lighthorne
STRATFORD-UPON-AVON
Tiddington
Alveston
Charlecote
Gaydon
Bidford-on-Avon
Salford Priors
Welford-on-Avon
Clifford Chambers
Kineton
Ettington
Harvington
Cleeve Prior
Long Marston
Pillerton Hersey
Fladbury
Offenham
Pebworth
Lower Quinton
Ratley
A422
A3400
A429
A46
A435
A441
A4189
A452
A45
A34
A38
A41
A5

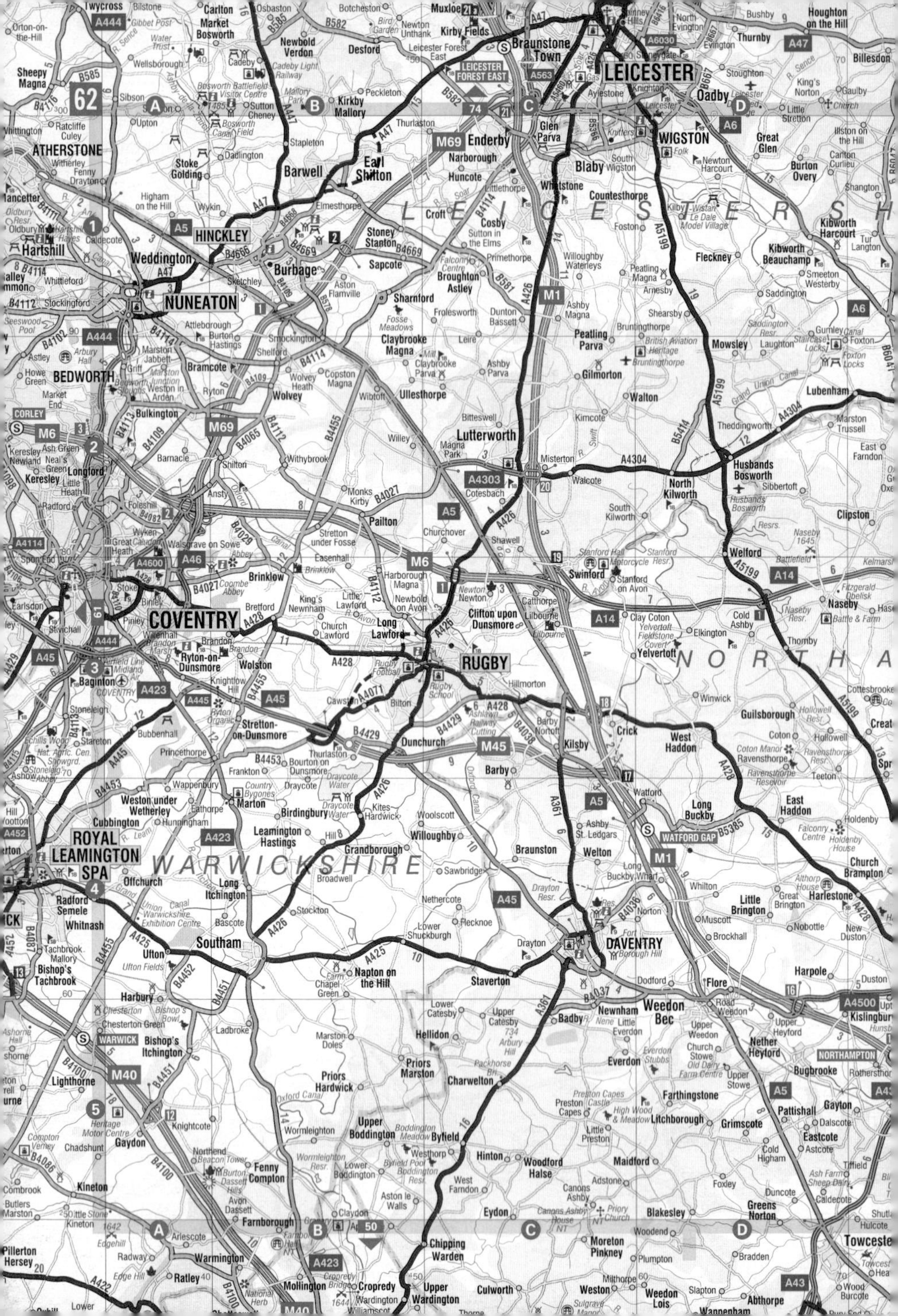
62
LEICESTER
COVENTRY
RUGBY
NUNEATON
HINCKLEY
ROYAL LEAMINGTON SPA
DAVENTRY
WIGSTON
BEDWORTH
ATHERSTONE
Oadby
Braunstone Town
Enderby
Blaby
Lutterworth
Husbands Bosworth
Market Bosworth
Earl Shilton
Barwell
Burbage
Kenilworth
Southam
Long Buckby
Weedon Bec
Towcester
Kineton
Market Harborough
LEICESTERSH
NORTHA
WARWICKSHIRE
M1
M6
M69
M45
M40
A5
A14
A45
A426
A428
A4304
A5199
A444
A47
A6
A361
A423
A425
CORLEY
LEICESTER FOREST EAST
WATFORD GAP
WARWICK
NORTHAMPTON

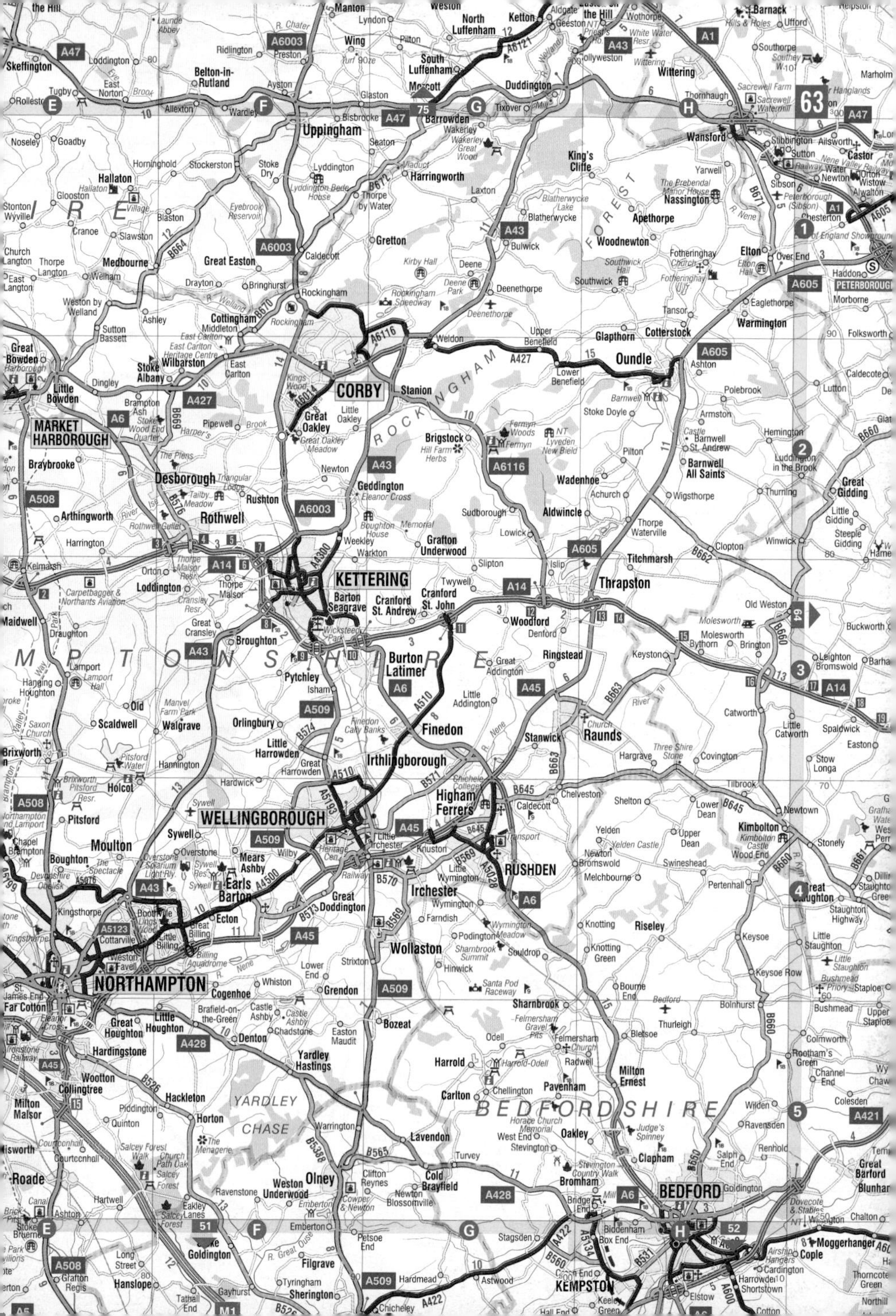
63
the Hill
Manton
Weston
Ketton
Aldgate
Geeston
Barnack
Hills & Holes
Ufford
Wothorpe
Lyndon
North
Luffenham
White Water Resr.
Wittering
Southorpe
Marholm
A47
Loddington
Launde Abbey
R. Chater
A6003
Preston
Wing
Pilton
A6121
A43
A1
Skeffington
Ridlington
Collyweston
Wittering
Belton-in-Rutland
East Norton
Ayston
South Luffenham
Morcott
Duddington
Sacrewell Farm
Sacrewell Watermill
Tugby
Rollesto
Allexton
Wardley
Glaston
Bisbrooke
Barrowden
Tixover
Thornhaugh
Noseley
Goadby
Uppingham
Seaton
Wakerley
Wakerley Great Wood
King's Cliffe
Wansford
Stibbington
Sutton
Ailsworth
Castor
Nene Valley Railway
Water Newton
Orton Wistow
Hallaton
Horninghold
Stockerston
Stoke Dry
Lyddington
Lyddington Bede House
Harringworth
Yarwell
The Prebendal Manor House
Nassington
Sibson
Peterborough (Sibson)
Alwalton
Glooston
Village
Eyebrook Reservoir
Thorpe by Water
Laxton
Blatherwycke Lake
Blatherwycke
Apethorpe
FOREST
Chesterton
Stonton Wyville
Blaston
Cranoe
Slawston
Gretton
Bulwick
Woodnewton
East of England Showground
Church Langton
Thorpe Langton
Medbourne
Great Easton
A6003
Caldecott
Kirby Hall
Deene
Deene Park
Fotheringhay
Fotheringhay Church
Elton
Elton Hall
Over End
East Langton
Welham
Drayton
Bringhurst
Rockingham
Rockingham Speedway
Deenethorpe
Southwick
Southwick Hall
Haddon
PETERBOROUGH
A605
Weston by Welland
R. Welland
Cottingham
Rockingham
Eaglethorpe
Morborne
Sutton Bassett
Ashley
Middleton
East Carlton
East Carlton Industrial Heritage Centre
A6116
Weldon
Upper Benefield
Glapthorn
Tansor
Cotterstock
Warmington
Folksworth
Great Bowden
Harborough
Wilbarston
Stoke Albany
East Carlton
A427
Lower Benefield
Oundle
Ashton
Caldecote
Little Bowden
Dingley
Kings Wood
CORBY
Stanion
ROCKINGHAM
Barnwell
Polebrook
Lutton
MARKET HARBOROUGH
A6
Brampton Ash
Stoke Wood End Quarter
Pipewell
Harper's Brook
Great Oakley
Great Oakley Meadow
Little Oakley
Brigstock
Hill Farm Herbs
Fermyn Woods
NT Lyveden New Bield
Stoke Doyle
Armston
Barnwell St. Andrew
Barnwell All Saints
Hemington
Luddington in the Brook
Braybrooke
The Plens
Desborough
Triangular Lodge
Talby Meadow
Newton
A43
Geddington
Eleanor Cross
A6116
Pilton
Wadenhoe
Achurch
Thurning
Great Gidding
A508
Arthingworth
Rothwell
Rushton
A6003
Boughton House
Memorial
Sudborough
Aldwincle
Wigsthorpe
Little Gidding
Steeple Gidding
Harrington
Rothwell Gullet
Weekley
Warkton
Grafton Underwood
Lowick
Thorpe Waterville
Titchmarsh
Clopton
Winwick
Kelmarsh
Orton
A14
Thorpe Malsor
A4300
Slipton
A605
Islip
Loddington
Carpetbagger & Northants Aviation
KETTERING
Twywell
Thrapston
Barton Seagrave
Cransley Resr.
Cranford St. Andrew
Cranford St. John
Woodford
Denford
Old Weston
Molesworth
Maidwell
Draughton
Great Cransley
Wicksteed Park
Bythorn
Brington
Buckworth
Broughton
A43
Burton Latimer
Great Addington
Ringstead
Keyston
Leighton Bromswold
Lamport
Lamport Hall
Pytchley
Isham
A6
A45
Hanging Houghton
Old
Manvel Farm Park
A509
A510
Little Addington
B663
Catworth
Little Catworth
Spaldwick
Scaldwell
Walgrave
Orlingbury
Finedon
Finedon Cally Banks
Stanwick
Raunds
Easton
Saxon Church
Brixworth
Little Harrowden
Great Harrowden
Irthlingborough
Hargrave
Three Shire Stone
Covington
Stow Longa
Pitsford Water
Hannington
Hardwick
Chichele College
Higham Ferrers
Caldecott
Chelveston
Shelton
Lower Dean
Tilbrook
Newtown
Holcot
Brixworth Pitsford Resr.
Sywell
WELLINGBOROUGH
B645
Yelden
Yelden Castle
Upper Dean
Kimbolton
Kimbolton Castle
Wood End
Stonely
Pitsford
Moulton
Sywell
A509
Overstone
Mears Ashby
Wilby
Little Irchester
Heritage Cen.
Knuston
Transport
RUSHDEN
Newton Bromswold
Swineshead
Melchbourne
Pertenhall
Great Staughton
Chapel Brampton
Boughton
The Spectacle
Devonshire Obelisk
Overstone Solarium
Sywell
Earls Barton
Railway
B570
Little Wymington
Irchester
Wymington
Staughton Highway
A43
A5076
Kingsthorpe
Boothville
Ecton
Great Doddington
Farndish
Knotting
Riseley
Keysoe
Little Staughton
A5123
Cottarville
Little Billing
Great Billing
Billing Aquadrome
A45
Podington
Wymington Meadow
Sharnbrook Summit
Souldrop
Knotting Green
Wollaston
Hinwick
Strixton
Little Staughton
Bushmead Priory
Staploe
Weston Favell
NORTHAMPTON
R. Nene
Whiston
Cogenhoe
Lower End
Grendon
A509
Santa Pod Raceway
Bourne End
Bedford
Keysoe Row
Bushmead
Far Cotton
James End
Eleanor Cross
Little Houghton
Brafield-on-the-Green
Castle Ashby
Chadstone
Easton Maudit
Bozeat
Sharnbrook
Felmersham Gravel Pits
Felmersham Church
Thurleigh
Bolnhurst
Upper Staploe
Great Houghton
A428
Denton
Yardley Hastings
Odell
Radwell
Bletsoe
Colmworth
Hardingstone
A45
Harrold
Harrold-Odell
Milton Ernest
Rootham's Green
Channel End
Wootton
Collingtree
B526
Hackleton
Carlton
Chellington
Pavenham
Milton Malsor
Piddington
Horton
YARDLEY CHASE
BEDFORDSHIRE
Wilden
Ravensden
Colesden
Quinton
Warrington
Horace Church Memorial
West End
Stevington
Oakley
Judge's Spinney
Salcey Forest Walk
Church Path Oak
Salcey Forest
The Menagerie
Lavendon
B5388
B565
Turvey
Clapham
Renhold
Salph End
Great Barford
Blunham
Roade
Olney
Weston Underwood
Clifton Reynes
Cold Brayfield
Newton Blossomville
A428
Stevington Country Walk
Bromham
Goldington
BEDFORD
Ravenstone
Hartwell
Eakley Lanes
Emberton
Cowper & Newton
Bridge End
Mill
A6
Dovecote & Stables
Willington
Chalton
Canal
Ashton
Stoke Bruerne
Emberton
Petsoe End
Stagsden
Biddenham
Box End
A5134
A422
A600
Moggerhanger
Cople
Airship Hangers
Cardington
A508
Long Street
Goldington
R. Great Ouse
Filgrave
B560
B531
Kempston
Harrowden
Shortstown
Thorncote Green
Grafton Regis
Hanslope
Tathall End
Tyringham
Sherington
A509
Hardmead
Astwood
KEMPSTON
Keele Green
Elstow
Northill
Chicheley
A422
M1
A5
Cotton
Hall End
51
52
64
75

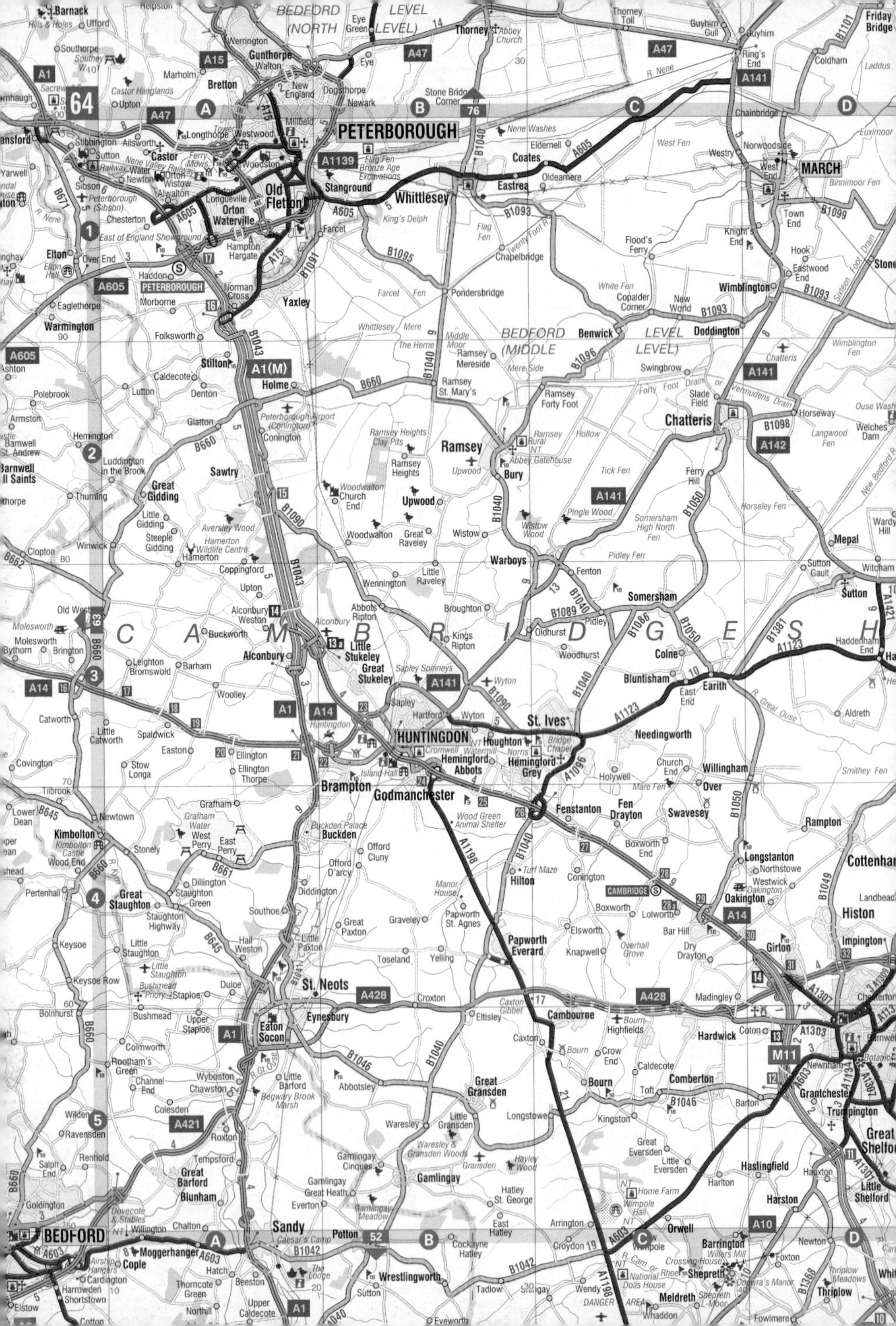

64
Barnack
Hills & Holes
Ufford
Helpston
BEDFORD (NORTH LEVEL)
LEVEL
Eye Green
Thorney
Abbey Church
Thorney Toll
Guyhirn Gull
Guyhirn
B1101
Friday Bridge
Southorpe
Southey W.
Werrington
A15
Gunthorpe
Walton
Eye
A47
30
Ring's End
Coldham
Laddus
A1
Sacrewell
Marholm
Castor Hanglands
Bretton
New England
Dogsthorpe
Stone Bridge Corner
R. Nene
A141
Wansford
Upton
A
Millfield
Newark
B
76
C
D
Chainbridge
Euximoor
A47
Tower
Longthorpe
Westwood
PETERBOROUGH
Nene Washes
Stibbington
Ailsworth
Castor
Sutton
Ferry Mdws.
Nene Valley Railway
Water Newton
Orton Wistow
Woodston
A1139
Flag Fen Bronze Age Excavations
Eldernell
Coates
A605
West Fen
Westry
Norwoodside
West End
MARCH
Yarwell
Sibson
Peterborough (Sibson)
Alwalton
Orton Longueville
Old Fletton
Stanground
Whittlesey
Eastrea
Oldeamere
Binnimoor Fen
B671
R. Nene
Chesterton
A605
Orton Waterville
King's Delph
B1093
Town End
B1099
East of England Showground
Hampton Hargate
Farcet
Flag Fen
Twenty Foot R.
Flood's Ferry
Knight's End
Elton
Elton Hall
Over End
Haddon
PETERBOROUGH
A15
B1091
B1095
Chapelbridge
Hook
Eastwood End
Stonea
A605
Norman Cross
Yaxley
Farcet Fen
Pondersbridge
White Fen
Copalder Corner
New World
Wimblington
B1093
Sixteen Foot Drain
Morborne
Eaglethorpe
Warmington
Folksworth
Whittlesey Mere
The Herne
Middle Moor
BEDFORD (MIDDLE LEVEL)
Benwick
B1093
Doddington
A605
Ashton
Stilton
B1043
Ramsey Mereside
Mere Side
B1096
Wimblington Fen
Chatteris
A1(M)
Caldecote
Denton
Swingbrow
A141
Polebrook
Lutton
Holme
B660
B1040
Ramsey St. Mary's
Ramsey Forty Foot
Forty Foot Drain or Vermudens Drain
Slade Field
Horseway
Ouse Washes
Armston
Glatton
Peterborough Airport (Conington)
Conington
Chatteris
B1098
Welches Dam
Barnwell St. Andrew
Hemington
Ramsey Heights Clay Pits
Ramsey
Ramsey Rural NT
Hollow
A142
Langwood Fen
Barnwell All Saints
Luddington in the Brook
B660
Ramsey Heights
Upwood
Abbey Gatehouse
Bury
Tick Fen
Ferry Hill
New Bedford River
Sawtry
Thurning
Great Gidding
Woodwalton Church End
Upwood
B1040
A141
Pingle Wood
Somersham High North Fen
B1050
Horseley Fen
Wardy Hill
Little Gidding
Steeple Gidding
Aversley Wood
Hamerton Wildlife Centre
B1090
Woodwalton
Great Raveley
Wistow
Wistow Wood
Mepal
Clopton
Winwick
Hamerton
Coppingford
B1043
Little Raveley
Warboys
Pidley Fen
Fenton
Sutton Gault
Witcham
B662
Upton
Wennington
Somersham
Sutton
A1421
Old Weston
Alconbury Weston
Abbots Ripton
Broughton
B1089
Pidley
B1040
B1086
B1050
B1381
Haddenham End
Molesworth
Buckworth
Alconbury
Kings Ripton
Oldhurst
A1123
CAMBRIDGESHIRE
Bythorn
Brington
B660
Leighton Bromswold
Barham
Alconbury
Little Stukeley
Great Stukeley
Woodhurst
Colne
A14
Sapley Spinneys
A141
Wyton
B1090
Bluntisham
Earith
Catworth
Woolley
A1
A14
Sapley
Hartford
Wyton
B1040
East End
R. Great Ouse
Aldreth
Little Catworth
Spaldwick
Huntingdon
HUNTINGDON
Houghton
St. Ives
A1123
Needingworth
Covington
Easton
Ellington
Cromwell
Watermill NT
Norris
Bridge Chapel
Church End
Willingham
Smithey Fen
Stow Longa
Ellington Thorpe
Hemingford Abbots
Hemingford Grey
A1096
Holywell
Tilbrook
Island Hall
Brampton
Godmanchester
Mare Fen
Over
Lower Dean
B645
Grafham
Newtown
Grafham Water
Wood Green Animal Shelter
Fenstanton
Fen Drayton
Swavesey
B1050
Rampton
Kimbolton
Kimbolton Castle
Buckden Palace
Buckden
Boxworth End
Wood End
Stonely
West Perry
East Perry
Offord Cluny
A1198
B1040
Longstanton
Cottenham
Pertenhall
B660
B661
Offord D'arcy
Manor House
Hilton
Turf Maze
Conington
Northstowe
Westwick
Oakington
Dillington
Great Staughton
Staughton Green
Diddington
CAMBRIDGE
Oakington
B1049
Landbeach
Staughton Highway
Southoe
Papworth St. Agnes
Boxworth
Lolworth
A14
Histon
Keysoe
Graveley
Great Paxton
Papworth Everard
Elsworth
Bar Hill
Overhall Grove
Dry Drayton
Impington
Little Staughton
B645
Hail Weston
Little Paxton
Toseland
Yelling
Knapwell
Girton
Little Staughton
Keysoe Row
Bushmead Priory
Staploe
Duloe
St. Neots
A428
Croxton
Caxton Gibbet
A428
Madingley
A1307
Bolnhurst
Bushmead
Upper Staploe
Eaton Socon
Eynesbury
Eltisley
Cambourne
Bourn Highfields
Chesterton
B660
A1
Caxton
Hardwick
Coton
A1303
Colmworth
B1040
Bourn
Crow End
M11
Barnwell
Botanic
Rootham's Green
R. Gt. Ouse
B1046
Caldecote
Newnham
Channel End
Wyboston
Chawston
Little Barford
Abbotsley
Great Gransden
Bourn
Comberton
Toft
B1046
Barton
Grantchester
A1134
A603
Begwary Brook Marsh
Wilden
Colesden
Longstowe
Kingston
Trumpington
Ravensden
A421
Roxton
Waresley
Little Gransden
A1307
Great Shelford
Renhold
Tempsford
Waresley & Gransden Woods
Gransden
Hayley Wood
Great Eversden
Little Eversden
Haslingfield
Salph End
Great Barford
Gamlingay Cinques
Gamlingay
Hatley St. George
Harlton
Hauxton
Little Shelford
B660
Blunham
Gamlingay Great Heath
Home Farm
A1301
Goldington
Dovecote & Stables
Everton
Gamlingay Meadow
Wimpole Hall
Harston
BEDFORD
Willington
Chalton
Sandy
Potton
52
B
East Hatley
Arrington
Orwell
A10
D
A603
Moggerhanger
A603
Caesar's Camp
B1042
Cockayne Hatley
Croydon
A603
C
Wimpole
Barrington
Newton
Cople
Airship Hangars
Cardington
The Lodge
Wrestlingworth
B1042
R. Cam or Rhee
Crossing House
Willers Mill
Foxton
Harrowden
Shortstown
Hatch
Thorncote Green
Beeston
Sutton
Tadlow
Shingay
Wendy
A1198
National Dolls House
Shepreth
Docwra's Manor
Thriplow Meadows
B1368
Elstow
Northill
Upper Caldecote
A1
Eyeworth
DANGER AREA
Meldreth
Shepreth L-Moor
Thriplow
Whaddon
Fowlmere

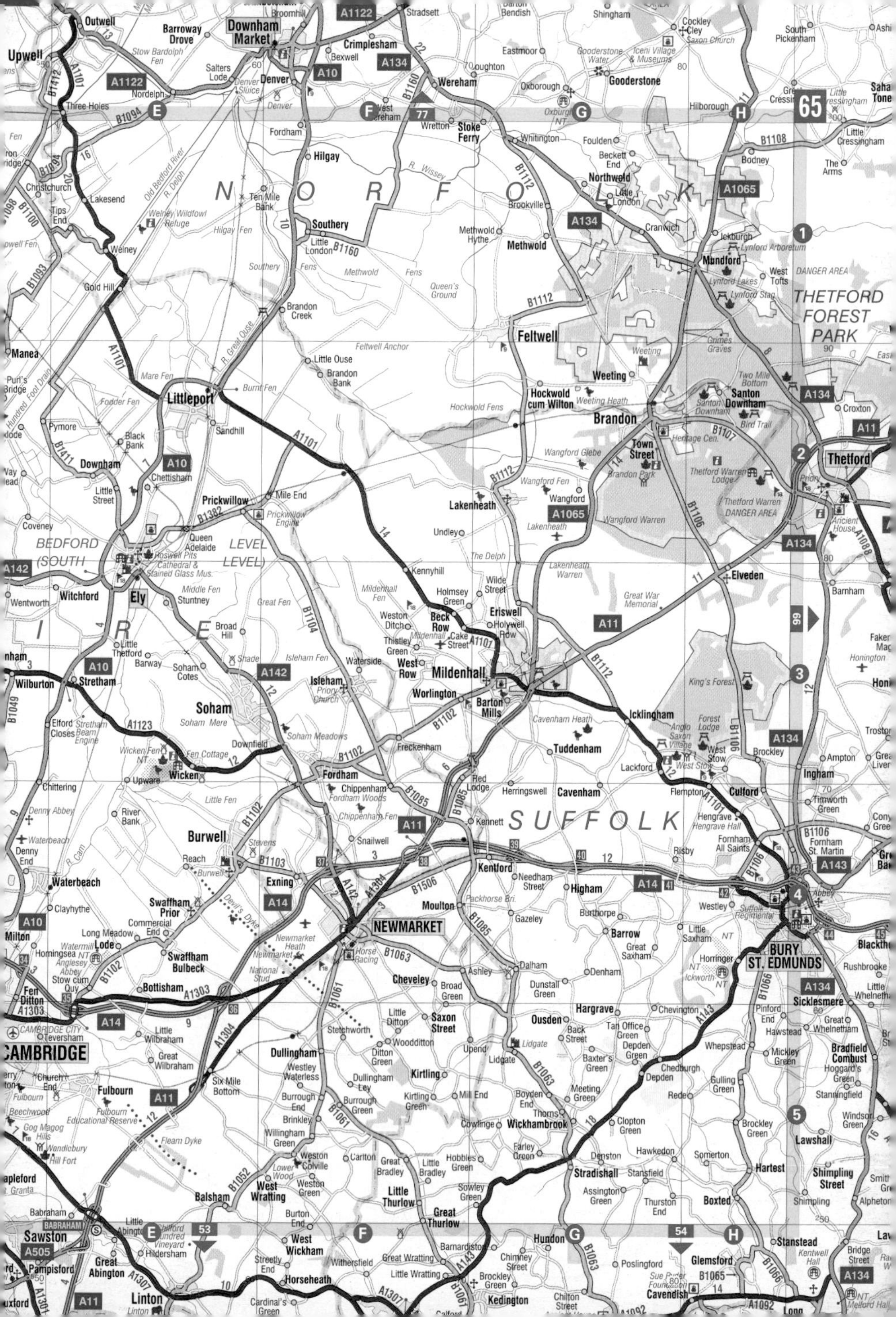
65
NORFOLK
SUFFOLK
Outwell
Upwell
Barroway Drove
Downham Market
Stradsett
Crimplesham
Bexwell
Denver
Salters Lode
Nordelph
Stow Bardolph Fen
Denver Sluice
Wereham
West Dereham
Wretton
Stoke Ferry
Whittington
Fordham
Hilgay
Southery
Little London
Ten Mile Bank
Welney
Welney Wildfowl Refuge
Hilgay Fen
Southery Fens
Methwold Fens
Queen's Ground
Lakesend
Tips End
Christchurch
Three Holes
Gold Hill
Brandon Creek
Little Ouse
Brandon Bank
Feltwell Anchor
Feltwell
Methwold Hythe
Methwold
Brookville
Northwold
Cranwich
Mundford
Ickburgh
Lynford Arboretum
Lynford Lakes
Lynford Stag
West Tofts
DANGER AREA
THETFORD FOREST PARK
Grimes Graves
Two Mile Bottom
Santon Downham
Bird Trail
Weeting
Weeting Heath
Hockwold cum Wilton
Hockwold Fens
Brandon
Town Street
Brandon Park
Heritage Cen.
Thetford Warren Lodge
Thetford Warren
Thetford
Priory
Ancient House
Croxton
Barnham
Elveden
Wangford Glebe
Wangford Fen
Wangford
Wangford Warren
Lakenheath
Lakenheath Warren
Undley
The Delph
Great War Memorial
Manea
Littleport
Mare Fen
Burnt Fen
Fodder Fen
Sandhill
Black Bank
Downham
Little Street
Pymore
Chettisham
Prickwillow
Prickwillow Engine
Mile End
Queen Adelaide
Coveney
BEDFORD (SOUTH LEVEL)
LEVEL
Roswell Pits
Cathedral & Stained Glass Mus.
Ely
Witchford
Wentworth
Middle Fen
Stuntney
Great Fen
Broad Hill
Little Thetford
Barway
Soham Cotes
Soham
Soham Mere
Shade
Isleham Fen
Isleham
Priory Church
Mildenhall Fen
Kennyhill
Holmsey Green
Wilde Street
Eriswell
Holywell Row
Beck Row
Weston Ditch
Thistley Green
Cake Street
West Row
Waterside
Mildenhall
Worlington
Barton Mills
Cavenham Heath
Icklingham
Tuddenham
King's Forest
Forest Lodge
Anglo Saxon Village
West Stow
Lackford
Flempton
Culford
Brockley
Ingham
Ampton
Timworth Green
Hengrave
Hengrave Hall
Fornham All Saints
Fornham St. Martin
Risby
Wilburton
Stretham
Elford Closes
Stretham Beam Engine
Wicken Fen
Wicken
Fen Cottage
Upware
Downfield
Soham Meadows
Chittering
Denny Abbey
Waterbeach
Denny End
River Bank
Little Fen
Burwell
Reach
Devil's Dyke
Fordham
Chippenham
Chippenham Fen
Fordham Woods
Freckenham
Red Lodge
Herringswell
Cavenham
Kennett
Snailwell
Kentford
Needham Street
Higham
Packhorse Bri.
Moulton
Gazeley
Exning
Newmarket
Newmarket Heath
Horse Racing
National Stud
Swaffham Prior
Commercial End
Long Meadow
Lode
Swaffham Bulbeck
Anglesey Abbey
Stow cum Quy
Horningsea
Clayhythe
Milton
Fen Ditton
Bottisham
CAMBRIDGE
Cambridge City
Teversham
Little Wilbraham
Great Wilbraham
Fulbourn
Fulbourn Educational Reserve
Cherry Hinton
Church End
Gog Magog Hills
Wandlebury Hill Fort
Fleam Dyke
Six Mile Bottom
Dullingham
Westley Waterless
Stetchworth
Woodditton
Ditton Green
Little Ditton
Cheveley
Broad Green
Saxon Street
Ashley
Dalham
Denham
Dunstall Green
Barrow
Great Saxham
Little Saxham
Burthorpe
Westley
Suffolk Regimental
Horringer
Ickworth
BURY ST. EDMUNDS
Abbey
Blackthorpe
Rushbrooke
Sicklesmere
Great Whelnetham
Little Whelnetham
Bradfield Combust
Hawstead
Pinford End
Mickley Green
Whepstead
Chevington
Hargrave
Ousden
Back Street
Tan Office Green
Depden Green
Lidgate
Upend
Kirtling
Kirtling Green
Dullingham Ley
Burrough End
Burrough Green
Brinkley
Willingham Green
Mill End
Cowlinge
Wickhambrook
Boyden End
Thorns
Baxter's Green
Meeting Green
Depden
Chedburgh
Rede
Gulling Green
Clopton Green
Farley Green
Hobbles Green
Little Bradley
Great Bradley
Carlton
Weston Colville
Weston Green
West Wratting
Balsham
Little Thurlow
Great Thurlow
Sowley Green
Stradishall
Denston
Stansfield
Hawkedon
Somerton
Assington Green
Thurston End
Boxted
Hartest
Brockley Green
Lawshall
Shimpling Street
Shimpling
Stanstead
Babraham
Sawston
Little Abington
Great Abington
Hildersham
Chilford Hundred Vineyard
Pampisford
Linton
Horseheath
Streetly End
West Wickham
Burton End
Withersfield
Great Wratting
Little Wratting
Barnardiston
Hundon
Chimney Street
Brockley Green
Kedington
Poslingford
Glemsford
Cavendish
Sue Ryder Foundation
Kentwell Hall
Bridge Street
Melford Hall
A10
A11
A14
A134
A142
A143
A1065
A1101
A1122
A1123
A1303
A1304
A1307
A505
B1106
B1112
B1102
B1085
B1061
B1063
B1160
B1094

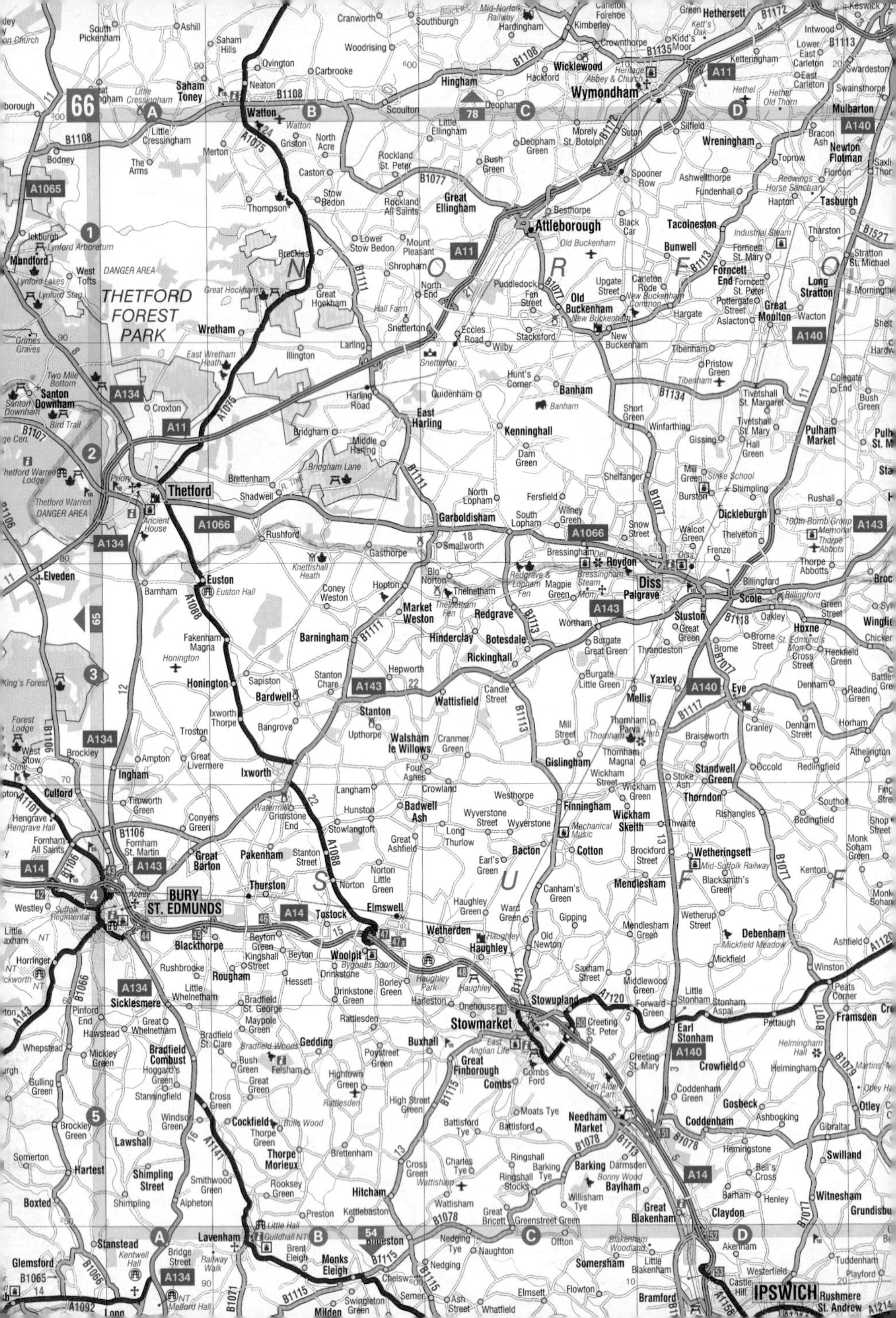
66
Cranworth
Southburgh
Mid-Norfolk Railway
Hardingham
Kimberley
Carleton Forehoe
Hethersett
B1172
Keswick
South Pickenham
Ashill
Saham Hills
Ovington
Woodrising
Crownthorpe
Kidd's Moor
Intwood
Carbrooke
B1108
Wicklewood
B1135
Ketteringham
Lower East Carleton
East Carleton
Swardeston
Saham Toney
Neaton
Hingham
Hackford
Wymondham
A11
Swainsthorpe
Little Cressingham
Watton
B1108
Scoulton
Deopham
Hethel
Hethel Old Thorn
Mulbarton
A
B
C
D
78
Little Ellingham
Silfield
A140
Little Cressingham
Griston
North Acre
Morely St. Botolph
Suton
Wreningham
Bracon Ash
Newton Flotman
B1108
Merton
Deopham Green
Bodney
The Arms
Caston
Rockland St. Peter
Bush Green
Spooner Row
Ashwellthorpe
Toprow
Redwings Horse Sanctuary
Flordon
A1065
B1077
Stow Bedon
Rockland All Saints
Fundenhall
Hapton
Tasburgh
Thompson
Great Ellingham
Besthorpe
Attleborough
Black Car
Tacolneston
Tharston
B1527
Ickburgh
Lynford Arboretum
Lower Stow Bedon
Mount Pleasant
A11
Old Buckenham
Bunwell
Forncett St. Mary
Stratton St. Michael
Mundford
Breckles
Lynford Lakes
West Tofts
DANGER AREA
Shropham
Forncett End
Forncett St. Peter
Long Stratton
Lynford Stag
THETFORD FOREST PARK
Great Hockham
Great Hockham
North End
Puddledock
Upgate Street
Carleton Rode
New Buckenham Common
Hall Farm
Fen Street
Old Buckenham
Pottergate Street
Great Moulton
Wretham
Snetterton
Eccles Road
New Buckenham
Hargate
Aslacton
Wacton
Grimes Graves
Larling
Wilby
Stacksford
New Buckenham
Tibenham
A140
Illington
East Wretham Heath
Snetterton
Pristow Green
Tibenham
Two Mile Bottom
Hunt's Corner
Banham
Colegate End
Santon Downham
A134
Croxton
Harling Road
Quidenham
Banham
B1134
Tivetshall St. Margaret
Bush Green
Bird Trail
A11
East Harling
Short Green
Winfarthing
Tivetshall St. Mary
Pulham Market
B1107
Bridgham
Middle Harling
Kenninghall
Gissing
Hall Green
Thetford Warren Lodge
Dam Green
Bridgham Lane
B1111
Shelfanger
Mill Green
Strike School
Shimpling
Brettenham
North Lopham
Fersfield
Burston
Rushall
Thetford
Shadwell
Wilney Green
Dickleburgh
Thetford Warren DANGER AREA
Ancient House
A1066
Garboldisham
South Lopham
Snow Street
Walcot Green
Thelveton
100th Bomb Group Memorial
A143
A134
Rushford
Smallworth
A1066
Frenze
Thorpe Abbotts
Gasthorpe
Bressingham
Roydon
Diss
Elveden
Knettishall Heath
Blo' Norton
Redgrave & Lopham Fen
Bressingham Steam
Diss
Billingford
Euston
Euston Hall
Coney Weston
Hopton
Thelnetham
Magpie Green
Palgrave
Scole
Barnham
Market Weston
Thelnetham Fen
Redgrave
A143
Wortham
Stuston
Oakley
Green Street
65
A1088
Fakenham Magna
Barningham
Hinderclay
Botesdale
Burgate Great Green
Thrandeston
Great Green
Brome
Brome Street
Hoxne
Honington
Rickinghall
Heckfield Green
Hepworth
Burgate Little Green
Yaxley
Eye
Denham
Honington
Sapiston
Stanton Chare
A143
Wattisfield
Candle Street
Mellis
A140
Reading Green
Bardwell
B1113
B1117
Cranley
Denham Street
Horham
Forest Lodge
Stanton
Thornham Parva
Ixworth Thorpe
Upthorpe
Mill Street
Thornham Herb
Braiseworth
West Stow
A134
Troston
Bangrove
Walsham le Willows
Cranmer Green
Thornham Magna
Athelington
Brockley
Ampton
Great Livermere
Gislingham
Standwell Green
Occold
Redlingfield
Ingham
Ixworth
Four Ashes
Wickham Street
Stoke Ash
Culford
Langham
Crowland
Westhorpe
Wickham Green
Thorndon
Timworth Green
Hunston
Badwell Ash
Finningham
Wickham Skeith
Thwaite
Rishangles
Southolt
Hengrave
Hengrave Hall
Grimstone End
Wyverstone Street
Wyverstone
Mechanical Music
Bedingfield
Conyers Green
Stowlangtoft
Long Thurlow
Cotton
Wetheringsett
B1106
Fornham St. Martin
Great Ashfield
Bacton
Brockford Street
Mid-Suffolk Railway
Monk Soham Green
Fornham All Saints
Great Barton
Pakenham
Stanton Street
Earl's Green
Mendlesham
Blacksmith's Green
Kenton
A14
A143
Norton Little Green
B1077
Westley
BURY ST. EDMUNDS
Thurston
Norton
Canham's Green
Suffolk Regimental
A14
Tostock
Elmswell
Haughley Green
Ward Green
Gipping
Wetherup Street
Debenham
Little Saxham
Beyton Green
Beyton
Wetherden
Haughley
Mendlesham Green
Ashfield
Blackthorpe
Kingshall Street
Woolpit
Old Newton
Mickfield Meadow
Mickfield
Horringer
Ickworth
Rushbrooke
Rougham
Drinkstone
Bygones Room
Haughley Park
Saxham Street
Winston
A1120
A134
Hessett
Borley Green
Haughley
Middlewood Green
Peats Corner
Little Whelnetham
Drinkstone Green
Harleston
Onehouse
Stowupland
Little Stonham
Sicklesmere
Bradfield St. George
Stonham Aspal
Framsden
Pinford End
Great Whelnetham
Maypole Green
Rattlesden
Stowmarket
Creeting St. Peter
Forward Green
Pettaugh
Hawstead
Bradfield St. Clare
Gedding
Buxhall
Earl Stonham
Whepstead
Mickley Green
Bradfield Woods
Poystreet Green
Anglian Life
A140
Helmingham Hall
Bradfield Combust
Felsham
Great Finborough
Creeting St. Mary
Crowfield
Helmingham
Hoggard's Green
Bush Green
Hightown Green
Combs
Combs Ford
Fen Alder Carr
Gulling Green
Great Green
Rattlesden
Coddenham Green
Gosbeck
Otley
Stanningfield
Cross Green
High Street Green
Moats Tye
Needham Market
Coddenham
Ashbocking
Brockley Green
Windsor Green
Cockfield
Bulls Wood
Battisford Tye
Battisford
Gibraltar
Lawshall
Thorpe Green
Hemingstone
B1078
Swilland
Somerton
Hartest
Brettenham
Thorpe Morieux
Cross Green
Charles Tye
Ringshall
Barking
Darmsden
Bell's Cross
A14
Shimpling Street
Smithwood Green
Rooksey Green
Ringshall Stocks
Barking Tye
Bonny Wood
Baylham
Barham
Henley
Witnesham
Grundisburgh
Boxted
Shimpling
Alpheton
Hitcham
Wattisham
Willisham Tye
Great Blakenham
Claydon
Little Hall
Preston
Kettlebaston
Great Bricett
Greenstreet Green
Offton
Stanstead
Lavenham
Guildhall NT
54
Bildeston
Nedging Tye
Naughton
Blakenham Woodland
Akenham
Kentwell Hall
Bridge Street
Railway Walk
Brent Eleigh
Monks Eleigh
B1115
Nedging
Somersham
Little Blakenham
Tuddenham
Glemsford
B1065
A134
Westerfield
Playford
Chelsworth
Flowton
Elmsett
Castle Hill
IPSWICH
Rushmere St. Andrew
A1092
Long Melford
Melford Hall NT
B1071
B1115
Milden
Swingleton Green
Semer
Ash Street
Whatfield
Bramford
A1156
A1214

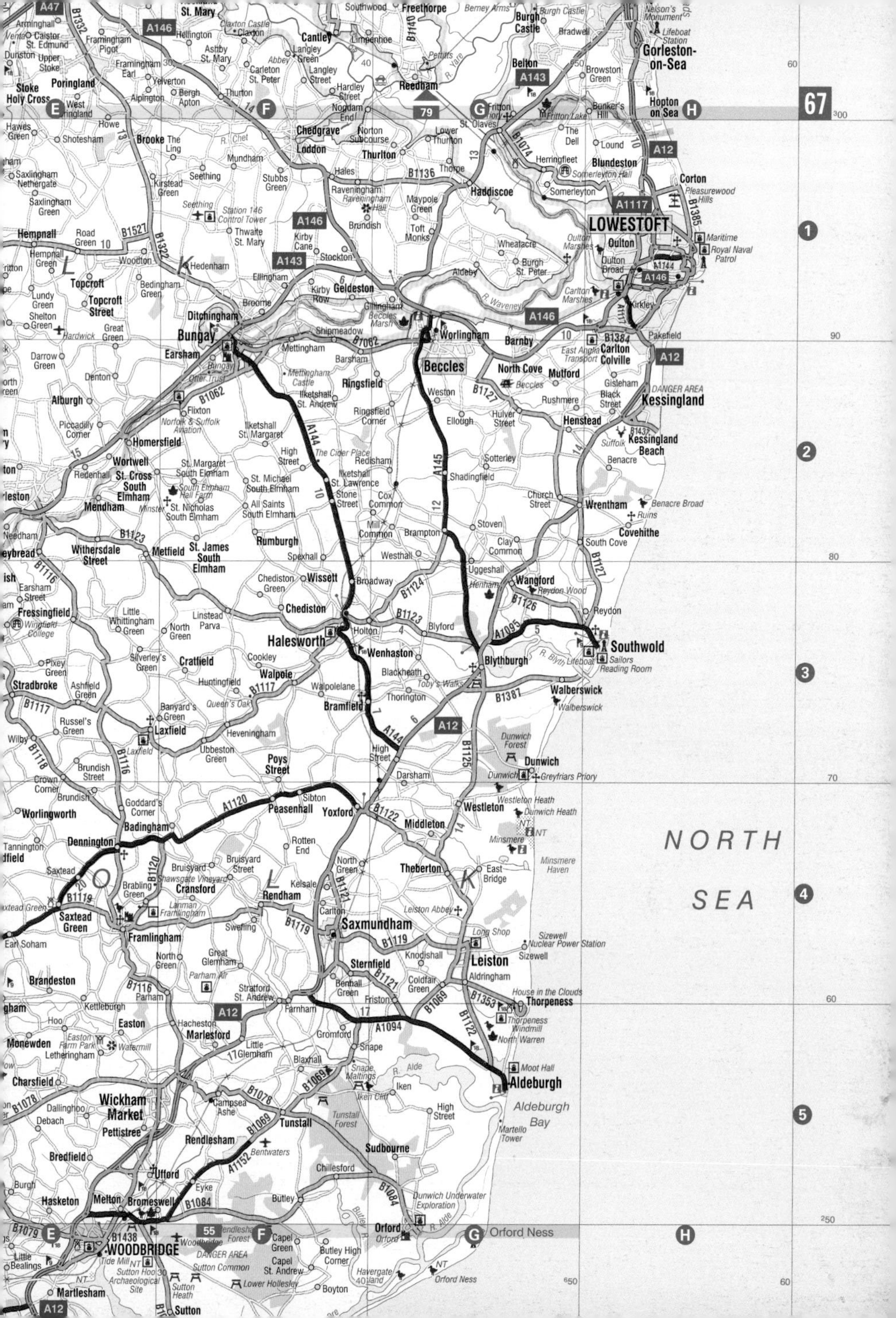

A47
St. Mary
Southwood
Freethorpe
Berney Arms
Burgh Castle
Burgh Castle
Nelson's Monument
Arminghall
A146
Hellington
Claxton Castle
Claxton
Cantley
Limpenhoe
B1140
Bradwell
Lifeboat Station
Venta Caistor St. Edmund
B1332
Framingham Pigot
Ashby St. Mary
Langley Green
Gorleston-on-Sea
Dunston
Upper Stoke
Framingham Earl
Yelverton
Abbey
Carleton St. Peter
Langley Street
Pettitts
R. Yare
Belton
Browston Green
Stoke Holy Cross
Poringland
Alpington
Bergh Apton
Thurton
Hardley Street
Reedham
A143
West Poringland
Howe
Nogdam End
Norton Subcourse
79
Fritton Priory
Fritton Lake
Bunker's Hill
Hopton on Sea
67
Hawes Green
Shotesham
Brooke
The Ling
R. Chet
Chedgrave
Loddon
Thurlton
Lower Thurlton
St. Olaves
B1074
The Dell
Lound
A12
Saxlingham Nethergate
Mundham
Seething
Stubbs Green
Hales
B1136
Thorpe
Herringfleet
Somerleyton Hall
Blundeston
Corton
Pleasurewood Hills
Saxlingham Green
Kirstead Green
Raveningham
Raveningham Hall
Haddiscoe
Somerleyton
Seething
Station 146 Control Tower
Maypole Green
Brundish
A1117
B1385
A146
LOWESTOFT
Maritime
Royal Naval Patrol
Hempnall
Road Green
B1527
Thwaite St. Mary
Kirby Cane
Toft Monks
Oulton Marshes
Oulton
Oulton Broad
Hempnall Green
Woodton
Hedenham
A143
Stockton
Wheatacre
Burgh St. Peter
A1144
Topcroft
Ellingham
Aldeby
Bedingham Green
Geldeston
Kirby Row
Carlton Marshes
Kirkley
Lundy Green
Topcroft Street
Broome
Gillingham
R. Waveney
A146
Shelton Green
Ditchingham
Beccles Marsh
Great Green
Hardwick
Bungay
Shipmeadow
Worlingham
Pakefield
B1384
Carlton Colville
Barnby
East Anglia Transport
Earsham
Mettingham
B1062
Barsham
Beccles
A12
Darrow Green
Bungay Otter Trust
Mettingham Castle
Ringsfield
North Cove
Mutford
Gisleham
Denton
Weston
Beccles
Black Street
DANGER AREA
Kessingland
Alburgh
B1062
Ilketshall St. Andrew
B1127
Rushmere
Flixton
Ringsfield Corner
Norfolk & Suffolk Aviation
Ellough
Hulver Street
Henstead
Piccadilly Corner
Ilketshall St. Margaret
A144
Suffolk
Kessingland Beach
B1437
Homersfield
High Street
The Cider Place
Redisham
A145
Sotterley
Benacre
Wortwell
St. Margaret South Elmham
Redenhall
St. Cross South Elmham
St. Michael South Elmham
Ilketshall St. Lawrence
Shadingfield
South Elmham Hall Farm
Mendham
Minster
St. Nicholas South Elmham
All Saints South Elmham
Stone Street
Cox Common
Church Street
Wrentham
Benacre Broad
Ruins
Needham
Mill Common
Stoven
Covehithe
B1123
Brampton
Clay Common
Withersdale Street
Metfield
St. James South Elmham
Rumburgh
South Cove
Spexhall
Westhall
B1127
B1116
Uggeshall
Earsham Street
Chediston Green
Wissett
Broadway
Henham
Wangford
Reydon Wood
Fressingfield
Little Whittingham Green
Linstead Parva
Chediston
B1124
B1126
Reydon
Wingfield College
B1123
Blyford
A1095
Southwold
North Green
Halesworth
Holton
Wenhaston
Lifeboat
Sailors Reading Room
Silverley's Green
Cookley
Blythburgh
R. Blyth
Pixey Green
Cratfield
Walpole
Blackheath
Toby's Walks
Stradbroke
Ashfield Green
Huntingfield
B1117
Walpolelane
Thorington
B1387
Walberswick
Walberswick
B1117
Banyard's Green
Queen's Oak
Bramfield
A12
Russel's Green
Laxfield
Heveningham
A144
Dunwich Forest
Wilby
B1118
Laxfield
Ubbeston Green
High Street
Dunwich
Brundish Street
B1116
Poys Street
B1125
Darsham
Greyfriars Priory
Crown Corner
Brundish
Sibton
Westleton Heath
Goddard's Corner
A1120
Peasenhall
Yoxford
Westleton
Dunwich Heath
Worlingworth
Badingham
B1122
Middleton
NT
Minsmere
Tannington
Dennington
Rotten End
NORTH
Saxtead
B1120
Bruisyard
Bruisyard Street
North Green
Theberton
East Bridge
Minsmere Haven
Brabling Green
Shawsgate Vineyard
Cransford
Kelsale
B1121
SEA
B1119
Rendham
Saxtead Green
Lanman Framlingham
Carlton
Leiston Abbey
Framlingham
Swefling
B1119
Saxmundham
Long Shop
Sizewell Nuclear Power Station
Earl Soham
Knodishall
Sizewell
North Green
Great Glemham
Sternfield
Leiston
Brandeston
Parham Air
B1121
Coldfair Green
Aldringham
B1116
Parham
Benhall Green
B1069
House in the Clouds
Stratford St. Andrew
Friston
B1353
Thorpeness
Kettleburgh
A12
Farnham
17
B1122
Thorpeness Windmill
Hoo
Easton
Hachestone
Marlesford
A1094
Easton Farm Park
Watermill
Gromford
North Warren
Monewden
Letheringham
Little Glemham
Snape
Moot Hall
Charsfield
Blaxhall
Snape Maltings
Aldeburgh
B1078
Iken Cliff
Iken
Wickham Market
Campsea Ashe
B1078
Aldeburgh Bay
Dallinghoo
B1069
High Street
Debach
Pettistree
Tunstall
Tunstall Forest
Martello Tower
Rendlesham
B1069
Bentwaters
Bredfield
A1152
Sudbourne
Ufford
Chillesford
Burgh
Eyke
B1084
Dunwich Underwater Exploration
Hasketon
Melton
Bromeswell
B1084
Butley
B1079
B1438
Orford
R. Alde
55
Rendlesham Forest
Capel Green
Orford
Orford Ness
WOODBRIDGE
Woodbridge
DANGER AREA
Butley High Corner
Little Bealings
Tide Mill
Sutton Hoo Archaeological Site
Sutton Common
Capel St. Andrew
Havergate Island
NT
Orford Ness
Sutton Heath
Lower Hollesley
Boyton
Martlesham
A12
Sutton

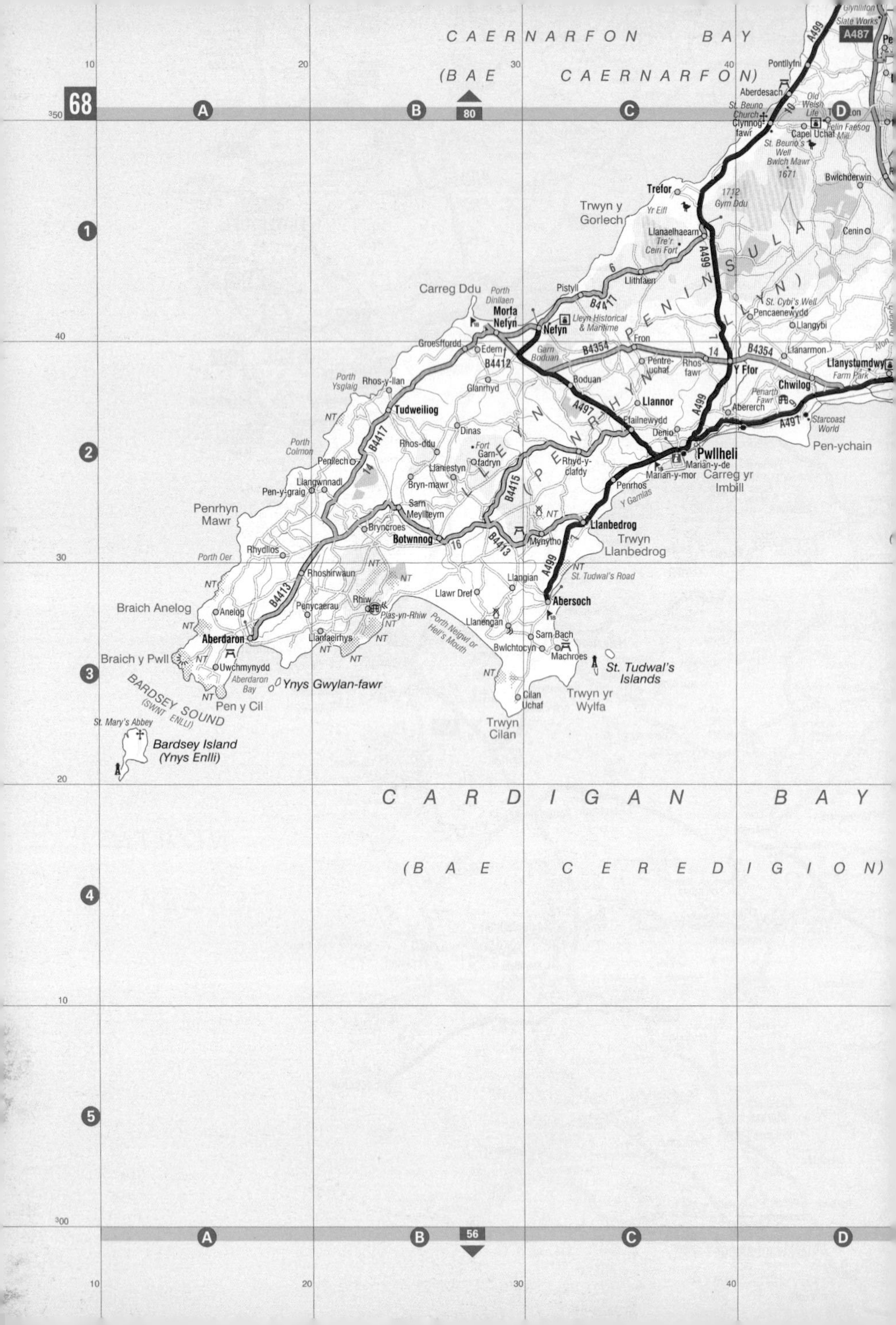
CAERNARFON BAY
(BAE CAERNARFON)
CARDIGAN BAY
(BAE CEREDIGION)
LLEYN PENINSULA
(PENRHYN LLEYN)
A
B
C
D
80
56
1
2
3
4
5
10
20
30
40
350
300
Glynllifon Slate Works
A487
A499
A497
B4354
B4412
B4417
B4415
B4413
Pontllyfni
Aberdesach
St. Beuno Church
Clynnog-fawr
Old Welsh Life
Felin Faesog Mill
Capel Uchaf
St. Beuno's Well
Bwlch Mawr 1671
Bwlchderwin
Trefor
Yr Eifl
1712 Gyrn Ddu
Trwyn y Gorlech
Llanaelhaearn
Tre'r Ceiri Fort
Cenin
Llithfaen
Pistyll
Carreg Ddu
Porth Dinllaen
Morfa Nefyn
Nefyn
Lleyn Historical & Maritime
St. Cybi's Well
Pencaenewydd
Llangybi
Groesffordd
Edern
Garn Boduan
Fron
Pentre-uchaf
Rhos-fawr
Y Ffor
Llanarmon
Llanystumdwy
Farm Park
Chwilog
Porth Ysglaig
Rhos-y-llan
Glanrhyd
Boduan
Llannor
Penarth Fawr
Abererch
Starcoast World
Tudweiliog
Dinas
Efailnewydd
Denio
Pwllheli
Pen-ychain
Porth Colmon
Rhos-ddu
Fort Garn fadryn
Rhyd-y-clafdy
Marian-y-de
Marian-y-mor
Carreg yr Imbill
Penllech
Llaniestyn
Llangwnnadl
Bryn-mawr
Penrhos
Pen-y-graig
Y Gamlas
Penrhyn Mawr
Sarn Meyllteyrn
Bryncroes
Botwnnog
Mynytho
Llanbedrog
Trwyn Llanbedrog
Rhydlios
Porth Oer
Rhoshirwaun
NT
Llangian
St. Tudwal's Road
Braich Anelog
Anelog
Penycaerau
Rhiw
Plas-yn-Rhiw
Llawr Dref
Abersoch
Porth Neigwl or Hell's Mouth
Llanengan
Aberdaron
Llanfaelrhys
Sarn Bach
Bwlchtocyn
Machroes
Braich y Pwll
Uwchmynydd
St. Tudwal's Islands
Aberdaron Bay
Ynys Gwylan-fawr
BARDSEY SOUND
(SWNT ENLLI)
Pen y Cil
Cilan Uchaf
Trwyn yr Wylfa
Trwyn Cilan
St. Mary's Abbey
Bardsey Island
(Ynys Enlli)

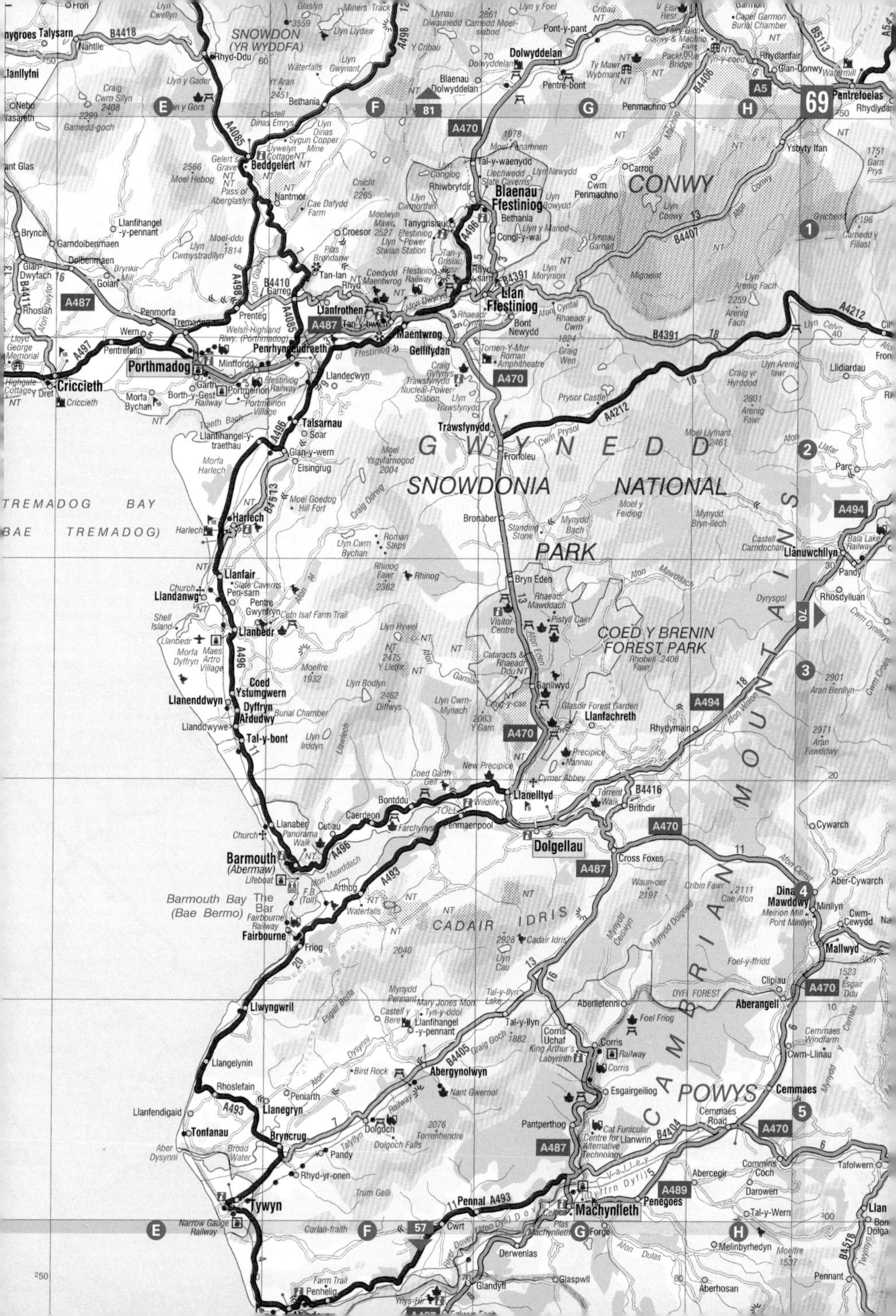

69
SNOWDON (YR WYDDFA)
Fron
Talysarn
Nantlle
Rhyd-Ddu
Llanllyfni
Nebo
Nasareth
Garnedd-goch
Craig Cwm Silyn
Llyn Cwellyn
Llyn y Gader
Glaslyn
Miners' Track
Llyn Llydaw
Y Cribau
Llyn Gwynant
Waterfalls
Yr Aran
Bethania
Sygun Copper Mine
Dinas Emrys
Llyn Dinas
Beddgelert
Gelert's Grave
Llywelyn Cottage
Moel Hebog
Pass of Aberglaslyn
Nantmor
Cae Dafydd Farm
Cnicht
Llanfihangel -y-pennant
Bryncir
Garndolbenmaen
Dolbenmaen
Golan
Brynkir Mill
Glan-Dwyfach
Rhoslan
Moel-ddu
Llyn Cwmystradllyn
Croesor
Plas Brondanw
Tan-lan
Garreg
Prenteg
Tremadog
Penmorfa
Wern
Pentrefelin
Criccieth
Lloyd George Memorial
Highgate Cottage
Y Dref
Porthmadog
Minffordd
Penrhyndeudraeth
Welsh Highland Rhwy. (Porthmadog)
Borth-y-Gest
Morfa Bychan
Portmeirion
Portmeirion Village
Ffestiniog Railway
Llanfrothen
Tan-y-bwlch
Maentwrog
Gellilydan
Llandecwyn
Rhyd
Coedydd Maentwrog
Tanygrisiau
Ffestiniog Power Station
Llyn Stwlan
Moelwyn Mawr
Llyn Cwmorthin
Rhiwbryfdir
Blaenau Ffestiniog
Bethania
Congl-y-wal
Llyn y Manod
Llechwedd Slate Caverns
Tal-y-waenydd
Llyn Conglog
Moel Penamnen
Llan Ffestiniog
Bont Newydd
Rhaeadr Cynfal
Rhaeadr y Cwm
Graig Wen
Tomen-Y-Mur Roman Amphitheatre
Craig Gyfynys
Trawsfynydd Nuclear Power Station
Llyn Trawsfynydd
Trawsfynydd
Fronoleu
Prysor Castle
Cwm Prysol
Afon Cynfal
Llyn Morynion
Dolwyddelan
Blaenau Dolwyddelan
Llynau Diwaunedd
Carnedd Moel-siabod
Llyn y Foel
Pont-y-pant
Pentre-bont
Ty Mawr Wybrnant
Penmachno
Cwm Penmachno
Carrog
Llyn Conwy
CONWY
Migneint
Cribau
Fairy Glen
Conwy & Machno Falls
Packhorse Bridge
Tyn-y-coed
Capel Garmon Burial Chamber
Rhydlanfair
Glan-Conwy
Watermill
Pentrefoelas
Rhydlydan
Ysbyty Ifan
Garn Prys
Gylchedd
Carnedd y Filiast
Llyn Arenig Fach
Arenig Fach
Llyn Celyn
Llyn Arenig fawr
Arenig Fawr
Craig yr Hyrddod
Llidiardau
Moel Llyfnant
Afon Llafar
Parc
GWYNEDD
SNOWDONIA NATIONAL PARK
Moel y Feidiog
Mynydd Bryn-llech
Castell Carndochan
Llanuwchllyn
Bala Lake Railway
Pandy
Rhosdylluan
Cwm Cynllwyd
Bronaber
Standing Stone
Mynydd Bach
Bryn Eden
Rhaeadr Mawddach
Pistyll Cain
Visitor Centre
Afon Mawddach
COED Y BRENIN FOREST PARK
Rhobell Fawr
Dyrysgol
Cataracts & Rhaeadr Ddu
Ganllwyd
Glasdir Forest Garden
Llanfachreth
Rhydymain
Afon Wnion
Aran Benllyn
Aran Fawddwy
Precipice Nannau
New Precipice
Cymer Abbey
Llanelltyd
Torrent Walk
Brithdir
Dolgellau
Cross Foxes
Cywarch
CAMBRIAN MOUNTAINS
Talsarnau
Soar
Llanfihangel-y-traethau
Traeth Bach
Glan-y-wern
Eisingrug
Morfa Harlech
Moel Ysgyfarnogod
Moel Goedog Hill Fort
Craig Ddrwg
TREMADOG BAY
(BAE TREMADOG)
Harlech
Llyn Cwm Bychan
Roman Steps
Rhinog Fawr
Rhinog
Llanfair
Slate Caverns
Pen-sarn
Llandanwg
Church
Shell Island
Pentre Gwynfryn
Cefn Isaf Farm Trail
Llanbedr
Maes Artro Village
Morfa Dyffryn
Llyn Hywel
Y Llethr
Moelfre
Llyn Bodlyn
Diffwys
Coed Ystumgwern
Llanenddwyn
Dyffryn Ardudwy
Burial Chamber
Llanddwywe
Tal-y-bont
Llyn Irddyn
Llyn Cwm-Mynach
Y Garn
Craig-y-cae
Gamlan
Coed Garth Gell
Bontddu
Caerdeon
Cutiau
Llanaber
Panorama Walk
Barmouth
(Abermaw)
Lifeboat
Penmaenpool
Farchynys
Wildlife
Afon Mawddach
Arthog
Waterfalls
Barmouth Bay
(Bae Bermo)
The Bar
Fairbourne
Fairbourne Railway
Friog
CADAIR IDRIS
Cadair Idris
Llyn Cau
Waun-oer
Cribin Fawr
Cae Afon
Mynydd Ceiswyn
Mynydd Dolgoed
Dinas Mawddwy
Aber-Cywarch
Minllyn
Meirion Mill
Pont Minllyn
Cwm-Cewydd
Mallwyd
Foel-y-ffridd
Clipiau
Aberangell
Egair Ddu
DYFI FOREST
Aberllefenni
Foel Friog
Tal-y-llyn Lake
Tal-y-llyn
Corris Uchaf
Corris
King Arthur's Labyrinth
Railway
Esgairgeiliog
Cemmaes Windfarm
Cwm-Llinau
Cemmaes
Cemmaes Road
POWYS
Llwyngwril
Mynydd Pennant
Mary Jones Mon
Tyn-y-ddol
Castell y Bere
Llanfihangel -y-pennant
Craig Goch
Dysynni
Bird Rock
Abergynolwyn
Nant Gwernol
Llangelynin
Rhoslefain
Peniarth
Llanegryn
Llanfendigaid
Tonfanau
Bryncrug
Dolgoch
Dolgoch Falls
Talyllyn Railway
Torrenhendre
Pantperthog
Cat Funicular
Centre for Alternative Technology
Llanwrin
Aber Dysynni
Broad Water
Pandy
Rhyd-yr-onen
Trum Gelli
Tywyn
Narrow Gauge Railway
Corlan-fraith
Pennal
Cwrt
Machynlleth
Dyfi Valley
Plas Machynlleth
Forge
Penegoes
Abercegir
Commins Coch
Darowen
Tafolwern
Tal-y-Wern
Llan
Melinbyrhedyn
Moelfre
River Dovey (Afon Dyfi)
Derwenlas
Afon Dulas
Glandyfi
Glaspwll
Aberhosan
Pennant
Farm Trail
Penhelig
Ynys-Hir

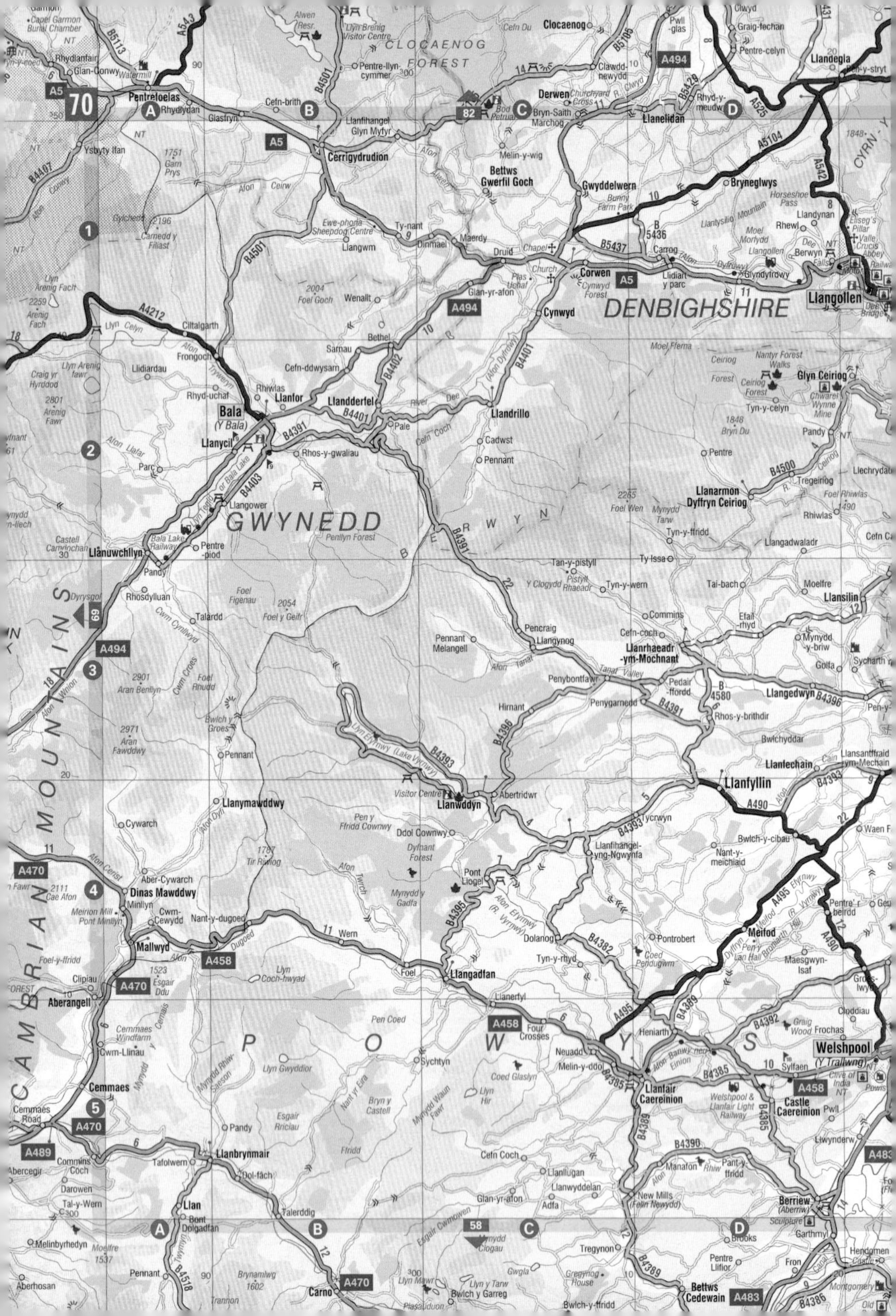
70
69
82
58
A
B
C
D
1
2
3
4
5
DENBIGHSHIRE
GWYNEDD
P O W Y S
CAMBRIAN MOUNTAINS
BERWYN
CLOCAENOG FOREST
Capel Garmon Burial Chamber
Rhydlanfair
Glan-Conwy
Watermill
Pentrefoelas
Rhydlydan
Glasfryn
Cefn-brith
Llanfihangel Glyn Myfyr
Cerrigydrudion
Ysbyty Ifan
1751 Garn Prys
Afon Ceirw
Gylchedd 2196
Carnedd y Filiast
Alwen Resr.
Llyn Brenig Visitor Centre
Pentre-llyn-cymmer
Cefn Du
Clocaenog
Clawdd-newydd
Derwen
Churchyard Cross
Bod Petrual
Bryn-Saith Marchog
Melin-y-wig
Bettws Gwerfil Goch
Pwll-glas
Llanelidan
Rhyd-y-meudwy
Graig-fechan
Pentre-celyn
Llandegla
Pen-y-stryt
Gwyddelwern
Bunny Farm Park
Bryneglwys
Horseshoe Pass
Llantysilio Mountain
Moel Morfydd
Llandynan
Rhewl
Eliseg's Pillar
Valle Crucis Abbey
Berwyn
Llangollen
Dee Bridge
Ewe-phoria Sheepdog Centre
Ty-nant
Llangwm
Dinmael
Maerdy
Druid
Chapel
Carrog
Corwen
Cynwyd Forest
Plas Uchaf
Church
Llidiart y parc
Glyndyfrdwy
Glan-yr-afon
Cynwyd
Wenallt
2004 Foel Goch
Llyn Arenig Fach
2259 Arenig Fach
Llyn Celyn
Ciltalgarth
Frongoch
Llyn Arenig fawr
Craig yr Hyrddod
2801 Arenig Fawr
Llidiardau
Rhyd-uchaf
Rhiwlas
Llanfor
Bala (Y Bala)
Llanycil
Afon Llafar
Parc
Sarnau
Bethel
Cefn-ddwysarn
Llandderfel
Pale
River Dee
Llandrillo
Cefn Coch
Cadwst
Pennant
Rhos-y-gwaliau
Llyn Tegid or Bala Lake
Llangower
Bala Lake Railway
Pentre-piod
Llanuwchllyn
Castell Carndochan
Pentlyn Forest
Moel Fferna
Ceiriog Forest
Nantyr Forest Walks
Glyn Ceiriog
Chwarel Wynne Mine
Tyn-y-celyn
1848 Bryn Du
Pandy
Pentre
Tregeiriog
Llechrydau
Llanarmon Dyffryn Ceiriog
Foel Rhiwlas
1490
Rhiwlas
2265 Foel Wen
Mynydd Tarw
Tyn-y-ffridd
Llangadwaladr
Ty Issa
Tan-y-pistyll
Y Clogydd
Pistyll Rhaeadr
Tyn-y-wern
Tai-bach
Moelfre
Llansilin
Dyrysgol
Pandy
Rhosdylluan
Talardd
Foel Figenau
2054 Foel y Geifr
Cwm Cynllwyd
Pencraig
Llangynog
Commins
Cefn-coch
Efail-rhyd
Llanrhaeadr-ym-Mochnant
Mynydd-y-briw
Golfa
Sycharth
Pennant Melangell
Afon Tanat
Tanat Valley
Penybontfawr
Pedair-ffordd
Llangedwyn
2901 Aran Benllyn
Cwm Croes
Foel Rhudd
Bwlch y Groes
2971 Aran Fawddwy
Pennant
Hirnant
Penygarnedd
Rhos-y-brithdir
Bwlchyddar
Llyn Efyrnwy (Lake Vyrnwy)
Llanfechain
Llansantffraid-ym-Mechain
Llanymawddwy
Visitor Centre
Llanwddyn
Abertridwr
Llanfyllin
Tycrwyn
Cywarch
Pen y Ffridd Cownwy
Ddol Cownwy
Dyfnant Forest
Bwlch-y-cibau
Waen Fawr
Nant-y-meichiaid
Llanfihangel-yng-Ngwynfa
1787 Tir Rhiwiog
Aber-Cywarch
2111 Cae Afon
Dinas Mawddwy
Meirion Mill
Pont Minllyn
Minllyn
Cwm-Cewydd
Nant-y-dugoed
Afon Twrch
Mynydd y Gadfa
Pont Llogel
Afon Efyrnwy (R. Vyrnwy)
Pentre'r beirdd
Meifod
Dyffryn Meifod
Pen-y-Lan Hall
Broniarth Hill
Mallwyd
Dugoed
Wern
Dolanog
Pontrobert
Coed Pendugwm
Tyn-y-rhyd
Foel-y-ffridd
1523 Esgair Ddu
Llyn Coch-hwyad
Foel
Llangadfan
Maesgwyn-Isaf
Groes-lwyd
Clipiau
Aberangell
Llanerfyl
Heniarth
Cloddiau
Graig Wood
Frochas
Cemmaes Windfarm
Pen Coed
Four Crosses
Welshpool (Y Trallwng)
Cwm-Llinau
Llyn Gwyddior
Sychtyn
Neuadd
Melin-y-ddol
Sylfaen
Clive of India
Powis Castle
Cemmaes
Mynydd Rhiw-Saeson
Nant yr Eira
Bryn y Castell
Coed Glaslyn
Llyn Hir
Mynydd Waun Fawr
Llanfair Caereinion
Welshpool & Llanfair Light Railway
Castle Caereinion
Pwll
Cemmaes Road
Esgair Rhiciau
Pandy
Llwynderw
Commins Coch
Abercegir
Llanbrynmair
Tafolwern
Ffridd
Cefn Coch
Llanllugan
Manafon
Pant-y-ffridd
Darowen
Dol-fâch
Llanwyddelan
Berriew (Aberriw)
Tal-y-Wern
Llan
Bont Dolgadfan
Talerddig
Glan-yr-afon
Adfa
New Mills (Felin Newydd)
Sculpture
Garthmyl
Melinbyrhedyn
Moelfre 1537
Mynydd Clogau
Esgair Cwmowen
Tregynon
Brooks
Hendomen
Pennant
Brynamlwg 1602
Gwgia
Gregynog House
Pentre Llifior
Fron
Castle
Montgomery
Aberhosan
Trannon
Carno
Llyn Mawr
Llyn y Tarw
Bwlch y Garreg
Plasauduon
Bwlch-y-ffridd
Bettws Cedewain
A5
A543
A494
A525
A5104
A542
A4212
A458
A470
A489
A483
A490
A495
B5113
B4501
B5105
B5429
B5436
B5437
B4407
B4402
B4401
B4391
B4403
B4500
B4580
B4396
B4393
B4395
B4382
B4389
B4392
B4385
B4390
B4518
B4386

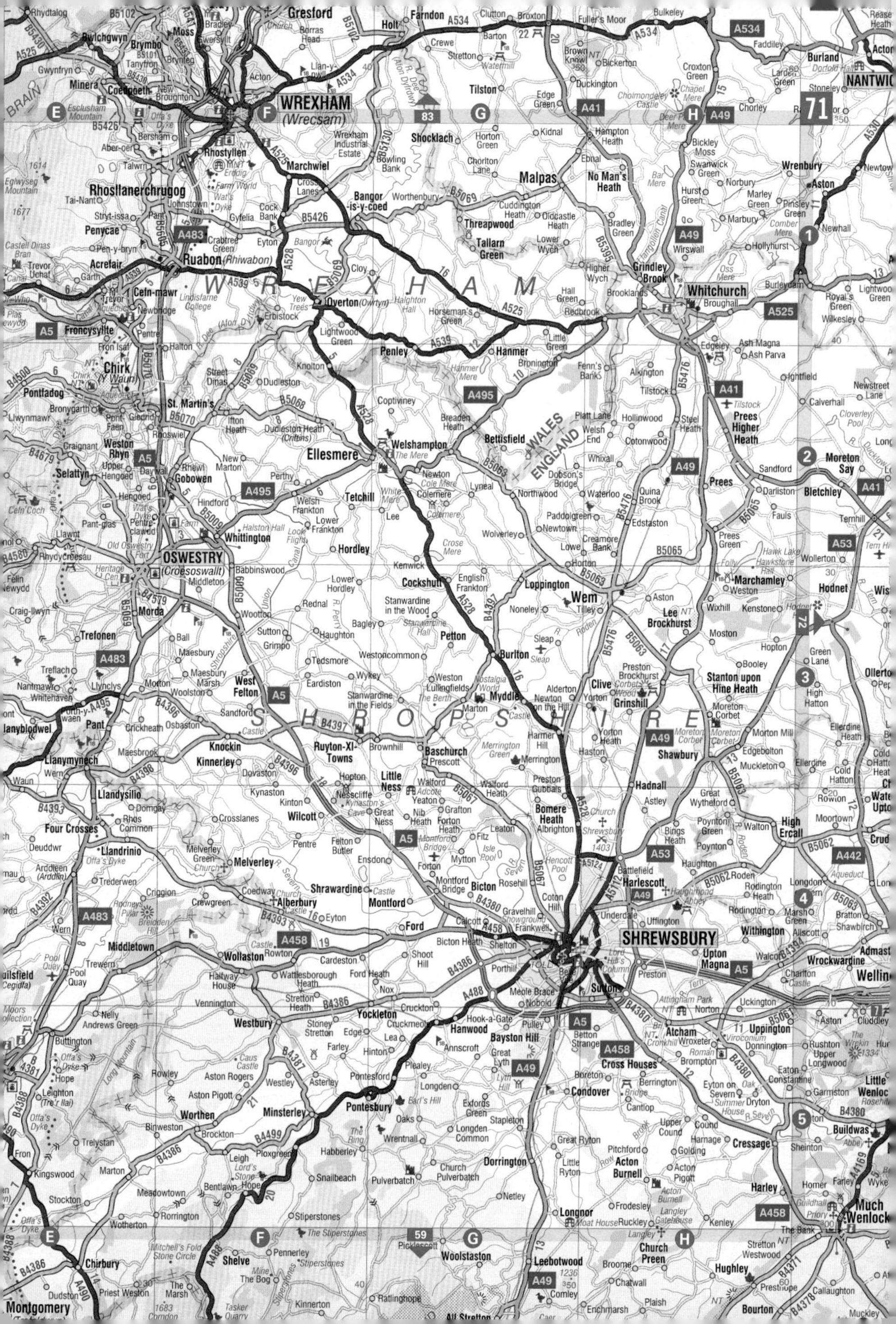

71
WREXHAM
(Wrecsam)
W R E X H A M
S H R O P S H I R E
WALES
ENGLAND
OSWESTRY
(Croesoswallt)
SHREWSBURY
NANTWICH
Whitchurch
Ellesmere
Wem
Malpas
Ruabon (Rhiwabon)
Chirk
(Y Waun)
Overton (Owrtyn)
Bangor-is-y-coed
Rhosllanerchrugog
Penycae
Acrefair
Cefn-mawr
Froncysyllte
Pontfadog
St. Martin's
Weston Rhyn
Gobowen
Whittington
Selattyn
Morda
Trefonen
Llanymynech
Llandysilio
Four Crosses
Llandrinio
Melverley
Alberbury
Middletown
Wollaston
Westbury
Worthen
Minsterley
Pontesbury
Chirbury
Montgomery
Shelve
Woolstaston
Leebotwood
Church Preen
Hughley
Much Wenlock
Harley
Cressage
Buildwas
Acton Burnell
Condover
Dorrington
Longnor
Bayston Hill
Hanwood
Yockleton
Cross Houses
Atcham
Uppington
Upton Magna
Withington
High Ercall
Harlescott
Hadnall
Shawbury
Grinshill
Clive
Myddle
Burlton
Baschurch
Ruyton-XI-Towns
Little Ness
Knockin
Kinnerley
West Felton
Cockshutt
Petton
Loppington
Lee Brockhurst
Marchamley
Hodnet
Prees
Prees Higher Heath
Moreton Say
Bletchley
Stanton upon Hine Heath
Welshampton
Bettisfield
Hanmer
Penley
Tetchill
Hordley
Shocklach
Tilston
Farndon
Holt
Gresford
Marchwiel
Threapwood
Tallarn Green
No Man's Heath
Grindley Brook
Wrenbury
Aston
Burland
Bulkeley
Brymbo
Minera
Bwlchgwyn
Coedpoeth
Rhostyllen
Montford
Bicton
Shrawardine
Ford
Wilcott
Bomere Heath
A5
A41
A49
A53
A442
A458
A483
A488
A495
A525
A528
A534
A539
B4380
B4386
B5063
B5065
B5069
B5476
83
59
72
E
F
G
H
1
2
3
4
5

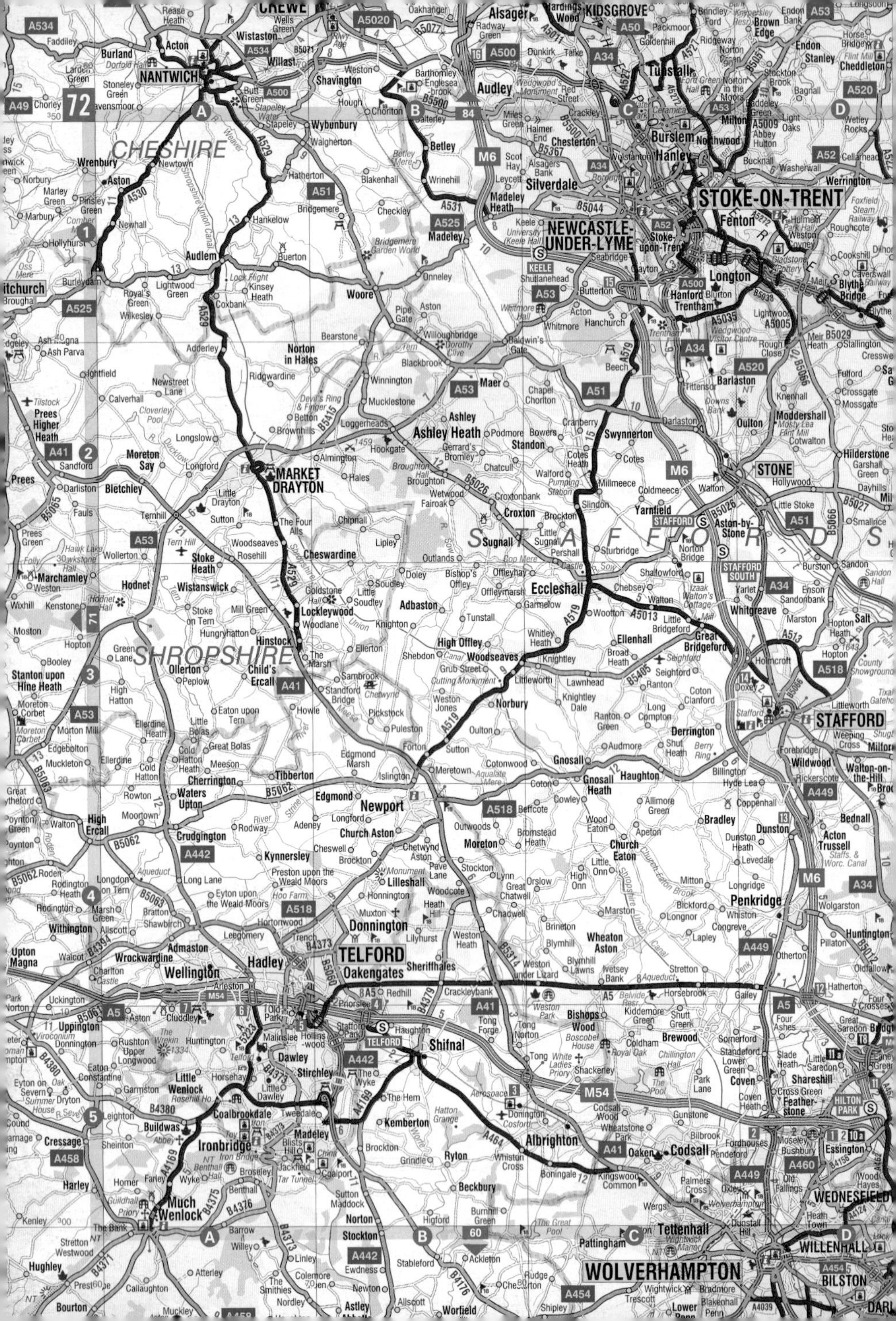

72
CHESHIRE
SHROPSHIRE
STAFFORDSHIRE
NANTWICH
Crewe
Alsager
Kidsgrove
Wistaston
Willaston
Acton
Burland
Shavington
Wybunbury
Audley
Tunstall
Burslem
Hanley
Northwood
Stoke-on-Trent
Fenton
Longton
Newcastle-under-Lyme
Stoke-upon-Trent
Silverdale
Chesterton
Madeley Heath
Madeley
Betley
Wrinehill
Keele
Wrenbury
Aston
Newhall
Audlem
Hankelow
Buerton
Whitchurch
Woore
Trentham
Blurton
Barlaston
Meir Heath
Blythe Bridge
Norton in Hales
Adderley
Maer
Ashley
Ashley Heath
Loggerheads
Market Drayton
Swynnerton
Stone
Yarnfield
Aston-by-Stone
Eccleshall
Croxton
Sugnall
Slindon
Millmeece
Prees
Moreton Say
Bletchley
Hodnet
Marchamley
Stoke Heath
Wistanswick
Cheswardine
Lockleywood
Hinstock
Child's Ercall
Adbaston
High Offley
Woodseaves
Norbury
Great Bridgeford
Stafford
Derrington
Gnosall
Haughton
Sutton
Forton
Newport
Edgmond
Tibberton
Church Aston
Lilleshall
Donnington
Telford
Oakengates
Hadley
Wellington
High Ercall
Crudgington
Waters Upton
Penkridge
Dunston
Acton Trussell
Bradley
Church Eaton
Wheaton Aston
Brewood
Coven
Shifnal
Albrighton
Codsall
Tettenhall
Wolverhampton
Wednesfield
Willenhall
Bilston
Dawley
Madeley
Ironbridge
Coalbrookdale
Buildwas
Much Wenlock
Broseley
Kemberton
Ryton
Beckbury
Pattingham
Wightwick
Worfield
Astley Abbotts
Hughley
Bourton
Cressage
Harley
Uppington
Wroxeter
M6
M54
A5
A41
A53
A51
A34
A500
A518
A519
A529
A442
A449
A454
A458
A520
A525
A534
A5020
Hilton Park
Stafford South
Stafford North

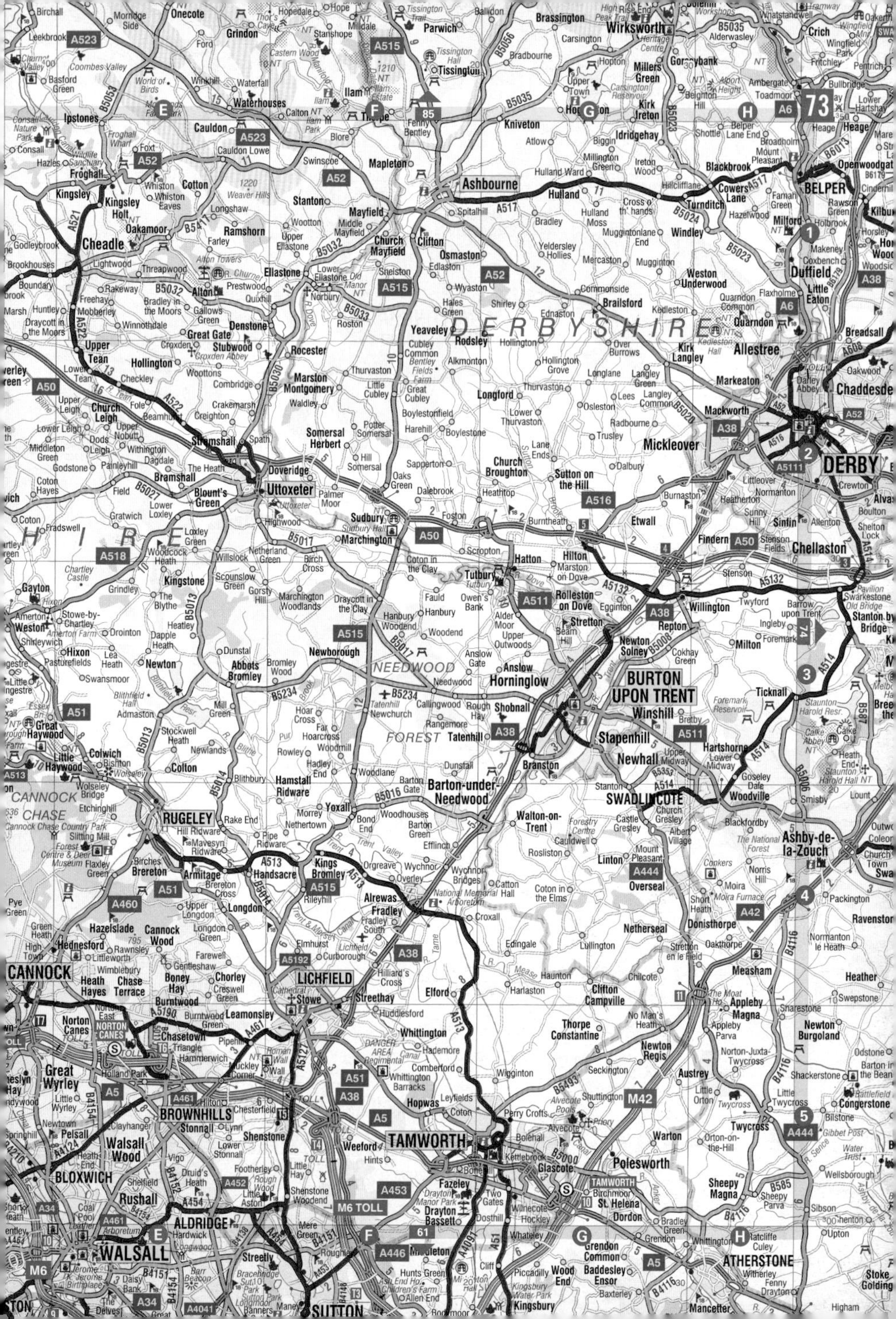

73
Onecote
Grindon
Hopedale
Parwich
Ballidon
Brassington
Wirksworth
Whatstandwell
Crich
Leekbrook
A523
Morridge Side
Alstonefield
Milldale
Stanshope
Tissington
Carsington
Bradbourne
Heritage Centre
Gorseybank
Alderwasley
B5035
Wingfield Park
Fritchley
Pentrich
Basford Green
Coombes Valley
World of Birds
Winkhill
Waterfall
Waterhouses
Ilam
Thorpe
Fenny Bentley
85
Kniveton
Hognaston
Kirk Ireton
Millers Green
Belper Lane End
Ambergate
Toadmoor
A6
Bullbridge
Heage
Ipstones
Cauldon
Cauldon Lowe
Calton
Blore
Atlow
Biggin
Idridgehay
Shottle
Broadholm
Consall
Foxt
A52
Swinscoe
Mapleton
Ashbourne
Hulland Ward
Millington Green
Ireton Wood
Mount Pleasant
Blackbrook
Openwoodgate
Hazles
Froghall
Whiston
Cotton
Weaver Hills
Stanton
Hulland
A517
Hillcliffiane
Turnditch
Cowers Lane
BELPER
Kingsley
Kingsley Holt
Whiston Eaves
Longshaw
Mayfield
Middle Mayfield
Spitalhill
Bradley
Hulland Moss
Cross o' th' hands
Famah Green
Hazelwood
Milford
Holbrook
Oakamoor
Ramshorn
Wootton
Upper Ellastone
Church Mayfield
Clifton
Osmaston
Yeldersley Hollies
Muggintonlane End
Windley
Makeney
Duffield
Coxbench
Cheadle
Farley
Alton Towers
Ellastone
B5032
Lightwood
Threapwood
Prestwood
Lower Ellastone
Shelston
Edlaston
Mercaston
Mugginton
Weston Underwood
Little Eaton
A38
Boundary
Alton
Rakeway
Quixhill
Norbury
Wyaston
Commonside
Brailsford
Flaxholme
Freehay
Mobberley
Bradley in the Moors
Gallows Green
A515
B5033
Roston
Hales Green
Shirley
Ednaston
Kedleston
Quarndon Common
Quarndon
Draycott in the Moors
Huntley
Winnothdale
Great Gate
Denstone
Yeaveley
Rodsley
DERBYSHIRE
Hollington
Kedleston Hall
Breadsall
Croxden
Stubwood
Rocester
Cubley Common
Alkmonton
Over Burrows
Kirk Langley
Allestree
Upper Tean
Tean
Hollington
Woottons
Croxden Abbey
Bentley Fields
Hollington Grove
Longlane
Langley Green
Oakwood
A50
Checkley
Cambridge
B5030
Thurvaston
Marston Montgomery
Little Cubley
Great Cubley
Longford
Lower Thurvaston
Lees
Langley Common
Markeaton
Darley Abbey
Chaddesden
Upper Leigh
Church Leigh
Fole
A522
Beamhurst
Crakemarsh
Creighton
Waldley
Boylestonfield
Harehill
Boylestone
Osleston
Radbourne
Mackworth
A52
Lower Leigh
Dods Leigh
Upper Nobutt
Withington
Dagdale
Stramshall
Spath
Somersal Herbert
Potter Somersal
Hill Somersal
Lane Ends
Trusley
Mickleover
DERBY
Middleton Green
Godstone
Painleyhill
Bramshall
The Heath
Doveridge
Sapperton
Church Broughton
Sutton on the Hill
Dalbury
A5111
Coton Hayes
Field
B5027
Blount's Green
Uttoxeter
Palmer Moor
Oaks Green
Dalebrook
Heathtop
Littleover
Normanton
Crewton
Lower Loxley
Burnaston
Heatherton
Alvaston
Gratwich
Highwood
Sudbury
Foston
Burntheath
A516
Etwall
Sunny Hill
Sinfin
Allenton
Boulton
Fradswell
Loxley Green
Marchington
Sudbury Hall
Findern
Stenson Fields
Shelton Lock
Chellaston
A518
Woodcock Heath
Willslock
Netherland Green
B5017
Birch Cross
Coton in the Clay
Scropton
Hatton
Hilton
Marston on Dove
Stenson
A514
Chartley Castle
Kingstone
Scounslow Green
Gorsty Hill
Tutbury
A5132
Twyford
Swarkestone
Gayton
Grindley
The Blythe
Marchington Woodlands
Draycott in the Clay
Fauld
Hanbury
Owen's Bank
A511
Rolleston on Dove
Egginton
Willington
Barrow upon Trent
Stanton by Bridge
Amerton
Stowe-by-Chartley
Weston
Amerton Farm
Drointon
Heatley
Dapple Heath
Hanbury Woodend
Woodend
Alder Moor
Stretton
Beam Hill
Repton
Ingleby
Foremark
Shirleywich
Hixon
Pasturefields
Lea Heath
Newton
Dunstal
Newborough
Upper Outwoods
Newton Solney
B5008
Cokhay Green
Milton
Swansmoor
Abbots Bromley
Bromley Wood
NEEDWOOD
Anslow Gate
Anslow
Horninglow
BURTON UPON TRENT
Ticknall
Blithfield
Needwood
B5234
Tatenhill
Newchurch
Callingwood
Rough Hay
Shobnall
Winshill
Bretby
Foremark Reservoir
Staunton Harold Resr.
A51
Admaston
Mill Green
Hoar Cross
Far Hoarcross
Rangemore
Tatenhill
Stapenhill
A511
Hartshorne
Calke
Calke Abbey
Great Haywood
Stockwell Heath
B5013
Woodmill
FOREST
Branston
Newhall
Upper Midway
Lower Midway
Little Haywood
Colwich
Bishton
Wolseley
Newlands
Colton
Rowley
Hadley End
Dunstall
Heath End
Staunton Harold Hall
A513
Wolseley Bridge
Blithbury
B5014
Hamstall Ridware
Woodlane
Barton Gate
Barton-under-Needwood
Stanton
B5353
Goseley Dale
Smisby
CANNOCK CHASE
Etchinghill
Cannock Chase Country Park
RUGELEY
Rake End
Morrey
Yoxall
Nethertown
B5016
Woodhouses
Barton Green
Walton-on-Trent
SWADLINCOTE
Church Gresley
Castle Gresley
Woodville
Blackfordby
Slitting Mill
Hill Ridware
Mavesyn Ridware
Pipe Ridware
Bond End
Efflinch
Forestry Centre
Cauldwell
Albert Village
The National Forest
Ashby-de-la-Zouch
Forest Centre & Deer Museum
Flaxley Green
Birches
Brereton
Armitage
Handsacre
Kings Bromley
Orgreave
Wychnor
Wychnor Bridges
Rosliston
Linton
Mount Pleasant
A444
Cokers
Norris Hill
Brereton Cross
Longdon
Rileyhill
Overley
National Memorial Arboretum
Catton Hall
Coton in the Elms
Overseal
Moira
Moira Furnace
Packington
A460
Upper Longdon
Alrewas
Fradley
Fradley South
Croxall
Short Heath
Donisthorpe
A42
Ravenstone
Pye Green
Hazelslade
Cannock Wood
Longdon Green
Green Heath
Hednesford
Rawnsley
Littleworth
Farewell
Gentleshaw
Elmhurst
Curborough
Edingale
Lullington
Netherseal
Oakthorpe
Stretton en le Field
Normanton le Heath
CANNOCK
Wimblebury
Heath Hayes
Chase Terrace
Boney Hay
Burntwood
Chorley
Creswell Green
A5192
LICHFIELD
Stowe
Hilliard's Cross
Streethay
Elford
Haunton
Harlaston
Clifton Campville
Chilcote
Measham
Heather
The Moat Ho.
Appleby Magna
Swepstone
Norton East
Norton Canes
Burntwood Green
Leamonsley
Huddlesford
No Man's Heath
Sharestone
Chasetown
Triangle
Hammerwich
Pipehill
Whittington
Hademore
Thorpe Constantine
Appleby Parva
Newton Burgoland
Great Wyrley
Holland Park
Muckley Corner
Wall
DANGER AREA
Comberford
Seckington
Newton Regis
Norton-Juxta-Twycross
Odstone
Cheslyn Hay
A5
Little Wyrley
A461
Hilton
Chesterfield
Whittington Barracks
Wigginton
Austrey
Shackerstone
Barton in the Beans
BROWNHILLS
Stonnall
Lynn
Hopwas
Leyfields
Coton
Perry Crofts
Shuttington
Alvecote Pools
Alvecote
Little Orton
Twycross
Little Twycross
Congerstone
Battlefield
Pelsall
Clayhanger
Newtown
Shenstone
Weeford
TAMWORTH
Bolehall
Kettlebrook
Glascote
Warton
Orton-on-the-Hill
Bilstone
Gibbet Post
Walsall Wood
Lower Stonnall
Vigo
Hints
Little Hay
Bone Hill
Polesworth
A444
Water Trust
B5000
BLOXWICH
Shelfield
Footherley
Druid's Heath
A452
Rough Wood
Little Aston
Shenstone Woodend
A453
Fazeley
Drayton Manor Park
Two Gates
Wilnecote
Birchmoor
St. Helena
Dordon
Sheepy Magna
Sheepy Parva
B585
Wellsborough
Sibson
Rushall
A454
M6 TOLL
Coal Pool
ALDRIDGE
Hardwick
Mere Green
Drayton Bassett
Dosthill
Hockley
Whateley
Bradley Green
Grendon
Whittington
Ratcliffe Culey
Upton
Sheepy
A34
WALSALL
Arboretum
Streetly
Roughley
A446
Middleton
Grendon Common
Baddesley Ensor
ATHERSTONE
Witherley
Fenny Drayton
Stoke Golding
M6
St Jerome Birthplace
Daisy Bank
Barr Beacon
B4151
Bracebridge
Hunts Green
Allen End
Clifft
Piccadilly
Wood End
Kingsbury
Kingsbury Water Park
Baxterley
Mancetter
A5
A4091
A4041
The Delves
Banners
SUTTON
Bodymoor
Higham
M42
B4116
A453
61

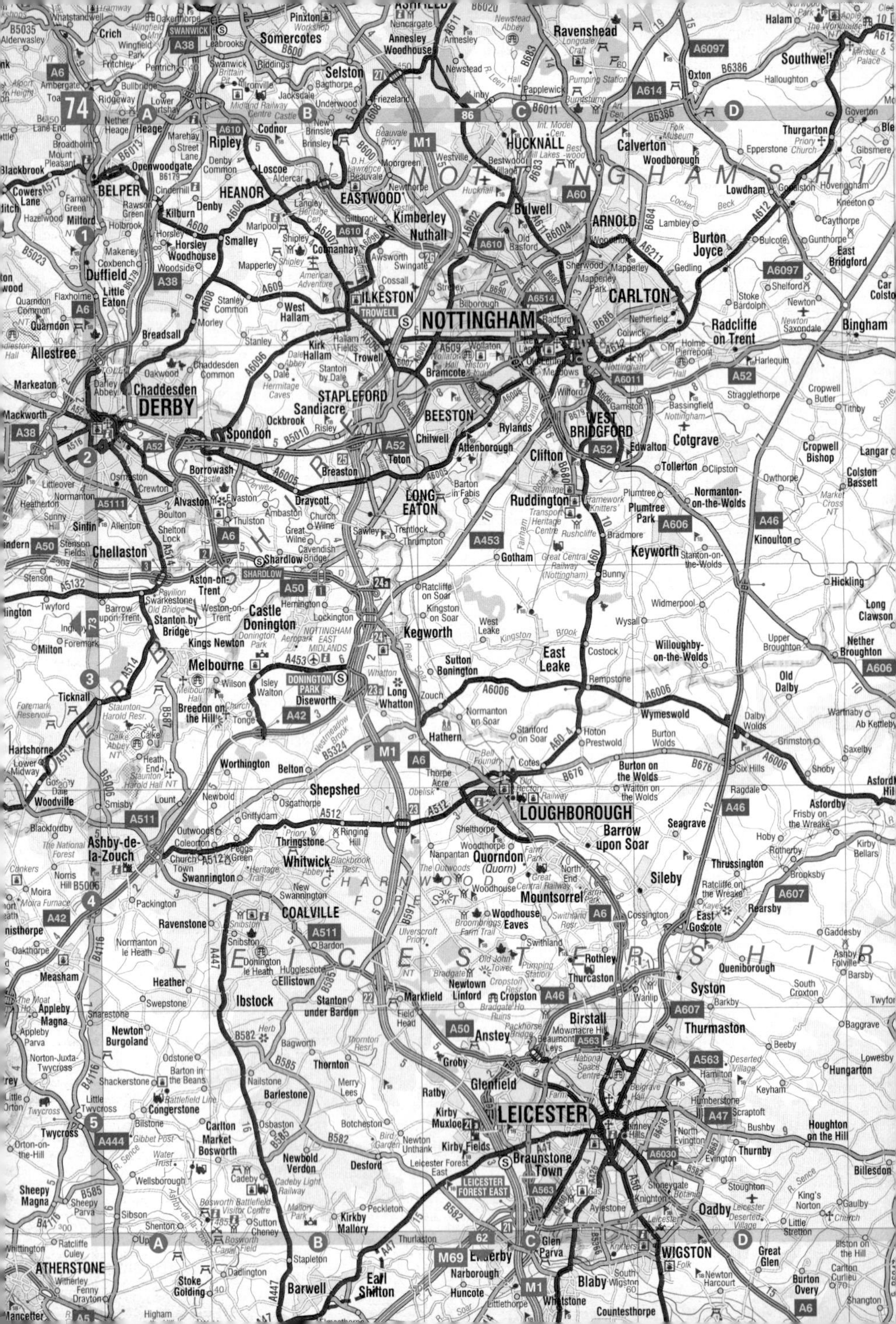

74
73
Whatstandwell
Crich
Oakerthorpe
SWANWICK
Pinxton
Somercotes
Annesley
Annesley Woodhouse
Newstead Abbey
Ravenshead
Halam
Southwell
B5035
Alderwasley
Wingfield Park
Fritchley
Pentrich
Leabrooks
Swanwick
Riddings
Selston
Newstead
Papplewick
Oxton
A6097
B6386
Halloughton
A6
Ambergate
Toad
Ridgeway
Bullbridge
Lower Hartshay
Ironville
Jacksdale
Bagthorpe
Underwood
Friezeland
Linby
Pumping Station
A614
Heage
Nether Heage
Midland Railway Centre
New Brinsley
Brinsley
86
B6011
Int. Model Cen.
Folk Museum
Goverton
Thurgarton
Priory Church
Lane End
Broadholm
Mount Pleasant
Marehay
Ripley
Codnor
Beauvale Priory
M1
HUCKNALL
Calverton
Woodborough
Epperstone
Gibsmere
Street Lane
Denby Common
Westville
Bestwood
B6013
Openwoodgate
Loscoe
D.H. Lawrence
Moorgreen
Beauvale
NOTTINGHAMSHI
Blackbrook
Cowers Lane
BELPER
Rawson Green
Cinderhill
Kilburn
HEANOR
Denby
Aldercar
Langley
Newthorpe
EASTWOOD
Hucknall
Bulwell
A60
ARNOLD
Lowdham
Gonalston
Hoveringham
Farnah Green
Hazelwood
Milford
Holbrook
A609
A608
Smalley
Marlpool
Gilltbrook
Kimberley
Nuthall
Lambley
Burton Joyce
Caythorpe
Kneeton
Makeney
Coxbench
Horsley
Horsley Woodhouse
Woodside
Shipley
Cotmanhay
A6096
A610
Old Basford
B6004
Woodthorpe
A6211
Gedling
Bulcote
Gunthorpe
East Bridgford
Duffield
Little Eaton
A38
Mapperley
American Adventure
Awsworth
Swingate
Cossall
Sherwood
Mapperley
Mapperley Park
A6097
Shelford
Car Colston
Flaxholme
Quarndon Common
A6
Quarndon
Stanley Common
West Hallam
ILKESTON
TROWELL
Strelley
Bilborough
A6514
CARLTON
Stoke Bardolph
Newton
Radford
Netherfield
Colwick
Radcliffe on Trent
Saxondale
Bingham
Breadsall
Morley
Stanley
Kirk Hallam
Hallam Fields
Trowell
NOTTINGHAM
Wollaton
Lenton
Holme Pierrepont
Harlequin
Allestree
Chaddesden
Chaddesden Common
Oakwood
Dale Abbey
Dale
Hermitage Caves
Stanton by Dale
Bramcote
History Lace
Wollaton Hall
Meadows
A6011
A52
Cropwell Butler
Markeaton
Darley Abbey
Chaddesden
DERBY
Ockbrook
Risley
Sandiacre
STAPLEFORD
BEESTON
Rylands
Wilford
WEST BRIDGFORD
Gamston
Bassingfield
Stragglethorpe
Tithby
Mackworth
A38
Spondon
B5010
Chilwell
Attenborough
Edwalton
Cotgrave
Langar
Cropwell Bishop
A516
A52
A52
Toton
Clifton
Tollerton
Clipston
Osmaston
Borrowash
Breaston
Colston Bassett
Littleover
Crewton
Normanton
A6005
Owthorpe
Heatherton
Alvaston
Elvaston
Draycott
LONG EATON
Barton in Fabis
Ruddington
Plumtree
Normanton-on-the-Wolds
A5111
Boulton
Ambaston
Church Wilne
Framework Knitters'
Plumtree Park
Sunny Hill
Sinfin
Allenton
Thulston
Great Wilne
Sawley
Trentlock
Thrumpton
Transport Heritage Centre
Rushcliffe
Bradmore
A606
Kinoulton
A46
Shelton Lock
A6
Cavendish Bridge
Fairham
Great Central Railway (Nottingham)
Keyworth
Stanton-on-the-Wolds
Sindern
A50
Stenson Fields
Chellaston
A514
Shardlow
SHARDLOW
A453
Gotham
Bunny
Stenson
A5132
Aston-on-Trent
A50
Ratcliffe on Soar
Hickling
Pavilion
Swarkestone
Weston-on-Trent
Hemington
Kingston on Soar
Widmerpool
Long Clawson
Twyford
Barrow upon Trent
Stanton by Bridge
Castle Donington
Lockington
West Leake
Wysall
Kings Newton
Donington Park
Kegworth
NOTTINGHAM EAST MIDLANDS
Aeropark
Kingston
Brook
Costock
Upper Broughton
Nether Broughton
Ingleby
Milton
Foremark
East Leake
Willoughby-on-the-Wolds
A606
Melbourne
A453
Sutton Bonington
Rempstone
Old Dalby
Ticknall
Wilson
Isley Walton
DONINGTON PARK
Diseworth
Whatton
Long Whatton
A6006
Foremark Reservoir
Staunton Harold Resr.
Melbourne Hall
Breedon on the Hill
Tonge
A42
Zouch
Normanton on Soar
Wymeswold
Wartnaby
Ab Kettleby
Calke Abbey
Calke
B587
Hathern
Stanford on Soar
Hoton
Prestwold
Burton Wolds
Dalby Wolds
Grimston
Saxelby
Hartshorne
Lower Midway
Heath End
Staunton Harold Hall
Worthington
Belton
B5324
M1
A6
Cotes
A60
Burton on the Wolds
Six Hills
Shoby
Asfordby Hill
Gorsley Dale
Woodville
Smisby
Lount
Newbold
Osgathorpe
Shepshed
Thorpe Acre
B676
Walton on the Wolds
Ragdale
Asfordby
Frisby on the Wreake
A511
Blackfordby
Griffydam
A512
LOUGHBOROUGH
Barrow upon Soar
Seagrave
A46
The National Forest
Ashby-de-la-Zouch
Outwoods
Coleorton
Thringstone
Ringing Hill
Shelthorpe
Woodthorpe
Hoby
Kirby Bellars
Conkers
Church Town
Peggs Green
Whitwick
Blackbrook Resr.
Nanpantan
Quorndon (Quorn)
Rotherby
Brooksby
Norris Hill
B5006
Swannington
CHARNWOOD FOREST
North End
Thrussington
Sileby
Moira
Moira Furnace
New Swannington
Ratcliffe on the Wreake
A607
Rearsby
Packington
COALVILLE
Woodhouse
Mountsorrel
Cossington
East Goscote
A42
Ravenstone
Snibston
A511
Woodhouse Eaves
Broombriggs Farm Trail
Swithland Resr.
A6
Gaddesby
Donisthorpe
Oakthorpe
Normanton le Heath
Bardon
Ulverscroft Priory
Swithland
Rothley
LEICESTERSHIR
Ashby Folville
Barsby
Measham
Donington le Heath
Hugglescote
Ellistown
Bradgate
Old John Tower
Thurcaston
Queniborough
South Croxton
Heather
Ibstock
Newtown Linford
Cropston
A46
Syston
Twyford
The Moat
Appleby Magna
Swepstone
Stanton under Bardon
Markfield
Field Head
Bradgate Ho. Ruins
Wanlip
Barkby
Snarestone
Birstall
A607
Thurmaston
Appleby Parva
Newton Burgoland
A50
Anstey
Mowmacre Hill
Beaumont Leys
A563
Baggrave
Norton-Juxta-Twycross
Odstone
Barton in the Beans
Bagworth
Thornton Resr.
Thornton
Groby
National Space Centre
Beeby
Lowesby
A563
Deserted Village
Hungarton
Shackerstone
Nailstone
Merry Lees
Glenfield
Hamilton
Keyham
Battlefield Line
Barlestone
Ratby
Belgrave Hall
Little Orton
Little Twycross
Twycross
Congerstone
Kirby Muxloe
LEICESTER
Humberstone
Scraptoft
A47
Bilstone
Carlton
Osbaston
Botcheston
Market Bosworth
Bird Garden
Newton Unthank
Kirby Fields
Spinney Hills
North Evington
Bushby
Houghton on the Hill
Twycross
A444
Gibbet Post
A47
Braunstone Town
Thurnby
Orton-on-the-Hill
Water Trust
B582
Newbold Verdon
Desford
Leicester Forest East
LEICESTER FOREST EAST
A6030
Evington
Billesdon
Wellsborough
Cadeby
Cadeby Light Railway
A563
Stoneygate
Botanic
Stoughton
King's Norton
Sheepy Magna
Sheepy Parva
Bosworth Battlefield Visitor Centre
Peckleton
Aylestone
Leicester Deserted Village
Oadby
Gaulby
Sibson
Mallory Park
Kirkby Mallory
Sutton Cheney
Little Stretton
Shenton
Bosworth Field
Thurlaston
Glen Parva
Knighton
Wigston
WIGSTON
Great Glen
Illston on the Hill
Whittington
Ratcliffe Culey
Stapleton
A47
M69
Enderby
Newton Harcourt
Carlton Curlieu
ATHERSTONE
Witherley
Fenny Drayton
Stoke Golding
Dadlington
Barwell
Earl Shilton
Narborough
Huncote
M1
Blaby
South Wigston
Burton Overy
Shangton
Mancetter
Higham
Littlethorpe
Whetstone
Countesthorpe
A6

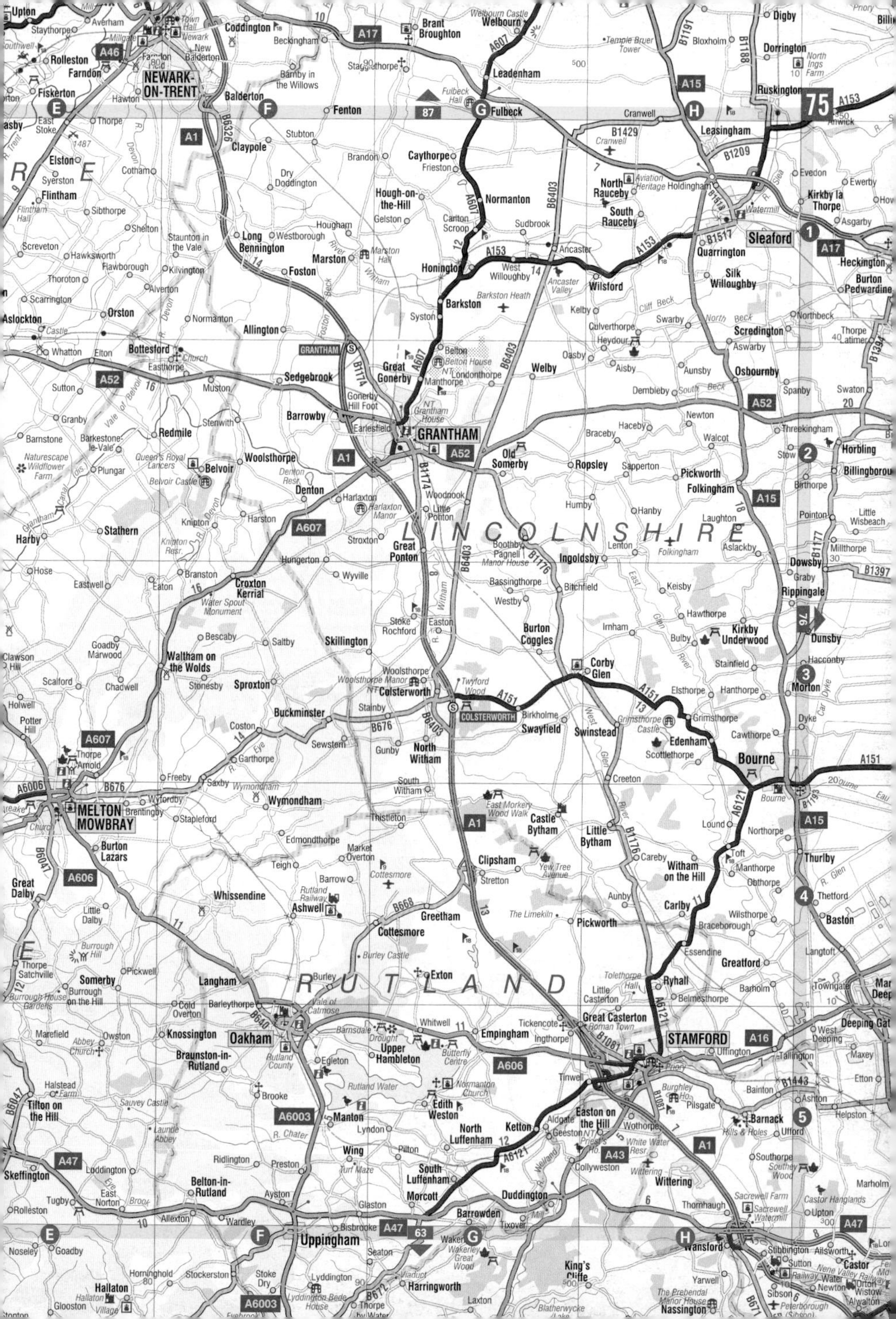

Upton
Staythorpe
Averham
Rolleston
Farndon
Fiskerton
East Stoke
Elston
Syerston
Flintham
Sibthorpe
Shelton
Screveton
Hawksworth
Flawborough
Thoroton
Scarrington
Aslockton
Orston
Whatton
Elton
Bottesford
Easthorpe
Sutton
Granby
Barnstone
Barkestone-le-Vale
Plungar
Redmile
Belvoir
Belvoir Castle
Woolsthorpe
Denton
Harby
Stathern
Harston
Knipton
Branston
Eaton
Eastwell
Hose
Croxton Kerrial
Water Spout Monument
Bescaby
Saltby
Goadby Marwood
Waltham on the Wolds
Stonesby
Sproxton
Chadwell
Scalford
Clawson Hill
Holwell
Potter Hill
Thorpe Arnold
Melton Mowbray
Brentingby
Wyfordby
Freeby
Saxby
Garthorpe
Coston
Buckminster
Sewstern
Wymondham
Stapleford
Burton Lazars
Great Dalby
Little Dalby
Whissendine
Burrough Hill
Thorpe Satchville
Somerby
Pickwell
Burrough on the Hill
Langham
Cold Overton
Barleythorpe
Oakham
Knossington
Owston
Marefield
Abbey Church
Braunston-in-Rutland
Halstead Farm
Tilton on the Hill
Sauvey Castle
Launde Abbey
Brooke
Skeffington
Loddington
East Norton
Tugby
Rolleston
Allexton
Wardley
Belton-in-Rutland
Ridlington
Preston
Ayston
Uppingham
Noseley
Goadby
Horninghold
Stockerston
Stoke Dry
Hallaton
Glooston
Lyddington
Seaton
Bisbrooke
Glaston
Morcott
South Luffenham
North Luffenham
Wing
Turf Maze
Pilton
Lyndon
Manton
Edith Weston
Rutland Water
Egleton
Upper Hambleton
Empingham
Whitwell
Barnsdale
Normanton Church
Ketton
Tinwell
Easton on the Hill
Collyweston
Duddington
Barrowden
Tixover
Wakerley
Wakerley Great Wood
Harringworth
King's Cliffe
Laxton
Wittering
Thornhaugh
Wansford
Yarwell
Nassington
Stamford
Burghley Ho.
Pilsgate
Barnack
Hills & Holes
Ufford
Southorpe
Bainton
Ashton
Helpston
Castor Hanglands
Marholm
Upton
Sutton
Stibbington
Ailsworth
Castor
Nene Valley Railway
Uffington
Tallington
West Deeping
Deeping Gate
Maxey
Etton
Ryhall
Belmesthorpe
Little Casterton
Great Casterton
Tickencote
Ingthorpe
Essendine
Greatford
Barholm
Braceborough
Wilsthorpe
Carlby
Witham on the Hill
Manthorpe
Toft
Obthorpe
Langtoft
Baston
Thetford
Thurlby
Northorpe
Lound
Bourne
Cawthorpe
Dyke
Morton
Hacconby
Dunsby
Rippingale
Dowsby
Millthorpe
Aslackby
Pointon
Little Wisbeach
Birthorpe
Billingborough
Horbling
Stow
Threekingham
Swaton
Spanby
Osbournby
Aswarby
Scredington
Northbeck
Burton Pedwardine
Heckington
Silk Willoughby
Quarrington
Sleaford
Kirkby la Thorpe
Asgarby
Evedon
Ewerby
Holdingham
Leasingham
Ruskington
Anwick
Dorrington
Digby
Bloxholm
Cranwell
North Rauceby
South Rauceby
Wilsford
Ancaster
Sudbrook
West Willoughby
Honington
Carlton Scroop
Normanton
Caythorpe
Frieston
Hough-on-the-Hill
Gelston
Fulbeck
Leadenham
Welbourn
Brant Broughton
Coddington
Beckingham
Stragglethorpe
Barnby in the Willows
Fenton
Balderton
Newark-on-Trent
Hawton
Thorpe
Claypole
Stubton
Brandon
Dry Doddington
Cotham
Staunton in the Vale
Long Bennington
Westborough
Hougham
Marston
Foston
Kilvington
Alverton
Normanton
Allington
Sedgebrook
Muston
Barrowby
Stenwith
Great Gonerby
Manthorpe
Londonthorpe
Belton
Belton House
Syston
Barkston
Barkston Heath
Grantham
Old Somerby
Ropsley
Welby
Oasby
Heydour
Aisby
Kelby
Culverthorpe
Swarby
Aunsby
Dembleby
Newton
Haceby
Braceby
Sapperton
Walcot
Pickworth
Folkingham
Laughton
Humby
Hanby
Lenton
Ingoldsby
Lincolnshire
Harlaxton
Harlaxton Manor
Little Ponton
Stroxton
Great Ponton
Boothby Pagnell
Hungerton
Wyville
Bassingthorpe
Westby
Bitchfield
Burton Coggles
Irnham
Keisby
Hawthorpe
Kirkby Underwood
Bulby
Stainfield
Corby Glen
Elsthorpe
Hanthorpe
Grimsthorpe
Grimsthorpe Castle
Edenham
Scottlethorpe
Swinstead
Swayfield
Birkholme
Colsterworth
Woolsthorpe
Woolsthorpe Manor
Twyford Wood
Stoke Rochford
Easton
Skillington
Stainby
Gunby
North Witham
South Witham
Thistleton
Edmondthorpe
Market Overton
Teigh
Barrow
Cottesmore
Ashwell
Greetham
Exton
Burley
Rutland
Clipsham
Stretton
Castle Bytham
Little Bytham
Creeton
Careby
Aunby
Pickworth
The Limekiln
Yew Tree Avenue
A1
A6003
A47
A52
A606
A607
A15
A153
A17
A151
A16
A43
A46
A6121
A6006
B6403
B1174
B1176
B676
B668
87
63
76

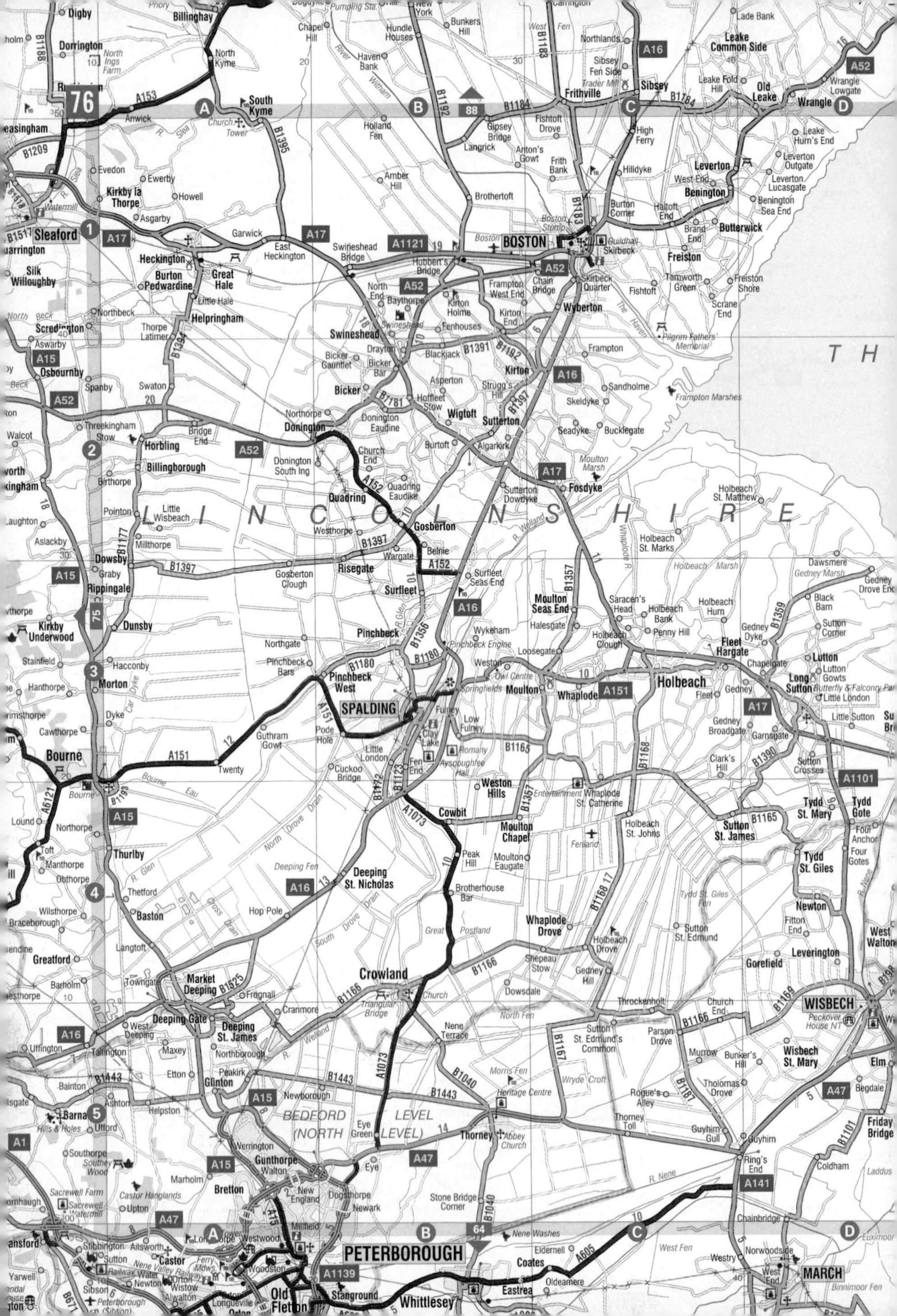

76
Digby
Billinghay
Priory
Pumping Sta.
New York
Carrington
Lade Bank
Dorrington
North Ings Farm
Chapel Hill
Hundle Houses
Bunkers Hill
West Fen
B1183
Northlands
A16
Leake Common Side
North Kyme
Haven Bank
River Witham
Sibsey Fen Side
Trader Mill
Sibsey
Leake Fold Hill
Old Leake
A52
Wrangle Lowgate
Wrangle
A153
Anwick
South Kyme
Church
Tower
B1192
88
B1184
Frithville
B1784
A
B
C
D
Holland Fen
Gipsey Bridge
Fishtoft Drove
High Ferry
Leake Hurn's End
Leverton Outgate
Leasingham
B1209
R. Slea
B1395
Langrick
Anton's Gowt
Frith Bank
Hilldyke
Leverton
Evedon
Ewerby
Amber Hill
West End
Leverton Lucasgate
Kirkby la Thorpe
Howell
Brothertoft
Burton Corner
Haltoft End
Benington
Benington Sea End
Watermill
Asgarby
Boston Stump
B1183
Brand End
Butterwick
Sleaford
B1517
A17
Garwick
East Heckington
Swineshead Bridge
A1121
Boston
BOSTON
Guildhall
Skirbeck
Quarrington
Heckington
Great Hale
Hubbert's Bridge
A52
Chain Bridge
Freiston
Silk Willoughby
Burton Pedwardine
Little Hale
North End
Baythorpe
Frampton West End
Skirbeck Quarter
Fishtoft
Tamworth Green
Freiston Shore
Northbeck
Helpringham
Kirton Holme
Kirton End
Wyberton
Scrane End
Scredington
Swineshead
Fenhouses
The Haven
Aswarby
Thorpe Latimer
Drayton
Blackjack
B1391
B1192
Frampton
Pilgrim Fathers' Memorial
A15
B1394
Bicker Gauntlet
Bicker Bar
Kirton
A16
T H
Osbournby
Spanby
Swaton
Bicker
Asperton
Strugg's Hill
Sandholme
Frampton Marshes
Hoffleet Stow
B1181
Skeldyke
A52
Northorpe
Donington Eaudine
Wigtoft
Sutterton
Threekingham Stow
Bridge End
Donington
Seadyke
Bucklegate
Walcot
Horbling
A52
Burtoft
Algarkirk
B1397
Church End
Moulton Marsh
Billingborough
Donington South Ing
A17
Birthorpe
A152
Quadring Eaudike
Sutterton Dowdyke
Fosdyke
Quadring
Holbeach St. Matthew
Pointon
Little Wisbeach
L I N C O L N S H I R E
Laughton
Gosberton
R. Welland
Whaplode R.
B1177
Westhorpe
Millthorpe
Holbeach St. Marks
Aslackby
B1397
Belnie
Wargate
Dowsby
Graby
B1397
Risegate
A152
Surfleet Seas End
B1357
Holbeach Marsh
Dawsmere
Gedney Marsh
Gosberton Clough
Surfleet
Gedney Drove End
Rippingale
Moulton Seas End
Saracen's Head
Holbeach Bank
Holbeach Hurn
Black Barn
B1359
A16
Kirkby Underwood
75
Dunsby
Pinchbeck
Wykeham
Halesgate
Penny Hill
Gedney Dyke
Sutton Corner
R. Glen
B1356
Pinchbeck Engine
Loosegate
Holbeach Clough
Fleet Hargate
Northgate
Stainfield
Hacconby
Pinchbeck Bars
B1180
Weston
Owl Centre
Chapelgate
Lutton
Lutton Gowts
Long Sutton
Butterfly & Falconry Park
Little London
Pinchbeck West
Morton
Moulton
Whaplode
A151
Holbeach
Fleet
Gedney
Hanthorpe
Springfields
SPALDING
Fulney
A17
Car Dyke
Dyke
A151
Pode Hole
Low Fulney
Clay Lake
Gedney Broadgate
Garnsgate
Little Sutton
Cawthorpe
Guthram Gowt
Romany
B1165
Bourne
Little London
Fen End
Ayscoughfee Hall
B1168
Clark's Hill
B1390
Sutton Crosses
A151
Twenty
Cuckoo Bridge
A1101
Bourne
Bourne Eau
B1193
B1123
Weston Hills
B1357
Entertainment
Whaplode St. Catherine
Tydd St. Mary
Tydd Gote
A6121
B1172
Cowbit
B1165
Lound
Northorpe
A15
A1073
North Drove Drain
Moulton Chapel
Holbeach St. Johns
Sutton St. James
Four Anchor
Toft
Thurlby
Peak Hill
Moulton Eaugate
Fenland
Four Gotes
Manthorpe
Obthorpe
Deeping Fen
Tydd St. Giles
R. Glen
Deeping St. Nicholas
A16
Brotherhouse Bar
B1168
Tydd St. Giles Fen
Thetford
Newton
Baston
Hop Pole
Cross Drain
South Drove Drain
Whaplode Drove
Holbeach Drove
Fitton End
Wilsthorpe
Braceborough
Great Postland
Sutton St. Edmund
West Walton
Langtoft
Greatford
Leverington
Gorefield
Market Deeping
B1525
Crowland
B1166
Shepeau Stow
Gedney Hill
Towngate
Barholm
Frognall
Dowsdale
Church End
Throckenholt
B1169
WISBECH
Peckover House NT
Triangular Bridge
Church
North Fen
B1166
Cranmore
Deeping Gate
Deeping St. James
West Deeping
Nene Terrace
Sutton St. Edmund's Common
Parson Drove
Wisbech St. Mary
A16
R. Welland
B1167
Murrow
Bunker's Hill
Elm
Uffington
Tallington
Maxey
Northborough
Wryde Croft
Etton
Peakirk
B1443
A1073
B1040
Morris Fen
Heritage Centre
Tholomas Drove
Bainton
B1443
Glinton
Newborough
B1443
Rogue's Alley
B1187
A47
Begdale
Ashton
A15
Barnack
Hills & Holes
Ufford
Helpston
BEDFORD (NORTH LEVEL)
LEVEL
Thorney Toll
Eye Green
Thorney
Abbey Church
Guyhirn Gull
Guyhirn
Friday Bridge
B1101
A1
Southorpe
Southey Wood
Werrington
Gunthorpe
Walton
A15
Eye
A47
Ring's End
Coldham
Laddus
Marholm
Bretton
R. Nene
A141
Sacrewell Farm
Sacrewell Watermill
Castor Hanglands
New England
Dogsthorpe
Newark
Stone Bridge Corner
B1040
Upton
Chainbridge
A47
A15
Millfield
Longthorpe
Westwood
64
Nene Washes
Eldernell
Norwoodside
Euximoor
Stamford
Stibbington
Ailsworth
PETERBOROUGH
A605
West Fen
Castor
Ferry Mdws
Woodston
Coates
Westry
Sutton
Nene Valley Railway
A1139
West End
MARCH
Wansford
Water Newton
Orton
Oldeamere
Binnimoor Fen
Yarwell
Sibson
Wistow
Alwalton
Peterborough Airport (Sibson)
Longueville
Orton
Old Fletton
Stanground
Eastrea
Whittlesey
B671

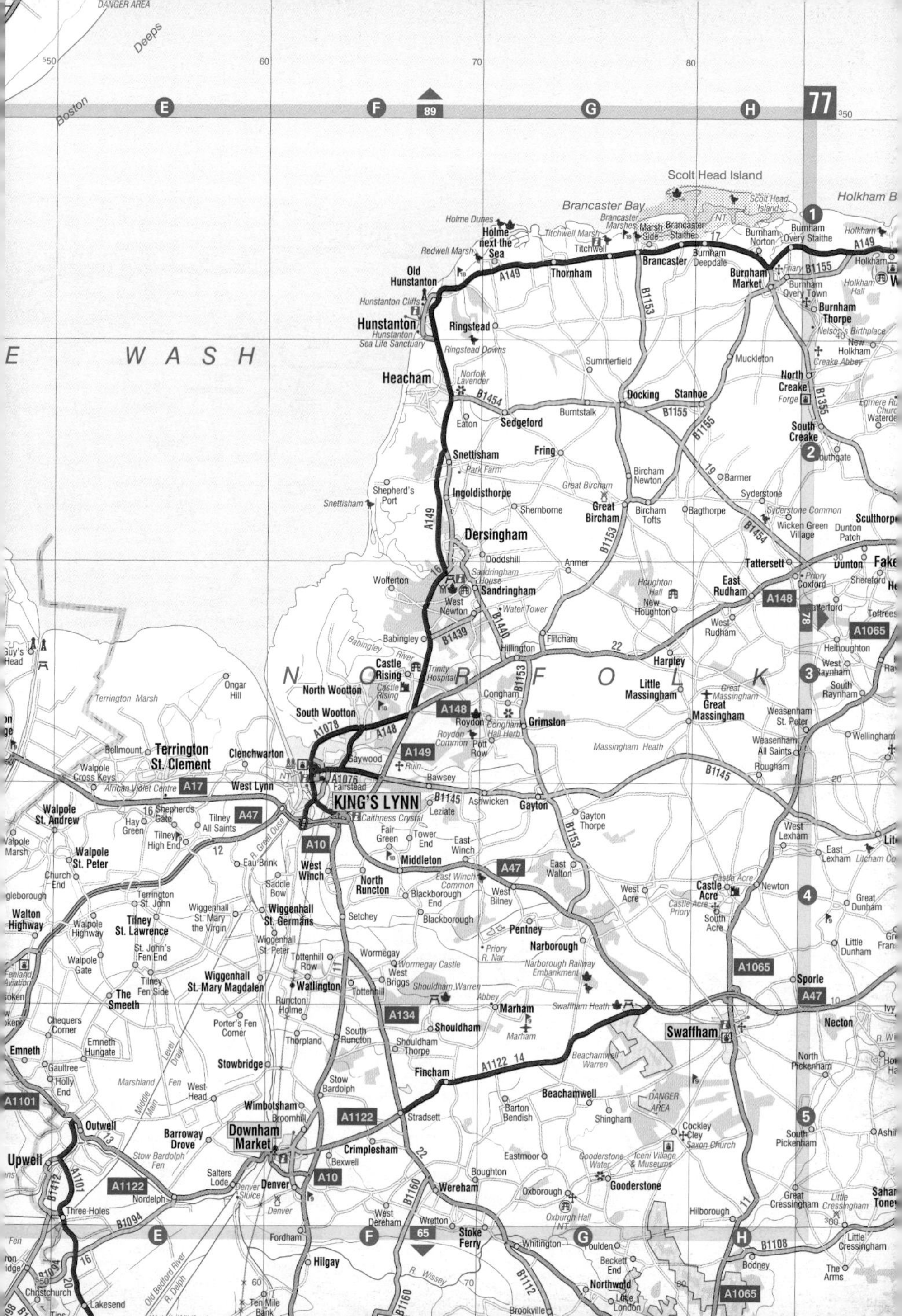
DANGER AREA
Deeps
Boston
E
F
89
G
H
550
60
70
80
350
Scolt Head Island
Brancaster Bay
Holkham B
Scolt Head Island
1
Holme Dunes
Holme next the Sea
Brancaster Marshes
Marsh Side
Brancaster Staithe
Titchwell Marsh
Titchwell
Burnham Norton
Burnham Overy Staithe
Holkham
A149
Redwell Marsh
Brancaster
Burnham Deepdale
17
Holkham
Old Hunstanton
Thornham
Burnham Market
Friary
B1155
Burnham Overy Town
Holkham Hall
Hunstanton Cliffs
Burnham Thorpe
Hunstanton
Hunstanton Sea Life Sanctuary
Ringstead
Ringstead Downs
B1153
Nelson's Birthplace
New Holkham
Creake Abbey
W A S H
Summerfield
Muckleton
North Creake
Forge
Heacham
Norfolk Lavender
B1454
Docking
Stanhoe
B1355
Burntstalk
B1155
Eaton
Sedgeford
South Creake
2
Southgate
Snettisham
Fring
Park Farm
Bircham Newton
Barmer
19
Great Bircham
Shepherd's Port
Snettisham
Ingoldisthorpe
Syderstone
Shernborne
Great Bircham
Bircham Tofts
Bagthorpe
Syderstone Common
Wicken Green Village
Dunton Patch
Sculthorpe
A149
Dersingham
B1454
B1153
Doddshill
Anmer
Tattersett
Dunton
Fake
Sandringham House
Houghton Hall
Priory
Coxford
Shereford
Wolferton
16
Sandringham
East Rudham
West Newton
New Houghton
A148
Tatterford
Toftrees
78
Water Tower
B1440
West Rudham
A1065
Babingley
B1439
Flitcham
Hillington
22
Helhoughton
Babingley River
Trinity Hospital
Harpley
West Raynham
Guy's Head
Castle Rising
3
N O R F O L K
Ongar Hill
North Wootton
Castle Rising
B1153
Little Massingham
Great Massingham
South Raynham
Terrington Marsh
South Wootton
A148
Congham
Great Massingham
Weasenham St. Peter
A1078
Roydon
Grimston
Congham Hall Herbs
Roydon Common
Pott Row
Wellingham
Bellmount
Terrington St. Clement
A148
Weasenham All Saints
Clenchwarton
Massingham Heath
Walpole Cross Keys
Gaywood
A149
Ruin
Rougham
African Violet Centre
A17
NT
A1076
Bawsey
B1145
West Lynn
Fairstead
20
KING'S LYNN
B1145
Ashwicken
Gayton
Walpole St. Andrew
16
Shepherds Gate
A47
Tilney All Saints
Leziate
Caithness Crystal
B1153
Gayton Thorpe
West Lexham
Hay Green
Tilney High End
Fair Green
Tower End
East Winch
Walpole Marsh
12
R. Great Ouse
A10
Walpole St. Peter
Middleton
East Lexham
Litcham
Eau Brink
West Winch
A47
East Walton
Church End
Saddle Bow
North Runcton
East Winch Common
Castle Acre
Newton
Terrington St. John
Blackborough End
West Bilney
West Acre
Castle Acre
4
Great Dunham
Walton Highway
Wiggenhall St. Mary the Virgin
Wiggenhall St. Germans
Setchey
Blackborough
Castle Acre Priory
South Acre
Walpole Highway
Tilney St. Lawrence
Wiggenhall St. Peter
Pentney
Priory
R. Nar
Narborough
Little Dunham
Walpole Gate
St. John's Fen End
Tottenhill Row
Wormegay
Wormegay Castle
Narborough Railway Embankment
A1065
Sporle
Tilney Fen Side
Wiggenhall St. Mary Magdalen
West Briggs
Wallington
11
Tottenhill
Shouldham Warren
Abbey
A47
The Smeeth
Runcton Holme
A134
Marham
Swaffham Heath
10
Chequers Corner
Porter's Fen Corner
Shouldham
Marham
Swaffham
Necton
Emneth Hungate
Thorpland
South Runcton
Shouldham Thorpe
Emneth
Stowbridge
Beachamwell Warren
Gaultree
Fincham
A1122
14
North Pickenham
Holly End
Marshland
Fen
West Head
Middle Level Main Drain
Stow Bardolph
Beachamwell
A1101
Wimbotsham
Broomhill
A1122
Stradsett
Barton Bendish
DANGER AREA
Shingham
5
Outwell
13
Barroway Drove
Downham Market
Crimplesham
Cockley Cley
Saxon Church
South Pickenham
Upwell
Stow Bardolph Fen
Bexwell
22
Eastmoor
Gooderstone Water
Iceni Village & Museums
A1101
A1122
Salters Lode
Denver
A10
Boughton
Gooderstone
B1412
Nordelph
Denver Sluice
Denver
B1160
Wereham
Oxborough
Oxburgh Hall
Hilborough
Great Cressingham
Little Cressingham
Three Holes
B1094
West Dereham
Wretton
NT
11
Fen
E
Fordham
F
65
Stoke Ferry
Whittington
G
Foulden
H
B1108
Little Cressingham
16
Beckett End
Bodney
Hilgay
R. Wissey
The Arms
B1094
Old Bedford River
R. Delph
60
70
B1160
B1112
Northwold
80
Little London
A1065
Christchurch
Lakesend
Ten Mile Bank
Brookville

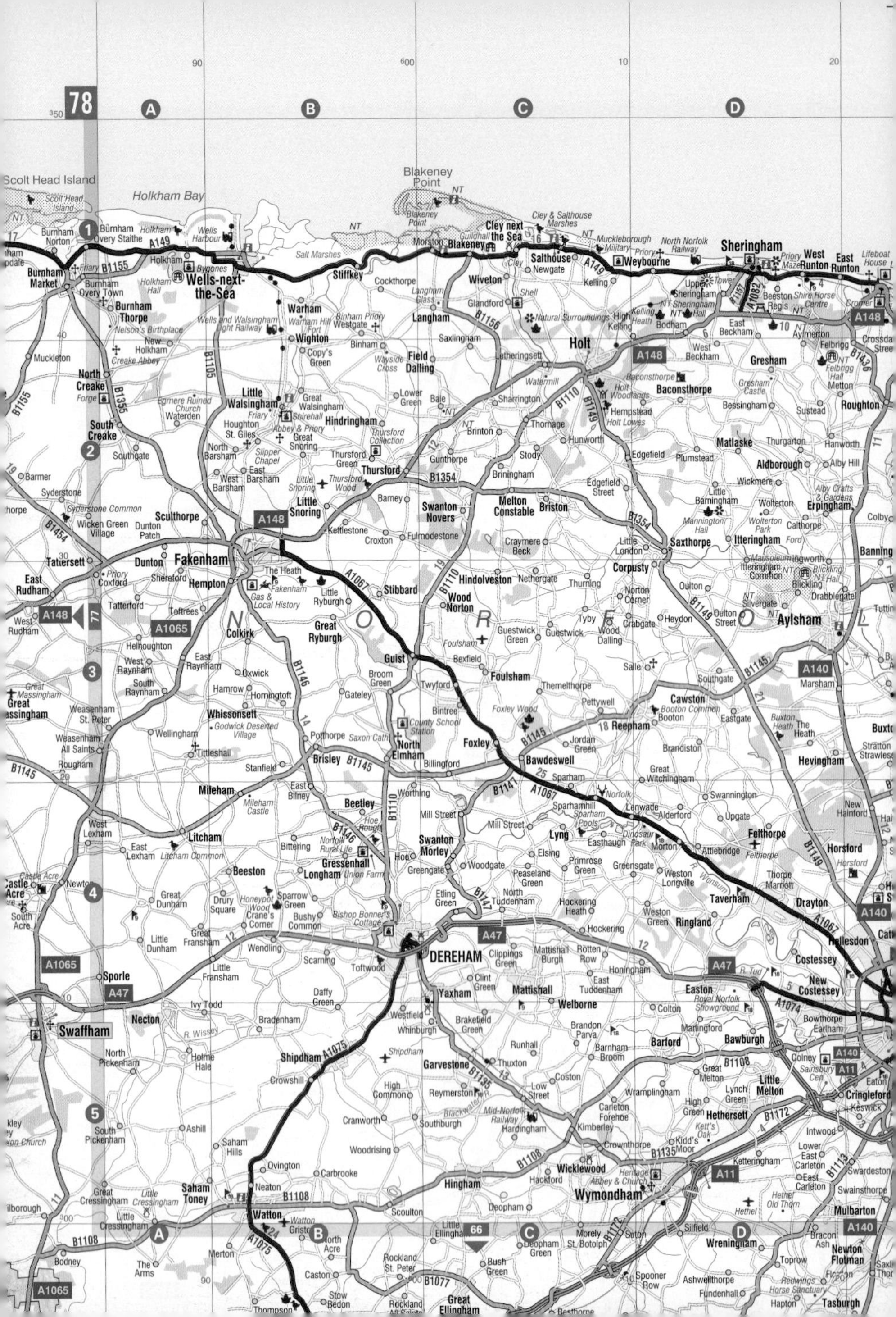
78
A
B
C
D
1
2
3
4
5
90
600
10
20
Scolt Head Island
Holkham Bay
Blakeney Point
Burnham Norton
Burnham Overy Staithe
Burnham Market
Burnham Overy Town
Burnham Thorpe
Nelson's Birthplace
Holkham
Holkham Hall
Wells Harbour
Wells-next-the-Sea
Bygones
Salt Marshes
Stiffkey
Morston
Blakeney
Cley next the Sea
Cley & Salthouse Marshes
Salthouse
Newgate
Muckleborough Military
Weybourne
North Norfolk Railway
Kelling
Sheringham
Upper Sheringham
Sheringham Hall
Beeston Regis
West Runton
East Runton
Shire Horse Centre
Cromer
Lifeboat House
Cockthorpe
Langham Glass
Langham
Wiveton
Glandford
Shell
Natural Surroundings
High Kelling
Kelling Heath
Bodham
East Beckham
West Beckham
Aylmerton
Felbrigg
Felbrigg Hall
Crossdale Street
Warham
Warham Hill Fort
Binham Priory
Westgate
Wells and Walsingham Light Railway
Wighton
Copy's Green
Binham
Wayside Cross
Field Dalling
Saxlingham
Letheringsett
Holt
Watermill
Gresham
Gresham Castle
Metton
Roughton
New Holkham
Creake Abbey
Muckleton
North Creake
Forge
South Creake
Southgate
Egmere Ruined Church
Waterden
Little Walsingham
Great Walsingham
Friary
Shirehall
Abbey & Priory
Houghton St. Giles
Slipper Chapel
North Barsham
West Barsham
East Barsham
Great Snoring
Little Snoring
Hindringham
Thursford Collection
Thursford Green
Thursford
Thursford Wood
Lower Green
Bale
Sharrington
Thornage
Brinton
Gunthorpe
Briningham
Stody
Hunworth
Holt Woodlands
Hempstead
Holt Lowes
Baconsthorpe
Bessingham
Sustead
Matlaske
Thurgarton
Hanworth
Plumstead
Edgefield
Edgefield Street
Aldborough
Alby Hill
Alby Crafts & Gardens
Wickmere
Barmer
Syderstone
Syderstone Common
Wicken Green Village
Sculthorpe
Dunton Patch
Barney
Swanton Novers
Melton Constable
Briston
Little Barningham
Mannington Hall
Wolterton
Wolterton Park
Erpingham
Calthorpe
Kettlestone
Croxton
Fulmodestone
Craymere Beck
Little London
Saxthorpe
Itteringham
Ford
Colby
Tattersett
Dunton
Fakenham
Priory
Coxford
Shereford
Hempton
The Heath
Fakenham
Gas & Local History
Stibbard
Little Ryburgh
Hindolveston
Nethergate
Thurning
Corpusty
Norton Corner
Mausoleum
Itteringham Common
Ingworth
Blickling
Blickling Hall
Drabblegate
Banningham
East Rudham
West Rudham
Tatterford
Toftrees
Colkirk
Great Ryburgh
Wood Norton
Guestwick Green
Guestwick
Tyby
Wood Dalling
Crabgate
Heydon
Oulton
Oulton Street
Silvergate
Aylsham
Helhoughton
West Raynham
East Raynham
South Raynham
Oxwick
Hamrow
Horningtoft
Guist
Foulsham
Bexfield
Broom Green
Twyford
Themelthorpe
Salle
Southgate
Marsham
Great Massingham
Weasenham St. Peter
Weasenham All Saints
Whissonsett
Godwick Deserted Village
Wellingham
Tittleshall
Gateley
Potthorpe
Saxon Cath
County School Station
North Elmham
Bintree
Foxley Wood
Foxley
Pettywell
Cawston
Booton Common
Booton
Eastgate
Reepham
Jordan Green
Brandiston
Buxton Heath
The Heath
Buxton
Stratton Strawless
Hevingham
Rougham
Stanfield
Brisley
Billingford
Bawdeswell
Sparham
Norfolk
Great Witchingham
Swannington
Mileham
Mileham Castle
East Bilney
Beetley
Worthing
Mill Street
Sparhamhill
Sparham Pools
Lenwade
Alderford
Upgate
New Hainford
West Lexham
Litcham
Litcham Common
East Lexham
Bittering
Norfolk Rural Life
Hoe Rough
Swanton Morley
Hoe
Mill Street
Lyng
Easthaugh
Dinosaur Park
Morton
Attlebridge
Felthorpe
Horsford
Castle Acre
Newton
South Acre
Beeston
Longham
Gressenhall
Union Farm
Greengate
Woodgate
Elsing
Primrose Green
Peaseland Green
Greensgate
Weston Longville
R. Wensum
Thorpe Marriott
Great Dunham
Drury Square
Honeypot Wood
Crane's Corner
Sparrow Green
Bushy Common
Bishop Bonner's Cottage
Etling Green
North Tuddenham
Hockering Heath
Weston Green
Ringland
Taverham
Drayton
Little Dunham
Great Fransham
Wendling
Scarning
Toftwood
DEREHAM
Clippings Green
Mattishall Burgh
Rotten Row
Hockering
Honingham
Hellesdon
Costessey
Sporle
Little Fransham
Daffy Green
Clint Green
Yaxham
Mattishall
East Tuddenham
Easton
R. Tud
Royal Norfolk Showground
New Costessey
Bowthorpe
Earlham
Swaffham
Necton
Ivy Todd
Bradenham
R. Wissey
Westfield
Whinburgh
Brakefield Green
Welborne
Colton
Marlingford
Brandon Parva
Bawburgh
North Pickenham
Holme Hale
Shipdham
Garvestone
Thuxton
Runhall
Barnham Broom
Barford
Colney
Sainsbury Cen
Crowshill
High Common
Reymerston
Low Street
Coston
Great Melton
Little Melton
Eaton
Cringleford
Keswick
South Pickenham
Ashill
Cranworth
Southburgh
Blackwater
Mid-Norfolk Railway
Hardingham
Carleton Forehoe
Wramplingham
Lynch Green
High Green
Hethersett
Kett's Oak
Intwood
Saxon Church
Saham Hills
Woodrising
Kimberley
Crownthorpe
Kidd's Moor
Lower East Carleton
Ovington
Carbrooke
Hingham
Hackford
Wicklewood
Heritage Abbey & Church
Wymondham
Ketteringham
East Carleton
Swardeston
Great Cressingham
Little Cressingham
Saham Toney
Neaton
Deopham
Hethel
Hethel Old Thorn
Swainsthorpe
Mulbarton
Little Cressingham
Watton
Watton
Griston
Scoulton
Little Ellingham
66
Deopham Green
Morley St. Botolph
Suton
Silfield
Wreningham
Bracon Ash
Newton Flotman
Merton
North Acre
Rockland St. Peter
Bush Green
Spooner Row
Ashwellthorpe
Toprow
Redwings Horse Sanctuary
Fundenhall
Flordon
Hapton
Tasburgh
Bodney
The Arms
Caston
Stow Bedon
Rockland All Saints
Great Ellingham
Besthorpe
Thompson
NT
N O R F O L
A149
A148
A1065
A1067
A47
A1075
A140
A11
A1074
A1082
B1155
B1355
B1105
B1156
B1110
B1149
B1354
B1146
B1145
B1147
B1135
B1108
B1172
B1113
B1436
B1077
B1454
77
350
300

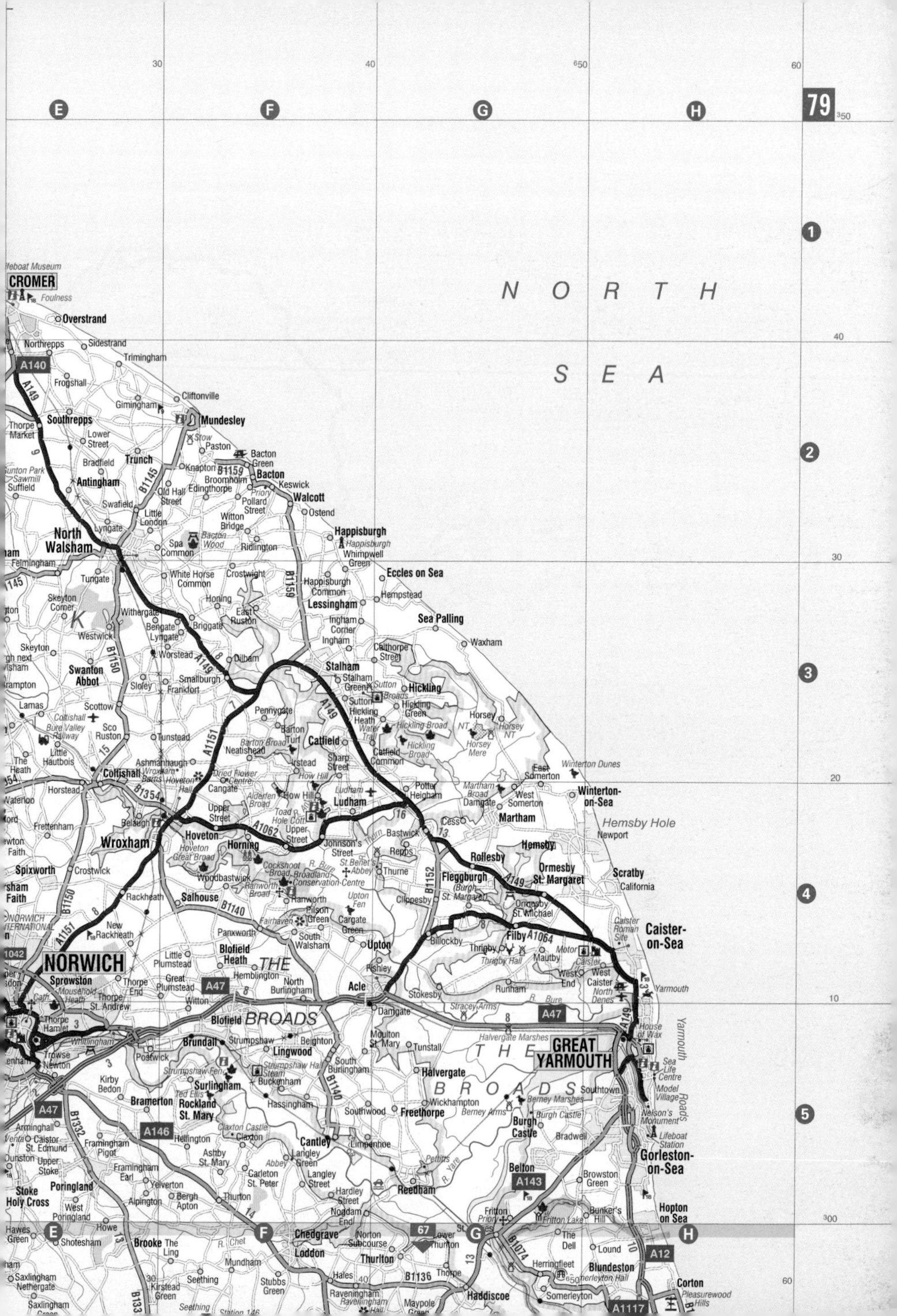
NORTH SEA
CROMER
Overstrand
Northrepps
Sidestrand
Trimingham
A140
Frogshall
Cliftonville
Gimingham
Mundesley
Southrepps
Thorpe Market
Lower Street
Stow
Paston
Bacton Green
Bradfield
Trunch
Knapton
B1159
Bacton
Gunton Park Sawmill
Suffield
Antingham
B1145
Old Hall Street
Broomholm
Edingthorpe
Keswick
Walcott
Ostend
Swafield
Pollard Street
Little London
Witton Bridge
North Walsham
Lyngate
Bacton Wood
Spa Common
Ridlington
Happisburgh
Whimpwell Green
Felmingham
Tungate
White Horse Common
Crostwight
Eccles on Sea
Happisburgh Common
Hempstead
Lessingham
Skeyton Corner
Honing
East Ruston
Sea Palling
Withergate
Bengate
Briggate
Ingham Corner
Ingham
Westwick
Lyngate
Waxham
Skeyton
Worstead
A149
Dilham
Calthorpe Street
Swanton Abbot
B1150
Smallburgh
Stalham
Stalham Green
Sloley
Frankfort
Sutton Broads
Hickling
Scottow
Sutton
Hickling Heath
Hickling Green
Lamas
Coltishall
Bure Valley Railway
Sco Ruston
Pennygate
Barton Turf
Hickling Broad
Horsey
Horsey NT
Horsey Mere
Tunstead
A1151
Catfield
Little Hautbois
Neatishead
Barton Broad
Catfield Common
Winterton Dunes
The Heath
Coltishall
Ashmanhaugh
Irstead
Sharp Street
East Somerton
Wroxham Barns
Dried Flower Centre
How Hill
Potter Heigham
Martham Broad
West Somerton
Winterton-on-Sea
Horstead
Cangate
Hoveton Hall
B1354
Ludham
Damgate
Upper Street
Martham
Hemsby Hole
Belaugh
Toad Hole Cott.
Cess
Newport
Frettenham
A1062
Bastwick
Wroxham
Hoveton
Horning
Upper Street
Hemsby
Johnson's Street
Repps
Rollesby
Spixworth
Crostwick
Hoveton Great Broad
Cockshoot Broad
St. Benet's Abbey
Thurne
Ormesby St. Margaret
Scratby
California
Woodbastwick
Broadland Conservation Centre
B1152
Fleggburgh
Ranworth Broad
Ranworth
Clippesby
Ormesby St. Michael
Rackheath
Salhouse
Upton Fen
Caister Roman Site
Caister-on-Sea
B1140
Pilson Green
Cargate Green
Fairhaven
New Rackheath
Panxworth
South Walsham
Billockby
Filby
A1064
Thrigby
Thrigby Hall
Mautby
Motor Museum
Caister Castle
West End
West Caister
NORWICH
Blofield Heath
THE BROADS
Upton
Little Plumstead
Sprowston
Thorpe End
Great Plumstead
Hemblington
North Burlingham
Pilshley
Acle
Stokesby
Runham
North Denes
Yarmouth
A47
Mousehold Heath
Thorpe St. Andrew
Witton
Damgate
R. Bure
Stracey Arms
Thorpe Hamlet
Blofield
Moulton St. Mary
Tunstall
Halvergate Marshes
GREAT YARMOUTH
House of Wax
Yarmouth Roads
Trowse Newton
Whittlingham
Brundall
Strumpshaw
Beighton
Lingwood
South Burlingham
Halvergate
Sea Life Centre
Model Village
Postwick
Strumpshaw Fen
Strumpshaw Hall Steam Museum
Buckenham
Southtown
Kirby Bedon
Surlingham
Ted Ellis
Hassingham
B1140
Wickhampton
Berney Marshes
Nelson's Monument
Bramerton
Rockland St. Mary
Southwood
Freethorpe
Berney Arms
Burgh Castle
Lifeboat Station
Arminghall
B1332
Claxton Castle
Claxton
Cantley
Limpenhoe
Bradwell
Caistor St. Edmund
A146
Hellington
Langley Green
Gorleston-on-Sea
Framingham Pigot
Ashby St. Mary
Abbey
Dunston
Upper Stoke
Framingham Earl
Carleton St. Peter
Langley Street
Pettitts
R. Yare
Belton
Browston Green
Stoke Holy Cross
Poringland
Yelverton
Bergh Apton
Reedham
A143
Hardley Street
Alpington
Thurton
West Poringland
Bunker's Hill
Hopton on Sea
Nogdam End
Fritton Priory
Fritton Lake
Hawes Green
Howe
Shotesham
Brooke
The Ling
Chedgrave
Norton Subcourse
Lower Thurlton
Loddon
Thurlton
The Dell
Lound
A12
R. Chet
B1074
Mundham
Herringfleet
Blundeston
Saxlingham Nethergate
Seething
Kirstead Green
Stubbs Green
Hales
B1136
Thorpe
Haddiscoe
Somerleyton Hall
Corton
Pleasurewood Hills
Saxlingham Green
Raveningham
Raveningham Hall
Maypole Green
Somerleyton
A1117

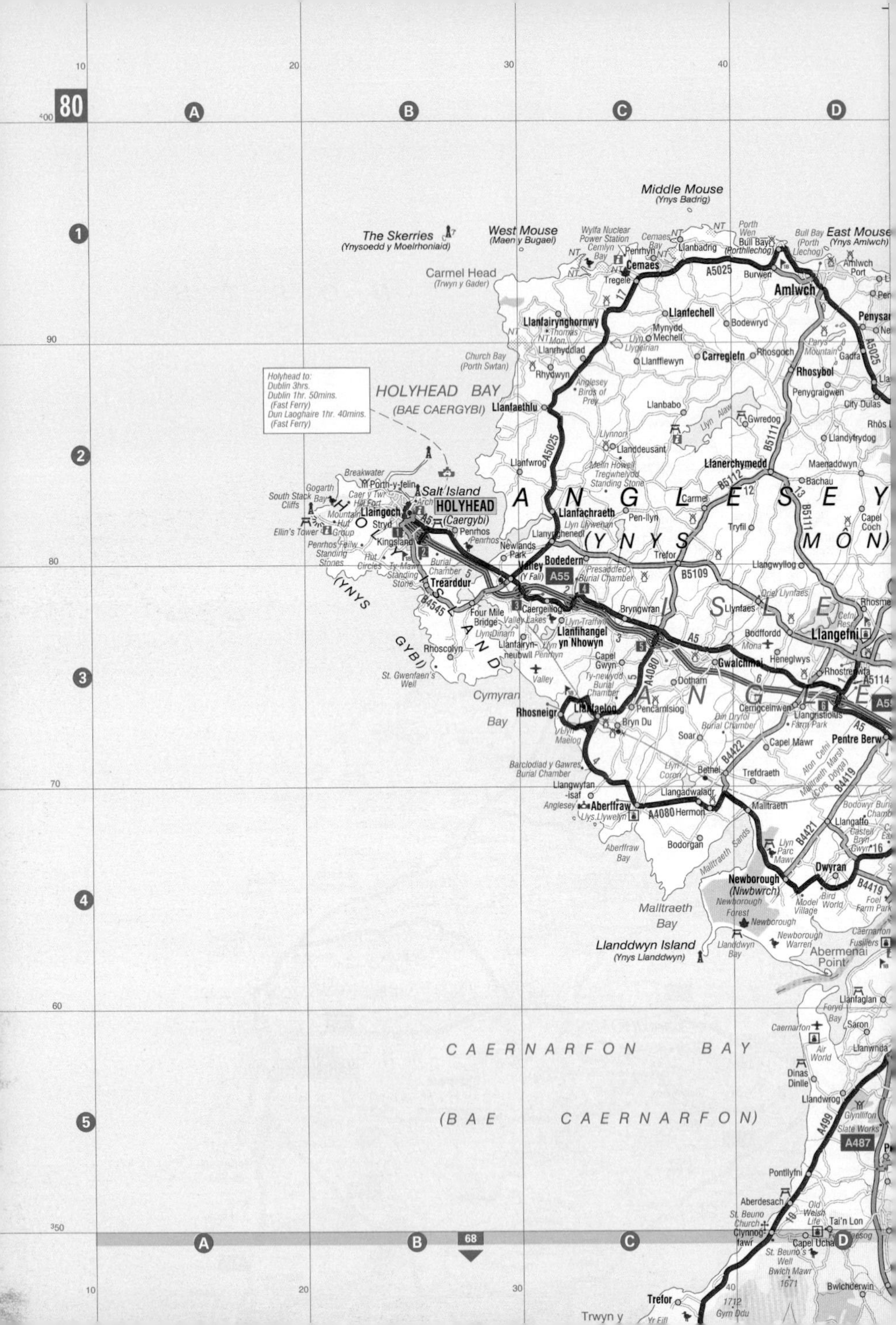

Middle Mouse
(Ynys Badrig)
The Skerries
(Ynysoedd y Moelrhoniaid)
West Mouse
(Maen y Bugael)
East Mouse
(Ynys Amlwch)
Wylfa Nuclear Power Station
Cemlyn Bay
Cemaes Bay
Cemaes
Tregele
Llanbadrig
Porth Wen
Bull Bay
(Porthllechog)
Bull Bay (Porth Llechog)
Burwen
Amlwch
Amlwch Port
Penysarn
A5025
Carmel Head
(Trwyn y Gader)
Llanfairynghornwy
Llanfechell
Mynydd Mechell
Bodewryd
Llyn Llygeirian
Llanfflewyn
Carreglefn
Rhosgoch
Parys Mountain
Rhosybol
Church Bay
(Porth Swtan)
Llanrhyddlad
Rhydwyn
Holyhead to:
Dublin 3hrs.
Dublin 1hr. 50mins.
(Fast Ferry)
Dun Laoghaire 1hr. 40mins.
(Fast Ferry)
HOLYHEAD BAY
(BAE CAERGYBI)
Llanfaethlu
Anglesey Birds of Prey
Llanbabo
Llyn Alaw
Gwredog
Penygraigwen
City Dulas
Llynnon
Llanddeusant
Melin Howell
Tregwhelydd Standing Stone
Llanfwrog
A5025
B5111
B5112
Llanerchymedd
Llandyfrydog
Maenaddwyn
Bachau
Breakwater
Porth-y-felin
Salt Island
Gogarth Bay
South Stack Cliffs
Caer y Twr Hill Fort
Holyhead Mountain Hut Group
Ellin's Tower
Penrhos Feilw Standing Stones
Llaingoch
Stryd
HOLYHEAD
(Caergybi)
Penrhos
Kingsland
ANGLESEY
(YNYS MÔN)
Llanfachraeth
Llyn Llywenan
Pen-llyn
Carmel
Tryfil
Capel Coch
Llanynghenedl
Newlands Park
Bodedern
Trefor
B5109
Llangwyllog
Hut Circles
Ty-Mawr Standing Stone
Burial Chamber
Valley
(Y Fali)
A55
Presaddfed Burial Chamber
Trearddur
HOLY ISLAND
(YNYS GYBI)
B4545
Four Mile Bridge
Valley Lakes
Caergeiliog
Llyn Traffwll
Bryngwran
Llynfaes
Llyn Dinam
Llanfihangel yn Nhowyn
Llanfairyn-neubwll
Penrhyn
Rhoscolyn
St. Gwenfaen's Well
Capel Gwyn
Ty-newydd Burial Chamber
A5
A4080
Gwalchmai
Bodffordd
Mona
Heneglwys
Llangefni
Rhosmeirch
Rhostrehwfa
A5114
Cymyran Bay
Rhosneigr
Llanfaelog
Llyn Maelog
Pencarnisiog
Bryn Du
Dotham
Cerrigceinwen
Llangristiolus
Din Dryfol Burial Chamber
Soar
Capel Mawr
Pentre Berw
Barclodiad y Gawres Burial Chamber
Llyn Coron
Bethel
B4422
Trefdraeth
Malltraeth Marsh
(Cors Ddyga)
Afon Cefni
B4419
Llangwyfan-isaf
Anglesey
Aberffraw
Llys Llywelyn
A4080
Hermon
Llangadwaladr
Malltraeth
Llangaffo
Bodorgan
Aberffraw Bay
Malltraeth Sands
Llyn Parc Mawr
B4421
Newborough
(Niwbwrch)
Dwyran
Newborough Forest
Model Village
Bird World
Foel Farm Park
B4419
Malltraeth Bay
Llanddwyn Island
(Ynys Llanddwyn)
Llanddwyn Bay
Newborough Warren
Caernarfon Fusiliers
Abermenai Point
Llanfaglan
Foryd Bay
Saron
Caernarfon
Air World
Llanwnda
CAERNARFON BAY
(BAE CAERNARFON)
Dinas Dinlle
Llandwrog
Glynllifon
Slate Works
A499
A487
Pontllyfni
Aberdesach
St. Beuno Church
Clynnog-fawr
Old Welsh Life
Tal'n Lon
Capel Uchaf
St. Beuno's Well
Bwlch Mawr
1671
Bwlchderwin
1712
Gyrn Ddu
Trefor
Trwyn y
Yr Eifl
A
B
C
D
1
2
3
4
5
10
20
30
40
400
90
80
70
60
350
68

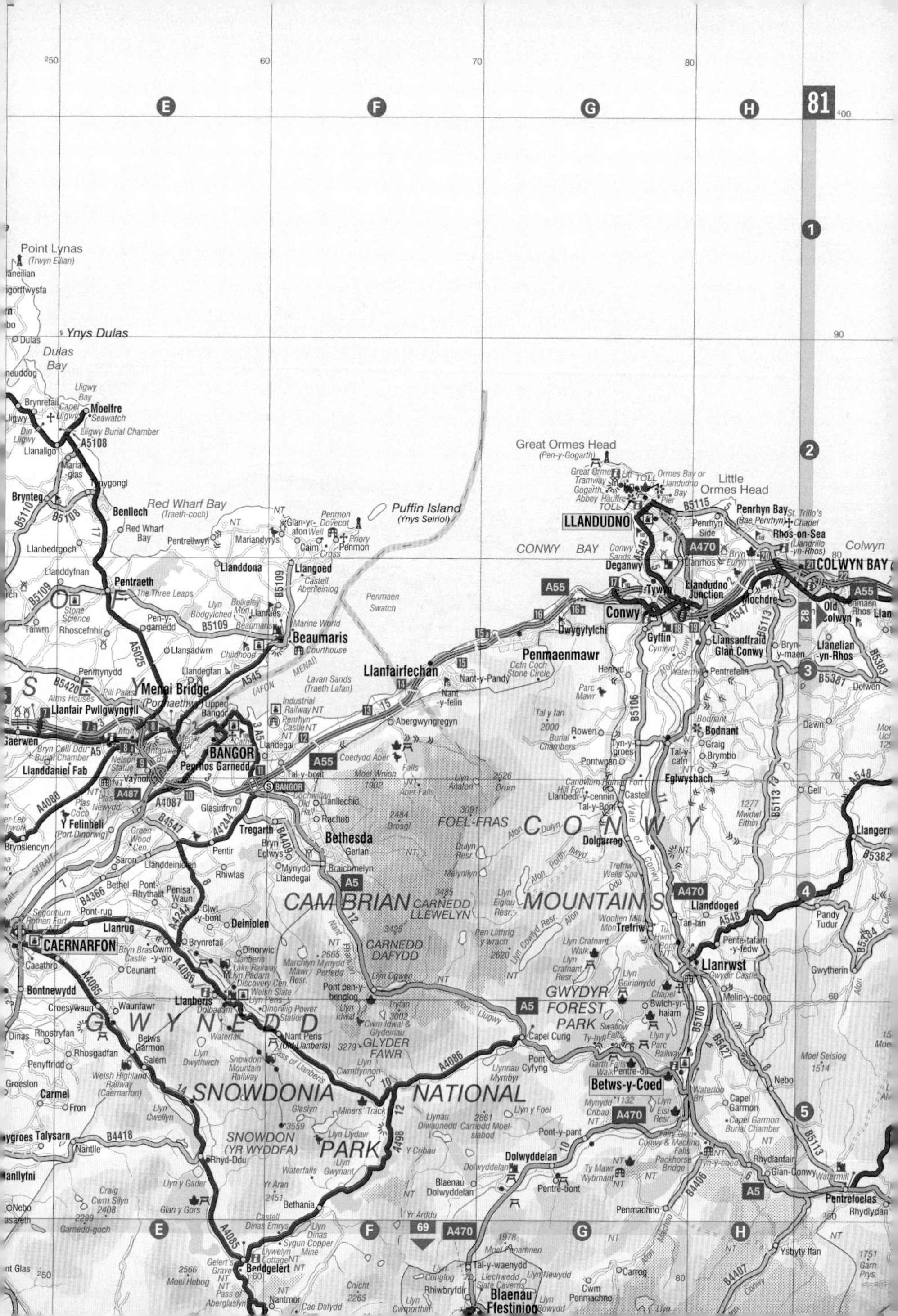
250
60
70
80
E
F
G
H
400
1
2
3
4
5
90
Point Lynas
(Trwyn Eilian)
Ynys Dulas
Dulas
Dulas Bay
Lligwy Bay
Brynrefail
Moelfre
Seawatch
Lligwy Burial Chamber
A5108
Llanallgo
Brynteg
Benllech
Red Wharf Bay
(Traeth-coch)
Red Wharf Bay
Pentrellwyn
Llanbedrgoch
Llanddyfnan
Pentraeth
The Three Leaps
Llanddona
Puffin Island
(Ynys Seiriol)
Penmon
Penmon Dovecot
Priory
Glan-yr-afon
Mariandyrys
Llangoed
Castell Aberlleiniog
Penmaen Swatch
B5109
Stone Science
Talwrn
Rhoscefnhir
Pen-y-garnedd
Llansadwrn
Beaumaris
Courthouse
Marine World
Childhood
A5025
Penmynydd
B5420
Pili Palas
Menai Bridge
(Porthaethwy)
Llanfair Pwllgwyngyll
Alms Houses
Llandegfan
A545
Upper Bangor
BANGOR
Penrhyn Castle NT
Industrial Railway NT
Llandegai
Gaerwen
Bryn Celli Ddu Burial Chamber
Llanddaniel Fab
Nelson Statue
Vaynol
Penrhos Garnedd
A487
A4080
A4087
Felinheli
(Port Dinorwig)
Plas Newydd
Brynsiencyn
Glasinfryn
Green Wood Cen.
B4547
A4244
Tregarth
Pentir
Llanddeiniolen
Saron
Rhiwlas
Bethel
B4366
Pont-Rhythallt
Penisa'r Waun
Clwt-y-bont
Pont-rug
Deiniolen
Segontium Roman Fort
CAERNARFON
Llanrug
Brynrefail
Dinorwic
Bryn Bras Castle
Cwm-y-glo
Caeathro
Ceunant
Llanberis Lake Railway
Llyn Padarn
Discovery Cen.
Welsh Slate
Bontnewydd
A4085
A4086
Llanberis
Dolbadarn
Dinorwig Power Station
Croesywaun
Waunfawr
GWYNEDD
Rhostryfan
Dinas
Betws Garmon
Rhosgadfan
Salem
Llyn Dwythwch
Waterfall
Nant Peris
(Old Llanberis)
Pass of Llanberis
Penyffridd
Welsh Highland Railway
(Caernarfon)
Snowdon Mountain Railway
SNOWDONIA
NATIONAL
PARK
Groeslon
Carmel
Fron
Llyn Cwellyn
Glaslyn
Miners' Track
3559
SNOWDON
(YR WYDDFA)
Llyn Llydaw
Talysarn
B4418
Nantlle
Rhyd-Ddu
Llyn y Gader
Craig Cwm Silyn
2408
Glan y Gors
Yr Aran
2451
Waterfalls
Llyn Gwynant
Bethania
A4498
Y Cribau
Nebo
2299
Garnedd-goch
Castell Dinas Emrys
Llyn Dinas
Sygun Copper Mine
Llywelyn Cottage NT
Beddgelert
Gelert's Grave
2566
Moel Hebog
Pass of Aberglaslyn
Nantmor
Cae Dafydd
Cnicht
2265
Llanfairfechan
Lavan Sands
(Traeth Lafan)
A55
Coedydd Aber
Abergwyngregyn
Nant-y-Pandy
Nant-y-felin
Aber Falls
Moel Wnion
1902
Llanllechid
Rachub
Bethesda
Gerlan
Bryn Eglwys
B4409
Mynydd Llandegai
Braichmelyn
A5
2484
Drosgl
3091
FOEL-FRAS
2526
Drum
Llyn Anafon
CAMBRIAN
CARNEDD LLEWELYN
3485
MOUNTAINS
3425
CARNEDD DAFYDD
Marchlyn Mawr Resr.
Mynydd Perfedd
2665
Pont pen-y-benglog
Llyn Ogwen
Llyn Idwal
Tryfan
3002
Cwm Idwal & Glyderiau
3279
GLYDER FAWR
Llyn Cwmffynnon
A4086
Capel Curig
Pont Cyfyng
Llynnau Mymbyr
Llynau Diwaunedd
2861
Carnedd Moel-siabod
Llyn y Foel
Dolwyddelan
Blaenau Dolwyddelan
Yr Arddu
69
A470
1978
Moel Penamnen
Tal-y-waenydd
Llyn Conglog
Llechwedd Slate Caverns
Llyn Newydd
Rhiwbryfdir
Blaenau Ffestiniog
Llyn Cwmorthin
Cwm Penmachno
Carrog
Penmaenmawr
Cefn Coch Stone Circle
Dwygyfylchi
Great Ormes Head
(Pen-y-Gogarth)
Great Orme Tramway
Gogarth Abbey
Haulfre
Ormes Bay or Llandudno Bay
Pier
TOLL
Little Ormes Head
LLANDUDNO
CONWY BAY
Conwy Sands
Deganwy
A546
B5115
Penrhyn Bay
(Bae Penrhyn)
St. Trillo's Chapel
Penrhyn Side
Rhos-on-Sea
(Llandrillo-yn-Rhos)
A470
Bryn Euryn
Llanrhos
COLWYN BAY
Colwyn
Conwy
Tywyn
Llandudno Junction
Mochdre
Old Colwyn
Penmaen Rhos
Gyffin
Cymryd
Afon Conwy
A547
Llansanffraid Glan Conwy
Bryn-y-maen
Llanelian-yn-Rhos
B5113
B5383
B5381
Dolwen
Henryd
Parc Mawr
Pentrefelin
Tal y fan
2000
Burial Chambers
Rowen
B5106
Tyn-y-groes
Bodnant
Graig
Brymbo
Dawn
Pontwgan
Tal-y-cafn
Eglwysbach
Canovium Roman Fort
Hill Fort
Llanbedr-y-cennin
Tal-y-Bont
Castell
Vale of Conwy
1277
Mwdwl Eithin
Gell
A548
Llangernyw
CONWY
Afon Dulyn
Dulyn Resr.
Melynllyn
Dolgarrog
Afon Porth-llwyd
Trefriw Wells Spa
Llyn Eigiau Resr.
Afon Ddu
Llyn Cowlyd Resr.
Pen Llithrig y wrach
2620
Woollen Mill
Trefriw
Llanddoged
B5382
Pandy Tudur
Tan-lan
Pente-tafarn-y-fedw
Llyn Crafnant Walk
Llyn Crafnant Resr.
Llyn Geirionydd
Chapel
Llanrwst
Gwydir Castle
GWYDYR FOREST PARK
Bwlch-yr-haiarn
Melin-y-coed
Gwytherin
Swallow Falls
Ty-hyll
Llyn y Parc
Railway
B5427
Moel Seisiog
1514
Garth Falls Walk
Pentre-du
Betws-y-Coed
Nebo
Mynydd Cribau
1132
Llyn Elsi Resr.
Waterloo Bri.
Capel Garmon
Capel Garmon Burial Chamber
B5113
Pont-y-pant
Fairy Glen
Conwy & Machno Falls
Packhorse Bridge
Tyn-y-coed
Rhydlanfair
Glan-Conwy
Watermill
Ty Mawr Wybrnant
Pentre-bont
B4406
Penmachno
Afon Machno
Pentrefoelas
Rhydlydan
Ysbyty Ifan
B4407
1751
Garn Prys
82

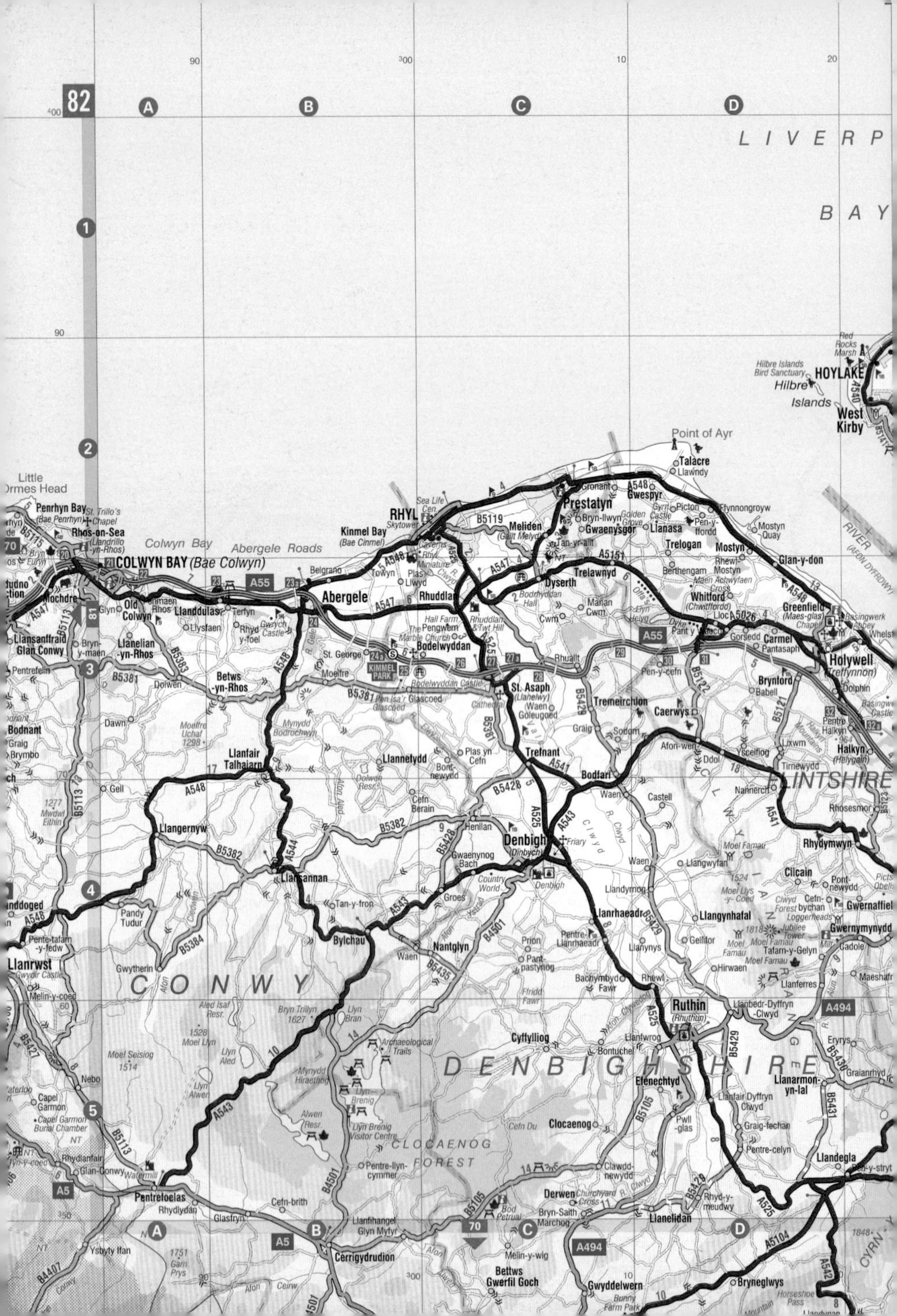
A
B
C
D
1
2
3
4
5
LIVERP
BAY
Red Rocks Marsh
Hilbre Islands Bird Sanctuary
HOYLAKE
Hilbre Islands
West Kirby
Point of Ayr
Talacre
Llawndy
Little Ormes Head
Penrhyn Bay (Bae Penrhyn)
St. Trillo's Chapel
Rhos-on-Sea (Llandrillo -yn-Rhos)
Colwyn Bay
Abergele Roads
COLWYN BAY (Bae Colwyn)
Mochdre
Old Colwyn
Llanddulas
Llysfaen
Rhyd y-foel
Gwrych Castle
Terfyn
Llansanffraid Glan Conwy
Bryn-y-maen
Llanelian -yn-Rhos
Pentrefelin
Dolwen
Betws -yn-Rhos
Bodnant
Graig
Brymbo
Dawn
Moelfre Uchaf 1298
Llanfair Talhaiarn
Gell
Mwdwl Eithin
Llangernyw
Llansannan
Pandy Tudur
Gwytherin
Llanddoged
Llanrwst
Gwydir Castle
Pente-tafarn -y-fedw
Melin-y-coed
Nebo
Capel Garmon
Capel Garmon Burial Chamber
Rhydlanfair
Glan-Conwy
Watermill
Pentrefoelas
Rhydlydan
Glasfryn
Cefn-brith
Ysbyty Ifan
Garn Prys
Cerrigydrudion
Llanfihangel Glyn Myfyr
CONWY
Aled Isaf Resr.
Moel Llyn
Llyn Aled
Moel Seisiog
Llyn Alwen
Bryn Trillyn 1627
Llyn Bran
Archaeological Trails
Mynydd Hiraethog
Llyn Brenig
Llyn Brenig Visitor Centre
Alwen Resr.
CLOCAENOG FOREST
Pentre-llyn-cymmer
Bylchau
Tan-y-fron
Groes
Nantglyn
Waen
RHYL
Sea Life Cen.
Skytower
Kinmel Bay (Bae Cinmel)
Caverns
Rhyl Miniature
Towyn
Plas Llwyd
Belgrano
Abergele
Rhuddlan
Hall Farm
Pengwern
The Marble Church
Bodelwyddan
St. George
KIMMEL PARK
Moelfre
Bodelwyddan Castle
Pen-isa'r Glascoed
Mynydd Bodrochwyn
Llannefydd
Plas yn Cefn
Bont-newydd
Dolwen Resr.
Cefn Berain
Henllan
Gwaenynog Bach
Country World
Denbigh (Dinbych)
Friary
Meliden (Gallt Melyd)
Prestatyn
Gronant
Gwespyr
Bryn-llwyn
Gwaenysgor
Golden Grove
Llanasa
Picton
Pen-y-ffordd
Ffynnongroyw
Mostyn Quay
Trelogan
Mostyn
Glan-y-don
Tan-yr-allt
Dyserth
Trelawnyd
Berthengam
Rhewl-Mostyn
Maen Achwyfaen Cross
Whitford (Chwitffordd)
Bodrhyddan Hall
Marian Cwm
Cwm
Rhuddlan Twt Hill
Greenfield (Maes-glas)
Basingwerk Abbey
Lloc
Pant y Wacco
Gorsedd
Carmel
Pantasaph
Holywell (Treffynnon)
Rhuallt
Pen-y-cefn
Brynford
Babell
Dolphin
St. Asaph (Llanelwy)
Cathedral
Waen Goleugoed
Tremeirchion
Caerwys
Graig
Sodom
Pentre Halkyn
Halkyn (Helygain)
Lixwm
Afon-wen
Ddol
Ysceifiog
Trefnant
Bodfari
Waen
Castell
Nannerch
FLINTSHIRE
Rhosesmor
Rhydymwyn
Moel Famau
Llangwyfan
Cilcain
Pont-newydd
Cefn-bychan
Gwernaffield
Loggerheads
Jubilee Tower
Gwernymynydd
Llandyrnog
Llanrhaeadr
Llangynhafal
Pentre-Llanrhaeadr
Llanynys
Gellifor
Prion
Pant-pastynog
Hirwaen
Tafarn-y-Gelyn
Cadole
Llanferres
Maeshafn
Bachymbyd Fawr
Rhewl
Ffridd Fawr
Ruthin (Rhuthun)
Llanbedr-Dyffryn -Clwyd
Cyffylliog
Bontuchel
Llanfwrog
Eryrys
DENBIGHSHIRE
Efenechtyd
Llanarmon-yn-Ial
Graianrhyd
Llanfair Dyffryn Clwyd
Cefn Du
Clocaenog
Pwll-glas
Graig-fechan
Pentre-celyn
Llandegla
Clawdd-newydd
Derwen
Churchyard Cross
Bryn-Saith Marchog
Llanelidan
Rhyd-y-meudwy
Bod Petrual
Melin-y-wig
Bettws Gwerfil Goch
Gwyddelwern
Bunny Farm Park
Bryneglwys
Horseshoe Pass
RIVER (AFON DYFRDWY)
A55
A547
A548
A544
A543
A525
A541
A5151
A5026
A5
A494
A5104
A542
A540
B5115
B5113
B5381
B5383
B5382
B5384
B5119
B5429
B5381
B5428
B5435
B4501
B5105
B5122
B5121
B5429
B5430
B5431
B5427
B4407
B5123
A5025
81
70

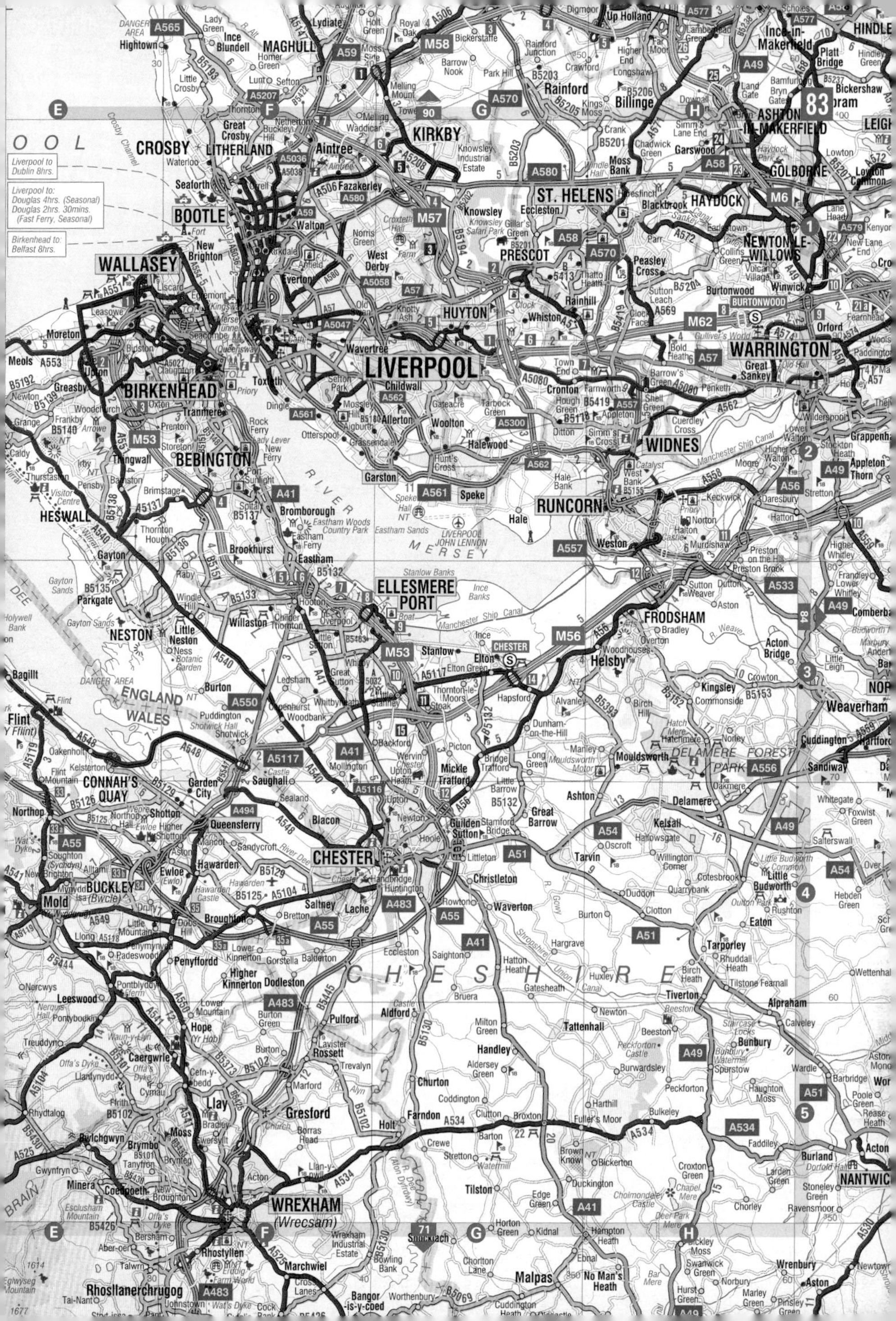
83
90
71
84
Liverpool to Dublin 8hrs.
Liverpool to: Douglas 4hrs. (Seasonal) Douglas 2hrs. 30mins. (Fast Ferry, Seasonal)
Birkenhead to: Belfast 8hrs.
LIVERPOOL
BIRKENHEAD
WALLASEY
BOOTLE
CROSBY
LITHERLAND
MAGHULL
KIRKBY
ST. HELENS
PRESCOT
HUYTON
WIDNES
RUNCORN
WARRINGTON
ELLESMERE PORT
CHESTER
WREXHAM
(Wrecsam)
Mold
BUCKLEY
CONNAH'S QUAY
Flint
HESWALL
NESTON
BEBINGTON
FRODSHAM
Helsby
Weaverham
Tarporley
Malpas
Gresford
Llay
Hope
Queensferry
Hawarden
Broughton
Saltney
Blacon
Speke
Hale
Garston
Halewood
Woolton
Allerton
Childwall
Wavertree
West Derby
Walton
Aintree
Fazakerley
Rainford
Billinge
Haydock
Golborne
NEWTON-LE-WILLOWS
ASHTON-IN-MAKERFIELD
Ince-in-Makerfield
Up Holland
Lydiate
Hightown
Moreton
Meols
Upton
Greasby
Thingwall
Heswall
Parkgate
Willaston
Hooton
Eastham
Bromborough
Stanlow
Elton
Ince
Kelsall
Tarvin
Delamere
DELAMERE FOREST
Mouldsworth
Tattenhall
Farndon
Holt
Churton
Aldford
Pulford
Rossett
Marford
Caergwrle
Leeswood
Penyffordd
Brymbo
Coedpoeth
Minera
Rhosllanerchrugog
Marchwiel
Bangor-is-y-coed
No Man's Heath
Bunbury
Alpraham
Wrenbury
Burland
NANTWICH
Little Budworth
Cuddington
Sandiway
Acton Bridge
Daresbury
Preston Brook
Sutton Weaver
Kingsley
Crowton
Norley
CHESHIRE
ENGLAND
WALES
RIVER MERSEY
DEE
Manchester Ship Canal
Shropshire Union Canal
LIVERPOOL JOHN LENNON
M53
M56
M57
M58
M62
M6
A41
A49
A51
A54
A55
A56
A57
A58
A59
A483
A534
A550
A556
A557
A561
A562
A570
A580
A5117
E
F
G
H

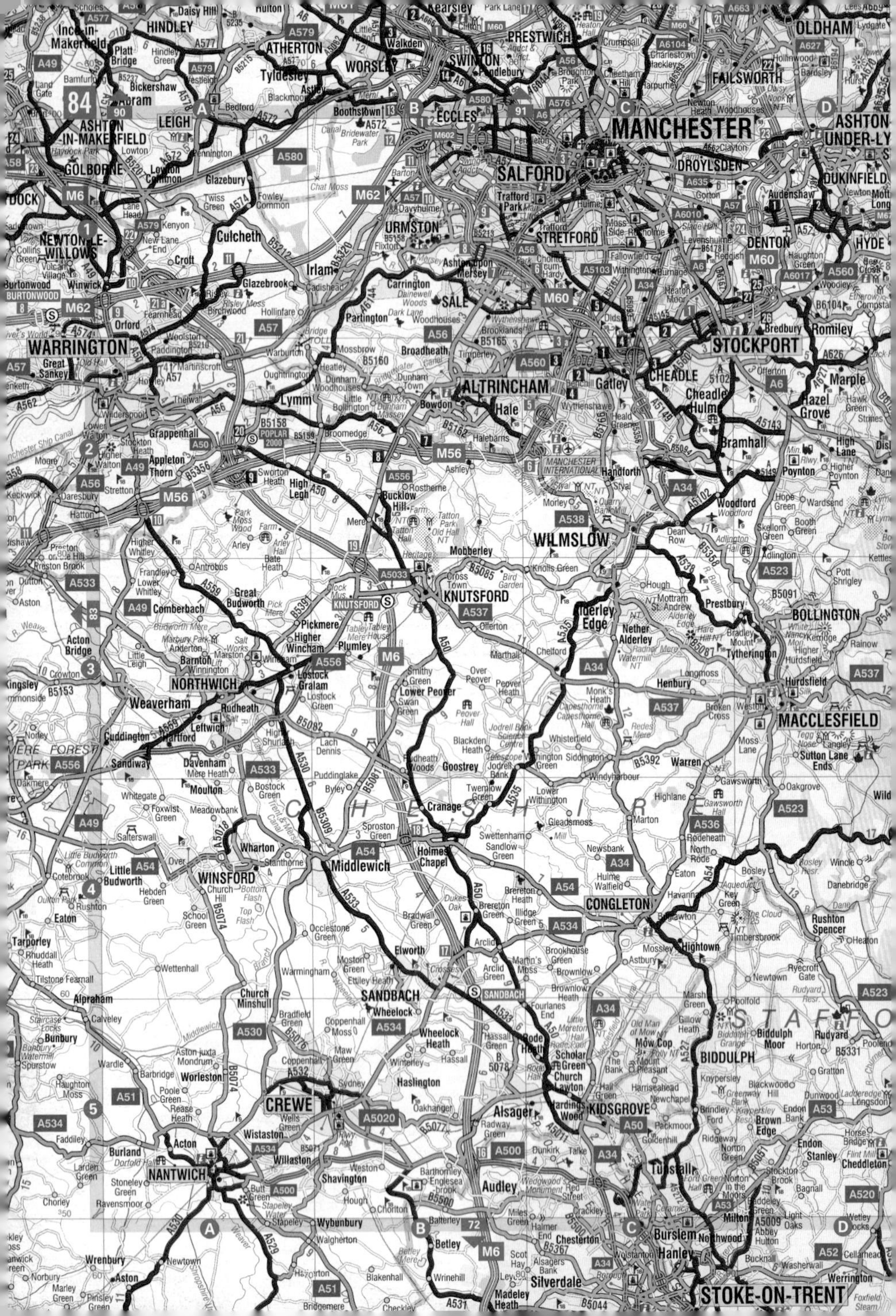
84
90
HINDLEY
ATHERTON
WORSLEY
PRESTWICH
OLDHAM
Ince-in-Makerfield
Platt Bridge
Tyldesley
SWINTON
FAILSWORTH
Abram
LEIGH
Boothstown
ECCLES
MANCHESTER
ASHTON-UNDER-LYNE
ASHTON-IN-MAKERFIELD
SALFORD
DROYLSDEN
GOLBORNE
DUKINFIELD
Glazebury
URMSTON
Trafford Park
Culcheth
STRETFORD
NEWTON-LE-WILLOWS
DENTON
HYDE
Irlam
Croft
Winwick
Carrington
SALE
Burtonwood
Partington
Orford
WARRINGTON
STOCKPORT
Romiley
Great Sankey
Lymm
ALTRINCHAM
Hale
Gatley
CHEADLE
Cheadle Hulme
Marple
Hazel Grove
Grappenhall
Appleton Thorn
Bowdon
Bramhall
High Lane
Poynton
Handforth
MANCHESTER INTERNATIONAL
High Legh
Styal
Woodford
Daresbury
WILMSLOW
Mobberley
Preston Brook
KNUTSFORD
Alderley Edge
Prestbury
Comberbach
Great Budworth
BOLLINGTON
Acton Bridge
Plumley
Nether Alderley
NORTHWICH
Weaverham
Lostock Gralam
Rudheath
MACCLESFIELD
Cuddington
Hartford
Lower Peover
Goostrey
Sandiway
Davenham
Moulton
Cranage
Middlewich
Holmes Chapel
Wharton
WINSFORD
Little Budworth
CONGLETON
Tarporley
Elworth
SANDBACH
Church Minshull
Alpraham
Bunbury
Wheelock
Biddulph Moor
Worleston
Haslington
BIDDULPH
CREWE
Alsager
KIDSGROVE
Acton
Wistaston
NANTWICH
Audley
Tunstall
Wybunbury
Betley
Burslem
Hanley
Silverdale
Wrenbury
Madeley Heath
STOKE-ON-TRENT
CHESHIRE
STAFFO

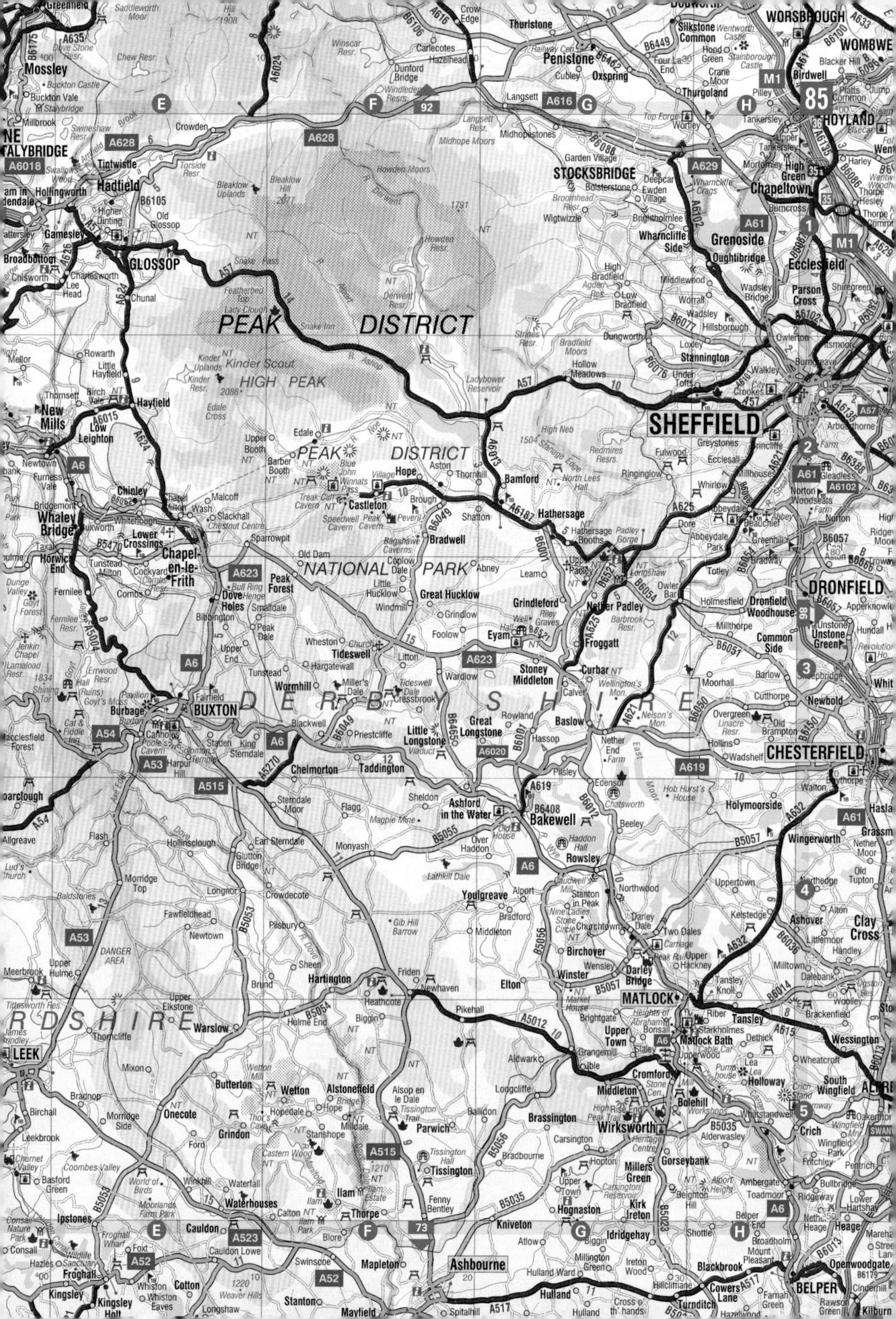

85
Greenfield
Saddleworth Moor
Mossley
Buckton Vale
Stalybridge
Millbrook
Tintwistle
Hadfield
Hollingworth
Gamesley
Broadbottom
Charlesworth
GLOSSOP
Old Glossop
Chunal
Crowden
Torside Resr.
Bleaklow Uplands
Bleaklow Hill 2077
Snake Pass
Featherbed Top
Lady Clough
Snake Inn
PEAK DISTRICT
Kinder Scout
Kinder Uplands
Kinder Resr.
HIGH PEAK
2086
Edale Cross
Rowarth
Little Hayfield
Mellor
Thornsett
Birch Vale
Hayfield
New Mills
Low Leighton
Newtown
Furness Vale
Bridgemont
Whaley Bridge
Chinley
Chapel Milton
Wash
Malcoff
Slackhall
Whitehough
Buxworth
Lower Crossings
Chapel-en-le-Frith
Horwich End
Taxal
Tunstead Milton
Cockyard
Combs
Combs Resr.
Fernilee
Fernilee Resr.
Errwood Resr.
Goyt's Moss
Shining Tor
1834
Pavilion
Burbage
BUXTON
Fairfield
Dove Holes
Bibbington
Sparrowpit
Peak Forest
Smalldale
Peak Dale
Upper End
Tunstead
Wormhill
Miller's Dale
Tideswell
Wheston
Hargatewall
Litton
Cressbrook
Tideswell Dale
Blackwell
Priestcliffe
Chelmorton
Taddington
King Sterndale
Staden
Harpur Hill
Poole's Cavern
Solomon's Temple
Cat & Fiddle Inn
Macclesfield Forest
Wildboarclough
Allgreave
Flash
Hollinsclough
Earl Sterndale
Glutton Bridge
Sterndale Moor
Longnor
Crowdecote
Morridge Top
Fawfieldhead
Newtown
Pilsbury
Sheen
Brund
Hartington
Heathcote
Biggin
Friden
Newhaven
Pikehall
Upper Elkstone
Warslow
Upper Hulme
Meerbrook
Tittesworth Resr.
LEEK
Thorncliffe
Mixon
Bradnop
Birchall
Leekbrook
Morridge Side
Onecote
Butterton
Wetton
Alstonefield
Hope
Hopedale
Milldale
Grindon
Stanshope
Thor's Cave
Ford
Winkhill
Waterfall
Waterhouses
Calton
Ilam
Ilam Park
Thorpe
Blore
Cauldon
Cauldon Lowe
Ipstones
Basford Green
Coombes Valley
Froghall
Foxt
Consall
Kingsley
Kingsley Holt
Whiston
Whiston Eaves
Cotton
Hazles
Swinscoe
Mapleton
Ashbourne
Stanton
Mayfield
Longshaw
Spitalhill
Alsop en le Dale
Tissington
Tissington Hall
Parwich
Fenny Bentley
Ballidon
Bradbourne
Kniveton
Atlow
Hognaston
Hopton
Carsington
Carsington Reservoir
Brassington
Longcliffe
Aldwark
Grangemill
Ible
Elton
Winster
Wensley
Birchover
Middleton
Youlgreave
Alport
Bradford
Stanton in Peak
Nine Ladies Stone Circle
Lathkill Dale
Over Haddon
Monyash
Flagg
Magpie Mine
Sheldon
Ashford in the Water
Bakewell
Great Longstone
Little Longstone
Monsal Viaduct
Rowland
Hassop
Pilsley
Edensor
Chatsworth
Beeley
Haddon Hall
Rowsley
Northwood
Darley Dale
Two Dales
Churchtown
Darley Bridge
MATLOCK
Matlock Bath
Upper Town
Bonsall
Riber
Starkholmes
Tansley
Tansley Knoll
Upper Hackney
Cromford
Middleton
Wirksworth
Bolehill
Gorseybank
Millers Green
Kirk Ireton
Idridgehay
Ireton Wood
Hulland Ward
Hulland
Biggin
Lea
Holloway
Dethick
Crich
Whatstandwell
Alderwasley
Ambergate
Shottle
Belper
BELPER
Blackbrook
Cowers Lane
Turnditch
Heage
Wingfield Park
Fritchley
Bullbridge
South Wingfield
Wessington
Brackenfield
Woolley
Ashover
Kelstedge
Clay Cross
Wingerworth
Holymoorside
Walton
Old Brampton
CHESTERFIELD
Wadshelf
Newbold
Barlow
Cutthorpe
Common Side
Unstone Green
Unstone
Dronfield Woodhouse
DRONFIELD
Holmesfield
Millthorpe
Owler Bar
Totley
Dore
Abbeydale
Beauchief
Bradway
Greenhill
Norton
Fulwood
Ecclesall
Ringinglow
Whirlow
Greystones
SHEFFIELD
Crookes
Walkley
Hillsborough
Loxley
Stannington
Dungworth
Owlerton
Wadsley
Wadsley Bridge
Parson Cross
Ecclesfield
Grenoside
Oughtibridge
Middlewood
Worrall
Wharncliffe Side
Wharncliffe Crags
High Bradfield
Low Bradfield
Agden Res.
Strines Resr.
Bradfield Moors
Hollow Meadows
Under Tofts
Ladybower Reservoir
Derwent Resr.
Howden Resr.
Howden Moors
Midhope Moors
Langsett
Langsett Resr.
Midhopestones
Garden Village
STOCKSBRIDGE
Bolsterstone
Deepcar
Ewden Village
Broomhead Resr.
Wigtwizzle
Brightholmlee
Thurlstone
Penistone
Oxspring
Cubley
Thurgoland
Wortley
Silkstone Common
Hood Green
Crane Moor
Pilley
Tankersley
Upper Tankersley
Mortomley
High Green
Chapeltown
Burncross
Birdwell
HOYLAND
WORSBROUGH
Dunford Bridge
Carlecotes
Hazelhead
Crow Edge
Winscar Resr.
Windleden Resrs.
Chew Resr.
Edale
Upper Booth
Barber Booth
Castleton
Blue John
Winnats Pass
Treak Cliff Cavern
Speedwell Cavern
Peak Cavern
Peveril
Hope
Aston
Thornhill
Brough
Bamford
Shatton
Bradwell
Bagshawe Caverns
Coplow Dale
Little Hucklow
Great Hucklow
Abney
Grindlow
Foolow
Windmill
Eyam
Riley Graves
Grindleford
Leam
Hathersage
Hathersage Booths
Padley Gorge
Upper Padley
Nether Padley
Froggatt
Curbar
Calver
Stoney Middleton
Baslow
Nether End
High Neb
Stanage Edge
Redmires Resrs.
North Lees Hall
NATIONAL PARK
DERBYSHIRE
STAFFORDSHIRE
Old Dam
DANGER AREA

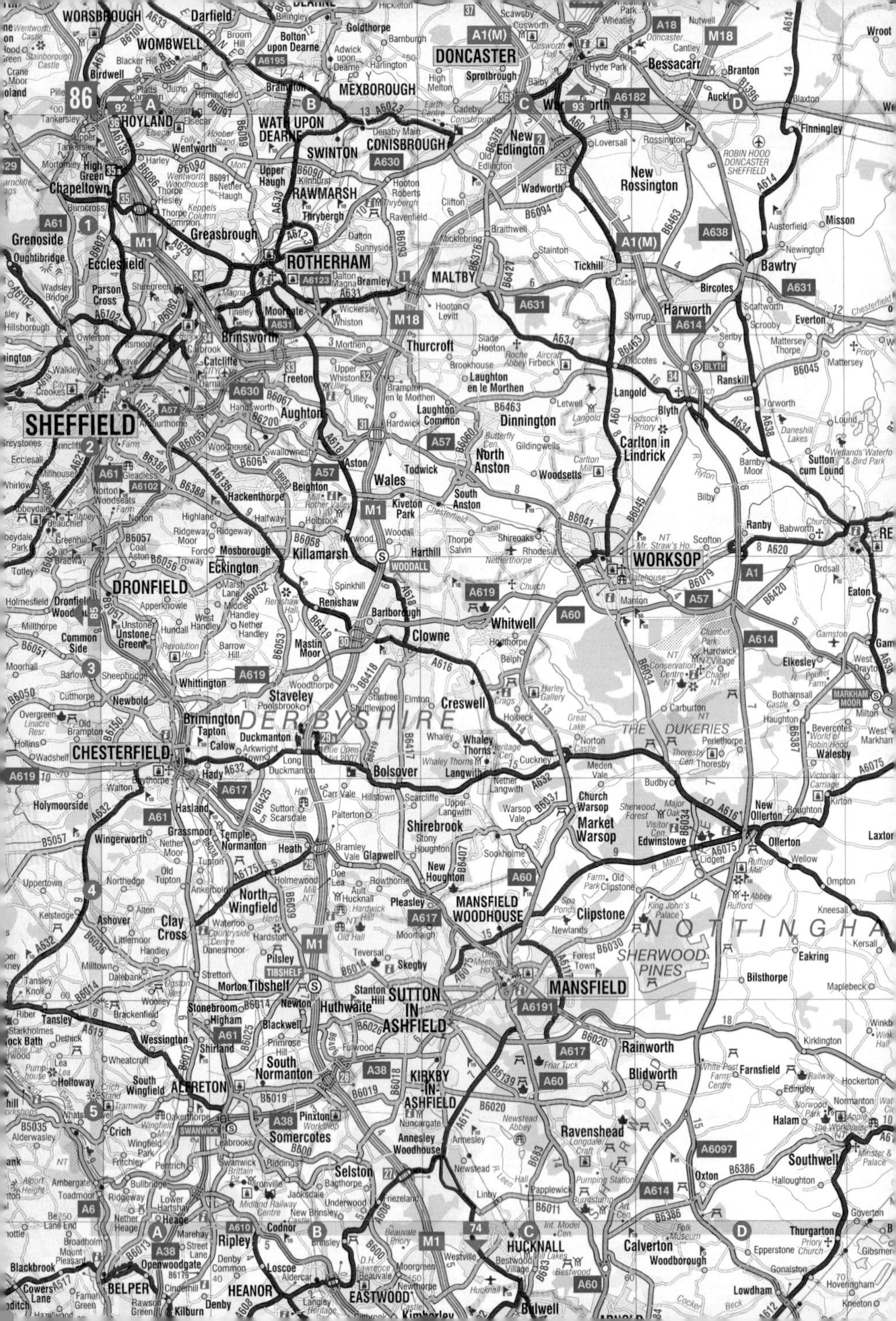
86
WORSBROUGH
Darfield
WOMBWELL
Bolton upon Dearne
Goldthorpe
Barnburgh
Scawsby
Cusworth
A1(M)
DONCASTER
Wheatley
A18
Nutwell
M18
Cantley
Bessacarr
Branton
Wroot
Birdwell
Hoyland
Platts Common
Jump
Hemingfield
Brampton
MEXBOROUGH
Sprotbrough
Warmsworth
Auckley
Blaxton
Finningley
92
93
A
B
C
D
Tankersley
HOYLAND
Elsecar
WATH UPON DEARNE
SWINTON
CONISBROUGH
Denaby Main
Cadeby
Earth Centre
New Edlington
Loversall
Rossington
ROBIN HOOD DONCASTER SHEFFIELD
Wentworth
Harley
Upper Haugh
Kilnhurst
Hooton Roberts
Old Edlington
Wadworth
New Rossington
Chapeltown
High Green
Thorpe Hesley
Keppels Column
RAWMARSH
Thrybergh
Ravenfield
Clifton
Grenoside
Greasbrough
Dalton
Sunnyside
Braithwell
Micklebring
Stainton
Austerfield
Misson
Newington
Ecclesfield
Oughtibridge
ROTHERHAM
Bramley
MALTBY
Tickhill
Bawtry
Wadsley Bridge
Parson Cross
Shiregreen
Magna
Wickersley
Hooton Levitt
Castle
Bircotes
Hillsborough
Owlerton
Tinsley
Moorgate
Whiston
Brinsworth
Thurcroft
Slade Hooton
Roche Abbey
Styrrup
Harworth
Scaftworth
Scrooby
Everton
Catcliffe
Treeton
Morthen
Brookhouse
Laughton en le Morthen
Firbeck
Oldcotes
Serlby
Mattersey Thorpe
Mattersey
Walkley
Crookes
Upper Whiston
Ulley
Brampton en le Morthen
Langold
Blyth
Ranskill
SHEFFIELD
Handsworth
Aughton
Laughton Common
Dinnington
Letwell
Hodsock Priory
Torworth
Greystones
Ecclesall
Millhouses
Woodhouse
Swallownest
Hardwick
Butterfly Cen.
Gildingwells
Carlton in Lindrick
Daneshill Lakes
Lound
Gleadless
Aston
Todwick
North Anston
Woodsetts
Barnby Moor
Sutton cum Lound
Wetlands Waterfowl & Bird Park
Norton Woodseats
Hackenthorpe
Beighton
Rother Valley
Wales
Kiveton Park
South Anston
Ryton
Bilby
Abbeydale
Beauchief
Norton
Highlane
Halfway
Holbrook
Chesterfield Canal
Woodall
Thorpe Salvin
Shireoaks
Scofton
Ranby
Babworth
Greenhill
Ridgeway Moor
Ridgeway
Mosborough
Killamarsh
Harthill
Rhodesia
Mr. Straw's Ho.
WORKSOP
Coal Aston
Ford
Troway
Eckington
WOODALL
Netherthorpe
Ordsall
Totley
Bradway
DRONFIELD
Marsh Lane
Spinkhill
Renishaw
Church
Gatehouse
Manton
Eaton
Holmesfield
Dronfield Woodhouse
85
Apperknowle
Middle Handley
West Handley
Nether Handley
Renishaw Hall
Barlborough
Clowne
Whitwell
Clumber Park
Hardwick Village
Millthorpe
Common Side
Unstone
Unstone Green
Hundall
Revolution Ho.
Barrow Hill
Mastin Moor
Hodthorpe
Belph
Conservation Centre
Chapel
Elkesley
West Drayton
Moorhall
Barlow
Sheepbridge
Whittington
Woodthorpe
Staveley
Stanfree
Elmton
Creswell
Crags
Harley Gallery
Poulter Forest
Bothamsall
MARKHAM MOOR
Cutthorpe
Newbold
Poolsbrook
Shuttlewood
Holbeck
Carburton
Milton
Overgreen
Linacre Resr.
Old Brampton
Brimington
Tapton
DERBYSHIRE
Duckmanton
Arkwright Town
Whaley
Whaley Thorns
Heritage Cen.
Great Lake
Norton
THE DUKERIES
Perlethorpe
Haughton
Bevercotes
World of Robin Hood
West Markham
Hollins
Wadshelf
CHESTERFIELD
Calow
Long Duckmanton
Bolsover
Langwith
Cuckney
Meden Vale
Thoresby
Walesby
Victorian Carriage
Kirton
Walton
Hady
Hasland
Sutton Scarsdale
Carr Vale
Hillstown
Scarcliffe
Upper Langwith
Nether Langwith
Church Warsop
Budby
Boughton
New Ollerton
Holymoorside
Grassmoor
Temple Normanton
Palterton
Shirebrook
Stony Houghton
Warsop Vale
Market Warsop
Sherwood Forest
Major Oak
Visitor Cen.
Edwinstowe
Ollerton
Laxton
Wingerworth
Nether Moor
Tupton
Heath
Bramley Vale
Glapwell
Sookholme
Lidgett
Rufford Mill
Wellow
Old Tupton
Northedge
Ankerbold
Doe Lea
Holmewood
Ault Hucknall
Hardwick Hall
Rowthorne
New Houghton
Farm Park
Old Clipstone
Rufford Abbey
Ompton
Uppertown
North Wingfield
Pleasley
MANSFIELD WOODHOUSE
Clipstone
Spa Ponds
King John's Palace
Kneesall
Kelstedge
Ashover
Alton
Clay Cross
Waterloo
Countryside Centre
Hardstoft
Old Hall
Moorhaigh
Newlands
NOTTINGHAM
Littlemoor
Handley
Danesmoor
Teversal
Skegby
Forest Town
SHERWOOD PINES
Eakring
Kersall
Milltown
Dalebank
Stretton
Pilsley
TIBSHELF
Oldi Meeting Ho.
MANSFIELD
Bilsthorpe
Tansley Knoll
Ogston Res.
Morton
Tibshelf
Stanton Hill
SUTTON IN ASHFIELD
Maplebeck
Riber
Tansley
Woolley
Brackenfield
Stonebroom
Higham
Newton
Huthwaite
Starkholmes
Lock Bath
Dethick
Lea
Holloway
Wessington
Shirland
Blackwell
Primrose Hill
Fulwood
Rainworth
Kirklington
Winkburn
Wheatcroft
South Wingfield
ALFRETON
South Normanton
KIRKBY IN ASHFIELD
Friar Tuck
Blidworth
White Post Farm Centre
Farnsfield
Railway
Hockerton
Edingley
Crich
Crich Stand
Tramway
Oakerthorpe
Pinxton
Workshop
Normanton
Norwood Park
Apple
The Workhouse
Halam
Whatstandwell
Alderwasley
Wingfield Park
SWANWICK
Somercotes
Nuncargate
Annesley
Newstead Abbey
Ravenshead
Longdale Craft
Fritchley
Pentrich
Leabrooks
Swanwick
Riddings
Annesley Woodhouse
Newstead
Pumping Station
Southwell
Minster & Palace
Ambergate
Toadmoor
Bullbridge
Ridgeway
Lower Hartshay
Butterley
Ironville
Midland Railway Centre
Selston
Bagthorpe
Jacksdale
Underwood
Linby
Papplewick
Oxton
Halloughton
Nether Heage
Heage
Codnor
New Brinsley
Brinsley
Friezeland
Hucknall
Calverton
Burnstump
Art Cen.
Folk Museum
Goverton
Ripley
Marehay
Street Lane
Broadholm
Mount Pleasant
Openwoodgate
Denby Common
Beauvale Priory
Westville
HUCKNALL
Int. Model Cen.
Woodborough
Epperstone
Thurgarton
Priory Church
Gibsmere
Blackbrook
BELPER
Cinderhill
Loscoe
Aldercar
D.H. Lawrence
Moorgreen
Bestwood Village
Mill Lakes
Bestwood
Gonalston
Hoveringham
Cowers Lane
Farnah Green
Rawson Green
Kilburn
Denby
HEANOR
Langley
EASTWOOD
Newthorpe
Bulwell
Lowdham
Kneeton
74
M1
A1
A38
A57
A60
A61
A614
A616
A617
A619
A630
A631
A632
A6097
A6191

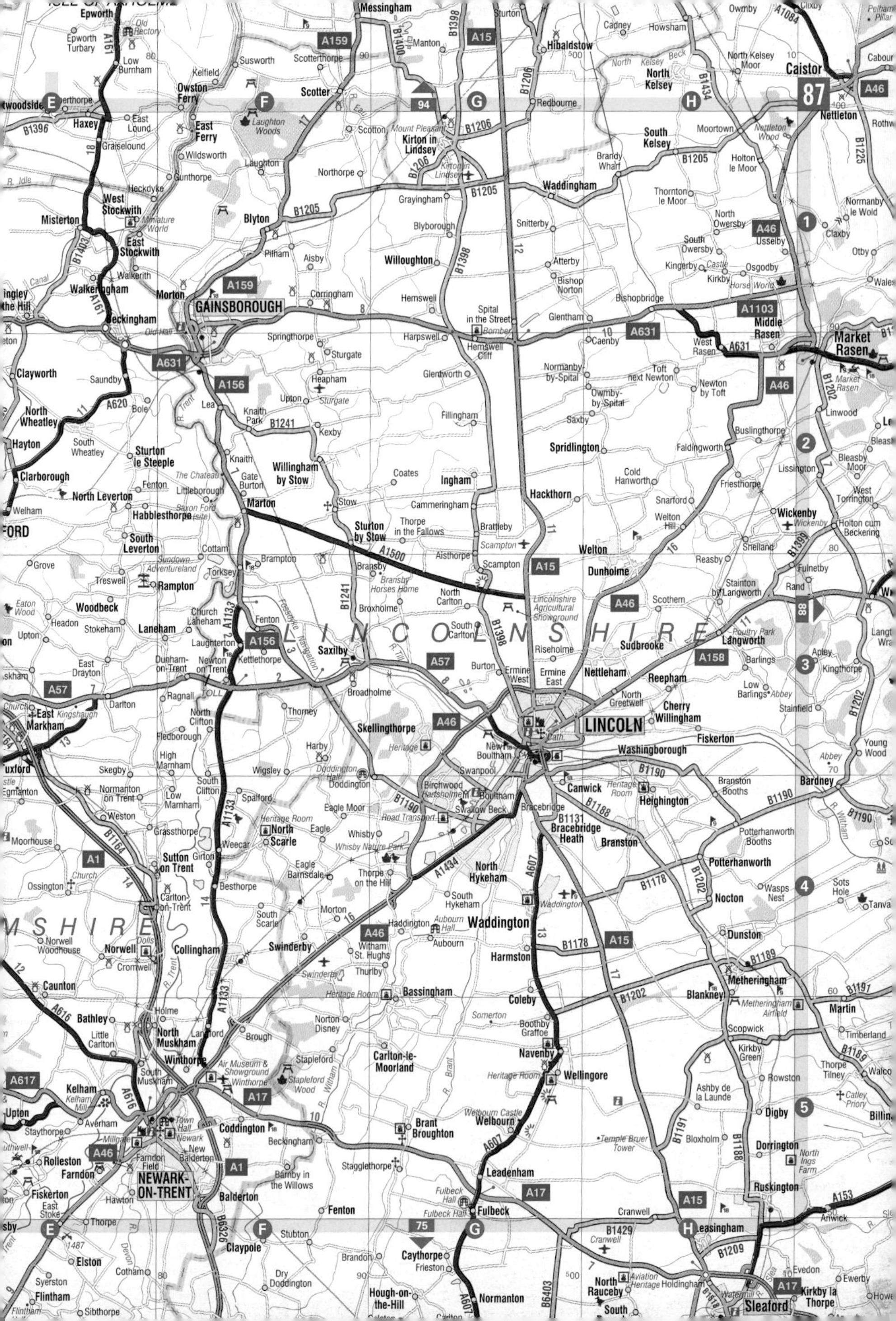

87
Epworth
Old Rectory
Epworth Turbary
Low Burnham
Messingham
Manton
A159
A15
Hibaldstow
Cadney
Howsham
Owmby
Clixby
North Kelsey Moor
Caistor
Cabourne
North Kelsey Beck
North Kelsey
A1084
A46
Nettleton
Rothwell
Scotterthorpe
Susworth
Kelfield
Owston Ferry
Scotter
Redbourne
Haxey
East Lound
Graiselound
East Ferry
Wildsworth
Laughton Woods
Laughton
Scotton
Mount Pleasant
Kirkton in Lindsey
B1206
B1205
South Kelsey
Moortown
Nettleton Wood
Holton le Moor
B1225
Brandy Wharf
R. Idle
Gunthorpe
Heckdyke
Northorpe
Grayingham
Waddingham
Thornton le Moor
Normanby le Wold
West Stockwith
Miniature World
Misterton
Blyton
Blyborough
Snitterby
North Owersby
Claxby
East Stockwith
Pilham
Aisby
Willoughton
B1398
Atterby
South Owersby
Usselby
Otby
Kingerby
Castle
Osgodby
Walkerith
Walkeringham
Morton
Canal
Corringham
Hemswell
Bishop Norton
Kirkby
Horse World
Bishopbridge
Wales
Gringley on the Hill
A161
B1403
A159
GAINSBOROUGH
Beckingham
Old Hall
Springthorpe
Sturgate
Heapham
Spital in the Street
Bomber
Glentham
Caenby
A631
A1103
Middle Rasen
West Rasen
Market Rasen
Harpswell
Hemswell Cliff
Glentworth
Normanby-by-Spital
Toft next Newton
Newton by Toft
Owmby-by-Spital
Clayworth
Saundby
A620
A156
Bole
Lea
Upton
Knaith Park
B1241
Kexby
Fillingham
Saxby
Linwood
B1202
North Wheatley
Hayton
South Wheatley
Sturton le Steeple
Knaith
Gate Burton
Willingham by Stow
Coates
Ingham
Spridlington
Faldingworth
Buslingthorpe
Lissington
Bleasby Moor
Clarborough
North Leverton
Habblesthorpe
Fenton
Littleborough
The Chateau
Saxon Ford (site)
Marton
Stow
Cammeringham
Hackthorn
Cold Hanworth
Friesthorpe
Snarford
Welton Hill
Wickenby
West Torrington
Holton cum Beckering
Welham
FORD
South Leverton
Sturton by Stow
Thorpe in the Fallows
Brattleby
Scampton
Welton
Snelland
B1399
Grove
Treswell
Cottam
Sundown Adventureland
Rampton
Torksey
Brampton
A1500
Aisthorpe
Dunholme
Reasby
Fulnetby
Rand
Eaton Wood
Woodbeck
Headon
Upton
Bransby
Bransby Horses Home
North Carlton
Lincolnshire Agricultural Showground
A46
Scothern
Stainton by Langworth
88
Church Laneham
Laneham
Stokeham
Fenton
Fossdyke Navigation
Broxholme
South Carlton
LINCOLNSHIRE
Sudbrooke
Poultry Park
Langworth
Apley
Kingthorpe
East Drayton
Dunham-on-Trent
Laughterton
Newton on Trent
Kettlethorpe
A156
A1133
Saxilby
A57
Burton
Riseholme
Ermine West
Ermine East
Nettleham
Reepham
A158
Barlings
Low Barlings
Abbey
Stainfield
Darlton
Ragnall
Broadholme
North Greetwell
Cherry Willingham
LINCOLN
Cath.
East Markham
Kingshaugh
North Clifton
Thorney
Skellingthorpe
Heritage
Harby
New Boultham
Washingborough
Fiskerton
Young Wood
Tuxford
Fledborough
High Marnham
Skegby
South Clifton
Wigsley
Doddington Hall
Doddington
Swanpool
Boultham
Canwick
Heritage Room
Branston Booths
Bardney
Abbey
Egmanton
Normanton on Trent
Low Marnham
Spalford
Eagle Moor
Birchwood
Hartsholme
Swallow Beck
B1190
Bracebridge
B1131
Bracebridge Heath
B1188
Heighington
Branston
R. Witham
Moorhouse
Weston
Grassthorpe
Heritage Room
North Scarle
Eagle
Whisby
Road Transport
Whisby Nature Park
Potterhanworth Booths
Potterhanworth
B1202
A1
B1164
Sutton on Trent
Girton
Weecar
A1133
Eagle Barnsdale
Thorpe on the Hill
A1434
North Hykeham
A607
B1178
Nocton
Wasps Nest
Sots Hole
Tanvats
Ossington
Church
Carlton-on-Trent
Besthorpe
South Hykeham
Waddington
Haddington
Aubourn Hall
Aubourn
Morton
South Scarle
A46
Waddington
Harmston
B1178
A15
Dunston
B1189
Metheringham
MSHIRE
Norwell Woodhouse
Norwell
Dolls
Cromwell
Collingham
Swinderby
Witham St. Hughs
Thurlby
Swinderby
Bassingham
Heritage Room
Coleby
B1202
Blankney
Metheringham Airfield
Martin
B1191
Caunton
A616
Bathley
Little Carlton
Holme
North Muskham
Langford
Brough
Norton Disney
Somerton
Boothby Graffoe
Scopwick
Timberland
Kirkby Green
Thorpe Tilney
Walcott
A617
Kelham
Kelham Mill
South Muskham
Winthorpe
Air Museum & Showground
Winthorpe
Stapleford
Stapleford Wood
Carlton-le-Moorland
R. Brant
Navenby
Heritage Room
Wellingore
Rowston
Catley Priory
Ashby de la Launde
Upton
Staythorpe
Averham
A616
Town Hall
Newark
A17
Coddington
Beckingham
R. Witham
Brant Broughton
Welbourn Castle
Welbourn
Digby
Billinghay
Southwell
Rolleston
Farndon
A46
Millgate
Farndon Field
New Balderton
A1
Barnby in the Willows
Stragglethorpe
Leadenham
Temple Bruer Tower
B1191
Bloxholm
B1188
Dorrington
North Ings Farm
Ruskington
NEWARK-ON-TRENT
Balderton
Hawton
Fiskerton
East Stoke
Fenton
Fulbeck Hall
Fulbeck
A17
Cranwell
A15
A153
Anwick
Thorpe
1487
Claypole
Stubton
75
B1429
Cranwell
Leasingham
B1209
Elston
B6326
Devon
Cotham
Brandon
Caythorpe
Frieston
Dry Doddington
Syerston
Flintham
Flintham
Sibthorpe
Hough-on-the-Hill
A607
Normanton
B6403
North Rauceby
Aviation Heritage
Holdingham
South Rauceby
Sleaford
A17
Evedon
Ewerby
Kirkby la Thorpe
Howell

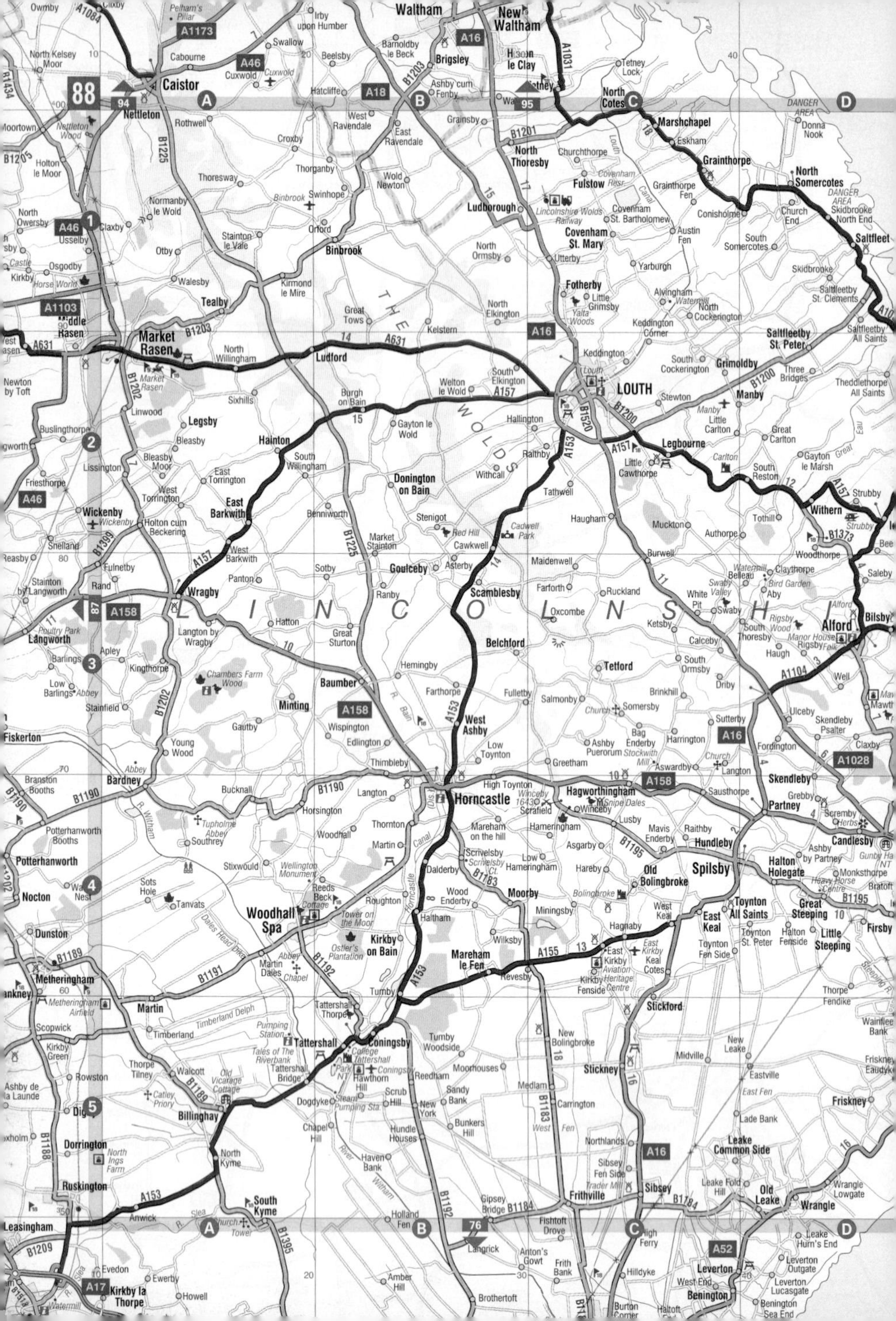
Owmby
Clixby
A1084
Pelham's Pillar
A1173
Irby upon Humber
Waltham
New Waltham
A16
A1031
Swallow
Barnoldby le Beck
Brigsley
Humberston
Holton le Clay
Tetney Lock
North Kelsey Moor
Cabourne
A46
Beelsby
B1434
Caistor
Cuxwold
Ashby cum Fenby
Tetney
North Cotes
Hatcliffe
A18
B1203
94
95
A
B
C
D
DANGER AREA
Donna Nook
Nettleton
Moortown
Nettleton Wood
Rothwell
West Ravendale
East Ravendale
Grainsby
Waithe
Marshchapel
Eskham
B1201
B1205
Holton le Moor
B1225
Croxby
North Thoresby
Churchthorpe
Grainthorpe
Thoresway
Thorganby
Fulstow
Covenham Resr.
Louth Canal
Grainthorpe Fen
North Somercotes
Normanby le Wold
Wold Newton
Binbrook
Swinhope
Ludborough
Lincolnshire Wolds Railway
Covenham St. Bartholomew
Conisholme
DANGER AREA
Church End
Skidbrooke North End
North Owersby
A46
Claxby
Usselby
Stainton le Vale
Orford
Covenham St. Mary
Austin Fen
Saltfleet
South Somercotes
Otby
Binbrook
North Ormsby
Utterby
Castle
Osgodby
Kirkby
Horse World
Walesby
Kirmond le Mire
Yarburgh
Skidbrooke
Fotherby
Alvingham
Watermill
Little Grimsby
North Cockerington
Saltfleetby St. Clements
Tealby
THE WOLDS
A1103
Middle Rasen
Great Tows
North Elkington
Yalta Woods
Keddington Corner
B1203
A16
Market Rasen
Kelstern
Saltfleetby St. Peter
Saltfleetby All Saints
A631
14
A631
North Willingham
Ludford
Keddington
West Rasen
South Cockerington
Grimoldby
Market Rasen
B1202
South Elkington
Three Bridges
Theddlethorpe All Saints
Newton by Toft
Welton le Wold
A157
LOUTH
B1200
Stewton
Manby
Linwood
Sixhills
Burgh on Bain
15
Legsby
Hallington
B1520
Little Carlton
Manby
Gayton le Wold
Buslingthorpe
Bleasby
Hainton
Raithby
A153
A157
Legbourne
Great Carlton
South Willingham
Little Cawthorpe
Carlton
Gayton le Marsh
Great Eau
Bleasby Moor
Lissington
East Torrington
Withcall
Donington on Bain
South Reston
Friesthorpe
West Torrington
12
A157
Strubby
A46
East Barkwith
Tathwell
Wickenby
Benniworth
Haugham
Withern
Tothill
Holton cum Beckering
Stenigot
Red Hill
Cadwell Park
Mucktom
Authorpe
Strubby
Snelland
B1399
West Barkwith
Market Stainton
Cawkwell
B1373
Reasby
80
A157
Burwell
Woodthorpe
Fulnetby
Asterby
Goulceby
Sotby
Maidenwell
Claythorpe
Watermill
Belleau
Bird Garden
Saleby
Stainton by Langworth
Rand
14
Farforth
Ruckland
Aby
Wragby
Panton
Ranby
Scamblesby
White Pit
Swaby Valley
Swaby
Alford
A158
LINCOLNSHIRE
Oxcombe
Rigsby Wood
Bilsby
11
Langworth
Poultry Park
Langton by Wragby
Hatton
Great Sturton
Belchford
Ketsby
South Thoresby
Manor House
Folk
Alford
Apley
Barlings
10
Calceby
Rigsby
Haugh
Kingthorpe
Hemingby
South Ormsby
Tetford
A1104
Well
Low Barlings
Abbey
Chambers Farm Wood
Baumber
Farthorpe
Driby
Brinkhill
Stainfield
Minting
A158
Fulletby
Salmonby
Somersby
Church
Ulceby
Skendleby Psalter
Mawthorpe
B1202
Gautby
Wispington
R. Bain
A153
West Ashby
Bag Enderby
Harrington
Sutterby
A16
Fiskerton
Young Wood
Edlington
Low Toynton
Ashby Puerorum
Stockwith Mill
Fordington
Claxby
Abbey
Thimbleby
Greetham
Aswardby
Church
Langton
A1028
70
Branston Booths
Bardney
Bucknall
B1190
Langton
High Toynton
10
A158
Skendleby
Horncastle
Winceby 1643
Scrafield
Hagworthingham
Snipe Dales
Sausthorpe
Partney
Grebby
Scremby
Herbs
B1190
Horsington
Winceby
Lusby
Raithby
R. Witham
Tupholme Abbey
Thornton
Mareham on the hill
Hameringham
Mavis Enderby
Hundleby
Candlesby
Potterhanworth Booths
Southrey
Woodhall
Martin
Asgarby
B1195
Ashby by Partney
Gunby Hall NT
Potterhanworth
Stixwould
Wellington Monument
Scrivelsby
Scrivelsby Ct.
Low Hameringham
Hareby
Old Bolingbroke
Spilsby
Halton Holegate
Monksthorpe
Heavy Horse Centre
Bratoft
Nocton
Wasps Nest
Sots Hole
Tanvats
Reeds Beck
Cottage
Dalderby
B1183
Horncastle Canal
Wood Enderby
Moorby
Bolingbroke
West Keal
Toynton All Saints
Great Steeping
B1195
Firsby
Woodhall Spa
Roughton
Tower on the Moor
Haltham
Miningsby
Hagnaby
East Keal
Toynton St. Peter
Halton Fenside
Little Steeping
Dunston
Dales Head Dike
Kirkby on Bain
Ostler's Plantation
Wilksby
Toynton Fen Side
B1189
Abbey
Martin Dales
Chapel
B1192
A153
Mareham le Fen
A155
13
East Kirkby
East Kirkby Aviation Heritage Centre
Keal Cotes
Metheringham
B1191
Revesby
Kirkby Fenside
Thorpe Fendike
60
Metheringham Airfield
Tumby
Stickford
Martin
Tattershall Thorpe
Wainfleet Bank
Timberland Delph
Pumping Station
Scopwick
Timberland
Tattershall
Coningsby
Tumby Woodside
New Bolingbroke
Tales of The Riverbank
College
Tattershall
Kirkby Green
Thorpe Tilney
Walcott
Tattershall Bridge
Coningsby
Hawthorn Hill
Moorhouses
Midville
New Leake
Rowston
Old Vicarage Cottage
Park NT
Reedham
Stickney
Eastville
Friskney Eaudyke
B1189
18
16
Ashby de la Launde
Catley Priory
Medlam
East Fen
Dogdyke
Steam Pumping Sta.
Scrub Hill
Sandy Bank
Billinghay
B1183
New York
Carrington
Friskney
Digby
Chapel Hill
Bunkers Hill
West Fen
Lade Bank
Hundle Houses
Dorrington
North Ings Farm
Northlands
Leake Common Side
B1188
North Kyme
Haven Bank
A16
16
River Witham
Sibsey Fen Side
Ruskington
Trader Mill
Leake Fold Hill
Wrangle Lowgate
B1192
Gipsey Bridge
Sibsey
Old Leake
Wrangle
A153
South Kyme
Holland Fen
B1184
Frithville
B1184
Leasingham
Anwick
Slea
Church
Tower
76
Fishtoft Drove
High Ferry
Leake Hurn's End
B1395
B1209
Langrick
Anton's Gowt
A52
Evedon
Ewerby
20
Frith Bank
Leverton
Leverton Outgate
A17
Kirkby la Thorpe
Howell
Amber Hill
30
Hilldyke
West End
Leverton Lucasgate
Brothertoft
Benington
B1518
Watermill
Burton Corner
Benington Sea End

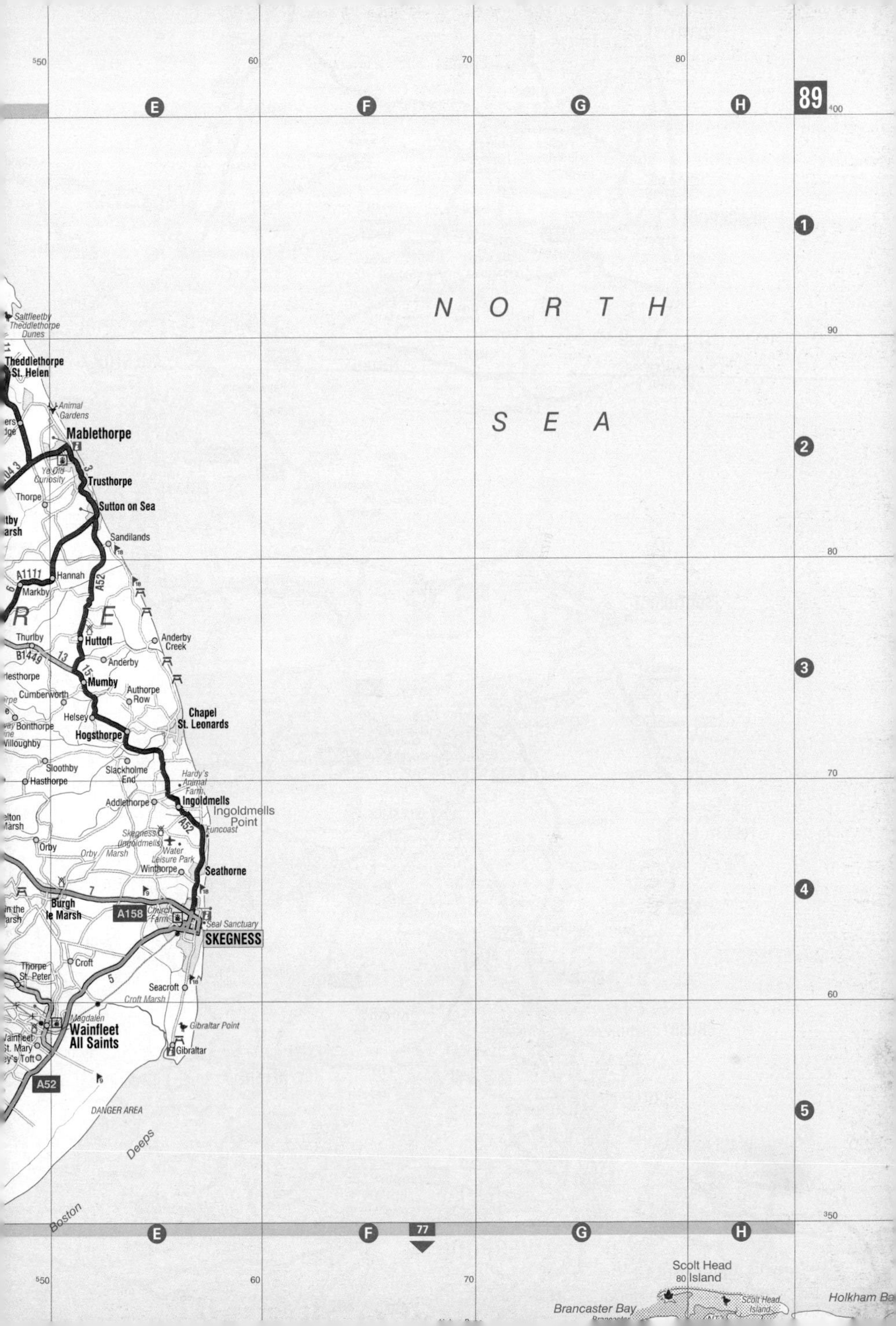
N O R T H
S E A
Saltfleetby Theddlethorpe Dunes
Theddlethorpe St. Helen
Animal Gardens
Mablethorpe
Ye Olde Curiosity
Trusthorpe
Thorpe
Sutton on Sea
Sandilands
A1111
Hannah
Markby
A52
Thurlby
B1449
Huttoft
Anderby Creek
Anderby
Mumby
Cumberworth
Authorpe Row
Helsey
Bonthorpe
Hogsthorpe
Chapel St. Leonards
Willoughby
Sloothby
Hasthorpe
Slackholme End
Hardy's Animal Farm
Addlethorpe
Ingoldmells
Ingoldmells Point
Funcoast
Skegness (Ingoldmells)
Orby
Orby Marsh
Water Leisure Park
Winthorpe
Seathorne
Burgh le Marsh
A158
Church Farm
Seal Sanctuary
SKEGNESS
Thorpe St. Peter
Croft
Seacroft
Croft Marsh
Magdalen
Wainfleet All Saints
Gibraltar Point
Gibraltar
A52
DANGER AREA
Deeps
Boston
Scolt Head Island
Brancaster Bay
Holkham Ba

77

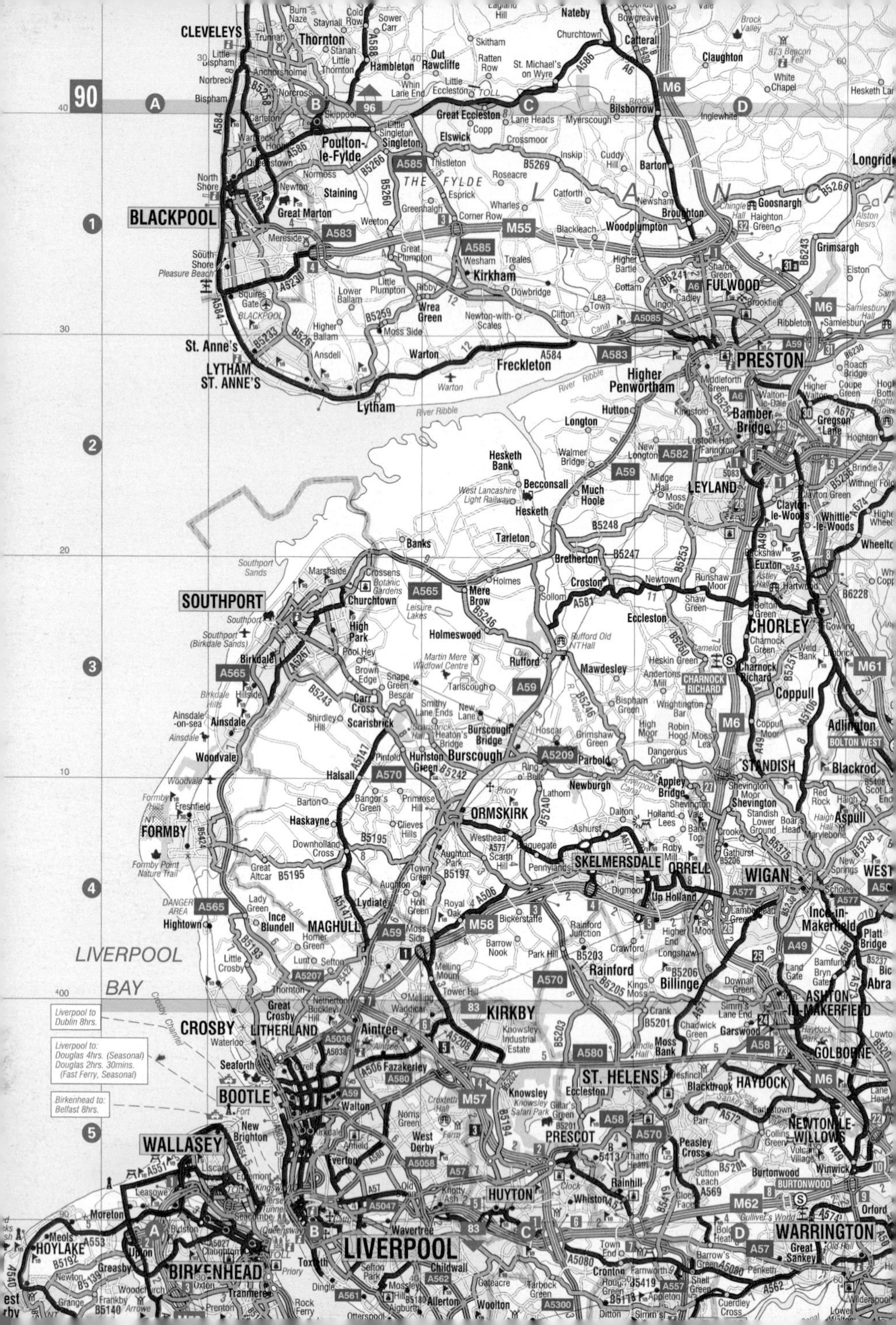

90
A
B
C
D
96
83
1
2
3
4
5
CLEVELEYS
Thornton
Hambleton
Out Rawcliffe
Nateby
Catterall
Claughton
Bilsborrow
Great Eccleston
Poulton-le-Fylde
Singleton
Elswick
THE FYLDE
BLACKPOOL
Great Marton
Staining
Kirkham
Wrea Green
Warton
Freckleton
St. Anne's
LYTHAM ST. ANNE'S
Lytham
River Ribble
Higher Penwortham
PRESTON
FULWOOD
Longridge
Goosnargh
Grimsargh
Bamber Bridge
Hutton
Longton
Hesketh Bank
Becconsall
Much Hoole
LEYLAND
Tarleton
Banks
Bretherton
Croston
SOUTHPORT
Churchtown
Mere Brow
Holmeswood
Rufford
Mawdesley
Eccleston
CHORLEY
Coppull
Adlington
Birkdale
Ainsdale
Woodvale
Scarisbrick
Burscough
Halsall
FORMBY
Haskayne
ORMSKIRK
Lathom
Newburgh
Parbold
Appley Bridge
STANDISH
Blackrod
Aspull
SKELMERSDALE
ORRELL
WIGAN
Ince-in-Makerfield
Up Holland
Billinge
Rainford
Hightown
Ince Blundell
MAGHULL
Lydiate
LIVERPOOL BAY
Liverpool to Dublin 8hrs.
Liverpool to: Douglas 4hrs. (Seasonal) Douglas 2hrs. 30mins. (Fast Ferry, Seasonal)
Birkenhead to: Belfast 8hrs.
CROSBY
LITHERLAND
Aintree
KIRKBY
ASHTON-IN-MAKERFIELD
GOLBORNE
HAYDOCK
ST. HELENS
BOOTLE
Walton
Fazakerley
Knowsley
PRESCOT
Rainhill
NEWTON-LE-WILLOWS
WALLASEY
New Brighton
Everton
West Derby
HUYTON
Whiston
Burtonwood
WARRINGTON
Great Sankey
HOYLAKE
Moreton
BIRKENHEAD
LIVERPOOL
Wavertree
Toxteth
Childwall
Woolton
Widnes
M6
M55
M58
M57
M62
M61
A583
A585
A565
A59
A570
A580
A58
A49
A57

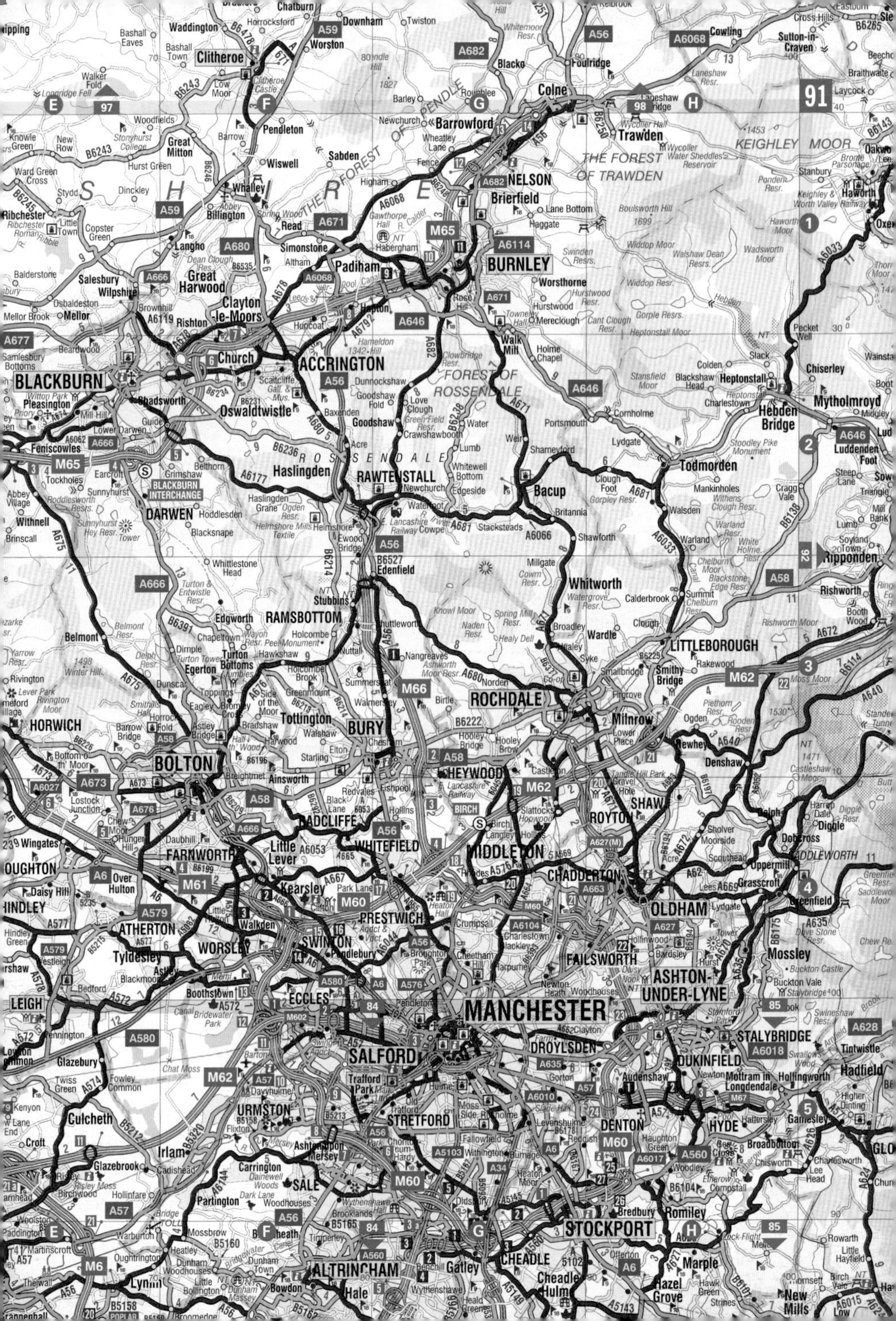
Chatburn
Waddington
Horrocksford
Downham
Twiston
Bashall Eaves
Bashall Town
Clitheroe
Clitheroe Castle
Worston
Cowling
Sutton-in-Craven
Cross Hills
Eastburn
Colne
Foulridge
Blacko
Laneshaw Bridge
Laneshaw Resr.
Barley
Roughlee
Barrowford
Newchurch
Pendleton
Longridge Fell
Walker Fold
Low Moor
Woodfields
Knowle Green
New Row
Stonyhurst College
Great Mitton
Barrow
Trawden
THE FOREST OF TRAWDEN
THE FOREST OF PENDLE
Wycoller Hall
KEIGHLEY MOOR
Wheatley Lane
Sabden
Fence
Wiswell
Hurst Green
Ward Green Cross
Stydd
Dinckley
Whalley
Higham
NELSON
Brierfield
Lane Bottom
Haggate
Boulsworth Hill
Stanbury
Oakworth
Haworth
Keighley & Worth Valley Railway
Ponden Resr.
Ribchester
Ribchester Roman Ribble
Little Town
Copster Green
Billington
Read
Gawthorpe Hall
Simonstone
Habergham
Langho
Altham
Padiham
BURNLEY
Worsthorne
Widdop Moor
Walshaw Dean Resrs.
Wadsworth Moor
Haworth Moor
Oxenhope
Balderstone
Salesbury
Wilpshire
Great Harwood
Clayton-le-Moors
Osbaldeston
Mellor Brook
Mellor
Brownhill
Rishton
Huncoat
Hapton
Rose Hill
Towneley Hall
Hurstwood
Mereclough
Cant Clough Resr.
Gorple Resrs.
Heptonstall Moor
Pecket Well
Beardwood
Samlesbury Bottoms
BLACKBURN
Church
ACCRINGTON
Hameldon
Clowbridge Resr.
Walk Mill
Holme Chapel
FOREST OF ROSSENDALE
Slack
Colden
Heptonstall
Chiserley
Mytholmroyd
Witton Park
Pleasington
Shadsworth
Oswaldtwistle
Scaitcliffe
Dunnockshaw
Goodshaw Fold
Love Clough
Stansfield Moor
Blackshaw Head
Charlestown
Hebden Bridge
Cornholme
Portsmouth
Mill Hill
Lower Darwen
Guide
Baxenden
Goodshaw
Crawshawbooth
Water
Weir
Lumb
Lydgate
Stoodley Pike Monument
Luddenden Foot
Feniscowles
Eachill
Bellhorn
Grimshaw
BLACKBURN INTERCHANGE
Haslingden
ROSSENDALE
Acre
RAWTENSTALL
Newchurch
Whitewell Bottom
Edgeside
Sharneyford
Bacup
Todmorden
Clough Foot
Mankinholes
Cragg Vale
Tockholes
Sunnyhurst
Abbey Village
Withnell
Brinscall
DARWEN
Hoddlesden
Haslingden Grane
Ogden Resr.
Helmshore
Waterfoot
Cowpe
Stacksteads
Britannia
Walsden
Gorpley Resr.
Withens Clough Resr.
Blacksnape
Ewood Bridge
Edenfield
Shawforth
Warland
Soyland Town
Ripponden
Whittlestone Head
Millgate
Whitworth
Summit
Calderbrook
Rishworth
Turton & Entwistle Resr.
Stubbins
RAMSBOTTOM
Edgworth
Chapeltown
Shuttleworth
Holcombe
Broadley
Wardle
Clough
LITTLEBOROUGH
Belmont
Dimple
Turton Bottoms
Egerton
Nuttall
Hawkshaw
Nangreaves
Healey
Rakewood
Smithy Bridge
Smallbridge
Winter Hill
Rivington
HORWICH
Holcombe Brook
Summerseat
Birtle
Norden
ROCHDALE
Moss Moor
Dunscar
Greenmount
Toppings
Eagley
Tottington
Walmersley
BURY
Milnrow
Ogden
Denshaw
Barrow Bridge
Astley Bridge
Bradshaw
Walshaw
Elton
Hooley Bridge
Hooley Brow
Rowhey
BOLTON
Harwood
Starling
Breightmet
Ainsworth
HEYWOOD
Castleton
Lostock Junction
Redvales
Fishpool
Hollins
Slattocks
ROYTON
SHAW
Delph
Diggle
Wingates
Chew Moor
Hunger Hill
Daubhill
Black Lane
RADCLIFFE
WHITEFIELD
Birch
MIDDLETON
Sholver
Moorside
Dobcross
SADDLEWORTH
FARNWORTH
Little Lever
CHADDERTON
Oppermill
Grasscroft
WESTHOUGHTON
Over Hulton
Kearsley
Rhodes
Lees
Greenfield
Daisy Hill
HINDLEY
Park Lane
OLDHAM
ATHERTON
Little Hulton
Walkden
PRESTWICH
Crumpsall
Heaton Hall
Charlestown
Blackley
Tyldesley
WORSLEY
SWINTON
Pendlebury
Broughton Park
Cheetham
Harpurhey
FAILSWORTH
Hollinwood
Bardsley
Mossley
Astley
Blackmoor
Bedford
Boothstown
Hurst
LEIGH
ECCLES
Pendleton
MANCHESTER
ASHTON-UNDER-LYNE
Buckton Vale
STALYBRIDGE
Tintwistle
Pennington
SALFORD
Clayton
DROYLSDEN
DUKINFIELD
Hadfield
Glazebury
Barton
Chat Moss
Trafford Park
Hulme
Gorton
Audenshaw
Mottram in Longdendale
Hollingworth
Twiss Green
Fowley Common
Davyhulme
Kenyon
URMSTON
Old Trafford
Moss Side
Rusholme
Levenshulme
DENTON
HYDE
Gamesley
Culcheth
Flixton
STRETFORD
Fallowfield
Withington
Reddish
Hattersley
Broadbottom
Croft
Irlam
Ashton upon Mersey
Chorlton-cum-Hardy
Burnage
Haughton Green
Charlesworth
Glazebrook
Cadishead
Carrington
SALE
Heaton Moor
Woodley
Gee Cross
Chisworth
Risley
Birchwood
Hollinfare
Partington
Dark Lane
Woodhouses
Brooklands
Didsbury
Bredbury
Compstall
Romiley
Woolston
Warburton
Mossbray
Timperley
STOCKPORT
Martinscroft
Oughtrington
Heatley
CHEADLE
Offerton
Marple
Rowarth
Little Hayfield
Dunham Woodhouses
Dunham Town
ALTRINCHAM
Gatley
Cheadle Hulme
Thelwall
Lymm
Little Bollington
Bowdon
Hale
Wythenshawe
Hazel Grove
Hawk Green
New Mills
Birch Vale
M65
M66
M62
M61
M60
M602
M6
M67
A59
A56
A682
A6068
A680
A666
A671
A6114
A646
A677
A58
A673
A6027
A676
A6053
A57
A6
A579
A580
A576
A627(M)
A663
A6104
A635
A6010
A5103
A6017
A560
A34
A6018
A628
A572
A577
A640
A672
A6033
A62
97
98
84
85
92
E
F
G
H

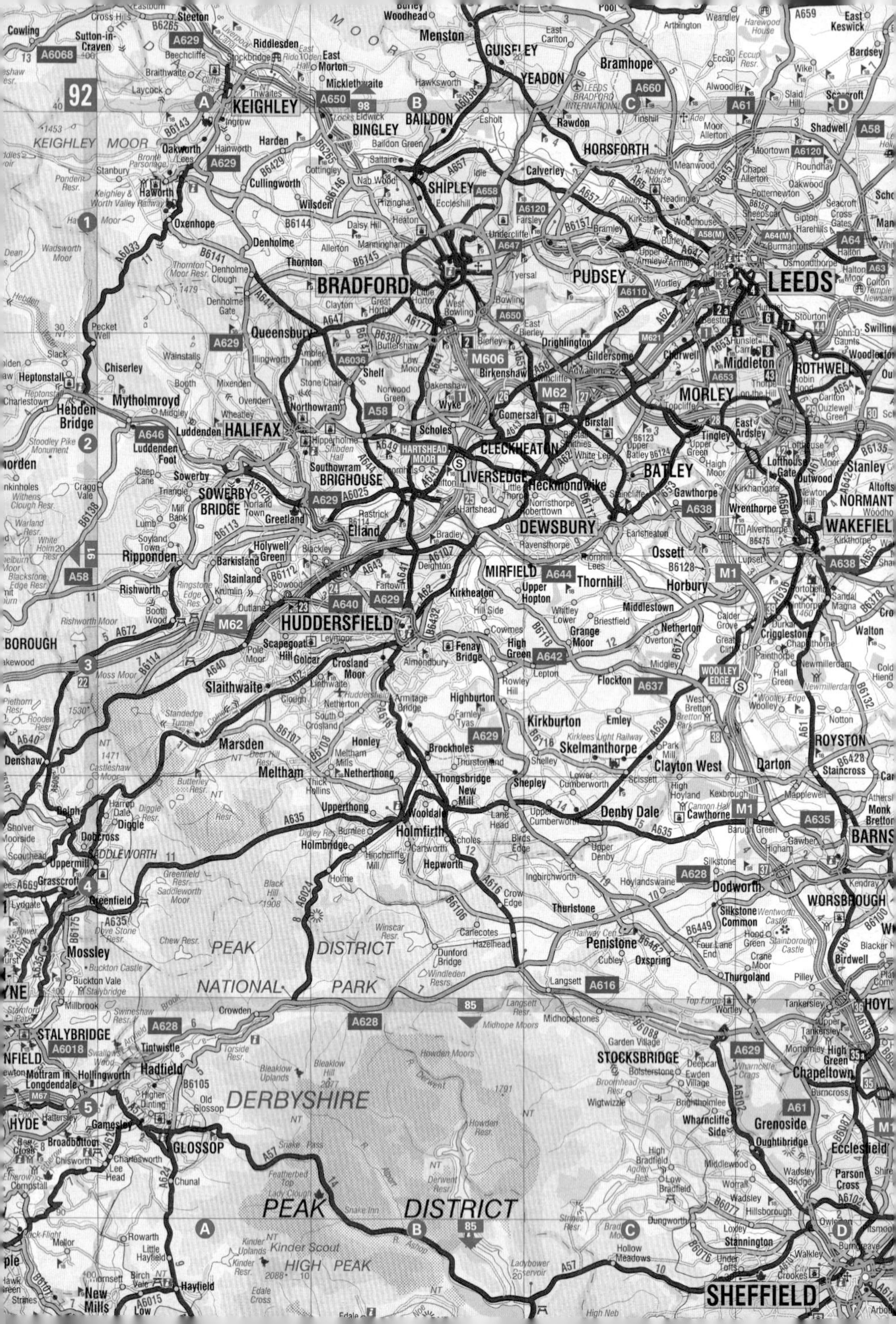

92
98
91
85
KEIGHLEY
BINGLEY
BAILDON
GUISELEY
YEADON
Menston
Bramhope
HORSFORTH
SHIPLEY
BRADFORD
PUDSEY
LEEDS
Keighley Moor
Haworth
Oxenhope
Oakworth
Cullingworth
Wilsden
Denholme
Thornton
Queensbury
HALIFAX
Mytholmroyd
Hebden Bridge
Heptonstall
Luddenden
Luddenden Foot
SOWERBY BRIDGE
Ripponden
Rishworth
Brighouse
Elland
Greetland
CLECKHEATON
LIVERSEDGE
Heckmondwike
DEWSBURY
BATLEY
MORLEY
ROTHWELL
Middleton
Birstall
Gomersal
MIRFIELD
Thornhill
Ossett
Horbury
WAKEFIELD
HUDDERSFIELD
Slaithwaite
Marsden
Meltham
Honley
Holmfirth
Kirkburton
Skelmanthorpe
Clayton West
Denby Dale
Darton
ROYSTON
BARNSLEY
Dodworth
WORSBROUGH
Penistone
STOCKSBRIDGE
Grenoside
Chapeltown
Ecclesfield
SHEFFIELD
Mossley
STALYBRIDGE
HYDE
Hadfield
GLOSSOP
Hayfield
New Mills
Denshaw
Delph
Diggle
Uppermill
SADDLEWORTH
Greenfield
PEAK DISTRICT NATIONAL PARK
DERBYSHIRE
PEAK DISTRICT
HIGH PEAK
Kinder Scout
Howden Moors
Bleaklow Hill
Black Hill
M62
M1
M606
M621
M67
A629
A650
A6068
A660
A61
A58
A6120
A657
A658
A647
A6110
A641
A644
A646
A6036
A6025
A640
A642
A637
A638
A635
A628
A616
A6018
A57
A653
A636
A6024

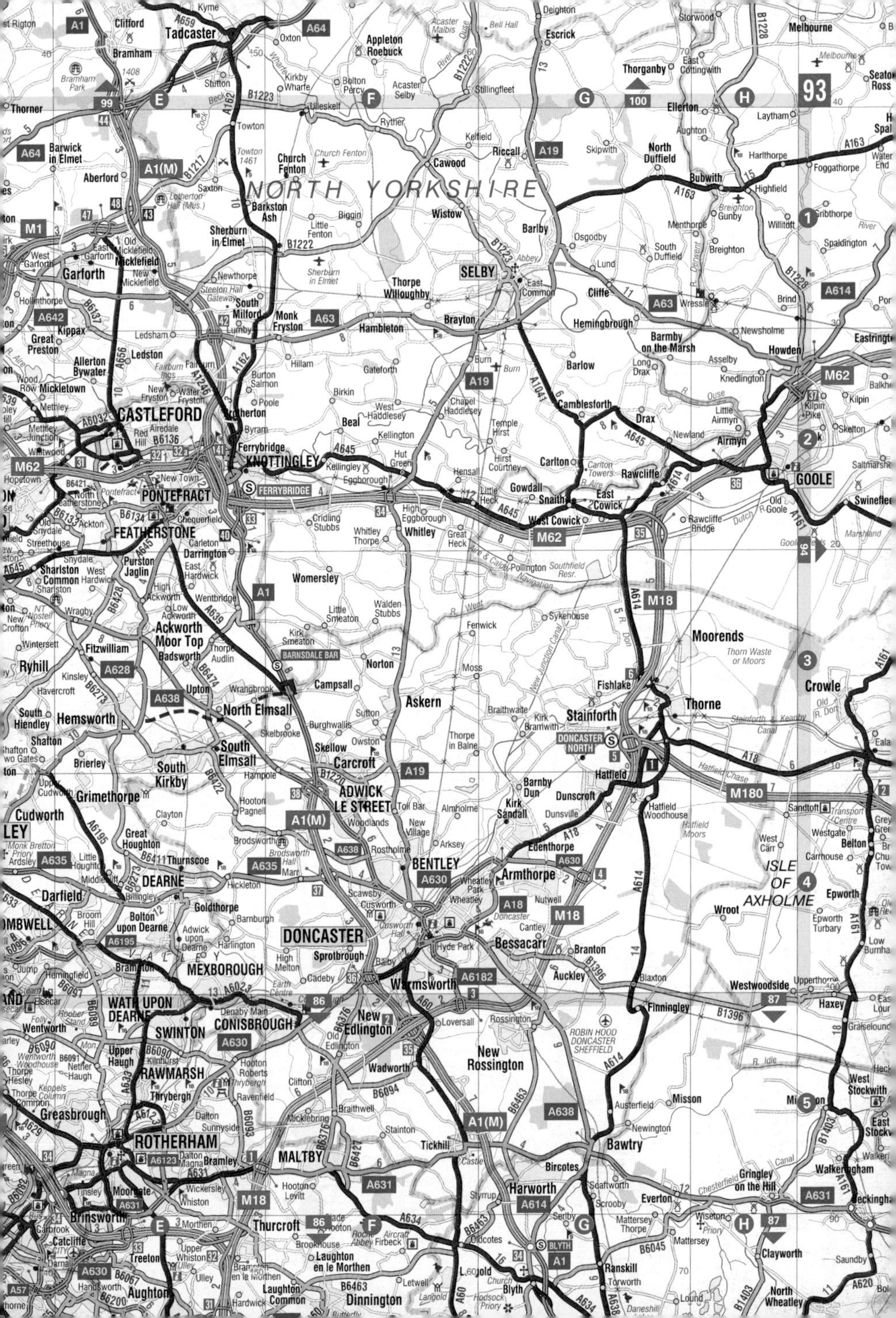

93
NORTH YORKSHIRE
Tadcaster
Clifford
Bramham
Bramham Park
Kyme
Oxton
Appleton Roebuck
Acaster Malbis
Bell Hall
Deighton
Escrick
Storwood
Melbourne
Thorganby
East Cottingwith
Stutton
Kirkby Wharfe
Bolton Percy
Acaster Selby
Stillingfleet
Ulleskelf
Ryther
Thorner
Towton
Barwick in Elmet
Church Fenton
Cawood
Kelfield
Riccall
Skipwith
North Duffield
Ellerton
Aughton
Laytham
Harlthorpe
Foggathorpe
Bubwith
Highfield
Aberford
Saxton
Lotherton Hall (Mus.)
Barkston Ash
Biggin
Wistow
Barlby
Osgodby
South Duffield
Menthorpe
Gunby
Breighton
Gribthorpe
Willitoft
Spaldington
Little Fenton
Sherburn in Elmet
Garforth
Micklefield
Newthorpe
Steeton Hall Gateway
South Milford
Monk Fryston
Hambleton
Thorpe Willoughby
SELBY
Abbey
East Common
Brayton
Lund
Cliffe
Hemingbrough
Wressle
Barmby on the Marsh
Newsholme
Brind
Howden
Eastrington
Kippax
Great Preston
Ledsham
Lumby
Allerton Bywater
Ledston
Fairburn
Fairburn Ings
Hillam
Gateforth
Burn
Barlow
Long Drax
Asselby
Knedlington
Mickletown
Methley
Burton Salmon
Birkin
Poole
New Fryston
Water Fryston
Beal
West Haddlesey
Chapel Haddlesey
Temple Hirst
Camblesforth
Drax
Little Airmyn
Airmyn
Kilpin
Kilpin Pike
Skelton
CASTLEFORD
Airedale
Red Hill
Brotherton
Byram
Ferrybridge
KNOTTINGLEY
Kellington
Hut Green
Kellingley
Eggborough
Hirst Courtney
Carlton
Carlton Towers
Rawcliffe
Newland
GOOLE
Saltmarshe
Swinefleet
Old Goole
PONTEFRACT
New Town
FERRYBRIDGE
Hensall
Little Heck
Gowdall
Snaith
East Cowick
West Cowick
Rawcliffe Bridge
FEATHERSTONE
Ackton
Chequerfield
Cridling Stubbs
Whitley Thorpe
High Eggborough
Whitley
Great Heck
Pollington
Southfield Resr.
Aire & Calder Navigation
Marshland
Carleton
Darrington
East Hardwick
Purston Jaglin
Streethouse
Sharlston Common
West Hardwick
Sharlston
Nostell Priory
Wragby
High Ackworth
Low Ackworth
Wentbridge
Womersley
Little Smeaton
Walden Stubbs
Fenwick
Sykehouse
Moorends
Thorn Waste or Moors
Ackworth Moor Top
Fitzwilliam
Kirk Smeaton
Thorpe Audlin
Badsworth
BARNSDALE BAR
Norton
Moss
Ryhill
Havercroft
Upton
Wrangbrook
Campsall
Askern
New Junction Canal
Fishlake
Thorne
Crowle
South Hiendley
Hemsworth
North Elmsall
Sutton
Burghwallis
Braithwaite
Kirk Bramwith
Stainforth
Stainforth & Keadby Canal
Shafton
Skelbrooke
Skellow
Owston
Thorpe in Balne
DONCASTER NORTH
Brierley
South Elmsall
South Kirkby
Hampole
Carcroft
Hatfield
Hatfield Chase
Cudworth
Grimethorpe
Clayton
Hooton Pagnell
ADWICK LE STREET
Toll Bar
Almholme
Barnby Dun
Dunscroft
Kirk Sandall
Dunsville
Hatfield Woodhouse
Hatfield Moors
Sandtoft
Transport Centre
Westgate
Belton
West Carr
Carrhouse
Woodlands
New Village
Arksey
Great Houghton
Little Houghton
Brodsworth
Brodsworth Hall
Thurnscoe
Marr
Rostholme
BENTLEY
Edenthorpe
Armthorpe
ISLE OF AXHOLME
Epworth
Epworth Turbary
Wroot
Darfield
DEARNE
Hickleton
Goldthorpe
Barnburgh
Scawsby
Cusworth
Cusworth Hall
Wheatley Park
Wheatley
Nutwell
Cantley
Bolton upon Dearne
Adwick upon Dearne
Harlington
DONCASTER
Sprotbrough
Hyde Park
Bessacarr
Branton
Low Burnham
MEXBOROUGH
High Melton
Cadeby
Balby
Warmsworth
Earth Centre
Auckley
Blaxton
Westwoodside
Upperthorpe
Haxey
WATH UPON DEARNE
Denaby Main
CONISBROUGH
New Edlington
Old Edlington
Loversall
Rossington
Finningley
ROBIN HOOD DONCASTER SHEFFIELD
Wentworth
SWINTON
Upper Haugh
Kilnhurst
Hooton Roberts
Thrybergh
Wadworth
New Rossington
West Stockwith
RAWMARSH
Ravenfield
Clifton
Braithwell
Austerfield
Misson
Greasbrough
Dalton
Sunnyside
Micklebring
Stainton
Newington
ROTHERHAM
Dalton Magna
Bramley
MALTBY
Tickhill
Bawtry
Walkeringham
Wickersley
Whiston
Hooton Levitt
Styrrup
Harworth
Bircotes
Scaftworth
Scrooby
Everton
Gringley on the Hill
Chesterfield Canal
Beckingham
Brinsworth
Morthen
Thurcroft
Slade Hooton
Roche Abbey
Firbeck
Oldcotes
Serlby
BLYTH
Mattersey Thorpe
Wiseton
Mattersey
Clayworth
Catcliffe
Treeton
Upper Whiston
Ulley
Brookhouse
Laughton en le Morthen
Letwell
Langold
Blyth
Ranskill
Torworth
Saundby
Aughton
Handsworth
Laughton Common
Dinnington
Hodsock Priory
Daneshill
Lound
North Wheatley

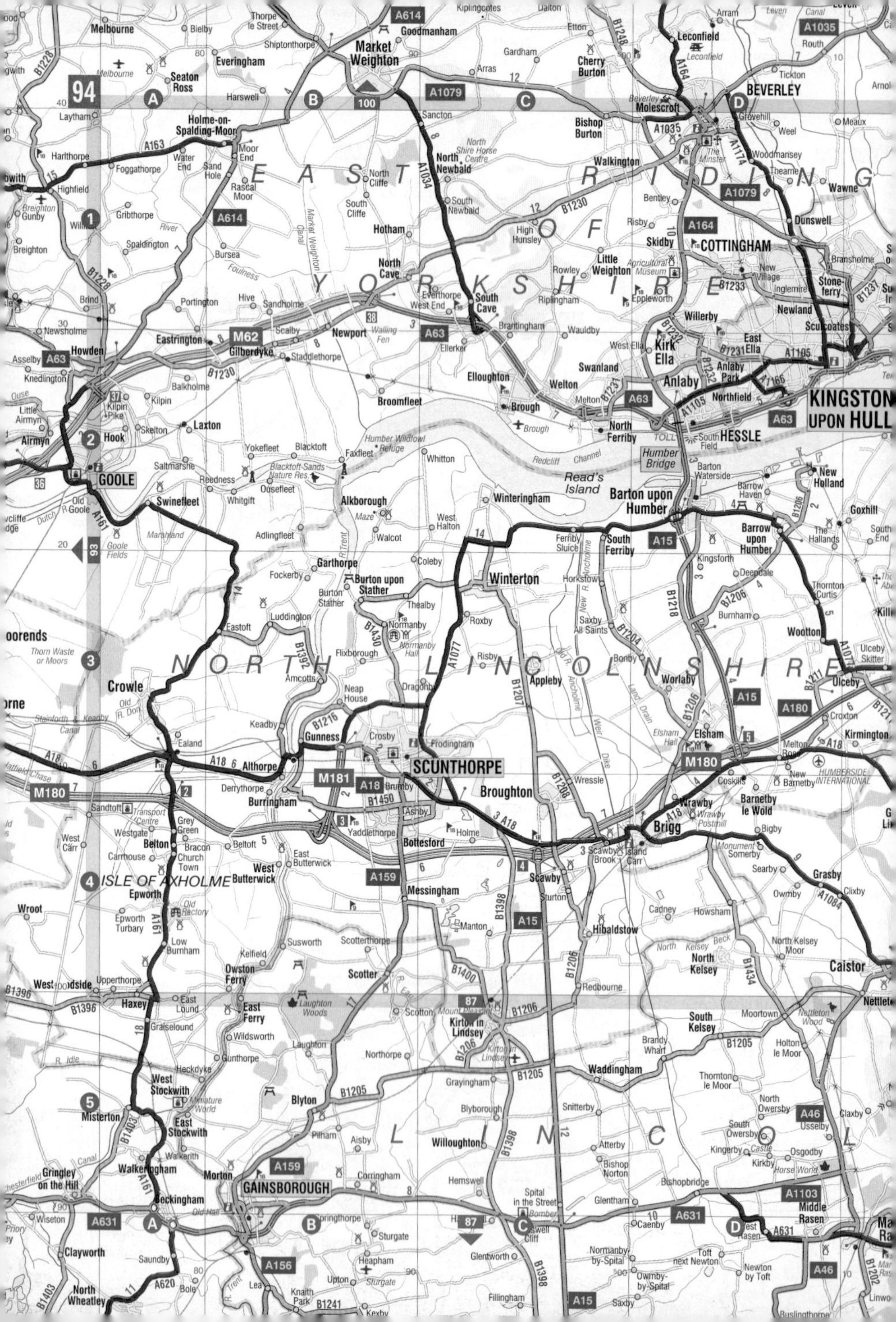
94
EAST RIDING OF YORKSHIRE
NORTH LINCOLNSHIRE
LINCOL
KINGSTON UPON HULL
BEVERLEY
COTTINGHAM
HESSLE
GOOLE
SCUNTHORPE
GAINSBOROUGH
Market Weighton
Melbourne
Bielby
Thorpe le Street
Goodmanham
Kiplingcotes
Dalton
Etton
Leconfield
Arram
Leven Canal
Routh
Tickton
Arnold
Shiptonthorpe
Everingham
Seaton Ross
Harswell
Gardham
Arras
Cherry Burton
Molescroft
Laytham
Holme-on-Spalding-Moor
Sancton
Bishop Burton
Grovehill
Weel
Meaux
Harlthorpe
Foggathorpe
Water End
Moor End
Sand Hole
Rascal Moor
North Newbald
South Newbald
North Shire Horse Centre
North Cliffe
South Cliffe
Walkington
Woodmansey
Thearne
Wawne
Highfield
Breighton
Gunby
Willitoft
Gribthorpe
Spaldington
Bursea
Foulness
Market Weighton Canal
Hotham
High Hunsley
Risby
Bentley
Skidby
Dunswell
North Cave
Rowley
Little Weighton
Agricultural Museum
Riplingham
Eppleworth
New Village
Bransholme
Inglemire
Stoneferry
Brind
Portington
Hive
Sandholme
Everthorpe
West End
South Cave
Willerby
Newland
Newsholme
Scalby
Newport
Walling Fen
Brantingham
Wauldby
West Ella
Kirk Ella
East Ella
Sculcoates
Howden
Asselby
Knedlington
Eastrington
Gilberdyke
Staddlethorpe
Ellerker
Swanland
Anlaby
Anlaby Park
Balkholme
Kilpin
Kilpin Pike
Elloughton
Welton
Melton
Northfield
Broomfleet
Brough
North Ferriby
Little Airmyn
Airmyn
Hook
Skelton
Laxton
Yokefleet
Blacktoft
Faxfleet
Humber Wildfowl Refuge
Whitton
Saltmarshe
Reedness
Blacktoft Sands Nature Res.
Ousefleet
Whitgift
Redcliff Channel
Read's Island
Humber Bridge
Barton Waterside
Barton upon Humber
Barrow Haven
New Holland
South Field
Old Goole
Swinefleet
Alkborough
Maze
Winteringham
Goxhill
Marshland
Goole Fields
Adlingfleet
Walcot
West Halton
Ferriby Sluice
South Ferriby
Barrow upon Humber
The Hallands
South End
Fockerby
Garthorpe
Coleby
Winterton
Horkstow
Kingsforth
Deepdale
Burton upon Stather
Burton Stather
Thealby
Normanby
Normanby Hall
Thornton Curtis
Eastoft
Luddington
Roxby
Saxby All Saints
Burnham
Wootton
Thorne Waste or Moors
Flixborough
Risby
Bonby
Ulceby Skitter
Ulceby
Crowle
Amcotts
Appleby
Worlaby
Dragonby
Neap House
Old R. Don
Stainforth & Keadby Canal
Keadby
Gunness
Crosby
Frodingham
Elsham
Elsham Hall
Croxton
Kirmington
Ealand
Althorpe
Wressle
Melton Ross
Hatfield Chase
Derrythorpe
Burringham
Brumby
Broughton
Coskills
New Barnetby
Barnetby le Wold
Humberside International
Sandtoft
Transport Centre
Grey Green
Westgate
Belton
Bracon
Church Town
Beltoft
East Butterwick
West Butterwick
Ashby
Yaddlethorpe
Bottesford
Holme
Wrawby
Wrawby Postmill
Brigg
Scawby Brook
Island Carr
Bigby
West Carr
Carrhouse
Isle of Axholme
Epworth
Old Rectory
Messingham
Scawby
Sturton
Monument
Somerby
Searby
Grasby
Clixby
Owmby
Wroot
Epworth Turbary
Manton
Cadney
Howsham
Hibaldstow
Low Burnham
Susworth
Scotterthorpe
North Kelsey Moor
North Kelsey
North Kelsey Beck
Kelfield
Owston Ferry
Scotter
Redbourne
Caistor
Upperthorpe
Westwoodside
Haxey
East Lound
East Ferry
Laughton Woods
Scotton
Mount Pleasant
Kirton in Lindsey
Moortown
Nettleton Wood
Nettleton
Graiselound
Wildsworth
Laughton
Northorpe
Kirton in Lindsey
South Kelsey
Brandy Wharf
Holton le Moor
R. Idle
Gunthorpe
Heckdyke
West Stockwith
Miniature World
Grayingham
Waddingham
Thornton le Moor
Blyton
Blyborough
Snitterby
North Owersby
Claxby
Misterton
East Stockwith
Pilham
Aisby
Willoughton
Atterby
South Owersby
Usselby
Walkerith
Bishop Norton
Kingerby
Castle
Osgodby
Kirkby
Horse World
Gringley on the Hill
Chesterfield Canal
Walkeringham
Morton
Corringham
Hemswell
Bishopbridge
Beckingham
Spital in the Street
Glentham
Middle Rasen
Wiseton
Old Hall
Springthorpe
Sturgate
Caenby
West Rasen
Market Rasen
Clayworth
Saundby
Heapham
Glentworth
Normanby-by-Spital
Toft next Newton
Newton by Toft
Bole
Upton
Owmby-by-Spital
North Wheatley
Lea
Knaith Park
Fillingham
Saxby
Kexby
Linwood
Buslingthorpe
A614
A1035
A164
A1079
A1034
A1174
A163
A63
M62
A161
A1077
A15
A18
M180
M181
A159
A46
A1084
A1103
A631
A156
A620
B1228
B1230
B1233
B1231
B1232
B1206
B1218
B1204
B1207
B1208
B1392
B1430
B1216
B1450
B1398
B1400
B1396
B1205
B1434
B1403
B1241
B1202
B1211
B1237
B1248
87
93
100

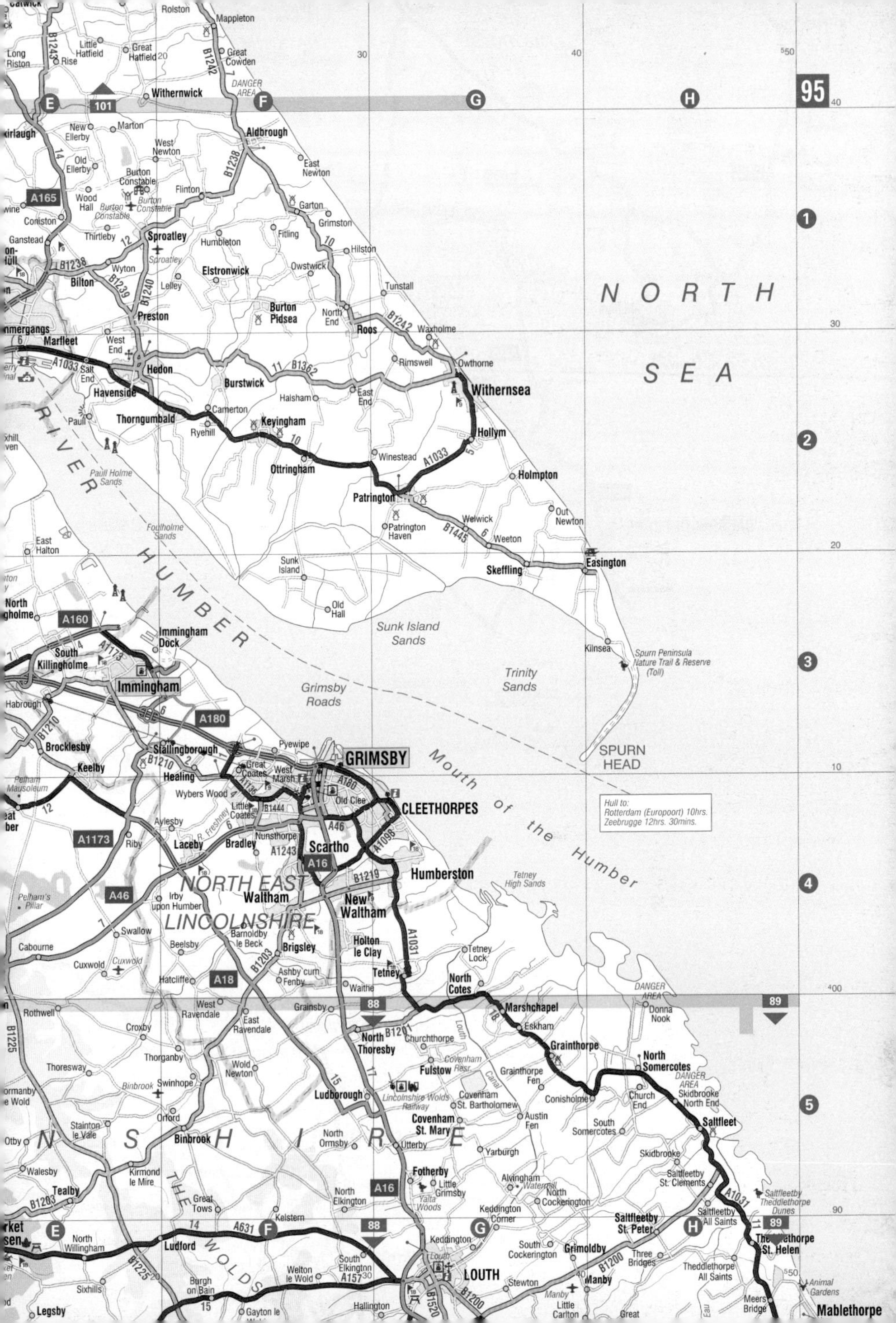
95
NORTH SEA
RIVER HUMBER
Mouth of the Humber
Rolston
Mappleton
Little Hatfield
Great Hatfield
Great Cowden
Long Riston
Rise
Withernwick
DANGER AREA
101
Aldbrough
Marton
New Ellerby
West Newton
East Newton
Old Ellerby
Burton Constable
Flinton
Wood Hall
Garton
Grimston
Coniston
A165
Thirtleby
Sproatley
Humbleton
Fitling
Hilston
Ganstead
Wyton
Bilton
Elstronwick
Owstwick
Lelley
Tunstall
Preston
Burton Pidsea
North End
Roos
Waxholme
Marfleet
West End
Hedon
Salt End
Rimswell
Owthorne
Burstwick
Halsham
East End
Withernsea
Havenside
Paull
Thorngumbald
Camerton
Ryehill
Keyingham
Hollym
Ottringham
Winestead
Holmpton
Paull Holme Sands
Patrington
Patrington Haven
Welwick
Out Newton
Weeton
Foulholme Sands
East Halton
Sunk Island
Skeffling
Easington
Old Hall
Sunk Island Sands
North Killingholme
A160
Immingham Dock
Kilnsea
Spurn Peninsula Nature Trail & Reserve (Toll)
South Killingholme
Trinity Sands
Immingham
Grimsby Roads
Habrough
A180
Brocklesby
Stallingborough
Pyewipe
GRIMSBY
SPURN HEAD
Keelby
Great Coates
West Marsh
Healing
Pelham Mausoleum
Wybers Wood
Old Clee
CLEETHORPES
Little Coates
Hull to:
Rotterdam (Europoort) 10hrs.
Zeebrugge 12hrs. 30mins.
Aylesby
R. Freshney
Nunsthorpe
A46
A1173
Riby
Laceby
Bradley
Scartho
A16
Humberston
NORTH EAST LINCOLNSHIRE
Tetney High Sands
Pelham's Pillar
Irby upon Humber
Waltham
New Waltham
Swallow
Barnoldby le Beck
Cabourne
Beelsby
Brigsley
Holton le Clay
Tetney Lock
Cuxwold
Hatcliffe
A18
Ashby cum Fenby
Tetney
North Cotes
Waithe
DANGER AREA
Rothwell
West Ravendale
Grainsby
88
Marshchapel
89
Donna Nook
East Ravendale
Eskham
Croxby
North Thoresby
Churchthorpe
Grainthorpe
Thorganby
Covenham Resr.
North Somercotes
Thoresway
Wold Newton
Fulstow
Grainthorpe Fen
Binbrook
Swinhope
Ludborough
Lincolnshire Wolds Railway
Covenham St. Bartholomew
Conisholme
Church End
Skidbrooke North End
Orford
Covenham St. Mary
Austin Fen
South Somercotes
Saltfleet
Stainton le Vale
North Ormsby
Utterby
Yarburgh
Binbrook
Skidbrooke
Walesby
Kirmond le Mire
Fotherby
Little Grimsby
Alvingham
Saltfleetby St. Clements
Tealby
A16
North Elkington
Yalta Woods
North Cockerington
Saltfleetby Theddlethorpe Dunes
Great Tows
Keddington Corner
Saltfleetby All Saints
Kelstern
Saltfleetby St. Peter
89
Theddlethorpe St. Helen
North Willingham
Ludford
A631
88
Keddington
South Cockerington
Grimoldby
Three Bridges
South Elkington
Theddlethorpe All Saints
Sixhills
Burgh on Bain
Welton le Wold
LOUTH
Stewton
Manby
Animal Gardens
Legsby
Gayton le Wold
Hallington
Little Carlton
Great Carlton
Meers Bridge
Mablethorpe
THE WOLDS
LINCOLNSHIRE

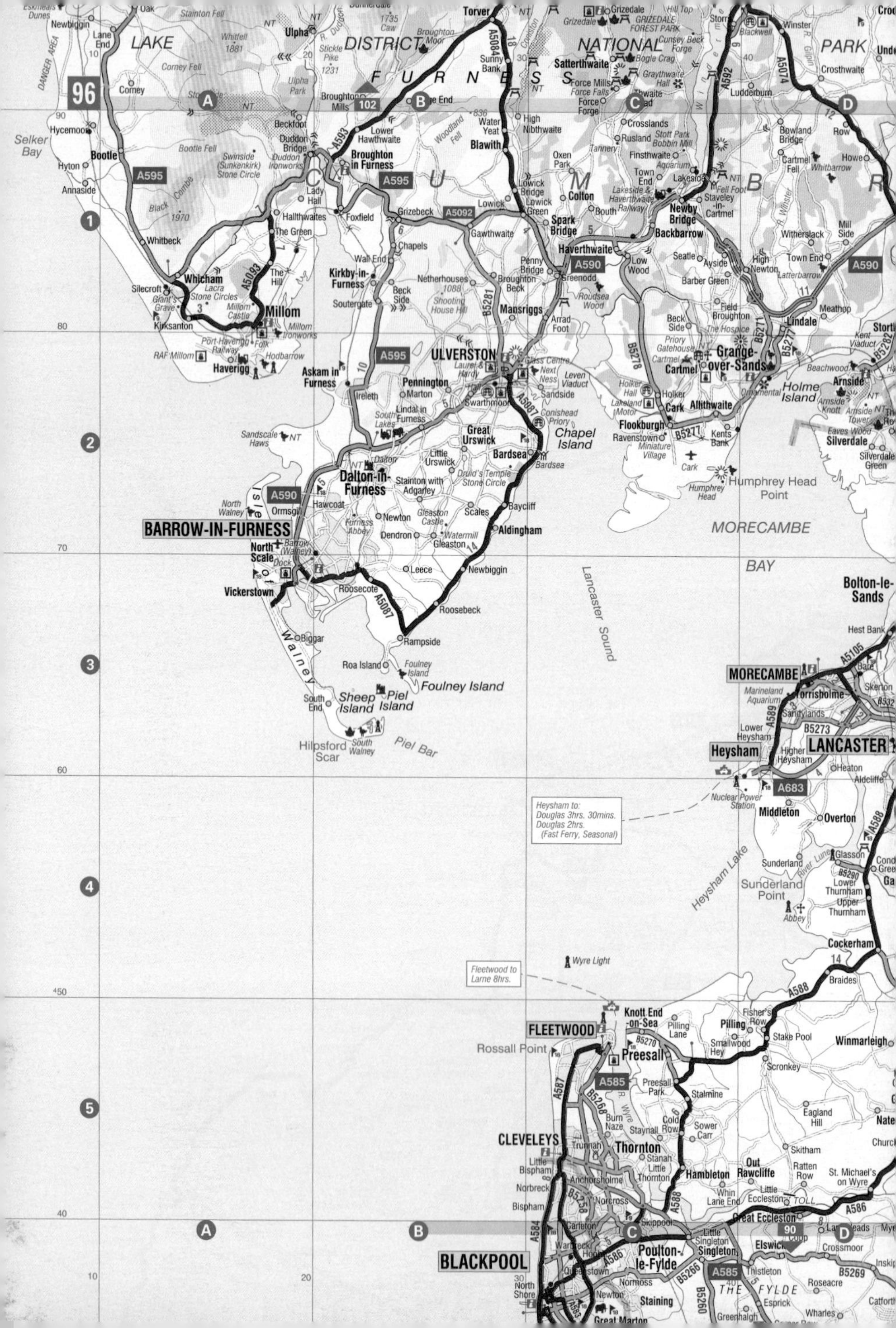

96
102
90
A
B
C
D
1
2
3
4
5
LAKE
DISTRICT
NATIONAL
PARK
FURNESS
CUMBRIA
Newbiggin
Lane End
Stainton Fell
Whitfell 1881
Ulpha
Dunnerdale
Torver
Grizedale
GRIZEDALE FOREST PARK
Hill Top
Winster
Corney Fell
Stickle Pike 1231
Broughton Moor
Cunsey Beck Forge
Satterthwaite
Bogle Crag
Graythwaite Hall
Crosthwaite
Corney
Ulpha Park
Sunny Bank
Force Mills
Force Falls
Force Forge
Thwaite Head
Ludderburn
Broughton Mills
Hycemoor
Selker Bay
Beckfoot
Water Yeat
High Nibthwaite
Crosslands
Bowland Bridge
Row
Bootle
Bootle Fell
Lower Hawthwaite
Woodland Fell
Blawith
Rusland
Stott Park Bobbin Mill
Cartmel Fell
Whitbarrow
Howe
Hyton
Duddon Bridge
Swinside (Sunkenkirk) Stone Circle
Duddon Ironworks
Broughton in Furness
Oxen Park
Finsthwaite
Annaside
A595
Black Combe 1970
Lady Hall
Lowick Bridge
Lowick Green
Lowick
Colton
Bouth
Town End
Lakeside
Lakeside & Haverthwaite Railway
Newby Bridge
Fell Foot
Staveley-in-Cartmel
Hallthwaites
Foxfield
Grizebeck
A5092
Gawthwaite
Spark Bridge
Backbarrow
Witherslack
Mill Side
The Green
Chapels
Haverthwaite
Low Wood
High Newton
Town End
A590
Whitbeck
Wall End
Penny Bridge
Seatle
Ayside
Latterbarrow
Whicham
Lacra Stone Circles
The Hill
A5093
Kirkby-in-Furness
Netherhouses 1088
Broughton Beck
Greenodd
Roudsea Wood
Barber Green
Silecroft
Giant's Grave
Millom Castle
Millom
Beck Side
Shooting House Hill
Field Broughton
Meathop
Soutergate
B5281
Mansriggs
Arrad Foot
Beck Side
Lindale
Kirksanton
Millom Ironworks
The Hospice
Kent Viaduct
Port Haverigg Railway
RAF Millom
Hodbarrow
Haverigg
Priory Gatehouse
Cartmel
Grange-over-Sands
B5278
B5277
B5282
Beachwood
Askam in Furness
ULVERSTON
Laurel & Hardy
Glass Centre
Next Ness
Leven Viaduct
Arnside
Holme Island
Ireleth
Pennington
Marton
Swarthmoor
Sandside
Holker Hall
Holker
Lakeland Motor
Cark
Allithwaite
Ornamental
Arnside Knott
Arnside Tower
Lindal in Furness
South Lakes
A5087
Conishead Priory
Chapel Island
Flookburgh
Ravenstown
Miniature Village
Kents Bank
Eaves Wood
Silverdale
Sandscale Haws
Great Urswick
Bardsea
Little Urswick
Silverdale Green
Dalton-in-Furness
Stainton with Adgarley
Druid's Temple Stone Circle
Humphrey Head
Humphrey Head Point
Isle of Walney
North Walney
A590
Ormsgill
Hawcoat
Baycliff
Scales
Gleaston Castle
Newton
Furness Abbey
BARROW-IN-FURNESS
Aldingham
MORECAMBE
Dendron
Watermill
Gleaston
North Scale
Barrow (Walney)
Dock
Leece
Newbiggin
BAY
Vickerstown
Roosecote
Lancaster Sound
Bolton-le-Sands
Roosebeck
Hest Bank
Biggar
Rampside
A5105
Roa Island
Foulney Island
MORECAMBE
Torrisholme
Marineland Aquarium
Skerton
Walney
South End
Sheep Island
Piel Island
Sandylands
A589
B5273
B5321
Lower Heysham
Hilpsford Scar
South Walney
Piel Bar
Heysham
Higher Heysham
LANCASTER
Heaton
Aldcliffe
Nuclear Power Station
A683
Heysham to:
Douglas 3hrs. 30mins.
Douglas 2hrs.
(Fast Ferry, Seasonal)
Middleton
Overton
A588
Heysham Lake
Sunderland
River Lune
Glasson
B5290
Lower Thurnham
Sunderland Point
Upper Thurnham
Abbey
Cockerham
Wyre Light
Fleetwood to
Larne 8hrs.
Braides
A588
Knott End-on-Sea
FLEETWOOD
Pilling Lane
Pilling
Fisher's Row
Stake Pool
Winmarleigh
B5270
Rossall Point
Preesall
Smallwood Hey
Scronkey
A585
Preesall Park
Stalmine
A587
B5268
River Wyre
Burn Naze
Staynall
Cold Row
Sower Carr
Eagland Hill
CLEVELEYS
Thornton
Trunnah
Stanah
Skitham
Little Bispham
Little Thornton
Hambleton
Out Rawcliffe
Ratten Row
St. Michael's on Wyre
Anchorsholme
Norbreck
Norcross
Whin Lane End
Little Eccleston
TOLL
Bispham
A588
Great Eccleston
A586
Skippool
Carleton
A584
Little Singleton
Elswick
Crossmoor
Warbreck
Hoohe
A586
Singleton
Poulton-le-Fylde
BLACKPOOL
B5266
A585
Thistleton
Roseacre
B5269
Queenstown
North Shore
Normoss
Newton
Staining
B5260
THE FYLDE
Esprick
Wharles
Greenhalgh
Great Marton
Inskip
Catforth
80
70
60
450
40
10
20
30

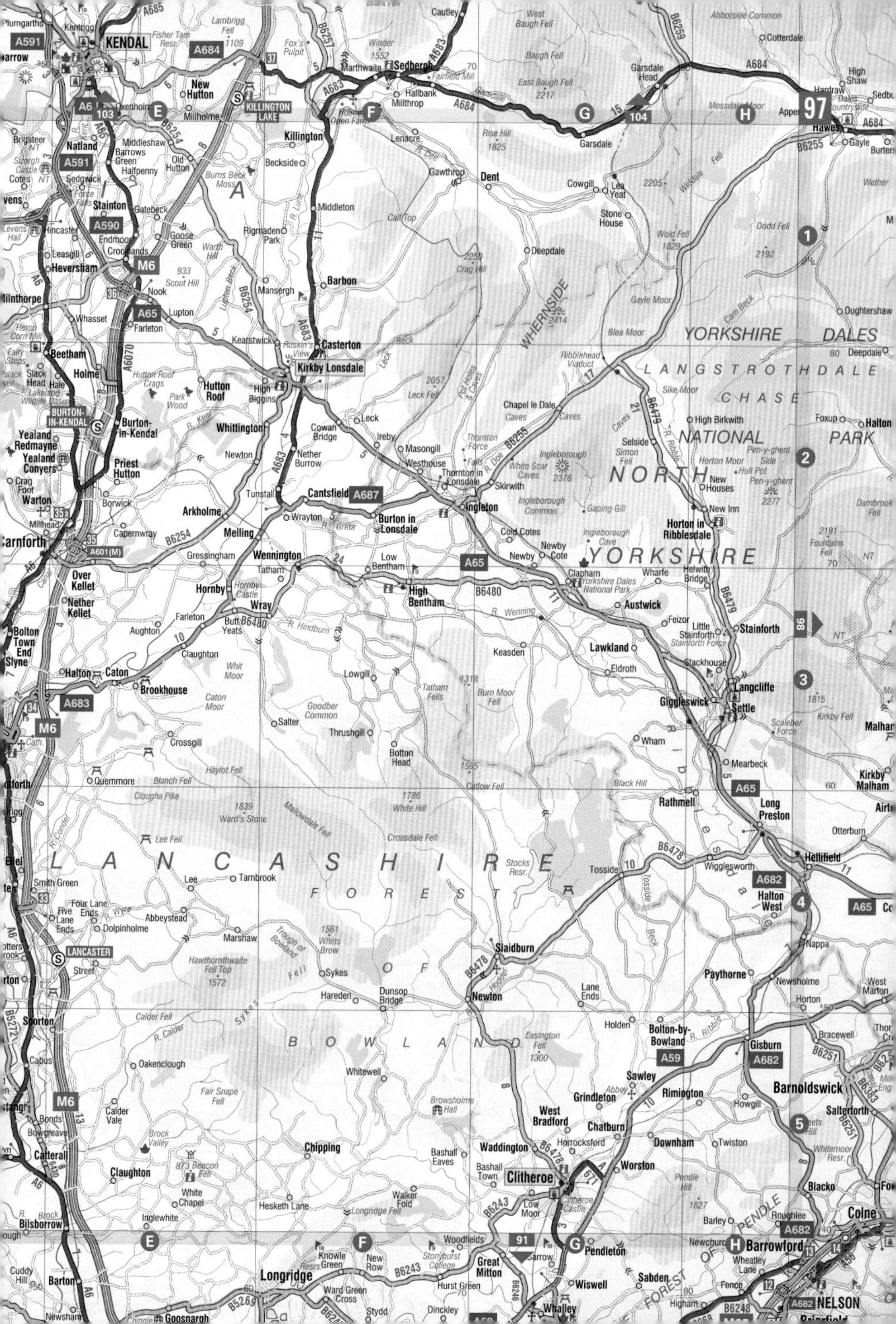
97
KENDAL
A591
A684
A685
A6
103
Plumgarths
Kentrigg
Fisher Tarn Resr.
Lambrigg Fell 1109
New Hutton
Oxenholme
Millholme
KILLINGTON LAKE
37
Fox's Pulpit
Winder 1552
B6257
Marthwaite
Sedbergh
A683
Fairfield Mill
Hallbank
Millthrop
Holme Open Farm
Cautley
West Baugh Fell
Baugh Fell
East Baugh Fell 2217
Garsdale
Garsdale Head
B6259
Abbotside Common
Cotterdale
High Shaw
Hardraw
Hawes
Gayle
A684
104
Mossdale Moor
Rise Hill 1825
Lenacre
R. Dee
Gawthrop
Dent
Cowgill
Lea Yeat
Stone House
Widdale Fell
2205
B6255
Wether
Dodd Fell 2192
Wold Fell 1829
Gayle Moor
Cam Beck
Oughtershaw
Brigsteer
Natland
A591
Middleshaw
Barrows Green
Halfpenny
Old Hutton
B6254
Sizergh Castle NT
Cotes
Sedgwick
Force Falls
Stainton
A590
Gatebeck
Burns Beck Moss
Killington
Beckside
Middleton
Levens
Levens Hall
Hincaster
Endmoor
Crooklands
Goose Green
Rigmaden Park
Calf Top
Leasgill
Heversham
M6
933 Scout Hill
Warth Hill
Crag Hill 2250
Deepdale
Milnthorpe
36
Nook
A65
Lupton
Lupton Beck
Mansergh
Barbon
WHERNSIDE 2414
Whasset
Farleton
Heron Corn Mill
Beetham
A6070
Kearstwick
Ruskin's View
Casterton
Kirkby Lonsdale
Leck Beck
Blea Moor
Ribblehead Viaduct
YORKSHIRE DALES
Deepdale
Fairy Steps
Slack Head
Hale
Lakeland Wildlife Oasis
Holme
Hutton Roof Crags
Park Wood
Hutton Roof
High Biggins
2057
Leck Fell
Pot Holes & Caves
Chapel le Dale
Caves
LANGSTROTHDALE CHASE
Sike Moor
BURTON-IN-KENDAL
Burton-in-Kendal
R. Keer
Whittington
Cowan Bridge
Leck
Ireby
Masongill
Thornton Force
Ingleborough 2376
Selside
Simon Fell
High Birkwith
NATIONAL
PARK
Foxup
Halton
Yealand Redmayne
Yealand Conyers
Priest Hutton
Newton
Nether Burrow
Westhouse
Thornton in Lonsdale
White Scar Caves
Skirwith
Horton Moor
Pen-y-ghent Side
Hull Pot
Pen-y-ghent 2277
NORTH
New Houses
Crag Foot
Warton
Borwick
Arkholme
Tunstall
Cantsfield
A687
Ingleton
Ingleborough Common
Gaping Gill
New Inn
Horton in Ribblesdale
Dambrook Fell
35a
Millhead
Capernwray
Melling
Wrayton
R. Greta
Burton in Lonsdale
Cold Cotes
Ingleborough Cave
Carnforth
35
A601(M)
B6254
Gressingham
Wennington
Tatham
Low Bentham
Newby
Newby Cote
YORKSHIRE
2191 Fountains Fell
NT
Over Kellet
Nether Kellet
Hornby
Hornby Castle
Wray
High Bentham
B6480
Clapham
Yorkshire Dales National Park
Wharfe
Helwith Bridge
B6479
Austwick
Bolton Town End
Slyne
Aughton
Farleton
Butt Yeats
R. Hindburn
R. Wenning
Feizor
Little Stainforth
Stainforth Force
Stainforth
98
Claughton
Keasden
Lawkland
Eldroth
Stackhouse
Halton
Caton
Brookhouse
Whit Moor
Lowgill
Tatham Fells
1318
Burn Moor Fell
Langcliffe
Giggleswick
Settle
1815
Kirkby Fell
Malham
34
A683
M6
Caton Moor
Salter
Goodber Common
Thrushgill
Botton Head
Wham
Scaleber Force
Cath.
Crossgill
Quernmore
Blanch Fell
Haylot Fell
1595
Mearbeck
Clougha Pike
1839 Ward's Stone
Mallowdale Fell
1786 White Hill
Catlow Fell
Black Hill
Rathmell
A65
Long Preston
Kirkby Malham
Otterburn
Lee Fell
Croasdale Fell
Stocks Resr.
B6478
Wigglesworth
Hellifield
LANCASHIRE
FOREST OF BOWLAND
Lee
Tarnbrook
Tosside
Halton West
A682
Smith Green
33
Four Lane Ends
Five Lane Ends
R. Wyre
Abbeystead
Dolphinholme
Marshaw
Trough of Bowland
1561 Whins Brow
Slaidburn
Nappa
A65
LANCASTER
Street
Hawthornthwaite Fell Top 1572
Sykes
Sykes Fell
Hareden
Dunsop Bridge
Newton
R. Hodder
Lane Ends
Paythorne
Newsholme
West Marton
Horton
Scorton
B5272
Calder Fell
R. Calder
Holden
Bolton-by-Bowland
R. Ribble
Easington Fell 1300
Gisburn
A682
Bracewell
A59
B6251
Cabus
Oakenclough
Whitewell
Sawley
Abbey
Barnoldswick
B6383
Fair Snape Fell
Browsholme Hall
Grindleton
Rimington
Howgill
Salterforth
M6
Bonds
Bowgreave
Calder Vale
West Bradford
Chatburn
Downham
Twiston
Weets Hill
Whitemoor Resr.
Brock Valley
Chipping
Bashall Eaves
Waddington
Horrocksford
Catterall
Claughton
873 Beacon Fell
Bashall Town
Clitheroe
Worston
Pendle Hill 1827
Blacko
White Chapel
Hesketh Lane
Walker Fold
Longridge Fell
B6243
Low Moor
Clitheroe Castle
Barley
Roughlee
Colne
Bilsborrow
Inglewhite
PENDLE
A682
Knowle Green
New Row
Woodfields
Stonyhurst College
91
Great Mitton
Barrow
Pendleton
Newchurch
Barrowford
Longridge
B6243
Hurst Green
Wiswell
Sabden
FOREST OF PENDLE
Wheatley Lane
Fence
Cuddy Hill
Barton
Ward Green Cross
B5269
Dinckley
Whalley
B6246
Higham
B6248
A682
NELSON
Newsham
Goosnargh
Stydd
Brierfield

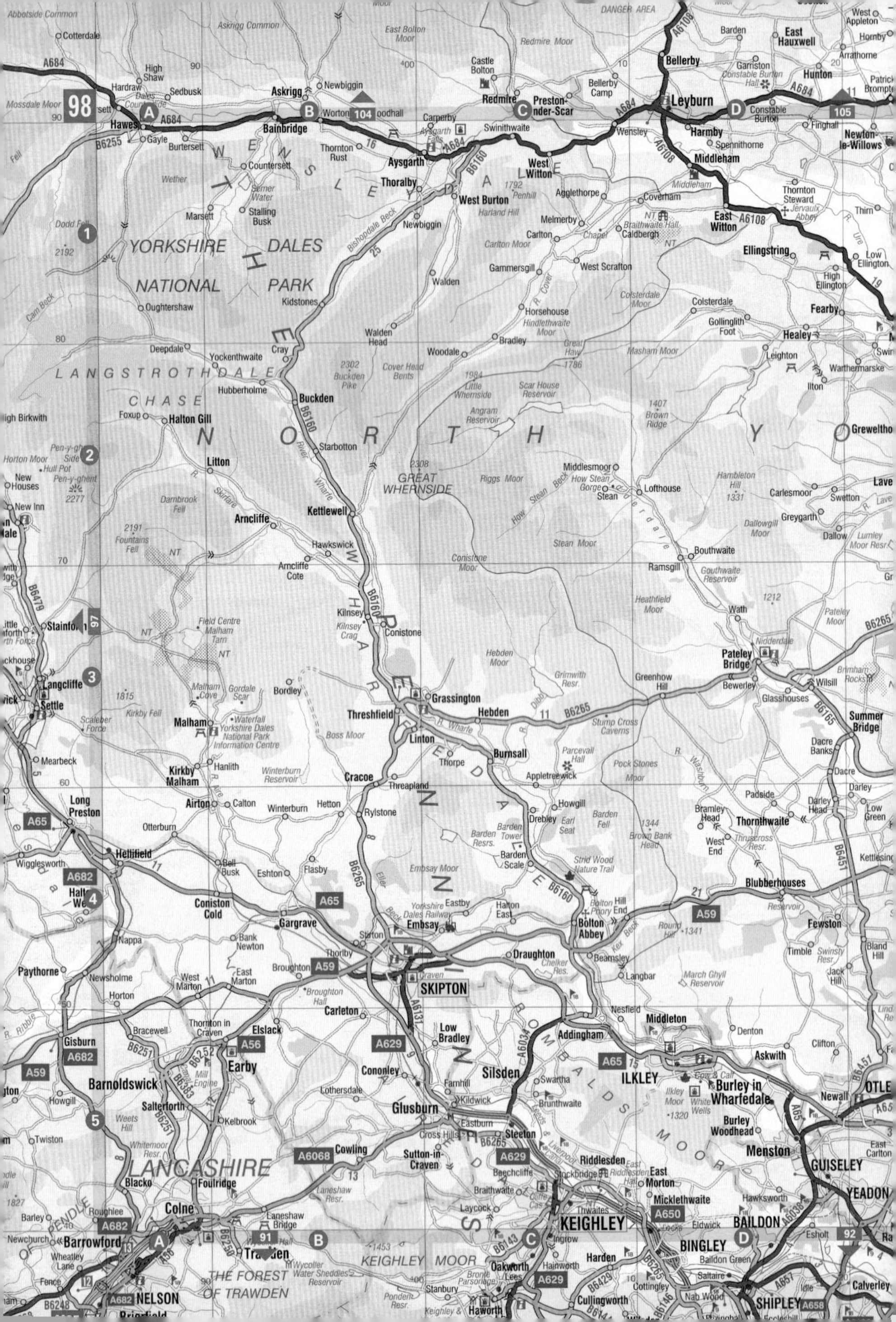

98
Abbotside Common
Cotterdale
Askrigg Common
East Bolton Moor
DANGER AREA
Redmire Moor
A6108
Barden
East Hauxwell
West Appleton
Hornby
Arrathorne
A684
High Shaw
Hardraw
Sedbusk
Askrigg
Newbiggin
Castle Bolton
Bellerby
Bellerby Camp
Garriston
Constable Burton Hall
Hunton
Patrick Brompton
Mossdale Moor
Hawes
Bainbridge
Worton
104
Woodhall
Carperby
Aysgarth Falls
Redmire
Preston-under-Scar
Leyburn
Constable Burton
105
Gayle
Burtersett
Thornton Rust
Aysgarth
Swinithwaite
Wensley
Harmby
Finghall
Newton-le-Willows
B6255
Countersett
W E N S L E Y D A L E
B6160
West Witton
Spennithorne
Middleham
Wether
Semer Water
Thoralby
1792 Penhill
Agglethorpe
Coverham
Thornton Steward
Marsett
Stalling Busk
West Burton
Harland Hill
Melmerby
Braithwaite Hall
East Witton
A6108
Jervaulx Abbey
Thirn
Dodd Fell
2192
Bishopdale Beck
Newbiggin
Carlton
Caldbergh
Carlton Moor
Chapel
YORKSHIRE DALES NATIONAL PARK
Ellingstring
Low Ellington
Gammersgill
West Scrafton
High Ellington
Cam Beck
Walden
Colsterdale Moor
Colsterdale
Fearby
Oughtershaw
Kidstones
Horsehouse
Hindlethwaite Moor
Gollinglith Foot
Healey
Deepdale
Yockenthwaite
Cray
Walden Head
Woodale
Bradley
Great Haw 1786
Masham Moor
Leighton
Warthermarske
LANGSTROTHDALE CHASE
2302 Buckden Pike
Cover Head Bents
1984 Little Whernside
Scar House Reservoir
Ilton
Hubberholme
Buckden
Angram Reservoir
1407 Brown Ridge
Foxup
Halton Gill
High Birkwith
N O R T H Y O
Grewelthorpe
Horton Moor
Hull Pot
Pen-y-ghent Side
Pen-y-ghent 2277
Starbotton
2308 GREAT WHERNSIDE
Riggs Moor
Middlesmoor
How Stean Gorge
Stean
Lofthouse
Hambleton Hill 1331
Carlesmoor
Swetton
Lave
Litton
New Houses
New Inn
Darnbrook Fell
Kettlewell
Stean Moor
Greygarth
Dallowgill Moor
Dallow
Lumley Moor Resr.
Arncliffe
2191 Fountains Fell
Hawkswick
Conistone Moor
Bouthwaite
Arncliffe Cote
Ramsgill
Gouthwaite Reservoir
B6479
Heathfield Moor
1212
Pateley Moor
Stainforth
97
Field Centre Malham Tarn
Kilnsey
Kilnsey Crag
Conistone
Wath
B6265
Hebden Moor
Nidderdale
Pateley Bridge
Brimham Rocks
Langcliffe
Settle
1815
Kirkby Fell
Malham Cove
Gordale Scar
Bordley
Grimwith Resr.
Greenhow Hill
Bewerley
Wilsill
Glasshouses
Scaleber Force
Malham
Waterfall Yorkshire Dales National Park Information Centre
Threshfield
Grassington
Hebden
B6265
Summer Bridge
B6165
Boss Moor
Linton
Stump Cross Caverns
Mearbeck
Kirkby Malham
Hanlith
Thorpe
Burnsall
Parcevall Hall
Pock Stones Moor
Dacre Banks
Winterburn Reservoir
Cracoe
Threapland
Appletreewick
Dacre
Long Preston
Airton
Calton
Winterburn
Hetton
Rylstone
Howgill
Drebley
Barden Fell
Padside
Bramley Head
Darley
Darley Head
Low Green
A65
Otterburn
Earl Seat
Barden Tower
Barden Resrs.
1344 Brown Bank Head
Thornthwaite
West End
Thruscross Resr.
B6451
Hellifield
Wigglesworth
A682
Bell Busk
Eshton
Flasby
Embsay Moor
B6265
Barden Scale
Strid Wood Nature Trail
B6160
Kettlesing
Blubberhouses
Halton West
Coniston Cold
A65
Yorkshire Dales Railway
Eastby
Halton East
Bolton Priory
Hill End
A59
Reservoir
Fewston
Nappa
Gargrave
Embsay
Bolton Abbey
Round Hill 1341
Kex Beck
Bank Newton
Skipton
Draughton
Beamsley
Timble
Swinsty Resr.
Bland Hill
Paythorne
Newsholme
West Marton
East Marton
Broughton
A59
Thorlby
Chelker Res.
Langbar
March Ghyll Reservoir
Jack Hill
Horton
Broughton Hall
SKIPTON
A6131
Nesfield
Middleton
Denton
R. Ribble
Thornton in Craven
Carleton
Low Bradley
A6034
Addingham
Bracewell
Elslack
A56
A629
Clifton
Gisburn
A682
B6251
B6252
Earby
Mill Engine
Cononley
Silsden
A65
ILKLEY
Cow & Calf
Burley in Wharfedale
Askwith
A59
Barnoldswick
Farnhill
Swartha
Kildwick
Brunthwaite
Ilkley Moor
White Wells
1320
Newall
OTLEY
Howgill
Salterforth
Lothersdale
Glusburn
Burley Woodhead
Weets Hill
Kelbrook
Eastburn
Cross Hills
Steeton
B6265
Twiston
Whitemoor Reservoir
A6068
Cowling
Sutton-in-Craven
A629
Riddlesden
East Morton
Menston
GUISELEY
East Carlton
LANCASHIRE
Blacko
Foulridge
Beechcliffe
Stockbridge
East Riddlesden Hall
Micklethwaite
YEADON
1827
Roughlee
Colne
Laneshaw Resr.
Laneshaw Bridge
Braithwaite
Laycock
Thwaites
A650
Hawksworth
Barley
A682
KEIGHLEY
Eldwick
BAILDON
A6038
Newchurch
Barrowford
B6250
91
B
Trawden
1453
Ingrow
B6143
Esholt
92
Wheatley Lane
Wycoller
KEIGHLEY MOOR
Water Sheddles Reservoir
Oakworth
Lees
Harden
Hainworth
BINGLEY
Baildon Green
Saltaire
FOREST OF PENDLE
THE FOREST OF TRAWDEN
Bronte Parsonage
A629
B6429
Cottingley
B6265
A657
Idle
Calverley
Fence
B6248
NELSON
A682
Brierfield
Ponden Resr.
Stanbury
Haworth
Keighley &
Cullingworth
Nab Wood
SHIPLEY
A658

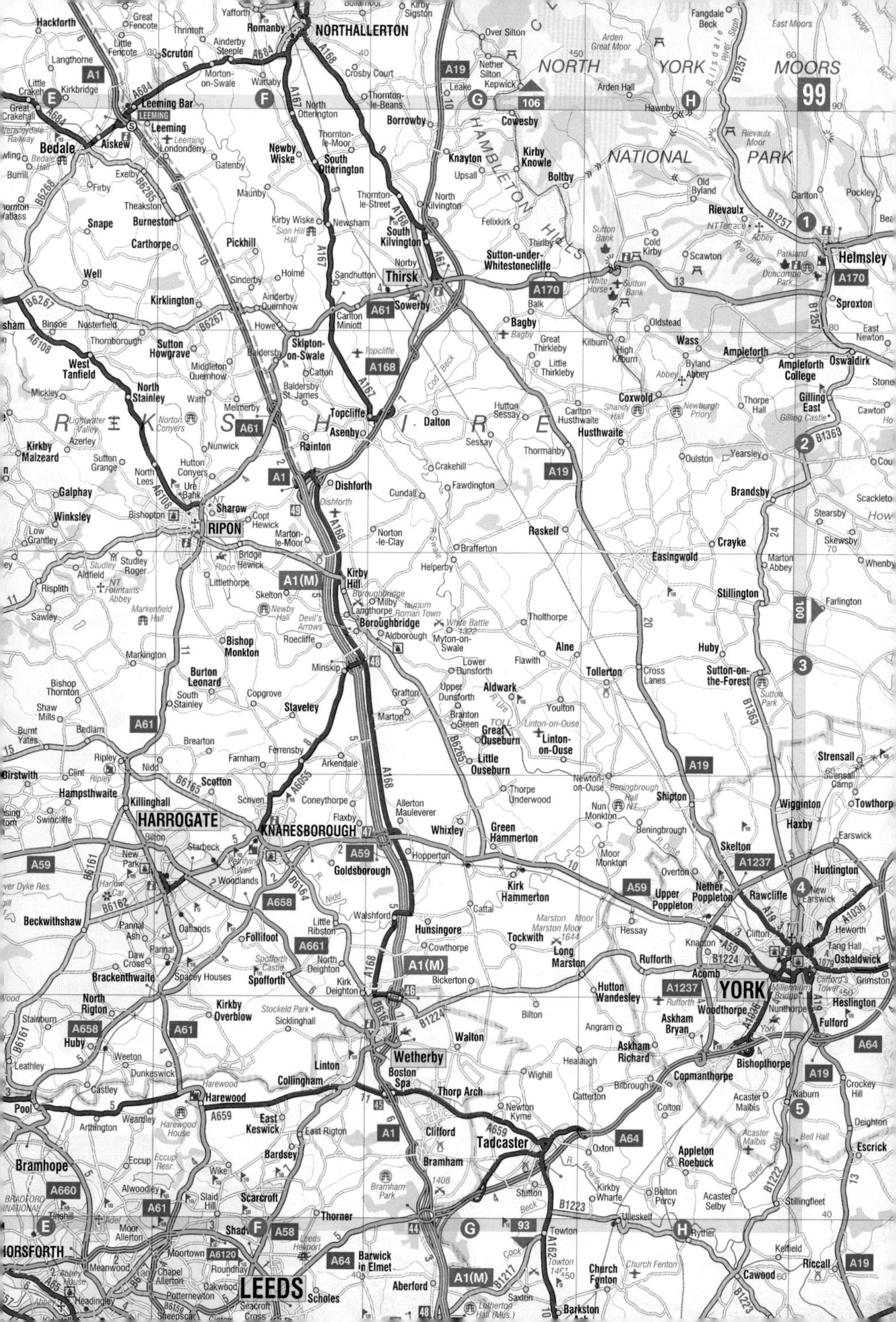

Hackforth
Great Fencote
Thrintoft
Yafforth
Romanby
NORTHALLERTON
Kirby Sigston
Over Silton
Fangdale Beck
East Moors
Little Fencote
Scruton
Ainderby Steeple
Arden Great Moor
NORTH
YORK
MOORS
99
Langthorne
A1
Morton-on-Swale
Warlaby
Crosby Court
A19
Nether Silton
Kepwick
Little Crakehall
Kirkbridge
E
F
Thornton-le-Beans
Leake
G
106
Arden Hall
Hawnby
H
Great Crakehall
Leeming Bar
LEEMING
North Otterington
Borrowby
Cowesby
Bedale
Aiskew
Leeming
Londonderry
Newby Wiske
Thornton-le-Moor
South Otterington
Knayton
Kirby Knowle
NATIONAL
PARK
Rievaulx Moor
Bedale Hall
Gatenby
Upsall
Boltby
Exelby
Old Byland
Burrill
Firby
HAMBLETON
Carlton
Pockley
Maunby
Thornton-le-Street
North Kilvington
Rievaulx
Theakston
Snape
Burneston
Kirby Wiske
Newsham
South Kilvington
Felixkirk
NT Terrace
Sion Hill Hall
Sutton Bank
HILLS
Cold Kirby
Helmsley
Carthorpe
Pickhill
Thirlby
Sutton-under-Whitestonecliffe
Scawton
Parkland
Duncombe Park
Norby
Well
Holme
Sandhutton
Thirsk
White Horse
A170
Sinderby
Sowerby
Sutton Bank
Kirklington
Ainderby Quernhow
Carlton Miniott
A61
Balk
Spoxton
B6267
Binsoe
Nosterfield
Howe
Bagby
Great Thirkleby
Oldstead
Thornborough
Sutton Howgrave
Baldersby
Skipton-on-Swale
Topcliffe
Kilburn
Wass
Ampleforth
East Newton
West Tanfield
Middleton Quernhow
Catton
A168
Little Thirkleby
High Kilburn
Byland Abbey
Ampleforth College
Oswaldkirk
Baldersby St. James
Cod Beck
Gilling East
Mickley
North Stainley
Wath
Melmerby
Topcliffe
Dalton
Hutton Sessay
Carlton Husthwaite
Coxwold
Shandy Hall
Newburgh Priory
Thorpe Hall
Gilling Castle
Cawton
Lightwater Valley
Norton Conyers
Asenby
Sessay
Husthwaite
Kirkby Malzeard
Azerley
Nunwick
Rainton
Thormanby
Oulston
Yearsley
Sutton Grange
Hutton Conyers
Crakehill
A19
Brandsby
North Lees
Ure Bank
Dishforth
Fawdington
Galphay
Sharow
Cundall
Scackleton
Winksley
Bishopton
RIPON
Copt Hewick
Raskelf
Stearsby
Low Grantley
Marton-le-Moor
Norton-le-Clay
Crayke
Skewsby
Studley Roger
Bridge Hewick
Brafferton
Easingwold
Marton Abbey
Studley
Aldfield
Ripon
Helperby
Whenby
Risplith
NT Fountains Abbey
Littlethorpe
A1(M)
Kirby Hill
Stillington
Farlington
Skelton
Boroughbridge
Milby
Isurium Roman Town
100
Sawley
Markenfield Hall
Newby Hall
Langthorpe
Devil's Arrows
White Battle 1322
Tholthorpe
Bishop Monkton
Roecliffe
Aldborough
Mynton-on-Swale
Markington
Alne
Huby
Minskip
Lower Dunsforth
Flawith
Tollerton
Cross Lanes
Sutton-on-the-Forest
Burton Leonard
Bishop Thornton
Aldwark
Upper Dunsforth
Grafton
South Stainley
Copgrove
Staveley
Youlton
Sutton Park
Shaw Mills
Marton
Branton Green
Linton-on-Ouse
Bedlam
Great Ouseburn
Burnt Yates
Brearton
Ferrensby
Arkendale
Little Ouseburn
Strensall
Ripley
Farnham
Strensall Camp
Nidd
Birstwith
Clint
Scotton
A19
Newton-on-Ouse
Beningbrough Hall
Hampsthwaite
Coneythorpe
Thorpe Underwood
Shipton
Wigginton
Towthorpe
Killinghall
Scriven
Allerton Mauleverer
Nun Monkton
Swincliffe
HARROGATE
Flaxby
Whixley
Green Hammerton
Beningbrough
Haxby
KNARESBOROUGH
Earswick
Bilton
Starbeck
A59
Hopperton
Moor Monkton
Skelton
Huntington
New Park
Goldsborough
A1237
Petrifying Well
Overton
Woodlands
Kirk Hammerton
Upper Poppleton
Nether Poppleton
Rawcliffe
New Earswick
Beckwithshaw
A658
Cattal
Walshford
Marston Moor
Hessay
Clifton
Heworth
Pannal Ash
Oatlands
Little Ribston
Hunsingore
Marston Moor 1644
Follifoot
Tockwith
Knapton
Tang Hall
Pannal
Daw Cross
A661
Cowthorpe
Long Marston
Rufforth
Osbaldwick
North Deighton
Acomb
Brackenthwaite
Spacey Houses
Spofforth Castle
A1(M)
Bickerton
YORK
Grimston
Spofforth
Kirk Deighton
Hutton Wandesley
Millennium Bridge
Clifford's Tower
North Rigton
Kirkby Overblow
Stockeld Park
Sicklinghall
Rufforth
Heslington
Bilton
Askham Bryan
Woodthorpe
Nunthorpe
Stainburn
B1224
Walton
Angram
Fulford
Huby
A64
Weeton
Wetherby
Askham Richard
Bishopthorpe
Leathley
Dunkeswick
Linton
Healaugh
Boston Spa
Copmanthorpe
Harewood
Collingham
Wighill
Crockey Hill
Castley
Thorp Arch
Bilbrough
Pool
Harewood
Catterton
Acaster Malbis
Naburn
A659
Newton Kyme
Colton
Deighton
Arthington
Weardley
Harewood House
East Keswick
East Rigton
Clifford
Acaster Malbis
Bell Hall
A1
Tadcaster
Oxton
Escrick
Bramhope
Eccup
Eccup Resr.
Bardsey
Appleton Roebuck
Bramham
A660
Wike
1408
Bramham Park
Alwoodley
Kirkby Wharfe
Bolton Percy
Stillingfleet
Slaid Hill
Scarcroft
Stutton
Acaster Selby
Thorner
B1223
Moor Allerton
Shadwell
A58
93
Ulleskelf
Ryther
Towton
HORSFORTH
Moortown
A6120
Leeds Heliport
Barwick in Elmet
Kelfield
Meanwood
Chapel Allerton
Roundhay
A64
Towton 1461
Church Fenton
Riccall
Cawood
LEEDS
Oakwood
A1(M)
Aberford
Potternewton
Scholes
Headingley
Seacroft
Cross
Lotherton Hall (Mus.)
Saxton
Barkston

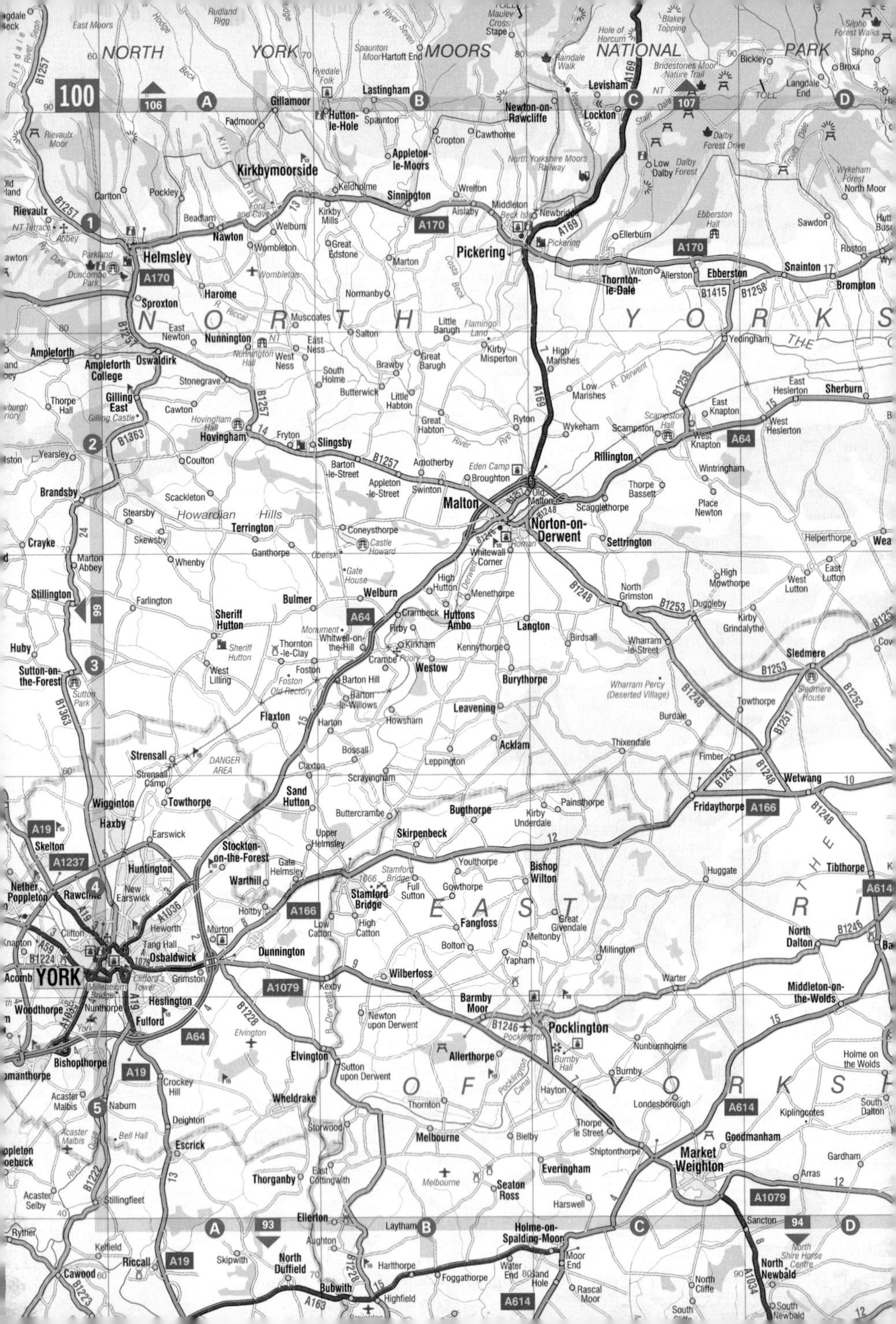
100
NORTH
YORK
MOORS
NATIONAL
PARK
106
107
A
B
C
D
East Moors
Rudland Rigg
Hodge Beck
Bilsdale
River Seph
B1257
Ryedale Folk
Spaunton Moor
Hartoft End
Mauley Cross
Stape
Hole of Horcum
Blakey Topping
Bridestones Moor Nature Trail
Silpho Forest Walks
Silpho
Bickley
Broxa
Langdale End
TOLL
Raindale Walk
Newton Dale
Levisham
Lockton
Newton-on-Rawcliffe
A169
Stain Dale
NT
Dalby Forest Drive
Low Dalby
Dalby Forest
Troutsdale
Wykeham Forest
North Moor
Gillamoor
Fadmoor
Hutton-le-Hole
Lastingham
Spaunton
Cropton
Cawthorne
Appleton-le-Moors
North Yorkshire Moors Railway
Rievaulx Moor
Kirkbymoorside
Kirk Dale
Old Byland
Carlton
Pockley
Keldholme
Sinnington
Wrelton
Middleton
Beck Isle
Newbridge
Rievaulx
NT Terrace
Abbey
Rye Dale
Beadlam
Ford and Cave
Kirkby Mills
Aislaby
A170
Ebberston Hall
Sawdon
Hutton Buscel
Helmsley
Nawton
Welburn
Wombleton
Great Edstone
Pickering
Ellerburn
Roston
Parkland
Duncombe Park
Marton
Costa Beck
Wilton
Allerston
Ebberston
Snainton
Brompton
Thornton-le-Dale
B1415
B1258
Harome
Sproxton
Normanby
River Riccal
NORTH
YORKS
Muscoates
Little Barugh
Flamingo Land
East Newton
Nunnington
Salton
East Ness
Great Barugh
Kirby Misperton
High Marishes
Yedingham
THE
Ampleforth
Ampleforth College
Oswaldirk
Nunnington Hall
West Ness
Brawby
B1251
Stonegrave
South Holme
Low Marishes
R. Derwent
East Heslerton
Sherburn
Thorpe Hall
Gilling East
Gilling Castle
Cawton
Butterwick
Little Habton
East Knapton
Scampston Hall
Hovingham Hall
Hovingham
B1363
B1257
Great Habton
Ryton
Wykeham
Scampston
West Knapton
West Heslerton
A64
Yearsley
Fryton
Slingsby
River Rye
Rillington
Coulton
Barton-le-Street
Amotherby
Eden Camp
Broughton
Wintringham
Brandsby
Scackleton
Appleton-le-Street
Swinton
Malton
Old Malton
Thorpe Bassett
Scagglethorpe
Place Newton
Stearsby
Howardian Hills
B1248
Norton-on-Derwent
Crayke
Skewsby
Terrington
Coneysthorpe
Castle Howard
Settrington
Helperthorpe
Weaverthorpe
Marton Abbey
Ganthorpe
Obelisk
Whitewall Corner
Roman
Whenby
Gate House
High Mowthorpe
West Lutton
East Lutton
Stillington
Farlington
Bulmer
Welburn
High Hutton
Menethorpe
B1253
North Grimston
Duggleby
Kirby Grindalythe
Sheriff Hutton
Crambeck
Huttons Ambo
Langton
Monument
Whitwell-on-the-Hill
Thornton-le-Clay
Firby
Kirkham
Priory
Birdsall
Wharram-le-Street
Huby
Sheriff Hutton
Crambe
Westow
Kennythorpe
Sledmere
Sutton-on-the-Forest
West Lilling
Foston
Barton Hill
Foston Old Rectory
Burythorpe
Wharram Percy (Deserted Village)
Sledmere House
B1252
Sutton Park
Barton-le-Willows
Howsham
Leavening
Towthorpe
Burdale
Flaxton
Harton
B1251
B1363
Bossall
Acklam
Thixendale
Strensall
DANGER AREA
Fimber
Strensall Camp
Claxton
Leppington
Scrayingham
Wetwang
Wigginton
Towthorpe
Sand Hutton
Bugthorpe
Painsthorpe
Fridaythorpe
A166
Haxby
Buttercrambe
Kirby Underdale
Upper Helmsley
Skirpenbeck
A19
Skelton
Earswick
Stockton-on-the-Forest
A1237
Gate Helmsley
Youlthorpe
Bishop Wilton
Huggate
Tibthorpe
Huntington
Warthill
1066
Stamford Bridge
Full Sutton
Gowthorpe
Nether Poppleton
Rawcliffe
New Earswick
Holtby
A166
EAST
RIDING
A614
Clifton
A1036
Low Catton
High Catton
Fangfoss
Great Givendale
North Dalton
Heworth
Murton
Meltonby
B1246
Knapton
Tang Hall
Bolton
Millington
B1224
A59
Osbaldwick
Dunnington
Yapham
Acomb
YORK
Millennium Bridge
Clifford's Tower
Grimston
A1079
Kexby
Wilberfoss
Warter
Middleton-on-the-Wolds
Heslington
Barmby Moor
Woodthorpe
Nunthorpe
A1036
Newton upon Derwent
R. Derwent
Fulford
A64
B1228
Elvington
B1246
Pocklington
Holme on the Wolds
Bishopthorpe
Pocklington Canal
Burnby Hall
Nunburnholme
Copmanthorpe
Elvington
Sutton upon Derwent
Allerthorpe
Burnby
A19
Crockey Hill
OF
YORKS
Acaster Malbis
Naburn
Wheldrake
Thornton
Hayton
Londesborough
South Dalton
A614
Kiplingcotes
Deighton
Storwood
Bell Hall
Melbourne
Thorpe le Street
Bielby
Goodmanham
Market Weighton
Appleton Roebuck
Escrick
Shiptonthorpe
River Ouse
B1222
Everingham
Gardham
Thorganby
East Cottingwith
Melbourne
Seaton Ross
Arras
Acaster Selby
Stillingfleet
Harswell
A1079
Ellerton
Laytham
93
Holme-on-Spalding-Moor
Sancton
94
Ryther
Kelfield
Aughton
North Shire Horse Centre
Riccall
A19
Skipwith
North Duffield
B1228
Harlthorpe
Moor End
North Newbald
Cawood
Water End
Sand Hole
North Cliffe
B1223
Bubwith
Foggathorpe
A1034
A163
Highfield
A614
Rascal Moor
South Cliffe
South Newbald

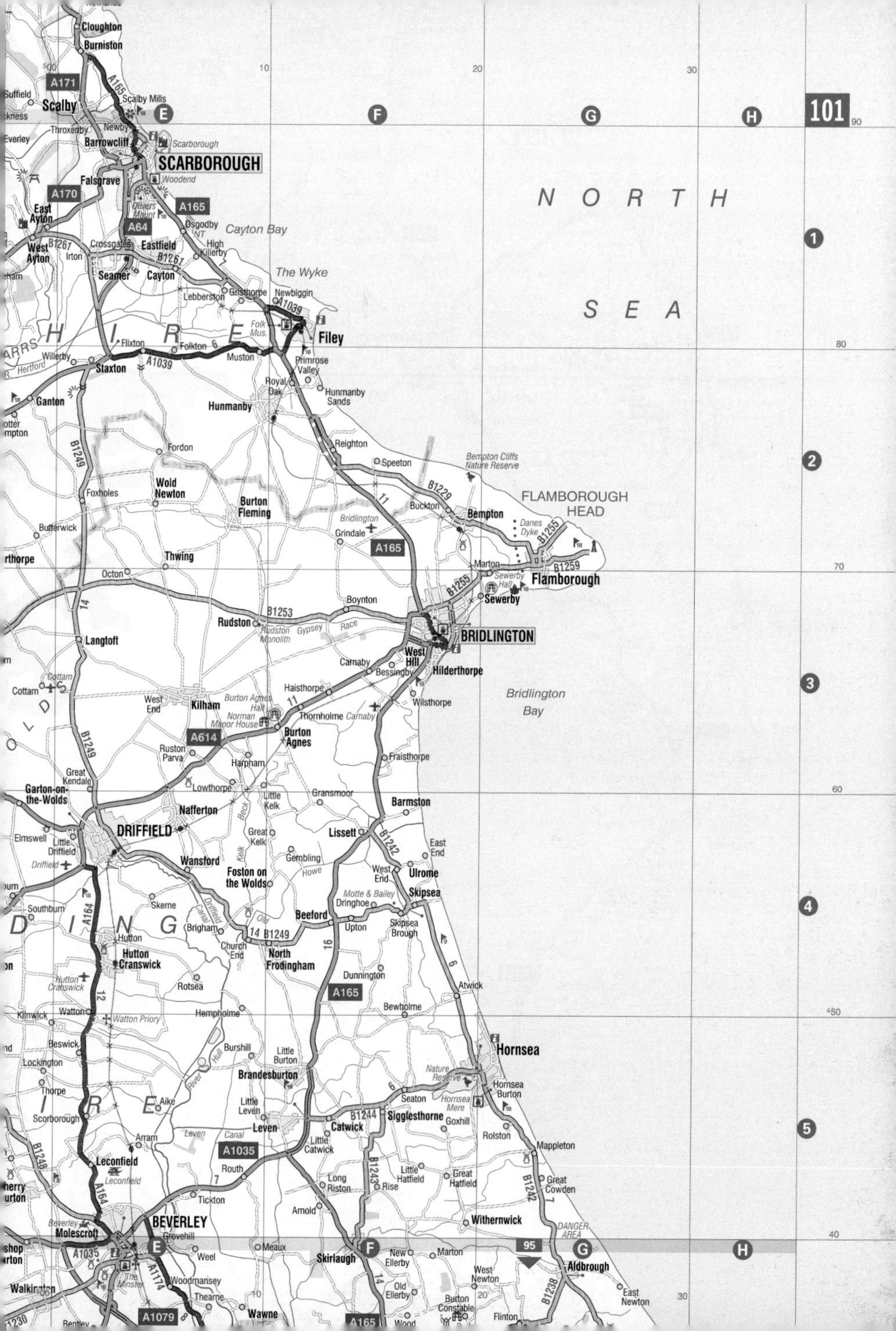
NORTH
SEA
Cloughton
Burniston
A171
A165
Scalby Mills
Suffield
Scalby
E
F
G
H
Throxenby
Newby
Barrowcliff
Scarborough
SCARBOROUGH
Woodend
Falsgrave
A170
A165
East Ayton
A64
Osgodby
Cayton Bay
High Killerby
Crossgates
Eastfield
West Ayton
Irton
B1261
Seamer
Cayton
The Wyke
Lebberston
Gristhorpe
Newbiggin
A1039
Folk Mus.
Filey
Flixton
Folkton
Willerby
Staxton
A1039
Muston
Primrose Valley
R. Hertford
Ganton
Royal Oak
Hunmanby
Hunmanby Sands
Reighton
Fordon
Speeton
Bempton Cliffs Nature Reserve
B1229
B1249
Foxholes
Wold Newton
Burton Fleming
Buckton
Bempton
FLAMBOROUGH HEAD
Butterwick
Bridlington
Grindale
Danes Dyke
B1255
A165
Thwing
Marton
B1259
Octon
Sewerby Hall
Flamborough
B1255
Sewerby
Boynton
B1253
Rudston
Rudston Monolith
Gypsey
Race
BRIDLINGTON
Langtoft
Carnaby
West Hill
Hilderthorpe
Bessingby
Cottam
Haisthorpe
Wilsthorpe
Bridlington Bay
West End
Kilham
Burton Agnes Hall
Norman Manor House
Thornholme
Carnaby
A614
Burton Agnes
B1249
Ruston Parva
Harpham
Fraisthorpe
Great Kendale
Garton-on-the-Wolds
Lowthorpe
Little Kelk
Gransmoor
Barmston
Nafferton
Great Kelk
Lissett
Elmswell
Little Driffield
DRIFFIELD
B1242
East End
Driffield
Wansford
Gembling
West End
Ulrome
Foston on the Wolds
Howe
Skipsea
Motte & Bailey
Dringhoe
Southburn
Skerne
Driffield Canal
Beeford
Upton
Skipsea Brough
A164
Brigham
B1249
Hutton
Church End
North Frodingham
Hutton Cranswick
Dunnington
Atwick
Hutton Cranswick
Rotsea
A165
Bewholme
Kilnwick
Watton
Watton Priory
Hempholme
Beswick
Burshill
Hornsea
Little Burton
Lockington
River Hull
Brandesburton
Nature Reserve
Hornsea Burton
Thorpe
Seaton
Aike
Little Leven
Hornsea Mere
Scorborough
B1244
Sigglesthorne
Goxhill
Leven
Catwick
Rolston
Arram
Leven Canal
Little Catwick
B1248
A1035
Mappleton
Leconfield
Little Hatfield
Great Hatfield
Routh
Long Riston
B1243
Rise
B1242
Great Cowden
Leconfield
A164
Tickton
Arnold
Withernwick
BEVERLEY
DANGER AREA
Molescroft
Grovehill
Meaux
95
A1035
Weel
Skirlaugh
New Ellerby
Marton
Aldbrough
Woodmansey
West Newton
A1174
The Minster
Old Ellerby
B1238
Walkington
Thearne
East Newton
Burton Constable
A1079
Wawne
Bentley
A165
Wood
Flinton
10
20
30
90
80
70
60
450
40
1
2
3
4
5

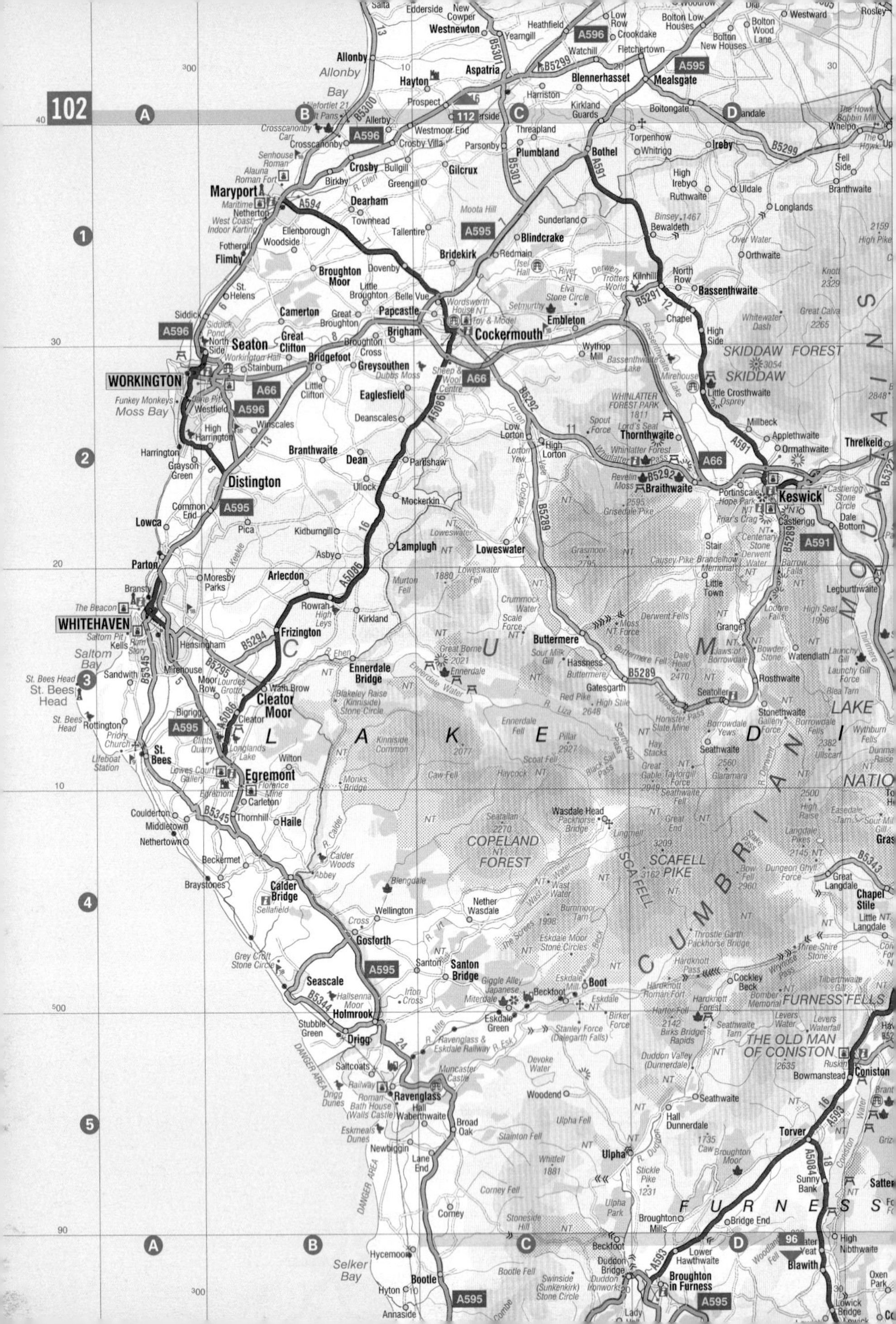

Allonby
Allonby Bay
Westnewton
Aspatria
Hayton
Blennerhasset
Mealsgate
Crookdake
Bolton Low Houses
Westward
Allerby
Crosscanonby
Crosby
Gilcrux
Plumbland
Bothel
Torpenhow
Ireby
Maryport
Dearham
Netherton
Ellenborough
Flimby
Blindcrake
Bridekirk
Broughton Moor
Dovenby
Papcastle
Cockermouth
Embleton
Camerton
Seaton
Great Clifton
Brigham
Bridgefoot
Greysouthen
Eaglesfield
WORKINGTON
Moss Bay
Harrington
Distington
Branthwaite
Dean
Lowca
Parton
WHITEHAVEN
Saltom Bay
St. Bees Head
St. Bees
Moresby Parks
Arlecdon
Frizington
Cleator Moor
Egremont
Haile
Thornhill
Beckermet
Braystones
Calder Bridge
Gosforth
Seascale
Holmrook
Drigg
Ravenglass
Bootle
Selker Bay
Lamplugh
Loweswater
Buttermere
Ennerdale Bridge
Wasdale Head
Santon Bridge
Boot
Eskdale Green
Ulpha
Broughton in Furness
Coniston
Torver
Blawith
Keswick
Portinscale
Braithwaite
Thornthwaite
Bassenthwaite
Threlkeld
Grange
Rosthwaite
Seatoller
Seathwaite
Chapel Stile
Great Langdale
SKIDDAW FOREST
SKIDDAW
COPELAND FOREST
SCAFELL PIKE
THE OLD MAN OF CONISTON
FURNESS FELLS
L A K E   D I S T R I C T
C U M B R I A N   M O U N T A I N S
LAKE DISTRICT NATIONAL PARK
A596
A595
A594
A66
A591
A5086
A593
A5084
B5300
B5299
B5301
B5291
B5292
B5289
B5294
B5295
B5345
B5344
B5343
B5322
112
96

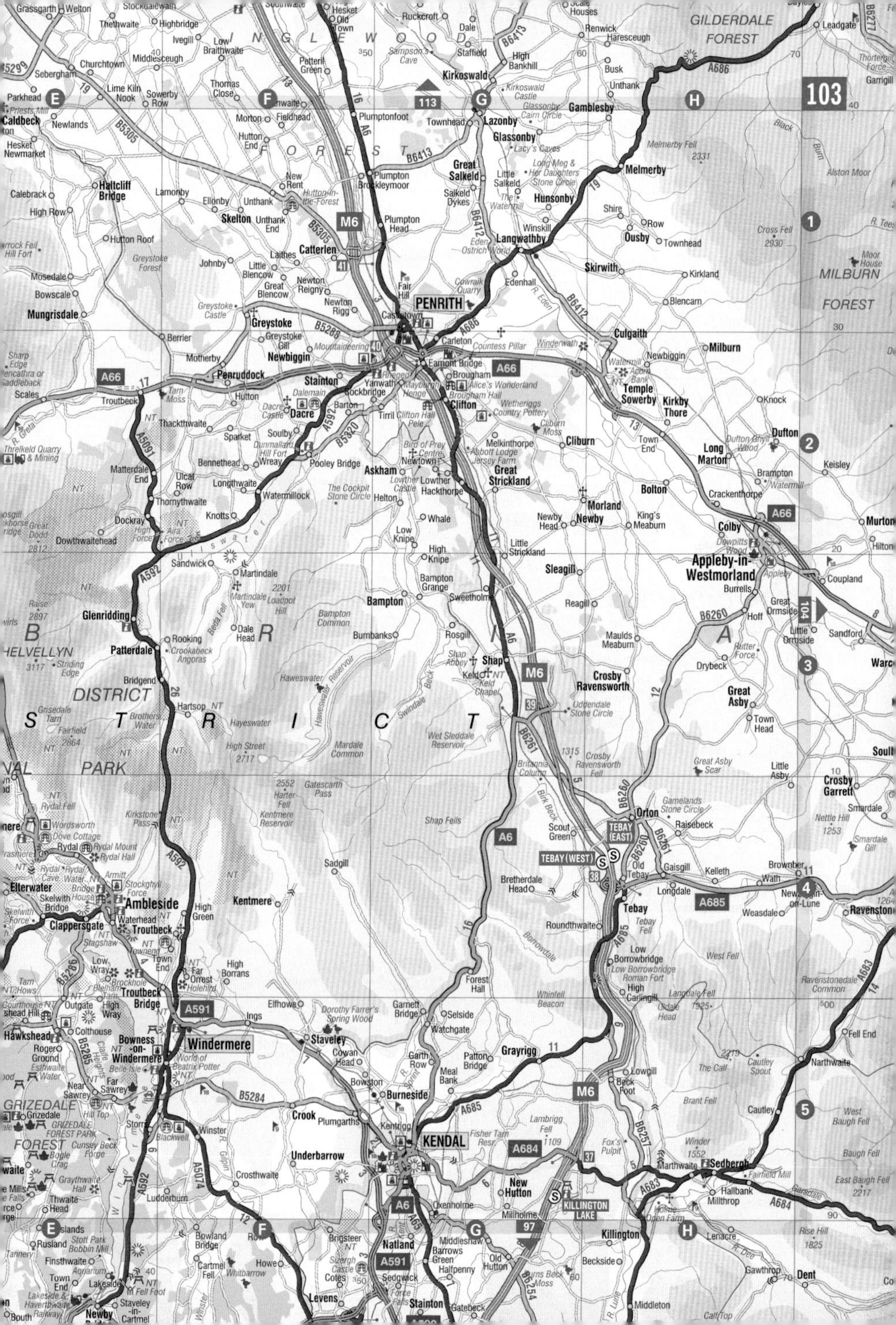
103
INGLEWOOD FOREST
GILDERDALE FOREST
MILBURN FOREST
Melmerby Fell
2331
Alston Moor
Cross Fell
2930
Moor House
Welton
Hesket
Ruckcroft
Dale
Scale Houses
Renwick
Haresceugh
Leadgate
Thethwaite
Highbridge
Ivegill
Low Braithwaite
Middlesceugh
Churchtown
Sebergham
Lime Kiln Nook
Thomas Close
Sowerby Row
Petteril Green
Sampson's Cave
Staffield
High Bankhill
Busk
Unthank
Kirkoswald
Kirkoswald Castle
Parkhead
Caldbeck
Newlands
Hesket Newmarket
Morton
Fieldhead
Hutton End
Plumptonfoot
Townhead
Lazonby
Glassonby
Gamblesby
Glassonby Cairn Circle
Lacy's Caves
Long Meg & Her Daughters Stone Circle
Melmerby
Great Salkeld
Little Salkeld
Salkeld Dykes
The Watermill
Hunsonby
Winskill
Langwathby
Eden Ostrich World
Shire
Row
Ousby
Townhead
Haltcliff Bridge
Calebrack
High Row
Lamonby
Ellonby
Unthank
Skelton
Unthank End
New Rent
Hutton-in-the-Forest
Plumpton
Brockleymoor
Plumpton Head
Hutton Roof
Greystoke Forest
Catterlen
Laithes
Johnby
Little Blencow
Great Blencow
Newton Reigny
Newton Rigg
Fair Hill
PENRITH
Castletown
Cowraik Quarry
Edenhall
Skirwith
Kirkland
Blencarn
Mosedale
Bowscale
Mungrisdale
Greystoke Castle
Greystoke
Greystoke Gill
Berrier
Mountaineering
Carleton
Countess Pillar
Winderwath
Culgaith
Milburn
Newbiggin
Sharp Edge
Blencathra or Saddleback
Motherby
Newbiggin
Penruddock
Stainton
Eamont Bridge
Brougham
Alice's Wonderland
Acorn Bank
Watermill
Temple Sowerby
Kirkby Thore
Knock
Scales
Troutbeck
Tarn Moss
Hutton
Dalemain
Dacre Castle
Dacre
Sockbridge
Yanwath
Mayburgh Henge
Brougham Hall
Clifton
Wetheriggs Country Pottery
Rheged
Barton
Tirril
Clifton Hall Pele
Thackthwaite
Sparket
Soulby
Cliburn Moss
Cliburn
Town End
Long Marton
Dufton
Dufton Ghyll Wood
Threlkeld Quarry & Mining
Matterdale End
Bennethead
Dunmallard Hill Fort
Wreay
Pooley Bridge
Bird of Prey Centre
Newtown
Melkinthorpe
Abbott Lodge Jersey Farm
Brampton
Keisley
Askham
Lowther Castle
Lowther
Hackthorpe
Great Strickland
Bolton
Ulcat Row
Longthwaite
Watermillock
The Cockpit Stone Circle
Helton
Morland
Crackenthorpe
Thornythwaite
Knotts
Whale
Newby Head
Newby
King's Meaburn
Colby
Murton
Dockray
Aira Force
High Force
Great Dodd
2812
Dowthwaitehead
Ullswater
Low Knipe
High Knipe
Little Strickland
Dowpitts Wood
Appleby-in-Westmorland
Appleby
Hilton
Sandwick
Martindale
Sleagill
Coupland
Martindale Yew
2201
Loadpot Hill
Bampton Grange
Sweetholme
Reagill
Burrells
Great Ormside
Raise
2897
Glenridding
Bampton
Bampton Common
Hoff
Little Ormside
Sandford
Rooking
Dale Head
Beda Fell
Burnbanks
Rosgill
Maulds Meaburn
Patterdale
Crookabeck Angoras
HELVELLYN
3117
Striding Edge
Shap Abbey
Shap
Haweswater
Haweswater Reservoir
Swindale Beck
Keld
Keld Chapel
Drybeck
Rutter Force
Crosby Ravensworth
Bridgend
DISTRICT
Great Asby
Grisedale Tarn
Hartsop
Brothers Water
Hayeswater
Uddendale Stone Circle
Fairfield
2864
Mardale Common
Wet Sleddale Reservoir
Town Head
High Street
2717
Crosby Ravensworth Fell
Britannia Column
Great Asby Scar
Little Asby
PARK
2552
Harter Fell
Gatescarth Pass
Kentmere Reservoir
Crosby Garrett
Smardale
Rydal Fell
Kirkstone Pass
Birk Beck
Orton
Gamelands Stone Circle
Raisebeck
Nettle Hill
1253
Smardale Gill
Wordsworth
Dove Cottage
Rydal
Rydal Mount
Rydal Hall
Shap Fells
Scout Green
TEBAY (EAST)
TEBAY (WEST)
Old Tebay
Gaisgill
Kelleth
Brownber
Wath
Newbiggin-on-Lune
Rydal Water
Rydal Cave
Armitt
Stockghyll Force
Sadgill
Bretherdale Head
Longdale
Weasdale
Ravenstonedale
Elterwater
Skelwith Bridge
Ambleside
Kentmere
High Green
Tebay
Tebay Fell
Skelwith Force
Clappersgate
Waterhead
Troutbeck
Stagshaw
Townend
Roundthwaite
Borrowdale
West Fell
Low Wray
Brockhole
Town End
Far Orrest
Holehird
High Borrans
Low Borrowbridge
Low Borrowbridge Roman Fort
Langdale Fell
Ravenstonedale Common
Tarn Hows
Forest Hall
High Carlingill
Uldale Head
1925
Courthouse
Hawkshead Hill
Outgate
High Wray
Troutbeck Bridge
Elfhowe
Garnett Bridge
Selside
Whinfell Beacon
Hawkshead
Colthouse
Bowness-on-Windermere
Windermere
Ings
Dorothy Farrer's Spring Wood
Staveley
Watchgate
Grayrigg
Fell End
Roger Ground
Esthwaite Water
Belle Isle
World of Beatrix Potter
Claife Heights
Cowan Head
Garth Row
Patton Bridge
Meal Bank
2219
The Calf
Cautley Spout
Narthwaite
Near Sawrey
Far Sawrey
Bowston
Burneside
Lowgill
Beck Foot
Brant Fell
GRIZEDALE FOREST
GRIZEDALE FOREST PARK
Grizedale
Hill Top
Storrs
Crook
Plumgarths
Kentrigg
KENDAL
Lambrigg Fell
Fisher Tarn Resr.
1109
Fox's Pulpit
Cautley
West Baugh Fell
Cunsey Beck Forge
Bogle Crag
Blackwell
Winster
Underbarrow
Whinfell
1552
Marthwaite
Sedbergh
Baugh Fell
Graythwaite Hall
Crosthwaite
New Hutton
Fairfield Mill
Hallbank
Millthrop
Garsdale
East Baugh Fell
2217
Thwaite Head
Lindeth
Ludderburn
Oxenholme
Millholme
KILLINGTON LAKE
Holme Open Farm
Rusland
Bowland Bridge
Natland
Middleshaw
Killington
Lenacre
Rise Hill
1825
Stott Park Bobbin Mill
Brigsteer
Barrows Green
Old Hutton
Beckside
Finsthwaite
Cartmel Fell
Whitbarrow
Howe
Sizergh Castle
Halfpenny
Aquarium
Town End
Lakeside
Fell Foot
Cotes
Sedgwick
Burns Beck Moss
Gawthrop
Dent
Lakeside & Haverthwaite Railway
Levens
Force Falls
Stainton
Gatebeck
Middleton
Newby Bridge
Staveley-in-Cartmel
Calf Top
Bouth
Windermere
R. Eden
R. Kent
R. Sprint
R. Lune
R. Dee
R. Gilpin
R. Greta
M6
A6
A66
A686
A592
A5091
B5320
B5288
B5305
B6413
B6412
A591
A685
A684
A683
B6260
B6261
B6257
B6254
B5284
B5286
B5285
A5074
A65
B5299
40
41
39
38
37
113
104
97

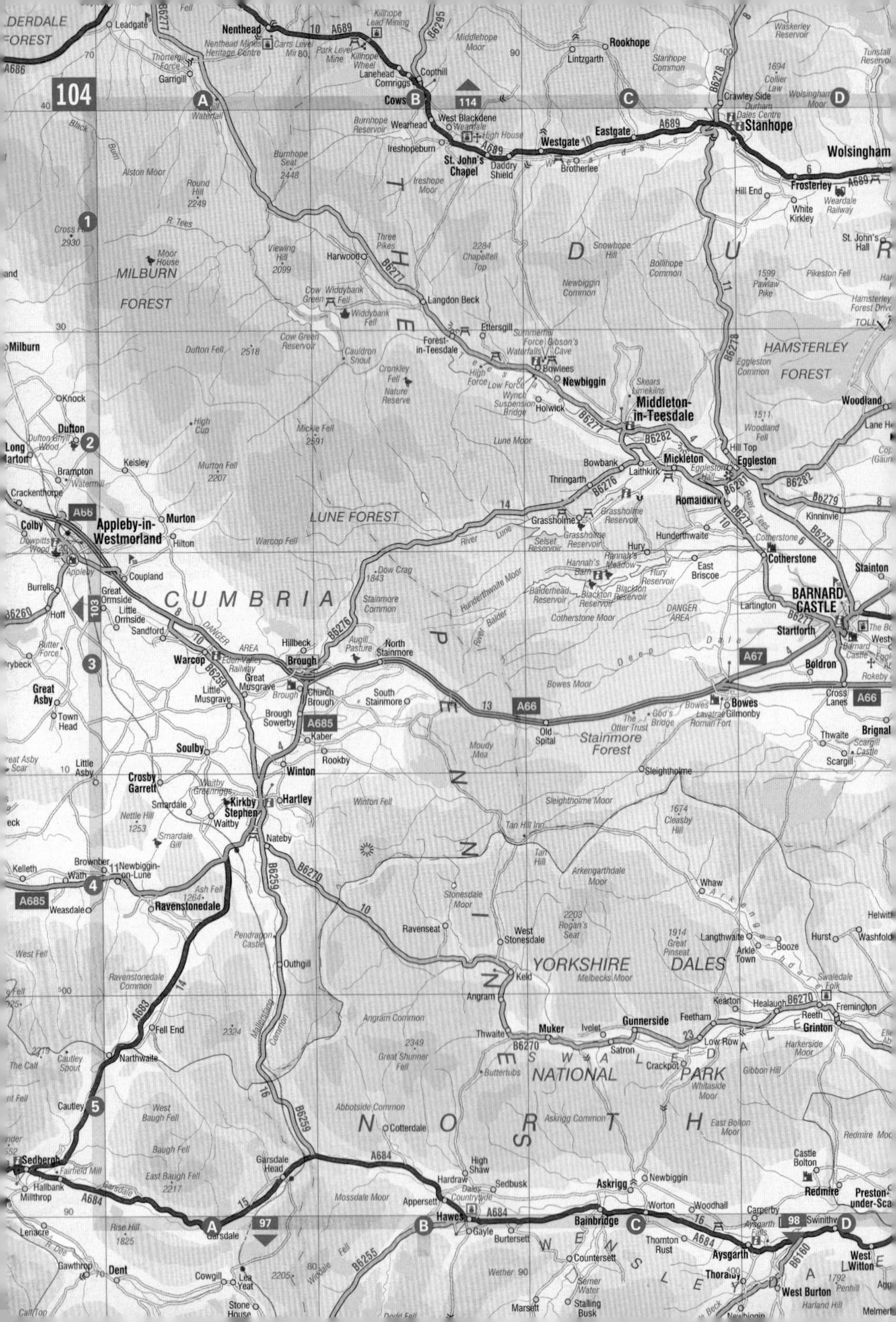

104
ALDERDALE
FOREST
A686
Leadgate
Nenthead
Nenthead Mines Heritage Centre
Carrs Level Mine
Killhope Lead Mining
A689
Park Level Mine
Killhope Wheel
Lanehead
Cornriggs
Copthill
B6295
Middlehope Moor
Rookhope
Lintzgarth
Stanhope Common
Waskerley Reservoir
Tunstall Reservoir
Thortergill Force
Garrigill
Cows
114
Crawley Side
Durham Dales Centre
Stanhope
Wolsingham Moor
1694 Collier Law
Waterfall
Black Burn
Burnhope Reservoir
Wearhead
West Blackdene
Weardale
High House
Westgate
Eastgate
Ireshopeburn
St. John's Chapel
Daddry Shield
Brotherlee
Wolsingham
Frosterley
Weardale Railway
Hill End
White Kirkley
B6278
Alston Moor
Burnhope Seat 2448
Round Hill 2249
Ireshope Moor
R. Tees
Cross Fell 2930
Moor House
MILBURN
FOREST
Viewing Hill 2099
Three Pikes
Harwood
B6277
2284 Chapelfell Top
Snowhope Hill
Bollihope Common
St. John's Hall
1599 Pawlaw Pike
Pikeston Fell
Hamsterley Forest Drive
TOLL
Cow Green
Widdybank Fell
Langdon Beck
Newbiggin Common
Ettersgill
Forest-in-Teesdale
Summerhill Force
Gibson's Cave
Waterfalls
Bowlees
Newbiggin
High Force
Low Force
Wynch Suspension Bridge
Holwick
HAMSTERLEY
FOREST
Eggleston Common
Milburn
Dufton Fell
2518
Cow Green Reservoir
Cauldron Snout
Cronkley Fell Nature Reserve
Skears Limekilns
Middleton-in-Teesdale
Woodland
Knock
Dufton
Dufton Ghyll Wood
Long Marton
High Cup
Mickle Fell 2591
Lune Moor
B6282
1511 Woodland Fell
Lane Head
Hill Top
Eggleston
Mickleton
Bowbank
Laithkirk
Eggleston Hall
Thringarth
B6276
Romaldkirk
Brampton
Keisley
Murton Fell 2207
Watermill
Crackenthorpe
A66
Appleby-in-Westmorland
Murton
Hilton
Colby
Dowpitts Wood
Appleby
LUNE FOREST
Warcop Fell
Grassholme
Grassholme Reservoir
Selset Reservoir
River Lune
Hury
Hunderthwaite
Cotherstone
Kinninvie
B6279
B6278
Coupland
Burrells
Dow Crag 1843
Hannah's Barn
Hannah's Meadow
Hury Reservoir
East Briscoe
Stainton
Great Ormside
CUMBRIA
Hunderthwaite Moor
Balderhead Reservoir
Blackton Reservoir
Cotherstone Moor
River Balder
DANGER AREA
Lartington
BARNARD CASTLE
Startforth
B6260
Hoff
103
Little Ormside
Stainmore Common
Sandford
Rutter Force
Warcop
Eden Valley Railway
Hillbeck
Augill Pasture
North Stainmore
Brough
Deepdale
A67
Boldron
Barnard Castle
Rokeby
Great Asby
Great Musgrave
Little Musgrave
Church Brough
South Stainmore
Bowes Moor
Bowes
Bowes Lavatrae Roman Fort
Gilmonby
Cross Lanes
God's Bridge
The Otter Trust
Old Spital
Stainmore Forest
Town Head
Brough Sowerby
A685
Kaber
Moudy Mea
Thwaite
Brignal
Scargill Castle
Scargill
Great Asby Scar
Little Asby
Soulby
Winton
Rookby
Sleightholme
Crosby Garrett
Waitby Greenriggs
Smardale
Kirkby Stephen
Hartley
Winton Fell
Sleightholme Moor
1674 Cleasby Hill
Nettle Hill 1253
Waitby
Nateby
Tan Hill Inn
Tan Hill
Arkengarthdale Moor
Smardale Gill
Brownber
Newbiggin-on-Lune
Wath
Kelleth
B6259
B6270
Whaw
Stonesdale Moor
Ash Fell 1264
Ravenstonedale
Weasdale
Ravenseat
West Stonesdale
2203 Rogan's Seat
1914 Great Pinseat
Langthwaite
Arkle Town
Booze
Hurst
Helwith
Washfold
Pendragon Castle
YORKSHIRE
DALES
West Fell
Outhgill
Keld
Melbecks Moor
Swaledale Folk
Ravenstonedale Common
Angram
Kearton
Healaugh
Fremington
Reeth
Grinton
A683
Mallerstang Common
Angram Common
Muker
Ivelet
Gunnerside
Feetham
Fell End
2324
Low Row
Harkerside Moor
The Calf
Cautley Spout
Narthwaite
2349 Great Shunner Fell
Satron
Crackpot
Buttertubs
NATIONAL
PARK
Gibbon Hill
Whitaside Moor
Cautley
West Baugh Fell
Abbotside Common
Askrigg Common
East Bolton Moor
Redmire Moor
NORTH
Cotterdale
Castle Bolton
Sedbergh
Baugh Fell
Garsdale Head
High Shaw
A684
Hardraw
Sedbusk
Askrigg
Newbiggin
Redmire
Preston-under-Scar
Fairfield Mill
Hallbank
Millthrop
East Baugh Fell 2217
Garsdale
Mossdale Moor
Appersett
Dales Countryside
Worton
Woodhall
Carperby
Hawes
Bainbridge
Aysgarth Falls
Swinithwaite
97
98
Rise Hill 1825
Gayle
Burtersett
Thornton Rust
Aysgarth
Lenacre
R. Dee
Widdale Fell
B6255
Countersett
West Witton
Gawthrop
Dent
Cowgill
Lea Yeat
Wether Fell
Semer Water
Thoralby
West Burton
1792 Penhill
Harland Hill
Stone House
Marsett
Stalling Busk
Newbiggin
B6160
Calf Top
WENSLEY DALE

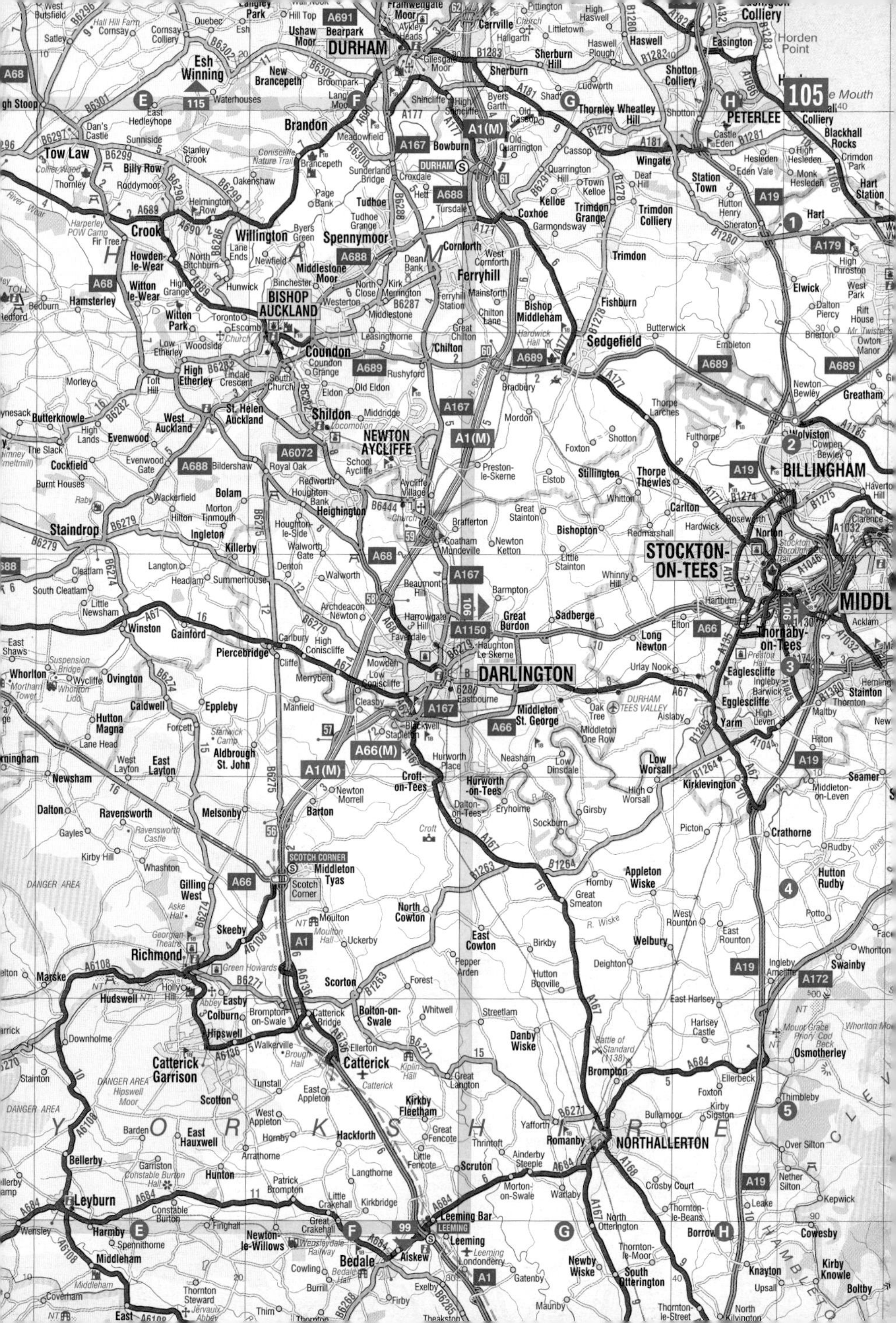
105
DURHAM
Esh Winning
Brandon
Tow Law
Crook
Willington
Spennymoor
Ferryhill
BISHOP AUCKLAND
Coundon
Shildon
NEWTON AYCLIFFE
Sedgefield
PETERLEE
Easington Colliery
Horden Point
Blackhall Colliery
Blackhall Rocks
Hart Station
Wingate
Trimdon
Fishburn
BILLINGHAM
STOCKTON-ON-TEES
MIDDL
Thornaby-on-Tees
Yarm
Eaglescliffe
DARLINGTON
Middleton St. George
DURHAM TEES VALLEY
Staindrop
Cockfield
Gainford
Piercebridge
Winston
Richmond
SCOTCH CORNER
Middleton Tyas
Catterick
Catterick Garrison
NORTHALLERTON
Romanby
Brompton
Bedale
Leeming
Leeming Bar
Leyburn
Middleham
Osmotherley
Hutton Rudby
Crathorne
Great Smeaton
Appleton Wiske
North Cowton
Croft-on-Tees
Hurworth-on-Tees
Barton
Melsonby
Skeeby
Scorton
Bolton-on-Swale
Hackforth
Scruton
Y O R K S H I R E
A1(M)
A1
A19
A66
A66(M)
A67
A68
A167
A177
A181
A684
A688
A689
A6108
A1150
A172
A179

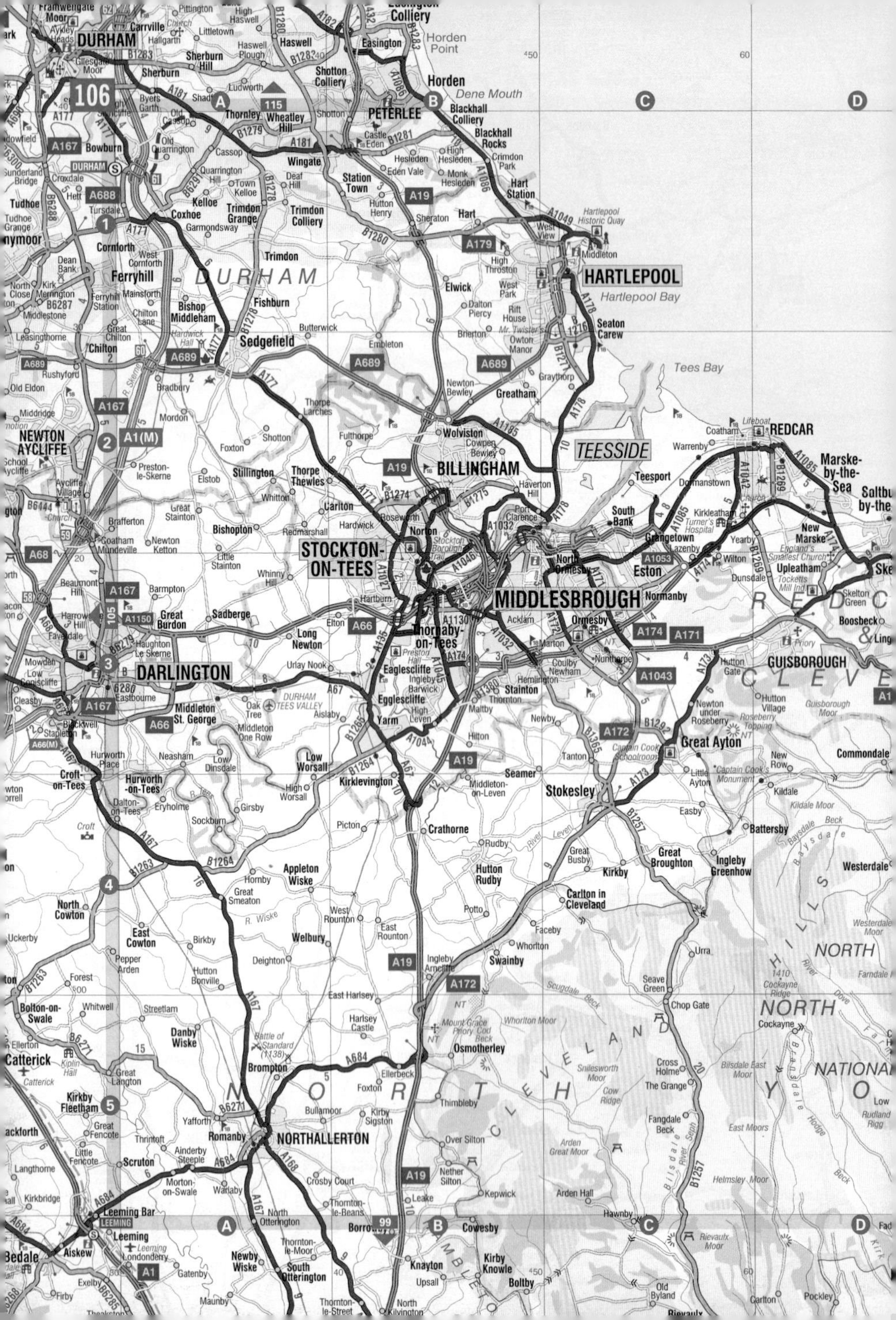

106
115
105
99
DURHAM
Sherburn Hill
Sherburn
Haswell
Haswell Plough
Easington
Easington Colliery
Horden
Horden Point
Dene Mouth
Shotton Colliery
PETERLEE
Blackhall Colliery
Blackhall Rocks
Crimdon Park
Castle Eden
Thornley
Wheatley Hill
Wingate
Station Town
Hesleden
High Hesleden
Monk Hesleden
Eden Vale
Hart Station
Hart
Hutton Henry
Sheraton
Bowburn
Cassop
Quarrington Hill
Kelloe
Trimdon Grange
Trimdon Colliery
Trimdon
Coxhoe
Tursdale
Cornforth
West Cornforth
Ferryhill
Bishop Middleham
Fishburn
Sedgefield
Butterwick
Embleton
Chilton
Tudhoe
Spennymoor
DURHAM
HARTLEPOOL
Hartlepool Bay
Hartlepool Historic Quay
Middleton
West View
High Throston
Elwick
West Park
Dalton Piercy
Rift House
Brierton
Owton Manor
Seaton Carew
Tees Bay
Graythorp
Greatham
Newton Bewley
Wolviston
Cowpen Bewley
BILLINGHAM
TEESSIDE
Haverton Hill
Port Clarence
Teesport
South Bank
Grangetown
Eston
Normanby
Dormanstown
Coatham
REDCAR
Warrenby
Marske-by-the-Sea
Saltburn-by-the-Sea
New Marske
Kirkleatham
Yearby
Lazenby
Wilton
Upleatham
Dunsdale
Skelton Green
Boosbeck
Lingdale
GUISBOROUGH
Hutton Gate
Hutton Village
Guisborough Moor
Roseberry Topping
Newton under Roseberry
Great Ayton
Little Ayton
Captain Cook's Monument
Commondale
Kildale
Kildale Moor
Battersby
Easby
Ingleby Greenhow
Great Broughton
Kirkby
Great Busby
Stokesley
Westerdale
Westerdale Moor
Baysdale
Farndale Moor
Cockayne Ridge
Cockayne
Bransdale
Chop Gate
Seave Green
Urra
Carlton in Cleveland
Faceby
Whorlton
Swainby
Scugdale Beck
Whorlton Moor
Osmotherley
Snilesworth Moor
Cow Ridge
Cross Holme
The Grange
Fangdale Beck
Bilsdale East Moor
East Moors
Helmsley Moor
Arden Great Moor
Arden Hall
Hawnby
Rievaulx Moor
Old Byland
Carlton
Pockley
Low
Rudland Rigg
NORTH
NORTH YORK MOORS NATIONAL PARK
CLEVELAND HILLS
NORTH YORKSHIRE
REDCAR & CLEVELAND
STOCKTON-ON-TEES
MIDDLESBROUGH
Norton
Roseworth
Hardwick
Carlton
Redmarshall
Thorpe Thewles
Thorpe Larches
Fulthorpe
Stillington
Whitton
Bishopton
Little Stainton
Whinny Hill
Elstob
Great Stainton
Hartburn
Elton
Long Newton
Thornaby-on-Tees
Preston Hall
Eaglescliffe
Egglescliffe
Ingleby Barwick
High Leven
Yarm
Aislaby
Urlay Nook
Acklam
Ormesby
Marton
Nunthorpe
Coulby Newham
Hemlington
Stainton
Thornton
Maltby
Newby
Hilton
Tanton
Seamer
Middleton-on-Leven
Captain Cook Schoolroom
Kirklevington
Crathorne
Rudby
Hutton Rudby
Potto
Picton
Low Worsall
High Worsall
NEWTON AYCLIFFE
Aycliffe Village
School Aycliffe
Middridge
Old Eldon
Rushyford
Preston-le-Skerne
Bradbury
Mordon
Foxton
Shotton
Great Burdon
Sadberge
Barmpton
Brafferton
Coatham Mundeville
Newton Ketton
Beaumont Hill
Harrowgate Hill
Faverdale
Haughton Le Skerne
DARLINGTON
Mowden
Low Coniscliffe
Cleasby
Eastbourne
Blackwell
Stapleton
Middleton St. George
Oak Tree
DURHAM TEES VALLEY
Middleton One Row
Low Dinsdale
Neasham
Hurworth Place
Hurworth-on-Tees
Croft-on-Tees
Dalton-on-Tees
Eryholme
Girsby
Sockburn
Croft
Hornby
Great Smeaton
Appleton Wiske
West Rounton
East Rounton
Welbury
Deighton
Ingleby Arncliffe
East Harlsey
Harlsey Castle
Mount Grace Priory
North Cowton
East Cowton
Birkby
Pepper Arden
Hutton Bonville
Forest
Whitwell
Bolton-on-Swale
Streetlam
Danby Wiske
Battle of Standard (1138)
Brompton
Ellerbeck
Foxton
Thimbleby
Bullamoor
Kirby Sigston
Over Silton
Nether Silton
Kepwick
Catterick
Kiplin Hall
Great Langton
Kirkby Fleetham
Great Fencote
Little Fencote
Yafforth
Romanby
NORTHALLERTON
Thrintoft
Ainderby Steeple
Scruton
Morton-on-Swale
Warlaby
Crosby Court
Thornton-le-Beans
North Otterington
Langthorne
Kirkbridge
Leeming Bar
Leeming
Aiskew
Bedale
Londonderry
Gatenby
Exelby
Firby
Newby Wiske
Thornton-le-Moor
South Otterington
Maunby
Borrowby
Leake
Cowesby
Knayton
Upsall
Kirby Knowle
Boltby
Thornton-le-Street
North Kilvington
A1(M)
A19
A66
A67
A167
A171
A172
A173
A174
A177
A179
A181
A684
A688
A689
A1043
A1053
A1130
A1150
A1185

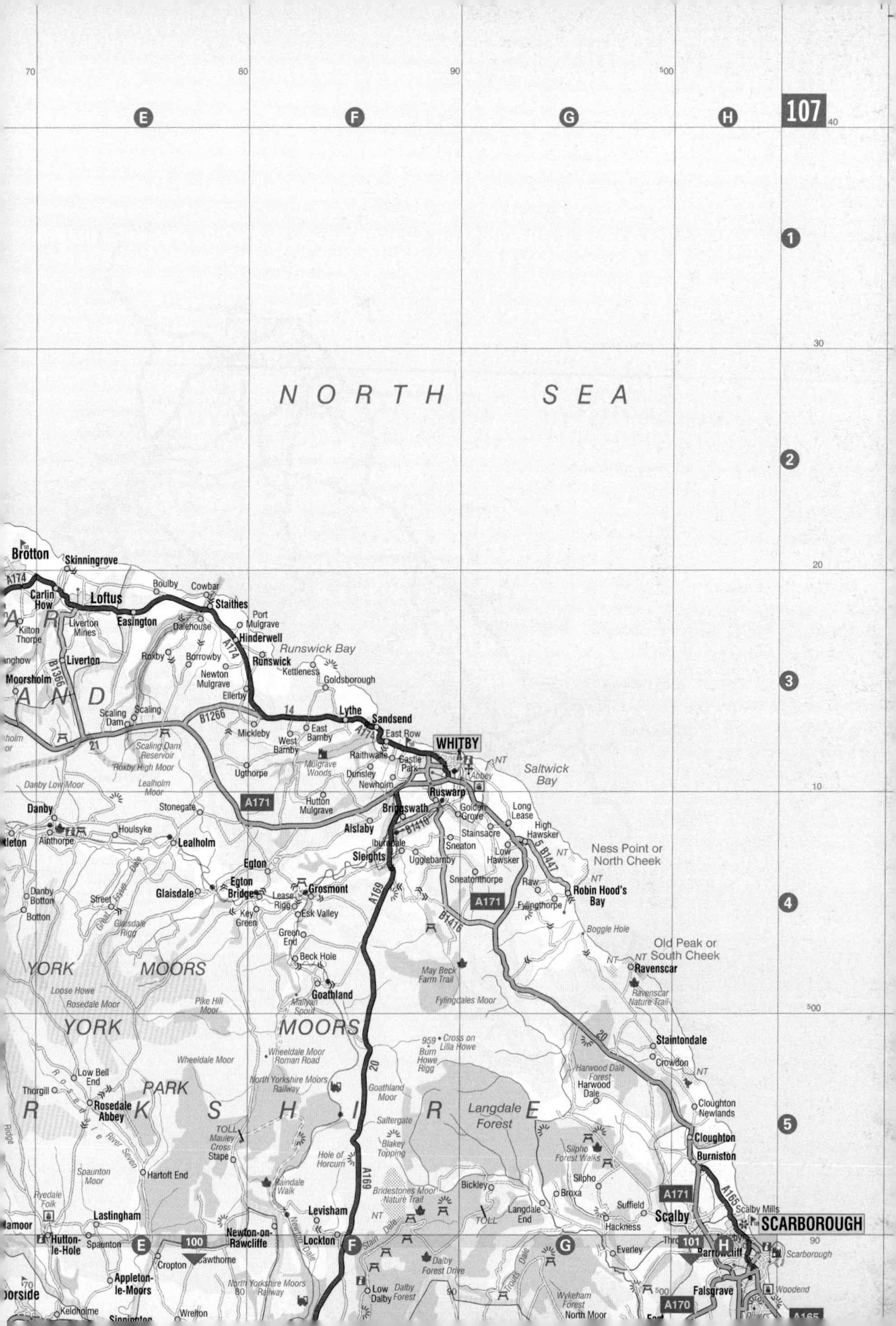

NORTH SEA
Brotton
Skinningrove
Carlin How
Loftus
Boulby
Cowbar
Staithes
Port Mulgrave
Kilton Thorpe
Liverton Mines
Easington
Dalehouse
Hinderwell
Runswick Bay
Liverton
Roxby
Borrowby
Runswick
Kettleness
Goldsborough
Moorsholm
Newton Mulgrave
Ellerby
Scaling Dam
Scaling
Lythe
Sandsend
East Row
WHITBY
Mickleby
East Barnby
West Barnby
Scaling Dam Reservoir
Roxby High Moor
Mulgrave Woods
Raithwaite
Castle Park
Abbey
Saltwick Bay
Ugthorpe
Dunsley
Newholm
Danby Low Moor
Lealholm Moor
Hutton Mulgrave
Ruswarp
Danby
Stonegate
Briggswath
Golden Grove
Long Lease
High Hawsker
Ness Point or North Cheek
Ainthorpe
Houlsyke
Lealholm
Aislaby
Stainsacre
Sneaton
Low Hawsker
Iburndale
Sleights
Ugglebarnby
Egton
Sneatonthorpe
Raw
Robin Hood's Bay
Danby Botton
Botton
Street
Glaisdale
Egton Bridge
Lease Rigg
Grosmont
Key Green
Esk Valley
Fylingthorpe
Glaisdale Rigg
Boggle Hole
Green End
Old Peak or South Cheek
Beck Hole
Ravenscar
YORK MOORS
May Beck Farm Trail
Ravenscar Nature Trail
Loose Howe
Rosedale Moor
Pike Hill Moor
Goathland
Mallyan Spout
Fylingdales Moor
YORK MOORS
959 Cross on Lilla Howe
Staintondale
Wheeldale Moor
Wheeldale Moor Roman Road
Burn Howe Rigg
Crowdon
Low Bell End
North Yorkshire Moors Railway
Harwood Dale Forest
Harwood Dale
PARK
Thorgill
Goathland Moor
Rosedale Abbey
Langdale Forest
Cloughton Newlands
R K S H I R E
Saltergate
TOLL
Mauley Cross
Stape
Blakey Topping
Cloughton
Hole of Horcum
Silpho Forest Walks
Burniston
Spaunton Moor
Hartoft End
Raindale Walk
Bridestones Moor Nature Trail
Bickley
Silpho
Broxa
Ryedale Folk
Suffield
Scalby
Scalby Mills
Lastingham
Levisham
Langdale End
Hackness
SCARBOROUGH
Hutton-le-Hole
Spaunton
Newton-on-Rawcliffe
Lockton
Newton Dale
Stain Dale
Everley
Barrowcliff
Scarborough
Cropton
Cawthorne
Dalby Forest Drive
Troutsdale
Appleton-le-Moors
North Yorkshire Moors Railway
Low Dalby
Dalby Forest
Wykeham Forest
Falsgrave
Woodend
Keldholme
Wrelton
North Moor
A174
A171
A169
A170
A165
B1366
B1266
B1410
B1416
B1447
100
101

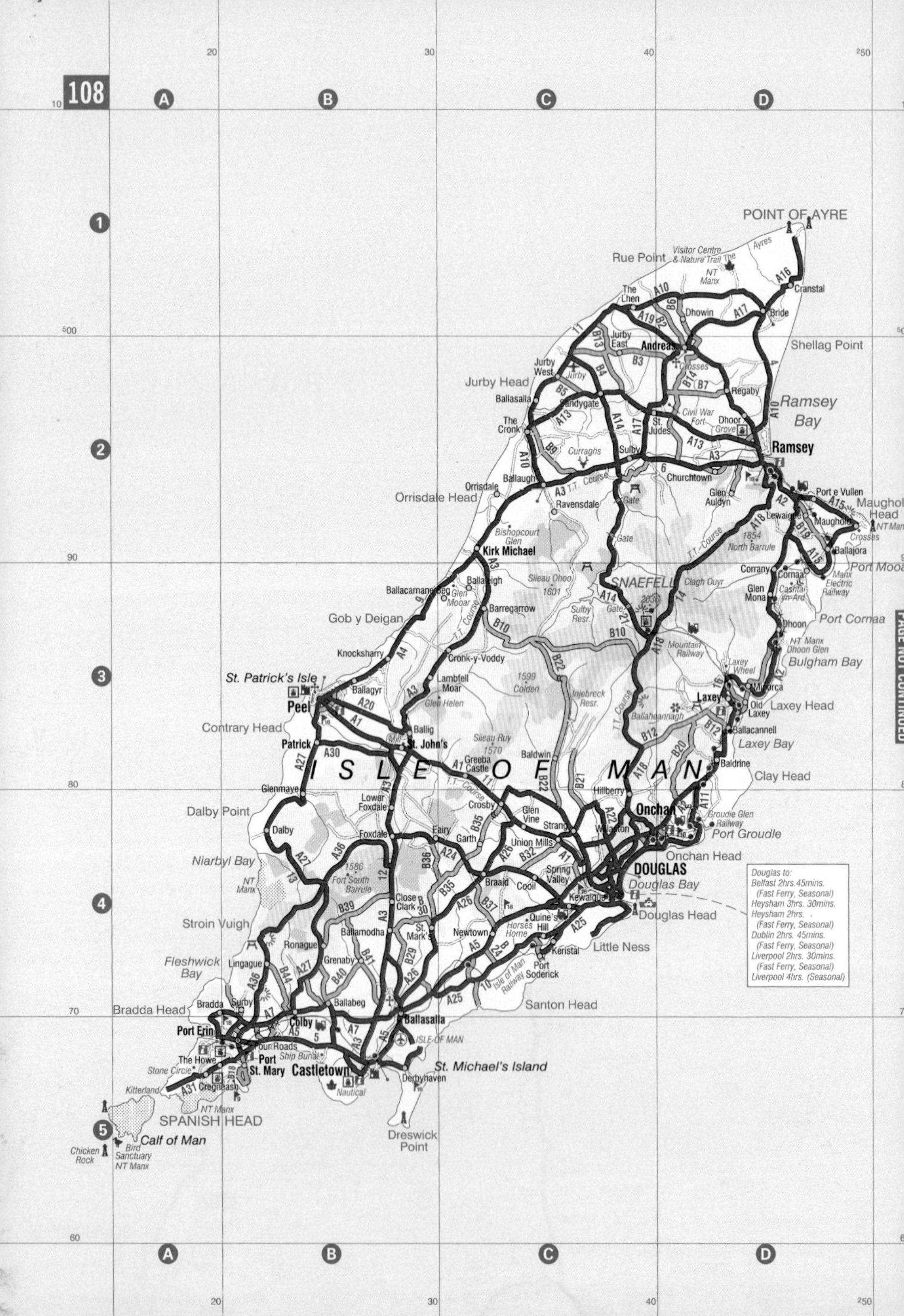

A
B
C
D
1
2
3
4
5
20
30
40
250
10
500
90
80
70
60
POINT OF AYRE
Rue Point
Visitor Centre & Nature Trail
The Ayres
NT Manx
Cranstal
The Lhen
Dhowin
Bride
Jurby East
Andreas
Shellag Point
Jurby West
Jurby
Crosses
Jurby Head
Regaby
Ballasalla
Sandygate
Civil War Fort
Ramsey Bay
The Cronk
St. Judes
Dhoor
Grove
Curraghs
Sulby
Ramsey
Churchtown
Orrisdale
Ballaugh
T.T. Course
Glen Auldyn
Port e Vullen
Orrisdale Head
Ravensdale
Gate
Lewaigue
Maughold Head
Maughold
NT Manx
1854 North Barrule
Crosses
Bishopcourt Glen
Ballajora
Kirk Michael
Port Mooar
Corrany
Cornaa
Manx Electric Railway
Ballaleigh
Sleau Dhoo 1601
SNAEFELL
Clagh Ouyr
Ballacarnane Beg
Glen Mooar
Glen Mona
Castal-yn-Ard
2036
Barregarrow
Sulby Resr.
Gate
Port Cornaa
Gob y Deigan
Dhoon
NT Manx Dhoon Glen
Mountain Railway
Knocksharry
Cronk-y-Voddy
Bulgham Bay
Laxey Wheel
St. Patrick's Isle
1599 Colden
Injebreck Resr.
Minorca
Ballagyr
Lambfell Moar
Laxey
Peel
Glen Helen
Old Laxey
Laxey Head
Ballaheannagh
Contrary Head
Ballig
Ballacanneil
Mill
St. John's
Slieau Ruy 1570
Laxey Bay
Patrick
Baldwin
Greeba Castle
Baldrine
ISLE OF MAN
Clay Head
Glenmaye
Hillberry
Lower Foxdale
Crosby
Onchan
Dalby Point
Glen Vine
Groudle Glen Railway
Willaston
Strang
Port Groudle
Dalby
Foxdale
Fairy Garth
Union Mills
Onchan Head
Niarbyl Bay
DOUGLAS
1586 Fort South Barrule
Spring Valley
Braaid
Cooil
Douglas Bay
NT Manx
Kewaigue
Close Clark
Douglas Head
Stroin Vuigh
Quine's Hill
Ballamodha
St. Mark's
Newtown
Horses Home
Little Ness
Ronague
Keristal
Fleshwick Bay
Lingague
Grenaby
Port Soderick
Isle of Man Railway
Santon Head
Bradda
Surby
Ballabeg
Bradda Head
Colby
Ballasalla
Port Erin
Four Roads
ISLE OF MAN
The Howe
Port St. Mary
Ship Burial
Castletown
St. Michael's Island
Stone Circle
Derbyhaven
Kitterland
Cregneash
Nautical
NT Manx
SPANISH HEAD
Calf of Man
Dreswick Point
Chicken Rock
Bird Sanctuary NT Manx
Douglas to:
Belfast 2hrs.45mins. (Fast Ferry, Seasonal)
Heysham 3hrs. 30mins.
Heysham 2hrs. (Fast Ferry, Seasonal)
Dublin 2hrs. 45mins. (Fast Ferry, Seasonal)
Liverpool 2hrs. 30mins. (Fast Ferry, Seasonal)
Liverpool 4hrs. (Seasonal)
PAGE NOT CONTINUED

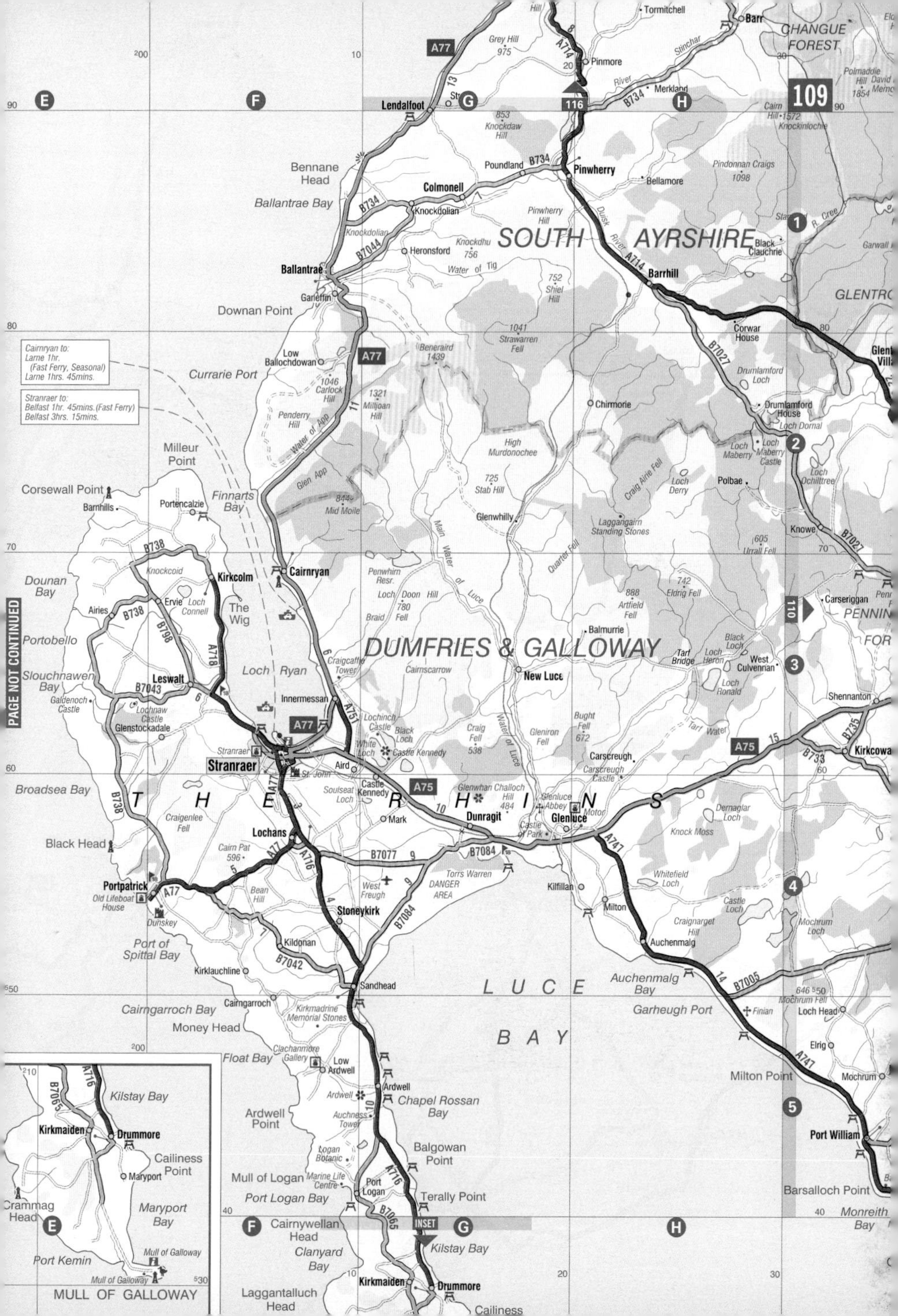

109
CHANGUE FOREST
Barr
Tormitchell
Pinmore
Grey Hill 975
Merkland
Lendalfoot
Knockdaw Hill
Poundland
Pinwherry
Bellamore
Pindonnan Craigs 1098
Cairn Hill 1572
Knockinlochie
Polmaddie Hill
Bennane Head
Colmonell
Ballantrae Bay
Knockdolian
Heronsford
Knockdhu 756
Water of Tig
Pinwherry Hill
SOUTH AYRSHIRE
Black Clauchrie
Barrhill
Ballantrae
Garleffin
Downan Point
752 Shiel Hill
1041 Strawarren Fell
Corwar House
GLENTROOL
Cairnryan to:
Larne 1hr. (Fast Ferry, Seasonal)
Larne 1hrs. 45mins.
Stranraer to:
Belfast 1hr. 45mins.(Fast Ferry)
Belfast 3hrs. 15mins.
Low Ballochdowan
Currarie Port
Beneraird 1439
1046 Carlock Hill
1321 Milljoan Hill
Penderry Hill
Drumlamford Loch
Chirmorie
Drumlamford House
Loch Dornal
Milleur Point
High Murdonochee
Loch Maberry
Loch Maberry Castle
Corsewall Point
Barnhills
Portencalzie
Finnarts Bay
Glen App
844 Mid Moile
725 Stab Hill
Craig Airie Fell
Loch Derry
Polbae
Loch Ochiltree
Glenwhilly
Laggangairn Standing Stones
Knowe
605 Urrall Fell
Dounan Bay
Knockcoid
Kirkcolm
Cairnryan
Penwhirn Resr.
Loch Doon Hill 780 Fell
Braid Fell
888 Artfield Fell
742 Eldrig Fell
Carseriggan
Airies
Ervie
Loch Connell
The Wig
Portobello
Balmurrie
PAGE NOT CONTINUED
DUMFRIES & GALLOWAY
Black Loch
Slouchnawen Bay
Leswalt
Loch Ryan
Craigcaffie Tower
Cairnscarrow
New Luce
Tarf Bridge
Loch Heron
West Culvennan
Loch Ronald
Galdenoch Castle
Lochnaw Castle
Glenstockadale
Innermessan
Lochinch Castle
Black Loch
White Loch
Castle Kennedy
Craig Fell 538
Gleniron Fell
Bught Fell 672
Tarf Water
Shennanton
Kirkcowan
Stranraer
St. John
Aird
Carscreugh
Carscreugh Castle
Broadsea Bay
Soulseat Loch
Castle Kennedy
Glenwhan Challoch
Hill 484
Glenluce Abbey
THE RHINS
Craigenlee Fell
Mark
Dunragit
Castle of Park
Glenluce
Dernaglar Loch
Lochans
Knock Moss
Black Head
Cairn Pat 596
Torrs Warren
DANGER AREA
Portpatrick
Old Lifeboat House
Dunskey
Bean Hill
West Freugh
Kilfillan
Milton
Whitefield Loch
Castle Loch
Mochrum Loch
Stoneykirk
Port of Spittal Bay
Kildonan
Craignarget Hill
Auchenmalg
Kirklauchline
Sandhead
LUCE
Auchenmalg Bay
Cairngarroch Bay
Cairngarroch
Kirkmadrine Memorial Stones
Garheugh Port
Finian
646 Mochrum Fell
Loch Head
Money Head
BAY
Elrig
Float Bay
Clachanmore Gallery
Low Ardwell
Milton Point
Mochrum
Ardwell
Chapel Rossan Bay
Ardwell Point
Auchness Tower
Port William
Balgowan Point
Logan Botanic
Mull of Logan
Marine Life Centre
Port Logan
Port Logan Bay
Terally Point
Barsalloch Point
Monreith Bay
Cairnywellan Head
INSET
Kilstay Bay
Clanyard Bay
Kirkmaiden
Drummore
Laggantalluch Head
Cailiness
Kilstay Bay
Kirkmaiden
Drummore
Cailiness Point
Maryport
Crammag Head
Maryport Bay
Mull of Galloway
Port Kemin
Mull of Galloway
MULL OF GALLOWAY
A77
A714
B734
B7044
A751
A75
A718
B738
B798
B7043
A716
B7077
B7084
B7042
A747
B7005
B7027
B733
B735
B7065
116
110

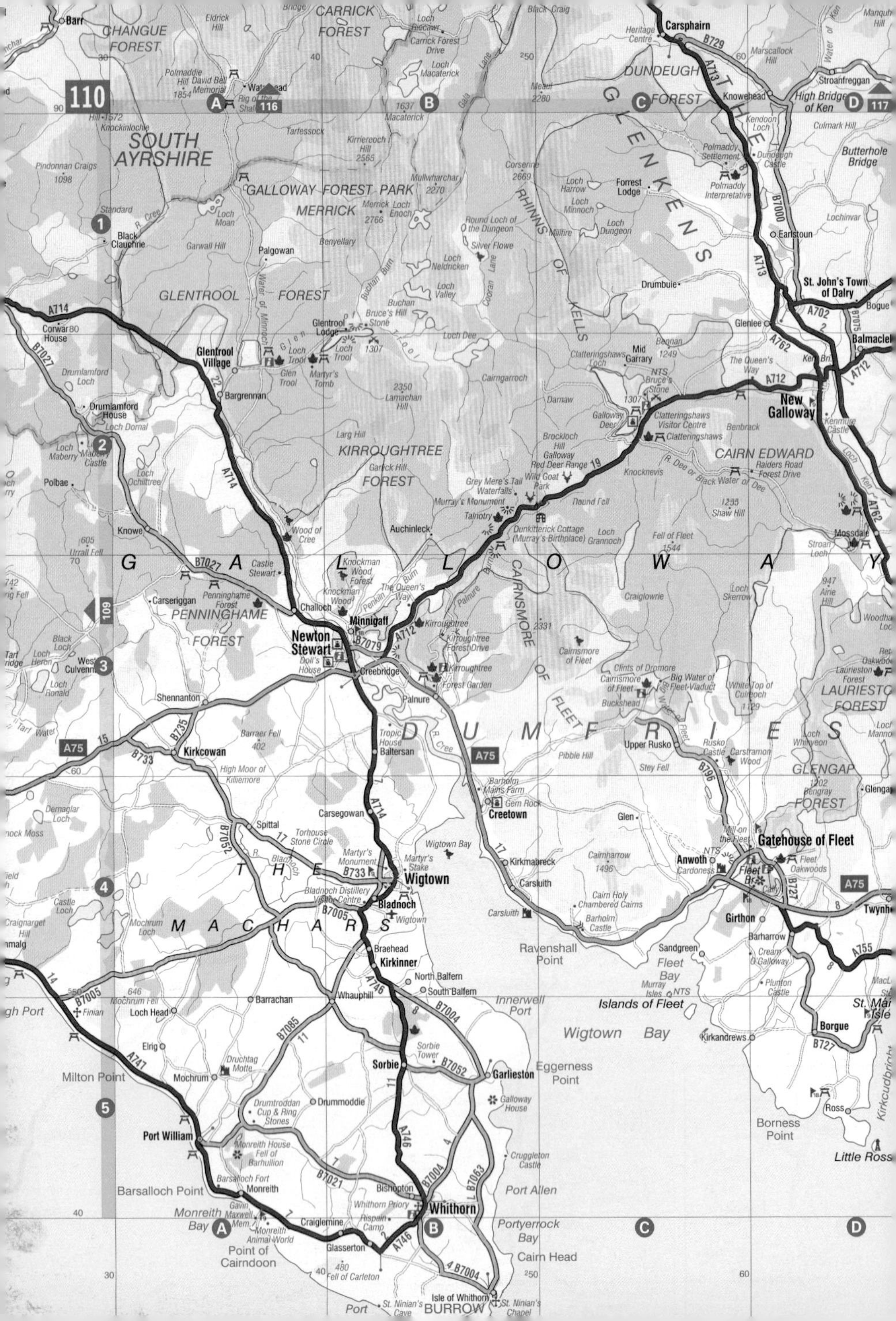

110
116
117
109
Barr
CHANGUE FOREST
CARRICK FOREST
Eldrick Hill
Loch Riecawr
Carrick Forest Drive
Loch Macaterick
Black Craig
Carsphairn
Heritage Centre
B729
Marscallock Hill
Manquhill
Water of Ken
Polmaddie Hill
David Bell Memorial
Waterhead
Rig of the Shalloch
1854
1637
Macaterick
Meaul
2280
DUNDEUGH FOREST
Knowehead
Stroanfreggan
High Bridge of Ken
Culmark Hill
Hill 1572
Knockinlochie
SOUTH AYRSHIRE
Tarfessock
Kirriereoch Hill
2565
Kendoon Loch
Polmaddy Settlement
Dundeugh Castle
Butterhole Bridge
Pindonnan Craigs
1098
GALLOWAY FOREST PARK
MERRICK
Merrick
2766
Loch Enoch
Mullwharchar
2270
Corserine
2669
Loch Harrow
Forrest Lodge
Loch Minnoch
Polmaddy Interpretative
B7000
Lochinvar
THE GLENKENS
Standard
R. Cree
Loch Moan
Black Clauchrie
Garwall Hill
Round Loch of the Dungeon
Millfire
Loch Dungeon
Earlstoun
Palgowan
Benyellary
Silver Flowe
RHINNS OF KELLS
Loch Neldricken
Buchan Burn
Water of Minnoch
Cooran Lane
Loch Valley
Drumbuie
A713
St. John's Town of Dalry
GLENTROOL FOREST
A714
Corwar House
80
Buchan
Glentrool Lodge
Bruce's Hill Stone
Glen Trool
Loch Dee
Glenlee
A702
Bogue
B7075
B7027
Glentrool Village
Loch Trool
1307
Glen Trool
Martyr's Tomb
Clatteringshaws Loch
Mid Garrary
Bennan
1249
NTS Bruce's Stone
The Queen's Way
A762
Balmaclellan
Ken Bridge
A712
Drumlamford Loch
Bargrennan
Cairngarroch
2350
Lamachan Hill
Darnaw
Galloway Deer
Clatteringshaws Visitor Centre
Clatteringshaws
New Galloway
Kenmure Castle
Benbrack
Drumlamford House
Loch Dornal
Loch Maberry
Maberry Castle
Larg Hill
KIRROUGHTREE FOREST
Garlick Hill
Brockloch Hill
Galloway Red Deer Range
Wild Goat Park
CAIRN EDWARD
Raiders Road Forest Drive
Knocknevis
R. Dee or Black Water of Dee
Polbae
Loch Ochiltree
Grey Mere's Tail Waterfalls
Murray's Monument
Talnotry
Round Fell
1235
Shaw Hill
Loch Ken
Wood of Cree
Auchinleck
Dunkitterick Cottage (Murray's Birthplace)
Loch Grannoch
Fell of Fleet
1544
Mossdale
Stroan Loch
Knowe
605
Urrall Fell
70
GALLOWAY
Castle Stewart
Knockman Wood Forest
Penkiln Burn
The Queen's Way
CAIRNSMORE OF FLEET
Palnure Burn
Loch Skerrow
Craiglowrie
947
Airie Hill
742
Carseriggan
Penninghame Forest
PENNINGHAME FOREST
Challoch
Knockman Wood
Minnigaff
Newton Stewart
B7079
Kirroughtree
Kirroughtree Forest Drive
2331
Cairnsmore of Fleet
Black Loch
Loch Heron
West Culvennan
Loch Ronald
Doll's House
Creebridge
Forest Garden
Palnure
Clints of Dromore
Cairnsmore of Fleet
Big Water of Fleet Viaduct
Buckshead
White Top of Culreoch
1129
Laurieston Forest
LAURIESTON FOREST
Shennanton
Tarf Water
B735
Barraer Fell
402
Tropic House
Baltersan
R. Cree
DUMFRIES
A75
Pibble Hill
Upper Rusko
Rusko Castle
Carstramon Wood
Loch Whinyeon
GLENGAP FOREST
A75
15
B733
Kirkcowan
60
High Moor of Killiemore
Stey Fell
B796
1202
Bengray
Glengap
Demaglar Loch
Barholm Mains Farm
Gem Rock
Creetown
Glen
Spittal
Carsegowan
Torhouse Stone Circle
17
B7052
R. Bladnoch
THE MACHARS
Wigtown Bay
Martyr's Monument
Martyr's Stake
B733
Wigtown
Bladnoch Distillery Visitor Centre
Bladnoch
Wigtown
Kirkmabreck
Carsluith
Cairnharrow
1496
Cairn Holy Chambered Cairns
Carsluith
Barholm Castle
Mill on the Fleet
Gatehouse of Fleet
NTS
Anwoth
Cardoness
Fleet Oakwoods
B727
Girthon
Barharrow
Cream O'Galloway
Twynholm
A755
Castle Loch
Mochrum Loch
B7005
Braehead
Kirkinner
North Balfern
South Balfern
Ravenshall Point
Sandgreen
Fleet Bay
Murray Isles
Islands of Fleet
Plunton Castle
14
B7005
Finian
646
Mochrum Fell
Barrachan
Loch Head
Whauphill
A746
B7004
Innerwell Port
Wigtown Bay
Kirkandrews
Borgue
St. Mary's Isle
B727
Milton Point
A747
Elrig
B7085
11
Druchtag Motte
Mochrum
Sorbie Tower
Sorbie
B7052
Garlieston
Eggerness Point
Drumtroddan Cup & Ring Stones
Drummoddie
Galloway House
Ross
Borness Point
Port William
Monreith House
Fell of Barhullion
Cruggleton Castle
Little Ross
Kirkcudbright
Barsalloch Fort
Barsalloch Point
Monreith
B7021
Bishopton
Whithorn Priory
Whithorn
B7063
Port Allen
Monreith Bay
Gavin Maxwell Mem.
Monreith Animal World
Craiglemine
Rispain Camp
Portyerrock Bay
Point of Cairndoon
Glasserton
A746
Cairn Head
480
Fell of Carleton
B7004
Isle of Whithorn
St. Ninian's Chapel
Port
St. Ninian's Cave
BURROW
A
B
C
D
1
2
3
4
5
30
40
250
60
90

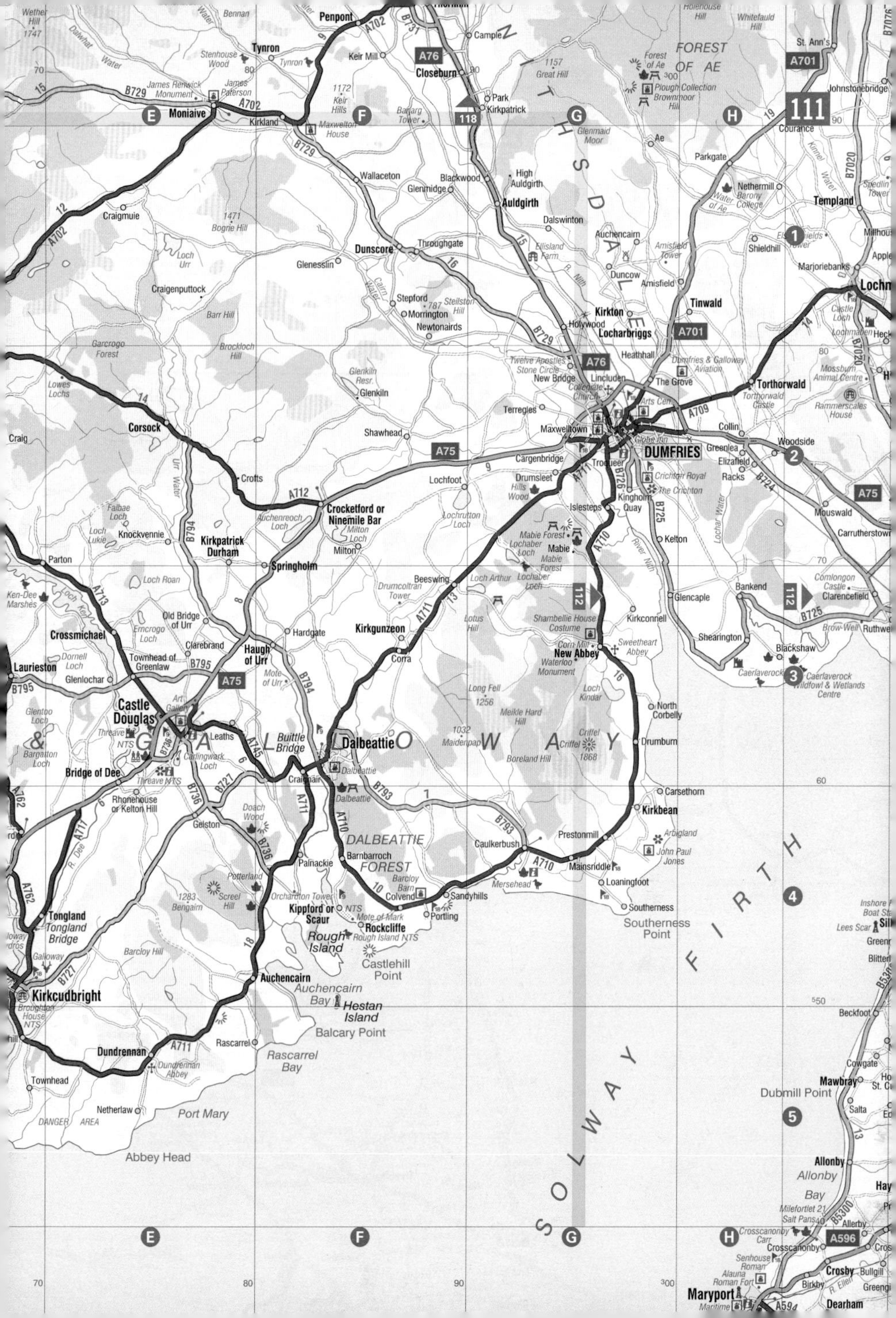

111
Wether Hill 1747
Bennan
Penpont
A702
B731
Dalwhat Water
Tynron
Stenhouse Wood
Keir Mill
A76
Closeburn
Campleton
Forest of Ae
FOREST OF AE
1157 Great Hill
Plough Collection
Brownmoor Hill
Whitefauld Hill
St. Ann's
A701
Johnstonebridge
B729
James Renwick Monument
James Paterson
Moniaive
Kirkland
1172 Keir Hills
Maxwelton House
Barjarg Tower
Park
Kirkpatrick
118
E
F
G
H
Glenmaid Moor
Ae
Courance
Kinnel Water
Parkgate
B7020
Wallaceton
Blackwood
Glenmidge
High Auldgirth
Auldgirth
Nethermill
Barony College
Water of Ae
Templand
Spedlin Tower
Craigmuie
1471 Bogrie Hill
Dalswinton
Auchencairn
Amisfield Tower
Elshieshields Tower
Shieldhill
Marjoriebanks
Loch Urr
Dunscore
Throughgate
Glenesslin
Ellisland Farm
R. Nith
Duncow
Amisfield
Lochmaben
Craigenputtock
Cairn Water
Stepford
787 Steilston Hill
Morrington
Newtonairds
Barr Hill
Kirkton
Holywood
Locharbriggs
Tinwald
A701
Castle Loch
Garcrogo Forest
Brockloch Hill
B729
Twelve Apostles Stone Circle
A76
New Bridge
Lincluden Collegiate Church
Heathhall
Dumfries & Galloway Aviation
The Grove
Mossburn Animal Centre
Torthorwald
Torthorwald Castle
Rammerscales House
Lowes Lochs
Glenkiln Resr.
Glenkiln
Terregles
Arts Centre
A709
Corsock
Craig
Shawhead
Maxwelltown
Globe Inn
DUMFRIES
Collin
Woodside
Greenlea
Elizafield
Racks
B724
A75
Crofts
Cargenbridge
Troqueer
B726
Crichton Royal
The Crichton
A75
Lochfoot
Drumsleet
Hills Wood
Kingholm Quay
B725
Mouswald
A712
Crocketford or Ninemile Bar
Auchenreoch Loch
Falbae Loch
Lochrutton Loch
Islesteps
Milton Loch
Milton
Loch Lukie
Knockvennie
B794
Kirkpatrick Durham
Mabie Forest
Lochaber Loch
Mabie
A710
River Nith
Kelton
Lochar Water
Carrutherstown
Parton
Springholm
Loch Roan
Beeswing
Drumcoltran Tower
Loch Arthur
Lochaber Loch
112
Bankend
Comlongon Castle
Clarencefield
Ken-Dee Marshes
Loch Ken
A713
Old Bridge of Urr
Glencaple
B725
Lotus Hill
Kirkgunzeon
Shambellie House Costume
Kirkconnell
Brow Well
Ruthwell
Crossmichael
Erncrogo Loch
Hardgate
Clarebrand
Haugh of Urr
Corn Mill
New Abbey
Sweetheart Abbey
Shearington
Blackshaw
Laurieston
Dornell Loch
Townhead of Greenlaw
B795
A75
Mote of Urr
Corra
Waterloo Monument
Caerlaverock
Caerlaverock Wildfowl & Wetlands Centre
Glenlochar
Loch Kindar
Long Fell 1256
North Corbelly
Glentoo Loch
Castle Douglas
Art Gallery
Meikle Hard Hill
Threave
NTS
GALLOWAY
Leaths
A745
Buittle Bridge
Dalbeattie
1032 Maidenpap
Criffel 1868
Boreland Hill
Drumburn
Bargatton Loch
Carlingwark Loch
B727
Craignair
Bridge of Dee
Threave NTS
Rhonehouse or Kelton Hill
B736
B793
Carsethorn
Kirkbean
Doach Wood
Gelston
Dalbeattie Forest
Preston Mill
Arbigland
John Paul Jones
A762
A711
Caulkerbush
R. Dee
A717
Palnackie
Barnbarroch
FOREST
A710
Mainsriddle
Mersehead
Loaningfoot
Potterland
Barcloy Barn
Colvend
Sandyhills
Southerness
Southerness Point
1283 Bengairn
Screel Hill
Orchardton Tower
Kippford or Scaur
Mote of Mark
Portling
Rockcliffe
Inshore Rescue Boat Station
Lees Scar
Tongland
Tongland Bridge
Rough Island
Rough Island NTS
Castlehill Point
Barcloy Hill
Galloway Hydros
B727
Auchencairn
Auchencairn Bay
Hestan Island
Kirkcudbright
Broughton House NTS
Balcary Point
SOLWAY FIRTH
Beckfoot
B5300
Dundrennan
Dundrennan Abbey
A711
Rascarrel
Rascarrel Bay
Townhead
Cowgate
Mawbray
Dubmill Point
Netherlaw
Port Mary
DANGER AREA
Salta
Abbey Head
Allonby
Allonby Bay
Milefortlet 21 Salt Pans
Allerby
A596
Crosscanonby Carr
Crosscanonby
Senhouse Roman Museum
Alauna Roman Fort
Crosby
Bullgill
Birkby
R. Ellen
Maryport
Maritime
A594
Dearham
1
2
3
4
5
70
80
90
300
60
550

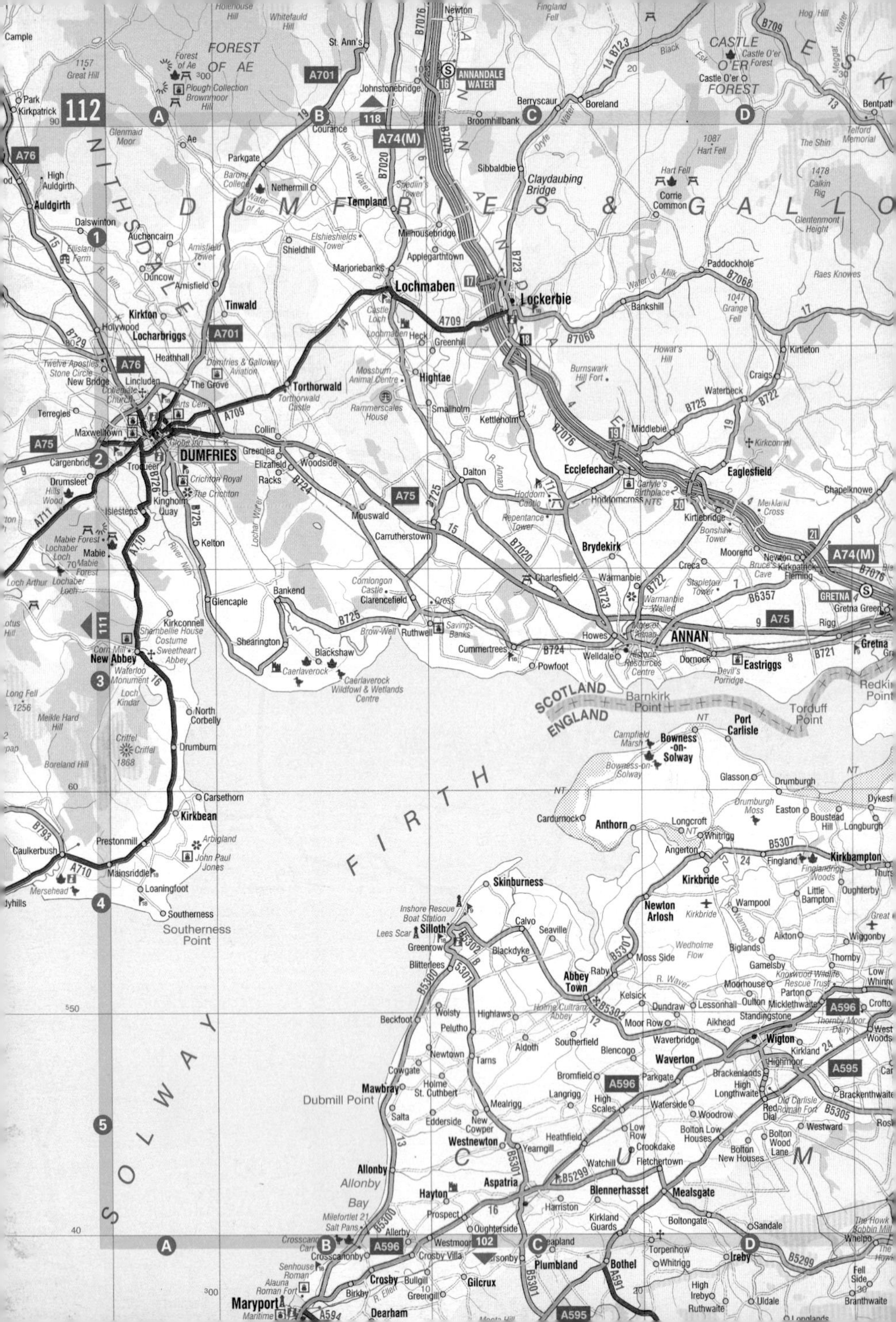
112
FOREST OF AE
Forest of Ae
Plough Collection
Brownmoor Hill
1157 Great Hill
Cample
Park
Kirkpatrick
Holehouse Hill
Whitefauld Hill
St. Ann's
A701
Johnstonebridge
118
A74(M)
ANNANDALE WATER
Newton
B7076
Fingland Fell
Berryscaur
Boreland
Broomhillbank
CASTLE O'ER FOREST
Castle O'er Forest
Castle O'er
Hog Hill
Bentpath
Telford Memorial
The Shin
1087 Hart Fell
1478 Calkin Rig
Glentenmont Height
Hart Fell
Corrie Common
Glenmaid Moor
Ae
Courance
Parkgate
Barony College
Water of Ae
Nethermill
Kinnel Water
B7020
Spedlin's Tower
Templand
Sibbaldbie
Claydaubing Bridge
Dryfe Water
NITHSDALE
DUMFRIES & GALLOWAY
A76
High Auldgirth
Auldgirth
Dalswinton
Auchencairn
Ellisland Farm
Amisfield Tower
Duncow
Amisfield
Elshieshields Tower
Shieldhill
Millhousebridge
Applegarthtown
Marjoriebanks
Lochmaben
Castle Loch
Lochmaben Castle
Lockerbie
B723
Paddockhole
B7068
Water of Milk
Raes Knowes
Bankshill
1047 Grange Fell
Tinwald
Kirkton
Holywood
Locharbriggs
A701
B729
A709
Heck
Greenhill
Howat's Hill
Kirtleton
Twelve Apostles Stone Circle
New Bridge
Heathhall
Dumfries & Galloway Aviation
Lincluden Collegiate Church
The Grove
Torthorwald
Torthorwald Castle
Mossburn Animal Centre
Rammerscales House
Hightae
Smallholm
Burnswark Hill Fort
Craigs
Waterbeck
B725
B722
Terregles
Maxwelltown
Arts Centre
Globe Inn
DUMFRIES
Collin
Kettleholm
Middlebie
Kirkconnel
A75
Cargenbridge
Drumsleet
Hills Wood
Troqueer
Greenlea
Elizafield
Racks
Woodside
B724
Crichton Royal
The Crichton
Dalton
Ecclefechan
Carlyle's Birthplace NTC
Hoddom Castle
Hoddomcross
Eaglesfield
Chapelknowe
Merkland Cross
A711
Kingholm Quay
B726
Islesteps
Mabie Forest
Lochaber Loch
Mabie
Mabie Forest
A710
Loch Arthur
Lochaber Loch
Kelton
River Nith
Lochar Water
Mouswald
Carrutherstown
Repentance Tower
B7020
Brydekirk
Kirtlebridge
Bonshaw Tower
Moorend
Newton
Kirkpatrick Fleming
Bruce's Cave
A74(M)
B7076
Creca
Stapleton Tower
B6357
GRETNA
Gretna Green
Rigg
Gretna
Charlesfield
Warmanbie
Warmanbie Walled
Glencaple
Bankend
Comlongon Castle
Clarencefield
Cross
Savings Banks
Brow Well
Ruthwell
B725
Kirkconnell
Shambellie House Costume
Sweetheart Abbey
Corn Mill
New Abbey
Shearington
Blackshaw
Caerlaverock
Caerlaverock Wildfowl & Wetlands Centre
Cummertrees
Powfoot
Howes
Welldale
Historic Resources Centre
ANNAN
Dornock
Devil's Porridge
Eastriggs
B721
Waterloo Monument
Loch Kindar
Long Fell
1256
Meikle Hard Hill
North Corbelly
Criffel
1868
Boreland Hill
Drumburn
SCOTLAND
ENGLAND
Barnkirk Point
Torduff Point
Redkirk Point
Campfield Marsh
Bowness-on-Solway
Port Carlisle
Glasson
Drumburgh
Drumburgh Moss
Easton
Boustead Hill
Longburgh
Dykesfield
Cardurnock
Anthorn
Longcroft
Whitrigg
Angerton
B5307
Fingland
Finglandrigg Woods
Kirkbampton
Carsethorn
Kirkbean
Arbigland
John Paul Jones
Prestonmill
Mainsriddle
Caulkerbush
B793
A710
Mersehead
Loaningfoot
Southerness
Southerness Point
SOLWAY FIRTH
Skinburness
Inshore Rescue Boat Station
Lees Scar
Silloth
Greenrow
Blitterlees
B5302
B5300
Calvo
Seaville
Blackdyke
Kirkbride
Newton Arlosh
Wampool
Little Bampton
Oughterby
Aikton
Wiggonby
Biglands
Wedholme Flow
Moss Side
Gamelsby
Thornby
Raby
Abbey Town
Holme Cultram Abbey
Kelsick
Dundraw
Lessonhall
Moorhouse
Knoxwood Wildlife Rescue Trust
Parton
Oulton
Micklethwaite
A596
Beckfoot
Wolsty
Highlaws
Pelutho
Aldoth
Southerfield
Blencogo
Moor Row
Aikhead
Waverbridge
Standingstone
Wigton
Kirkland
Newtown
Tarns
Waverton
Highmoor
Brackenlands
A595
Cowgate
Holme St. Cuthbert
Mawbray
Bromfield
Langrigg
High Scales
Parkgate
High Longthwaite
Brackenthwaite
Dubmill Point
Mealrigg
Waterside
Woodrow
Red Dial
Old Carlisle Roman Fort
B5305
Salta
Edderside
New Cowper
Low Row
Bolton Low Houses
Westward
Westnewton
Yearngill
Heathfield
Crookdake
Bolton New Houses
Bolton Wood Lane
Allonby
Allonby Bay
Watchill
Fletchertown
B5299
CUMBRIA
Hayton
Aspatria
Blennerhasset
Mealsgate
Harriston
Kirkland Guards
Boltongate
Sandale
Milefortlet 21 Salt Pans
Prospect
Oughterside
Allerby
Crosscanonby Carr
Crosscanonby
Westmoor
A596
102
Crosby Villa
Parsonby
Plumbland
Bothel
Torpenhow
Whitrigg
Ireby
Whelpo
B5299
Senhouse Roman Museum
Alauna Roman Fort
Crosby
Bullgill
Birkby
Greengill
Gilcrux
B5301
A591
High Ireby
Ruthwaite
Uldale
Fell Side
Branthwaite
Maryport
Maritime
Dearham
A594
A595
R. Ellen

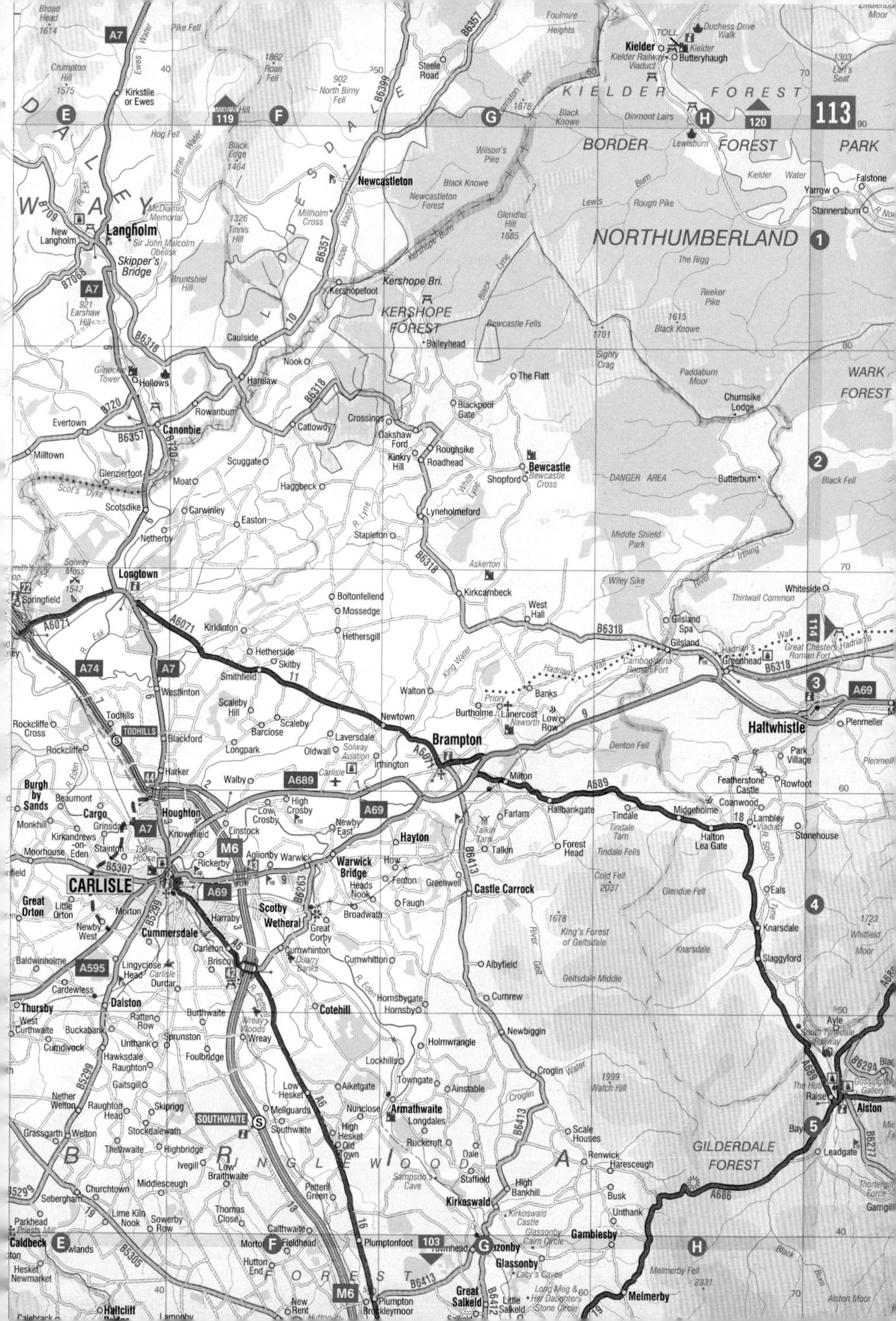
113
Broad Head 1614
A7
Pike Fell
Ewes Water
Crumpton Hill 1575
1862 Roan Fell
902 North Birny Fell
B6357
B6399
Steele Road
Foulmire Heights
Kielder
TOLL
Duchess Drive Walk
Kielder Railway Viaduct
Butteryhaugh
1303 Earl's Seat
Kirkstile or Ewes
KIELDER FOREST
Watch Hill
119
Tarras Water
Larriston Fells 1678
Black Knowe
Dinmont Lairs
120
E
F
G
H
Hog Fell
Black Edge 1464
Wilson's Pike
BORDER FOREST
PARK
Lewisburn
Kielder Water
Lewis Burn
Rough Pike
Falstone
Yarrow
Stannersburn
R. North Tyne
DALEY
WAY
LIDDESDALE
B7709
R. Esk
McDiamid Memorial
1326 Tinnis Hill
Millholm Cross
Liddel Water
Newcastleton
Black Knowe
Newcastleton Forest
Glendhu Hill 1685
NORTHUMBERLAND
1
New Langholm
Langholm
Sir John Malcolm Obelisk
Skipper's Bridge
B7068
B6357
Kershope Burn
Black Lyne
The Rigg
Kershope Bri.
Kershopefoot
Bruntshiel Hill
A7
921 Earshaw Hill
KERSHOPE FOREST
Reeker Pike
Bewcastle Fells
1615 Black Knowe
B6318
Caulside
Baileyhead
1701
Sighty Crag
Nook
Gilnockie Tower
Hollows
Harelaw
B6318
The Flatt
Paddaburn Moor
WARK FOREST
Churnsike Lodge
Evertown
B720
Rowanburn
Catlowdy
Crossings
Blackpool Gate
Canonbie
B6357
B6120
Oakshaw Ford
Roughsike
Milltown
Scuggate
Kinkry Hill
Roadhead
Bewcastle
Bewcastle Cross
Shopford
DANGER AREA
Butterburn
2
Black Fell
Glenzierfoot
Moat
Haggbeck
Scot's Dyke
White Lyne
Scotsdike
Carwinley
Easton
R. Lyne
Lyneholmeford
Netherby
Stapleton
Middle Shield Park
River Irthing
Solway Moss 1542
Longtown
Askerton
Wiley Sike
22
Springfield
Kirkcambeck
Whiteside
Boltonfellend
Mossedge
West Hall
Thirlwall Common
A6071
Gilsland Spa
114
Kirklinton
Hethersgill
B6318
Gilsland
Hadrian's Wall
Great Chesters Roman Fort
Hetherside
Camboglanna Roman Fort
Greenhead
B6318
A74
A7
Skitby
Smithfield
King Water
3
Westlinton
Walton
A69
Scaleby Hill
Scaleby
Priory
Banks
Todhills
Barclose
Newtown
Burtholme
Lanercost
Naworth
Low Row
Haltwhistle
Plenmeller
Rockcliffe Cross
TODHILLS
Laversdale
Brampton
Blackford
Longpark
Oldwall
Solway Aviation
Denton Fell
Park Village
Rockcliffe
Irthington
R. Eden
Carlisle
Harker
Walby
A689
Milton
Featherstone Castle
Rowfoot
Burgh by Sands
Beaumont
A689
44
Cargo
Grinsdale
Houghton
Low Crosby
High Crosby
Hallbankgate
Tindale
Midgeholme
Coanwood
Lambley Viaduct
Monkhill
Linstock
A69
Farlam
Tindale Tarn
18
Kirkandrews-on-Eden
A7
Knowefield
Newby East
Talkin Tarn
Halton Lea Gate
Stonehouse
Stainton
M6
Hayton
Talkin
Forest Head
Tindale Fells
R. South Tyne
Moorhouse
Tullie House
Rickerby
Aglionby
Warwick
How
B5307
43
Warwick Bridge
Heads Nook
Fenton
Greenwell
B6413
Cold Fell 2037
CARLISLE
A69
Castle Carrock
Glendue Fell
Eals
Great Orton
Little Orton
B5299
Morton
Scotby
Wetheral
B6263
Faugh
Broadwath
4
Newby West
Harraby
Great Corby
1678
Tyne
Knarsdale
1723 Whitfield Moor
Cummersdale
Carleton
A6
King's Forest of Geltsdale
River Gelt
Knarsdale
Baldwinholme
Brisco
Cumwhinton
Quarry Banks
Cumwhitton
Slaggyford
A595
Lingyclose Head
Carlisle Durdar
42
Albyfield
Geltsdale Middle
Cardewlees
R. Petteril
R. Eden
Dalston
Hornsbygate
Hornsby
Cumrew
Thursby
Cotehill
West Curthwaite
Ratten Row
Burthwaite
Wreay Woods
Ayle
Buckabank
Sprunston
Wreay
Newbiggin
South Tynedale Railway
Cumdivock
Unthank
Holmwrangle
Hawksdale
Raughton
Foulbridge
Lockhills
B5299
Croglin Water
A689
B6294
Gaitsgill
Low Hesket
Towngate
Aiketgate
Ainstable
1999 Watch Hill
The Hub
Gossipgate Gallery
Nether Welton
Raughton Head
Skiprigg
Mellguards
A6
Nunclose
Armathwaite
Longdales
Croglin
Raise
Alston
SOUTHWAITE
Stockdalewath
Southwaite
High Hesket
Old Town
B6413
Scale Houses
5
Grassgarth
Welton
Thethwaite
Highbridge
Ruckcroft
Bayles
B6277
Ivegill
Low Braithwaite
Dale
Renwick
Harescough
Leadgate
INGLEWOOD
GILDERDALE FOREST
Middlesceugh
Staffield
Sampson's Cave
Sebergham
Churchtown
Petteril Green
High Bankhill
Busk
Thortergill Force
Kirkoswald
A686
Lime Kiln Nook
Thomas Close
Kirkoswald Castle
Unthank
Garrigill
Parkhead
Priests Mill
Sowerby Row
Calthwaite
Glassonby Cairn Circle
Gamblesby
Caldbeck
Howlands
Morton
Fieldhead
Plumptonfoot
103
Townhead
Lazonby
Hesket Newmarket
B5305
Hutton End
Glassonby
Lacy's Caves
Melmerby Fell 2331
Black Burn
FOREST
B6413
M6
Plumpton
Brockleymoor
Great Salkeld
B6412
Little Salkeld
Long Meg & Her Daughters Stone Circle
Melmerby
Alston Moor
Haltcliff
Calebrack
New Rent

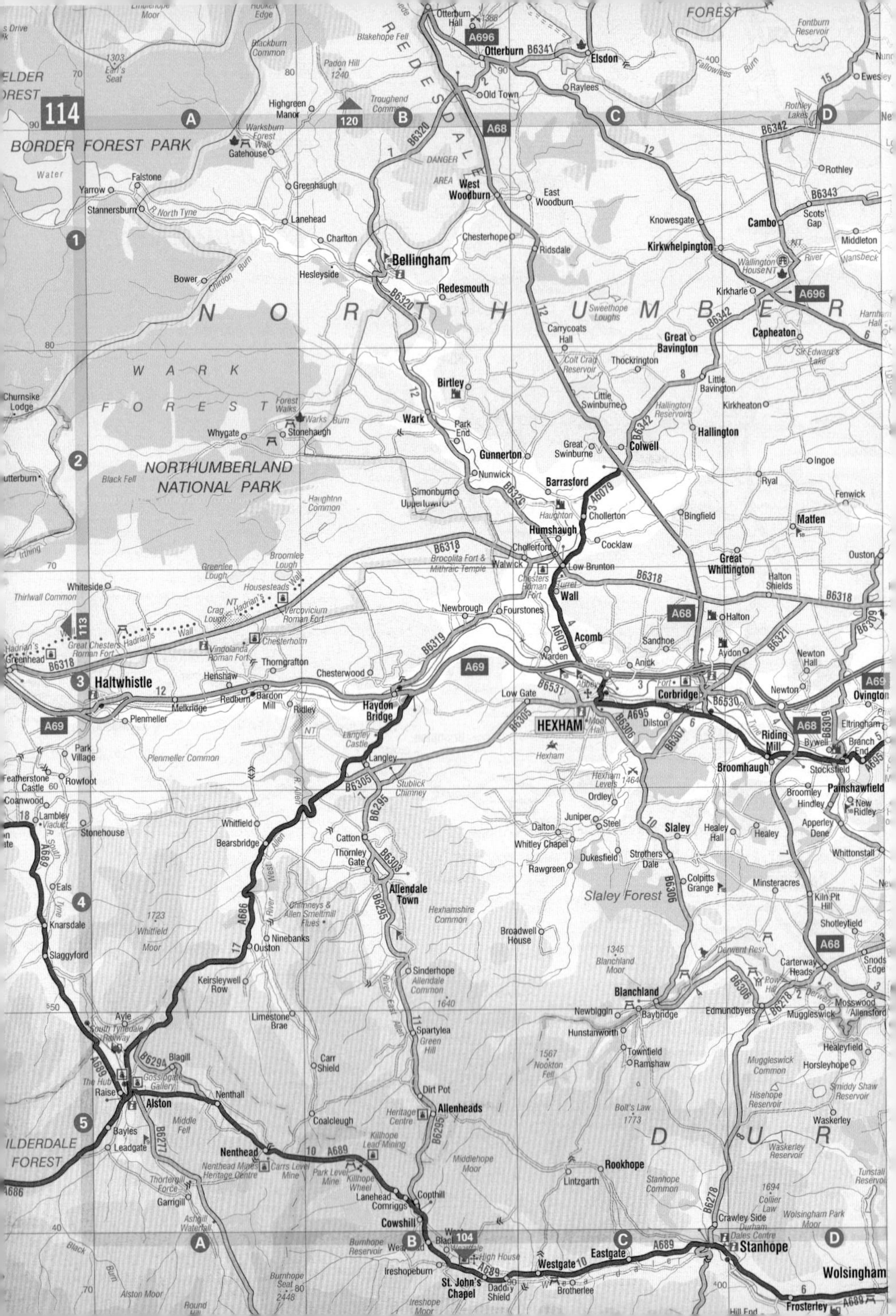

114
120
113
104
A
B
C
D
1
2
3
4
5
Otterburn Hall
Otterburn
A696
B6341
Elsdon
Blakehope Fell
Padon Hill 1240
Blackburn Common
Hooker Edge
Earl's Seat
1303
KIELDER FOREST
BORDER FOREST PARK
FOREST
Fontburn Reservoir
Fallowlees Burn
Ewesley
Old Town
Raylees
Highgreen Manor
Troughend Common
REDESDALE
A68
B6320
Warksburn Forest Walk
Gatehouse
Rothley Lakes
B6342
Rothley
Falstone
Yarrow
Stannersburn
R. North Tyne
Water
Greenhaugh
DANGER AREA
West Woodburn
East Woodburn
B6343
Cambo
Scots' Gap
Lanehead
Knowesgate
Kirkwhelpington
Middleton
Charlton
Chesterhope
Ridsdale
Wallington House NT
River Wansbeck
Bellingham
Hesleyside
Bower
Chirdon Burn
Redesmouth
Kirkharle
NORTHUMBERLAND
Sweethope Loughs
Capheaton
Carrycoats Hall
Great Bavington
Sir Edward's Lake
Colt Crag Reservoir
Thockrington
Little Bavington
WARK FOREST
Birtley
Little Swinburne
Hallington Reservoirs
Kirkheaton
Churnsike Lodge
Forest Walks
Warks Burn
Stonehaugh
Whygate
Wark
Park End
Hallington
Colwell
Great Swinburne
Gunnerton
Ingoe
Black Fell
NORTHUMBERLAND NATIONAL PARK
Nunwick
Ryal
Barrasford
Simonburn
Uppertown
Fenwick
Haughton Common
A6079
Haughton
Chollerton
Bingfield
Matfen
Humshaugh
Cocklaw
Irthing
Broomlee Lough
B6318
Chollerford
Brocolita Fort & Mithraic Temple
Walwick
Great Whittington
Ouston
Greenlee Lough
Low Brunton
Chesters Roman Fort
Turret
Whiteside
Housesteads
Hadrian's Wall
Halton Shields
Thirlwall Common
Wall
NT
Crag Lough
Vercovicium Roman Fort
Newbrough
Fourstones
Halton
Great Chesters Roman Fort
Vindolanda Roman Fort
Chesterholm
Acomb
Sandhoe
B6321
Greenhead
Warden
Anick
Aydon
Newton Hall
Thorngrafton
B6319
A69
Haltwhistle
Henshaw
Chesterwood
Abbey
Fort
Corbridge
Newton
Ovington
Melkridge
Redburn
Bardon Mill
Ridley
Haydon Bridge
Low Gate
B6531
B6530
HEXHAM
Moot Hall
Dilston
Plenmeller
B6305
B6306
B6307
Riding Mill
Eltringham
Bywell
Langley Castle
Park Village
Plenmeller Common
Langley
Hexham
Broomhaugh
Branch End
Stocksfield
Featherstone Castle
Rowfoot
Stublick Chimney
Hexham Levels
1464
Painshawfield
Coanwood
Broomley
Hindley
New Ridley
Lambley
Lambley Viaduct
R. South Tyne
Whitfield
Ordley
Stonehouse
Juniper
Steel
Apperley Dene
A689
Bearsbridge
Catton
Dalton
Slaley
Healey Hall
Healey
Whittonstall
Whitley Chapel
Thornley Gate
B6303
Dukesfield
Strothers Dale
Rawgreen
Allendale Town
Colpitts Grange
Minsteracres
Eals
Chimneys & Allen Smeltmill Flues
Slaley Forest
Kiln Pit Hill
Hexhamshire Common
Knarsdale
1723
Whitfield Moor
Broadwell House
Shotleyfield
A686
Ninebanks
Ouston
Slaggyford
1345
Blanchland Moor
Derwent Resr
Sinderhope
Allendale Common
Carterway Heads
Snods Edge
Keirsleywell Row
Blanchland
Pow Hill
1640
Newbiggin
Baybridge
Edmundbyers
B6278
Muggleswick
Mosswood
Allensford
Ayle
South Tynedale Railway
Limestone Brae
Spartylea
Green Hill
Hunstanworth
Townfield
Ramshaw
Healeyfield
B6294
Blagill
Carr Shield
1567
Nookton Fell
Muggleswick Common
Horsleyhope
Gossipgate Gallery
The Hub
Raise
Alston
Nenthall
Dirt Pot
Hisehope Reservoir
Smiddy Shaw Reservoir
Allenheads
Heritage Centre
Bolt's Law
1773
Middle Fell
Coalcleugh
B6295
Waskerley
Bayles
B6277
Killhope Lead Mining
Leadgate
Nenthead
DURHAM
Waskerley Reservoir
ALDERDALE FOREST
Nenthead Mines Heritage Centre
Carrs Level Mine
Park Level Mine
Killhope Wheel
Middlehope Moor
Rookhope
Tunstall Reservoir
Thortergill Force
Lintzgarth
Stanhope Common
1694
Collier Law
Garrigill
Lanehead
Copthill
Comriggs
Ashgill Waterfall
Cowshill
Crawley Side
Durham Dales Centre
Wolsingham Park Moor
Stanhope
Burnhope Reservoir
Wearhead
West Blackdene
Weardale
High House
Eastgate
Westgate
Wolsingham
Black Burn
Ireshopeburn
St. John's Chapel
Daddry Shield
Brotherlee
Burnhope Seat
2448
Alston Moor
Round Hill
Ireshope Moor
Hill End
Frosterley

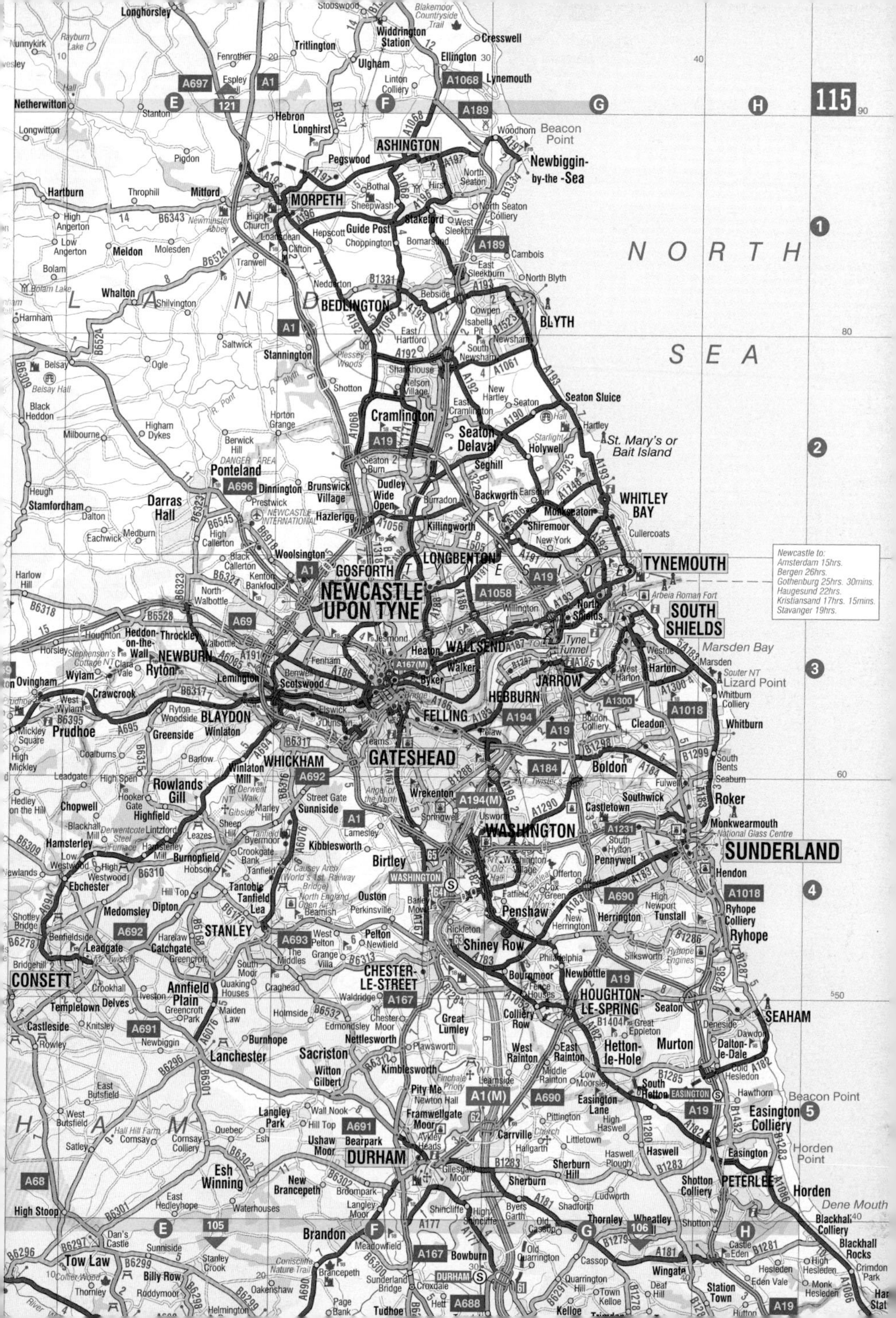
NORTH SEA
Newcastle to:
Amsterdam 15hrs.
Bergen 26hrs.
Gothenburg 25hrs. 30mins.
Haugesund 22hrs.
Kristiansand 17hrs. 15mins.
Stavanger 19hrs.
Longhorsley
Stobswood
Blakemoor Countryside Trail
Widdrington Station
Cresswell
Tritlington
Ulgham
Ellington
Lynemouth
Linton Colliery
Fenrother
Espley
Netherwitton
Stanton
Hebron
Longhirst
Longwitton
Pigdon
Pegswood
ASHINGTON
Woodhorn
Beacon Point
Newbiggin-by-the-Sea
North Seaton
Bothal
Sheepwash
Hartburn
Throphill
Mitford
MORPETH
Newminster Abbey
High Church
North Seaton Colliery
Stakeford
West Sleekburn
High Angerton
Low Angerton
Meldon
Molesden
Hepscott
Guide Post
Choppington
Bomarsund
Cambois
Bolam
Tranwell
Clifton
East Sleekburn
Bolam Lake
Whalton
Shilvington
Nedderton
BEDLINGTON
Bebside
North Blyth
Cowpen
Isabella Pit
BLYTH
Newsham
South Newsham
East Hartford
Harnham
Saltwick
Stannington
Plessey Woods
Belsay
Belsay Hall
Ogle
Shankhouse
Nelson Village
Shotton
Seaton Sluice
New Hartley
Seaton
Black Heddon
East Cramlington
Hartley
Cramlington
Horton Grange
Higham Dykes
Milbourne
Berwick Hill
Seaton Delaval
Starlight
Holywell
St. Mary's or Bait Island
DANGER AREA
Ponteland
Seaton Burn
Seghill
Heugh
Dinnington
Brunswick Village
Dudley
Wide Open
Burradon
Backworth
Earsdon
WHITLEY BAY
Stamfordham
Darras Hall
Prestwick
NEWCASTLE INTERNATIONAL
Hazlerigg
Monkseaton
Shiremoor
Cullercoats
Dalton
Killingworth
New York
Eachwick
Medburn
High Callerton
Woolsington
LONGBENTON
TYNEMOUTH
Black Callerton
GOSFORTH
Kenton Bankfoot
Harlow Hill
North Walbottle
NEWCASTLE UPON TYNE
Willington
North Shields
Arbeia Roman Fort
SOUTH SHIELDS
Houghton
Heddon-on-the-Wall
Throckley
Walbottle
Jesmond
Heaton
WALLSEND
Tyne Tunnel
Marsden Bay
Horsley
Stephenson's Cottage NT
NEWBURN
Westoe
Marsden
Fenham
Walker
Harton
Ovingham
Wylam
Clara Vale
Ryton
Lemington
Benwell
Byker
JARROW
West Harton
Souter NT
Lizard Point
Crawcrook
Scotswood
HEBBURN
Whitburn Colliery
West Wylam
Ryton Woodside
BLAYDON
Elswick
Dunston
FELLING
Mickley Square
Prudhoe
Greenside
Winlaton
Pelaw
Boldon Colliery
Cleadon
Whitburn
Teams
GATESHEAD
High Mickley
Coalburns
Barlow
WHICKHAM
Boldon
South Bents
Seaburn
Leadgate
High Spen
Hooker Gate
Rowlands Gill
Winlaton Mill
Derwent Walk
Street Gate
Sunniside
Angel of the North
Wrekenton
Mr. Twister's
Fulwell
Roker
Hedley on the Hill
Chopwell
Highfield
Gibside
Marley Hill
Springwell
Usworth
Castletown
Southwick
Blackhall Mill
Derwentcote Steel Furnace
Sheep Hill
Lintzford
Tanfield Byermoor
Lamesley
WASHINGTON
Monkwearmouth
National Glass Centre
Hamsterley
Leazes
SUNDERLAND
Low Westwood
Hamsterley Mill
Burnopfield
Crookgate Bank
Kibblesworth
South Hylton
Pennywell
High Westwood
Hobson
Tanfield
Causey Arch (World's 1st Railway Bridge)
Birtley
Washington Old Hall
Offerton
Hendon
Newlands
Ebchester
Tantobie
Tanfield Lea
Cox Green
High Newport
Tunstall
Hill Top
Dipton
North England Open Air Museum Beamish
Ouston
Barley Mow
Fatfield
Penshaw
Herrington
Ryhope Colliery
Shotley Bridge
Medomsley
Perkinsville
New Herrington
Ryhope
Benfieldside
Harelaw
STANLEY
West Pelton
Pelton
Newfield
Rickleton
Shiney Row
Philadelphia
Silksworth
Ryhope Engines
Leadgate
Catchgate
Greencroft
The Middles
Grange Villa
Bridgehill
CONSETT
South Moor
CHESTER-LE-STREET
Bournmoor
Newbottle
Fence Houses
Crookhall
Annfield Plain
Quaking Houses
Craghead
Waldridge
HOUGHTON-LE-SPRING
Templetown
Delves
Iveston
Greencroft Park
Maiden Law
Holmside
Chester Moor
Great Lumley
Colliery Row
Seaton
SEAHAM
Castleside
Knitsley
Edmondsley
Great Eppleton
Deneside
Dawdon
Rowley
Newbiggin
Burnhope
Nettlesworth
Plawsworth
West Rainton
East Rainton
Hetton-le-Hole
Murton
Dalton-le-Dale
Lanchester
Sacriston
Kimblesworth
Middle Rainton
Low Moorsley
Cold Hesleden
Witton Gilbert
Finchale Priory
Leamside
South Hetton
East Butsfield
Pity Me
Newton Hall
Hawthorn
Beacon Point
West Butsfield
Langley Park
Wall Nook
Framwellgate Moor
Easington Lane
High Haswell
Easington Colliery
Hill Top
Pittington
Hall Hill Farm
Quebec
Cornsay
Cornsay Colliery
Esh
Carrville
Church
Littletown
Horden Point
Satley
Ushaw Moor
Bearpark
Ayykley Heads
Hallgarth
Haswell
Easington
DURHAM
Gilesgate Moor
Sherburn Hill
Haswell Plough
Esh Winning
New Brancepeth
Broompark
Sherburn
Shotton Colliery
PETERLEE
Horden
Dene Mouth
High Stoop
East Hedleyhope
Waterhouses
Langley Moor
Shincliffe
High Shincliffe
Byers Garth
Shadforth
Ludworth
Thornley
Wheatley Hill
Shotton
Blackhall Colliery
Dan's Castle
Sunniside
Brandon
Meadowfield
Old Cassop
Blackhall Rocks
Stanley Crook
Castle Eden
Tow Law
Billy Row
Brancepeth
Bowburn
Old Quarrington
Cassop
Wingate
Crimdon Park
High Hesleden
Hesleden
Collier Wood
Coniscliffe Nature Trail
Quarrington Hill
Deaf Hill
Eden Vale
Thornley
Roddymoor
Oakenshaw
Sunderland Bridge
Croxdale
Town Kelloe
Kelloe
Station Town
Monk Hesleden
River
Page Bank
Tudhoe
Hett
Helmington
A697
A1
A1068
A189
A197
A192
A196
B6343
B6524
B1331
A193
B1523
A1061
A190
B1325
A1148
A186
A191
A696
B6323
B6545
B6918
A1056
B1318
A188
B1505
A19
A1058
A187
B6324
B6318
B6528
A69
A6085
A167(M)
B1297
A185
B6317
B6395
A695
A694
A1300
A1018
A194
A1290
B1288
B1298
B1299
A184
A194(M)
A195
A692
A6076
B6315
B6316
A1231
A183
A182
A690
A693
B6173
B6168
B6310
B6309
B6278
A691
A167
B6313
B6532
B1286
B1285
B1287
B1404
B1284
B6296
B6301
B6312
A1(M)
B1283
B1280
B1432
A1086
B6302
A181
A68
A177
B6300
B6297
B6299
B6298
B1281
B1279
A688
B6291
B1278
121
105
106
S
WASHINGTON
EASINGTON
DURHAM

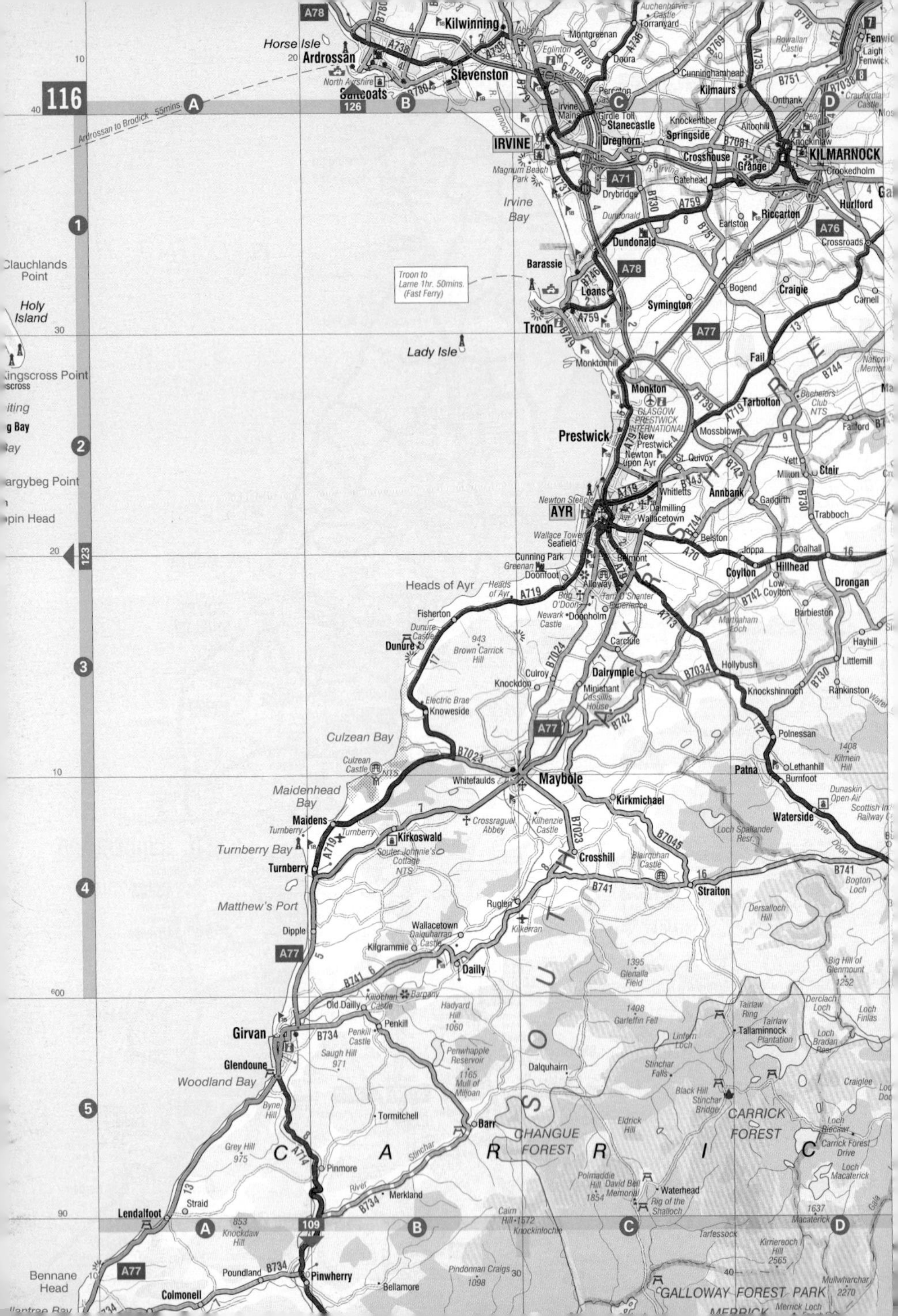
A78
Kilwinning
Horse Isle
Ardrossan
Montgreenan
Torranyard
Auchenharvie Castle
Doura
Rowallan Castle
Fenwick
Laigh Fenwick
Stevenston
North Ayrshire
Saltcoats
126
Cunninghamhead
Kilmaurs
Perceton
Onthank
Craufurdland Castle
A
B
C
D
Ardrossan to Brodick 55mins.
Irvine Mains
Girdle Toll
Stanecastle
Knockentiber
Springside
Altonhill
Knockinlaw
IRVINE
Dreghorn
B7081
Crosshouse
Grange
KILMARNOCK
Crookedholm
Magnum Beach Park
A71
Drybridge
Gatehead
Hurlford
Irvine Bay
Dundonald
Earlston
Riccarton
A76
Crossroads
Clauchlands Point
Holy Island
Barassie
Troon to Larne 1hr. 50mins. (Fast Ferry)
A78
Loans
Symington
Bogend
Craigie
Carnell
Troon
A759
A77
Lady Isle
Monktonhill
Fail
Kingscross Point
Monkton
GLASGOW PRESTWICK INTERNATIONAL
Tarbolton
Bachelors' Club NTS
Prestwick
New Prestwick
Mossblown
Fairlford
Newton upon Ayr
St. Quivox
Yett
Milton
Stair
Whitletts
Annbank
Newton Steeple
AYR
Dalmilling
Wallacetown
Gadgirth
Trabboch
Wallace Tower
Seafield
Belston
Joppa
Coalhall
Cunning Park
Greenan
Belmont
Coylton
Hillhead
Drongan
Doonfoot
Heads of Ayr
Alloway
Low Coylton
Bog O'Doon
Tam O'Shanter Experience
Barbieston
Newark Castle
Doonholm
Fisherton
Dunure Castle
Dunure
943
Brown Carrick Hill
Carcluie
Hayhill
Littlemill
Hollybush
B7034
Culroy
Knockdon
Dalrymple
Minishant
Cassillis House
Knockshinnoch
Rankinston
Electric Brae
Knoweside
A77
B742
Polnessan
Culzean Bay
B7023
Culzean Castle
NTS
Lethanhill
Burnfoot
Patna
Whitefaulds
Maybole
Maidenhead Bay
Kirkmichael
Dunaskin Open Air
Maidens
Crossraguel Abbey
Kilhenzie Castle
Waterside
Turnberry
Kirkoswald
B7045
Loch Spallander Resr.
Turnberry Bay
Souter Johnnie's Cottage NTS
Crosshill
Blairquhan Castle
Turnberry
B741
Straiton
Bogton Loch
Matthew's Port
Ruglen
Kilkerran
Dersalloch Hill
Dipple
Wallacetown
Dalquharran Castle
A77
Kilgrammie
Dailly
1395 Glenalla Fell
Big Hill of Glenmount 1252
B741
Bargany
Old Dailly
Killochan Castle
Hadyard Hill 1060
1408 Garleffin Fell
Tairlaw Ring
Derclach Loch
Tallaminnock
Loch Finlas
Girvan
B734
Penkill
Penkill Castle
Linfern Loch
Loch Bradan Resr.
Saugh Hill 971
Penwhapple Reservoir
Glendoune
Dalquhairn
Stinchar Falls
Woodland Bay
1165 Mull of Miljoan
Black Hill
Stinchar Bridge
Craiglee
Byne Hill
Tormitchell
CARRICK FOREST
Eldrick Hill
Loch Riecawr
Barr
CHANGUE FOREST
Carrick Forest Drive
Grey Hill 975
A714
C A R R I C K
Loch Macaterick
Pinmore
Stinchar
Polmaddie Hill 1854
David Bell Memorial
Waterhead
Rig of the Shalloch
Merkland
B734
Lendalfoot
Straid
Cairn Hill 1572
Knockinlochie
Macaterick
1637
853 Knockdaw Hill
109
Tarfessock
Kirriereoch Hill 2565
Bennane Head
A77
Poundland
B734
Pinwherry
Pindonnan Craigs 1098
Mullwharchar 2270
Bellamore
Colmonell
GALLOWAY FOREST PARK
Merrick Loch
SOUTH AYRSHIRE
123

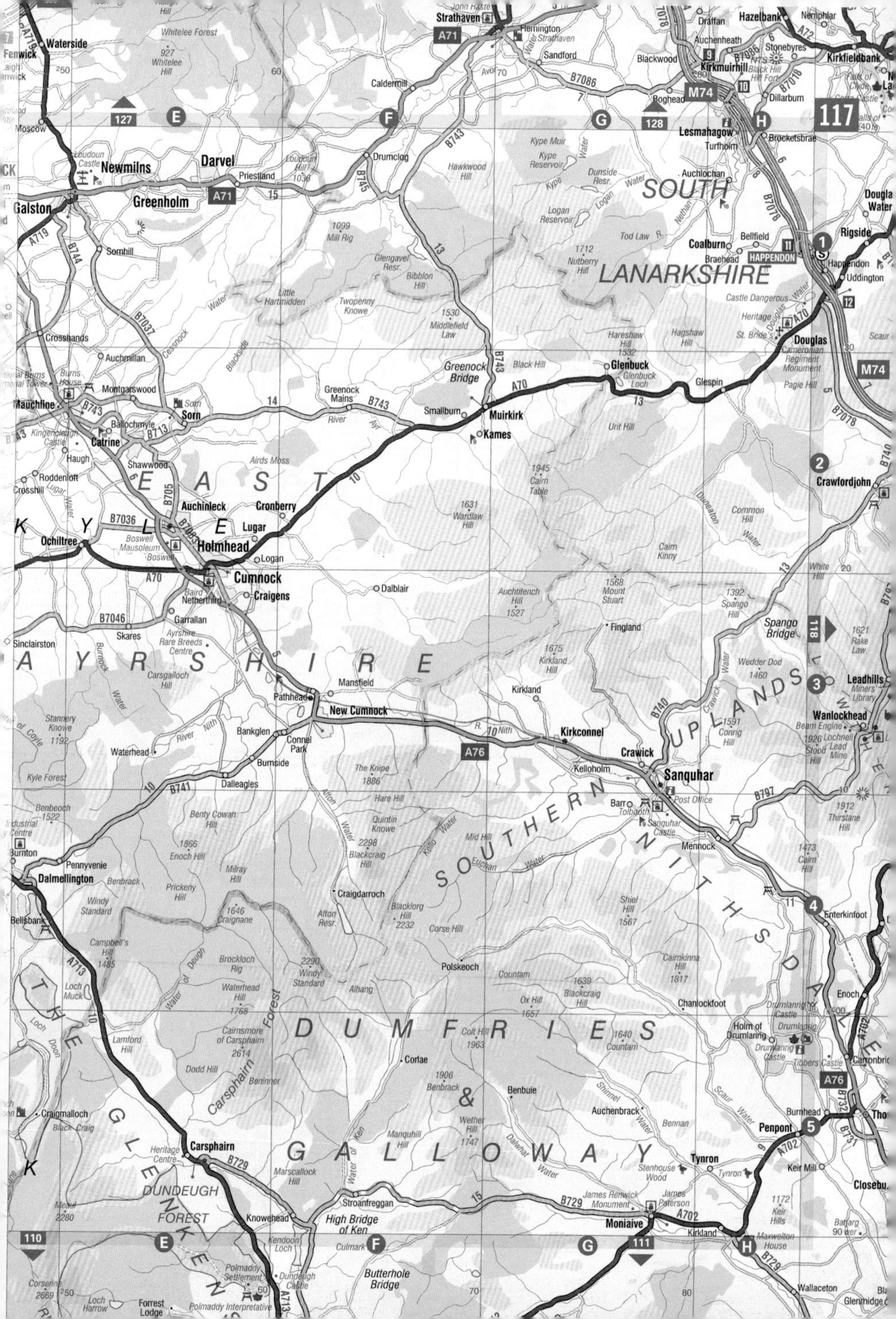
117
127
128
118
110
111
E
F
G
H
1
2
3
4
5
Strathaven
Flemington
Draffan
Hazelbank
Nemphlar
Waterside
Fenwick
Whitelee Forest
927
Whitelee
Hill
Auchenheath
Stonebyres
Kirkfieldbank
Sandford
Blackwood
Kirkmuirhill
Black Hill
Hill Fort
Falls of Clyde
Caldermill
Boghead
Dillarburn
Moscow
M74
A71
A72
A719
B7086
B7078
B7018
B743
B745
Lesmahagow
Brocketsbrae
Turfholm
Kype Muir
Kype
Reservoir
Dunside
Resr.
Hawkwood
Hill
Drumclog
Loudoun
Castle
Newmilns
Darvel
Priestland
Loudoun
Hill
1036
Auchlochan
SOUTH
Galston
Greenholm
Logan
Reservoir
Douglas
Water
Rigside
1099
Mill Rig
Tod Law
Coalburn
Bellfield
Braehead
HAPPENDON
Happendon
Uddington
Sornhill
Glengavel
Resr.
Bibblon
Hill
1712
Nutberry
Hill
LANARKSHIRE
Castle Dangerous
Little
Hartmidden
Twopenny
Knowe
Heritage
St. Bride's
1530
Middlefield
Law
Hareshaw
Hill
1532
Hagshaw
Hill
Crossbands
Douglas
Cameronian
Regiment
Monument
Auchmillan
Glenbuck
Glenbuck
Loch
Greenock
Bridge
Black Hill
Burns
House
Montgarswood
Glespin
Pagie Hill
Greenock
Mains
Mauchline
Sorn
Smallburn
Muirkirk
Ballochmyle
River
Ayr
Kames
Urit Hill
Catrine
Kingencleugh
Castle
Haugh
Shawwood
Airds Moss
Roddenloft
EAST
1945
Cairn
Table
Crawfordjohn
Crosshill
Auchinleck
Cronberry
1631
Wardlaw
Hill
Duneaton
Water
Common
Hill
KYLE
Ochiltree
Lugar
Boswell
Mausoleum
Holmhead
Logan
Cairn
Kinny
A70
Cumnock
White
Hill
Baird
Netherthird
Craigens
Dalblair
Auchtitench
Hill
1527
1568
Mount
Stuart
1392
Spango
Hill
B7046
Garrallan
Skares
Fingland
Spango
Bridge
1621
Rake
Law
Sinclairston
Ayrshire
Rare Breeds
Centre
1675
Kirkland
Hill
AYRSHIRE
Carsgalloch
Hill
Wedder Dod
1460
Leadhills
Miners'
Library
Mansfield
Kirkland
UPLANDS
Pathhead
New Cumnock
Wanlockhead
Beam Engine
Lochnell
Lead
Mine
Stannery
Knowe
1192
Bankglen
Connel
Park
R. Nith
Kirkconnel
Crawick
1591
Conrig
Hill
1926
Stood
Hill
Waterhead
River
Nith
A76
Burnside
Kelloholm
Sanquhar
Kyle Forest
The Knipe
1886
Dalleagles
B741
Post Office
Barr
Tolbooth
Sanquhar
Castle
B797
Benbeoch
1522
Hare Hill
1912
Thirstane
Hill
Industrial
Centre
Benty Cowan
Hill
Quintin
Knowe
Mid Hill
SOUTHERN
Mennock
Burnton
Pennyvenie
1866
Enoch Hill
Afton
Water
2298
Blackcraig
Hill
Kello Water
Euchan Water
1473
Cairn
Hill
Dalmellington
Benbrack
Milray
Hill
Prickeny
Hill
Craigdarroch
NITHSDALE
Enterkinfoot
Windy
Standard
1646
Craignane
Afton
Resr.
Blacklorg
Hill
2232
Corse Hill
Shiel
Hill
1567
Bellsbank
Campbell's
Hill
1485
Brockloch
Rig
2290
Windy
Standard
Polskeoch
Countam
Cairnkinna
Hill
1817
A713
Loch
Muck
Water of Deugh
Waterhead
Hill
1768
Alhang
1639
Blackcraig
Hill
Ox Hill
1657
Chanlockfoot
Enoch
THE GLENKENS
Loch
Doon
Carsphairn Forest
Cairnsmore
of Carsphairn
2614
DUMFRIES
Colt Hill
1963
1640
Countam
Holm of
Drumlanrig
Drumlanrig
Castle
Tibbers Castle
Carronbridge
Lamford
Hill
Dodd Hill
Beninner
Corlae
1906
Benbrack
Benbuie
Shinnel Water
Scaur Water
Craigmalloch
Black Craig
&
Auchenbrack
Bennan
Burnhead
Penpont
A702
Keir Mill
Closeburn
Carsphairn
Heritage
Centre
B729
GALLOWAY
Water of Ken
Manquhill
Hill
Wether
Hill
1747
Dalwhat Water
Tynron
Stenhouse
Wood
DUNDEUGH
FOREST
Marscallock
Hill
James Renwick
Monument
James
Paterson
Meaul
2280
Knowehead
Stroanfreggan
High Bridge
of Ken
Moniaive
Kirkland
1172
Keir
Hills
Kendoon
Loch
Culmark
Maxwelton
House
Barjarg
Tower
Corserine
2669
Polmaddy
Settlement
Dundeugh
Castle
Butterhole
Bridge
Wallaceton
Loch
Harrow
Forrest
Lodge
Polmaddy Interpretative
Glenmidge

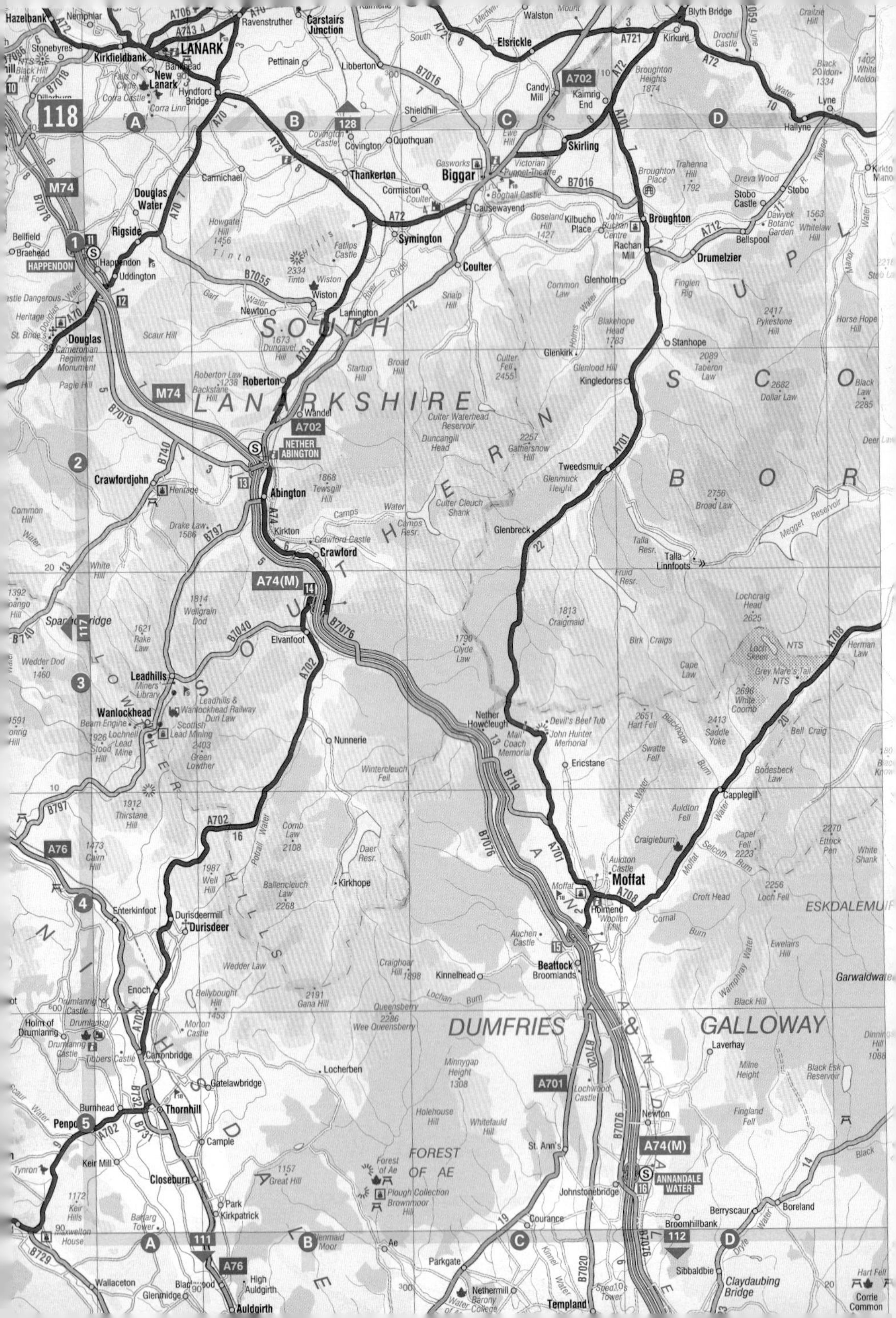

118
Hazelbank
Nemphlar
Stonebyres
Kirkfieldbank
LANARK
New Lanark
Falls of Clyde
Corra Castle
Corra Linn
Bankhead
Ravenstruther
Carstairs Junction
Hyndford Bridge
Pettinain
Libberton
Walston
Elsrickle
Blyth Bridge
Kirkurd
Drochil Castle
Broughton Heights 1874
Candy Mill
Kaimrig End
Black Dod 1334
White Meldon
Lyne
Hallyne
Shieldhill
Covington Castle
Covington
Quothquan
Skirling
Thankerton
Gasworks
Biggar
Victorian Puppet Theatre
Boghall Castle
Trahenna Hill 1792
Broughton Place
Dreva Wood
Stobo
Stobo Castle
Carmichael
Douglas Water
Cormiston
Coulter
Causewayend
Goseland Hill 1427
Kilbucho Place
John Buchan Centre
Broughton
Dawyck Botanic Garden
Bellspool
Whitelaw Hill
Rigside
Howgate Hill 1456
Tinto Hills
Fatlips Castle
Symington
Rachan Mill
Drumelzier
Belfield
Braehead
HAPPENDON
Happendon
Uddington
2334 Tinto
Wiston
Coulter
Glenholm
Common Law
Finglen Rig
Castle Dangerous
Heritage
St. Bride's
Douglas
Cameronian Regiment Monument
Garf Water
Newton
Lamington
Snaip Hill
Blakehope Head 1783
Pykestone Hill
Horse Hope Hill
Scaur Hill
SOUTH
1673 Dungavel Hill
Stanhope
Glenkirk
2089 Taberon Law
Roberton Law 1238
Backstane Hill
Roberton
Startup Hill
Broad Hill
Culter Fell 2455
Glenlood Hill
Kingledores
Pagie Hill
LANARKSHIRE
Wandel
2682 Dollar Law
Black Law 2285
Culter Waterhead Reservoir
NETHER ABINGTON
Duncangill Head
2257 Gathersnow Hill
Crawfordjohn
Heritage
1868 Tewsgill Hill
Abington
Glenmuck Height
Tweedsmuir
2756 Broad Law
Megget Reservoir
Common Hill
Drake Law 1586
Kirkton
Camps Water
Camps Resr.
Culter Cleuch Shank
Glenbreck
Crawford Castle
Crawford
Talla Resr.
Talla Linnfoots
Fruid Resr.
White Hill
SOUTHERN UPLANDS
SCOTTISH BORDERS
Sparabridge
1814 Wellgrain Dod
1621 Rake Law
Elvanfoot
1813 Craigmaid
1790 Clyde Law
Lochcraig Head 2625
Birk Craigs
Loch Skeen
NTS
Grey Mare's Tail NTS
Herman Law
Wedder Dod 1460
Leadhills
Miners' Library
Leadhills & Wanlockhead Railway
Wanlockhead
Beam Engine
Lochnell Lead Mine
1926 Stood Hill
Scottish Lead Mining
Dun Law
2403 Green Lowther
Cape Law
2651 Hart Fell
Devil's Beef Tub
Nether Howcleugh
Mail Coach Memorial
John Hunter Memorial
2696 White Coomb
2413 Saddle Yoke
Bell Craig
Nunnerie
Wintercleuch Fell
Ericstane
Swatte Fell
Bodesbeck Law
Capplegill
1912 Thirstane Hill
Comb Law 2108
Daer Resr.
Auldton Fell
Craigieburn
Capel Fell 2223
2270 Ettrick Pen
White Shank
1473 Cairn Hill
1987 Well Hill
Ballencleuch Law 2268
Kirkhope
Auldton Castle
Moffat
Holmend
Woollen Mill
2256 Loch Fell
Croft Head
ESKDALEMUIR
Enterkinfoot
Durisdeermill
Durisdeer
Auchen Castle
Beattock
Broomlands
Cornal Burn
Ewelairs Hill
Wedder Law
Craighoar Hill 1898
Kinnelhead
Lochan Burn
Garwaldwater
Enoch
Drumlanrig Castle
Holm of Drumlanrig
Bellybought Hill 1453
2191 Gana Hill
Queensberry 2286
Wee Queensberry
Black Hill
Morton Castle
DUMFRIES & GALLOWAY
Laverhay
Tibbers Castle
Carronbridge
Locherben
Minnygap Height 1308
Milne Height
Black Esk Reservoir
Gatelawbridge
Lochwood Castle
Burnhead
Thornhill
Penpont
Cample
Holehouse Hill
Whitefauld Hill
Newton
Fingland Fell
Keir Mill
FOREST OF AE
Forest of Ae
St. Ann's
ANNANDALE WATER
Tynron
1157 Great Hill
Plough Collection
Brownmoor Hill
Closeburn
Johnstonebridge
1172 Keir Hills
Park
Kirkpatrick
Courance
Broomhillbank
Berryscaur
Boreland
Barjarg Tower
Maxwelton House
Glenmaid Moor
Ae
Sibbaldbie
Parkgate
Claydaubing Bridge
Hart Fell
Wallaceton
Blackwood
High Auldgirth
Glenmidge
Auldgirth
Nethermill
Barony College
Templand
Spedlo's Tower
Corrie Common
M74
A74(M)
A70
A73
A72
A702
A701
A721
A708
A712
A76
B7078
B7055
B7016
B740
B797
B7040
B7076
B7020
B729
B732
B731
B719
111
112
117
128

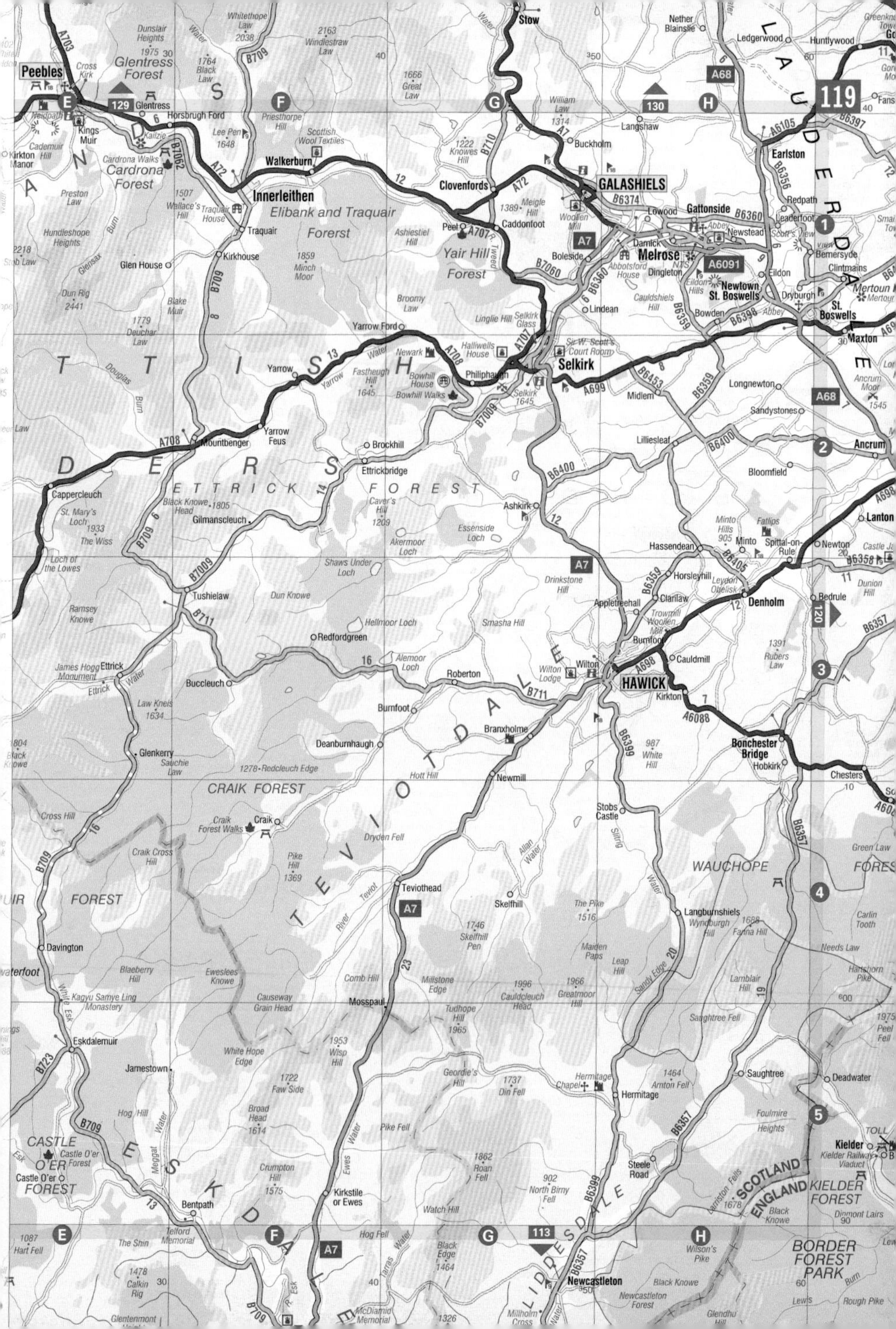

119
Peebles
Cross Kirk
Glentress Forest
Dunslair Heights
1975
Whitehope Law 2038
2163 Windlestraw Law
1764 Black Law
1666 Great Law
Stow
Nether Blainslie
Ledgerwood
Huntlywood
LAUDERDALE
129
130
E
F
G
H
Glentress
Horsbrugh Ford
Priesthorpe Hill
William Law 1314
Langshaw
A68
A6105
B6397
Neidpath
Kings Muir
Kailzie
Lee Pen 1648
Scottish Wool Textiles
1222 Knowes Hill
Buckholm
Earlston
Kirkton Manor
Cademuir Hill
Cardrona Walks
B7062
Cardrona Forest
Walkerburn
A72
A7
B710
Clovenfords
GALASHIELS
B6356
Preston Law
1507 Wallace's Hill
Traquair House
Innerleithen
Elibank and Traquair Forerst
1389 Meigle Hill
B6374
Woollen Mill
Lowood
Gattonside
B6360
Redpath
Leaderfoot
Scott's View
Hundleshope Heights
Traquair
Peel
A707
Caddonfoot
Ashiestiel Hill
Darnick
Abbey
Newstead
Bemersyde
2218 Stob Law
Kirkhouse
Glen House
1859 Minch Moor
Yair Hill Forest
R. Tweed
Boleside
Melrose
A6091
Clintmains
Abbotsford House
Dingleton
NTS
Eildon
Eildon Hills
Newtown St. Boswells
Dryburgh
Mertoun
St. Boswells
Glensax
B709
Blake Muir
Dun Rig 2441
B7060
B6360
Lindean
Cauldshiels Hill
B6359
Broomy Law
Linglie Hill
Selkirk Glass
Bowden
B6398
Maxton
1779 Deuchar Law
Yarrow Ford
Halliwells House
Sir W. Scott's Court Room
Newark
Selkirk
A708
Yarrow
Yarrow Water
Fastheugh Hill 1645
Bowhill House
Bowhill Walks
Philiphaugh
Selkirk 1645
A699
B6453
Midlem
Longnewton
Ancrum Moor 1545
Douglas Burn
Sandystones
Yarrow Feus
Mountbenger
Lilliesleaf
B6400
Ancrum
Brockhill
Ettrickbridge
Bloomfield
Cappercleuch
ETTRICK FOREST
BORDERS
Black Knowe Head
1805
Cavers Hill 1209
Ashkirk
St. Mary's Loch
1933
The Wiss
Gilmanscleuch
Essenside Loch
Akermoor Loch
Minto Hills 905
Minto
Fatlips
Spittal-on-Rule
Lanton
Newton
Castle Ja
Loch of the Lowes
B7009
Shaws Under Loch
Hassendean
B6405
B6358
Dunion Hill
Drinkstone Hill
Horsleyhill
Leyden Obelisk
Denholm
Bedrule
120
Ramsey Knowe
Tushielaw
Dun Knowe
Appletreehall
Clarilaw
Trowmill Woollen Mill
B711
Smasha Hill
Hellmoor Loch
Redfordgreen
Burnfoot
B6357
Cauldmill
1391 Rubers Law
Alemoor Loch
Wilton
Wilton Lodge
A698
HAWICK
James Hogg Monument
Ettrick
Ettrick Water
Buccleuch
Roberton
Kirkton
A6088
Law Kneis 1634
Burnfoot
TEVIOTDALE
Branxholme
B6399
987 White Hill
1804 Black Knowe
Glenkerry
Sauchie Law
Deanburnhaugh
Bonchester Bridge
Hobkirk
Chesters
1278 Redcleuch Edge
Hott Hill
Newmill
CRAIK FOREST
Cross Hill
Craik Forest Walks
Craik
Stobs Castle
Slitrig
Dryden Fell
Green Law
Craik Cross Hill
Pike Hill 1369
Allan Water
WAUCHOPE FOREST
B709
FOREST
River Teviot
Teviothead
Skelfhill
The Pike 1516
Langburnshiels
Wyndburgh Hill
1688 Fanna Hill
Carlin Tooth
Needs Law
Davington
1746 Skelfhill Pen
Maiden Paps
Leap Hill
Waterfoot
Blaeberry Hill
Eweslees Knowe
Comb Hill
Millstone Edge
1996 Cauldcleuch Head
1966 Greatmoor Hill
Sandy Edge
Lamblair Hill
Hartshorn Pike
White Esk
Kagyu Samye Ling Monastery
Causeway Grain Head
Mosspaul
Tudhope Hill 1965
Saughtree Fell
1975 Peel Fell
Eskdalemuir
B723
1953 Wisp Hill
White Hope Edge
Jamestown
1722 Faw Side
Geordie's Hill
1737 Din Fell
Hermitage Chapel
Hermitage
1464 Arnton Fell
Saughtree
Deadwater
Hog Hill
Meggat Water
Broad Head 1614
Pike Fell
Foulmire Heights
Kielder
TOLL
CASTLE O'ER FOREST
Castle O'er Forest
Castle O'er
Crumpton Hill 1575
Ewes Water
1862 Roan Fell
Steele Road
Kielder Railway Viaduct
SCOTLAND
ENGLAND
KIELDER FOREST
Larriston Fells 1678
Black Knowe
Dinmont Lairs
ESKDALE
Kirkstile or Ewes
902 North Birny Fell
LIDDESDALE
Bentpath
Watch Hill
1087 Hart Fell
Telford Memorial
The Shin
113
Hog Fell
Black Edge 1464
Wilson's Pike
BORDER FOREST PARK
Tarras Water
1478 Calkin Rig
Newcastleton
Black Knowe
Newcastleton Forest
Burn
R. Esk
Lewis
Rough Pile
Glentenmont
McDiamid Memorial
1326
Millholm Cross
Glendhu Hill

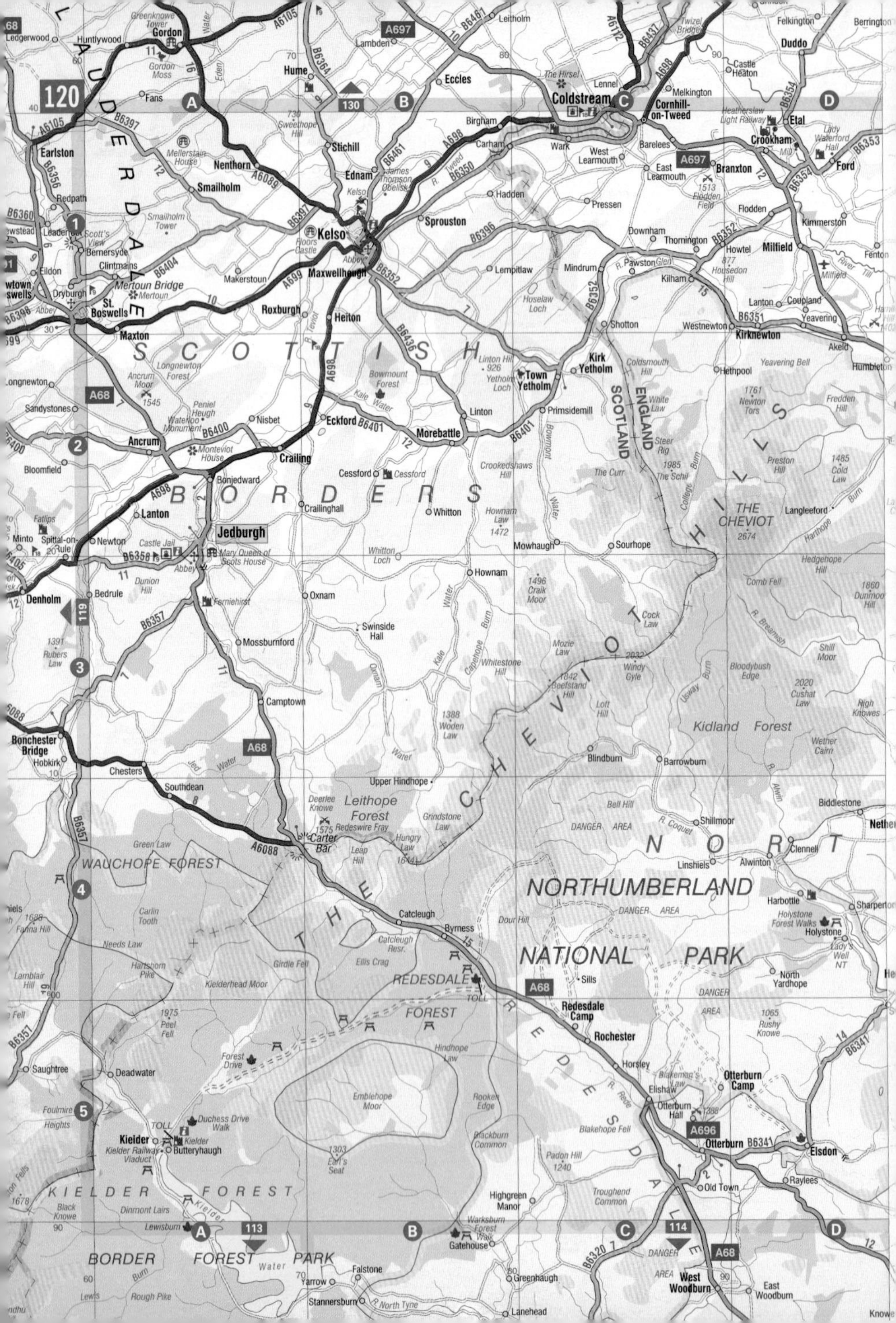
120
LAUDERDALE
Ledgerwood
Huntlywood
Greenknowe Tower
Gordon
Gordon Moss
Fans
Earlston
Mellerstain House
Nenthorn
Smailholm
Redpath
Leaderfoot
Scott's View
Bemersyde
Smailholm Tower
Eildon
Clintmains
Mertoun Bridge
Mertoun
Makerstoun
Dryburgh
St. Boswells
Newtown St. Boswells
Abbey
Maxton
Hume
Lambden
Eccles
Leitholm
Sweethope Hill
Stichill
Ednam
James Thomson Obelisk
Kelso
Floors Castle
Abbey
Maxwellheugh
Roxburgh
Heiton
Birgham
Carham
Wark
The Hirsel
Lennel
Coldstream
Cornhill-on-Tweed
Twizel Bridge
Melkington
Castle Heaton
Felkington
Duddo
Berrington
Heatherslaw Light Railway
Etal
Crookham
Lady Waterford Hall
Ford
Barelees
West Learmouth
East Learmouth
Branxton
1513 Flodden Field
Flodden
Kimmerston
Hadden
Pressen
Sprouston
Downham
Thornington
Howtel
Milfield
Fenton
Lempitlaw
Mindrum
Pawston
Kilham
Housedon Hill
Hoselaw Loch
Lanton
Coupland
Yeavering
Shotton
Westnewton
Kirknewton
Akeld
Humbleton
SCOTTISH
BORDERS
Longnewton Forest
Longnewton
Ancrum Moor
1545
Sandystones
Peniel Heugh
Waterloo Monument
Nisbet
Bowmount Forest
Kale Water
Linton Hill 926
Yetholm Loch
Town Yetholm
Kirk Yetholm
Coldsmouth Hill
Hethpool
Yeavering Bell
Eckford
Linton
Primsidemill
Morebattle
Ancrum
Monteviot House
Crailing
Bonjedward
Bloomfield
Cessford
SCOTLAND
ENGLAND
White Law
Steer Rig
1761 Newton Tors
Fredden Hill
Preston Hill
1485 Cold Law
Crookedshaws Hill
Bowmont Water
The Curr
1985 The Schil
College Burn
THE CHEVIOT 2674
Langleeford
Harthope Burn
Crailinghall
Whitton
Hownam Law 1472
Lanton
Fatlips
Minto
Spittal-on-Rule
Newton
Castle Jail
Jedburgh
Mary Queen of Scots House
Abbey
Dunion Hill
Bedrule
Denholm
Whitton Loch
Mowhaugh
Sourhope
Hownam
1496 Craik Moor
Hedgehope Hill
Comb Fell
1860 Dunmoor Hill
Oxnam
Ferniehirst
Swinside Hall
Cock Law
R. Breamish
1391 Rubers Law
Mossburnford
Capehope Burn
Kale Water
Oxnam Water
Whitestone Hill
Mozie Law
2032 Windy Gyle
Shill Moor
Bloodybush Edge
Usway Burn
2020 Cushat Law
High Knowes
Camptown
1842 Beefstand Hill
Loft Hill
Kidland Forest
Bonchester Bridge
Hobkirk
1388 Woden Law
Wether Cairn
Chesters
Jed Water
Blindburn
Barrowburn
Upper Hindhope
Southdean
Deerlee Knowe
Leithope Forest
1575 Redeswire Fray
Carter Bar
Grindstone Law
Hungry Law
1644
Bell Hill
Shillmoor
R. Coquet
R. Alwin
Biddlestone
Green Law
WAUCHOPE FOREST
Leap Hill
DANGER AREA
Linshiels
Alwinton
Clennell
THE CHEVIOT HILLS
NORTHUMBERLAND
NATIONAL PARK
Catcleugh
Byrness
Catcleugh Resr.
Carlin Tooth
1688 Fanna Hill
Needs Law
Dour Hill
Harbottle
Holystone Forest Walks
Holystone
Lady's Well NT
Sharperton
Hartshorn Pike
Ellis Crag
Girdle Fell
Lamblair Hill
Kielderhead Moor
REDESDALE
FOREST
TOLL
Sills
North Yardhope
1975 Peel Fell
Redesdale Camp
Rochester
1065 Rushy Knowe
Forest Drive
Hindhope Law
Saughtree
Deadwater
Horsley
Blakeman's Law
Otterburn Camp
Emblehope Moor
Rooken Edge
Elishaw
R. Rede
Otterburn Hall
1388
Foulmire Heights
Duchess Drive Walk
Blakehope Fell
Kielder
Kielder Railway Viaduct
Butteryhaugh
Blackburn Common
Otterburn
Elsdon
1303 Earl's Seat
Padon Hill 1240
KIELDER FOREST
1678
Black Knowe
Dinmont Lairs
Highgreen Manor
Troughend Common
Old Town
Raylees
Lewisburn
Warksburn Forest Walk
Gatehouse
BORDER FOREST PARK
Falstone
Yarrow
Stannersburn
R. North Tyne
Greenhaugh
Lanehead
Lewis Burn
Rough Pike
DANGER AREA
West Woodburn
East Woodburn
Knowe
REDESDALE
113
114
119
130

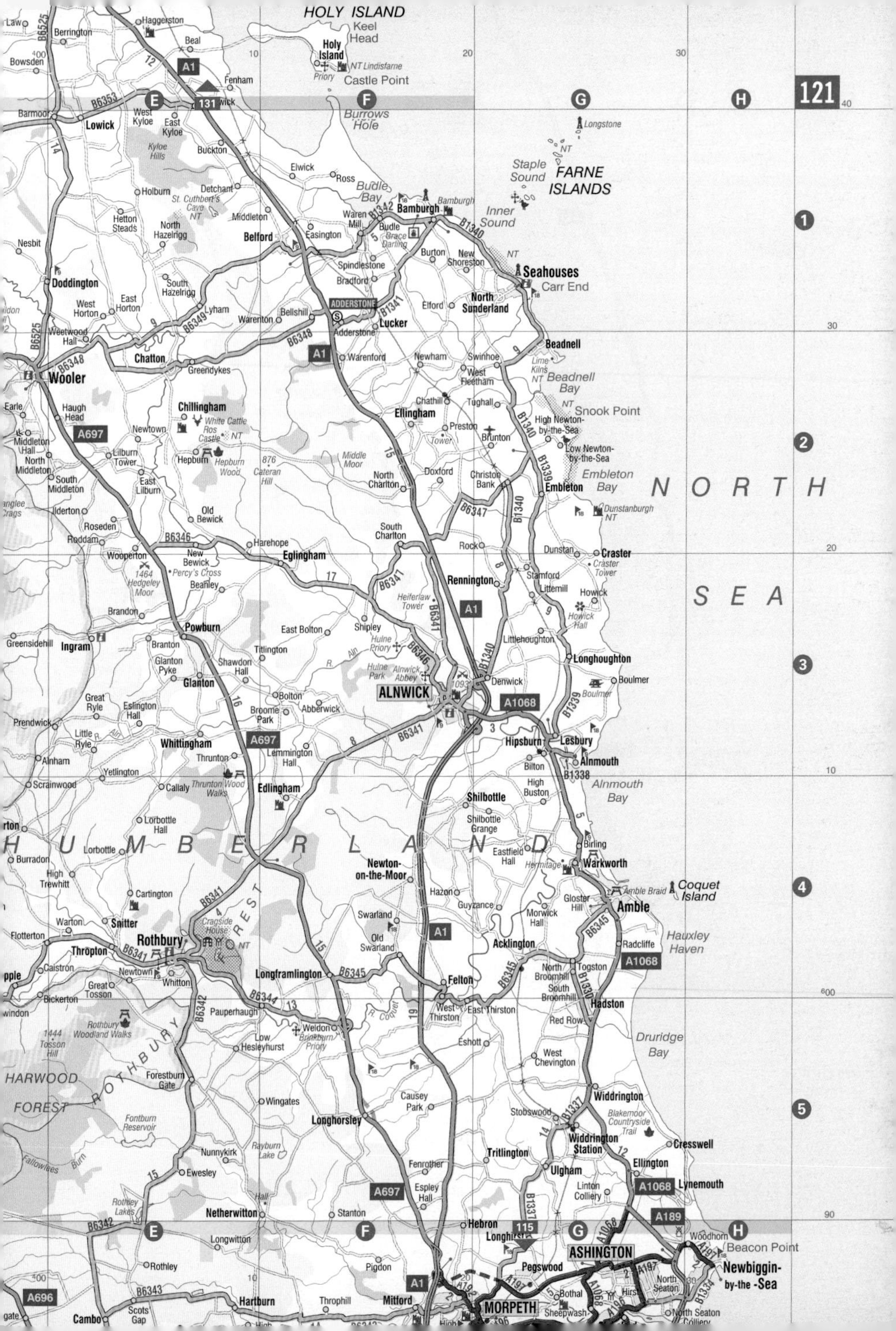
HOLY ISLAND
Keel Head
Holy Island
NT Lindisfarne
Priory
Castle Point
Burrows Hole
Longstone
Staple Sound
FARNE ISLANDS
Inner Sound
Budle Bay
Bamburgh
Waren Mill
Budle
Grace Darling
Seahouses
Carr End
North Sunderland
Beadnell
Lime Kilns NT
Beadnell Bay
Snook Point
High Newton-by-the-Sea
Low Newton-by-the-Sea
Embleton Bay
Embleton
NORTH SEA
Dunstanburgh NT
Craster
Craster Tower
Howick
Howick Hall
Longhoughton
Boulmer
Lesbury
Alnmouth
Alnmouth Bay
Hipsburn
Bilton
Birling
Warkworth
Hermitage
Coquet Island
Amble Braid
Amble
Gloster Hill
Morwick Hall
Hauxley Haven
Radcliffe
Togston
North Broomhill
South Broomhill
Hadston
Red Row
Druridge Bay
West Chevington
Widdrington
Blakemoor Countryside Trail
Widdrington Station
Cresswell
Ellington
Lynemouth
Linton Colliery
Ulgham
Woodhorn
Beacon Point
Newbiggin-by-the-Sea
ASHINGTON
North Seaton
North Seaton Colliery
Hirst
Bothal
Sheepwash
Pegswood
Longhirst
Hebron
MORPETH
Mitford
Pigdon
Throphill
Hartburn
Scots Gap
Cambo
Rothley
Longwitton
Netherwitton
Stanton
Espley Hall
Fenrother
Tritlington
Stobswood
Causey Park
Longhorsley
Wingates
Nunnykirk
Ewesley
Rayburn Lake
Rothley Lakes
Fontburn Reservoir
Fallowlees Burn
HARWOOD FOREST
ROTHBURY FOREST
Forestburn Gate
Low Hesleyhurst
Weldon
Brinkburn Priory
Pauperhaugh
Whitton
Rothbury
Rothbury Woodland Walks
1444 Tosson Hill
Great Tosson
Newtown
Bickerton
Caistron
Thropton
Flotterton
Warton
Snitter
Cragside House NT
Cartington
High Trewhitt
Burradon
Lorbottle
Lorbottle Hall
Callaly
Thrunton Wood Walks
Thrunton
Yetlington
Scrainwood
Alnham
Little Ryle
Prendwick
Great Ryle
Eslington Hall
Whittingham
Glanton
Glanton Pyke
Branton
Shawdon Hall
Powburn
Ingram
Greensidehill
Brandon
Beanley
1464 Hedgeley Moor
Percy's Cross
New Bewick
Wooperton
Roddam
Roseden
Ilderton
South Middleton
North Middleton
Middleton Hall
Earle
Haugh Head
Wooler
Lilburn Tower
East Lilburn
Old Bewick
Harehope
Eglingham
Newtown
Chillingham
White Cattle
Ros Castle NT
Hepburn
Hepburn Wood
876 Cateran Hill
Middle Moor
Chatton
Greendykes
Weetwood Hall
Doddington
West Horton
East Horton
Lyham
South Hazelrigg
North Hazelrigg
Hetton Steads
Holburn
Nesbit
Kyloe Hills
West Kyloe
East Kyloe
Lowick
Barmoor
Bowsden
Berrington
Haggerston
Beal
Fenham
Buckton
Detchant
St. Cuthbert's Cave NT
Middleton
Belford
Elwick
Ross
Easington
Spindlestone
Bradford
Burton
New Shoreston
Elford
ADDERSTONE
Adderstone
Bellshill
Warenton
Lucker
Warenford
Newham
Swinhoe
West Fleetham
Chathill
Tughall
Ellingham
Preston
Preston Tower
Brunton
Doxford
Christon Bank
North Charlton
South Charlton
Rock
Rennington
Dunstan
Stamford
Littemill
Littlehoughton
Heiferlaw Tower
Shipley
East Bolton
Titlington
Hulne Priory
Hulne Park
Alnwick Abbey
ALNWICK
Denwick
Bolton
Abberwick
Broome Park
Lemmington Hall
Edlingham
Shilbottle
Shilbottle Grange
High Buston
Eastfield Hall
Newton-on-the-Moor
Hazon
Guyzance
Swarland
Old Swarland
Acklington
Longframlington
Felton
West Thirston
East Thirston
Eshott
NORTHUMBERLAND
A1
A697
A1068
A189
A196
A197
A696
B6525
B6353
B6348
B6349
B1342
B1341
B1340
B1339
B6347
B6346
B6341
B6345
B6344
B6342
B6343
B1337
B1338
B1334
B1330
131
115
E
F
G
H
1
2
3
4
5
10
20
30
40
90
600
100

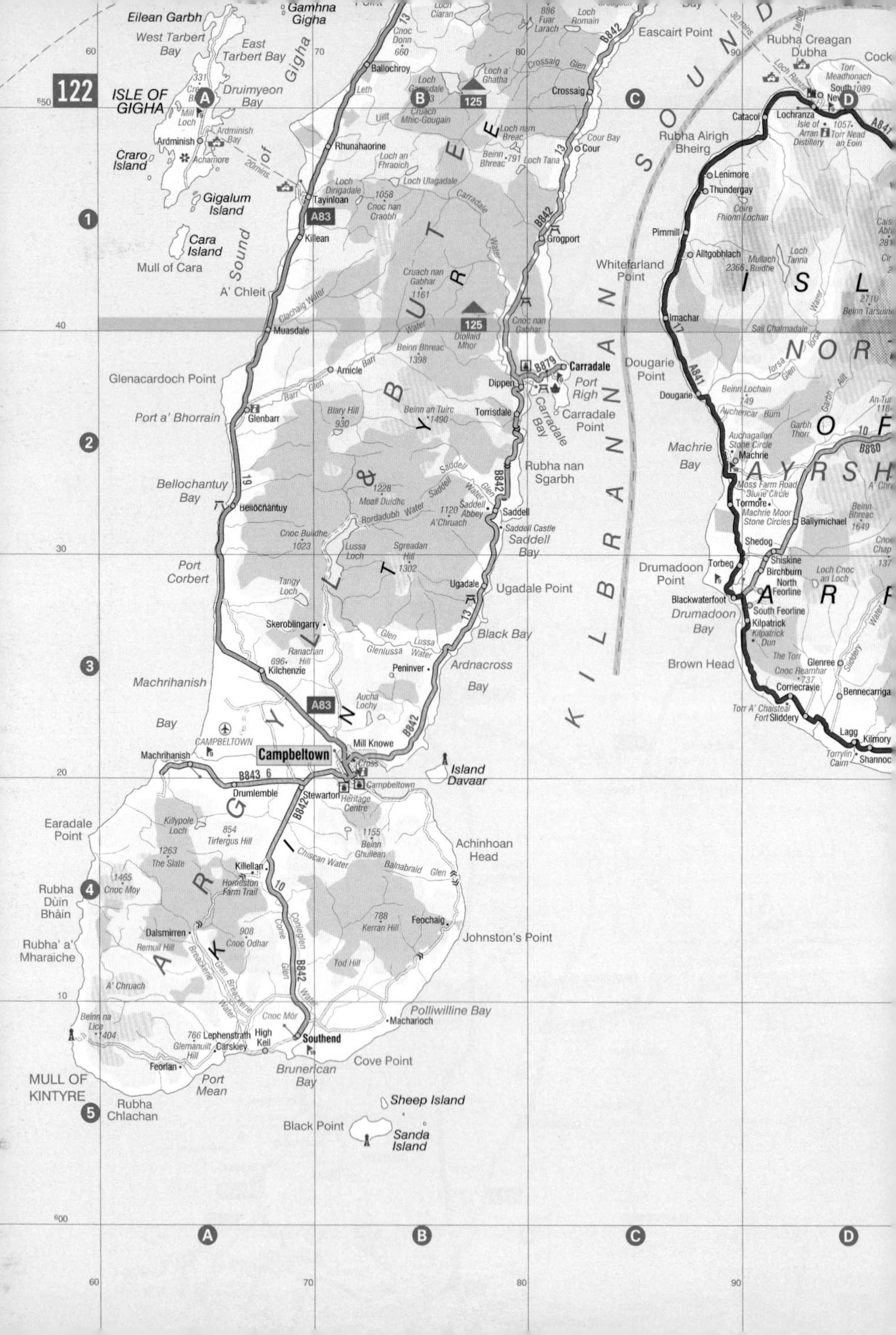

ISLE OF GIGHA
Eilean Garbh
West Tarbert Bay
East Tarbert Bay
Gamhna Gigha
Druimyeon Bay
Ardminish
Craro Island
Gigalum Island
Cara Island
Mull of Cara
Sound of Gigha
A' Chleit
Ballochroy
Rhunahaorine
Tayinloan
Killean
Muasdale
Glenacardoch Point
Glenbarr
Port a' Bhorrain
Bellochantuy Bay
Bellochantuy
Port Corbert
Skeroblingarry
Kilchenzie
Machrihanish Bay
Machrihanish
Campbeltown
Drumlemble
Stewarton
Mill Knowe
Island Davaar
Earadale Point
Rubha Dùin Bhàin
Rubha' a' Mharaiche
Dalsmirren
Killellan
Achinhoan Head
Feochaig
Johnston's Point
Polliwilline Bay
Macharioch
Southend
Lephenstrath
Carskiey
Feorlan
MULL OF KINTYRE
Rubha Chlachan
Port Mean
Brunerican Bay
Cove Point
Sheep Island
Black Point
Sanda Island
Peninver
Ardnacross Bay
Black Bay
Ugadale
Ugadale Point
Saddell
Saddell Bay
Torrisdale
Dippen
Carradale
Port Righ
Carradale Bay
Carradale Point
Rubha nan Sgarbh
Grogport
Cour
Cour Bay
Crossaig
Eascairt Point
ARGYLL & BUTE
KILBRANNAN SOUND
Whitefarland Point
Dougarie Point
Drumadoon Point
Drumadoon Bay
Brown Head
Machrie Bay
Rubha Creagan Dubha
Rubha Airigh Bheirg
Catacol
Lochranza
Lenimore
Thundergay
Pirnmill
Alltgobhlach
Imachar
Dougarie
Machrie
Tormore
Shedog
Shiskine
Birchburn
Torbeg
Blackwaterfoot
Kilpatrick
Corriecravie
Sliddery
Lagg
Kilmory
Glenree
Bennecarrigan
Ballymichael
ISLE OF ARRAN
NORTH AYRSHIRE
A83
B842
B843
B879
A841
B880

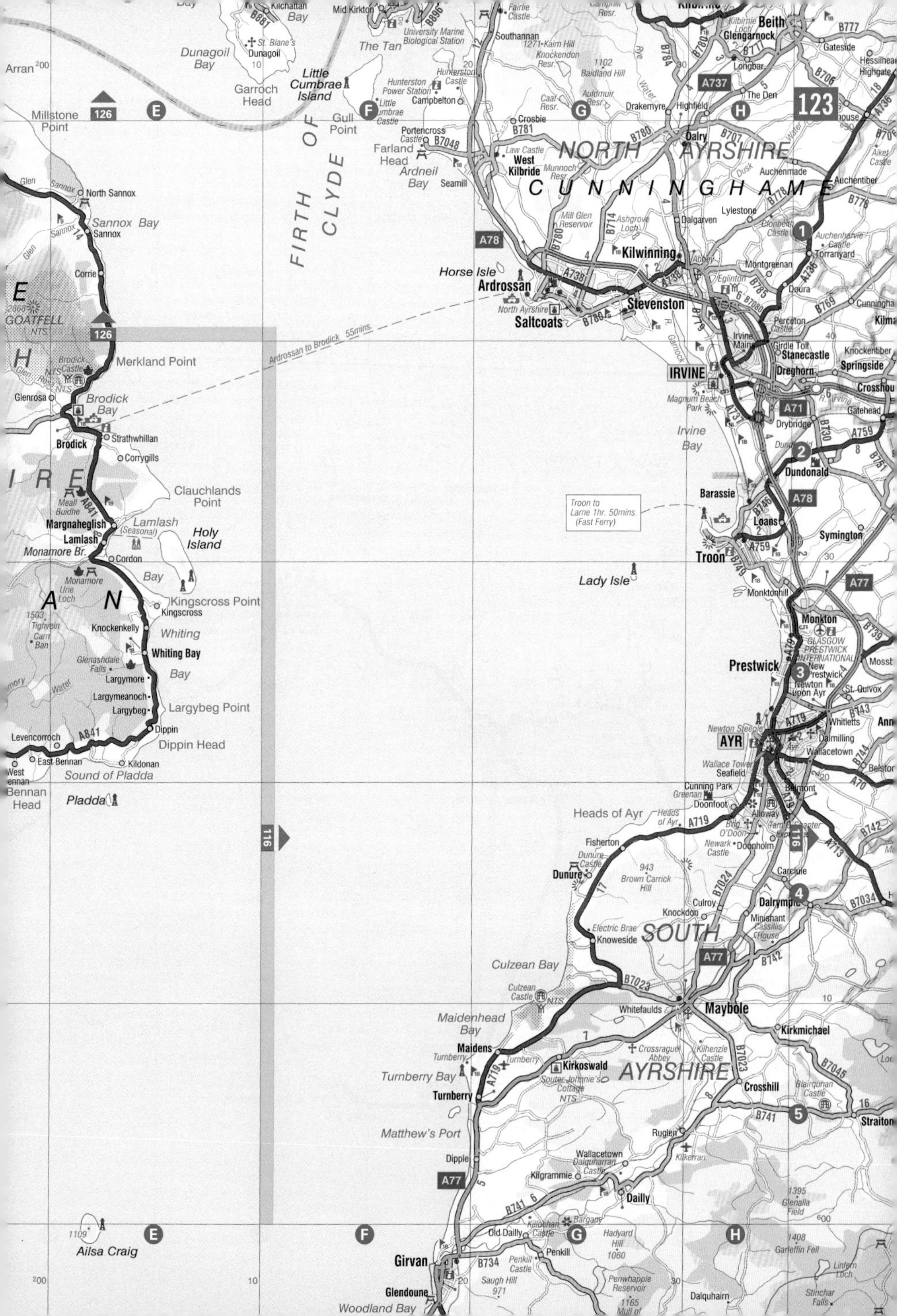
123
NORTH AYRSHIRE
CUNNINGHAME
SOUTH AYRSHIRE
FIRTH OF CLYDE
ARRAN
Little Cumbrae Island
Holy Island
Lady Isle
Ailsa Craig
Pladda
Horse Isle
Ardrossan
Saltcoats
Stevenston
Kilwinning
IRVINE
Troon
Prestwick
AYR
Maybole
Girvan
Brodick
Lamlash
Whiting Bay
West Kilbride
Dalry
Beith
Kilbirnie
Dundonald
Monkton
Kirkoswald
Turnberry
Maidens
Dailly
Ardrossan to Brodick 55mins.
Troon to Larne 1hr. 50mins. (Fast Ferry)
Culzean Bay
Maidenhead Bay
Turnberry Bay
Irvine Bay
Heads of Ayr
Sound of Pladda
Brodick Bay
Lamlash Bay
Whiting Bay
Sannox Bay
Dunagoil Bay
GOATFELL
Culzean Castle
Brodick Castle
GLASGOW PRESTWICK INTERNATIONAL
Hunterston Power Station
University Marine Biological Station
A78
A77
A71
A737
A719
A759
A841
126
116

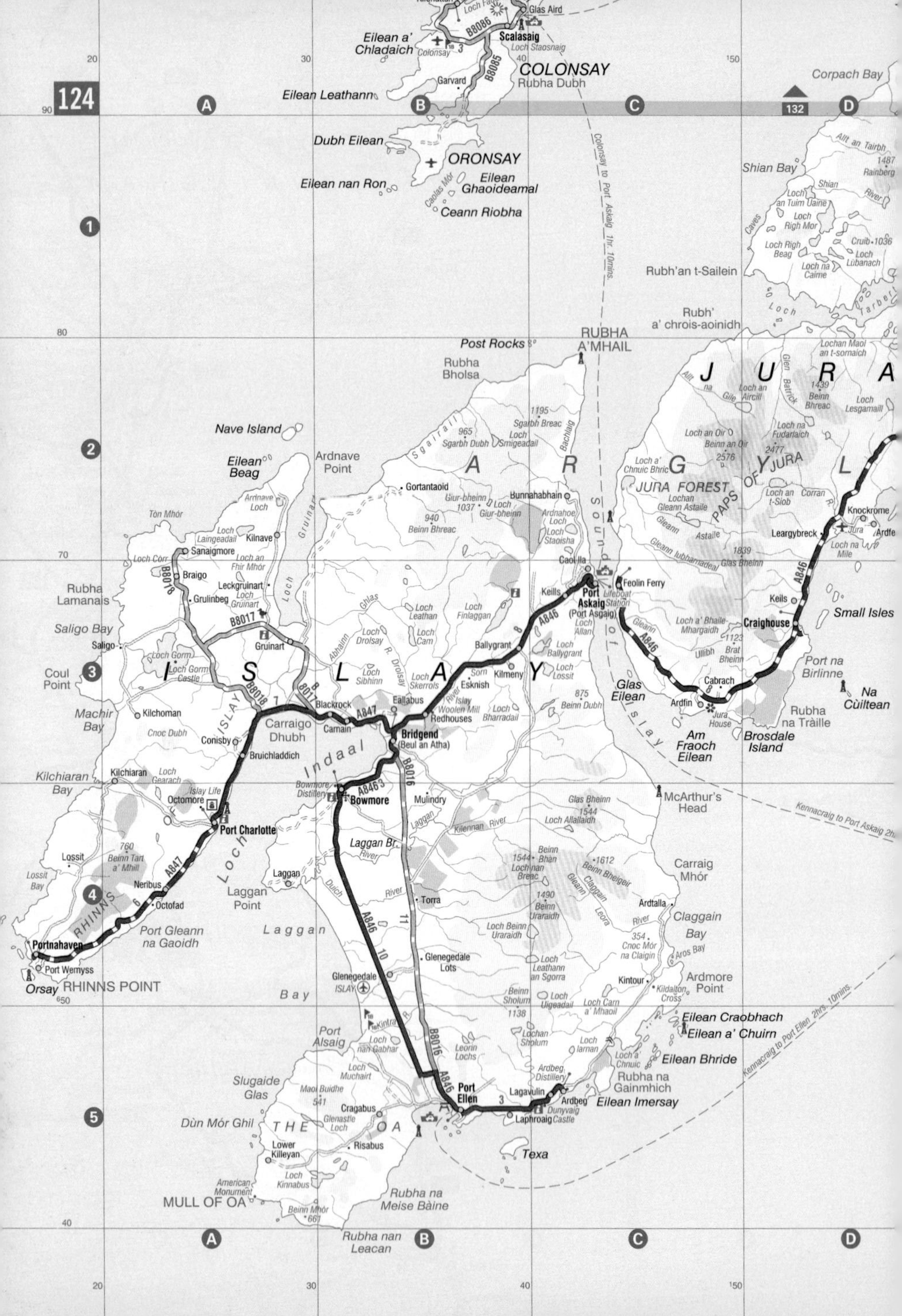

COLONSAY
Scalasaig
Glas Aird
Eilean a' Chladaich
Garvard
Rubha Dubh
Eilean Leathann
Corpach Bay
132
Dubh Eilean
ORONSAY
Eilean nan Ron
Eilean Ghaoideamal
Ceann Riobha
Colonsay to Port Askaig 1hr. 10mins.
Shian Bay
Rubh'an t-Sailein
Rubh' a' chrois-aoinidh
Post Rocks
RUBHA A'MHAIL
Rubha Bholsa
JURA
Nave Island
Eilean Beag
Ardnave Point
ARGYLL
JURA FOREST
PAPS OF JURA
Knockrome
Leargybreck
Rubha Lamanais
Saligo Bay
Saligo
Coul Point
ISLAY
Gruinart
Caol Ila
Port Askaig (Port Asgaig)
Feolin Ferry
Keills
Small Isles
Craighouse
Port na Birlinne
Na Cùiltean
Machir Bay
Kilchoman
Carraigo Dhubh
Bridgend (Beul an Atha)
Glas Eilean
Ardfin
Am Fraoch Eilean
Brosdale Island
Rubha na Tràille
Kilchiaran Bay
Bowmore
Port Charlotte
McArthur's Head
Kennacraig to Port Askaig 2hrs
Lossit Bay
RHINNS
Port Gleann na Gaoidh
Laggan Point
Laggan Bay
Carraig Mhór
Claggain Bay
Portnahaven
Port Wemyss
Orsay
RHINNS POINT
Ardmore Point
Eilean Craobhach
Eilean a' Chuirn
Eilean Bhride
Port Ellen
Lagavulin
Ardbeg
Laphroaig
Rubha na Gainmhich
Eilean Imersay
Kennacraig to Port Ellen 2hrs. 10mins.
Slugaide Glas
Dùn Mór Ghil
THE OA
Texa
MULL OF OA
Rubha na Meise Bàine
Rubha nan Leacan

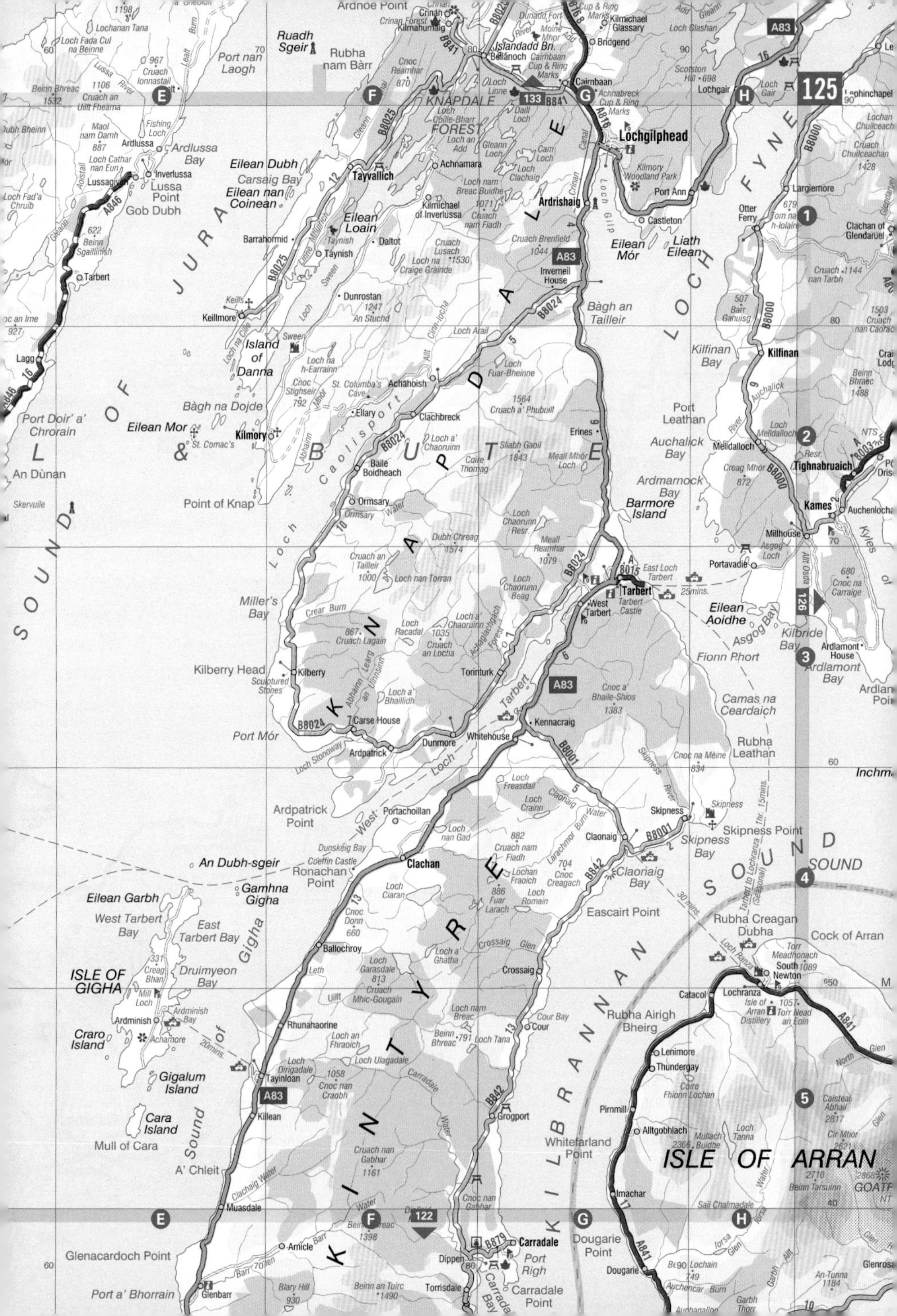

125
Ardnoe Point
Crinan
Crinan Forest
Kilmahumaig
Dunadd Fort
Cup & Ring Marks
Kilmichael Glassary
Bridgend
Loch Glashan
A83
Lochanan Tana
Loch Fada Cul na Beinne
Ruadh Sgeir
Rubha nam Bàrr
Port nan Laogh
967 Cruach Ionnastail
Beinn Bhreac 1532
1106 Cruach an Uillt Fhearna
Islandadd Bri.
Bellanoch
Cnoc Reamhar 870
Cairnbaan Cup & Ring Marks
Cairnbaan
Loch Linne
KNAPDALE
FOREST
133
B841
Achnabreck Cup & Ring Marks
Scotston Hill 698
Lochgair
Loch Gair
Lephinchapel
Dubh Bheinn
Maol nam Damh 887
Fishing Loch
Ardlussa
Ardlussa Bay
Loch Cathar nan Eun
Lussagiven
Inverlussa
Lussa Point
Gob Dubh
Loch Fad'a Chruib
A846
622 Beinn Sgaillinish
Tarbert
Lagg
Eilean Dubh
Carsaig Bay
Eilean nan Coinean
B8025
Tayvallich
Achnamara
Loch Coille-Bhar
Loch an Add
Gleann Loch
Daill Loch
Cam Loch
Loch Clachaig
Lochgilphead
Kilmory Woodland Park
Port Ann
Largiemore
Otter Ferry
679 Tom na h-Iolaire
Clachan of Glendaruel
Lochan Chuilceachan
Cruach Chuilceachan 1428
B8000
Eilean Loain
Taynish
Daltot
Barrahormid
Loch nam Breac Buidhe
Kilmichael of Inverlussa
1071 Cruach nam Fiadh
Ardrishaig
Loch Gilp
Castleton
Eilean Mór
Liath Eilean
Cruach Brenfield 1044
Cruach Lusach 1530
Loch na Craige Grainde
A83
Inverneil House
Cruach 1144 nan Tarbh
JURA
Keills
Keillmore
Dunrostan
1247 An Stuchd
Bàgh an Tailleir
LOCH FYNE
507 Barr Ganuisg
1503 Cruach nan Caorach
Cnoc an Ime 927
Island of Danna
Sween
Loch Arail
B8024
Loch na h-Earrainn
Cnoc Stighseir 792
St. Columba's Cave
Achahoish
Loch Fuar-Bheinne
Kilfinan Bay
Kilfinan
Beinn Bhreac 1488
Bàgh na Dojde
Ellary
Clachbreck
1564 Cruach a' Phubuill
Port Leathan
Loch Melldalloch
Melldalloch
Port Doir' a' Chrorain
Eilean Mor
Kilmory
St. Comac's
Loch Caolisport
Loch a' Chaoruinn
Sliabh Gaoil 1843
Coire Thomag
Erines
Meall Mhór Loch
Auchalick Bay
Creag Mhór 872
Tighnabruaich
SOUND OF JURA
KNAPDALE
An Dùnan
Baile Boidheach
Skervuile
Point of Knap
Ormsary
Ormsary Water
Loch Chaorunn Resr.
Ardmarnock Bay
Barmore Island
Kames
Auchenlochan
Millhouse
Dubh Chreag 1574
Meall Reamhar 1079
Asgog Loch
Portavadie
Kyles of
Cruach an Tailleir 1000
Loch nan Torran
Loch Chaorunn Beag
East Loch Tarbert
Tarbert
25mins.
Tarbert Castle
West Tarbert
Miller's Bay
Crear Burn
Eilean Aoidhe
Asgog Bay
680 Cnoc na Carraige
126
867 Cruach Lagain
Loch Racadal
1035 Cruach an Locha
Loch a' Chaoruinn
Achaglachgach Forest
Kilbride Bay
Ardlamont House
Fionn Phort
Ardlamont Bay
Kilberry Head
Sculptured Stones
Kilberry
Abhainn Learg an Uinnsinn
Loch a' Bhaillidh
Torinturk
A83
Cnoc a' Bhaile-Shios 1383
Camas na Ceardaich
Carse House
Port Mór
Dunmore
Whitehouse
Kennacraig
B8001
Rubha Leathan
Loch Stonoway
Ardpatrick
West Loch Tarbert
Cnoc na Mèine 834
Inchmarnock
Loch Freasdail
Loch Crainn
Claonaig Water
Skipness River
Ardpatrick Point
Portachoillan
Loch nan Gad
Skipness
Skipness Point
Tarbert to Lochranza 1hr. 15mins. (Seasonal)
882 Cruach nam Fiadh
Larachmor Burn
Claonaig
Skipness Bay
Dunskeig Bay
Coeffin Castle
An Dubh-sgeir
Ronachan Point
Clachan
Lochan Fraoich
704 Cnoc Creagach
B842
Claonaig Bay
SOUND
Gamhna Gigha
Loch Ciaran
886 Fuar Larach
Loch Romain
30 mins.
Eilean Garbh
West Tarbert Bay
East Tarbert Bay
Cnoc Donn 660
Eascairt Point
Rubha Creagan Dubha
Cock of Arran
Ballochroy
Loch a' Ghatha
Crossaig Glen
Loch Ranza
Torr Meadhonach 1089
South Newton
331 Creag Bhan
Druimyeon Bay
ISLE OF GIGHA
Loch Garasdale 813
Cruach Mhic-Gougain
Crossaig
Catacol
Lochranza
Isle of Arran Distillery
1057 Torr Nead an Eoin
A841
Mill Loch
Ardminish
Ardminish Bay
Achamore
Craro Island
Rhunahaorine
Loch nam Breac
Cour Bay
Cour
Rubha Airigh Bheirg
Loch an Fhraoich
Beinn Bhreac 791
Loch Tana
Lenimore
Thundergay
North Glen
20mins.
Loch Dirigadale
Loch Ulagadale
Carradale
Coire Fhionn Lochan
Gigalum Island
Tayinloan
1058 Cnoc nan Craobh
A83
Caisteal Abhail 2817
Killean
B842
Grogport
Pirnmill
Cara Island
Mull of Cara
Sound of Gigha
Whitefarland Point
Alltgobhlach
Loch Tanna
Mullach Buidhe 2366
Cir Mhòr 2621
ISLE OF ARRAN
Cruach nan Gabhar 1161
A' Chleit
Clachaig Water
Cnoc nan Gabhar
2710 Beinn Tarsuinn
2868
GOATF
Imachar
Sail Chalmadale
KINTYRE
KILBRANNAN SOUND
Muasdale
122
Beinn Bhreac 1398
Iorsa Water
Dougarie Point
Glenacardoch Point
Amicle Barr
B879
Carradale
Port Righ
Dippen
Iorsa Glen
A841
Dougarie
Lochain 749
Auchencar Burn
An Tunna 1184
Glenrosa
Port a' Bhorrain
Glenbarr
Blary Hill 930
Beinn an Tuirc 1490
Torrisdale
Carradale Bay
Carradale Point
Garbh Thorr

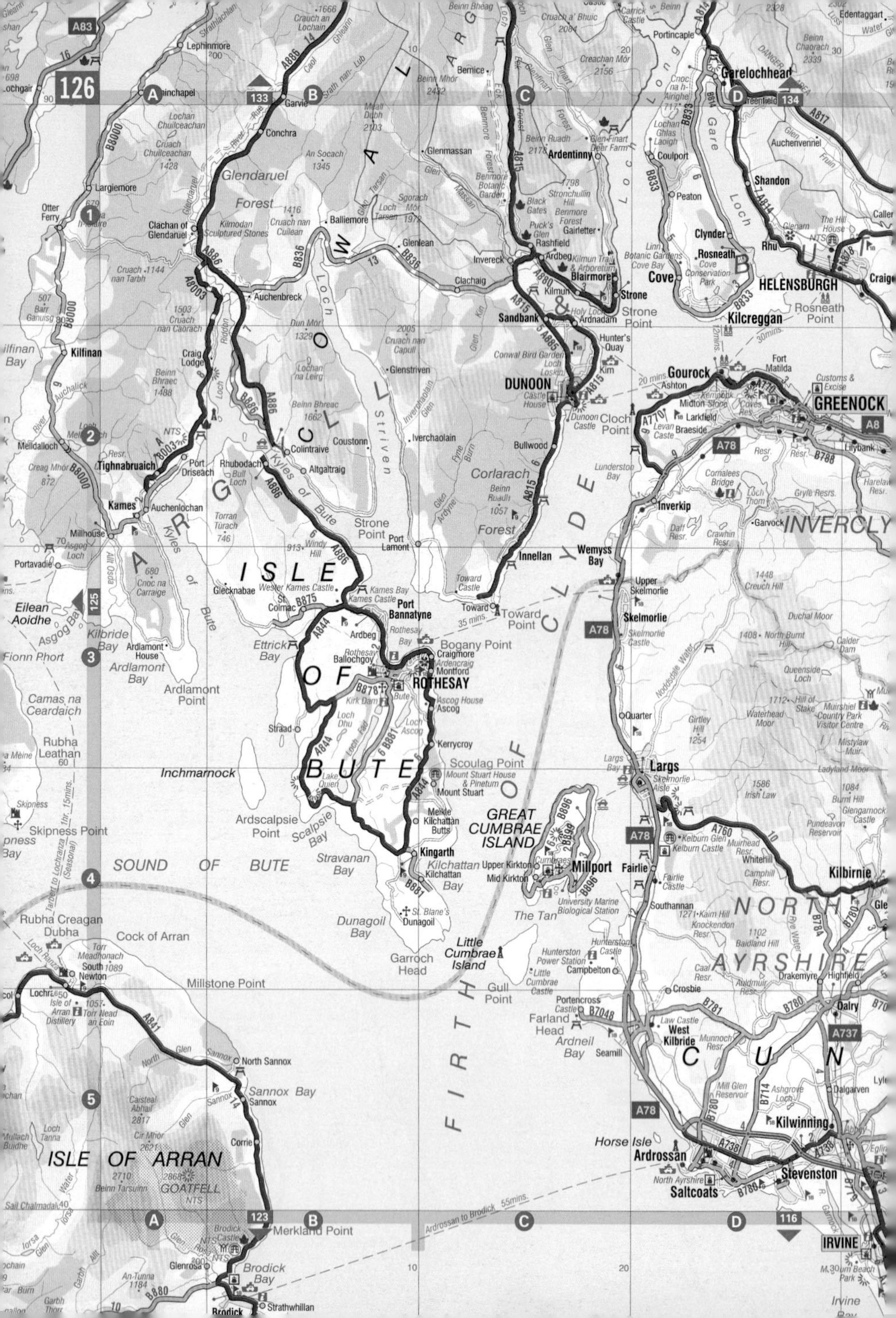

126
133
134
125
123
116
A
B
C
D
1
2
3
4
5
10
20
A83
A886
A815
A880
A885
A8
A78
A770
A760
A737
A738
A841
A844
A814
A817
B8000
B836
B875
B878
B881
B833
B896
B7048
B780
B781
B714
B788
Lephinmore
Strathlachlan
Crauch an Lochain
Beinn Bheag
Bernice
Beinn Mhòr
Garvie
Conchra
Glendaruel Forest
Largiemore
Otter Ferry
Clachan of Glendaruel
Kilmodan Sculptured Stones
Balliemore
Glenlean
Glenmassan
Benmore Botanic Garden
Ardentinny
Glen Finart Deer Farm
Portincaple
Garelochhead
Coulport
Peaton
Clynder
Rosneath
Shandon
Rhu
HELENSBURGH
Cove
Kilcreggan
Rosneath Point
Loch Long
Gare Loch
Auchenbreck
Kilfinan
Craig Lodge
Melldalloch
Tighnabruaich
Kames
Millhouse
Portavadie
Auchenlochan
Port Driseach
Rhubodach
Colintraive
Altgaltraig
Coustonn
Iverchaolain
Glenstriven
Loch Striven
Kyles of Bute
Clachaig
Invereck
Rashfield
Puck's Glen
Ardbeg
Blairmore
Kilmun
Strone
Strone Point
Sandbank
Holy Loch
Ardnadam
Hunter's Quay
Kirn
DUNOON
Dunoon Castle
Cloch Point
Bullwood
Corlarach Forest
Innellan
Toward
Toward Castle
Toward Point
Gourock
Ashton
Fort Matilda
GREENOCK
Larkfield
Levan Castle
Braeside
Lilybank
Inverkip
Wemyss Bay
INVERCLYDE
Upper Skelmorlie
Skelmorlie
Skelmorlie Castle
Quarter
Largs
Fairlie
Southannan
Kilbirnie
NORTH AYRSHIRE
ISLE OF BUTE
Port Bannatyne
Kames Castle
Wester Kames Castle
Glecknabae
St. Colmac
Ardbeg
Ettrick Bay
Rothesay Bay
Bogany Point
Craigmore
Ardencraig
Montford
ROTHESAY
Ballochgoy
Ascog
Ascog House
Straad
Kerrycroy
Scoulag Point
Mount Stuart House & Pinetum
Mount Stuart
Inchmarnock
Ardscalpsie Point
Scalpsie Bay
Meikle Kilchattan Butts
Kingarth
Kilchattan
Kilchattan Bay
St. Blane's
Dunagoil
Dunagoil Bay
Garroch Head
Stravanan Bay
SOUND OF BUTE
GREAT CUMBRAE ISLAND
Millport
Upper Kirkton
Mid Kirkton
University Marine Biological Station
The Tan
Little Cumbrae Island
Hunterston Castle
Hunterston Power Station
Campbelton
Portencross Castle
Farland Head
Ardneil Bay
Seamill
West Kilbride
Law Castle
Crosbie
Dalry
Drakemyre
Highfield
Kilwinning
Dalgarven
Ardrossan
Horse Isle
Saltcoats
Stevenston
IRVINE
FIRTH OF CLYDE
Ardlamont Point
Ardlamont House
Ardlamont Bay
Kilbride Bay
Asgog Bay
Eilean Aoidhe
Fionn Phort
Camas na Ceardaich
Rubha Leathan
Skipness Point
Rubha Creagan Dubha
Cock of Arran
South Newton
Lochranza
Millstone Point
Isle of Arran Distillery
North Sannox
Sannox Bay
Sannox
Corrie
ISLE OF ARRAN
GOATFELL
Merkland Point
Brodick Castle
Brodick Bay
Glenrosa
Strathwhillan
Brodick
Ardrossan to Brodick 55mins.

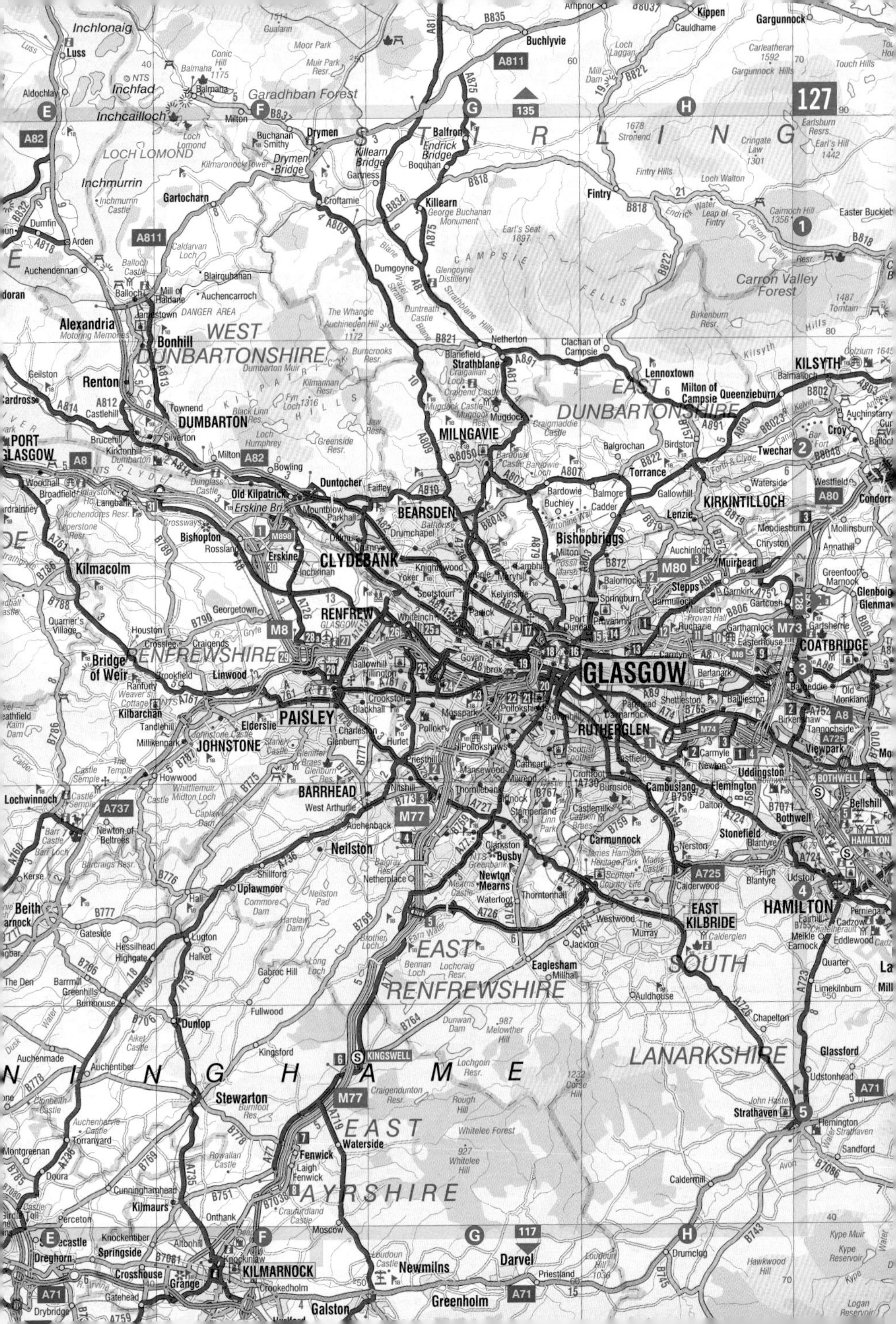

127
135
117
Kippen
Gargunnock
Buchlyvie
Inchlonaig
Luss
Inchfad
Balmaha
Conic Hill 1175
Garadhban Forest
Inchcailloch
Milton
Aldochlay
Drymen
Balfron
Killearn Bridge
Endrick Bridge
Boquhan
Gartness
LOCH LOMOND
Inchmurrin
Gartocharn
Croftamie
Killearn
George Buchanan Monument
Fintry
Fintry Hills
Loch Walton
Cairnoch Hill 1356
Leap of Fintry
Carron Valley Forest
Earl's Seat 1897
CAMPSIE FELLS
S T I R L I N G
Dumfin
Arden
Auchendennan
Balloch
Mill of Haldane
Blairquhanan
Auchencarroch
Jamestown
Alexandria
Bonhill
WEST DUNBARTONSHIRE
Dumgoyne
Glengoyne Distillery
Duntreath Castle
The Whangie
Auchineden Hill 1172
Blanefield
Strathblane
Netherton
Clachan of Campsie
Lennoxtown
Milton of Campsie
Queenzieburn
KILSYTH
Balmalloch
Croy
Twechar
Renton
Geilston
Cardross
Castlehill
Townend
DUMBARTON
Silverton
Milton
Bowling
Duntocher
Faifley
Old Kilpatrick
Erskine Bri.
Mountblow
Parkhall
BEARSDEN
MILNGAVIE
Mugdock
Mugdock Castle
Craigmaddie Castle
EAST DUNBARTONSHIRE
Balgrochan
Birdston
Torrance
Bardowie
Balmore
Buchley
Cadder
Bishopbriggs
KIRKINTILLOCH
Lenzie
Gallowhill
Waterside
Westfield
Condorrat
PORT GLASGOW
Kirktonhill
Woodhall
Broadfield
Langbank
Bishopton
Rossland
Erskine
CLYDEBANK
Drumchapel
Dalmuir
Inchinnan
Knightswood
Yoker
Scotstoun
RENFREW
Whiteinch
Partick
Kelvinside
Maryhill
Lambhill
Milton
Springburn
Balornock
Stepps
Muirhead
Chryston
Moodiesburn
Mollinsburn
Annathill
Greenfoot
Marnock
Glenboig
Gartcosh
Garnkirk
Barmulloch
Millerston
Provan Hall
Ruchazie
Garthamlock
Easterhouse
Gartsherrie
COATBRIDGE
Kilmacolm
Quarrier's Village
Houston
Crosslee
Craigends
Georgetown
RENFREWSHIRE
Bridge of Weir
Ranfurly
Brookfield
Linwood
Kilbarchan
Weaver's Cottage
Gallowhill
Hillington
Crookston
PAISLEY
Blackhall
Charleston
Glenburn
Elderslie
JOHNSTONE
Tandlehill
Millikenpark
Howwood
Castle Semple
Lochwinnoch
Govan
Ibrox
Mosspark
Pollok
Pollokshields
Pollokshaws
Govanhill
GLASGOW
Port Dundas
Provanmill
Carntyne
Barlanark
Shettleston
Parkhead
Dalmarnock
Baillieston
RUTHERGLEN
Eastfield
Carmyle
Newton
Uddingston
Viewpark
Tannochside
Birkenshaw
Old Monkland
Barrhead
BARRHEAD
West Arthurlie
Nitshill
Priesthill
Hurlet
Mansewood
Cathcart
Muirend
Thornliebank
Giffnock
Stamperland
Croftfoot
Burnside
Cambuslang
Flemington
Dalton
Castlemilk
Carmunnock
Bothwell
Bellshill
HAMILTON
Stonefield
Blantyre
Nerston
High Blantyre
Calderwood
Udston
EAST KILBRIDE
Calderglen
Westwood
The Murray
Jackton
Eaglesham
Millhall
Auldhouse
Auchenback
Neilston
Newton of Beltrees
Shillford
Uplawmoor
Netherplace
Clarkston
Busby
Newton Mearns
Thorntonhall
Waterfoot
Beith
Kerse
Hall
Lugton
Halket
Gateside
Hessilhead
Highgate
Barrmill
Greenhills
Burnhouse
Gabroc Hill
Fullwood
Dunlop
Kingsford
KINGSWELL
EAST RENFREWSHIRE
Eaglesham Moor
Melowther Hill 987
Lochgoin Resr.
Craigendunton Resr.
Rough Hill
Whitelee Forest
Whitelee Hill 927
SOUTH LANARKSHIRE
Chapelton
Quarter
Limekilnburn
Glassford
Udstonhead
Strathaven
Flemington
Sandford
Ferniegair
Eddlewood
Meikle Earnock
Cadzow
Chatelherault
Auchenmade
Auchentiber
N I N G H A M E
Stewarton
Montgreenan
Torranyard
Doura
Cunninghamhead
Kilmaurs
Perceton
Onthank
Fenwick
Laigh Fenwick
Waterside
EAST AYRSHIRE
Craufurdland Castle
Moscow
Caldermill
Drumclog
Hawkwood Hill
Kype Muir
Kype Reservoir
Logan Reservoir
Stanecastle
Dreghorn
Knockentiber
Springside
Altonhill
Crosshouse
Knockinlaw
KILMARNOCK
Grange
Gatehead
Crookedholm
Drybridge
Galston
Newmilns
Loudoun Castle
Darvel
Priestland
Loudoun Hill 1036
Greenholm
M8
M77
M80
M73
M74
M898
A82
A811
A81
A809
A875
A803
A891
A807
A8
A80
A737
A736
A735
A77
A726
A725
A723
A71
A761
A812
A813
A814
A818
A89
A752
A724
B818
B822
B835
B837
B834
B8050
B8049
B819
B757
B802
B8048
B806
B790
B789
B788
B786
B775
B774
B773
B769
B767
B764
B759
B776
B777
B778
B706
B751
B7081
B7038
B7071
B743
B7086
E
F
G
H
1
2
3
4
5

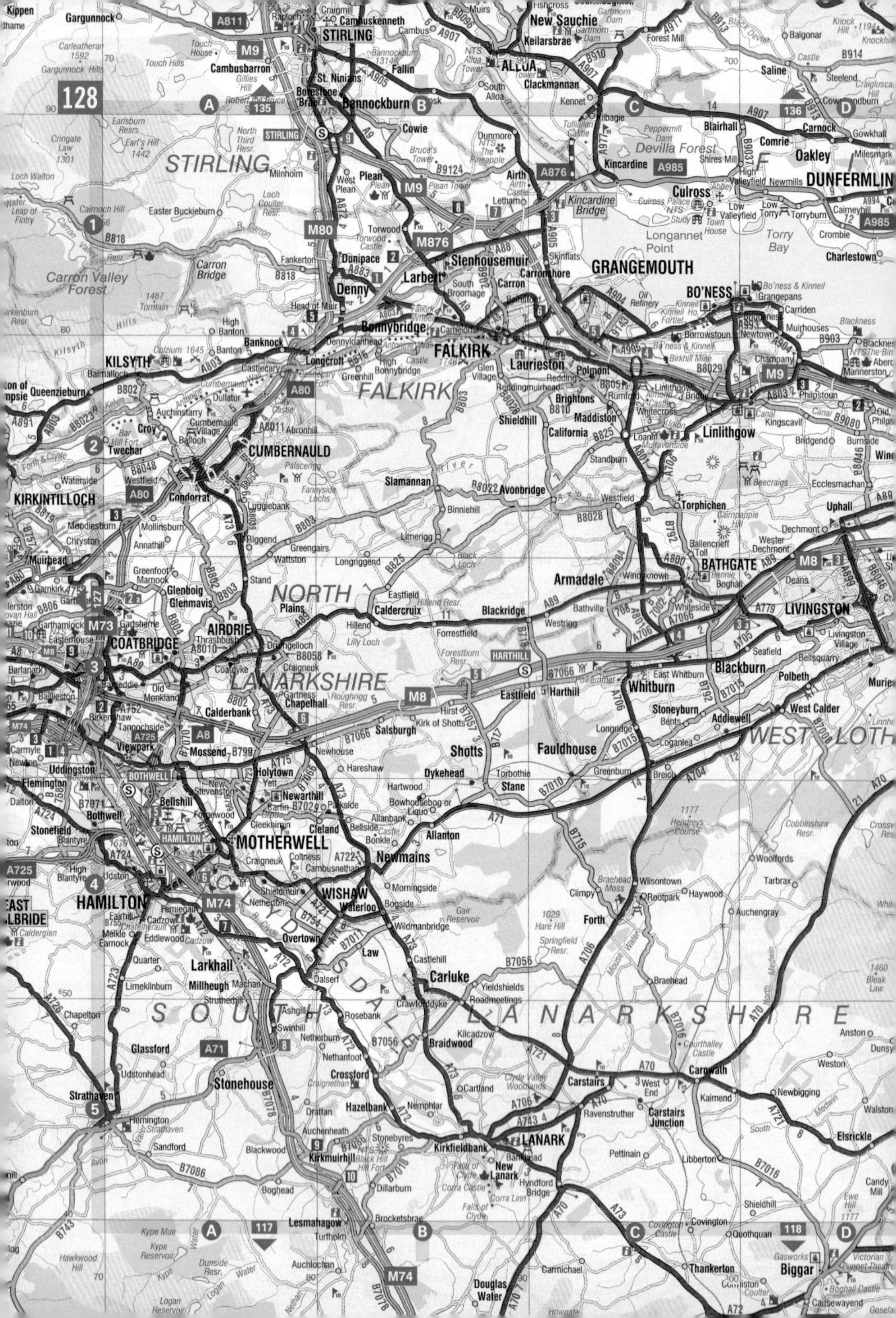
128
135
136
117
118
A
B
C
D
1
2
3
4
5
STIRLING
FALKIRK
NORTH LANARKSHIRE
SOUTH LANARKSHIRE
CLYDESDALE
WEST LOTH
Kippen
Gargunnock
Raploch
Craigmill
Cambuskenneth
Cambus
Fishcross
New Sauchie
Keilarsbrae
Forest Mill
Balgonar
Knock Hill
Knockhill
Saline
Steelend
Cowstrandburn
Carleatheran
Touch House
Touch Hills
Gargunnock Hills
Cambusbarron
Gillies Hill
St. Ninians
Fallin
Bannockburn
Alloa
Alloa Tower
Clackmannan
South Alloa
Kennet
Kilbagie
Tulliallan Castle
Peppermill Dam
Devilla Forest
Blairhall
Comrie
Carnock
Gowkhall
Oakley
Shires Mill
Milesmark
Borestone Brae
Cowie
Dunmore
Bruce's Tower
The Pineapple
Airth
Airth Castle
Kincardine
Kincardine Bridge
High Valleyfield
Newmills
DUNFERMLINE
Culross
Culross Palace
Low Valleyfield
Low Torry
Torryburn
Cairneyhill
Crombie
Charlestown
Torry Bay
Longannet Point
Earlsburn Resrs.
Earl's Hill
Cringate Law
North Third Resr.
Milnholm
Plean
West Plean
Plean Tower
Letham
Loch Walton
Leap of Fintry
Cairnoch Hill
Easter Buckieburn
Loch Coulter Resr.
Carron Valley Resr.
Carron Valley Forest
Carron Bridge
Tomtain
Torwood
Torwood Castle
Dunipace
Fankerton
Denny
Larbert
Stenhousemuir
South Broomage
Carron
Carronshore
Skinflats
GRANGEMOUTH
Oil Refinery
BO'NESS
Grangepans
Carriden
Bo'ness & Kinneil
Kinneil Ho.
Kinneil Fortlet
Borrowstoun
Newtown
Muirhouses
Blackness
Birkhill Mine
Champany
Mannerston
Head of Muir
High Banton
Banton
Banknock
Bonnybridge
Camelon
Falkirk Wheel
Dennyloanhead
Longcroft
High Bonnybridge
Greenhill
Castlecary
Glen Village
Laurieston
Polmont
Redding
Reddingmuirhead
Rumford
Brightons
Shieldhill
Maddiston
California
Linlithgow
Linlithgow Bridge
Whitecross
Kingscavil
Philpstoun
Bridgend
Burnside
Muiravonside
Loanie
Beecraigs
Ecclesmachan
KILSYTH
Colzium
Balmalloch
Queenzieburn
Dullatur
Auchinstarry
Croy
Twechar
Cumbernauld Village
Balloch
Abronhill
CUMBERNAULD
Palacerigg
Fannyside Lochs
Slamannan
Avonbridge
Standburn
Westfield
Torphichen
Cairnpapple Hill
Uphall
Dechmont
Wester Dechmont
Waterside
Westfield
Condorrat
KIRKINTILLOCH
Luggiebank
Moodiesburn
Mollinsburn
Chryston
Annathill
Riggend
Greengairs
Wattston
Binniehill
Limerigg
Black Loch
Longriggend
Ballencrieff Toll
BATHGATE
Boghall
Deans
LIVINGSTON
Armadale
Windyknowe
Bathville
Westrigg
Whiteside
Blackridge
Muirhead
Greenfoot
Marnock
Glenboig
Glenmavis
Stand
Eastfield
Caldercruix
Hillend Resr.
Plains
Hillend
Forrestfield
Lilly Loch
Gartsherrie
COATBRIDGE
AIRDRIE
Thrashbush
Drumgelloch
Craigneuk
Coatdyke
Old Monkland
Gartness
Chapelhall
Roughrigg Resr.
Forestburn Resr.
HARTHILL
Eastfield
Harthill
Polkemmet
East Whitburn
Whitburn
Blackburn
Seafield
Livingston Village
Bellsquarry
Polbeth
West Calder
Addiewell
Stoneybriggs
Bents
Longridge
Loganlea
Fauldhouse
Shotts
Kirk of Shotts
Hirst
Salsburgh
Calderbank
Newhouse
Hareshaw
Dykehead
Torbothie
Stane
Greenburn
Breich
Baillieston
Birkenshaw
Tannochside
Viewpark
Mossend
Holytown
New Stevenston
Newarthill
Carfin
Hartwood
Bowhousebog or Liquo
Allanbank
Uddingston
BOTHWELL
Bellshill
Forgewood
Cleekhimin
Cleland
Bellside
Bonkle
Allanton
Newmains
Hendreys Course
Cobbinshaw Resr.
Bothwell
Flemington
Dalton
Stonefield
Blantyre
High Blantyre
HAMILTON
MOTHERWELL
Craigneuk
Coltness
Cambusnethan
Shieldmuir
Netherton
WISHAW
Waterloo
Bogside
Morningside
Gair Reservoir
Braehead Moss
Climpy
Wilsontown
Rootpark
Haywood
Woolfords
Tarbrax
Auchengray
Forth
Hare Hill
Springfield Resr.
EAST KILBRIDE
Calderglen
Udston
Fairhill
Cadzow
Chatelherault
Perniegair
Meikle Earnock
Eddlewood
Wildmanbridge
Overtown
Law
Castlehill
Carluke
Yieldshields
Roadmeetings
Braehead
Bleak Law
Quarter
Larkhall
Millheugh
Machan
Limekilnburn
Dalserf
Chapelton
Strutherhill
Ashgill
Rosebank
Crawforddyke
Swinhill
Netherburn
Kilcadzow
Braidwood
Anston
Dunsyre
Glassford
Nethanfoot
Courthalley Castle
Weston
Udstonhead
Stonehouse
Crossford
Craignethan
Cartland
Clyde Valley Woodlands
Carstairs
West End
Carnwath
Newbigging
Kaimend
Walston
Strathaven
Flemington
Draffan
Hazelbank
Nemphlar
Ravenstruther
Carstairs Junction
Elsrickle
Sandford
Auchenheath
Stonebyres
Kirkfieldbank
LANARK
Bankhead
Blackwood
Kirkmuirhill
Pettinain
Libberton
New Lanark
Falls of Clyde
Corra Castle
Corra Linn
Hyndford Bridge
Candy Mill
Ewe Hill
Boghead
Dillarbun
Shieldhill
Lesmahagow
Brocketsbrae
Turfholm
Covington
Covington Castle
Quothquan
Kype Muir
Kype Reservoir
Dunside Resr.
Hawkwood Hill
Auchlochan
Carmichael
Thankerton
Biggar
Gasworks
Victorian Puppet Theatre
Boghall Castle
Douglas Water
Coulter
Causewayend
M9
M80
M876
M73
M8
M74
A811
A905
A907
A977
A985
A876
A88
A9
A803
A80
A8011
A73
A89
A706
A800
A779
A705
A71
A72
A70
A704
A721
A723
A726
A724
A725
A752
A8
A743
A743
B912
B913
B914
B910
B9124
B818
B802
B8023
B8048
B803
B8022
B8028
B825
B8058
B7066
B7057
B717
B7010
B7015
B792
B7071
B7029
B754
B7011
B7056
B7016
B7078
B7086
B743
B8029
B903
B9080
B8046
B715

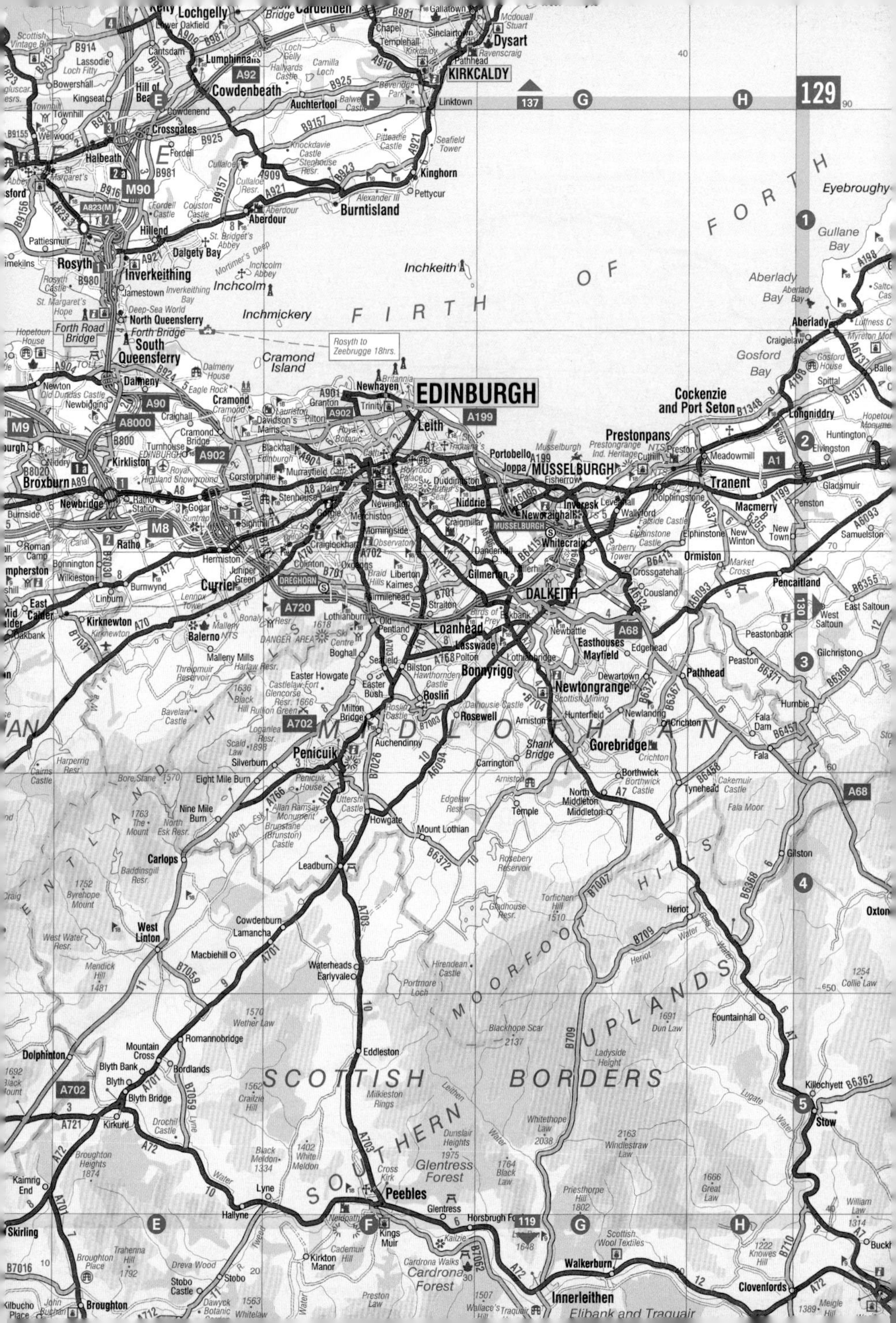
Lochgelly
Cardenden
Dysart
Lower Oakfield
Chapel
Sinclairtown
Templehall
Ravenscraig
Scottish Vintage Bus
Lassodie
Loch Fitty
Cantsdam
Lumphinnans
Loch Gelly
Camilla Loch
Pathhead
KIRKCALDY
Bowershall
Hill of Beath
Cowdenbeath
Kingseat
Auchtertool
Beveridge Park
Balwearie Castle
Linktown
Townhill
Cowdenend
Crossgates
Wellwood
Halbeath
Fordell
Knockdavie Castle
Stenhouse Resr.
Pitteadie Castle
Seafield Tower
Kinghorn
Pettycur
Cullaloe
Cullaloe Resr.
Alexander III
Burntisland
St. Margaret's
Fordell Castle
Couston Castle
Aberdour
Pattiesmuir
Hillend
St. Bridget's Abbey
Dalgety Bay
Mortimer's Deep
Inchcolm Abbey
Inchcolm
Inchkeith
Rosyth
Inverkeithing
Jamestown
Rosyth Castle
St. Margaret's Hope
Deep-Sea World
North Queensferry
Forth Road Bridge
Forth Bridge
Inchmickery
South Queensferry
Hopetoun House
Rosyth to Zeebrugge 18hrs.
Cramond Island
Dalmeny
Dalmeny House
Newton
Old Dundas Castle
Newbigging
Eagle Rock
Cramond
Cramond Fort
Lauriston Castle
Davidson's Mains
Craighall
Cramond Bridge
Turnhouse
EDINBURGH
Kirkliston
Niddry
Broxburn
Newbridge
Royal Highland Showground
Corstorphine
Murrayfield
Ratho Station
Gogar
Suntrap
Sighthill
Ratho
Roman Camp
Bonnington
Wilkieston
Hermiston
Juniper Green
Currie
Burnwynd
Linburn
Lennox Tower
East Calder
Kirknewton
Oakbank
Balerno
Malleny NTS
Bonaly
Malleny Mills
Harlaw Resr.
Threipmuir Reservoir
Newhaven
Britannia
Granton
Trinity
Pilton
Leith
Royal Botanic Garden
Blackhall
Edinburgh Zoo
Dalry
Stenhouse
Gorgie
Merchiston
Holyrood Palace
Duddingston
Arthur's Seat
Newington
Morningside
Observatory
Craiglockhart
Colinton
Oxgangs
Braid Hills
Liberton
Kaimes
Craigmillar
Niddrie
Danderhall
Gilmerton
Straiton
Fairmilehead
Lothianburn
Dreghorn
Portobello
Joppa
MUSSELBURGH
Fisherrow
Newcraighall
Inveresk
Whitecraig
Wallyford
Levenhall
Millerhill
DALKEITH
Eskbank
Birds of Prey
Loanhead
Lasswade
Polton
Bonnyrigg
Old Pentland
Hillend
Ski Centre
Danger Area
Boghall
Seafield
Bilston
Hawthornden Castle
Roslin
Roslin Castle
Easter Howgate
Easter Bush
Castlelaw Fort
Glencorse Resr.
Black Hill
Rullion Green
Bavelaw Castle
Loganlea Resr.
Scald Law
Milton Bridge
Rosewell
Dalhousie Castle
Newbattle
Easthouses
Mayfield
Lothianbridge
Newtongrange
Scottish Mining
Hunterfield
Arniston
Dewartown
Edgehead
Pathhead
Newlandrig
Crichton
Gorebridge
Crichton Castle
Shank Bridge
Carrington
Arniston
Borthwick
Borthwick Castle
North Middleton
Middleton
Temple
Tynehead
Cakemuir Castle
Fala Moor
Penicuik
Penicuik House
Auchendinny
Silverburn
Harperrig Resr.
Cairns Castle
Bore Stane
Eight Mile Burn
Nine Mile Burn
The Mount
North Esk Resr.
Allan Ramsay Monument
Uttershill Castle
Brunstane (Brunston) Castle
Howgate
Mount Lothian
Edgelaw Resr.
Rosebery Reservoir
Carlops
Baddinsgill Resr.
Byrehope Mount
Leadburn
West Linton
West Water Resr.
Cowdenburn
Lamancha
Macbiehill
Mendick Hill
Waterheads
Earlyvale
Portmore Loch
Hirendean Castle
Gladhouse Resr.
Torfichen Hill
Heriot
Heriot Water
Wether Law
Romannobridge
Mountain Cross
Bordlands
Dolphinton
Black Mount
Blyth Bank
Blyth
Blyth Bridge
Eddleston
Blackhope Scar
Ladyside Height
Dun Law
Fountainhall
Collie Law
Kirkurd
Drochil Castle
Crailzie Hill
Milkieston Rings
Whitehope Law
Windlestraw Law
Killochyett
Stow
Lugate Water
Broughton Heights
Black Meldon
White Meldon
Dunslair Heights
Glentress Forest
Black Law
Great Law
Kaimrig End
Cross Kirk
Peebles
Glentress
Lyne
Hallyne
Neidpath
Kings Muir
Horsburgh Ford
Priesthorpe Hill
Scottish Wool Textiles
Knowes Hill
William Law
Skirling
Trahenna Hill
Broughton Place
Kirkton Manor
Cademuir Hill
Kailzie
Cardrona Walks
Cardrona Forest
Dreva Wood
Stobo Castle
Stobo
Walkerburn
Clovenfords
Meigle Hill
Broughton
John Buchan
Kilbucho Place
Dawyck Botanic Garden
Whitelaw
Preston Law
Wallace's Hill
Traquair
Innerleithen
Elibank and Traquair
Eyebroughy
Gullane Bay
Aberlady Bay
Aberlady
Craigielaw
Luffness Castle
Myreton Motor Museum
Gosford Bay
Gosford House
Spittal
Ballencrieff
Cockenzie and Port Seton
Longniddry
Hopetoun Monument
Huntington
Elvingston
Prestonpans
Prestongrange Ind. Heritage
Musselburgh
Preston
Cuthill
Meadowmill
Tranent
Gladsmuir
Dolphingstone
Macmerry
Penston
Falside Castle
Elphinstone
Elphinstone Castle
New Winton
New Town
Samuelston
Carberry Tower
Crossgatehall
Ormiston
Market Cross
Cousland
Pencaitland
East Saltoun
West Saltoun
Peastonbank
Peaston
Gilchriston
Humbie
Fala Dam
Fala
Gilston
Oxton
FIRTH OF FORTH
MIDLOTHIAN
PENTLAND HILLS
MOORFOOT HILLS
SCOTTISH BORDERS
SOUTHERN UPLANDS
137
119
130
129

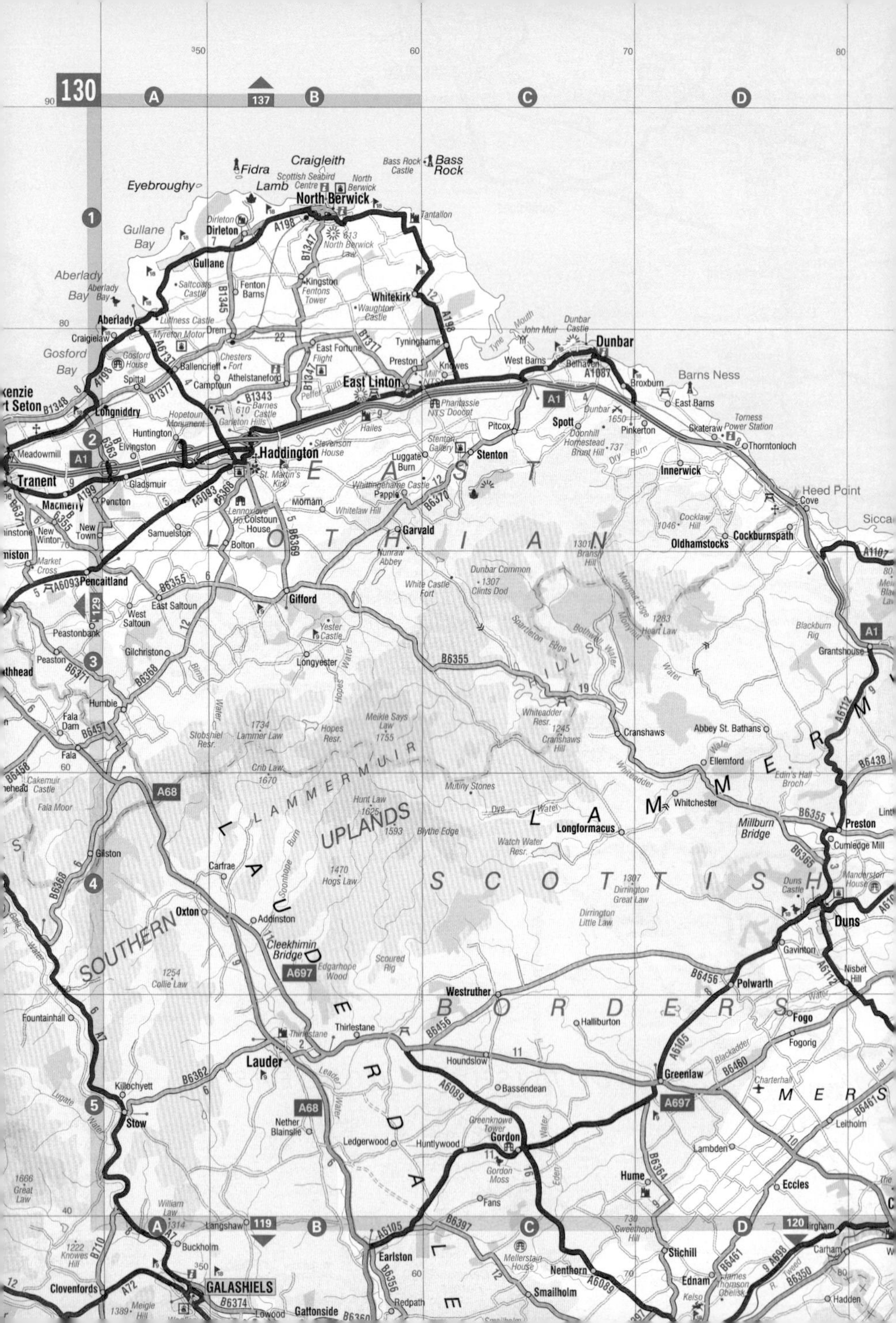
A
137
B
C
D
Craigleith
Bass Rock Castle
Bass Rock
Fidra
Scottish Seabird Centre
North Berwick
Lamb
Eyebroughy
North Berwick
Tantallon
Dirleton
Gullane Bay
Dirleton
613 North Berwick Law
Gullane
Aberlady Bay
Aberlady Bay
Saltcoats Castle
Fenton Barns
Kingston
Fentons Tower
Whitekirk
Waughton Castle
Luffness Castle
Aberlady
Craigielaw
Myreton Motor
Drem
Gosford Bay
Gosford House
Chesters Fort
Ballencrieff
Spittal
Athelstaneford
Camptoun
East Fortune Flight
Tyninghame
Preston
Knowes
John Muir
Dunbar Castle
Dunbar
West Barns
Belhaven
A1087
Broxburn
Barns Ness
East Barns
East Linton
Phantassie NTS Doocot
Hailes
kenzie
rt Seton
Longniddry
Hopetoun Monument
Barnes Castle
610 Garleton Hills
Huntington
Elvingston
Meadowmill
Tranent
Gladsmuir
Haddington
St. Martin's Kirk
Stevenson House
Luggate Burn
Stenton Gallery
Stenton
Pitcox
Spott
Doonhill Homestead
Brunt Hill
Dunbar 1650
Pinkerton
Skateraw
Torness Power Station
Thorntonloch
Innerwick
Heed Point
Cove
Macmerry
Penston
New Winton
New Town
Samuelston
Lennoxlove Ho.
Colstoun House
Morham
Whitelaw Hill
Whittingehame Castle
Papple
Garvald
Cocklaw Hill
1046
Oldhamstocks
Cockburnspath
Siccar
EAST LOTHIAN
Bolton
Nunraw Abbey
1301 Bransly Hill
Market Cross
Pencaitland
East Saltoun
West Saltoun
Gifford
White Castle Fort
Dunbar Common
1307 Clints Dod
Monynut Edge
1283 Heart Law
Peastonbank
Yester Castle
Spartleton Edge
Bothwell Water
Blackburn Rig
A1
Grantshouse
Gilchriston
Peaston
Longyester
B6355
HILLS
Whiteadder Resr.
1245 Cranshaws Hill
Cranshaws
Abbey St. Bathans
Humbie
Fala Dam
Fala
1734 Lammer Law
Stobshiel Resr.
Hopes Resr.
Meikle Says Law 1755
Crib Law 1670
Ellemford
Edin's Hall Broch
Cakemuir Castle
Fala Moor
A68
LAMMERMUIR
Hunt Law 1625
Mutiny Stones
Whitchester
Millburn Bridge
Preston
Cumledge Mill
UPLANDS
1593
Blythe Edge
Dye Water
Watch Water Resr.
Longformacus
LAMMER
Gilston
Carfrae
1470 Hogs Law
SCOTTISH
1307 Dirrington Great Law
Dirrington Little Law
Duns Castle
Manderston House
Duns
Oxton
Addinston
Cleekhimin Bridge
SOUTHERN
1254 Collie Law
A697
Edgarhope Wood
Scoured Rig
Gavinton
Nisbet Hill
Westruther
Polwarth
BORDERS
Fountainhall
Thirlestane
Thirlestane
Halliburton
Fogo
Fogorig
Houndslow
Lauder
Greenlaw
Killochyett
Bassendean
Charterhall
MERS
LAUDERDALE
Stow
Nether Blainslie
Greenknowe Tower
Gordon
Leitholm
Ledgerwood
Huntlywood
Gordon Moss
Lambden
1666 Great Law
Hume
Eccles
Fans
William Law
1314
Langshaw
119
Sweethope Hill
120
Buckholm
1222 Knowes Hill
Earlston
Mellerstain House
Stichill
Carham
Nenthorn
Ednam
James Thomson Obelisk
Clovenfords
GALASHIELS
Smailholm
Kelso
1389 Meigle Hill
Lowood
Gattonside
Redpath
Hadden
129

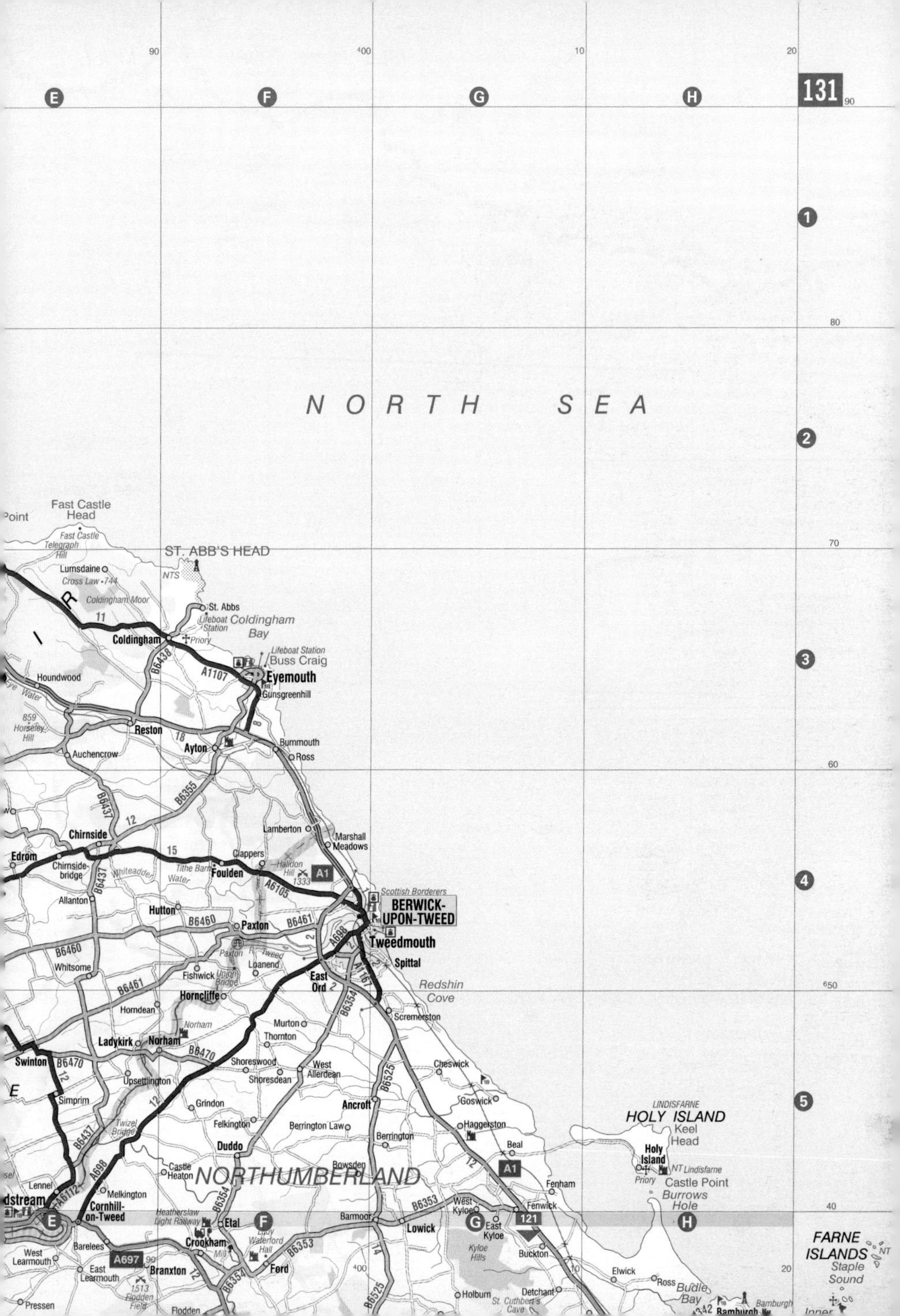

90
400
10
20
E
F
G
H
1
2
3
4
5
80
70
60
650
40
NORTH SEA
Fast Castle Head
Fast Castle
Telegraph Hill
ST. ABB'S HEAD
NTS
Lumsdaine
Cross Law 744
Coldingham Moor
St. Abbs
Lifeboat Station
Coldingham Bay
Coldingham
Priory
Lifeboat Station
Buss Craig
Eyemouth
Gunsgreenhill
Houndwood
Eye Water
859 Horseley Hill
Reston
Ayton
Burnmouth
Ross
Auchencrow
B6438
A1107
B6355
B6437
Chirnside
Lamberton
Marshall Meadows
Edrom
Chirnside-bridge
Whiteadder Water
Tithe Barn
Foulden
Clappers
Halidon Hill 1333
A1
A6105
Allanton
Hutton
B6460
Paxton
B6461
Scottish Borderers
BERWICK-UPON-TWEED
Tweedmouth
Spittal
A698
A1167
Whitsome
Fishwick
Union Bridge
Loanend
East Ord
Redshin Cove
Horncliffe
Horndean
Norham
Scremerston
Murton
Thornton
Ladykirk
B6470
Swinton
Shoreswood
Shoresdean
West Allerdean
Cheswick
Upsettlington
B6525
Goswick
Simprim
Grindon
Ancroft
LINDISFARNE
HOLY ISLAND
Keel Head
Felkington
Berrington Law
Haggerston
Twizel Bridge
Berrington
Beal
Duddo
Holy Island
Castle Heaton
NORTHUMBERLAND
Bowsden
NT Lindisfarne
Priory
Castle Point
Lennel
Melkington
B6354
Fenham
Burrows Hole
Coldstream
A6112
Cornhill-on-Tweed
Heatherslaw Light Railway
Etal
Barmoor
B6353
Lowick
West Kyloe
East Kyloe
Fenwick
121
Crookham
Lady Waterford Hall
Kyloe Hills
FARNE ISLANDS
Staple Sound
West Learmouth
Barelees
A697
Buckton
East Learmouth
Branxton
Ford
Elwick
Ross
Budle Bay
1513 Flodden Field
Pressen
Flodden
Holburn
St. Cuthbert's Cave
Detchant
Bamburgh

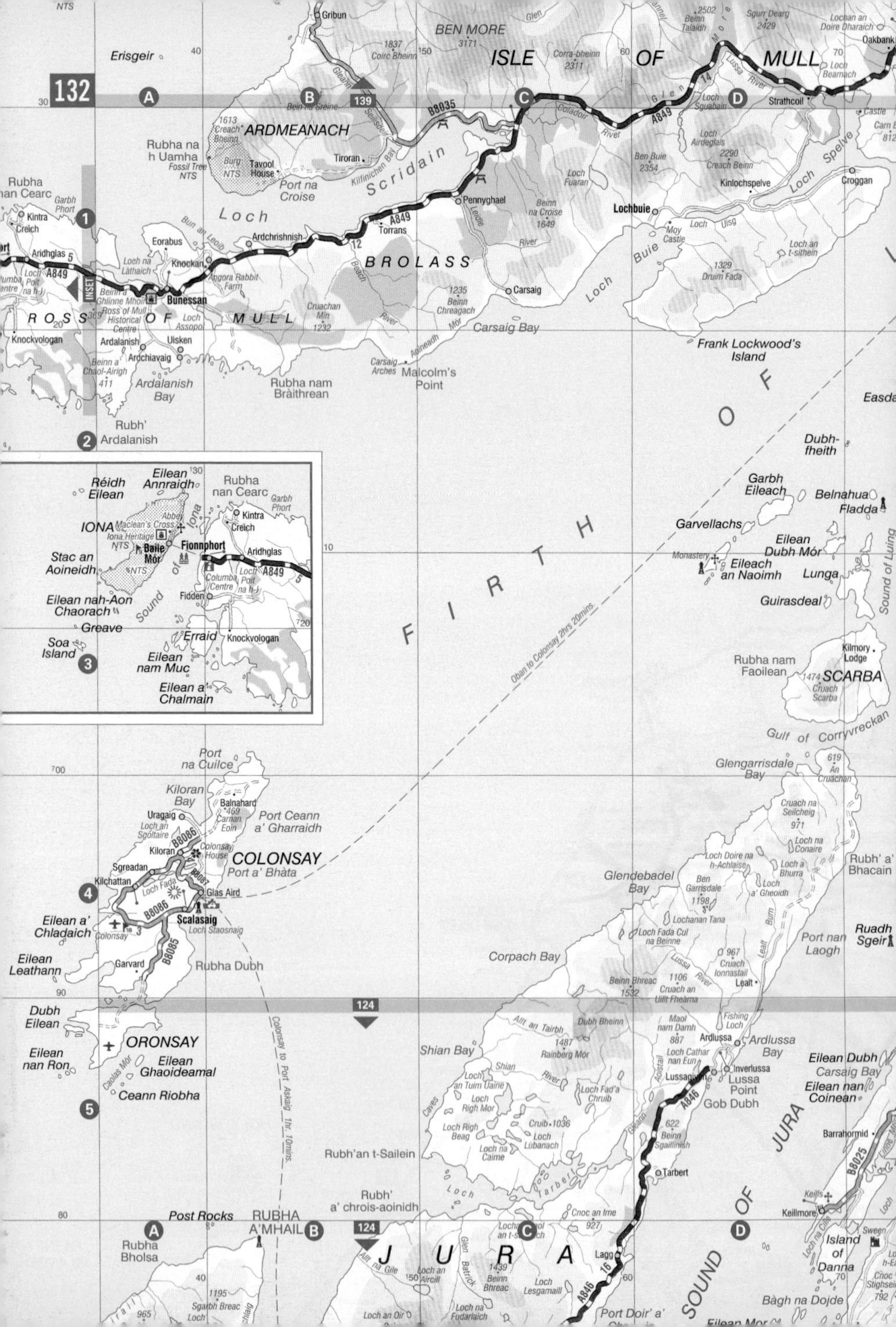
ISLE OF MULL
BEN MORE
3171
ARDMEANACH
BROLASS
ROSS OF MULL
Loch Scridain
Bunessan
Pennyghael
Lochbuie
Carsaig
Carsaig Bay
Ardalanish Bay
Rubh' Ardalanish
Frank Lockwood's Island
FIRTH OF LORN
Garvellachs
Eileach an Naoimh
Lunga
SCARBA
Gulf of Corryvreckan
IONA
Fionnphort
Baile Mór
Sound of Iona
Erraid
COLONSAY
Scalasaig
Kiloran Bay
ORONSAY
JURA
SOUND OF JURA
Lussagiven
Ardlussa
Tarbert
Lagg
Loch Tarbert
Corpach Bay
Glengarrisdale Bay
Oban to Colonsay 2hrs 20mins.
Colonsay to Port Askaig 1hr. 10mins.
A849
A846
B8035
B8086
B8085
B8025
INSET
139
124

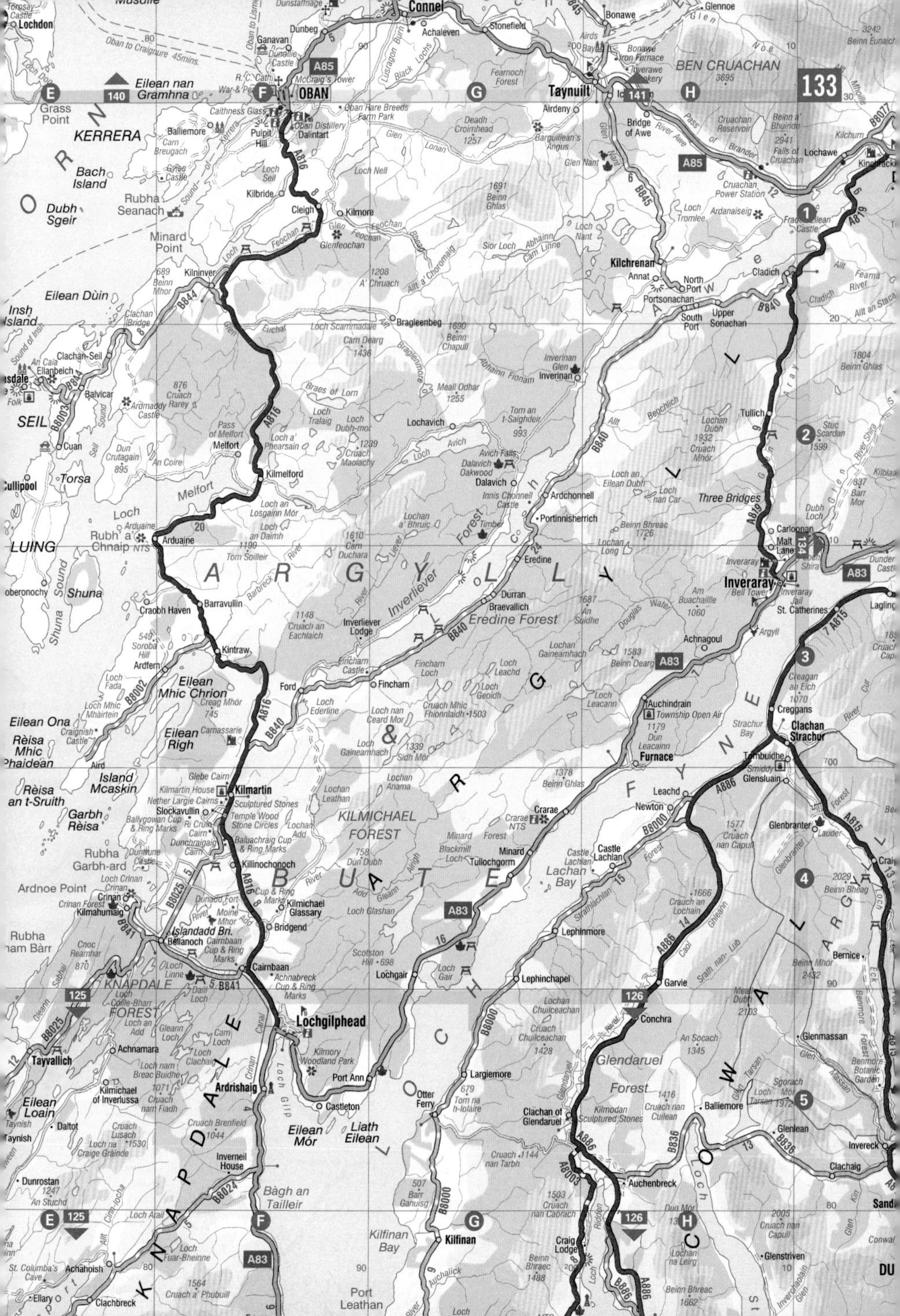

133
Lochdon
Connel
Dunbeg
Achaleven
Stonefield
Bonawe
Glennoe
Ganavan
Dunollie Castle
Oban to Lismore
Oban to Craignure 45mins.
Black Lochs
Lusragan Burn
A85
McCaig's Tower
R. C. Cath.
War & Peace
Eilean nan Gramhna
140
OBAN
Fearnoch Forest
Airds Bay
Bonawe Iron Furnace
Inverawe Smokery
BEN CRUACHAN
3695
Taynuilt
141
Grass Point
KERRERA
Caithness Glass
Oban Rare Breeds Farm Park
Oban Distillery
Dalintart
Pulpit Hill
Balliemore
Airdeny
Deadh Croimhead
1257
Barguillean's Angus
Bridge of Awe
River Awe
Pass of Brander
Cruachan Reservoir
Beinn a' Bhuiridh
2941
Falls of Cruachan
Lochawe
Kilchurn
B8077
Carn Breugach
Glen Lonan
Bach Island
Gylen Castle
A816
Loch Seil
Loch Nell
Glen Nant
Cruachan Power Station
A85
Kilbride
Dubh Sgeir
Rubha Seanach
Cleigh
Kilmore
1691
Beinn Ghlas
B845
Loch Tromlee
Ardanaiseig
Fraoch Eilean Castle
A819
Minard Point
Glen Feochan
Glenfeochan
Loch Feochan
Loch Nant
Sior Loch
Abhainn Cam Linne
Kilchrenan
Annat
North Port
Cladich
689
Beinn Mhor
Kilninver
1208
A' Chruach
Allt a' Chromaig
Portsonachan
Eilean Dùin
B844
Clachan Bridge
Insh Island
Sound of Insh
Glen Euchar
Loch Scammadale
Bragleenbeg
1690
Beinn Chapull
South Port
Upper Sonachan
B840
Allt an Stacain
Clachan-Seil
An Cala
Ellanbeich
Carn Dearg
1436
Braglenmore
Abhainn Fionam
Inverinan Glen
Inverinan
1804
Beinn Ghlas
876
Cruach Rarey
Ardmaddy Castle
Balvicar
Braes of Lorn
Meall Odhar
1255
SEIL
B8003
Cuan
Loch Tralaig
Loch Dubh-mor
Tom an t-Saighdeir
993
Lochavich
Pass of Melfort
Loch a' Phearsain
1239
Cruach Maolachy
Loch Avich
Tullich
Lochan Dubh
1932
Cruach Mhòr
Stuc Scardan
1599
Melfort
Dun Crutagain
895
An Coire
Kilmelford
Avich Falls
Dalavich Oakwood
Dalavich
Loch an Eilean Dubh
Loch nan Car
Three Bridges
837
Barr Mor
Cullipool
Torsa
Loch Melfort
Loch an Losgainn Mòr
Lochan a' Bhruic
Innis Chonnell Castle
Ardchonnell
Portinnisherrich
Dubh Loch
Rubh' a' Chnaip
Arduaine
NTS
20
Loch an Daimh
1610
Carn Duchara
Forest
Timber
Beinn Bhreac
1726
Carloonan
Malt Lane
134
LUING
1199
Tom Soilleir
Barbreck River
River Liever
Eredine
Lochan Long
Inveraray
Inveraray Jail
Bell Tower
INVERARAY
A83
ARGYLL
Shuna
Shuna Sound
Cobberonochy
Craobh Haven
Barravullin
Inverliever
Durran
Braevallich
Eredine Forest
1687
An Suidhe
Am Buachaille
1060
St. Catherines
A815
1148
Cruach an Eachlaich
Inverliever Lodge
Douglas Water
Achnagoul
549
Soroba Hill
Ardfern
Kintraw
Fincharn Castle
Fincharn
Fincharn Loch
Loch Leachd
Lochan Gaineamhach
1583
Beinn Dearg
Loch Fada
B8002
Eilean Mhic Chrion
Creag Mhòr
745
Ford
Loch Ederline
Loch nan Ceard Mor
Cruach Mhic Fhionnlaidh 1503
Loch Geoidh
Loch Leacann
Auchindrain
Township Open Air
1179
Dùn Leacainn
Creagan an Eich
Creggans
Clachan Strachur
Strachur Bay
Loch Mhic Mhàirtein
Craignish Castle
Eilean Ona
Rèisa Mhic Phaidean
Aird
Eilean Righ
Carnassarie
B840
Loch Gaineamhach
1339
Sidh Mòr
Furnace
Tomnbuidhe
Smiddy
Glensluain
700
Island Mcaskin
Glebe Cairn
Kilmartin House
Kilmartin
Nether Largie Cairns
Sculptured Stones
Slockavullin
Temple Wood Stone Circles
Ri Cruin Cairn
Lochan Anama
Lochan Leathan
1378
Beinn Ghlas
Leachd
Newton
A886
Rèisa an t-Sruith
Garbh Rèisa
Ballygowan Cup & Ring Marks
Dunchraigaig Cairn
Baluachraig Cup & Ring Marks
Lochan Add
KILMICHAEL FOREST
Crarae
Crarae NTS
B8000
Glenbranter
Lauder
Rubha Garbh-ard
Dunttrune Castle
Killinochonoch
758
Dùn Dubh
Minard Forest
Blackmill Loch
Tullochgorm
Minard
Castle Lachlan
Lachan Bay
1577
Cruach nan Capull
Glenbranter Forest
Loch Crinan
Ardnoe Point
Crinan
Crinan Forest
Kilmahumaig
B8025
Dunadd Fort
Moine Mhor
River Add
Cup & Ring Marks
Kilmichael Glassary
Gleann Airigh
Loch Glashan
A83
Strathlachlan
1666
Crauch an Lochain
2029
Beinn Bhreac
B841
Islandadd Bri.
Bellanoch
Cairnbaan Cup & Ring Marks
Bridgend
Scotston Hill 698
Lephinmore
Caol Ghleann
Strath nan Lub
Bernice
Rubha nam Bàrr
Cnoc Reamhar
870
Loch Linne
Dail Loch
KNAPDALE
Cairnbaan
Achnabreck Cup & Ring Marks
Lochgair
Loch Gair
Lephinchapel
Garvie
Beinn Mhòr
2432
125
Loch Coille-Bharr
FOREST
Loch an Add
Lochgilphead
Crinan Canal
126
Conchra
Lochan Chuilceachan
Meall Dubh
2103
Benmore Forest
Gleann Loch
Cam Loch
Loch Clachaig
Achnamara
Kilmory Woodland Park
Cruach Chuilceachan
1428
An Socach
1345
Glenmassan
B8025
Tayvallich
Loch nam Breac Buidhe
1071
Cruach nam Fiadh
Kilmichael of Inverlussa
Ardrishaig
Loch Gilp
Port Ann
Castleton
Largiemore
Otter Ferry
679
Tom na h-Ioiaire
Glendaruel Forest
1416
Cruach nan Cuilean
Sgorach Mòr
1972
Loch Tarsan
Glen Tarsan
Benmore Botanic Garden
Eilean Loain
Taynish
Daltot
Cruach Lusach
1530
Loch na Craige Grainde
Cruach Brenfield
1044
Eilean Mòr
Liath Eilean
Clachan of Glendaruel
Kilmodan Sculptured Stones
Balliemore
Glenlean
B836
Invereck
Clachaig
Dunrostan
1247
An Stuchd
Inverneil House
B8024
Bàgh an Tailleir
507
Barr Ganuisg
Cruach nan Tarbh 1144
A8003
Auchenbreck
Loch Striven
1503
Cruach nan Caorach
Dun Mòr
2005
Cruach nan Capull
Glen Kin
Sandbank
Loch Arail
Allt Cinn-locha
Kilfinan
Kilfinan Bay
Craig Lodge
River Ruel
Lochan na Leirg
Glenstriven
Achahoish
Loch Fuar-Bheinne
1564
Cruach a' Phubuill
Beinn Bhreac
1488
St. Columba's Cave
Ellary
Clachbreck
Port Leathan
Auchalick
Beinn Bhreac
1662
Inverchaolain Glen
B8000
B886
A886

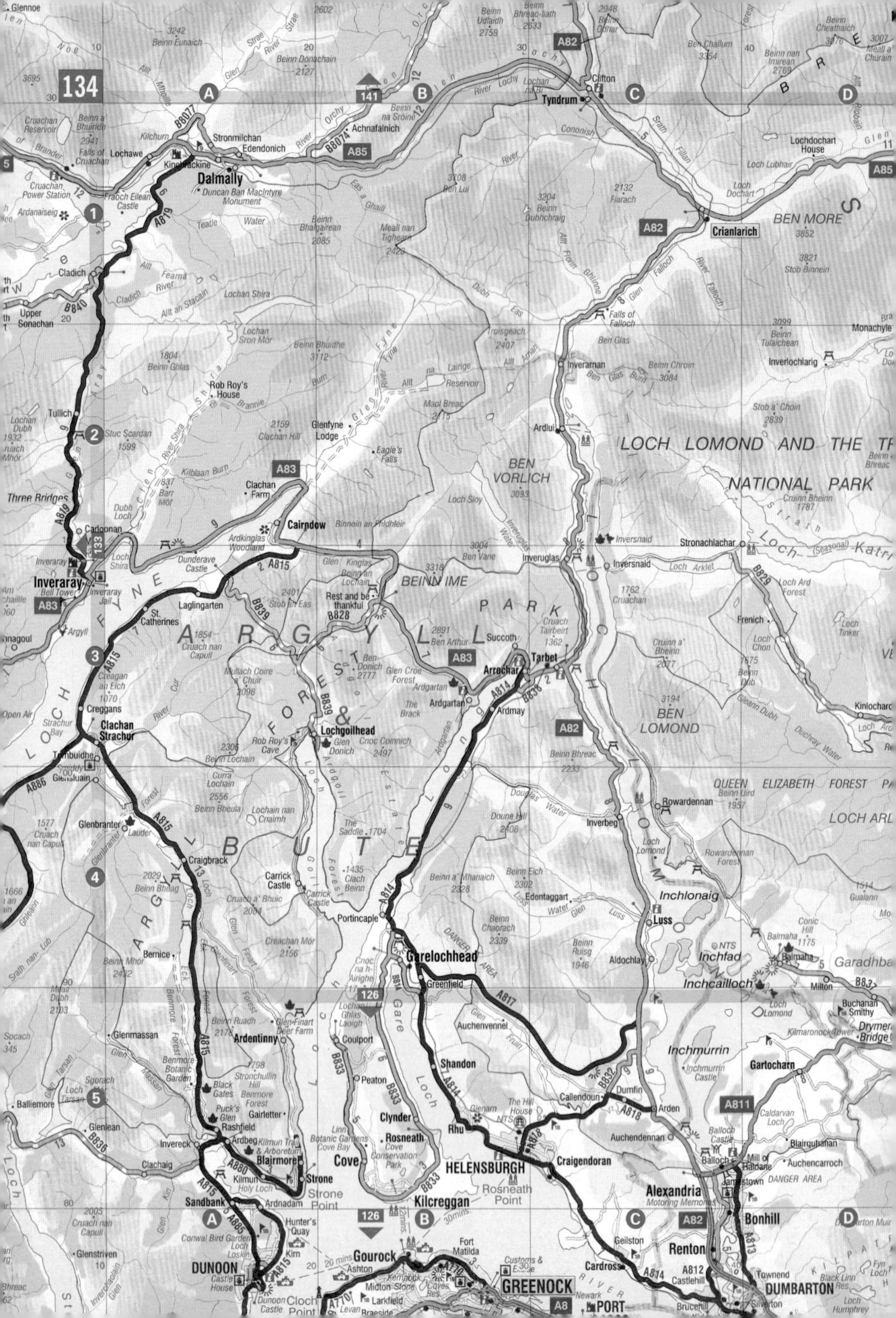
Glennoe
Beinn Eunaich
3242
Beinn Udlaidh
2759
Beinn Bhreac-liath
2633
Beinn Odhar
2948
A82
Ben Challum
3354
Beinn Cheathaich
3076
Meall a' Churain
3007
Beinn nan Imirean
2769
Beinn Donachain
2127
141
Cruachan Reservoir
Beinn a' Bhuiridh
2941
Falls of Cruachan
Cruachan Power Station
Stronmilchan
Edendonich
Kilchurn
Lochawe
Kinchrackine
Achnafalnich
Beinn na Sroine
B8077
B8074
A85
Tyndrum
Clifton
River Lochy
Lochan na Bi
Cononish
Lochdochart House
Loch Lubhair
Loch Dochart
Dalmally
Duncan Ban MacIntyre Monument
Fraoch Eilean Castle
Ardanaiseig
A819
Teatle Water
Beinn Bhalgairean
2085
Meall nan Tighearn
2423
3708
Ben Lui
3204
Beinn Dubhchraig
2132
Fiarach
A82
Crianlarich
BEN MORE
3852
3821
Stob Binnein
Cladich
Cladich River
Allt Fearna
Allt an Stacain
Lochan Shira
Upper Sonachan
B840
Glen Falloch
River Falloch
Falls of Falloch
Troisgeach
2407
Ben Glas
Beinn Chroin
3084
3099
Beinn Tulaichean
Monachyle
Inverlochlarig
Lochan Sron Mòr
Beinn Bhuidhe
3112
1804
Beinn Ghlas
Rob Roy's House
Allt na Lairige
Reservoir
Inverarnan
Glen Fyne
Tullich
Stuc Scardan
1599
2159
Clachan Hill
Glenfyne Lodge
Eagle's Falls
Maol Breac
2215
Ardlui
Stob a' Choin
2839
LOCH LOMOND AND THE TR
NATIONAL PARK
Lochan Dubh
1932
Kilblaan Burn
A83
BEN VORLICH
3093
837
Barr Mòr
Three Bridges
Clachan Farm
Loch Sloy
Cruinn Bheinn
1787
Dubh Loch
Cairndow
Binnein an Fhidhleir
Cadoonan
Ardkinglas Woodland
Inveruglas Water
133
Inveraray
Loch Shira
Dunderave Castle
3004
Ben Vane
Inveruglas
Inversnaid
Stronachlachar
Loch Katrine
Loch Arklet
B829
Loch Ard Forest
Inveraray Bell Tower
Inveraray Jail
A815
Glen Kinglas
Beinn an Lochain
3318
BEINN IME
PARK
1762
Cruachan
A83
Laglingarten
St. Catherines
Argyll
B839
2401
Stob an Eas
Rest and be thankful
B828
Frenich
Loch Tinker
Loch Chon
LOCH FYNE
ARGYLL
1854
Cruach nan Capull
2891
Ben Arthur
Succoth
Cruach Tairbeirt
1362
Cruinn a' Bheinn
2077
1675
Beinn Dubh
Mullach Coire a' Chuir
2098
Ben Donich
2777
Glen Croe Forest
A83
Arrochar
Tarbet
1070
Creagan an Eich
FOREST
Ardgartan
The Brack
A814
B838
Ardmay
3194
BEN LOMOND
Gleann Dubh
Duchray Water
Kinlochard
Creggans
Clachan Strachur
Strachur Bay
Lochgoilhead
Glen Donich
Cnoc Coinnich
2497
A82
Tombuidhe
Glenshuain
A886
2306
Beinn Lochain
Rob Roy's Cave
Beinn Bhreac
2233
QUEEN ELIZABETH FOREST PA
Beinn Uird
1957
Curra Lochain
2556
Beinn Bheula
Lochain nan Cnaimh
Douglas Water
Doune Hill
2408
Rowardennan
Inverbeg
LOCH ARD
Glenbranter
Lauder
1577
Cruach nan Capull
The Saddle 1704
BUTE
Loch Long
Loch Lomond
Rowardennan Forest
Craigbrack
2029
Beinn Bheag
Carrick Castle
1435
Clach Bheinn
Beinn a' Mhanaich
2328
Beinn Eich
2302
1514
Gualann
Cruach a' Bhuic
2084
Edentaggart
Glen Luss
Inchlonaig
1666
Portincaple
Beinn Chaorach
2339
Luss
Conic Hill
1175
Balmaha
Bernice
Beinn Mhor
2432
Creachan Mòr
2156
Garelochhead
DANGER AREA
Beinn Ruisg
1946
Aldochlay
Inchfad
Inchcailloch
Garadhban
Milton
B837
Meall Dubh
2103
Greenfield
126
A817
Buchanan Smithy
Drymen
Glenmassan
Beinn Ruadh
2178
Glen Finart Deer Farm
Lochan Ghlas Laoigh
Coulport
Auchenvennel
Loch Lomond
Kilmaronock Tower
Bridge
Ardentinny
Shandon
Inchmurrin
Inchmurrin Castle
Gartocharn
Benmore Botanic Garden
1798
Stronchullin Hill
Benmore Forest
Peaton
B833
Gare Loch
A814
B832
Dumfin
Loch Tarsan
Black Gates
Glenarn
Callendoun
Arden
A811
Balliemore
Puck's Glen
Gairletter
Clynder
The Hill House
A818
Caldarvan Loch
Glenlean
Rashfield
Linn Botanic Gardens
Cove Bay
Rosneath
Rhu
Auchendennan
Balloch Castle
Blairquhanan
B836
Invereck
Ardbeg
Kilmun Trail & Arboretum
Blairmore
Cove
Cove Conservation Park
HELENSBURGH
Craigendoran
Balloch
Mill of Haldane
Auchencarroch
Clachaig
A880
Kilmun
Holy Loch
Strone
Strone Point
Rosneath Point
Jamestown
DANGER AREA
Sandbank
Ardnadam
Kilcreggan
Alexandria
Motoring Memories
A815
A885
Hunter's Quay
126
12mins
30mins
A82
Bonhill
2005
Cruach nan Capull
Conwal Bird Garden
Loch Loskin
Kirn
Gourock
Fort Matilda
Customs & Excise
Geilston
Renton
A813
Glenstriven
DUNOON
Castle House
Dunoon Castle
20 mins
Ashton
Kempock Stone
Midton
Larkfield
Cloch Point
Levan
Braeside
A770
A78
GREENOCK
A8
PORT
Cardross
A814
A812
Castlehill
Newark
Townend
DUMBARTON
Black Linn Res
Silverton
Brucehill
Loch Humphrey

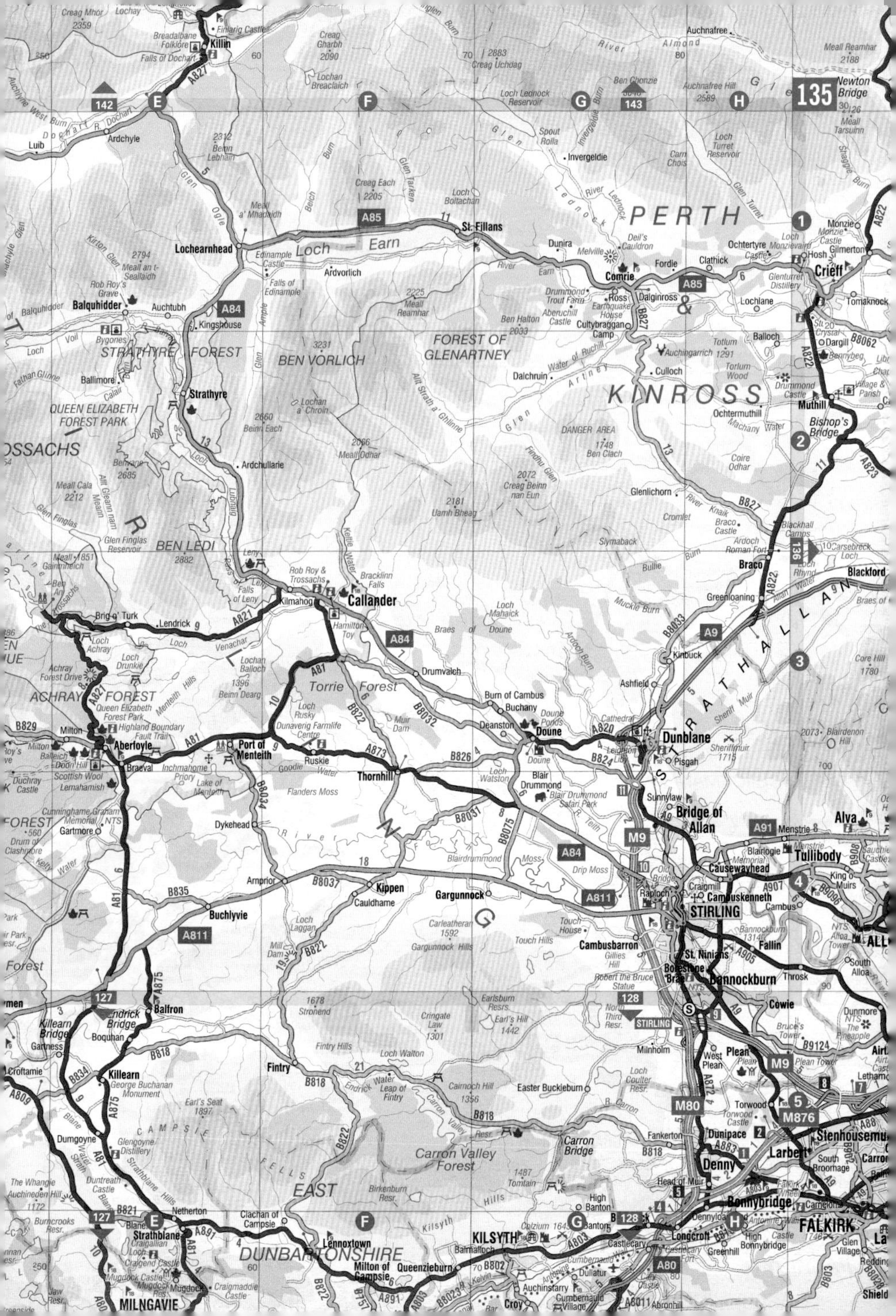

135
142
143
136
127
128
PERTH
&
KINROSS
STIRLING
EAST
DUNBARTONSHIRE
Killin
Finlarig Castle
Breadalbane Folklore
Falls of Dochart
Creag Mhor 2359
Lochay
Creag Gharbh 2090
Lochan Breaclaich
2883 Creag Uchdag
Loch Lednock Reservoir
Ben Chonzie
Auchnafree
Auchnafree Hill 2589
River Almond
Meall Reamhar 2188
Newton Bridge
Meall Tarsuinn
Loch Turret Reservoir
Carn Chois
Spout Rolla
Invergeldie
Glen Lednock
Glen Turret
Shaggie Burn
Luib
Ardchyle
Glen Dochart
Auchlyne West Burn
2312 Beinn Leabhain
Glen Ogle
Creag Each 2205
Glen Tarken
Loch Boltachan
Beich Burn
Meall a' Mhadaidh
Lochearnhead
St. Fillans
Loch Earn
Edinample Castle
Falls of Edinample
Ardvorlich
2225 Meall Reamhar
River Earn
Dunira
Melville
Deil's Cauldron
Comrie
Ross
Dalginross
Fordie
Clathick
Ochtertyre
Loch Monzievaird
Monzie
Monzie Castle
Gilmerton
Crieff
Hosh
Glenturret Distillery
Lochlane
Tomaknock
Drummond Trout Farm
Earthquake House
Aberuchill Castle
Cultybraggan Camp
Ben Halton 2033
FOREST OF GLENARTNEY
Auchingarrich
Totlum 1291
Torlum Wood
Balloch
Stuart Crystal
Dargill
Bennybeg
Drummond Castle
Muthill
Village & Parish
Bishop's Bridge
Ochtermuthill
Machany Water
Culloch
Dalchruin
Water of Ruchill
Glen Artney
Allt Strath a' Ghlinne
DANGER AREA
1748 Ben Clach
Findhu Glen
2072 Creag Beinn nan Eun
2181 Uamh Bheag
Coire Odhar
Glenlichorn
River Knaik
Cromlet
Braco Castle
Blackhall Camps
Ardoch Roman Fort
Braco
Carsebreck Loch
Loch Rhynd
Blackford
Slymaback
Bullie Burn
Greenloaning
Allan Water
Muckle Burn
Ardoch Burn
Kinbuck
Ashfield
STRATHALLAN
Core Hill 1780
Blairdenon Hill 2073
Sheriff Muir
Sheriffmuir 1715
Pisgah
Dunblane
Cathedral
Leighton Liby
Balquhidder
Auchtubh
Rob Roy's Grave
Kingshouse
Loch Voil
Bygones
STRATHYRE FOREST
Ballimore
Fathan Glinne
Calair
Strathyre
QUEEN ELIZABETH FOREST PARK
TROSSACHS
Kirton Glen
2794 Meall an t-Seallaidh
BEN VORLICH 3231
Lochan a' Chroin
2660 Beinn Each
2666 Meall Odhar
Ardchullarie
Loch Lubnaig
Benvane 2685
Meall Cala 2212
Allt Gleann nam Meann
Glen Finglas
Glen Finglas Reservoir
BEN LEDI 2882
Meall a' Chinn 1851 Gainmheich
Leny
Falls of Leny
Pass of Leny
Keltie Water
Rob Roy & Trossachs
Bracklinn Falls
Kilmahog
Callander
Hamilton Toy
Loch Mahaick
Braes of Doune
Ben A'an
The Trossachs
Brig o' Turk
Lendrick
Loch Achray
Loch Venachar
Loch Drunkie
Achray Forest Drive
ACHRAY FOREST
Lochan Balloch
1396 Beinn Dearg
Menteith Hills
Torrie Forest
Drumvaich
Burn of Cambus
Buchany
Doune Ponds
Deanston
Doune
Queen Elizabeth Forest Park
Highland Boundary Fault Trail
Loch Rusky
Dunaverig Farmlife Centre
Muir Dam
Milton
Aberfoyle
Braeval
Doon Hill
Scottish Wool
Lernahamish
Duchray Castle
Port of Menteith
Inchmahome Priory
Lake of Menteith
Ruskie
Goodie Water
Thornhill
Flanders Moss
Loch Watston
Blair Drummond
Blair Drummond Safari Park
Cunninghame Graham Memorial
Gartmore
Drum of Clashmore
Kelty Water
Dykehead
River Forth
Blairdrummond Moss
Drip Moss
R. Teith
Sunnylaw
Bridge of Allan
Menstrie
Alva
Blairlogie
Tullibody
Causewayhead
Craigmill
Cambuskenneth
Old Bridge
Raploch
STIRLING
King o' Muirs
Cambus
Arnprior
Kippen
Cauldhame
Gargunnock
Buchlyvie
Loch Laggan
Mill Dam
Carleatheran 1592
Gargunnock Hills
Touch House
Touch Hills
Cambusbarron
Gillies Hill
St. Ninians
Borestone Brae
Bannockburn
Bannockburn 1314
Fallin
Throsk
NTS Alloa Tower
South Alloa
Robert the Bruce Statue
North Third Resr.
Earlsburn Resrs.
Earl's Hill 1442
1678 Stronend
Cringate Law 1301
Fintry Hills
Loch Walton
Fintry
Endrick Water
Leap of Fintry
Cairnoch Hill 1356
Carron Valley Resr.
Carron Valley Forest
Carron Bridge
Easter Buckieburn
Loch Coulter Resr.
Milnholm
Cowie
Bruce's Tower
Dunmore
The Pineapple
Plean
West Plean
Plean Tower
Torwood
Torwood Castle
Fankerton
Dunipace
Denny
Larbert
Stenhousemuir
South Broomage
Head of Muir
High Banton
Banton
Bonnybridge
Dennyloanhead
Longcroft
High Bonnybridge
Greenhill
Castlecary
Castlecary Fort
FALKIRK
Camelon
Glen Village
Redding
Shieldhill
Killearn Bridge
Gartness
Endrick Bridge
Balfron
Boquhan
Killearn
George Buchanan Monument
Croftamie
Earl's Seat 1897
CAMPSIE FELLS
Dumgoyne
Blane Water
Strathblane Hills
Glengoyne Distillery
The Whangie
Auchineden Hill 1172
Duntreath Castle
Burncrooks Resr.
Strathblane
Craigallian Loch
Craigend Castle
Mugdock Castle
Mugdock Resr.
Craigmaddie Castle
Milngavie
Netherton
Clachan of Campsie
Lennoxtown
Milton of Campsie
Queenzieburn
Balmalloch
KILSYTH
Colzium 1643
Kilsyth Hills
1487 Tomtain
Birkenburn Resr.
Croy
Dullatur
Auchinstarry
Cumbernauld
Abronhill
Antonine Wall
A85
A84
A821
A81
A873
A811
A9
A822
A823
A827
A820
A91
A907
A905
A872
A883
A803
A891
A80
A809
A875
A88
B827
B8033
B8062
B822
B8032
B826
B824
B8031
B8075
B8034
B8037
B835
B829
B818
B834
B821
B802
B9124
B908
B8023
B757
B803
B816
M9
M80
M876
STIRLING

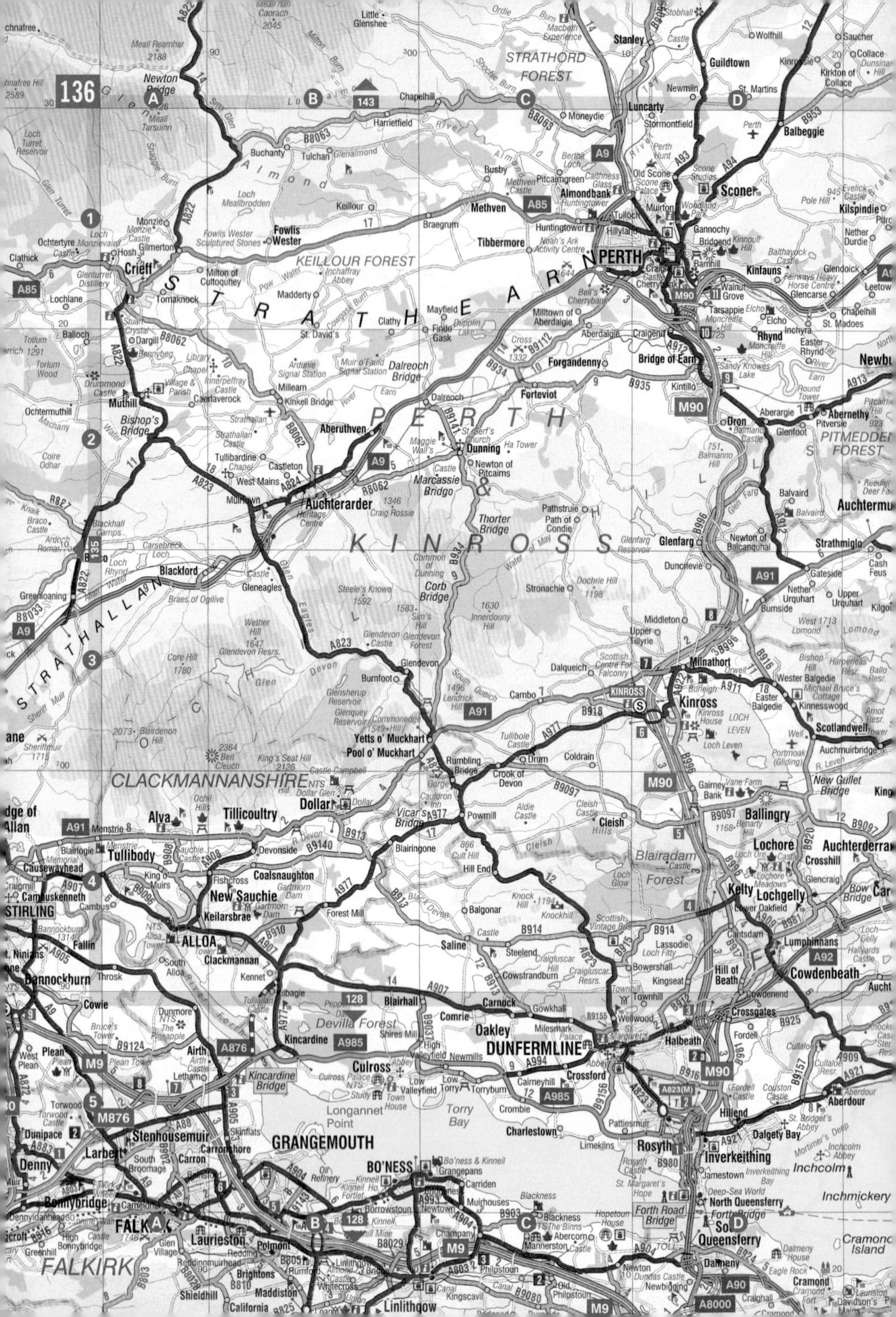
136
143
128
STRATHORD FOREST
KEILLOUR FOREST
STRATHEARN
PERTH & KINROSS
STRATHALLAN
CLACKMANNANSHIRE
PITMEDDEN FOREST
Devilla Forest
Blairadam Forest
FALKIRK
PERTH
STIRLING
ALLOA
DUNFERMLINE
GRANGEMOUTH
BO'NESS
FALKIRK
Newton Bridge
Little Glenshee
Chapelhill
Harrietfield
Moneydie
Stanley
Luncarty
Stormontfield
Guildtown
Wolfhill
Saucher
Collace
Kinrossie
Kirkton of Collace
St. Martins
Newmiln
Balbeggie
Buchanty
Tulchan
Glenalmond
Busby
Pitcairngreen
Almondbank
Huntingtower
Methven
Tibbermore
Keillour
Braegrum
Fowlis Wester
Monzie
Gilmerton
Crieff
Clathick
Ochtertyre
Hosh
Lochlane
Balloch
Tomaknock
Milton of Cultoquhey
Madderty
Mayfield
Clathy
Findo Gask
St. David's
Dargill
Muthill
Drummond Castle
Innerpeffray Castle
Caerlaverock
Millearn
Kinkell Bridge
Dalreoch Bridge
Ochtermuthill
Bishop's Bridge
Aberuthven
Dunning
Forteviot
Forgandenny
Bridge of Earn
Kintillo
Aberdalgie
Milltown of Aberdalgie
Craigend
Scone
Old Scone
Scone Palace
Muirton
Gannochy
Bridgend
Barnhill
Kinfauns
Kilspindie
Glendoick
Glencarse
Chapelhill
St. Madoes
Elcho
Rhynd
Inchyra
Walnut Grove
Tarsappie
Cherrybank
Craigie
Tullibardine
Castleton
West Mains
Muirtown
Auchterarder
Craig Rossie
Marcassie Bridge
Newton of Pitcairns
Pathstruie
Path of Condie
Thorter Bridge
Glenfarg
Dron
Aberargie
Abernethy
Glenfoot
Balvaird
Auchtermuchty
Strathmiglo
Newton of Balcanquhal
Duncrievie
Gateside
Braco
Blackford
Gleneagles
Greenloaning
Common of Dunning
Corb Bridge
Stronachie
Middleton
Upper Tillyrie
Milnathort
Kinross
Dalqueich
Glendevon
Burnfoot
Cambo
Yetts o' Muckhart
Pool o' Muckhart
Rumbling Bridge
Crook of Devon
Drum
Coldrain
Tullibole Castle
Scotlandwell
Kinnesswood
Wester Balgedie
Easter Balgedie
Auchmuirbridge
Loch Leven
Gairney Bank
Ballingry
Lochore
Crosshill
Auchterderran
Glencraig
Kelty
Lochgelly
Lumphinnans
Cowdenbeath
Bow Bridge
Dollar
Castle Campbell
Tillicoultry
Alva
Menstrie
Bridge of Allan
Causewayhead
Tullibody
Blairlogie
Devonside
Coalsnaughton
Fishcross
New Sauchie
Keilarsbrae
Cambuskenneth
Cambus
Fallin
St. Ninians
Bannockburn
Throsk
Clackmannan
Kennet
Cowie
Powmill
Vicar's Bridge
Blairingone
Hill End
Forest Mill
Balgonar
Saline
Steelend
Cowstrandburn
Knockhill
Bowershall
Kingseat
Hill of Beath
Townhill
Crossgates
Cowdenend
Halbeath
Wellwood
Gowkhall
Carnock
Oakley
Blairhall
Comrie
Milesmark
Kilbagie
Kincardine
Shires Mill
High Valleyfield
Newmills
Culross
Low Valleyfield
Low Torry
Torryburn
Cairneyhill
Crossford
Crombie
Charlestown
Limekilns
Pattiesmuir
Rosyth
Inverkeithing
Jamestown
North Queensferry
Dalgety Bay
Aberdour
Hillend
Fordell
Inchcolm
Inchmickery
Cramond Island
Queensferry
Dalmeny
Cramond
Plean
West Plean
Airth
Letham
Dunmore
Kincardine Bridge
Torwood
Dunipace
Denny
Larbert
Stenhousemuir
Carron
Carronshore
Skinflats
South Broomage
Longannet Point
Torry Bay
Grangepans
Carriden
Kinneil
Muirhouses
Blackness
Newtown
Borrowstoun
Champany
Bonnybridge
Camelon
Laurieston
Polmont
Redding
Reddingmuirhead
Brightons
Rumford
Maddiston
Whitecross
Linlithgow
Linlithgow Bridge
Philpstoun
Old Philpstoun
Kingscavil
California
Shieldhill
Greenhill
High Bonnybridge
Dennyloanhead
Newton
Newbigging
Dundas Castle
Forth Road Bridge
Forth Bridge
Hopetoun House
Abercorn
Mannerston
A9
A85
A822
A823
A824
A91
A93
A94
A912
A913
A977
A907
A905
A876
A985
A994
A904
A993
A803
A92
A909
A921
A90
A8000
A823(M)
M9
M90
M876
B8063
B8062
B934
B935
B9141
B9112
B8033
B827
B9097
B996
B918
B919
B913
B9140
B908
B910
B914
B915
B9037
B9155
B9156
B980
B903
B8029
B9080
B9124
B916
B920
B925
B981
B9157
B810
B825

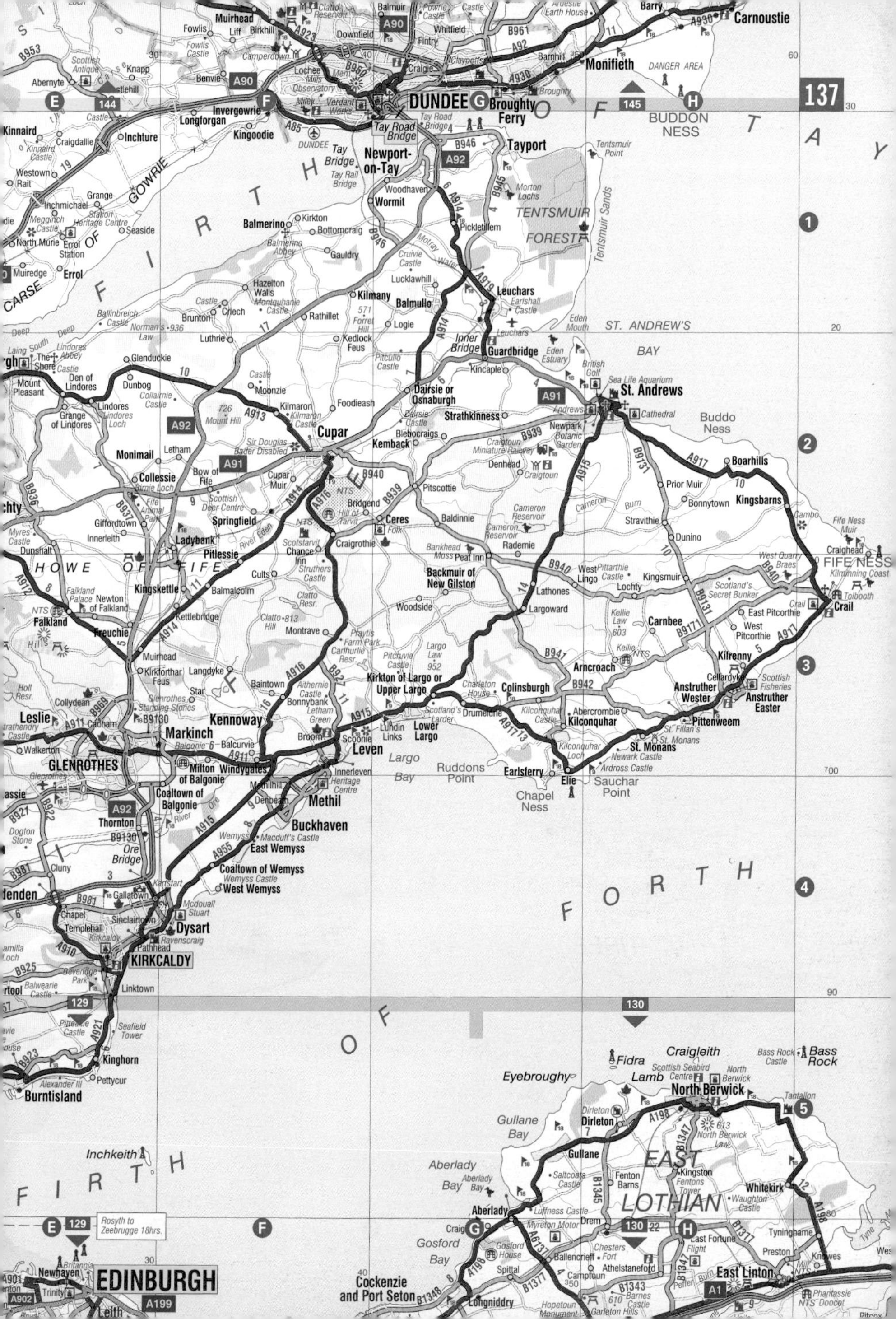

137
DUNDEE
Broughty Ferry
Carnoustie
Monifieth
Barry
BUDDON NESS
DANGER AREA
Muirhead
Fowlis
Liff
Birkhill
Downfield
Balmuir
Fintry
Whitfield
Camperdown
Lochee
Craigie
Benvie
Knapp
Abernyte
Invergowrie
Longforgan
Kingoodie
Inchture
Kinnaird
Craigdallie
Westown
Rait
Inchmichael
Grange
Megginch Castle
Seaside
North Muirie
Errol Station
Errol
Muiredge
CARSE OF GOWRIE
FIRTH OF TAY
Tay Road Bridge
Tay Bridge
Tay Rail Bridge
Newport-on-Tay
Tayport
Tentsmuir Point
Woodhaven
Wormit
Balmerino
Kirkton
Bottomcraig
Balmerino Abbey
Gauldry
Morton Lochs
TENTSMUIR FOREST
Tentsmuir Sands
Pickletillem
Cruivie Castle
Motray Water
Lucklawhill
Leuchars
Earlshall Castle
Hazelton Walls
Kilmany
Balmullo
Rathillet
Brunton
Criech
Logie
Luthrie
Kedlock Feus
Norman's Law
Ballinbreich Castle
Lindores Abbey
The Shore
Glenduckie
Den of Lindores
Mount Pleasant
Dunbog
Collairnie Castle
Grange of Lindores
Lindores
Lindores Loch
Moonzie
Kilmaron Castle
Foodieash
Mount Hill
Cupar
Inner Bridge
Guardbridge
Eden Estuary
Eden Mouth
ST. ANDREW'S BAY
British Golf
Sea Life Aquarium
St. Andrews
Cathedral
Kincaple
Dairsie or Osnaburgh
Dairsie Castle
Strathkinness
Blebocraigs
Kemback
Craigtoun Miniature Railway
Newpark Botanic Garden
Denhead
Craigtoun
Buddo Ness
Boarhills
Prior Muir
Bonnytown
Kingsbarns
Cambo
Fife Ness Muir
Craighead
FIFE NESS
Kilminning Coast
Monimail
Letham
Collessie
Birnie Loch
Bow of Fife
Cupar Muir
Sir Douglas Bader Disabled
Scottish Deer Centre
Fife Animal Park
Springfield
Giffordtown
Innerleith
Ladybank
Pitlessie
Myres Castle
Dunshalt
HOWE OF FIFE
Kingskettle
Falkland
Falkland Palace
Newton of Falkland
Freuchie
Kettlebridge
Balmalcolm
Cults
Scotstarvit
Chance Inn
Struthers Castle
Craigrothie
Bridgend
Hill of Tarvit
Ceres
Pitscottie
Baldinnie
Cameron Reservoir
Rademie
Bankhead Moss
Peat Inn
Backmuir of New Gilston
West Lingo
Pittarthie Castle
Lochty
Kingsmuir
Lathones
Largoward
Stravithie
Dunino
West Quarry Braes
Scotland's Secret Bunker
Crail
Tolbooth
East Pitcorthie
West Pitcorthie
Carnbee
Kellie Law
Kellie
Arncroach
Kilrenny
Cellardyke
Scottish Fisheries
Anstruther Wester
Anstruther Easter
Pittenweem
St. Monans
St. Fillan's
Newark Castle
Ardross Castle
Kilconquhar
Kilconquhar Loch
Abercrombie
Colinsburgh
Charleton House
Drumeldrie
Earlsferry
Elie
Chapel Ness
Sauchar Point
Ruddons Point
Largo Bay
Lower Largo
Lundin Links
Scotland's Larder
Kirkton of Largo or Upper Largo
Largo Law
Pitcruvie Castle
Woodside
Montrave
Praytis Farm Park
Carlhurlie Resr.
Clatto Resr.
Clatto Hill
Baintown
Aithernie Castle
Bonnybank
Letham Green
Broom
Scoonie
Leven
Innerleven
Methilhill
Methil
Denbeath
Buckhaven
Wemyss
Macduff's Castle
East Wemyss
Coaltown of Wemyss
Wemyss Castle
West Wemyss
Kennoway
Balcurvie
Windygates
Milton of Balgonie
Markinch
Balgonie
Coaltown of Balgonie
Muirhead
Kirkforthar Feus
Langdyke
Star
Glenrothes Standing Stones
Collydean
Leslie
Cadham
Walkerton
GLENROTHES
Holl Resr.
Thornton
River Ore
Dogton Stone
Ore Bridge
Cluny
Kirkstart
Gallatown
Chapel
Templehall
Sinclairtown
Dysart
Ravenscraig
Pathhead
KIRKCALDY
Mcdouall Stuart
Beveridge Park
Balwearie Castle
Linktown
Pitteadie Castle
Seafield Tower
Kinghorn
Pettycur
Burntisland
Alexander III
FIRTH OF FORTH
Inchkeith
Rosyth to Zeebrugge 18hrs.
Newhaven
Britannia
Trinity
EDINBURGH
Leith
Cockenzie and Port Seton
Gosford Bay
Gosford House
Craig
Aberlady Bay
Aberlady
Luffness Castle
Myreton Motor
Spittal
Longniddry
Ballencrieff
Chesters Fort
Camptoun
Athelstaneford
Drem
Hopetoun Monument
Garleton Hills
Barnes Castle
Gullane Bay
Gullane
Saltcoats Castle
Fenton Barns
Dirleton
Dirleton Castle
Eyebroughy
Fidra
Lamb
Craigleith
Scottish Seabird Centre
North Berwick
North Berwick Law
Bass Rock Castle
Bass Rock
Tantallon
EAST LOTHIAN
Kingston
Fentons Tower
Whitekirk
Waughton Castle
East Fortune Flight
Tyninghame
Preston
Knowes
East Linton
Phantassie NTS Doocot
Peffer Burn
Tyne
Pitcox

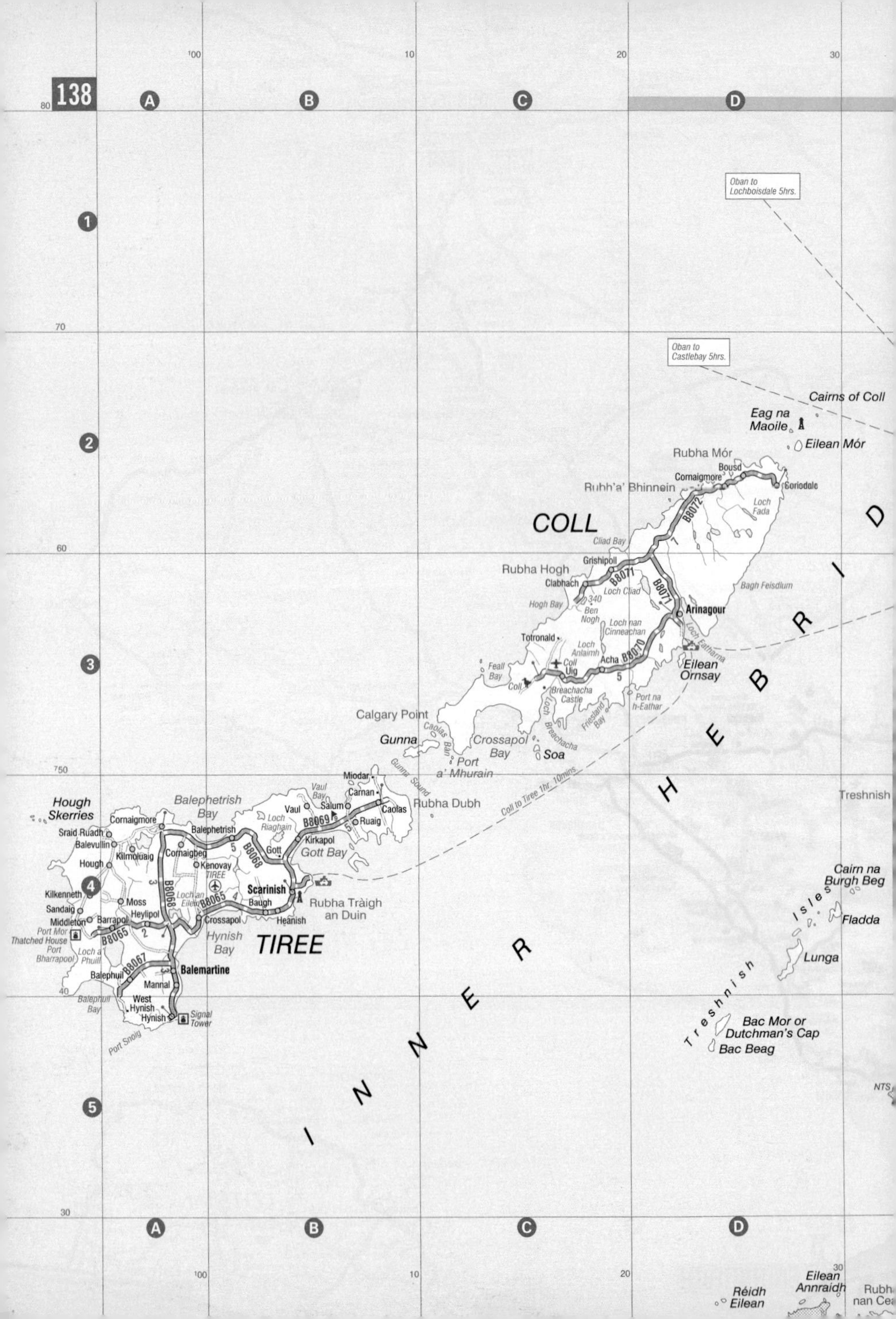

COLL

TIRE

INNER HEBRIDES

Treshnish Isles

Oban to Lochboisdale 5hrs.

Oban to Castlebay 5hrs.

Cairns of Coll

Eag na Maoile

Eilean Mór

Rubha Mór

Bousd

Cornaigmore

Sorisdale

Rubh'a' Bhinnein

Loch Fada

Cliad Bay

Grishipoll

Rubha Hogh

Clabhach

Loch Cliad

Bagh Feisdlum

340 Ben Nogh

Arinagour

Hogh Bay

Loch nan Cinneachan

Totronald

Loch Anlaimh

Acha

Coll Uig

Eilean Ornsay

Feall Bay

Coll

5

Breachacha Castle

Port na h-Eathar

Calgary Point

Caolas Bay

Gunna

Crossapol Bay

Soa

Breachacha

Friesland Bay

Port a' Mhurain

Gunna Sound

Treshnish

Miodar

Carnan

Coll to Tiree 1hr 10mins

Hough Skerries

Vaul Bay

Vaul

Salum

Rubha Dubh

Balephetrish Bay

Loch Riaghain

Ruaig

Caolas

Cornaigmore

Balephetrish

Kirkapol

Cairn na Burgh Beg

Sraid Ruadh

Cornaigbeg

Gott

Gott Bay

Fladda

Balevullin

Kilmoluaig

Kenovay

TIREE

Hough

Loch a' Eilein

Scarinish

Rubha Tràigh an Duin

Lunga

Kilkenneth

Moss

Baugh

Sandaig

Heylipol

Crossapol

Heanish

Middleton

Barrapol

Bac Mor or Dutchman's Cap

Port Mor

Thatched House

Loch a' Phuill

Hynish Bay

TIREE

Bac Beag

Port Bharrapol

2

Balephuil

Mannal

Balemartine

Balephuil Bay

West Hynish

Signal Tower

Port Snoig

NTS

Réidh Eilean

Eilean Annraidh

Rubha nan Cea

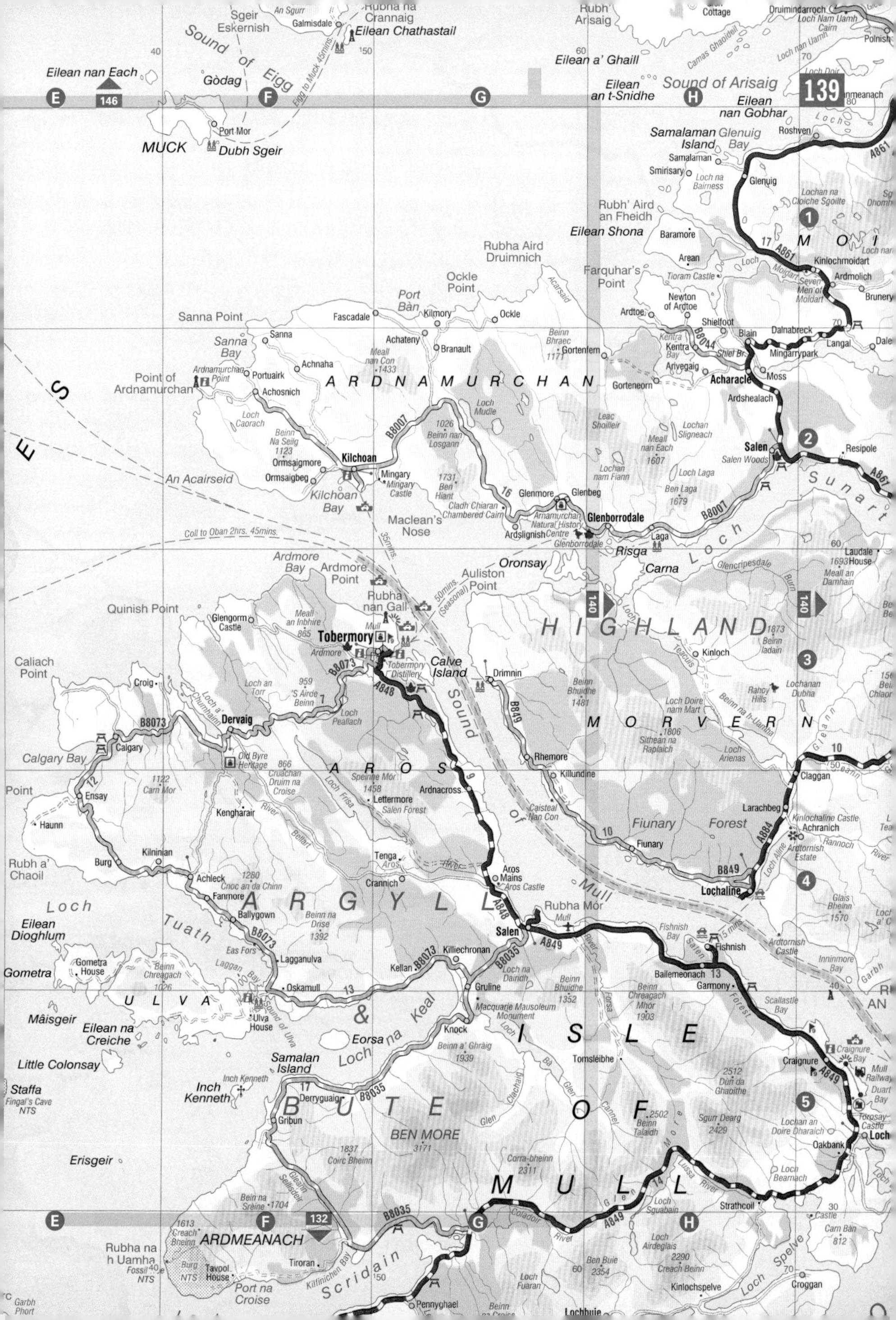
Sound of Eigg
Eilean Chathastail
Galmisdale
Sgeir Eskernish
Eilean nan Each
Gòdag
Egg to Muck 45mins.
146
MUCK
Port Mor
Dubh Sgeir
Eilean a' Ghaill
Sound of Arisaig
Eilean an t-Snidhe
Eilean nan Gobhar
Samalaman Island
Glenuig Bay
Samalaman
Smirisary
Glenuig
Roshven
Lochan na Bairness
Rubh' Aird an Fheidh
Eilean Shona
Baramore
Arean
Tioram Castle
Kinlochmoidart
Ardmolich
Brunery
Seven Men of Moidart
MOIDART
Rubha Aird Druimnich
Farquhar's Point
Ockle Point
Port Bàn
Newton of Ardtoe
Ardtoe
Shielfoot
Blain
Dalnabreck
Langal
Kentra Bay
Kentra
Arivegaig
Shiel Br.
Mingarrypark
Moss
Acharacle
Ardshealach
Salen
Salen Woods
Resipole
Loch Sunart
Sanna Point
Sanna Bay
Sanna
Fascadale
Kilmory
Ockle
Achateny
Branault
Meall nan Con 1433
Beinn Bhraec 1171
Gortenfern
Gorteneorn
Point of Ardnamurchan
Ardnamurchan Point
Portuairk
Achnaha
Achosnich
ARDNAMURCHAN
Loch Caorach
Beinn Na Seilg 1123
Ormsaigmore
Ormsaigbeg
Kilchoan
Kilchoan Bay
Mingary
Mingary Castle
An Acairseid
Loch Mudle
Beinn nan Losgann 1026
Ben Hiant 1731
Leac Shoilleir
Lochan Sligneach
Meall nan Each 1607
Lochan nam Fiann
Loch Laga
Ben Laga 1679
Glenmore
Glenbeg
Cladh Chiaran Chambered Cairn
Ardnamurchan Natural History Centre
Ardslignish
Glenborrodale
Laga
Maclean's Nose
Coll to Oban 2hrs. 45mins.
Risga
Carna
Oronsay
Auliston Point
Glencripesdale
Laudale House
Meall an Damhain 1693
Ardmore Bay
Ardmore Point
Rubha nan Gall
Quinish Point
Glengorm Castle
Meall an Inbhire 865
Tobermory
Ardmore
Tobermory Distillery
Calve Island
Drimnin
140
HIGHLAND
Beinn Iadain 1873
Kinloch
Caliach Point
Croig
Loch an Torr
'S Airde Beinn 959
Loch Peallach
Dervaig
Loch a' Chumhainn
Calgary
Calgary Bay
Old Byre Heritage
Cruachan Druim na Croise 866
Sound of Mull
Beinn Bhuidhe 1481
Loch Doire nam Mart
MORVERN
Sithean na Raplaich 1806
Rahoy Hills
Lochanan Dubha
Loch Teacuis
Loch Arienas
Rhemore
Killundine
Claggan
Larachbeg
Kinlochaline Castle
Achranich
Ardtornish Estate
Fiunary Forest
Fiunary
Caisteal Nan Con
Lochaline
Ensay
Carn Mor 1122
Haunn
Kengharair
AROS
Speinne Mòr 1458
Lettermore
Salen Forest
Loch Frisa
Ardnacross
Rubh a' Chaoil
Burg
Kilninian
Achleck
Cnoc an da Chinn 1260
Tenga
Crannich
Aros Mains
Aros Castle
Rubha Mòr
Salen
Glais Bheinn 1570
Fishnish Bay
Fishnish
Ardtornish Castle
Inninmore Bay
Loch Tuath
Eilean Dioghlum
Fanmore
Ballygown
ARGYLL
Beinn na Drise 1392
Eas Fors
Lagganulva
Killiechronan
Kellan
Loch na Dairidh
Gruline
Gometra
Gometra House
Beinn Chreagach 1026
Laggan Bay
Oskamull
Bailemeanach
Garmony
Salen Forest
Beinn Bhuidhe 1352
Beinn Chreagach Mhor 1903
Scallastle Bay
ULVA
Ulva House
Sound of Ulva
Macquarie Mausoleum Monument
Màisgeir
Eilean na Creiche
Loch na Keal
Eorsa
Knock
ISLE
Little Colonsay
Samalan Island
Beinn a' Ghràig 1939
Tomsléibhe
Craignure
Craignure Bay
Mull Railway
Duart Bay
Dùn da Ghaoithe 2512
Staffa
Fingal's Cave NTS
Inch Kenneth
Derryguaig
Gribun
BUTE
OF
Beinn Talaidh 2502
Sgurr Dearg 2429
Lochan an Doire Dharaich
Torosay Castle
Oakbank
BEN MORE 3171
Coirc Bheinn 1837
Corra-bheinn 2311
Glen Clachaig
Erisgeir
Glen Seilisdeir
Glen More
Lussa River
Loch Bearnach
MULL
Bein na Sreine 1704
Loch Squabain
Strathcoil
Castle
Carn Bàn 812
Creach Bheinn 1613
ARDMEANACH
132
Coladoir River
Loch Airdeglais
Creach Beinn 2290
Ben Buie 2354
Loch Spelve
Rubha na h Uamha
Fossil Tree NTS
Burg NTS
Tavool House
Tiroran
Port na Croise
Loch Scridain
Kilfinichen Bay
Pennyghael
Loch Fuaran
Kinlochspelve
Croggan
Lochbuie

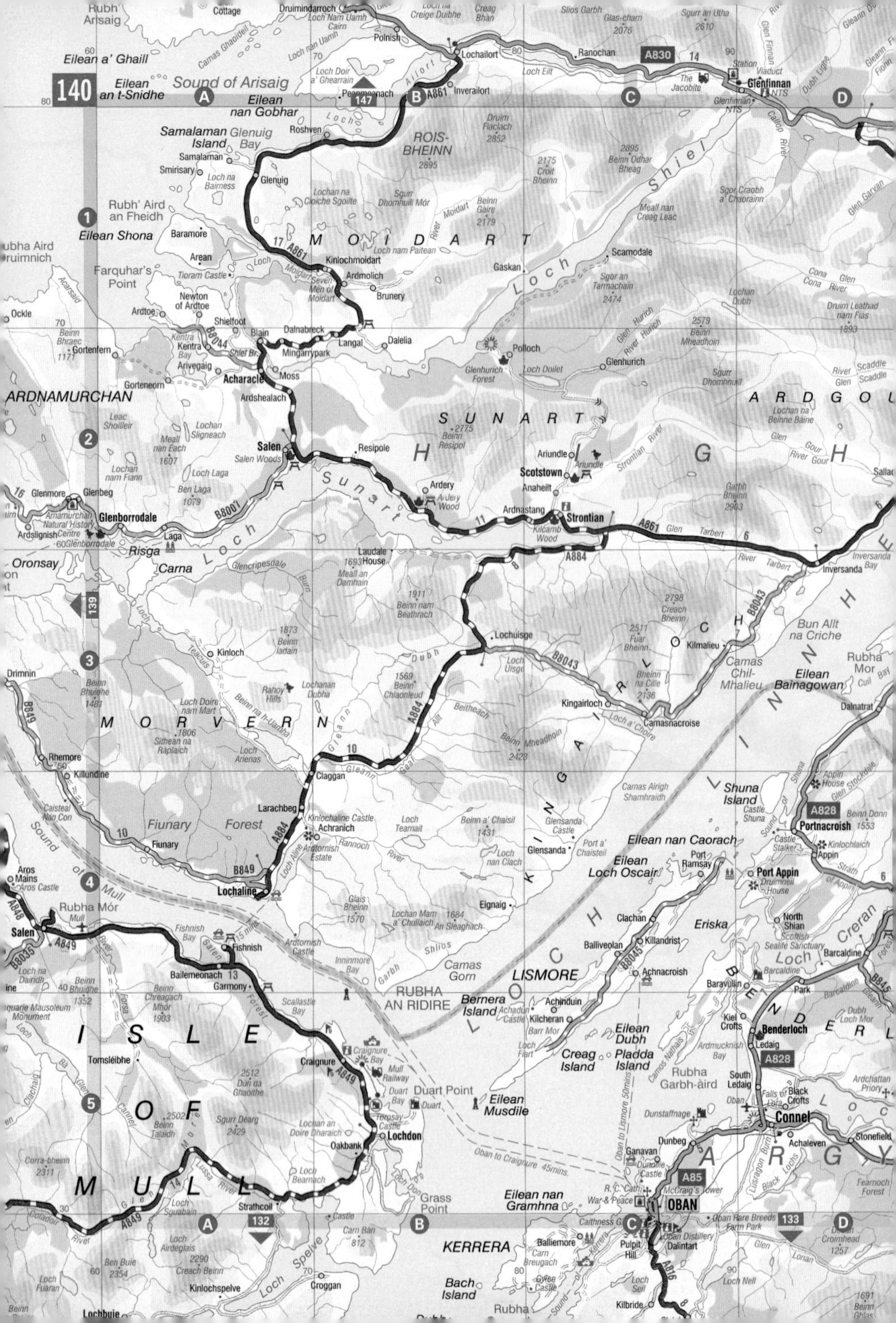
140
Sound of Arisaig
Eilean a' Ghaill
Eilean an t-Snidhe
Eilean nan Gobhar
Rubh' Arisaig
Cottage
Druimindarroch
Loch Nam Uamh Cairn
Loch nan Uamh
Polnish
Loch na Creige Duibhe
Creag Bhàn
Slios Garbh
Glas-charn 2076
Sgurr an Utha 2610
Lochailort
Ranochan
Loch Eilt
A830
Glenfinnan
Station
Viaduct
The Jacobite
NTS
Glen Finnan
Loch Doir a' Ghearrain
147
Peanmeanach
Inverailort
A861
Samalaman Island
Glenuig Bay
Samalaman
Smirisary
Roshven
Glenuig
Loch na Bairness
ROIS-BHEINN 2895
Druim Fiaclach 2852
2175 Croit Bheinn
2895 Beinn Odhar Bheag
Callop River
Dubh Lighe
Rubh' Aird an Fheidh
Eilean Shona
Lochan na Cloiche Sgoilte
Sgurr Dhomhuill Mór
Beinn Gaire 2179
River Moidart
Loch Shiel
Sgor Craobh a' Chaorainn
Meall nan Creag Leac
Glen Garvan
Baramore
M O I D A R T
Loch nam Paitean
Rubha Aird Druimnich
Arean
Tioram Castle
Farquhar's Point
Newton of Ardtoe
Ardtoe
Ockle
Kinlochmoidart
Ardmolich
Brunery
Seven Men of Moidart
Gaskan
Scamodale
Sgor an Tarmachain 2474
Cona Glen
Cona River
Lochan Dubh
Druim Leathad nam Fias 1893
Acarsaid
Beinn Bhraec 1171
Gortenfern
Kentra
Kentra Bay
Shielfoot
B8044
Blain
Dalnabreck
Langal
Dalelia
Arivegaig
Shiel Br.
Mingarrypark
Moss
Acharacle
Gorteneorn
Polloch
Glenhurich Forest
Loch Doilet
Glen Hurich
River Hurich
Glenhurich
2579 Beinn Mheadhoin
Sgurr Dhomhnuill
River Scaddle
Glen Scaddle
ARDNAMURCHAN
Ardshealach
Leac Shoilleir
Lochan Sligneach
Meall nan Each 1607
SUNART
2775 Beinn Resipol
ARDGOUR
Lochan na Beinne Bàine
Salen
Salen Woods
Resipole
Ariundle
Scotstown
Anaheilt
Strontian River
Glen Gour
River Gour
Lochan nam Fiann
Loch Laga
Ben Laga 1079
Loch Sunart
Ardery
Ardery Wood
Garbh Bheinn 2903
Glenmore
Glenbeg
Glenborrodale
Amamurchan Natural History Centre
Ardslignish
Laga
B8001
Ardnastang
Strontian
Kilcamb Wood
A861
Glen Tarbert
Risga
Carna
Oronsay
Glencripesdale
Laudale House
1693 Meall an Damhain
A884
River Tarbert
Inversanda
Inversanda Bay
139
Loch Teacuis
1911 Beinn nam Beathrach
2798 Creach Bheinn
B8043
Bun Allt na Criche
Kinloch
1873 Beinn Iadain
Lochuisge
Loch Uisge
2511 Fuar Bheinn
Kilmalieu
Camas Chil-Mhalieu
Rubha Mor
Eilean Bainagowan
Cuil Bay
Drimnin
Beinn Bhuidhe 1481
Rahoy Hills
Lochanan Dubha
1569 Beinn Chlaonleud
Bheinn na Cille 2136
Kingairloch
Camasnacroise
Loch a' Choire
Dalnatrat
Loch Doire nam Mart
B849
M O R V E R N
Beinn na h-Uamha
Gleann Dubh
Beitheach
1806 Sithean na Raplaich
Loch Arienas
Beinn Mheadhoin 2423
K I N G A I R L O C H
L I N N H E
Rhemore
Killundine
Claggan
Gleann Geal
Camas Airigh Shamhraidh
Shuna Island
Castle Shuna
Sound of Shuna
Appin House
Glen Stockdale
A828
Beinn Donn 1553
Portnacroish
Kinlochlaich
Castle Stalker
Appin
Caisteal Nan Con
Larachbeg
Kinlochaline Castle
Achranich
Loch Tearnait
Beinn a' Chaisil 1431
Glensanda Castle
Fiunary Forest
Fiunary
Ardtornish Estate
Rannoch River
Loch nan Clach
Glensanda
Port a' Chaisteil
Eilean nan Caorach
Eilean Loch Oscair
Port Ramsay
Port Appin
Druimneil House
Strath of Appin
Sound of Mull
Aros Mains
Aros Castle
Lochaline
Loch Aline
Glais Bheinn 1570
Lochan Mam a' Chullaich
1684 An Sleaghach
Eignaig
Clachan
North Shian
Scottish Sealife Sanctuary
Loch Creran
Barcaldine
Rubha Mór
Salen
A848
A849
B8035
Fishnish Bay
Fishnish
Ardtornish Castle
Inninmore Bay
Garbh Shlios
Balliveolan
Killandrist
B8045
Eriska
Loch na Dairidh
Beinn Bhuidhe 1352
Bailemeonach
Garmony
Camas Gorn
RUBHA AN RIDIRE
LISMORE
Achnacroish
Baravullin
Barcaldine
Park
B845
Macquarie Mausoleum Monument
Beinn Chreagach Mhòr 1903
Forsa
Scallastle Bay
Bernera Island
Achinduin
Kilcheran
Barr Mor
Kiel Crofts
Benderloch
Ledaig
Dubh Loch Mor
BENDERLOCH
I S L E
O F
M U L L
Tomsléibhe
Craignure
Craignure Bay
Mull Railway
Duart Bay
Duart
Duart Point
Eilean Dubh
Pladda Island
Creag Island
Loch Fiart
Camas Nathais
Ardmucknish Bay
Rubha Garbh-àird
A828
South Ledaig
Falls of Lora
Black Crofts
Ardchattan Priory
2512 Dùn da Ghaoithe
Eilean Musdile
Dunstaffnage
Connel
2502 Beinn Talaidh
Sgurr Dearg 2429
Lochan an Doire Dharaich
Torosay Castle
Lochdon
Oakbank
Dunbeg
Achaleven
Stonefield
Corra-bheinn 2311
Ganavan
Dunollie Castle
A85
Oban to Craignure 45mins.
Oban to Lismore 50mins
Lusragan Burn
Black Lochs
Fearnoch Forest
A R G Y L L
Loch Beannach
Loch Don
Grass Point
R. C. Cath.
War & Peace
McCaig's Tower
OBAN
Eilean nan Gramhna
Glen Lussa
Lussa River
A849
Loch Sguabain
Strathcoil
132
Coladoir River
Caithness Glass
Oban Rare Breeds Farm Park
Oban Distillery
133
Dalintart
Doire Croimhead 1257
Loch Airdeglais
2290 Creach Beinn
Ben Buie 2354
Carn Ban 812
Loch Spelve
Balliemore
Carn Breugach
Pulpit Hill
KERRERA
Gylen Castle
A816
Loch Nell
Loch Fuaran
Kinlochspelve
Croggan
Bach Island
Loch Seil
Kilbride
Lochbuie
1691 Beinn Ghlas

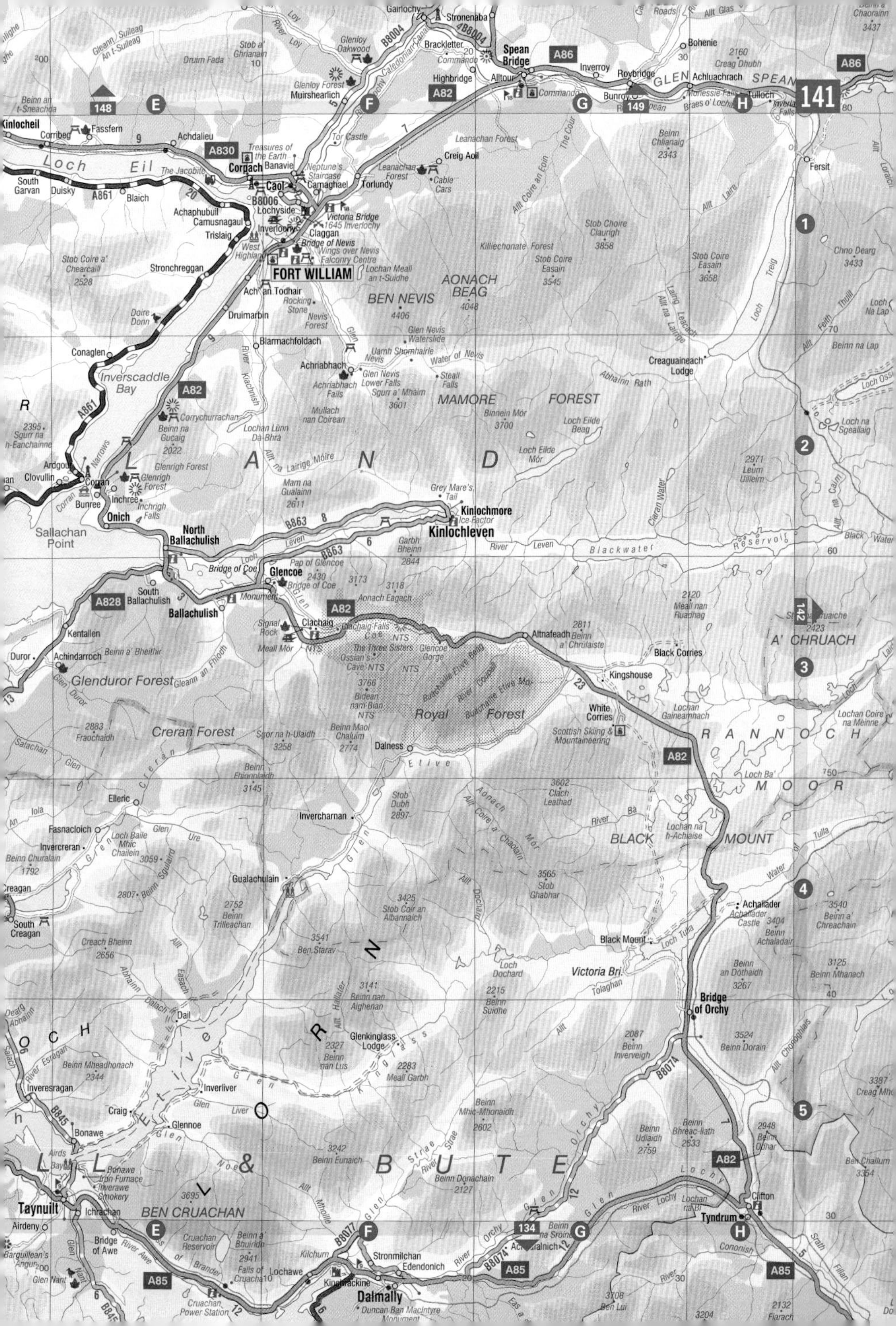
141
Gairlochy
Stronenaba
B8004
Spean Bridge
A86
Bohenie
Allt Glas
Chaorainn
3437
Gleann Suileag
An t-Suileag
Stob a' Ghrianain
Druim Fada
River Loy
Glenloy Oakwood
Glenloy Forest
Muirshearlich
Brackletter
Commando
Highbridge
A82
Alltour
Commando
Inverroy
Roybridge
Achluachrach
2160
Creag Dhubh
GLEN SPEAN
Bunroy
Monessie Falls
Braes o' Lochaber
Tulloch
Inverlair Falls
Beinn an t-Sneachda
148
E
F
G
149
H
Kinlocheil
Corribeg
Fassfern
Achdalieu
A830
Loch Eil
Treasures of the Earth
Corpach
Banavie
Neptune's Staircase
Caol
Camaghael
Torlundy
Tor Castle
Leanachan Forest
Creig Aoil
Cable Cars
The Jacobite
South Garvan
Duisky
A861
Blaich
B8006
Lochyside
Victoria Bridge
1645 Inverlochy
Achaphubuil
Camusnagaul
Trislaig
Inverlochy
Claggan
Bridge of Nevis
Wings over Nevis
Falconry Centre
West Highland
FORT WILLIAM
Lochan Meall an t-Suidhe
Stob Coire a' Chearcaill
2528
Stronchreggan
Ach an Todhair
Rocking Stone
Nevis Forest
Glen Nevis
BEN NEVIS
4406
AONACH BEAG
4048
Stob Choire Claurigh
3858
Killiechonate Forest
Stob Coire Easain
3545
Stob Coire Easain
3658
Beinn Chlianaig
2343
Fersit
Chno Dearg
3433
Loch Treig
Loch Na Lap
Beinn na Lap
Doire Donn
Druimarbin
Blarmachfoldach
Glen Nevis Waterslide
Uamh Shomhairle
Water of Nevis
Achriabhach
Glen Nevis Lower Falls
Achriabhach Falls
Steall Falls
Sgurr a' Mhaim
3601
Conaglen
Inverscaddle Bay
A82
River Kiachnish
Creaguaineach Lodge
Abhainn Rath
MAMORE FOREST
Binnein Mòr
3700
Loch Eilde Beag
Loch Eilde Mòr
Loch Ossian
Loch na Sgeallaig
A861
Corrychurrachan
Beinn na Gucaig
2022
Mullach nan Coirean
Lochan Lùnn Dà-Bhrà
2395
Sgurr na h-Eanchainne
Ardgour
Clovullin
Corran Narrows
Corran
Bunree
Inchree
Glenrigh Forest
Inchrigh Falls
Onich
Sallachan Point
Mam na Gualainn
2611
A N D
2971
Leum Uilleim
Ciaran Water
Grey Mare's Tail
Kinlochmore
Ice Factor
Kinlochleven
B863
North Ballachulish
Garbh Bheinn
2844
River Leven
Blackwater Reservoir
Black Water
Bridge of Coe
Glencoe
Pap of Glencoe
2430
3173
3118
Aonach Eagach
A828
South Ballachulish
Ballachulish
Monument
A82
2120
Meall nan Ruadhag
142
Stob na Cruaiche
2423
A' CHRUACH
Kentallen
Signal Rock
Clachaig
Clachaig Falls
Meall Mòr
NTS
The Three Sisters
Glencoe Gorge
Ossian's Cave
Altnafeadh
2811
Beinn a' Chrùlaiste
Black Corries
Duror
Achindarroch
Beinn a' Bheithir
Glenduror Forest
Gleann an Fhiodh
3766
Bidean nam Bian
Buachaille Etive Beag
River Coupall
Buachaille Etive Mòr
Royal Forest
Kingshouse
White Corries
Scottish Skiing & Mountaineering
Lochan Gaineamhach
Lochan Coire na Meinne
RANNOCH MOOR
2883
Fraochaidh
Creran Forest
Sgor na h-Ulaidh
3258
Beinn Maol Chaluim
2774
Dalness
Etive
A82
Loch Ba'
Beinn Fhionnlaidh
3145
Elleric
3602
Clach Leathad
Aonach Mòr
River Bà
Lochan na h-Achlaise
BLACK MOUNT
Fasnacloich
Invercreran
Loch Baile Mhic Chailein
Glen Ure
3059
Invercharnan
Stob Dubh
2897
Beinn Churalain
1792
Creagan
2807
Beinn Sgulaird
Gualachulain
3565
Stob Ghabhar
Water of Tulla
2752
Beinn Trilleachan
3425
Stob Coir an Albannaich
Achallader
Achallader Castle
3404
Beinn Achaladair
3540
Beinn a' Chreachain
South Creagan
Creach Bheinn
2656
3541
Ben Starav
Black Mount
Loch Tulla
Loch Dochard
Victoria Bri.
Tolaghan
Abhainn Dalach
3141
Beinn nan Aighenan
2215
Beinn Suidhe
Beinn an Dòthaidh
3267
3125
Beinn Mhanach
Bridge of Orchy
Dail
Glenkinglass Lodge
2327
Beinn nan Lus
2087
Beinn Inverveigh
3524
Beinn Dorain
River Esragan
Beinn Mheadhonach
2344
2283
Meall Garbh
B8074
Allt Chonoghlais
3387
Creag Mhor
Inveresragan
Inverliver
Glen Liver
Beinn Mhic-Mhonaidh
2602
Glen Orchy
Craig
B845
Bonawe
Glennoe
Glen Noe
Beinn Udlaidh
2759
Beinn Bhreac-liath
2633
2948
Beinn Odhar
Airds Bay
Bonawe Iron Furnace
Inverawe Smokery
3242
Beinn Eunaich
Glen Strae
River Strae
A82
Ben Challum
3354
3695
BEN CRUACHAN
Beinn Donachain
2127
River Lochy
Lochan na Bì
Clifton
Tyndrum
Taynuilt
Ichrachan
Airdeny
Cruachan Reservoir
Beinn a' Bhuiridh
2941
Falls of Cruachan
Allt Mhoille
B8077
Beinn na Sròine
134
Achrainalnich
Bridge of Awe
River Awe
Pass of Brander
Kilchurn
Stronmilchan
Edendonich
River Orchy
Cononish
A85
Barguillean's Angus
Glen Nant
A85
Lochawe
Kinchrackine
Dalmally
Duncan Ban MacIntyre Monument
3708
Ben Lui
3204
2132
Fiarach
Strath Fillan
A85
Cruachan Power Station
A R G Y L L & B U T E
L O C H A B E R
1
2
3
4
5

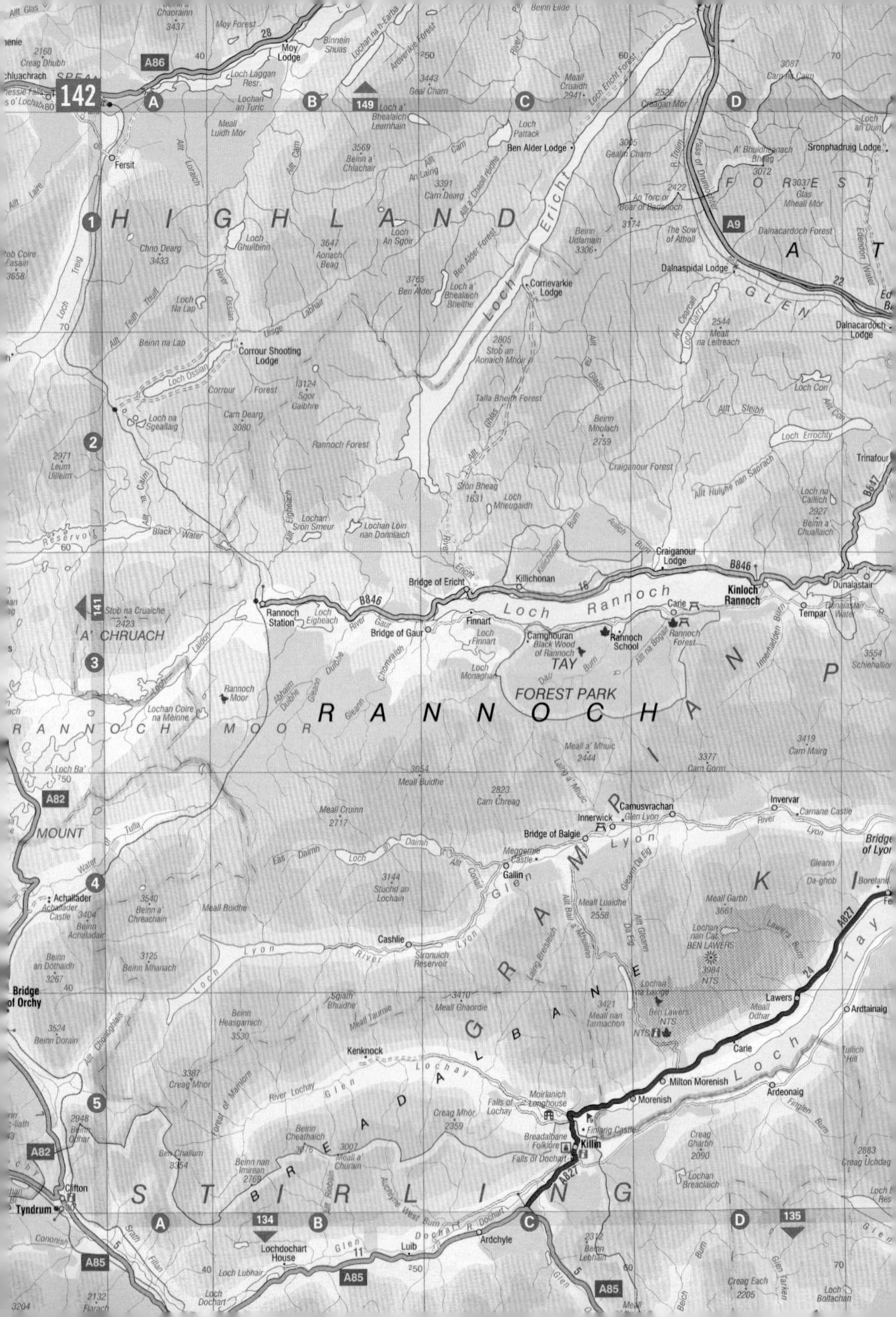

142
149
141
134
135
A
B
C
D
1
2
3
4
5
H I G H L A N D
R A N N O C H
M O O R
G R A M P I A N
B R E A D A L B A N E
S T I R L I N G
F O R E S T
A T
Chaorainn
3437
Moy Forest
28
Moy Lodge
Binnein Shuas
Lochan na h-Earba
Ardverikie Forest
Beinn Eilde
River Pattack
Loch Ericht Forest
2160
Creag Dhubh
A86
40
Loch Laggan Resr.
Lochan an Turic
3443
Geal Charn
Meall Cruaidh
2941
2522
Creagan Mór
3087
Carn na Caim
70
Loch a' Bhealaich Leamhain
Loch Pattack
Ben Alder Lodge
3005
Geal-Charn
Pass of Drumochter
A' Bhuidheanach Bheag
3072
Sronphadruig Lodge
Loch an Duin
Fersit
Meall Luidh Mór
Allt Loraich
Allt Cam
3569
Beinn a' Chlachair
An Lairig
3391
Carn Dearg
Allt a' Chaoil-reidhe
Loch Ericht
2422
An Torc or Boar of Badenoch
3037
Glas Mheall Mór
A9
Dalnacardoch Forest
Edendon Water
Allt Laire
Chno Dearg
3433
Loch Ghuilbinn
3647
Aonach Beag
Loch An Sgòir
Ben Alder Forest
3174
Beinn Udlamain
3306
The Sow of Atholl
Dalnaspidal Lodge
22
Loch Treig
Stob Coire Fasain
3658
Loch Na Lap
River Ossian
3765
Ben Alder
Loch a' Bhealaich Bheithe
Corrievarkie Lodge
Loch Garry
An Cearcall
2544
Meall na Leitreach
GLEN
Dalnacardoch Lodge
Allt Feith Thuill
Labhair
Uisge
Beinn na Lap
Corrour Shooting Lodge
Loch Ossian
Corrour
Forest
3124
Sgor Gaibhre
2805
Stob an Aonaich Mhóir
Allt na Glaise
Loch Con
Allt Con
Carn Dearg
3080
Loch na Sgeallaig
Talla Bheith Forest
Allt Sleibh
Beinn Mholach
2759
Loch Errochty
Rannoch Forest
Allt Ghlas
Trinafour
2971
Leum Uilleim
Allt na Cailm
Craiganour Forest
Allt Hulyhe nan Saorach
B847
Sròn Bheag
1631
Loch Mheugaidh
Loch na Caillich
2927
Beinn a' Chuallaich
Allt Eigheach
Lochan Sròn Smeur
Lochan Lòin nan Donnlaich
Reservoir
60
Black Water
River Ericht
Killichonan Burn
Aulich Burn
Craiganour Lodge
B846
Bridge of Ericht
Killichonan
16
Loch Rannoch
Kinloch Rannoch
Dunalastair
Stob na Cruaiche
2423
A' CHRUACH
Rannoch Station
Loch Eigheach
River Gaur
Bridge of Gaur
Finnart
Carie
Tempar
Dunalastair Water
Loch Finnart
Camghouran
Black Wood of Rannoch
Rannoch School
Allt na Bogair
Rannoch Forest
Innerhadden Burn
3554
Schiehallion
Loch Laidon
Rannoch Moor
Abhainn Duibhe
Gleann Duibhe
Gleann Chomraidh
Loch Monaghan
TAY
Dall Burn
FOREST PARK
Lochan Coire na Mèinne
Meall a' Mhuic
2444
3419
Carn Mairg
Loch Ba'
750
3054
Meall Buidhe
Lairig a' Mhuic
3377
Carn Gorm
A82
2823
Carn Chreag
Meall Cruinn
2717
Camusvrachan
Innerwick
Glen Lyon
Invervar
Carnane Castle
River Lyon
MOUNT
Tulla
Bridge of Balgie
Bridge of Lyon
Water
Eas Daimh
Loch an Daimh
Meggernie Castle
Gallin
Allt Conait
Gleann Da Eig
Gleann Da-ghob
Boreland
Achallader
Achallader Castle
3540
Beinn a' Chreachain
3404
Beinn Achaladair
Meall Buidhe
3144
Stùchd an Lochain
Meall Luaidhe
2558
Meall Garbh
3661
Lochan nan Cat
BEN LAWERS
Lawers Burn
A827
Tay
Allt Bail a' Mhuilinn
Allt Gleann Da Eig
Cashlie
Stronuich Reservoir
Loch Lyon
River Lyon
Lairig Breisleich
Beinn an Dòthaidh
3267
3125
Beinn Mhanach
3984
NTS
24
Lawers
Bridge of Orchy
40
Sgiath Bhuidhe
3410
Meall Ghaordie
3421
Meall nan Tarmachan
Lochan na Lairige
Ben Lawers NTS
Meall Odhar
Ardtainaig
3524
Beinn Dorain
Beinn Heasgarnich
3530
Meall Taurnie
NTS
Carie
Tullich Hill
Allt Chonoghlais
Kenknock
Loch Tay
3387
Creag Mhór
Forest of Mamlorn
River Lochay
Glen Lochay
Milton Morenish
Morenish
Ardeonaig
Moirlanich Longhouse
Falls of Lochay
Creag Mhór
2359
Fingfen Burn
2948
Beinn Odhar
Beinn Cheathaich
3076
3007
Meall a' Churain
Finlarig Castle
Breadalbane Folklore
Killin
Falls of Dochart
Creag Gharbh
2090
2883
Creag Uchdag
Ben Challum
3354
Beinn nan Imirean
2769
Allt Riobain
Auchlyne West Burn
A827
Lochan Breaclaich
Clifton
Tyndrum
Loch Res
Cononish
Strath Fillan
A85
5
R. Dochart
Glen Dochart
Ardchyle
2312
Beinn Lebhain
Lochdochart House
Luib
11
250
40
Loch Lubhair
A85
Glen Ogle
60
Beich Burn
Glen Tarken
Creag Each
2205
70
2132
Fiarach
3204
Loch Dochart
Meall
Loch Boltachan

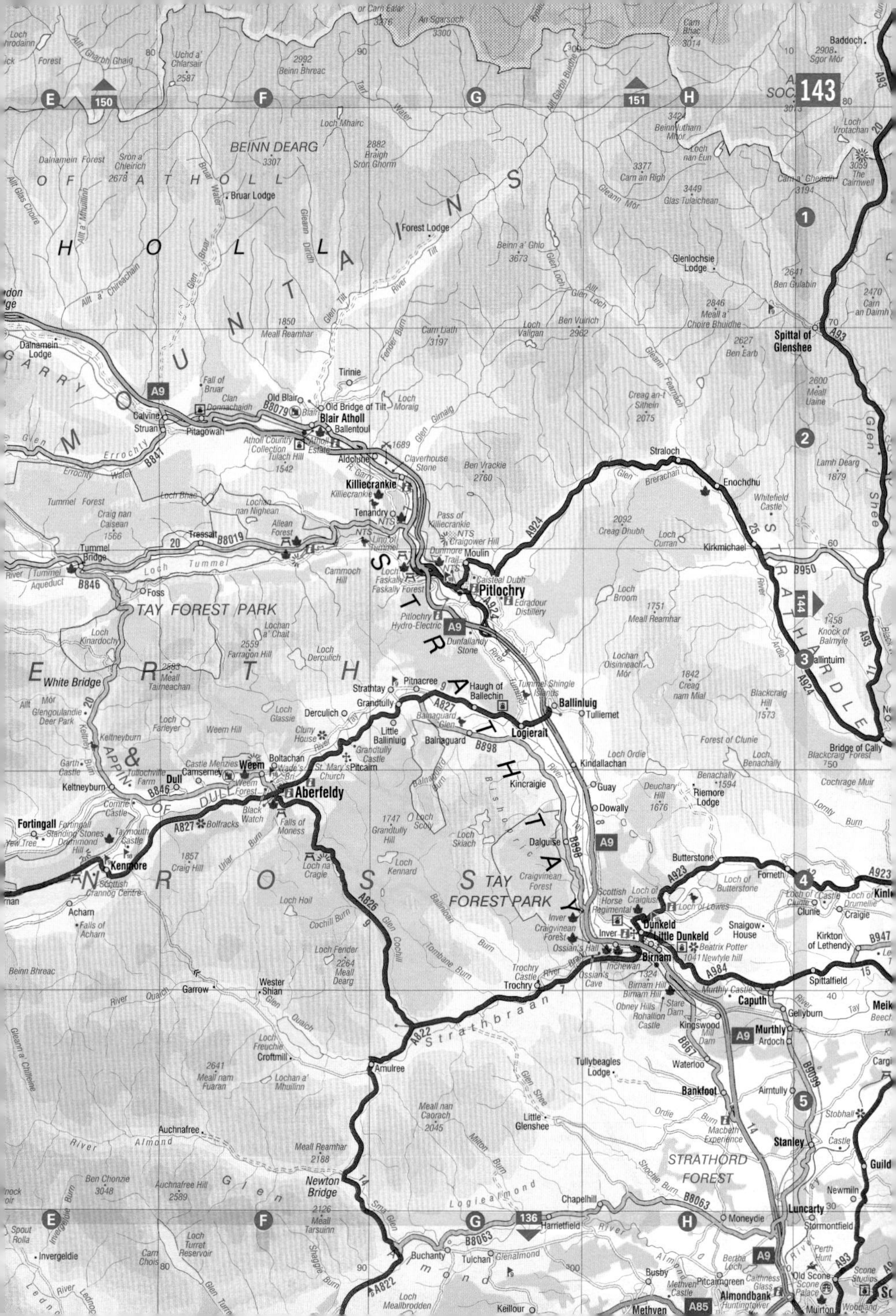

Loch Ghrodainn
Forest
Allt Gharbh Ghaig
Uchd a' Chlarsair
2587
or Carn Ealar 3276
An Sgarsoch 3300
2992 Beinn Bhreac
Cam Bhac 3014
Baddoch
2908 Sgor Mòr
150
151
143
Loch Mhairc
Tarf Water
2882 Braigh Sron Ghorm
BEINN DEARG 3307
Dalnamein Forest
Sron a' Chleirich 2678
O F A T H O L L
Bruar Lodge
Allt Glas Choire
3424 Beinn Iutharn Mhòr
Loch nan Eun
3377 Carn an Rìgh
3449 Glas Tulaichean
Loch Vrotachan
3059 The Cairnwell
Carn a' Gheoidh 3194
Gleann Mòr
H O U N T A I N S
M O U N T A I N S
Forest Lodge
River Tilt
Glen Tilt
Beinn a' Ghlo 3673
Glen Loch
Glenlochsie Lodge
2641 Ben Gulabin
2470 Carn an Daimh
2846 Meall a' Choire Bhuidhe
Spittal of Glenshee
A93
Allt a' Chireachain
Glen Bruar
Gleann Diridh
1850 Meall Reamhar
Carn Liath 3197
Loch Valigan
Ben Vuirich 2962
2627 Ben Earb
Dalnamein Lodge
GARRY
A9
Fall of Bruar
Clan Donnachaidh
Old Blair
B8079
Blair Atholl
Old Bridge of Tilt
Tirinie
Loch Moraig
Glen Girnaig
Creag an-t Sithein 2075
2600 Meall Uaine
Calvine
Struan
Pitagowan
Ballentoul
Atholl Country Collection
Atholl Estate
Tulach Hill 1542
1689
Glen Errochty
B841
Aldclune
Claverhouse Stone
Ben Vrackie 2760
Straloch
Glen Brerachan
Enochdhu
Lamh Dearg 1879
Whitefield Castle
Glen Shee
Killiecrankie
Tummel Forest
Craig nan Caisean 1566
Loch Bhac
Lochan nan Nighean
Allean Forest
Tenandry
Pass of Killiecrankie
NTS
Craigower Hill
A924
2092 Creag Dhubh
Loch Curran
Kirkmichael
S T R A T H A R D L E
B950
144
Tressait
B8019
Linn of Tummel
Dunmore Trail
Moulin
Tummel Bridge
River Tummel
Loch Tummel
Aqueduct
B846
Foss
Cammoch Hill
Loch Faskally
Faskally Forest
Caisteal Dubh
Pitlochry
Edradour Distillery
Loch Broom
1751 Meall Reamhar
1458 Knock of Balmyle
TAY FOREST PARK
Loch Kinardochy
Lochan a' Chait
2559 Farragon Hill
Loch Derculich
Pitlochry Hydro-Electric
Dunfallandy Stone
Lochan Oisinneach Mòr
Ballintuim
E R T H
White Bridge
2583 Meall Tairneachan
S T R A T H T A Y
Strathtay
Pitnacree
Haugh of Ballechin
Tummel Shingle Islands
Ballinluig
Tulliemet
1842 Creag nam Mial
Blackcraig Hill 1573
Allt Mòr
Glengoulandie Deer Park
Loch Glassie
Derculich
Grandtully
A827
Logierait
Loch Farleyer
Weem Hill
Cluny House
Little Ballinluig
Balnaguard
Balnaguard Glen
B898
Forest of Clunie
Keltneyburn
APPIN &
Grandtully Castle
St. Mary's Church
Pitcairn
Kindallachan
Loch Ordie
Loch Benachally
Bridge of Cally
Blackcraig Forest 750
Garth Castle
Castle Menzies
Tullochville Farm
Camserney
Weem
Boltachan
Wade's Bri
Dull
Keltneyburn
Weem Forest
B846
Aberfeldy
Kincraigie
Guay
Benachally 1594
Deuchary Hill 1676
Riemore Lodge
Cochrage Muir
OF DULL
Comrie Castle
Black Watch
Falls of Moness
Dowally
Lornty Burn
Fortingall
Fortingall Standing Stones
Yew Tree
A827 Bolfracks
Taymouth Castle
Drummond Hill
1747 Grandtully Hill
Loch Scoly
Loch Skiach
Dalguise
B898
A9
Kenmore
1857 Craig Hill
Urlar Burn
Loch na Craige
Loch Kennard
Butterstone
Forneth
A923
Loch of Butterstone
Scottish Crannog Centre
N R O S S
TAY FOREST PARK
Craigvinean Forest
Scottish Horse Regimental
Loch of Craiglush
Loch of Clunie
Loch of Drumellie
Clunie
Craigie
Kinloch
Acharn
Loch Hoil
A826
Loch of Lowes
Falls of Acharn
Cochill Burn
Glen Cochill
Ballinloan Burn
Inver
Dunkeld
Little Dunkeld
Snaigow House
Kirkton of Lethendy
B947
Loch Fender
2264 Meall Dearg
Tombane Burn
Craigvinean Forest
Ossian's Hall
Birnam
Beatrix Potter
1041 Newtyle hill
Beinn Bhreac
Trochry Castle
River Braan
Inchewan
Ossian's Cave
1324 Birnam Hill
A984
Spittalfield
Garrow
River Quaich
Wester Shian
Glen Quaich
Trochry
Obney Hills
Rohallion Castle
Stare Dam
Murthly Castle
Caputh
Gellyburn
River Tay
Meikleour
A822
Strathbraan
Kingswood
Mill Dam
Murthly
Ardoch
Gleann a' Chilleine
Loch Freuchie
Croftmill
Amulree
Lochan a' Mhuillinn
2641 Meall nam Fuaran
Tullybeagles Lodge
Glen Shee
B867
Waterloo
B9099
Bankfoot
Airntully
Meall nan Caorach 2045
Little Glenshee
Ordie Burn
Macbeth Experience
Stobhall
Auchnafree
River Almond
Meall Reamhar 2188
Milton Burn
STRATHORD FOREST
Stanley
Castle
Shochie Burn
Guildtown
Ben Chonzie 3048
Auchnafree Hill 2589
Glen Almond
Newton Bridge
Logiealmond
Chapelhill
B8063
Newmiln
Luncarty
Invergeldie Burn
2126 Meall Tarsuinn
Sma' Glen
136
Harrietfield
Moneydie
Stormontfield
Spout Rolla
Invergeldie
Loch Turret Reservoir
Carn Chois
Buchanty
B8063
Tulchan
Glenalmond
River Almond
Bertha Loch
A9
Perth Hunt
A93
Scone Studios
Shaggie Burn
Glen Turret
River Lednock
A822
Loch Meallbrodden
Keillour
Busby
Methven Castle
Pitcairngreen
Caithness Glass
Old Scone
Scone Palace
Almondbank
Huntingtower
Murton
Methven
A85

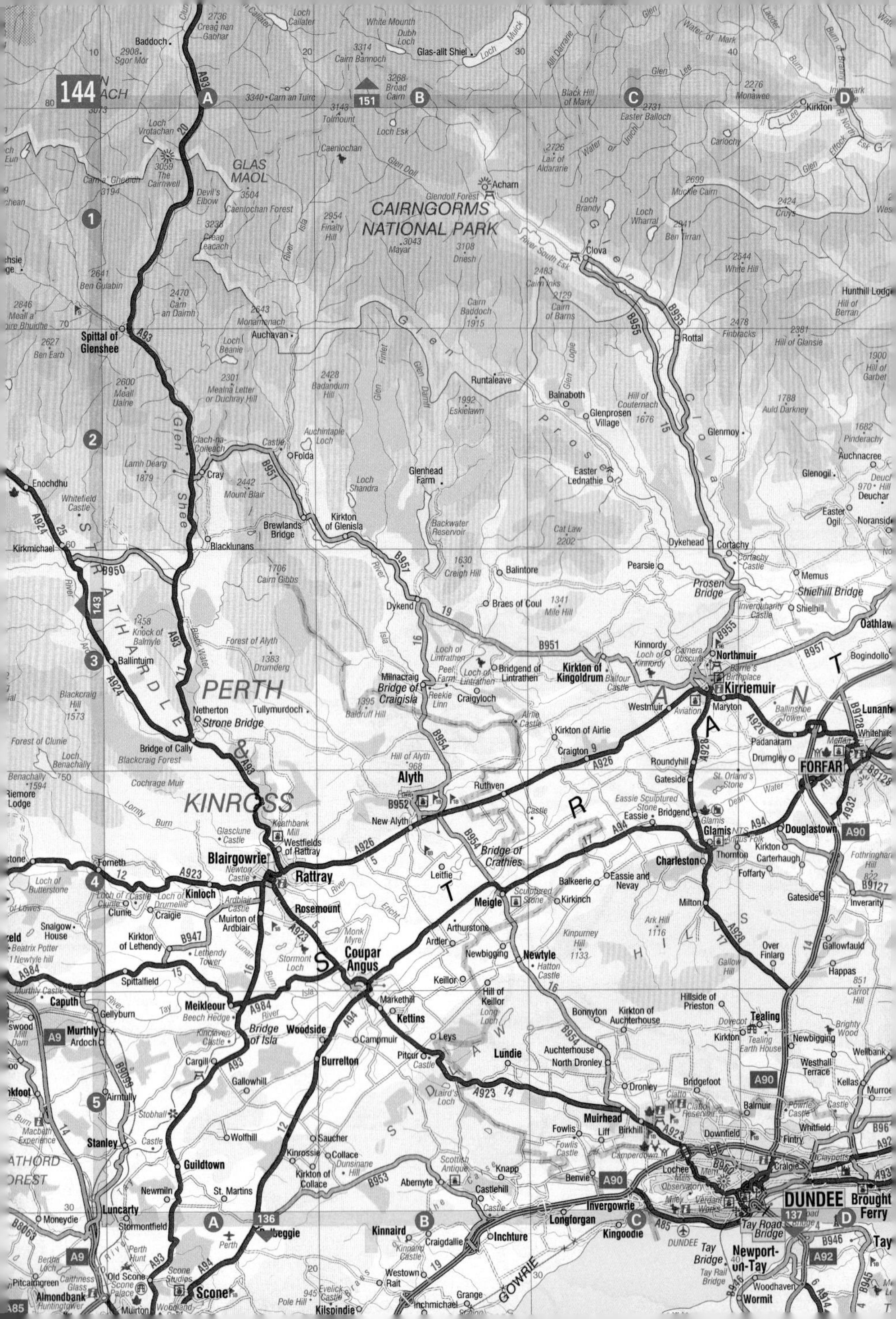

144
151
143
136
137
CAIRNGORMS
NATIONAL PARK
PERTH
&
KINROSS
GLAS
MAOL
Loch Callater
White Mounth
Dubh Loch
Glas-allt Shiel
Loch Muick
Baddoch
Creag nan Gabhar
Sgor Mór
Cairn Bannoch
Broad Cairn
Carn an Tuirc
Tolmount
Loch Esk
Black Hill of Mark
Easter Balloch
Monawee
Kirkton
Loch Vrotachan
The Cairnwell
Caenlochan
Glen Doll
Glendoll Forest
Acharn
Lair of Aldararie
Muckle Cairn
Loch Brandy
Loch Wharral
Ben Tirran
Cruys
Devil's Elbow
Caenlochan Forest
Creag Leacach
Finalty Hill
Mayar
Driesh
Clova
White Hill
Hunthill Lodge
Hill of Berran
Ben Gulabin
Carn an Daimh
Monamenach
Cairn Inks
Cairn of Barns
Cairn Baddoch
Spittal of Glenshee
Auchavan
Loch Beanie
Rottal
Finbracks
Hill of Glansie
Hill of Garbet
Ben Earb
Meall Uaine
Mealna Letter or Duchray Hill
Badandum Hill
Glen Finlet
Glen Damff
Runtaleave
Balnaboth
Glenprosen Village
Hill of Couternach
Eskielawn
Auld Darkney
Glenmoy
Pinderachy
Auchnacree
Glen Shee
Clach-na-Coileach
Castle
Folda
Auchintaple Loch
Lamh Dearg
Cray
Mount Blair
Glenhead Farm
Loch Shandra
Easter Lednathie
Glenogil
Deuchar
Enochdhu
Whitefield Castle
Brewlands Bridge
Kirkton of Glenisla
Backwater Reservoir
Cat Law
Easter Ogil
Noranside
Kirkmichael
Blacklunans
Cairn Gibbs
Creigh Hill
Balintore
Dykehead
Cortachy
Cortachy Castle
Pearsie
Memus
Dykend
Braes of Coul
Mile Hill
Prosen Bridge
Inverquharity Castle
Shielhill Bridge
Shielhill
Oathlaw
Knock of Balmyle
Forest of Alyth
Drumderg
Loch of Lintrathen
Peel Farm
Bridgend of Lintrathen
Kirkton of Kingoldrum
Balfour Castle
Kinnordy
Loch of Kinnordy
Camera Obscura
Northmuir
Barrie's Birthplace
Kirriemuir
Bogindollo
Ballintuim
Milnacraig
Bridge of Craigisla
Reekie Linn
Craigyloch
Baldruff Hill
Airlie Castle
Westmuir
Aviation
Maryton
Lunanhead
Blackcraig Hill
Netherton
Strone Bridge
Tullymurdoch
Kirkton of Airlie
Ballinshoe Tower
Whitehills
Forest of Clunie
Loch Benachally
Bridge of Cally
Blackcraig Forest
Hill of Alyth
Craigton
Padanaram
Drumgley
Mettan
FORFAR
Benachally
Riemore Lodge
Cochrage Muir
Alyth
Ruthven
Roundyhill
Gateside
St. Orland's Stone
New Alyth
Eassie Sculptured Stone
Eassie
Bridgend
Glamis
Dean Water
Douglastown
Lornty Burn
Glasclune Castle
Keathbank Mill
Westfields of Rattray
Bridge of Crathies
Angus Folk
Thornton
Kirkton
Carterhaugh
Fothringham Hill
Blairgowrie
Newton Castle
Rattray
Leitfie
Charleston
Foffarty
Forneth
Loch of Butterstone
Kinloch
Loch of Drumellie
Meigle
Sculptured Stone
Balkeerie
Eassie and Nevay
Kirkinch
Gateside
Inverarity
Loch of Clunie
Clunie
Craigie
Ardblair Castle
Muirton of Ardblair
Rosemount
Milton
Snaigow House
Kirkton of Lethendy
Lethendy Tower
Monk Myre
Arthurstone
Ark Hill
Beatrix Potter
Newtyle hill
Stormont Loch
Coupar Angus
Ardler
Newbigging
Newtyle
Hatton Castle
Kinpurney Hill
Over Finlarg
Gallowfauld
Gallow Hill
Happas
Spittalfield
Keillor
Hill of Keillor
Murthly Castle
Caputh
Gellyburn
Meikleour
Beech Hedge
Markethill
Kettins
Long Loch
Bonnyton
Kirkton of Auchterhouse
Hillside of Prieston
Carrot Hill
Murthly
Ardoch
Kinclaven Castle
Bridge of Isla
Woodside
Campmuir
Leys
Auchterhouse
North Dronley
Dovecot
Tealing
Tealing Earth House
Brighty Wood
Newbigging
Wellbank
Burrelton
Pitcur Castle
Lundie
Westhall Terrace
Kellas
Cargill
Gallowhill
Laird's Loch
Dronley
Bridgefoot
Balmuir
Powrie Castle
Murroes
Airntully
Stobhall
Clatto Reservoir
Whitfield
Muirhead
Birkhill
Fowlis
Fowlis Castle
Liff
Downfield
Fintry
Macbeth Experience
Stanley
Wolfhill
Saucher
Castle
Camperdown
Kinrossie
Collace
Dunsinane Hill
Scottish Antiques
Knapp
Claypotts
Guildtown
Kirkton of Collace
Abernyte
Castlehill
Benvie
Lochee
Mills Observatory
Craigie
Newmiln
St. Martins
Invergowrie
Longforgan
Kingoodie
Verdant Works
Mills
DUNDEE
Broughty Ferry
Luncarty
Stormontfield
Moneydie
Balbeggie
Perth
Kinnaird
Craigdallie
Kinnaird Castle
Inchture
DUNDEE
Tay Bridge
Tay Road Bridge
Newport-on-Tay
Tay
Perth Hunt
Scone Studios
Old Scone
Scone Palace
Caithness Glass
Pitcairngreen
Westown
Rait
Tay Rail Bridge
Woodhaven
Almondbank
Huntingtower
Muirton
Scone
Pole Hill
Evelick Castle
Kilspindie
Inchmichael
Grange
Wormit
GOWRIE
STRATHARDLE
ANGUS
STRATHMORE
SIDLAW HILLS
A93
A924
B950
B951
A926
B954
B952
A923
A984
A94
A928
B955
B957
A932
A90
B9128
B9127
B947
B9099
A9
B953
A85
B960
A92
B946
B8063
A914

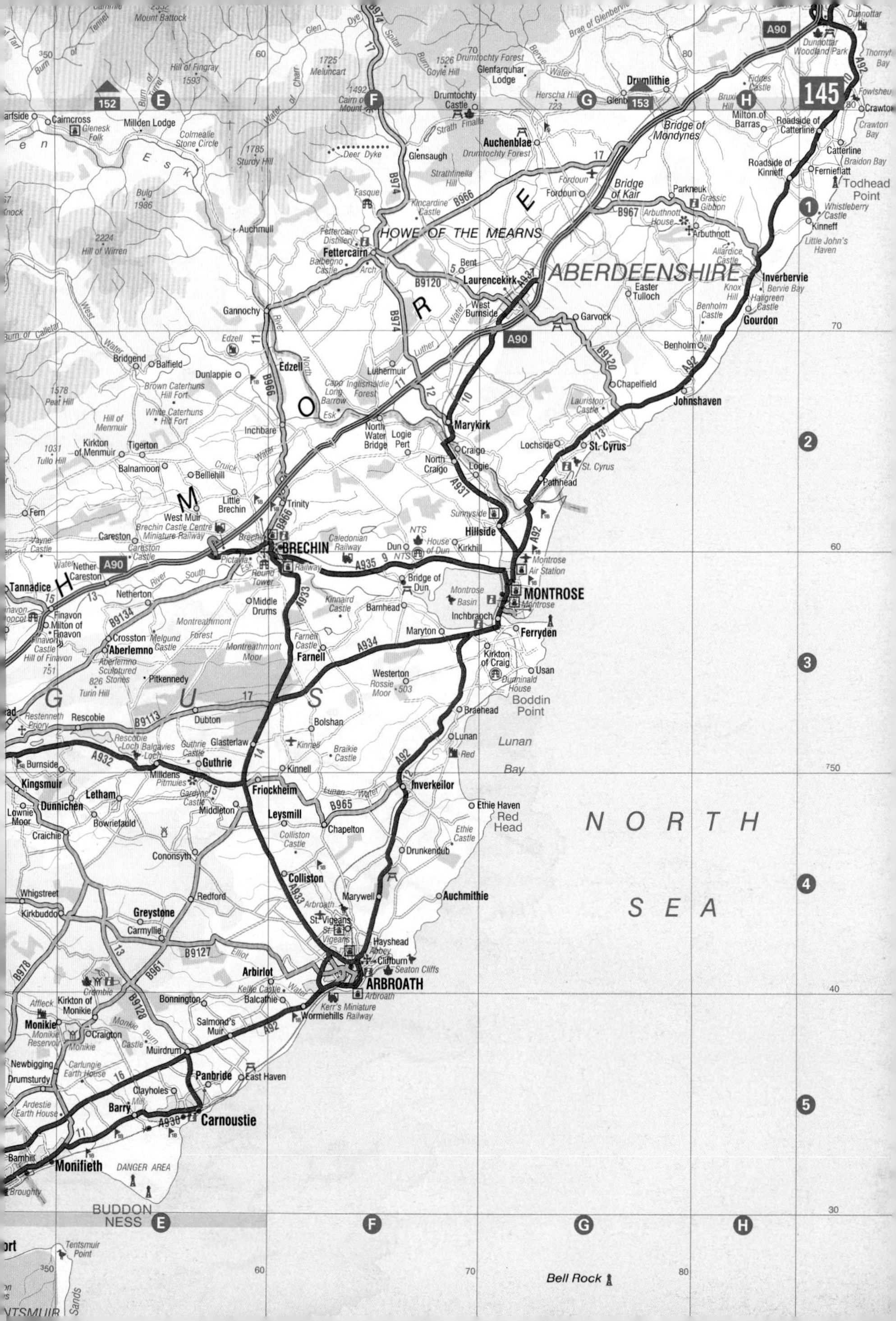

145
Mount Battock
Glen Dye
B974
Spital
Brae of Glenbervie
A90
Dunnottar
Dunnottar Woodland Park
Thornyhall Bay
A92
Fowlsheugh
Crawton
Crawton Bay
350
Burn of Tennet
60
1725 Mount Cairn
1725 Meluncart
1526 Goyle Hill
70
Drumtochty Forest
Glenfarquhar Lodge
Bervie Water
80
Hill of Fingray
1593
152
E
Cairn o' Mount
1492
F
Drumtochty Castle
Herscha Hill
723
G
Glenbervie
Drumlithie
153
Fiddes Castle
Bruxie Hill
H
Milton of Barras
Roadside of Catterline
Bridge of Mondynes
Catterline
Braidon Bay
Roadside of Kinneff
Fernieflatt
Todhead Point
Cairncross
Glenesk Folk
Millden Lodge
Colmeallie Stone Circle
Strath Finalla
Auchenblae
Drumtochty Forest
Deer Dyke
1785 Sturdy Hill
Glensaugh
Strathfinella Hill
17
Fordoun
Bridge of Kair
Parkneuk
Grassic Gibbon
Whistleberry Castle
Kinneff
Little John's Haven
Bulg
1986
Fasque
Kincardine Castle
B966
B967
Arbuthnott House
Arbuthnott
2224 Hill of Wirren
Auchmull
Fettercairn Distillery
HOWE OF THE MEARNS
Fettercairn
Balbegno Castle
Arch
Bent
Allardice Castle
Inverbervie
Bervie Bay
5
B9120
Laurencekirk
A937
ABERDEENSHIRE
Easter Tulloch
Knox Hill
Hallgreen Castle
Gannochy
West Burnside
Benholm Castle
Gourdon
Garvock
A90
Burn of Calletar
Edzell
West Water
Bridgend
Balfield
Dunlappie
Edzell
B974
Luthermuir
Luther Water
Benholm
Mill
Chapelfield
1578 Peat Hill
Brown Caterthun Hill Fort
White Caterthun Hill Fort
B966
Capo Long Barrow
Inglismaldie Forest
North Esk
11
12
10
Lauriston Castle
Johnshaven
Hill of Menmuir
Inchbare
North Water Bridge
Logie Pert
Marykirk
13
1031 Tullo Hill
Kirkton of Menmuir
Tigerton
Cruick Water
Craigo
North Craigo
Logie
Lochside
St. Cyrus
St. Cyrus
Balnamoon
Bellehill
A937
Pathhead
Fern
Little Brechin
West Muir
Trinity
Sunnyside
Careston
Brechin Castle Centre Miniature Railway
Caledonian Railway
NTS
House of Dun
Hillside
A92
Vayne Castle
Careston Castle
Brechin
BRECHIN
Dun
Kirkhill
Montrose Air Station
Nether Careston
A90
Pictavia
Round Tower
Railway
A935
9
Bridge of Dun
MONTROSE
Tannadice
15
13
River South Esk
Netherton
Montrose Basin
Montrose
Finavon
Milton of Finavon
B9134
Middle Drums
Kinnaird Castle
A933
Barnhead
Inchbraoch
Ferryden
Crosston
Aberlemno
Finavon Castle
Hill of Finavon
751
Montreathmont Forest
Melgund Castle
Montreathmont Moor
Farnell Castle
Farnell
A934
Maryton
Kirkton of Craig
Usan
Aberlemno Sculptured Stones
826 Turin Hill
Pitkennedy
Westerton
Rossie Moor
503
Dunninald House
Boddin Point
Restenneth Priory
Rescobie
B9113
Dubton
17
Braehead
Bolshan
Rescobie Loch
Balgavies Loch
Guthrie Castle
Glasterlaw
Kinnell
Braikie Castle
Lunan
Lunan Bay
Red Castle
Burnside
A932
Guthrie
Milldens
Pitmuies
14
A92
Kinnell
Kingsmuir
Letham
Gardyne Castle
15
Friockheim
Lunan Water
Inverkeilor
Dunnichen
Lownie Moor
Bowriefauld
Middleton
Leysmill
B965
Chapelton
Ethie Haven
Red Head
Ethie Castle
NORTH
SEA
Craichie
Colliston Castle
Cononsyth
Drunkendub
Colliston
A933
Whigstreet
Kirkbuddo
Redford
Marywell
Auchmithie
Greystone
Carmyllie
Arbroath
St. Vigeans
Hayshead
Abbey
Cliffburn
Seaton Cliffs
B978
B961
B9127
Elliot Water
Arbirlot
ARBROATH
Crombie
B9128
Kelly Castle
Balcathie
Kerr's Miniature Railway
Affleck
Kirkton of Monikie
Bonnington
Wormiehills
Monikie
Monikie Reservoir
Craigton
Monikie Burn
Castle
Salmond's Muir
A92
Muirdrum
Newbigging
Carlungie Earth House
Panbride
East Haven
Drumsturdy
16
Clayholes
Ardestie Earth House
Barry
Mill
A930
Carnoustie
11
Barnhill
Monifieth
DANGER AREA
Broughty
BUDDON NESS
E
F
G
H
Tentsmuir Point
350
60
70
Bell Rock
80
Sands
1
2
3
4
5
70
60
750
40
30

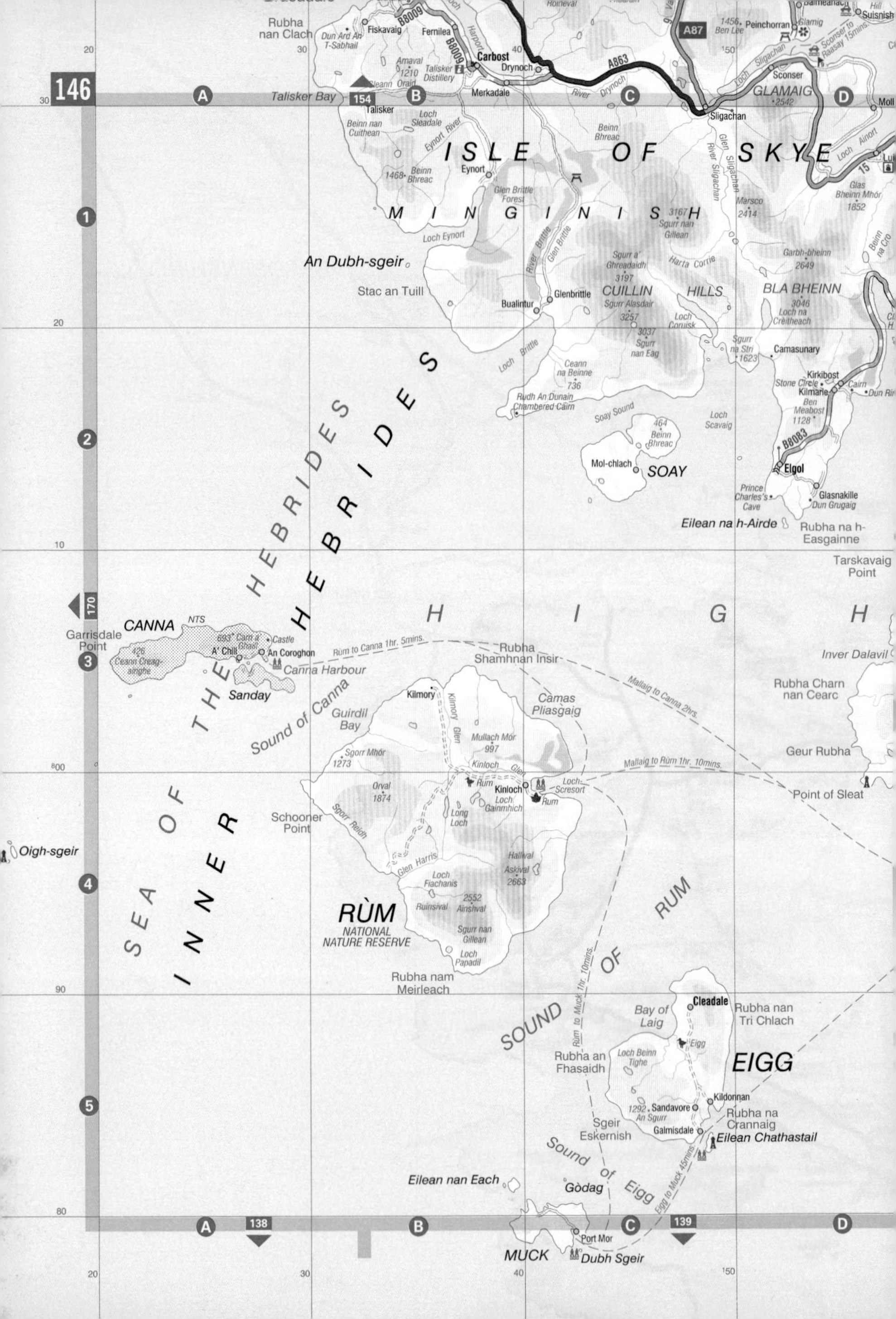
Rubha nan Clach
Dun Ard An T-Sabhail
Fiskavaig
Fernilea
B8009
Amaval 1210
Talisker Distillery
Carbost
Drynoch
A863
Roineval
Harport
A87
1456 Ben Lee
Peinchorran
Glamig
Balmeanach
Hill
Suisnish
Sconser to Raasay 15mins.
Sconser
Loch Sligachan
Glen Oraid
154
Talisker Bay
Talisker
Merkadale
River Drynoch
GLAMAIG 2542
Sligachan
Moll
Beinn nan Cuithean
Loch Sleadale
Eynort River
Beinn Bhreac
Glen Sligachan
River Sligachan
ISLE OF SKYE
Loch Ainort
1468 Beinn Bhreac
Eynort
Glen Brittle Forest
Glas Bheinn Mhór 1852
MINGINISH
3167 Sgurr nan Gillean
Marsco 2414
Loch Eynort
River Brittle
Glen Brittle
Sgurr a' Ghreadaidh 3197
Harta Corrie
Garbh-bheinn 2649
Beinn na Cro
An Dubh-sgeir
Stac an Tuill
Bualintur
Glenbrittle
CUILLIN HILLS
BLA BHEINN 3046
Sgurr Alasdair 3257
Loch Coruisk
Loch na Creitheach
3037 Sgurr nan Eag
Sgurr na Stri 1623
Camasunary
Loch Brittle
Ceann na Beinne 736
Stone Circle
Kirkibost
Kilmarie
Cairn
Dun Ringill
Rudh An Dunain Chambered Cairn
Ben Meabost 1128
Soay Sound
Loch Scavaig
464 Beinn Bhreac
B8083
Mol-chlach
SOAY
Elgol
Glasnakille
Dun Grugaig
Prince Charles's Cave
Eilean na h-Airde
Rubha na h-Easgainne
Tarskavaig Point
SEA OF THE HEBRIDES
INNER HEBRIDES
HIGHLAND
170
CANNA
NTS
Garrisdale Point
426 Ceann Creag-aighe
693 Carn a' Ghaill
Castle
A' Chill
An Coroghon
Rùm to Canna 1hr. 5mins.
Canna Harbour
Sanday
Rubha Shamhnan Insir
Mallaig to Canna 2hrs.
Inver Dalavil
Rubha Charn nan Cearc
Kilmory
Kilmory Glen
Camas Pliasgaig
Guirdil Bay
Sound of Canna
Mullach Mor 997
Sgorr Mhòr 1273
Kinloch Glen
Geur Rubha
Mallaig to Rùm 1hr. 10mins.
Rum
Kinloch
Loch Scresort
Orval 1874
Point of Sleat
Schooner Point
Sgorr Reidh
Long Loch
Loch Gainmhich
Oigh-sgeir
Glen Harris
Hallival
Askival 2663
Loch Fiachanis
2552 Ainshval
Ruinsival
RÙM
NATIONAL NATURE RESERVE
Sgurr nan Gillean
Loch Papadil
SOUND OF RUM
Rùm to Muck 1hr. 10mins.
Rubha nam Meirleach
Cleadale
Bay of Laig
Rubha nan Tri Chlach
Eigg
Rubha an Fhasaidh
Loch Beinn Tighe
EIGG
Kildonnan
1292 An Sgurr
Sandavore
Rubha na Crannaig
Galmisdale
Sgeir Eskernish
Eilean Chathastail
Sound of Eigg
Eigg to Muck 45mins.
Eilean nan Each
Gòdag
138
139
Port Mor
MUCK
Dubh Sgeir
A
B
C
D
1
2
3
4
5
20
30
40
150
10
800
90
80

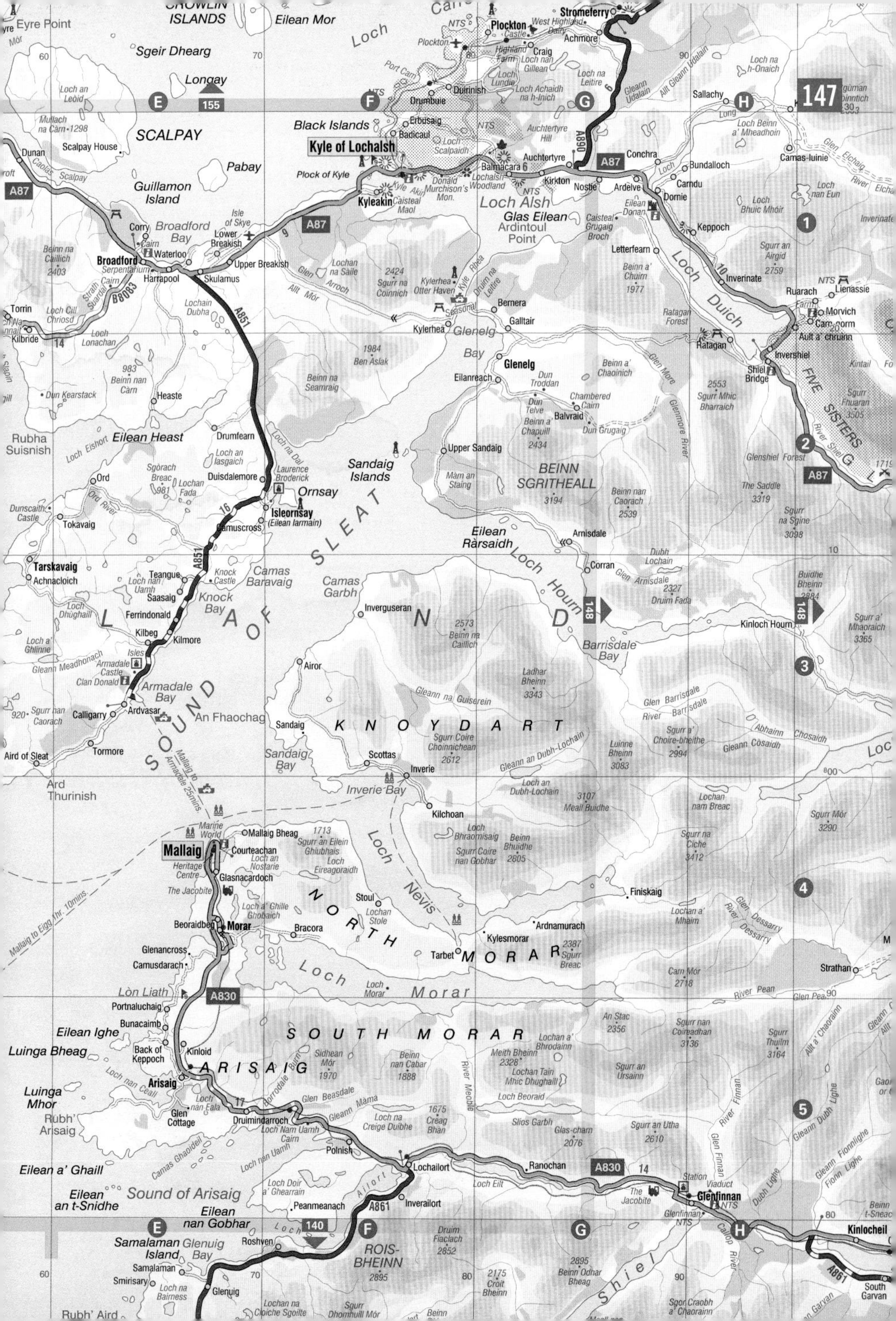

Eyre Point
ISLANDS
Eilean Mor
Stromeferry
Plockton
West Highland Dairy
Achmore
Sgeir Dhearg
Loch
Plockton
Castle
Craig
Highland Farm
Loch nan Gillean
Loch na h-Oinich
Longay
155
Port Cam
Loch Lundie
Loch na Leitire
Duirinish
Loch Achaidh na h-Inich
Gleann Udalain
Allt Gleann Udalain
Sallachy
147
Loch an Leòid
Drumbuie
Mullach na Càrn 1298
Black Islands
Erbusaig
Long
Loch Beinn a' Mheadhoin
SCALPAY
Badicaul
Loch Scalpaidh
Auchtertyre Hill
A890
Camas-luinie
Dunan
Scalpay House
Kyle of Lochalsh
Auchtertyre
A87
Conchra
Glen Elchaig
Caolas Scalpay
Pabay
Plock of Kyle
Balmacara
Bundalloch
River Elchaig
Kyle Akin
Donald Murchison's Mon.
Lochalsh Woodland
Kirkton
Nostie
Ardelve
Carndu
Loch nan Eun
A87
Guillamon Island
Kyleakin
Caisteal Maol
Loch Alsh
NTS
Dornie
Loch Bhuic Mhòir
Glas Eilean
Eilean Donan
Isle of Skye
Broadford Bay
Corry
Cairn
Lower Breakish
A87
Ardintoul Point
Caisteal Grugaig Broch
Keppoch
Beinn na Caillich 2403
Broadford
Waterloo
Upper Breakish
Letterfearn
Sgurr an Airgid 2759
Serpentarium
Harrapool
Skulamus
Lochan na Saile
2424 Sgurr na Coinnich
Kylerhea Otter Haven
Kyle Rhea
Druim na Leitire
Beinn a' Chuirn 1977
Loch Duich
Invernate
Strath Suardal
Cairn
B8083
Glen Arroch
Allt Mòr
NTS
Lienassie
Ruarach
Torrin
Loch Cill Chriosd
Lochain Dubha
A851
Bernera
Ratagan Forest
Farm
Morvich
Kilbride
Loch Lonachan
Kylerhea
Seasonal
Galltair
Glenelg
Carn-gorm
Ault a' chruinn
Ratagan
1984 Ben Aslak
Bay
Glenelg
Invershiel
Shiel Bridge
983 Beinn nan Càrn
Dun Kearstack
Heaste
Beinn na Seamraig
Eilanreach
Dun Troddan
Beinn a' Chaoinich
Glen More
Kintail
2553 Sgurr Mhic Bharraich
Dun Telve
Chambered Cairn
Balvraid
Beinn a' Chapuill 2434
Dun Grugaig
Glenmore River
FIVE SISTERS
Sgurr Fhuaran 3505
Rubha Suisnish
Eilean Heast
Drumfearn
Loch na Dal
River Shiel
Loch Eishort
Loch an Iasgaich
Sandaig Islands
Upper Sandaig
Glenshiel Forest
Sgòrach Breac 981
Lochan Fada
Ord
Duisdalemore
Laurence Broderick
Ornsay
Màm an Staing
BEINN SGRITHEALL
A87
The Saddle 3319
Ord River
16
Isleornsay (Eilean Iarmain)
3194
Beinn nan Caorach 2539
Dunscaith Castle
Tokavaig
Camuscross
Sgurr na Sgine 3098
Eilean Rarsaidh
Arnisdale
SLEAT
Tarskavaig
Achnacloich
Teangue
A851
Knock Castle
Camas Baravaig
Loch Hourn
Corran
Dubh Lochain
Buidhe Bheinn 2884
Loch nan Uamh
Saasaig
Knock Bay
Camas Garbh
Glen Arnisdale
2327 Druim Fada
148
148
Loch Dhughaill
Ferrindonald
Inverguseran
Kinloch Hourn
Sgurr a' Mhaoraich 3365
Loch a' Ghlinne
Kilbeg
Kilmore
2573 Beinn na Caillich
Barrisdale Bay
Isles
Gleann Meadhonach
Armadale Castle
Clan Donald
Airor
Ladhar Bheinn 3343
Armadale Bay
Gleann na Guiserein
Glen Barrisdale
River Barrisdale
920 Sgurr nan Caorach
Calligarry
Ardvasar
An Fhaochag
Sandaig
KNOYDART
Sgurr Coire Choinnichean 2612
Sgurr a' Choire-bheithe 2994
Abhainn Chosaidh
Gleann Cosaidh
Tormore
SOUND
Sandaig Bay
Scottas
Luinne Bheinn 3083
Aird of Sleat
Mallaig to Armadale 25mins
Inverie
Gleann an Dubh-Lochain
Ard Thurinish
Inverie Bay
Loch an Dubh-Lochain
3107 Meall Buidhe
Lochan nam Breac
Sgurr Mòr 3290
Kilchoan
Marine World
Mallaig Bheag
1713 Sgurr an Eilein Ghiubhais
Loch Bhraomisaig
Beinn Bhuidhe 2605
Mallaig
Courteachan
Loch an Nostarie
Loch Eireagoraidh
Sgurr Coire nan Gobhar
Sgurr na Ciche 3412
Heritage Centre
Glasnacardoch
Loch Nevis
The Jacobite
NORTH
Finiskaig
Loch a' Ghille Ghobaich
Stoul
Lochan Stole
Lochan a' Mhaim
Glen Dessarry
River Dessarry
Mallaig to Eigg 1hr. 10mins.
Beoraidbeg
Morar
Bracora
Ardnamurach
Kylesmorar
2387 Sgurr Breac
Glenancross
Tarbet
MORAR
Strathan
Camusdarach
Loch
Loch Morar
Carn Mòr 2718
Lòn Liath
A830
Morar
River Pean
Glen Pean
Portnaluchaig
Bunacaimb
An Stac 2356
Eilean Ighe
SOUTH MORAR
Lochan a' Bhrodainn
Sgurr nan Coireadhan 3136
Sgurr Thuilm 3164
Allt a' Chaorainn
Luinga Bheag
Back of Keppoch
Kinloid
Sidhean Mòr 1970
Beinn nan Cabar 1888
River Meoble
Meith Bheinn 2328
Lochan Tain Mhic Dhughaill
Sgurr an Ursainn
Arisaig
ARISAIG
Borrodale Burn
Loch nan Ceall
Luinga Mhor
Loch nan Eala
Glen Beasdale
Loch Beoraid
Rubh' Arisaig
Glen Cottage
17
Druimindarroch
Gleann Mama
Loch na Creige Duibhe
1675 Creag Bhan
Slios Garbh
Glas-charn 2076
Sgurr an Utha 2610
River Finnan
Gleann Dubh Lighe
Loch Nam Uamh Cairn
Polnish
Camas Ghaoideil
Loch nan Uamh
Glen Finnan
Gleann Fionnlighe
Eilean a' Ghaill
Lochailort
Ranochan
A830
14
Station
Viaduct
Dubh Lighe
Fionn Lighe
Loch Doir a' Ghearrain
Ailort
Loch Eilt
The Jacobite
Glenfinnan
NTS
Eilean an t-Snidhe
Sound of Arisaig
Eilean nan Gobhar
Peanmeanach
A861
Inverailort
Glenfinnan NTS
Beinn t-Sneac
Samalaman Island
Glenuig Bay
Loch
140
Roshven
Druim Fiaclach 2852
Callop River
Kinlocheil
ROIS-BHEINN 2895
2895 Beinn Odhar Bheag
Shiel
Samalaman
Smirisary
Loch na Bairness
Glenuig
2175 Croit Bheinn
A861
South Garvan
Lochan na Cloiche Sgoilte
Sgurr Dhomhnuill Mòr
Sgor Craobh a' Chaorainn
Rubh' Aird

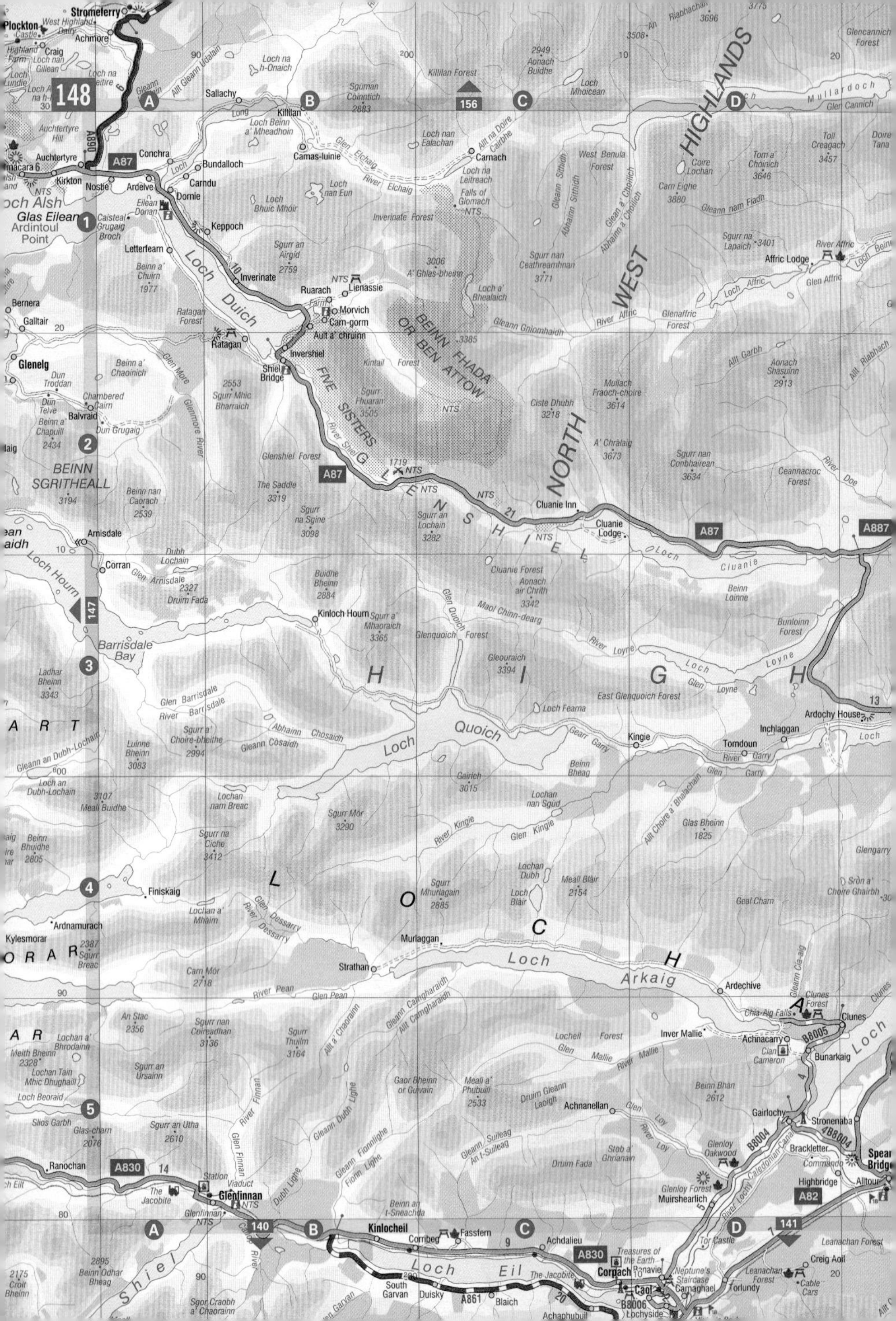

148
Stromeferry
Plockton
West Highland Dairy
Achmore
Craig
Loch nan Gillean
Loch na Beitire
A890
Auchtertyre Hill
Auchtertyre
Kirkton
Nostie
Loch Alsh
Glas Eilean
Ardintoul Point
A87
Conchra
Bundalloch
Ardelve
Carndu
Dornie
Eilean Donan
Caisteal Grugaig Broch
Keppoch
Letterfearn
Loch Duich
Beinn a' Chuirn 1977
Inverinate
Sgurr an Airgid 2759
Loch Bhuic Mhòir
Loch nan Eun
Bernera
Galltair
Ratagan Forest
Ratagan
Glenelg
Dun Troddan
Dun Telve
Chambered Cairn
Balvraid
Dun Grugaig
Beinn a' Chaoinich
Glen More
Glenmore River
2553 Sgurr Mhic Bharraich
Beinn a Chapuill 2434
BEINN SGRITHEALL 3194
Beinn nan Caorach 2539
Amisdale
Corran
Loch Hourn
147
Barrisdale Bay
Ladhar Bheinn 3343
Glen Barrisdale
River Barrisdale
Sallachy
Killilan
Loch Beinn a' Mheadhoin
Camas-luinie
Glen Elchaig
River Elchaig
Killilan Forest
156
Sgùman Coinntich 2883
Loch na h-Onaich
Allt Gleann Udalain
Loch nan Ealachan
Carnach
Allt na Doire Gairbhe
Loch na Leitreach
Falls of Glomach NTS
Inverinate Forest
3006 A' Ghlas-bheinn
Loch a' Bhealaich
Ruarach
Lienassie
Morvich
Carn-gorm
Ault a' chruinn
Invershiel
Shiel Bridge
BEINN FHADA OR BEN ATTOW
3385
Kintail Forest
FIVE SISTERS
Sgurr Fhuaran 3505
River Shiel
Glenshiel Forest
The Saddle 3319
Sgurr na Sgine 3098
Sgurr an Lochain 3282
GLEN SHIEL
NTS
2949 Aonach Buidhe
Loch Mhoicean
Gleann Sithidh
Abhainn Sithidh
West Benula Forest
Glean a' Choilich
Abhainn a' Choilich
Sgurr nan Ceathreamhnan 3771
Gleann Gniomhaidh
River Affric
Glenaffric Forest
NORTH WEST HIGHLANDS
Mullach Fraoch-choire 3614
Ciste Dhubh 3218
A' Chràlaig 3673
Cluanie Inn
Cluanie Lodge
Loch Cluanie
An Riabhachan 3696
3508
3775
Glencannich Forest
Loch Mullardoch
Glen Cannich
Coire Lochan
Carn Eighe 3880
Tom a' Chòinich 3646
Toll Creagach 3457
Doire Tana
Gleann nam Fiadh
Sgurr na Lapaich 3401
River Affric
Affric Lodge
Loch Affric
Glen Affric
Loch Beinn
Allt Garbh
Aonach Shasuinn 2913
Allt Riabhach
Sgurr nan Conbhairean 3634
Ceannacroc Forest
River Doe
A887
Dubh Lochain
Glen Arnisdale
2327 Druim Fada
Buidhe Bheinn 2884
Kinloch Hourn
Sgurr a' Mhaoraich 3365
Glen Quoich
Glenquoich Forest
Maol Chinn-dearg
Cluanie Forest
Aonach air Chrith 3342
Beinn Loinne
Bunloinn Forest
River Loyne
Loch Loyne
Glen Loyne
Gleouraich 3394
HIGH
East Glenquoich Forest
Loch Fearna
Ardochy House
Inchlaggan
Tomdoun
Kingie
Loch Quoich
Gearr Garry
River Garry
Glen Garry
Beinn Bheag
Gairich 3015
Lochan nan Sgùd
Abhainn Chosaidh
Gleann Còsaidh
Sgurr a' Choire-bheithe 2994
Luinne Bheinn 3083
Gleann an Dubh-Lochain
ART
Loch an Dubh-Lochain
3107 Meall Buidhe
Lochan nam Breac
Sgurr Mòr 3290
River Kingie
Glen Kingie
Allt Choire a' Bhalachain
Glas Bheinn 1825
Glengarry
Beinn Bhuidhe 2805
Sgurr na Ciche 3412
Finiskaig
Lochan a' Mhaim
Glen Dessarry
River Dessarry
LOCHABER
Sgurr Mhurlagain 2885
Lochan Dubh
Loch Blàir
Meall Blàir 2154
Geal Charn
Sròn a' Choire Ghairbh
Ardnamurach
Kylesmorar
ORAR
2387 Sgurr Breac
Carn Mòr 2718
Murlaggan
Strathan
Loch Arkaig
Ardechive
Gleann Cia-aig
River Pean
Glen Pean
Gleann Camgharaidh
Allt Camgharaidh
Allt a' Chaorainn
Clunes Forest
Chia-Aig Falls
Clunes
An Stac 2356
Lochan a' Bhrodainn
Meith Bheinn 2328
Lochan Tain Mhic Dhughaill
Loch Beoraid
Sgurr nan Coireadhan 3136
Sgurr Thuilm 3164
Sgurr an Ursainn
Locheil Forest
Glen Mallie
River Mallie
Inver Mallie
Achnacarry
Clan Cameron
B8005
Bunarkaig
Loch Lochy
Gaor Bheinn or Gulvain
Meall a' Phubuill 2533
Druim Gleann Laoigh
Achnanellan
Glen Loy
River Loy
Beinn Bhan 2612
Gairlochy
Stronenaba
Slios Garbh
Glas-charn 2076
Sgurr an Utha 2610
River Finnan
Glen Finnan
Gleann Dubh Lighe
Gleann Fionnlighe
Fionn Lighe
Gleann Suileag
An t-Suileag
Stob a' Ghrianain
Druim Fada
Glenloy Oakwood
Glenloy Forest
B8004
Caledonian Canal
Brackletter
Commando
Spean Bridge
Highbridge
Alltour
A82
Muirshearlich
River Lochy
Ranochan
A830
Station
Viaduct
The Jacobite
Glenfinnan
Glenfinnan NTS
Dubh Lighe
Beinn an t-Sneachda
140
Kinlocheil
Corribeg
Fassfern
Achdalieu
Treasures of the Earth
Corpach
Banavie
Neptune's Staircase
Caol
Camaghael
Tor Castle
141
Leanachan Forest
Creig Aoil
Torlundy
Cable Cars
Loch Shiel
Callop River
2895 Beinn Odhar Bheag
2175 Croit Bheinn
Sgor Craobh a' Chaorainn
Loch Eil
South Garvan
Duisky
A861
Blaich
B8006
Lochyside
Achaphubuil

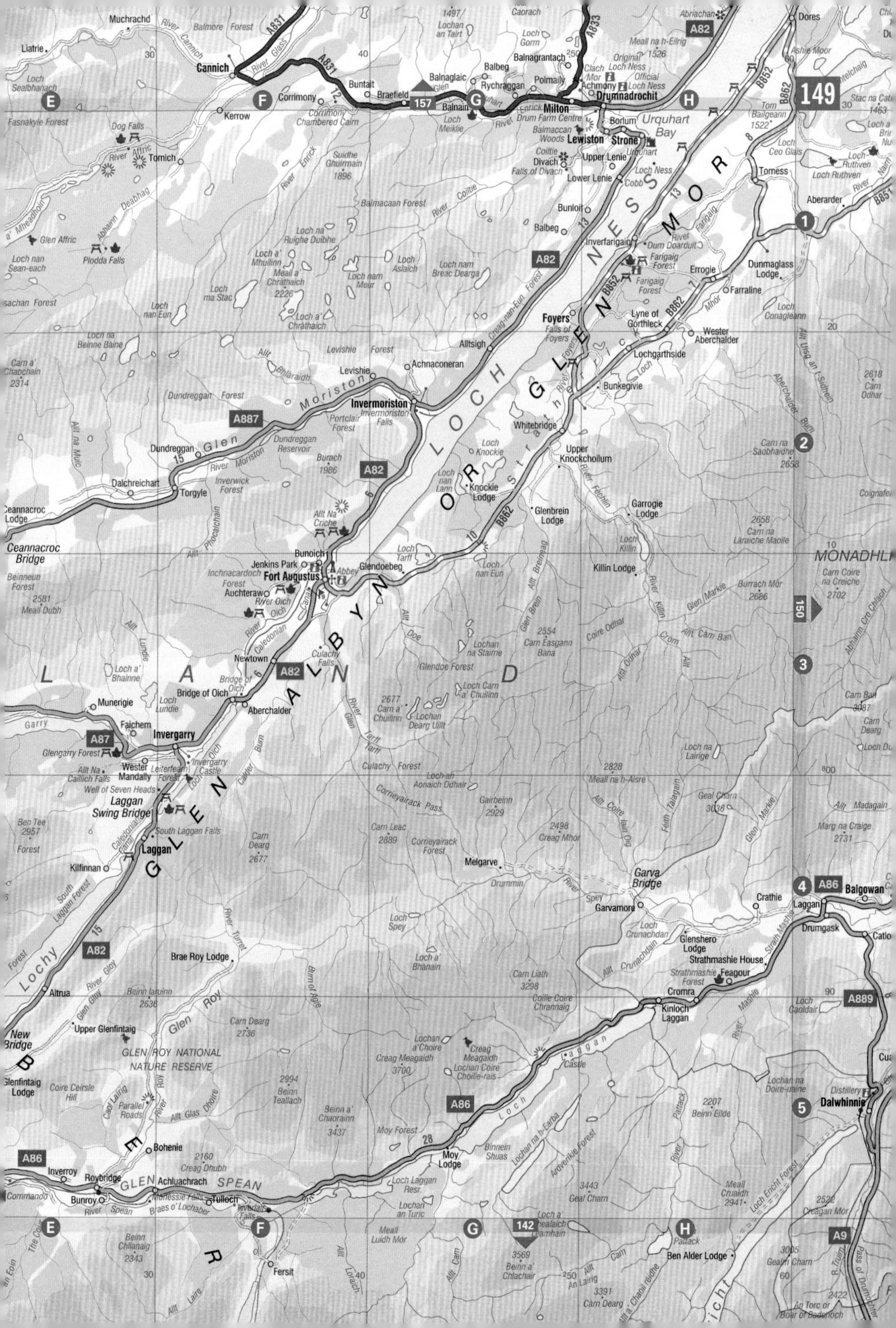
149
Muchrachd
Balmore Forest
River Cannich
A831
Liatrie
Cannich
River Glass
Loch Sealbhanach
E
F
G
H
Corrimony
Corrimony Chambered Cairn
Buntait
Braefield
157
Balnaglaic
Balnain
Loch Meiklie
Balbeg
Rychraggan
Balnagrantach
Polmaily
Loch Gorm
Lochan an Tairt
Caorach
1497
A833
Abriachan
A82
Meall na h-Eilrig 1526
Original Loch Ness
Clach Mor
Achmony
Official Loch Ness
Drumnadrochit
Milton
Drum Farm Centre
Balmaccan Woods
Lewiston
Strone
Borlum
Urquhart Bay
Urquhart
Coiltie
Divach
Falls of Divach
Upper Lenie
Lower Lenie
Cobb
Loch Ness
Dores
Ashie Moor
B852
B862
Torn Baileann 1522
Stac na Cat 1463
Loch Ceo Glais
Torness
Loch Ruthven
Aberarder
B851
1
Kerrow
Fasnakyle Forest
Dog Falls
River Affric
Tomich
Abhainn Deabhag
Glen Affric
Loch nan Sean-each
Plodda Falls
Suidhe Ghuirmain 1896
River Enrick
River Coiltie
Balmacaan Forest
Bunloit
Balbeg
Inverfarigaig
Dum Doarduil
Farigaig Forest
River Farigaig
Errogie
Dunmaglass Lodge
Farraline
Loch na Ruighe Duibhe
Loch a' Mhuilinn
Meall a' Chrathaich 2226
Loch nam Mear
Loch Aslaich
Loch nam Breac Dearga
Loch ma Stac
Loch nan Eun
Loch a' Chrathaich
Creag-nan-Eun Forest
LOCH NESS
OR
GLEN MOR
Foyers
Falls of Foyers
Lyne of Gorthleck
Wester Aberchalder
Lochgarthside
Loch Conagleann
Loch na Beinne Baine
Carn a' Chaochain 2314
Levishie Forest
Alltsigh
Achnaconeran
Levishie
Bunkegivie
River Foyers
Strath Errick
Dundreggan Forest
Invermoriston
Invermoriston Falls
Portclair Forest
A887
Whitebridge
Dundreggan
Glen Moriston
Dundreggan Reservoir
River Moriston
Burach 1986
A82
Loch Knockie
Upper Knockchoilum
Carn na Saobhaidhe 2658
2
2618 Carn Odhar
Allt na Muic
Dalchreichart
Torgyle
Inverwick Forest
Loch nan Lann
Knockie Lodge
River Fechlin
Garrogie Lodge
Coignafearn
Ceannacroc Lodge
Ceannacroc Bridge
Allt Na Criche
Glenbrein Lodge
Loch Killin
2658 Carn na Laraiche Maoile
MONADHLI
Beinneun Forest
2581 Meall Dubh
Jenkins Park
Bunoich
Fort Augustus
Abbey
Glendoebeg
Loch Tarff
Loch nan Eun
Inchnacardoch Forest
Auchterawe
River Oich
Caledonian Canal
Killin Lodge
Glen Markie
Burrach Mór 2686
Carn Coire na Creiche 2702
150
Allt Doe
2554 Carn Easgann Bana
Coire Odhar
Allt Cam Ban
Lochan na Stairne
Culachy Falls
Glendoe Forest
3
L A G G A N
A L B Y N
D
Newtown
Loch a' Bhainne
Bridge of Oich
Loch Lundie
Loch Carn a' Chuilinn
2677 Carn a' Chuilinn
Lochan Dearg Uillt
Carn Ban 3087
Munerigie
Aberchalder
River Tarff
Glen Tarff
Garry
Faichem
Invergarry
Carn Dearg
Loch Duv
A87
Glengarry Forest
Wester Mandally
Allt Na Caillich Falls
Leiterfearn Forest
Invergarry Castle
Loch Oich
Culachy Forest
Loch na Lairige
2828 Meall na h-Aisre
Loch an Aonaich Odhair
Well of Seven Heads
Laggan Swing Bridge
Corrieyairack Pass
Gairbeinn 2929
Allt Coire Iain Oig
Feith Talagain
Geal Charn 3036
Allt Madagain
Marg na Craige 2731
Ben Tee 2957
Forest
South Laggan Falls
Laggan
GLEN
Carn Dearg 2677
Carn Leac 2889
Corrieyairack Forest
2498 Creag Mhór
Kilfinnan
Melgarve
Drummin
River Spey
Garva Bridge
Garvamore
4
A86
Balgowan
Crathie
Laggan
Drumgask
South Laggan Forest
Loch Spey
Loch Crunachdan
Glenshero Lodge
Strathmashie House
Strath Mashie
Lochy
A82
Brae Roy Lodge
River Turret
Loch a' Bhanain
Allt Crunachdain
Carn Liath 3298
Strathmashie Forest
Feagour
River Gloy
Burn of Agie
Coille Coire Chrannaig
Cromra
Kinloch Laggan
A889
Loch Caoldair
Altrua
Beinn Iaruinn 2636
Glen Roy
Carn Dearg 2736
New Bridge
Glen Gloy
Upper Glenfintaig
GLEN ROY NATIONAL NATURE RESERVE
Lochan a' Choire
Creag Meagaidh 3700
Creag Meagaidh
Lochan Coire Choille-rais
Loch Laggan
Castle
River Mashie
Glenfintaig Lodge
Coire Ceirsle Hill
Caol Laing
Parallel Roads
Allt Glas Dhoire
2994 Beinn Teallach
Beinn a' Chaorainn 3437
Lochan na Doire-uaine
Distillery
Dalwhinnie
5
A86
Moy Forest
Lochan na h-Earba
Ardverikie Forest
2207 Beinn Eilde
River Pattack
Bohenie
2160 Creag Dhubh
28
Moy Lodge
Binnein Shuas
Loch Ericht Forest
A86
Inverroy
Roybridge
GLEN SPEAN
Achluachrach
Commando
Bunroy
River Spean
Monessie Falls
Braes o' Lochaber
Tulloch
Inverlair Falls
Loch Laggan Resr.
Lochan an Turic
3443 Geal Charn
Meall Cruaidh 2941
2522 Creagan Mor
142
Loch a' Bhealaich Leamhain
Pattack
Ben Alder Lodge
A9
Beinn Chlianaig 2343
Meall Luidh Mór
Fersit
Allt Loraich
Allt Cam
3569 Beinn a' Chlachair
Allt An Lairig
3391 Carn Dearg
Allt a' Chaoil-reidhe
3005 Gealm Charn
R. Truim
Pass of Drumochter
2422 An Torc or Boar of Badenoch
The Coire
Allt Laire
R

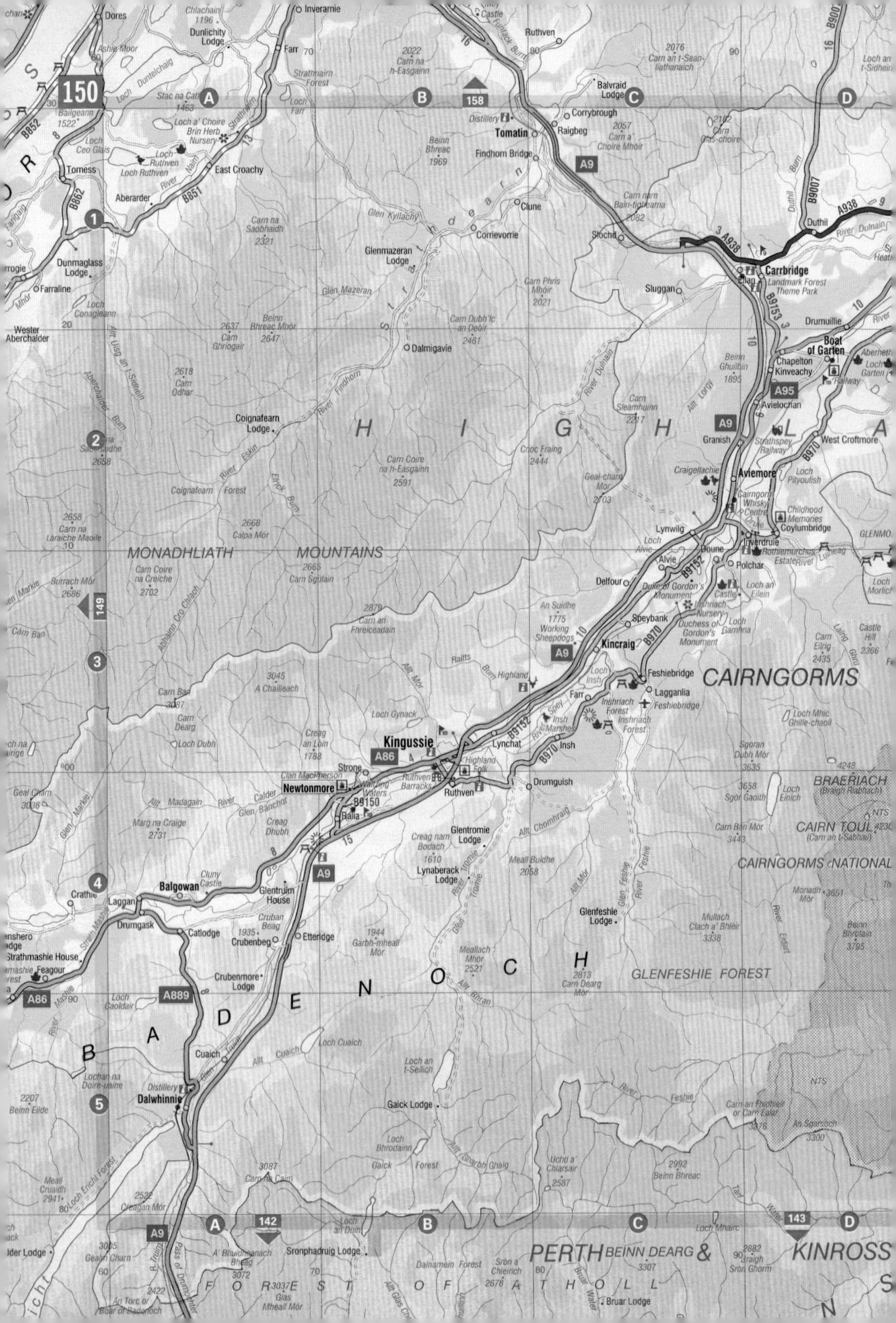
150
158
149
142
143
Inverarnie
Dores
Chlachain 1196
Dunlichity Lodge
Ashie Moor
Farr
Strathnairn Forest
Loch Duntelchaig
Stac na Cathaig 1463
Bailgeann 1522
B852
Loch a' Choire
Brin Herb Nursery
Loch Ceo Glais
Loch Ruthven
Torness
B862
East Croachy
Aberarder
River Nairn
B851
Dunmaglass Lodge
Farraline
Loch Conagleann
Wester Aberchalder
Allt Uisg an t-Sidhein
Abercahalder Burn
2022 Carn na h-Easgainn
Castle
Ruthven
Balvraid Lodge
Corrybrough
Raigbeg
Distillery
Tomatin
2057 Carn a' Choire Mhòir
Findhorn Bridge
A9
Beinn Bhreac 1969
Clune
Corrievorrie
Glen Kyllachy
Carn na Saobhaidh 2321
Glenmazeran Lodge
Glen Mazeran
Strathdearn
Carn nam Bain-tighearna 2082
Slochd
2076 Carn an t-Sean-liathanaich
2162 Carn Glas-choire
B9007
Duthil
Duthil Burn
A938
River Dulnain
Carrbridge
Ellan
Landmark Forest Theme Park
Sluggan
Carn Phris Mhòir 2021
B9153
Drumuillie
Boat of Garten
Chapelton
Kinveachy
Beinn Ghuilbin 1895
A95
Avielochan
Loch Garten
Railway
Cam Dubh 'lc an Deòir 2461
Dalmigavie
2637 Carn Ghriogair
Beinn Bhreac Mhòr 2647
2618 Carn Odhar
River Findhorn
River Dulnain
Allt Lorgy
Carn Sleamhuinn 2217
Coignafearn Lodge
H I G H L A
Granish
Strathspey Railway
West Croftmore
B970
Aviemore
Craigellachie
Cairngorm Whisky Centre
Loch Pityoulish
Childhood Memories
Coylumbridge
Carn na Saobhaidhe 2658
River Eskin
Elrick Burn
Carn Coire na h-Easgainn 2591
Cnoc Fraing 2444
Geal-charn Mòr 2703
Coignafearn Forest
2668 Calpa Mòr
2658 Carn na Laraiche Maoile
MONADHLIATH MOUNTAINS
Lynwilg
Loch Alvie
Alvie
Doune
Inverdruie
Rothiemurchus Estate
River Luineag
GLENMORE
Polchar
2665 Carn Sgùlain
Carn Coire na Creiche 2702
Burrach Mòr 2686
Delfour
B9152
Duke of Gordon's Monument
Castle
Loch an Eilein
Inshriach Nursery
Loch Gamhna
Duchess of Gordon's Monument
An Suidhe 1775
Working Sheepdogs
Speybank
Kincraig
Carn Eilrig 2435
Castle Hill 2366
Abhainn Cro Chlach
2879 Carn an Fhreiceadain
Raitts Burn
Allt Mòr
Highland
Loch Insh
Feshiebridge
CAIRNGORMS
Lagganlia
3045 A Chailleach
Carn Ban
Carn Bad 3087
Carn Dearg
Loch Dubh
Loch Gynack
Creag an Loin 1788
Kingussie
Lynchat
Farr
River Spey
Insh Marshes
Inshriach Forest
Insh
Loch Mhic Ghille-chaoil
Sgoran Dubh Mòr 3635
4248
BRAERIACH (Braigh Riabhach)
A86
Strone
Clan MacPherson
Newtonmore
Wildlife Waters
Highland Folk
Ruthven Barracks
Ruthven
Drumguish
3658 Sgòr Gaoith
Loch Einich
Geal Charn 3036
Glen Markie
Allt Madagain
River Calder
Glen Banchor
B9150
Ralia
Marg na Craige 2731
Creag Dhubh
Allt Chomhraig
Carn Ban Mòr 3443
CAIRN TOUL 4236 (Carn an t-Sabhail)
NTS
Creag nam Bodach 1610
Glentromie Lodge
Meall Buidhe 2058
CAIRNGORMS NATIONAL
Cluny Castle
Balgowan
Glentruim House
Lynaberack Lodge
River Tromie
Allt Mòr
Glen Feshie
River Feshie
Monadh Mòr 3651
Crathie
Laggan
Drumgask
Catlodge
Cruban Beag
1935 Crubenbeg
Etteridge
1944 Garbh-mheall Mòr
Glenfeshie Lodge
Mullach Clach a' Bhleir 3338
River Eidart
Beinn Bhrotain 3795
Strathmashie House
Strath Mashie
Feagour
Crubenmore Lodge
Meallach Mhòr 2521
2813 Carn Dearg Mòr
GLENFESHIE FOREST
A889
Loch Caoldair
River Mashie
B A D E N O C H
Allt Bhran
Cuaich
Loch Cuaich
Allt Cuaich
Loch an t-Seilich
Lochan na Doire-uaine
Distillery
Dalwhinnie
2207 Beinn Eilde
Gaick Lodge
River Feshie
Carn an Fhidhleir or Carn Ealar 3276
An Sgarsoch 3300
Loch Bhrodainn
Gaick Forest
Allt Gharbh Ghaig
Meall Cruaidh 2941
Loch Ericht Forest
3087 Carn na Caim
2522 Creagan Mòr
Uchd a' Chlarsair 2587
2992 Beinn Bhreac
Tarf Water
3005 Gealm Charn
A' Bhuidheanach Bheag 3072
Loch an Doin
Sronphadruig Lodge
Loch Mhairc
2882 Braigh Sròn Ghorm
PERTH
BEINN DEARG 3307
& KINROSS
Dalnamein Forest
Sròn a' Chleirich 2678
Bruar Water
Bruar Lodge
Pass of Drumochter
2422 An Torc or Boar of Badenoch
3037 Glas Mheall Mòr
Allt Glas Choire
F O R E S T O F A T H O L L
A B C D

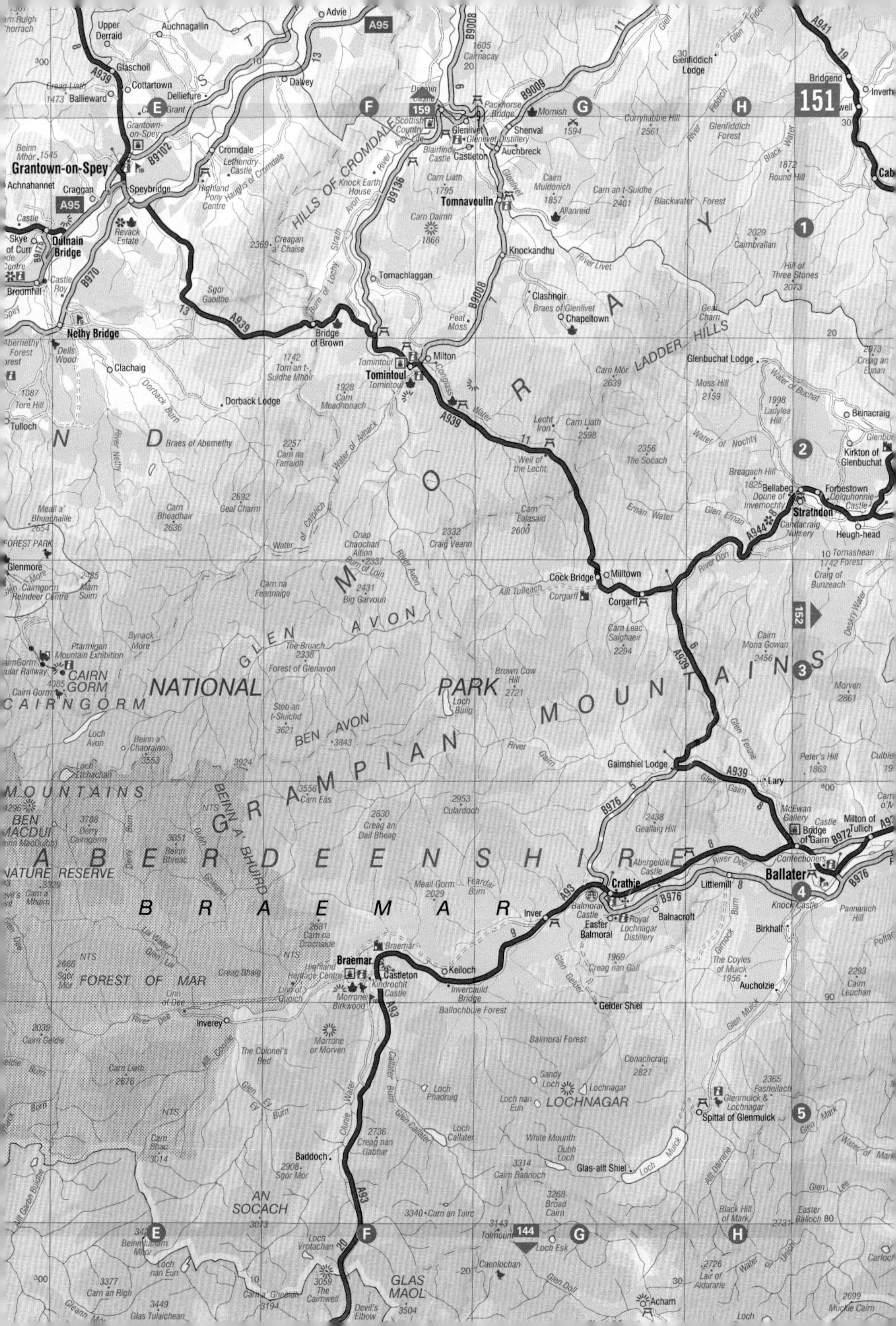
151
Upper Derraid
Auchnagallin
Advie
A95
B9008
1605 Carnacay
Glenfiddich Lodge
Glen Fiddich
A941
Bridgend
Glaschoil
Cottartown
Dellifure
Dalvey
Creag Liath 1473
Ballieward
E
F
G
H
159
Scottish Country Life
Packhorse Bridge
Glenlivet
Mornish
1594
Corryhabbie Hill 2561
Glenfiddich Forest
Grantown-on-Spey
Cromdale
Lethendry Castle
Glenlivet Distillery
Shenval
Blairfindy Castle
Castleton
Auchbreck
Black Water
1872 Round Hill
B9102
Beinn Mhòr 1545
Achnahannet
Craggan
Speybridge
Highland Pony Centre
HILLS OF CROMDALE
Haughs of Cromdale
Knock Earth House
Carn Liath 1795
Tomnavoulin
Cairn Muldonich 1857
Carn an t-Suidhe 2401
Blackwater Forest
A95
B9136
River Avon
Carn Daimh 1866
Allanreid
Castle
Skye of Curr
Dulnain Bridge
Revack Estate
2369 Creagan a' Chaise
Strath Avon
Knockandhu
River Livet
1
2029 Cairnbrallan
Hill of Three Stones 2073
B970
Broomhill
Castle Roy
Tomachlaggan
Clashnoir
Braes of Glenlivet
Chapeltown
Sgòr Gaoithe
A939
13
Burn of Lochy
B9008
Peat Moss
Geal Charn
Nethy Bridge
Bridge of Brown
LADDER HILLS
Abernethy Forest
Dells Wood
1742 Tom an t-Suidhe Mhòr
Milton
Tomintoul
Glenbuchat Lodge
2073 Creag an Eunan
Clachaig
Carn Mòr 2639
Moss Hill 2159
Water of Buchat
1087 Tore Hill
Dorback Burn
Dorback Lodge
1928 Carn Meadhonach
Conglass Water
1998 Ladylea Hill
Belnacraig
Tulloch
Lecht Iron
Carn Liath 2598
Water of Nochty
Kirkton of Glenbuchat
River Nethy
Braes of Abernethy
Water of Ailnack
2257 Carn na Farraidh
11
Well of the Lecht
2356 The Socach
2
Breagach Hill 1825
Bellabeg
Doune of Invernochty
Forbestown
Colquhonnie Castle
Strathdon
2692 Geal Charm
Carn Bheadhair 2636
Water of Caiplich
2332 Craig Veann
Carn Ealasaid 2600
Ernan Water
Glen Ernan
A944
Candacraig Nursery
Heugh-head
Meall a' Bhuachaille 2654
FOREST PARK
Cnap Chaochan Aitinn
2337
Burn of Loin
River Avon
10
Tornashean Forest
1742 Craig of Bunzeach
Glenmore
2485 Màm Suim
Cairngorm Reindeer Centre
Carn na Feannaige
2431 Big Garvoun
Cock Bridge
Milltown
Allt Tuileach
Corgarff
River Don
Deskry Water
GLEN AVON
152
Bynack More
The Bruach 2338
Forest of Glenavon
Carn Leac Saighaeir 2294
A939
Cairn Mona Gowan 2456
Ptarmigan Mountain Exhibition
CAIRN GORM
4085
Cairn Gorm
CAIRNGORM
NATIONAL
PARK
Brown Cow Hill 2721
Loch Builg
MOUNTAINS
3
Morven 2861
Stob an t-Sluichd 3621
BEN AVON
3843
Loch Avon
Beinn a' Chaorainn 3553
3924
GRAMPIAN
River Gairn
Glen Fenzie
Gairnshiel Lodge
Peter's Hill 1863
Loch Etchachan
MOUNTAINS
3556 Carn Eas
2953 Culardoch
A939
Lary
Glen Gairn
BEN MACDUI
3788 Derry Cairngorm
BEINN A' BHUIRD
3051 Beinn Bhreac
2830 Creag an Dail Bheag
B976
2438 Geallaig Hill
McEwan Gallery
Bridge of Gairn
Castle
Milton of Tullich
B972
ABERDEENSHIRE
NATURE RESERVE
Abergeldie Castle
River Dee
Confectioners
Ballater
3329
Carn a' Mhàim
Meall Gorm 2029
Feardar Burn
Crathie
Littlemill
4
Knock Castle
Balmoral Castle
B976
Balnacroft
Pannanich Hill
BRAEMAR
Inver
A93
Easter Balmoral
Royal Lochnagar Distillery
Birkhall
2681 Carn na Drochaide
Braemar
Glen Gelder
1969 Creag nan Gall
Girnock Burn
The Coyles of Muick 1956
2293 Cairn Leuchan
2666 Sgòr Mòr
FOREST OF MAR
Creag Bhaig
Braemar
Highland Heritage Centre
Castleton
Kindrochit Castle
Keiloch
Invercauld Bridge
Aucholzie
Linn of Dee
Linn of Quoich
Morrone Birkwood
Ballochbuie Forest
Gelder Shiel
River Dee
Inverey
A93
Glen Muick
2039 Carn Geldie
Morrone or Morven
Balmoral Forest
The Colonel's Bed
Conachcraig 2827
Carn Liath 2676
Callater Burn
Sandy Loch
Lochnagar
Loch Phadruig
Loch nan Eun
LOCHNAGAR
2365 Fasheilach
Glenmuick & Lochnagar
Spittal of Glenmuick
5
Glen Mark
Glen Ey
Ey Burn
Clunie Water
Glen Callater
2736 Creag nan Gabhar
Loch Callater
White Mouth
Dubh Loch
Carn Bhac 3014
Baddoch
2908 Sgòr Mòr
3314 Cairn Bannoch
Glas-allt Shiel
Loch Muick
Allt Darrarie
Water of Mark
Allt Garbh Buidhe
AN SOCACH
3073
A93
3268 Broad Cairn
Glen Lee
3340 Carn an Tuirc
Black Hill of Mark
Easter Balloch
2731
E
F
144
G
H
Beinn Iutharn Mhòr
Loch Vrotachan
3143 Tolmount
Loch Esk
Loch nan Eun
3059 The Cairnwell
Caenlochan
Glen Doll
Water of Unich
2726 Lair of Aldararie
3377 Carn an Righ
Carn a' Gheoidh 3194
GLAS MAOL 3504
3449 Glas Tulaichean
Devil's Elbow
Acharn
2699 Muckle Cairn

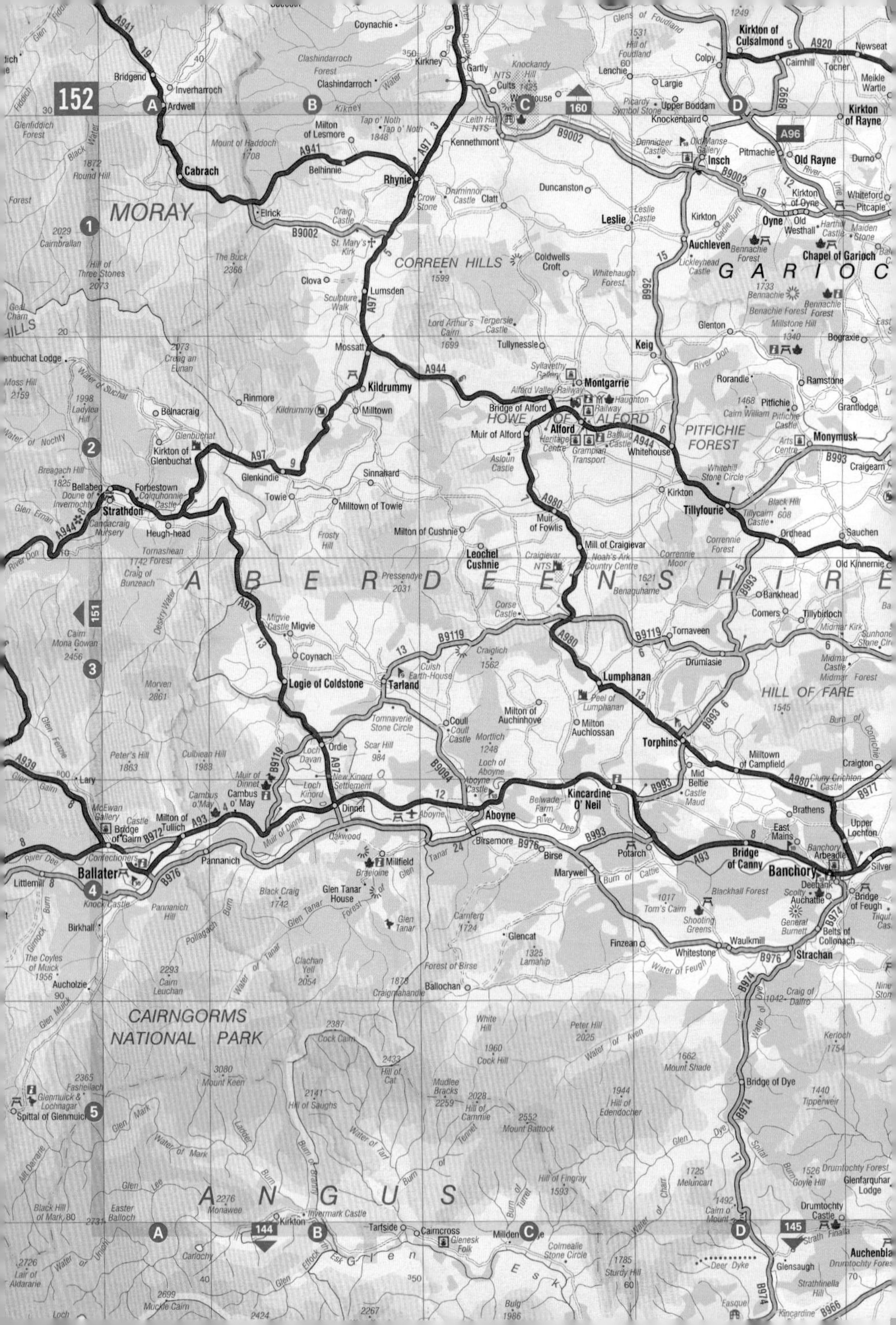
152
Coynachie
Glens of Foudland
1249
Kirkton of Culsalmond
A920
Newseat
A941
19
40
Clashindarroch Forest
350
Kirkney
Gartly
Knockandy Hill
1531 Hill of Foudland
Lenchie
Colpy
Cairnhill
Tocher
Meikle Wartle
Bridgend
Inverharroch
Clashindarroch
NTS Cults
Wardhouse
160
Largie
Picardy Symbol Stone
Upper Boddam
B992
Kirkton of Rayne
A
Ardwell
B
Kildrummy
C
D
30
Glenfiddich Forest
Black Water
Milton of Lesmore
Tap o' Noth 1848
Leith Hall NTS
Kennethmont
B9002
Knockenbaird
Dunnideer Castle
Old Manse Gallery
A96
Mount of Haddoch 1708
A941
A97
Belhinnie
Pitmachie
Old Rayne
Durno
Insch
1872 Round Hill
Cabrach
Rhynie
Druminnor Castle
Clatt
Duncanston
B9002
River Urie
Whiteford
Pitcaple
Forest
MORAY
Crow Stone
Craig Castle
Elrick
Leslie
Leslie Castle
Kirkton
Kirkton of Oyne
Oyne
Old Westhall
Harthill Castle
Maiden Stone
1
2029 Cairnbrallan
B9002
St. Mary's Kirk
Gadie Burn
Auchleven
Bennachie Forest
Chapel of Garioch
Hill of Three Stones 2073
The Buck 2366
CORREEN HILLS
Coldwells Croft
15
Lickleyhead Castle
GARIOCH
Clova
Lumsden
Whitehaugh Forest
1599
1733 Bennachie
HILLS
Sculpture Walk
B992
Benachie Forest
Bennachie Forest
Lord Arthur's Cairn 1699
Terpersie Castle
Glenton
Millstone Hill 1340
20
2073 Creag an Eunan
Mossatt
Tullynessle
Keig
Bograxie
Glenbuchat Lodge
Water of Buchat
A944
Syllavethy Gallery
Montgarrie
River Don
Rorandle
Ramstone
Moss Hill 2159
1998 Ladylea Hill
Rinmore
Kildrummy
Alford Valley Railway
Haughton
1468 Pitfichie
Belnacraig
Kildrummy
Milltown
Bridge of Alford
HOWE OF ALFORD
Cairn William
Pitfichie Castle
Grantlodge
Water of Nochty
2
Glenbuchat
Kirkton of Glenbuchat
Muir of Alford
Alford
Heritage Centre
Grampian Transport
Balfluig Castle
A944
Whitehouse
6
PITFICHIE FOREST
Arts Centre
Monymusk
B993
A97
9
Asloun Castle
Craigearn
Breagach Hill 1825
Glenkindie
Sinnahard
Whitehill Stone Circle
Bellabeg
Forbestown
Doune of Invernochty
Colquhonnie Castle
Towie
Milltown of Towie
Kirkton
Black Hill 608
Glen Ernan
Strathdon
Candacraig Nursery
A980
Muir of Fowlis
Tillyfourie
Tillycairn Castle
A944
Heugh-head
Frosty Hill
Milton of Cushnie
Ordhead
Sauchen
River Don
10
Tornashean Forest 1742
Leochel Cushnie
Mill of Craigievar
Craigievar NTS
Noah's Ark Country Centre
Corrennie Forest
Corrennie Moor
Old Kinnernie
Craig of Bunzeach
ABERDEENSHIRE
Pressendye 2031
1621 Benaquhame
5
B993
151
Deskry Water
Corse Castle
Bankhead
Comers
Tillybirloch
A97
Migvie Castle
Migvie
B9119
Tornaveen
Midmar Kirk
Sunhoney Stone Circle
Cairn Mona Gowan 2456
13
Coynach
13
Craiglich 1562
A980
6
Drumlasie
6
Midmar Castle
Midmar Forest
3
Cush Earth-House
Logie of Coldstone
Tarland
Lumphanan
Peel of Lumphanan
13
HILL OF FARE
1545
Morven 2861
Milton of Auchinhove
Burn of Corrichie
Tomnaverie Stone Circle
Coull
Coull Castle
Milton Auchlossan
Torphins
B993
Glen Fenzie
Peter's Hill 1863
Culblean Hill 1983
Loch Davan
Ordie
Scar Hill 984
Mortlich 1248
Milltown of Campfield
Craigton
A939
B9119
A97
B9094
Loch of Aboyne
Mid Beltie
Castle Maud
Cluny Crichton Castle
A980
B977
800
Lary
Muir of Dinnet
New Kinord Settlement
Aboyne Castle
Kincardine O' Neil
B993
Glen Gairn
8
Cambus o' May
Cambus o' May
Loch Kinord
12
Belwade Farm
Brathens
McEwan Gallery
Castle
Milton of Tullich
A93
4
Dinnet
Aboyne
Aboyne
River Dee
Upper Lochton
8
Bridge of Gairn
B972
Muir of Dinnet
Oakwood
24
Birsemore
B976
Birse
B993
Potarch
8
East Mains
Banchory Arbeadie
River Dee
Confectioners
Pannanich
Tanar
Bridge of Canny
A93
Silver
Ballater
B976
Millfield
Marywell
Burn of Cattie
Banchory
Deebank
Littlemill
8
4
Knock Castle
Braeloine
Glen Tanar
Scolty
Auchattie
Bridge of Feugh
Black Craig 1742
Glen Tanar House
Forest of Glen Tanar
1017 Tom's Cairn
Blackhall Forest
Pannanich Hill
Birkhall
Pollagach Burn
Glen Tanar
Glen Tanar
Carnferg 1724
Glencat
Shooting Greens
General Burnett
B974
Belts of Collonach
Girnock Burn
Finzean
Whitestone
Waulkmill
Strachan
Water of Tanar
1325 Lamahip
Clachan Yell 2054
The Coyles of Muick 1956
2293 Cairn Leuchan
Forest of Birse
Water of Feugh
B976
Aucholzie
90
1878 Craigmahandle
Ballochan
B974
1042 Craig of Dalfro
Glen Muick
CAIRNGORMS NATIONAL PARK
2387
White Hill
Peter Hill 2025
Water of Dye
Kerloch 1754
Cock Cairn
2433 Hill of Cat
1960 Cock Hill
Water of Aven
1662 Mount Shade
3080 Mount Keen
2365 Fasheilach
Mudlee Bracks 2259
2141 Hill of Saughs
2028 Hill of Cammie
1944 Hill of Edendocher
Bridge of Dye
1440 Tipperweir
Glenmuick & Lochnagar
2552 Mount Battock
Spittal of Glenmuick
5
Glen Mark
Water of Mark
Ladder Burn
Water of Tarf
Tennet
Burn of Brany
Burn of Turret
Glen Dye
B974
Spital Burn
Drumtochty Forest
Allt Darrarie
Glen Lee
17
1526 Goyle Hill
Glenfarquhar Lodge
Hill of Fingray 1593
1725 Meluncart
Water of Charr
ANGUS
2276 Monawee
Black Hill of Mark
Easter Balloch
Invermark Castle
1492 Cairn o' Mount
Drumtochty Castle
2731
80
Kirkton
144
Tartside
Craincross
Glenesk Folk
Millden Lodge
C
145
Finalla
Strath
Auchenblae
Colmeallie Stone Circle
Deer Dyke
Glensaugh
Drumtochty Forest
Carlochy
Glen Esk
1785 Sturdy Hill
2726 Lair of Aldararie
Water of Unich
40
Glen Effock
350
60
Strathfinella Hill
70
B974
2699 Muckle Cairn
2267
2424
Bulg 1986
Fasque
Kincardine
B966
Loch

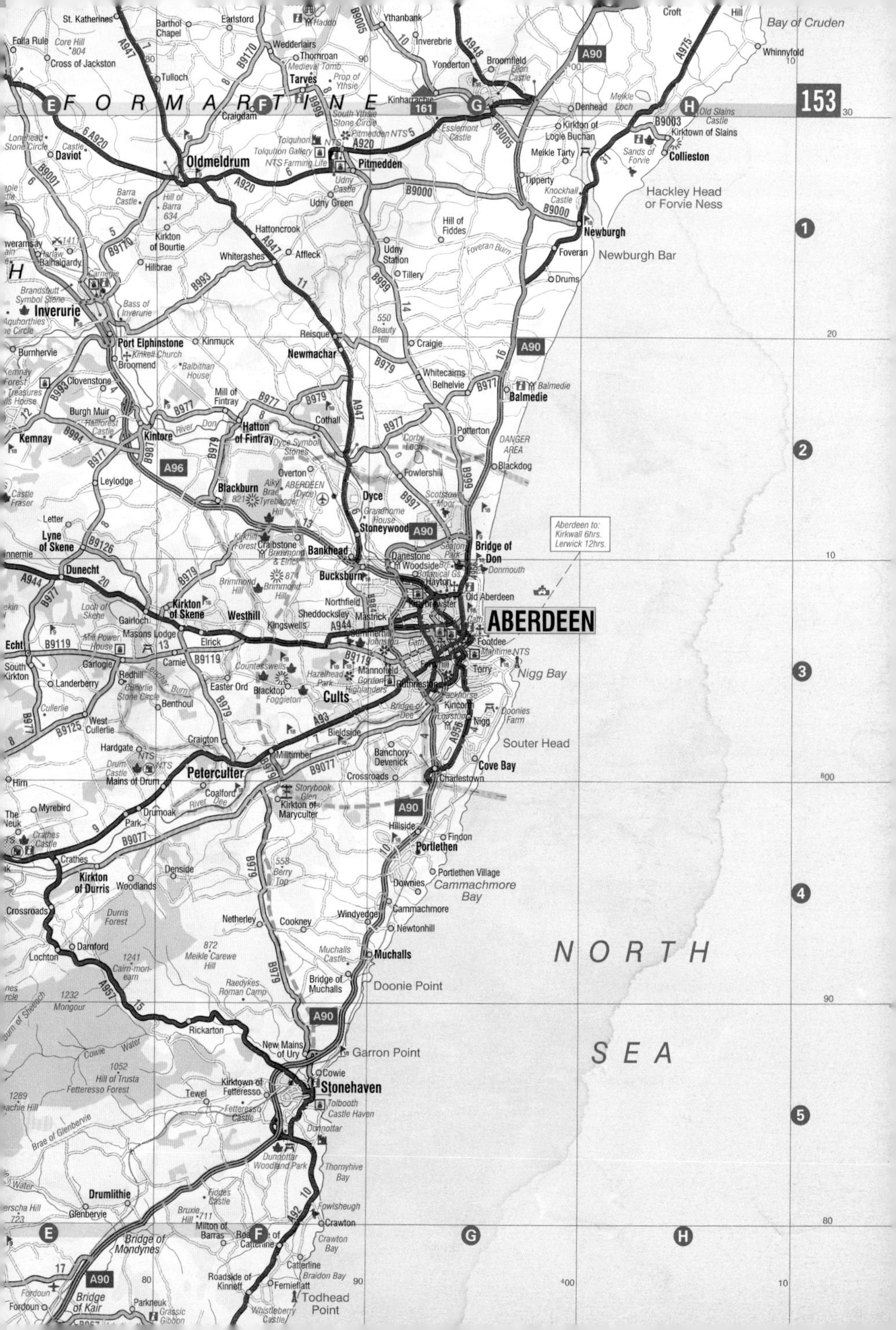

FORMARTINE
ABERDEEN
NORTH
SEA
Bay of Cruden
Whinnyfold
Croft
Hill
St. Katherines
Barthol Chapel
Earlsford
Haddo
Ythanbank
Folla Rule
Core Hill 804
Cross of Jackston
Wedderlairs
Thornroan
Medieval Tomb
Inverebrie
Yonderton
Broomfield
Ellon Castle
Tulloch
Tarves
Prop of Ythsie
Kinharrachie
Denhead
Meikle Loch
Old Slains Castle
Craigdam
South Ythsie Stone Circle
Pitmedden NTS
Esslemont Castle
Kirkton of Logie Buchan
Kirktown of Slains
Collieston
Lonehead Stone Circle
Daviot
Tolquhon
Tolquhon Gallery
NTS Farming Life
Pitmedden
Meikle Tarty
Sands of Forvie
Oldmeldrum
Udny Castle
Tipperty
Knockhall Castle
Hackley Head or Forvie Ness
Barra Castle
Hill of Barra 634
Udny Green
Newburgh
Hill of Fiddes
Inveramsay
Harlaw
Balhalgardy
Kirkton of Bourtie
Hattoncrook
Foveran Burn
Foveran
Newburgh Bar
Whiterashes
Affleck
Udny Station
Tillery
Hillbrae
Carnegie
Drums
Brandsbutt Symbol Stone
Inverurie
Bass of Inverurie
Aquhorthies Stone Circle
550 Beauty Hill
Reisque
Port Elphinstone
Kinmuck
Craigie
Burnhervie
Kinkell Church
Broomend
Newmachar
Kemnay Forest
Clovenstone
Balbithan House
Whitecairns
Belhelvie
Balmedie
Treasures House
Mill of Fintray
Burgh Muir
Hallforest Castle
Cothall
Kemnay
Kintore
River Don
Hatton of Fintray
Dyce Symbol Stones
Corby Loch
Potterton
DANGER AREA
Blackdog
Leylodge
Overton
Fowlershill
Castle Fraser
Blackburn
Aiky Brae
ABERDEEN (Dyce)
Dyce
Scotstown Moor
821 Tyrebagger Hill
Grandhome House
Letter
Stoneywood
Aberdeen to: Kirkwall 6hrs. Lerwick 12hrs.
Lyne of Skene
Kirkhill Forest
Craibstone
Brimmond & Elrick
Bankhead
Danestone
Bridge of Don
Seaton Park
Woodside
Botanical Gs.
Donmouth
Dunecht
Brimmond Hill
874
Bucksburn
Hayton
Old Aberdeen
Loch of Skene
Kirkton of Skene
Northfield
Kittybrewster
Sheddocksley
Mastrick
Gairloch
Westhill
Kingswells
Masons Lodge
Mill Power House
Elrick
Summerhill
Johnston
Footdee
Maritime NTS
Echt
Garlogie
Carnie
Countesswells
Torry
Nigg Bay
South Kirkton
Redhill
Hazlehead Park
Mannofield
Gordon Highlanders
Ruthrieston
Landerberry
Cullerlie Stone Circle
Easter Ord
Blacktop
Foggieton
Cults
Benthoul
Bridge of Dee
Kincorth
Loirston
Doonies Farm
Nigg
Cullerlie
West Cullerlie
Bieldside
Souter Head
Craigton
Hardgate
Banchory-Devenick
Cove Bay
Drum Castle
Milltimber
Peterculter
Mains of Drum
Crossroads
Charlestown
Hirn
Coalford
Storybook Glen
Kirkton of Maryculter
Myrebird
Drumoak
River Dee
Park
Hillside
The Neuk
Crathes Castle
Findon
Portlethen
Crathes
558 Berry Top
Kirkton of Durris
Denside
Woodlands
Portlethen Village
Downies
Cammachmore Bay
Cammachmore
Crossroads
Durris Forest
Netherley
Cookney
Windyedge
Newtonhill
Durnford
Lochton
872 Meikle Carewe Hill
Muchalls Castle
Muchalls
1241 Cairn-mon-earn
Bridge of Muchalls
Doonie Point
Raedykes Roman Camp
1232 Mongour
Rickarton
Cowie Water
New Mains of Ury
Garron Point
Cowie
1052 Hill of Trusta
Fetteresso Forest
Kirktown of Fetteresso
Stonehaven
1289
Tewel
Fetteresso Castle
Tolbooth
Castle Haven
Dunnottar
Brae of Glenbervie
Dunnottar Woodland Park
Thornyhive Bay
Drumlithie
Fiddes Castle
Fowlsheugh
Glenbervie
Bruxie Hill 711
Crawton
Milton of Barras
Crawton Bay
Bridge of Mondynes
Roadside of Catterline
Catterline
Braidon Bay
Roadside of Kinneff
Fernieflatt
Todhead Point
Fordoun
Bridge of Kair
Parkneuk
Grassic Gibbon
Whistleberry Castle

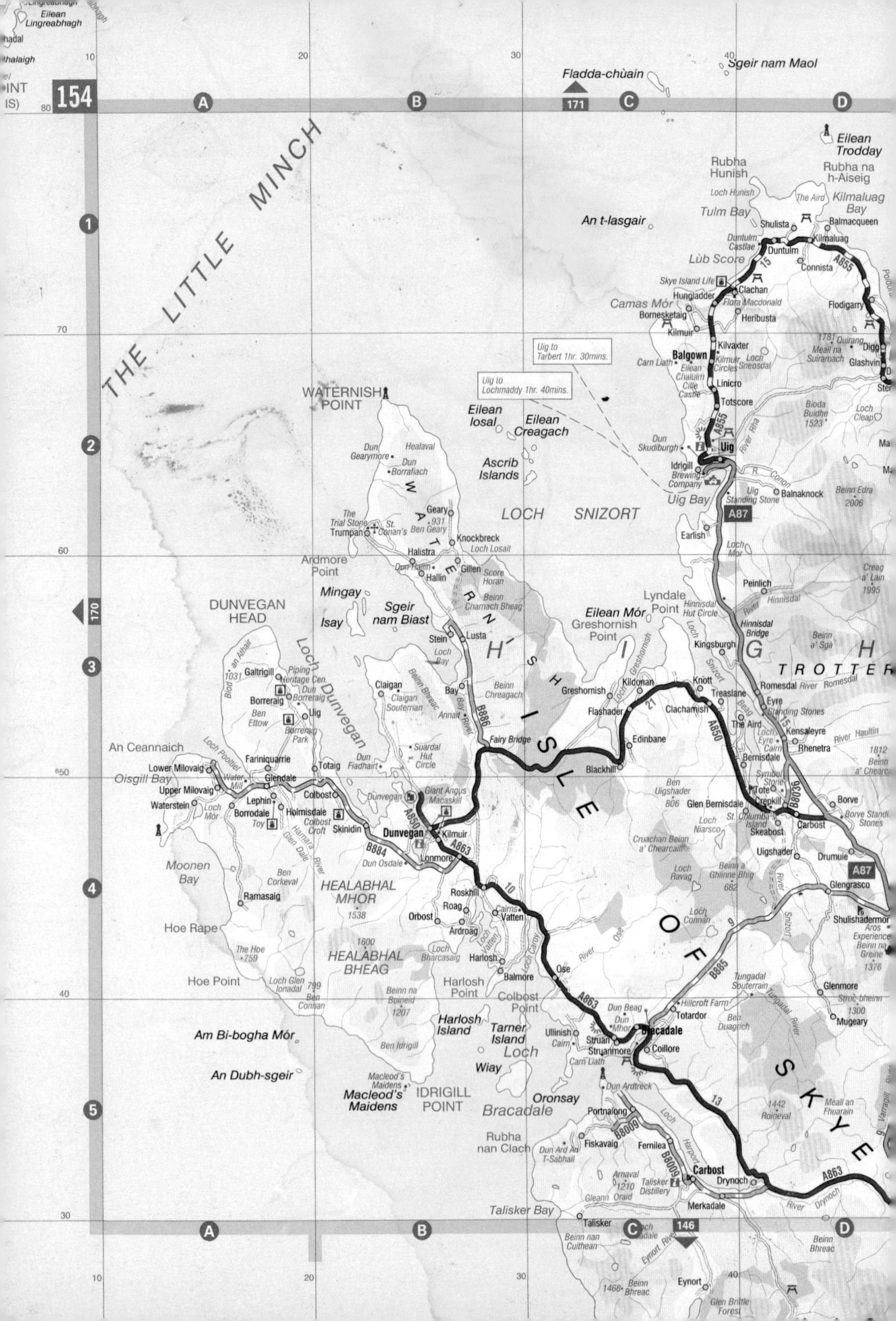
THE LITTLE MINCH
Fladda-chùain
171
170
146
Sgeir nam Maol
Eilean Trodday
Rubha Hunish
Rubha na h-Aiseig
Loch Hunish
The Aird
Kilmaluag Bay
Tulm Bay
Shulista
Balmacqueen
An t-Iasgair
Duntulm Castle
Duntulm
Kilmaluag
Lùb Score
Connista
A855
Skye Island Life
Clachan
Camas Mór
Hungladder
Flora Macdonald
Flodigarry
Bornesketaig
Heribusta
Kilmuir
Kilvaxter
Quirang
Meall na Suiramach
Digg
Glashvin
Balgown
Carn Liath
Eilean Chaluim Cille Castle
Kilmuir Circles
Loch Sneosdal
Linicro
Totscore
Bioda Buidhe
Loch Cleap
Uig to Tarbert 1hr. 30mins.
Uig to Lochmaddy 1hr. 40mins.
WATERNISH POINT
Eilean Iosal
Eilean Creagach
Ascrib Islands
Dun Skudiburgh
Uig
Idrigill
Brewing Company
River Rha
R. Conon
Uig Standing Stone
Balnaknock
Beinn Edra
Uig Bay
A87
Dun Gearymore
Healaval
Dun Borrafiach
LOCH SNIZORT
WATERNISH
The Trial Stone
Trumpan
St. Conan's
Geary
Ben Geary
Knockbreck
Loch Losait
Earlish
Loch Mor
Halistra
Dun Hallin
Hallin
Gillen
Score Horan
Ardmore Point
Beinn Chamach Bheag
Peinlich
Hinnisdal
Creag a' Lain
Mingay
Sgeir nam Biast
Isay
Eilean Mór
Lyndale Point
Hinnisdal Hut Circle
Greshornish Point
Hinnisdal Bridge
DUNVEGAN HEAD
Stein
Lusta
Loch Bay
Loch Greshornish
Kingsburgh
Loch Snizort
Beinn a' Sga
TROTTER
Blod an Athair
Galtrigill
Piping Heritage Cen.
Dun Borreraig
Borreraig
Ben Ettow
Loch Dunvegan
Claigan
Claigan Souterrain
Beinn Bhreac
Bay
Beinn Chreagach
Greshornish
Kildonan
Knott
Treaslane
Romesdal
River Romesdal
Eyre
Standing Stones
Uig
Borreraig Park
Annait
Bay River
B886
Flashader
Clachamish
The Aird
Kensaleyre
Rhenetra
River Haultin
An Ceannaich
Loch Pooltiel
Fariniquarrie
Totaig
Dun Fiadhairt
Suardal Hut Circle
Fairy Bridge
Edinbane
A850
Loch Eyre
Cairn
Bernisdale
Beinn a' Chearcall
Lower Milovaig
Oisgill Bay
Water Mill
Glendale
Blackhill
Ben Uigshader
Symbol Stone
Upper Milovaig
Lephin
Colbost
Dunvegan
Giant Angus Macaskill
Tote
Skeabost
B8036
Borve
Borve Standing Stones
Waterstein
Loch Mór
Borrodale
Holmisdale
Toy
Colbost Croft
Skinidin
Glen Bernisdale
St. Columba's Island
Carbost
Dunvegan
Kilmuir
Loch Niarsco
Uigshader
Drumuie
B884
Glen Dale
Hamara River
Lonmore
A863
Dun Osdale
Cruachan Beinn a' Chearcaill
Moonen Bay
Ben Corkeval
HEALABHAL MHOR
Roskhill
Roag
Loch Ravag
Beinn a' Ghlinne Bhig
Glengrasco
Ramasaig
Orbost
Cairns
Vatten
Ardroag
Loch Vatten
Loch Connan
River Snizort
Shulishadermor
Aros Experience
Beinn na Greine
Hoe Rape
The Hoe
HEALABHAL BHEAG
Loch Bharcasaig
Harlosh
Loch Caroy
River Ose
Balmore
Ose
B885
Tungadal Souterrain
Tungadal River
Glenmore
Hoe Point
Loch Glen Ionadal
Ben Connan
Beinn na Boineid
Harlosh Point
Colbost Point
Dun Beag
Hillcroft Farm
Totardor
Ben Duagrich
Stroc-bheinn
Mugeary
Am Bi-bogha Mór
Harlosh Island
Tarner Island
Ullinish
Cairn
Dun Mhor
Bracadale
Struan
Struanmore
Coillore
Ben Idrigill
Loch
Wiay
Carn Liath
An Dubh-sgeir
Macleod's Maidens
IDRIGILL POINT
Oronsay
Dun Ardtreck
Bracadale
ISLE OF SKYE
Portnalong
Loch Harport
B8009
Roineval
Meall an Fhuarain
Rubha nan Clach
Dun Ard an T-Sabhail
Fiskavaig
Fernilea
Carbost
Drynoch
Arnaval
Talisker Distillery
Gleann Oraid
Merkadale
River Drynoch
Talisker Bay
Talisker
Beinn nan Cuithean
Eynort River
Beinn Bhreac
Eynort
Glen Brittle Forest
A B C D
1 2 3 4 5
10 20 30 40
30 40 50 60 70 80
Eilean Lingreabhagh

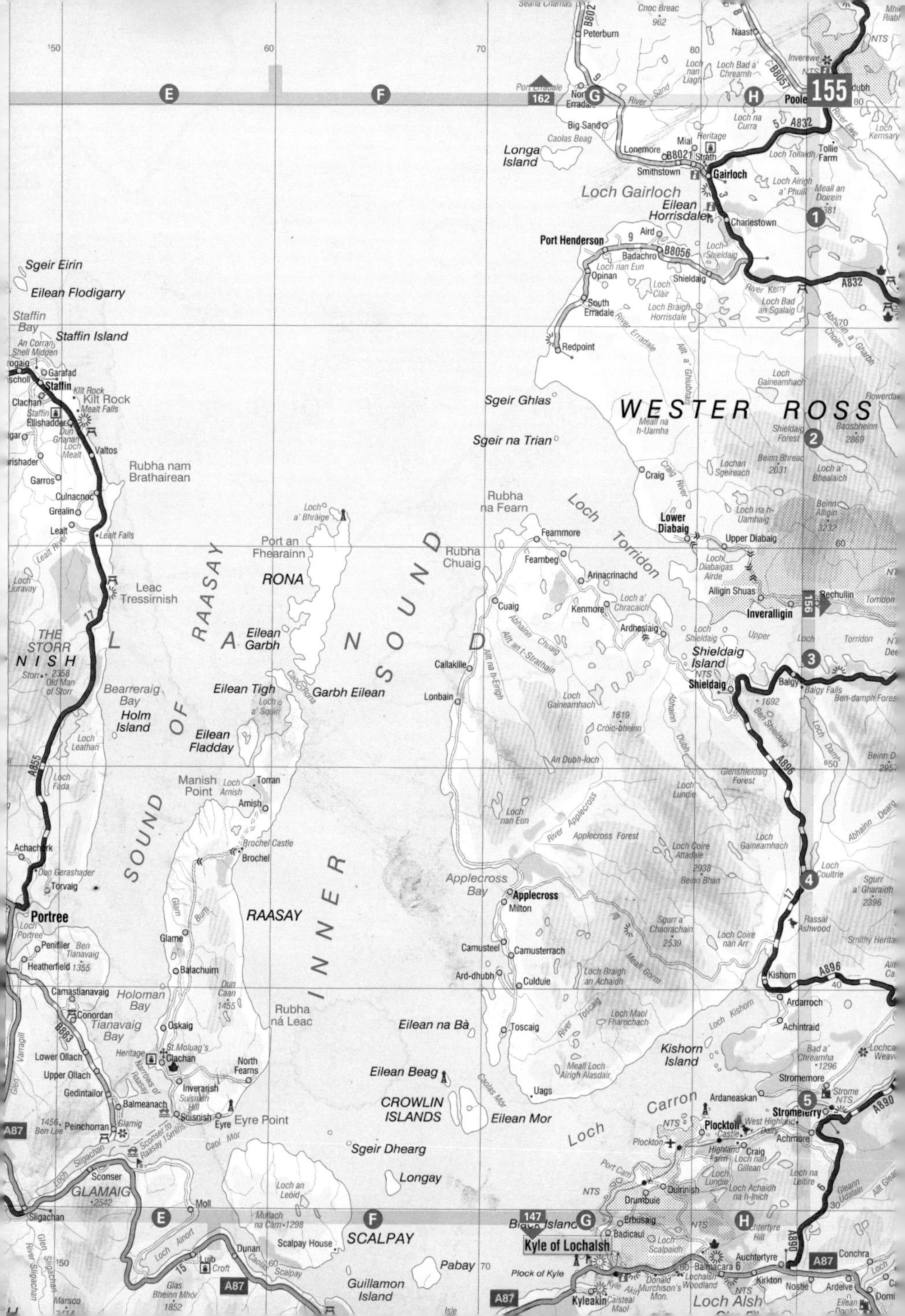
E
F
G
H
162
147
156
Peterburn
Cnoc Breac
962
Naast
Inverewe
NTS
Loch nan Liagh
Loch Bad a' Chreamh
Port Erradale
North Erradale
River Sand
Poolewe
Big Sand
Caolas Beag
Loch na Curra
Longa Island
Mial
Heritage
Lonemore
B8021
Strath
Smithstown
Gairloch
Tollie Farm
Loch Tollaidh
Loch Airigh a' Phuill
Meall an Doirein
Loch Gairloch
Eilean Horrisdale
Charlestown
Port Henderson
Aird
Badachro
B8056
Loch Shieldaig
Loch nan Eun
Opinan
Shieldaig
A832
River Kerry
Loch Clàir
Loch Bad an Sgalaig
South Erradale
River Erradale
Loch Braigh Horrisdale
Redpoint
Allt a' Ghiubhais
Loch Gaineamhach
Sgeir Ghlas
WESTER ROSS
Meall na h-Uamha
Shieldaig Forest
Baosbheinn
2869
Sgeir na Trian
Beinn Bhreac
2031
Lochan Sgeireach
Loch a' Bhealaich
Craig
Craig River
Rubha na Fearn
Loch Torridon
Lower Diabaig
Loch na h-Uamhaig
Beinn Alligin
3232
Upper Diabaig
Loch Diabaigas Airde
Fearnmore
Fearnbeg
Arinacrinachd
Rubha Chuaig
Alligin Shuas
Torridon
Inveralligin
Cuaig
Loch a' Chracaich
Kenmore
Ardheslaig
Abhainn Chuaig
Allt an t-Strathain
Upper Loch Torridon
Shieldaig Island
Callakille
Allt na h-Eiregh
NTS
Shieldaig
Balgy
Balgy Falls
Ben-damph Forest
Lonbain
Loch Gaineamhach
1619
Croic-bheinn
1692
Ben Shieldaig
Loch Damh
An Dubh-loch
A896
Glenshieldaig Forest
Loch Lundie
Loch nan Eun
River Applecross
Applecross Forest
Loch Gaineamhach
Loch Coire Attadale
2938
Beinn Bhan
Abhainn Deargh
Loch Coultrie
Sgurr a' Gharaidh
2396
Applecross Bay
Applecross
Milton
Sgurr a' Chaorachain
2539
Rassal Ashwood
Loch Coire nan Arr
Camusteel
Camusterrach
Meall Gorm
Loch Braigh an Achaidh
Ard-dhubh
Culduie
Kishorn
A896
Ardarroch
Loch Kishorn
Loch Maol Fharochach
Achintraid
Toscaig
River Toscaig
Eilean na Bà
Kishorn Island
Bad a' Chreamha
1296
Meall Loch Airigh Alasdair
Stromemore
Uags
Eilean Beag
Caolas Mòr
CROWLIN ISLANDS
Eilean Mor
Loch Carron
Ardaneaskan
Stromeferry
Strome NTS
A890
NTS
Plockton
West Highland Dairy
Castle
Achmore
Highland Farm
Craig
Loch nan Gillean
Sgeir Dhearg
Port Cam
Loch na Leitire
Longay
Loch Lundie
Duirinish
Loch Achaidh na h-Inich
Drumbuie
Gleann Udalain
Erbusaig
Black Island
Badicaul
Loch Scalpaidh
Kyle of Lochalsh
Auchtertyre
A87
Conchra
Plock of Kyle
Balmacara
Lochalsh Woodland
Kirkton
Nostie
Ardelve
Kyleakin
Kyle Akin
Caisteal Maol
Donald Murchison's Mon.
Loch Alsh
Pabay
A87
Sgeir Eirin
Eilean Flodigarry
Staffin Bay
Staffin Island
An Corran Shell Midden
Garafad
Staffin
Kilt Rock
Mealt Falls
Clachan
Staffin
Ellishadder
Dun Gnanan
Loch Mealt
Valtos
Rubha nam Brathairean
Garros
Culnacnoc
Grealin
Lealt
Lealt Falls
Leac Tressirnish
Loch a' Bhràige
Port an Fhearainn
RONA
SOUND OF RAASAY
INNER SOUND
THE STORR
Storr 2358
Old Man of Storr
Eilean Garbh
Bearreraig Bay
Holm Island
Eilean Tigh
Caol Rona
Garbh Eilean
Loch a' Squir
Eilean Fladday
Loch Leathan
A855
Loch Fada
Manish Point
Loch Arnish
Torran
Arnish
Brochel Castle
Brochel
Achachork
Dun Gerashader
Torvaig
Portree
Loch Portree
Glam Burn
Glame
RAASAY
Penifiler
Ben Tianavaig
1355
Heatherfield
Balachuirn
Dun Caan
1455
Camastianavaig
Holoman Bay
Conordan
Tianavaig Bay
Rubha ná Leac
B883
Oskaig
St. Moluag's
Heritage
Clachan
Lower Ollach
Upper Ollach
Narrows of Raasay
North Fearns
Inverarish
Gedintailor
Balmeanach
Suisnish Hill
Suisnish
Eyre
Eyre Point
Glamaig
1456 Ben Lee
Peinchorran
A87
Sconser to Raasay 15mins
Caol Mòr
Loch Sligachan
Sconser
GLAMAIG
2542
Loch an Leòid
Mullach na Càrn 1298
Sligachan
Moll
SCALPAY
Scalpay House
Loch Ainort
Dunan
Caolas Scalpay
Luib
Croft
Glen Sligachan
River Sligachan
Glas Bheinn Mhòr
1852
Marsco
Guillamon Island
Isle
A87
A87
A832
A890

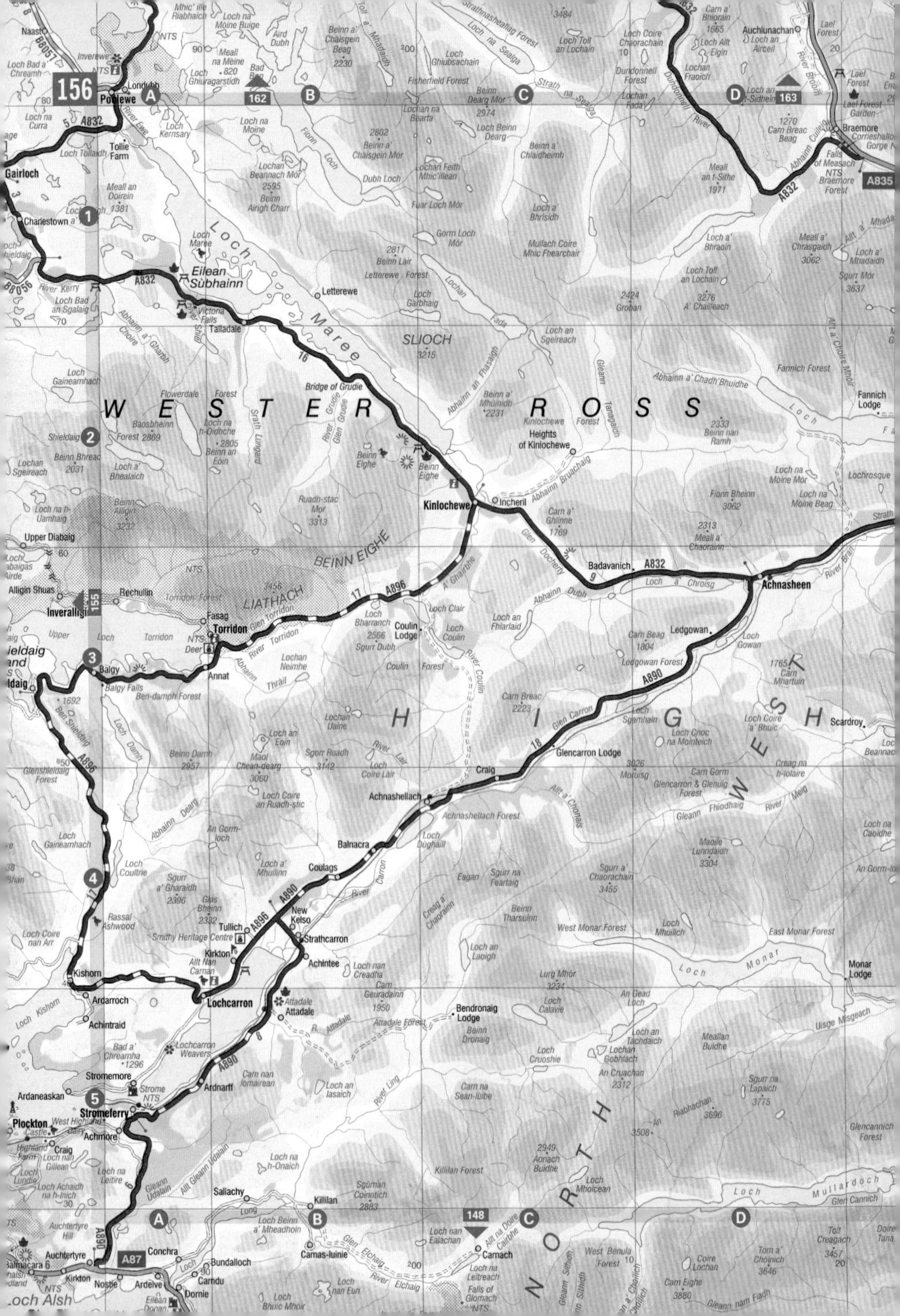
156
Naast
B8057
Mhic' ille Riabhaich
Inverewe
NTS
Loch Bad a' Chreamh
Londubh
Poolewe
A
Loch na Moine Buige
Aird Dubh
Meall na Meine
820
Loch Ghiuragarstidh
Bad Bog
162
B
Beinn a' Chaisgein Beag
2230
Toll a' Mhadaidh
Loch Ghiubsachain
Fisherfield Forest
Strathnasheallag Forest
Loch na Sealga
3484
Loch Toll an Lochain
Beinn Dearg Mòr
2974
C
Strath na Sealga
Loch Coire Chaorachain
Dundonnell Forest
Lochan Fada
Dundonnell River
Carn a' Bhiorain
1665
Loch Allt Eigin
Lochan Fraoich
Auchlunachan
Loch an Airceil
Lael Forest
D
Loch an t-Sidhein
163
Lael Forest
Lael Forest Garden
Braemore
Corrieshalloch Gorge
Falls of Measach
NTS
Braemore Forest
A835
1270
Carn Breac Beag
River Broom
Abhainn Cuileig
A832
Loch na Curra
A832
River Ewe
Loch Kernsary
Tollie Farm
Loch Tollaidh
Gairloch
Loch na Moine
Fionn Loch
Lochan na Bearta
2802
Beinn a' Chaisgein Mòr
Loch Beinn Dearg
Beinn a' Chlaidheimh
Lochan Beannach Mòr
2595
Beinn Airigh Charr
Dubh Loch
Lochan Feith Mhic'illean
Fuar Loch Mòr
Meall an t-Sithe
1971
Meall an Doirein
1381
Charlestown
1
Loch Maree
Loch Maree
Eilean Sùbhainn
Gorm Loch Mòr
Loch a' Bhrisidh
Mullach Coire Mhic Fhearchair
Loch a' Bhraoin
Meall a' Chrasgaidh
3062
Loch a' Mhadaidh
Allt a' Mhadaidh
2817
Beinn Làir
Letterewe Forest
Letterewe
Loch Garbhaig
Lochan Fada
Loch Toll an Lochain
3276
A' Chailleach
2424
Groban
Sgurr Mòr
3637
B8056
River Kerry
Loch Bad an Sgalaig
A832
Victoria Falls
River Shiel
Talladale
Abhainn a' Gharbh Choire
Loch Gaineamhach
SLIOCH
3215
Loch an Sgeireach
Gleann Tanagaidh
Fannich Forest
Allt a' Chaorainn Mhòir
Abhainn a' Chadh' Bhuidhe
Bridge of Grudie
Flowerdale Forest
Abhainn an Fhasaigh
WESTER ROSS
Beinn a' Mhùinidh
2231
Kinlochewe Forest
Fannich Lodge
Loch Fannich
Shieldaig
2
Baosbheinn
2869
Loch na h-Oidhche
2805
Beinn an Eoin
Strath Lungard
River Grudie
Glen Grudie
Beinn Eighe
Beinn Eighe
Heights of Kinlochewe
Abhainn Bruachaig
2333
Beinn nan Ramh
Lochan Sgeireach
Beinn Bhreac
2031
Loch a' Bhealaich
Loch na Moine Mòr
Lochrosque
Loch na h-Uamhaig
Beinn Alligin
3232
Ruadh-stac Mor
3313
Kinlochewe
Incheril
Carn a' Ghlinne
1769
Fionn Bheinn
3062
Loch na Moine Beag
Upper Diabaig
2313
Meall a' Chaorainn
Strath Bran
60
BEINN EIGHE
NTS
Glen Docherty
Badavanich
A832
Loch a' Chroisg
Achnasheen
River Bran
Alligin Shuas
155
Inveralligin
Rechullin
Torridon Forest
1456
LIATHACH
A896
A' Ghairbhe
Abhainn Dubh
Loch an Fhiarlaid
Upper Loch Torridon
Fasag
Torridon
NTS
Deer
Glen Torridon
River Torridon
Loch Bharranch
2566
Sgurr Dubh
Coulin Lodge
Loch Clair
Loch Coulin
River Coulin
Carn Beag
1804
Ledgowan
Loch Gowan
Ledgowan Forest
Shieldaig Island
3
Balgy
Balgy Falls
Annat
Abhainn Thrail
Lochan Neimhe
Coulin Forest
1765
Carn Mhartuin
A890
Ben-damph Forest
1692
Ben Shieldaig
Loch Damh
Lochan Uaine
Carn Breac
2223
HIGH
Glen Carron
Loch Sgamhain
Loch Coire a' Bhuic
Scardroy
Loch Cnoc na Mointeich
Loch an Eoin
River Lair
Glencarron Lodge
18
A896
Glenshieldaig Forest
Beinn Damh
2957
Maol Chean-dearg
3060
Sgorr Ruadh
3142
Loch Coire Lair
Craig
3026
Moruisg
Carn Gorm
Glencarron & Glenuig Forest
Creag na h-Iolaire
Beannach
Loch Coire an Ruadh-stac
Achnashellach
Allt a' Chonais
WEST
Abhainn Dearg
An Gorm-loch
Achnashellach Forest
Gleann Fhiodhaig
River Meig
Loch na Caoidhe
Loch Gaineamhach
Balnacra
Loch Dùghaill
Maoile Lunndaidh
3304
An Gorm-loch
Loch Coultrie
Loch a' Mhuilinn
Coulags
River Carron
Eagan
Sgurr na Feartaig
Sgurr a' Chaorachain
3455
4
Sgurr a' Gharaidh
2396
Glas Bheinn
2332
A890
New Kelso
Creag a' Chaorainn
Beinn Tharsuinn
Rassal Ashwood
Tullich
A896
Smithy Heritage Centre
Strathcarron
West Monar Forest
Loch Mhuilich
East Monar Forest
Loch Coire nan Arr
Kirkton
Allt Nan Carnan
Achintee
Loch an Laoigh
Loch nan Creadha
Loch Monar
Monar Lodge
Kishorn
Ardarroch
Lochcarron
Attadale
Attadale
Carn Geuradainn
1950
Lurg Mhòr
3234
Loch Calavie
An Gead Loch
Loch Kishorn
Achintraid
Bendronaig Lodge
Attadale Forest
R. Attadale
Beinn Dronaig
Loch an Tachdaich
Meallan Buidhe
Uisge Misgeach
Bad a' Chreamha
1296
Lochcarron Weavers
A890
Carn nan Iomairean
Loch Cruoshie
Lochan Gobhlach
An Cruachan
2312
Sgurr na Lapaich
3775
Stromemore
Strome
NTS
Ardnarff
Loch an Iasaich
River Ling
Carn na Sean-lùibe
5
Ardaneaskan
Stromeferry
Plockton
West Highland Dairy
Castle
Achmore
Highland Farm
Craig
Loch nan Gillean
An Riabhachan
3696
3508
NORTH
Glencannich Forest
Loch Lundie
Loch Achaidh na h-Inich
30
Loch na Leitire
Gleann Udalain
Allt Gleann Udalain
Loch na h-Onaich
Killilan Forest
2949
Aonach Buidhe
Loch Mhoicean
Loch Mullardoch
Glen Cannich
Sallachy
Killilan
Sgùman Coinntich
2883
A
Long
B
148
C
Allt na Doire Cairbhe
D
Auchtertyre Hill
Loch Beinn a' Mheadhoin
Loch nan Ealachan
A890
Auchtertyre
Conchra
Camas-luinie
Glen Elchaig
Carnach
West Benula Forest
Coire Lochan
Toll Creagach
3457
Doire Tana
Balmacara
A87
Bundalloch
Kirkton
NTS
Nostie
Ardelve
Loch Long
Carndu
Dornie
River Elchaig
Loch na Leitreach
Falls of Glomach
NTS
Loch nan Eun
Loch Bhuic Mhòir
Gleann Sithidh
Carn Eighe
3880
Tom a' Choinich
3646
Gleann nam Fiadh
Loch Alsh
Eilean Donan

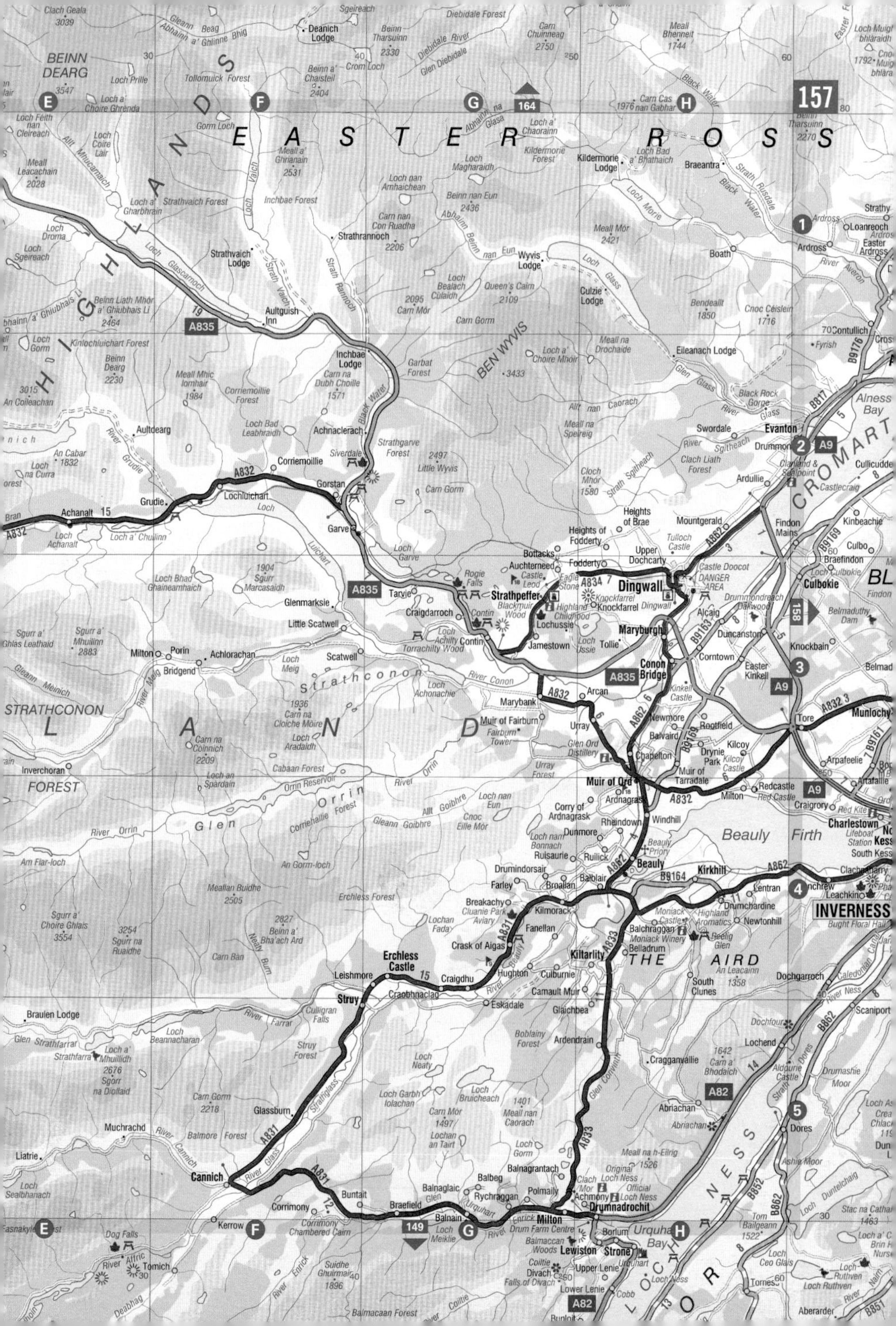

157
EASTER ROSS
HIGHLANDS
LAND
164
149
158
Clach Geala 3039
Sgeireach
Diebidale Forest
Gleann Beag
Abhainn a' Ghlinne Bhig
Deanich Lodge
Beinn Tharsuinn 2330
Diebidale River
Carn Chuinneag 2750
Meall Bhenneit 1744
Loch Muigh bhlàraidh
BEINN DEARG 3547
Loch Prille
Crom Loch
Glen Diebidale
Beinn a' Chaisteil 2404
Tollomuick Forest
Black Water
Loch a' Choire Ghrenda
Carn Cas nan Gabhar 1976
Beinn Tharsuinn 2270
Loch Féith nan Cleireach
Gorm Loch
Abhainn na Glasa
Loch a' Chaorainn
Loch Coire Làir
Allt Mhucarnaich
Meall a' Ghrianain 2531
Kildermorie Forest
Kildermorie Lodge
Loch Bad a' Bhathaich
Braeantra
Meall Leacachain 2028
Loch Magharaidh
Strath Rusdale
Loch nan Amhaichean
Loch Vaich
Loch a' Gharbhrain
Strathvaich Forest
Inchbae Forest
Beinn nan Eun 2436
Loch Morie
Strathy
Ardross
Loanreoch
Easter Ardross
Loch Droma
Carn nan Con Ruadha 2206
Abhainn Beinn nan Eun
Meall Mór 2421
Boath
Loch Sgeireach
Loch Glascarnoch
Strathrannoch
Strathvaich Lodge
Wyvis Lodge
Loch Glass
River Averon
Strath Vaich
Strath Rannoch
Loch Bealach Culaidh
Culzie Lodge
Beinn Liath Mhòr a' Ghiubhais Li 2464
Queen's Cairn 2109
Bendeallt 1850
Cnoc Céislein 1716
2095 Carn Mór
Carn Gorm
Aultguish Inn
A835
Loch Gorm
Kinlochluichart Forest
BEN WYVIS 3433
Loch a' Choire Mhóir
Meall na Drochaide
Contullich
Fyrish
Inchbae Lodge
Carn na Dubh Choille 1571
Garbat Forest
Eileanach Lodge
B9176
Beinn Dearg 2230
Meall Mhic Iomhair 1984
Corriemoillie Forest
3015 An Coileachan
Black Water
Glen Glass
Black Rock Gorge
Alness Bay
Allt nan Caorach
River Glass
B817
Loch Bad Leabhraidh
Aultdearg
Achnaclerach
Meall na Speireig
Swordale
Evanton
Drummond
A9
CROMARTY
River Grudie
An Cabar 1832
Loch na Curra
Strathgarve Forest
Siverdale
2497 Little Wyvis
River Sgitheach
Clach Liath Forest
Clanland & Sealpoint
Cullicudden
Corriemoillie
Carn Gorm
Cloch Mhòr 1580
Strath Sgitheach
Castlecraig
A832
Lochluichart
Gorstan
Ardullie
Grudie
Achanalt
Loch Achanalt
Loch a' Chuilinn
Garve
Heights of Brae
Mountgerald
Findon Mains
Kinbeachie
Heights of Fodderty
Tulloch Castle
Culbo
Luichart
Loch Garve
Bottacks
Upper Dochcarty
Braefindon
B9169
Loch Bhad Ghaineamhaich
1904 Sgurr Marcasaidh
Auchterneed
Castle Leod
Fodderty
Castle Doocot
Loch Culbokie
A862
A834
Dingwall
DANGER AREA
Culbokie
Eagle Stone
Knockfarrel
Rogie Falls
Tarvie
Strathpeffer
Blackmuir Wood
Highland Childhood
Dingwall
Drummondreach Oakwood
Findon
Glenmarksie
Craigdarroch
Contin
Lochussie
Alcaig
Belmaduthy Dam
Little Scatwell
Loch Achilty
Torrachilty Wood
Jamestown
Loch Ussie
Tollie
Maryburgh
B9163
Duncanston
Sgurr a' Ghlas Leathaid
Sgurr a' Mhuilinn 2883
Knockbain
Milton
Porin
Achlorachan
Loch Meig
Scatwell
Corntown
Easter Kinkell
Belmaduthy
Bridgend
Strathconon
River Conon
A835
Conon Bridge
Gleann Meinich
Loch Achonachie
Kinkell Castle
A832
Arcan
Tore
Munlochy
STRATHCONON
River Meig
1936 Carn na Cloiche Móire
Marybank
Urray
Newmore
Rootfield
Muir of Fairburn
Fairburn Tower
Balvaird
Drynie Park
Kilcoy
Kilcoy Castle
B9161
Carn na Coinnich 2209
Loch Aradaidh
Glen Ord Distillery
Chapelton
Arpafeelie
Inverchoran
FOREST
Cabaan Forest
Urray Forest
Loch an Spardain
River Orrin
Orrin Reservoir
Muir of Ord
Muir of Tarradale
Redcastle
Red Castle
Artafallie
Orrin
Corriehallie Forest
Allt Goibhre
Loch nan Eun
Ardnagrask
Milton
A9
Glen
Gleann Goibhre
Cnoc Eille Mór
Corry of Ardnagrask
Windhill
Craigrory
Red Kite
River Orrin
Rheindown
Charlestown
Lifeboat Station
Beauly Firth
Dunmore
Loch nam Bonnach
Beauly Priory
South Kessock
Am Fiar-loch
An Gorm-loch
Ruisaurie
Ruilick
Beauly
Meallan Buidhe 2505
Drumindorsair
Balblair
B9164
Kirkhill
A862
Clachnaharry
Farley
Broallan
Lentran
Inchrew
Leachkin
Erchless Forest
Breakachy
Cluanie Park Aviary
Kilmorack
Drumchardine
INVERNESS
Bught Floral Hall
Sgurr a' Choire Ghlais 3554
3254 Sgurr na Ruaidhe
2827 Beinn a' Bha'ach Ard
Lochan Fada
Fanellan
Moniack Castle
Highland Aromatics
Newtonhill
Neaty Burn
A831
Balchraggan
Moniack Winery
Reelig Glen
Carn Bàn
Crask of Aigas
Belladrum
Kiltarlity
A833
THE AIRD
Erchless Castle
River Beauly
An Leacainn 1358
Leishmore
Craigdhu
Hughton
Culburnie
South Clunes
Dochgarroch
Caledonian Canal
Struy
Craobhnaclag
Eskadale
Camault Muir
River Ness
Braulen Lodge
Culligran Falls
River Farrar
Glaichbea
Scaniport
Glen Strathfarrar
Loch Beannacharan
Boblainy Forest
Dochfour
B862
Strathfarrar
Loch a' Mhuillidh
Struy Forest
Ardendrain
Lochend
2676 Sgòrr na Diollaid
Loch Neaty
Cragganvallie
1642 Carn a' Bhodaich
Aldourie Castle
Strath Dores
Drumashie Moor
A82
Loch Garbh Iolachan
Loch Bruicheach
Glen Convinth
Carn Gorm 2218
1401 Meall nan Caorach
Abriachan
Glassburn
Carn Mór 1497
Dores
Muchrachd
River Cannich
Balmore Forest
Strathglass
Lochan an Tairt
Meall na h-Eilrig 1526
Ashie Moor
Liatrie
Loch Gorm
LOCH NESS
Balnagrantach
Clach Mor
Original Loch Ness
Official Loch Ness
Loch Duntelchaig
Loch Sealbhanach
Cannich
River Glass
Balbeg
Balnaglaic
Rychraggan
Polmaily
Achmony
B852
Buntait
Glen Urquhart
Drumnadrochit
Stac na Cathaig 1463
Corrimony
Braefield
Balnain
Milton
Tom Bailgeann 1522
Kerrow
Corrimony Chambered Cairn
Loch Meiklie
River Enrick
Drum Farm Centre
Urquhart Bay
Borlum
Fasnakyle Forest
Dog Falls
Balmaccan Woods
Lewiston
Strone
Urquhart
Loch Ceo Glais
Loch Ruthven
River Affric
Tomich
Suidhe Ghuirmain 1896
Coiltie
Divach
Upper Lenie
Falls of Divach
Lower Lenie
Cobb
Torness
River Enrick
River Coiltie
Balmacaan Forest
Deabhag
A82
Bunloit
Aberarder
River Nairn
B851

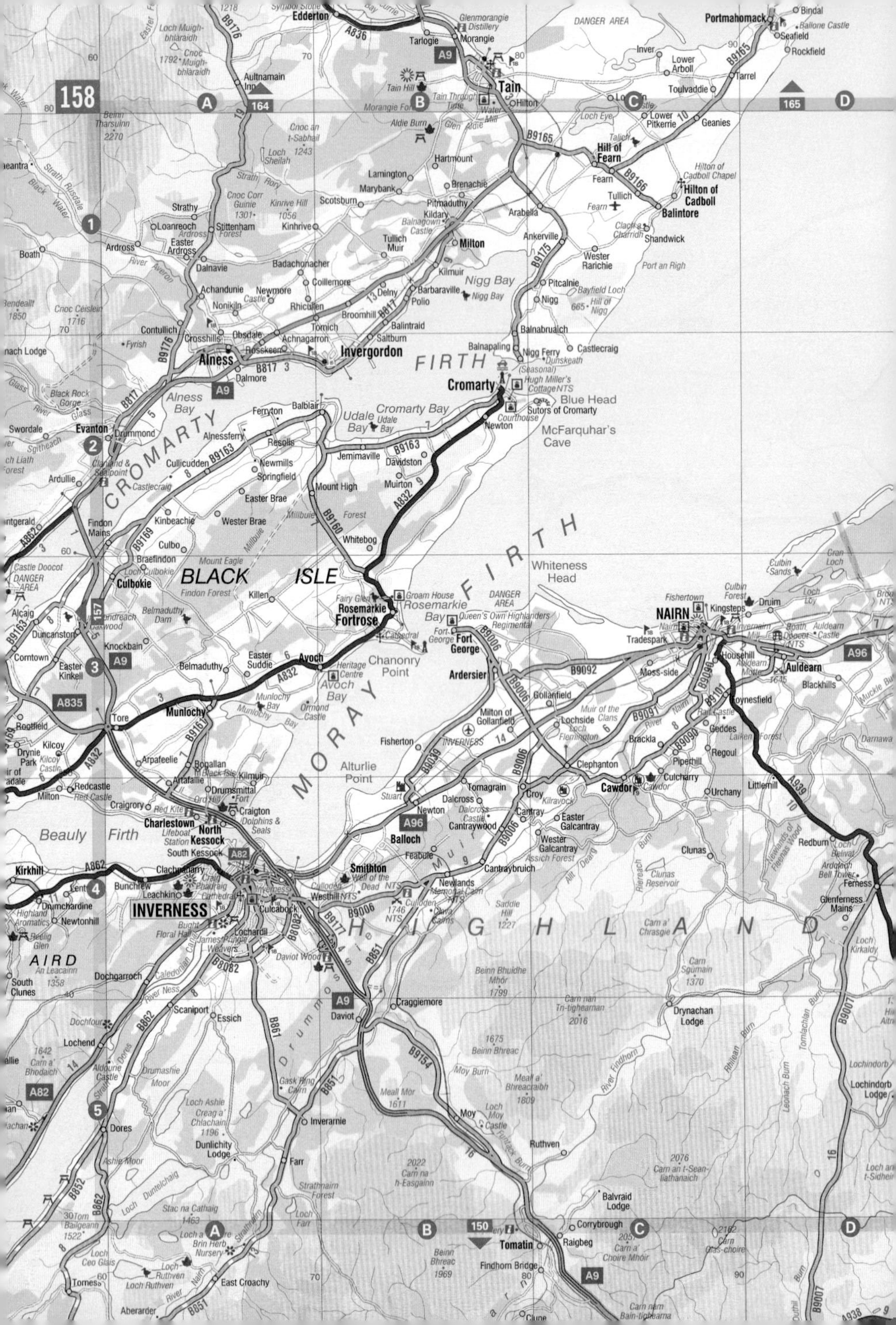

158
164
165
150
A
B
C
D
Edderton
Glenmorangie Distillery
Tarlogie
Morangie
A836
A9
B9176
Loch Muigh-bhlàraidh
Cnoc Muigh-bhlàraidh
1792
Aultnamain Inn
Tain Hill
Tain
Tain Through Time
Morangie Forest
Water Mill
Hilton
Glen Aldie
Aldie Burn
Beinn Tharsuinn
2270
Cnoc an t-Sabhail
1243
Loch Sheilah
Strath Rory
Hartmount
Lamington
Marybank
Brenachie
Pitmaduthy
Kildary
Balnagown Castle
Scotsburn
Kinrive Hill
1056
Cnoc Corr Guinie
1301
Strathy
Loanreoch
Stittenham
Ardross Forest
Kinkhrive
Ardross
Easter Ardross
Boath
River Averon
Dalnavie
Strath Rusdale
Black Water
Badachonacher
Coillemore
Tullich Muir
Milton
Kilmuir
Nigg Bay
Barbaraville
Polio
Delny
Newmore Castle
Rhicullen
Achandunie
Nonikiln
Broomhill
B817
Tomich
Balintraid
Saltburn
Cnoc Ceislein
1716
Contullich
Crosshills
Obsdale
Achnagarron
Rosskeen
Invergordon
Alness
Dalmore
Fyrish
B9176
Black Rock Gorge
Glass
Alness Bay
Ferryton
Balblair
Udale Bay
Cromarty Bay
Cromarty
Hugh Miller's Cottage NTS
Courthouse
Sutors of Cromarty
Blue Head
McFarquhar's Cave
Newton
Evanton
Drummond
Swordale
CROMARTY
FIRTH
Alnessferry
Resolis
B9163
Jemimaville
Davidston
Cullicudden
Newmills
Springfield
Castlecraig
Ardullie
Clarland & Seapoint
Muirton
A832
Mount High
Easter Brae
Wester Brae
Kinbeachie
Findon Mains
B9169
B9160
Millbuie Forest
Whitebog
Culbo
Braefindon
Mount Eagle
Loch Culbokie
Culbokie
BLACK
ISLE
Findon Forest
Castle Doocot
DANGER AREA
A862
Killen
Fairy Glen
Groam House
Rosemarkie
Fortrose
Cathedral
Rosemarkie Bay
MORAY
FIRTH
Whiteness Head
Queen's Own Highlanders Regimental
Fort George
B9006
Ardersier
Chanonry Point
Alcaig
Duncanston
Belmaduthy Dam
Knockbain
Cornton
Easter Kinkell
A835
Belmaduthy
Easter Suddie
Avoch
Heritage Centre
Avoch Bay
Ormond Castle
Munlochy Bay
Munlochy
Tore
Rootfield
Kilcoy
Drynie Park
Kilcoy Castle
Redcastle
Red Castle
Milton
B9161
Arpafeelie
Bogallan
Artafallie
Kilmuir
Drumsmittal
Ord Hill
Craigton
Dolphins & Seals
Red Kite
Craigrory
Charlestown
North Kessock
Lifeboat Station
South Kessock
Beauly Firth
A82
Kirkhill
Clachnaharry
Bunchrew
Leachkin
Craig Phadraig
Cathedral
Lentran
Drumchardine
Highland Aromatics
Newtonhill
INVERNESS
Culcabock
Bught Floral Hall
James Pringle Weavers
Lochardil
B8082
Reelig Glen
AIRD
An Leacainn
1358
South Clunes
Dochgarroch
Caledonian Canal
River Ness
Scaniport
Essich
Dochfour
Lochend
B862
Dores
Aldourie Castle
Drumashie Moor
Loch Ashie
Creag a' Chlachain
1196
Dunlichity Lodge
Ashie Moor
Carn a' Bhodaich
1642
Loch Duntelchaig
B852
Stac na Cathaig
1463
Loch a' Bhrin Herb Nursery
Torn Baileann
1522
Loch Ceo Glais
Loch Ruthven
Torness
East Croachy
Aberarder
River Nairn
B851
Strathnairn
Strathnairn Forest
Loch Farr
Farr
Inverarnie
Gask Ring Cairn
Meall Mòr
1611
Drummossie Muir
B861
B9154
Daviot Wood
Daviot
Craggiemore
B9177
B9006
Westhill
Culloden
Well of the Dead NTS
Smithton
Culloden 1746 NTS
Clava Cairns
Memorial Cairn NTS
Newlands
Feabuie
Balloch
A96
Cantraybruich
Saddle Hill
1227
HIGHLAND
Cantraywood
Cantray
Dalcross Castle
Dalcross
Tomagrain
Croy
Kilravock
Easter Galcantray
Wester Galcantray
Assich Forest
Stuart
Fisherton
Alturlie Point
B9039
INVERNESS
Milton of Gollanfield
Gollanfield
Lochside
Loch Flemington
Muir of the Clans
Clephanton
B9091
B9092
Moss-side
Tradespark
NAIRN
Fishertown
Kingsteps
Culbin Forest
Culbin Sands
Druim
Loch Loy
Cran Loch
Invernairn Mill
Boath Doocot NTS
Auldearn
Auldearn Castle
Househill
Auldearn Motte
1645
Blackhills
B9090
B9101
Boynesfield
Rait Castle
Geddes
Lethen Forest
Brackla
Piperhill
Regoul
Cawdor
Culcharry
Urchany
Littlemill
A939
Clunas
Clunas Reservoir
Redburn
Loch Belivat
Ardclach Bell Tower
Newlands of Fleenas Wood
Ferness
Glenferness Mains
Loch Kirkaldy
Càrn a' Chrasgie
Càrn Sgumain
1370
Beinn Bhuidhe Mhòr
1799
Càrn nan Tri-tighearnan
2016
Drynachan Lodge
1675
Beinn Bhreac
Moy Burn
Meall a' Bhreacraibh
1809
River Findhorn
Rhilean Burn
Leonach Burn
Tomlachan Burn
B9007
Lochindorb
Lochindorb Lodge
Moy
Loch Moy
Castle
Ruthven
Funtack Burn
2022
Càrn na h-Easgainn
2076
Càrn an t-Sean-liathanaich
Balvraid Lodge
Corrybrough
Raigbeg
Tomatin
2037
Càrn a' Choire Mhòir
2162
Càrn Glas-choire
Beinn Bhreac
1969
Findhorn Bridge
Clune
Càrn nam Bain-tighearna
A938
Portmahomack
Bindal
Ballone Castle
Seafield
Rockfield
DANGER AREA
Inver
Lower Arboll
Tarrel
B9165
Toulvaddie
Loch Eye
Lower Pitkerrie
Geanies
Hill of Fearn
B9166
Fearn
Tullich
Hilton of Cadboll Chapel
Hilton of Cadboll
Balintore
Arabella
Clach a' Charridh
Shandwick
Ankerville
B9175
Wester Rarichie
Port an Righ
Pitcalnie
Bayfield Loch
Hill of Nigg
665
Nigg
Balnabruaich
Balnapaling
Nigg Ferry
Dunskeath
Castlecraig
(Seasonal)

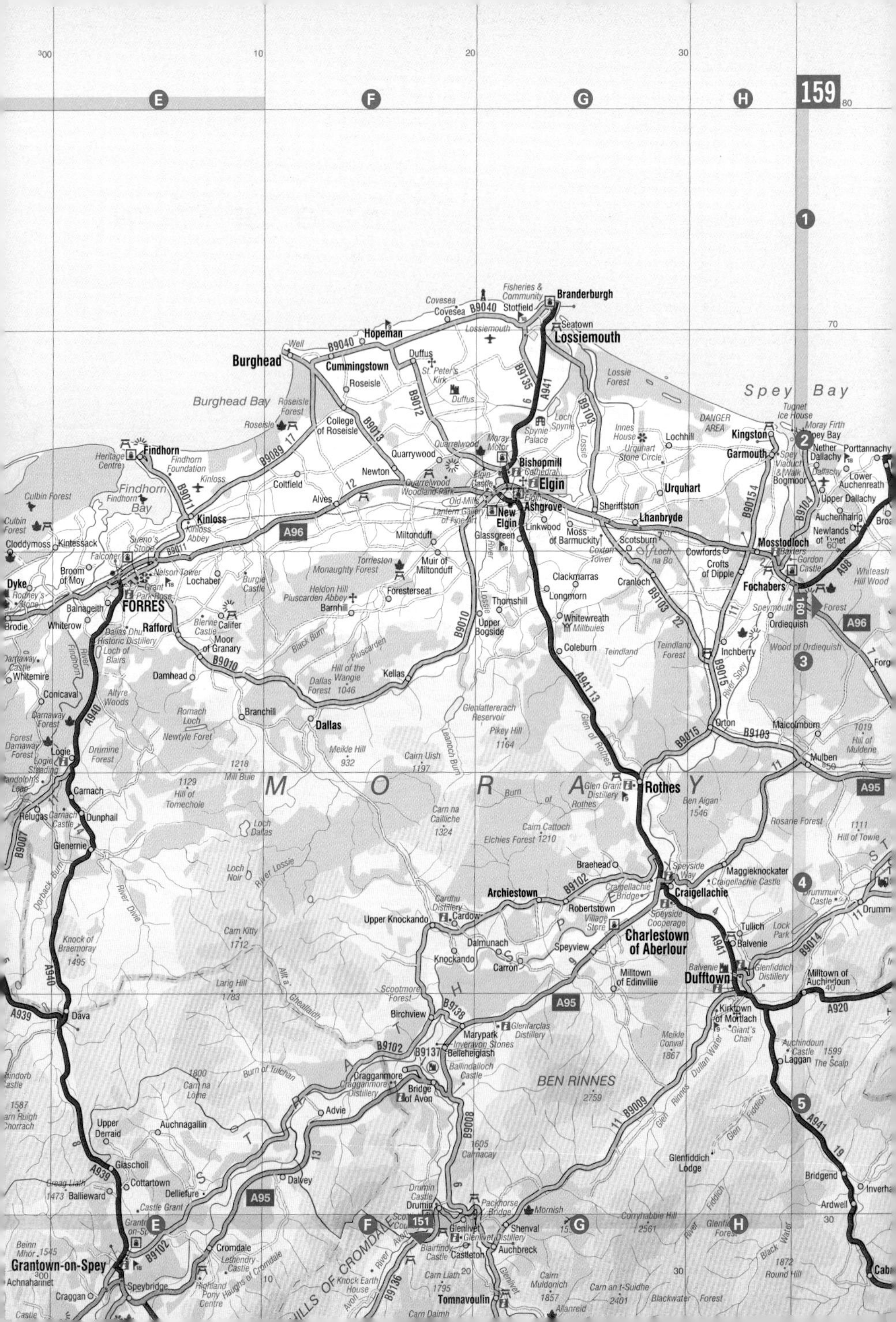
E
F
G
H
1
2
3
4
5
Fisheries & Community
Branderburgh
Covesea
Stotfield
B9040
Seatown
Lossiemouth
Hopeman
Burghead
Well
Cummingstown
Duffus
St. Peter's Kirk
Roseisle
Duffus
Burghead Bay
Roseisle Forest
Roseisle
College of Roseisle
B9012
B9013
B9135
A941
B9103
Lossie Forest
Spey Bay
Tugnet Ice House
Moray Firth
Spey Bay
Loch Spynie
Spynie Palace
Innes House
Urquhart Stone Circle
Lochhill
DANGER AREA
Kingston
Garmouth
Spey Viaduct & Walk
Nether Dallachy
Porttannachy
Dallachy
Lower Auchenreath
Bogmoor
Upper Dallachy
Auchenhalrig
Newlands of Tynet
Findhorn
Heritage Centre
Findhorn Foundation
Kinloss
B9089
Quarrywood
Moray Motor
Bishopmill
Cathedral
Elgin
Elgin Castle
Newton
Coltfield
Quarrelwood Woodland Park
Old Mills
Lantern Gallery of Fine Art
Ashgrove
New Elgin
Urquhart
Sheriffston
Lhanbryde
B90154
B9104
Culbin Forest
Findhorn Bay
Culbin Forest
Alves
Kinloss
Kinloss Abbey
A96
Linkwood
Moss of Barmuckity
Scotsburn
Loch na Bo
Mosstodloch
Baxters
Gordon Castle
A98
Whiteash Hill Wood
Cloddymoss
Kintessack
Sueno's Stone
B9011
Falconer
Miltonduff
Glassgreen
Coxton Tower
Cowfords
Crofts of Dipple
Broom of Moy
Nelson Tower
Lochaber
Grant Park
Rose
Burgie Castle
Torrieston
Monaughty Forest
Muir of Miltonduff
Clackmarras
Cranloch
Fochabers
Dyke
Rodney's Stone
Heldon Hill
Pluscarden Abbey
Foresterseat
Thomshill
Longmorn
B9103
Spey
Forest
Balnageith
FORRES
Barnhill
Brodie
Whiterow
Rafford
Blervie Castle
Califer
B9010
Upper Bogside
Whitewreath
Millbuies
Spey mouth
Ordiequish
A96
Dallas Dhu Historic Distillery
Moor of Granary
Coleburn
Teindland
Teindland Forest
Inchberry
Wood of Ordiequish
Loch of Blairs
Black Burn
Pluscarden
Forge
Darnaway Castle
Whitemire
Damhead
Hill of the Wangie 1046
Kellas
B9015
River Spey
Dallas Forest
A941
Conicaval
Altyre Woods
Glenlatterach Reservoir
Darnaway Forest
A940
Romach Loch
Branchill
Dallas
Leanoch Burn
Pikey Hill 1164
Glen of Rothes
Orton
B9103
Malcolmburn
1019 Hill of Mulderie
Newtyle Forest
Forest Darnaway Forest
Drumine Forest
Meikle Hill 932
Cairn Uish 1197
Logie
Logie Steading
1218 Mill Buie
Mulben
A95
Randolph's Leap
1129 Hill of Tomechole
M O R A Y
Burn of Rothes
Glen Grant Distillery
Rothes
Carnach
Ben Aigan 1546
Relugas
Carnach Castle
Dunphail
Carn na Cailliche 1324
Cairn Cattoch
Elchies Forest 1210
Rosarie Forest
1111 Hill of Towie
B9007
Loch Dallas
Glenernie
Loch Noir
River Lossie
Braehead
Speyside Way
Maggieknockater
Craigellachie Castle
River Divie
Dorback Burn
Craigellachie Bridge
Craigellachie
Drummuir Castle
Archiestown
B9102
Robertstown
Cardhu Distillery
Upper Knockando
Cardow
Village Store
Speyside Cooperage
Charlestown of Aberlour
Tullich
Lock Park
B9014
Carn Kitty 1712
Dalmunach
Speyview
Knockando
Carron
A941
Balvenie
Knock of Braemoray 1495
Balvenie
Glenfiddich Distillery
Milltown of Auchindoun
Milltown of Edinvillie
Dufftown
Larig Hill 1783
Allt a' Gheallaidh
Scootmore Forest
A95
A940
Birchview
B9138
Kirktown of Mortlach
Giant's Chair
A920
A939
Dava
Marypark
Glenfarclas Distillery
Inveravon Stones
B9102
B9137
Bellehiglash
Meikle Conval 1867
Auchindoun Castle
1599 The Scalp
Laggan
Ballindalloch Castle
Dullan Water
Dorb Castle
1800 Carn na Loine
Burn of Tulchan
Cragganmore
Cragganmore Distillery
Bridge of Avon
BEN RINNES 2759
1587 Carn Ruigh Chorrach
Upper Derraid
Auchnagallin
Advie
B9008
B9009
Glen Rinnes
Glen Fiddich
A941
1605 Carnacay
Glenfiddich Lodge
Glaschoil
A939
Creag Liath 1473
Ballieward
Cottartown
Delliefure
Dalvey
A95
Drumin Castle
Drumin
Packhorse Bridge
Mornish
Corryhabbie Hill 2561
Bridgend
Inverha
Ardwell
Castle Grant
Grantown-on-Spey
151
Glenlivet
Glenlivet Distillery
Shenval
Glenfiddich Forest
River Fiddich
Black Water
Beinn Mhor 1545
B9102
Cromdale
Lethendry Castle
Hills of Cromdale
Blairfindy Castle
Castleton
Auchbreck
1872 Round Hill
Grantown-on-Spey
Achnahannet
Speybridge
Highland Pony Centre
Haughs of Cromdale
Knock Earth House
River Avon
Carn Liath 1795
Glenlivet
Cairn Muldonich 1857
Carn an t-Suidhe 2401
Blackwater Forest
Craggan
B9136
Tomnavoulin
Allanreid
Carn Daimh
300
10
20
30
80
70
60
50
40
30

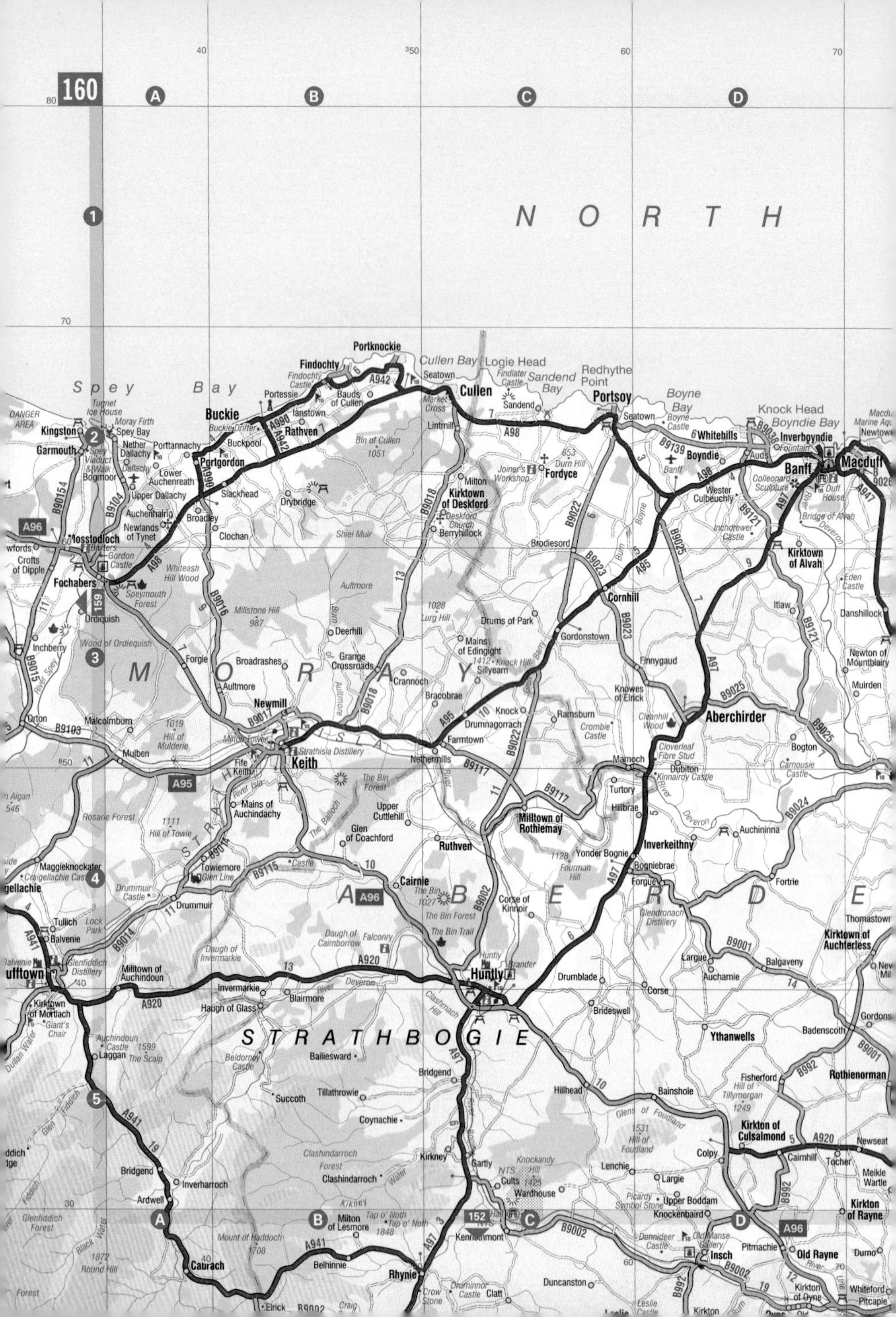

160
A
B
C
D
1
2
3
4
5
N O R T H
Spey Bay
Portknockie
Findochty
Cullen Bay
Logie Head
Findochty Castle
A942
Seatown
Cullen
Findlater Castle
Sandend Bay
Redhythe Point
Portsoy
Boyne Bay
Knock Head
Boyndie Bay
Macduff
Portessie
Bauds of Cullen
Buckie
Buckie Drifter
Ianstown
Rathven
A990
Tugnet Ice House
Moray Firth
Spey Bay
Kingston
Garmouth
DANGER AREA
Nether Dallachy
Porttannachy
Buckpool
Portgordon
Lower Auchenreath
Upper Dallachy
Bogmoor
Slackhead
Auchenhalrig
Newlands of Tynet
Broadley
Clochan
Drybridge
Bin of Cullen 1051
Lintmill
Market Cross
Sandend
Seatown
Boyne Castle
Whitehills
Inverboyndie
Boyndie
Banff
B9139
Fordyce
Joiner's Workshop
653 Durn Hill
Milton
Kirktown of Deskford
Deskford Church
Berryhillock
Shiel Muir
Brodiesord
Wester Culbeuchly
Colleonard Sculpture
Duff House
Bridge of Alvah
Inchdrewer Castle
Kirktown of Alvah
Eden Castle
Danshillock
Itlaw
Mosstodloch
Baxters
Gordon Castle
Crofts of Dipple
Fochabers
Whiteash Hill Wood
Speymouth Forest
Ordiquish
Wood of Ordiequish
Inchberry
Millstone Hill 987
Aultmore
Deerhill
1028 Lurg Hill
Drums of Park
Cornhill
Gordonstown
Mains of Edingight
1412 Knock Hill
Sillyearn
Grange Crossroads
Broadrashes
Forgie
Crannoch
Bracobrae
Finnygaud
Knowes of Elrick
Newton of Mountblairy
Muirden
M O R A Y
Aultmore
Newmill
Knock
Drumnagorrach
Ramsburn
Crombie Castle
Cleanhill Wood
Aberchirder
Orton
Malcolmburn
1019 Hill of Mulderie
Milton Tower
Strathisla Distillery
Keith
Fife Keith
Farmtown
Nethermills
Mulben
A95
Bogton
Carnousie Castle
Marnoch
Cloverleaf Fibre Stud
Dubiton
Kinnairdy Castle
Turtory
Hillbrae
The Bin Forest
Mains of Auchindachy
Upper Cuttlehill
Milltown of Rothiemay
Rosarie Forest
1111 Hill of Towie
The Balloch
Glen of Coachford
Ruthven
Auchininna
Inverkeithny
Yonder Bognie
1128 Fourman Hill
Bogniebrae
Forgue
Fortrie
Maggieknockater
Craigellachie Castle
Towiemore
Glen Line
Castle
Cairnie
A B E R D E E N
Drummuir Castle
Drummuir
The Bin 1027
Corse of Kinnoir
Glendronach Distillery
Thomastown
Tullich
Lock Park
Balvenie
Daugh of Cairnborrow
Falconry
The Bin Forest
The Bin Trail
Kirktown of Auchterless
Daugh of Invermarkie
Glenfiddich Distillery
Milltown of Auchindoun
A920
Huntly
Brander
Largue
Auchamie
Balgaveny
Dufftown
Invermarkie
Blairmore
Haugh of Glass
Deveron
Clashmach Hill
Drumblade
Corse
Brideswell
Kirktown of Mortlach
Giant's Chair
Auchindoun Castle
1599 The Scalp
Laggan
S T R A T H B O G I E
Ythanwells
Badenscoth
Beldorney Castle
Bailiesward
Bridgend
Fisherford
Hill of Tillymorgan 1249
Rothienorman
Succoth
Tillathrowie
Hillhead
Bainshole
Glens of Foudland
Coynachie
1531 Hill of Foudland
Kirkton of Culsalmond
Newseat
Cairnhill
Tocher
Meikle Wartle
Glen Fiddich
Bridgend
Clashindarroch Forest
Clashindarroch
Kirkney
Gartly
NTS
Knockandy Hill 1425
Cults
Wardhouse
Lenchie
Largie
Colpy
Picardy Symbol Stone
Upper Boddam
Knockenbaird
Inverharroch
Ardwell
Glenfiddich Forest
Milton of Lesmore
Tap o' Noth 1848
152
Kennethmont
B9002
Dunnideer Castle
Old Manse Gallery
Insch
Pitmachie
Old Rayne
Kirkton of Rayne
Durno
Mount of Haddoch 1708
A941
Belhinnie
Black Water
1872 Round Hill
Cabrach
Rhynie
Duncanston
Kirkton of Oyne
Whiteford
Pitcaple
Crow Stone
Druminnor Castle
Clatt
Leslie Castle
Kirkton
Elrick
Craig
Forest
A96
A97
A98
A941
A920
B9022
B9023
B9025
B9018
B9016
B9015
B9103
B9117
B9115
B9014
B9002
B9001
B992
B9024
B9121
B9038
B9104
B90154

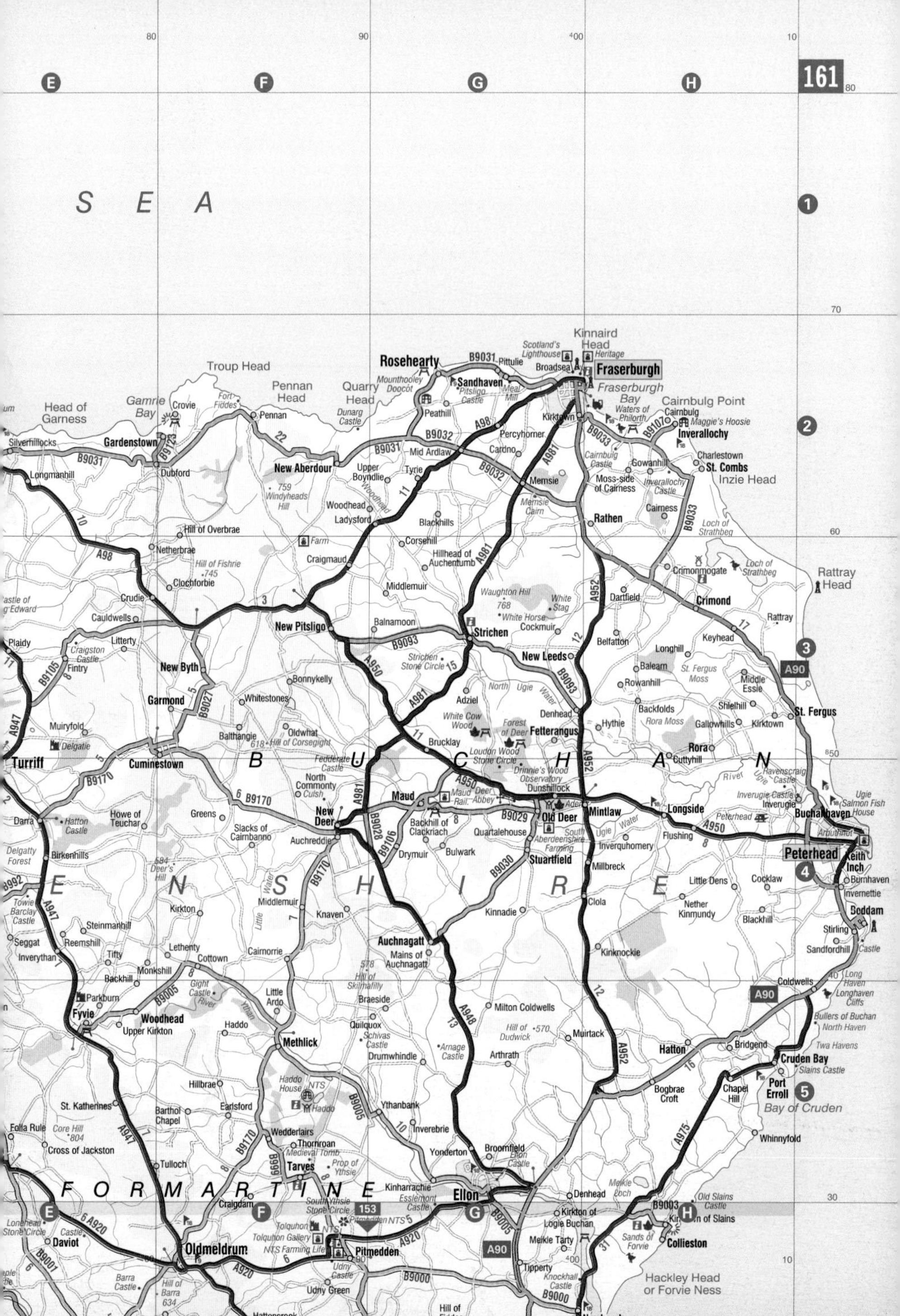
80
90
400
10
E
F
G
H
80
S E A
1
70
Kinnaird Head
Scotland's Lighthouse
Heritage
Troup Head
Rosehearty
B9031
Pittulie
Broadsea
Fraserburgh
Pennan Head
Quarry Head
Mounthooley Doocot
Sandhaven
Pitsligo Castle
Meal Mill
Fraserburgh Bay
Waters of Philorth
Cairnbulg Point
Head of Garness
Gamrie Bay
Crovie
Fort Fiddes
Pennan
Dunarg Castle
Peathill
Kirktown
Cairnbulg
Maggie's Hoosie
Inverallochy
2
Silverhillocks
Gardenstown
B9123
22
B9032
A98
Percyhorner
Cardno
A981
B9033
B9107
B9031
Mid Ardlaw
Charlestown
St. Combs
Cairnbulg Castle
Gowanhill
Inzie Head
Longmanhill
Dubford
New Aberdour
Upper Boyndlie
Tyrie
B9032
Memsie
Moss-side of Cairness
Inverallochy Castle
759 Windyheads Hill
Woodhead
Memsie Cairn
Cairness
B9033
10
Ladysford
11
Blackhills
Rathen
Loch of Strathbeg
Hill of Overbrae
60
Farm
Corsehill
Netherbrae
A98
Craigmaud
Hillhead of Auchentumb
A981
Crimonmogate
Loch of Strathbeg
Hill of Fishrie 745
Rattray Head
Clochforbie
Middlemuir
A952
Dartfield
Castle of Edward
Crudie
3
Waughton Hill 768
White Stag
White Horse
Crimond
Cauldwells
Balnamoon
New Pitsligo
Strichen
Cockmuir
Rattray
17
Plaidy
Craigston Castle
Litterty
B9093
Belfatton
Keyhead
3
Fintry
New Byth
Strichen Stone Circle
15
New Leeds
12
Longhill
A90
B9105
8
A950
Balearn
St. Fergus Moss
Middle Essie
Bonnykelly
A981
North Ugie Water
B9093
Rowanhill
Garmond
B9027
5
Whitestones
Adziel
Denhead
Backfolds
Shielhill
St. Fergus
A947
White Cow Wood
Forest of Deer
Fetterangus
Hythie
Rora Moss
Gallowhills
Kirktown
Muiryfold
Oldwhat
Balthangie
618 Hill of Corsegight
Bruckley
Delgatie
Rora
Cuttyhill
B U C H A N
Turriff
Cuminestown
Federate Castle
Loudon Wood Stone Circle
Drinnie's Wood Observatory
A952
850
Havenscraig Castle
River Ugie
5
11
North Commonty
Dunshillock
B9170
Inverugie Castle
Inverugie
Ugie Salmon Fish House
6
B9170
Cuish
A981
Maud
A950
Deer Abbey
Maud Rail.
Aden
Mintlaw
Longside
Buchanhaven
Howe of Teuchar
Greens
New Deer
Backhill of Clackriach
8
B9029
Old Deer
Peterhead
Darra
Hatton Castle
Slacks of Cairnbanno
B9028
B9106
Quartalehouse
South Ugie Water
A950
Flushing
Auchreddie
Aberdeenshire Farming
Arbuthnot
Delgatty Forest
Birkenhills
Drymuir
Bulwark
Inverquhomery
8
Peterhead
Keith Inch
684 Deer's Hill
B9170
Stuartfield
B9030
Millbreck
4
Burnhaven
B992
E N S H I R E
Little Dens
Cocklaw
Invernettie
Towie Barclay Castle
A947
Middlemuir
Water
Nether Kinmundy
Boddam
Kirkton
Clola
Knaven
Kinnadie
Blackhill
Little
7
Stirling
Seggat
Steinmanhill
Auchnagatt
Castle
Reemshill
Mains of Auchnagatt
Sandfordhill
Inverythan
Tifty
Lethenty
Cairnorrie
Kinknockie
Cottown
Monkshill
578 Hill of Skillmafilly
40
Long Haven
Backhill
8
Coldwells
Gight Castle
Little Ardo
A90
Longhaven Cliffs
Parkburn
B9005
Braeside
12
Ythan
River
A948
Milton Coldwells
Fyvie
Woodhead
Quilquox
Bullers of Buchan
Haddo
13
North Haven
Upper Kirkton
Schivas Castle
Hill of Dudwick
570
Muirtack
Twa Havens
Methlick
Arnage Castle
A952
Hatton
Bridgend
Drumwhindle
Arthrath
Cruden Bay
Slains Castle
16
Hillbrae
Haddo House
NTS
Chapel Hill
Port Erroll
Haddo
B9005
Bogbrae Croft
5
St. Katherines
Barthol Chapel
Earlsford
Ythanbank
Bay of Cruden
Folla Rule
Core Hill 804
A947
Wedderlairs
10
Inverebrie
A975
Cross of Jackston
Thornroan
Medieval Tomb
B9170
Whinnyfold
Tulloch
B999
Tarves
Prop of Ythsie
Yonderton
Broomfield
Ellon Castle
8
Meikle Loch
F O R M A R T I N E
Kinharrachie
Ellon
Denhead
Old Slains Castle
Craigdam
Esslemont Castle
B9003
30
South Ythsie Stone Circle
153
Kirkton of Logie Buchan
Kirkton of Slains
E
F
G
H
6
A920
Tolquhon
Pitmedden NTS
5
B9005
Lonehead Stone Circle
Castle
Tolquhon Gallery
NTS
A920
Meikle Tarty
Sands of Forvie
Collieston
Daviot
NTS Farming Life
A90
Oldmeldrum
Pitmedden
31
B9001
6
A920
Udny Castle
400
10
Barra Castle
Hill of Barra 634
B9000
Tipperty
Knockhall Castle
Hackley Head or Forvie Ness
Udny Green
B9000
Hill of Fiddes
Hattoncrook
Newburgh

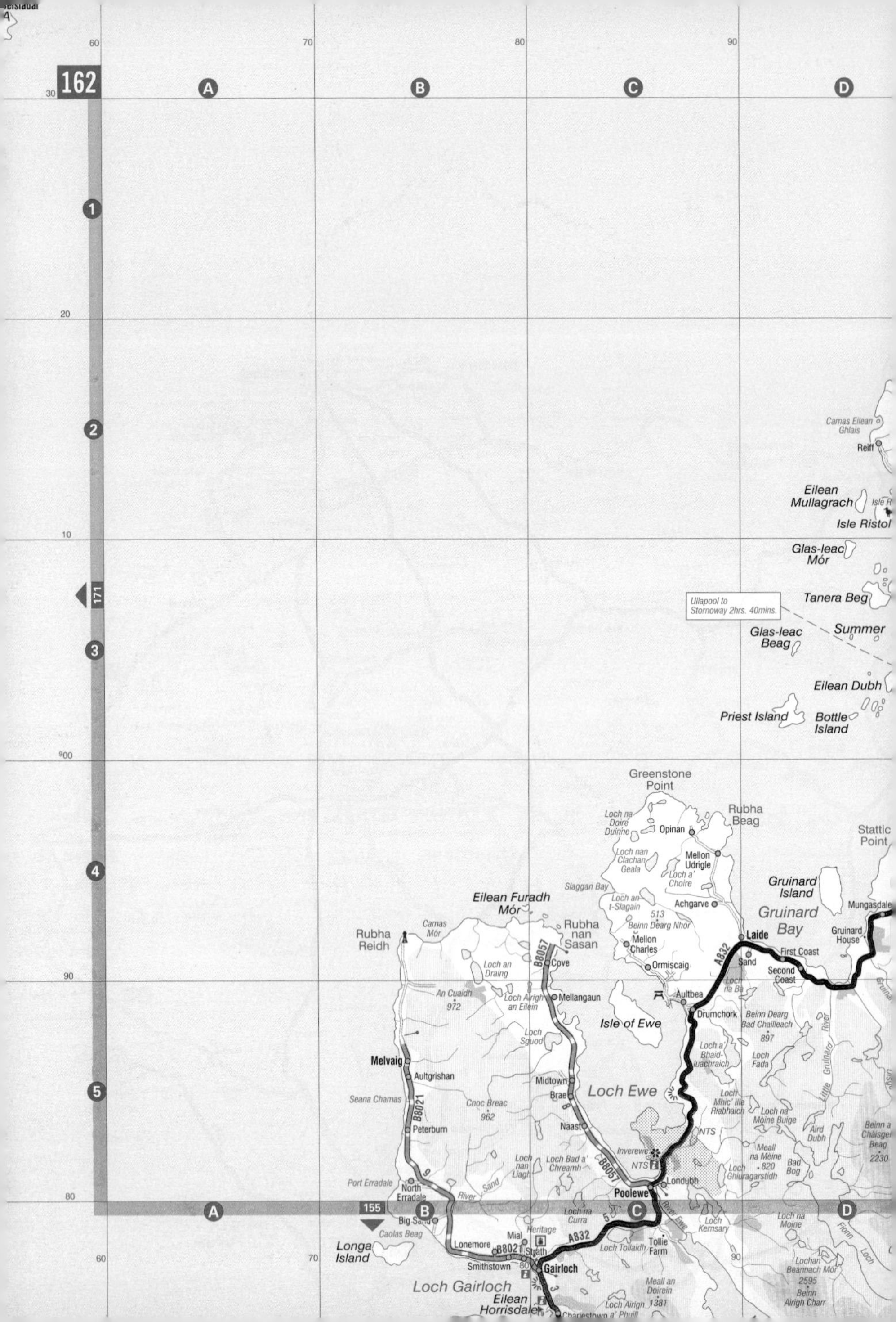

Ullapool to Stornoway 2hrs. 40mins.
Camas Eilean Ghlais
Reiff
Eilean Mullagrach
Isle Ristol
Glas-leac Mór
Tanera Beg
Glas-leac Beag
Summer
Eilean Dubh
Priest Island
Bottle Island
Greenstone Point
Loch na Doire Duinne
Opinan
Rubha Beag
Mellon Udrigle
Loch nan Clachan Geala
Loch a' Choire
Stattic Point
Slaggan Bay
Achgarve
Gruinard Island
Gruinard Bay
Mungasdale
Gruinard House
Loch an t-Slagain
513
Beinn Dearg Nhor
Mellon Charles
Laide
Sand
First Coast
Second Coast
Ormiscaig
Eilean Furadh Mór
Camas Mór
Rubha nan Sasan
Rubha Reidh
B8057
Cove
Loch an Draing
An Cuaidh 972
Loch Airigh an Eilein
Mellangaun
Aultbea
Drumchork
Loch na Ba
Beinn Dearg Bad Chailleach 897
Isle of Ewe
Loch Sguod
Loch a' Bhaid-luachraich
Loch Fada
Melvaig
Aultgrishan
Midtown
Brae
Loch Ewe
Seana Chamas
B8021
Cnoc Breac 962
Loch Mhic' ille Riabhaich
Loch na Moine Buige
Peterburn
Naast
NTS
Aird Dubh
Beinn a Chàisgein Beag 2230
Inverewe
Meall na Meine 820
Loch nan Liagh
Loch Bad a' Chreamh
B8057
Loch Ghiuragarstidh
Bad Bog
Port Erradale
North Erradale
River Sand
Londubh
Poolewe
Big Sand
Loch na Curra
River Ewe
Loch Kernsary
Loch na Moine
Fionn Loch
Longa Island
Caolas Beag
Mial
Heritage
Lonemore
B8021
Strath
A832
Loch Tollaidh
Tollie Farm
Lochan Beannach Mór 2595
Beinn Airigh Charr
Smithstown
Gairloch
Loch Gairloch
Meall an Doirein 1381
Eilean Horrisdale
Loch Airigh
Charlestown
A832
Little Gruinard River

171
155

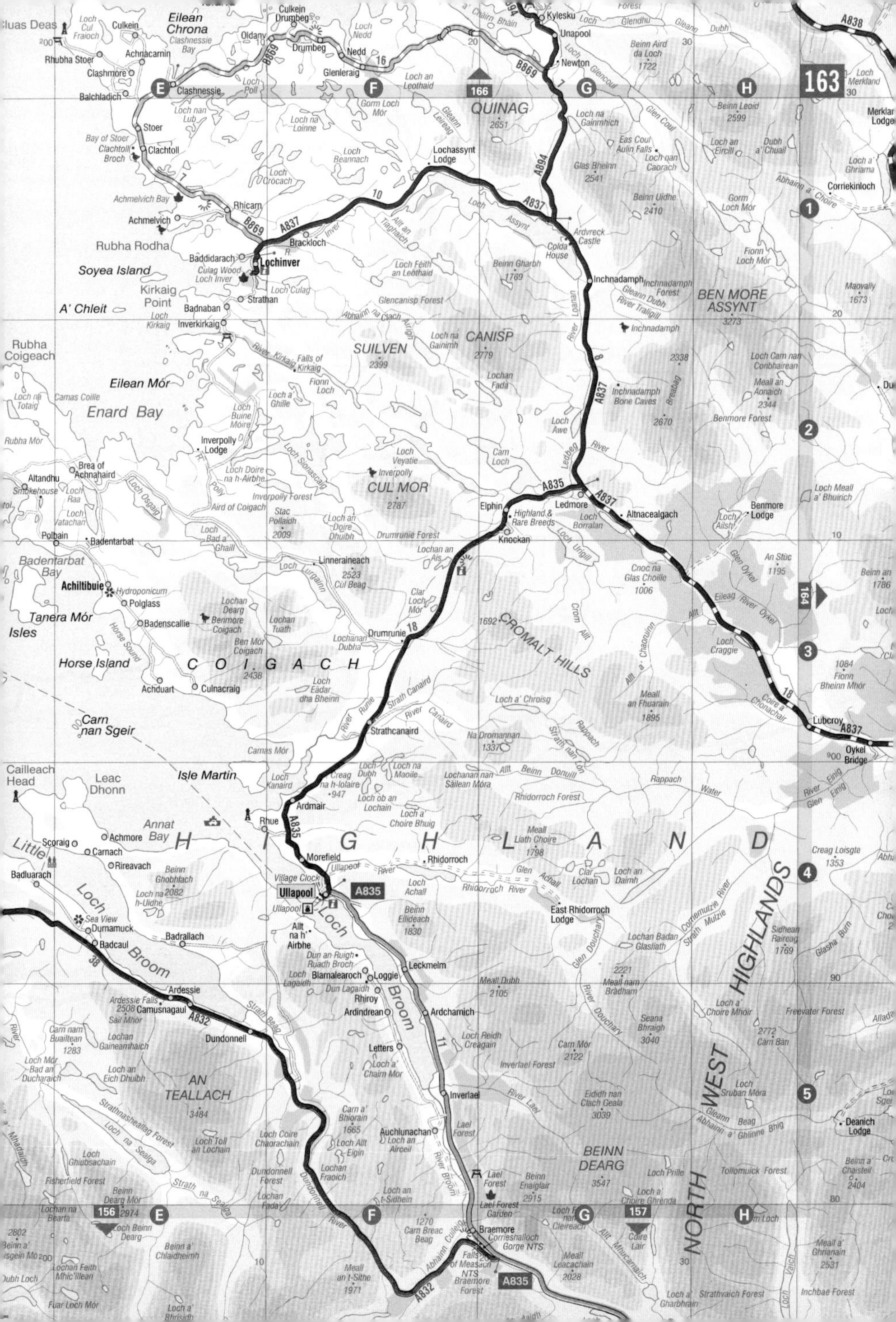
Kylesku
Unapool
Loch Glendhu
Gleann Dubh
A838
A894
Culkein Drumbeg
Culkein
Loch Cul Fraioch
Eilean Chrona
Clashnessie Bay
Oldany
Drumbeg
Loch Nedd
Nedd
Glenleraig
Rhubha Stoer
Achnacarnin
Clashmore
Balchladich
Clashnessie
Loch Poll
Loch nan Lub
Loch an Leothaid
Gorm Loch Mór
Newton
Loch Glencoul
Beinn Aird da Loch 1722
163
Loch Merkland
Merklan Lodge
166
QUINAG 2651
Gleann Leireag
Loch na Loinne
Stoer
Bay of Stoer
Clachtoll Broch
Clachtoll
Loch Beannach
Loch Crocach
Lochassynt Lodge
Loch na Gainmhich
Glen Coul
Eas Coul Aulin Falls
Loch nan Caorach
Beinn Leoid 2599
Loch an Eircill
Dubh a' Chuail
Loch a' Ghriama
Glas Bheinn 2541
Abhainn a' Choire
Corriekinloch
Achmelvich Bay
Rhicarn
Achmelvich
B869
A837
Loch Assynt
Beinn Uidhe 2410
Gorm Loch Mór
Rubha Rodha
Brackloch
Allt an Tiaghaich
Ardvreck Castle
Colda House
Fionn Loch Mór
Baddidarach
Culag Wood Loch Inver
Lochinver
Soyea Island
Kirkaig Point
Loch Culag
Loch Feith an Leothaid
Beinn Gharbh 1769
Inchnadamph
Inchnadamph Forest
Gleann Dubh
River Traligill
BEN MORE ASSYNT 3273
Maovally 1673
Strathan
Glencanisp Forest
A' Chleit
Badnaban
Loch Kirkaig
Inverkirkaig
Abhainn na Clach Airigh
Loch na Gainimh
CANISP 2779
River Loanan
SUILVEN 2399
Rubha Coigeach
River Kirkaig
Falls of Kirkaig
Fionn Loch
Lochan Fada
2338
Loch Carn nan Conbhairean
Meall an Aonaich 2344
Eilean Mór
Loch na Totaig
Camas Coille
Enard Bay
Loch a' Ghille
Loch Buine Móire
Inchnadamph Bone Caves
Breabag
2670
Benmore Forest
Rubha Mór
Inverpolly Lodge
Loch Sionascaig
Loch Veyatie
Inverpolly
Loch Awe
Ledbeg River
Cam Loch
Altandhu
Brea of Achnahaird
Smokehouse
Loch Raa
Loch Vatachan
Loch Osgaig
Loch Doire na h-Airbhe
Polly
Inverpolly Forest
Aird of Coigach
CUL MOR 2787
A835
Elphin
Highland & Rare Breeds
Ledmore
Loch Borralan
Altnacealgach
Loch Meall a' Bhuirich
Benmore Lodge
Loch Ailsh
Polbain
Badentarbat
Badentarbat Bay
Loch Bad a' Ghaill
Stac Pollaidh 2009
Loch an Doire Dhuibh
Drumrunie Forest
Knockan
Loch Urigill
Lochan an Ais
Linneraineach
Loch Lurgainn
2523 Cùl Beag
Cnoc na Glas Choille 1006
Glen Oykel
An Stùc 1195
Beinn an 1786
Achiltibuie
Hydroponicum
Polglass
Lochan Dearg
Benmore Coigach
Clar Loch Mór
Eileag
River Oykel
164
Tanera Mór
Isles
Badenscallie
Lochan Tuath
1692
CROMALT HILLS
Crom Allt
Drumrunie
Lochanan Dubha
Loch Craggie
Horse Sound
Ben Mór Coigach 2438
Horse Island
COIGACH
Allt a' Chaoruinn
1084 Fionn Bheinn Mhór
Achduart
Culnacraig
Loch Eadar dha Bheinn
Strath Canaird
Loch a' Chroisg
Meall an Fhuarain 1895
Coire a' Chonachair
Lubcroy
Carn nan Sgeir
River Runie
River Canaird
Strathcanaird
Na Dromannan 1337
Strath nan Lon
Rappach
Oykel Bridge
Camas Mór
Cailleach Head
Leac Dhonn
Isle Martin
Loch Kanaird
Loch Dubh
Creag na h-Iolaire 947
Loch na Maoile
Lochanan nan Sàilean Móra
Allt Beinn Donuill
Rappach Water
River Einig
Glen Einig
Rhidorroch Forest
Ardmair
Loch ob an Lochain
Loch a' Choire Bhuig
Rhue
Annat Bay
Meall Liath Choire 1798
Creag Loisgte 1353
HIGHLAND
Scoraig
Achmore
Little
Carnach
Rireavach
Morefield
Rhidorroch
Ullapool River
Glen Achall
Clar Lochan
Loch an Daimh
Beinn Ghobhlach 2082
Village Clock
Ullapool
Loch Achall
Rhidorroch River
Badluarach
Loch na h-Uidhe
Beinn Eilideach 1830
East Rhidorroch Lodge
Cormuizie River
Strath Mulzie
Sea View
Dumamuck
Badcaul
Badrallach
Allt na h' Airbhe
Loch Broom
Dun an Ruigh Ruadh Broch
Loggie
Leckmelm
Glen Douchary
Lochan Badan Glasliath
2221 Meall nam Bradham
Sidhean Raireag 1769
Glasha Burn
38
Ardessie
Ardessie Falls
2508 Sàil Mhór
Camusnagaul
A832
Loch Lagaidh
Biarnalearoch
Dun Lagaidh
Rhiroy
Ardindrean
Ardcharnich
Meall Dubh 2105
Loch a' Choire Mhóir
Freevater Forest
NORTH WEST HIGHLANDS
Strath Beag
Dundonnell
Carn nam Buailtean 1283
Lochan Gaineamhaich
Letters
Loch Reidh Creagain
River Douchary
Seana Bhraigh 3040
2772 Carn Ban
Loch Mór Bad an Ducharaich
Loch an Eich Dhuibh
AN TEALLACH 3484
Loch a' Chairn Mor
Carn Mór 2122
Inverlael Forest
Inverlael
River Lael
Eididh nan Clach Geala 3039
Loch Sruban Móra
Gleann Beag
Abhainn a' Ghlinne Bhig
Deanich Lodge
Strathnasheallag Forest
Loch na Sealga
Loch Toll an Lochain
Loch Coire Chaorachain
Carn a' Bhiorain 1665
Auchlunachan
Loch an Airceil
Lael Forest
Loch Allt Eigin
Loch Ghiubsachain
Dundonnell Forest
Lochan Fraoich
River Broom
BEINN DEARG 3547
Loch Prille
Tollomuick Forest
Beinn a' Chaisteil 2404
Fisherfield Forest
Beinn Dearg Mór 2974
Strath na Sealga
Lochan Fada
Loch an t-Sidhein
Lael Forest Garden
Beinn Enaiglair 2915
Loch a' Choire Ghrànda
Lochan na Bearta
156
Loch Beinn Dearg
Dundonnell River
1270 Carn Breac Beag
Abhainn Cuileig
Braemore
Corrieshalloch Gorge NTS
Loch nan Cleireach
Allt Mhucarnaich
157
Coire Lair
Meall a' Ghrianain 2531
Beinn a' Chlaidheimh
Lochan Feith Mhic'illean
Meall an t-Sithe 1971
Falls of Measach NTS
Braemore Forest
Meall Leacachain 2028
Loch Vaich
Dubh Loch
Fuar Loch Mór
Loch a' Bhrisidh
Loch a' Gharbhrain
Strathvaich Forest
Inchbae Forest
E
F
G
H
1
2
3
4
5

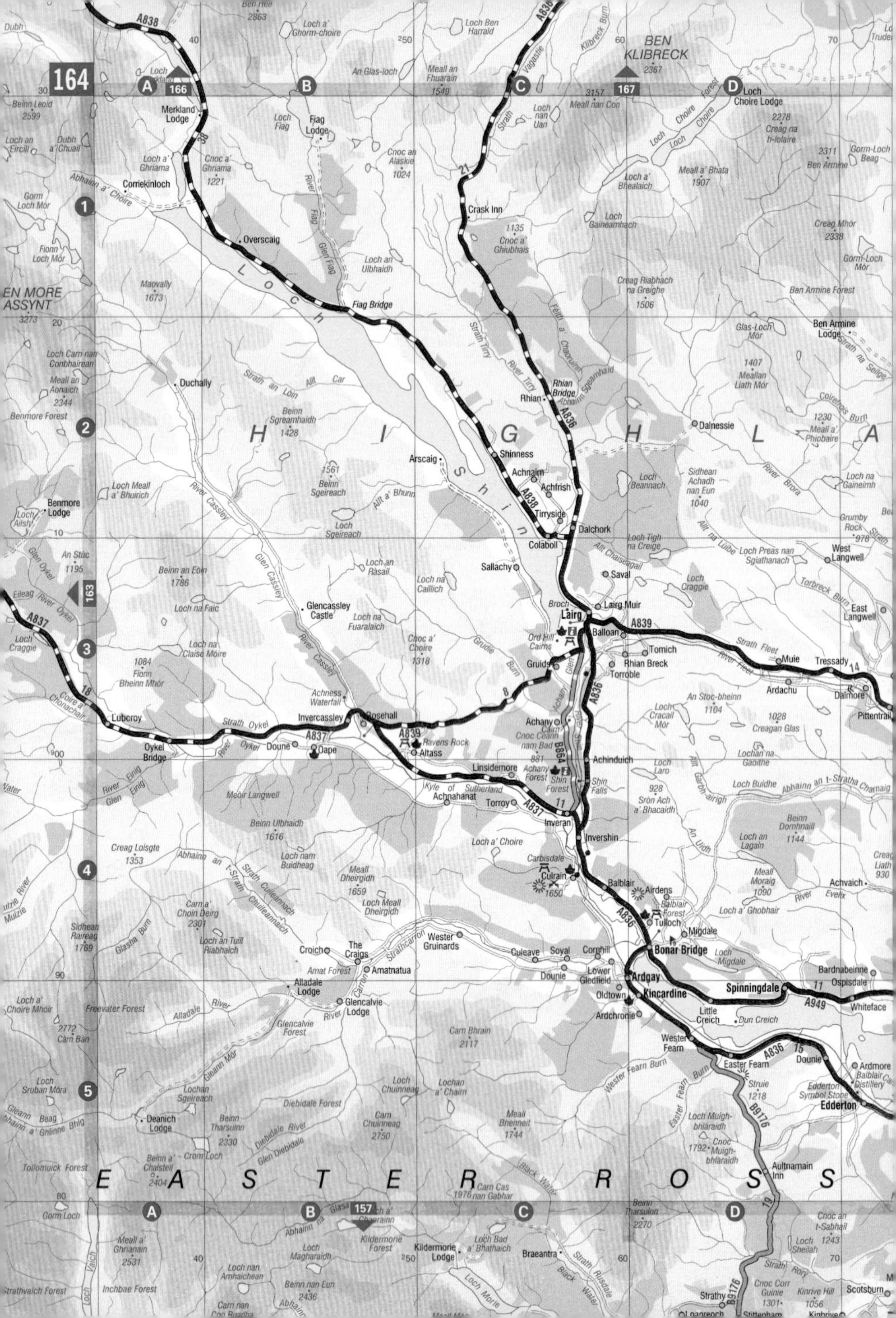
A838
Loch a' Ghorm-choire
Loch Ben Harrald
BEN KLIBRECK
2367
166
167
A
B
C
D
Merkland Lodge
Loch Fiag
Fiag Lodge
An Glas-loch
Meall an Fhuarain
1549
Strath Vagastie
Meall nan Con
3157
Loch Choire Lodge
Loch Choire Forest
Beinn Leoid
2599
Loch an Eircill
Dubh a' Chuail
Loch a' Ghriama
Cnoc a' Ghriama
1221
Cnoc an Alaskie
1024
Loch nan Uan
Creag na h-Iolaire
2278
Corriekinloch
Abhainn a' Choire
Gorm Loch Mór
River Fiag
Loch a' Bhealaich
Meall a' Bhata
1907
Ben Armine
2311
Gorm-Loch Beag
Crask Inn
Loch Gaineamhach
Creag Mhór
2338
Overscaig
Fionn Loch Mór
Glen Fiag
Loch an Ulbhaidh
1135
Cnoc a' Ghiubhais
Gorm-Loch Mór
Loch Shin
Maovally
1673
BEN MORE ASSYNT
3273
Fiag Bridge
Creag Riabhach na Greighe
1506
Ben Armine Forest
Loch Carn nan Conbhairean
Meall an Aonaich
2344
Strath Tirry
River Tirry
Glas-Loch Mór
Ben Armine Lodge
Strath na Seilge
Duchally
Strath an Lòin
Allt Car
Rhian Bridge
Rhian
1407
Meallan Liath Mór
Benmore Forest
Beinn Sgreamhaidh
1428
A836
Dalnessie
Coirefrois Burn
Meall a' Phiobaire
1230
H I G H L A
Arscaig
Shinness
Loch Beannach
River Brora
Loch na Gaineimh
1561
Beinn Sgeireach
Achnairn
Achfrish
Sidhean Achadh nan Eun
1040
Loch Meall a' Bhuirich
River Cassley
Allt a' Bhunn
Benmore Lodge
Loch Ailsh
Tirryside
Grumby Rock
976
Loch Sgeireach
Dalchork
Colaboll
Loch Tigh na Creige
Allt Chaiseagail
Allt na Luibe
Loch Preas nan Sgiathanach
West Langwell
An Stùc
1195
Glen Oykel
Loch an Rasail
Sallachy
Saval
Beinn an Eòin
1786
Glen Cassley
Loch na Caillich
Loch Craggie
163
Torbreck Burn
East Langwell
Eileag
River Oykel
Loch na Faic
Glencassley Castle
Broch
Lairg
Lairg Muir
A837
Loch na Fuaralaich
Balloan
A839
Loch Craggie
Loch na Claise Moire
Cnoc a' Choire
1318
Ord Hill Cairns
Tomich
Strath Fleet
Grudie Burn
Gruids
Rhian Breck
River Fleet
Muie
Tressady
1084
Fionn Bheinn Mhór
Torroble
Ardachu
Dalmore
Achness Waterfall
An Stoc-bheinn
1104
Pittentrail
Coire a' Chonachair
Lubcroy
Invercassley
Rosehall
Achany
Loch Cracail Mór
1028
Creagan Glas
Strath Oykel
Cnoc Ceann nam Bad
Oykel Bridge
Doune
Oape
Ravens Rock
Altass
B864
Achinduich
Lochan na Gaoithe
River Einig
Glen Einig
Linsidemore
Achany Forest
881
Shin Forest
Loch Laro
Shin Falls
Allt Garbh-airigh
Loch Buidhe
Abhainn an t-Stratha Chárnaig
Meoir Langwell
Kyle of Sutherland
Achnahanat
Torroy
Inveran
928
Sròn Ach a' Bhacaidh
Beinn Domhnaill
1144
Beinn Ulbhaidh
1616
Invershin
Loch a' Choire
Loch an Lagain
Creag Loisgte
1353
Abhainn an t-Strath
Loch nam Buidheag
An Uidh
Carbisdale
Culrain
1650
Meall Dheirgidh
1659
Strath Chuileannach
Balblair
Airdens
Meall Moraig
1090
Achvaich
River Evelix
Loch Meall Dheirgidh
Carn a' Choin Deirg
2301
Balblair Forest
Loch a' Ghobhair
Sidhean Raireag
1769
Loch an Tuill Riabhaich
Glasha Burn
Wester Gruinards
Tulloch
Migdale
Croich
The Craigs
Strathcarron
Culeave
Soyal
Corghill
Bonar Bridge
Loch Migdale
Amat Forest
Amatnatua
Dounie
Lower Gledfield
Ardgay
Bardnabeinne
Ospisdale
Alladale Lodge
Glencalvie Lodge
River Carron
Oldtown
Kincardine
Spinningdale
A949
Whiteface
Loch a' Choire Mhóir
Freevater Forest
Alladale River
Glencalvie Forest
Ardchronie
Little Creich
Dun Creich
2772
Càrn Bàn
Carn Bhrain
2117
Wester Fearn
A836
Dounie
Ardmore
Balblair Distillery
Easter Fearn
Struie
1218
Edderton Symbol Stone
Edderton
Loch Sruban Móra
Gleann Mór
Lochan Sgeireach
Loch Chuinneag
Lochan a' Chairn
Wester Fearn Burn
Easter Fearn Burn
Diebidale Forest
Deanich Lodge
Gleann Beag
Abhainn a' Ghlinne Bhig
Beinn Tharsuinn
2330
Carn Chuinneag
2750
Diebidale River
Meall Bhenneit
1744
Loch Muigh-bhlàraidh
1792
Cnoc Muigh-bhlàraidh
B9176
Glen Diebidale
Crom Loch
Beinn a' Chaisteil
2404
Tollomuick Forest
Black Water
Aultnamain Inn
E A S T E R R O S S
Carn Cas nan Gabhar
1976
Beinn Tharsuinn
2270
157
Gorm Loch
Abhainn na Glasa
Loch a' Chairainn
Kildermorie Forest
Cnoc an t-Sabhail
1243
Meall a' Ghrianain
2531
Loch Magharaidh
Kildermorie Lodge
Loch Bad a' Bhathaich
Braeantra
Strath Rusdale
Loch Sheilah
Loch nan Amhaichean
Strath Rory
Beinn nan Eun
2436
Loch Morie
Black Water
Strathvaich Forest
Inchbae Forest
Loch Vaich
Carn nan Coo Ruadha
Strathy
Cnoc Corr Guinie
1301
Kinrive Hill
1056
Scotsburn
Loanreoch
Stittenham
Kinbrive

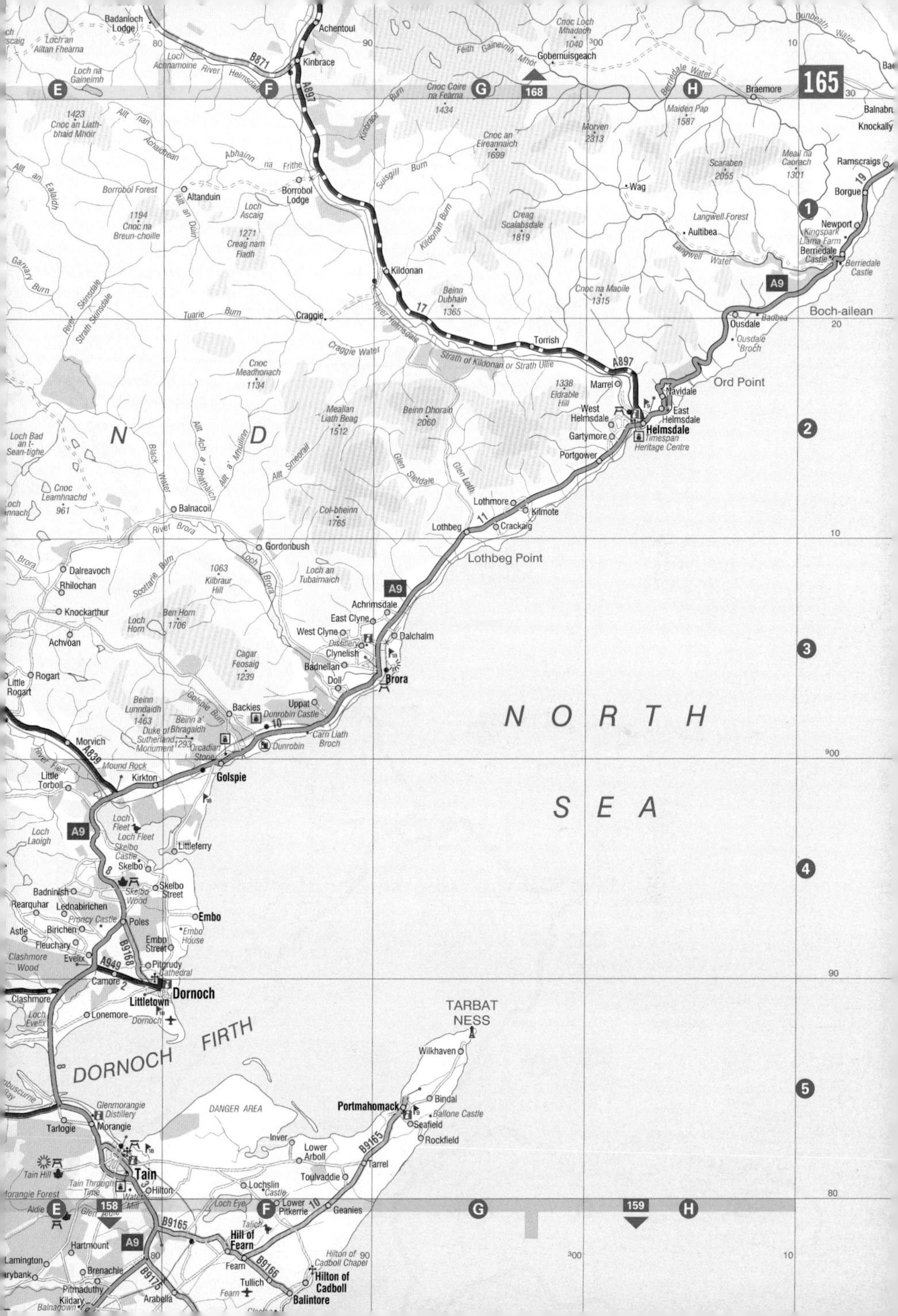
Badanloch Lodge
Loch an Alltan Fhearna
Achentoul
Kinbrace
B871
A897
Loch Achnamoine
River Helmsdale
Loch na Gaineimh
Cnoc Loch Mhadadh 1040
Feith Gaineimh Mhor
Gobernuisgeach
Dunbeath Water
Berriedale Water
Braemore
Cnoc Coire na Fearna 1434
168
1423 Cnoc an Liath-bhaid Mhoir
Allt nan Achaidhean
Abhainn na Frithe
Kinbrace Burn
Cnoc an Eireannaich 1699
Morven 2313
Maiden Pap 1587
Scaraben 2055
Meall na Caorach 1301
Balnabruich
Knockally
Ramscraigs
Borgue
Allt an Ealaidh
Borrobol Forest
Altanduin
Borrobol Lodge
Suisgill Burn
Wag
1194 Cnoc na Breun-choille
Allt an Duin
Loch Ascaig
1271 Creag nam Fiadh
Kildonan Burn
Creag Scalabsdale 1819
Langwell Forest
Aultibea
Newport
Kingspark Llama Farm
Berriedale Castle
Langwell Water
Garvary Burn
Kildonan
Beinn Dubhain 1365
Cnoc na Maoile 1315
A9
Boch-ailean
River Skinsdale
Strath Skinsdale
Tuarie Burn
Craggie
River Helmsdale
Ousdale
Badbea
Ousdale Broch
Craggie Water
Torrish
Strath of Kildonan or Strath Ullie
A897
Cnoc Meadhonach 1134
Marrel
1338 Eldrable Hill
Navidale
Ord Point
East Helmsdale
Helmsdale
Timespan Heritage Centre
West Helmsdale
Gartymore
Portgower
Meallan Liath Beag 1512
Beinn Dhorain 2060
Loch Bad an t-Sean-tighe
N
D
Black Water
Allt Ach a' Bhathaich
Allt a' Mhuilinn
Allt Smeorail
Glen Sletdale
Glen Loth
Cnoc Leamhnachd 961
Balnacoil
Col-bheinn 1765
Lothmore
Kilmote
Lothbeg
Crackaig
River Brora
Gordonbush
Lothbeg Point
Brora
Dalreavoch
Rhilochan
Scottarie Burn
1063 Kilbraur Hill
Loch Brora
Loch an Tubairnaich
Knockarthur
Loch Horn
Ben Horn 1706
Achrimsdale
East Clyne
West Clyne
Dalchalm
Achvoan
Distillery
Clynelish
Cagar Feosaig 1239
Badnellan
Doll
Rogart
Little Rogart
Beinn Lunndaidh 1463
Golspie Burn
Backies
Uppat
Dunrobin Castle
NORTH
Beinn a' Bhragaidh 1293
Duke of Sutherland Monument
Carn Liath Broch
Morvich
A839
Orcadian Stone
Dunrobin
River Fleet
Mound Rock
Kirkton
Golspie
Little Torboll
SEA
Loch Fleet
Loch Laoigh
Littleferry
Skelbo Castle
Skelbo
Badninish
Skelbo Wood
Skelbo Street
Rearquhar
Lednabirichen
Proncy Castle
Embo
Astle
Birichen
Poles
Embo House
Fleuchary
B9168
Embo Street
Clashmore Wood
Evelix
A949
Pitgrudy
Cathedral
Camore
Dornoch
Clashmore
Littletown
Loch Evelix
Lonemore
Dornoch
TARBAT NESS
DORNOCH FIRTH
Wilkhaven
Glenmorangie Distillery
DANGER AREA
Bindal
Portmahomack
Ballone Castle
Seafield
Tarlogie
Morangie
Rockfield
Inver
Lower Arboll
B9165
Tarrel
Tain Hill
Tain
Tain Through Time
Toulvaddie
Lochslin Castle
Hilton
Water Mill
Morangie Forest
158
Loch Eye
Lower Pitkerrie
Geanies
159
Aldie
Glen Aldie
B9165
Talich
Hill of Fearn
Hartmount
A9
Hilton of Cadboll Chapel
Lamington
Fearn
B9166
Brenachie
Hilton of Cadboll
Tullich
Pitmaduthy
B9175
Kildary
Arabella
Fearn
Balintore
Balnagown

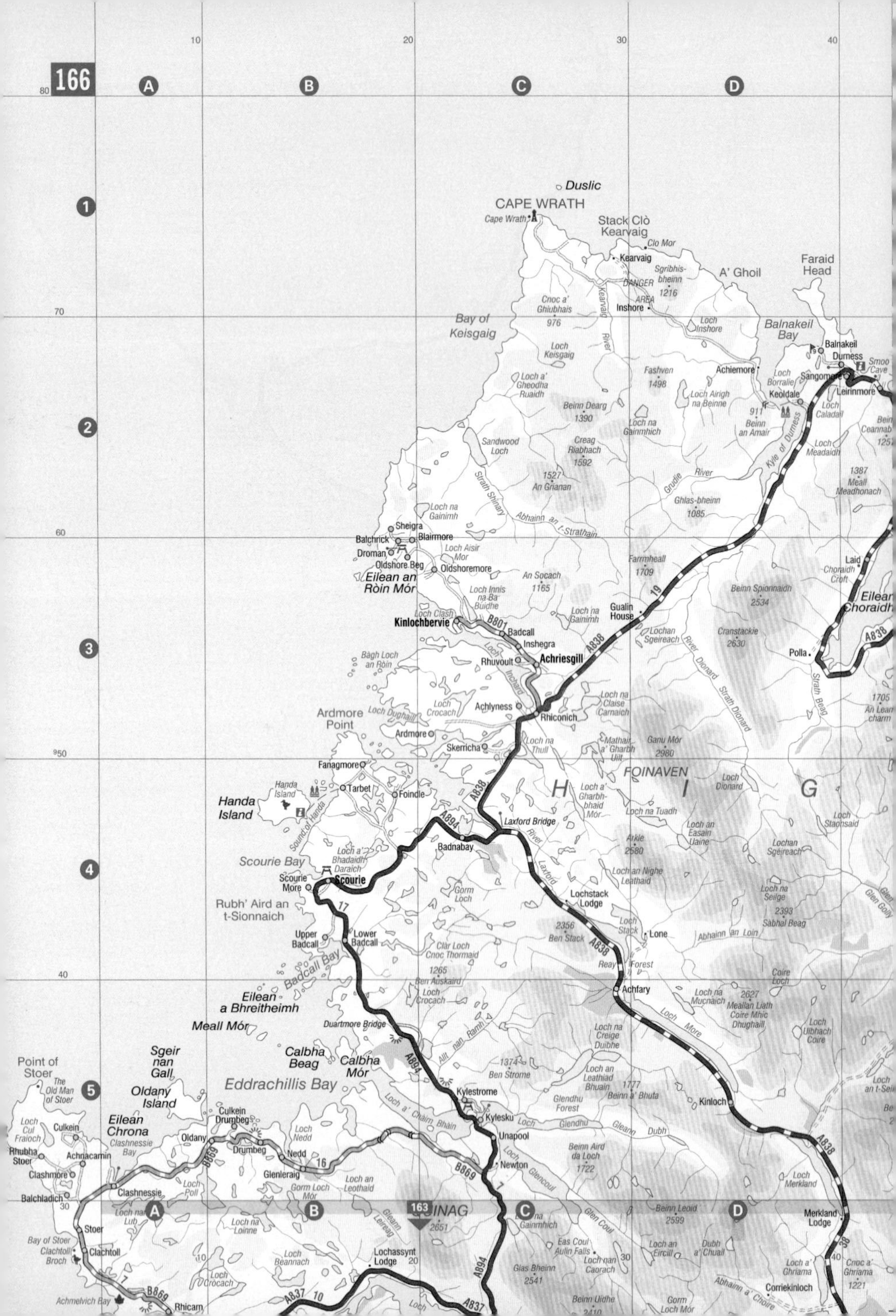
Duslic
CAPE WRATH
Cape Wrath
Stack Clò Kearvaig
Clo Mor
Kearvaig
Sgribhis-bheinn 1216
DANGER AREA
A' Ghoil
Faraid Head
Cnoc a' Ghiubhais 976
Inshore
Loch Inshore
Balnakeil Bay
Bay of Keisgaig
Loch Keisgaig
Balnakeil
Durness
Smoo Cave
Fashven 1498
Achiemore
Loch Borralie
Sangomore
Leirinmore
Loch a' Gheodha Ruaidh
Beinn Dearg 1390
Loch Airigh na Beinne
Keoldale
Loch Caladail
911 Beinn an Amair
Sandwood Loch
Creag Riabhach 1592
Loch na Gainmhich
Kyle of Durness
Loch Meadaidh
1527 An Grianan
Grudie River
1387 Meall Meadhonach
Strath Shinary
Ghlas-bheinn 1085
Loch na Gainimh
Abhainn an t-Strathain
Sheigra
Balchrick
Blairmore
Droman
Loch Aisir Mor
Oldshore Beg
Oldshoremore
Farrmheall 1709
Laid
Choraidh Croft
Eilean an Ròin Mór
An Socach 1165
Beinn Spionnaidh 2534
Loch Innis na Ba Buidhe
Loch Clash
Kinlochbervie
B801
Badcall
Loch na Gainimh
Gualin House
19
Inshegra
Lochan Sgeireach
Cranstackie 2630
Bàgh Loch an Ròin
Rhuvoult
Achriesgill
A838
Loch Inchard
River Dionard
Polla
Strath Dionard
Strath Beag
Ardmore Point
Loch Dughaill
Loch Crocach
Achlyness
Loch na Claise Carnaich
Rhiconich
1705 An Lean charn
Ardmore
Skerricha
Loch na Thull
Mathair a' Gharbh Uilt
Ganu Mór 2980
FOINAVEN
Fanagmore
Loch Dionard
Handa Island
Tarbet
Foindle
H
I
G
Handa Island
Sound of Handa
Loch a' Gharbh-bhaid Mór
Laxford Bridge
Loch na Tuadh
Loch Staonsaid
A894
Badnabay
River Laxford
Loch an Easain Uaine
Arkle 2580
Lochan Sgèireach
Loch a' Bhadaidh Daraich
Scourie Bay
Scourie More
Scourie
Loch an Nighe Leathaid
Loch na Seilge
Gorm Loch
Lochstack Lodge
2393 Sabhal Beag
Rubh' Aird an t-Sionnaich
17
Glen Golly
2356 Ben Stack
Loch Stack
Lone
Abhainn an Loin
Upper Badcall
Lower Badcall
Clar Loch Cnoc Thormaid
Reay Forest
Badcall Bay
1265 Ben Auskaird
Coire Loch
Eilean a Bhreitheimh
Loch Crocach
Achfary
Loch na Mucnaich
2627 Meallan Liath Coire Mhic Dhughaill
Loch Ulbhach Coire
Loch More
Meall Mór
Duartmore Bridge
Loch na Creige Duibhe
Allt nan Ramh
Sgeir nan Gall
Calbha Beag
Calbha Mór
1374 Ben Strome
Point of Stoer
The Old Man of Stoer
Oldany Island
Eddrachillis Bay
Kylestrome
Loch an Leathiad Bhuain
1777 Beinn a' Bhuta
Loch an t-Seilg
Glendhu Forest
Kinloch
Loch Cul Fraoich
Culkein
Eilean Chrona
Culkein Drumbeg
Loch Nedd
Loch a' Chàirn Bhàin
Kylesku
Loch Glendhu
Gleann Dubh
Clashnessie Bay
Oldany
Unapool
Rhubha Stoer
Achnacarnin
B869
Drumbeg
Nedd
16
Beinn Aird da Loch 1722
A838
Clashmore
Glenleraig
B869
Newton
Loch Glencoul
Loch Merkland
Balchladich
Clashnessie
Loch Poll
Gorm Loch Mór
Loch an Leothaid
30
A
B
C
D
163
Loch nan Lub
Loch na Loinne
Gleann Leireag
2651
Loch na Gainmhich
Glen Coul
Beinn Leoid 2599
Merkland Lodge
Stoer
Bay of Stoer
Clachtoll
Clachtoll Broch
Loch Beannach
Lochassynt Lodge
Eas Coul Aulin Falls
Loch nan Caorach
Loch an Eircill
Dubh a' Chuail
Loch a' Ghriama
Cnoc a' Ghriama 1221
Loch Crocach
Glas Bheinn 2541
Achmelvich Bay
B869
Rhicarn
A837
10
Loch
A837
Beinn Uidhe
Gorm Loch Mór
Abhainn a' Choire
Corriekinloch
A894
7
38
10
20
30
40
80
70
60
50
40
1
2
3
4
5

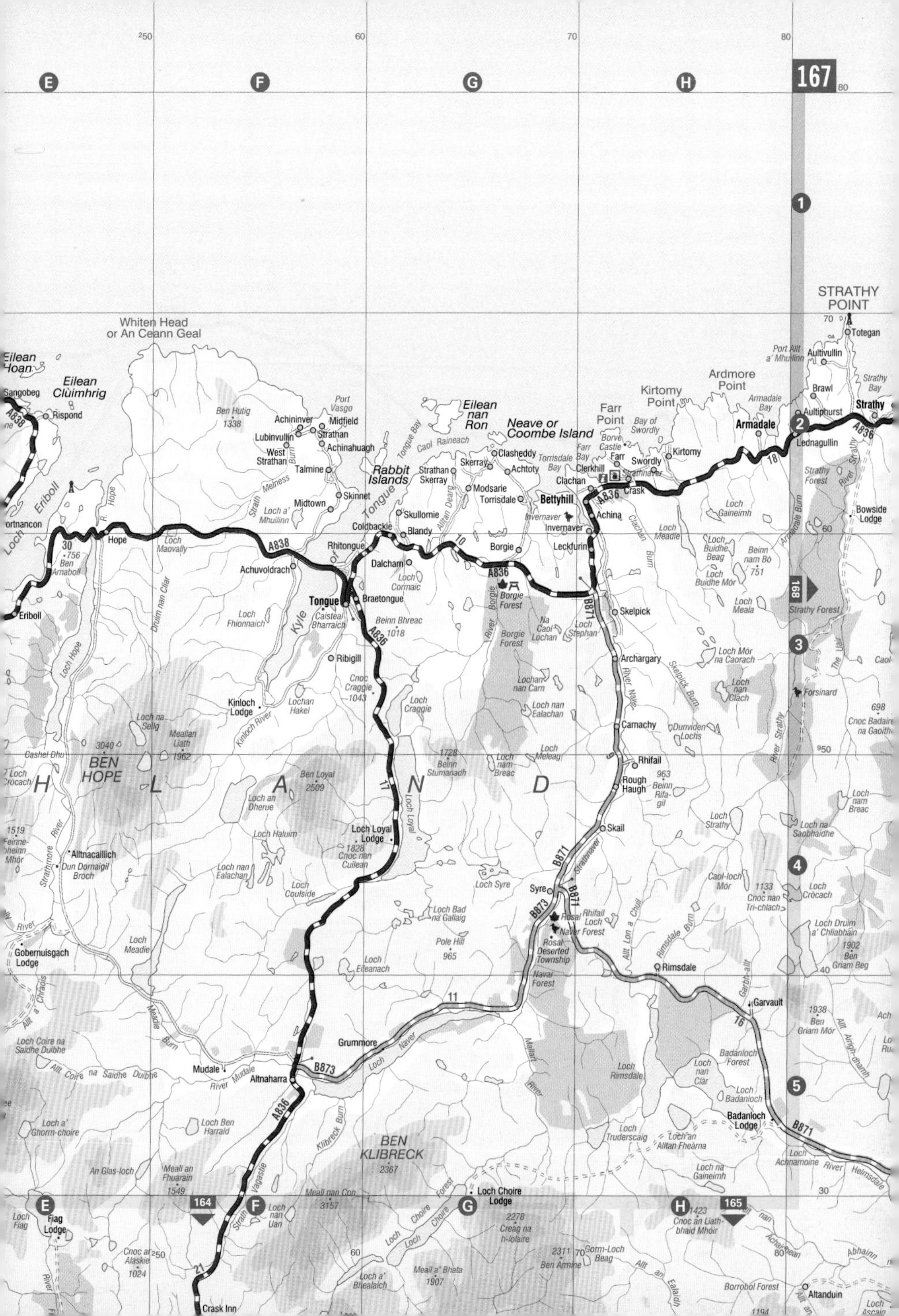

E
F
G
H
STRATHY POINT
Whiten Head or An Ceann Geal
Eilean Hoan
Eilean Clùimhrig
Eilean nan Ron
Neave or Coombe Island
Rabbit Islands
Farr Point
Kirtomy Point
Ardmore Point
Sangobeg
Rispond
Ben Hutig 1338
Achininver
Midfield
Lubinvullin
Strathan
West Strathan
Achinahuagh
Talmine
Skinnet
Midtown
Portnancon
Hope
Loch Eriboll
Eriboll
Coldbackie
Rhitongue
Achuvoldrach
Tongue
Braetongue
Dalcharn
Kyle of Tongue
Caisteal Bharraich
Ribigill
Kinloch Lodge
Strathan Skerray
Skerray
Clasheddy
Achtoty
Modsarie
Torrisdale
Skullomie
Blandy
Borgie
Bettyhill
Invernaver
Achina
Leckfurin
Clachan
Clerkhill
Farr
Crask
Swordly
Kirtomy
Armadale
Strathy
Lednagullin
Aultiphurst
Brawl
Aultivullin
Totegan
Bowside Lodge
Borgie Forest
Skelpick
Archargary
Carnachy
Rhifail
Rough Haugh
Skail
Syre
Rosal
Naver Forest
Rosal Deserted Township
Rimsdale
Garvault
Badanloch Lodge
Strathy Forest
Forsinard
BEN HOPE 3040
Ben Loyal 2509
Beinn Stumanadh 1728
Loch Loyal Lodge
Loch Loyal
Loch Naver
Altnaharra
Mudale
Grummore
Alltnacaillich
Dun Dornaigil Broch
Gobernuisgach Lodge
Loch Choire Lodge
BEN KLIBRECK 2367
Crask Inn
Altanduin
Badanloch Forest
Borrobol Forest
Ben Griam Beg 1902
Ben Griam Mór 1938
A838
A836
B871
B873
H L A N D
168
164
165
1
2
3
4
5

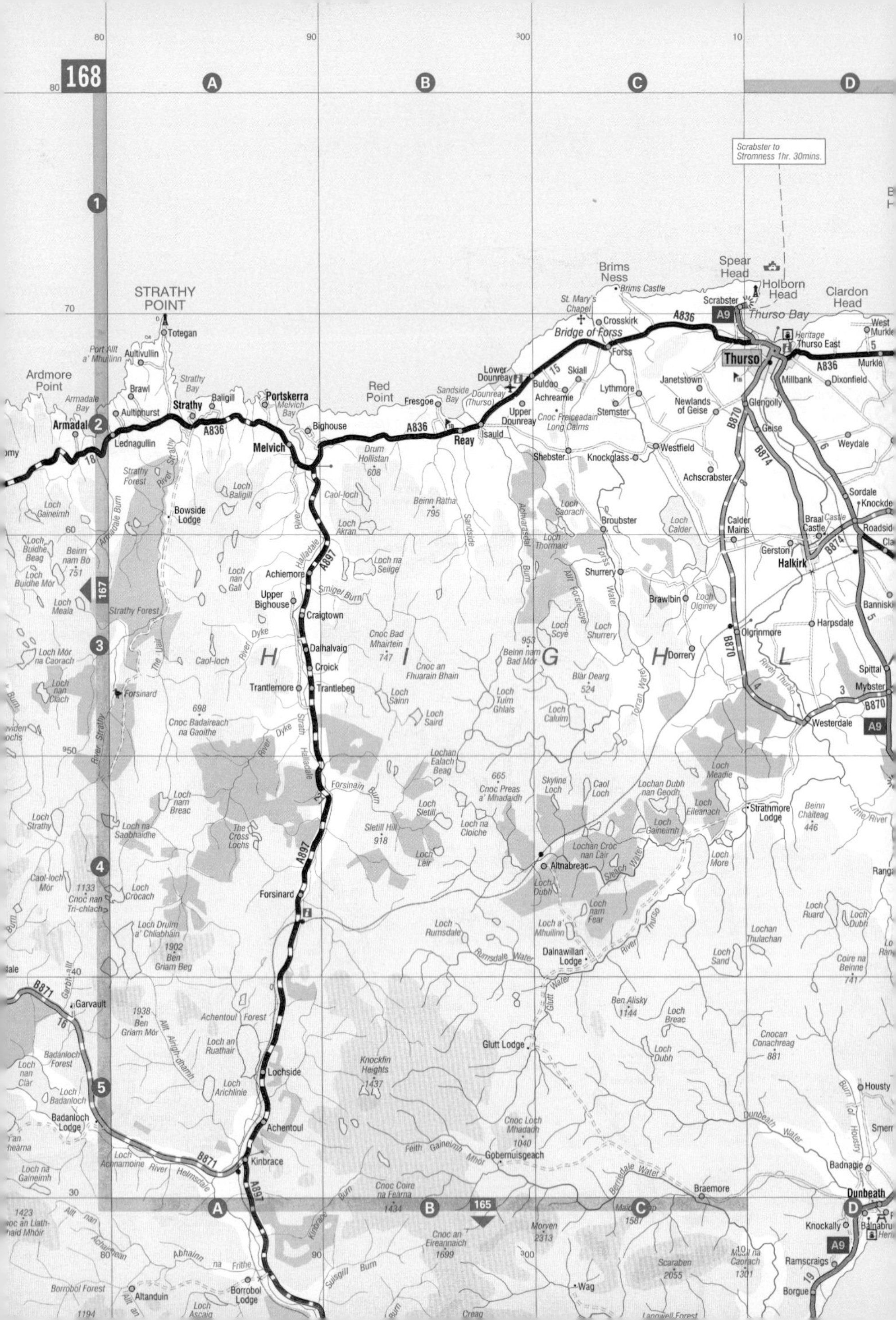
168
A
B
C
D
Scrabster to Stromness 1hr. 30mins.
STRATHY POINT
Totegan
Port Allt a' Mhuilinn
Aultivullin
Strathy Bay
Ardmore Point
Brawl
Armadale Bay
Aultiphurst
Strathy
Baligill
Portskerra
Melvich Bay
Armadale
Lednagullin
A836
Melvich
Bighouse
Red Point
Fresgoe
Sandside Bay
Dounreay (Thurso)
Reay
Isauld
Lower Dounreay
Buldoo
Achreamie
Upper Dounreay
Cnoc Freiceadain Long Cairns
Skiall
St. Mary's Chapel
Crosskirk
Bridge of Forss
Forss
Brims Ness
Brims Castle
Spear Head
Holborn Head
Scrabster
Thurso Bay
Clardon Head
A9
Heritage
Thurso East
Thurso
Millbank
Dixonfield
West Murkle
Murkle
Janetstown
Lythmore
Stemster
Newlands of Geise
Glengolly
Geise
Weydale
Shebster
Knockglass
Westfield
Achscrabster
B870
B874
Sordale
Knockdee
Roadside
Braal Castle
Calder Mains
Gerston
Halkirk
B874
Broubster
Loch Calder
Loch Saorach
Loch Thormaid
Shurrery
Brawlbin
Loch Olginey
Olgrinmore
Harpsdale
Banniskirk
Loch Scye
Loch Shurrery
Dorrery
Forss Water
Allt Forsiescye
Achvarasdal Burn
Sandside
953
Beinn nam Bad Mòr
Blàr Dearg
524
Torran Water
River Thurso
Spittal
Mybster
B870
Westerdale
A9
H
I
G
H
L
Strathy Forest
River Strathy
Armadale Burn
Bowside Lodge
Loch Baligill
Loch Gaineimh
Loch Buidhe Beag
Beinn nam Bò
751
Loch Buidhe Mòr
Loch Meala
167
Strathy Forest
Loch nan Gall
Drum Hollistan
608
Caol-loch
Loch Akran
Beinn Ratha
795
Loch na Seilge
Halladale River
A897
Achiemore
Upper Bighouse
Craigtown
Smigel Burn
Dalhalvaig
Croick
Trantlemore
Trantlebeg
Cnoc Bad Mhairtein
747
Cnoc an Fhuarain Bhain
Loch Sainn
Loch Saird
Loch Tuim Ghlais
Loch Caluim
Loch Mòr na Caorach
Loch nan Clach
Caol-loch
River Dyke
The Uair
Forsinard
698
Cnoc Badaireach na Gaoithe
Strath Halladale
Lochan Ealach Beag
665
Cnoc Preas a' Mhadaidh
Skyline Loch
Caol Loch
Lochan Dubh nan Geodh
Loch Meadie
Loch Eileanach
Strathmore Lodge
Beinn Châiteag
446
Little River
Loch Strathy
Loch nam Breac
Loch na Saobhaidhe
The Cross Lochs
Forsinain Burn
Loch Sletill
Sletill Hill
918
Loch na Cloiche
Loch Leir
Lochan Cròc nan Làir
Loch Gaineimh
Altnabreac
Sleach Water
Loch More
Caol-loch Mòr
1133
Cnoc nan Tri-chlach
Loch Crocach
Forsinard
Loch Dubh
Loch nam Fear
Loch Ruard
Loch Dubh
Loch Druim a' Chliabhain
1902
Ben Griam Beg
Loch Rumsdale
Loch a' Mhuilinn
Rumsdale Water
Dalnawillan Lodge
Lochan Thulachan
Loch Sand
Coire na Beinne
741
B871
Garbh-allt
Garvault
1938
Ben Griam Mòr
Achentoul Forest
Allt Airigh-dhamh
Loch an Ruathair
Glutt Water
Ben Alisky
1144
Loch Breac
Cnocan Conachreag
881
Glutt Lodge
Loch Dubh
Badanloch Forest
Loch nan Clàr
Loch Badanloch
Badanloch Lodge
Loch Arichlinie
Lochside
Knockfin Heights
1437
Cnoc Loch Mhadadh
1040
Housty
Burn of Housty
Dunbeath Water
Achentoul
Feith Gaineimh Mhòr
Gobernuisgeach
Badnagie
Loch Achnamoine
River Helmsdale
B871
Kinbrace
Loch na Gaineimh
Berriedale Water
Braemore
Dunbeath
Cnoc Coire na Fearna
1434
165
Maiden Pap
1587
Knockally
Balnabruich
A9
1423
Cnoc an Liath-bhaid Mhòir
Allt nan Achaidhean
Abhainn na Frithe
Kinbrace Burn
Cnoc an Eireannaich
1699
Morven
2313
Meall na Caorach
1301
Scaraben
2055
Ramscraigs
Suisgill Burn
Borrobol Forest
Altanduin
Borrobol Lodge
Wag
Borgue
Loch Ascaig
Creag
Langwell Forest
1194
80
90
300
10
70
60
50
40
30
1
2
3
4
5

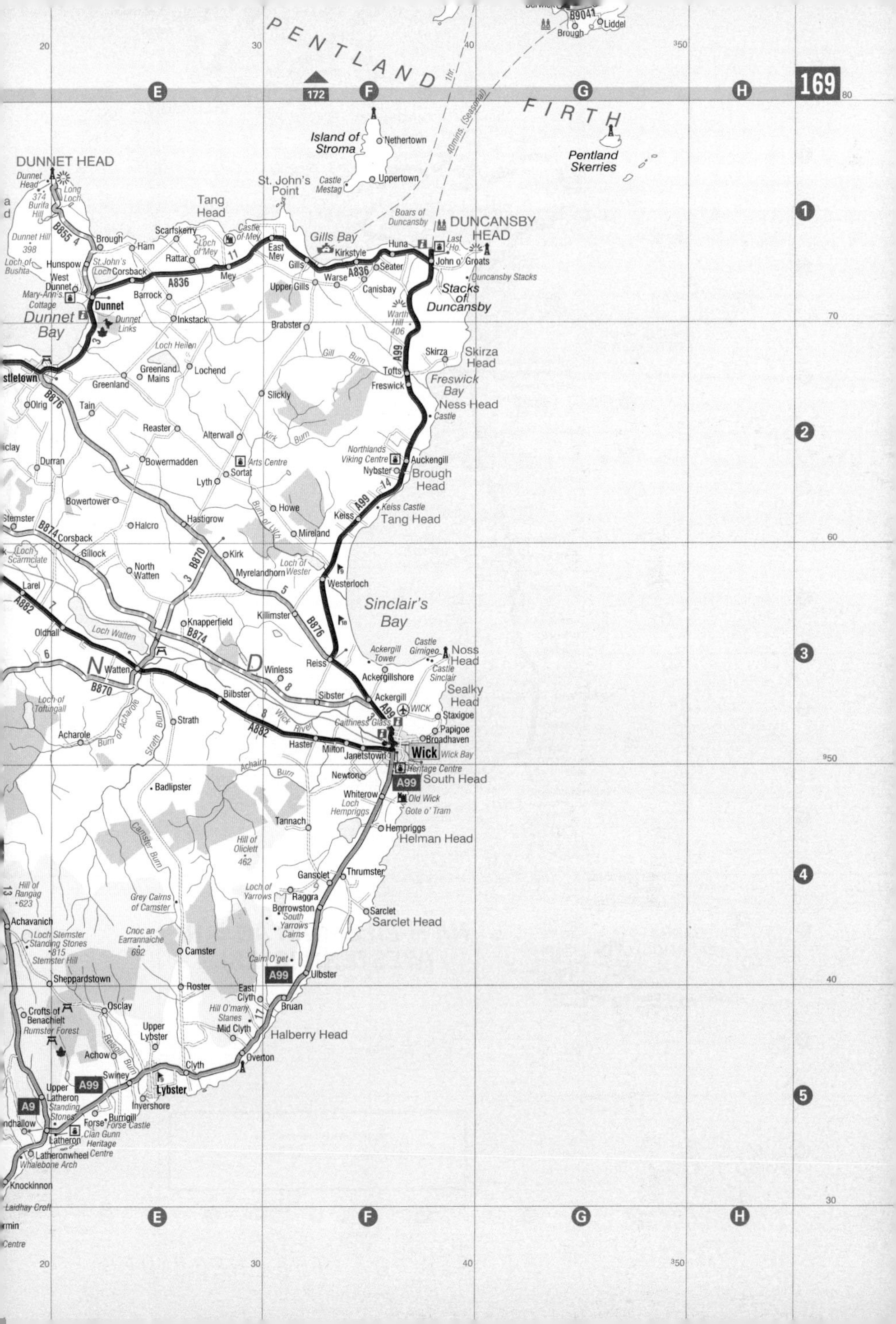
PENTLAND FIRTH
Island of Stroma
Nethertown
Uppertown
Castle Mestag
Pentland Skerries
DUNNET HEAD
Dunnet Head
Dunnet Bay
Dunnet
St. John's Point
Tang Head
Gills Bay
DUNCANSBY HEAD
John o' Groats
Stacks of Duncansby
Huna
Canisbay
Mey
Castle of Mey
Brough
Scarfskerry
Ham
Rattar
Barrock
Inkstack
Brabster
Skirza
Skirza Head
Freswick Bay
Freswick
Tofts
Ness Head
Lochend
Greenland
Slickly
Reaster
Alterwall
Bowermadden
Northlands Viking Centre
Auckengill
Nybster
Brough Head
Lyth
Sortat
Arts Centre
Keiss
Keiss Castle
Tang Head
Howe
Mireland
Hastigrow
Bowertower
Halcro
Durran
Olrig
Tain
Kirk
North Watten
Myrelandhorn
Loch of Wester
Westerloch
Sinclair's Bay
Killimster
Knapperfield
Loch Watten
Watten
Oldhall
Reiss
Ackergill Tower
Castle Girnigeo
Noss Head
Ackergillshore
Ackergill
Sealky Head
Staxigoe
Papigoe
Broadhaven
Winless
Bilbster
Sibster
Strath
Wick
Wick Bay
Heritage Centre
South Head
Janetstown
Milton
Haster
Newton
Whiterow
Old Wick
Gote o' Tram
Hempriggs
Helman Head
Tannach
Badlipster
Acharole
Hill of Oliclett 462
Thrumster
Gansclet
Raggra
Borrowston
South Yarrows Cairns
Sarclet
Sarclet Head
Grey Cairns of Camster
Camster
Cnoc an Earrannaiche 692
Achavanich
Loch Stemster
Stemster Hill
Sheppardstown
Roster
East Clyth
Ulbster
Bruan
Oscaly
Hill O'many Stanes
Mid Clyth
Halberry Head
Upper Lybster
Achow
Clyth
Overton
Swiney
Lybster
Upper Latheron
Latheron
Inveshore
Forse
Burrigill
Forse Castle
Clan Gunn Heritage Centre
Latheronwheel
Whalebone Arch
Knockinnon
Laidhay Croft
A99
A9
A836
A882
B855
B874
B870
B876
E F G H
1 2 3 4 5
172

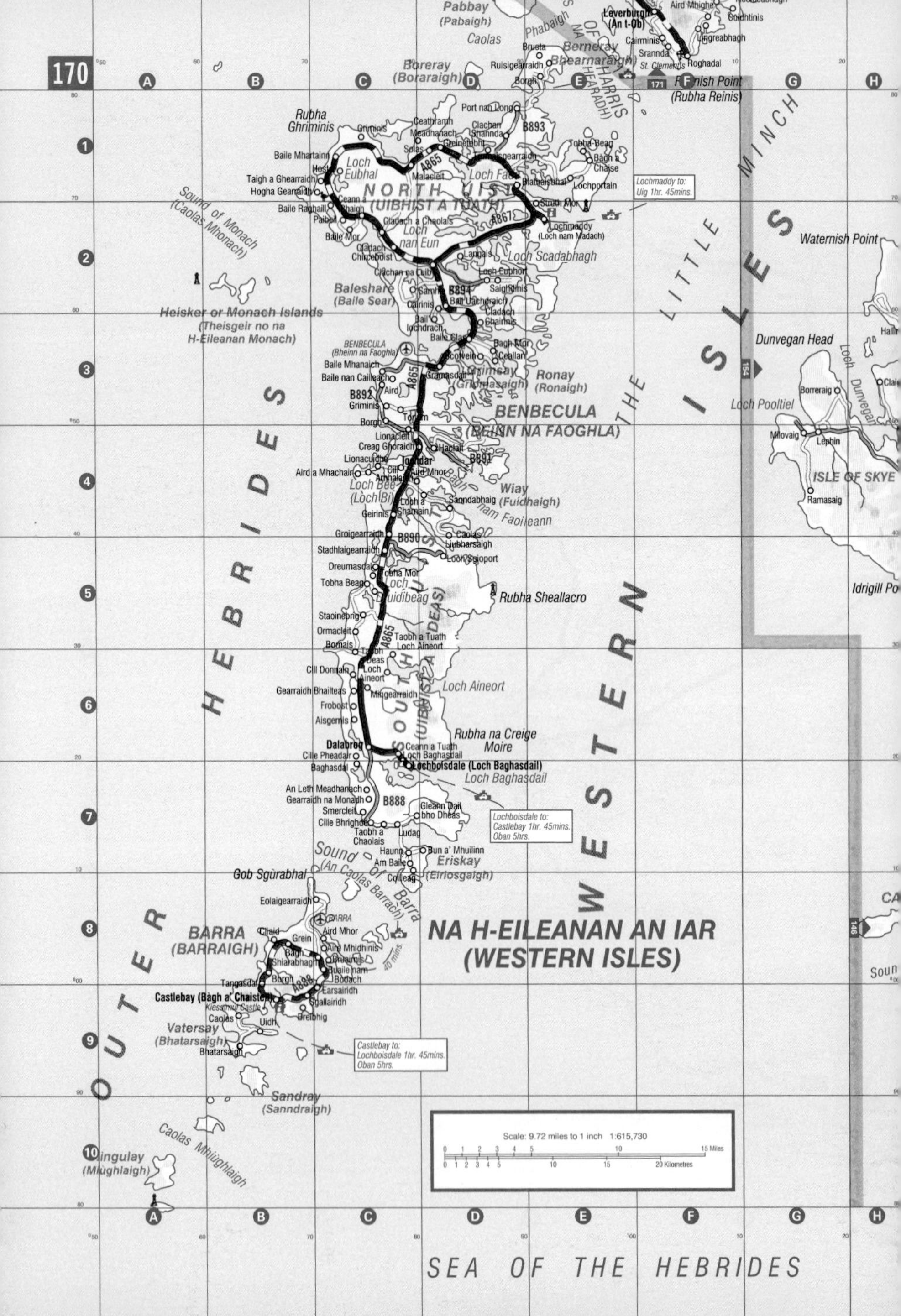
OUTER HEBRIDES
THE LITTLE MINCH
WESTERN ISLES
NA H-EILEANAN AN IAR
(WESTERN ISLES)
NORTH UIST
(UIBHIST A TUATH)
SOUTH UIST
(UIBHIST A DEAS)
BENBECULA
(BEINN NA FAOGHLA)
BARRA
(BARRAIGH)
ISLE OF SKYE
Heisker or Monach Islands
(Theisgeir no na
H-Eileanan Monach)
Sound of Monach
(Caolas Mhonach)
Pabbay
(Pabaigh)
Boreray
(Boraraigh)
Berneray
(Bearnaraigh)
Leverburgh
(An t-Ob)
Renish Point
(Rubha Reinis)
Rubha Ghriminis
Lochmaddy
(Loch nam Madadh)
Lochmaddy to:
Uig 1hr. 45mins.
Waternish Point
Dunvegan Head
Loch Pooltiel
Loch Scadabhagh
Ronay
(Ronaigh)
Wiay
(Fuidhaigh)
Rubha Sheallacro
Idrigill Point
Rubha na Creige
Moire
Lochboisdale (Loch Baghasdail)
Loch Baghasdail
Lochboisdale to:
Castlebay 1hr. 45mins.
Oban 5hrs.
Eriskay
(Eiriosgaigh)
Sound of Barra
(An Caolas Barrach)
Gob Sgùrabhal
Castlebay (Bàgh a' Chaisteil)
Castlebay to:
Lochboisdale 1hr. 45mins.
Oban 5hrs.
Vatersay
(Bhatarsaigh)
Sandray
(Sanndraigh)
Mingulay
(Miughlaigh)
Caolas Mhiùghlaigh
Loch Aineort
Loch Bee
(Loch Bi)
Scale: 9.72 miles to 1 inch 1:615,730
SEA OF THE HEBRIDES

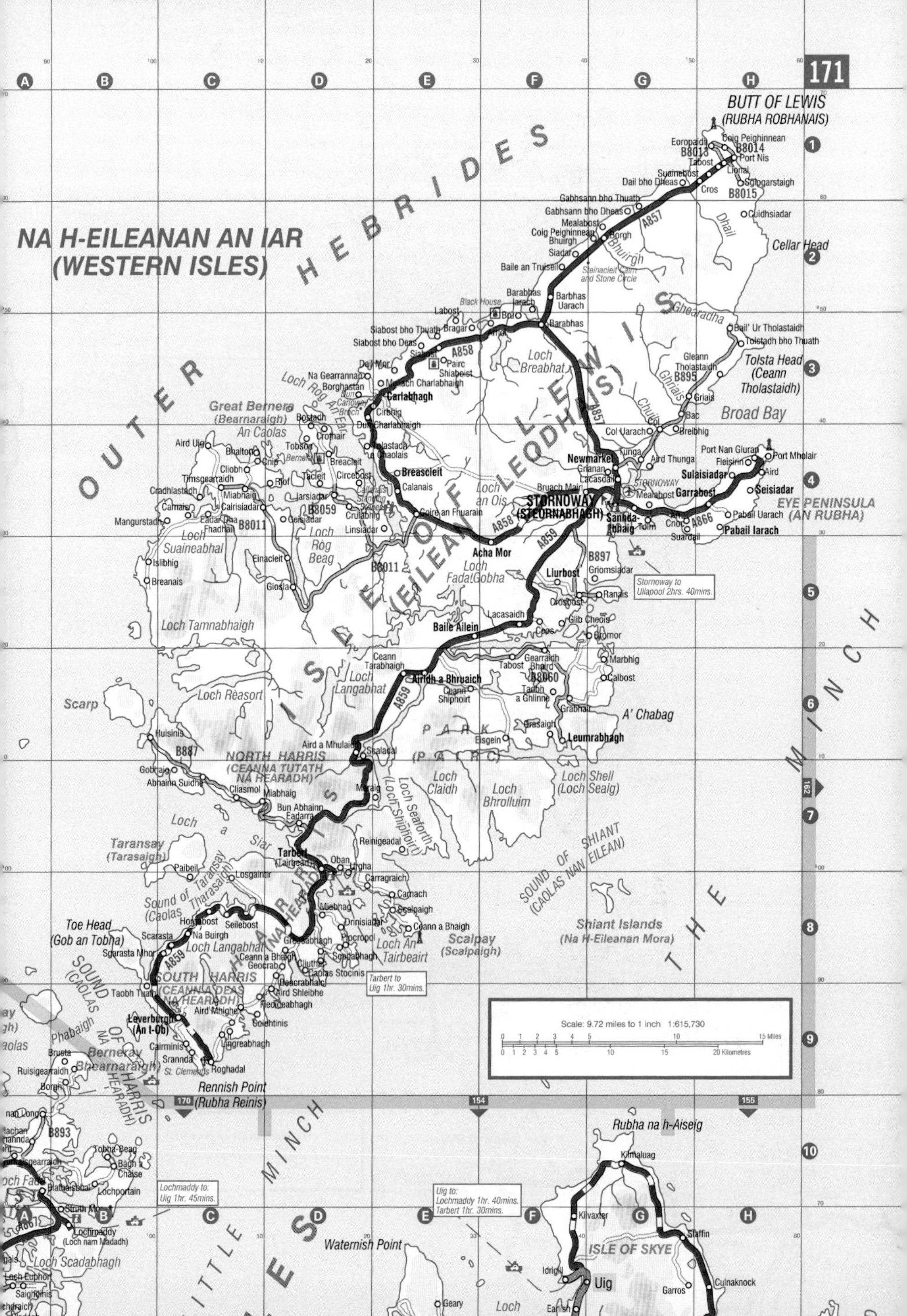

BUTT OF LEWIS
(RUBHA ROBHANAIS)

Na H-EILEANAN AN IAR
(WESTERN ISLES)

OUTER HEBRIDES

ISLE OF LEWIS (EILEAN LEODHAIS)

Cellar Head

Tolsta Head
(Ceann
Tholastaidh)

Broad Bay

EYE PENINSULA
(AN RUBHA)

Great Berneray
(Bearnaraigh)

An Caolas

Loch Roag

NEWMARKET
STORNOWAY
(STEORNABHAGH)

Acha Mor

Loch
Fada/Gobha

Liurbost

Loch
Suaineabhal

Loch Tamnabhaigh

Loch
Rog
Beag

Loch Reasort

Loch Seaforth
(Loch Shiphoirt)

A' Chabag

Leumrabhagh

Scarp

Stornoway to
Ullapool 2hrs. 40mins.

NORTH HARRIS
(CEANNA TUATH
NA HEARADH)

Taransay
(Tarasaigh)

Loch Claidh

Loch
Bhrolluim

Loch Shell
(Loch Sealg)

SOUND OF SHIANT
(CAOLAS NAN EILEAN)

Shiant Islands
(Na H-Eileanan Mora)

Tarbert
(Tairbeart)

Scalpay
(Scalpaigh)

Toe Head
(Gob an Tobha)

SOUTH HARRIS
(CEANNA DEAS
NA HEARADH)

Leverburgh
(An t-Ob)

Loch An
Tairbeairt

Tarbert to
Uig 1hr. 30mins.

Scale: 9.72 miles to 1 inch 1:615,730

0 ... 15 Miles

0 ... 20 Kilometres

Rennish Point
(Rubha Reinis)

170

154

155

Lochmaddy to:
Uig 1hr. 45mins.

Rubha na h-Aiseig

Kilmaluag

Uig to:
Lochmaddy 1hr. 40mins.
Tarbert 1hr. 30mins.

Kilvaxter

ISLE OF SKYE

Staffin

Lochmaddy
(Loch nam Madadh)

Waternish Point

Idrigil

Uig

Garros

Culnaknock

Earlish

THE MINCH

LITTLE MINCH

SOUND OF HARRIS (CAOLAS NA HEARADH)

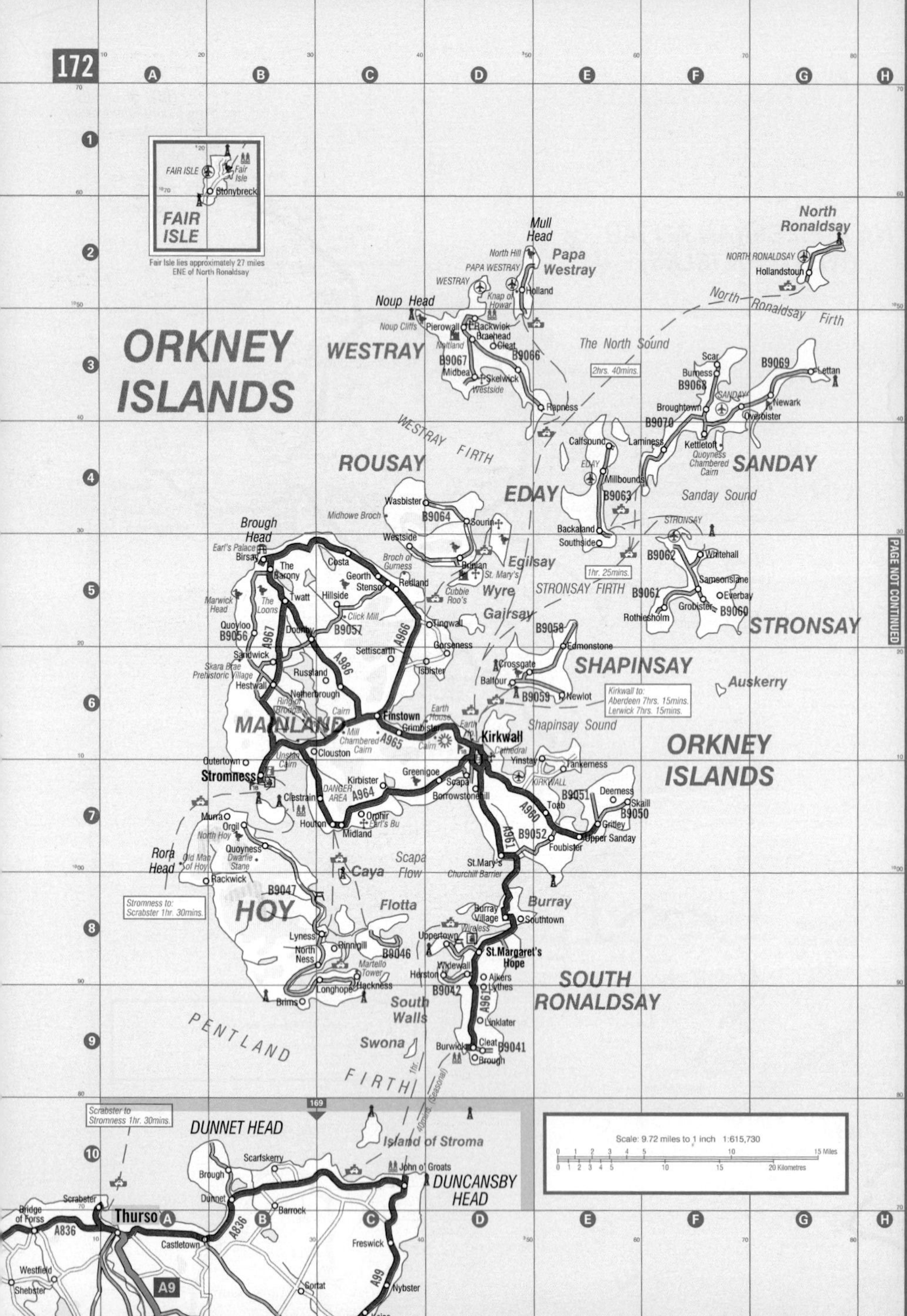
ORKNEY ISLANDS
FAIR ISLE
Fair Isle
Stonybreck
Fair Isle lies approximately 27 miles ENE of North Ronaldsay
Mull Head
North Hill
Papa Westray
PAPA WESTRAY
WESTRAY
Knap of Howar
Holland
North Ronaldsay
NORTH RONALDSAY
Hollandstoun
North Ronaldsay Firth
Noup Head
Noup Cliffs
Pierowall
Backaskaill
Braehead
Cleat
Noltland
B9067
Midbea
Skelwick
Westside
B9066
WESTRAY
The North Sound
2hrs. 40mins.
Rapness
Scar
Burness
B9068
B9069
Lettan
SANDAY
Broughtown
Newark
Overbister
B9070
Laminess
Kettletoft
Quoyness Chambered Cairn
SANDAY
WESTRAY FIRTH
ROUSAY
Calfsound
EDAY
Millbounds
B9063
EDAY
Sanday Sound
Wasbister
Midhowe Broch
B9064
Sourin
Westside
Backaland
Southside
STRONSAY
Whitehall
B9062
Brough Head
Earl's Palace
Birsay
The Barony
Costa
Broch of Gurness
Egilsay
Trumland
St. Mary's
1hr. 25mins.
STRONSAY FIRTH
Samsonslane
Everbay
B9061
Grobister
B9060
Rothiesholm
STRONSAY
Georth
Stenso
Redland
Cubbie Roo's
Wyre
Marwick Head
The Loons
Twatt
Hillside
Click Mill
B9057
Tingwall
Gairsay
B9058
Quoyloo
B9056
A967
Dounby
A966
Gorseness
Edmonstone
Sandwick
Skara Brae Prehistoric Village
Settiscarth
A986
Isbister
Crossgate
SHAPINSAY
Balfour
Russland
Hestwall
Netherbrough
Ring of Brodgar
B9059
Newlot
Kirkwall to: Aberdeen 7hrs. 15mins. Lerwick 7hrs. 15mins.
Auskerry
Cairn
Finstown
Earth House
Shapinsay Sound
MAINLAND
Grimbister
Maeshowe Chambered Cairn
A965
Kirkwall
Cathedral
Outertown
Clouston
Unstan Cairn
Yinstay
Tankerness
ORKNEY ISLANDS
Stromness
Kirbister
Greenigoe
Scapa
Clestrain
DANGER AREA
A964
Borrowstonehill
KIRKWALL
B9051
Deerness
Skaill
B9050
Toab
Murra
Orgil
Houton
Orphir
Earl's Bu
A960
A961
Gritley
North Hoy
Midland
B9052
Upper Sanday
Quoyness
Foubister
Rora Head
Old Man of Hoy
Dwarfie Stane
Scapa Flow
St.Mary's
Churchill Barrier
Rackwick
Caya
Stromness to: Scrabster 1hr. 30mins.
B9047
HOY
Flotta
Burray
Burray Village
Southtown
Lyness
Uppertown
Wireless
North Ness
Rinnigill
B9046
St.Margaret's Hope
Martello Tower
Widewall
Herston
Hackness
Aikers
Lythes
Longhope
B9042
SOUTH RONALDSAY
Brims
South Walls
A961
Linklater
PENTLAND
Swona
Burwick
Cleat
B9041
Brough
FIRTH
1hr.
40mins. (Seasonal)
169
Scrabster to Stromness 1hr. 30mins.
DUNNET HEAD
Island of Stroma
Scale: 9.72 miles to 1 inch 1:615,730
0 1 2 3 4 5 10 15 Miles
0 1 2 3 4 5 10 15 20 Kilometres
Scarfskerry
John o' Groats
Brough
DUNCANSBY HEAD
Dunnet
Scrabster
Barrock
Bridge of Forss
Thurso
A836
A836
Castletown
Freswick
Westfield
Shebster
A9
Sortat
A99
Nybster
Keiss
PAGE NOT CONTINUED
A B C D E F G H
1 2 3 4 5 6 7 8 9 10

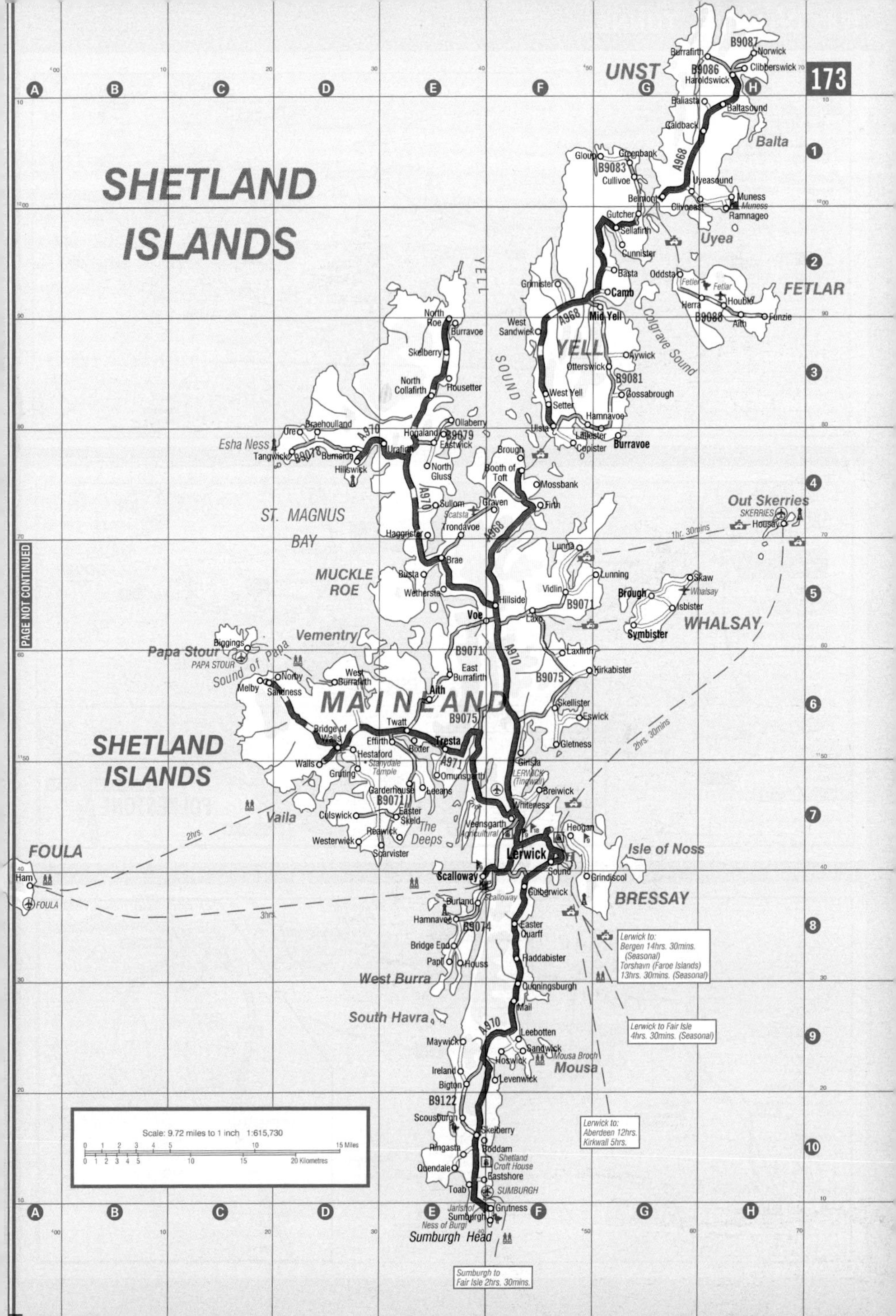
SHETLAND ISLANDS
UNST
Burrafirth
B9087
Norwick
B9086
Haroldswick
Clibberswick
Baliasta
Baltasound
Caldback
Balta
A968
Gloup
Greenbank
B9083
Cullivoe
Uyeasound
Belmont
Muness
Clivocast
Ramnageo
Gutcher
Sellafirth
Uyea
Cunnister
Basta
Oddsta
FETLAR
Fetlar
Grimister
Camb
Houbie
Herra
Mid Yell
Funzie
B9088
Aith
West Sandwick
YELL
Colgrave Sound
Aywick
Otterswick
B9081
Gossabrough
West Yell
Setter
Hamnavoe
Ulsta
Littlester
Copister
Burravoe
YELL SOUND
North Roe
Burravoe
Skelberry
North Collafirth
Housetter
Ollaberry
Braehoulland
Ure
Hogaland
B9079
Eastwick
Esha Ness
Tangwick
B9078
Burnside
A970
Urafirth
Hillswick
North Gluss
Brough
Booth of Toft
Mossbank
Sullom
Graven
Scatsta
Firth
Out Skerries
SKERRIES
Housay
1hr. 30mins
ST. MAGNUS BAY
Haggrister
Trondavoe
A968
Lunna
Brae
MUCKLE ROE
Busta
Wethersta
Lunning
Skaw
Vidlin
Brough
Whalsay
B9071
Isbister
Hillside
Voe
Laxo
WHALSAY
Symbister
Vementry
Biggings
Papa Stour
PAPA STOUR
Sound of Papa
B9071
Laxfirth
Kirkabister
Norby
West Burrafirth
East Burrafirth
B9075
Melby
Sandness
Aith
MAINLAND
Skellister
Eswick
SHETLAND ISLANDS
Bridge of Walls
Twatt
B9075
Effirth
Tresta
Gletness
2hrs. 30mins
Walls
Hestaford
Bixter
A971
Girlsta
Gruting
Stanydale Temple
Omunsgarth
LERWICK (Tingwall)
Garderhouse
Leeans
Breiwick
B9071
Whiteness
Vaila
Culswick
Easter Skeld
Veensgarth Agricultural
Heogan
2hrs.
The Deeps
Reawick
Westerwick
Scarvister
Lerwick
Isle of Noss
FOULA
Sound
Scalloway
Grindiscol
Ham
FOULA
3hrs.
Burland
Scalloway
Gulberwick
BRESSAY
Hamnavoe
B9074
Easter Quarff
Lerwick to: Bergen 14hrs. 30mins. (Seasonal) Torshavn (Faroe Islands) 13hrs. 30mins. (Seasonal)
Bridge End
Papil
Houss
Fladdabister
West Burra
Cunningsburgh
Mail
South Havra
Lerwick to Fair Isle 4hrs. 30mins. (Seasonal)
A970
Leebotten
Maywick
Sandwick
Hoswick
Mousa Broch
Mousa
Ireland
Bigton
Levenwick
B9122
Lerwick to: Aberdeen 12hrs. Kirkwall 5hrs.
Scousburgh
Skelberry
Scale: 9.72 miles to 1 inch 1:615,730
0 1 2 3 4 5 10 15 Miles
0 1 2 3 4 5 10 15 20 Kilometres
Ringasta
Boddam
Shetland Croft House
Quendale
Eastshore
Toab
SUMBURGH
Jarlshof
Grutness
Sumburgh
Ness of Burgi
Sumburgh Head
Sumburgh to Fair Isle 2hrs. 30mins.
PAGE NOT CONTINUED

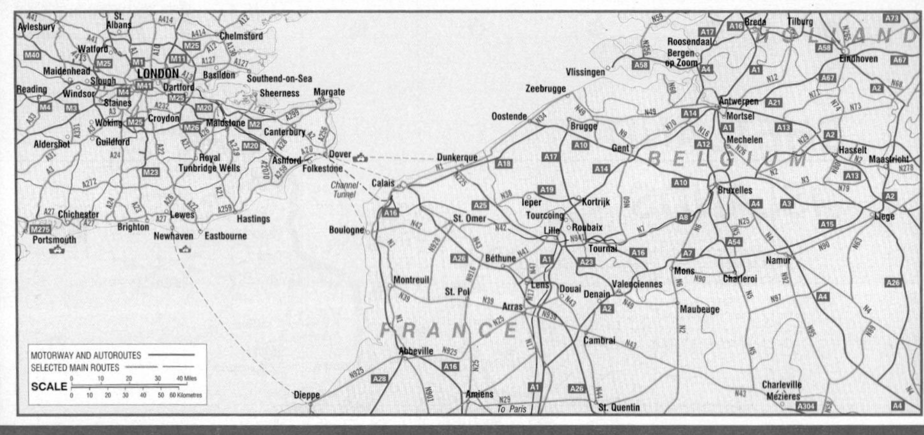

LONDON
Aylesbury
St. Albans
Chelmsford
Watford
Maidenhead
Slough
Reading
Windsor
Staines
Dartford
Basildon
Southend-on-Sea
Sheerness
Margate
Woking
Croydon
Guildford
Aldershot
Maidstone
Canterbury
Dover
Ashford
Folkestone
Royal Tunbridge Wells
Chichester
Brighton
Lewes
Hastings
Portsmouth
Newhaven
Eastbourne
Channel Tunnel
Calais
Boulogne
Dunkerque
Oostende
Zeebrugge
Brugge
Gent
Vlissingen
Roosendaal
Bergen op Zoom
Breda
Tilburg
Eindhoven
HOLLAND
Antwerpen
Mortsel
Mechelen
BELGIUM
Hasselt
Maastricht
Bruxelles
Liège
Ieper
Kortrijk
Tourcoing
Roubaix
Lille
Tournai
St. Omer
Béthune
Mons
Charleroi
Namur
Montreuil
St. Pol
Lens
Douai
Denain
Valenciennes
Maubeuge
Arras
FRANCE
Cambrai
Abbeville
Amiens
To Paris
St. Quentin
Charleville Mézières
Dieppe
MOTORWAY AND AUTOROUTES
SELECTED MAIN ROUTES
SCALE
0 10 20 30 40 Miles
0 10 20 30 40 50 60 Kilometres

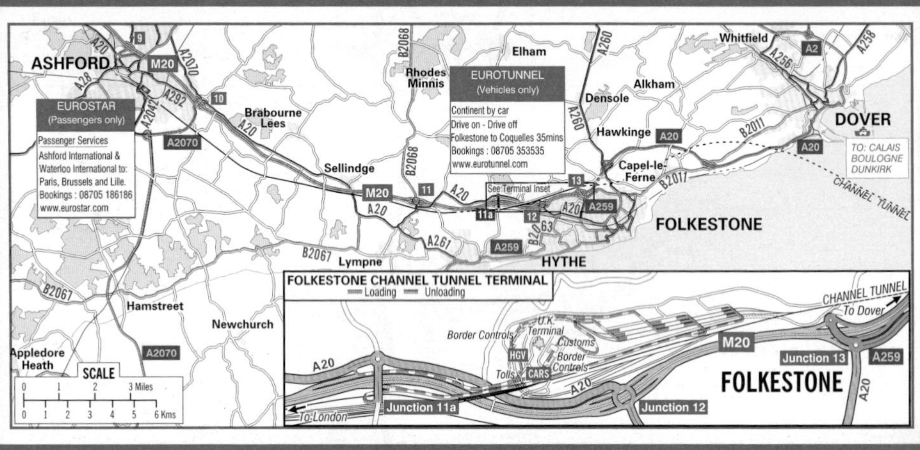

ASHFORD
EUROSTAR
(Passengers only)
Passenger Services
Ashford International & Waterloo International to: Paris, Brussels and Lille.
Bookings : 08705 186186
www.eurostar.com
EUROTUNNEL
(Vehicles only)
Continent by car
Drive on - Drive off
Folkestone to Coquelles 35mins
Bookings : 08705 353535
www.eurotunnel.com
Brabourne Lees
Rhodes Minnis
Elham
Densole
Alkham
Whitfield
Hawkinge
Capel-le-Ferne
DOVER
TO: CALAIS BOULOGNE DUNKIRK
CHANNEL TUNNEL
Sellindge
See Terminal Inset
FOLKESTONE
Lympne
HYTHE
Hamstreet
Newchurch
Appledore Heath
SCALE
0 1 2 3 Miles
0 1 2 3 4 5 6 Kms
FOLKESTONE CHANNEL TUNNEL TERMINAL
Loading
Unloading
CHANNEL TUNNEL
To Dover
Border Controls
U.K. Terminal
Customs
Border Controls
HGV
Tolls
CARS
Junction 11a
Junction 12
Junction 13
To London
FOLKESTONE

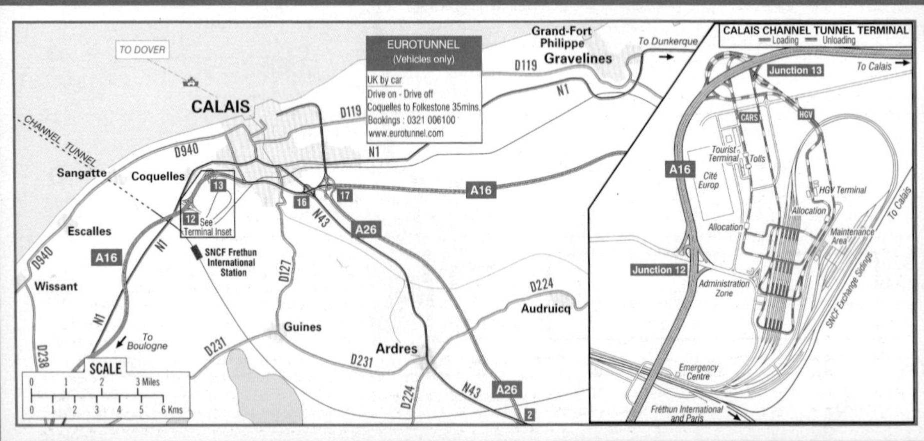

TO DOVER
EUROTUNNEL
(Vehicles only)
UK by car
Drive on - Drive off
Coquelles to Folkestone 35mins.
Bookings : 0321 006100
www.eurotunnel.com
Grand-Fort Philippe
Gravelines
To Dunkerque
CALAIS
CHANNEL TUNNEL
Sangatte
Coquelles
See Terminal Inset
Escalles
SNCF Frethun International Station
Wissant
To Boulogne
Guines
Ardres
Audruicq
SCALE
0 1 2 3 Miles
0 1 2 3 4 5 6 Kms
CALAIS CHANNEL TUNNEL TERMINAL
Loading
Unloading
Junction 13
To Calais
CARS
HGV
Tourist Terminal
Tolls
Cité Europ
HGV Terminal
Allocation
Allocation
Maintenance Area
Junction 12
Administration Zone
SNCF Exchange Sidings
Emergency Centre
Fréthun International and Paris

Mileage Chart

The distances for the mileage chart have been compiled by using a combination of Primary Routes and Motorways between any two towns shown.

To find the distance between any two towns shown, follow the horizontal line of one town and the vertical line of the other; at the intersection read off the mileage.

ie : Horizontal - LONDON

Intersection 216 miles

Vertical - LIVERPOOL

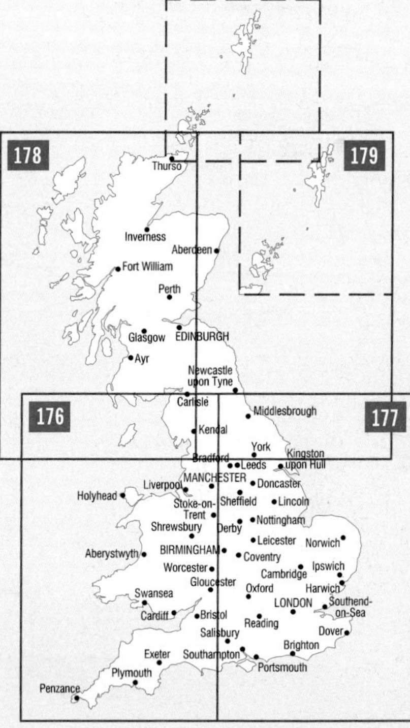

Key to Route Planning Map Pages

PRIMARY ROUTES, shown in green throughout this Atlas, are a national network of recommended through routes which complement the motorway system. Selected places of major traffic importance are known as Primary Route Destinations and, on road signs, have a green background.

ABERDEEN
449 ABERYSTWYTH
181 324 AYR
400 114 272 BIRMINGHAM
330 159 196 124 BRADFORD
562 258 441 169 263 BRIGHTON
503 122 375 88 215 129 BRISTOL
447 198 366 102 156 117 167 CAMBRIDGE
505 106 377 106 233 168 42 201 CARDIFF
217 232 89 183 107 345 286 256 288 CARLISLE
437 134 297 18 124 157 102 84 129 200 COVENTRY
397 137 269 41 88 188 134 99 159 180 43 DERBY
340 192 239 95 40 232 184 117 210 150 94 57 DONCASTER
558 315 477 195 284 81 194 118 233 393 180 208 244 DOVER
125 340 75 284 198 466 377 326 379 91 303 266 212 444 EDINBURGH
553 199 425 161 282 170 75 232 107 336 166 213 257 244 439 EXETER
148 430 136 391 305 568 478 456 486 198 415 387 345 591 131 549 FORT WILLIAM
148 322 36 291 203 468 378 355 384 96 313 282 245 491 46 449 100 GLASGOW
445 109 317 53 171 152 35 132 53 228 59 93 149 189 331 107 435 324 GLOUCESTER
520 258 411 170 224 130 203 64 234 323 152 167 185 129 397 262 524 419 171 HARWICH
443 96 315 151 158 330 204 252 209 226 167 156 169 358 316 279 423 323 189 331 HOLYHEAD
107 492 198 449 353 620 536 490 540 258 458 421 369 607 63 162 496 554 481 INVERNESS
505 268 420 156 210 125 206 54 240 311 138 155 171 127 381 264 510 409 177 21 307 538 IPSWICH
269 182 139 151 62 324 235 215 232 50 170 136 99 344 141 307 248 146 200 279 180 310 268 KENDAL
357 235 255 139 68 243 228 134 239 165 123 94 37 254 230 290 367 255 195 204 218 387 189 127 KINGSTON UPON HULL
316 171 198 119 9 256 209 144 226 111 117 74 32 275 190 279 309 208 167 217 162 345 197 72 60 LEEDS
407 155 294 43 99 163 118 70 140 214 24 30 73 183 282 189 412 312 83 146 182 431 155 166 98 97 LEICESTER
376 208 249 87 80 207 170 88 192 178 76 53 41 206 247 241 376 274 135 152 204 402 124 140 46 72 52 LINCOLN
327 120 199 99 67 267 180 179 169 110 113 90 89 294 201 240 308 213 142 265 95 370 236 75 126 73 110 118 LIVERPOOL
321 128 204 87 37 252 167 159 188 117 99 58 51 273 208 239 315 215 132 230 120 363 211 72 96 42 95 87 34 MANCHESTER
273 233 181 174 69 316 265 196 287 92 175 130 84 316 147 337 279 192 230 266 226 306 253 77 88 54 127 134 106 MIDDLESBROUGH
230 266 146 209 98 345 300 232 312 58 209 165 115 350 104 369 237 153 263 297 257 263 287 88 130 96 188 153 167 134 106 NEWCASTLE UPON TYNE
476 270 348 163 185 174 234 62 256 280 142 146 142 169 351 284 478 378 193 72 289 505 44 249 145 178 112 103 222 177 221 252 NORWICH
381 155 267 54 78 191 140 84 165 188 52 15 48 210 256 218 386 286 108 165 177 410 140 141 92 72 27 37 107 68 128 159 118 NOTTINGHAM
485 151 335 68 167 106 73 92 106 267 57 101 138 142 358 151 465 365 47 101 134 208 515 126 223 175 162 76 223 159 104 OXFORD
680 301 552 269 394 279 184 343 218 463 278 316 369 355 551 109 663 561 217 374 388 715 375 419 432 391 310 359 353 344 449 481 393 323 261 PENZANCE
87 366 85 336 245 509 412 370 422 134 346 309 254 485 43 487 103 59 362 439 360 113 424 184 273 233 326 290 244 254 191 148 394 299 404 598 PERTH
589 232 461 203 325 206 111 274 159 372 209 254 300 285 485 43 592 490 150 305 322 648 305 348 326 323 231 284 299 281 379 412 327 255 193 75 529 PLYMOUTH
575 231 440 147 274 50 95 132 138 357 132 184 231 137 448 127 555 455 114 161 303 603 158 308 268 245 166 209 254 237 315 360 200 191 83 235 486 170 PORTSMOUTH
526 180 399 103 213 79 77 90 112 309 90 133 184 115 402 168 184 378 137 265 230 132 187 213 208 287 318 200 162 65 201 443 132 43 57 SALISBURY
529 178 383 121 245 82 53 140 101 312 113 159 207 158 400 91 510 408 73 177 262 569 177 265 251 230 132 187 213 208 287 318 200 162 65 201 443 132 43 57 SALISBURY
355 173 235 79 40 225 163 121 193 154 75 35 21 268 230 245 352 250 139 185 164 387 176 102 66 33 68 46 74 40 102 133 144 37 137 361 273 293 228 160 203 SHEFFIELD
388 73 260 47 100 216 116 140 107 171 64 67 114 249 262 175 369 267 77 215 104 424 195 125 163 102 79 123 59 67 166 203 196 86 105 286 309 218 195 147 150 85 SHREWSBURY
547 213 401 128 235 64 75 129 122 330 114 167 201 150 433 106 528 426 98 157 287 590 162 276 249 230 136 189 235 215 288 320 190 162 66 217 476 149 20 47 23 206 175 SOUTHAMPTON
520 258 431 152 220 85 177 64 211 342 129 168 185 89 395 226 548 438 152 57 303 549 57 283 200 213 139 156 255 225 262 299 99 160 105 337 439 269 117 98 132 197 173 126 SOUTHEND-ON-SEA
374 108 243 47 75 217 127 137 140 150 64 41 74 236 241 202 348 248 95 201 122 410 179 121 117 78 55 87 56 36 142 173 171 55 118 311 287 241 201 147 168 50 35 183 199 STOKE-ON-TRENT
496 76 368 124 220 209 80 236 41 279 150 184 244 264 370 154 477 375 91 279 172 578 279 249 262 229 174 226 168 187 323 286 178 144 266 446 196 175 147 136 202 124 159 245 159 SWANSEA
213 584 304 557 461 728 644 589 640 352 552 529 475 706 262 715 169 268 604 657 589 108 654 402 492 453 544 510 463 471 410 367 613 519 621 823 220 758 709 662 664 506 523 682 659 502 631 THURSO
437 96 309 29 135 162 62 119 73 220 46 68 124 197 306 136 418 311 28 168 151 480 174 169 146 146 72 118 108 101 203 229 180 85 57 244 350 177 145 95 101 103 49 124 150 65 97 572 WORCESTER
312 193 201 129 34 269 227 151 237 116 129 84 33 269 187 289 314 214 181 232 185 344 200 81 38 24 108 76 96 65 48 83 176 84 174 400 230 331 257 217 244 54 132 244 214 114 268 450 164 YORK
501 206 390 118 203 53 118 58 150 305 97 128 165 76 373 171 503 403 101 79 264 527 76 264 188 196 102 143 216 200 246 278 114 130 55 282 416 214 74 39 84 161 160 78 43 160 187 636 110 203 LONDON

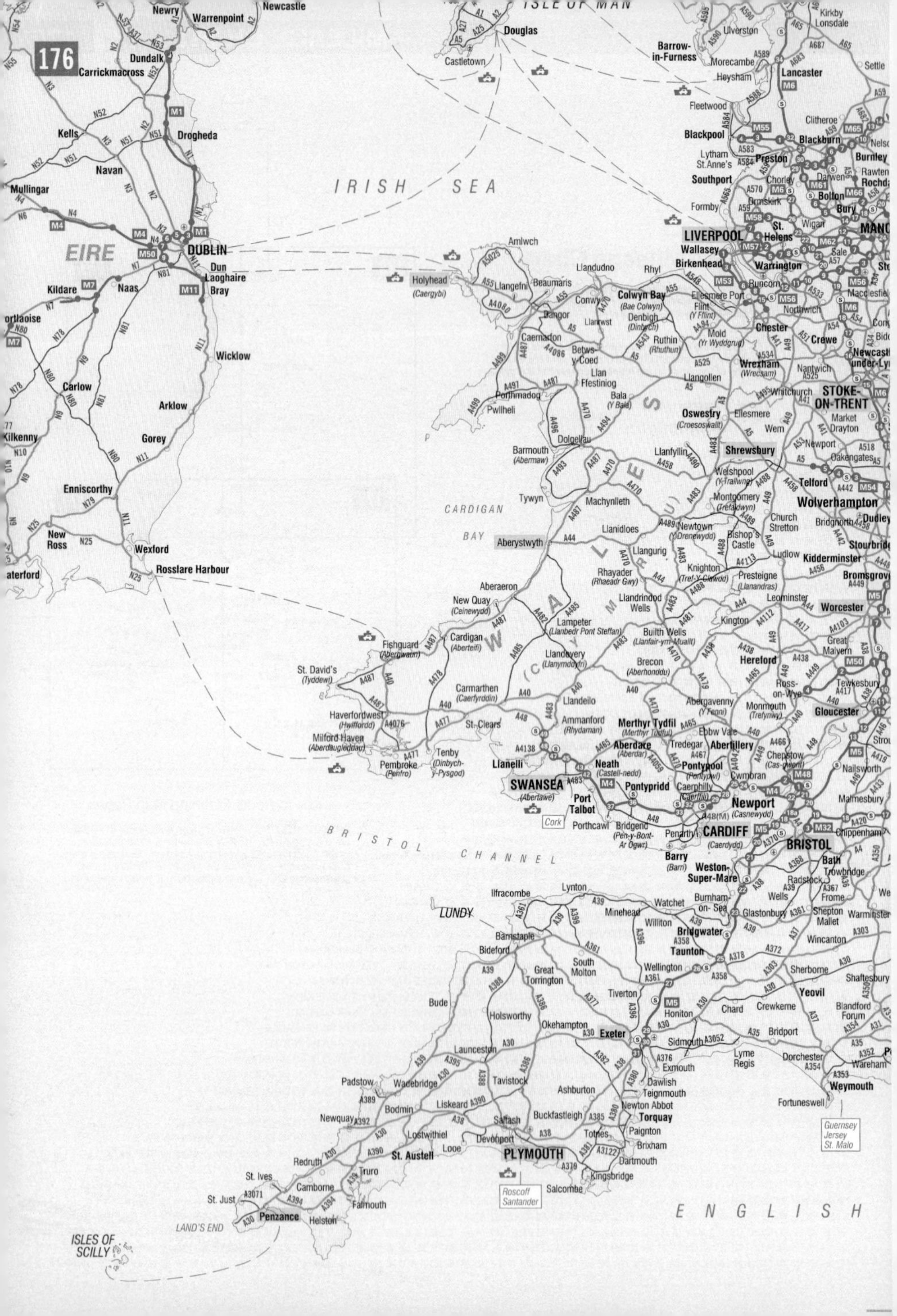
ISLE OF MAN
Douglas
Castletown
Newry
Warrenpoint
Newcastle
Dundalk
Carrickmacross
Kells
Drogheda
Navan
Mullingar
EIRE
DUBLIN
Dun Laoghaire
Bray
Kildare
Naas
Portlaoise
Carlow
Wicklow
Arklow
Kilkenny
Gorey
Enniscorthy
New Ross
Wexford
Rosslare Harbour
Waterford
IRISH SEA
Amlwch
Holyhead
(Caergybi)
Llangefni
Beaumaris
Bangor
Caernarfon
Llandudno
Conwy
Llanrwst
Colwyn Bay
(Bae Colwyn)
Rhyl
Denbigh
(Dinbych)
Flint
(Y Fflint)
Mold
(Yr Wyddgrug)
Ruthin
(Rhuthun)
Betws-y-Coed
Llan Ffestiniog
Porthmadog
Pwllheli
Bala
(Y Bala)
Llangollen
Wrexham
(Wrecsam)
Chester
Oswestry
(Croesoswallt)
Dolgellau
Barmouth
(Abermaw)
Llanfyllin
Welshpool
(Y Trallwng)
Shrewsbury
Tywyn
Machynlleth
Montgomery
(Trefaldwyn)
Newtown
(Y Drenewydd)
Llanidloes
CARDIGAN BAY
Aberystwyth
Llangurig
Rhayader
(Rhaeadr Gwy)
Knighton
(Tref-Y-Clawdd)
Presteigne
(Llanandras)
Bishop's Castle
Church Stretton
Ludlow
Aberaeron
New Quay
(Ceinewydd)
Llandrindod Wells
Lampeter
(Llanbedr Pont Steffan)
WALES
(CYMRU)
Builth Wells
(Llanfair-ym-Muallt)
Cardigan
(Aberteifi)
Fishguard
(Abergwaun)
Llandovery
(Llanymddyfri)
Brecon
(Aberhonddu)
Hereford
Leominster
Kington
St. David's
(Tyddewi)
Carmarthen
(Caerfyrddin)
Llandeilo
Abergavenny
(Y Fenni)
Monmouth
(Trefynwy)
Ross-on-Wye
Haverfordwest
(Hwlffordd)
St. Clears
Ammanford
(Rhydaman)
Merthyr Tydfil
(Merthyr Tudful)
Ebbw Vale
Tredegar
Abertillery
Aberdare
(Aberdar)
Milford Haven
(Aberdaugleddau)
Pembroke
(Penfro)
Tenby
(Dinbych-y-Pysgod)
Llanelli
Neath
(Castell-nedd)
Pontypool
(Pontypwl)
Cwmbran
Chepstow
(Cas-gwent)
SWANSEA
(Abertawe)
Port Talbot
Pontypridd
Caerphilly
(Caerffili)
Newport
(Casnewydd)
Cork
Porthcawl
Bridgend
(Pen-y-Bont-Ar Ogwr)
Penarth
CARDIFF
(Caerdydd)
Barry
(Barri)
BRISTOL
BRISTOL CHANNEL
Weston-Super-Mare
Lundy
Ilfracombe
Lynton
Minehead
Watchet
Williton
Burnham-on-Sea
Bridgwater
Taunton
Barnstaple
Bideford
Great Torrington
South Molton
Wellington
Tiverton
Bude
Holsworthy
Okehampton
Exeter
Honiton
Launceston
Tavistock
Padstow
Wadebridge
Bodmin
Liskeard
Saltash
Newquay
Lostwithiel
Devonport
St. Austell
Looe
PLYMOUTH
Redruth
Truro
St. Ives
Camborne
St. Just
Falmouth
Penzance
Helston
LAND'S END
ISLES OF SCILLY
Roscoff
Santander
Salcombe
Kingsbridge
Dartmouth
Totnes
Brixham
Paignton
Torquay
Newton Abbot
Buckfastleigh
Ashburton
Teignmouth
Dawlish
Exmouth
Sidmouth
Lyme Regis
Bridport
Dorchester
Weymouth
Fortuneswell
Wareham
Guernsey
Jersey
St. Malo
ENGLISH
Chard
Crewkerne
Yeovil
Sherborne
Wincanton
Shepton Mallet
Glastonbury
Wells
Frome
Radstock
Bath
Trowbridge
Chippenham
Malmesbury
Nailsworth
Gloucester
Tewkesbury
Great Malvern
Worcester
Bromsgrove
Kidderminster
Stourbridge
Bridgnorth
Dudley
Wolverhampton
Telford
Oakengates
Newport
Market Drayton
Wem
Ellesmere
Whitchurch
Nantwich
STOKE-ON-TRENT
Newcastle-under-Lyme
Crewe
Northwich
Macclesfield
Runcorn
Ellesmere Port
Warrington
Birkenhead
Wallasey
LIVERPOOL
St. Helens
Wigan
Bolton
Bury
Ormskirk
Formby
Southport
Chorley
Darwen
Lytham St.Anne's
Preston
Blackpool
Blackburn
Burnley
Clitheroe
Fleetwood
Heysham
Morecambe
Lancaster
Barrow-in-Furness
Ulverston
Kirkby Lonsdale
Settle
Sale

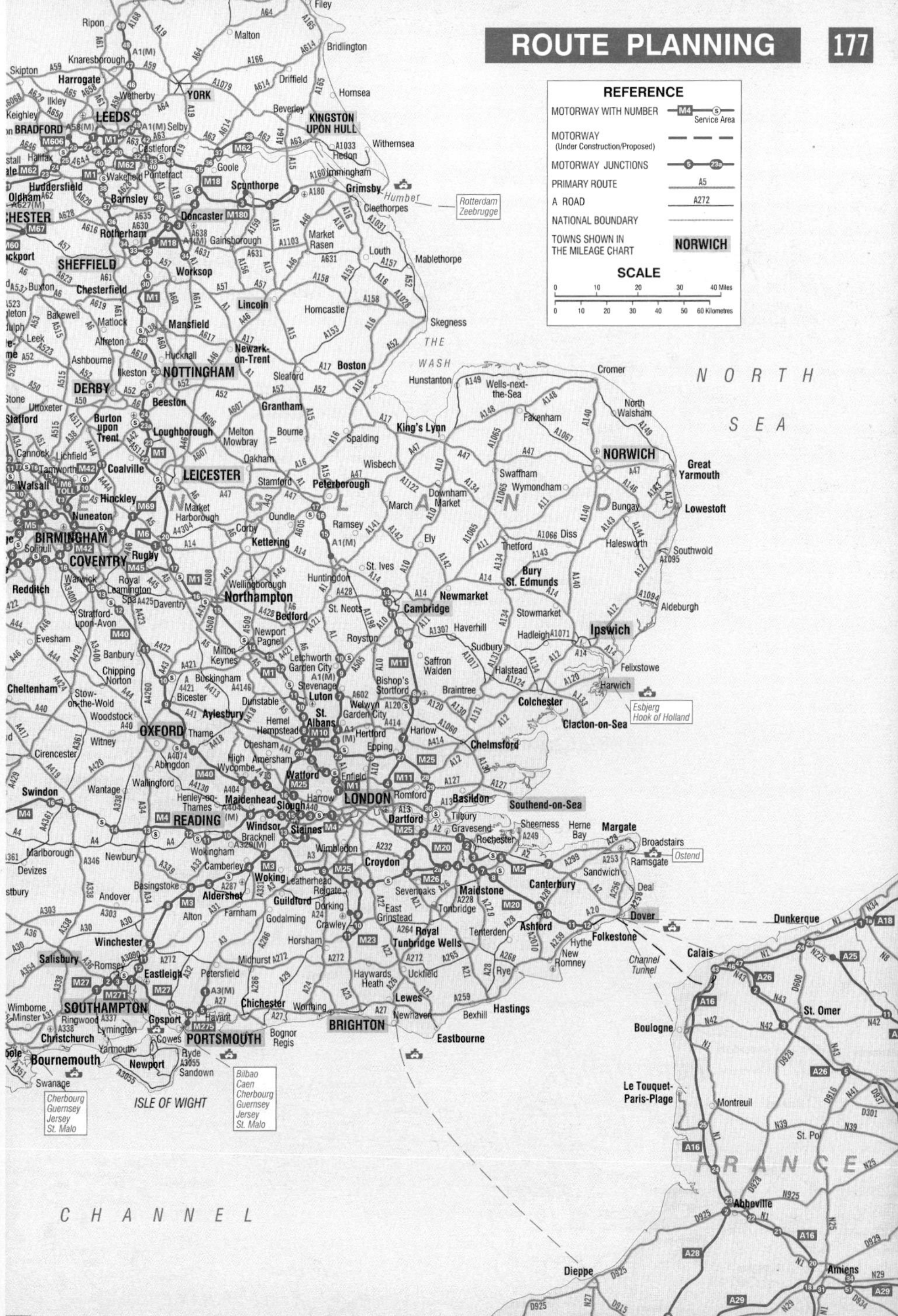
REFERENCE
MOTORWAY WITH NUMBER M4 S Service Area
MOTORWAY (Under Construction/Proposed)
MOTORWAY JUNCTIONS 5 23a
PRIMARY ROUTE A5
A ROAD A272
NATIONAL BOUNDARY
TOWNS SHOWN IN THE MILEAGE CHART NORWICH
SCALE
0 10 20 30 40 Miles
0 10 20 30 40 50 60 Kilometres
NORTH SEA
ENGLAND
FRANCE
CHANNEL
THE WASH
Humber
ISLE OF WIGHT
Rotterdam Zeebrugge
Esbjerg Hook of Holland
Ostend
Channel Tunnel
Cherbourg Guernsey Jersey St. Malo
Bilbao Caen Cherbourg Guernsey Jersey St. Malo
Ripon
Filey
Malton
Bridlington
Knaresborough
Skipton
Harrogate
Driffield
Hornsea
Ilkley
Wetherby
YORK
Keighley
LEEDS
Beverley
KINGSTON UPON HULL
BRADFORD
Selby
Withernsea
Halifax
Castleford
Goole
Hedon
Huddersfield
Wakefield
Pontefract
Immingham
Oldham
Barnsley
Scunthorpe
Grimsby
Cleethorpes
Doncaster
Rotherham
Gainsborough
Market Rasen
Louth
Mablethorpe
SHEFFIELD
Worksop
Buxton
Chesterfield
Lincoln
Horncastle
Skegness
Bakewell
Matlock
Mansfield
Leek
Alfreton
Newark-on-Trent
Ashbourne
Hucknall
Boston
Ilkeston
NOTTINGHAM
Sleaford
Hunstanton
Cromer
DERBY
Beeston
Wells-next-the-Sea
Uttoxeter
Grantham
North Walsham
Stafford
Burton upon Trent
Loughborough
Melton Mowbray
Bourne
Fakenham
Spalding
King's Lynn
Cannock
Lichfield
Oakham
NORWICH
Great Yarmouth
Tamworth
Coalville
LEICESTER
Wisbech
Swaffham
Walsall
Stamford
Peterborough
Downham Market
Wymondham
Hinckley
Market Harborough
March
Bungay
Lowestoft
Nuneaton
Oundle
Corby
Ramsey
Ely
Diss
BIRMINGHAM
Kettering
Thetford
Halesworth
Solihull
Rugby
Southwold
COVENTRY
St. Ives
Bury St. Edmunds
Redditch
Warwick
Royal Leamington Spa
Wellingborough
Huntingdon
Daventry
Northampton
Newmarket
Stratford-upon-Avon
Bedford
St. Neots
Cambridge
Stowmarket
Aldeburgh
Haverhill
Evesham
Newport Pagnell
Royston
Hadleigh
Ipswich
Sudbury
Banbury
Milton Keynes
Letchworth Garden City
Saffron Walden
Felixstowe
Chipping Norton
Buckingham
Halstead
Cheltenham
Stow-on-the-Wold
Bicester
Stevenage
Bishop's Stortford
Braintree
Harwich
Dunstable
Luton
Colchester
Woodstock
Aylesbury
Welwyn Garden City
Hemel Hempstead
St. Albans
Hertford
Harlow
Clacton-on-Sea
OXFORD
Thame
Witney
Chesham
Epping
Chelmsford
Cirencester
Abingdon
High Wycombe
Amersham
Watford
Enfield
Wallingford
Wantage
Swindon
Henley-on-Thames
Maidenhead
Harrow
LONDON
Romford
Basildon
Southend-on-Sea
READING
Slough
Dartford
Tilbury
Windsor
Staines
Gravesend
Sheerness
Herne Bay
Margate
Bracknell
Rochester
Broadstairs
Marlborough
Newbury
Wokingham
Wimbledon
Croydon
Ramsgate
Devizes
Camberley
Woking
Leatherhead
Sandwich
Basingstoke
Aldershot
Reigate
Sevenoaks
Maidstone
Canterbury
Deal
Andover
Guildford
Dorking
East Grinstead
Tonbridge
Dover
Alton
Farnham
Godalming
Crawley
Ashford
Dunkerque
Winchester
Horsham
Royal Tunbridge Wells
Tenterden
Hythe
Folkestone
Salisbury
Romsey
Eastleigh
Petersfield
Midhurst
Uckfield
Rye
New Romney
Calais
Haywards Heath
Wimborne Minster
SOUTHAMPTON
Ringwood
Gosport
Chichester
Worthing
Lewes
Newhaven
Bexhill
Hastings
St. Omer
Christchurch
Lymington
Havant
PORTSMOUTH
BRIGHTON
Eastbourne
Boulogne
Bognor Regis
Yarmouth
Cowes
Ryde
Bournemouth
Newport
Sandown
Swanage
Le Touquet-Paris-Plage
Montreuil
St. Pol
Abbeville
Dieppe
Amiens

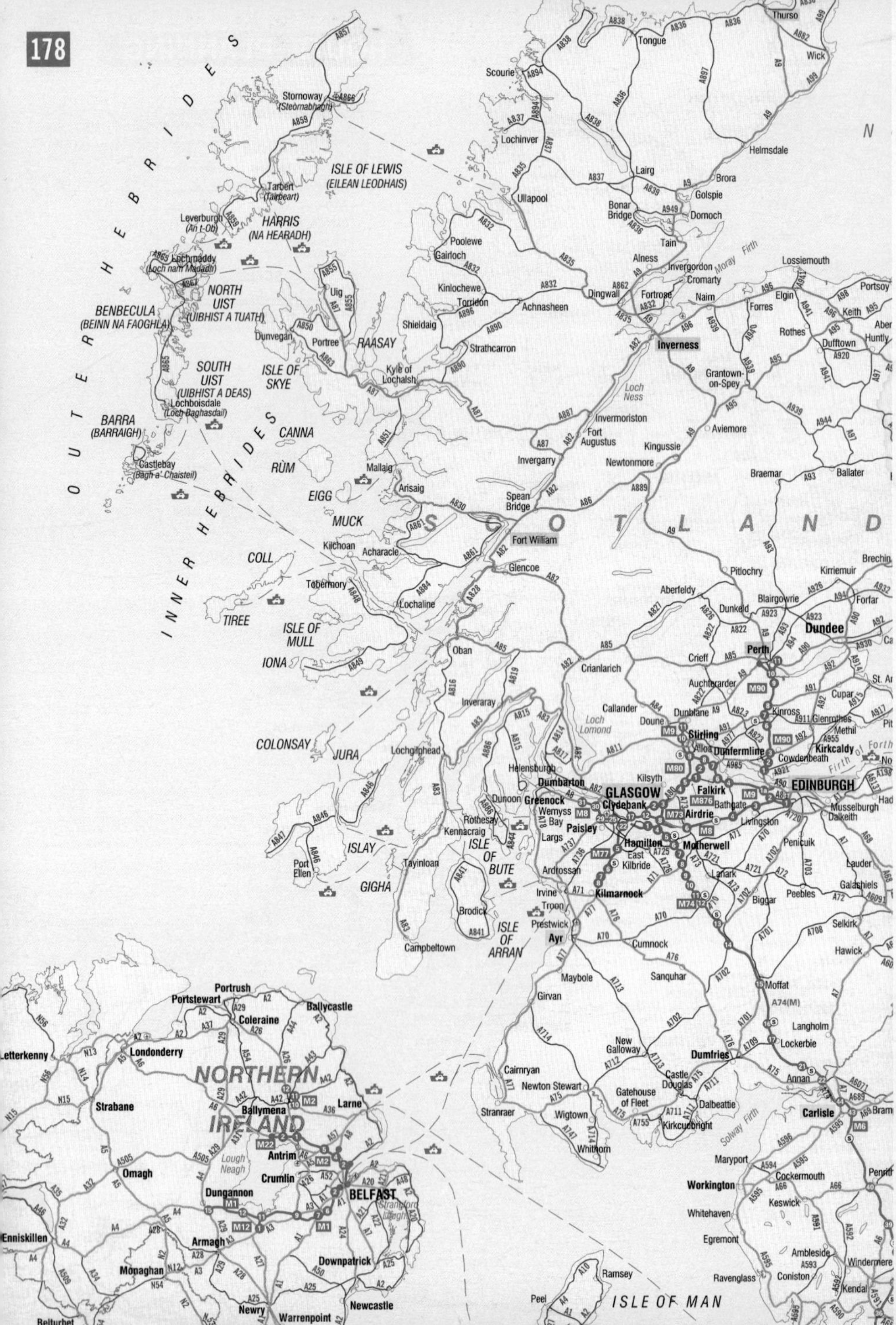
OUTER HEBRIDES
INNER HEBRIDES
SCOTLAND
NORTHERN IRELAND
ISLE OF MAN
Thurso
Tongue
Wick
Scourie
Lochinver
Helmsdale
Lairg
Brora
Golspie
Bonar Bridge
Dornoch
Tain
Ullapool
Stornoway
(Steornabhagh)
ISLE OF LEWIS
(EILEAN LEODHAIS)
Tarbert
(Tairbeart)
Leverburgh
(An t-Ob)
HARRIS
(NA HEARADH)
Lochmaddy
(Loch nam Madadh)
NORTH UIST
(UIBHIST A TUATH)
BENBECULA
(BEINN NA FAOGHLA)
SOUTH UIST
(UIBHIST A DEAS)
Lochboisdale
(Loch Baghasdail)
BARRA
(BARRAIGH)
Castlebay
(Bagh a' Chaisteil)
Poolewe
Gairloch
Kinlochewe
Torridon
Achnasheen
Alness
Invergordon
Cromarty
Moray Firth
Lossiemouth
Dingwall
Fortrose
Nairn
Forres
Elgin
Keith
Portsoy
Rothes
Dufftown
Huntly
Uig
Shieldaig
Dunvegan
Portree
RAASAY
Strathcarron
Inverness
Kyle of Lochalsh
ISLE OF SKYE
Grantown-on-Spey
Loch Ness
Invermoriston
Fort Augustus
Aviemore
Kingussie
Newtonmore
Invergarry
CANNA
RÙM
Mallaig
Arisaig
EIGG
MUCK
Spean Bridge
Braemar
Ballater
Fort William
Kilchoan
Acharacle
COLL
Tobermory
Glencoe
Pitlochry
Kirriemuir
Brechin
Aberfeldy
Dunkeld
Blairgowrie
Forfar
TIREE
Lochaline
ISLE OF MULL
Dundee
IONA
Oban
Perth
Crieff
Crianlarich
Auchterarder
Cupar
Inveraray
Callander
Dunblane
Kinross
Glenrothes
Methil
Doune
Stirling
Loch Lomond
COLONSAY
JURA
Lochgilphead
Alloa
Dunfermline
Kirkcaldy
Cowdenbeath
Firth of Forth
Helensburgh
Kilsyth
Dumbarton
Falkirk
GLASGOW
Clydebank
EDINBURGH
Dunoon
Greenock
Wemyss Bay
Airdrie
Bathgate
Musselburgh
Dalkeith
Livingston
Paisley
Rothesay
Kennacraig
Largs
Hamilton
Motherwell
Penicuik
ISLAY
Port Ellen
Tayinloan
ISLE OF BUTE
East Kilbride
Lanark
Lauder
Ardrossan
GIGHA
Irvine
Kilmarnock
Peebles
Galashiels
Troon
Biggar
Brodick
Prestwick
Selkirk
ISLE OF ARRAN
Ayr
Campbeltown
Cumnock
Hawick
Sanquhar
Maybole
Girvan
Moffat
Langholm
Lockerbie
New Galloway
Dumfries
Annan
Cairnryan
Newton Stewart
Castle Douglas
Gatehouse of Fleet
Dalbeattie
Carlisle
Stranraer
Wigtown
Kirkcudbright
Solway Firth
Whithorn
Maryport
Cockermouth
Penrith
Workington
Keswick
Whitehaven
Egremont
Ambleside
Windermere
Coniston
Ravenglass
Kendal
Ramsey
Peel
Portrush
Portstewart
Ballycastle
Coleraine
Letterkenny
Londonderry
Strabane
Ballymena
Larne
Antrim
Lough Neagh
Omagh
Crumlin
Dungannon
BELFAST
Strangford Lough
Enniskillen
Armagh
Downpatrick
Monaghan
Newry
Warrenpoint
Newcastle
Belturbet

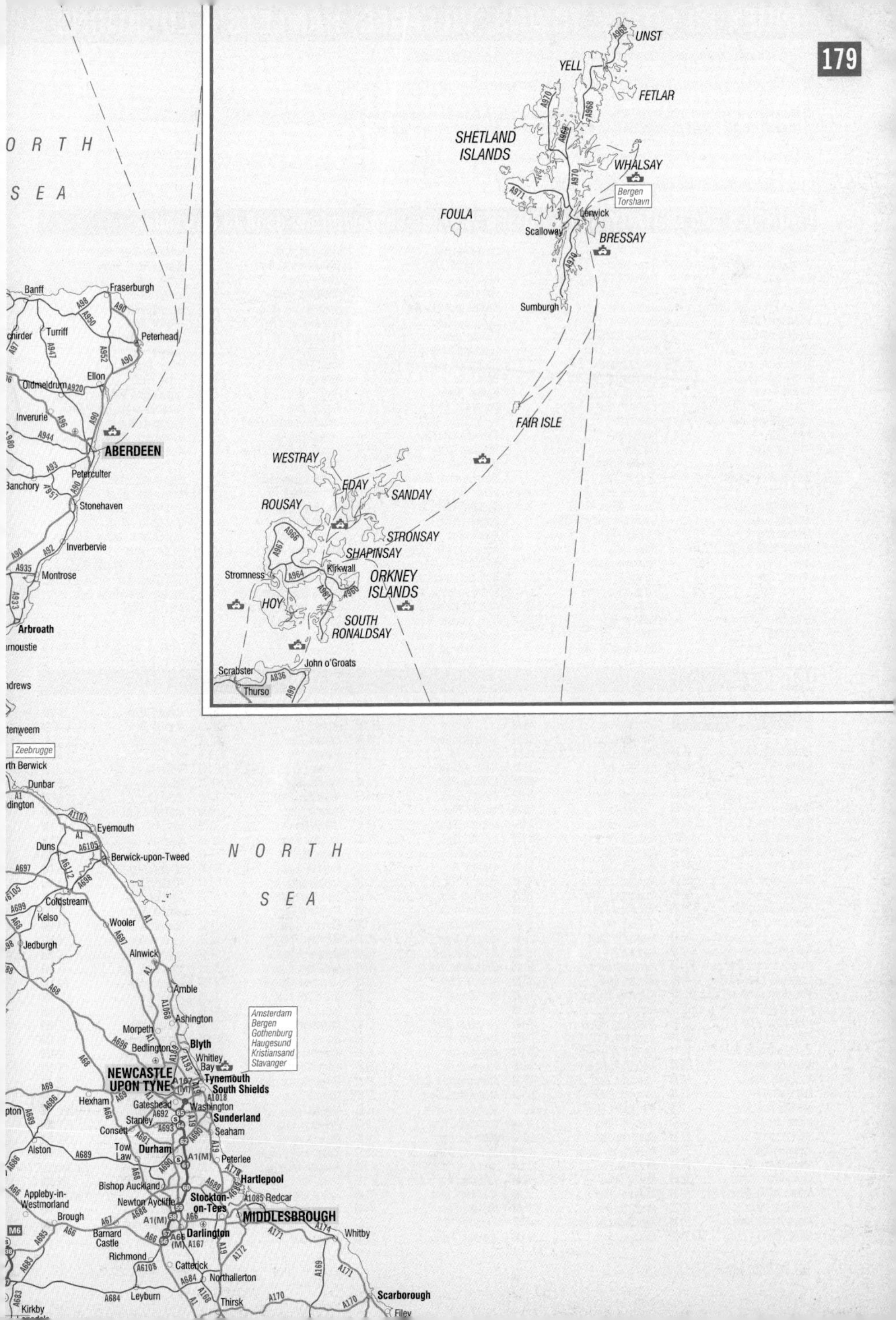

UNST

YELL

FETLAR

SHETLAND ISLANDS

WHALSAY

Bergen
Torshavn

FOULA

Lerwick

Scalloway

BRESSAY

Sumburgh

FAIR ISLE

WESTRAY

EDAY SANDAY

ROUSAY

STRONSAY

SHAPINSAY

Stromness Kirkwall

ORKNEY
ISLANDS

HOY

SOUTH
RONALDSAY

Scrabster John o'Groats

Thurso

NORTH SEA

Banff Fraserburgh

Turriff Peterhead

Oldmeldrum Ellon

Inverurie

ABERDEEN

Peterculter

Banchory Stonehaven

Inverbervie

Montrose

Arbroath

rmoustie

ndrews

tenweem

Zeebrugge

rth Berwick

Dunbar

dington Eyemouth

Duns Berwick-upon-Tweed

Coldstream

Kelso Wooler

Jedburgh Alnwick

Amble

Ashington

Morpeth

Bedlington Blyth

Whitley Bay

NEWCASTLE
UPON TYNE Tynemouth

South Shields

Hexham Gateshead Washington

Stanley Sunderland

Consett Seaham

Tow Law Durham

Peterlee

Alston

Bishop Auckland Hartlepool

Appleby-in-
Westmorland Newton Aycliffe Stockton-
on-Tees Redcar

Brough MIDDLESBROUGH

Barnard
Castle Darlington Whitby

Richmond

Catterick

Leyburn Northallerton

Kirkby Thirsk

Scarborough

Filey

NORTH SEA

Amsterdam
Bergen
Gothenburg
Haugesund
Kristiansand
Stavanger

INDEX TO CITIES, TOWNS, VILLAGES, HAMLETS & LOCATIONS

(1) A strict alphabetical order is used e.g Abbotstone follows Abbot's Salford but precedes Abbots Worthy.

(2) The map reference given refers to the actual map square in which the town spot or built-up area is located and not to the place name.

(3) Where two or more places of the same name occur in the same County or Unitary Authority, the nearest large town is also given; e.g. Achiemore. *High* . . . .2D **166** (nr. Durness) indicates that Achiemore is located in square 2D on page **166** and is situated near Durness in the Unitary Authority of Highland.

(4) Only one reference is given although due to page overlaps the place may appear on more than one page.

(5) Major towns are shown in bold, i.e. **Abercynon.** *Rhon* 2D **32**

COUNTIES and UNITARY AUTHORITIES with the abbreviations used in this index

Aberdeen : *Aber*
Aberdeenshire : *Abers*
Angus : *Ang*
Argyll & Bute : *Arg*
Bath & N E Somerset : *Bath*
Bedfordshire : *Beds*
Blackburn with Darwen : *Bkbn*
Blackpool : *Bkpl*
Blaenau Gwent : *Blae*
Bournemouth : *Bour*
Bracknell Forest : *Brac*
Bridgend : *B'end*
Brighton & Hove : *Brig*
Bristol : *Bris*
Buckinghamshire : *Buck*
Caerphilly : *Cphy*
Cambridgeshire : *Cambs*
Cardiff : *Card*
Carmarthenshire : *Carm*
Ceredigion : *Cdgn*
Cheshire : *Ches*
Clackmannanshire : *Clac*
Conwy : *Cnwy*
Cornwall : *Corn*
Cumbria : *Cumb*
Darlington : *Darl*
Denbighshire : *Den*
Derby : *Derb*
Derbyshire : *Derbs*
Devon : *Devn*
Dorset : *Dors*
Dumfries & Galloway : *Dum*
Dundee : *D'dee*
Durham : *Dur*
East Ayrshire : *E Ayr*
East Dunbartonshire : *E Dun*
East Lothian : *E Lot*
East Renfrewshire : *E Ren*
East Riding of Yorkshire : *E Yor*
East Sussex : *E Sus*
Edinburgh : *Edin*
Essex : *Essx*
Falkirk : *Falk*
Fife : *Fife*
Flintshire : *Flin*
Glasgow : *Glas*
Gloucestershire : *Glos*
Greater London : *G Lon*
Greater Manchester : *G Man*
Gwynedd : *Gwyn*
Halton : *Hal*
Hampshire : *Hants*
Hartlepool : *Hart*
Herefordshire : *Here*
Hertfordshire : *Herts*
Highland : *High*
Inverclyde : *Inv*
Isle of Anglesey : *IOA*
Isle of Man : *IOM*
Isle of Wight : *IOW*
Isles of Scilly : *IOS*
Kent : *Kent*
Kingston upon Hull : *Hull*
Lancashire : *Lanc*
Leicester : *Leic*
Leicestershire : *Leics*
Lincolnshire : *Linc*
Luton : *Lutn*
Medway : *Medw*
Merseyside : *Mers*
Merthyr Tydfil : *Mer T*
Middlesbrough : *Midd*
Midlothian : *Midl*
Milton Keynes : *Mil*
Monmouthshire : *Mon*
Moray : *Mor*
Neath Port Talbot : *Neat*
Newport : *Newp*
Norfolk : *Norf*
Northamptonshire : *Nptn*
North Ayrshire : *N Ayr*
North East Lincolnshire : *NE Lin*
North Lanarkshire : *N Lan*
North Lincolnshire : *N Lin*
North Somerset : *N Som*
Northumberland : *Nmbd*
North Yorkshire : *N Yor*
Nottingham : *Nott*
Nottinghamshire : *Notts*
Orkney : *Orkn*
Oxfordshire : *Oxon*
Pembrokeshire : *Pemb*
Perth & Kinross : *Per*
Peterborough : *Pet*
Plymouth : *Plym*
Poole : *Pool*
Portsmouth : *Port*
Powys : *Powy*
Reading : *Read*
Redcar & Cleveland : *Red C*
Renfrewshire : *Ren*
Rhondda Cynon Taff : *Rhon*
Rutland : *Rut*
Scottish Borders : *Bord*
Shetland : *Shet*
Shropshire : *Shrp*
Slough : *Slo*
Somerset : *Som*
Southampton : *Sotn*
South Ayrshire : *S Ayr*
Southend-on-Sea : *S'end*
South Gloucestershire : *S Glo*
South Lanarkshire : *S Lan*
South Yorkshire : *S Yor*
Staffordshire : *Staf*
Stirling : *Stir*
Stockton-on-Tees : *Stoc T*
Stoke-on-Trent : *Stoke*
Suffolk : *Suff*
Surrey : *Surr*
Swansea : *Swan*
Swindon : *Swin*
Telford & Wrekin : *Telf*
Thurrock : *Thur*
Torbay : *Torb*
Torfaen : *Torf*
Tyne & Wear : *Tyne*
Vale of Glamorgan, The : *V Glam*
Warrington : *Warr*
Warwickshire : *Warw*
West Berkshire : *W Ber*
West Dunbartonshire : *W Dun*
Western Isles : *W Isl*
West Lothian : *W Lot*
West Midlands : *W Mid*
West Sussex : *W Sus*
West Yorkshire : *W Yor*
Wiltshire : *Wilts*
Windsor & Maidenhead : *Wind*
Wokingham : *Wok*
Worcestershire : *Worc*
Wrexham : *Wrex*
York : *York*

INDEX

A

Abbas Combe. *Som* . . . 4C **22**
Abberley. *Worc* . . . 4B **60**
Abberley Common. *Worc* . . . 4B **60**
Abberton. *Essx* . . . 4D **54**
Abberton. *Worc* . . . 5D **61**
Abberwick. *Nmbd* . . . 3F **121**
Abbess Roding. *Essx* . . . 4F **53**
Abbey. *Devn* . . . 1E **13**
Abbey-cwm-hir. *Powy* . . . 3C **58**
Abbeydale. *S Yor* . . . 2H **85**
Abbeydale Park. *S Yor* . . . 2H **85**
Abbey Dore. *Here* . . . 2G **47**
Abbey Gate. *Devn* . . . 3F **13**
Abbey Hulton. *Stoke* . . . 1D **72**
Abbey St Bathans. *Bord* . . . 3D **130**
Abbeystead. *Lanc* . . . 4E **97**
Abbey Town. *Cumb* . . . 4C **112**
Abbey Village. *Lanc* . . . 2E **91**
Abbey Wood. *G Lon* . . . 3F **39**
Abbots Ann. *Hants* . . . 2B **24**
Abbots Bickington. *Devn* . . . 1D **11**
Abbots Bromley. *Staf* . . . 3E **73**
Abbotsbury. *Dors* . . . 4A **14**
Abbotsham. *Devn* . . . 4E **19**
Abbotskerswell. *Devn* . . . 2E **9**
Abbots Langley. *Herts* . . . 5A **52**
Abbots Leigh. *N Som* . . . 4A **34**
Abbotsley. *Cambs* . . . 5B **64**
Abbots Morton. *Worc* . . . 5E **61**
Abbots Ripton. *Cambs* . . . 3B **64**
Abbot's Salford. *Warw* . . . 5E **61**
Abbotstone. *Hants* . . . 3D **24**
Abbots Worthy. *Hants* . . . 3C **24**
Abcott. *Shrp* . . . 3F **59**
Abdon. *Shrp* . . . 2H **59**
Abenhall. *Glos* . . . 4B **48**
Aber. *Cdgn* . . . 1E **45**
Aberaeron. *Cdgn* . . . 4D **56**
Aberafan. *Neat* . . . 3G **31**
Aberaman. *Rhon* . . . 5D **46**
Aberangell. *Powy* . . . 4H **69**
Aberarad. *Carm* . . . 1H **43**
Aberarder. *High* . . . 1A **150**
Aberargie. *Per* . . . 2D **136**
Aberarth. *Cdgn* . . . 4D **57**
Aberavon. *Neat* . . . 3G **31**
Aber-banc. *Cdgn* . . . 1D **44**
Aberbargoed. *Cphy* . . . 2E **33**
Aberbechan. *Powy* . . . 1D **58**
Aberbeeg. *Blae* . . . 5F **47**
Aberbowlan. *Carm* . . . 2G **45**
Aberbran. *Powy* . . . 3C **46**
Abercanaid. *Mer T* . . . 5D **46**
Abercarn. *Cphy* . . . 2F **33**
Abercastle. *Pemb* . . . 1C **42**
Abercegir. *Powy* . . . 5H **69**
Aberchalder. *High* . . . 3F **149**
Aberchirder. *Abers* . . . 3D **160**
Abercorn. *W Lot* . . . 2D **129**
Abercraf. *Powy* . . . 4B **46**
Abercregan. *Neat* . . . 2B **32**
Abercrombie. *Fife* . . . 3H **137**
Abercwmboi. *Rhon* . . . 2D **32**
Abercych. *Pemb* . . . 1C **44**
Abercynon. *Rhon* . . . 2D **32**
Aber-Cywarch. *Gwyn* . . . 4A **70**
Aberdalgie. *Per* . . . 1C **136**
Aberdâr. *Rhon* . . . 5C **46**
Aberdare. *Rhon* . . . 5C **46**
Aberdaron. *Gwyn* . . . 3A **68**
Aberdaugleddau. *Pemb* . . . 4D **42**
Aberdeen. *Aber* . . . 3G **153**
Aberdeen (Dyce) Airport. *Aber* . . . 2F **153**
Aberdesach. *Gwyn* . . . 5D **80**
Aberdour. *Fife* . . . 1E **129**
Aberdovey. *Gwyn* . . . 1F **57**
Aberdulais. *Neat* . . . 5A **46**
Aberdyfi. *Gwyn* . . . 1F **57**
Aberedw. *Powy* . . . 1D **46**
Abereiddy. *Pemb* . . . 1B **42**
Abererch. *Gwyn* . . . 2C **68**
Aberfan. *Mer T* . . . 5D **46**
Aberfeldy. *Per* . . . 4F **143**
Aberffraw. *IOA* . . . 4C **80**
Aberffrwd. *Cdgn* . . . 3F **57**
Aberford. *W Yor* . . . 1E **93**
Aberfoyle. *Stir* . . . 3E **135**
Abergarw. *B'end* . . . 3C **32**
Abergarwed. *Neat* . . . 5B **46**
Abergavenny. *Mon* . . . 4G **47**
Abergele. *Cnwy* . . . 3B **82**
Aber-Giar. *Carm* . . . 1F **45**
Abergorlech. *Carm* . . . 2F **45**
Abergwaun. *Pemb* . . . 1D **42**
Abergwesyn. *Powy* . . . 5A **58**
Abergwili. *Carm* . . . 3E **45**
Abergwynfi. *Neat* . . . 2B **32**
Abergwyngregyn. *Gwyn* . . . 3F **81**
Abergynolwyn. *Gwyn* . . . 5F **69**
Aberhafesp. *Powy* . . . 1C **58**
Aberhonddu. *Powy* . . . 3D **46**
Aberhosan. *Powy* . . . 1H **57**
Aberkenfig. *B'end* . . . 3B **32**
Aberlady. *E Lot* . . . 2A **130**
Aberlemno. *Ang* . . . 3E **145**
Aberllefenni. *Gwyn* . . . 5G **69**
Abermaw. *Gwyn* . . . 4F **69**
Abermeurig. *Cdgn* . . . 5E **57**
Aber-miwl. *Powy* . . . 1D **58**
Abermule. *Powy* . . . 1D **58**
Abernant. *Carm* . . . 2H **43**
Abernant. *Rhon* . . . 5D **46**
Abernethy. *Per* . . . 2D **136**
Abernyte. *Per* . . . 5B **144**
Aber-oer. *Wrex* . . . 1E **71**
Aberpennar. *Rhon* . . . 2D **32**
Aberporth. *Cdgn* . . . 5B **56**
Aberriw. *Powy* . . . 5D **70**
Abersoch. *Gwyn* . . . 3C **68**
Abersychan. *Torf* . . . 5F **47**
Abertawe. *Swan* . . . 3F **31**
Aberteifi. *Cdgn* . . . 1B **44**
Aberthin. *V Glam* . . . 4D **32**
Abertillery. *Blae* . . . 5F **47**
Abertridwr. *Cphy* . . . 3E **32**
Abertridwr. *Powy* . . . 4C **70**
Abertyleri. *Blae* . . . 5F **47**
Abertysswg. *Cphy* . . . 5E **47**
Aberuthven. *Per* . . . 2B **136**
Aber Village. *Powy* . . . 3E **46**
Aberyscir. *Powy* . . . 3D **46**
Aberystwyth. *Cdgn* . . . 2E **57**
Abhainn Suidhe. *W Isl* . . . 7C **171**
Abingdon. *Oxon* . . . 2C **36**
Abinger Common. *Surr* . . . 1C **26**
Abinger Hammer. *Surr* . . . 1B **26**
Abington. *S Lan* . . . 2B **118**
Abington Pigotts. *Cambs* . . . 1D **52**
Ab Kettleby. *Leics* . . . 3E **74**
Ab Lench. *Worc* . . . 5E **61**
Ablington. *Glos* . . . 5G **49**
Ablington. *Wilts* . . . 2G **23**
Abney. *Derbs* . . . 3F **85**
Aboyne. *Abers* . . . 4C **152**
Abram. *G Man* . . . 4E **90**
Abriachan. *High* . . . 5H **157**
Abridge. *Essx* . . . 1F **39**
Abronhill. *N Lan* . . . 2A **128**
Abson. *S Glo* . . . 4C **34**
Abthorpe. *Nptn* . . . 1E **51**
Aby. *Linc* . . . 3D **88**
Acaster Malbis. *York* . . . 5H **99**
Acaster Selby. *N Yor* . . . 5H **99**
Accott. *Devn* . . . 3G **19**
Accrington. *Lanc* . . . 2F **91**
Acha. *Arg* . . . 3C **138**
Achachork. *High* . . . 4D **155**
Achahoish. *Arg* . . . 2F **125**
Achaleven. *Arg* . . . 5D **140**
Achallader. *Arg* . . . 4H **141**
Acha Mor. *W Isl* . . . 5F **171**
Achanalt. *High* . . . 2E **157**
Achandunie. *High* . . . 1A **158**
Ach'an Todhair. *High* . . . 1E **141**
Achany. *High* . . . 3C **164**
Achaphubuil. *High* . . . 1E **141**
Acharacle. *High* . . . 2A **140**
Acharn. *Ang* . . . 1B **144**
Acharn. *Per* . . . 4E **143**
Acharole. *High* . . . 3E **169**
Achateny. *High* . . . 2G **139**
Achavanich. *High* . . . 4D **169**
Achdalieu. *High* . . . 1E **141**
Achduart. *High* . . . 3E **163**
Achentoul. *High* . . . 5A **168**
Achfary. *High* . . . 5C **166**
Achfrish. *High* . . . 2C **164**
Achgarve. *High* . . . 4C **162**
Achiemore. *High* . . . 2D **166** (nr. Durness)
Achiemore. *High* . . . 3A **168** (nr. Thurso)
A'Chill. *High* . . . 3A **146**
Achiltibuie. *High* . . . 3E **163**
Achina. *High* . . . 2H **167**

Achinahuagh. *High* 2F 167
Achindarroch. *High* 3E 141
Achinduich. *High* 3C 164
Achinduin. *Arg* 5C 140
Achininver. *High* 2F 167
Achintee. *High* 4B 156
Achintraid. *High* 5H 155
Achleck. *Arg* 4F 139
Achlorachan. *High* 3F 157
Achluachrach. *High* 5E 149
Achlyness. *High* 3C 166
Achmelvich. *High* 1E 163
Achmony. *High* 5H 157
Achmore. *High* 5A 156
(nr. Stromeferry)
Achmore. *High* 4E 163
(nr. Ullapool)
Achnacarnin. *High* 1E 163
Achnacarry. *High* 5D 148
Achnaclerach. *High* 2G 157
Achnacloich. *High* 3D 147
Achnaconeran. *High* 2G 149
Achnacroish. *Arg* 4C 140
Achnafalnich. *Arg* 1B 134
Achnagarron. *High* 1A 158
Achnaha. *High* 2F 139
Achnahanat. *High* 4C 164
Achnahannet. *High* 1D 151
Achnairn. *High* 2C 164
Achnamara. *Arg* 1F 125
Achnanellan. *High* 5C 148
Achnangoul. *Arg* 3H 133
Achnasheen. *High* 3D 156
Achnashellach. *High* 4C 156
Achosnich. *High* 2F 139
Achow. *High* 5E 169
Achranich. *High* 4B 140
Achreamie. *High* 2C 168
Achriabhach. *High* 2F 141
Achriesgill. *High* 3C 166
Achrimsdale. *High* 3G 165
Achscrabster. *High* 2C 168
Achtoty. *High* 2G 167
Achurch. *Nptn* 2H 63
Achuvoldrach. *High* 3F 167
Achvaich. *High* 4E 164
Achvoan. *High* 3E 165
Ackergill. *High* 3F 169
Ackergillshore. *High* 3F 169
Acklam. *Midd* 3B 106
Acklam. *N Yor* 3B 100
Ackleton. *Shrp* 1B 60
Acklington. *Nmbd* 4G 121
Ackton. *W Yor* 2E 93
Ackworth Moor Top.
W Yor 3E 93
Acle. *Norf* 4G 79
Acocks Green. *W Mid* 2F 61
Acol. *Kent* 4H 41
Acomb. *Nmbd* 3C 114
Acomb. *York* 4H 99
Aconbury. *Here* 2A 48
Acre. *G Man* 4H 91
Acre. *Lanc* 2F 91
Acrefair. *Wrex* 1E 71
Acrise. *Kent* 1F 29
Acton. *Ches* 5A 84
Acton. *Dors* 5E 15
Acton. *G Lon* 2C 38
Acton. *Shrp* 2F 59
Acton. *Staf* 1C 72
Acton. *Suff* 1B 54
Acton. *Worc* 4C 60
Acton. *Wrex* 5F 83
Acton Beauchamp. *Here* 5A 60
Acton Bridge. *Ches* 3H 83
Acton Burnell. *Shrp* 5H 71
Acton Green. *Here* 5A 60
Acton Pigott. *Shrp* 5H 71
Acton Round. *Shrp* 1A 60
Acton Scott. *Shrp* 2G 59
Acton Trussell. *Staf* 4D 72
Acton Turville. *S Glo* 3D 34
Adam's Hill. *Worc* 3D 60
Adbaston. *Staf* 3B 72
Adber. *Dors* 4B 22
Adderbury. *Oxon* 2C 50
Adderley. *Shrp* 2A 72
Adderstone. *Nmbd* 1F 121
Addiewell. *W Lot* 3C 128
Addingham. *W Yor* 5C 98
Addington. *Buck* 3F 51
Addington. *G Lon* 4E 39
Addington. *Kent* 5A 40
Addinston. *Bord* 4B 130
Addiscombe. *G Lon* 4E 39
Addlestone. *Surr* 4B 38
Addlethorpe. *Linc* 4E 89
Adeney. *Telf* 4B 72
Adfa. *Powy* 5C 70
Adforton. *Here* 3G 59
Adgestone. *IOW* 4D 16
Adisham. *Kent* 5G 41
Adlestrop. *Glos* 3H 49
Adlingfleet. *E Yor* 2B 94
Adlington. *Ches* 2D 84
Adlington. *Lanc* 3E 90
Admaston. *Staf* 3E 73
Admaston. *Telf* 4A 72
Admington. *Warw* 1G 49
Adpar. *Cdgn* 1D 44
Adsborough. *Som* 4F 21
Adstock. *Buck* 2F 51
Adstone. *Nptn* 5C 62
Adversane. *W Sus* 3B 26
Advie. *High* 5F 159
Adwalton. *W Yor* 2C 92
Adwell. *Oxon* 2E 37
Adwick le Street. *S Yor* 4F 93
Adwick upon Dearne. *S Yor* 4E 93
Adziel. *Abers* 3G 161
Ae. *Dum* 1A 112
Affleck. *Abers* 1F 153
Affpuddle. *Dors* 3D 14
Affric Lodge. *High* 1D 148
Afon-wen. *Flin* 3D 82
Agglethorpe. *N Yor* 1C 98
Aglionby. *Cumb* 4F 113
Aigburth. *Mers* 2F 83
Aike. *E Yor* 5E 101
Aikers. *Orkn* 8D 172
Aiketgate. *Cumb* 5F 113
Aikhead. *Cumb* 5D 112
Aikton. *Cumb* 4D 112
Ailey. *Here* 1G 47
Ailsworth. *Pet* 1A 64
Ainderby Quernhow. *N Yor* 1F 99
Ainderby Steeple. *N Yor* 5A 106
Aingers Green. *Essx* 3E 54
Ainsdale. *Mers* 3B 90
Ainsdale-on-Sea. *Mers* 3B 90
Ainstable. *Cumb* 5G 113
Ainsworth. *G Man* 3F 91
Ainthorpe. *N Yor* 4E 107
Aintree. *Mers* 1F 83
Aird. *Arg* 3E 133
Aird. *Dum* 3F 109
Aird. *High* 1G 155
Aird. *W Isl* 3C 170
(on Benbecula)
Aird. *W Isl* 4H 171
(on Isle of Lewis)
Aird a Mhachair. *W Isl* 4C 170
Aird a Mhulaidh. *W Isl* 6D 171
Airdens. *High* 4D 164
Airdeny. *Arg* 1G 133
Aird Mhidhinis. *W Isl* 8C 170
Aird Mhighe. *W Isl* 8D 171
(nr. Ceann a Bhaigh)
Aird Mhighe. *W Isl* 9C 171
(nr. Fionnsabhagh)
Aird Mhor. *W Isl* 8C 170
(on Barra)
Aird Mhor. *W Isl* 4D 170
(on South Uist)
Aird of Sleat. *High* 3D 147
Airdrie. *N Lan* 3A 128
Aird Shleibhe. *W Isl* 9D 171
Aird, The. *High* 3D 154
Aird Thunga. *W Isl* 4G 171
Aird Uig. *W Isl* 4C 171
Airedale. *W Yor* 2E 93
Airidh a Bhruaich. *W Isl* 6E 171
Airies. *Dum* 3E 109
Airmyn. *E Yor* 2H 93
Airntully. *Per* 5H 143
Airor. *High* 3F 147
Airth. *Falk* 1C 128
Airton. *N Yor* 4B 98
Aisby. *Linc* 1F 87
(nr. Gainsborough)
Aisby. *Linc* 2H 75
(nr. Grantham)
Aisgernis. *W Isl* 6C 170
Aish. *Devn* 2C 8
(nr. Buckfastleigh)
Aish. *Devn* 3E 9
(nr. Totnes)
Aisholt. *Som* 3E 21
Aiskew. *N Yor* 1E 99
Aislaby. *N Yor* 1B 100
(nr. Pickering)
Aislaby. *N Yor* 4F 107
(nr. Whitby)
Aislaby. *Stoc T* 3B 106
Aisthorpe. *Linc* 2G 87
Aith. *Shet* 2H 173
(on Fetlar)
Aith. *Shet* 6E 173
(on Mainland)
Akeld. *Nmbd* 2D 120
Akeley. *Buck* 2F 51
Akenham. *Suff* 1E 55
Albaston. *Corn* 5E 11
Alberbury. *Shrp* 4F 71
Albert Town. *Pemb* 3D 42
Albert Village. *Leics* 4H 73
Albourne. *W Sus* 4D 26
Albrighton. *Shrp* 4G 71
(nr. Shrewsbury)
Albrighton. *Shrp* 5C 72
(nr. Telford)
Alburgh. *Norf* 2E 67
Albury. *Herts* 3E 53
Albury. *Surr* 1B 26
Albyfield. *Cumb* 4G 113
Alby Hill. *Norf* 2D 78
Alcaig. *High* 3H 157
Alcaston. *Shrp* 2G 59
Alcester. *Warw* 5E 61
Alciston. *E Sus* 5G 27
Alcombe. *Som* 2C 20
Alconbury. *Cambs* 3A 64
Alconbury Weston. *Cambs* 3A 64
Aldborough. *Norf* 2D 78
Aldborough. *N Yor* 3G 99
Aldbourne. *Wilts* 4A 36
Aldbrough. *E Yor* 1F 95
Aldbrough St John. *N Yor* 3F 105
Aldbury. *Herts* 4H 51
Aldcliffe. *Lanc* 3D 96
Aldclune. *Per* 2G 143
Aldeburgh. *Suff* 5G 67
Aldeby. *Norf* 1G 67
Aldenham. *Herts* 1C 38
Alderbury. *Wilts* 4G 23
Aldercar. *Derbs* 1B 74
Alderford. *Norf* 4D 78
Alderholt. *Dors* 1G 15
Alderley. *Glos* 2C 34
Alderley Edge. *Ches* 3C 84
Aldermaston. *W Ber* 5D 36
Aldermaston Stoke. *W Ber* 5E 36
Aldermaston Wharf. *W Ber* 5E 36
Alderminster. *Warw* 1H 49
Alder Moor. *Staf* 3G 73
Aldersey Green. *Ches* 5G 83
Aldershot. *Hants* 1G 25
Alderton. *Glos* 2E 49
Alderton. *Nptn* 1F 51
Alderton. *Shrp* 3G 71
Alderton. *Suff* 1G 55
Alderton. *Wilts* 3D 34
Alderton Fields. *Glos* 2F 49
Alderwasley. *Derbs* 5H 85
Aldfield. *N Yor* 3E 99
Aldford. *Ches* 5G 83
Aldgate. *Rut* 5G 75
Aldham. *Essx* 3C 54
Aldham. *Suff* 1D 54
Aldingbourne. *W Sus* 5A 26
Aldingham. *Cumb* 2B 96
Aldington. *Kent* 2E 29
Aldington. *Worc* 1F 49
Aldochlay. *Arg* 4C 134
Aldon. *Shrp* 3G 59
Aldoth. *Cumb* 5C 112
Aldreth. *Cambs* 3D 64
Aldridge. *W Mid* 5E 73
Aldringham. *Suff* 4G 67
Aldsworth. *Glos* 4G 49
Aldsworth. *W Sus* 2F 17
Aldwark. *Derbs* 5G 85
Aldwark. *N Yor* 3G 99
Aldwick. *W Sus* 3H 17
Aldwincle. *Nptn* 2H 63
Aldworth. *W Ber* 4D 36
Alexandria. *W Dun* 1E 127
Aley. *Som* 3E 21
Aley Green. *Beds* 4A 52
Alfardisworthy. *Devn* 1C 10
Alfington. *Devn* 3E 12
Alfold. *Surr* 2B 26
Alfold Bars. *W Sus* 2B 26
Alfold Crossways. *Surr* 2B 26
Alford. *Abers* 2C 152
Alford. *Linc* 3D 88
Alford. *Som* 3B 22
Alfreton. *Derbs* 5B 86
Alfrick. *Worc* 5B 60
Alfrick Pound. *Worc* 5B 60
Alfriston. *E Sus* 5G 27
Algarkirk. *Linc* 2B 76
Alhampton. *Som* 3B 22
Aline Lodge. *W Isl* 6D 171
Alkborough. *N Lin* 2B 94
Alkerton. *Oxon* 1B 50
Alkham. *Kent* 1G 29
Alkington. *Shrp* 2H 71
Alkmonton. *Derbs* 2F 73
Alladale Lodge. *High* 5B 164
Allaleigh. *Devn* 3E 9
Allanbank. *N Lan* 4B 128
Allanton. *N Lan* 4B 128
Allanton. *Bord* 4E 131
Allaston. *Glos* 5B 48
Allbrook. *Hants* 4C 24
All Cannings. *Wilts* 5F 35
Allendale Town. *Nmbd* 4B 114
Allen End. *Warw* 1F 61
Allenheads. *Nmbd* 5B 114
Allensford. *Dur* 5D 115
Allen's Green. *Herts* 4E 53
Allensmore. *Here* 2H 47
Allenton. *Derb* 2A 74
Aller. *Som* 4H 21
Allerby. *Cumb* 1B 102
Allercombe. *Devn* 3D 12
Allerford. *Som* 2C 20
Allerston. *N Yor* 1C 100
Allerthorpe. *E Yor* 5B 100
Allerton. *Mers* 2G 83
Allerton. *W Yor* 1B 92
Allerton Bywater. *W Yor* 2E 93
Allerton Mauleverer. *N Yor* 4G 99
Allesley. *W Mid* 2G 61
Allestree. *Derb* 2H 73
Allet. *Corn* 4B 6
Allexton. *Leics* 5F 75
Allgreave. *Ches* 4D 84
Allhallows. *Medw* 3C 40
Allhallows-on-Sea. *Medw* 3C 40
Alligin Shuas. *High* 3H 155
Allimore Green. *Staf* 4C 72
Allington. *Kent* 5B 40
Allington. *Linc* 1F 75
Allington. *Wilts* 3H 23
(nr. Amesbury)
Allington. *Wilts* 5F 35
(nr. Devizes)
Allithwaite. *Cumb* 2C 96
Alloa. *Clac* 4A 136
Allonby. *Cumb* 5B 112
Alloway. *S Ayr* 3C 116
Allowenshay. *Som* 1G 13
All Saints South Elmham.
Suff 2F 67
Allscott. *Shrp* 1B 60
Allscott. *Telf* 4A 72
All Stretton. *Shrp* 1G 59
Allt. *Carm* 5F 45
Alltami. *Flin* 4E 83
Alltgobhlach. *N Ayr* 5G 125
Alltmawr. *Powy* 1D 46
Alltnacaillich. *High* 4E 167
Allt na h-Airbhe. *High* 4F 163
Alltour. *High* 5E 148
Alltsigh. *High* 2G 149
Alltwalis. *Carm* 2E 45
Alltwen. *Neat* 5H 45
Alltyblacca. *Cdgn* 1F 45
Allt-y-goed. *Pemb* 1B 44
Almeley. *Here* 5F 59
Almeley Wooton. *Here* 5F 59
Almer. *Dors* 3E 15
Almholme. *S Yor* 4F 93
Almington. *Staf* 2B 72
Alminstone Cross. *Devn* 4D 18
Almodington. *W Sus* 3G 17
Almondbank. *Per* 1C 136
Almondbury. *W Yor* 3B 92
Almondsbury. *S Glo* 3B 34
Alne. *N Yor* 3G 99
Alness. *High* 2A 158
Alnessferry. *High* 2A 158
Alnham. *Nmbd* 3D 121
Alnmouth. *Nmbd* 3G 121
Alnwick. *Nmbd* 3F 121
Alphamstone. *Essx* 2B 54
Alpheton. *Suff* 5A 66
Alphington. *Devn* 3C 12
Alpington. *Norf* 5E 79
Alport. *Derbs* 4G 85
Alport. *Powy* 1E 59
Alpraham. *Ches* 5H 83
Alresford. *Essx* 3D 54
Alrewas. *Staf* 4F 73
Alsager. *Ches* 5B 84
Alsagers Bank. *Staf* 1C 72
Alsop en le Dale. *Derbs* 5F 85
Alston. *Cumb* 5A 114
Alstone. *Glos* 2E 49
Alstone. *Som* 2G 21
Alstonefield. *Staf* 5F 85
Alston Sutton. *Som* 1H 21
Alswear. *Devn* 4H 19
Altandhu. *High* 2D 163
Altanduin. *High* 1F 165
Altarnun. *Corn* 4C 10
Altass. *High* 3B 164
Alterwall. *High* 2E 169
Altgaltraig. *Arg* 2B 126
Altham. *Lanc* 1F 91
Althorne. *Essx* 1D 40
Althorpe. *N Lin* 4B 94
Altnabreac. *High* 4C 168
Altnacealgach. *High* 2G 163
Altnafeadh. *High* 3G 141
Altnaharra. *High* 5F 167
Altofts. *W Yor* 2D 92
Alton. *Derbs* 4A 86
Alton. *Hants* 3F 25
Alton. *Staf* 1E 73
Alton Barnes. *Wilts* 5G 35
Altonhill. *E Ayr* 1D 116
Alton Pancras. *Dors* 2C 14
Alton Priors. *Wilts* 5G 35
Altrincham. *G Man* 2B 84
Altrua. *High* 4E 149
Alva. *Clac* 4A 136

Alvanley—Ashley

Alvanley. *Ches* 3G **83**
Alvaston. *Derb* 2A **74**
Alvechurch. *Worc* 3E **61**
Alvecote. *Warw* 5G **73**
Alvediston. *Wilts* 4E **23**
Alveley. *Shrp* 2B **60**
Alverdiscott. *Devn* 4F **19**
Alverstoke. *Hants* 3D **16**
Alverstone. *IOW* 4D **16**
Alverthorpe. *W Yor* 2D **92**
Alverton. *Notts* 1E **75**
Alves. *Mor* 2F **159**
Alvescot. *Oxon* 5A **50**
Alveston. *S Glo* 3B **34**
Alveston. *Warw* 5G **61**
Alvie. *High* 3C **150**
Alvingham. *Linc* 1C **88**
Alvington. *Glos* 5B **48**
Alwalton. *Cambs* 1A **64**
Alweston. *Dors* 1B **14**
Alwington. *Devn* 4E **19**
Alwinton. *Nmbd* 4D **120**
Alwoodley. *W Yor* 5E **99**
Alyth. *Per* 4B **144**
Amatnatua. *High* 4B **164**
Am Baile. *W Isl* 7C **170**
Ambaston. *Derbs* 2B **74**
Ambergate. *Derbs* 5H **85**
Amber Hill. *Linc* 1B **76**
Amberley. *Glos* 5D **48**
Amberley. *W Sus* 4B **26**
Amble. *Nmbd* 4G **121**
Amblecote. *W Mid* 2C **60**
Ambler Thorn. *W Yor* 2A **92**
Ambleside. *Cumb* 4E **103**
Ambleston. *Pemb* 2E **43**
Ambrosden. *Oxon* 4E **50**
Amcotts. *N Lin* 3B **94**
Amersham. *Buck* 1A **38**
Amerton. *Staf* 3D **73**
Amesbury. *Wilts* 2G **23**
Amisfield. *Dum* 1B **112**
Amlwch. *IOA* 1D **80**
Amlwch Port. *IOA* 1D **80**
Ammanford. *Carm* 4G **45**
Amotherby. *N Yor* 2B **100**
Ampfield. *Hants* 4B **24**
Ampleforth. *N Yor* 2H **99**
Ampleforth College. *N Yor* 2H **99**
Ampney Crucis. *Glos* 5F **49**
Ampney St Mary. *Glos* 5F **49**
Ampney St Peter. *Glos* 5F **49**
Amport. *Hants* 2A **24**
Ampthill. *Beds* 2A **52**
Ampton. *Suff* 3A **66**
Amroth. *Pemb* 4F **43**
Amulree. *Per* 5G **143**
Amwell. *Herts* 4B **52**
Anaheilt. *High* 2C **140**
Ancaster. *Linc* 1G **75**
Anchor. *Shrp* 2D **58**
Anchorsholme. *Bkpl* 5C **96**
An Cnoc. *W Isl* 4G **171**
An Coroghon. *High* 3A **146**
Ancroft. *Nmbd* 5G **131**
Ancrum. *Bord* 2A **120**
Ancton. *W Sus* 5A **26**
Anderby. *Linc* 3E **89**
Anderby Creek. *Linc* 3E **89**
Anderson. *Dors* 3D **15**
Anderton. *Ches* 3A **84**
Andertons Mill. *Lanc* 3D **90**
Andover. *Hants* 2B **24**
Andover Down. *Hants* 2B **24**
Andoversford. *Glos* 4F **49**
Andreas. *IOM* 2D **108**
Andwell. *Hants* 1E **25**
Anelog. *Gwyn* 3A **68**
Anfield. *Mers* 1F **83**
Angarrack. *Corn* 3C **4**
Angelbank. *Shrp* 3H **59**
Angerton. *Cumb* 4D **112**
Angle. *Pemb* 4C **42**
Angmering. *W Sus* 5B **26**
Angmering-on-Sea. *W Sus* 5B **26**
Angram. *N Yor* 5B **104** (nr. Keld)
Angram. *N Yor* 5H **99** (nr. York)
Anick. *Nmbd* 3C **114**
Ankerbold. *Derbs* 4A **86**
Ankerville. *High* 1C **158**
Anlaby. *E Yor* 2D **94**
Anlaby Park. *Hull* 2D **94**
An Leth Meadhanach. *W Isl* 7C **170**
Anmer. *Norf* 3G **77**
Anmore. *Hants* 1E **17**
Annan. *Dum* 3D **112**
Annaside. *Cumb* 1A **96**
Annat. *Arg* 1H **133**
Annat. *High* 3A **156**
Annathill. *N Lan* 2A **128**
Anna Valley. *Hants* 2B **24**
Annbank. *S Ayr* 2D **116**
Annesley. *Notts* 5C **86**
Annesley Woodhouse. *Notts* 5C **86**
Annfield Plain. *Dur* 4E **115**
Annscroft. *Shrp* 5G **71**
Ansdell. *Lanc* 2B **90**
Ansford. *Som* 3B **22**
Ansley. *Warw* 1G **61**
Anslow. *Staf* 3G **73**
Anslow Gate. *Staf* 3F **73**
Ansteadbrook. *Surr* 2A **26**
Anstey. *Herts* 2E **53**
Anstey. *Leics* 5C **74**
Anston. *S Lan* 5D **128**
Anstruther Easter. *Fife* 3H **137**
Anstruther Wester. *Fife* 3H **137**
Ansty. *Warw* 2A **62**
Ansty. *W Sus* 3D **27**
Ansty. *Wilts* 4E **23**
Anthill Common. *Hants* 1E **17**
Anthorn. *Cumb* 4C **112**
Antingham. *Norf* 2E **79**
An t-Ob. *W Isl* 9C **171**
Anton's Gowt. *Linc* 1B **76**
Antony. *Corn* 3A **8**
Antrobus. *Ches* 3A **84**
Anvil Corner. *Devn* 2D **10**
Anwick. *Linc* 5A **88**
Anwoth. *Dum* 4C **110**
Apethorpe. *Nptn* 1H **63**
Apeton. *Staf* 4C **72**
Apley. *Linc* 3A **88**
Apperknowle. *Derbs* 3A **86**
Apperley. *Glos* 3D **48**
Apperley Dene. *Nmbd* 4D **114**
Appersett. *N Yor* 5B **104**
Appin. *Arg* 4D **140**
Appleby. *N Lin* 3C **94**
Appleby-in-Westmorland. *Cumb* 2H **103**
Appleby Magna. *Leics* 5H **73**
Appleby Parva. *Leics* 5H **73**
Applecross. *High* 4G **155**
Appledore. *Devn* 3E **19** (nr. Bideford)
Appledore. *Devn* 1D **12** (nr. Tiverton)
Appledore. *Kent* 3D **28**
Appledore Heath. *Kent* 2D **28**
Appleford. *Oxon* 2D **36**
Applegarthtown. *Dum* 1C **112**
Applemore. *Hants* 2B **16**
Appleshaw. *Hants* 2B **24**
Applethwaite. *Cumb* 2D **102**
Appleton. *Hal* 2H **83**
Appleton. *Oxon* 5C **50**
Appleton-le-Moors. *N Yor* 1B **100**
Appleton-le-Street. *N Yor* 2B **100**
Appleton Roebuck. *N Yor* 5H **99**
Appleton Thorn. *Warr* 2A **84**
Appleton Wiske. *N Yor* 4A **106**
Appletree. *Nptn* 1C **50**
Appletreehall. *Bord* 3H **119**
Appletreewick. *N Yor* 3C **98**
Appley. *Som* 4D **20**
Appley Bridge. *Lanc* 4D **90**
Apse Heath. *IOW* 4D **16**
Apsley End. *Beds* 2B **52**
Apuldram. *W Sus* 2G **17**
Arabella. *High* 1C **158**
Arbeadie. *Abers* 4D **152**
Arberth. *Pemb* 3F **43**
Arbirlot. *Ang* 4F **145**
Arborfield. *Wok* 5F **37**
Arborfield Cross. *Wok* 5F **37**
Arborfield Garrison. *Wok* 5F **37**
Arbourthorne. *S Yor* 2A **86**
Arbroath. *Ang* 4F **145**
Arbuthnott. *Abers* 1H **145**
Arcan. *High* 3H **157**
Archargary. *High* 3H **167**
Archdeacon Newton. *Darl* 3F **105**
Archiestown. *Mor* 4G **159**
Arclid. *Ches* 4B **84**
Arclid Green. *Ches* 4B **84**
Ardachu. *High* 3D **164**
Ardalanish. *Arg* 2A **132**
Ardaneaskan. *High* 5H **155**
Ardarroch. *High* 5H **155**
Ardbeg. *Arg* 1C **126** (nr. Dunoon)
Ardbeg. *Arg* 5C **124** (on Islay)
Ardbeg. *Arg* 3B **126** (on Isle of Bute)
Ardcharnich. *High* 5F **163**
Ardchiavaig. *Arg* 2A **132**
Ardchonnell. *Arg* 2G **133**
Ardchrishnish. *Arg* 1B **132**
Ardchronie. *High* 5D **164**
Ardchullarie. *Stir* 2E **135**
Ardchyle. *Stir* 1E **135**
Ard-dhubh. *High* 4G **155**
Arddleen. *Powy* 4E **71**
Arddlîn. *Powy* 4E **71**
Ardechive. *High* 4D **148**
Ardeley. *Herts* 3D **52**
Ardelve. *High* 1A **148**
Arden. *Arg* 1E **127**
Ardendrain. *High* 5H **157**
Arden Hall. *N Yor* 5C **106**
Ardens Grafton. *Warw* 5F **61**
Ardentinny. *Arg* 1C **126**
Ardeonaig. *Stir* 5D **142**
Ardersier. *High* 3B **158**
Ardery. *High* 2B **140**
Ardessie. *High* 5E **163**
Ardfern. *Arg* 3F **133**
Ardfernal. *Arg* 2D **124**
Ardfin. *Arg* 3C **124**
Ardgartan. *Arg* 3B **134**
Ardgay. *High* 4C **164**
Ardgour. *High* 2E **141**
Ardheslaig. *High* 3G **155**
Ardindrean. *High* 5F **163**
Ardingly. *W Sus* 3E **27**
Ardington. *Oxon* 3C **36**
Ardlamont House. *Arg* 3A **126**
Ardleigh. *Essx* 3D **54**
Ardler. *Per* 4B **144**
Ardley. *Oxon* 3D **50**
Ardlui. *Arg* 2C **134**
Ardlussa. *Arg* 1E **125**
Ardmair. *High* 4F **163**
Ardmay. *Arg* 3B **134**
Ardminish. *Arg* 5E **125**
Ardmolich. *High* 1B **140**
Ardmore. *High* 3C **166** (nr. Kinlochbervie)
Ardmore. *High* 5E **164** (nr. Tain)
Ardnacross. *Arg* 4G **139**
Ardnadam. *Arg* 1C **126**
Ardnagrask. *High* 4H **157**
Ardnamurach. *High* 4G **147**
Ardnarff. *High* 5A **156**
Ardnastang. *High* 2C **140**
Ardoch. *Per* 5H **143**
Ardochy House. *High* 3E **148**
Ardpatrick. *Arg* 3F **125**
Ardrishaig. *Arg* 1G **125**
Ardroag. *High* 4B **154**
Ardross. *High* 1A **158**
Ardrossan. *N Ayr* 5D **126**
Ardshealach. *High* 2A **140**
Ardsley. *S Yor* 4D **93**
Ardslignish. *High* 2G **139**
Ardtalla. *Arg* 4C **124**
Ardtalnaig. *Per* 5E **142**
Ardtoe. *High* 1A **140**
Arduaine. *Arg* 2E **133**
Ardullie. *High* 2H **157**
Ardvasar. *High* 3E **147**
Ardvorlich. *Per* 1F **135**
Ardwell. *Dum* 5G **109**
Ardwell. *Mor* 5A **160**
Arean. *High* 1A **140**
Areley Common. *Worc* 3C **60**
Areley Kings. *Worc* 3B **60**
Arford. *Hants* 3G **25**
Argoed. *Cphy* 2E **33**
Argoed Mill. *Powy* 4B **58**
Aridhglas. *Arg* 2B **132**
Arinacrinachd. *High* 3G **155**
Arinagour. *Arg* 3D **138**
Arisaig. *High* 5E **147**
Ariundle. *High* 2C **140**
Arivegaig. *High* 2A **140**
Arkendale. *N Yor* 3F **99**
Arkesden. *Essx* 2E **53**
Arkholme. *Lanc* 2E **97**
Arkle Town. *N Yor* 4D **104**
Arkley. *G Lon* 1D **38**
Arksey. *S Yor* 4F **93**
Arkwright Town. *Derbs* 3B **86**
Arlecdon. *Cumb* 3B **102**
Arlescote. *Warw* 1B **50**
Arlesey. *Beds* 2B **52**
Arleston. *Telf* 4A **72**
Arley. *Ches* 2A **84**
Arlingham. *Glos* 4C **48**
Arlington. *Devn* 2G **19**
Arlington. *E Sus* 5G **27**
Arlington. *Glos* 5G **49**
Arlington Beccott. *Devn* 2G **19**
Armadale. *High* 2H **167**
Armadale. *W Lot* 3C **128**
Armathwaite. *Cumb* 5G **113**
Arminghall. *Norf* 5E **79**
Armitage. *Staf* 4E **73**
Armitage Bridge. *W Yor* 3B **92**
Armley. *W Yor* 1C **92**
Armscote. *Warw* 1H **49**
Arms, The. *Norf* 1A **66**
Armston. *Nptn* 2H **63**
Armthorpe. *S Yor* 4G **93**
Arncliffe. *N Yor* 2B **98**
Arncliffe Cote. *N Yor* 2B **98**
Arncroach. *Fife* 3H **137**
Arne. *Dors* 4E **15**
Arnesby. *Leics* 1D **62**
Arnicle. *Arg* 2B **122**
Arnisdale. *High* 2G **147**
Arnish. *High* 4E **155**
Arniston. *Midl* 3G **129**
Arnol. *W Isl* 3F **171**
Arnold. *E Yor* 5F **101**
Arnold. *Notts* 1C **74**
Arnprior. *Stir* 4F **135**
Arnside. *Cumb* 2D **96**
Aros Mains. *Arg* 4G **139**
Arpafeelie. *High* 3A **158**
Arrad Foot. *Cumb* 1C **96**
Arram. *E Yor* 5E **101**
Arras. *E Yor* 5D **100**
Arrathorne. *N Yor* 5E **105**
Arreton. *IOW* 4D **16**
Arrington. *Cambs* 5C **64**
Arrochar. *Arg* 3B **134**
Arrow. *Warw* 5E **61**
Arscaig. *High* 2C **164**
Artafallie. *High* 4A **158**
Arthington. *W Yor* 5E **99**
Arthingworth. *Nptn* 2E **63**
Arthog. *Gwyn* 4F **69**
Arthrath. *Abers* 5G **161**
Arthurstone. *Per* 4B **144**
Arundel. *W Sus* 5B **26**
Asby. *Cumb* 2B **102**
Ascog. *Arg* 3C **126**
Ascot. *Wind* 4A **38**
Ascott-under-Wychwood. *Oxon* 4B **50**
Asenby. *N Yor* 2F **99**
Asfordby. *Leics* 4E **74**
Asfordby Hill. *Leics* 4E **74**
Asgarby. *Linc* 4C **88** (nr. Horncastle)
Asgarby. *Linc* 1A **76** (nr. Sleaford)
Ash. *Devn* 4E **9**
Ash. *Dors* 1D **14**
Ash. *Kent* 5G **41** (nr. Sandwich)
Ash. *Kent* 4H **39** (nr. Swanley)
Ash. *Som* 4H **21**
Ash. *Surr* 1G **25**
Ashampstead. *W Ber* 4D **36**
Ashbocking. *Suff* 5D **66**
Ashbourne. *Derbs* 1F **73**
Ashbrittle. *Som* 4D **20**
Ashbrook. *Shrp* 1G **59**
Ashburton. *Devn* 2D **8**
Ashbury. *Devn* 3F **11**
Ashbury. *Oxon* 3A **36**
Ashby. *N Lin* 4B **94**
Ashby by Partney. *Linc* 4D **88**
Ashby cum Fenby. *NE Lin* 4F **95**
Ashby de la Launde. *Linc* 5H **87**
Ashby-de-la-Zouch. *Leics* 4A **74**
Ashby Folville. *Leics* 4E **74**
Ashby Magna. *Leics* 1C **62**
Ashby Parva. *Leics* 2C **62**
Ashby Puerorum. *Linc* 3C **88**
Ashby St Ledgars. *Nptn* 4C **62**
Ashby St Mary. *Norf* 5F **79**
Ashcombe. *Devn* 5C **12**
Ashcott. *Som* 3H **21**
Ashcurch. *Glos* 2E **49**
Ashdon. *Essx* 1F **53**
Ashe. *Hants* 1D **24**
Asheldham. *Essx* 5C **54**
Ashen. *Essx* 1H **53**
Ashendon. *Buck* 4F **51**
Ashey. *IOW* 4D **16**
Ashfield. *Hants* 1B **16**
Ashfield. *Here* 3A **48**
Ashfield. *Shrp* 2H **59**
Ashfield. *Stir* 3G **135**
Ashfield. *Suff* 4E **66**
Ashfield Green. *Suff* 3E **67**
Ashfold Crossways. *W Sus* 3D **26**
Ashford. *Devn* 3F **19** (nr. Barnstaple)
Ashford. *Devn* 4C **8** (nr. Kingsbridge)
Ashford. *Hants* 1G **15**
Ashford. *Kent* 1E **28**
Ashford. *Surr* 3B **38**
Ashford Bowdler. *Shrp* 3H **59**
Ashford Carbonel. *Shrp* 3H **59**
Ashford Hill. *Hants* 5D **36**
Ashford in the Water. *Derbs* 4F **85**
Ashgill. *S Lan* 5A **128**
Ash Green. *Warw* 2H **61**
Ashgrove. *Mor* 2G **159**
Ashill. *Devn* 1D **12**
Ashill. *Norf* 5A **78**
Ashill. *Som* 1G **13**
Ashingdon. *Essx* 1C **40**
Ashington. *Nmbd* 1F **115**
Ashington. *W Sus* 4C **26**
Ashkirk. *Bord* 2G **119**
Ashlett. *Hants* 2C **16**
Ashleworth. *Glos* 3D **48**
Ashley. *Cambs* 4F **65**

Ashley—Bagley

Ashley. *Ches* 2B **84**
Ashley. *Dors* 2G **15**
Ashley. *Glos* 2E **35**
Ashley. *Hants* 3A **16**
(nr. New Milton)
Ashley. *Hants* 3B **24**
(nr. Winchester)
Ashley. *Kent* 1H **29**
Ashley. *Nptn* 1E **63**
Ashley. *Staf* 2B **72**
Ashley. *Wilts* 5D **34**
Ashley Green. *Buck* 5H **51**
Ashley Heath. *Dors* 2G **15**
Ashley Heath. *Staf* 2B **72**
Ashley Moor. *Here* 4G **59**
Ash Magna. *Shrp* 2H **71**
Ashmanhaugh. *Norf* 3F **79**
Ashmansworth. *Hants* 1C **24**
Ashmansworthy. *Devn* 1D **10**
Ashmead Green. *Glos* 2C **34**
Ashmill. *Devn* 3D **11**
(nr. Holsworthy)
Ash Mill. *Devn* 4A **20**
(nr. South Molton)
Ashmore. *Dors* 1E **15**
Ashmore Green. *W Ber* 5D **36**
Ashorne. *Warw* 5H **61**
Ashover. *Derbs* 4A **86**
Ashow. *Warw* 3H **61**
Ash Parva. *Shrp* 2H **71**
Ashperton. *Here* 1B **48**
Ashprington. *Devn* 3E **9**
Ash Priors. *Som* 4E **21**
Ashreigney. *Devn* 1G **11**
Ash Street. *Suff* 1D **54**
Ashtead. *Surr* 5C **38**
Ash Thomas. *Devn* 1D **12**
Ashton. *Ches* 4H **83**
Ashton. *Corn* 4D **4**
Ashton. *Here* 4H **59**
Ashton. *Inv* 2D **126**
Ashton. *Nptn* 2H **63**
(nr. Oundle)
Ashton. *Nptn* 1F **51**
(nr. Roade)
Ashton. *Pet* 5A **76**
Ashton Common. *Wilts* 1E **23**
Ashton-in-Makerfield.
G Man 4D **90**
Ashton Keynes. *Wilts* 2F **35**
Ashton under Hill. *Worc* 2E **49**
Ashton-under-Lyne. *G Man* 1D **84**
Ashton upon Mersey. *G Man* 1B **84**
Ashurst. *Hants* 1B **16**
Ashurst. *Kent* 2G **27**
Ashurst. *Lanc* 4C **90**
Ashurst. *W Sus* 4C **26**
Ashurstwood. *W Sus* 2F **27**
Ash Vale. *Surr* 1G **25**
Ashwater. *Devn* 3D **11**
Ashwell. *Herts* 2C **52**
Ashwell. *Rut* 4F **75**
Ashwellthorpe. *Norf* 1D **66**
Ashwick. *Som* 2B **22**
Ashwicken. *Norf* 4G **77**
Ashwood. *Staf* 2C **60**
Askam in Furness. *Cumb* 2B **96**
Askern. *S Yor* 3F **93**
Askerswell. *Dors* 3A **14**
Askett. *Buck* 5G **51**
Askham. *Cumb* 2G **103**
Askham. *Notts* 3E **87**
Askham Bryan. *York* 5H **99**
Askham Richard. *York* 5H **99**
Askrigg. *N Yor* 5C **104**
Askwith. *N Yor* 5D **98**
Aslackby. *Linc* 2H **75**
Aslacton. *Norf* 1D **66**
Aslockton. *Notts* 1E **75**
Aspatria. *Cumb* 5C **112**
Aspenden. *Herts* 3D **52**
Asperton. *Linc* 2B **76**
Aspley Guise. *Beds* 2H **51**
Aspley Heath. *Beds* 2H **51**
Aspull. *G Man* 4E **90**
Asselby. *E Yor* 2H **93**
Assington. *Suff* 2C **54**
Assington Green. *Suff* 5G **65**
Astbury. *Ches* 4C **84**
Astcote. *Nptn* 5D **62**
Asterby. *Linc* 3B **88**
Asterley. *Shrp* 5F **71**
Asterton. *Shrp* 1F **59**
Asthall. *Oxon* 4A **50**
Asthall Leigh. *Oxon* 4B **50**
Astle. *High* 4E **165**
Astley. *G Man* 4F **91**
Astley. *Shrp* 4H **71**
Astley. *Warw* 2H **61**
Astley. *Worc* 4B **60**
Astley Abbotts. *Shrp* 1B **60**
Astley Bridge. *G Man* 3F **91**
Astley Cross. *Worc* 4C **60**
Aston. *Ches* 3H **83**
(nr. Frodsham)
Aston. *Ches* 1A **72**
(nr. Nantwich)
Aston. *Derbs* 2F **85**
Aston. *Flin* 4F **83**
Aston. *Here* 4G **59**
Aston. *Herts* 3C **52**
Aston. *Oxon* 5B **50**
Aston. *Shrp* 1C **60**
(nr. Bridgnorth)
Aston. *Shrp* 3H **71**
(nr. Wem)
Aston. *S Yor* 2B **86**
Aston. *Staf* 1B **72**
Aston. *Telf* 5A **72**
Aston. *W Mid* 1E **61**
Aston. *Wok* 3F **37**
Aston Abbotts. *Buck* 3G **51**
Aston Botterell. *Shrp* 2A **60**
Aston-by-Stone. *Staf* 2D **72**
Aston Cantlow. *Warw* 5F **61**
Aston Clinton. *Buck* 4G **51**
Aston Crews. *Here* 3B **48**
Aston Cross. *Glos* 2E **49**
Aston End. *Herts* 3C **52**
Aston Eyre. *Shrp* 1A **60**
Aston Fields. *Worc* 4D **60**
Aston Flamville. *Leics* 1B **62**
Aston Ingham. *Here* 3B **48**
Aston juxta Mondrum. *Ches* 5A **84**
Astonlane. *Shrp* 1A **60**
Aston le Walls. *Nptn* 5B **62**
Aston Magna. *Glos* 2G **49**
Aston Munslow. *Shrp* 2H **59**
Aston on Carrant. *Glos* 2E **49**
Aston on Clun. *Shrp* 2F **59**
Aston-on-Trent. *Derbs* 3B **74**
Aston Pigott. *Shrp* 5F **71**
Aston Rogers. *Shrp* 5F **71**
Aston Rowant. *Oxon* 2F **37**
Aston Sandford. *Buck* 5F **51**
Aston Somerville. *Worc* 2F **49**
Aston Subedge. *Glos* 1G **49**
Aston Tirrold. *Oxon* 3D **36**
Aston Upthorne. *Oxon* 3D **36**
Astrop. *Nptn* 2D **50**
Astwick. *Beds* 2C **52**
Astwood. *Mil* 1H **51**
Astwood Bank. *Worc* 4E **61**
Aswarby. *Linc* 2H **75**
Aswardby. *Linc* 3C **88**
Atcham. *Shrp* 5H **71**
Atch Lench. *Worc* 5E **61**
Athelhampton. *Dors* 3C **14**
Athelington. *Suff* 3E **66**
Athelney. *Som* 4G **21**
Athelstaneford. *E Lot* 2B **130**
Atherfield Green. *IOW* 5C **16**
Atherington. *Devn* 4F **19**
Atherington. *W Sus* 5B **26**
Athersley. *S Yor* 4D **92**
Atherstone. *Warw* 1H **61**
Atherstone on Stour. *Warw* 5G **61**
Atherton. *G Man* 4E **91**
Atlow. *Derbs* 1G **73**
Attadale. *High* 5B **156**
Attenborough. *Notts* 2C **74**
Atterby. *Linc* 1G **87**
Atterley. *Shrp* 1A **60**
Attleborough. *Norf* 1C **66**
Attleborough. *Warw* 1A **62**
Attlebridge. *Norf* 4D **78**
Atwick. *E Yor* 4F **101**
Atworth. *Wilts* 5D **34**
Auberrow. *Here* 1H **47**
Aubourn. *Linc* 4G **87**
Aucharnie. *Abers* 4D **160**
Auchattie. *Abers* 4D **152**
Auchavan. *Ang* 2A **144**
Auchbreck. *Mor* 1G **151**
Auchenback. *E Ren* 4G **127**
Auchenblae. *Abers* 1G **145**
Auchenbrack. *Dum* 5G **117**
Auchenbreck. *Arg* 1B **126**
Auchencairn. *Dum* 4E **111**
(nr. Dalbeattie)
Auchencairn. *Dum* 1A **112**
(nr. Dumfries)
Auchencarroch. *W Dun* 1F **127**
Auchencrow. *Bord* 3E **131**
Auchendennan. *W Dun* 1E **127**
Auchendinny. *Midl* 3F **129**
Auchengray. *S Lan* 4C **128**
Auchenhalrig. *Mor* 2A **160**
Auchenheath. *S Lan* 5B **128**
Auchenlochan. *Arg* 2A **126**
Auchenmade. *N Ayr* 5E **127**
Auchenmaig. *Dum* 4H **109**
Auchentiber. *N Ayr* 5E **127**
Auchenvennel. *Arg* 1D **126**
Auchindrain. *Arg* 3H **133**
Auchininna. *Abers* 4D **160**
Auchinleck. *Dum* 2B **110**
Auchinleck. *E Ayr* 2E **117**
Auchinloch. *N Lan* 2H **127**
Auchinstarry. *N Lan* 2A **128**
Auchleven. *Abers* 1D **152**
Auchlochan. *S Lan* 1H **117**
Auchlunachan. *High* 5F **163**
Auchmillan. *E Ayr* 2E **117**
Auchmithie. *Ang* 4F **145**
Auchmuirbridge. *Per* 3E **136**
Auchmull. *Ang* 1E **145**
Auchnacree. *Ang* 2D **144**
Auchnafree. *Per* 5F **143**
Auchnagallin. *High* 5E **159**
Auchnagatt. *Abers* 4G **161**
Aucholzie. *Abers* 4H **151**
Auchreddie. *Abers* 4F **161**
Auchterarder. *Per* 2B **136**
Auchteraw. *High* 3F **149**
Auchterderran. *Fife* 4E **136**
Auchterhouse. *Ang* 5C **144**
Auchtermuchty. *Fife* 2E **137**
Auchterneed. *High* 3G **157**
Auchtertool. *Fife* 4E **136**
Auchtertyre. *High* 1G **147**
Auchtubh. *Stir* 1E **135**
Auckengill. *High* 2F **169**
Auckley. *S Yor* 4G **93**
Audenshaw. *G Man* 1D **84**
Audlem. *Ches* 1A **72**
Audley. *Staf* 5B **84**
Audley End. *Essx* 2F **53**
Audmore. *Staf* 3C **72**
Auds. *Abers* 2D **160**
Aughton. *E Yor* 1H **93**
Aughton. *Lanc* 3E **97**
(nr. Lancaster)
Aughton. *Lanc* 4B **90**
(nr. Ormskirk)
Aughton. *S Yor* 2B **86**
Aughton. *Wilts* 1H **23**
Aughton Park. *Lanc* 4C **90**
Auldearn. *High* 3D **158**
Aulden. *Here* 5G **59**
Auldgirth. *Dum* 1G **111**
Auldhouse. *S Lan* 4H **127**
Ault a' chruinn. *High* 1B **148**
Aultbea. *High* 5C **162**
Aultdearg. *High* 2E **157**
Aultgrishan. *High* 5B **162**
Aultguish Inn. *High* 1F **157**
Ault Hucknall. *Derbs* 4B **86**
Aultibea. *High* 1H **165**
Aultiphurst. *High* 2A **168**
Aultivullin. *High* 2A **168**
Aultmore. *Mor* 3B **160**
Aultnamain Inn. *High* 5D **164**
Aunby. *Linc* 4H **75**
Aunsby. *Linc* 2H **75**
Aust. *S Glo* 3A **34**
Austerfield. *S Yor* 1D **86**
Austin Fen. *Linc* 1C **88**
Austrey. *Warw* 5G **73**
Austwick. *N Yor* 3G **97**
Authorpe. *Linc* 2D **88**
Authorpe Row. *Linc* 3E **89**
Avebury. *Wilts* 5G **35**
Avebury Trusloe. *Wilts* 5F **35**
Aveley. *Thur* 2G **39**
Avening. *Glos* 2D **35**
Averham. *Notts* 5E **87**
Aveton Gifford. *Devn* 4C **8**
Avielochan. *High* 2D **150**
Aviemore. *High* 2C **150**
Avington. *Hants* 3D **24**
Avoch. *High* 3B **158**
Avon. *Hants* 3G **15**
Avonbridge. *Falk* 2C **128**
Avon Dassett. *Warw* 5B **62**
Avonmouth. *Bris* 4A **34**
Avonwick. *Devn* 3D **8**
Awbridge. *Hants* 4B **24**
Awliscombe. *Devn* 2E **13**
Awre. *Glos* 5C **48**
Awsworth. *Notts* 1B **74**
Axbridge. *Som* 1H **21**
Axford. *Hants* 2E **24**
Axford. *Wilts* 5H **35**
Axminster. *Devn* 3F **13**
Axmouth. *Devn* 3F **13**
Aycliffe Village. *Dur* 2F **105**
Aydon. *Nmbd* 3D **114**
Aykley Heads. *Dur* 5F **115**
Aylburton. *Glos* 5B **48**
Aylburton Common. *Glos* 5B **48**
Ayle. *Nmbd* 5A **114**
Aylesbeare. *Devn* 3D **12**
Aylesbury. *Buck* 4G **51**
Aylesby. *NE Lin* 4F **95**
Aylescott. *Devn* 1G **11**
Aylesford. *Kent* 5B **40**
Aylesham. *Kent* 5G **41**
Aylestone. *Leic* 5C **74**
Aylmerton. *Norf* 2D **78**
Aylsham. *Norf* 3D **78**
Aylton. *Here* 2B **48**
Aylworth. *Glos* 3G **49**
Aymestrey. *Here* 4G **59**
Aynho. *Nptn* 2D **50**
Ayot Green. *Herts* 4C **52**
Ayot St Lawrence. *Herts* 4B **52**
Ayot St Peter. *Herts* 4C **52**
Ayr. *S Ayr* 2C **116**
Ayreville. *Torb* 2E **9**
Aysgarth. *N Yor* 1C **98**
Ayshford. *Devn* 1D **12**
Ayside. *Cumb* 1C **96**
Ayston. *Rut* 5F **75**
Ayton. *Bord* 3F **131**
Aywick. *Shet* 3G **173**
Azerley. *N Yor* 2E **99**

B

Babbacombe. *Torb* 2F **9**
Babbinswood. *Shrp* 3F **71**
Babb's Green. *Herts* 4D **53**
Babcary. *Som* 4A **22**
Babel. *Carm* 2B **46**
Babell. *Flin* 3D **82**
Babingley. *Norf* 3F **77**
Babraham. *Cambs* 5E **65**
Babworth. *Notts* 2D **86**
Bac. *W Isl* 3G **171**
Bachau. *IOA* 2D **80**
Bacheldre. *Powy* 1E **59**
Bachymbyd Fawr. *Den* 4C **82**
Backaland. *Orkn* 4E **172**
Backbarrow. *Cumb* 1C **96**
Backe. *Carm* 3G **43**
Backfolds. *Abers* 3H **161**
Backford. *Ches* 3G **83**
Backhill. *Abers* 5E **161**
Backhill of Clackriach. *Abers* 4G **161**
Backies. *High* 3F **165**
Backmuir of New Gilston.
Fife 3G **137**
Back of Keppoch. *High* 5E **147**
Back Street. *Suff* 5G **65**
Backwell. *N Som* 5H **33**
Backworth. *Tyne* 2G **115**
Bacon End. *Essx* 4G **53**
Baconsthorpe. *Norf* 2D **78**
Bacton. *Here* 2G **47**
Bacton. *Norf* 2F **79**
Bacton. *Suff* 4C **66**
Bacton Green. *Norf* 2F **79**
Bacup. *Lanc* 2G **91**
Badachonacher. *High* 1A **158**
Badachro. *High* 1G **155**
Badanloch Lodge. *High* 5H **167**
Badavanich. *High* 3D **156**
Badbury. *Swin* 3G **35**
Badby. *Nptn* 5C **62**
Badcall. *High* 3C **166**
Badcaul. *High* 4E **163**
Baddeley Green. *Stoke* 5D **84**
Baddesley Clinton. *W Mid* 3G **61**
Baddesley Ensor. *Warw* 1G **61**
Baddidarach. *High* 1E **163**
Baddoch. *Abers* 5F **151**
Badenscallie. *High* 3E **163**
Badenscoth. *Abers* 5E **160**
Badentarbat. *High* 2E **163**
Badgall. *Corn* 4C **10**
Badgers Mount. *Kent* 4F **39**
Badgeworth. *Glos* 4E **49**
Badgworth. *Som* 1G **21**
Badicaul. *High* 1F **147**
Badingham. *Suff* 4F **67**
Badlesmere. *Kent* 5E **40**
Badlipster. *High* 4E **169**
Badluarach. *High* 4D **163**
Badminton. *S Glo* 3D **34**
Badnaban. *High* 1E **163**
Badnabay. *High* 4C **166**
Badnagie. *High* 5D **168**
Badnellan. *High* 3F **165**
Badninish. *High* 4E **165**
Badrallach. *High* 4E **163**
Badsey. *Worc* 1F **49**
Badshot Lea. *Surr* 2G **25**
Badsworth. *W Yor* 3E **93**
Badwell Ash. *Suff* 4B **66**
Bae Cinmel. *Cnwy* 2B **82**
Bae Colwyn. *Cnwy* 3A **82**
Bae Penrhyn. *Cnwy* 2H **81**
Bagby. *N Yor* 1G **99**
Bag Enderby. *Linc* 3C **88**
Bagendon. *Glos* 5F **49**
Bagginswood. *Shrp* 2A **60**
Baggrave. *Leics* 5D **74**
Bàgh a Chàise. *W Isl* 1E **170**
Bàgh a' Chaisteil. *W Isl* 9B **170**
Bagham. *Kent* 5E **41**
Baghasdal. *W Isl* 7C **170**
Bagh Mor. *W Isl* 3D **170**
Bagh Shiarabhagh. *W Isl* 8C **170**
Bagillt. *Flin* 3E **83**
Baginton. *Warw* 3H **61**
Baglan. *Neat* 2A **32**
Bagley. *Shrp* 3G **71**
Bagley. *Som* 2H **21**

Bagnall. *Staf* 5D **84**
Bagnor. *W Ber* 5C **36**
Bagshot. *Surr* 4A **38**
Bagshot. *Wilts* 5B **36**
Bagstone. *S Glo* 3B **34**
Bagthorpe. *Norf* 2G **77**
Bagthorpe. *Notts* 5B **86**
Bagworth. *Leics* 5B **74**
Bagwy Llydiart. *Here* 3H **47**
Baildon. *W Yor* 1B **92**
Baildon Green. *W Yor* 1B **92**
Baile. *W Isl* 1E **170**
Baile Ailein. *W Isl* 5E **171**
Baile an Truiseil. *W Isl* 2F **171**
Baile Boidheach. *Arg* 2F **125**
Baile Glas. *W Isl* 3D **170**
Bailemeonach. *Arg* 4A **140**
Baile Mhanaich. *W Isl* 3C **170**
Baile Mhartainn. *W Isl* 1C **170**
Baile Mor. *Arg* 2A **132**
Baile Mor. *W Isl* 2C **170**
Baile nan Cailleach. *W Isl* 3C **170**
Baile Raghaill. *W Isl* 2C **170**
Bailey Green. *Hants* 4E **25**
Baileyhead. *Cumb* 1G **113**
Bailiesward. *Abers* 5B **160**
Bail' Iochdrach. *W Isl* 3D **170**
Baillieston. *Glas* 3H **127**
Bailrigg. *Lanc* 4D **97**
Bail' Uachdraich. *W Isl* 2D **170**
Bail Ur Tholastaidh. *W Isl* 3H **171**
Bainbridge. *N Yor* 5C **104**
Bainsford. *Falk* 1B **128**
Bainshole. *Abers* 5D **160**
Bainton. *E Yor* 4D **100**
Bainton. *Oxon* 3D **50**
Bainton. *Pet* 5H **75**
Baintown. *Fife* 3F **137**
Baker Street. *Thur* 2H **39**
Bakewell. *Derbs* 4G **85**
Bala. *Gwyn* 2B **70**
Balachuirn. *High* 4E **155**
Balbeg. *High* 5G **157** (nr. Cannich)
Balbeg. *High* 1G **149** (nr. Loch Ness)
Balbeggie. *Per* 1D **136**
Balblair. *High* 4C **164** (nr. Bonar Bridge)
Balblair. *High* 2B **158** (nr. Invergordon)
Balblair. *High* 4H **157** (nr. Inverness)
Balby. *S Yor* 4F **93**
Balcathie. *Ang* 5F **145**
Balchladich. *High* 1E **163**
Balchraggan. *High* 4H **157**
Balchrick. *High* 3B **166**
Balcombe. *W Sus* 2E **27**
Balcombe Lane. *W Sus* 2E **27**
Balcurvie. *Fife* 3F **137**
Baldersby. *N Yor* 2F **99**
Baldersby St James. *N Yor* 2F **99**
Balderstone. *Lanc* 1E **91**
Balderton. *Ches* 4F **83**
Balderton. *Notts* 5F **87**
Baldinnie. *Fife* 2G **137**
Baldock. *Herts* 2C **52**
Baldrine. *IOM* 3D **108**
Baldslow. *E Sus* 4C **28**
Baldwin. *IOM* 3C **108**
Baldwinholme. *Cumb* 4E **113**
Baldwin's Gate. *Staf* 2B **72**
Bale. *Norf* 2C **78**
Balearn. *Abers* 3H **161**
Balemartine. *Arg* 4A **138**
Balephretrish. *Arg* 4B **138**
Balephuil. *Arg* 4A **138**
Balerno. *Edin* 3E **129**
Balevullin. *Arg* 4A **138**
Balfield. *Ang* 2E **145**
Balfour. *Orkn* 6D **172**
Balfron. *Stir* 1G **127**
Balgaveny. *Abers* 4D **160**
Balgonar. *Fife* 4C **136**
Balgowan. *High* 4A **150**
Balgown. *High* 2C **154**
Balgrochan. *E Dun* 2H **127**
Balgy. *High* 3H **155**
Balhalgardy. *Abers* 1E **153**
Baliasta. *Shet* 1H **173**
Baligill. *High* 2A **168**
Balintore. *Ang* 3B **144**
Balintore. *High* 1C **158**
Balintraid. *High* 1B **158**
Balk. *N Yor* 1G **99**
Balkeerie. *Ang* 4C **144**
Balkholme. *E Yor* 2A **94**
Ball. *Shrp* 3F **71**
Ballabeg. *IOM* 4B **108**
Ballacannell. *IOM* 3D **108**
Ballacarnane Beg. *IOM* 3C **108**
Ballachulish. *High* 3E **141**
Ballagyr. *IOM* 3B **108**
Ballajora. *IOM* 2D **108**
Ballaleigh. *IOM* 3C **108**
Ballamodha. *IOM* 4B **108**
Ballantrae. *S Ayr* 1F **109**
Ballards Gore. *Essx* 1D **40**
Ballasalla. *IOM* 4B **108** (nr. Castletown)
Ballasalla. *IOM* 2C **108** (nr. Kirk Michael)
Ballater. *Abers* 4A **152**
Ballaugh. *IOM* 2C **108**
Ballencrieff. *E Lot* 2A **130**
Ballencrieff Toll. *W Lot* 2C **128**
Ballentoul. *Per* 2F **143**
Ball Hill. *Hants* 5C **36**
Ballidon. *Derbs* 5G **85**
Balliemore. *Arg* 1B **126** (nr. Dunoon)
Balliemore. *Arg* 1F **133** (nr. Oban)
Ballieward. *High* 5E **159**
Ballig. *IOM* 3B **108**
Ballimore. *Stir* 2E **135**
Ballingdon. *Suff* 1B **54**
Ballinger Common. *Buck* 5H **51**
Ballingham. *Here* 2A **48**
Ballingry. *Fife* 4D **136**
Ballinluig. *Per* 3G **143**
Ballintuim. *Per* 3A **144**
Balliveolan. *Arg* 4C **140**
Balloan. *High* 3C **164**
Balloch. *High* 4B **158**
Balloch. *N Lan* 2A **128**
Balloch. *Per* 2H **135**
Balloch. *W Dun* 1E **127**
Ballochan. *Abers* 4C **152**
Ballochgoy. *Arg* 3B **126**
Ballochmyle. *E Ayr* 2E **117**
Ballochroy. *Arg* 4F **125**
Balls Cross. *W Sus* 3A **26**
Ball's Green. *E Sus* 2F **27**
Ballygown. *Arg* 4F **139**
Ballygrant. *Arg* 3B **124**
Ballymichael. *N Ayr* 2D **122**
Balmacara. *High* 1G **147**
Balmaclellan. *Dum* 2D **110**
Balmacqueen. *High* 1D **154**
Balmaha. *Stir* 4D **134**
Balmalcolm. *Fife* 3F **137**
Balmalloch. *N Lan* 2A **128**
Balmeanach. *High* 5E **155**
Balmedie. *Abers* 2G **153**
Balmerino. *Fife* 1F **137**
Balmerlawn. *Hants* 2B **16**
Balmore. *E Dun* 2H **127**
Balmore. *High* 4B **154**
Balmuir. *Ang* 5D **144**
Balmullo. *Fife* 1G **137**
Balmurrie. *Dum* 3H **109**
Balnaboth. *Ang* 2C **144**
Balnabruaich. *High* 1B **158**
Balnabruich. *High* 5D **168**
Balnacoil. *High* 2F **165**
Balnacra. *High* 4B **156**
Balnacroft. *Abers* 4G **151**
Balnageith. *Mor* 3E **159**
Balnaglaic. *High* 5G **157**
Balnagrantach. *High* 5G **157**
Balnaguard. *Per* 3G **143**
Balnahard. *Arg* 4B **132**
Balnain. *High* 5G **157**
Balnakeil. *High* 2D **166**
Balnaknock. *High* 2D **154**
Balnamoon. *Abers* 3G **161**
Balnamoon. *Ang* 2E **145**
Balnapaling. *High* 2B **158**
Balornock. *Glas* 3H **127**
Balquhidder. *Stir* 1E **135**
Balsall. *W Mid* 3G **61**
Balsall Common. *W Mid* 3G **61**
Balscote. *Oxon* 1B **50**
Balsham. *Cambs* 5E **65**
Balstonia. *Thur* 2A **40**
Baltasound. *Shet* 1H **173**
Balterley. *Staf* 5B **84**
Baltersan. *Dum* 3B **110**
Balthangie. *Abers* 3F **161**
Baltonsborough. *Som* 3A **22**
Balvaird. *High* 3H **157**
Balvaird. *Per* 2D **136**
Balvenie. *Mor* 4H **159**
Balvicar. *Arg* 2E **133**
Balvraid. *High* 2G **147**
Balvraid Lodge. *High* 5C **158**
Bamber Bridge. *Lanc* 2D **90**
Bamber's Green. *Essx* 3F **53**
Bamburgh. *Nmbd* 1F **121**
Bamford. *Derbs* 2G **85**
Bamfurlong. *G Man* 4D **90**
Bampton. *Cumb* 3G **103**
Bampton. *Devn* 4C **20**
Bampton. *Oxon* 5B **50**
Bampton Grange. *Cumb* 3G **103**
Banavie. *High* 1F **141**
Banbury. *Oxon* 1C **50**
Bancffosfelen. *Carm* 4E **45**
Banchory. *Abers* 4D **152**
Banchory-Devenick. *Abers* 3G **153**
Bancycapel. *Carm* 4E **45**
Bancyfelin. *Carm* 3H **43**
Banc-y-ffordd. *Carm* 2E **45**
Banff. *Abers* 2D **160**
Bangor. *Gwyn* 3E **81**
Bangor-is-y-coed. *Wrex* 1F **71**
Bangors. *Corn* 3C **10**
Bangor's Green. *Lanc* 4B **90**
Bangrove. *Suff* 3B **66**
Banham. *Norf* 2C **66**
Bank. *Hants* 2A **16**
Bankend. *Dum* 3B **112**
Bankfoot. *Per* 5H **143**
Bankglen. *E Ayr* 3E **117**
Bankhead. *Aber* 2F **153**
Bankhead. *Abers* 3D **152**
Bankhead. *S Lan* 5B **128**
Bankland. *Som* 4G **21**
Bank Newton. *N Yor* 4B **98**
Banknock. *Falk* 2A **128**
Banks. *Cumb* 3G **113**
Banks. *Lanc* 2B **90**
Bankshill. *Dum* 1C **112**
Bank Street. *Worc* 4A **60**
Bank, The. *Ches* 5C **84**
Bank, The. *Shrp* 1A **60**
Bank Top. *Lanc* 4D **90**
Banners Gate. *W Mid* 1E **61**
Banningham. *Norf* 3E **78**
Banniskirk. *High* 3D **168**
Bannister Green. *Essx* 3G **53**
Bannockburn. *Stir* 4H **135**
Banstead. *Surr* 5D **38**
Bantham. *Devn* 4C **8**
Banton. *N Lan* 2A **128**
Banwell. *N Som* 1G **21**
Banyard's Green. *Suff* 3F **67**
Bapchild. *Kent* 4D **40**
Bapton. *Wilts* 3E **23**
Barabhas. *W Isl* 2F **171**
Barabhas Iarach. *W Isl* 3F **171**
Baramore. *High* 1A **140**
Barassie. *S Ayr* 1C **116**
Baravullin. *Arg* 4D **140**
Barbaraville. *High* 1B **158**
Barber Booth. *Derbs* 2F **85**
Barber Green. *Cumb* 1C **96**
Barbhas Uarach. *W Isl* 2F **171**
Barbieston. *S Ayr* 3D **116**
Barbon. *Cumb* 1F **97**
Barbourne. *Worc* 5C **60**
Barbridge. *Ches* 5A **84**
Barbrook. *Devn* 2H **19**
Barby. *Nptn* 3C **62**
Barby Nortoft. *Nptn* 3C **62**
Barcaldine. *Arg* 4D **140**
Barcheston. *Warw* 1A **50**
Barclose. *Cumb* 3F **113**
Barcombe. *E Sus* 4F **27**
Barcombe Cross. *E Sus* 4F **27**
Barden. *N Yor* 5E **105**
Barden Scale. *N Yor* 4C **98**
Bardfield End Green. *Essx* 2G **53**
Bardfield Saling. *Essx* 3G **53**
Bardnabeinne. *High* 4E **164**
Bardney. *Linc* 4A **88**
Bardon. *Leics* 4B **74**
Bardon Mill. *Nmbd* 3A **114**
Bardowie. *E Dun* 2G **127**
Bardrainney. *Inv* 2E **127**
Bardsea. *Cumb* 2C **96**
Bardsey. *W Yor* 5F **99**
Bardsley. *G Man* 4H **91**
Bardwell. *Suff* 3B **66**
Bare. *Lanc* 3D **96**
Barelees. *Nmbd* 1C **120**
Barewood. *Here* 5F **59**
Barford. *Hants* 3G **25**
Barford. *Norf* 5D **78**
Barford. *Warw* 4G **61**
Barford St John. *Oxon* 2C **50**
Barford St Martin. *Wilts* 3F **23**
Barford St Michael. *Oxon* 2C **50**
Barfrestone. *Kent* 5G **41**
Bargeddie. *N Lan* 3A **128**
Bargod. *Cphy* 2E **33**
Bargoed. *Cphy* 2E **33**
Bargrennan. *Dum* 2A **110**
Barham. *Cambs* 3A **64**
Barham. *Kent* 5G **41**
Barham. *Suff* 5D **66**
Barharrow. *Dum* 4D **110**
Bar Hill. *Cambs* 4C **64**
Barholm. *Linc* 4H **75**
Barkby. *Leics* 4D **74**
Barkestone-le-Vale. *Leics* 2E **75**
Barkham. *Wok* 5F **37**
Barking. *G Lon* 2F **39**
Barking. *Suff* 5C **66**
Barkingside. *G Lon* 2F **39**
Barking Tye. *Suff* 5C **66**
Barkisland. *W Yor* 3A **92**
Barkston. *Linc* 1G **75**
Barkston Ash. *N Yor* 1E **93**
Barkway. *Herts* 2D **53**
Barlanark. *Glas* 3H **127**
Barlaston. *Staf* 2C **72**
Barlavington. *W Sus* 4A **26**
Barlborough. *Derbs* 3B **86**
Barlby. *N Yor* 1G **93**
Barlestone. *Leics* 5B **74**
Barley. *Herts* 2D **53**
Barley. *Lanc* 5H **97**
Barley Mow. *Tyne* 4F **115**
Barleythorpe. *Rut* 5F **75**
Barling. *Essx* 2D **40**
Barlings. *Linc* 3H **87**
Barlow. *Derbs* 3H **85**
Barlow. *N Yor* 2G **93**
Barlow. *Tyne* 3E **115**
Barmby Moor. *E Yor* 5B **100**
Barmby on the Marsh. *E Yor* 2G **93**
Barmer. *Norf* 2H **77**
Barming. *Kent* 5B **40**
Barming Heath. *Kent* 5B **40**
Barmoor. *Nmbd* 1E **121**
Barmouth. *Gwyn* 4F **69**
Barmpton. *Darl* 3A **106**
Barmston. *E Yor* 4F **101**
Barmulloch. *Glas* 3H **127**
Barnack. *Pet* 5H **75**
Barnacle. *Warw* 2A **62**
Barnard Castle. *Dur* 3D **104**
Barnard Gate. *Oxon* 4C **50**
Barnardiston. *Suff* 1H **53**
Barnbarroch. *Dum* 4F **111**
Barnburgh. *S Yor* 4E **93**
Barnby. *Suff* 2G **67**
Barnby Dun. *S Yor* 4G **93**
Barnby in the Willows. *Notts* 5F **87**
Barnby Moor. *Notts* 2D **86**
Barnes. *G Lon* 3D **38**
Barnes Street. *Kent* 1H **27**
Barnet. *G Lon* 1D **38**
Barnetby le Wold. *N Lin* 4D **94**
Barney. *Norf* 2B **78**
Barnham. *Suff* 3A **66**
Barnham. *W Sus* 5A **26**
Barnham Broom. *Norf* 5C **78**
Barnhead. *Ang* 3F **145**
Barnhill. *D'dee* 5D **145**
Barnhill. *Mor* 3F **159**
Barnhill. *Per* 1D **136**
Barnhills. *Dum* 2E **109**
Barningham. *Dur* 3D **105**
Barningham. *Suff* 3B **66**
Barnoldby le Beck. *NE Lin* 4F **95**
Barnoldswick. *Lanc* 5A **98**
Barns Green. *W Sus* 3C **26**
Barnsley. *Glos* 5F **49**
Barnsley. *Shrp* 1B **60**
Barnsley. *S Yor* 4D **92**
Barnstaple. *Devn* 3F **19**
Barnston. *Essx* 4G **53**
Barnston. *Mers* 2E **83**
Barnstone. *Notts* 2E **75**
Barnt Green. *Worc* 3E **61**
Barnton. *Ches* 3A **84**
Barnwell. *Cambs* 5D **64**
Barnwell All Saints. *Nptn* 2H **63**
Barnwell St Andrew. *Nptn* 2H **63**
Barnwood. *Glos* 4D **48**
Barons Cross. *Here* 5G **59**
Barony, The. *Orkn* 5B **172**
Barr. *Dum* 4G **117**
Barr. *S Ayr* 5B **116**
Barra Airport. *W Isl* 8C **170**
Barrachan. *Dum* 5A **110**
Barraglom. *W Isl* 4D **171**
Barrahormid. *Arg* 1F **125**
Barrapol. *Arg* 4A **138**
Barrasford. *Nmbd* 2C **114**
Barravullin. *Arg* 3F **133**
Barregarrow. *IOM* 3C **108**
Barrhead. *E Ren* 4G **127**
Barrhill. *S Ayr* 1H **109**
Barri. *V Glam* 5E **32**
Barrington. *Cambs* 1D **53**
Barrington. *Som* 1G **13**
Barripper. *Corn* 3D **4**
Barrmill. *N Ayr* 4E **127**
Barrock. *High* 1E **169**
Barrow. *Lanc* 1F **91**
Barrow. *Rut* 4F **75**
Barrow. *Shrp* 5A **72**
Barrow. *Som* 3C **22**
Barrow. *Suff* 4G **65**
Barroway Drove. *Norf* 5E **77**
Barrow Bridge. *G Man* 3E **91**
Barrowburn. *Nmbd* 3C **120**
Barrowby. *Linc* 2F **75**
Barrowcliff. *N Yor* 1E **101**
Barrow Common. *N Som* 5A **34**
Barrowden. *Rut* 5G **75**
Barrowford. *Lanc* 1G **91**
Barrow Gurney. *N Som* 5A **34**
Barrow Haven. *N Lin* 2D **94**
Barrow Hill. *Derbs* 3B **86**

Barrow-in-Furness. *Cumb* 3B 96
Barrow Nook. *Lanc* 4C 90
Barrows Green. *Cumb* 1E 97
Barrow's Green. *Hal* 2H 83
Barrow Street. *Wilts* 3D 22
Barrow upon Humber. *N Lin* 2D 94
Barrow upon Soar. *Leics* 4C 74
Barrow upon Trent. *Derbs* 3A 74
Barry. *Ang* 5E 145
Barry. *V Glam* 5E 32
Barry Island. *V Glam* 5E 32
Barsby. *Leics* 4D 74
Barsham. *Suff* 2F 67
Barston. *W Mid* 3G 61
Bartestree. *Here* 1A 48
Barthol Chapel. *Abers* 5F 161
Bartholomew Green. *Essx* 3H 53
Barthomley. *Ches* 5B 84
Bartley. *Hants* 1B 16
Bartley Green. *W Mid* 2E 61
Bartlow. *Cambs* 1F 53
Barton. *Cambs* 5D 64
Barton. *Ches* 5G 83
Barton. *Cumb* 2F 103
Barton. *Glos* 3F 49
Barton. *IOW* 4D 16
Barton. *Lanc* 4B 90
(nr. Ormskirk)
Barton. *Lanc* 1D 90
(nr. Preston)
Barton. *N Som* 1G 21
Barton. *N Yor* 4F 105
Barton. *Oxon* 5D 50
Barton. *Torb* 2F 9
Barton. *Warw* 5F 61
Barton Bendish. *Norf* 5G 77
Barton Gate. *Staf* 4F 73
Barton Green. *Staf* 4F 73
Barton Hartshorn. *Buck* 2E 51
Barton Hill. *N Yor* 3B 100
Barton in Fabis. *Notts* 2C 74
Barton in the Beans. *Leics* 5A 74
Barton-le-Clay. *Beds* 2A 52
Barton-le-Street. *N Yor* 2B 100
Barton-le-Willows. *N Yor* 3B 100
Barton Mills. *Suff* 3G 65
Barton on Sea. *Hants* 3H 15
Barton-on-the-Heath. *Warw* 2A 50
Barton St David. *Som* 3A 22
Barton Seagrave. *Nptn* 3F 63
Barton Stacey. *Hants* 2C 24
Barton Town. *Devn* 2G 19
Barton Turf. *Norf* 3F 79
Barton-under-Needwood. *Staf* 4F 73
Barton-upon-Humber. *N Lin* 2D 94
Barton Waterside. *N Lin* 2D 94
Barugh Green. *S Yor* 4D 92
Barway. *Cambs* 3E 65
Barwell. *Leics* 1B 62
Barwick. *Herts* 4D 53
Barwick. *Som* 1A 14
Barwick in Elmet. *W Yor* 1D 93
Baschurch. *Shrp* 3G 71
Bascote. *Warw* 4B 62
Basford Green. *Staf* 5D 85
Bashall Eaves. *Lanc* 5F 97
Bashall Town. *Lanc* 5G 97
Bashley. *Hants* 3H 15
Basildon. *Essx* 2B 40
Basingstoke. *Hants* 1E 25
Baslow. *Derbs* 3G 85
Bason Bridge. *Som* 2G 21
Bassaleg. *Newp* 3F 33
Bassendean. *Bord* 5C 130
Bassenthwaite. *Cumb* 1D 102
Bassett. *Sotn* 1C 16
Bassingbourn. *Cambs* 1D 52
Bassingfield. *Notts* 2D 74
Bassingham. *Linc* 5G 87
Bassingthorpe. *Linc* 3G 75
Bassus Green. *Herts* 3D 52
Basta. *Shet* 2G 173
Baston. *Linc* 4A 76
Bastonford. *Worc* 5C 60
Bastwick. *Norf* 4G 79
Batchley. *Worc* 4E 61
Batchworth. *Herts* 1B 38
Batcombe. *Dors* 2B 14
Batcombe. *Som* 3B 22
Bate Heath. *Ches* 3A 84
Bath. *Bath* 5C 34
Bathampton. *Bath* 5C 34
Bathealton. *Som* 4D 20
Batheaston. *Bath* 5C 34
Bathford. *Bath* 5C 34
Bathgate. *W Lot* 3C 128
Bathley. *Notts* 5E 87
Bathpool. *Corn* 5C 10
Bathpool. *Som* 4F 21
Bathville. *W Lot* 3C 128
Bathway. *Som* 1A 22
Batley. *W Yor* 2C 92
Batsford. *Glos* 2G 49
Batson. *Devn* 5D 8
Battersby. *N Yor* 4C 106
Battersea. *G Lon* 3D 39
Battisborough Cross. *Devn* 4C 8
Battisford. *Suff* 5C 66
Battisford Tye. *Suff* 5C 66
Battle. *E Sus* 4B 28
Battle. *Powy* 2D 46
Battleborough. *Som* 1G 21
Battledown. *Glos* 3E 49
Battlefield. *Shrp* 4H 71
Battlesbridge. *Essx* 1B 40
Battlesden. *Beds* 3H 51
Battlesea Green. *Suff* 3E 66
Battleton. *Som* 4C 20
Battramsley. *Hants* 3B 16
Batt's Corner. *Surr* 2G 25
Bauds of Cullen. *Mor* 2B 160
Baugh. *Arg* 4B 138
Baughton. *Worc* 1D 49
Baughurst. *Hants* 5D 36
Baulking. *Oxon* 2B 36
Baumber. *Linc* 3B 88
Baunton. *Glos* 5F 49
Baverstock. *Wilts* 3F 23
Bawburgh. *Norf* 5D 78
Bawdeswell. *Norf* 3C 78
Bawdrip. *Som* 3G 21
Bawdsey. *Suff* 1G 55
Bawdsey Manor. *Suff* 2G 55
Bawsey. *Norf* 4F 77
Bawtry. *S Yor* 1D 86
Baxenden. *Lanc* 2F 91
Baxterley. *Warw* 1G 61
Baxter's Green. *Suff* 5G 65
Baybridge. *Hants* 4D 24
Baybridge. *Nmbd* 4C 114
Baycliff. *Cumb* 2B 96
Baydon. *Wilts* 4A 36
Bayford. *Herts* 5D 52
Bayford. *Som* 4C 22
Bayles. *Cumb* 5A 114
Baylham. *Suff* 5D 66
Baynard's Green. *Oxon* 3D 50
Bayston Hill. *Shrp* 5G 71
Baythorn End. *Essx* 1H 53
Baythorpe. *Linc* 1B 76
Bayton. *Worc* 3A 60
Bayton Common. *Worc* 3B 60
Bayworth. *Oxon* 5D 50
Beach. *S Glo* 4C 34
Beachampton. *Buck* 2F 51
Beachamwell. *Norf* 5G 77
Beachley. *Glos* 2A 34
Beacon. *Devn* 2E 13
Beacon End. *Essx* 3C 54
Beacon Hill. *Surr* 3G 25
Beacon's Bottom. *Buck* 2F 37
Beaconsfield. *Buck* 1A 38
Beacontree. *G Lon* 2F 39
Beacrabhaicg. *W Isl* 8D 171
Beadlam. *N Yor* 1A 100
Beadnell. *Nmbd* 2G 121
Beaford. *Devn* 1F 11
Beal. *Nmbd* 5G 131
Beal. *N Yor* 2F 93
Bealsmill. *Corn* 5D 10
Beam Hill. *Staf* 3G 73
Beamhurst. *Staf* 2E 73
Beaminster. *Dors* 2H 13
Beamish. *Dur* 4F 115
Beamond End. *Buck* 1A 38
Beamsley. *N Yor* 4C 98
Bean. *Kent* 3G 39
Beanacre. *Wilts* 5E 35
Beanley. *Nmbd* 3E 121
Beanshanger. *Nptn* 2F 51
Beardwood. *Bkbn* 2E 91
Beare Green. *Surr* 1C 26
Bearley. *Warw* 4F 61
Bearpark. *Dur* 5F 115
Bearsbridge. *Nmbd* 4A 114
Bearsden. *E Dun* 2G 127
Bearsted. *Kent* 5B 40
Bearstone. *Shrp* 2B 72
Bearwood. *Pool* 3F 15
Bearwood. *W Mid* 2E 61
Beattock. *Dum* 4C 118
Beauchamp Roding. *Essx* 5F 53
Beauchief. *S Yor* 2H 85
Beaufort. *Blae* 4E 47
Beaulieu. *Hants* 2B 16
Beauly. *High* 4H 157
Beaumaris. *IOA* 3F 81
Beaumont. *Cumb* 4E 113
Beaumont. *Essx* 3E 55
Beaumont Hill. *Darl* 3F 105
Beaumont Leys. *Leic* 5C 74
Beausale. *Warw* 3G 61
Beauvale. *Notts* 1B 74
Beauworth. *Hants* 4D 24
Beaworthy. *Devn* 3E 11
Beazley End. *Essx* 3H 53
Bebington. *Mers* 2F 83
Bebside. *Nmbd* 1F 115
Beccles. *Suff* 2G 67
Becconsall. *Lanc* 2C 90
Beckbury. *Shrp* 5B 72
Beckenham. *G Lon* 4E 39
Beckermet. *Cumb* 4B 102
Beckett End. *Norf* 1G 65
Beckfoot. *Cumb* 1A 96
(nr. Broughton in Furness)
Beck Foot. *Cumb* 5H 103
(nr. Kendal)
Beckfoot. *Cumb* 4C 102
(nr. Seascale)
Beckfoot. *Cumb* 5B 112
(nr. Silloth)
Beckford. *Worc* 2E 49
Beckhampton. *Wilts* 5F 35
Beck Hole. *N Yor* 4F 107
Beckingham. *Linc* 5F 87
Beckingham. *Notts* 1E 87
Beckington. *Som* 1D 22
Beckley. *E Sus* 3C 28
Beckley. *Hants* 3H 15
Beckley. *Oxon* 4D 50
Beck Row. *Suff* 3F 65
Beck Side. *Cumb* 1C 96
(nr. Cartmel)
Beckside. *Cumb* 1F 97
(nr. Sedbergh)
Beck Side. *Cumb* 1B 96
(nr. Ulverston)
Beckton. *G Lon* 2F 39
Beckwithshaw. *N Yor* 4E 99
Becontree. *G Lon* 2F 39
Bedale. *N Yor* 1E 99
Bedburn. *Dur* 1E 105
Bedchester. *Dors* 1D 14
Beddau. *Rhon* 3D 32
Beddgelert. *Gwyn* 1E 69
Beddingham. *E Sus* 5F 27
Beddington. *G Lon* 4D 39
Bedfield. *Suff* 4E 66
Bedford. *Beds* 1A 52
Bedford. *G Man* 4E 91
Bedham. *W Sus* 3B 26
Bedhampton. *Hants* 2F 17
Bedingfield. *Suff* 4D 66
Bedingham Green. *Norf* 1E 67
Bedlam. *N Yor* 3E 99
Bedlar's Green. *Essx* 4F 53
Bedlington. *Nmbd* 1F 115
Bedlinog. *Mer T* 5D 46
Bedminster. *Bris* 4A 34
Bedmond. *Herts* 5A 52
Bednall. *Staf* 4D 72
Bedrule. *Bord* 3A 120
Bedstone. *Shrp* 3F 59
Bedwas. *Cphy* 3E 33
Bedwellty. *Cphy* 5E 47
Bedworth. *Warw* 2A 62
Beeby. *Leics* 5D 74
Beech. *Hants* 3E 25
Beech. *Staf* 2C 72
Beechcliffe. *W Yor* 5C 98
Beech Hill. *W Ber* 5E 37
Beechingstoke. *Wilts* 1F 23
Beedon. *W Ber* 4C 36
Beeford. *E Yor* 4F 101
Beeley. *Derbs* 4G 85
Beelsby. *NE Lin* 4F 95
Beenham. *W Ber* 5D 36
Beeny. *Corn* 3B 10
Beer. *Devn* 4F 13
Beer. *Som* 3H 21
Beer Crocombe. *Som* 4G 21
Beer Hackett. *Dors* 1B 14
Beesands. *Devn* 4E 9
Beesby. *Linc* 2D 88
Beeson. *Devn* 4E 9
Beeston. *Beds* 1B 52
Beeston. *Ches* 5H 83
Beeston. *Norf* 4B 78
Beeston. *Notts* 2C 74
Beeston. *W Yor* 1C 92
Beeston Regis. *Norf* 1D 78
Beeswing. *Dum* 3F 111
Beetham. *Cumb* 2D 97
Beetham. *Som* 1F 13
Beetley. *Norf* 4B 78
Beffcote. *Staf* 4C 72
Began. *Card* 3F 33
Begbroke. *Oxon* 4C 50
Begdale. *Cambs* 5D 76
Begelly. *Pemb* 4F 43
Beggar Hill. *Essx* 5G 53
Beggar's Bush. *Powy* 4E 59
Beggearn Huish. *Som* 3D 20
Beguildy. *Powy* 3D 58
Beighton. *Norf* 5F 79
Beighton. *S Yor* 2B 86
Beighton Hill. *Derbs* 5G 85
Beith. *N Ayr* 4E 127
Bekesbourne. *Kent* 5F 41
Belaugh. *Norf* 4E 79
Belbroughton. *Worc* 3D 60
Belchalwell. *Dors* 2C 14
Belchalwell Street. *Dors* 2C 14
Belchamp Otten. *Essx* 1B 54
Belchamp St Paul. *Essx* 1A 54
Belchamp Walter. *Essx* 1B 54
Belchford. *Linc* 3B 88
Belfatton. *Abers* 3H 161
Belford. *Nmbd* 1F 121
Belgrano. *Cnwy* 3B 82
Belhaven. *E Lot* 2C 130
Belhelvie. *Abers* 2G 153
Belhinnie. *Abers* 1B 152
Bellabeg. *Abers* 2A 152
Belladrum. *High* 4H 157
Bellamore. *S Ayr* 1H 109
Bellanoch. *Arg* 4F 133
Bell Busk. *N Yor* 4B 98
Belleau. *Linc* 3D 88
Belleheiglash. *Mor* 5F 159
Bell End. *Worc* 3D 60
Bellerby. *N Yor* 5E 105
Bellerby Camp. *N Yor* 5D 105
Bellever. *Devn* 5G 11
Belle Vue. *Cumb* 1C 102
Belle Vue. *Shrp* 4G 71
Bellfield. *S Lan* 1H 117
Belliehill. *Ang* 2E 145
Bellingdon. *Buck* 5H 51
Bellingham. *Nmbd* 1B 114
Bellmount. *Norf* 3E 77
Bellochantuy. *Arg* 2A 122
Bellsbank. *E Ayr* 4D 117
Bell's Cross. *Suff* 5D 66
Bellshill. *N Lan* 4A 128
Bellshill. *Nmbd* 1F 121
Bellside. *N Lan* 4B 128
Bellspool. *Bord* 1D 118
Bellsquarry. *W Lot* 3D 128
Bells Yew Green. *E Sus* 2H 27
Belmaduthy. *High* 3A 158
Belmesthorpe. *Rut* 4H 75
Belmont. *Bkbn* 3E 91
Belmont. *Shet* 1G 173
Belmont. *S Ayr* 3C 116
Belnacraig. *Abers* 2A 152
Belnie. *Linc* 2B 76
Belowda. *Corn* 2D 6
Belper. *Derbs* 1A 74
Belper Lane End. *Derbs* 1H 73
Belph. *Derbs* 3C 86
Belsay. *Nmbd* 2E 115
Belsford. *Devn* 3D 8
Belsize. *Herts* 5A 52
Belstead. *Suff* 1E 55
Belston. *S Ayr* 2C 116
Belstone. *Devn* 3G 11
Belstone Corner. *Devn* 3G 11
Belthorn. *Lanc* 2F 91
Beltinge. *Kent* 4F 41
Beltoft. *N Lin* 4B 94
Belton. *Leics* 3B 74
Belton. *Linc* 2G 75
Belton. *Norf* 5G 79
Belton. *N Lin* 4A 94
Belton-in-Rutland. *Rut* 5F 75
Beltring. *Kent* 1A 28
Belts of Collonach. *Abers* 4D 152
Belvedere. *G Lon* 3F 39
Belvoir. *Leics* 2F 75
Bembridge. *IOW* 4E 17
Bemersyde. *Bord* 1H 119
Bemerton. *Wilts* 3G 23
Bempton. *E Yor* 2F 101
Benacre. *Suff* 2H 67
Ben Alder Lodge. *High* 1C 142
Ben Armine Lodge. *High* 2E 164
Benbuie. *Dum* 5G 117
Benchill. *G Man* 2C 84
Benderloch. *Arg* 5D 140
Bendish. *Herts* 3B 52
Bendronaig Lodge. *High* 5C 156
Benenden. *Kent* 2C 28
Benera. *High* 1G 147
Benfieldside. *Dur* 4D 115
Bengate. *Norf* 3F 79
Bengeworth. *Worc* 1F 49
Bengrove. *Glos* 2E 49
Benhall Green. *Suff* 4F 67
Benholm. *Abers* 2H 145
Benington. *Herts* 3C 52
Benington. *Linc* 1C 76
Benington Sea End. *Linc* 1D 76
Benllech. *IOA* 2E 81
Benmore Lodge. *High* 2H 163
Bennacott. *Corn* 3D 10
Bennah. *Devn* 4B 12
Bennecarrigan. *N Ayr* 3D 122
Bennethead. *Cumb* 2F 103
Benningbrough. *N Yor* 4H 99
Benniworth. *Linc* 2B 88
Benover. *Kent* 1B 28
Benson. *Oxon* 2E 36
Bent. *Abers* 1F 145
Benthall. *Shrp* 5A 72
Bentham. *Glos* 4E 49
Benthoul. *Aber* 3F 153
Bentlawn. *Shrp* 5F 71
Bentley. *E Yor* 1D 94

Bentley—Bittering

Bentley. *Hants* 2F 25
Bentley. *S Yor* 4F 93
Bentley. *Suff* 2E 54
Bentley. *Warw* 1G 61
Bentley. *W Mid* 1D 61
Bentley Heath. *Herts* 1D 38
Bentley Heath. *W Mid* 3F 61
Bentpath. *Dum* 5F 119
Bents. *W Lot* 3C 128
Bentworth. *Hants* 2E 25
Benvie. *D'dee* 5C 144
Benville. *Dors* 2A 14
Benwell. *Tyne* 3F 115
Benwick. *Cambs* 1C 64
Beoley. *Worc* 4E 61
Beoraidbeg. *High* 4E 147
Bepton. *W Sus* 1G 17
Berden. *Essx* 3E 53
Bere Alston. *Devn* 2A 8
Bere Ferrers. *Devn* 2A 8
Berepper. *Corn* 4D 4
Bere Regis. *Dors* 3D 14
Bergh Apton. *Norf* 5F 79
Berinsfield. *Oxon* 2D 36
Berkeley. *Glos* 2B 34
Berkhamsted. *Herts* 5H 51
Berkley. *Som* 2D 22
Berkswell. *W Mid* 3G 61
Bermondsey. *G Lon* 3E 39
Bernice. *Arg* 4A 134
Bernisdale. *High* 3D 154
Berrick Salome. *Oxon* 2E 36
Berriedale. *High* 1H 165
Berrier. *Cumb* 2F 103
Berriew. *Powy* 5D 70
Berrington. *Nmbd* 5G 131
Berrington. *Shrp* 5H 71
Berrington. *Worc* 4H 59
Berrington Green. *Worc* 4H 59
Berrington Law. *Nmbd* 5F 131
Berrow. *Som* 1G 21
Berrow Green. *Worc* 5B 60
Berry Cross. *Devn* 1E 11
Berry Down Cross. *Devn* 2F 19
Berry Hill. *Glos* 4A 48
Berry Hill. *Pemb* 1A 44
Berryhillock. *Mor* 2C 160
Berrynarbor. *Devn* 2F 19
Berry Pomeroy. *Devn* 2E 9
Berryscaur. *Dum* 5D 118
Berry's Green. *G Lon* 5F 39
Bersham. *Wrex* 1F 71
Berthengam. *Flin* 3D 82
Berwick. *E Sus* 5G 27
Berwick Bassett. *Wilts* 4G 35
Berwick Hill. *Nmbd* 2E 115
Berwick St James. *Wilts* 3F 23
Berwick St John. *Wilts* 4E 23
Berwick St Leonard. *Wilts* 3E 23
Berwick-upon-Tweed. *Nmbd* 4G 131
Berwyn. *Den* 1D 70
Bescaby. *Leics* 3F 75
Bescar. *Lanc* 3B 90
Besford. *Worc* 1E 49
Bessacarr. *S Yor* 4G 93
Bessels Leigh. *Oxon* 5C 50
Bessingby. *E Yor* 3F 101
Bessingham. *Norf* 2D 78
Best Beech Hill. *E Sus* 2H 27
Besthorpe. *Norf* 1C 66
Besthorpe. *Notts* 4F 87
Bestwood Village. *Notts* 1C 74
Beswick. *E Yor* 5E 101
Betchworth. *Surr* 5D 38
Bethania. *Cdgn* 4E 57
Bethania. *Gwyn* 1G 69 (nr. Blaenau Ffestiniog)
Bethania. *Gwyn* 5F 81 (nr. Caernarfon)
Bethel. *Gwyn* 2B 70 (nr. Bala)
Bethel. *Gwyn* 4E 81 (nr. Caernarfon)
Bethel. *IOA* 3C 80
Bethersden. *Kent* 1D 28
Bethesda. *Gwyn* 4F 81
Bethesda. *Pemb* 3E 43
Bethlehem. *Carm* 3G 45
Bethnal Green. *G Lon* 2E 39
Betishill. *N Lan* 3A 128
Betley. *Staf* 1B 72
Betsham. *Kent* 3H 39
Betteshanger. *Kent* 5H 41
Bettiscombe. *Dors* 3H 13
Bettisfield. *Wrex* 2G 71
Betton. *Shrp* 2A 72
Betton Strange. *Shrp* 5H 71
Bettws. *B'end* 3C 32
Bettws. *Newp* 2F 33
Bettws Bledrws. *Cdgn* 5E 57
Bettws Cedewain. *Powy* 1D 58
Bettws Gwerfil Goch. *Den* 1C 70
Bettws Ifan. *Cdgn* 1D 44
Bettws Newydd. *Mon* 5G 47
Bettyhill. *High* 2H 167
Betws. *Carm* 4G 45
Betws Garmon. *Gwyn* 5E 81
Betws-y-Coed. *Cnwy* 5G 81
Betws-yn-Rhos. *Cnwy* 3B 82
Beulah. *Cdgn* 1C 44
Beulah. *Powy* 5B 58
Beul an Atha. *Arg* 3B 124
Bevendean. *Brig* 5E 27
Bevercotes. *Notts* 3E 86
Beverley. *E Yor* 1D 94
Beverston. *Glos* 2D 34
Bevington. *Glos* 2B 34
Bewaldeth. *Cumb* 1D 102
Bewcastle. *Cumb* 2G 113
Bewdley. *Worc* 3B 60
Bewerley. *N Yor* 3D 98
Bewholme. *E Yor* 4F 101
Bexfield. *Norf* 3C 78
Bexhill. *E Sus* 5B 28
Bexley. *G Lon* 3F 39
Bexleyheath. *G Lon* 3F 39
Bexleyhill. *W Sus* 3A 26
Bexwell. *Norf* 5F 77
Beyton. *Suff* 4B 66
Beyton Green. *Suff* 4B 66
Bhalton. *W Isl* 4C 171
Bhatarsaigh. *W Isl* 9B 170
Bibbington. *Derbs* 3E 85
Bibury. *Glos* 5G 49
Bicester. *Oxon* 3D 50
Bickenhall. *Som* 1F 13
Bickenhill. *W Mid* 2F 61
Bicker. *Linc* 2B 76
Bicker Bar. *Linc* 2B 76
Bicker Gauntlet. *Linc* 2B 76
Bickershaw. *G Man* 4E 91
Bickerstaffe. *Lanc* 4C 90
Bickerton. *Ches* 5H 83
Bickerton. *Nmbd* 4D 121
Bickerton. *N Yor* 4G 99
Bickford. *Staf* 4C 72
Bickington. *Devn* 3F 19 (nr. Barnstaple)
Bickington. *Devn* 5B 12 (nr. Newton Abbot)
Bickleigh. *Devn* 2B 8 (nr. Plymouth)
Bickleigh. *Devn* 2C 12 (nr. Tiverton)
Bickleton. *Devn* 3F 19
Bickley. *N Yor* 5G 107
Bickley Moss. *Ches* 1H 71
Bickmarsh. *Warw* 5F 61
Bicknacre. *Essx* 5A 54
Bicknoller. *Som* 3E 20
Bicknor. *Kent* 5C 40
Bickton. *Hants* 1G 15
Bicton. *Here* 4G 59
Bicton. *Shrp* 2E 59 (nr. Bishop's Castle)
Bicton. *Shrp* 4G 71 (nr. Shrewsbury)
Bicton Heath. *Shrp* 4G 71
Bidborough. *Kent* 1G 27
Biddenden. *Kent* 2C 28
Biddenden Green. *Kent* 1C 28
Biddenham. *Beds* 1A 52
Biddestone. *Wilts* 4D 34
Biddisham. *Som* 1G 21
Biddlesden. *Buck* 1E 51
Biddlestone. *Nmbd* 4D 120
Biddulph. *Staf* 5C 84
Biddulph Moor. *Staf* 5D 84
Bideford. *Devn* 4E 19
Bidford-on-Avon. *Warw* 5E 61
Bidlake. *Devn* 4F 11
Bidston. *Mers* 2E 83
Bielby. *E Yor* 5B 100
Bieldside. *Aber* 3F 153
Bierley. *IOW* 5D 16
Bierley. *W Yor* 1B 92
Bierton. *Buck* 4G 51
Bigbury. *Devn* 4C 8
Bigbury-on-Sea. *Devn* 4C 8
Bigby. *Linc* 4D 94
Biggar. *Cumb* 3A 96
Biggar. *S Lan* 1C 118
Biggin. *Derbs* 5F 85 (nr. Hartington)
Biggin. *Derbs* 1G 73 (nr. Hulland)
Biggin. *N Yor* 1F 93
Biggings. *Shet* 5C 173
Biggin Hill. *G Lon* 5F 39
Biggin Hill (London) Airport. *G Lon* 4F 39
Biggleswade. *Beds* 1B 52
Bighouse. *High* 2A 168
Bighton. *Hants* 3E 24
Biglands. *Cumb* 4D 112
Bignor. *W Sus* 4A 26
Bigrigg. *Cumb* 3B 102
Big Sand. *High* 1G 155
Bigton. *Shet* 9E 173
Bilberry. *Corn* 2E 6
Bilborough. *Nott* 1C 74
Bilbrook. *Som* 2D 20
Bilbrook. *Staf* 5C 72
Bilbrough. *N Yor* 5H 99
Bilbster. *High* 3E 169
Bilby. *Notts* 2D 86
Bildershaw. *Dur* 2F 105
Bildeston. *Suff* 1C 54
Billericay. *Essx* 1A 40
Billesdon. *Leics* 5E 74
Billesley. *Warw* 5F 61
Billingborough. *Linc* 2A 76
Billinge. *Mers* 4D 90
Billingford. *Norf* 3C 78 (nr. Dereham)
Billingford. *Norf* 3D 66 (nr. Diss)
Billingham. *Stoc T* 2B 106
Billinghay. *Linc* 5A 88
Billingley. *S Yor* 4E 93
Billingshurst. *W Sus* 3B 26
Billingsley. *Shrp* 2B 60
Billington. *Beds* 3H 51
Billington. *Lanc* 1F 91
Billington. *Staf* 3C 72
Billockby. *Norf* 4G 79
Billy Row. *Dur* 1E 105
Bilsborrow. *Lanc* 5E 97
Bilsby. *Linc* 3D 88
Bilsham. *W Sus* 5A 26
Bilsington. *Kent* 2E 29
Bilson Green. *Glos* 4B 48
Bilsthorpe. *Notts* 4D 86
Bilston. *Midl* 3F 129
Bilston. *W Mid* 1D 60
Bilstone. *Leics* 5A 74
Bilting. *Kent* 1E 29
Bilton. *E Yor* 1E 95
Bilton. *Nmbd* 3G 121
Bilton. *N Yor* 4E 99 (nr. Harrogate)
Bilton. *N Yor* 5G 99 (nr. York)
Bilton. *Warw* 3B 62
Binbrook. *Linc* 1B 88
Binchester. *Dur* 1F 105
Bincombe. *Dors* 4B 14
Bindal. *High* 5G 165
Binegar. *Som* 2B 22
Bines Green. *W Sus* 4C 26
Binfield. *Brac* 4G 37
Binfield Heath. *Oxon* 4F 37
Bingfield. *Nmbd* 2C 114
Bingham. *Notts* 1E 74
Bingham's Melcombe. *Dors* 2C 14
Bingley. *W Yor* 1B 92
Bings Heath. *Shrp* 4H 71
Binham. *Norf* 2B 78
Binley. *Hants* 1C 24
Binley. *W Mid* 3A 62
Binnegar. *Dors* 4D 15
Binniehill. *Falk* 2B 128
Binsoe. *N Yor* 2E 99
Binstead. *IOW* 3D 16
Binstead. *W Sus* 5A 26
Binsted. *Hants* 2F 25
Binton. *Warw* 5F 61
Bintree. *Norf* 3C 78
Binweston. *Shrp* 5F 71
Birch. *Essx* 4C 54
Birchall. *Staf* 5D 85
Bircham Newton. *Norf* 2G 77
Bircham Tofts. *Norf* 2G 77
Birchanger. *Essx* 3F 53
Birchburn. *N Ayr* 3D 122
Birch Cross. *Staf* 2F 73
Bircher. *Here* 4G 59
Birch Green. *Essx* 4C 54
Birchgrove. *Card* 4E 33
Birchgrove. *Swan* 3G 31
Birch Heath. *Ches* 4H 83
Birch Hill. *Ches* 3H 83
Birchington. *Kent* 4G 41
Birch Langley. *G Man* 4G 91
Birchley Heath. *Warw* 1G 61
Birchmoor. *Warw* 5G 73
Birchmoor Green. *Beds* 2H 51
Birchover. *Derbs* 4G 85
Birch Vale. *Derbs* 2E 85
Birchview. *Mor* 5F 159
Birchwood. *Linc* 4G 87
Birchwood. *Som* 1F 13
Birchwood. *Warr* 1A 84
Bircotes. *Notts* 1D 86
Birdbrook. *Essx* 1H 53
Birdham. *W Sus* 2G 17
Birdingbury. *Warw* 4B 62
Birdlip. *Glos* 4E 49
Birdsall. *N Yor* 3C 100
Birds Edge. *W Yor* 4C 92
Birds Green. *Essx* 5F 53
Birdsgreen. *Shrp* 2B 60
Birdsmoor Gate. *Dors* 2G 13
Birdston. *E Dun* 2H 127
Birdwell. *S Yor* 4D 92
Birdwood. *Glos* 4C 48
Birgham. *Bord* 1B 120
Birichen. *High* 4E 165
Birkby. *Cumb* 1B 102
Birkby. *N Yor* 4A 106
Birkdale. *Mers* 3B 90
Birkenhead. *Mers* 2F 83
Birkenhills. *Abers* 4E 161
Birkenshaw. *N Lan* 3H 127
Birkenshaw. *W Yor* 2C 92
Birkhall. *Abers* 4H 151
Birkhill. *Ang* 5C 144
Birkholme. *Linc* 3G 75
Birkin. *N Yor* 2F 93
Birley. *Here* 5G 59
Birling. *Kent* 4A 40
Birling. *Nmbd* 4G 121
Birling Gap. *E Sus* 5G 27
Birlingham. *Worc* 1E 49
Birmingham. *W Mid* 2E 61
Birmingham International Airport. *Mid* 2F 61
Birnam. *Per* 4H 143
Birsay. *Orkn* 5B 172
Birse. *Abers* 4C 152
Birsemore. *Abers* 4C 152
Birstall. *Leics* 5C 74
Birstall. *W Yor* 2C 92
Birstall Smithies. *W Yor* 2C 92
Birstwith. *N Yor* 4E 99
Birthorpe. *Linc* 2A 76
Birtle. *Lanc* 3G 91
Birtley. *Here* 4F 59
Birtley. *Nmbd* 2B 114
Birtley. *Tyne* 4F 115
Birtsmorton. *Worc* 2D 48
Birts Street. *Worc* 2C 48
Bisbrooke. *Rut* 1F 63
Bisham. *Wind* 3G 37
Bishampton. *Worc* 5D 61
Bish Mill. *Devn* 4H 19
Bishop Auckland. *Dur* 2F 105
Bishopbridge. *Linc* 1H 87
Bishopbriggs. *E Dun* 2H 127
Bishop Burton. *E Yor* 1C 94
Bishopdown. *Wilts* 3G 23
Bishop Middleham. *Dur* 1A 106
Bishopmill. *Mor* 2G 159
Bishop Monkton. *N Yor* 3F 99
Bishop Norton. *Linc* 1G 87
Bishopsbourne. *Kent* 5F 41
Bishops Cannings. *Wilts* 5F 35
Bishop's Castle. *Shrp* 2F 59
Bishop's Caundle. *Dors* 1B 14
Bishop's Cleeve. *Glos* 3E 49
Bishop's Down. *Dors* 1B 14
Bishop's Frome. *Here* 1B 48
Bishop's Green. *Essx* 4G 53
Bishop's Green. *Hants* 5D 36
Bishop's Hull. *Som* 4F 21
Bishop's Itchington. *Warw* 5A 62
Bishop's Lydeard. *Som* 4E 21
Bishop's Norton. *Glos* 3D 48
Bishop's Nympton. *Devn* 4A 20
Bishop's Offley. *Staf* 3B 72
Bishop's Stortford. *Herts* 3E 53
Bishops Sutton. *Hants* 3E 24
Bishop's Tachbrook. *Warw* 4H 61
Bishop's Tawton. *Devn* 3F 19
Bishopsteignton. *Devn* 5C 12
Bishopstoke. *Hants* 1C 16
Bishopston. *Swan* 4E 31
Bishopstone. *Buck* 4G 51
Bishopstone. *E Sus* 5F 27
Bishopstone. *Here* 1H 47
Bishopstone. *Swin* 3H 35
Bishopstone. *Wilts* 4F 23
Bishopstrow. *Wilts* 2D 23
Bishop Sutton. *Bath* 1A 22
Bishop's Waltham. *Hants* 1D 16
Bishopswood. *Som* 1F 13
Bishops Wood. *Staf* 5C 72
Bishopsworth. *Bris* 5A 34
Bishop Thornton. *N Yor* 3E 99
Bishopthorpe. *York* 5H 99
Bishopton. *Darl* 2A 106
Bishopton. *Dum* 5B 110
Bishopton. *N Yor* 2E 99
Bishopton. *Ren* 2F 127
Bishopton. *Warw* 5F 61
Bishop Wilton. *E Yor* 4B 100
Bishton. *Newp* 3G 33
Bishton. *Staf* 3E 73
Bisley. *Glos* 5E 49
Bisley. *Surr* 5A 38
Bispham. *Bkpl* 5C 96
Bispham Green. *Lanc* 3C 90
Bissoe. *Corn* 4B 6
Bisterne. *Hants* 2G 15
Bisterne Close. *Hants* 2H 15
Bitchfield. *Linc* 3G 75
Bittadon. *Devn* 2F 19
Bittaford. *Devn* 3C 8
Bittering. *Norf* 4B 78

Bitterley. *Shrp* 3H **59**
Bitterne. *Sotn* 1C **16**
Bitteswell. *Leics* 2C **62**
Bitton. *S Glo* 5B **34**
Bix. *Oxon* 3F **37**
Bixter. *Shet* 6E **173**
Blaby. *Leics* 1C **62**
Blackawton. *Devn* 3E **9**
Black Bank. *Cambs* 2E **65**
Black Barn. *Linc* 3D **76**
Blackborough. *Devn* 2D **12**
Blackborough. *Norf* 4F **77**
Blackborough End. *Norf* 4F **77**
Black Bourton. *Oxon* 5A **50**
Blackboys. *E Sus* 3G **27**
Blackbrook. *Derbs* 1H **73**
Blackbrook. *Mers* 1H **83**
Blackbrook. *Staf* 2B **72**
Blackbrook. *Surr* 1C **26**
Blackburn. *Abers* 2F **153**
Blackburn. *Bkbn* 2E **91**
Blackburn. *W Lot* 3C **128**
Black Callerton. *Tyne* 3E **115**
Black Car. *Norf* 1C **66**
Black Clauchrie. *S Ayr* 1H **109**
Black Corries. *High* 3G **141**
Black Crofts. *Arg* 5D **140**
Black Cross. *Corn* 2D **6**
Blackden Heath. *Ches* 3B **84**
Blackditch. *Oxon* 5C **50**
Blackdog. *Abers* 2G **153**
Black Dog. *Devn* 2B **12**
Blackdown. *Dors* 2G **13**
Blackdyke. *Cumb* 4C **112**
Blacker Hill. *S Yor* 4D **92**
Blackfen. *G Lon* 3F **39**
Blackfield. *Hants* 2C **16**
Blackford. *Cumb* 3E **113**
Blackford. *Per* 3A **136**
Blackford. *Shrp* 2H **59**
Blackford. *Som* 2H **21**
(nr. Burnham-on-Sea)
Blackford. *Som* 4B **22**
(nr. Wincanton)
Blackfordby. *Leics* 4H **73**
Blackgang. *IOW* 5C **16**
Blackhall. *Edin* 2F **129**
Blackhall. *Ren* 3F **127**
Blackhall Colliery. *Dur* 1B **106**
Blackhall Mill. *Tyne* 4E **115**
Blackhall Rocks. *Dur* 1B **106**
Blackham. *E Sus* 2F **27**
Blackheath. *Essx* 3D **54**
Blackheath. *G Lon* 3E **39**
Blackheath. *Suff* 3G **67**
Blackheath. *Surr* 1B **26**
Blackheath. *W Mid* 2D **61**
Black Heddon. *Nmbd* 2D **115**
Blackhill. *Abers* 4H **161**
Blackhill. *High* 3C **154**
Black Hill. *Warw* 5G **61**
Blackhills. *Abers* 2G **161**
Blackhills. *High* 3D **158**
Blackjack. *Linc* 2B **76**
Blackland. *Wilts* 5F **35**
Black Lane. *G Man* 4F **91**
Blackleach. *Lanc* 1C **90**
Blackley. *G Man* 4G **91**
Blackley. *W Yor* 3B **92**
Blacklunans. *Per* 2A **144**
Blackmill. *B'end* 3C **32**
Blackmoor. *G Man* 4E **91**
Blackmoor. *Hants* 3F **25**
Blackmoor Gate. *Devn* 2G **19**
Blackmore. *Essx* 5G **53**
Blackmore End. *Essx* 2H **53**
Blackmore End. *Herts* 4B **52**
Black Mount. *Arg* 4G **141**
Blackness. *Falk* 2D **128**
Blacknest. *Hants* 2F **25**
Blackney. *Dors* 3H **13**
Blacknoll. *Dors* 4D **14**
Black Notley. *Essx* 3A **54**
Blacko. *Lanc* 5A **98**
Black Pill. *Swan* 3F **31**
Blackpool. *Bkpl* 1B **90**
Blackpool. *Devn* 4E **9**
Blackpool Airport. *Lanc* 1B **90**
Blackpool Corner. *Devn* 3G **13**
Blackpool Gate. *Cumb* 2G **113**
Blackridge. *W Lot* 3C **128**
Blackrock. *Arg* 3B **124**
Blackrock. *Mon* 4F **47**
Blackrod. *G Man* 3E **90**
Blackshaw. *Dum* 3B **112**
Blackshaw Head. *W Yor* 2H **91**
Blacksmith's Green. *Suff* 4D **66**
Blacksnape. *Bkbn* 2F **91**
Blackstone. *W Sus* 4D **26**
Black Street. *Suff* 2H **67**
Black Tar. *Pemb* 4D **43**
Blackthorn. *Oxon* 4E **50**
Blackthorpe. *Suff* 4B **66**
Blacktoft. *E Yor* 2B **94**
Blacktop. *Aber* 3F **153**
Black Torrington. *Devn* 2E **11**
Blacktown. *Newp* 3F **33**
Blackwall Tunnel. *G Lon* 2E **39**
Blackwater. *Corn* 4B **6**
Blackwater. *Hants* 1G **25**
Blackwater. *IOW* 4D **16**
Blackwater. *Som* 1F **13**
Blackwaterfoot. *N Ayr* 3C **122**
Blackwell. *Darl* 3F **105**
Blackwell. *Derbs* 5B **86**
(nr. Alfreton)
Blackwell. *Derbs* 3F **85**
(nr. Buxton)
Blackwell. *Som* 4D **20**
Blackwell. *Warw* 1H **49**
Blackwell. *Worc* 3D **61**
Blackwood. *Cphy* 2E **33**
Blackwood. *Dum* 1G **111**
Blackwood. *S Lan* 5A **128**
Blackwood Hill. *Staf* 5D **84**
Blacon. *Ches* 4F **83**
Bladnoch. *Dum* 4B **110**
Bladon. *Oxon* 4C **50**
Blaenannerch. *Cdgn* 1C **44**
Blaenau Dolwyddelan. *Cnwy* 5F **81**
Blaenau Ffestiniog. *Gwyn* 1G **69**
Blaenavon. *Torf* 5F **47**
Blaenawey. *Mon* 4F **47**
Blaen Celyn. *Cdgn* 5C **56**
Blaen Clydach. *Rhon* 2C **32**
Blaendulais. *Neat* 5B **46**
Blaenffos. *Pemb* 1F **43**
Blaengarw. *B'end* 2C **32**
Blaen-geuffordd. *Cdgn* 2F **57**
Blaengwrach. *Neat* 5B **46**
Blaengwynfi. *Neat* 2B **32**
Blaenllechau. *Rhon* 2D **32**
Blaenpennal. *Cdgn* 4F **57**
Blaenplwyf. *Cdgn* 3E **57**
Blaenporth. *Cdgn* 1C **44**
Blaenrhondda. *Rhon* 2C **32**
Blaenwaun. *Carm* 2G **43**
Blaen-y-coed. *Carm* 2H **43**
Blaenycwm. *Rhon* 2C **32**
Blagdon. *N Som* 1A **22**
Blagdon. *Torb* 2E **9**
Blagdon Hill. *Som* 1F **13**
Blagill. *Cumb* 5A **114**
Blaguegate. *Lanc* 4C **90**
Blaich. *High* 1E **141**
Blain. *High* 2A **140**
Blaina. *Blae* 5F **47**
Blair Atholl. *Per* 2F **143**
Blair Drummond. *Stir* 4G **135**
Blairgowrie. *Per* 4A **144**
Blairhall. *Fife* 1D **128**
Blairingone. *Per* 4B **136**
Blairlogie. *Stir* 4H **135**
Blairmore. *Abers* 5B **160**
Blairmore. *Arg* 1C **126**
Blairmore. *High* 3B **166**
Blairquhanan. *W Dun* 1F **127**
Blaisdon. *Glos* 4C **48**
Blakebrook. *Worc* 3C **60**
Blakedown. *Worc* 3C **60**
Blake End. *Essx* 3H **53**
Blakemere. *Here* 1G **47**
Blakeney. *Glos* 5B **48**
Blakeney. *Norf* 1C **78**
Blakenhall. *Ches* 1B **72**
Blakenhall. *W Mid* 1C **60**
Blakeshall. *Worc* 2C **60**
Blakesley. *Nptn* 5D **62**
Blanchland. *Nmbd* 4C **114**
Blandford Camp. *Dors* 2E **15**
Blandford Forum. *Dors* 2D **15**
Blandford St Mary. *Dors* 2D **15**
Bland Hill. *N Yor* 4E **98**
Blandy. *High* 3G **167**
Blanefield. *Stir* 2G **127**
Blankney. *Linc* 4H **87**
Blantyre. *S Lan* 4H **127**
Blarmachfoldach. *High* 2E **141**
Blarnalearoch. *High* 4F **163**
Blashford. *Hants* 2G **15**
Blaston. *Leics* 1F **63**
Blatchbridge. *Som* 2C **22**
Blathaisbhal. *W Isl* 1D **170**
Blatherwycke. *Nptn* 1G **63**
Blawith. *Cumb* 1B **96**
Blaxhall. *Suff* 5F **67**
Blaxton. *S Yor* 4G **93**
Blaydon. *Tyne* 3E **115**
Bleadney. *Som* 2H **21**
Bleadon. *N Som* 1G **21**
Blean. *Kent* 4F **41**
Bleasby. *Linc* 2A **88**
Bleasby. *Notts* 1E **74**
Bleasby Moor. *Linc* 2A **88**
Blebocraigs. *Fife* 2G **137**
Bleddfa. *Powy* 4E **58**
Bledington. *Glos* 3H **49**
Bledlow. *Buck* 5F **51**
Bledlow Ridge. *Buck* 2F **37**
Blencarn. *Cumb* 1H **103**
Blencogo. *Cumb* 5C **112**
Blendworth. *Hants* 1F **17**
Blenheim. *Oxon* 5D **50**
Blennerhasset. *Cumb* 5C **112**
Bletchingdon. *Oxon* 4D **50**
Bletchingley. *Surr* 5E **39**
Bletchley. *Mil* 2G **51**
Bletchley. *Shrp* 2A **72**
Bletherston. *Pemb* 2E **43**
Bletsoe. *Beds* 5H **63**
Blewbury. *Oxon* 3D **36**
Blickling. *Norf* 3D **78**
Blidworth. *Notts* 5C **86**
Blindburn. *Nmbd* 3C **120**
Blindcrake. *Cumb* 1C **102**
Blindley Heath. *Surr* 1E **27**
Blisland. *Corn* 5A **10**
Blissford. *Hants* 1G **15**
Bliss Gate. *Worc* 3B **60**
Blists Hill. *Telf* 5A **72**
Blisworth. *Nptn* 5E **63**
Blithbury. *Staf* 3E **73**
Blitterlees. *Cumb* 4C **112**
Blockley. *Glos* 2G **49**
Blofield. *Norf* 5F **79**
Blofield Heath. *Norf* 4F **79**
Blo' Norton. *Norf* 3C **66**
Bloomfield. *Bord* 2H **119**
Blore. *Staf* 1F **73**
Blount's Green. *Staf* 2E **73**
Bloxham. *Oxon* 2C **50**
Bloxholm. *Linc* 5H **87**
Bloxwich. *W Mid* 5E **73**
Bloxworth. *Dors* 3D **15**
Blubberhouses. *N Yor* 4D **98**
Blue Anchor. *Som* 2D **20**
Blue Anchor. *Swan* 3E **31**
Blue Bell Hill. *Kent* 4B **40**
Blue Row. *Essx* 4D **54**
Bluetown. *Kent* 5D **40**
Blundeston. *Suff* 1H **67**
Blunham. *Beds* 5A **64**
Blunsdon St Andrew. *Swin* 3G **35**
Bluntington. *Worc* 3C **60**
Bluntisham. *Cambs* 3C **64**
Blunts. *Corn* 2H **7**
Blurton. *Stoke* 1C **72**
Blyborough. *Linc* 1G **87**
Blyford. *Suff* 3G **67**
Blymhill. *Staf* 4C **72**
Blymhill Lawns. *Staf* 4C **72**
Blyth. *Nmbd* 1G **115**
Blyth. *Notts* 2D **86**
Blyth. *Bord* 5E **129**
Blyth Bank. *Bord* 5E **129**
Blyth Bridge. *Bord* 5E **129**
Blythburgh. *Suff* 3G **67**
Blythe Bridge. *Staf* 1D **72**
Blythe Marsh. *Staf* 1D **72**
Blythe, The. *Staf* 3E **73**
Blyton. *Linc* 1F **87**
Boarhills. *Fife* 2H **137**
Boarhunt. *Hants* 2E **16**
Boarshead. *E Sus* 2G **27**
Boar's Head. *G Man* 4D **90**
Boars Hill. *Oxon* 5C **50**
Boarstall. *Buck* 4E **51**
Boasley Cross. *Devn* 3F **11**
Boath. *High* 1H **157**
Boat of Garten. *High* 2D **150**
Bobbing. *Kent* 4C **40**
Bobbington. *Staf* 1C **60**
Bobbingworth. *Essx* 5F **53**
Bocaddon. *Corn* 3F **7**
Bocking. *Essx* 3A **54**
Bocking Churchstreet. *Essx* 3A **54**
Boddam. *Abers* 4H **161**
Boddam. *Shet* 10E **173**
Boddington. *Glos* 3D **49**
Bodedern. *IOA* 2C **80**
Bodelwyddan. *Den* 3C **82**
Bodenham. *Here* 5H **59**
Bodenham. *Wilts* 4G **23**
Bodewryd. *IOA* 1C **80**
Bodfari. *Den* 3C **82**
Bodffordd. *IOA* 3D **80**
Bodham. *Norf* 1D **78**
Bodiam. *E Sus* 3B **28**
Bodicote. *Oxon* 2C **50**
Bodieve. *Corn* 1D **6**
Bodinnick. *Corn* 3F **7**
Bodle Street Green. *E Sus* 4A **28**
Bodmin. *Corn* 2E **7**
Bodnant. *Cnwy* 3H **81**
Bodney. *Norf* 1H **65**
Bodorgan. *IOA* 4C **80**
Bodrane. *Corn* 2G **7**
Bodsham Green. *Kent* 1F **29**
Boduan. *Gwyn* 2C **68**
Bodymoor Heath. *Warw* 1F **61**
Bogallan. *High* 3A **158**
Bogbrae Croft. *Abers* 5H **161**
Bogend. *S Ayr* 1C **116**
Boghall. *Midl* 3F **129**
Boghall. *W Lot* 3C **128**
Boghead. *S Lan* 5A **128**
Bogindollo. *Ang* 3D **144**
Bogmoor. *Mor* 2A **160**
Bogniebrae. *Abers* 4C **160**
Bognor Regis. *W Sus* 3H **17**
Bograxie. *Abers* 2E **152**
Bogside. *N Lan* 4B **128**
Bog, The. *Shrp* 1F **59**
Bogton. *Abers* 3D **160**
Bogue. *Dum* 1D **110**
Bohenie. *High* 5E **149**
Bohortha. *Corn* 5C **6**
Bokiddick. *Corn* 2E **7**
Bolam. *Dur* 2E **105**
Bolam. *Nmbd* 1D **115**
Bolberry. *Devn* 5C **8**
Bold Heath. *Mers* 2H **83**
Boldon. *Tyne* 3G **115**
Boldon Colliery. *Tyne* 3G **115**
Boldre. *Hants* 3B **16**
Boldron. *Dur* 3D **104**
Bole. *Notts* 2E **87**
Bolehall. *Staf* 5G **73**
Bolehill. *Derbs* 5G **85**
Bolenowe. *Corn* 5A **6**
Boleside. *Bord* 1G **119**
Bolham. *Devn* 1C **12**
Bolham Water. *Devn* 1E **13**
Bolingey. *Corn* 3B **6**
Bollington. *Ches* 3D **84**
Bolney. *W Sus* 3D **26**
Bolnhurst. *Beds* 5H **63**
Bolshan. *Ang* 3F **145**
Bolsover. *Derbs* 3B **86**
Bolsterstone. *S Yor* 1G **85**
Bolstone. *Here* 2A **48**
Boltachan. *Per* 3F **143**
Boltby. *N Yor* 1G **99**
Bolton. *Cumb* 2H **103**
Bolton. *E Lot* 2B **130**
Bolton. *E Yor* 4B **100**
Bolton. *G Man* 4F **91**
Bolton. *Nmbd* 3F **121**
Bolton Abbey. *N Yor* 4C **98**
Bolton-by-Bowland. *Lanc* 5G **97**
Boltonfellend. *Cumb* 3F **113**
Boltongate. *Cumb* 5D **112**
Bolton Green. *Lanc* 3D **90**
Bolton-le-Sands. *Lanc* 3D **97**
Bolton Low Houses. *Cumb* 5D **112**
Bolton New Houses. *Cumb* 5D **112**
Bolton-on-Swale. *N Yor* 5F **105**
Bolton Percy. *N Yor* 5H **99**
Bolton Town End. *Lanc* 3D **97**
Bolton upon Dearne. *S Yor* 4E **93**
Bolton Wood Lane. *Cumb* 5D **112**
Bolventor. *Corn* 5B **10**
Bomarsund. *Nmbd* 1F **115**
Bomere Heath. *Shrp* 4G **71**
Bonar Bridge. *High* 4D **164**
Bonawe. *Arg* 5E **141**
Bonby. *N Lin* 3D **94**
Boncath. *Pemb* 1G **43**
Bonchester Bridge. *Bord* 3H **119**
Bonchurch. *IOW* 5D **16**
Bond End. *Staf* 4F **73**
Bondleigh. *Devn* 2G **11**
Bonds. *Lanc* 5D **97**
Bonehill. *Devn* 5H **11**
Bonehill. *Staf* 5F **73**
Bo'ness. *Falk* 1C **128**
Boney Hay. *Staf* 4E **73**
Bonham. *Wilts* 3C **22**
Bonhill. *W Dun* 2E **127**
Boningale. *Shrp* 5C **72**
Bonjedward. *Bord* 2A **120**
Bonkle. *N Lan* 4B **128**
Bonnington. *Ang* 5E **145**
Bonnington. *Edin* 3E **129**
Bonnington. *Kent* 2E **29**
Bonnybank. *Fife* 3F **137**
Bonnybridge. *Falk* 1B **128**
Bonnykelly. *Abers* 3F **161**
Bonnyrigg. *Midl* 3G **129**
Bonnyton. *Ang* 5C **144**
Bonnytown. *Fife* 2H **137**
Bonsall. *Derbs* 5G **85**
Bont. *Mon* 4G **47**
Bontddu. *Gwyn* 4F **69**
Bont Dolgadfan. *Powy* 5A **70**
Bontgoch. *Cdgn* 2F **57**
Bonthorpe. *Linc* 3D **89**
Bontnewydd. *Cdgn* 4F **57**
Bont-newydd. *Cnwy* 3C **82**
Bontnewydd. *Gwyn* 4D **81**
(nr. Caernarfon)
Bont Newydd. *Gwyn* 1G **69**
(nr. Llan Ffestiniog)
Bontuchel. *Den* 5C **82**
Bonvilston. *V Glam* 4D **32**
Bon-y-maen. *Swan* 3F **31**
Booker. *Buck* 2G **37**
Booley. *Shrp* 3H **71**
Boorley Green. *Hants* 1D **16**
Boosbeck. *Red C* 3D **106**

Boot—Brampton en le Morthen

Boot. *Cumb* 4C **102**
Booth. *W Yor* 2A **92**
Boothby Graffoe. *Linc* 5G **87**
Boothby Pagnell. *Linc* 2G **75**
Booth Green. *Ches* 2D **84**
Booth of Toft. *Shet* 4F **173**
Boothstown. *G Man* 4F **91**
Boothville. *Nptn* 4E **63**
Booth Wood. *W Yor* 3A **92**
Bootle. *Cumb* 1A **96**
Bootle. *Mers* 1F **83**
Booton. *Norf* 3D **78**
Booze. *N Yor* 4D **104**
Boquhan. *Stir* 1G **127**
Boraston. *Shrp* 3A **60**
Borden. *Kent* 4C **40**
Borden. *W Sus* 4G **25**
Bordlands. *Bord* 5E **129**
Bordley. *N Yor* 3B **98**
Bordon. *Hants* 3G **25**
Boreham. *Essx* 5A **54**
Boreham. *Wilts* 2D **23**
Boreham Street. *E Sus* 4A **28**
Borehamwood. *Herts* 1C **38**
Boreland. *Dum* 5D **118**
Boreston. *Devn* 3D **8**
Borestone Brae. *Stir* 4H **135**
Boreton. *Shrp* 5H **71**
Borgh. *W Isl* 8B **170** (on Barra)
Borgh. *W Isl* 3C **170** (on Benbecula)
Borgh. *W Isl* 1E **170** (on Berneray)
Borgh. *W Isl* 2G **171** (on Isle of Lewis)
Borghastan. *W Isl* 3D **171**
Borgie. *High* 3G **167**
Borgue. *Dum* 5D **110**
Borgue. *High* 1H **165**
Borley. *Essx* 1B **54**
Borley Green. *Essx* 1B **54**
Borley Green. *Suff* 4B **66**
Borlum. *High* 1H **149**
Bornais. *W Isl* 6C **170**
Bornesketaig. *High* 1C **154**
Boroughbridge. *N Yor* 3F **99**
Borough Green. *Kent* 5H **39**
Borras Head. *Wrex* 5F **83**
Borreraig. *High* 3A **154**
Borrobol Lodge. *High* 1F **165**
Borrodale. *High* 4A **154**
Borrowash. *Derb* 2B **74**
Borrowby. *N Yor* 1G **99** (nr. Northallerton)
Borrowby. *N Yor* 3E **107** (nr. Whitby)
Borrowston. *High* 4F **169**
Borrowstonehill. *Orkn* 7D **172**
Borrowstoun. *Falk* 1C **128**
Borstal. *Medw* 4B **40**
Borth. *Cdgn* 2F **57**
Borthwick. *Midl* 4G **129**
Borth-y-Gest. *Gwyn* 2E **69**
Borve. *High* 4D **154**
Borwick. *Lanc* 2E **97**
Bosbury. *Here* 1B **48**
Boscastle. *Corn* 3A **10**
Boscombe. *Bour* 3G **15**
Boscombe. *Wilts* 3H **23**
Boscoppa. *Corn* 3E **7**
Bosham. *W Sus* 2G **17**
Bosherston. *Pemb* 5D **42**
Bosley. *Ches* 4D **84**
Bossall. *N Yor* 3B **100**
Bossiney. *Corn* 4A **10**
Bossingham. *Kent* 1F **29**
Bossington. *Som* 2B **20**
Bostadh. *W Isl* 3D **171**
Bostock Green. *Ches* 4A **84**
Boston. *Linc* 1C **76**
Boston Spa. *W Yor* 5G **99**
Boswarthen. *Corn* 3B **4**
Boswinger. *Corn* 4D **6**
Botallack. *Corn* 3A **4**
Botany Bay. *G Lon* 1D **39**
Botcheston. *Leics* 5B **74**
Botesdale. *Suff* 3C **66**
Bothal. *Nmbd* 1F **115**
Bothampstead. *W Ber* 4D **36**
Bothamsall. *Notts* 3D **86**
Bothel. *Cumb* 1C **102**
Bothenhampton. *Dors* 3H **13**
Bothwell. *S Lan* 4H **127**
Botley. *Buck* 5H **51**
Botley. *Hants* 1D **16**
Botley. *Oxon* 5C **50**
Botloe's Green. *Glos* 3C **48**
Botolph Claydon. *Buck* 3F **51**
Botolphs. *W Sus* 5C **26**
Bottacks. *High* 2G **157**
Bottesford. *Leics* 2F **75**
Bottesford. *N Lin* 4B **94**
Bottisham. *Cambs* 4E **65**
Bottlesford. *Wilts* 1G **23**
Bottomcraig. *Fife* 1F **137**
Bottom o' th' Moor. *G Man* 3E **91**
Botton. *N Yor* 4D **107**
Botton Head. *Lanc* 3F **97**
Bottreaux Mill. *Devn* 4B **20**
Botusfleming. *Corn* 2A **8**
Botwnnog. *Gwyn* 2B **68**
Bough Beech. *Kent* 1F **27**
Boughrood. *Powy* 2E **47**
Boughspring. *Glos* 2A **34**
Boughton. *Norf* 5F **77**
Boughton. *Nptn* 4E **63**
Boughton. *Notts* 4D **86**
Boughton Aluph. *Kent* 1E **29**
Boughton Green. *Kent* 5B **40**
Boughton Lees. *Kent* 1E **28**
Boughton Malherbe. *Kent* 1C **28**
Boughton Monchelsea. *Kent* 5B **40**
Boughton under Blean. *Kent* 5E **41**
Boulby. *Red C* 3E **107**
Bouldnor. *IOW* 4B **16**
Bouldon. *Shrp* 2H **59**
Boulmer. *Nmbd* 3G **121**
Boulston. *Pemb* 3D **42**
Boultham. *Linc* 4G **87**
Boulton. *Derb* 2A **74**
Boundary. *Staf* 1D **73**
Bounds. *Here* 2B **48**
Bourn. *Cambs* 5C **64**
Bournbrook. *W Mid* 2E **61**
Bourne. *Linc* 3H **75**
Bourne End. *Beds* 1H **51** (nr. Cranfield)
Bourne End. *Beds* 4H **63** (nr. Sharnbrook)
Bourne End. *Buck* 3G **37**
Bourne End. *Herts* 5A **52**
Bournemouth. *Bour* 3F **15**
Bournemouth Airport. *Dors* 3G **15**
Bournes Green. *Glos* 5E **49**
Bournes Green. *S'end* 2D **40**
Bourne, The. *Surr* 2G **25**
Bournheath. *Worc* 3D **60**
Bournmoor. *Dur* 4G **115**
Bournville. *W Mid* 2E **61**
Bourton. *Dors* 3C **22**
Bourton. *N Som* 5G **33**
Bourton. *Oxon* 3H **35**
Bourton. *Shrp* 1H **59**
Bourton. *Wilts* 5F **35**
Bourton on Dunsmore. *Warw* 3B **62**
Bourton-on-the-Hill. *Glos* 2G **49**
Bourton-on-the-Water. *Glos* 3G **49**
Bousd. *Arg* 2D **138**
Boustead Hill. *Cumb* 4D **112**
Bouth. *Cumb* 1C **96**
Bouthwaite. *N Yor* 2D **98**
Boveney. *Buck* 3A **38**
Boveridge. *Dors* 1F **15**
Boverton. *V Glam* 5C **32**
Bovey Tracey. *Devn* 5B **12**
Bovingdon. *Herts* 5A **52**
Bovingdon Green. *Buck* 3G **37**
Bovinger. *Essx* 5F **53**
Bovington Camp. *Dors* 4D **14**
Bow. *Devn* 2H **11**
Bowbank. *Dur* 2C **104**
Bow Brickhill. *Mil* 2H **51**
Bowbridge. *Glos* 5D **48**
Bowburn. *Dur* 1A **106**
Bowcombe. *IOW* 4C **16**
Bowd. *Devn* 4E **12**
Bowden. *Devn* 4E **9**
Bowden. *Bord* 1H **119**
Bowden Hill. *Wilts* 5E **35**
Bowdon. *G Man* 2B **84**
Bower. *Nmbd* 1A **114**
Bowerchalke. *Wilts* 4F **23**
Bowerhill. *Wilts* 5E **35**
Bower Hinton. *Som* 1H **13**
Bowermadden. *High* 2E **169**
Bowers. *Staf* 2C **72**
Bowers Gifford. *Essx* 2B **40**
Bowershall. *Fife* 4C **136**
Bowertower. *High* 2E **169**
Bowes. *Dur* 3C **104**
Bowgreave. *Lanc* 5D **97**
Bowhousebog. *N Lan* 4B **128**
Bowithick. *Corn* 4B **10**
Bowland Bridge. *Cumb* 1D **96**
Bowlees. *Dur* 2C **104**
Bowley. *Here* 5H **59**
Bowlhead Green. *Surr* 2A **26**
Bowling. *W Dun* 2F **127**
Bowling. *W Yor* 1B **92**
Bowling Bank. *Wrex* 1F **71**
Bowling Green. *Worc* 5C **60**
Bowlish. *Som* 2B **22**
Bowmanstead. *Cumb* 5E **102**
Bowmore. *Arg* 4B **124**
Bowness-on-Solway. *Cumb* 3D **112**
Bowness-on-Windermere. *Cumb* 5F **103**
Bow of Fife. *Fife* 2F **137**
Bowriefauld. *Ang* 4E **145**
Bowscale. *Cumb* 1E **103**
Bowsden. *Nmbd* 5F **131**
Bowside Lodge. *High* 2A **168**
Bowston. *Cumb* 5F **103**
Bow Street. *Cdgn* 2F **57**
Bowthorpe. *Norf* 5D **78**
Box. *Glos* 5D **48**
Box. *Wilts* 5D **34**
Boxbush. *Glos* 3B **48**
Box End. *Beds* 1A **52**
Boxford. *Suff* 1C **54**
Boxford. *W Ber* 4C **36**
Boxgrove. *W Sus* 5A **26**
Boxley. *Kent* 5B **40**
Box's Shop. *Corn* 2C **10**
Boxted. *Essx* 2C **54**
Boxted. *Suff* 5H **65**
Boxted Cross. *Essx* 2D **54**
Boxworth. *Cambs* 4C **64**
Boxworth End. *Cambs* 4C **64**
Boyden End. *Suff* 5G **65**
Boyden Gate. *Kent* 4G **41**
Boylestone. *Derbs* 2F **73**
Boylestonfield. *Derbs* 2F **73**
Boyndlie. *Abers* 2D **160**
Boynton. *E Yor* 3F **101**
Boys Hill. *Dors* 1B **14**
Boythorpe. *Derbs* 4A **86**
Boyton. *Corn* 3D **10**
Boyton. *Suff* 1G **55**
Boyton. *Wilts* 3E **23**
Boyton Cross. *Essx* 5G **53**
Boyton End. *Essx* 2G **53**
Boyton End. *Suff* 1H **53**
Bozeat. *Nptn* 5G **63**
Brù. *W Isl* 3F **171**
Braaid. *IOM* 4C **108**
Braal Castle. *High* 2D **168**
Brabling Green. *Suff* 4E **67**
Brabourne. *Kent* 1F **29**
Brabourne Lees. *Kent* 1E **29**
Brabster. *High* 2F **169**
Bracadale. *High* 5C **154**
Braceborough. *Linc* 4H **75**
Bracebridge. *Linc* 4G **87**
Bracebridge Heath. *Linc* 4G **87**
Braceby. *Linc* 2H **75**
Bracewell. *Lanc* 5A **98**
Brackenfield. *Derbs* 5A **86**
Brackenlands. *Cumb* 5D **112**
Brackenthwaite. *Cumb* 5D **112**
Brackenthwaite. *N Yor* 4E **99**
Brackla. *B'end* 4C **32**
Brackla. *High* 3C **158**
Bracklesham. *W Sus* 3G **17**
Brackletter. *High* 5D **148**
Brackley. *Nptn* 2D **50**
Brackley Hatch. *Nptn* 1E **51**
Brackloch. *High* 1F **163**
Bracknell. *Brac* 5G **37**
Braco. *Per* 3H **135**
Bracobrae. *Mor* 3C **160**
Bracon. *N Lin* 4A **94**
Bracon Ash. *Norf* 1D **66**
Bracora. *High* 4F **147**
Bradbourne. *Derbs* 5G **85**
Bradbury. *Dur* 2A **106**
Bradda. *IOM* 4A **108**
Bradden. *Nptn* 1E **51**
Bradenham. *Buck* 2G **37**
Bradenham. *Norf* 5B **78**
Bradenstoke. *Wilts* 4F **35**
Bradfield. *Essx* 2E **55**
Bradfield. *Norf* 2E **79**
Bradfield. *W Ber* 4E **36**
Bradfield Combust. *Suff* 5A **66**
Bradfield Green. *Ches* 5A **84**
Bradfield Heath. *Essx* 3E **55**
Bradfield St Clare. *Suff* 5B **66**
Bradfield St George. *Suff* 4B **66**
Bradford. *Derbs* 4G **85**
Bradford. *Devn* 2E **11**
Bradford. *Nmbd* 1F **121**
Bradford. *W Yor* 1B **92**
Bradford Abbas. *Dors* 1A **14**
Bradford Barton. *Devn* 1B **12**
Bradford Leigh. *Wilts* 5D **34**
Bradford-on-Avon. *Wilts* 5D **34**
Bradford-on-Tone. *Som* 4E **21**
Bradford Peverell. *Dors* 3B **14**
Bradiford. *Devn* 3F **19**
Brading. *IOW* 4E **16**
Bradley. *Ches* 3H **83**
Bradley. *Derbs* 1G **73**
Bradley. *Glos* 2C **34**
Bradley. *Hants* 2E **25**
Bradley. *NE Lin* 4F **95**
Bradley. *N Yor* 1C **98**
Bradley. *Staf* 4C **72**
Bradley. *W Mid* 1D **60**
Bradley. *W Yor* 2B **92**
Bradley. *Wrex* 5F **83**
Bradley Cross. *Som* 1H **21**
Bradley Green. *Ches* 1H **71**
Bradley Green. *Som* 3F **21**
Bradley Green. *Warw* 5G **73**
Bradley Green. *Worc* 4D **61**
Bradley in the Moors. *Staf* 1E **73**
Bradley Mount. *Ches* 3D **84**
Bradley Stoke. *S Glo* 3B **34**
Bradlow. *Here* 2C **48**
Bradmore. *Notts* 2C **74**
Bradmore. *W Mid* 1C **60**
Bradninch. *Devn* 2D **12**
Bradnop. *Staf* 5E **85**
Bradpole. *Dors* 3H **13**
Bradshaw. *G Man* 3F **91**
Bradstone. *Devn* 4D **11**
Bradwall Green. *Ches* 4B **84**
Bradway. *S Yor* 2H **85**
Bradwell. *Derbs* 2F **85**
Bradwell. *Essx* 3B **54**
Bradwell. *Mil* 2G **51**
Bradwell. *Norf* 5H **79**
Bradwell-on-Sea. *Essx* 5D **54**
Bradwell Waterside. *Essx* 5C **54**
Bradworthy. *Devn* 1D **10**
Brae. *High* 5C **162**
Brae. *Shet* 5E **173**
Braeantra. *High* 1H **157**
Braefield. *High* 5G **157**
Braefindon. *High* 3A **158**
Braegrum. *Per* 1C **136**
Braehead. *Ang* 3F **145**
Braehead. *Dum* 4B **110**
Braehead. *Mor* 4G **159**
Braehead. *Orkn* 3D **172**
Braehead. *S Lan* 1H **117** (nr. Coalburn)
Braehead. *S Lan* 4C **128** (nr. Forth)
Braehoulland. *Shet* 4D **173**
Braemar. *Abers* 4F **151**
Braemore. *High* 5C **168** (nr. Dunbeath)
Braemore. *High* 1D **156** (nr. Ullapool)
Brae of Achnahaird. *High* 2E **163**
Brae Roy Lodge. *High* 4F **149**
Braeside. *Abers* 5G **161**
Braeside. *Inv* 2D **126**
Braes of Coul. *Ang* 3B **144**
Braetongue. *High* 3F **167**
Braeval. *Stir* 3E **135**
Braevallich. *Arg* 3G **133**
Brafferton. *Darl* 2F **105**
Brafferton. *N Yor* 2G **99**
Brafield-on-the-Green. *Nptn* 5F **63**
Bragar. *W Isl* 3E **171**
Bragbury End. *Herts* 3C **52**
Bragleenbeg. *Arg* 1G **133**
Braichmelyn. *Gwyn* 4F **81**
Braides. *Lanc* 4D **96**
Braidwood. *S Lan* 5B **128**
Braigo. *Arg* 3A **124**
Brailsford. *Derbs* 1G **73**
Braintree. *Essx* 3A **54**
Braiseworth. *Suff* 3D **66**
Braishfield. *Hants* 4B **24**
Braithwaite. *Cumb* 2D **102**
Braithwaite. *S Yor* 3G **93**
Braithwaite. *W Yor* 5C **98**
Braithwell. *S Yor* 1C **86**
Brakefield Green. *Norf* 5C **78**
Bramber. *W Sus* 4C **26**
Brambledown. *Kent* 3D **40**
Brambridge. *Hants* 4C **24**
Bramcote. *Notts* 2C **74**
Bramcote. *Warw* 2B **62**
Bramdean. *Hants* 4E **24**
Bramerton. *Norf* 5E **79**
Bramfield. *Herts* 4C **52**
Bramfield. *Suff* 3F **67**
Bramford. *Suff* 1E **54**
Bramhall. *G Man* 2C **84**
Bramham. *W Yor* 5G **99**
Bramhope. *W Yor* 5E **99**
Bramley. *Hants* 1E **25**
Bramley. *S Yor* 1B **86**
Bramley. *Surr* 1B **26**
Bramley. *W Yor* 1C **92**
Bramley Green. *Hants* 1E **25**
Bramley Head. *N Yor* 4D **98**
Bramley Vale. *Derbs* 4B **86**
Bramling. *Kent* 5G **41**
Brampford Speke. *Devn* 3C **12**
Brampton. *Cambs* 3B **64**
Brampton. *Cumb* 2H **103** (nr. Appleby)
Brampton. *Cumb* 3G **113** (nr. Carlisle)
Brampton. *Linc* 3F **87**
Brampton. *Norf* 3E **78**
Brampton. *S Yor* 4E **93**
Brampton. *Suff* 2G **67**
Brampton Abbotts. *Here* 3B **48**
Brampton Ash. *Nptn* 2E **63**
Brampton Bryan. *Here* 3F **59**
Brampton en le Morthen. *S Yor* 2B **86**

Bramshall. *Staf* 2E 73
Bramshaw. *Hants* 1A 16
Bramshill. *Hants* 5F 37
Bramshott. *Hants* 3G 25
Branault. *High* 2G 139
Brancaster. *Norf* 1G 77
Brancaster Staithe. *Norf* 1G 77
Brancepeth. *Dur* 1F 105
Branch End. *Nmbd* 3D 114
Branchill. *Mor* 3E 159
Brand End. *Linc* 1C 76
Branderburgh. *Mor* 1G 159
Brandesburton. *E Yor* 5F 101
Brandeston. *Suff* 4E 67
Brand Green. *Glos* 3C 48
Brandhill. *Shrp* 3G 59
Brandis Corner. *Devn* 2E 11
Brandish Street. *Som* 2C 20
Brandiston. *Norf* 3D 78
Brandon. *Dur* 1F 105
Brandon. *Linc* 1G 75
Brandon. *Nmbd* 3E 121
Brandon. *Suff* 2G 65
Brandon. *Warw* 3B 62
Brandon Bank. *Cambs* 2F 65
Brandon Creek. *Norf* 1F 65
Brandon Parva. *Norf* 5C 78
Brandsby. *N Yor* 2H 99
Brandy Wharf. *Linc* 1H 87
Brane. *Corn* 4B 4
Bran End. *Essx* 3G 53
Branksome. *Pool* 3F 15
Bransbury. *Hants* 2C 24
Bransby. *Linc* 3G 87
Branscombe. *Devn* 4E 13
Bransford. *Worc* 5B 60
Bransgore. *Hants* 3G 15
Bransholme. *Hull* 1D 94
Bransley. *Shrp* 3A 60
Branston. *Leics* 3F 75
Branston. *Linc* 4H 87
Branston. *Staf* 3G 73
Branston Booths. *Linc* 4H 87
Branstone. *IOW* 4D 16
Bransty. *Cumb* 3A 102
Brant Broughton. *Linc* 5G 87
Brantham. *Suff* 2E 54
Branthwaite. *Cumb* 1D 102
(nr. Caldbeck)
Branthwaite. *Cumb* 2B 102
(nr. Workington)
Brantingham. *E Yor* 2C 94
Branton. *Nmbd* 3E 121
Branton. *S Yor* 4G 93
Branton Green. *N Yor* 3G 99
Branxholme. *Bord* 3G 119
Branxton. *Nmbd* 1C 120
Brassington. *Derbs* 5G 85
Brasted. *Kent* 5F 39
Brasted Chart. *Kent* 5F 39
Bratch, The. *Staf* 1C 60
Brathens. *Abers* 4D 152
Bratoft. *Linc* 4D 88
Brattleby. *Linc* 2G 87
Bratton. *Som* 2C 20
Bratton. *Telf* 4A 72
Bratton. *Wilts* 1E 23
Bratton Clovelly. *Devn* 3E 11
Bratton Fleming. *Devn* 3G 19
Bratton Seymour. *Som* 4B 22
Braughing. *Herts* 3D 53
Braulen Lodge. *High* 5E 157
Braunston. *Nptn* 4C 62
Braunstone Town. *Leic* 5C 74
Braunston-in-Rutland. *Rut* 5F 75
Braunton. *Devn* 3E 19
Brawby. *N Yor* 2B 100
Brawl. *High* 2A 168
Brawlbin. *High* 3C 168
Bray. *Wind* 3A 38
Braybrooke. *Nptn* 2E 63
Brayford. *Devn* 3G 19
Bray Shop. *Corn* 5D 10
Braystones. *Cumb* 4B 102
Brayton. *N Yor* 1G 93
Bray Wick. *Wind* 4G 37
Brazacott. *Corn* 3C 10
Brea. *Corn* 4A 6
Breach. *W Sus* 2F 17
Breachwood Green. *Herts* 3B 52
Breacleit. *W Isl* 4D 171
Breaden Heath. *Shrp* 2G 71
Breadsall. *Derbs* 1A 74
Breadstone. *Glos* 5C 48
Breage. *Corn* 4D 4
Breakachy. *High* 4G 157
Bream. *Glos* 5B 48
Breamore. *Hants* 1G 15
Bream's Meend. *Glos* 5B 48
Brean. *Som* 1F 21
Breanais. *W Isl* 5B 171
Brearton. *N Yor* 3F 99
Breascleit. *W Isl* 4E 171
Breaston. *Derbs* 2B 74
Brechfa. *Carm* 2F 45
Brechin. *Ang* 3F 145
Breckles. *Norf* 1B 66
Brecon. *Powy* 3D 46
Bredbury. *G Man* 1D 84
Brede. *E Sus* 4C 28
Bredenbury. *Here* 5A 60
Breden's Norton. *Worc* 2E 49
Bredfield. *Suff* 5E 67
Bredgar. *Kent* 4C 40
Bredhurst. *Kent* 4B 40
Bredicot. *Worc* 5D 60
Bredon. *Worc* 2E 49
Bredwardine. *Here* 1G 47
Breedon on the Hill. *Leics* 3B 74
Breibhig. *W Isl* 9B 170
(on Barra)
Breibhig. *W Isl* 4G 171
(on Isle of Lewis)
Breich. *W Lot* 3C 128
Breightmet. *G Man* 3F 91
Breighton. *E Yor* 1H 93
Breinton. *Here* 2H 47
Breinton Common. *Here* 2H 47
Breiwick. *Shet* 7F 173
Brelston Green. *Here* 3A 48
Bremhill. *Wilts* 4E 35
Brenachie. *High* 1B 158
Brenchley. *Kent* 1A 28
Brendon. *Devn* 2A 20
Brent Cross. *G Lon* 2D 38
Brent Eleigh. *Suff* 1C 54
Brentford. *G Lon* 3C 38
Brentingby. *Leics* 4E 75
Brent Knoll. *Som* 1G 21
Brent Pelham. *Herts* 2E 53
Brentwood. *Essx* 1H 39
Brenzett. *Kent* 3E 28
Brereton. *Staf* 4E 73
Brereton Cross. *Staf* 4E 73
Brereton Green. *Ches* 4B 84
Brereton Heath. *Ches* 4C 84
Bressingham. *Norf* 2C 66
Bretby. *Derbs* 3G 73
Bretford. *Warw* 3B 62
Bretforton. *Worc* 1F 49
Bretherdale Head. *Cumb* 4G 103
Bretherton. *Lanc* 2C 90
Brettenham. *Norf* 2B 66
Brettenham. *Suff* 5B 66
Bretton. *Flin* 4F 83
Bretton. *Pet* 5A 76
Brewer Street. *Surr* 5E 39
Brewlands Bridge. *Ang* 2A 144
Brewood. *Staf* 5C 72
Briantspuddle. *Dors* 3D 14
Bricket Wood. *Herts* 5B 52
Bricklehampton. *Worc* 1E 49
Bride. *IOM* 1D 108
Bridekirk. *Cumb* 1C 102
Bridell. *Pemb* 1B 44
Bridestowe. *Devn* 4F 11
Brideswell. *Abers* 5C 160
Bridford. *Devn* 4B 12
Bridfordmills. *Devn* 4B 12
Bridge. *Corn* 4A 6
Bridge. *Kent* 5F 41
Bridge End. *Beds* 5H 63
Bridge End. *Cumb* 5D 102
Bridge End. *Linc* 2A 76
Bridge End. *Shet* 8E 173
Bridgefoot. *Ang* 5C 144
Bridgefoot. *Cumb* 2B 102
Bridge Green. *Essx* 2E 53
Bridgehampton. *Som* 4A 22
Bridge Hewick. *N Yor* 2F 99
Bridgehill. *Dur* 4D 115
Bridgemary. *Hants* 2D 16
Bridgemere. *Ches* 1B 72
Bridgemont. *Derbs* 2E 85
Bridgend. *Abers* 5C 160
(nr. Huntly)
Bridgend. *Abers* 5H 161
(nr. Peterhead)
Bridgend. *Ang* 2E 145
(nr. Brechin)
Bridgend. *Ang* 4C 144
(nr. Kirriemuir)
Bridgend. *Arg* 4F 133
(nr. Lochgilphead)
Bridgend. *Arg* 3B 124
(on Islay)
Bridgend. *B'end* 3C 32
Bridgend. *Cumb* 3F 103
Bridgend. *Devn* 4B 8
Bridgend. *Fife* 2F 137
Bridgend. *High* 3F 157
Bridgend. *Mor* 5A 160
Bridgend. *Per* 1D 136
Bridgend. *W Lot* 2D 128
Bridgend of Lintrathen. *Ang* 3B 144
Bridgeness. *Falk* 1D 128
Bridge of Alford. *Abers* 2C 152
Bridge of Allan. *Stir* 4G 135
Bridge of Avon. *Mor* 5F 159
Bridge of Awe. *Arg* 1H 133
Bridge of Balgie. *Per* 4C 142
Bridge of Brown. *High* 1F 151
Bridge of Cally. *Per* 3A 144
Bridge of Canny. *Abers* 4D 152
Bridge of Dee. *Dum* 3E 111
Bridge of Don. *Aber* 2G 153
Bridge of Dun. *Ang* 3F 145
Bridge of Dye. *Abers* 5D 152
Bridge of Earn. *Per* 2D 136
Bridge of Ericht. *Per* 3C 142
Bridge of Feugh. *Abers* 4E 152
Bridge of Forss. *High* 2C 168
Bridge of Gairn. *Abers* 4A 152
Bridge of Gaur. *Per* 3C 142
Bridge of Muchalls. *Abers* 4F 153
Bridge of Oich. *High* 3F 149
Bridge of Orchy. *Arg* 5H 141
Bridge of Walls. *Shet* 6D 173
Bridge of Weir. *Ren* 3E 127
Bridge Reeve. *Devn* 1G 11
Bridgerule. *Devn* 2C 10
Bridge Sollers. *Here* 1H 47
Bridge Street. *Suff* 1B 54
Bridgetown. *Devn* 2E 9
Bridgetown. *Som* 3C 20
Bridge Town. *Warw* 5G 61
Bridge Trafford. *Ches* 3G 83
Bridgeyate. *S Glo* 4B 34
Bridgham. *Norf* 2B 66
Bridgnorth. *Shrp* 1B 60
Bridgtown. *Staf* 5D 73
Bridgwater. *Som* 3G 21
Bridlington. *E Yor* 3F 101
Bridport. *Dors* 3H 13
Bridstow. *Here* 3A 48
Brierfield. *Lanc* 1G 91
Brierley. *Glos* 4B 48
Brierley. *Here* 5G 59
Brierley. *S Yor* 3E 93
Brierley Hill. *W Mid* 2D 60
Brierton. *Hart* 1B 106
Briestfield. *W Yor* 3C 92
Brigg. *N Lin* 4D 94
Briggate. *Norf* 3F 79
Briggswath. *N Yor* 4F 107
Brigham. *Cumb* 1B 102
Brigham. *E Yor* 4E 101
Brighouse. *W Yor* 2B 92
Brighstone. *IOW* 4C 16
Brightgate. *Derbs* 5G 85
Brighthampton. *Oxon* 5B 50
Brightholmlee. *S Yor* 1G 85
Brightley. *Devn* 3G 11
Brightling. *E Sus* 3A 28
Brightlingsea. *Essx* 4D 54
Brighton. *Brig* 5E 27
Brighton. *Corn* 3D 6
Brighton Hill. *Hants* 2E 24
Brightons. *Falk* 2C 128
Brightwalton. *W Ber* 4C 36
Brightwalton Green. *W Ber* 4C 36
Brightwell. *Suff* 1F 55
Brightwell Baldwin. *Oxon* 2E 37
Brightwell-cum-Sotwell.
Oxon 2D 36
Brigmerston. *Wilts* 2G 23
Brignall. *Dur* 3D 104
Brig o'Turk. *Stir* 3E 135
Brigsley. *NE Lin* 4F 95
Brigsteer. *Cumb* 1D 97
Brigstock. *Nptn* 2G 63
Brill. *Buck* 4E 51
Brill. *Corn* 4E 5
Brilley. *Here* 1F 47
Brimaston. *Pemb* 2D 42
Brimfield. *Here* 4H 59
Brimington. *Derbs* 3B 86
Brimley. *Devn* 5B 12
Brimpsfield. *Glos* 4E 49
Brimpton. *W Ber* 5D 36
Brims. *Orkn* 9B 172
Brimscombe. *Glos* 5D 48
Brimstage. *Mers* 2F 83
Brincliffe. *S Yor* 2H 85
Brind. *E Yor* 1H 93
Brindle. *Lanc* 2E 90
Brindley Ford. *Stoke* 5C 84
Brineton. *Staf* 4C 72
Bringhurst. *Leics* 1F 63
Brington. *Cambs* 3H 63
Brinian. *Orkn* 5D 172
Briningham. *Norf* 2C 78
Brinkhill. *Linc* 3C 88
Brinkley. *Cambs* 5F 65
Brinklow. *Warw* 3B 62
Brinkworth. *Wilts* 3F 35
Brinscall. *Lanc* 2E 91
Brinscombe. *Som* 1H 21
Brinsley. *Notts* 1B 74
Brinsty Common. *Here* 5A 60
Brinsworth. *S Yor* 2B 86
Brinton. *Norf* 2C 78
Brisco. *Cumb* 4F 113
Brisley. *Norf* 3B 78
Brislington. *Bris* 4B 34
Brissenden Green. *Kent* 2D 28
Bristol. *Bris* 4A 34
Bristol International Airport.
N Som 5A 34
Briston. *Norf* 2C 78
Britannia. *Lanc* 2G 91
Britford. *Wilts* 4G 23
Brithdir. *Cphy* 5E 47
Brithdir. *Cdgn* 1D 44
Brithdir. *Gwyn* 4G 69
Briton Ferry. *Neat* 3G 31
Britwell Salome. *Oxon* 2E 37
Brixham. *Torb* 3F 9
Brixton. *Devn* 3B 8
Brixton. *G Lon* 3E 39
Brixton Deverill. *Wilts* 3D 22
Brixworth. *Nptn* 3E 63
Brize Norton. *Oxon* 5B 50
Brize Norton Airport. *Oxon* 5A 50
Broad Alley. *Worc* 4C 60
Broad Blunsdon. *Swin* 2G 35
Broadbottom. *G Man* 1D 85
Broadbridge. *W Sus* 2G 17
Broadbridge Heath. *W Sus* 2C 26
Broad Campden. *Glos* 2G 49
Broad Chalke. *Wilts* 4F 23
Broadclyst. *Devn* 3C 12
Broadfield. *Inv* 2E 127
Broadfield. *Pemb* 4F 43
Broadfield. *W Sus* 2D 26
Broadford. *High* 1E 147
Broadford Bridge. *W Sus* 3B 26
Broad Green. *Beds* 1H 51
Broad Green. *Cambs* 5F 65
Broad Green. *Worc* 3D 61
(nr. Bromsgrove)
Broad Green. *Worc* 5B 60
(nr. Worcester)
Broadhaven. *High* 3F 169
Broad Haven. *Pemb* 3C 42
Broadheath. *G Man* 2B 84
Broad Heath. *Staf* 3C 72
Broadheath. *Worc* 4A 60
Broadhembury. *Devn* 2E 12
Broadhempston. *Devn* 2E 9
Broad Hill. *Cambs* 3E 65
Broad Hinton. *Wilts* 4G 35
Broadholm. *Derbs* 1A 74
Broadholme. *Linc* 3F 87
Broadlay. *Carm* 5D 44
Broad Laying. *Hants* 5C 36
Broadley. *Lanc* 3G 91
Broadley. *Mor* 2A 160
Broadley Common. *Essx* 5E 53
Broad Marston. *Worc* 1G 49
Broadmayne. *Dors* 4C 14
Broadmere. *Hants* 2E 24
Broadmoor. *Pemb* 4E 43
Broad Oak. *Carm* 3F 45
Broad Oak. *Cumb* 5C 102
Broad Oak. *Devn* 3D 12
Broadoak. *Dors* 3H 13
Broad Oak. *Dors* 1C 14
Broad Oak. *E Sus* 4C 28
(nr. Hastings)
Broad Oak. *E Sus* 3H 27
(nr. Heathfield)
Broadoak. *Glos* 4B 48
Broadoak. *Hants* 1C 16
Broad Oak. *Here* 3H 47
Broad Oak. *Kent* 4F 41
Broadrashes. *Mor* 3B 160
Broadsea. *Abers* 2G 161
Broad's Green. *Essx* 4G 53
Broadshard. *Som* 1H 13
Broadstairs. *Kent* 4H 41
Broadstone. *Pool* 3F 15
Broadstone. *Shrp* 2H 59
Broad Street. *E Sus* 4C 28
Broad Street. *Kent* 1F 29
(nr. Ashford)
Broad Street. *Kent* 5C 40
(nr. Maidstone)
Broad Street Green. *Essx* 5B 54
Broad, The. *Here* 4G 59
Broad Town. *Wilts* 4F 35
Broadwas. *Worc* 5B 60
Broadwath. *Cumb* 4F 113
Broadway. *Carm* 5D 45
(nr. Kidwelly)
Broadway. *Carm* 3G 43
(nr. Laugharne)
Broadway. *Pemb* 3C 42
Broadway. *Som* 1G 13
Broadway. *Suff* 3F 67
Broadway. *Worc* 2G 49
Broadwell. *Glos* 4A 48
(nr. Cinderford)
Broadwell. *Glos* 3H 49
(nr. Stow-on-the-Wold)
Broadwell. *Oxon* 5A 50
Broadwell. *Warw* 4B 62
Broadwell House. *Nmbd* 4C 114
Broadwey. *Dors* 4B 14
Broadwindsor. *Dors* 2H 13

Broadwoodkelly. *Devn* 2G **11**
Broadwoodwidger. *Devn* 4E **11**
Broallan. *High* 4G **157**
Brobury. *Here* 1G **47**
Brochel. *High* 4E **155**
Brockamin. *Worc* 5B **60**
Brockbridge. *Hants* 1E **16**
Brockdish. *Norf* 3E **66**
Brockencote. *Worc* 3C **60**
Brockenhurst. *Hants* 2A **16**
Brocketsbrae. *S Lan* 1H **117**
Brockford Street. *Suff* 4D **66**
Brockhall. *Nptn* 4D **62**
Brockham. *Surr* 1C **26**
Brockhampton. *Glos* 3E **49**
(nr. Bishop's Cleeve)
Brockhampton. *Glos* 3F **49**
(nr. Sevenhampton)
Brockhampton. *Here* 2A **48**
Brockhill. *Bord* 2F **119**
Brockholes. *W Yor* 3B **92**
Brockhouse. *S Yor* 2C **86**
Brockhurst. *Hants* 2D **16**
Brocklesby. *Linc* 3E **95**
Brockley. *N Som* 5H **33**
Brockley. *Suff* 3H **65**
Brockley Green. *Suff* 1H **53**
(nr. Bury St Edmunds)
Brockley Green. *Suff* 5H **65**
(nr. Haverhill)
Brockleymoor. *Cumb* 1F **103**
Brockmoor. *W Mid* 2C **60**
Brockton. *Shrp* 2F **59**
(nr. Bishop's Castle)
Brockton. *Shrp* 5B **72**
(nr. Madeley)
Brockton. *Shrp* 1H **59**
(nr. Much Wenlock)
Brockton. *Shrp* 5F **71**
(nr. Pontesbury)
Brockton. *Staf* 2C **72**
Brockton. *Telf* 4B **72**
Brockweir. *Glos* 5A **48**
Brockworth. *Glos* 4D **49**
Brocton. *Staf* 4D **72**
Brodick. *N Ayr* 2E **123**
Brodie. *Mor* 3D **159**
Brodiesord. *Abers* 3C **160**
Brodsworth. *S Yor* 4F **93**
Brogaig. *High* 2D **154**
Brogborough. *Beds* 2H **51**
Brokenborough. *Wilts* 3E **35**
Broken Cross. *Ches* 3C **84**
Bromborough. *Mers* 2F **83**
Bromdon. *Shrp* 2A **60**
Brome. *Suff* 3D **66**
Brome Street. *Suff* 3D **66**
Bromeswell. *Suff* 5F **67**
Bromfield. *Cumb* 5C **112**
Bromfield. *Shrp* 3G **59**
Bromford. *W Mid* 1F **61**
Bromham. *Beds* 5H **63**
Bromham. *Wilts* 5E **35**
Bromley. *G Lon* 4F **39**
Bromley. *Herts* 3E **53**
Bromley. *Shrp* 1B **60**
Bromley Cross. *G Man* 3F **91**
Bromley Green. *Kent* 2D **28**
Bromley Wood. *Staf* 3F **73**
Brompton. *Medw* 4B **40**
Brompton. *N Yor* 5A **106**
(nr. Northallerton)
Brompton. *N Yor* 1D **100**
(nr. Scarborough)
Brompton. *Shrp* 5H **71**
Brompton-on-Swale. *N Yor* 5F **105**
Brompton Ralph. *Som* 3D **20**
Brompton Regis. *Som* 3C **20**
Bromsash. *Here* 3B **48**
Bromsberrow. *Glos* 2C **48**
Bromsberrow Heath. *Glos* 2C **48**
Bromsgrove. *Worc* 3D **60**
Bromstead Heath. *Staf* 4B **72**
Bromyard. *Here* 5A **60**
Bromyard Downs. *Here* 5A **60**
Bronaber. *Gwyn* 2G **69**
Broncroft. *Shrp* 2H **59**
Brongest. *Cdgn* 1D **44**
Brongwyn. *Cdgn* 1C **44**
Bronington. *Wrex* 2G **71**
Bronllys. *Powy* 2E **47**
Bronnant. *Cdgn* 4F **57**
Bronwydd Arms. *Carm* 3E **45**
Bronydd. *Powy* 1F **47**
Bronygarth. *Shrp* 2E **71**
Brook. *Carm* 4G **43**
Brook. *Devn* 5E **11**
Brook. *Hants* 1A **16**
(nr. Cadnam)
Brook. *Hants* 4B **24**
(nr. Romsey)
Brook. *IOW* 4B **16**
Brook. *Kent* 1E **29**
Brook. *Surr* 1B **26**
(nr. Guildford)
Brook. *Surr* 2A **26**
(nr. Haslemere)
Brooke. *Norf* 1E **67**
Brooke. *Rut* 5F **75**
Brookend. *Glos* 5B **48**
Brook End. *Worc* 1D **48**
Brookfield. *Lanc* 1D **90**
Brookfield. *Ren* 3F **127**
Brookhouse. *Lanc* 3E **97**
Brookhouse Green. *Ches* 4C **84**
Brookhouses. *Staf* 1D **73**
Brookhurst. *Mers* 2F **83**
Brookland. *Kent* 3D **28**
Brooklands. *G Man* 1B **84**
Brooklands. *Shrp* 1H **71**
Brookmans Park. *Herts* 5C **52**
Brooks. *Powy* 1D **58**
Brooksby. *Leics* 4D **74**
Brooks Green. *W Sus* 3C **26**
Brook Street. *Essx* 1G **39**
Brook Street. *Kent* 2D **28**
Brook Street. *W Sus* 3E **27**
Brookthorpe. *Glos* 4D **48**
Brookville. *Norf* 1G **65**
Brookwood. *Surr* 5A **38**
Broom. *Beds* 1B **52**
Broom. *Fife* 3F **137**
Broom. *Warw* 5E **61**
Broome. *Norf* 1F **67**
Broome. *Shrp* 1H **59**
(nr. Cardington)
Broome. *Shrp* 2G **59**
(nr. Craven Arms)
Broome. *Worc* 3D **60**
Broomedge. *Warr* 2B **84**
Broomend. *Abers* 2E **153**
Broome Park. *Nmbd* 3F **121**
Broomer's Corner. *W Sus* 3C **26**
Broomfield. *Abers* 5G **161**
Broomfield. *Essx* 4H **53**
Broomfield. *Kent* 4F **41**
(nr. Herne Bay)
Broomfield. *Kent* 5C **40**
(nr. Maidstone)
Broomfield. *Som* 3F **21**
Broomfleet. *E Yor* 2B **94**
Broom Green. *Norf* 3B **78**
Broomhall. *Wind* 4A **38**
Broomhaugh. *Nmbd* 3D **114**
Broomhill. *Bris* 4B **34**
Broom Hill. *Dors* 2F **15**
Broomhill. *High* 1D **151**
(nr. Grantown-on-Spey)
Broomhill. *High* 1B **158**
(nr. Invergordon)
Broomhill. *Norf* 5F **77**
Broom Hill. *S Yor* 4E **93**
Broom Hill. *Worc* 3D **60**
Broomhillbank. *Dum* 5D **118**
Broomholm. *Norf* 2F **79**
Broomlands. *Dum* 4C **118**
Broomley. *Nmbd* 3D **114**
Broom of Moy. *Mor* 3E **159**
Broompark. *Dur* 5F **115**
Broom's Green. *Glos* 2C **48**
Brora. *High* 3G **165**
Broseley. *Shrp* 5A **72**
Brotherhouse Bar. *Linc* 4B **76**
Brotheridge Green. *Worc* 1D **48**
Brotherlee. *Dur* 1C **104**
Brothertoft. *Linc* 1B **76**
Brotherton. *N Yor* 2E **93**
Brotton. *Red C* 2D **107**
Broubster. *High* 2C **168**
Brough. *Cumb* 3A **104**
Brough. *Derbs* 2F **85**
Brough. *E Yor* 2C **94**
Brough. *High* 1E **169**
Brough. *Notts* 5F **87**
Brough. *Orkn* 9D **172**
Brough. *Shet* 4F **173**
(nr. Booth of Toft)
Brough. *Shet* 5G **173**
(on Whalsay)
Broughall. *Shrp* 1H **71**
Brougham. *Cumb* 2G **103**
Brough Sowerby. *Cumb* 3A **104**
Broughton. *Cambs* 3B **64**
Broughton. *Flin* 4F **83**
Broughton. *Hants* 3B **24**
Broughton. *Lanc* 1D **90**
Broughton. *Mil* 2G **51**
Broughton. *Nptn* 3F **63**
Broughton. *N Lin* 4C **94**
Broughton. *N Yor* 2B **100**
(nr. Malton)
Broughton. *N Yor* 4B **98**
(nr. Skipton)
Broughton. *Oxon* 2C **50**
Broughton. *Bord* 1D **118**
Broughton. *Staf* 2B **72**
Broughton. *V Glam* 4C **32**
Broughton Astley. *Leics* 1C **62**
Broughton Beck. *Cumb* 1B **96**
Broughton Cross. *Cumb* 1B **102**
Broughton Gifford. *Wilts* 5D **35**
Broughton Green. *Worc* 4D **60**
Broughton Hackett. *Worc* 5D **60**
Broughton in Furness. *Cumb* 1B **96**
Broughton Mills. *Cumb* 5D **102**
Broughton Moor. *Cumb* 1B **102**
Broughton Park. *G Man* 4G **91**
Broughton Poggs. *Oxon* 5H **49**
Broughtown. *Orkn* 3F **172**
Broughty Ferry. *D'dee* 5D **144**
Brownber. *Cumb* 4A **104**
Brownbread Street. *E Sus* 4A **28**
Brown Candover. *Hants* 3D **24**
Brown Edge. *Lanc* 3B **90**
Brown Edge. *Staf* 5D **84**
Brownhill. *Bkbn* 1E **91**
Brownhill. *Shrp* 3G **71**
Brownhills. *Shrp* 2A **72**
Brownhills. *W Mid* 5E **73**
Brown Knowl. *Ches* 5G **83**
Brownlow. *Ches* 4C **84**
Brownlow Heath. *Ches* 4C **84**
Brown's Green. *W Mid* 1E **61**
Brownshill. *Glos* 5D **49**
Brownston. *Devn* 3C **8**
Brownstone. *Devn* 2A **12**
Browston Green. *Norf* 5G **79**
Broxa. *N Yor* 5G **107**
Broxbourne. *Herts* 5D **52**
Broxburn. *E Lot* 2C **130**
Broxburn. *W Lot* 2D **129**
Broxholme. *Linc* 3G **87**
Broxted. *Essx* 3F **53**
Broxton. *Ches* 5G **83**
Broxwood. *Here* 5F **59**
Broyle Side. *E Sus* 4F **27**
Bruach Mairi. *W Isl* 4G **171**
Bruairnis. *W Isl* 8C **170**
Bruan. *High* 5F **169**
Bruar Lodge. *Per* 1F **143**
Brucehill. *W Dun* 2E **127**
Brucklay. *Abers* 3G **161**
Bruera. *Ches* 4G **83**
Bruern Abbey. *Oxon* 3A **50**
Bruichladdich. *Arg* 3A **124**
Bruisyard. *Suff* 4F **67**
Bruisyard Street. *Suff* 4F **67**
Brumby. *N Lin* 4B **94**
Brund. *Staf* 4F **85**
Brundall. *Norf* 5F **79**
Brundish. *Norf* 1F **67**
Brundish. *Suff* 4E **67**
Brundish Street. *Suff* 3E **67**
Brunery. *High* 1B **140**
Brunswick Village. *Tyne* 2F **115**
Brunthwaite. *W Yor* 5C **98**
Bruntingthorpe. *Leics* 1D **62**
Brunton. *Fife* 1F **137**
Brunton. *Nmbd* 2G **121**
Brunton. *Wilts* 1H **23**
Brushford. *Devn* 2G **11**
Brushford. *Som* 4C **20**
Brusta. *W Isl* 1E **170**
Bruton. *Som* 3B **22**
Bryanston. *Dors* 2D **15**
Bryant's Bottom. *Buck* 2G **37**
Brydekirk. *Dum* 2C **112**
Brymbo. *Cnwy* 3H **81**
Brymbo. *Wrex* 5E **83**
Brympton D'Evercy. *Som* 1A **14**
Bryn. *Carm* 5F **45**
Bryn. *G Man* 4D **90**
Bryn. *Neat* 2B **32**
Bryn. *Shrp* 2E **59**
Brynamman. *Carm* 4H **45**
Brynberian. *Pemb* 1F **43**
Brynbryddan. *Neat* 2A **32**
Bryncae. *Rhon* 3C **32**
Bryncethin. *B'end* 3C **32**
Bryncir. *Gwyn* 1D **69**
Bryn-coch. *Neat* 3G **31**
Bryncroes. *Gwyn* 2B **68**
Bryncrug. *Gwyn* 5F **69**
Bryn Du. *IOA* 3C **80**
Bryn Eden. *Gwyn* 3G **69**
Bryneglwys. *Den* 1D **70**
Bryn Eglwys. *Gwyn* 4F **81**
Brynford. *Flin* 3D **82**
Bryn Gates. *G Man* 4D **90**
Bryn Golau. *Rhon* 3D **32**
Bryngwran. *IOA* 3C **80**
Bryngwyn. *Mon* 5G **47**
Bryngwyn. *Powy* 1E **47**
Bryn-henllan. *Pemb* 1E **43**
Brynhoffnant. *Cdgn* 5C **56**
Bryn-llwyn. *Flin* 2C **82**
Brynllywarch. *Powy* 2D **58**
Bryn-mawr. *Blae* 4E **47**
Bryn-mawr. *Gwyn* 2B **68**
Brynmenyn. *B'end* 3C **32**
Brynmill. *Swan* 3F **31**
Brynna. *Rhon* 3C **32**
Brynrefail. *Gwyn* 4E **81**
Brynrefail. *IOA* 2D **81**
Brynsadler. *Rhon* 3D **32**
Bryn-Saith Marchog. *Den* 5C **82**
Brynsiencyn. *IOA* 4D **81**
Brynteg. *IOA* 2D **81**
Brynteg. *Wrex* 5F **83**
Brynygwenyn. *Mon* 4G **47**
Bryn-y-maen. *Cnwy* 3H **81**
Buaile nam Bodach. *W Isl* 8C **170**
Bualintur. *High* 1C **146**
Bubbenhall. *Warw* 3A **62**
Bubwith. *E Yor* 1H **93**
Buccleuch. *Bord* 3F **119**
Buchanan Smithy. *Stir* 1F **127**
Buchanhaven. *Abers* 4H **161**
Buchanty. *Per* 1B **136**
Buchany. *Stir* 3G **135**
Buchley. *E Dun* 2G **127**
Buchlyvie. *Stir* 4E **135**
Buckabank. *Cumb* 5E **113**
Buckden. *Cambs* 4A **64**
Buckden. *N Yor* 2B **98**
Buckenham. *Norf* 5F **79**
Buckerell. *Devn* 2E **13**
Buckfast. *Devn* 2D **8**
Buckfastleigh. *Devn* 2D **8**
Buckhaven. *Fife* 4F **137**
Buckholm. *Bord* 1G **119**
Buckholt. *Here* 4A **48**
Buckhorn Weston. *Dors* 4C **22**
Buckhurst Hill. *Essx* 1F **39**
Buckie. *Mor* 2B **160**
Buckingham. *Buck* 2E **51**
Buckland. *Buck* 4G **51**
Buckland. *Devn* 4C **8**
Buckland. *Glos* 2F **49**
Buckland. *Here* 5H **59**
Buckland. *Herts* 2D **52**
Buckland. *Kent* 1H **29**
Buckland. *Oxon* 2B **36**
Buckland. *Surr* 5D **38**
Buckland Brewer. *Devn* 4E **19**
Buckland Common. *Buck* 5H **51**
Buckland Dinham. *Som* 1C **22**
Buckland Filleigh. *Devn* 2E **11**
Buckland in the Moor. *Devn* 5H **11**
Buckland Monachorum. *Devn* 2A **8**
Buckland Newton. *Dors* 2B **14**
Buckland Ripers. *Dors* 4B **14**
Buckland St Mary. *Som* 1F **13**
Buckland-tout-Saints. *Devn* 4D **8**
Bucklebury. *W Ber* 4D **36**
Bucklegate. *Linc* 2C **76**
Buckleigh. *Devn* 4E **19**
Bucklers Hard. *Hants* 3C **16**
Bucklesham. *Suff* 1F **55**
Buckley. *Flin* 4E **83**
Buckley Green. *Warw* 4F **61**
Buckley Hill. *Mers* 1F **83**
Bucklow Hill. *Ches* 2B **84**
Buckminster. *Leics* 3F **75**
Bucknall. *Linc* 4A **88**
Bucknall. *Stoke* 1D **72**
Bucknell. *Oxon* 3D **50**
Bucknell. *Shrp* 3F **59**
Buckpool. *Mor* 2B **160**
Bucksburn. *Aber* 3F **153**
Buck's Cross. *Devn* 4D **18**
Bucks Green. *W Sus* 2B **26**
Buckshaw. *Lanc* 2D **90**
Bucks Hill. *Herts* 5A **52**
Bucks Horn Oak. *Hants* 2G **25**
Buck's Mills. *Devn* 4D **18**
Buckton. *E Yor* 2F **101**
Buckton. *Here* 3F **59**
Buckton. *Nmbd* 1E **121**
Buckton Vale. *G Man* 4H **91**
Buckworth. *Cambs* 3A **64**
Budby. *Notts* 4D **86**
Bude. *Corn* 2C **10**
Budge's Shop. *Corn* 3H **7**
Budlake. *Devn* 2C **12**
Budle. *Nmbd* 1F **121**
Budleigh Salterton. *Devn* 4D **12**
Budock Water. *Corn* 5B **6**
Buerton. *Ches* 1A **72**
Buffler's Holt. *Buck* 2E **51**
Bugbrooke. *Nptn* 5D **62**
Buglawton. *Ches* 4C **84**
Bugle. *Corn* 3E **6**
Bugthorpe. *E Yor* 4B **100**
Buildwas. *Shrp* 5A **72**
Builth Road. *Powy* 5C **58**
Builth Wells. *Powy* 5C **58**
Bulbourne. *Herts* 4H **51**
Bulby. *Linc* 3H **75**
Bulcote. *Notts* 1D **74**
Buldoo. *High* 2B **168**
Bulford. *Wilts* 2G **23**
Bulford Camp. *Wilts* 2G **23**
Bulkeley. *Ches* 5H **83**
Bulkington. *Warw* 2A **62**
Bulkington. *Wilts* 1E **23**
Bulkworthy. *Devn* 1D **11**
Bullamoor. *N Yor* 5A **106**
Bull Bay. *IOA* 1D **80**
Bullbridge. *Derbs* 5A **86**

Bullgill. *Cumb* 1B **102**
Bull Hill. *Hants* 3B **16**
Bullinghope. *Here* 2A **48**
Bull's Green. *Herts* 4C **52**
Bullwood. *Arg* 2C **126**
Bulmer. *Essx* 1B **54**
Bulmer. *N Yor* 3A **100**
Bulmer Tye. *Essx* 2B **54**
Bulphan. *Thur* 2H **39**
Bulverhythe. *E Sus* 5B **28**
Bulwark. *Abers* 4G **161**
Bulwell. *Nott* 1C **74**
Bulwick. *Nptn* 1G **63**
Bumble's Green. *Essx* 5E **53**
Bun Abhainn Eadarra. *W Isl* 7D **171**
Bunacaimb. *High* 5E **147**
Bun a' Mhuillinn. *W Isl* 7C **170**
Bunarkaig. *High* 5D **148**
Bunbury. *Ches* 5H **83**
Bunchrew. *High* 4A **158**
Bundalloch. *High* 1A **148**
Bunessan. *Arg* 1A **132**
Bungay. *Suff* 2F **67**
Bunkegivie. *High* 2H **149**
Bunker's Hill. *Cambs* 5D **76**
Bunkers Hill. *Linc* 5B **88**
Bunker's Hill. *Suff* 5H **79**
Bunloit. *High* 1H **149**
Bunnahabhain. *Arg* 2C **124**
Bunny. *Notts* 3C **74**
Bunoich. *High* 3F **149**
Bunree. *High* 2E **141**
Bunroy. *High* 5E **149**
Buntait. *High* 5F **157**
Buntingford. *Herts* 3D **52**
Buntings Green. *Essx* 2B **54**
Bunwell. *Norf* 1D **66**
Burbage. *Derbs* 3E **85**
Burbage. *Leics* 1B **62**
Burbage. *Wilts* 5H **35**
Burcher. *Here* 4F **59**
Burchett's Green. *Wind* 3G **37**
Burcombe. *Wilts* 3F **23**
Burcot. *Oxon* 2D **36**
Burcote. *Shrp* 1B **60**
Burcott. *Buck* 3G **51**
Burcott. *Som* 2A **22**
Burdale. *N Yor* 3C **100**
Burdrop. *Oxon* 2B **50**
Bures. *Suff* 2C **54**
Burford. *Oxon* 4A **50**
Burford. *Shrp* 4H **59**
Burf, The. *Worc* 4C **60**
Burg. *Arg* 4E **139**
Burgate Great Green. *Suff* 3C **66**
Burgate Little Green. *Suff* 3C **66**
Burgess Hill. *W Sus* 4E **27**
Burgh. *Suff* 5E **67**
Burgh by Sands. *Cumb* 4E **113**
Burgh Castle. *Norf* 5G **79**
Burghclere. *Hants* 5C **36**
Burghead. *Mor* 2F **159**
Burghfield. *W Ber* 5E **37**
Burghfield Common. *W Ber* 5E **37**
Burghfield Hill. *W Ber* 5E **37**
Burgh Heath. *Surr* 5D **38**
Burghill. *Here* 1H **47**
Burgh le Marsh. *Linc* 4E **89**
Burgh Muir. *Abers* 2E **153**
Burgh next Aylsham. *Norf* 3E **78**
Burgh on Bain. *Linc* 2B **88**
Burgh St Margaret. *Norf* 4G **79**
Burgh St Peter. *Norf* 1G **67**
Burghwallis. *S Yor* 3F **93**
Burgie. *Mor* 3E **159**
Burham. *Kent* 4B **40**
Buriton. *Hants* 4F **25**
Burland. *Ches* 5A **84**
Burland. *Shet* 8E **173**
Burlawn. *Corn* 2D **6**
Burleigh. *Brac* 3A **38**
Burleigh. *Glos* 5D **48**
Burlescombe. *Devn* 1D **12**
Burleston. *Dors* 3C **14**
Burlestone. *Devn* 4E **9**
Burley. *Hants* 2H **15**
Burley. *Rut* 4F **75**
Burley. *W Yor* 1C **92**
Burley Gate. *Here* 1A **48**
Burley in Wharfedale. *W Yor* 5D **98**
Burley Street. *Hants* 2H **15**
Burley Woodhead. *W Yor* 5D **98**
Burlingjobb. *Powy* 5E **59**
Burlton. *Shrp* 3G **71**
Burmantofts. *W Yor* 1D **92**
Burmarsh. *Kent* 2F **29**
Burmington. *Warw* 2A **50**
Burn. *N Yor* 2F **93**
Burnage. *G Man* 1C **84**
Burnaston. *Derbs* 2G **73**
Burnbanks. *Cumb* 3G **103**
Burnby. *E Yor* 5C **100**
Burncross. *S Yor* 1H **85**
Burneside. *Cumb* 5G **103**
Burness. *Orkn* 3F **172**
Burneston. *N Yor* 1F **99**
Burnett. *Bath* 5B **34**
Burnfoot. *E Ayr* 4D **116**
Burnfoot. *Per* 3B **136**
Burnfoot. *Bord* 3H **119**
(nr. Hawick)
Burnfoot. *Bord* 3G **119**
(nr. Roberton)
Burngreave. *S Yor* 2A **86**
Burnham. *Buck* 2A **38**
Burnham. *N Lin* 3D **94**
Burnham Deepdale. *Norf* 1H **77**
Burnham Green. *Herts* 4C **52**
Burnham Market. *Norf* 1H **77**
Burnham Norton. *Norf* 1H **77**
Burnham-on-Crouch. *Essx* 1D **40**
Burnham-on-Sea. *Som* 2G **21**
Burnham Overy Staithe. *Norf* 1H **77**
Burnham Overy Town. *Norf* 1H **77**
Burnham Thorpe. *Norf* 1A **78**
Burnhaven. *Abers* 4H **161**
Burnhead. *Dum* 5A **118**
Burnhervie. *Abers* 2E **153**
Burnhill Green. *Staf* 5B **72**
Burnhope. *Dur* 5E **115**
Burnhouse. *N Ayr* 4E **127**
Burniston. *N Yor* 5H **107**
Burnlee. *W Yor* 4B **92**
Burnley. *Lanc* 1G **91**
Burnleydam. *Wrex* 1A **72**
Burnmouth. *Bord* 3F **131**
Burn Naze. *Lanc* 5C **96**
Burn of Cambus. *Stir* 3G **135**
Burnopfield. *Dur* 4E **115**
Burnsall. *N Yor* 3C **98**
Burnside. *Ang* 3E **145**
Burnside. *E Ayr* 3E **117**
Burnside. *Per* 3D **136**
Burnside. *Shet* 4D **173**
Burnside. *S Lan* 4H **127**
Burnside. *W Lot* 2D **129**
(nr. Broxburn)
Burnside. *W Lot* 2D **128**
(nr. Winchburgh)
Burntcommon. *Surr* 5B **38**
Burntheath. *Derbs* 2G **73**
Burnt Heath. *Essx* 3D **54**
Burnt Hill. *W Ber* 4D **36**
Burnt Houses. *Dur* 2E **105**
Burntisland. *Fife* 1F **129**
Burnt Oak. *G Lon* 1D **38**
Burnton. *E Ayr* 4D **117**
Burntstalk. *Norf* 2G **77**
Burntwood. *Staf* 5E **73**
Burntwood Green. *Staf* 5E **73**
Burnt Yates. *N Yor* 3E **99**
Burnwynd. *Edin* 3E **129**
Burpham. *Surr* 5B **38**
Burpham. *W Sus* 5B **26**
Burradon. *Nmbd* 4D **121**
Burradon. *Tyne* 2F **115**
Burrafirth. *Shet* 1H **173**
Burras. *Corn* 5A **6**
Burraton. *Corn* 3A **8**
Burravoe. *Shet* 3E **173**
Burray Village. *Orkn* 8D **172**
Burrells. *Cumb* 3H **103**
Burrelton. *Per* 5A **144**
Burridge. *Devn* 2G **13**
Burridge. *Hants* 1D **16**
Burrigill. *High* 5E **169**
Burrill. *N Yor* 1E **99**
Burringham. *N Lin* 4B **94**
Burrington. *Devn* 1G **11**
Burrington. *Here* 3G **59**
Burrington. *N Som* 1H **21**
Burrough End. *Cambs* 5F **65**
Burrough Green. *Cambs* 5F **65**
Burrough on the Hill. *Leics* 4E **75**
Burrow. *Devn* 4D **12**
Burrow. *Som* 2C **20**
Burrowbridge. *Som* 4G **21**
Burrowhill. *Surr* 4A **38**
Burry. *Swan* 3D **30**
Burry Green. *Swan* 3D **30**
Burry Port. *Carm* 5E **45**
Burscough. *Lanc* 3C **90**
Burscough Bridge. *Lanc* 3C **90**
Bursea. *E Yor* 1B **94**
Burshill. *E Yor* 5E **101**
Bursledon. *Hants* 2C **16**
Burslem. *Stoke* 1C **72**
Burstall. *Suff* 1D **54**
Burstock. *Dors* 2H **13**
Burston. *Devn* 2H **11**
Burston. *Norf* 2D **66**
Burston. *Staf* 2D **72**
Burstow. *Surr* 1E **27**
Burstwick. *E Yor* 2F **95**
Burtersett. *N Yor* 1A **98**
Burtholme. *Cumb* 3G **113**
Burthorpe. *Suff* 4G **65**
Burthwaite. *Cumb* 5F **113**
Burtle. *Som* 2H **21**
Burtoft. *Linc* 2B **76**
Burton. *Ches* 4H **83**
(nr. Kelsall)
Burton. *Ches* 3F **83**
(nr. Neston)
Burton. *Dors* 3G **15**
(nr. Christchurch)
Burton. *Dors* 3B **14**
(nr. Dorchester)
Burton. *Linc* 3G **87**
Burton. *Nmbd* 1F **121**
Burton. *Pemb* 4D **43**
Burton. *Som* 2E **21**
Burton. *Wilts* 4D **34**
(nr. Chippenham)
Burton. *Wilts* 3D **22**
(nr. Warminster)
Burton. *Wrex* 5F **83**
Burton Agnes. *E Yor* 3F **101**
Burton Bradstock. *Dors* 4H **13**
Burton Coggles. *Linc* 3G **75**
Burton Constable. *E Yor* 1E **95**
Burton Corner. *Linc* 1C **76**
Burton End. *Cambs* 1G **53**
Burton End. *Essx* 3F **53**
Burton Fleming. *E Yor* 2E **101**
Burton Green. *W Mid* 3G **61**
Burton Green. *Wrex* 5F **83**
Burton Hastings. *Warw* 2B **62**
Burton-in-Kendal. *Cumb* 2E **97**
Burton in Lonsdale. *N Yor* 2F **97**
Burton Joyce. *Notts* 1D **74**
Burton Latimer. *Nptn* 3G **63**
Burton Lazars. *Leics* 4E **75**
Burton Leonard. *N Yor* 3F **99**
Burton on the Wolds. *Leics* 3C **74**
Burton Overy. *Leics* 1D **62**
Burton Pedwardine. *Linc* 1A **76**
Burton Pidsea. *E Yor* 1F **95**
Burton Salmon. *N Yor* 2E **93**
Burton's Green. *Essx* 3B **54**
Burton Stather. *N Lin* 3B **94**
Burton upon Stather. *N Lin* 3B **94**
Burton upon Trent. *Staf* 3G **73**
Burton Wolds. *Leics* 3D **74**
Burtonwood. *Warr* 1H **83**
Burwardsley. *Ches* 5H **83**
Burwarton. *Shrp* 2A **60**
Burwash. *E Sus* 3A **28**
Burwash Common. *E Sus* 3H **27**
Burwash Weald. *E Sus* 3A **28**
Burwell. *Cambs* 4E **65**
Burwell. *Linc* 3C **88**
Burwen. *IOA* 1D **80**
Burwick. *Orkn* 9D **172**
Bury. *Cambs* 2B **64**
Bury. *G Man* 3G **91**
Bury. *Som* 4C **20**
Bury. *W Sus* 4B **26**
Bury End. *Worc* 2F **49**
Bury Green. *Herts* 3E **53**
Bury Hill. *S Glo* 3C **34**
Bury St Edmunds. *Suff* 4A **66**
Burythorpe. *N Yor* 3B **100**
Busbridge. *Surr* 1A **26**
Busby. *E Ren* 4G **127**
Busby. *Per* 1C **136**
Buscot. *Oxon* 2H **35**
Bush. *Corn* 2C **10**
Bush Bank. *Here* 5G **59**
Bushbury. *W Mid* 5D **72**
Bushby. *Leics* 5D **74**
Bushey. *Dors* 4E **15**
Bushey. *Herts* 1C **38**
Bushey Heath. *Herts* 1C **38**
Bush Green. *Norf* 1C **66**
(nr. Attleborough)
Bush Green. *Norf* 2E **66**
(nr. Harleston)
Bush Green. *Suff* 5B **66**
Bushley. *Worc* 2D **48**
Bushley Green. *Worc* 2D **48**
Bushmead. *Beds* 4A **64**
Bushmoor. *Shrp* 2G **59**
Bushton. *Wilts* 4F **35**
Bushy Common. *Norf* 4B **78**
Busk. *Cumb* 5H **113**
Buslingthorpe. *Linc* 2H **87**
Bussage. *Glos* 5D **49**
Bussex. *Som* 3G **21**
Busta. *Shet* 5E **173**
Bustard Green. *Essx* 3G **53**
Butcher's Cross. *E Sus* 3G **27**
Butcombe. *N Som* 5A **34**
Bute Town. *Cphy* 5E **46**
Butleigh. *Som* 3A **22**
Butleigh Wootton. *Som* 3A **22**
Butlers Marston. *Warw* 5H **61**
Butley. *Suff* 5F **67**
Butley High Corner. *Suff* 1G **55**
Butterburn. *Cumb* 2H **113**
Buttercrambe. *N Yor* 4B **100**
Butterknowle. *Dur* 2E **105**
Butterleigh. *Devn* 2C **12**
Buttermere. *Cumb* 3C **102**
Buttermere. *Wilts* 5B **36**
Buttershaw. *W Yor* 2B **92**
Butterstone. *Per* 4H **143**
Butterton. *Staf* 5E **85**
(nr. Leek)
Butterton. *Staf* 1C **72**
(nr. Stoke-on-Trent)
Butterwick. *Dur* 2A **106**
Butterwick. *Linc* 1C **76**
Butterwick. *N Yor* 2B **100**
(nr. Malton)
Butterwick. *N Yor* 2D **101**
(nr. Weaverthorpe)
Butteryhaugh. *Nmbd* 5A **120**
Butt Green. *Ches* 5A **84**
Buttington. *Powy* 5E **71**
Buttonbridge. *Shrp* 3B **60**
Buttonoak. *Shrp* 3B **60**
Buttsash. *Hants* 2C **16**
Butt's Green. *Essx* 5A **54**
Butt Yeats. *Lanc* 3E **97**
Buxhall. *Suff* 5C **66**
Buxted. *E Sus* 3F **27**
Buxton. *Derbs* 3E **85**
Buxton. *Norf* 3E **79**
Buxworth. *Derbs* 2E **85**
Bwcle. *Flin* 4E **83**
Bwlch. *Powy* 3E **47**
Bwlchderwin. *Gwyn* 1D **68**
Bwlchgwyn. *Wrex* 5E **83**
Bwlch-Llan. *Cdgn* 5E **57**
Bwlchnewydd. *Carm* 3D **44**
Bwlchtocyn. *Gwyn* 3C **68**
Bwlch-y-cibau. *Powy* 4D **70**
Bwlchyddar. *Powy* 3D **70**
Bwlch-y-fadfa. *Cdgn* 1E **45**
Bwlch-y-ffridd. *Powy* 1C **58**
Bwlch y Garreg. *Powy* 1C **58**
Bwlch-y-groes. *Pemb* 1G **43**
Bwlch-yr-haiarn. *Cnwy* 5G **81**
Bwlch-y-sarnau. *Powy* 3C **58**
Bybrook. *Kent* 1E **28**
Byermoor. *Tyne* 4E **115**
Byers Garth. *Dur* 5G **115**
Byers Green. *Dur* 1F **105**
Byfield. *Nptn* 5C **62**
Byfleet. *Surr* 4B **38**
Byford. *Here* 1G **47**
Bygrave. *Herts* 2C **52**
Byker. *Tyne* 3F **115**
Byland Abbey. *N Yor* 2H **99**
Bylchau. *Cnwy* 4B **82**
Byley. *Ches* 4B **84**
Bynea. *Carm* 3E **31**
Byram. *N Yor* 2E **93**
Byrness. *Nmbd* 4B **120**
Bystock. *Devn* 4D **12**
Bythorn. *Cambs* 3H **63**
Byton. *Here* 4F **59**
Bywell. *Nmbd* 3D **114**
Byworth. *W Sus* 3A **26**

C

Cabourne. *Linc* 4E **95**
Cabrach. *Arg* 3C **124**
Cabrach. *Mor* 1A **152**
Cabus. *Lanc* 5D **97**
Cadbury. *Devn* 2C **12**
Cadder. *E Dun* 2H **127**
Caddington. *Beds* 4A **52**
Caddonfoot. *Bord* 1G **119**
Cadeby. *Leics* 5B **74**
Cadeby. *S Yor* 4F **93**
Cadeleigh. *Devn* 2C **12**
Cade Street. *E Sus* 3H **27**
Cadgwith. *Corn* 5E **5**
Cadham. *Fife* 3E **137**
Cadishead. *G Man* 1B **84**
Cadle. *Swan* 3F **31**
Cadley. *Lanc* 1D **90**
Cadley. *Wilts* 1H **23**
(nr. Ludgershall)
Cadley. *Wilts* 5H **35**
(nr. Marlborough)
Cadmore End. *Buck* 2F **37**
Cadnam. *Hants* 1A **16**
Cadney. *N Lin* 4D **94**
Cadole. *Flin* 4E **82**
Cadoxton-Juxta-Neath. *Neat* 2A **32**
Cadwell. *Herts* 2B **52**
Cadwst. *Den* 2C **70**
Cadzow. *S Lan* 4A **128**
Caeathro. *Gwyn* 4E **81**
Caehopkin. *Powy* 4B **46**
Caenby. *Linc* 2H **87**
Caenn-na-Cleithe. *W Isl* 8D **171**
Caerau. *B'end* 2B **32**
Caerau. *Card* 4E **33**
Cae'r-bont. *Powy* 4B **46**
Cae'r-bryn. *Carm* 4F **45**
Caerdeon. *Gwyn* 4F **69**
Caerdydd. *Card* 4E **33**
Caerfarchell. *Pemb* 2B **42**
Caerffili. *Cphy* 3E **33**

Caerfyrddin—Carrhouse

Caerfyrddin. *Carm* 4E 45
Caergeiliog. *IOA* 3C 80
Caergwrle. *Flin* 5F 83
Caergybi. *IOA* 2B 80
Caerlaverock. *Per* 2A 136
Caerleon. *Newp* 2G 33
Caerlleon. *Carm* 2G 43
Caerllion. *Newp* 2G 33
Caernarfon. *Gwyn* 4D 81
Caerphilly. *Cphy* 3E 33
Caersws. *Powy* 1C 58
Caerwedros. *Cdgn* 5C 56
Caerwent. *Mon* 2H 33
Caerwys. *Flin* 3D 82
Caim. *IOA* 2F 81
Caio. *Carm* 2G 45
Cairinis. *W Isl* 2D 170
Cairisiadar. *W Isl* 4D 171
Cairminis. *W Isl* 9C 171
Cairnbaan. *Arg* 4F 133
Cairnbulg. *Abers* 2H 161
Cairncross. *Ang* 1D 145
Cairndow. *Arg* 2A 134
Cairness. *Abers* 2H 161
Cairneyhill. *Fife* 1D 128
Cairngarroch. *Dum* 5F 109
Cairnhill. *Abers* 5D 160
Cairnie. *Abers* 4B 160
Cairnorrie. *Abers* 4F 161
Cairnryan. *Dum* 3F 109
Caister-on-Sea. *Norf* 4H 79
Caister St Edmund. *Norf* 5E 79
Caistor. *Linc* 4E 95
Caistron. *Nmbd* 4D 121
Cakebole. *Worc* 3C 60
Cake Street. *Suff* 3F 65
Calais Street. *Suff* 1C 54
Calanais. *W Isl* 4E 171
Calbost. *W Isl* 6G 171
Calbourne. *IOW* 4C 16
Calceby. *Linc* 3C 88
Calcot. *Glos* 4F 49
Calcot Row. *W Ber* 4E 37
Calcott. *Kent* 4F 41
Calcott. *Shrp* 4G 71
Caldback. *Shet* 1H 173
Caldbeck. *Cumb* 1E 102
Caldbergh. *N Yor* 1C 98
Caldecote. *Cambs* 5C 64
(nr. Cambridge)
Caldecote. *Cambs* 2A 64
(nr. Peterborough)
Caldecote. *Herts* 2C 52
Caldecote. *Warw* 1A 62
Caldecott. *Nptn* 4G 63
Caldecott. *Oxon* 2C 36
Caldecott. *Rut* 1F 63
Calderbank. *N Lan* 3A 128
Calder Bridge. *Cumb* 4B 102
Calderbrook. *G Man* 3H 91
Caldercruix. *N Lan* 3B 128
Calder Grove. *W Yor* 3D 92
Calder Mains. *High* 3C 168
Caldermill. *S Lan* 5H 127
Calder Vale. *Lanc* 5E 97
Calderwood. *S Lan* 4H 127
Caldescote. *Nptn* 5D 62
Caldicot. *Mon* 3H 33
Caldwell. *N Yor* 3E 105
Caldy. *Mers* 2E 83
Calebrack. *Cumb* 1E 103
Caledfwlch. *Carm* 3G 45
Calford Green. *Suff* 1G 53
Calfsound. *Orkn* 4E 172
Calgary. *Arg* 3E 139
Califer. *Mor* 3E 159
California. *Falk* 2C 128
California. *Norf* 4H 79
California. *Suff* 1E 55
Calke. *Derbs* 3A 74
Callakille. *High* 3F 155
Callaly. *Nmbd* 4E 121
Callander. *Stir* 3F 135
Callaughton. *Shrp* 1A 60
Callendoun. *Arg* 1E 127
Callestick. *Corn* 3B 6
Calligarry. *High* 3E 147
Callington. *Corn* 2H 7
Callingwood. *Staf* 3F 73
Callow. *Here* 2H 47
Callowell. *Glos* 5D 48
Callow End. *Worc* 1D 48
Callow Hill. *Wilts* 3F 35
Callow Hill. *Worc* 3B 60
(nr. Bewdley)
Callow Hill. *Worc* 4E 61
(nr. Redditch)
Calmore. *Hants* 1B 16
Calmsden. *Glos* 5F 49
Calne. *Wilts* 4E 35
Calow. *Derbs* 3B 86
Calshot. *Hants* 2C 16
Calstock. *Corn* 2A 8
Calstone Wellington. *Wilts* 5F 35
Calthorpe. *Norf* 2D 78
Calthorpe Street. *Norf* 3G 79
Calthwaite. *Cumb* 5F 113
Calton. *N Yor* 4B 98
Calton. *Staf* 5F 85
Calveley. *Ches* 5H 83
Calver. *Derbs* 3G 85
Calverhall. *Shrp* 2A 72
Calverleigh. *Devn* 1C 12
Calverley. *W Yor* 1C 92
Calvert. *Buck* 3E 51
Calverton. *Mil* 2F 51
Calverton. *Notts* 1D 74
Calvine. *Per* 2F 143
Calvo. *Cumb* 4C 112
Cam. *Glos* 2C 34
Camaghael. *High* 1F 141
Camas-luinie. *High* 1B 148
Camasnacroise. *High* 3C 140
Camastianavaig. *High* 5E 155
Camasunary. *High* 2D 146
Camault Muir. *High* 4H 157
Camb. *Shet* 2G 173
Camber. *E Sus* 4D 28
Camberley. *Surr* 5G 37
Camberwell. *G Lon* 3E 39
Camblesforth. *N Yor* 2G 93
Cambo. *Nmbd* 1D 114
Cambois. *Nmbd* 1G 115
Camborne. *Corn* 3D 4
Cambourne. *Cambs* 5C 64
Cambridge. *Cambs* 5D 64
Cambridge. *Glos* 5C 48
Cambridge City Airport. *Cambs* 5D 65
Cambrose. *Corn* 4A 6
Cambus. *Clac* 4A 136
Cambusbarron. *Stir* 4G 135
Cambuskenneth. *Stir* 4H 135
Cambuslang. *S Lan* 3H 127
Cambusnethan. *N Lan* 4B 128
Cambus o'May. *Abers* 4B 152
Camden Town. *G Lon* 2D 39
Cameley. *Bath* 1B 22
Camelford. *Corn* 4B 10
Camelon. *Falk* 1B 128
Camelsdale. *Surr* 2A 26
Camer's Green. *Worc* 2C 48
Camerton. *Bath* 1B 22
Camerton. *Cumb* 1B 102
Camerton. *E Yor* 2F 95
Camghouran. *Per* 3C 142
Cammachmore. *Abers* 4G 153
Cammeringham. *Linc* 2G 87
Camore. *High* 4E 165
Campbelton. *N Ayr* 4C 126
Campbeltown. *Arg* 3B 122
Campbeltown Airport. *Arg* 3A 122
Cample. *Dum* 5B 118
Campmuir. *Per* 5B 144
Campsall. *S Yor* 3F 93
Campsea Ashe. *Suff* 5F 67
Camps End. *Cambs* 1G 53
Camp, The. *Glos* 5E 49
Campton. *Beds* 2B 52
Camptoun. *E Lot* 2B 130
Camptown. *Bord* 3A 120
Camrose. *Pemb* 2D 42
Camserney. *Per* 4F 143
Camster. *High* 4E 169
Camuscross. *High* 2E 147
Camusdarach. *High* 4E 147
Camusnagaul. *High* 1E 141
(nr. Fort William)
Camusnagaul. *High* 5E 163
(nr. Little Loch Broom)
Camusteel. *High* 4G 155
Camusterrach. *High* 4G 155
Camusvrachan. *Per* 4D 142
Canada. *Hants* 1A 16
Canadia. *E Sus* 4B 28
Canaston Bridge. *Pemb* 3E 43
Candlesby. *Linc* 4D 88
Candle Street. *Suff* 3C 66
Candy Mill. *S Lan* 5D 128
Cane End. *Oxon* 4E 37
Canewdon. *Essx* 1C 40
Canford Cliffs. *Pool* 4F 15
Canford Heath. *Pool* 3F 15
Canford Magna. *Pool* 3F 15
Cangate. *Norf* 3F 79
Canham's Green. *Suff* 4C 66
Canholes. *Derbs* 3E 85
Canisbay. *High* 1F 169
Canley. *W Mid* 3H 61
Cann. *Dors* 4D 22
Cann Common. *Dors* 4D 23
Cannich. *High* 5F 157
Cannington. *Som* 3F 21
Cannock. *Staf* 4D 73
Cannock Wood. *Staf* 4E 73
Canonbie. *Dum* 2E 113
Canon Bridge. *Here* 1H 47
Canon Frome. *Here* 1B 48
Canon Pyon. *Here* 1H 47
Canons Ashby. *Nptn* 5C 62
Canonstown. *Corn* 3C 4
Canterbury. *Kent* 5F 41
Cantley. *Norf* 5F 79
Cantley. *S Yor* 4G 93
Cantlop. *Shrp* 5H 71
Canton. *Card* 4E 33
Cantray. *High* 4B 158
Cantraybruich. *High* 4B 158
Cantraywood. *High* 4B 158
Cantsdam. *Fife* 4D 136
Cantsfield. *Lanc* 2F 97
Canvey Island. *Essx* 2B 40
Canwick. *Linc* 4G 87
Canworthy Water. *Corn* 3C 10
Caol. *High* 1F 141
Caolas. *W Isl* 9B 170
Caolas Liubharsaigh. *W Isl* 4D 170
Caolas Stocinis. *W Isl* 8D 171
Caoles. *Arg* 4B 138
Caol Ila. *Arg* 3C 124
Capel. *Kent* 1H 27
Capel. *Surr* 1C 26
Capel Bangor. *Cdgn* 2F 57
Capel Betws Lleucu. *Cdgn* 5F 57
Capel Coch. *IOA* 2D 80
Capel Curig. *Cnwy* 5G 81
Capel Cynon. *Cdgn* 1D 45
Capel Dewi. *Carm* 3E 45
Capel Dewi. *Cdgn* 2F 57
(nr. Aberystwyth)
Capel Dewi. *Cdgn* 1E 45
(nr. Llandysul)
Capel Garmon. *Cnwy* 5H 81
Capel Green. *Suff* 1G 55
Capel Gwyn. *IOA* 3C 80
Capel Gwynfe. *Carm* 3H 45
Capel Hendre. *Carm* 4F 45
Capel Isaac. *Carm* 3F 45
Capel Iwan. *Carm* 1G 43
Capel-le-Ferne. *Kent* 2G 29
Capel Llanilterne. *Card* 4D 32
Capel Mawr. *IOA* 3D 80
Capel Newydd. *Pemb* 1G 43
Capel St Andrew. *Suff* 1G 55
Capel St Mary. *Suff* 2D 54
Capel Seion. *Carm* 4F 45
Capel Seion. *Cdgn* 3F 57
Capel Uchaf. *Gwyn* 1D 68
Capel-y-ffin. *Powy* 2F 47
Capenhurst. *Ches* 3F 83
Capernwray. *Lanc* 2E 97
Capheaton. *Nmbd* 1D 114
Cappercleuch. *Bord* 2E 119
Capplegill. *Dum* 4D 118
Capton. *Devn* 3E 9
Capton. *Som* 3D 20
Caputh. *Per* 5H 143
Caradon Town. *Corn* 5C 10
Carbis Bay. *Corn* 3C 4
Carbost. *High* 5C 154
(nr. Loch Harport)
Carbost. *High* 4D 154
(nr. Portree)
Carbrook. *S Yor* 2A 86
Carbrooke. *Norf* 5B 78
Carburton. *Notts* 3D 86
Carcluie. *S Ayr* 3C 116
Car Colston. *Notts* 1E 74
Carcroft. *S Yor* 3F 93
Cardenden. *Fife* 4E 136
Cardeston. *Shrp* 4F 71
Cardewlees. *Cumb* 4E 113
Cardiff. *Card* 4E 33
Cardiff International Airport. *V Glam* 5D 32
Cardigan. *Cdgn* 1B 44
Cardinal's Green. *Cambs* 1G 53
Cardington. *Beds* 1A 52
Cardington. *Shrp* 1H 59
Cardinham. *Corn* 2F 7
Cardno. *Abers* 2G 161
Cardow. *Mor* 4F 159
Cardross. *Arg* 2E 127
Cardurnock. *Cumb* 4C 112
Careby. *Linc* 4H 75
Careston. *Ang* 2E 145
Carew. *Pemb* 4E 43
Carew Cheriton. *Pemb* 4E 43
Carew Newton. *Pemb* 4E 43
Carey. *Here* 2A 48
Carfin. *N Lan* 4A 128
Carfrae. *Bord* 4B 130
Cargate Green. *Norf* 4F 79
Cargenbridge. *Dum* 2G 111
Cargill. *Per* 5A 144
Cargo. *Cumb* 4E 113
Cargreen. *Corn* 2A 8
Carham. *Nmbd* 1B 120
Carhampton. *Som* 2D 20
Carharrack. *Corn* 4B 6
Carie. *Per* 3D 142
(nr. Loch Rannah)
Carie. *Per* 5D 142
(nr. Loch Tay)
Carisbrooke. *IOW* 4C 16
Cark. *Cumb* 2C 96
Carkeel. *Corn* 2A 8
Carlabhagh. *W Isl* 3E 171
Carland Cross. *Corn* 3C 6
Carlbury. *Darl* 3F 105
Carlby. *Linc* 4H 75
Carlecotes. *S Yor* 4B 92
Carleen. *Corn* 4D 4
Carlesmoor. *N Yor* 2D 98
Carleton. *Cumb* 4F 113
(nr. Carlisle)
Carleton. *Cumb* 4B 102
(nr. Egremont)
Carleton. *Cumb* 2G 103
(nr. Penrith)
Carleton. *Lanc* 1B 90
Carleton. *N Yor* 5B 98
Carleton. *W Yor* 2E 93
Carleton Forehoe. *Norf* 5C 78
Carleton Rode. *Norf* 1D 66
Carleton St Peter. *Norf* 5F 79
Carlidnack. *Corn* 4E 5
Carlingcott. *Bath* 1B 22
Carlin How. *Red C* 3E 107
Carlisle. *Cumb* 4F 113
Carloonan. *Arg* 2H 133
Carlops. *Bord* 4E 129
Carlton. *Beds* 5G 63
Carlton. *Cambs* 5F 65
Carlton. *Leics* 5A 74
Carlton. *N Yor* 1A 100
(nr. Helmsley)
Carlton. *N Yor* 1C 98
(nr. Middleham)
Carlton. *N Yor* 2G 93
(nr. Selby)
Carlton. *Notts* 1D 74
Carlton. *S Yor* 3D 92
Carlton. *Stoc T* 2A 106
Carlton. *Suff* 4F 67
Carlton. *W Yor* 2D 92
Carlton Colville. *Suff* 1H 67
Carlton Curlieu. *Leics* 1D 62
Carlton Husthwaite. *N Yor* 2G 99
Carlton in Cleveland. *N Yor* 4C 106
Carlton in Lindrick. *Notts* 2C 86
Carlton-le-Moorland. *Linc* 5G 87
Carlton Miniott. *N Yor* 1F 99
Carlton-on-Trent. *Notts* 4F 87
Carlton Scroop. *Linc* 1G 75
Carluke. *S Lan* 4B 128
Carlyon Bay. *Corn* 3E 7
Carmarthen. *Carm* 4E 45
Carmel. *Carm* 4F 45
Carmel. *Flin* 3D 82
Carmel. *Gwyn* 5D 81
Carmel. *IOA* 2C 80
Carmichael. *S Lan* 1B 118
Carmunnock. *Glas* 4H 127
Carmyle. *S Lan* 3H 127
Carmyllie. *Ang* 4E 145
Carnaby. *E Yor* 3F 101
Carnach. *High* 1C 148
(nr. Lochcarron)
Carnach. *High* 4E 163
(nr. Ullapool)
Carnach. *Mor* 4E 159
Carnach. *W Isl* 8E 171
Carnachy. *High* 3H 167
Carnain. *Arg* 3B 124
Carnais. *W Isl* 4C 171
Carnan. *Arg* 4B 138
Carnan. *W Isl* 4C 170
Carnbee. *Fife* 3H 137
Carnbo. *Per* 3C 136
Carn Brea Village. *Corn* 4A 6
Carndu. *High* 1A 148
Carne. *Corn* 5D 6
Carnell. *S Ayr* 1D 116
Carnforth. *Lanc* 2E 97
Carn-gorm. *High* 1B 148
Carnhedryn. *Pemb* 2B 42
Carnhell Green. *Corn* 3D 4
Carnie. *Abers* 3F 153
Carnkie. *Corn* 5B 6
(nr. Falmouth)
Carnkie. *Corn* 5A 6
(nr. Redruth)
Carnkief. *Corn* 3B 6
Carno. *Powy* 1B 58
Carnock. *Fife* 1D 128
Carnon Downs. *Corn* 4B 6
Carnoustie. *Ang* 5E 145
Carntyne. *Glas* 3H 127
Carnwath. *S Lan* 5C 128
Carnyorth. *Corn* 3A 4
Carol Green. *W Mid* 3G 61
Carpalla. *Corn* 3D 6
Carperby. *N Yor* 1C 98
Carradale. *Arg* 2C 122
Carragraich. *W Isl* 8D 171
Carrbridge. *High* 1D 150
Carr Cross. *Lanc* 3B 90
Carreglefn. *IOA* 2C 80
Carrhouse. *N Lin* 4A 94

Carrick Castle. *Arg* 4A 134
Carriden. *Falk* 1D 128
Carrington. *G Man* 1B 84
Carrington. *Linc* 5C 88
Carrington. *Midl* 3G 129
Carrog. *Cnwy* 1G 69
Carrog. *Den* 1D 70
Carron. *Falk* 1B 128
Carron. *Mor* 4G 159
Carronbridge. *Dum* 5A 118
Carronshore. *Falk* 1B 128
Carrow Hill. *Mon* 2H 33
Carr Shield. *Nmbd* 5B 114
Carrutherstown. *Dum* 2C 112
Carr Vale. *Derbs* 4B 86
Carrville. *Dur* 5G 115
Carrycoats Hall. *Nmbd* 2C 114
Carsaig. *Arg* 1C 132
Carscreugh. *Dum* 3H 109
Carsegowan. *Dum* 4B 110
Carse House. *Arg* 3F 125
Carseriggan. *Dum* 3A 110
Carsethorn. *Dum* 4A 112
Carshalton. *G Lon* 4D 38
Carsington. *Derbs* 5G 85
Carskiey. *Arg* 5A 122
Carsluith. *Dum* 4B 110
Carsphairn. *Dum* 5E 117
Carstairs. *S Lan* 5C 128
Carstairs Junction. *S Lan* 5C 128
Cartbridge. *Surr* 5B 38
Carterhaugh. *Ang* 4D 144
Carter's Clay. *Hants* 4B 24
Carterton. *Oxon* 5A 50
Carterway Heads. *Nmbd* 4D 114
Carthew. *Corn* 3E 6
Carthorpe. *N Yor* 1F 99
Cartington. *Nmbd* 4E 121
Cartland. *S Lan* 5B 128
Cartmel. *Cumb* 2C 96
Cartmel Fell. *Cumb* 1D 96
Cartworth. *W Yor* 4B 92
Carwath. *Cumb* 5E 112
Carway. *Carm* 5E 45
Carwinley. *Cumb* 2F 113
Cascob. *Powy* 4E 59
Cas-gwent. *Mon* 2A 34
Cash Feus. *Fife* 3E 136
Cashlie. *Per* 4B 142
Cashmoor. *Dors* 1E 15
Cas-Mael. *Pemb* 2E 43
Casnewydd. *Newp* 3G 33
Cassington. *Oxon* 4C 50
Cassop. *Dur* 1A 106
Castell. *Cnwy* 4G 81
Castell. *Den* 4D 82
Castell Hendre. *Pemb* 2E 43
Castell-nedd. *Neat* 2A 32
Castell Newydd Emlyn. *Carm* 1D 44
Castell-y-bwch. *Torf* 2F 33
Casterton. *Cumb* 2F 97
Castle. *Som* 2A 22
Castle Acre. *Norf* 4H 77
Castle Ashby. *Nptn* 5F 63
Castlebay. *W Isl* 9B 170
Castle Bolton. *N Yor* 5D 104
Castle Bromwich. *W Mid* 2F 61
Castle Bytham. *Linc* 4G 75
Castlebythe. *Pemb* 2E 43
Castle Caereinion. *Powy* 5D 70
Castle Camps. *Cambs* 1G 53
Castle Carrock. *Cumb* 4G 113
Castlecary. *N Lan* 2A 128
Castle Cary. *Som* 3B 22
Castle Combe. *Wilts* 4D 34
Castlecraig. *High* 2C 158
Castle Donington. *Leics* 3B 74
Castle Douglas. *Dum* 3E 111
Castle Eaton. *Swin* 2G 35
Castle Eden. *Dur* 1B 106
Castleford. *W Yor* 2E 93
Castle Frome. *Here* 1B 48
Castle Green. *Surr* 4A 38
Castle Green. *Warw* 3G 61
Castle Gresley. *Derbs* 4G 73
Castle Heaton. *Nmbd* 5F 131
Castle Hedingham. *Essx* 2A 54
Castle Hill. *Kent* 1A 28
Castlehill. *Per* 5B 144
Castlehill. *S Lan* 4B 128
Castle Hill. *Suff* 1E 55
Castlehill. *W Dun* 2E 127
Castle Kennedy. *Dum* 4G 109
Castle Lachlan. *Arg* 4H 133
Castlemartin. *Pemb* 5D 42
Castlemilk. *Glas* 4H 127
Castlemorris. *Pemb* 1D 42
Castlemorton. *Worc* 2C 48
Castle O'er. *Dum* 5E 119
Castle Park. *N Yor* 3F 107
Castlerigg. *Cumb* 2D 102
Castle Rising. *Norf* 3F 77
Castleside. *Dur* 5D 115
Castlethorpe. *Mil* 1F 51
Castleton. *Abers* 4F 151
Castleton. *Arg* 1G 125
Castleton. *Derbs* 2F 85
Castleton. *G Man* 3G 91
Castleton. *Mor* 1F 151
Castleton. *Newp* 3F 33
Castleton. *N Yor* 4D 107
Castleton. *Per* 2B 136
Castletown. *Cumb* 1G 103
Castletown. *Dors* 5B 14
Castletown. *High* 2D 169
Castletown. *IOM* 5B 108
Castletown. *Tyne* 4G 115
Castley. *N Yor* 5E 99
Caston. *Norf* 1B 66
Castor. *Pet* 1A 64
Caswell. *Swan* 4E 31
Catacol. *N Ayr* 5H 125
Catbrook. *Mon* 5A 48
Catchems End. *Worc* 3B 60
Catchgate. *Dur* 4E 115
Catcleugh. *Nmbd* 4B 120
Catcliffe. *S Yor* 2B 86
Catcott. *Som* 3G 21
Caterham. *Surr* 5E 39
Catfield. *Norf* 3F 79
Catfield Common. *Norf* 3F 79
Catford. *G Lon* 3E 39
Catforth. *Lanc* 1C 90
Cathcart. *Glas* 3G 127
Cathedine. *Powy* 3E 47
Catherine-de-Barnes. *W Mid* 2F 61
Catherington. *Hants* 1E 17
Catherston Leweston. *Dors* 3G 13
Catherton. *Shrp* 3A 60
Catisfield. *Hants* 2D 16
Catlodge. *High* 4A 150
Catlowdy. *Cumb* 2F 113
Catmore. *W Ber* 3C 36
Caton. *Devn* 5A 12
Caton. *Lanc* 3E 97
Catrine. *E Ayr* 2E 117
Cat's Ash. *Newp* 2G 33
Catsfield. *E Sus* 4B 28
Catsgore. *Som* 4A 22
Catshill. *Worc* 3D 60
Cattal. *N Yor* 4G 99
Cattawade. *Suff* 2E 54
Catterall. *Lanc* 5D 97
Catterick. *N Yor* 5F 105
Catterick Bridge. *N Yor* 5F 105
Catterick Garrison. *N Yor* 5E 105
Catterlen. *Cumb* 1F 103
Catterline. *Abers* 1H 145
Catterton. *N Yor* 5H 99
Catteshall. *Surr* 1A 26
Catthorpe. *Leics* 3C 62
Cattistock. *Dors* 3A 14
Catton. *Norf* 4E 78
Catton. *Nmbd* 4B 114
Catton. *N Yor* 2F 99
Catton Hall. *Derbs* 4G 73
Catwick. *E Yor* 5F 101
Catworth. *Cambs* 3H 63
Caudle Green. *Glos* 4E 49
Caulcott. *Oxon* 3D 50
Cauldhame. *Stir* 4F 135
Cauldmill. *Bord* 3H 119
Cauldon. *Staf* 1E 73
Cauldon Lowe. *Staf* 1E 73
Cauldwell. *Derbs* 4G 73
Cauldwells. *Abers* 3E 161
Caulkerbush. *Dum* 4G 111
Caulside. *Dum* 1F 113
Caunsall. *Worc* 2C 60
Caunton. *Notts* 4E 87
Causewayend. *S Lan* 1C 118
Causewayhead. *Stir* 4H 135
Causey Park. *Nmbd* 5F 121
Caute. *Devn* 1E 11
Cautley. *Cumb* 5H 103
Cavendish. *Suff* 1B 54
Cavendish Bridge. *Derbs* 2B 74
Cavenham. *Suff* 4G 65
Caversfield. *Oxon* 3D 50
Caversham. *Read* 4F 37
Caversham Heights. *Read* 4E 37
Caverswall. *Staf* 1D 72
Cawdor. *High* 4C 158
Cawkwell. *Linc* 2B 88
Cawood. *N Yor* 1F 93
Cawsand. *Corn* 3A 8
Cawston. *Norf* 3D 78
Cawston. *Warw* 3B 62
Cawthorne. *N Yor* 1B 100
Cawthorne. *S Yor* 4C 92
Cawthorpe. *Linc* 3H 75
Cawton. *N Yor* 2A 100
Caxton. *Cambs* 5C 64
Caynham. *Shrp* 3H 59
Caythorpe. *Linc* 1G 75
Caythorpe. *Notts* 1D 74
Cayton. *N Yor* 1E 101
Ceallan. *W Isl* 3D 170
Ceann a Bhaigh. *W Isl* 2C 170 (on North Uist)
Ceann a Bhaigh. *W Isl* 8E 171 (on Scalpay)
Ceann a Bhàigh. *W Isl* 9C 171 (on Harris)
Ceannacroc Lodge. *High* 2E 149
Ceann a Tuath Loch Baghasdail. *W Isl* 6C 170
Ceann Shiphoirt. *W Isl* 6E 171
Ceann Tarabhaigh. *W Isl* 6E 171
Ceathramh Meadhanach. *W Isl* 1C 170
Cefn Berain. *Cnwy* 4B 82
Cefn-brith. *Cnwy* 5B 82
Cefn-bryn-brain. *Carm* 4H 45
Cefn Bychan. *Cphy* 2F 33
Cefn-bychan. *Flin* 4D 82
Cefncaeau. *Carm* 3E 31
Cefn Canol. *Powy* 2E 71
Cefn-coch. *Powy* 3D 70
Cefn Coch. *Powy* 5C 70
Cefn-coed-y-cymmer. *Mer T* 5D 46
Cefn Cribwr. *B'end* 3B 32
Cefn-ddwysarn. *Gwyn* 2B 70
Cefn Einion. *Shrp* 2E 59
Cefneithin. *Carm* 4F 45
Cefn Glas. *B'end* 3B 32
Cefngorwydd. *Powy* 1C 46
Cefn Llwyd. *Cdgn* 2F 57
Cefn-mawr. *Wrex* 1E 71
Cefn-y-bedd. *Flin* 5F 83
Cefn-y-coed. *Powy* 1D 58
Cefn-y-pant. *Carm* 2F 43
Cegidfa. *Powy* 4E 70
Ceinewydd. *Cdgn* 5C 56
Cellan. *Cdgn* 1G 45
Cellardyke. *Fife* 3H 137
Cellarhead. *Staf* 1D 72
Cemaes. *IOA* 1C 80
Cemmaes. *Powy* 5H 69
Cemmaes Road. *Powy* 5H 69
Cenarth. *Carm* 1C 44
Cenin. *Gwyn* 1D 68
Ceos. *W Isl* 5F 171
Ceres. *Fife* 2G 137
Ceri. *Powy* 2D 58
Cerist. *Powy* 2B 58
Cerne Abbas. *Dors* 2B 14
Cerney Wick. *Glos* 2F 35
Cerrigceinwen. *IOA* 3D 80
Cerrigydrudion. *Cnwy* 1B 70
Cess. *Norf* 4G 79
Cessford. *Bord* 2B 120
Ceunant. *Gwyn* 4E 81
Chaceley. *Glos* 2D 48
Chacewater. *Corn* 4B 6
Chackmore. *Buck* 2E 51
Chacombe. *Nptn* 1C 50
Chadderton. *G Man* 4H 91
Chaddesden. *Derb* 2A 74
Chaddesden Common. *Derb* 2A 74
Chaddesley Corbett. *Worc* 3C 60
Chaddlehanger. *Devn* 5E 11
Chaddleworth. *W Ber* 4C 36
Chadlington. *Oxon* 3B 50
Chadshunt. *Warw* 5H 61
Chadstone. *Nptn* 5F 63
Chad Valley. *W Mid* 2E 61
Chadwell. *Leics* 3E 75
Chadwell. *Shrp* 4B 72
Chadwell Heath. *G Lon* 2F 39
Chadwell St Mary. *Thur* 3H 39
Chadwick End. *W Mid* 3G 61
Chadwick Green. *Mers* 1H 83
Chaffcombe. *Som* 1G 13
Chafford Hundred. *Thur* 3H 39
Chagford. *Devn* 4H 11
Chailey. *E Sus* 4E 27
Chainbridge. *Cambs* 5D 76
Chain Bridge. *Linc* 1C 76
Chainhurst. *Kent* 1B 28
Chalbury. *Dors* 2F 15
Chalbury Common. *Dors* 2F 15
Chaldon. *Surr* 5E 39
Chaldon Herring. *Dors* 4C 14
Chale. *IOW* 5C 16
Chale Green. *IOW* 5C 16
Chalfont Common. *Buck* 1B 38
Chalfont St Giles. *Buck* 1A 38
Chalfont St Peter. *Buck* 2B 38
Chalford. *Glos* 5D 49
Chalgrove. *Oxon* 2E 37
Chalk. *Kent* 3A 40
Chalk End. *Essx* 4G 53
Chalk Hill. *Glos* 3G 49
Challaborough. *Devn* 4C 8
Challacombe. *Devn* 2G 19
Challoch. *Dum* 3A 110
Challock. *Kent* 5E 40
Chalton. *Beds* 5A 64 (nr. Bedford)
Chalton. *Beds* 3A 52 (nr. Luton)
Chalton. *Hants* 1F 17
Chalvington. *E Sus* 5G 27
Champany. *Falk* 2D 128
Chance Inn. *Fife* 2F 137
Chancery. *Cdgn* 3E 57
Chandler's Cross. *Herts* 1B 38
Chandler's Cross. *Worc* 2C 48
Chandler's Ford. *Hants* 4C 24
Chanlockfoot. *Dum* 4G 117
Channel End. *Beds* 5A 64
Channel Tunnel. *Kent* 2F 29
Chantry. *Som* 2C 22
Chantry. *Suff* 1E 55
Chapel. *Cumb* 1D 102
Chapel. *Fife* 4E 137
Chapel Allerton. *Som* 1H 21
Chapel Allerton. *W Yor* 1D 92
Chapel Amble. *Corn* 1D 6
Chapel Brampton. *Nptn* 4E 63
Chapelbridge. *Cambs* 1B 64
Chapel Chorlton. *Staf* 2C 72
Chapel Cleeve. *Som* 2D 20
Chapel End. *Beds* 1A 52
Chapel-en-le-Frith. *Derbs* 2E 85
Chapelfield. *Abers* 2G 145
Chapelgate. *Linc* 3D 76
Chapel Green. *Warw* 2G 61 (nr. Coventry)
Chapel Green. *Warw* 4B 62 (nr. Southam)
Chapel Haddlesey. *N Yor* 2F 93
Chapelhall. *N Lan* 3A 128
Chapel Hill. *Abers* 5H 161
Chapel Hill. *Linc* 5B 88
Chapel Hill. *Mon* 5A 48
Chapelhill. *Per* 1E 136 (nr. Glencarse)
Chapelhill. *Per* 5H 143 (nr. Harrietfield)
Chapelknowe. *Dum* 2E 112
Chapel Lawn. *Shrp* 3F 59
Chapel le Dale. *N Yor* 2G 97
Chapel Milton. *Derbs* 2E 85
Chapel of Garioch. *Abers* 1E 152
Chapel Row. *W Ber* 5D 36
Chapels. *Cumb* 1B 96
Chapel St Leonards. *Linc* 3E 89
Chapel Stile. *Cumb* 4E 102
Chapelthorne. *W Yor* 3D 92
Chapelton. *Ang* 4F 145
Chapelton. *Devn* 4F 19
Chapelton. *High* 2D 150 (nr. Grantown-on-Spey)
Chapelton. *High* 3H 157 (nr. Inverness)
Chapelton. *S Lan* 5H 127
Chapeltown. *Bkbn* 3F 91
Chapel Town. *Corn* 3C 6
Chapeltown. *Mor* 1G 151
Chapeltown. *S Yor* 1H 85
Chapmanslade. *Wilts* 2D 22
Chapmans Well. *Devn* 3D 10
Chapmore End. *Herts* 4D 52
Chappel. *Essx* 3B 54
Chard. *Som* 2G 13
Chard Junction. *Dors* 2G 13
Chardstock. *Devn* 2G 13
Charfield. *S Glo* 2C 34
Charing. *Kent* 1D 28
Charing Heath. *Kent* 1D 28
Charing Hill. *Kent* 5D 40
Charingworth. *Glos* 2H 49
Charlbury. *Oxon* 4B 50
Charlcombe. *Bath* 5C 34
Charlcutt. *Wilts* 4E 35
Charlecote. *Warw* 5G 61
Charles. *Devn* 3G 19
Charlesfield. *Dum* 3C 112
Charleshill. *Surr* 2G 25
Charleston. *Ang* 4C 144
Charleston. *Ren* 3F 127
Charlestown. *Aber* 3G 153
Charlestown. *Abers* 2H 161
Charlestown. *Corn* 3E 7
Charlestown. *Dors* 5B 14
Charlestown. *Fife* 1D 128
Charlestown. *G Man* 4G 91
Charlestown. *High* 1H 155 (nr. Gairloch)
Charlestown. *High* 4A 158 (nr. Inverness)
Charlestown. *W Yor* 2H 91
Charlestown of Aberlour. *Mor* 4G 159
Charles Tye. *Suff* 5C 66
Charlesworth. *Derbs* 1E 85
Charlton. *G Lon* 3F 39
Charlton. *Hants* 2B 24
Charlton. *Herts* 3B 52
Charlton. *Nptn* 2D 50
Charlton. *Nmbd* 1B 114
Charlton. *Oxon* 3C 36
Charlton. *Som* 1B 22 (nr. Radstock)
Charlton. *Som* 2B 22 (nr. Shepton Mallet)
Charlton. *Telf* 4H 71
Charlton. *W Sus* 1G 17

Charlton—Church Preen

Charlton. *Wilts* 3E **35** (nr. Malmesbury)
Charlton. *Wilts* 1G **23** (nr. Pewsey)
Charlton. *Wilts* 4G **23** (nr. Salisbury)
Charlton. *Wilts* 4E **23** (nr. Shaftesbury)
Charlton. *Worc* 1F **49** (nr. Evesham)
Charlton. *Worc* 3C **60** (nr. Stourport-on-Severn)
Charlton Abbots. *Glos* 3F **49**
Charlton Adam. *Som* 4A **22**
Charlton Down. *Dors* 3B **14**
Charlton Horethorne. *Som* 4B **22**
Charlton Kings. *Glos* 3E **49**
Charlton Mackrell. *Som* 4A **22**
Charlton Marshall. *Dors* 2E **15**
Charlton Musgrove. *Som* 4C **22**
Charlton-on-Otmoor. *Oxon* 4D **50**
Charlton on the Hill. *Dors* 2D **15**
Charlwood. *Hants* 3E **25**
Charlwood. *Surr* 1D **26**
Charlynch. *Som* 3F **21**
Charminster. *Dors* 3B **14**
Charmouth. *Dors* 3G **13**
Charndon. *Buck* 3E **51**
Charney Bassett. *Oxon* 2B **36**
Charnock Green. *Lanc* 3D **90**
Charnock Richard. *Lanc* 3D **90**
Charsfield. *Suff* 5E **67**
Chart Corner. *Kent* 5B **40**
Charter Alley. *Hants* 1D **24**
Charterhouse. *Som* 1H **21**
Charterville Allotments. *Oxon* 4B **50**
Chartham. *Kent* 5F **41**
Chartham Hatch. *Kent* 5F **41**
Chartridge. *Buck* 5H **51**
Chart Sutton. *Kent* 5B **40**
Chart, The. *Kent* 5F **39**
Charvil. *Wok* 4F **37**
Charwelton. *Nptn* 5C **62**
Chase Terrace. *Staf* 5E **73**
Chasetown. *Staf* 5E **73**
Chastleton. *Oxon* 3H **49**
Chasty. *Devn* 2D **10**
Chatburn. *Lanc* 5G **97**
Chatcull. *Staf* 2B **72**
Chatham. *Medw* 4B **40**
Chatham Green. *Essx* 4H **53**
Chathill. *Nmbd* 2F **121**
Chatley. *Worc* 4C **60**
Chattenden. *Medw* 3B **40**
Chatteris. *Cambs* 2C **64**
Chattisham. *Suff* 1D **54**
Chatton. *Nmbd* 2E **121**
Chatwall. *Shrp* 1H **59**
Chaulden. *Herts* 5A **52**
Chaul End. *Beds* 3A **52**
Chawleigh. *Devn* 1H **11**
Chawley. *Oxon* 5C **50**
Chawston. *Beds* 5A **64**
Chawton. *Hants* 3F **25**
Chaxhill. *Glos* 4C **48**
Cheadle. *G Man* 2C **84**
Cheadle. *Staf* 1E **73**
Cheadle Hulme. *G Man* 2C **84**
Cheam. *Surr* 4D **38**
Cheapside. *Wind* 4A **38**
Chearsley. *Buck* 4F **51**
Chebsey. *Staf* 3C **72**
Checkendon. *Oxon* 3E **37**
Checkley. *Ches* 1B **72**
Checkley. *Here* 2A **48**
Checkley. *Staf* 2E **73**
Chedburgh. *Suff* 5G **65**
Cheddar. *Som* 1H **21**
Cheddington. *Buck* 4H **51**
Cheddleton. *Staf* 5D **84**
Cheddon Fitzpaine. *Som* 4F **21**
Chedglow. *Wilts* 2E **35**
Chedgrave. *Norf* 1F **67**
Chedington. *Dors* 2H **13**
Chediston. *Suff* 3F **67**
Chediston Green. *Suff* 3F **67**
Chedworth. *Glos* 4F **49**
Chedzoy. *Som* 3G **21**
Cheeseman's Green. *Kent* 2E **29**
Cheetham Hill. *G Man* 4G **91**
Cheglinch. *Devn* 2F **19**
Cheldon. *Devn* 1H **11**
Chelford. *Ches* 3C **84**
Chellaston. *Derb* 2A **74**
Chellington. *Beds* 5G **63**
Chelmarsh. *Shrp* 2B **60**
Chelmick. *Shrp* 1G **59**
Chelmondiston. *Suff* 2F **55**
Chelmorton. *Derbs* 4F **85**
Chelmsford. *Essx* 5H **53**
Chelsea. *G Lon* 3D **39**
Chelsfield. *G Lon* 4F **39**
Chelsham. *Surr* 5E **39**
Chelston. *Som* 4E **21**
Chelsworth. *Suff* 1C **54**
Cheltenham. *Glos* 3E **49**
Chelveston. *Nptn* 4G **63**
Chelvey. *N Som* 5H **33**
Chelwood. *Bath* 5B **34**
Chelwood Common. *E Sus* 3F **27**
Chelwood Gate. *E Sus* 3F **27**
Chelworth. *Wilts* 2E **35**
Chelworth Lower Green. *Wilts* 2F **35**
Chelworth Upper Green. *Wilts* 2F **35**
Chelynch. *Som* 2B **22**
Cheney Longville. *Shrp* 2G **59**
Chenies. *Buck* 1B **38**
Chepstow. *Mon* 2A **34**
Chequerfield. *W Yor* 2E **93**
Chequers Corner. *Norf* 5D **77**
Cherhill. *Wilts* 4F **35**
Cherington. *Glos* 2E **35**
Cherington. *Warw* 2A **50**
Cheriton. *Devn* 2H **19**
Cheriton. *Hants* 4D **24**
Cheriton. *Kent* 2G **29**
Cheriton. *Pemb* 5D **43**
Cheriton. *Swan* 3D **30**
Cheriton Bishop. *Devn* 3A **12**
Cheriton Cross. *Devn* 3A **12**
Cheriton Fitzpaine. *Devn* 2B **12**
Cherrington. *Telf* 3A **72**
Cherrybank. *Per* 1D **136**
Cherry Burton. *E Yor* 5D **101**
Cherry Green. *Herts* 3D **52**
Cherry Hinton. *Cambs* 5D **65**
Cherry Willingham. *Linc* 3H **87**
Chertsey. *Surr* 4B **38**
Cheselbourne. *Dors* 3C **14**
Chesham. *Buck* 5H **51**
Chesham. *G Man* 3G **91**
Chesham Bois. *Buck* 1A **38**
Cheshunt. *Herts* 5D **52**
Cheslyn Hay. *Staf* 5D **73**
Chessetts Wood. *Warw* 3F **61**
Chessington. *G Lon* 4C **38**
Chester. *Ches* 4G **83**
Chesterblade. *Som* 2B **22**
Chesterfield. *Derbs* 3A **86**
Chesterfield. *Staf* 5F **73**
Chesterhope. *Nmbd* 1C **114**
Chester-le-Street. *Dur* 4F **115**
Chester Moor. *Dur* 5F **115**
Chesters. *Bord* 3A **120**
Chesterton. *Cambs* 4D **64** (nr. Cambridge)
Chesterton. *Cambs* 1A **64** (nr. Peterborough)
Chesterton. *Glos* 5F **49**
Chesterton. *Oxon* 3D **50**
Chesterton. *Shrp* 1B **60**
Chesterton. *Staf* 1C **72**
Chesterton Green. *Warw* 5H **61**
Chesterwood. *Nmbd* 3B **114**
Chestfield. *Kent* 4F **41**
Cheston. *Devn* 3C **8**
Cheswardine. *Shrp* 2B **72**
Cheswell. *Telf* 4B **72**
Cheswick. *Nmbd* 5G **131**
Cheswick Green. *W Mid* 3F **61**
Chetnole. *Dors* 2B **14**
Chettiscombe. *Devn* 1C **12**
Chettisham. *Cambs* 2E **65**
Chettle. *Dors* 1E **15**
Chetton. *Shrp* 1A **60**
Chetwode. *Buck* 3E **51**
Chetwynd Aston. *Telf* 4B **72**
Cheveley. *Cambs* 4F **65**
Chevening. *Kent* 5F **39**
Chevington. *Suff* 5G **65**
Chevithorne. *Devn* 1C **12**
Chew Magna. *Bath* 5A **34**
Chew Moor. *G Man* 4E **91**
Chew Stoke. *Bath* 5A **34**
Chewton Keynsham. *Bath* 5B **34**
Chewton Mendip. *Som* 1A **22**
Chichacott. *Devn* 3G **11**
Chicheley. *Mil* 1H **51**
Chichester. *W Sus* 2G **17**
Chickerell. *Dors* 4B **14**
Chickering. *Suff* 3E **66**
Chicklade. *Wilts* 3E **23**
Chickward. *Here* 5E **59**
Chidden. *Hants* 1E **17**
Chiddingfold. *Surr* 2A **26**
Chiddingly. *E Sus* 4G **27**
Chiddingstone. *Kent* 1F **27**
Chiddingstone Causeway. *Kent* 1G **27**
Chiddingstone Hoath. *Kent* 1F **27**
Chideock. *Dors* 3H **13**
Chidgley. *Som* 3D **20**
Chidham. *W Sus* 2F **17**
Chieveley. *W Ber* 4C **36**
Chignall St James. *Essx* 5G **53**
Chignall Smealy. *Essx* 4G **53**
Chigwell. *Essx* 1F **39**
Chigwell Row. *Essx* 1F **39**
Chilbolton. *Hants* 2B **24**
Chilcomb. *Hants* 4D **24**
Chilcombe. *Dors* 3A **14**
Chilcompton. *Som* 1B **22**
Chilcote. *Leics* 4G **73**
Childer Thornton. *Ches* 3F **83**
Child Okeford. *Dors* 1D **14**
Childrey. *Oxon* 3B **36**
Child's Ercall. *Shrp* 3A **72**
Childswickham. *Worc* 2F **49**
Childwall. *Mers* 2G **83**
Childwick Green. *Herts* 4B **52**
Chilfrome. *Dors* 3A **14**
Chilgrove. *W Sus* 1G **17**
Chilham. *Kent* 5E **41**
Chilhampton. *Wilts* 3F **23**
Chilla. *Devn* 2E **11**
Chilland. *Hants* 3D **24**
Chillaton. *Devn* 4E **11**
Chillenden. *Kent* 5G **41**
Chillerton. *IOW* 4C **16**
Chillesford. *Suff* 5F **67**
Chillingham. *Nmbd* 2E **121**
Chillington. *Devn* 4D **9**
Chillington. *Som* 1G **13**
Chilmark. *Wilts* 3E **23**
Chilmington Green. *Kent* 1D **28**
Chilson. *Oxon* 4B **50**
Chilsworthy. *Corn* 5E **11**
Chilsworthy. *Devn* 2D **10**
Chiltern Green. *Beds* 4B **52**
Chilthorne Domer. *Som* 1A **14**
Chilton. *Buck* 4E **51**
Chilton. *Devn* 2B **12**
Chilton. *Dur* 2F **105**
Chilton. *Oxon* 3C **36**
Chilton Candover. *Hants* 2D **24**
Chilton Cantelo. *Som* 4A **22**
Chilton Foliat. *Wilts* 4B **36**
Chilton Lane. *Dur* 1A **106**
Chilton Polden. *Som* 3G **21**
Chilton Street. *Suff* 1A **54**
Chilton Trinity. *Som* 3F **21**
Chilwell. *Notts* 2C **74**
Chilworth. *Hants* 1C **16**
Chilworth. *Surr* 1B **26**
Chimney. *Oxon* 5B **50**
Chimney Street. *Suff* 1H **53**
Chineham. *Hants* 1E **25**
Chingford. *G Lon* 1E **39**
Chinley. *Derbs* 2E **85**
Chinnor. *Oxon* 5F **51**
Chipley. *Som* 4E **20**
Chipnall. *Shrp* 2B **72**
Chippenham. *Cambs* 4F **65**
Chippenham. *Wilts* 4E **35**
Chipperfield. *Herts* 5A **52**
Chipping. *Herts* 2D **52**
Chipping. *Lanc* 5F **97**
Chipping Campden. *Glos* 2G **49**
Chipping Hill. *Essx* 4B **54**
Chipping Norton. *Oxon* 3B **50**
Chipping Ongar. *Essx* 5F **53**
Chipping Sodbury. *S Glo* 3C **34**
Chipping Warden. *Nptn* 1C **50**
Chipstable. *Som* 4D **20**
Chipstead. *Kent* 5G **39**
Chipstead. *Surr* 5D **38**
Chirbury. *Shrp* 1E **59**
Chirk. *Wrex* 2E **71**
Chirmorie. *S Ayr* 2H **109**
Chirnside. *Bord* 4E **131**
Chirnsidebridge. *Bord* 4E **131**
Chirton. *Wilts* 1F **23**
Chisbridge Cross. *Buck* 3G **37**
Chisbury. *Wilts* 5A **36**
Chiselborough. *Som* 1H **13**
Chiseldon. *Swin* 4G **35**
Chiserley. *W Yor* 2A **92**
Chislehampton. *Oxon* 2D **36**
Chislehurst. *G Lon* 4F **39**
Chislet. *Kent* 4G **41**
Chiswell. *Dors* 5B **14**
Chiswell Green. *Herts* 5B **52**
Chiswick. *G Lon* 3D **38**
Chisworth. *Derbs* 1D **85**
Chitcombe. *E Sus* 3C **28**
Chithurst. *W Sus* 4G **25**
Chittering. *Cambs* 4D **65**
Chitterley. *Devn* 2C **12**
Chitterne. *Wilts* 2E **23**
Chittlehamholt. *Devn* 4G **19**
Chittlehampton. *Devn* 4G **19**
Chittoe. *Wilts* 5E **35**
Chivelstone. *Devn* 5D **9**
Chivenor. *Devn* 3F **19**
Chobham. *Surr* 4A **38**
Cholderton. *Wilts* 2H **23**
Cholesbury. *Buck* 5H **51**
Chollerford. *Nmbd* 2C **114**
Chollerton. *Nmbd* 2C **114**
Cholsey. *Oxon* 3D **36**
Cholstrey. *Here* 5G **59**
Chop Gate. *N Yor* 5C **106**
Choppington. *Nmbd* 1F **115**
Chopwell. *Tyne* 4E **115**
Chorley. *Ches* 5H **83**
Chorley. *Lanc* 3D **90**
Chorley. *Shrp* 2A **60**
Chorley. *Staf* 4E **73**
Chorleywood. *Herts* 1B **38**
Chorlton. *Ches* 5B **84**
Chorlton-cum-Hardy. *G Man* 1C **84**
Chorlton Lane. *Ches* 1G **71**
Choulton. *Shrp* 2F **59**
Chrishall. *Essx* 2E **53**
Christchurch. *Cambs* 1D **65**
Christchurch. *Dors* 3G **15**
Christchurch. *Glos* 4A **48**
Christian Malford. *Wilts* 4E **35**
Christleton. *Ches* 4G **83**
Christmas Common. *Oxon* 2F **37**
Christon. *N Som* 1G **21**
Christon Bank. *Nmbd* 2G **121**
Christow. *Devn* 4B **12**
Chryston. *N Lan* 2H **127**
Chuck Hatch. *E Sus* 2F **27**
Chudleigh. *Devn* 5B **12**
Chudleigh Knighton. *Devn* 5B **12**
Chulmleigh. *Devn* 1G **11**
Chunal. *Derbs* 1E **85**
Church. *Lanc* 2F **91**
Churcham. *Glos* 4C **48**
Church Aston. *Telf* 4B **72**
Church Brampton. *Nptn* 4E **62**
Church Brough. *Cumb* 3A **104**
Church Broughton. *Derbs* 2G **73**
Church Common. *Hants* 4F **25**
Church Crookham. *Hants* 1G **25**
Churchdown. *Glos* 4D **48**
Church Eaton. *Staf* 4C **72**
Church End. *Beds* 3H **51** (nr. Dunstable)
Church End. *Beds* 2B **52** (nr. Stotfold)
Church End. *Beds* 2H **51** (nr. Woburn)
Church End. *Cambs* 5D **65** (nr. Cambridge)
Church End. *Cambs* 2B **64** (nr. Sawtry)
Church End. *Cambs* 3C **64** (nr. Willingham)
Church End. *Cambs* 5C **76** (nr. Wisbech)
Church End. *E Yor* 4E **101**
Church End. *Essx* 3H **53** (nr. Braintree)
Churchend. *Essx* 3G **53** (nr. Great Dunmow)
Church End. *Essx* 1F **53** (nr. Saffron Walden)
Churchend. *Essx* 1E **40** (nr. Southend)
Church End. *Glos* 5C **48**
Church End. *Hants* 1E **25**
Church End. *Linc* 2B **76** (nr. Donington)
Church End. *Linc* 1D **88** (nr. North Somercotes)
Church End. *Norf* 4E **77**
Church End. *Warw* 1G **61** (nr. Coleshill)
Church End. *Warw* 1G **61** (nr. Nuneaton)
Church End. *Wilts* 4F **35**
Church Enstone. *Oxon* 3B **50**
Church Fenton. *N Yor* 1F **93**
Church Green. *Devn* 3E **13**
Church Gresley. *Derbs* 4G **73**
Church Hanborough. *Oxon* 4C **50**
Church Hill. *Ches* 4A **84**
Church Hill. *Worc* 4E **61**
Church Hougham. *Kent* 1G **29**
Church Houses. *N Yor* 5D **106**
Churchill. *Devn* 2G **13** (nr. Axminster)
Churchill. *Devn* 2F **19** (nr. Barnstaple)
Churchill. *N Som* 1H **21**
Churchill. *Oxon* 3A **50**
Churchill. *Worc* 3C **60** (nr. Kidderminster)
Churchill. *Worc* 5D **60** (nr. Worcester)
Churchingford. *Som* 1F **13**
Church Knowle. *Dors* 4E **15**
Church Laneham. *Notts* 3F **87**
Church Langley. *Essx* 5E **53**
Church Langton. *Leics* 1E **62**
Church Lawford. *Warw* 3B **62**
Church Lawton. *Ches* 5C **84**
Church Leigh. *Staf* 2E **73**
Church Lench. *Worc* 5E **61**
Church Mayfield. *Staf* 1F **73**
Church Minshull. *Ches* 4A **84**
Church Norton. *W Sus* 3G **17**
Churchover. *Warw* 2C **62**
Church Preen. *Shrp* 1H **59**

Church Pulverbatch. *Shrp* 5G **71**
Churchstanton. *Som* 1E **13**
Church Stoke. *Powy* 1E **59**
Churchstow. *Devn* 4D **8**
Church Stowe. *Nptn* 5D **62**
Church Street. *Kent* 3B **40**
Church Street. *Suff* 2G **67**
Church Stretton. *Shrp* 1G **59**
Churchthorpe. *Linc* 1C **88**
Churchtown. *Cumb* 5E **113**
Churchtown. *Derbs* 4G **85**
Churchtown. *Devn* 2G **19**
Churchtown. *IOM* 2D **108**
Churchtown. *Lanc* 5D **97**
Church Town. *Leics* 4A **74**
Churchtown. *Mers* 3B **90**
Church Town. *N Lin* 4A **94**
Churchtown. *Shrp* 2E **59**
Church Village. *Rhon* 3D **32**
Church Warsop. *Notts* 4C **86**
Church Westcote. *Glos* 3H **49**
Church Wilne. *Derbs* 2B **74**
Churnsike Lodge. *Nmbd* 2H **113**
Churston Ferrers. *Torb* 3F **9**
Churt. *Surr* 3G **25**
Churton. *Ches* 5G **83**
Churwell. *W Yor* 2C **92**
Chute Standen. *Wilts* 1B **24**
Chwilog. *Gwyn* 2D **68**
Chwittffordd. *Flin* 3D **82**
Chyandour. *Corn* 3B **4**
Cilan Uchaf. *Gwyn* 3B **68**
Cilcain. *Flin* 4D **82**
Cilcennin. *Cdgn* 4E **57**
Cilfrew. *Neat* 5A **46**
Cilfynydd. *Rhon* 2D **32**
Cilgerran. *Pemb* 1B **44**
Cilgeti. *Pemb* 4F **43**
Cilgwyn. *Carm* 3H **45**
Cilgwyn. *Pemb* 1E **43**
Ciliau Aeron. *Cdgn* 5D **57**
Cill Amhlaidh. *W Isl* 4C **170**
Cill Donnain. *High* 1G **165**
Cill Donnain. *W Isl* 6C **170**
Cille Bhrighde. *W Isl* 7C **170**
Cille Pheadair. *W Isl* 7C **170**
Cilmaengwyn. *Neat* 5H **45**
Cilmeri. *Powy* 5C **58**
Cilmery. *Powy* 5C **58**
Cilrhedyn. *Pemb* 1G **43**
Cilsan. *Carm* 3F **45**
Ciltalgarth. *Gwyn* 1A **70**
Ciltwrch. *Powy* 1E **47**
Cilybebyll. *Neat* 5H **45**
Cilycwm. *Carm* 2A **46**
Cimla. *Neat* 2A **32**
Cinderford. *Glos* 4B **48**
Cinderhill. *Derbs* 1A **74**
Cippenham. *Slo* 2A **38**
Cippyn. *Pemb* 1B **44**
Cirbhig. *W Isl* 3D **171**
Circebost. *W Isl* 4D **171**
Cirencester. *Glos* 5F **49**
City. *Powy* 1E **58**
City. *V Glam* 4C **32**
City Dulas. *IOA* 2D **80**
City (London) Airport. *G Lon* 2F **39**
City of London. *G Lon* 2E **39**
City, The. *Buck* 2F **37**
Clabhach. *Arg* 3C **138**
Clachaig. *Arg* 1C **126**
Clachaig. *High* 3F **141** (nr. Kinlochleven)
Clachaig. *High* 2E **151** (nr. Nethy Bridge)
Clachamish. *High* 3C **154**
Clachan. *Arg* 4F **125** (on Kintyre)
Clachan. *Arg* 4C **140** (on Lismore)
Clachan. *High* 2H **167** (nr. Bettyhill)
Clachan. *High* 2D **155** (nr. Staffin)
Clachan. *High* 1C **154** (nr. Uig)
Clachan. *High* 5E **155** (on Raasay)
Clachan Farm. *Arg* 2A **134**
Clachan na Luib. *W Isl* 2D **170**
Clachan of Campsie. *E Dun* 2H **127**
Clachan of Glendaruel. *Arg* 1A **126**
Clachan-Seil. *Arg* 2E **133**
Clachan Shannda. *W Isl* 1D **170**
Clachan Strachur. *Arg* 3H **133**
Clachbreck. *Arg* 2F **125**
Clachnaharry. *High* 4A **158**
Clachtoll. *High* 1E **163**
Clackmannan. *Clac* 4B **136**
Clackmarras. *Mor* 3G **159**
Clacton-on-Sea. *Essx* 4E **55**
Cladach a Chaolais. *W Isl* 2C **170**
Cladach Chairinis. *W Isl* 3D **170**
Cladach Chirceboist. *W Isl* 2C **170**
Cladich. *Arg* 1H **133**
Cladswell. *Worc* 5E **61**
Claggan. *High* 1F **141** (nr. Fort William)
Claggan. *High* 4A **140** (nr. Lochaline)
Claigan. *High* 3B **154**
Clandown. *Bath* 1B **22**
Clanfield. *Hants* 1E **17**
Clanfield. *Oxon* 5A **50**
Clanville. *Hants* 2B **24**
Clanville. *Som* 3B **22**
Claonaig. *Arg* 4G **125**
Clapgate. *Dors* 2F **15**
Clapgate. *Herts* 3E **53**
Clapham. *Beds* 5H **63**
Clapham. *Devn* 4B **12**
Clapham. *G Lon* 3D **39**
Clapham. *N Yor* 3G **97**
Clapham. *W Sus* 5B **26**
Clap Hill. *Kent* 2E **29**
Clappers. *Bord* 4F **131**
Clappersgate. *Cumb* 4E **103**
Clapton. *Som* 2H **13** (nr. Crewkerne)
Clapton. *Som* 1B **22** (nr. Radstock)
Clapton-in-Gordano. *N Som* 4H **33**
Clapton-on-the-Hill. *Glos* 4G **49**
Clapworthy. *Devn* 4G **19**
Clara Vale. *Tyne* 3E **115**
Clarbeston. *Pemb* 2E **43**
Clarbeston Road. *Pemb* 2E **43**
Clarborough. *Notts* 2E **87**
Clare. *Suff* 1A **54**
Clarebrand. *Dum* 3E **111**
Clarencefield. *Dum* 3B **112**
Clarilaw. *Bord* 3H **119**
Clark's Green. *Surr* 2C **26**
Clark's Hill. *Linc* 3C **76**
Clarkston. *E Ren* 4G **127**
Clasheddy. *High* 2G **167**
Clashindarroch. *Abers* 5B **160**
Clashmore. *High* 5E **165** (nr. Dornoch)
Clashmore. *High* 1E **163** (nr. Stoer)
Clashnessie. *High* 5A **166**
Clashnoir. *Mor* 1G **151**
Clathick. *Per* 1H **135**
Clathy. *Per* 2B **136**
Clatt. *Abers* 1C **152**
Clatter. *Powy* 1B **58**
Clatterford. *IOW* 4C **16**
Clatworthy. *Som* 3D **20**
Claughton. *Lanc* 3E **97** (nr. Caton)
Claughton. *Lanc* 5E **97** (nr. Garstang)
Claughton. *Mers* 2F **83**
Claverdon. *Warw* 4F **61**
Claverham. *N Som* 5H **33**
Clavering. *Essx* 2E **53**
Claverley. *Shrp* 1B **60**
Claverton. *Bath* 5C **34**
Clawdd-coch. *V Glam* 4D **32**
Clawdd-newydd. *Den* 5C **82**
Clawson Hill. *Leics* 3E **75**
Clawton. *Devn* 3D **10**
Claxby. *Linc* 3D **88** (nr. Alford)
Claxby. *Linc* 1A **88** (nr. Market Rasen)
Claxton. *Norf* 5F **79**
Claxton. *N Yor* 4A **100**
Claybrooke Magna. *Leics* 2B **62**
Claybrooke Parva. *Leics* 2B **62**
Clay Common. *Suff* 2G **67**
Clay Coton. *Nptn* 3C **62**
Clay Cross. *Derbs* 4A **86**
Claydon. *Oxon* 5B **62**
Claydon. *Suff* 5D **66**
Clay End. *Herts* 3D **52**
Claygate. *Kent* 1B **28**
Claygate. *Surr* 4C **38**
Claygate Cross. *Kent* 5H **39**
Clayhall. *Hants* 3E **16**
Clayhanger. *Devn* 4D **20**
Clayhanger. *W Mid* 5E **73**
Clayhidon. *Devn* 1E **13**
Clay Hill. *Bris* 4B **34**
Clayhill. *E Sus* 3C **28**
Clayhill. *Hants* 2B **16**
Clayholes. *Ang* 5E **145**
Clayhythe. *Cambs* 4E **65**
Claylake. *Dors* 2F **15**
Clay Lake. *Linc* 3B **76**
Clayock. *High* 3D **168**
Claypits. *Glos* 5C **48**
Claypole. *Linc* 1F **75**
Claythorpe. *Linc* 3D **88**
Clayton. *G Man* 1C **84**
Clayton. *S Yor* 4E **93**
Clayton. *Staf* 1C **72**
Clayton. *W Sus* 4E **27**
Clayton. *W Yor* 1B **92**
Clayton Green. *Lanc* 2D **90**
Clayton-le-Moors. *Lanc* 1F **91**
Clayton-le-Woods. *Lanc* 2D **90**
Clayton West. *W Yor* 3C **92**
Clayworth. *Notts* 2E **87**
Cleadale. *High* 5C **146**
Cleadon. *Tyne* 3G **115**
Clearbrook. *Devn* 2B **8**
Clearwell. *Glos* 5A **48**
Cleasby. *N Yor* 3F **105**
Cleat. *Orkn* 3D **172** (nr. Braehead)
Cleat. *Orkn* 9D **172** (nr. St Margaret's Hope)
Cleatlam. *Dur* 3E **105**
Cleator. *Cumb* 3B **102**
Cleator Moor. *Cumb* 3B **102**
Cleckheaton. *W Yor* 2B **92**
Cleedownton. *Shrp* 2H **59**
Cleehill. *Shrp* 3H **59**
Cleekhimin. *N Lan* 4A **128**
Clee St Margaret. *Shrp* 2H **59**
Cleestanton. *Shrp* 3H **59**
Cleethorpes. *NE Lin* 4G **95**
Cleeton St Mary. *Shrp* 3A **60**
Cleeve. *N Som* 5H **33**
Cleeve. *Oxon* 3E **36**
Cleeve Hill. *Glos* 3E **49**
Cleeve Prior. *Worc* 1F **49**
Clehonger. *Here* 2H **47**
Cleigh. *Arg* 1F **133**
Cleish. *Per* 4C **136**
Cleland. *N Lan* 4B **128**
Clench Common. *Wilts* 5G **35**
Clenchwarton. *Norf* 3E **77**
Clennell. *Nmbd* 4D **120**
Clent. *Worc* 3D **60**
Cleobury Mortimer. *Shrp* 3A **60**
Cleobury North. *Shrp* 2A **60**
Clephanton. *High* 3C **158**
Clerkhill. *High* 2H **167**
Clestrain. *Orkn* 7C **172**
Clevancy. *Wilts* 4F **35**
Clevedon. *N Som* 4H **33**
Cleveley. *Oxon* 3B **50**
Cleveleys. *Lanc* 5C **96**
Clevelode. *Worc* 1D **48**
Cleverton. *Wilts* 3E **35**
Clewer. *Som* 1H **21**
Cley next the Sea. *Norf* 1C **78**
Cliaid. *W Isl* 8B **170**
Cliasmol. *W Isl* 7C **171**
Clibberswick. *Shet* 1H **173**
Cliburn. *Cumb* 2G **103**
Cliddesden. *Hants* 2E **25**
Clieves Hills. *Lanc* 4B **90**
Cliff. *Warw* 1G **61**
Cliffburn. *Ang* 4F **145**
Cliffe. *Medw* 3B **40**
Cliffe. *N Yor* 3F **105** (nr. Darlington)
Cliffe. *N Yor* 1G **93** (nr. Selby)
Cliff End. *E Sus* 4C **28**
Cliffe Woods. *Medw* 3B **40**
Clifford. *Here* 1F **47**
Clifford. *W Yor* 5G **99**
Clifford Chambers. *Warw* 5F **61**
Clifford's Mesne. *Glos* 3B **48**
Cliffs End. *Kent* 4H **41**
Clifton. *Beds* 2B **52**
Clifton. *Bris* 4A **34**
Clifton. *Cumb* 2G **103**
Clifton. *Derbs* 1F **73**
Clifton. *Devn* 2G **19**
Clifton. *G Man* 4F **91**
Clifton. *Lanc* 1C **90**
Clifton. *Nmbd* 1F **115**
Clifton. *N Yor* 5D **98**
Clifton. *Nott* 2C **74**
Clifton. *Oxon* 2C **50**
Clifton. *S Yor* 1C **86**
Clifton. *Stir* 5H **141**
Clifton. *W Yor* 2B **92**
Clifton. *Worc* 1D **48**
Clifton. *York* 4H **99**
Clifton Campville. *Staf* 4G **73**
Clifton Hampden. *Oxon* 2D **36**
Clifton Hill. *Worc* 4B **60**
Clifton Reynes. *Mil* 5G **63**
Clifton upon Dunsmore. *Warw* 3C **62**
Clifton-upon-Teme. *Worc* 4B **60**
Cliftonville. *Kent* 3H **41**
Cliftonville. *Norf* 2F **79**
Climping. *W Sus* 5A **26**
Climpy. *S Lan* 4C **128**
Clint. *N Yor* 4E **99**
Clint Green. *Norf* 4C **78**
Clintmains. *Bord* 1A **120**
Cliobh. *W Isl* 4C **171**
Clipiau. *Gwyn* 4H **69**
Clippesby. *Norf* 4G **79**
Clippings Green. *Norf* 4C **78**
Clipsham. *Rut* 4G **75**
Clipston. *Nptn* 2E **62**
Clipston. *Notts* 2D **74**
Clipstone. *Notts* 4C **86**
Clitheroe. *Lanc* 5G **97**
Cliuthar. *W Isl* 8D **171**
Clive. *Shrp* 3H **71**
Clivocast. *Shet* 1H **173**
Clixby. *Linc* 4D **94**
Clocaenog. *Den* 5C **82**
Clochan. *Mor* 2B **160**
Clochforbie. *Abers* 3F **161**
Clock Face. *Mers* 1H **83**
Cloddiau. *Powy* 5E **70**
Cloddymoss. *Mor* 2D **159**
Clodock. *Here* 3G **47**
Cloford. *Som* 2C **22**
Clola. *Abers* 4H **161**
Clophill. *Beds* 2A **52**
Clopton. *Nptn* 2H **63**
Clopton Corner. *Suff* 5E **66**
Clopton Green. *Suff* 5G **65**
Closeburn. *Dum* 5A **118**
Close Clark. *IOM* 4B **108**
Closworth. *Som* 1A **14**
Clothall. *Herts* 2C **52**
Clotton. *Ches* 4H **83**
Clough. *G Man* 3H **91**
Clough. *W Yor* 3A **92**
Clough Foot. *W Yor* 2H **91**
Cloughton. *N Yor* 5H **107**
Cloughton Newlands. *N Yor* 5H **107**
Clouston. *Orkn* 6B **172**
Clova. *Abers* 1B **152**
Clova. *Ang* 1C **144**
Clovelly. *Devn* 4D **18**
Clovenfords. *Bord* 1G **119**
Clovenstone. *Abers* 2E **153**
Clovullin. *High* 2E **141**
Clowne. *Derbs* 3B **86**
Clows Top. *Worc* 3B **60**
Cloy. *Wrex* 1F **71**
Cluanie Inn. *High* 2C **148**
Cluanie Lodge. *High* 2C **148**
Cluddley. *Telf* 5A **72**
Clun. *Shrp* 2F **59**
Clunas. *High* 4C **158**
Clunbury. *Shrp* 2F **59**
Clunderwen. *Carm* 3F **43**
Clune. *High* 1B **150**
Clunes. *High* 5E **148**
Clungunford. *Shrp* 3F **59**
Clunie. *Per* 4A **144**
Clunton. *Shrp* 2F **59**
Cluny. *Fife* 4E **137**
Clutton. *Bath* 1B **22**
Clutton. *Ches* 5G **83**
Clwt-y-bont. *Gwyn* 4E **81**
Clwydfagwyr. *Mer T* 5D **46**
Clydach. *Mon* 4F **47**
Clydach. *Swan* 5G **45**
Clydach Vale. *Rhon* 2C **32**
Clydebank. *W Dun* 2G **127**
Clydey. *Pemb* 1G **43**
Clyffe Pypard. *Wilts* 4F **35**
Clynder. *Arg* 1D **126**
Clyne. *Neat* 5B **46**
Clynelish. *High* 3F **165**
Clynnog-fawr. *Gwyn* 1D **68**
Clyro. *Powy* 1F **47**
Clyst Honiton. *Devn* 3C **12**
Clyst Hydon. *Devn* 2D **12**
Clyst St George. *Devn* 4C **12**
Clyst St Lawrence. *Devn* 2D **12**
Clyst St Mary. *Devn* 3C **12**
Clyth. *High* 5E **169**
Cnip. *W Isl* 4C **171**
Cnwcau. *Pemb* 1C **44**
Cnwch Coch. *Cdgn* 3F **57**
Coad's Green. *Corn* 5C **10**
Coal Aston. *Derbs* 3A **86**
Coalbrookdale. *Telf* 5A **72**
Coalbrookvale. *Blae* 5F **47**
Coalburn. *S Lan* 1H **117**
Coalburns. *Tyne* 3E **115**
Coalcleugh. *Nmbd* 5B **114**
Coaley. *Glos* 5C **48**
Coalford. *Abers* 4F **153**
Coalhall. *E Ayr* 3D **116**
Coalhill. *Essx* 1B **40**
Coalpit Heath. *S Glo* 3B **34**
Coal Pool. *W Mid* 5E **73**
Coalport. *Telf* 5B **72**
Coalsnaughton. *Clac* 4B **136**
Coaltown of Balgonie. *Fife* 4F **137**
Coaltown of Wemyss. *Fife* 4F **137**
Coalville. *Leics* 4B **74**
Coalway. *Glos* 4A **48**
Coanwood. *Nmbd* 4H **113**
Coat. *Som* 4H **21**
Coatbridge. *N Lan* 3A **128**
Coatdyke. *N Lan* 3A **128**
Coate. *Swin* 3G **35**
Coate. *Wilts* 5F **35**
Coates. *Cambs* 1C **64**
Coates. *Glos* 5E **49**

Coates. *Linc* 2G **87**
Coates. *W Sus* 4A **26**
Coatham. *Red C* 2C **106**
Coatham Mundeville. *Darl* 2F **105**
Cobbaton. *Devn* 4G **19**
Coberley. *Glos* 4E **49**
Cobhall Common. *Here* 2H **47**
Cobham. *Kent* 4A **40**
Cobham. *Surr* 4C **38**
Cobnash. *Here* 4G **59**
Coburg. *Devn* 5B **12**
Cockayne. *N Yor* 5D **106**
Cockayne Hatley. *Beds* 1C **52**
Cock Bank. *Wrex* 1F **71**
Cock Bridge. *Abers* 3G **151**
Cockburnspath. *Bord* 2D **130**
Cock Clarks. *Essx* 5B **54**
Cockenzie and Port Seton. *E Lot* 2H **129**
Cockerham. *Lanc* 4D **96**
Cockermouth. *Cumb* 1C **102**
Cockernhoe. *Herts* 3B **52**
Cockfield. *Dur* 2E **105**
Cockfield. *Suff* 5B **66**
Cockfosters. *G Lon* 1D **39**
Cock Gate. *Here* 4G **59**
Cock Green. *Essx* 4G **53**
Cocking. *W Sus* 1G **17**
Cocking Causeway. *W Sus* 1G **17**
Cockington. *Torb* 2F **9**
Cocklake. *Som* 2H **21**
Cocklaw. *Abers* 4H **161**
Cocklaw. *Nmbd* 2C **114**
Cockley Beck. *Cumb* 4D **102**
Cockley Cley. *Norf* 5G **77**
Cockmuir. *Abers* 3G **161**
Cockpole Green. *Wind* 3G **37**
Cockshutford. *Shrp* 2H **59**
Cockshutt. *Shrp* 3G **71**
Cockthorpe. *Norf* 1B **78**
Cockwood. *Devn* 4C **12**
Cockyard. *Derbs* 3E **85**
Cockyard. *Here* 2H **47**
Codda. *Corn* 5B **10**
Coddenham. *Suff* 5D **66**
Coddenham Green. *Suff* 5D **66**
Coddington. *Ches* 5G **83**
Coddington. *Here* 1C **48**
Coddington. *Notts* 5F **87**
Codford St Mary. *Wilts* 3E **23**
Codford St Peter. *Wilts* 3E **23**
Codicote. *Herts* 4C **52**
Codmore Hill. *W Sus* 3B **26**
Codnor. *Derbs* 1B **74**
Codrington. *S Glo* 4C **34**
Codsall. *Staf* 5C **72**
Codsall Wood. *Staf* 5C **72**
Coed Duon. *Cphy* 2E **33**
Coedely. *Rhon* 3D **32**
Coedglasson. *Powy* 4C **58**
Coedkernew. *Newp* 3F **33**
Coed Morgan. *Mon* 4G **47**
Coedpoeth. *Wrex* 5E **83**
Coedway. *Powy* 4F **71**
Coed-y-bryn. *Cdgn* 1D **44**
Coed-y-paen. *Mon* 2G **33**
Coed-yr-ynys. *Powy* 3E **47**
Coed Ystumgwern. *Gwyn* 3E **69**
Coelbren. *Powy* 4B **46**
Coffinswell. *Devn* 2E **9**
Cofton Hackett. *Worc* 3E **61**
Cogan. *V Glam* 4E **33**
Cogenhoe. *Nptn* 4F **63**
Cogges. *Oxon* 5B **50**
Coggeshall. *Essx* 3B **54**
Coggeshall Hamlet. *Essx* 3B **54**
Coggins Mill. *E Sus* 3G **27**
Coignafearn Lodge. *High* 2A **150**
Coig Peighinnean. *W Isl* 1H **171**
Coig Peighinnean Bhuirgh. *W Isl* 2G **171**
Coilleag. *W Isl* 7C **170**
Coilliemore. *High* 1A **158**
Coillore. *High* 5C **154**
Coire an Fhuarain. *W Isl* 4E **171**
Coity. *B'end* 3C **32**
Cokhay Green. *Derbs* 3G **73**
Col. *W Isl* 3G **171**
Colaboll. *High* 2C **164**
Colan. *Corn* 2C **6**
Colaton Raleigh. *Devn* 4D **12**
Colbost. *High* 4B **154**
Colburn. *N Yor* 5E **105**
Colby. *Cumb* 2H **103**
Colby. *IOM* 4B **108**
Colby. *Norf* 2E **78**
Colchester. *Essx* 3D **54**
Cold Ash. *W Ber* 5D **36**
Cold Ashby. *Nptn* 3D **62**
Cold Ashton. *S Glo* 4C **34**
Cold Aston. *Glos* 4G **49**
Coldbackie. *High* 3G **167**
Cold Blow. *Pemb* 3F **43**
Cold Brayfield. *Mil* 5G **63**
Cold Cotes. *N Yor* 2G **97**
Coldean. *Brig* 5E **27**
Coldeast. *Devn* 5B **12**
Colden. *W Yor* 2H **91**
Colden Common. *Hants* 4C **24**
Coldfair Green. *Suff* 4G **67**
Coldham. *Cambs* 5D **76**
Coldham. *Staf* 5C **72**
Cold Hanworth. *Linc* 2H **87**
Coldharbour. *Corn* 4B **6**
Cold Harbour. *Dors* 3E **15**
Coldharbour. *Glos* 5A **48**
Coldharbour. *Kent* 5G **39**
Coldharbour. *Surr* 1C **26**
Cold Hatton. *Telf* 3A **72**
Cold Hatton Heath. *Telf* 3A **72**
Cold Hesledon. *Dur* 5H **115**
Cold Hiendley. *W Yor* 3D **92**
Cold Higham. *Nptn* 5D **62**
Coldingham. *Bord* 3F **131**
Cold Kirby. *N Yor* 1H **99**
Coldmeece. *Staf* 2C **72**
Cold Northcott. *Corn* 4C **10**
Cold Norton. *Essx* 5B **54**
Cold Overton. *Leics* 4F **75**
Coldrain. *Per* 3C **136**
Coldred. *Kent* 1G **29**
Coldridge. *Devn* 2G **11**
Cold Row. *Lanc* 5C **96**
Coldstream. *Bord* 5E **131**
Coldwaltham. *W Sus* 4B **26**
Coldwell. *Here* 2H **47**
Coldwells. *Abers* 5H **161**
Coldwells Croft. *Abers* 1C **152**
Cole. *Som* 3B **22**
Colebatch. *Shrp* 2F **59**
Colebrook. *Devn* 2D **12**
Colebrooke. *Devn* 2A **12**
Coleburn. *Mor* 3G **159**
Coleby. *Linc* 4G **87**
Coleby. *N Lin* 3B **94**
Cole End. *Warw* 2G **61**
Coleford. *Devn* 2A **12**
Coleford. *Glos* 4A **48**
Coleford. *Som* 2B **22**
Colegate End. *Norf* 2D **66**
Cole Green. *Herts* 4C **52**
Cole Henley. *Hants* 1C **24**
Colehill. *Dors* 2F **15**
Coleman Green. *Herts* 4B **52**
Coleman's Hatch. *E Sus* 2F **27**
Colemere. *Shrp* 2G **71**
Colemore. *Hants* 3F **25**
Colemore Green. *Shrp* 1B **60**
Coleorton. *Leics* 4B **74**
Colerne. *Wilts* 4D **34**
Colesbourne. *Glos* 4E **49**
Colesden. *Beds* 5A **64**
Coles Green. *Worc* 5B **60**
Coleshill. *Buck* 1A **38**
Coleshill. *Oxon* 2H **35**
Coleshill. *Warw* 2G **61**
Colestocks. *Devn* 2D **12**
Colethrop. *Glos* 4D **48**
Coley. *Bath* 1A **22**
Colgate. *W Sus* 2D **26**
Colinsburgh. *Fife* 3G **137**
Colinton. *Edin* 3F **129**
Colintraive. *Arg* 2B **126**
Colkirk. *Norf* 3B **78**
Collace. *Per* 5B **144**
Collam. *W Isl* 8D **171**
Collaton. *Devn* 5D **8**
Collaton St Mary. *Torb* 2E **9**
College of Roseisle. *Mor* 2F **159**
Collessie. *Fife* 2E **137**
Collier Row. *G Lon* 1F **39**
Colliers End. *Herts* 3D **52**
Collier Street. *Kent* 1B **28**
Colliery Row. *Tyne* 5G **115**
Collieston. *Abers* 1H **153**
Collin. *Dum* 2B **112**
Collingbourne Ducis. *Wilts* 1H **23**
Collingbourne Kingston. *Wilts* 1H **23**
Collingham. *Notts* 4F **87**
Collingham. *W Yor* 5F **99**
Collingtree. *Nptn* 5E **63**
Collins Green. *Warr* 1H **83**
Collins Green. *Worc* 5B **60**
Colliston. *Ang* 4F **145**
Colliton. *Devn* 2D **12**
Collydean. *Fife* 3E **137**
Collyweston. *Nptn* 5G **75**
Colmonell. *S Ayr* 1G **109**
Colmworth. *Beds* 5A **64**
Colnbrook. *Slo* 3B **38**
Colne. *Cambs* 3C **64**
Colne. *Lanc* 5A **98**
Colne Engaine. *Essx* 2B **54**
Colney. *Norf* 5D **78**
Colney Heath. *Herts* 5C **52**
Colney Street. *Herts* 5B **52**
Coln Rogers. *Glos* 5F **49**
Coln St Aldwyns. *Glos* 5G **49**
Coln St Dennis. *Glos* 4F **49**
Colpitts Grange. *Nmbd* 4C **114**
Colpy. *Abers* 5D **160**
Colscott. *Devn* 1D **10**
Colsterdale. *N Yor* 1D **98**
Colsterworth. *Linc* 3G **75**
Colston Bassett. *Notts* 2D **74**
Colstoun House. *E Lot* 2B **130**
Coltfield. *Mor* 2F **159**
Colthouse. *Cumb* 5E **103**
Coltishall. *Norf* 4E **79**
Coltness. *N Lan* 4A **128**
Colton. *Cumb* 1C **96**
Colton. *Norf* 5D **78**
Colton. *N Yor* 5H **99**
Colton. *Staf* 3E **73**
Colton. *W Yor* 1D **92**
Colt's Hill. *Kent* 1H **27**
Col Uarach. *W Isl* 4G **171**
Colvend. *Dum* 4F **111**
Colwall Green. *Here* 1C **48**
Colwall Stone. *Here* 1C **48**
Colwell. *Nmbd* 2C **114**
Colwich. *Staf* 3E **73**
Colwick. *Notts* 1D **74**
Colwinston. *V Glam* 4C **32**
Colworth. *W Sus* 5A **26**
Colwyn Bay. *Cnwy* 3A **82**
Colyford. *Devn* 3F **13**
Colyton. *Devn* 3F **13**
Combe. *Devn* 2D **8**
Combe. *Here* 4F **59**
Combe. *Oxon* 4C **50**
Combe. *W Ber* 5B **36**
Combe Almer. *Dors* 3E **15**
Combebow. *Devn* 4E **11**
Combe Common. *Surr* 2A **26**
Combe Down. *Bath* 5C **34**
Combe Fishacre. *Devn* 2E **9**
Combe Florey. *Som* 3E **21**
Combe Hay. *Bath* 1C **22**
Combeinteignhead. *Devn* 5C **12**
Combe Martin. *Devn* 2F **19**
Combe Moor. *Here* 4F **59**
Combe Raleigh. *Devn* 2E **13**
Comberbach. *Ches* 3A **84**
Comberford. *Staf* 5F **73**
Comberton. *Cambs* 5C **64**
Comberton. *Here* 4G **59**
Combe St Nicholas. *Som* 1G **13**
Combpyne. *Devn* 3F **13**
Combridge. *Staf* 2E **73**
Combrook. *Warw* 5H **61**
Combs. *Derbs* 3E **85**
Combs. *Suff* 5C **66**
Combs Ford. *Suff* 5C **66**
Combwich. *Som* 2F **21**
Comers. *Abers* 3D **152**
Comhampton. *Worc* 4C **60**
Comins Coch. *Cdgn* 2F **57**
Comley. *Shrp* 1G **59**
Commercial End. *Cambs* 4E **65**
Commins. *Powy* 3D **70**
Commins Coch. *Powy* 5H **69**
Commondale. *N Yor* 3D **106**
Common End. *Cumb* 2B **102**
Common Hill. *Here* 2A **48**
Common Moor. *Corn* 2G **7**
Common Platt. *Wilts* 3G **35**
Commonside. *Ches* 3H **83**
Common Side. *Derbs* 3H **85** (nr. Chesterfield)
Commonside. *Derbs* 1G **73** (nr. Derby)
Common, The. *Wilts* 3H **23** (nr. Salisbury)
Common, The. *Wilts* 3F **35** (nr. Swindon)
Compstall. *G Man* 1D **84**
Compton. *Devn* 2E **9**
Compton. *Hants* 4C **24**
Compton. *Plym* 3A **8**
Compton. *Staf* 2C **60**
Compton. *Surr* 1A **26**
Compton. *W Ber* 3D **36**
Compton. *W Sus* 1F **17**
Compton. *Wilts* 1G **23**
Compton Abbas. *Dors* 1D **14**
Compton Abdale. *Glos* 4F **49**
Compton Bassett. *Wilts* 4F **35**
Compton Beauchamp. *Oxon* 3A **36**
Compton Bishop. *Som* 1G **21**
Compton Chamberlayne. *Wilts* 4F **23**
Compton Dando. *Bath* 5B **34**
Compton Dundon. *Som* 3H **21**
Compton Greenfield. *S Glo* 3A **34**
Compton Martin. *Bath* 1A **22**
Compton Pauncefoot. *Som* 4B **22**
Compton Valence. *Dors* 3A **14**
Comrie. *Fife* 1D **128**
Comrie. *Per* 1G **135**
Conaglen. *High* 2E **141**
Conchra. *Arg* 1B **126**
Conchra. *High* 1A **148**
Conder Green. *Lanc* 4D **96**
Conderton. *Worc* 2E **49**
Condicote. *Glos* 3G **49**
Condorrat. *N Lan* 2A **128**
Condover. *Shrp* 5G **71**
Coneyhurst Common. *W Sus* 3C **26**
Coneysthorpe. *N Yor* 2B **100**
Coneythorpe. *N Yor* 4F **99**
Coney Weston. *Suff* 3B **66**
Conford. *Hants* 3G **25**
Congdon's Shop. *Corn* 5C **10**
Congerstone. *Leics* 5A **74**
Congham. *Norf* 3G **77**
Congleton. *Ches* 4C **84**
Congl-y-wal. *Gwyn* 1G **69**
Congresbury. *N Som* 5H **33**
Congreve. *Staf* 4D **72**
Conham. *S Glo* 4B **34**
Conicaval. *Mor* 3D **159**
Coningsby. *Linc* 5B **88**
Conington. *Cambs* 4C **64** (nr. Fenstanton)
Conington. *Cambs* 2A **64** (nr. Sawtry)
Conisbrough. *S Yor* 1C **86**
Conisby. *Arg* 3A **124**
Conisholme. *Linc* 1D **88**
Coniston. *Cumb* 5E **102**
Coniston. *E Yor* 1E **95**
Coniston Cold. *N Yor* 4B **98**
Conistone. *N Yor* 3B **98**
Connah's Quay. *Flin* 4E **83**
Connel. *Arg* 5D **140**
Connel Park. *E Ayr* 3F **117**
Connista. *High* 1D **154**
Connor Downs. *Corn* 3C **4**
Conock. *Wilts* 1F **23**
Conon Bridge. *High* 3H **157**
Cononley. *N Yor* 5B **98**
Cononsyth. *Ang* 4E **145**
Conordan. *High* 5E **155**
Consall. *Staf* 1D **73**
Consett. *Dur* 4E **115**
Constable Burton. *N Yor* 5E **105**
Constantine. *Corn* 4E **5**
Constantine Bay. *Corn* 1C **6**
Contin. *High* 3G **157**
Contullich. *High* 1A **158**
Conwy. *Cnwy* 3G **81**
Conyer. *Kent* 4D **40**
Conyers Green. *Suff* 4A **66**
Cooden. *E Sus* 5B **28**
Cooil. *IOM* 4C **108**
Cookbury. *Devn* 2E **11**
Cookbury Wick. *Devn* 2D **11**
Cookham. *Wind* 3G **37**
Cookham Dean. *Wind* 3G **37**
Cookham Rise. *Wind* 3G **37**
Cookhill. *Worc* 5E **61**
Cookley. *Suff* 3F **67**
Cookley. *Worc* 2C **60**
Cookley Green. *Oxon* 2E **37**
Cookney. *Abers* 4F **153**
Cooksbridge. *E Sus* 4F **27**
Cooksey Corner. *Worc* 4D **60**
Cooksey Green. *Worc* 4D **60**
Cookshill. *Staf* 1D **72**
Cooksmill Green. *Essx* 5G **53**
Coolham. *W Sus* 3C **26**
Cooling. *Medw* 3B **40**
Cooling Street. *Medw* 3B **40**
Coombe. *Corn* 1C **10** (nr. Bude)
Coombe. *Corn* 3D **6** (nr. St Austell)
Coombe. *Corn* 4C **6** (nr. Truro)
Coombe. *Devn* 3E **12** (nr. Sidmouth)
Coombe. *Devn* 5C **12** (nr. Teignmouth)
Coombe. *Glos* 2C **34**
Coombe. *Hants* 4E **25**
Coombe. *Wilts* 1G **23**
Coombe Bissett. *Wilts* 4G **23**
Coombe Hill. *Glos* 3D **49**
Coombe Keynes. *Dors* 4D **14**
Coombes. *W Sus* 5C **26**
Coombe Street. *Som* 3C **22**
Coopersale Common. *Essx* 5E **53**
Coopersale Street. *Essx* 5E **53**
Cooper's Corner. *Kent* 1F **27**
Cooper Street. *Kent* 5H **41**
Cootham. *W Sus* 4B **26**
Copalder Corner. *Cambs* 1C **64**
Copdock. *Suff* 1E **54**
Copford. *Essx* 3C **54**
Copford Green. *Essx* 3C **54**
Copgrove. *N Yor* 3F **99**
Copister. *Shet* 4F **173**
Cople. *Beds* 1B **52**
Copley. *Dur* 2D **105**
Coplow Dale. *Derbs* 3F **85**
Copmanthorpe. *York* 5H **99**
Copp. *Lanc* 1C **90**
Coppathorne. *Corn* 2C **10**

Coppenhall. *Ches* 5B **84**
Coppenhall. *Staf* 4D **72**
Coppenhall Moss. *Ches* 5B **84**
Copperhouse. *Corn* 3C **4**
Coppicegate. *Shrp* 2B **60**
Coppingford. *Cambs* 2A **64**
Copplestone. *Devn* 2A **12**
Coppull. *Lanc* 3D **90**
Coppull Moor. *Lanc* 3D **90**
Copsale. *W Sus* 3C **26**
Copster Green. *Lanc* 1E **91**
Copston Magna. *Warw* 2B **62**
Copt Green. *Warw* 4F **61**
Copthall Green. *Essx* 5E **53**
Copt Heath. *W Mid* 3F **61**
Copt Hewick. *N Yor* 2F **99**
Copthill. *Dur* 5B **114**
Copthorne. *W Sus* 2E **27**
Coptiviney. *Shrp* 2G **71**
Copy's Green. *Norf* 2B **78**
Copythorne. *Hants* 1B **16**
Corbridge. *Nmbd* 3C **114**
Corby. *Nptn* 2F **63**
Corby Glen. *Linc* 3H **75**
Cordon. *N Ayr* 2E **123**
Coreley. *Shrp* 3A **60**
Corfe. *Som* 1F **13**
Corfe Castle. *Dors* 4E **15**
Corfe Mullen. *Dors* 3E **15**
Corfton. *Shrp* 2G **59**
Corgarff. *Abers* 3G **151**
Corhampton. *Hants* 4E **24**
Corlae. *Dum* 5F **117**
Corlannau. *Neat* 2A **32**
Corley. *Warw* 2H **61**
Corley Ash. *Warw* 2G **61**
Corley Moor. *Warw* 2G **61**
Cormiston. *S Lan* 1C **118**
Cornaa. *IOM* 3D **108**
Cornaigbeg. *Arg* 4A **138**
Cornaigmore. *Arg* 2D **138** (on Coll)
Cornaigmore. *Arg* 4A **138** (on Tiree)
Corner Row. *Lanc* 1C **90**
Corney. *Cumb* 5C **102**
Cornforth. *Dur* 1A **106**
Cornhill. *Abers* 3C **160**
Cornhill. *High* 4C **164**
Cornhill-on-Tweed. *Nmbd* 1C **120**
Cornholme. *W Yor* 2H **91**
Cornish Hall End. *Essx* 2G **53**
Cornriggs. *Dur* 5B **114**
Cornsay. *Dur* 5E **115**
Cornsay Colliery. *Dur* 5E **115**
Corntown. *High* 3H **157**
Corntown. *V Glam* 4C **32**
Cornwell. *Oxon* 3A **50**
Cornwood. *Devn* 3C **8**
Cornworthy. *Devn* 3E **9**
Corpach. *High* 1E **141**
Corpusty. *Norf* 3D **78**
Corra. *Dum* 3F **111**
Corran. *High* 2E **141** (nr. Arnisdale)
Corran. *High* 3A **148** (nr. Fort William)
Corrany. *IOM* 3D **108**
Corribeg. *High* 1D **141**
Corrie. *N Ayr* 5B **126**
Corrie Common. *Dum* 1D **112**
Corriecravie. *N Ayr* 3D **122**
Corriekinloch. *High* 1A **164**
Corriemoillie. *High* 2F **157**
Corrievarkie Lodge. *Per* 1C **142**
Corrievorrie. *High* 1B **150**
Corrimony. *High* 5F **157**
Corringham. *Linc* 1F **87**
Corringham. *Thur* 2B **40**
Corris. *Gwyn* 5G **69**
Corris Uchaf. *Gwyn* 5G **69**
Corrour Shooting Lodge. *High* 2B **142**
Corry. *High* 1E **147**
Corrybrough. *High* 1C **150**
Corrygills. *N Ayr* 2E **123**
Corry of Ardnagrask. *High* 4H **157**
Corsback. *High* 1E **169** (nr. Dunnet)
Corsback. *High* 3E **169** (nr. Halkirk)
Corscombe. *Dors* 2A **14**
Corse. *Abers* 4D **160**
Corse. *Glos* 3C **48**
Corsehill. *Abers* 3G **161**
Corse Lawn. *Worc* 2D **48**
Corse of Kinnoir. *Abers* 4C **160**
Corsham. *Wilts* 4D **34**
Corsley. *Wilts* 2D **22**
Corsley Heath. *Wilts* 2D **22**
Corsock. *Dum* 2E **111**
Corston. *Bath* 5B **34**
Corston. *Wilts* 3E **35**
Corstorphine. *Edin* 2F **129**
Cortachy. *Ang* 3C **144**
Corton. *Suff* 1H **67**
Corton. *Wilts* 2E **23**
Corton Denham. *Som* 4B **22**
Corwar House. *S Ayr* 1H **109**
Corwen. *Den* 1C **70**
Coryates. *Dors* 4B **14**
Coryton. *Devn* 4E **11**
Coryton. *Thur* 2B **40**
Cosby. *Leics* 1C **62**
Coscote. *Oxon* 3D **36**
Coseley. *W Mid* 1D **60**
Cosgrove. *Nptn* 1F **51**
Cosham. *Port* 2E **17**
Cosheston. *Pemb* 4E **43**
Coskills. *N Lin* 3D **94**
Cosmeston. *V Glam* 5E **33**
Cossall. *Notts* 1B **74**
Cossington. *Leics* 4D **74**
Cossington. *Som* 2G **21**
Costa. *Orkn* 5C **172**
Costessey. *Norf* 4D **78**
Costock. *Notts* 3C **74**
Coston. *Leics* 3F **75**
Coston. *Norf* 5C **78**
Cote. *Oxon* 5B **50**
Cotebrook. *Ches* 4H **83**
Cotehill. *Cumb* 4F **113**
Cotes. *Cumb* 1D **97**
Cotes. *Leics* 3C **74**
Cotes. *Staf* 2C **72**
Cotesbach. *Leics* 2C **62**
Cotes Heath. *Staf* 2C **72**
Cotgrave. *Notts* 2D **74**
Cothall. *Abers* 2F **153**
Cotham. *Notts* 1E **75**
Cothelstone. *Som* 3E **21**
Cotheridge. *Worc* 5B **60**
Cotherstone. *Dur* 3D **104**
Cothill. *Oxon* 2C **36**
Cotland. *Mon* 5A **48**
Cotleigh. *Devn* 2F **13**
Cotmanhay. *Derbs* 1B **74**
Coton. *Cambs* 5D **64**
Coton. *Nptn* 3D **62**
Coton. *Staf* 3C **72** (nr. Gnosall)
Coton. *Staf* 2D **73** (nr. Stone)
Coton. *Staf* 5F **73** (nr. Tamworth)
Coton Clanford. *Staf* 3C **72**
Coton Hayes. *Staf* 2D **73**
Coton Hill. *Shrp* 4G **71**
Coton in the Clay. *Staf* 3F **73**
Coton in the Elms. *Derbs* 4G **73**
Cotonwood. *Shrp* 2H **71**
Cotonwood. *Staf* 3C **72**
Cott. *Devn* 2D **9**
Cottam. *E Yor* 3D **101**
Cottam. *Lanc* 1D **90**
Cottam. *Notts* 3F **87**
Cottartown. *High* 5E **159**
Cottarville. *Nptn* 4E **63**
Cottenham. *Cambs* 4D **64**
Cotterdale. *N Yor* 5B **104**
Cottered. *Herts* 3D **52**
Cotterstock. *Nptn* 1H **63**
Cottesbrooke. *Nptn* 3E **62**
Cottesmore. *Rut* 4G **75**
Cotteylands. *Devn* 1C **12**
Cottingham. *E Yor* 1D **94**
Cottingham. *Nptn* 1F **63**
Cottingley. *W Yor* 1B **92**
Cottisford. *Oxon* 2D **50**
Cotton. *Staf* 1E **73**
Cotton. *Suff* 4C **66**
Cotton End. *Beds* 1A **52**
Cottown. *Abers* 4F **161**
Cotts. *Devn* 2A **8**
Cotwalton. *Staf* 2D **72**
Couch's Mill. *Corn* 3F **7**
Coughton. *Here* 3A **48**
Coughton. *Warw* 4E **61**
Coulags. *High* 4B **156**
Coulderton. *Cumb* 4A **102**
Coulin Lodge. *High* 3C **156**
Coull. *Abers* 3C **152**
Coulport. *Arg* 1D **126**
Coulsdon. *Surr* 5D **39**
Coulter. *S Lan* 1C **118**
Coultershaw Bridge. *W Sus* 4A **26**
Coultings. *Som* 2F **21**
Coulton. *N Yor* 2A **100**
Cound. *Shrp* 5H **71**
Coundon. *Dur* 2F **105**
Coundon Grange. *Dur* 2F **105**
Countersett. *N Yor* 1B **98**
Countess. *Wilts* 2G **23**
Countess Cross. *Essx* 2B **54**
Countesthorpe. *Leics* 1C **62**
Countisbury. *Devn* 2H **19**
Coupar Angus. *Per* 4B **144**
Coupe Green. *Lanc* 2D **90**
Coupland. *Cumb* 3A **104**
Coupland. *Nmbd* 1D **120**
Cour. *Arg* 5G **125**
Courance. *Dum* 5C **118**
Court-at-Street. *Kent* 2E **29**
Courteachan. *High* 4E **147**
Courteenhall. *Nptn* 5E **63**
Court Henry. *Carm* 3F **45**
Courtsend. *Essx* 1E **41**
Courtway. *Som* 3F **21**
Cousland. *Midl* 3G **129**
Cousley Wood. *E Sus* 2A **28**
Coustonn. *Arg* 2B **126**
Cove. *Arg* 1D **126**
Cove. *Devn* 1C **12**
Cove. *Hants* 1G **25**
Cove. *High* 4C **162**
Cove. *Bord* 2D **130**
Cove Bay. *Aber* 3G **153**
Covehithe. *Suff* 2H **67**
Coven. *Staf* 5D **72**
Coveney. *Cambs* 2D **65**
Covenham St Bartholomew. *Linc* 1C **88**
Covenham St Mary. *Linc* 1C **88**
Coven Heath. *Staf* 5D **72**
Coventry. *W Mid* 3H **61**
Coventry Airport. *Warw* 3A **62**
Coverack. *Corn* 5E **5**
Coverham. *N Yor* 1D **98**
Covesea. *Mor* 1F **159**
Covingham. *Swin* 3G **35**
Covington. *Cambs* 3H **63**
Covington. *S Lan* 1B **118**
Cowan Bridge. *Lanc* 2F **97**
Cowan Head. *Cumb* 5F **103**
Cowbar. *Red C* 3E **107**
Cowbeech. *E Sus* 4H **27**
Cowbit. *Linc* 4B **76**
Cowbridge. *V Glam* 4C **32**
Cowden. *Kent* 1F **27**
Cowdenbeath. *Fife* 4D **136**
Cowdenburn. *Bord* 4F **129**
Cowdenend. *Fife* 4D **136**
Cowers Lane. *Derbs* 1H **73**
Cowes. *IOW* 3C **16**
Cowesby. *N Yor* 1G **99**
Cowfold. *W Sus* 3D **26**
Cowfords. *Mor* 2H **159**
Cowgate. *Cumb* 5B **112**
Cowgill. *Cumb* 1G **97**
Cowie. *Abers* 5F **153**
Cowie. *Stir* 1B **128**
Cowlam. *E Yor* 3D **100**
Cowley. *Devn* 3C **12**
Cowley. *Glos* 4E **49**
Cowley. *G Lon* 2B **38**
Cowley. *Oxon* 5D **50**
Cowley. *Staf* 4C **72**
Cowleymoor. *Devn* 1C **12**
Cowling. *Lanc* 3D **90**
Cowling. *N Yor* 1E **99** (nr. Bedale)
Cowling. *N Yor* 5B **98** (nr. Glusburn)
Cowlinge. *Suff* 5G **65**
Cowmes. *W Yor* 3B **92**
Cowpe. *Lanc* 2G **91**
Cowpen. *Nmbd* 1F **115**
Cowpen Bewley. *Stoc T* 2B **106**
Cowplain. *Hants* 1E **17**
Cowshill. *Dur* 5B **114**
Cowslip Green. *N Som* 5H **33**
Cowstrandburn. *Fife* 4C **136**
Cowthorpe. *N Yor* 4G **99**
Coxall. *Here* 3F **59**
Coxbank. *Ches* 1A **72**
Coxbench. *Derbs* 1A **74**
Cox Common. *Suff* 2G **67**
Coxford. *Norf* 3H **77**
Coxgreen. *Staf* 2C **60**
Cox Green. *Surr* 2B **26**
Cox Green. *Tyne* 4G **115**
Coxheath. *Kent* 5B **40**
Coxhoe. *Dur* 1A **106**
Coxley. *Som* 2A **22**
Coxwold. *N Yor* 2H **99**
Coychurch. *V Glam* 3C **32**
Coylton. *S Ayr* 3D **116**
Coylumbridge. *High* 2D **150**
Coynach. *Abers* 3B **152**
Coynachie. *Abers* 5B **160**
Coytrahen. *B'end* 3B **32**
Crabbs Cross. *Worc* 4E **61**
Crabgate. *Norf* 3C **78**
Crab Orchard. *Dors* 2F **15**
Crabtree. *W Sus* 3D **26**
Crabtree Green. *Wrex* 1F **71**
Crackaig. *High* 2G **165**
Crackenthorpe. *Cumb* 2H **103**
Crackington Haven. *Corn* 3B **10**
Crackley. *Staf* 5C **84**
Crackley. *Warw* 3G **61**
Crackleybank. *Shrp* 4B **72**
Crackpot. *N Yor* 5C **104**
Cracoe. *N Yor* 3B **98**
Craddock. *Devn* 1D **12**
Cradhlastadh. *W Isl* 4C **171**
Cradley. *Here* 1C **48**
Cradley. *W Mid* 2D **60**
Cradoc. *Powy* 2D **46**
Crafthole. *Corn* 3H **7**
Crafton. *Buck* 4G **51**
Cragabus. *Arg* 5B **124**
Crag Foot. *Lanc* 2D **97**
Craggan. *High* 1E **151**
Cragganmore. *Mor* 5F **159**
Cragganvallie. *High* 5H **157**
Craggie. *High* 1F **165**
Craggiemore. *High* 5B **158**
Cragg Vale. *W Yor* 2A **92**
Craghead. *Dur* 4F **115**
Crai. *Powy* 3B **46**
Craibstone. *Aber* 2F **153**
Craichie. *Ang* 4E **145**
Craig. *Arg* 5E **141**
Craig. *Dum* 2D **111**
Craig. *High* 4C **156** (nr. Achnashellach)
Craig. *High* 2G **155** (nr. Lower Diabaig)
Craig. *High* 5H **155** (nr. Stromeferry)
Craiganour Lodge. *Per* 3D **142**
Craigbrack. *Arg* 4A **134**
Craig-cefn-parc. *Swan* 5G **45**
Craigdallie. *Per* 1E **137**
Craigdam. *Abers* 5F **161**
Craigdarroch. *E Ayr* 4F **117**
Craigdarroch. *High* 3G **157**
Craigdhu. *High* 4G **157**
Craigearn. *Abers* 2E **152**
Craigellachie. *Mor* 4G **159**
Craigend. *Per* 1D **136**
Craigendoran. *Arg* 1E **126**
Craigends. *Ren* 3F **127**
Craigenputtock. *Dum* 1E **111**
Craigens. *E Ayr* 3E **117**
Craighall. *Edin* 2E **129**
Craighead. *Fife* 2H **137**
Craighouse. *Arg* 3D **124**
Craigie. *Abers* 2G **153**
Craigie. *D'dee* 5D **144**
Craigie. *Per* 4A **144** (nr. Blairgowrie)
Craigie. *Per* 1D **136** (nr. Perth)
Craigie. *S Ayr* 1D **116**
Craigielaw. *E Lot* 2A **130**
Craiglemine. *Dum* 5B **110**
Craig-llwyn. *Shrp* 3E **71**
Craiglockhart. *Edin* 2F **129**
Craig Lodge. *Arg* 2B **126**
Craigmalloch. *E Ayr* 5D **117**
Craigmaud. *Abers* 3F **161**
Craigmill. *Stir* 4H **135**
Craigmillar. *Edin* 2F **129**
Craigmore. *Arg* 3C **126**
Craigmuie. *Dum* 1E **111**
Craignair. *Dum* 3F **111**
Craignant. *Shrp* 2E **71**
Craigneuk. *N Lan* 3A **128** (nr. Airdrie)
Craigneuk. *N Lan* 4A **128** (nr. Motherwell)
Craignure. *Arg* 5B **140**
Craigo. *Abers* 2F **145**
Craigrory. *High* 4A **158**
Craigrothie. *Fife* 2F **137**
Craigs. *Dum* 2D **112**
Craigshill. *W Lot* 3D **128**
Craigs, The. *High* 4B **164**
Craigton. *Aber* 3F **153**
Craigton. *Abers* 3E **152**
Craigton. *Ang* 5E **145** (nr. Carnoustie)
Craigton. *Ang* 3C **144** (nr. Kirriemuir)
Craigton. *High* 4A **158**
Craigtown. *High* 3A **168**
Craig-y-Duke. *Neat* 5H **45**
Craigyloch. *Ang* 3B **144**
Craig-y-nos. *Powy* 4B **46**
Craik. *Bord* 4F **119**
Crail. *Fife* 3H **137**
Crailing. *Bord* 2A **120**
Crailinghall. *Bord* 2A **120**
Crakehill. *N Yor* 2G **99**
Crakemarsh. *Staf* 2E **73**
Crambe. *N Yor* 3B **100**
Crambeck. *N Yor* 3B **100**
Cramlington. *Nmbd* 2F **115**
Cramond. *Edin* 2E **129**
Cramond Bridge. *Edin* 2E **129**
Cranage. *Ches* 4B **84**
Cranberry. *Staf* 2C **72**
Cranborne. *Dors* 1F **15**
Cranbourne. *Brac* 3A **38**
Cranbrook. *Kent* 2B **28**
Cranbrook Common. *Kent* 2B **28**
Crane Moor. *S Yor* 4D **92**

Crane's Corner—Cuddington

Crane's Corner. *Norf* 4B 78
Cranfield. *Beds* 1H 51
Cranford. *G Lon* 3B 38
Cranford St Andrew. *Nptn* 3G 63
Cranford St John. *Nptn* 3G 63
Cranham. *Glos* 4D 49
Cranham. *G Lon* 2G 39
Crank. *Mers* 1H 83
Cranleigh. *Surr* 2B 26
Cranley. *Suff* 3D 66
Cranloch. *Mor* 3G 159
Cranmer Green. *Suff* 3C 66
Cranmore. *IOW* 3B 16
Cranmore. *Linc* 5A 76
Crannich. *Arg* 4G 139
Crannoch. *Mor* 3B 160
Cranoe. *Leics* 1E 63
Cransford. *Suff* 4F 67
Cranshaws. *Bord* 3C 130
Cranstal. *IOM* 1D 108
Crantock. *Corn* 2B 6
Cranwell. *Linc* 5H 87
Cranwich. *Norf* 1G 65
Cranworth. *Norf* 5B 78
Craobh Haven. *Arg* 3E 133
Craobhnaclag. *High* 4G 157
Crapstone. *Devn* 2B 8
Crarae. *Arg* 4G 133
Crask. *High* 2H 167
Crask Inn. *High* 1C 164
Crask of Aigas. *High* 4G 157
Craster. *Nmbd* 3G 121
Cratfield. *Suff* 3F 67
Crathes. *Abers* 4E 153
Crathie. *Abers* 4G 151
Crathie. *High* 4H 149
Crathorne. *N Yor* 4B 106
Craven Arms. *Shrp* 2G 59
Crawcrook. *Tyne* 3E 115
Crawford. *Lanc* 4D 90
Crawford. *S Lan* 2B 118
Crawforddyke. *S Lan* 4B 128
Crawfordjohn. *S Lan* 2A 118
Crawick. *Dum* 3G 117
Crawley. *Devn* 2F 13
Crawley. *Hants* 3C 24
Crawley. *Oxon* 4B 50
Crawley. *W Sus* 2D 26
Crawley Down. *W Sus* 2E 27
Crawley Side. *Dur* 5C 114
Crawshawbooth. *Lanc* 2G 91
Crawton. *Abers* 5F 153
Cray. *N Yor* 2B 98
Cray. *Per* 2A 144
Crayford. *G Lon* 3G 39
Crayke. *N Yor* 2H 99
Craymere Beck. *Norf* 2C 78
Crays Hill. *Essx* 1B 40
Cray's Pond. *Oxon* 3E 37
Crazies Hill. *Wok* 3F 37
Creacombe. *Devn* 1B 12
Creagan. *Arg* 4D 141
Creag Aoil. *High* 1F 141
Creag Ghoraidh. *W Isl* 4C 170
Creaguaineach Lodge. *High* 2H 141
Creamore Bank. *Shrp* 2H 71
Creaton. *Nptn* 3E 62
Creca. *Dum* 2D 112
Credenhill. *Here* 1H 47
Crediton. *Devn* 2B 12
Creebridge. *Dum* 3B 110
Creech. *Dors* 4E 15
Creech Heathfield. *Som* 4F 21
Creech St Michael. *Som* 4F 21
Creed. *Corn* 4D 6
Creekmoor. *Pool* 3E 15
Creekmouth. *G Lon* 2F 39
Creeting St Mary. *Suff* 5C 66
Creeting St Peter. *Suff* 5C 66
Creeton. *Linc* 3H 75
Creetown. *Dum* 4B 110
Creggans. *Arg* 3H 133
Cregneash. *IOM* 5A 108
Cregrina. *Powy* 5D 58
Creich. *Arg* 2B 132
Creighton. *Staf* 2E 73
Creigiau. *Card* 3D 32
Cremyll. *Corn* 3A 8
Crendell. *Dors* 1F 15
Crepkill. *High* 4D 154
Cressage. *Shrp* 5H 71
Cressbrook. *Derbs* 3F 85
Cresselly. *Pemb* 4E 43
Cressing. *Essx* 3A 54
Cresswell. *Nmbd* 5G 121
Cresswell. *Staf* 2D 73
Cresswell Quay. *Pemb* 4E 43
Creswell. *Derbs* 3C 86
Creswell Green. *Staf* 4E 73
Cretingham. *Suff* 4E 67
Crewe. *Ches* 5G 83
(nr. Farndon)
Crewe. *Ches* 5B 84
(nr. Nantwich)
Crewgreen. *Powy* 4F 71
Crewkerne. *Som* 2H 13
Crews Hill. *G Lon* 5D 52
Crewton. *Derb* 2A 74
Crianlarich. *Stir* 1C 134
Cribbs Causeway. *S Glo* 3A 34
Cribyn. *Cdgn* 5E 57
Criccieth. *Gwyn* 2D 69
Crich. *Derbs* 5A 86
Crichton. *Midl* 3G 129
Crick. *Mon* 2H 33
Crick. *Nptn* 3C 62
Crickadarn. *Powy* 1D 46
Cricket Hill. *Hants* 5G 37
Cricket Malherbie. *Som* 1G 13
Cricket St Thomas. *Som* 2G 13
Crickham. *Som* 2H 21
Crickheath. *Shrp* 3E 71
Crickhowell. *Powy* 4F 47
Cricklade. *Wilts* 2F 35
Cricklewood. *G Lon* 2D 38
Cridling Stubbs. *N Yor* 2F 93
Criech. *Fife* 1F 137
Crieff. *Per* 1A 136
Criftins. *Shrp* 2F 71
Criggion. *Powy* 4E 71
Crigglestone. *W Yor* 3D 92
Crimchard. *Som* 2G 13
Crimdon Park. *Dur* 1B 106
Crimond. *Abers* 3H 161
Crimonmogate. *Abers* 3H 161
Crimplesham. *Norf* 5F 77
Crimscote. *Warw* 1H 49
Crinan. *Arg* 4E 133
Cringleford. *Norf* 5D 78
Crinow. *Pemb* 3F 43
Cripplesease. *Corn* 3C 4
Cripplestyle. *Dors* 1F 15
Cripp's Corner. *E Sus* 3B 28
Croanford. *Corn* 5A 10
Crockenhill. *Kent* 4G 39
Crocker End. *Oxon* 3F 37
Crockerhill. *Hants* 2D 16
Crockernwell. *Devn* 3A 12
Crocker's Ash. *Here* 4A 48
Crockerton. *Wilts* 2D 22
Crocketford. *Dum* 2F 111
Crockey Hill. *York* 5A 100
Crockham Hill. *Kent* 5F 39
Crockhurst Street. *Kent* 1H 27
Crockleford Heath. *Essx* 3D 54
Croeserw. *Neat* 2B 32
Croes-Goch. *Pemb* 1C 42
Croes Hywel. *Mon* 4G 47
Croes-lan. *Cdgn* 1D 45
Croesor. *Gwyn* 1F 69
Croesoswallt. *Shrp* 3E 71
Croesyceiliog. *Carm* 4E 45
Croesyceiliog. *Torf* 2F 33
Croes-y-mwyalch. *Torf* 2G 33
Croesywaun. *Gwyn* 5E 81
Croford. *Som* 4E 20
Croft. *Leics* 1C 62
Croft. *Linc* 4E 89
Croft. *Warr* 1A 84
Croftamie. *Stir* 1F 127
Croftfoot. *Glas* 3G 127
Croftmill. *Per* 5F 143
Crofton. *Cumb* 4E 112
Crofton. *W Yor* 3D 93
Crofton. *Wilts* 5A 36
Croft-on-Tees. *N Yor* 4F 105
Crofts. *Dum* 2E 111
Crofts of Benachielt. *High* 5D 169
Crofts of Dipple. *Mor* 3H 159
Crofty. *Swan* 3E 31
Croggan. *Arg* 1E 132
Croglin. *Cumb* 5G 113
Croich. *High* 4B 164
Croick. *High* 3A 168
Croig. *Arg* 3E 139
Cromarty. *High* 2B 158
Crombie. *Fife* 1D 128
Cromdale. *High* 1E 151
Cromer. *Herts* 3C 52
Cromer. *Norf* 1E 79
Cromford. *Derbs* 5G 85
Cromhall. *S Glo* 2B 34
Cromhall Common. *S Glo* 3B 34
Cromor. *W Isl* 5G 171
Cromra. *High* 5H 149
Cromwell. *Notts* 4E 87
Cronberry. *E Ayr* 2F 117
Crondall. *Hants* 2F 25
Cronk, The. *IOM* 2C 108
Cronk-y-Voddy. *IOM* 3C 108
Cronton. *Mers* 2G 83
Crook. *Cumb* 5F 103
Crook. *Dur* 1E 105
Crookdake. *Cumb* 5C 112
Crooke. *G Man* 4D 90
Crookedholm. *E Ayr* 1D 116
Crooked Soley. *Wilts* 4B 36
Crookes. *S Yor* 2H 85
Crookgate Bank. *Dur* 4E 115
Crookhall. *Dur* 4E 115
Crookham. *Nmbd* 1D 120
Crookham. *W Ber* 5D 36
Crookham Village. *Hants* 1F 25
Crooklands. *Cumb* 1E 97
Crook of Devon. *Per* 3C 136
Crookston. *Ren* 3G 127
Cropredy. *Oxon* 1C 50
Cropston. *Leics* 4C 74
Cropthorne. *Worc* 1E 49
Cropton. *N Yor* 1B 100
Cropwell Bishop. *Notts* 2D 74
Cropwell Butler. *Notts* 2D 74
Cros. *W Isl* 1H 171
Crosbie. *N Ayr* 5D 126
Crosbost. *W Isl* 5F 171
Crosby. *Cumb* 1B 102
Crosby. *IOM* 4C 108
Crosby. *Mers* 1F 83
Crosby. *N Lin* 3B 94
Crosby Court. *N Yor* 5A 106
Crosby Garrett. *Cumb* 4A 104
Crosby Ravensworth. *Cumb* 3H 103
Crosby Villa. *Cumb* 1B 102
Croscombe. *Som* 2A 22
Crosland Moor. *W Yor* 3B 92
Cross. *Som* 1H 21
Crossaig. *Arg* 4G 125
Crossapol. *Arg* 4A 138
Cross Ash. *Mon* 4H 47
Cross-at-Hand. *Kent* 1B 28
Crossbush. *W Sus* 5B 26
Crosscanonby. *Cumb* 1B 102
Crossdale Street. *Norf* 2E 79
Cross End. *Essx* 2B 54
Crossens. *Mers* 3B 90
Crossford. *Fife* 1D 128
Crossford. *S Lan* 5B 128
Cross Foxes. *Gwyn* 4G 69
Crossgate. *Orkn* 6D 172
Crossgate. *Staf* 2D 72
Crossgatehall. *E Lot* 3G 129
Crossgates. *Fife* 1E 129
Crossgates. *N Yor* 1E 101
Crossgates. *Powy* 4C 58
Cross Gates. *W Yor* 1D 92
Crossgill. *Lanc* 3E 97
Cross Green. *Devn* 4D 11
Cross Green. *Staf* 5D 72
Cross Green. *Suff* 5A 66
(nr. Cockfield)
Cross Green. *Suff* 5B 66
(nr. Hitcham)
Cross Hands. *Carm* 4F 45
(nr. Ammanford)
Crosshands. *Carm* 2F 43
(nr. Whitland)
Crosshands. *E Ayr* 1D 117
Crosshill. *E Ayr* 2D 117
Crosshill. *Fife* 4D 136
Cross Hill. *Glos* 2A 34
Crosshill. *S Ayr* 4C 116
Crosshills. *High* 1A 158
Cross Hills. *N Yor* 5C 98
Cross Holme. *N Yor* 5C 106
Crosshouse. *E Ayr* 1C 116
Cross Houses. *Shrp* 5H 71
Crossings. *Cumb* 2G 113
Cross in Hand. *E Sus* 3G 27
Cross Inn. *Cdgn* 4E 57
(nr. Aberaeron)
Cross Inn. *Cdgn* 5C 56
(nr. New Quay)
Cross Inn. *Rhon* 3D 32
Crosskeys. *Cphy* 2F 33
Crosskirk. *High* 2C 168
Crosslands. *Cumb* 1C 96
Cross Lane Head. *Shrp* 1B 60
Cross Lanes. *Corn* 4D 5
Cross Lanes. *Dur* 3D 104
Cross Lanes. *N Yor* 3H 99
Crosslanes. *Shrp* 4F 71
Cross Lanes. *Wrex* 1F 71
Crosslee. *Ren* 3F 127
Crossmichael. *Dum* 3E 111
Crossmoor. *Lanc* 1C 90
Cross Oak. *Powy* 3E 46
Cross of Jackston. *Abers* 5E 161
Cross o' th' Hands. *Derbs* 1G 73
Crossroads. *Abers* 3G 153
(nr. Aberdeen)
Crossroads. *Abers* 4E 153
(nr. Banchory)
Crossroads. *E Ayr* 1D 116
Cross Side. *Devn* 4B 20
Cross Street. *Suff* 3D 66
Crosston. *Ang* 3E 145
Cross Town. *Ches* 3B 84
Crossway. *Mon* 4H 47
Crossway. *Powy* 5C 58
Crossway Green. *Mon* 2A 34
Crossway Green. *Worc* 4C 60
Crossways. *Dors* 4C 14
Crosswell. *Pemb* 1F 43
Crosswood. *Cdgn* 3F 57
Crosthwaite. *Cumb* 5F 103
Croston. *Lanc* 3C 90
Crostwick. *Norf* 4E 79
Crostwight. *Norf* 3F 79
Crothair. *W Isl* 4D 171
Crouch. *Kent* 5H 39
Croucheston. *Wilts* 4F 23
Crouch Hill. *Dors* 1C 14
Croughton. *Nptn* 2D 50
Crovie. *Abers* 2F 161
Crow. *Hants* 2G 15
Crowan. *Corn* 3D 4
Crowborough. *E Sus* 2G 27
Crowcombe. *Som* 3E 21
Crowcroft. *Worc* 5B 60
Crowdecote. *Derbs* 4F 85
Crowden. *Derbs* 1E 85
Crowden. *Devn* 3E 11
Crowdhill. *Hants* 1C 16
Crowdon. *N Yor* 5G 107
Crow Edge. *S Yor* 4B 92
Crow End. *Cambs* 5C 64
Crowfield. *Nptn* 1E 50
Crowfield. *Suff* 5D 66
Crow Green. *Essx* 1G 39
Crow Hill. *Here* 3B 48
Crowhurst. *E Sus* 4B 28
Crowhurst. *Surr* 1E 27
Crowhurst Lane End. *Surr* 1E 27
Crowland. *Linc* 4B 76
Crowland. *Suff* 3C 66
Crowlas. *Corn* 3C 4
Crowle. *N Lin* 3A 94
Crowle. *Worc* 5D 60
Crowle Green. *Worc* 5D 60
Crowmarsh Gifford. *Oxon* 3E 36
Crown Corner. *Suff* 3E 67
Crownthorpe. *Norf* 5C 78
Crowntown. *Corn* 3D 4
Crows-an-wra. *Corn* 4A 4
Crowshill. *Norf* 5B 78
Crowthorne. *Brac* 5G 37
Crowton. *Ches* 3H 83
Croxall. *Staf* 4F 73
Croxby. *Linc* 1A 88
Croxdale. *Dur* 1F 105
Croxden. *Staf* 2E 73
Croxley Green. *Herts* 1B 38
Croxton. *Cambs* 4B 64
Croxton. *Norf* 2B 78
(nr. Fakenham)
Croxton. *Norf* 2A 66
(nr. Thetford)
Croxton. *N Lin* 3D 94
Croxton. *Staf* 2B 72
Croxtonbank. *Staf* 2B 72
Croxton Green. *Ches* 5H 83
Croxton Kerrial. *Leics* 3F 75
Croy. *High* 4B 158
Croy. *N Lan* 2A 128
Croyde. *Devn* 3E 19
Croydon. *Cambs* 1D 52
Croydon. *G Lon* 4E 39
Crubenbeg. *High* 4A 150
Crubenmore Lodge. *High* 4A 150
Cruckmeore. *Shrp* 5G 71
Cruckton. *Shrp* 4G 71
Cruden Bay. *Abers* 5H 161
Crudgington. *Telf* 4A 72
Crudie. *Abers* 3E 161
Crudwell. *Wilts* 2E 35
Cruft. *Devn* 3F 11
Crug. *Powy* 3D 58
Crughywel. *Powy* 4F 47
Crugmeer. *Corn* 1D 6
Crugybar. *Carm* 2G 45
Crug-y-byddar. *Powy* 2D 58
Crulabhig. *W Isl* 4D 171
Crumlin. *Cphy* 2F 33
Crumpsall. *G Man* 4G 91
Crumpsbrook. *Shrp* 3A 60
Crundale. *Kent* 1E 29
Crundale. *Pemb* 3D 42
Cruwys Morchard. *Devn* 1B 12
Crux Easton. *Hants* 1C 24
Cruxton. *Dors* 3B 14
Crwbin. *Carm* 4E 45
Cryers Hill. *Buck* 2G 37
Crymych. *Pemb* 1F 43
Crynant. *Neat* 5A 46
Crystal Palace. *G Lon* 3E 39
Cuaich. *High* 5A 150
Cuaig. *High* 3G 155
Cuan. *Arg* 2E 133
Cubbington. *Warw* 4H 61
Cubert. *Corn* 3B 6
Cubley. *S Yor* 4C 92
Cubley Common. *Derbs* 2F 73
Cublington. *Buck* 3G 51
Cublington. *Here* 2H 47
Cuckfield. *W Sus* 3E 27
Cucklington. *Som* 4C 22
Cuckney. *Notts* 3C 86
Cuckoo Bridge. *Linc* 3B 76
Cuddesdon. *Oxon* 5E 50
Cuddington. *Buck* 4F 51

Cuddington. *Ches* 3A **84**
Cuddington Heath. *Ches* 1G **71**
Cuddy Hill. *Lanc* 1C **90**
Cudham. *G Lon* 5F **39**
Cudlipptown. *Devn* 5F **11**
Cudworth. *Som* 1G **13**
Cudworth. *S Yor* 4D **93**
Cudworth. *Surr* 1D **26**
Cuerdley Cross. *Warr* 2H **83**
Cuffley. *Herts* 5D **52**
Cuidhsiadar. *W Isl* 2H **171**
Cuidhtinis. *W Isl* 9C **171**
Culbo. *High* 2A **158**
Culbokie. *High* 3A **158**
Culburnie. *High* 4G **157**
Culcabock. *High* 4A **158**
Culcharry. *High* 3C **158**
Culcheth. *Warr* 1A **84**
Culduie. *High* 4G **155**
Culeave. *High* 4C **164**
Culford. *Suff* 4H **65**
Culgaith. *Cumb* 2H **103**
Culham. *Oxon* 2D **36**
Culkein. *High* 1E **163**
Culkein Drumbeg. *High* 5B **166**
Culkerton. *Glos* 2E **35**
Cullen. *Mor* 2C **160**
Cullercoats. *Tyne* 2G **115**
Cullicudden. *High* 2A **158**
Cullingworth. *W Yor* 1A **92**
Cullipool. *Arg* 2E **133**
Cullivoe. *Shet* 1G **173**
Culloch. *Per* 2G **135**
Cullompton. *Devn* 2D **12**
Culm Davy. *Devn* 1E **13**
Culmington. *Shrp* 2G **59**
Culmstock. *Devn* 1E **12**
Culnacnoc. *High* 2E **155**
Culnacraig. *High* 3E **163**
Culrain. *High* 4C **164**
Culross. *Fife* 1C **128**
Culroy. *S Ayr* 3C **116**
Culswick. *Shet* 7D **173**
Cults. *Aber* 3F **153**
Cults. *Abers* 5C **160**
Cults. *Fife* 3F **137**
Cultybraggan Camp. *Per* 1G **135**
Culver. *Devn* 3B **12**
Culverlane. *Devn* 2D **8**
Culverstone Green. *Kent* 4H **39**
Culverthorpe. *Linc* 1H **75**
Culworth. *Nptn* 1D **50**
Culzie Lodge. *High* 1H **157**
Cumberlow Green. *Herts* 2D **52**
Cumbernauld. *N Lan* 2A **128**
Cumbernauld Village. *N Lan* 2A **128**
Cumberworth. *Linc* 3E **89**
Cumdivock. *Cumb* 5E **113**
Cuminestown. *Abers* 3F **161**
Cumledge Mill. *Bord* 4D **130**
Cummersdale. *Cumb* 4E **113**
Cummertrees. *Dum* 3C **112**
Cummingstown. *Mor* 2F **159**
Cumnock. *E Ayr* 3E **117**
Cumnor. *Oxon* 5C **50**
Cumrew. *Cumb* 4G **113**
Cumwhinton. *Cumb* 4F **113**
Cumwhitton. *Cumb* 4G **113**
Cundall. *N Yor* 2G **99**
Cunninghamhead. *N Ayr* 5E **127**
Cunning Park. *S Ayr* 3C **116**
Cunningsburgh. *Shet* 9F **173**
Cunnister. *Shet* 2G **173**
Cupar. *Fife* 2F **137**
Cupar Muir. *Fife* 2F **137**
Cupernham. *Hants* 4B **24**
Curbar. *Derbs* 3G **85**
Curborough. *Staf* 4F **73**
Curbridge. *Hants* 1D **16**
Curbridge. *Oxon* 5B **50**
Curdridge. *Hants* 1D **16**
Curdworth. *Warw* 1F **61**
Curland. *Som* 1F **13**
Curridge. *W Ber* 4C **36**
Currie. *Edin* 3E **129**
Curry Mallet. *Som* 4G **21**
Curry Rivel. *Som* 4G **21**
Curtisden Green. *Kent* 1B **28**
Curtisknowle. *Devn* 3D **8**
Cury. *Corn* 4D **5**
Cusgarne. *Corn* 4B **6**
Cusop. *Here* 1F **47**
Cusworth. *S Yor* 4F **93**
Cutcombe. *Som* 3C **20**
Cuthill. *E Lot* 2G **129**
Cutiau. *Gwyn* 4F **69**
Cutlers Green. *Essx* 2F **53**
Cutmadoc. *Corn* 2E **7**
Cutnall Green. *Worc* 4C **60**
Cutsdean. *Glos* 2F **49**
Cutthorpe. *Derbs* 3H **85**
Cuttivett. *Corn* 2H **7**
Cuttybridge. *Pemb* 3D **42**
Cuttyhill. *Abers* 3H **161**
Cuxham. *Oxon* 2E **37**
Cuxton. *Medw* 4B **40**
Cuxwold. *Linc* 4E **95**
Cwm. *Blae* 5E **47**
Cwm. *Den* 3C **82**
Cwm. *Powy* 1E **59**
Cwmafan. *Neat* 2A **32**
Cwmaman. *Rhon* 2C **32**
Cwmann. *Carm* 1F **45**
Cwmbach. *Carm* 2G **43**
Cwmbach. *Powy* 2E **47**
Cwmbach. *Rhon* 5D **46**
Cwmbach Llechryd. *Powy* 5C **58**
Cwmbelan. *Powy* 2B **58**
Cwmbran. *Torf* 2F **33**
Cwmbrwyno. *Cdgn* 2G **57**
Cwm Capel. *Carm* 5E **45**
Cwmcarn. *Cphy* 2F **33**
Cwmcarvan. *Mon* 5H **47**
Cwm-celyn. *Blae* 5F **47**
Cwmcerdinen. *Swan* 5G **45**
Cwm-Cewydd. *Gwyn* 4A **70**
Cwmcoy. *Cdgn* 1C **44**
Cwmcrawnon. *Powy* 4E **47**
Cwmcych. *Pemb* 1G **43**
Cwmdare. *Rhon* 5C **46**
Cwmdu. *Carm* 2G **45**
Cwmdu. *Powy* 3E **47**
Cwmduad. *Carm* 2D **45**
Cwm Dulais. *Swan* 5G **45**
Cwmerfyn. *Cdgn* 2F **57**
Cwmfelin. *B'end* 3B **32**
Cwmfelin Boeth. *Carm* 3F **43**
Cwmfelinfach. *Cphy* 2E **33**
Cwmfelin Mynach. *Carm* 2G **43**
Cwmffrwd. *Carm* 4E **45**
Cwmgiedd. *Powy* 4A **46**
Cwmgors. *Neat* 4H **45**
Cwmgwili. *Carm* 4F **45**
Cwmgwrach. *Neat* 5B **46**
Cwmhiraeth. *Carm* 1H **43**
Cwmifor. *Carm* 3G **45**
Cwmisfael. *Carm* 4E **45**
Cwm-Llinau. *Powy* 5H **69**
Cwmllynfell. *Neat* 4H **45**
Cwm-mawr. *Carm* 4F **45**
Cwm-miles. *Carm* 2F **43**
Cwmorgan. *Carm* 1G **43**
Cwmparc. *Rhon* 2C **32**
Cwm Penmachno. *Cnwy* 1G **69**
Cwmpennar. *Rhon* 5D **46**
Cwm Plysgog. *Pemb* 1B **44**
Cwmrhos. *Powy* 3E **47**
Cwmsychpant. *Cdgn* 1E **45**
Cwmsyfiog. *Cphy* 5E **47**
Cwmsymlog. *Cdgn* 2F **57**
Cwmtillery. *Blae* 5F **47**
Cwm-twrch Isaf. *Powy* 5A **46**
Cwm-twrch Uchaf. *Powy* 4A **46**
Cwmwysg. *Powy* 3B **46**
Cwm-y-glo. *Gwyn* 4E **81**
Cwmyoy. *Mon* 3G **47**
Cwmystwyth. *Cdgn* 3G **57**
Cwrt. *Gwyn* 1F **57**
Cwrtnewydd. *Cdgn* 1E **45**
Cwrt-y-Cadno. *Carm* 1G **45**
Cydweli. *Carm* 5E **45**
Cyffylliog. *Den* 5C **82**
Cymau. *Flin* 5E **83**
Cymer. *Neat* 2B **32**
Cymmer. *Neat* 2B **32**
Cymmer. *Rhon* 2D **32**
Cyncoed. *Card* 3E **33**
Cynghordy. *Carm* 2B **46**
Cynghordy. *Swan* 5G **45**
Cynheidre. *Carm* 5E **45**
Cynonville. *Neat* 2B **32**
Cynwyd. *Den* 1C **70**
Cynwyl Elfed. *Carm* 3D **44**
Cywarch. *Gwyn* 4A **70**

D

Dacre. *Cumb* 2F **103**
Dacre. *N Yor* 3D **98**
Dacre Banks. *N Yor* 3D **98**
Daddry Shield. *Dur* 1B **104**
Dadford. *Buck* 2E **51**
Dadlington. *Leics* 1B **62**
Dafen. *Carm* 5F **45**
Daffy Green. *Norf* 5B **78**
Dagdale. *Staf* 2E **73**
Dagenham. *G Lon* 2F **39**
Daggons. *Dors* 1G **15**
Daglingworth. *Glos* 5E **49**
Dagnall. *Buck* 4H **51**
Dagtail End. *Worc* 4E **61**
Dail. *Arg* 5E **141**
Dail bho Dheas. *W Isl* 1G **171**
Dailly. *S Ayr* 4B **116**
Dail Mor. *W Isl* 3E **171**
Dairsie. *Fife* 2G **137**
Daisy Bank. *W Mid* 1E **61**
Daisy Hill. *G Man* 4E **91**
Daisy Hill. *W Yor* 1B **92**
Dalabrog. *W Isl* 6C **170**
Dalavich. *Arg* 2G **133**
Dalbeattie. *Dum* 3F **111**
Dalblair. *E Ayr* 3F **117**
Dalbury. *Derbs* 2G **73**
Dalby. *IOM* 4B **108**
Dalby Wolds. *Leics* 3D **74**
Dalchalm. *High* 3G **165**
Dalcharn. *High* 3G **167**
Dalchork. *High* 2C **164**
Dalchreichart. *High* 2E **149**
Dalchruin. *Per* 2G **135**
Dalcross. *High* 4B **158**
Dalderby. *Linc* 4B **88**
Dale. *Cumb* 5G **113**
Dale. *Derbs* 2B **74**
Dale. *Pemb* 4C **42**
Dalebank. *Derbs* 4A **86**
Dale Bottom. *Cumb* 2D **102**
Dalebrook. *Derbs* 2F **73**
Dale Head. *Cumb* 3F **103**
Dalehouse. *N Yor* 3E **107**
Dalelia. *High* 2B **140**
Dale of Walls. *Shet* 6C **173**
Dalgarven. *N Ayr* 5D **126**
Dalgety Bay. *Fife* 1E **129**
Dalginross. *Per* 1G **135**
Dalguise. *Per* 4G **143**
Dalhalvaig. *High* 3A **168**
Dalham. *Suff* 4G **65**
Dalintart. *Arg* 1F **133**
Dalkeith. *Midl* 3G **129**
Dallas. *Mor* 3F **159**
Dalleagles. *E Ayr* 3E **117**
Dallinghoo. *Suff* 5E **67**
Dallington. *E Sus* 4A **28**
Dallow. *N Yor* 2D **98**
Dalmally. *Arg* 1A **134**
Dalmarnock. *Glas* 3H **127**
Dalmellington. *E Ayr* 4D **117**
Dalmeny. *Edin* 2E **129**
Dalmigavie. *High* 2B **150**
Dalmilling. *S Ayr* 2C **116**
Dalmore. *High* 2A **158** (nr. Alness)
Dalmore. *High* 3E **164** (nr. Rogart)
Dalmuir. *W Dun* 2F **127**
Dalmunach. *Mor* 4G **159**
Dalnabreck. *High* 2B **140**
Dalnacardoch Lodge. *Per* 1E **142**
Dalnamein Lodge. *Per* 2E **143**
Dalnaspidal Lodge. *Per* 1D **142**
Dalnatrat. *High* 3D **140**
Dalnavie. *High* 1A **158**
Dalnawillan Lodge. *High* 4C **168**
Dalness. *High* 3F **141**
Dalnessie. *High* 2D **164**
Dalqueich. *Per* 3C **136**
Dalquhairn. *S Ayr* 5C **116**
Dalreavoch. *High* 3E **165**
Dalreoch. *Per* 2C **136**
Dalry. *Edin* 2F **129**
Dalry. *N Ayr* 5D **126**
Dalrymple. *E Ayr* 3C **116**
Dalscote. *Nptn* 5D **62**
Dalserf. *S Lan* 4A **128**
Dalsmirren. *Arg* 4A **122**
Dalston. *Cumb* 4E **113**
Dalswinton. *Dum* 1G **111**
Dalton. *Dum* 2C **112**
Dalton. *Lanc* 4C **90**
Dalton. *Nmbd* 4C **114** (nr. Hexham)
Dalton. *Nmbd* 2E **115** (nr. Ponteland)
Dalton. *N Yor* 4E **105** (nr. Richmond)
Dalton. *N Yor* 2G **99** (nr. Thirsk)
Dalton. *S Lan* 4H **127**
Dalton. *S Yor* 1B **86**
Dalton-in-Furness. *Cumb* 2B **96**
Dalton-le-Dale. *Dur* 5H **115**
Dalton Magna. *S Yor* 1B **86**
Dalton-on-Tees. *N Yor* 4F **105**
Dalton Piercy. *Hart* 1B **106**
Daltot. *Arg* 1F **125**
Dalvey. *High* 5F **159**
Dalwhinnie. *High* 5A **150**
Dalwood. *Devn* 2F **13**
Damerham. *Hants* 1G **15**
Damgate. *Norf* 5G **79** (nr. Acle)
Damgate. *Norf* 4G **79** (nr. Martham)
Dam Green. *Norf* 2C **66**
Damhead. *Mor* 3E **159**
Danaway. *Kent* 4C **40**
Danbury. *Essx* 5A **54**
Danby. *N Yor* 4E **107**
Danby Botton. *N Yor* 4D **107**
Danby Wiske. *N Yor* 5A **106**
Danderhall. *Midl* 3G **129**
Danebank. *Ches* 2D **85**
Danebridge. *Ches* 4D **84**
Dane End. *Herts* 3D **52**
Danehill. *E Sus* 3F **27**
Danesford. *Shrp* 1B **60**
Daneshill. *Hants* 1E **25**
Danesmoor. *Derbs* 4A **86**
Danestone. *Aber* 2G **153**
Dangerous Corner. *Lanc* 3D **90**
Daniel's Water. *Kent* 1D **28**
Dan's Castle. *Dur* 1E **105**
Danshillock. *Abers* 3E **160**
Danzey Green. *Warw* 4F **61**
Dapple Heath. *Staf* 3E **73**
Daren. *Powy* 4F **47**
Darenth. *Kent* 3G **39**
Daresbury. *Hal* 2H **83**
Darfield. *S Yor* 4E **93**
Dargate. *Kent* 4E **41**
Dargill. *Per* 2A **136**
Darite. *Corn* 2G **7**
Darlaston. *Staf* 2C **72**
Darlaston. *W Mid* 1D **60**
Darley. *N Yor* 4E **98**
Darley Abbey. *Derb* 2A **74**
Darley Bridge. *Derbs* 4G **85**
Darley Dale. *Derbs* 4G **85**
Darley Head. *N Yor* 4D **98**
Darlingscott. *Warw* 1H **49**
Darlington. *Darl* 3F **105**
Darliston. *Shrp* 2H **71**
Darlton. *Notts* 3E **87**
Darmsden. *Suff* 5C **66**
Darnall. *S Yor* 2A **86**
Darnford. *Abers* 4E **153**
Darnick. *Bord* 1H **119**
Darowen. *Powy* 5H **69**
Darra. *Abers* 4E **161**
Darracott. *Devn* 3E **19**
Darras Hall. *Nmbd* 2E **115**
Darrington. *W Yor* 3E **93**
Darrow Green. *Norf* 2E **67**
Darsham. *Suff* 4G **67**
Dartfield. *Abers* 3H **161**
Dartford. *Kent* 3G **39**
Dartford Crossing. *Kent* 3G **39**
Dartington. *Devn* 2D **9**
Dartmeet. *Devn* 5G **11**
Dartmouth. *Devn* 3E **9**
Darton. *S Yor* 3D **92**
Darvel. *E Ayr* 1E **117**
Darwen. *Bkbn* 2E **91**
Dassels. *Herts* 3D **53**
Datchet. *Wind* 3A **38**
Datchworth. *Herts* 4C **52**
Datchworth Green. *Herts* 4C **52**
Daubhill. *G Man* 4F **91**
Dauntsey. *Wilts* 3E **35**
Dauntsey Green. *Wilts* 3E **35**
Dauntsey Lock. *Wilts* 3E **35**
Dava. *Mor* 5E **159**
Davenham. *Ches* 3A **84**
Daventry. *Nptn* 4C **62**
Davidson's Mains. *Edin* 2F **129**
Davidston. *High* 2B **158**
Davidstow. *Corn* 4B **10**
David's Well. *Powy* 3C **58**
Davington. *Dum* 4E **119**
Daviot. *Abers* 1E **153**
Daviot. *High* 5B **158**
Davyhulme. *G Man* 1B **84**
Daw Cross. *N Yor* 4E **99**
Dawdon. *Dur* 5H **115**
Dawesgreen. *Surr* 1D **26**
Dawley. *Telf* 5A **72**
Dawlish. *Devn* 5C **12**
Dawlish Warren. *Devn* 5C **12**
Dawn. *Cnwy* 3A **82**
Daws Heath. *Essx* 2C **40**
Dawshill. *Worc* 5C **60**
Daw's House. *Corn* 4D **10**
Dawsmere. *Linc* 2D **76**
Dayhills. *Staf* 2D **72**
Dayhouse Bank. *Worc* 3D **60**
Daylesford. *Glos* 3H **49**
Daywall. *Shrp* 2E **71**
Ddol. *Flin* 3D **82**
Ddol Cownwy. *Powy* 4C **70**
Deadwater. *Nmbd* 5A **120**
Deaf Hill. *Dur* 1A **106**
Deal. *Kent* 5H **41**
Dean. *Cumb* 2B **102**
Dean. *Devn* 2G **19** (nr. Combe Martin)
Dean. *Devn* 2F **19** (nr. Ilfracombe)
Dean. *Devn* 2H **19** (nr. Lynton)
Dean. *Dors* 1E **15**
Dean. *Hants* 1D **16** (nr. Bishop's Waltham)
Dean. *Hants* 3C **24** (nr. Winchester)
Dean. *Som* 2B **22**
Dean Bank. *Dur* 1F **105**
Deanburnhaugh. *Bord* 3F **119**

Deane—Downham

Deane. *Hants* 1D **24**
Deanich Lodge. *High* 5A **164**
Deanland. *Dors* 1E **15**
Deanlane End. *W Sus* 1F **17**
Dean Park. *Shrp* 4H **59**
Dean Prior. *Devn* 2D **8**
Dean Row. *Ches* 2C **84**
Deans. *W Lot* 3D **128**
Deanscales. *Cumb* 2B **102**
Deanshanger. *Nptn* 2F **51**
Deanston. *Stir* 3G **135**
Dearham. *Cumb* 1B **102**
Dearne. *S Yor* 4E **93**
Dearne Valley. *S Yor* 4D **93**
Debach. *Suff* 5E **67**
Debden. *Essx* 2F **53**
Debden Green. *Essx* 1F **39** (nr. Loughton)
Debden Green. *Essx* 2F **53** (nr. Saffron Walden)
Debenham. *Suff* 4D **66**
Dechmont. *W Lot* 2D **128**
Deddington. *Oxon* 2C **50**
Dedham. *Essx* 2D **54**
Dedham Heath. *Essx* 2D **54**
Deebank. *Abers* 4D **152**
Deene. *Nptn* 1G **63**
Deenethorpe. *Nptn* 1G **63**
Deepcar. *S Yor* 1G **85**
Deepcut. *Surr* 5A **38**
Deepdale. *Cumb* 1G **97**
Deepdale. *N Lin* 3D **94**
Deepdale. *N Yor* 2A **98**
Deeping Gate. *Pet* 5A **76**
Deeping St James. *Linc* 5A **76**
Deeping St Nicholas. *Linc* 4B **76**
Deerhill. *Mor* 3B **160**
Deerhurst. *Glos* 3D **48**
Deerhurst Walton. *Glos* 3D **49**
Deerness. *Orkn* 7E **172**
Defford. *Worc* 1E **49**
Defynnog. *Powy* 3C **46**
Deganwy. *Cnwy* 3G **81**
Deighton. *N Yor* 4A **106**
Deighton. *W Yor* 3B **92**
Deighton. *York* 5A **100**
Deiniolen. *Gwyn* 4E **81**
Delabole. *Corn* 4A **10**
Delamere. *Ches* 4H **83**
Delfour. *High* 3C **150**
Dellieture. *High* 5E **159**
Dell, The. *Suff* 1G **67**
Delly End. *Oxon* 4B **50**
Delny. *High* 1B **158**
Delph. *G Man* 4H **91**
Delves. *Dur* 5E **115**
Delves, The. *W Mid* 1E **61**
Delvin End. *Essx* 2A **54**
Dembleby. *Linc* 2H **75**
Demelza. *Corn* 2D **6**
Denaby Main. *S Yor* 1B **86**
Denbeath. *Fife* 4F **137**
Denbigh. *Den* 4C **82**
Denbury. *Devn* 2E **9**
Denby. *Derbs* 1A **74**
Denby Common. *Derbs* 1B **74**
Denby Dale. *W Yor* 4C **92**
Denchworth. *Oxon* 2B **36**
Dendron. *Cumb* 2B **96**
Deneside. *Dur* 5H **115**
Denford. *Nptn* 3G **63**
Dengie. *Essx* 5C **54**
Denham. *Buck* 2B **38**
Denham. *Suff* 4G **65** (nr. Bury St Edmunds)
Denham. *Suff* 3D **66** (nr. Eye)
Denham Green. *Buck* 2B **38**
Denham Street. *Suff* 3D **66**
Denhead. *Abers* 5G **161** (nr. Ellon)
Denhead. *Abers* 3G **161** (nr. Strichen)
Denhead. *Fife* 2G **137**
Denholm. *Bord* 3H **119**
Denholme. *W Yor* 1A **92**
Denholme Clough. *W Yor* 1A **92**
Denholme Gate. *W Yor* 1A **92**
Denio. *Gwyn* 2C **68**
Denmead. *Hants* 1E **17**
Dennington. *Suff* 4E **67**
Denny. *Falk* 1B **128**
Denny End. *Cambs* 4D **65**
Dennyloanhead. *Falk* 1B **128**
Den of Lindores. *Fife* 2E **137**
Denshaw. *G Man* 3H **91**
Denside. *Abers* 4F **153**
Densole. *Kent* 1G **29**
Denston. *Suff* 5G **65**
Denstone. *Staf* 1F **73**
Denstroude. *Kent* 4F **41**
Dent. *Cumb* 1G **97**
Den, The. *N Ayr* 4E **127**
Denton. *Cambs* 2A **64**
Denton. *Darl* 3F **105**
Denton. *E Sus* 5F **27**
Denton. *G Man* 1D **84**
Denton. *Kent* 1G **29**
Denton. *Linc* 2F **75**
Denton. *Norf* 2E **67**
Denton. *Nptn* 5F **63**
Denton. *N Yor* 5D **98**
Denton. *Oxon* 5D **50**
Denver. *Norf* 5F **77**
Denwick. *Nmbd* 3G **121**
Deopham. *Norf* 5C **78**
Deopham Green. *Norf* 1C **66**
Depden. *Suff* 5G **65**
Depden Green. *Suff* 5G **65**
Deptford. *G Lon* 3E **39**
Deptford. *Wilts* 3F **23**
Derby. *Derb* 2A **74**
Derbyhaven. *IOM* 5B **108**
Derculich. *Per* 3F **143**
Dereham. *Norf* 4B **78**
Deri. *Cphy* 5E **47**
Derril. *Devn* 2D **10**
Derringstone. *Kent* 1G **29**
Derrington. *Shrp* 1A **60**
Derrington. *Staf* 3C **72**
Derriton. *Devn* 2D **10**
Derryguaig. *Arg* 5F **139**
Derry Hill. *Wilts* 4E **35**
Derrythorpe. *N Lin* 4B **94**
Dersingham. *Norf* 2F **77**
Dervaig. *Arg* 3F **139**
Derwen. *Den* 5C **82**
Derwen Gam. *Cdgn* 5D **56**
Derwenlas. *Powy* 1G **57**
Desborough. *Nptn* 2F **63**
Desford. *Leics* 5B **74**
Detchant. *Nmbd* 1E **121**
Dethick. *Derbs* 5H **85**
Detling. *Kent* 5B **40**
Deuchar. *Ang* 2D **144**
Deuddwr. *Powy* 4E **71**
Devauden. *Mon* 2H **33**
Devil's Bridge. *Cdgn* 3G **57**
Devitts Green. *Warw* 1G **61**
Devizes. *Wilts* 5F **35**
Devonport. *Plym* 3A **8**
Devonside. *Clac* 4B **136**
Devoran. *Corn* 5B **6**
Dewartown. *Midl* 3G **129**
Dewlish. *Dors* 3C **14**
Dewsbury. *W Yor* 2C **92**
Dewshall Court. *Here* 2H **47**
Dexbeer. *Devn* 2C **10**
Dhoon. *IOM* 3D **108**
Dhoor. *IOM* 2D **108**
Dhowin. *IOM* 1D **108**
Dial Green. *W Sus* 3A **26**
Dial Post. *W Sus* 4C **26**
Dibberford. *Dors* 2H **13**
Dibden. *Hants* 2C **16**
Dibden Purlieu. *Hants* 2C **16**
Dickleburgh. *Norf* 2D **66**
Didbrook. *Glos* 2F **49**
Didcot. *Oxon* 2D **36**
Diddington. *Cambs* 4A **64**
Diddlebury. *Shrp* 2H **59**
Didley. *Here* 2H **47**
Didling. *W Sus* 1G **17**
Didmarton. *Glos* 3D **34**
Didsbury. *G Man* 1C **84**
Didworthy. *Devn* 2C **8**
Digby. *Linc* 5H **87**
Digg. *High* 2D **154**
Diggle. *G Man* 4A **92**
Digmoor. *Lanc* 4C **90**
Digswell. *Herts* 4C **52**
Dihewyd. *Cdgn* 5D **57**
Dilham. *Norf* 3F **79**
Dilhorne. *Staf* 1D **72**
Dillarburn. *S Lan* 5B **128**
Dillington. *Cambs* 4A **64**
Dilston. *Nmbd* 3C **114**
Dilton Marsh. *Wilts* 2D **22**
Dilwyn. *Here* 5G **59**
Dimmer. *Som* 3B **22**
Dimple. *G Man* 3F **91**
Dinas. *Carm* 1G **43**
Dinas. *Gwyn* 5D **81** (nr. Caernarfon)
Dinas. *Gwyn* 2B **68** (nr. Tudweiliog)
Dinas. *Pemb* 1E **43**
Dinas Dinlle. *Gwyn* 5D **80**
Dinas Mawddwy. *Gwyn* 4A **70**
Dinas Powys. *V Glam* 4E **33**
Dinbych. *Den* 4C **82**
Dinbych-y-Pysgod. *Pemb* 4F **43**
Dinckley. *Lanc* 1E **91**
Dinder. *Som* 2A **22**
Dinedor. *Here* 2A **48**
Dinedor Cross. *Here* 2A **48**
Dingestow. *Mon* 4H **47**
Dingle. *Mers* 2F **83**
Dingleden. *Kent* 2C **28**
Dingleton. *Bord* 1H **119**
Dingley. *Nptn* 2E **63**
Dingwall. *High* 3H **157**
Dinmael. *Cnwy* 1C **70**
Dinnet. *Abers* 4B **152**
Dinnington. *Som* 1H **13**
Dinnington. *S Yor* 2C **86**
Dinnington. *Tyne* 2F **115**
Dinorwic. *Gwyn* 4E **81**
Dinton. *Buck* 4F **51**
Dinton. *Wilts* 3F **23**
Dinworthy. *Devn* 1D **10**
Dipley. *Hants* 1F **25**
Dippen. *Arg* 2B **122**
Dippenhall. *Surr* 2G **25**
Dippertown. *Devn* 4E **11**
Dippin. *N Ayr* 3E **123**
Dipple. *S Ayr* 4B **116**
Diptford. *Devn* 3D **8**
Dipton. *Dur* 4E **115**
Dirleton. *E Lot* 1B **130**
Dirt Pot. *Nmbd* 5B **114**
Discoed. *Powy* 4E **59**
Diseworth. *Leics* 3B **74**
Dishforth. *N Yor* 2F **99**
Disley. *Ches* 2D **85**
Diss. *Norf* 3D **66**
Disserth. *Powy* 5C **58**
Distington. *Cumb* 2B **102**
Ditchampton. *Wilts* 3F **23**
Ditcheat. *Som* 3B **22**
Ditchingham. *Norf* 1F **67**
Ditchling. *E Sus* 4E **27**
Ditteridge. *Wilts* 5D **34**
Dittisham. *Devn* 3E **9**
Ditton. *Hal* 2G **83**
Ditton. *Kent* 5B **40**
Ditton Green. *Cambs* 5F **65**
Ditton Priors. *Shrp* 2A **60**
Divach. *High* 1G **149**
Dixonfield. *High* 2D **168**
Dixton. *Glos* 2E **49**
Dixton. *Mon* 4A **48**
Dizzard. *Corn* 3B **10**
Dobcross. *G Man* 4H **91**
Dobs Hill. *Flin* 4F **83**
Dobson's Bridge. *Shrp* 2G **71**
Dobwalls. *Corn* 2G **7**
Doccombe. *Devn* 4A **12**
Dochgarroch. *High* 4A **158**
Docking. *Norf* 2G **77**
Docklow. *Here* 5H **59**
Dockray. *Cumb* 2E **103**
Doc Penfro. *Pemb* 4D **42**
Dodbrooke. *Devn* 4D **8**
Doddenham. *Worc* 5B **60**
Doddinghurst. *Essx* 1G **39**
Doddington. *Cambs* 1C **64**
Doddington. *Kent* 5D **40**
Doddington. *Linc* 4G **87**
Doddington. *Nmbd* 1D **121**
Doddington. *Shrp* 3A **60**
Doddiscombsleigh. *Devn* 4B **12**
Doddshill. *Norf* 2G **77**
Dodford. *Nptn* 4D **62**
Dodford. *Worc* 3D **60**
Dodington. *Som* 2E **21**
Dodington. *S Glo* 4C **34**
Dodleston. *Ches* 4F **83**
Dods Leigh. *Staf* 2E **73**
Dodworth. *S Yor* 4D **92**
Doe Lea. *Derbs* 4B **86**
Dogdyke. *Linc* 5B **88**
Dogmersfield. *Hants* 1F **25**
Dogsthorpe. *Pet* 5B **76**
Dog Village. *Devn* 3C **12**
Dolanog. *Powy* 4C **70**
Dolau. *Powy* 4D **58**
Dolau. *Rhon* 3D **32**
Dolbenmaen. *Gwyn* 1E **69**
Doley. *Staf* 3B **72**
Dol-fach. *Powy* 5B **70** (nr. Llanbrynmair)
Dolfach. *Powy* 3B **58** (nr. Llanidloes)
Dolfor. *Powy* 2D **58**
Dolgarrog. *Cnwy* 4G **81**
Dolgellau. *Gwyn* 4G **69**
Dolgoch. *Gwyn* 5F **69**
Dol-gran. *Carm* 2E **45**
Dolhelfa. *Powy* 3B **58**
Doll. *High* 3F **165**
Dollar. *Clac* 4B **136**
Dolley Green. *Powy* 4E **59**
Dollwen. *Cdgn* 2F **57**
Dolphin. *Flin* 3D **82**
Dolphingstone. *E Lot* 2G **129**
Dolphinholme. *Lanc* 4E **97**
Dolphinton. *S Lan* 5E **129**
Dolton. *Devn* 1F **11**
Dolwen. *Cnwy* 3A **82**
Dolwyddelan. *Cnwy* 5G **81**
Dol-y-Bont. *Cdgn* 2F **57**
Dolyhir. *Powy* 5E **59**
Domgay. *Powy* 4E **71**
Doncaster. *S Yor* 4F **93**
Donhead St Andrew. *Wilts* 4E **23**
Donhead St Mary. *Wilts* 4E **23**
Doniford. *Som* 2D **20**
Donington. *Linc* 2B **76**
Donington. *Shrp* 5C **72**
Donington Eaudike. *Linc* 2B **76**
Donington le Heath. *Leics* 4B **74**
Donington on Bain. *Linc* 2B **88**
Donington South Ing. *Linc* 2B **76**
Donisthorpe. *Leics* 4H **73**
Donkey Town. *Surr* 4A **38**
Donna Nook. *Linc* 1D **88**
Donnington. *Glos* 3G **49**
Donnington. *Here* 2C **48**
Donnington. *Shrp* 5H **71**
Donnington. *Telf* 4B **72**
Donnington. *W Ber* 5C **36**
Donnington. *W Sus* 2G **17**
Donyatt. *Som* 1G **13**
Doomsday Green. *W Sus* 2C **26**
Doonfoot. *S Ayr* 3C **116**
Doonholm. *S Ayr* 3C **116**
Dorback Lodge. *High* 2E **151**
Dorchester. *Dors* 3B **14**
Dorchester. *Oxon* 2D **36**
Dordon. *Warw* 5G **73**
Dore. *S Yor* 2H **85**
Dores. *High* 5H **157**
Dorking. *Surr* 1C **26**
Dorking Tye. *Suff* 2C **54**
Dormansland. *Surr* 1F **27**
Dormans Park. *Surr* 1E **27**
Dormanstown. *Red C* 2C **106**
Dormington. *Here* 1A **48**
Dormston. *Worc* 5D **61**
Dorn. *Glos* 2H **49**
Dorney. *Buck* 3A **38**
Dornie. *High* 1A **148**
Dornoch. *High* 5E **165**
Dornock. *Dum* 3D **112**
Dorrery. *High* 3C **168**
Dorridge. *W Mid* 3F **61**
Dorrington. *Linc* 5H **87**
Dorrington. *Shrp* 5G **71**
Dorsington. *Warw* 1G **49**
Dorstone. *Here* 1G **47**
Dorton. *Buck* 4E **51**
Dotham. *IOA* 3C **80**
Dottery. *Dors* 3H **13**
Doublebois. *Corn* 2F **7**
Dougarie. *N Ayr* 2C **122**
Doughton. *Glos* 2D **35**
Douglas. *IOM* 4C **108**
Douglas. *S Lan* 1H **117**
Douglastown. *Ang* 4D **144**
Douglas Water. *S Lan* 1A **118**
Doulting. *Som* 2B **22**
Dounby. *Orkn* 5B **172**
Doune. *High* 3C **150** (nr. Kingussie)
Doune. *High* 3B **164** (nr. Lairg)
Doune. *Stir* 3G **135**
Dounie. *High* 4C **164** (nr. Bonar Bridge)
Dounie. *High* 5D **164** (nr. Tain)
Dounreay. *High* 2B **168**
Doura. *N Ayr* 5E **127**
Dousland. *Devn* 2B **8**
Dovaston. *Shrp* 3F **71**
Dove Holes. *Derbs* 3E **85**
Dovenby. *Cumb* 1B **102**
Dover. *Kent* 1H **29**
Dovercourt. *Essx* 2F **55**
Doverdale. *Worc* 4C **60**
Doveridge. *Derbs* 2F **73**
Doversgreen. *Surr* 1D **26**
Dowally. *Per* 4H **143**
Dowbridge. *Lanc* 1C **90**
Dowdeswell. *Glos* 4F **49**
Dowlais. *Mer T* 5D **46**
Dowland. *Devn* 1F **11**
Dowlands. *Devn* 3F **13**
Dowles. *Worc* 3B **60**
Dowlesgreen. *Wok* 5G **37**
Dowlish Wake. *Som* 1G **13**
Downall Green. *Mers* 4D **90**
Down Ampney. *Glos* 2F **35**
Downderry. *Corn* 3H **7** (nr. Looe)
Downderry. *Corn* 3D **6** (nr. St Austell)
Downe. *G Lon* 4F **39**
Downend. *IOW* 4D **16**
Downend. *S Glo* 4B **34**
Downend. *W Ber* 4C **36**
Downfield. *Cambs* 3F **65**
Downfield. *D'dee* 5C **144**
Downgate. *Corn* 5D **10** (nr. Kelly Bray)
Downgate. *Corn* 5C **10** (nr. Upton Cross)
Downham. *Essx* 1B **40**
Downham. *Lanc* 5G **97**

Downham. *Nmbd* 1C 120
Downham Market. *Norf* 5F 77
Down Hatherley. *Glos* 3D 48
Downhead. *Som* 2B 22
(nr. Frome)
Downhead. *Som* 4A 22
(nr. Yeovil)
Downholland Cross. *Lanc* 4B 90
Downholme. *N Yor* 5E 105
Downies. *Abers* 4G 153
Downley. *Buck* 2G 37
Down St Mary. *Devn* 2H 11
Downside. *Som* 1B 22
(nr. Chilcompton)
Downside. *Som* 2B 22
(nr. Shepton Mallet)
Downside. *Surr* 5C 38
Down, The. *Shrp* 1A 60
Down Thomas. *Devn* 3B 8
Downton. *Hants* 3A 16
Downton. *Wilts* 4G 23
Downton on the Rock. *Here* 3G 59
Dowsby. *Linc* 3A 76
Dowsdale. *Linc* 4B 76
Dowthwaitehead. *Cumb* 2E 103
Doxey. *Staf* 3D 72
Doxford. *Nmbd* 2F 121
Doynton. *S Glo* 4C 34
Drabblegate. *Norf* 3E 78
Draethen. *Cphy* 3F 33
Draffan. *S Lan* 5A 128
Dragonby. *N Lin* 3C 94
Dragons Green. *W Sus* 3C 26
Drakelow. *Worc* 2C 60
Drakemyre. *N Ayr* 4D 126
Drakes Broughton. *Worc* 1E 49
Drakes Cross. *Worc* 3E 61
Drakewalls. *Corn* 5E 11
Draughton. *Nptn* 3E 63
Draughton. *N Yor* 4C 98
Drax. *N Yor* 2G 93
Draycot. *Oxon* 5E 51
Draycote. *Warw* 4B 62
Draycot Foliat. *Swin* 4G 35
Draycott. *Derbs* 2B 74
Draycott. *Glos* 2G 49
Draycott. *Shrp* 1C 60
Draycott. *Som* 1H 21
(nr. Cheddar)
Draycott. *Som* 4A 22
(nr. Yeovil)
Draycott. *Worc* 1D 48
Draycott in the Clay. *Staf* 3F 73
Draycott in the Moors. *Staf* 1D 73
Drayford. *Devn* 1A 12
Drayton. *Leics* 1F 63
Drayton. *Linc* 2B 76
Drayton. *Norf* 4D 78
Drayton. *Nptn* 4C 62
Drayton. *Oxon* 2C 36
(nr. Abingdon)
Drayton. *Oxon* 1C 50
(nr. Banbury)
Drayton. *Port* 2E 17
Drayton. *Som* 4H 21
Drayton. *Warw* 5F 61
Drayton. *Worc* 3D 60
Drayton Bassett. *Staf* 5F 73
Drayton Beauchamp. *Buck* 4H 51
Drayton Parslow. *Buck* 3G 51
Drayton St Leonard. *Oxon* 2D 36
Drebley. *N Yor* 4C 98
Dreenhill. *Pemb* 3D 42
Drefach. *Carm* 4F 45
(nr. Meidrim)
Drefach. *Carm* 2D 44
(nr. Newcastle Emlyn)
Drefach. *Carm* 2G 43
(nr. Tumble)
Drefach. *Cdgn* 1E 45
Dreghorn. *N Ayr* 1C 116
Drellingore. *Kent* 1G 29
Drem. *E Lot* 2B 130
Dreumasdal. *W Isl* 5C 170
Drewsteignton. *Devn* 3H 11
Drewston. *Devn* 4H 11
Driby. *Linc* 3C 88
Driffield. *E Yor* 4E 101
Driffield. *Glos* 2F 35
Drift. *Corn* 4B 4
Drigg. *Cumb* 5B 102
Drighlington. *W Yor* 2C 92
Drimnin. *High* 3G 139
Drimpton. *Dors* 2H 13
Dringhoe. *E Yor* 4F 101
Drinisiadar. *W Isl* 8D 171
Drinkstone. *Suff* 4B 66
Drinkstone Green. *Suff* 4B 66
Drointon. *Staf* 3E 73
Droitwich Spa. *Worc* 4C 60
Droman. *High* 3B 166
Dron. *Per* 2D 136
Dronfield. *Derbs* 3A 86
Dronfield Woodhouse. *Derbs* 3H 85
Drongan. *E Ayr* 3D 116
Dronley. *Ang* 5C 144
Droop. *Dors* 2C 14
Drope. *V Glam* 4E 32
Droxford. *Hants* 1E 16
Droylsden. *G Man* 1C 84
Druggers End. *Worc* 2C 48
Druid. *Den* 1C 70
Druid's Heath. *W Mid* 5E 73
Druidston. *Pemb* 3C 42
Druim. *High* 3D 158
Druimarbin. *High* 1E 141
Druimindarroch. *High* 5E 147
Drum. *Per* 3C 136
Drumbeg. *High* 5B 166
Drumblade. *Abers* 4C 160
Drumbuie. *Dum* 1C 110
Drumbuie. *High* 5G 155
Drumburgh. *Cumb* 4D 112
Drumburn. *Dum* 3A 112
Drumchapel. *Glas* 2G 127
Drumchardine. *High* 4H 157
Drumchork. *High* 5C 162
Drumclog. *S Lan* 1F 117
Drumeldrie. *Fife* 3G 137
Drumelzier. *Bord* 1D 118
Drumfearn. *High* 2E 147
Drumgask. *High* 4A 150
Drumgelloch. *N Lan* 3A 128
Drumgley. *Ang* 3D 144
Drumguish. *High* 4B 150
Drumin. *Mor* 5F 159
Drumindorsair. *High* 4G 157
Drumlamford House. *S Ayr* 2H 109
Drumlasie. *Abers* 3D 152
Drumlemble. *Arg* 4A 122
Drumlithie. *Abers* 5E 153
Drummoddie. *Dum* 5A 110
Drummond. *High* 2A 158
Drummore. *Dum* 5E 109
Drummuir. *Mor* 4A 160
Drumnadrochit. *High* 5H 157
Drumnagorrach. *Mor* 3C 160
Drumoak. *Abers* 4E 153
Drumrunie. *High* 3F 163
Drumry. *W Dun* 2G 127
Drums. *Abers* 1G 153
Drumsleet. *Dum* 2G 111
Drumsmittal. *High* 4A 158
Drums of Park. *Abers* 3C 160
Drumsturdy. *Ang* 5D 145
Drumtochty Castle. *Abers* 5D 152
Drumuie. *High* 4D 154
Drumuillie. *High* 1D 150
Drumvaich. *Stir* 3F 135
Drumwhindle. *Abers* 5G 161
Drunkendub. *Ang* 4F 145
Drury. *Flin* 4E 83
Drury Square. *Norf* 4B 78
Drybeck. *Cumb* 3H 103
Drybridge. *Mor* 2B 160
Drybridge. *N Ayr* 1C 116
Drybrook. *Glos* 4B 48
Drybrook. *Here* 4A 48
Dryburgh. *Bord* 1H 119
Dry Doddington. *Linc* 1F 75
Dry Drayton. *Cambs* 4C 64
Drym. *Corn* 3D 4
Drymen. *Stir* 1F 127
Drymuir. *Abers* 4G 161
Drynachan Lodge. *High* 5C 158
Drynie Park. *High* 3H 157
Drynoch. *High* 5D 154
Dry Sandford. *Oxon* 5C 50
Dryslwyn. *Carm* 3F 45
Dry Street. *Essx* 2A 40
Dryton. *Shrp* 5H 71
Dubford. *Abers* 2E 161
Dubiton. *Abers* 3D 160
Dubton. *Ang* 3E 145
Duchally. *High* 2A 164
Duck End. *Essx* 3G 53
Duckington. *Ches* 5G 83
Ducklington. *Oxon* 5B 50
Duckmanton. *Derbs* 3B 86
Duck Street. *Hants* 2B 24
Dudbridge. *Glos* 5D 48
Duddenhoe End. *Essx* 2E 53
Duddingston. *Edin* 2F 129
Duddington. *Nptn* 5G 75
Duddleswell. *E Sus* 3F 27
Duddo. *Nmbd* 5F 131
Duddon. *Ches* 4H 83
Duddon Bridge. *Cumb* 1A 96
Dudleston. *Shrp* 2F 71
Dudleston Heath. *Shrp* 2F 71
Dudley. *Tyne* 2F 115
Dudley. *W Mid* 2D 60
Dudston. *Shrp* 1E 59
Dudwells. *Pemb* 2D 42
Duffield. *Derbs* 1H 73
Duffryn. *Neat* 2B 32
Dufftown. *Mor* 4H 159
Duffus. *Mor* 2F 159
Dufton. *Cumb* 2H 103
Duggleby. *N Yor* 3C 100
Duirinish. *High* 5G 155
Duisdalemore. *High* 2E 147
Duisky. *High* 1E 141
Dukesfield. *Nmbd* 4C 114
Dukestown. *Blae* 5E 47
Dukinfield. *G Man* 1D 84
Dulas. *IOA* 2D 81
Dulcote. *Som* 2A 22
Dulford. *Devn* 2D 12
Dull. *Per* 4F 143
Dullatur. *N Lan* 2A 128
Dullingham. *Cambs* 5F 65
Dullingham Ley. *Cambs* 5F 65
Dulnain Bridge. *High* 1D 151
Duloe. *Beds* 4A 64
Duloe. *Corn* 3G 7
Dulverton. *Som* 4C 20
Dulwich. *G Lon* 3E 39
Dumbarton. *W Dun* 2F 127
Dumbleton. *Glos* 2F 49
Dumfin. *Arg* 1E 127
Dumfries. *Dum* 2A 112
Dumgoyne. *Stir* 1G 127
Dummer. *Hants* 2D 24
Dumpford. *W Sus* 4G 25
Dun. *Ang* 2F 145
Dunagoil. *Arg* 4B 126
Dunalastair. *Per* 3E 142
Dunan. *High* 1D 147
Dunball. *Som* 2G 21
Dunbar. *E Lot* 2C 130
Dunbeath. *High* 5D 168
Dunbeg. *Arg* 5C 140
Dunblane. *Stir* 3G 135
Dunbog. *Fife* 2E 137
Dunbridge. *Hants* 4B 24
Duncanston. *Abers* 1C 152
Duncanston. *High* 3H 157
Dun Charlabhaigh. *W Isl* 3D 171
Dunchideock. *Devn* 4B 12
Dunchurch. *Warw* 3B 62
Duncote. *Nptn* 5D 62
Duncow. *Dum* 1A 112
Duncrievie. *Per* 3D 136
Duncton. *W Sus* 4A 26
Dundee. *D'dee* 5D 144
Dundee Airport. *D'dee* 1F 137
Dundon. *Som* 3H 21
Dundonald. *S Ayr* 1C 116
Dundonnell. *High* 5E 163
Dundraw. *Cumb* 5D 112
Dundreggan. *High* 2F 149
Dundrennan. *Dum* 5E 111
Dundridge. *Hants* 1D 16
Dundry. *N Som* 5A 34
Dunecht. *Abers* 3E 153
Dunfermline. *Fife* 1D 129
Dunford Bridge. *S Yor* 4B 92
Dungate. *Kent* 5D 40
Dunge. *Wilts* 1D 23
Dungeness. *Kent* 4E 29
Dungworth. *S Yor* 2G 85
Dunham-on-the-Hill. *Ches* 3G 83
Dunham-on-Trent. *Notts* 3F 87
Dunhampton. *Worc* 4C 60
Dunham Town. *G Man* 2B 84
Dunham Woodhouses. *G Man* 2B 84
Dunholme. *Linc* 3H 87
Dunino. *Fife* 2H 137
Dunipace. *Falk* 1B 128
Dunira. *Per* 1G 135
Dunkeld. *Per* 4H 143
Dunkerton. *Bath* 1C 22
Dunkeswell. *Devn* 2E 13
Dunkeswick. *N Yor* 5F 99
Dunkirk. *Kent* 5E 41
Dunkirk. *S Glo* 3C 34
Dunkirk. *Staf* 5C 84
Dunkirk. *Wilts* 5E 35
Dunk's Green. *Kent* 5H 39
Dunlappie. *Ang* 2E 145
Dunley. *Hants* 1C 24
Dunley. *Worc* 4B 60
Dunlichity Lodge. *High* 5A 158
Dunlop. *E Ayr* 5F 127
Dunmaglass Lodge. *High* 1H 149
Dunmore. *Arg* 3F 125
Dunmore. *Falk* 1B 128
Dunmore. *High* 4H 157
Dunnet. *High* 1E 169
Dunnichen. *Ang* 4E 145
Dunning. *Per* 2C 136
Dunnington. *E Yor* 4F 101
Dunnington. *Warw* 5E 61
Dunnington. *York* 4A 100
Dunnockshaw. *Lanc* 2G 91
Dunoon. *Arg* 2C 126
Dunphail. *Mor* 4E 159
Dunragit. *Dum* 4G 109
Dunrostan. *Arg* 1F 125
Duns. *Bord* 4D 130
Dunsby. *Linc* 3A 76
Dunscar. *G Man* 3F 91
Dunscore. *Dum* 1F 111
Dunscroft. *S Yor* 4G 93
Dunsdale. *Red C* 3D 106
Dunsden Green. *Oxon* 4F 37
Dunsfold. *Surr* 2B 26
Dunsford. *Devn* 4B 12
Dunshalt. *Fife* 2E 137
Dunshillock. *Abers* 4G 161
Dunsley. *N Yor* 3F 107
Dunsley. *Staf* 2C 60
Dunsmore. *Buck* 5G 51
Dunsop Bridge. *Lanc* 4F 97
Dunstable. *Beds* 3A 52
Dunstal. *Staf* 3E 73
Dunstall. *Staf* 3F 73
Dunstall Green. *Suff* 4G 65
Dunstall Hill. *W Mid* 1D 60
Dunstan. *Nmbd* 3G 121
Dunster. *Som* 2C 20
Duns Tew. *Oxon* 3C 50
Dunston. *Linc* 4H 87
Dunston. *Norf* 5E 79
Dunston. *Staf* 4D 72
Dunston. *Tyne* 3F 115
Dunstone. *Devn* 3B 8
Dunston Heath. *Staf* 4D 72
Dunsville. *S Yor* 4G 93
Dunswell. *E Yor* 1D 94
Dunsyre. *S Lan* 5D 128
Dunterton. *Devn* 5D 11
Duntisbourne Abbots. *Glos* 5E 49
Duntisbourne Leer. *Glos* 5E 49
Duntisbourne Rouse. *Glos* 5E 49
Duntish. *Dors* 2B 14
Duntocher. *W Dun* 2F 127
Dunton. *Beds* 1C 52
Dunton. *Buck* 3G 51
Dunton. *Norf* 2A 78
Dunton Bassett. *Leics* 1C 62
Dunton Green. *Kent* 5G 39
Dunton Patch. *Norf* 2A 78
Duntulm. *High* 1D 154
Dunure. *S Ayr* 3B 116
Dunvant. *Swan* 3E 31
Dunvegan. *High* 4B 154
Dunwich. *Suff* 3G 67
Dunwood. *Staf* 5D 84
Durdar. *Cumb* 4F 113
Durgates. *E Sus* 2H 27
Durham. *Dur* 5F 115
Durham Tees Valley Airport. *Darl* 3A 106
Durisdeer. *Dum* 4A 118
Durisdeermill. *Dum* 4A 118
Durkar. *W Yor* 3D 92
Durleigh. *Som* 3F 21
Durley. *Hants* 1D 16
Durley. *Wilts* 5H 35
Durley Street. *Hants* 1D 16
Durlow Common. *Here* 2B 48
Durnamuck. *High* 4E 163
Durness. *High* 2E 166
Durno. *Abers* 1E 152
Durns Town. *Hants* 3A 16
Duror. *High* 3D 141
Durran. *Arg* 3G 133
Durran. *High* 2D 169
Durrant Green. *Kent* 2C 28
Durrants. *Hants* 1F 17
Durrington. *W Sus* 5C 26
Durrington. *Wilts* 2G 23
Dursley. *Glos* 2C 34
Dursley Cross. *Glos* 4B 48
Durston. *Som* 4F 21
Durweston. *Dors* 2D 14
Duston. *Nptn* 4E 62
Duthil. *High* 1D 150
Dutlas. *Powy* 3E 58
Duton Hill. *Essx* 3G 53
Dutson. *Corn* 4D 10
Dutton. *Ches* 3H 83
Duxford. *Cambs* 1E 53
Duxford. *Oxon* 2B 36
Dwygyfylchi. *Cnwy* 3G 81
Dwyran. *IOA* 4D 80
Dyce. *Aber* 2F 153
Dyffryn. *B'end* 2B 32
Dyffryn. *Carm* 2H 43
Dyffryn. *Pemb* 1D 42
Dyffryn. *V Glam* 4D 32
Dyffryn Ardudwy. *Gwyn* 3E 69
Dyffryn Castell. *Cdgn* 2G 57
Dyffryn Ceidrych. *Carm* 3H 45
Dyffryn Cellwen. *Neat* 5B 46
Dyke. *Linc* 3A 76
Dyke. *Mor* 3D 159
Dykehead. *Ang* 2C 144
Dykehead. *N Lan* 3B 128
Dykehead. *Stir* 4E 135
Dykend. *Ang* 3B 144
Dykesfield. *Cumb* 4E 112
Dylife. *Powy* 1A 58
Dymchurch. *Kent* 3F 29

Dymock—East Stratton

Dymock. *Glos* 2C **48**
Dyrham. *S Glo* 4C **34**
Dysart. *Fife* 4F **137**
Dyserth. *Den* 3C **82**

E

Eachwick. *Nmbd* 2E **115**
Eadar Dha Fhadhail. *W Isl* 4C **171**
Eagland Hill. *Lanc* 5D **96**
Eagle. *Linc* 4F **87**
Eagle Barnsdale. *Linc* 4F **87**
Eagle Moor. *Linc* 4F **87**
Eaglescliffe. *Stoc T* 3B **106**
Eaglesfield. *Cumb* 2B **102**
Eaglesfield. *Dum* 2D **112**
Eaglesham. *E Ren* 4G **127**
Eaglethorpe. *Nptn* 1H **63**
Eagley. *G Man* 3F **91**
Eairy. *IOM* 4B **108**
Eakley Lanes. *Mil* 5F **63**
Eakring. *Notts* 4D **86**
Ealand. *N Lin* 3A **94**
Ealing. *G Lon* 2C **38**
Eallabus. *Arg* 3B **124**
Eals. *Nmbd* 4H **113**
Eamont Bridge. *Cumb* 2G **103**
Earby. *Lanc* 5B **98**
Earcroft. *Bkbn* 2E **91**
Eardington. *Shrp* 1B **60**
Eardisland. *Here* 5G **59**
Eardisley. *Here* 1G **47**
Eardiston. *Shrp* 3F **71**
Eardiston. *Worc* 4A **60**
Earith. *Cambs* 3C **64**
Earle. *Nmbd* 2D **121**
Earlesfield. *Linc* 2G **75**
Earlestown. *Mers* 1H **83**
Earley. *Wok* 4F **37**
Earlham. *Norf* 5D **78**
Earlish. *High* 2C **154**
Earls Barton. *Nptn* 4F **63**
Earls Colne. *Essx* 3B **54**
Earls Common. *Worc* 5D **60**
Earl's Croome. *Worc* 1D **48**
Earlsdon. *W Mid* 3H **61**
Earlsferry. *Fife* 3G **137**
Earlsford. *Abers* 5F **161**
Earl's Green. *Suff* 4C **66**
Earlsheaton. *W Yor* 2C **92**
Earl Shilton. *Leics* 1B **62**
Earl Soham. *Suff* 4E **67**
Earl Sterndale. *Derbs* 4E **85**
Earlston. *E Ayr* 1D **116**
Earlston. *Bord* 1H **119**
Earl Stonham. *Suff* 5D **66**
Earlstoun. *Dum* 1D **110**
Earlswood. *Mon* 2H **33**
Earlswood. *Warw* 3F **61**
Earlyvale. *Bord* 4F **129**
Earnley. *W Sus* 3G **17**
Earsairidh. *W Isl* 9C **170**
Earsdon. *Tyne* 2G **115**
Earsham. *Norf* 2F **67**
Earsham Street. *Suff* 3E **67**
Earswick. *York* 4A **100**
Eartham. *W Sus* 5A **26**
Earthcott Green. *S Glo* 3B **34**
Easby. *N Yor* 4C **106** (nr. Great Ayton)
Easby. *N Yor* 4E **105** (nr. Richmond)
Easdale. *Arg* 2E **133**
Easebourne. *W Sus* 4G **25**
Easenhall. *Warw* 3B **62**
Eashing. *Surr* 1A **26**
Easington. *Buck* 4E **51**
Easington. *Dur* 5H **115**
Easington. *E Yor* 3G **95**
Easington. *Nmbd* 1F **121**
Easington. *Oxon* 2C **50** (nr. Banbury)
Easington. *Oxon* 2E **37** (nr. Watlington)
Easington. *Red C* 3E **107**
Easington Colliery. *Dur* 5H **115**
Easington Lane. *Tyne* 5G **115**
Easingwold. *N Yor* 3H **99**
Easole Street. *Kent* 5G **41**
Eassie. *Ang* 4C **144**
Eassie and Nevay. *Ang* 4C **144**
East Aberthaw. *V Glam* 5D **32**
Eastacombe. *Devn* 4F **19**
Eastacott. *Devn* 4G **19**
East Allington. *Devn* 4D **8**
East Anstey. *Devn* 4B **20**
East Anton. *Hants* 2B **24**
East Appleton. *N Yor* 5F **105**
East Ardsley. *W Yor* 2D **92**
East Ashley. *Devn* 1G **11**
East Ashling. *W Sus* 2G **17**
East Aston. *Hants* 2C **24**
East Ayton. *N Yor* 1D **101**
East Bagborough. *Som* 3E **21**
East Barkwith. *Linc* 2A **88**
East Barnby. *N Yor* 3F **107**
East Barnet. *G Lon* 1D **39**
East Barns. *E Lot* 2D **130**
East Barsham. *Norf* 2B **78**
East Beach. *W Sus* 3G **17**
East Beckham. *Norf* 1D **78**
East Bedfont. *G Lon* 3B **38**
East Bennan. *N Ayr* 3D **123**
East Bergholt. *Suff* 2D **54**
East Bierley. *W Yor* 2B **92**
East Blatchington. *E Sus* 5F **27**
East Bliney. *Norf* 4B **78**
East Bloxworth. *Dors* 3D **15**
East Boldre. *Hants* 2B **16**
East Bolton. *Nmbd* 3F **121**
Eastbourne. *Darl* 3F **105**
Eastbourne. *E Sus* 5H **27**
East Brent. *Som* 1G **21**
East Bridge. *Suff* 4G **67**
East Bridgford. *Notts* 1D **74**
East Briscoe. *Dur* 3C **104**
East Buckland. *Devn* 3G **19**
East Budleigh. *Devn* 4D **12**
Eastburn. *W Yor* 5C **98**
East Burnham. *Buck* 2A **38**
East Burrafirth. *Shet* 6E **173**
East Burton. *Dors* 4D **14**
Eastbury. *Herts* 1B **38**
Eastbury. *W Ber* 4B **36**
East Butsfield. *Dur* 5E **115**
East Butterleigh. *Devn* 2C **12**
East Butterwick. *N Lin* 4B **94**
Eastby. *N Yor* 4C **98**
East Calder. *W Lot* 3D **129**
East Carleton. *Norf* 5D **78**
East Carlton. *Nptn* 2F **63**
East Carlton. *W Yor* 5E **98**
East Chaldon. *Dors* 4C **14**
East Challow. *Oxon* 3B **36**
East Charlton. *Devn* 4D **8**
East Chelborough. *Dors* 2A **14**
East Chiltington. *E Sus* 4E **27**
East Chinnock. *Som* 1H **13**
East Chisenbury. *Wilts* 1G **23**
Eastchurch. *Kent* 3D **40**
East Clandon. *Surr* 5B **38**
East Claydon. *Buck* 3F **51**
East Clevedon. *N Som* 4H **33**
East Clyne. *High* 3F **165**
East Clyth. *High* 5E **169**
East Coker. *Som* 1A **14**
Eastcombe. *Glos* 5D **49**
East Combe. *Som* 3E **21**
East Common. *N Yor* 1G **93**
East Compton. *Som* 2B **22**
East Cornworthy. *Devn* 3E **9**
Eastcote. *G Lon* 2C **38**
Eastcote. *Nptn* 5D **62**
Eastcote. *W Mid* 3F **61**
Eastcott. *Corn* 1C **10**
Eastcott. *Wilts* 1F **23**
East Cottingwith. *E Yor* 5B **100**
East Coulston. *Wilts* 1E **23**
Eastcourt. *Wilts* 5H **35** (nr. Pewsey)
Eastcourt. *Wilts* 2E **35** (nr. Tetbury)
East Cowes. *IOW* 3D **16**
East Cowick. *E Yor* 2G **93**
East Cowton. *N Yor* 4A **106**
East Cramlington. *Nmbd* 2F **115**
East Cranmore. *Som* 2B **22**
East Creech. *Dors* 4E **15**
East Croachy. *High* 1A **150**
East Dean. *E Sus* 5G **27**
East Dean. *Glos* 3B **48**
East Dean. *Hants* 4A **24**
East Dean. *W Sus* 4A **26**
East Down. *Devn* 2G **19**
East Drayton. *Notts* 3E **87**
East Dundry. *N Som* 5A **34**
East Ella. *Hull* 2D **94**
East End. *Cambs* 3C **64**
East End. *Dors* 3E **15**
East End. *E Yor* 4F **101** (nr. Ulrome)
East End. *E Yor* 2F **95** (nr. Withernsea)
East End. *Hants* 3B **16** (nr. Lymington)
East End. *Hants* 5C **36** (nr. Newbury)
East End. *Herts* 3E **53**
East End. *Kent* 3D **40** (nr. Minster)
East End. *Kent* 2C **28** (nr. Tenterden)
East End. *N Som* 4H **33**
East End. *Oxon* 4B **50**
East End. *Som* 1A **22**
East End. *Suff* 2E **54**
Easter Ardross. *High* 1A **158**
Easter Balgedie. *Per* 3D **136**
Easter Balmoral. *Abers* 4G **151**
Easter Brae. *High* 2A **158**
Easter Buckieburn. *Stir* 1A **128**
Easter Bush. *Midl* 3F **129**
Easter Compton. *S Glo* 3A **34**
Easter Fearn. *High* 5D **164**
Easter Galcantray. *High* 4C **158**
Eastergate. *W Sus* 5A **26**
Easterhouse. *Glas* 3H **127**
Easter Howgate. *Midl* 3F **129**
Easter Kinkell. *High* 3H **157**
Easter Lednathie. *Ang* 2C **144**
Easter Ogil. *Ang* 2D **144**
Easter Ord. *Abers* 3F **153**
Easter Quarff. *Shet* 8F **173**
Easter Rhynd. *Per* 2D **136**
Easter Skeld. *Shet* 7E **173**
Easter Suddie. *High* 3A **158**
Easterton. *Wilts* 1F **23**
Eastertown. *Som* 1G **21**
Easter Tulloch. *Abers* 1G **145**
East Everleigh. *Wilts* 1H **23**
East Farleigh. *Kent* 5B **40**
East Farndon. *Nptn* 2E **62**
East Ferry. *Linc* 1F **87**
Eastfield. *N Lan* 3B **128** (nr. Caldercruix)
Eastfield. *N Lan* 3B **128** (nr. Harthill)
Eastfield. *N Yor* 1E **101**
Eastfield. *S Lan* 3H **127**
Eastfield Hall. *Nmbd* 4G **121**
East Fortune. *E Lot* 2B **130**
East Garforth. *W Yor* 1E **93**
East Garston. *W Ber* 4B **36**
Eastgate. *Dur* 1C **104**
Eastgate. *Norf* 3D **78**
East Ginge. *Oxon* 3C **36**
East Gores. *Essx* 3B **54**
East Goscote. *Leics* 4D **74**
East Grafton. *Wilts* 5A **36**
East Grimstead. *Wilts* 4H **23**
East Grinstead. *W Sus* 2E **27**
East Guldeford. *E Sus* 3D **28**
East Haddon. *Nptn* 4D **62**
East Hagbourne. *Oxon* 3D **36**
East Halton. *N Lin* 2E **95**
East Ham. *G Lon* 2F **39**
Eastham. *Mers* 2F **83**
Eastham. *Worc* 4A **60**
Eastham Ferry. *Mers* 2F **83**
Easthampstead. *Brac* 5G **37**
Easthampton. *Here* 4G **59**
East Hanney. *Oxon* 2C **36**
East Hanningfield. *Essx* 5A **54**
East Hardwick. *W Yor* 3E **93**
East Harling. *Norf* 2B **66**
East Harlsey. *N Yor* 5B **106**
East Harnham. *Wilts* 4G **23**
East Harptree. *Bath* 1A **22**
East Hartford. *Nmbd* 2F **115**
East Harting. *W Sus* 1G **17**
East Hatch. *Wilts* 4E **23**
East Hatley. *Cambs* 5B **64**
Easthaugh. *Norf* 4C **78**
East Hauxwell. *N Yor* 5E **105**
East Haven. *Ang* 5E **145**
Eastheath. *Wok* 5G **37**
East Heckington. *Linc* 1A **76**
East Hedleyhope. *Dur* 5E **115**
East Helmsdale. *High* 2H **165**
East Hendred. *Oxon* 3C **36**
East Heslerton. *N Yor* 2D **100**
East Hoathly. *E Sus* 4G **27**
East Holme. *Dors* 4D **15**
Easthope. *Shrp* 1H **59**
Easthorpe. *Essx* 3C **54**
Easthorpe. *Leics* 2F **75**
East Horrington. *Som* 2A **22**
East Horsley. *Surr* 5B **38**
East Horton. *Nmbd* 1E **121**
Easthouses. *Midl* 3G **129**
East Howe. *Bour* 3F **15**
East Huntspill. *Som* 2G **21**
East Hyde. *Beds* 4B **52**
East Ilsley. *W Ber* 3C **36**
Eastington. *Devn* 2H **11**
Eastington. *Glos* 4G **49** (nr. Northleach)
Eastington. *Glos* 5C **48** (nr. Stonehouse)
East Keal. *Linc* 4C **88**
East Kennett. *Wilts* 5G **35**
East Keswick. *W Yor* 5F **99**
East Kilbride. *S Lan* 4H **127**
East Kirkby. *Linc* 4C **88**
East Knapton. *N Yor* 2C **100**
East Knighton. *Dors* 4D **14**
East Knowstone. *Devn* 4B **20**
East Knoyle. *Wilts* 3D **23**
East Kyloe. *Nmbd* 1E **121**
East Lambrook. *Som* 1H **13**
East Langdon. *Kent* 1H **29**
East Langton. *Leics* 1E **63**
East Langwell. *High* 3E **164**
East Lavant. *W Sus* 2G **17**
East Lavington. *W Sus* 4A **26**
East Layton. *N Yor* 4E **105**
Eastleach Martin. *Glos* 5H **49**
Eastleach Turville. *Glos* 5G **49**
East Leake. *Notts* 3C **74**
East Learmouth. *Nmbd* 1C **120**
Eastleigh. *Devn* 4E **19** (nr. Bideford)
East Leigh. *Devn* 2H **11** (nr. Crediton)
East Leigh. *Devn* 3C **8** (nr. Modbury)
Eastleigh. *Hants* 1C **16**
East Lexham. *Norf* 4A **78**
East Lilburn. *Nmbd* 2E **121**
Eastling. *Kent* 5D **40**
East Linton. *E Lot* 2B **130**
East Liss. *Hants* 4F **25**
East Lockinge. *Oxon* 3C **36**
East Looe. *Corn* 3G **7**
East Lound. *N Lin* 1E **87**
East Lulworth. *Dors* 4D **14**
East Lutton. *N Yor* 3D **100**
East Lydford. *Som* 3A **22**
East Mains. *Abers* 4D **152**
East Malling. *Kent* 5B **40**
East Marden. *W Sus* 1G **17**
East Markham. *Notts* 3E **87**
East Marton. *N Yor* 4B **98**
East Meon. *Hants* 4E **25**
East Mersea. *Essx* 4D **54**
East Mey. *High* 1F **169**
East Molesey. *Surr* 4C **38**
Eastmoor. *Norf* 5G **77**
East Morden. *Dors* 3E **15**
East Morton. *W Yor* 5D **98**
East Ness. *N Yor* 2A **100**
East Newton. *E Yor* 1F **95**
East Newton. *N Yor* 2A **100**
Eastney. *Port* 3E **17**
Eastnor. *Here* 2C **48**
East Norton. *Leics* 5E **75**
East Oakley. *Hants* 1D **24**
Eastoft. *N Lin* 3B **94**
East Ogwell. *Devn* 5B **12**
Easton. *Cambs* 3A **64**
Easton. *Cumb* 4D **112** (nr. Burgh by Sands)
Easton. *Cumb* 2F **113** (nr. Longtown)
Easton. *Devn* 4H **11**
Easton. *Dors* 5B **14**
Easton. *Hants* 3D **24**
Easton. *Linc* 3G **75**
Easton. *Norf* 4D **78**
Easton. *Som* 2A **22**
Easton. *Suff* 5E **67**
Easton. *Wilts* 4D **35**
Easton Grey. *Wilts* 3D **35**
Easton-in-Gordano. *N Som* 4A **34**
Easton Maudit. *Nptn* 5F **63**
Easton on the Hill. *Nptn* 5H **75**
Easton Royal. *Wilts* 5H **35**
East Orchard. *Dors* 1D **14**
East Ord. *Nmbd* 4F **131**
East Panson. *Devn* 3D **10**
East Peckham. *Kent* 1A **28**
East Pennard. *Som* 3A **22**
East Perry. *Cambs* 4A **64**
East Pitcorthie. *Fife* 3H **137**
East Portlemouth. *Devn* 5D **8**
East Prawle. *Devn* 5D **9**
East Preston. *W Sus* 5B **26**
East Putford. *Devn* 1D **10**
East Quantoxhead. *Som* 2E **21**
East Rainton. *Tyne* 5G **115**
East Ravendale. *NE Lin* 1B **88**
East Raynham. *Norf* 3A **78**
Eastrea. *Cambs* 1B **64**
East Rhidorroch Lodge. *High* 4G **163**
Eastriggs. *Dum* 3D **112**
East Rigton. *W Yor* 5F **99**
Eastrington. *E Yor* 1A **94**
East Rounton. *N Yor* 4B **106**
East Row. *N Yor* 3F **107**
East Rudham. *Norf* 3H **77**
East Runton. *Norf* 1D **78**
East Ruston. *Norf* 3F **79**
Eastry. *Kent* 5H **41**
East Saltoun. *E Lot* 3A **130**
East Shaws. *Dur* 3D **105**
East Shefford. *W Ber* 4B **36**
Eastshore. *Shet* 10E **173**
East Sleekburn. *Nmbd* 1F **115**
East Somerton. *Norf* 4G **79**
East Stockwith. *Linc* 1E **87**
East Stoke. *Dors* 4D **14**
East Stoke. *Notts* 1E **75**
East Stoke. *Som* 1H **13**
East Stour. *Dors* 4D **22**
East Stourmouth. *Kent* 4G **41**
East Stowford. *Devn* 4G **19**
East Stratton. *Hants* 2D **24**

East Studdal. Kent 1H 29
East Taphouse. Corn 2F 7
East-the-Water. Devn 4E 19
East Thirston. Nmbd 5F 121
East Tilbury. Thur 3A 40
East Tisted. Hants 3F 25
East Torrington. Linc 2A 88
East Tuddenham. Norf 4C 78
East Tytherley. Hants 4A 24
East Tytherton. Wilts 4E 35
East Village. Devn 2B 12
Eastville. Linc 5D 88
East Wall. Shrp 1H 59
East Walton. Norf 4G 77
East Week. Devn 3G 11
Eastwell. Leics 3E 75
East Wellow. Hants 4B 24
East Wemyss. Fife 4F 137
East Whitburn. W Lot 3C 128
Eastwick. Herts 4E 53
Eastwick. Shet 4E 173
East Williamston. Pemb 4E 43
East Winch. Norf 4F 77
East Winterslow. Wilts 3H 23
East Wittering. W Sus 3F 17
East Witton. N Yor 1D 98
Eastwood. Notts 1B 74
Eastwood. S'end 2C 40
East Woodburn. Nmbd 1C 114
Eastwood End. Cambs 1D 64
East Woodhay. Hants 5C 36
East Woodlands. Som 2C 22
East Worldham. Hants 3F 25
East Worlington. Devn 1A 12
East Youlstone. Devn 1C 10
Eathorpe. Warw 4A 62
Eaton. Ches 4C 84
(nr. Congleton)
Eaton. Ches 4H 83
(nr. Kelsall)
Eaton. Leics 3E 75
Eaton. Norf 2F 77
(nr. Heacham)
Eaton. Norf 5E 78
(nr. Norwich)
Eaton. Notts 3E 86
Eaton. Oxon 5C 50
Eaton. Shrp 2F 59
(nr. Bishop's Castle)
Eaton. Shrp 1H 59
(nr. Church Stretton)
Eaton Bishop. Here 2H 47
Eaton Bray. Beds 3H 51
Eaton Constantine. Shrp 5H 71
Eaton Hastings. Oxon 2A 36
Eaton Socon. Cambs 5A 64
Eaton upon Tern. Shrp 3A 72
Eau Brink. Norf 4E 77
Eaves Green. W Mid 2G 61
Ebberston. N Yor 1C 100
Ebbesbourne Wake. Wilts 4E 23
Ebblake. Dors 2G 15
Ebbw Vale. Blae 5E 47
Ebchester. Dur 4E 115
Ebford. Devn 4C 12
Ebley. Glos 5D 48
Ebnal. Ches 1G 71
Ebrington. Glos 1G 49
Ecchinswell. Hants 1D 24
Ecclefechan. Dum 2C 112
Eccles. G Man 1B 84
Eccles. Kent 4B 40
Eccles. Bord 5D 130
Ecclesall. S Yor 2H 85
Ecclesfield. S Yor 1A 86
Eccles Green. Here 1G 47
Eccleshall. Staf 3C 72
Eccleshill. W Yor 1B 92
Ecclesmachan. W Lot 2D 128
Eccles on Sea. Norf 3G 79
Eccles Road. Norf 1C 66
Eccleston. Ches 4G 83
Eccleston. Lanc 3D 90
Eccleston. Mers 1G 83
Eccup. W Yor 5E 99
Echt. Abers 3E 153
Eckford. Bord 2B 120
Eckington. Derbs 3B 86
Eckington. Worc 1E 49
Ecton. Nptn 4F 63
Edale. Derbs 2F 85
Eday Airport. Orkn 4E 172
Edburton. W Sus 4D 26
Edderside. Cumb 5C 112
Edderton. High 5E 164
Eddington. Kent 4F 41
Eddington. W Ber 5B 36
Eddleston. Bord 5F 129
Eddlewood. S Lan 4A 128
Edenbridge. Kent 1F 27
Edendonich. Arg 1A 134
Edenfield. Lanc 3G 91
Edenhall. Cumb 1G 103
Edenham. Linc 3H 75
Edensor. Derbs 4G 85
Edentaggart. Arg 4C 134
Edenthorpe. S Yor 4G 93
Eden Vale. Dur 1B 106
Edern. Gwyn 2B 68
Edgarley. Som 3A 22
Edgbaston. W Mid 2E 61
Edgcott. Buck 3E 51
Edgcott. Som 3B 20
Edge. Glos 5D 48
Edge. Shrp 5F 71
Edgebolton. Shrp 3H 71
Edge End. Glos 4A 48
Edgefield. Norf 2C 78
Edgefield Street. Norf 2C 78
Edge Green. Ches 5G 83
Edgehead. Midl 3G 129
Edgeley. Shrp 1H 71
Edgeside. Lanc 2G 91
Edgeworth. Glos 5E 49
Edgiock. Worc 4E 61
Edgmond. Telf 4B 72
Edgmond Marsh. Telf 3B 72
Edgton. Shrp 2F 59
Edgware. G Lon 1C 38
Edgworth. Bkbn 3F 91
Edinbane. High 3C 154
Edinburgh. Edin 2F 129
Edinburgh Airport. Edin 2E 129
Edingale. Staf 4G 73
Edingley. Notts 5D 86
Edingthorpe. Norf 2F 79
Edington. Som 3G 21
Edington. Wilts 1E 23
Edingworth. Som 1G 21
Edistone. Devn 4C 18
Edithmead. Som 2G 21
Edith Weston. Rut 5G 75
Edlaston. Derbs 1F 73
Edlesborough. Buck 4H 51
Edlingham. Nmbd 4F 121
Edlington. Linc 3B 88
Edmondsham. Dors 1F 15
Edmondsley. Dur 5F 115
Edmondthorpe. Leics 4F 75
Edmonstone. Orkn 5E 172
Edmonton. Corn 1D 6
Edmonton. G Lon 1E 39
Edmundbyers. Dur 4D 114
Ednam. Bord 1B 120
Ednaston. Derbs 1G 73
Edney Common. Essx 5G 53
Edrom. Bord 4E 131
Edstaston. Shrp 2H 71
Edstone. Warw 4F 61
Edwalton. Notts 2D 74
Edwardstone. Suff 1C 54
Edwardsville. Mer T 2D 32
Edwinsford. Carm 2G 45
Edwinstowe. Notts 4D 86
Edworth. Beds 1C 52
Edwyn Ralph. Here 5A 60
Edzell. Ang 2F 145
Efail-fach. Neat 2A 32
Efail Isaf. Rhon 3D 32
Efailnewydd. Gwyn 2C 68
Efail-rhyd. Powy 3D 70
Efailwen. Carm 2F 43
Efenechtyd. Den 5D 82
Effingham. Surr 5C 38
Effingham Common. Surr 5C 38
Effirth. Shet 6E 173
Efflinch. Staf 4F 73
Efford. Devn 2B 12
Egbury. Hants 1C 24
Egdon. Worc 5D 60
Egerton. G Man 3F 91
Egerton. Kent 1D 28
Egerton Forstal. Kent 1C 28
Eggborough. N Yor 2F 93
Eggbuckland. Plym 3A 8
Eggesford. Devn 1G 11
Eggington. Beds 3H 51
Egginton. Derbs 3G 73
Egglescliffe. Stoc T 3B 106
Eggleston. Dur 2C 104
Egham. Surr 3B 38
Egham Hythe. Surr 3B 38
Egleton. Rut 5F 75
Eglingham. Nmbd 3F 121
Egloshayle. Corn 5A 10
Egloskerry. Corn 4C 10
Eglwysbach. Cnwy 3H 81
Eglwys Brewis. V Glam 5D 32
Eglwys Fach. Cdgn 1F 57
Eglwyswrw. Pemb 1F 43
Egmanton. Notts 4E 87
Egremont. Cumb 3B 102
Egremont. Mers 1F 83
Egton. N Yor 4F 107
Egton Bridge. N Yor 4F 107
Egypt. Buck 2A 38
Egypt. Hants 2C 24
Eight Ash Green. Essx 3C 54
Eight Mile Burn. Midl 4E 129
Eignaig. High 4B 140
Eilanreach. High 2G 147
Eildon. Bord 1H 119
Eileanach Lodge. High 2H 157
Eilean Iarmain. High 2F 147
Einacleit. W Isl 5D 171
Eisgein. W Isl 6F 171
Eisingrug. Gwyn 2F 69
Elan Village. Powy 4B 58
Elberton. S Glo 3B 34
Elbridge. W Sus 5A 26
Elburton. Plym 3B 8
Elcho. Per 1D 136
Elcombe. Swin 3G 35
Elcot. W Ber 5B 36
Eldernell. Cambs 1C 64
Eldersfield. Worc 2D 48
Elderslie. Ren 3F 127
Elder Street. Essx 2F 53
Eldon. Dur 2F 105
Eldroth. N Yor 3G 97
Eldwick. W Yor 5D 98
Elfhowe. Cumb 5F 103
Elford. Nmbd 1F 121
Elford. Staf 4F 73
Elford Closes. Cambs 3D 65
Elgin. Mor 2G 159
Elgol. High 2D 146
Elham. Kent 1F 29
Elie. Fife 3G 137
Eling. Hants 1B 16
Eling. W Ber 4D 36
Elishaw. Nmbd 5C 120
Elizafield. Dum 2B 112
Elkesley. Notts 3D 86
Elkington. Nptn 3D 62
Elkins Green. Essx 5G 53
Elkstone. Glos 4E 49
Ellan. High 1C 150
Ellanbeich. Arg 2E 133
Elland. W Yor 2B 92
Ellary. Arg 2F 125
Ellastone. Staf 1F 73
Ellbridge. Corn 2A 8
Ellel. Lanc 4D 97
Ellemford. Bord 3D 130
Ellenborough. Cumb 1B 102
Ellenbrook. Herts 5C 52
Ellenhall. Staf 3C 72
Ellen's Green. Surr 2B 26
Ellerbec. N Yor 5B 106
Ellerburn. N Yor 1C 100
Ellerby. N Yor 3E 107
Ellerdine. Telf 3A 72
Ellerdine Heath. Telf 3A 72
Ellerhayes. Devn 2C 12
Elleric. Arg 4E 141
Ellerker. E Yor 2C 94
Ellerton. E Yor 1H 93
Ellerton. N Yor 5F 105
Ellerton. Shrp 3B 72
Ellesborough. Buck 5G 51
Ellesmere. Shrp 2F 71
Ellesmere Port. Ches 3G 83
Ellingham. Hants 2G 15
Ellingham. Norf 1F 67
Ellingham. Nmbd 2F 121
Ellingstring. N Yor 1D 98
Ellington. Cambs 3A 64
Ellington. Nmbd 5G 121
Ellington Thorpe. Cambs 3A 64
Ellisfield. Hants 2E 25
Ellishadder. High 2E 155
Ellistown. Leics 4B 74
Ellon. Abers 5G 161
Ellonby. Cumb 1F 103
Ellough. Suff 2G 67
Elloughton. E Yor 2C 94
Ellwood. Glos 5A 48
Elm. Cambs 5D 76
Elmbridge. Glos 4D 48
Elmbridge. Worc 4D 60
Elmdon. Essx 2E 53
Elmdon. W Mid 2F 61
Elmdon Heath. W Mid 2F 61
Elmesthorpe. Leics 1B 62
Elmfield. IOW 3D 16
Elm Hill. Dors 4D 22
Elmhurst. Staf 4F 73
Elmley Castle. Worc 1E 49
Elmley Lovett. Worc 4C 60
Elmore. Glos 4C 48
Elmore Back. Glos 4C 48
Elm Park. G Lon 2G 39
Elmscott. Devn 4C 18
Elmsett. Suff 1D 54
Elmstead. Essx 3D 54
Elmstead Heath. Essx 3D 54
Elmstead Market. Essx 3D 54
Elmsted. Kent 1F 29
Elmstone. Kent 4G 41
Elmstone Hardwicke. Glos 3E 49
Elmswell. E Yor 4D 101
Elmswell. Suff 4B 66
Elmton. Derbs 3C 86
Elphin. High 2G 163
Elphinstone. E Lot 2G 129
Elrick. Abers 3F 153
Elrick. Mor 1B 152
Elrig. Dum 5A 110
Elsdon. Nmbd 5D 120
Elsecar. S Yor 1A 86
Elsenham. Essx 3F 53
Elsfield. Oxon 4D 50
Elsham. N Lin 3D 94
Elsing. Norf 4C 78
Elslack. N Yor 5B 98
Elsrickle. S Lan 5D 128
Elstead. Surr 1A 26
Elsted. W Sus 1G 17
Elsted Marsh. W Sus 4G 25
Elsthorpe. Linc 3H 75
Elstob. Dur 2A 106
Elston. Devn 2A 12
Elston. Lanc 1E 90
Elston. Notts 1E 75
Elston. Wilts 2F 23
Elstone. Devn 1G 11
Elstow. Beds 1A 52
Elstree. Herts 1C 38
Elstronwick. E Yor 1F 95
Elswick. Lanc 1C 90
Elswick. Tyne 3F 115
Elsworth. Cambs 4C 64
Elterwater. Cumb 4E 103
Eltham. G Lon 3F 39
Eltisley. Cambs 5B 64
Elton. Cambs 1H 63
Elton. Ches 3G 83
Elton. Derbs 4G 85
Elton. Glos 4C 48
Elton. G Man 3F 91
Elton. Here 3G 59
Elton. Notts 2E 75
Elton. Stoc T 3B 106
Elton Green. Ches 3G 83
Eltringham. Nmbd 3D 115
Elvanfoot. S Lan 3B 118
Elvaston. Derbs 2B 74
Elveden. Suff 3H 65
Elvetham Heath. Hants 1F 25
Elvingston. E Lot 2A 130
Elvington. Kent 5G 41
Elvington. York 5B 100
Elwick. Hart 1B 106
Elwick. Nmbd 1F 121
Elworth. Ches 4B 84
Elworth. Dors 4A 14
Elworthy. Som 3D 20
Ely. Cambs 2E 65
Ely. Card 4E 33
Emberton. Mil 1G 51
Embleton. Cumb 1C 102
Embleton. Dur 2B 106
Embleton. Nmbd 2G 121
Embo. High 4F 165
Emborough. Som 1B 22
Embo Street. High 4F 165
Embsay. N Yor 4C 98
Emery Down. Hants 2A 16
Emley. W Yor 3C 92
Emmbrook. Wok 5F 37
Emmer Green. Read 4F 37
Emmington. Oxon 5F 51
Emneth. Norf 5D 77
Emneth Hungate. Norf 5E 77
Empingham. Rut 5G 75
Empshott. Hants 3F 25
Emsworth. Hants 2F 17
Enborne. W Ber 5C 36
Enborne Row. W Ber 5C 36
Enchmarsh. Shrp 1H 59
Enderby. Leics 1C 62
Endmoor. Cumb 1E 97
Endon. Staf 5D 84
Endon Bank. Staf 5D 84
Enfield. G Lon 1E 39
Enfield Wash. G Lon 1E 39
Enford. Wilts 1G 23
Engine Common. S Glo 3B 34
Englefield. W Ber 4E 36
Englefield Green. Surr 3A 38
Engleseabrook. Ches 5B 84
English Bicknor. Glos 4A 48
Englishcombe. Bath 5C 34
English Frankton. Shrp 3G 71
Enham Alamein. Hants 2B 24
Enmore. Som 3F 21
Ennerdale Bridge. Cumb 3B 102
Enniscaven. Corn 3D 6
Enoch. Dum 4A 118
Enochdhu. Per 2H 143
Ensay. Arg 4E 139
Ensbury. Bour 3F 15
Ensdon. Shrp 4G 71
Ensis. Devn 4F 19
Enson. Staf 3D 72
Enstone. Oxon 3B 50
Enterkinfoot. Dum 4A 118
Enville. Staf 2C 60
Eolaigearraidh. W Isl 8C 170

Eorabus—Felinwynt

Eorabus. *Arg* 1A 132
Eoropaidh. *W Isl* 1H 171
Epney. *Glos* 4C 48
Epperstone. *Notts* 1D 74
Epping. *Essx* 5E 53
Epping Green. *Essx* 5E 53
Epping Green. *Herts* 5C 52
Epping Upland. *Essx* 5E 53
Eppleby. *N Yor* 3E 105
Eppleworth. *E Yor* 1D 94
Epsom. *Surr* 4D 38
Epwell. *Oxon* 1B 50
Epworth. *N Lin* 4A 94
Epworth Turbary. *N Lin* 4A 94
Erbistock. *Wrex* 1F 71
Erbusaig. *High* 1F 147
Erchless Castle. *High* 4G 157
Erdington. *W Mid* 1F 61
Eredine. *Arg* 3G 133
Eriboll. *High* 3E 167
Ericstane. *Dum* 3C 118
Eridge Green. *E Sus* 2G 27
Erines. *Arg* 2G 125
Eriswell. *Suff* 3G 65
Erith. *G Lon* 3G 39
Erlestoke. *Wilts* 1E 23
Ermine East. *Linc* 3G 87
Ermine West. *Linc* 3G 87
Ermington. *Devn* 3C 8
Ernesettle. *Plym* 3A 8
Erpingham. *Norf* 2D 78
Erriottwood. *Kent* 5D 40
Errogie. *High* 1H 149
Errol. *Per* 1E 137
Errol Station. *Per* 1E 137
Erskine. *Ren* 2F 127
Erskine Bridge. *Ren* 2F 127
Ervie. *Dum* 3F 109
Erwarton. *Suff* 2F 55
Erwood. *Powy* 1D 46
Eryholme. *N Yor* 4A 106
Eryrys. *Den* 5E 82
Escalls. *Corn* 4A 4
Escomb. *Dur* 1E 105
Escrick. *N Yor* 5A 100
Esgair. *Carm* 3D 45
(nr. Carmarthen)
Esgair. *Carm* 3G 43
(nr. St Clears)
Esgairgeiliog. *Powy* 5G 69
Esh. *Dur* 5E 115
Esher. *Surr* 4C 38
Esholt. *W Yor* 5D 98
Eshott. *Nmbd* 5G 121
Eshton. *N Yor* 4B 98
Esh Winning. *Dur* 5E 115
Eskadale. *High* 5G 157
Eskbank. *Midl* 3G 129
Eskdale Green. *Cumb* 4C 102
Eskdalemuir. *Dum* 5E 119
Eskham. *Linc* 1C 88
Esknish. *Arg* 3B 124
Esk Valley. *N Yor* 4F 107
Eslington Hall. *Nmbd* 3E 121
Espley Hall. *Nmbd* 5F 121
Esprick. *Lanc* 1C 90
Essendine. *Rut* 4H 75
Essendon. *Herts* 5C 52
Essich. *High* 5A 158
Essington. *Staf* 5D 72
Eston. *Red C* 3C 106
Estover. *Plym* 3B 8
Eswick. *Shet* 6F 173
Etal. *Nmbd* 1D 120
Etchilhampton. *Wilts* 5F 35
Etchingham. *E Sus* 3B 28
Etchinghill. *Kent* 2F 29
Etchinghill. *Staf* 4E 73
Ethie Haven. *Ang* 4F 145
Etling Green. *Norf* 4C 78
Etloe. *Glos* 5B 48
Eton. *Wind* 3A 38
Eton Wick. *Wind* 3A 38
Etteridge. *High* 4A 150
Ettersgill. *Dur* 2B 104
Ettiley Heath. *Ches* 4B 84
Ettington. *Warw* 1A 50
Etton. *E Yor* 5D 101
Etton. *Pet* 5A 76
Ettrick. *Bord* 3E 119
Ettrickbridge. *Bord* 2F 119
Etwall. *Derbs* 2G 73
Eudon Burnell. *Shrp* 2B 60
Eudon George. *Shrp* 2A 60
Euston. *Suff* 3A 66
Euxton. *Lanc* 3D 90
Evanstown. *B'end* 3C 32
Evanton. *High* 2A 158
Evedon. *Linc* 1H 75
Evelix. *High* 4E 165
Evendine. *Here* 1C 48
Evenjobb. *Powy* 4E 59
Evenley. *Nptn* 2D 50
Evenlode. *Glos* 3H 49
Even Swindon. *Swin* 3G 35
Evenwood. *Dur* 2E 105
Evenwood Gate. *Dur* 2E 105
Everbay. *Orkn* 5F 172
Evercreech. *Som* 3B 22
Everdon. *Nptn* 5C 62
Everingham. *E Yor* 5C 100
Everleigh. *Wilts* 1H 23
Everley. *N Yor* 1D 100
Eversholt. *Beds* 2H 51
Evershot. *Dors* 2A 14
Eversley. *Hants* 5F 37
Eversley Cross. *Hants* 5F 37
Everthorpe. *E Yor* 1C 94
Everton. *Beds* 5B 64
Everton. *Hants* 3A 16
Everton. *Mers* 1F 83
Everton. *Notts* 1D 86
Evertown. *Dum* 2E 113
Evesbatch. *Here* 1B 48
Evesham. *Worc* 1F 49
Evington. *Leic* 5D 74
Ewden Village. *S Yor* 1G 85
Ewdness. *Shrp* 1B 60
Ewell. *Surr* 4D 38
Ewell Minnis. *Kent* 1G 29
Ewelme. *Oxon* 2E 37
Ewen. *Glos* 2F 35
Ewenny. *V Glam* 4C 32
Ewerby. *Linc* 1A 76
Ewes. *Dum* 5F 119
Ewesley. *Nmbd* 5E 121
Ewhurst. *Surr* 1B 26
Ewhurst Green. *E Sus* 3B 28
Ewhurst Green. *Surr* 2B 26
Ewlo. *Flin* 4F 83
Ewloe. *Flin* 4F 83
Ewood Bridge. *Lanc* 2F 91
Eworthy. *Devn* 3E 11
Ewshot. *Hants* 1G 25
Ewyas Harold. *Here* 3G 47
Exbourne. *Devn* 2G 11
Exbury. *Hants* 2C 16
Exceat. *E Sus* 5G 27
Exebridge. *Som* 4C 20
Exelby. *N Yor* 1E 99
Exeter. *Devn* 3C 12
Exeter International Airport.
Devn 3D 12
Exford. *Som* 3B 20
Exfords Green. *Shrp* 5G 71
Exhall. *Warw* 5F 61
Exlade Street. *Oxon* 3E 37
Exminster. *Devn* 4C 12
Exmouth. *Devn* 4D 12
Exning. *Suff* 4F 65
Exton. *Devn* 4C 12
Exton. *Hants* 4E 24
Exton. *Rut* 4G 75
Exton. *Som* 3C 20
Exwick. *Devn* 3C 12
Eyam. *Derbs* 3G 85
Eydon. *Nptn* 5C 62
Eye. *Here* 4G 59
Eye. *Pet* 5B 76
Eye. *Suff* 3D 66
Eye Green. *Pet* 5B 76
Eyemouth. *Bord* 3F 131
Eyeworth. *Beds* 1C 52
Eyhorne Street. *Kent* 5C 40
Eyke. *Suff* 5F 67
Eynesbury. *Cambs* 5A 64
Eynort. *High* 1B 146
Eynsford. *Kent* 4G 39
Eynsham. *Oxon* 5C 50
Eyre. *High* 3D 154
(on Isle of Skye)
Eyre. *High* 5E 155
(on Raasay)
Eythorne. *Kent* 1G 29
Eyton. *Here* 4G 59
Eyton. *Shrp* 2F 59
(nr. Bishop's Castle)
Eyton. *Shrp* 4F 71
(nr. Shrewsbury)
Eyton. *Wrex* 1F 71
Eyton on Severn. *Shrp* 5H 71
Eyton upon the Weald Moors.
Telf 4A 72

F

Faccombe. *Hants* 1B 24
Faceby. *N Yor* 4B 106
Faddiley. *Ches* 5H 83
Fadmoor. *N Yor* 1A 100
Fagwyr. *Swan* 5G 45
Faichem. *High* 3E 149
Faifley. *W Dun* 2G 127
Fail. *S Ayr* 2D 116
Failand. *N Som* 4A 34
Failford. *S Ayr* 2D 116
Failsworth. *G Man* 4H 91
Fairbourne. *Gwyn* 4F 69
Fairbourne Heath. *Kent* 5C 40
Fairburn. *N Yor* 2E 93
Fairfield. *Derbs* 3E 85
Fairfield. *Kent* 3D 28
Fairfield. *Worc* 3D 60
(nr. Bromsgrove)
Fairfield. *Worc* 1F 49
(nr. Evesham)
Fairford. *Glos* 5G 49
Fair Green. *Norf* 4F 77
Fair Hill. *Cumb* 1G 103
Fairhill. *S Lan* 4A 128
Fair Isle Airport. *Shet* 1B 172
Fairlands. *Surr* 5A 38
Fairlie. *N Ayr* 4D 126
Fairlight. *E Sus* 4C 28
Fairlight Cove. *E Sus* 4C 28
Fairmile. *Devn* 3D 12
Fairmile. *Surr* 4C 38
Fairmilehead. *Edin* 3F 129
Fair Oak. *Devn* 1D 12
Fair Oak. *Hants* 1C 16
(nr. Eastleigh)
Fair Oak. *Hants* 5D 36
(nr. Kingsclere)
Fairoak. *Staf* 2B 72
Fair Oak Green. *Hants* 5E 37
Fairseat. *Kent* 4H 39
Fairstead. *Essx* 4A 54
Fairstead. *Norf* 4F 77
Fairwarp. *E Sus* 3F 27
Fairwater. *Card* 4E 33
Fairy Cross. *Devn* 4E 19
Fakenham. *Norf* 3B 78
Fakenham Magna. *Suff* 3B 66
Fala. *Midl* 3H 129
Fala Dam. *Midl* 3H 129
Falcon. *Here* 2B 48
Faldingworth. *Linc* 2H 87
Falfield. *S Glo* 2B 34
Falkenham. *Suff* 2F 55
Falkirk. *Falk* 2B 128
Falkland. *Fife* 3E 137
Fallin. *Stir* 4H 135
Fallowfield. *G Man* 1C 84
Falmer. *E Sus* 5E 27
Falmouth. *Corn* 5C 6
Falsgrave. *N Yor* 1E 101
Falstone. *Nmbd* 1A 114
Fanagmore. *High* 4B 166
Fancott. *Beds* 3A 52
Fanellan. *High* 4G 157
Fangdale Beck. *N Yor* 5C 106
Fangfoss. *E Yor* 4B 100
Fankerton. *Falk* 1A 128
Fanmore. *Arg* 4F 139
Fanner's Green. *Essx* 4G 53
Fannich Lodge. *High* 2E 156
Fans. *Bord* 5C 130
Farcet. *Cambs* 1B 64
Far Cotton. *Nptn* 5E 63
Fareham. *Hants* 2D 16
Farewell. *Staf* 4E 73
Far Forest. *Worc* 3B 60
Farforth. *Linc* 3C 88
Far Green. *Glos* 5C 48
Far Hoarcross. *Staf* 3F 73
Faringdon. *Oxon* 2A 36
Farington. *Lanc* 2D 90
Farlam. *Cumb* 4G 113
Farleigh. *N Som* 5H 33
Farleigh. *Surr* 4E 39
Farleigh Hungerford. *Som* 1D 22
Farleigh Wallop. *Hants* 2E 24
Farleigh Wick. *Wilts* 5D 34
Farlesthorpe. *Linc* 3D 88
Farleton. *Cumb* 1E 97
Farleton. *Lanc* 3E 97
Farley. *High* 4G 157
Farley. *N Som* 4H 33
Farley. *Shrp* 5F 71
(nr. Shrewsbury)
Farley. *Shrp* 5A 72
(nr. Telford)
Farley. *Staf* 1E 73
Farley. *Wilts* 4H 23
Farley Green. *Suff* 5G 65
Farley Green. *Surr* 1B 26
Farley Hill. *Wok* 5F 37
Farley's End. *Glos* 4C 48
Farlington. *N Yor* 3A 100
Farlington. *Port* 2E 17
Farlow. *Shrp* 2A 60
Farmborough. *Bath* 5B 34
Farmcote. *Glos* 3F 49
Farmcote. *Shrp* 1B 60
Farmington. *Glos* 4G 49
Far Moor. *G Man* 4D 90
Farmoor. *Oxon* 5C 50
Farmtown. *Mor* 3C 160
Farnah Green. *Derbs* 1H 73
Farnborough. *G Lon* 4F 39
Farnborough. *Hants* 1G 25
Farnborough. *Warw* 1C 50
Farnborough. *W Ber* 3C 36
Farnborough Airport. *Surr* 1G 25
Farncombe. *Surr* 1A 26
Farndish. *Beds* 4G 63
Farndon. *Ches* 5G 83
Farndon. *Notts* 5E 87
Farnell. *Ang* 3F 145
Farnham. *Dors* 1E 15
Farnham. *Essx* 3E 53
Farnham. *N Yor* 3F 99
Farnham. *Suff* 4F 67
Farnham. *Surr* 2G 25
Farnham Common. *Buck* 2A 38
Farnham Green. *Essx* 3E 53
Farnham Royal. *Buck* 2A 38
Farnhill. *N Yor* 5C 98
Farningham. *Kent* 4G 39
Farnley. *N Yor* 5E 98
Farnley Tyas. *W Yor* 3B 92
Farnsfield. *Notts* 5D 86
Farnworth. *G Man* 4F 91
Farnworth. *Hal* 2H 83
Far Oakridge. *Glos* 5E 49
Far Orrest. *Cumb* 4F 103
Farr. *High* 2H 167
(nr. Bettyhill)
Farr. *High* 5A 158
(nr. Inverness)
Farr. *High* 3C 150
(nr. Kingussie)
Farraline. *High* 1H 149
Farringdon. *Devn* 3D 12
Farrington. *Dors* 1D 14
Farrington Gurney. *Bath* 1B 22
Far Sawrey. *Cumb* 5E 103
Farsley. *W Yor* 1C 92
Farthinghoe. *Nptn* 2D 50
Farthingstone. *Nptn* 5D 62
Farthorpe. *Linc* 3B 88
Fartown. *W Yor* 3B 92
Farway. *Devn* 3E 13
Fasag. *High* 3A 156
Fascadale. *High* 1G 139
Fasnacloich. *Arg* 4E 141
Fassfern. *High* 1E 141
Fatfield. *Tyne* 4G 115
Faugh. *Cumb* 4G 113
Fauld. *Staf* 3F 73
Fauldhouse. *W Lot* 3C 128
Faulkbourne. *Essx* 4A 54
Faulkland. *Som* 1C 22
Fauls. *Shrp* 2H 71
Faverdale. *Darl* 3F 105
Faversham. *Kent* 4E 40
Fawdington. *N Yor* 2G 99
Fawfieldhead. *Staf* 4E 85
Fawkham Green. *Kent* 4G 39
Fawler. *Oxon* 4B 50
Fawley. *Buck* 3F 37
Fawley. *Hants* 2C 16
Fawley. *W Ber* 3B 36
Fawley Chapel. *Here* 3A 48
Fawton. *Corn* 2F 7
Faxfleet. *E Yor* 2B 94
Faygate. *W Sus* 2D 26
Fazakerley. *Mers* 1F 83
Fazeley. *Staf* 5F 73
Feabuie. *High* 4B 158
Feagour. *High* 4H 149
Fearby. *N Yor* 1D 98
Fearn. *High* 1C 158
Fearnan. *Per* 4E 142
Fearnbeg. *High* 3G 155
Fearnhead. *Warr* 1A 84
Fearnmore. *High* 2G 155
Featherstone. *Staf* 5D 72
Featherstone. *W Yor* 2E 93
Featherstone Castle. *Nmbd* 3H 113
Feckenham. *Worc* 4E 61
Feering. *Essx* 3B 54
Feetham. *N Yor* 5C 104
Feizor. *N Yor* 3G 97
Felbridge. *Surr* 2E 27
Felbrigg. *Norf* 2E 78
Felcourt. *Surr* 1E 27
Felden. *Herts* 5A 52
Felhampton. *Shrp* 2G 59
Felindre. *Carm* 3F 45
(nr. Llandeilo)
Felindre. *Carm* 2G 45
(nr. Llandovery)
Felindre. *Carm* 2D 44
(nr. Newcastle Emlyn)
Felindre. *Powy* 2D 58
Felindre. *Swan* 5G 45
Felindre Farchog. *Pemb* 1F 43
Felinfach. *Cdgn* 5E 57
Felinfach. *Powy* 2D 46
Felinfoel. *Carm* 5F 45
Felingwmisaf. *Carm* 3F 45
Felingwmuchaf. *Carm* 3F 45
Felin Newydd. *Powy* 5C 70
(nr. Newtown)
Felin Newydd. *Powy* 3E 70
(nr. Oswestry)
Felin Wnda. *Cdgn* 1D 44
Felinwynt. *Cdgn* 5B 56

Felixkirk. N Yor 1G 99
Felixstowe. Suff 2F 55
Felixstowe Ferry. Suff 2G 55
Felkington. Nmbd 5F 131
Fell End. Cumb 5A 104
Felling. Tyne 3F 115
Fell Side. Cumb 1E 102
Felmersham. Beds 5G 63
Felmingham. Norf 3E 79
Felpham. W Sus 3H 17
Felsham. Suff 5B 66
Felsted. Essx 3G 53
Feltham. G Lon 3C 38
Felthamhill. Surr 3B 38
Felthorpe. Norf 4D 78
Felton. Here 1A 48
Felton. N Som 5A 34
Felton. Nmbd 4F 121
Felton Butler. Shrp 4F 71
Feltwell. Norf 1G 65
Fenay Bridge. W Yor 3B 92
Fence. Lanc 1G 91
Fence Houses. Tyne 4G 115
Fencott. Oxon 4D 50
Fen Ditton. Cambs 4D 65
Fen Drayton. Cambs 4C 64
Fen End. Linc 3B 76
Fen End. W Mid 3G 61
Fenham. Nmbd 5G 131
Fenham. Tyne 3F 115
Fenhouses. Linc 1B 76
Feniscowles. Bkbn 2E 91
Feniton. Devn 3D 12
Fenn Green. Shrp 2B 60
Fenn's Bank. Wrex 2H 71
Fenn Street. Medw 3B 40
Fenny Bentley. Derbs 5F 85
Fenny Bridges. Devn 3E 12
Fenny Compton. Warw 5B 62
Fenny Drayton. Leics 1A 62
Fenny Stratford. Mil 2G 51
Fenrother. Nmbd 5F 121
Fenstanton. Cambs 4C 64
Fen Street. Norf 1C 66
Fenton. Cambs 3C 64
Fenton. Cumb 4G 113
Fenton. Linc 5F 87 (nr. Caythorpe)
Fenton. Linc 3F 87 (nr. Saxilby)
Fenton. Nmbd 1D 120
Fenton. Notts 2E 87
Fenton. Stoke 1C 72
Fentonadle. Corn 5A 10
Fenton Barns. E Lot 1B 130
Fenwick. E Ayr 5F 127
Fenwick. Nmbd 5G 131 (nr. Berwick)
Fenwick. Nmbd 2D 114 (nr. Hexham)
Fenwick. S Yor 3F 93
Feochaig. Arg 4B 122
Feock. Corn 5C 6
Feolin Ferry. Arg 3C 124
Feorlan. Arg 5A 122
Feriniquarrie. High 3A 154
Fern. Ang 2D 145
Ferndale. Rhon 2C 32
Ferndown. Dors 2F 15
Ferness. High 4D 158
Fernham. Oxon 2A 36
Fernhill. W Sus 1D 27
Fernhill Heath. Worc 5C 60
Fernhurst. W Sus 4G 25
Ferniefl att. Abers 1H 145
Ferniegair. S Lan 4A 128
Fernilea. High 5C 154
Fernilee. Derbs 3E 85
Ferrensby. N Yor 3F 99
Ferriby Sluice. N Lin 2C 94
Ferrindonald. High 3E 147
Ferring. W Sus 5C 26
Ferrybridge. W Yor 2E 93
Ferryden. Ang 3G 145
Ferryhill. Aber 3G 153
Ferry Hill. Cambs 2C 64
Ferryhill. Dur 1F 105
Ferryhill Station. Dur 1F 105
Ferryside. Carm 4D 44
Ferryton. High 2A 158
Fersfield. Norf 2C 66
Fersit. High 1A 142
Feshiebridge. High 3C 150
Fetcham. Surr 5C 38
Fetterangus. Abers 3G 161
Fettercairn. Abers 1F 145
Fewcott. Oxon 3D 50
Fewston. N Yor 4D 98
Ffairfach. Carm 3G 45
Ffair Rhos. Cdgn 4G 57
Ffaldybrenin. Carm 1G 45
Ffarmers. Carm 1G 45
Ffawyddog. Powy 4F 47
Ffodun. Powy 5E 71
Ffont-y-gari. V Glam 5D 32
Fforest. Carm 5F 45
Fforest-fach. Swan 3F 31
Fforest Goch. Neat 5H 45
Ffostrasol. Cdgn 1D 44
Ffos-y-ffin. Cdgn 4D 56
Ffrith. Flin 5E 83
Ffrwdgrech. Powy 3D 46
Ffwl-y-mwn. V Glam 5D 32
Ffynnon-ddrain. Carm 3E 45
Ffynnongroyw. Flin 2D 82
Ffynnon Gynydd. Powy 1E 47
Ffynnonoer. Cdgn 5E 57
Fiag Lodge. High 1B 164
Fidden. Arg 2B 132
Fiddington. Glos 2E 49
Fiddington. Som 2F 21
Fiddleford. Dors 1D 14
Fiddlers Hamlet. Essx 5E 53
Field. Staf 2E 73
Field Assarts. Oxon 4B 50
Field Broughton. Cumb 1C 96
Field Dalling. Norf 2C 78
Fieldhead. Cumb 1F 103
Field Head. Leics 5B 74
Fifehead Magdalen. Dors 4C 22
Fifehead Neville. Dors 1C 14
Fifehead St Quintin. Dors 1C 14
Fife Keith. Mor 3B 160
Fifield. Oxon 4H 49
Fifield. Wilts 1G 23
Fifield. Wind 3A 38
Fifield Bavant. Wilts 4F 23
Figheldean. Wilts 2G 23
Filby. Norf 4G 79
Filey. N Yor 1F 101
Filford. Dors 3H 13
Filgrave. Mil 1G 51
Filkins. Oxon 5H 49
Filleigh. Devn 1H 11 (nr. Crediton)
Filleigh. Devn 4G 19 (nr. South Molton)
Fillingham. Linc 2G 87
Fillongley. Warw 2G 61
Filton. S Glo 4B 34
Fimber. E Yor 3C 100
Finavon. Ang 3D 145
Fincham. Norf 5F 77
Finchampstead. Wok 5F 37
Fincharn. Arg 3G 133
Finchdean. Hants 1F 17
Finchingfield. Essx 2G 53
Finchley. G Lon 1D 38
Findern. Derbs 2H 73
Findhorn. Mor 2E 159
Findhorn Bridge. High 1C 150
Findochty. Mor 2B 160
Findo Gask. Per 1C 136
Findon. Abers 4G 153
Findon. W Sus 5C 26
Findon Mains. High 2A 158
Findon Valley. W Sus 5C 26
Finedon. Nptn 3G 63
Fingal Street. Suff 3E 66
Fingest. Buck 2F 37
Finghall. N Yor 1D 98
Fingland. Cumb 4D 112
Fingland. Dum 3G 117
Finglesham. Kent 5H 41
Fingringhoe. Essx 3D 54
Finiskaig. High 4A 148
Finmere. Oxon 2E 51
Finnart. Per 3C 142
Finningham. Suff 4C 66
Finningley. S Yor 1D 86
Finnyguad. Abers 3D 160
Finsbury. G Lon 2E 39
Finstall. Worc 3D 61
Finsthwaite. Cumb 1C 96
Finstock. Oxon 4B 50
Finstown. Orkn 6C 172
Fintry. Abers 3E 161
Fintry. D'dee 5D 144
Fintry. Stir 1H 127
Finwood. Warw 4F 61
Finzean. Abers 4D 152
Fionnphort. Arg 2B 132
Fionnsabhagh. W Isl 9C 171
Firbeck. S Yor 2C 86
Firby. N Yor 1E 99 (nr. Bedale)
Firby. N Yor 3B 100 (nr. Malton)
Firgrove. G Man 3H 91
Firsdown. Wilts 3H 23
First Coast. High 4D 162
Firth. Shet 4F 173
Fir Tree. Dur 1E 105
Fishbourne. IOW 3D 16
Fishbourne. W Sus 2G 17
Fishburn. Dur 1A 106
Fishcross. Clac 4B 136
Fisherford. Abers 5D 160
Fisherrow. E Lot 2G 129
Fisher's Pond. Hants 4C 24
Fisher's Row. Lanc 5D 96
Fisherstreet. W Sus 2A 26
Fisherton. High 3B 158
Fisherton. S Ayr 3B 116
Fisherton de la Mere. Wilts 3E 23
Fishguard. Pemb 1D 42
Fishlake. S Yor 3G 93
Fishley. Norf 4G 79
Fishnish. Arg 4A 140
Fishpond Bottom. Dors 3G 13
Fishponds. Bris 4B 34
Fishpool. Glos 3B 48
Fishpool. G Man 4G 91
Fishpools. Powy 4D 58
Fishtoft. Linc 1C 76
Fishtoft Drove. Linc 1C 76
Fishwick. Bord 4F 131
Fiskavaig. High 5C 154
Fiskerton. Linc 3H 87
Fiskerton. Notts 5E 87
Fitling. E Yor 1F 95
Fittleton. Wilts 2G 23
Fittleworth. W Sus 4B 26
Fitton End. Cambs 4D 76
Fitz. Shrp 4G 71
Fitzhead. Som 4E 20
Fitzwilliam. W Yor 3E 93
Fiunary. High 4A 140
Five Ash Down. E Sus 3F 27
Five Ashes. E Sus 3G 27
Five Bells. Som 2D 20
Five Bridges. Here 1B 48
Fivehead. Som 4G 21
Five Lane Ends. Lanc 4E 97
Fivelanes. Corn 4C 10
Five Oak Green. Kent 1H 27
Five Oaks. W Sus 3B 26
Five Roads. Carm 5E 45
Five Ways. Warw 3G 61
Flack's Green. Essx 4A 54
Flackwell Heath. Buck 3G 37
Fladbury. Worc 1E 49
Fladdabister. Shet 8F 173
Flagg. Derbs 4F 85
Flamborough. E Yor 2G 101
Flamstead. Herts 4A 52
Flansham. W Sus 5A 26
Flasby. N Yor 4B 98
Flash. Staf 4E 85
Flashader. High 3C 154
Flatt, The. Cumb 2G 113
Flaunden. Herts 5A 52
Flawborough. Notts 1E 75
Flawith. N Yor 3G 99
Flax Bourton. N Som 5A 34
Flaxby. N Yor 4F 99
Flaxholme. Derbs 1H 73
Flaxley. Glos 4B 48
Flaxley Green. Staf 4E 73
Flaxpool. Som 3E 21
Flaxton. N Yor 3A 100
Fleckney. Leics 1D 62
Flecknoe. Warw 4C 62
Fledborough. Notts 3F 87
Fleet. Dors 4B 14
Fleet. Hants 1G 25 (nr. Farnborough)
Fleet. Hants 2F 17 (nr. South Hayling)
Fleet. Linc 3C 76
Fleet Hargate. Linc 3C 76
Fleetville. Herts 5B 52
Fleetwood. Lanc 5C 96
Fleggburgh. Norf 4G 79
Fleisirin. W Isl 4H 171
Flemingston. V Glam 4D 32
Flemington. S Lan 3H 127 (nr. Glasgow)
Flemington. S Lan 5A 128 (nr. Strathaven)
Flempton. Suff 4H 65
Fleoideabhagh. W Isl 9C 171
Fletcher's Green. Kent 1G 27
Fletchertown. Cumb 5D 112
Fletching. E Sus 3F 27
Fleuchary. High 4E 165
Flexbury. Corn 2C 10
Flexford. Surr 5A 38
Flimby. Cumb 1B 102
Flimwell. E Sus 2B 28
Flint. Flin 3E 83
Flintham. Notts 1E 75
Flint Mountain. Flin 3E 83
Flinton. E Yor 1F 95
Flintsham. Here 5F 59
Flishinghurst. Kent 2B 28
Flitcham. Norf 3G 77
Flitton. Beds 2A 52
Flitwick. Beds 2A 52
Flixborough. N Lin 3B 94
Flixton. G Man 1B 84
Flixton. N Yor 2E 101
Flixton. Suff 2F 67
Flockton. W Yor 3C 92
Flodden. Nmbd 1D 120
Flodigarry. High 1D 154
Flood's Ferry. Cambs 1C 64
Flookburgh. Cumb 2C 96
Flordon. Norf 1D 66
Flore. Nptn 4D 62
Flotterton. Nmbd 4E 121
Flowton. Suff 1D 54
Flushing. Abers 4H 161
Flushing. Corn 5C 6
Fluxton. Devn 3D 12
Flyford Flavell. Worc 5D 61
Fobbing. Thur 2B 40
Fochabers. Mor 3H 159
Fochriw. Cphy 5E 46
Fockerby. N Lin 3B 94
Fodderty. High 3H 157
Foddington. Som 4A 22
Foel. Powy 4B 70
Foffarty. Ang 4D 144
Foggathorpe. E Yor 1A 94
Fogo. Bord 5D 130
Fogorig. Bord 5D 130
Foindle. High 4B 166
Folda. Ang 2A 144
Fole. Staf 2E 73
Foleshill. W Mid 2A 62
Foley Park. Worc 3C 60
Folke. Dors 1B 14
Folkestone. Kent 2G 29
Folkingham. Linc 2H 75
Folkington. E Sus 5G 27
Folksworth. Cambs 1A 64
Folkton. N Yor 2E 101
Folla Rule. Abers 5E 161
Follifoot. N Yor 4F 99
Folly Cross. Devn 2E 11
Folly Gate. Devn 3F 11
Folly, The. Herts 4B 52
Folly, The. W Ber 5C 36
Fonmon. V Glam 5D 32
Fonthill Bishop. Wilts 3E 23
Fonthill Gifford. Wilts 3E 23
Fontmell Magna. Dors 1D 14
Fontwell. W Sus 5A 26
Font-y-gary. V Glam 5D 32
Foodieash. Fife 2F 137
Foolow. Derbs 3F 85
Footdee. Aber 3G 153
Footherley. Staf 5F 73
Foots Cray. G Lon 3F 39
Forbestown. Abers 2A 152
Force Forge. Cumb 5E 103
Force Mills. Cumb 5E 103
Forcett. N Yor 3E 105
Ford. Arg 3F 133
Ford. Buck 5F 51
Ford. Derbs 2B 86
Ford. Devn 4E 19 (nr. Bideford)
Ford. Devn 3C 8 (nr. Holbeton)
Ford. Devn 4D 9 (nr. Salcombe)
Ford. Glos 3F 49
Ford. Nmbd 1D 120
Ford. Plym 3A 8
Ford. Shrp 4G 71
Ford. Som 1A 22 (nr. Wells)
Ford. Som 4D 20 (nr. Wiveliscombe)
Ford. Staf 5E 85
Ford. W Sus 5B 26
Ford. Wilts 4D 34 (nr. Chippenham)
Ford. Wilts 3G 23 (nr. Salisbury)
Forda. Devn 3E 19
Ford Barton. Devn 1C 12
Fordcombe. Kent 1G 27
Fordell. Fife 1E 129
Forden. Powy 5E 71
Ford End. Essx 4G 53
Forder Green. Devn 2D 9
Ford Green. Lanc 5D 97
Fordham. Cambs 3F 65
Fordham. Essx 3C 54
Fordham. Norf 1F 65
Fordham Heath. Essx 3C 54
Ford Heath. Shrp 4G 71
Fordhouses. W Mid 5D 72
Fordie. Per 1G 135
Fordingbridge. Hants 1G 15
Fordington. Linc 3D 88
Fordon. E Yor 2E 101
Fordoun. Abers 1G 145
Ford Street. Essx 3C 54
Ford Street. Som 1E 13
Fordton. Devn 3B 12
Fordwells. Oxon 4B 50
Fordwich. Kent 5F 41
Fordyce. Abers 2C 160
Forebridge. Staf 3D 72
Foremark. Derbs 3H 73
Forest. N Yor 4F 105

Forestburn Gate. *Nmbd* 5E **121**
Foresterseat. *Mor* 3F **159**
Forest Green. *Glos* 2D **34**
Forest Green. *Surr* 1C **26**
Forest Hall. *Cumb* 4G **103**
Forest Head. *Cumb* 4G **113**
Forest Hill. *Oxon* 5D **50**
Forest-in-Teesdale. *Dur* 2B **104**
Forest Lodge. *Per* 1G **143**
Forest Mill. *Clac* 4B **136**
Forest Row. *E Sus* 2F **27**
Forestside. *W Sus* 1F **17**
Forest Town. *Notts* 4C **86**
Forfar. *Ang* 3D **144**
Forgandenny. *Per* 2C **136**
Forge. *Powy* 1G **57**
Forge Side. *Torf* 5F **47**
Forge, The. *Here* 5F **59**
Forgewood. *N Lan* 4A **128**
Forgie. *Mor* 3A **160**
Forgue. *Abers* 4D **160**
Formby. *Mers* 4A **90**
Forncett End. *Norf* 1D **66**
Forncett St Mary. *Norf* 1D **66**
Forncett St Peter. *Norf* 1D **66**
Forneth. *Per* 4H **143**
Fornham All Saints. *Suff* 4H **65**
Fornham St Martin. *Suff* 4A **66**
Forres. *Mor* 3E **159**
Forrestfield. *N Lan* 3B **128**
Forrest Lodge. *Dum* 1C **110**
Forsbrook. *Staf* 1D **72**
Forse. *High* 5E **169**
Forsinard. *High* 4A **168**
Forss. *High* 2C **168**
Forstal, The. *Kent* 2E **29**
Forston. *Dors* 3B **14**
Fort Augustus. *High* 3F **149**
Forteviot. *Per* 2C **136**
Fort George. *High* 3B **158**
Forth. *S Lan* 4C **128**
Forthampton. *Glos* 2D **48**
Forthay. *Glos* 2C **34**
Forth Road Bridge. *Fife* 2E **129**
Fortingall. *Per* 4E **143**
Fort Matilda. *Inv* 2D **126**
Forton. *Hants* 2C **24**
Forton. *Lanc* 4D **97**
Forton. *Shrp* 4G **71**
Forton. *Som* 2G **13**
Forton. *Staf* 3B **72**
Forton Heath. *Shrp* 4G **71**
Fortrie. *Abers* 4D **160**
Fortrose. *High* 3B **158**
Fortuneswell. *Dors* 5B **14**
Fort William. *High* 1F **141**
Forty Green. *Buck* 1A **38**
Forty Hill. *G Lon* 1E **39**
Forward Green. *Suff* 5C **66**
Fosbury. *Wilts* 1B **24**
Foscot. *Oxon* 3H **49**
Fosdyke. *Linc* 2C **76**
Foss. *Per* 3E **143**
Fossebridge. *Glos* 4F **49**
Foster Street. *Essx* 5E **53**
Foston. *Derbs* 2F **73**
Foston. *Leics* 1D **62**
Foston. *Linc* 1F **75**
Foston. *N Yor* 3A **100**
Foston on the Wolds. *E Yor* 4F **101**
Fotherby. *Linc* 1C **88**
Fothergill. *Cumb* 1B **102**
Fotheringhay. *Nptn* 1H **63**
Foubister. *Orkn* 7E **172**
Foula Airport. *Shet* 8A **173**
Foul Anchor. *Cambs* 4D **76**
Foulbridge. *Cumb* 5F **113**
Foulden. *Norf* 1G **65**
Foulden. *Bord* 4F **131**
Foul Mile. *E Sus* 4H **27**
Foulridge. *Lanc* 5A **98**
Foulsham. *Norf* 3C **78**
Fountainhall. *Bord* 5H **129**
Four Alls, The. *Shrp* 2A **72**
Four Ashes. *Staf* 5D **72**
(nr. Cannock)
Four Ashes. *Staf* 2C **60**
(nr. Kinver)
Four Ashes. *Suff* 3C **66**
Four Crosses. *Powy* 5C **70**
(nr. Llanerfyl)
Four Crosses. *Powy* 4E **71**
(nr. Llanymynech)
Four Crosses. *Staf* 5D **72**
Four Elms. *Kent* 1F **27**
Four Forks. *Som* 3F **21**
Four Gotes. *Cambs* 4D **76**
Four Lane End. *S Yor* 4C **92**
Four Lane Ends. *Lanc* 4E **97**
Four Lanes. *Corn* 5A **6**
Fourlanes End. *Ches* 5B **84**
Four Marks. *Hants* 3E **25**
Four Mile Bridge. *IOA* 3B **80**
Four Oaks. *E Sus* 3C **28**
Four Oaks. *Glos* 3B **48**
Four Oaks. *W Mid* 2G **61**
Four Roads. *Carm* 5E **45**
Four Roads. *IOM* 5B **108**
Fourstones. *Nmbd* 3B **114**
Four Throws. *Kent* 3B **28**
Fovant. *Wilts* 4F **23**
Foveran. *Abers* 1G **153**
Fowey. *Corn* 3F **7**
Fowlershill. *Abers* 2G **153**
Fowley Common. *Warr* 1A **84**
Fowlis. *Ang* 5C **144**
Fowlis Wester. *Per* 1B **136**
Fowlmere. *Cambs* 1E **53**
Fownhope. *Here* 2A **48**
Foxcombe Hill. *Oxon* 5C **50**
Fox Corner. *Surr* 5A **38**
Foxcote. *Glos* 4F **49**
Foxcote. *Som* 1C **22**
Foxdale. *IOM* 4B **108**
Foxearth. *Essx* 1B **54**
Foxfield. *Cumb* 1B **96**
Foxham. *Wilts* 4E **35**
Fox Hatch. *Essx* 1G **39**
Foxhole. *Corn* 3D **6**
Foxholes. *N Yor* 2E **101**
Foxhunt Green. *E Sus* 4G **27**
Fox Lane. *Hants* 1G **25**
Foxlediate. *Worc* 4E **61**
Foxley. *Norf* 3C **78**
Foxley. *Nptn* 5D **62**
Foxley. *Wilts* 3D **35**
Fox Street. *Essx* 3D **54**
Foxt. *Staf* 1E **73**
Foxton. *Cambs* 1E **53**
Foxton. *Dur* 2A **106**
Foxton. *Leics* 2D **62**
Foxton. *N Yor* 5B **106**
Foxup. *N Yor* 2A **98**
Foxwist Green. *Ches* 4A **84**
Foxwood. *Shrp* 3A **60**
Foy. *Here* 3A **48**
Foyers. *High* 1G **149**
Foynesfield. *High* 3C **158**
Fraddam. *Corn* 3C **4**
Fraddon. *Corn* 3D **6**
Fradley. *Staf* 4F **73**
Fradley South. *Staf* 4F **73**
Fradswell. *Staf* 2D **73**
Fraisthorpe. *E Yor* 3F **101**
Framfield. *E Sus* 3F **27**
Framingham Earl. *Norf* 5E **79**
Framingham Pigot. *Norf* 5E **79**
Framlingham. *Suff* 4E **67**
Frampton. *Dors* 3B **14**
Frampton. *Linc* 2C **76**
Frampton Cotterell. *S Glo* 3B **34**
Frampton Mansell. *Glos* 5E **49**
Frampton on Severn. *Glos* 5C **48**
Frampton West End. *Linc* 1B **76**
Framsden. *Suff* 5D **66**
Framwellgate Moor. *Dur* 5F **115**
Franche. *Worc* 3C **60**
Frandley. *Ches* 3A **84**
Frankby. *Mers* 2E **83**
Frankfort. *Norf* 3F **79**
Frankley. *Worc* 2D **61**
Frank's Bridge. *Powy* 5D **58**
Frankton. *Warw* 3B **62**
Frankwell. *Shrp* 4G **71**
Frant. *E Sus* 2G **27**
Fraserburgh. *Abers* 2G **161**
Frating Green. *Essx* 3D **54**
Fratton. *Port* 2E **17**
Freathy. *Corn* 3A **8**
Freckenham. *Suff* 3F **65**
Freckleton. *Lanc* 2C **90**
Freeby. *Leics* 3F **75**
Freefolk Priors. *Hants* 2C **24**
Freehay. *Staf* 1E **73**
Freeland. *Oxon* 4C **50**
Freethorpe. *Norf* 5G **79**
Freiston. *Linc* 1C **76**
Freiston Shore. *Linc* 1C **76**
Fremington. *Devn* 3F **19**
Fremington. *N Yor* 5D **104**
Frenchbeer. *Devn* 4G **11**
French Street. *Kent* 5F **39**
Frenich. *Stir* 3D **134**
Frensham. *Surr* 2G **25**
Frenze. *Norf* 2D **66**
Fresgoe. *High* 2B **168**
Freshfield. *Mers* 4A **90**
Freshford. *Bath* 5C **34**
Freshwater. *IOW* 4B **16**
Freshwater Bay. *IOW* 4B **16**
Freshwater East. *Pemb* 5E **43**
Fressingfield. *Suff* 3E **67**
Freston. *Suff* 2E **55**
Freswick. *High* 2F **169**
Fretherne. *Glos* 5C **48**
Frettenham. *Norf* 4E **79**
Freuchie. *Fife* 3E **137**
Freystrop. *Pemb* 3D **42**
Friar's Gate. *E Sus* 2F **27**
Friar Waddon. *Dors* 4B **14**
Friday Bridge. *Cambs* 5D **76**
Friday Street. *E Sus* 5H **27**
Friday Street. *Surr* 1C **26**
Fridaythorpe. *E Yor* 4C **100**
Friden. *Derbs* 4F **85**
Friern Barnet. *G Lon* 1D **39**
Friesthorpe. *Linc* 2H **87**
Frieston. *Linc* 1G **75**
Frieth. *Buck* 2F **37**
Friezeland. *Notts* 5B **86**
Frilford. *Oxon* 2C **36**
Frilsham. *W Ber* 4D **36**
Frimley. *Surr* 1G **25**
Frimley Green. *Surr* 1G **25**
Frindsbury. *Medw* 4B **40**
Fring. *Norf* 2G **77**
Fringford. *Oxon* 3E **50**
Frinsted. *Kent* 5C **40**
Frinton-on-Sea. *Essx* 4F **55**
Friockheim. *Ang* 4E **145**
Friog. *Gwyn* 4F **69**
Frisby. *Linc* 4D **88**
Frisby on the Wreake. *Leics* 4D **74**
Friskney. *Linc* 5D **88**
Friskney Eaudyke. *Linc* 5D **88**
Friston. *E Sus* 5G **27**
Friston. *Suff* 4G **67**
Fritchley. *Derbs* 5A **86**
Fritham. *Hants* 1H **15**
Frith Bank. *Linc* 1C **76**
Frith Common. *Worc* 4A **60**
Frithelstock. *Devn* 1E **11**
Frithelstock Stone. *Devn* 1E **11**
Frithsden. *Herts* 5A **52**
Frithville. *Linc* 5C **88**
Frittenden. *Kent* 1C **28**
Frittiscombe. *Devn* 4E **9**
Fritton. *Norf* 5G **79**
(nr. Great Yarmouth)
Fritton. *Norf* 1E **67**
(nr. Long Stratton)
Fritwell. *Oxon* 3D **50**
Frizinghall. *W Yor* 1B **92**
Frizington. *Cumb* 3B **102**
Frobost. *W Isl* 6C **170**
Frocester. *Glos* 5C **48**
Frochas. *Powy* 5D **70**
Frodesley. *Shrp* 5H **71**
Frodingham. *N Lin* 3C **94**
Frodsham. *Ches* 3H **83**
Froggat. *Derbs* 3G **85**
Froghall. *Staf* 1E **73**
Frogham. *Hants* 1G **15**
Frogham. *Kent* 5G **41**
Frogmore. *Devn* 4D **8**
Frogmore. *Hants* 5G **37**
Frogmore. *Herts* 5B **52**
Frognall. *Linc* 4A **76**
Frogshall. *Norf* 2E **79**
Frogwell. *Corn* 2H **7**
Frolesworth. *Leics* 1C **62**
Frome. *Som* 2C **22**
Fromefield. *Som* 2C **22**
Frome St Quintin. *Dors* 2A **14**
Fromes Hill. *Here* 1B **48**
Fron. *Carm* 2A **46**
Fron. *Gwyn* 5E **81**
(nr. Caernarfon)
Fron. *Gwyn* 2C **68**
(nr. Pwllheli)
Fron. *Powy* 4C **58**
(nr. Llandrindod Wells)
Fron. *Powy* 1D **58**
(nr. Newtown)
Fron. *Powy* 5E **71**
(nr. Welshpool)
Froncysyllte. *Wrex* 1E **71**
Frongoch. *Gwyn* 2B **70**
Fron Isaf. *Wrex* 1E **71**
Fronoleu. *Gwyn* 2G **69**
Frosterley. *Dur* 1D **104**
Froxfield. *Beds* 2H **51**
Froxfield. *Wilts* 5A **36**
Froxfield Green. *Hants* 4F **25**
Fryern Hill. *Hants* 4C **24**
Fryerning. *Essx* 5G **53**
Fryton. *N Yor* 2A **100**
Fugglestone St Peter. *Wilts* 3G **23**
Fulbeck. *Linc* 5G **87**
Fulbourn. *Cambs* 5E **65**
Fulbrook. *Oxon* 4A **50**
Fulflood. *Hants* 3C **24**
Fulford. *Som* 4F **21**
Fulford. *Staf* 2D **72**
Fulford. *York* 5A **100**
Fulham. *G Lon* 3D **38**
Fulking. *W Sus* 4D **26**
Fuller's Moor. *Ches* 5G **83**
Fuller Street. *Essx* 4H **53**
Fullerton. *Hants* 3B **24**
Fulletby. *Linc* 3B **88**
Full Sutton. *E Yor* 4B **100**
Fullwood. *E Ayr* 4F **127**
Fulmer. *Buck* 2A **38**
Fulmodestone. *Norf* 2B **78**
Fulnetby. *Linc* 3H **87**
Fulney. *Linc* 3B **76**
Fulstow. *Linc* 1C **88**
Fulthorpe. *Stoc T* 2B **106**
Fulwell. *Tyne* 4G **115**
Fulwood. *Lanc* 1D **90**
Fulwood. *Notts* 5B **86**
Fulwood. *Som* 1F **13**
Fulwood. *S Yor* 2G **85**
Fundenhall. *Norf* 1D **66**
Funtington. *W Sus* 2G **17**
Funtley. *Hants* 2D **16**
Funzie. *Shet* 2H **173**
Furley. *Devn* 2F **13**
Furnace. *Arg* 3H **133**
Furnace. *Carm* 5F **45**
Furnace. *Cdgn* 1F **57**
Furner's Green. *E Sus* 3F **27**
Furness Vale. *Derbs* 2E **85**
Furneux Pelham. *Herts* 3E **53**
Furzebrook. *Dors* 4E **15**
Furzehill. *Devn* 2H **19**
Furzehill. *Dors* 2F **15**
Furzeley Corner. *Hants* 1E **17**
Furzey Lodge. *Hants* 2B **16**
Furzley. *Hants* 1A **16**
Fyfield. *Essx* 5F **53**
Fyfield. *Glos* 5H **49**
Fyfield. *Hants* 2A **24**
Fyfield. *Oxon* 2C **36**
Fyfield. *Wilts* 5G **35**
Fylde, The. *Lanc* 1B **90**
Fylingthorpe. *N Yor* 4G **107**
Fyning. *W Sus* 4G **25**
Fyvie. *Abers* 5E **161**

G

Gabhsann bho Dheas. *W Isl* . . .2G **171**
Gabhsann bho Thuath.
W Isl 2G **171**
Gabroc Hill. *E Ayr* 4F **127**
Gadbrook. *Surr* 1D **26**
Gaddesby. *Leics* 4D **74**
Gadfa. *IOA* 2D **80**
Gadgirth. *S Ayr* 2D **116**
Gaer. *Powy* 3E **47**
Gaerwen. *IOA* 3D **81**
Gagingwell. *Oxon* 3C **50**
Gaick Lodge. *High* 5B **150**
Gailey. *Staf* 4D **72**
Gainford. *Dur* 3E **105**
Gainsborough. *Linc* 1F **87**
Gainsborough. *Suff* 1E **55**
Gainsford End. *Essx* 2H **53**
Gairletter. *Arg* 1C **126**
Gairloch. *Abers* 3E **153**
Gairloch. *High* 1H **155**
Gairlochy. *High* 5D **148**
Gairney Bank. *Per* 4D **136**
Gairnshiel Lodge. *Abers* 3G **151**
Gaisgill. *Cumb* 4H **103**
Gaitsgill. *Cumb* 5E **113**
Galashiels. *Bord* 1G **119**
Galgate. *Lanc* 4D **97**
Galhampton. *Som* 4B **22**
Gallatown. *Fife* 4E **137**
Galley Common. *Warw* 1H **61**
Galleyend. *Essx* 5H **53**
Galleywood. *Essx* 5H **53**
Gallin. *Per* 4C **142**
Gallowfauld. *Ang* 4D **144**
Gallowhill. *E Dun* 2H **127**
Gallowhill. *Per* 5A **144**
Gallowhill. *Ren* 3F **127**
Gallowhills. *Abers* 3H **161**
Gallows Green. *Staf* 1E **73**
Gallows Green. *Worc* 4D **60**
Gallowstree Common. *Oxon* 3E **37**
Galltair. *High* 1G **147**
Gallt Melyd. *Den* 2C **82**
Galmington. *Som* 4F **21**
Galmisdale. *High* 5C **146**
Galmpton. *Devn* 4C **8**
Galmpton. *Torb* 3E **9**
Galmpton Warborough. *Torb* 3E **9**
Galphay. *N Yor* 2E **99**
Galston. *E Ayr* 1D **117**
Galton. *Dors* 4C **14**
Galtrigill. *High* 3A **154**
Gamblesby. *Cumb* 1H **103**
Gamelsby. *Cumb* 4D **112**
Gamesley. *Derbs* 1E **85**
Gamlingay. *Cambs* 5B **64**
Gamlingay Cinques. *Cambs* 5B **64**
Gamlingay Great Heath.
Cambs 5B **64**
Gammaton. *Devn* 4E **19**
Gammersgill. *N Yor* 1C **98**
Gamston. *Notts* 2D **74**
(nr. Nottingham)
Gamston. *Notts* 3E **86**
(nr. Retford)
Ganarew. *Here* 4A **48**

Ganavan. *Arg* 5C 140
Ganborough. *Glos* 3G 49
Gang. *Corn* 2H 7
Ganllwyd. *Gwyn* 3G 69
Gannochy. *Ang* 1E 145
Gannochy. *Per* 1D 136
Gansclet. *High* 4F 169
Ganstead. *E Yor* 1E 95
Ganthorpe. *N Yor* 2A 100
Ganton. *N Yor* 2D 101
Gappah. *Devn* 5B 12
Garafad. *High* 2D 155
Garboldisham. *Norf* 2C 66
Garden City. *Flin* 4F 83
Gardeners Green. *Wok* 5G 37
Gardenstown. *Abers* 2F 161
Garden Village. *S Yor* 1G 85
Garden Village. *Swan* 3E 31
Garderhouse. *Shet* 7E 173
Gardham. *E Yor* 5D 100
Gare Hill. *Som* 2C 22
Garelochhead. *Arg* 4B 134
Garford. *Oxon* 2C 36
Garforth. *W Yor* 1E 93
Gargrave. *N Yor* 4B 98
Gargunnock. *Stir* 4G 135
Garleffin. *S Ayr* 1F 109
Garlieston. *Dum* 5B 110
Garlinge Green. *Kent* 5F 41
Garlogie. *Abers* 3E 153
Garmelow. *Staf* 3B 72
Garmond. *Abers* 3F 161
Garmondsway. *Dur* 1A 106
Garmony. *Arg* 4A 140
Garmouth. *Mor* 2H 159
Garmston. *Shrp* 5A 72
Garnant. *Carm* 4G 45
Garndiffaith. *Torf* 5F 47
Garndolbenmaen. *Gwyn* 1D 69
Garnett Bridge. *Cumb* 5G 103
Garnfadryn. *Gwyn* 2B 68
Garnkirk. *N Lan* 3H 127
Garnlydan. *Blae* 4E 47
Garnsgate. *Linc* 3D 76
Garnswllt. *Swan* 5G 45
Garn-yr-erw. *Torf* 4F 47
Garrabost. *W Isl* 4H 171
Garrallan. *E Ayr* 3E 117
Garras. *Corn* 4E 5
Garreg. *Gwyn* 1F 69
Garrigill. *Cumb* 5A 114
Garriston. *N Yor* 5E 105
Garrogie Lodge. *High* 2H 149
Garros. *High* 2D 155
Garrow. *Per* 4F 143
Garsdale. *Cumb* 1G 97
Garsdale Head. *Cumb* 5A 104
Garsdon. *Wilts* 3E 35
Garshall Green. *Staf* 2D 72
Garsington. *Oxon* 5D 50
Garstang. *Lanc* 5D 97
Garston. *Mers* 2G 83
Garswood. *Mers* 1H 83
Gartcosh. *N Lan* 3H 127
Garth. *B'end* 2B 32
Garth. *Cdgn* 2F 57
Garth. *Gwyn* 2E 69
Garth. *IOM* 4C 108
Garth. *Powy* 1C 46
(nr. Builth Wells)
Garth. *Powy* 3E 59
(nr. Knighton)
Garth. *Wrex* 1E 71
Garthamlock. *Glas* 3H 127
Garthbrengy. *Powy* 2D 46
Gartheli. *Cdgn* 5E 57
Garthmyl. *Powy* 1D 58
Garthorpe. *Leics* 3F 75
Garthorpe. *N Lin* 3B 94
Garth Owen. *Powy* 1D 58
Garth Row. *Cumb* 5G 103
Gartly. *Abers* 5C 160
Gartmore. *Stir* 4E 135
Gartness. *N Lan* 3A 128
Gartness. *Stir* 1G 127
Gartocharn. *W Dun* 1F 127
Garton. *E Yor* 1F 95
Garton-on-the-Wolds. *E Yor* 4D 101
Gartsherrie. *N Lan* 3A 128
Gartymore. *High* 2H 165
Garvald. *E Lot* 2B 130
Garvamore. *High* 4H 149
Garvard. *Arg* 4A 132
Garvault. *High* 5H 167
Garve. *High* 2F 157
Garvestone. *Norf* 5C 78
Garvie. *Arg* 4H 133
Garvock. *Abers* 1G 145
Garvock. *Inv* 2D 126
Garway. *Here* 3H 47
Garway Common. *Here* 3H 47
Garway Hill. *Here* 3H 47
Garwick. *Linc* 1A 76
Gaskan. *High* 1C 140
Gasper. *Wilts* 3C 22
Gastard. *Wilts* 5D 35
Gasthorpe. *Norf* 2B 66
Gatcombe. *IOW* 4C 16
Gateacre. *Mers* 2G 83
Gatebeck. *Cumb* 1E 97
Gate Burton. *Linc* 2F 87
Gateforth. *N Yor* 2F 93
Gatehead. *E Ayr* 1C 116
Gate Helmsley. *N Yor* 4A 100
Gatehouse. *Nmbd* 1A 114
Gatehouse of Fleet. *Dum* 4D 110
Gatelawbridge. *Dum* 5B 118
Gateley. *Norf* 3B 78
Gatenby. *N Yor* 1F 99
Gatesgarth. *Cumb* 3C 102
Gateshead. *Tyne* 3F 115
Gatesheath. *Ches* 4G 83
Gateside. *Ang* 4D 144
(nr. Forfar)
Gateside. *Ang* 4C 144
(nr. Kirriemuir)
Gateside. *Fife* 3D 136
Gateside. *N Ayr* 4E 127
Gathurst. *G Man* 4D 90
Gatley. *G Man* 2C 84
Gatton. *Surr* 5D 39
Gattonside. *Bord* 1H 119
Gatwick (London) Airport.
W Sus 1D 27
Gaufron. *Powy* 4B 58
Gaulby. *Leics* 5D 74
Gauldry. *Fife* 1F 137
Gaultree. *Norf* 5D 77
Gaunt's Common. *Dors* 2F 15
Gaunt's Earthcott. *S Glo* 3B 34
Gautby. *Linc* 3A 88
Gavinton. *Bord* 4D 130
Gawber. *S Yor* 4D 92
Gawcott. *Buck* 2E 51
Gawsworth. *Ches* 4C 84
Gawthorpe. *W Yor* 2C 92
Gawthrop. *Cumb* 1F 97
Gawthwaite. *Cumb* 1B 96
Gay Bowers. *Essx* 5A 54
Gaydon. *Warw* 5A 62
Gayhurst. *Mil* 1G 51
Gayle. *N Yor* 1A 98
Gayles. *N Yor* 4E 105
Gay Street. *W Sus* 3B 26
Gayton. *Mers* 2E 83
Gayton. *Norf* 4G 77
Gayton. *Nptn* 5E 62
Gayton. *Staf* 3D 73
Gayton le Marsh. *Linc* 2D 88
Gayton le Wold. *Linc* 2B 88
Gayton Thorpe. *Norf* 4G 77
Gaywood. *Norf* 3F 77
Gazeley. *Suff* 4G 65
Geanies. *High* 1C 158
Gearraidh Bhailteas. *W Isl* 6C 170
Gearraidh Bhaird. *W Isl* 6F 171
Gearraidh ma Monadh.
W Isl 7C 170
Geary. *High* 2B 154
Geddes. *High* 3C 158
Gedding. *Suff* 5B 66
Geddington. *Nptn* 2F 63
Gedintailor. *High* 5E 155
Gedling. *Notts* 1D 74
Gedney. *Linc* 3D 76
Gedney Broadgate. *Linc* 3D 76
Gedney Drove End. *Linc* 3D 76
Gedney Dyke. *Linc* 3D 76
Gedney Hill. *Linc* 4C 76
Gee Cross. *G Man* 1D 84
Geeston. *Rut* 5G 75
Geilston. *Arg* 2E 127
Geirinis. *W Isl* 4C 170
Geise. *High* 2D 168
Geisiadar. *W Isl* 4D 171
Gelder Shiel. *Abers* 5G 151
Geldeston. *Norf* 1F 67
Gell. *Cnwy* 4A 82
Gelli. *Pemb* 3E 43
Gelli. *Rhon* 2C 32
Gellifor. *Den* 4D 82
Gelligaer. *Cphy* 2E 33
Gellilydan. *Gwyn* 2F 69
Gellinudd. *Neat* 5H 45
Gellyburn. *Per* 5H 143
Gellywen. *Carm* 2G 43
Gelston. *Dum* 4E 111
Gelston. *Linc* 1G 75
Gembling. *E Yor* 4F 101
Geneva. *Cdgn* 5D 56
Gentleshaw. *Staf* 4E 73
Geocrab. *W Isl* 8D 171
George Green. *Buck* 2A 38
Georgeham. *Devn* 3E 19
George Nympton. *Devn* 4H 19
Georgetown. *Blae* 5E 47
Georgetown. *Ren* 3F 127
Georth. *Orkn* 5C 172
Gerlan. *Gwyn* 4F 81
Germansweek. *Devn* 3E 11
Germoe. *Corn* 4C 4
Gerrard's Bromley. *Staf* 2B 72
Gerrards Cross. *Buck* 2A 38
Gerston. *High* 3D 168
Gervans. *Corn* 5C 6
Gestingthorpe. *Essx* 2B 54
Gethsemane. *Pemb* 1A 44
Geuffordd. *Powy* 4E 70
Gibraltar. *Buck* 4F 51
Gibraltar. *Linc* 5E 89
Gibraltar. *Suff* 5D 66
Gibsmere. *Notts* 1E 74
Giddeahall. *Wilts* 4D 34
Gidea Park. *G Lon* 2G 39
Gidleigh. *Devn* 4G 11
Giffnock. *E Ren* 4G 127
Gifford. *E Lot* 3B 130
Giffordtown. *Fife* 2E 137
Giggetty. *Staf* 1C 60
Giggleswick. *N Yor* 3H 97
Gignog. *Pemb* 2C 42
Gilberdyke. *E Yor* 2B 94
Gilbert's End. *Worc* 1D 48
Gilbert's Green. *Warw* 3F 61
Gilchriston. *E Lot* 3A 130
Gilcrux. *Cumb* 1C 102
Gildersome. *W Yor* 2C 92
Gildingwells. *S Yor* 2C 86
Gilesgate Moor. *Dur* 5F 115
Gileston. *V Glam* 5D 32
Gilfach. *Cphy* 2E 33
Gilfach Goch. *Rhon* 2C 32
Gilfachreda. *Cdgn* 5D 56
Gillamoor. *N Yor* 5D 107
Gillan. *Corn* 4E 5
Gillar's Green. *Mers* 1G 83
Gillen. *High* 3B 154
Gilling East. *N Yor* 2A 100
Gillingham. *Dors* 4D 22
Gillingham. *Medw* 4B 40
Gillingham. *Norf* 1G 67
Gilling West. *N Yor* 4E 105
Gillock. *High* 3E 169
Gillow Heath. *Staf* 5C 84
Gills. *High* 1F 169
Gill's Green. *Kent* 2B 28
Gilmanscleuch. *Bord* 2F 119
Gilmerton. *Edin* 3F 129
Gilmerton. *Per* 1A 136
Gilmonby. *Dur* 3C 104
Gilmorton. *Leics* 2C 62
Gilsland. *Nmbd* 3H 113
Gilsland Spa. *Cumb* 3H 113
Gilston. *Midl* 4H 129
Giltbrook. *Notts* 1B 74
Gilwern. *Mon* 4F 47
Gimingham. *Norf* 2E 79
Giosla. *W Isl* 5D 171
Gipping. *Suff* 4C 66
Gipsey Bridge. *Linc* 1B 76
Gipton. *W Yor* 1D 92
Girdle Toll. *N Ayr* 5E 127
Girlsta. *Shet* 6F 173
Girsby. *N Yor* 4A 106
Girthon. *Dum* 4D 110
Girton. *Cambs* 4D 64
Girton. *Notts* 4F 87
Girvan. *S Ayr* 5A 116
Gisburn. *Lanc* 5H 97
Gisleham. *Suff* 2H 67
Gislingham. *Suff* 3C 66
Gissing. *Norf* 2D 66
Gittisham. *Devn* 3E 13
Gladestry. *Powy* 5E 59
Gladsmuir. *E Lot* 2A 130
Glaichbea. *High* 5H 157
Glais. *Swan* 5H 45
Glaisdale. *N Yor* 4E 107
Glame. *High* 4E 155
Glamis. *Ang* 4C 144
Glamisdale. *High* 5C 146
Glanaman. *Carm* 4G 45
Glan-Conwy. *Cnwy* 5H 81
Glandford. *Norf* 1C 78
Glan Duar. *Carm* 1F 45
Glandwr. *Blae* 5F 47
Glandwr. *Pemb* 2F 43
Glan-Dwyfach. *Gwyn* 1D 69
Glandy Cross. *Carm* 2F 43
Glandyfi. *Cdgn* 1F 57
Glangrwyney. *Powy* 4F 47
Glanmule. *Powy* 1D 58
Glanrhyd. *Gwyn* 2B 68
Glanrhyd. *Pemb* 1B 44
(nr. Cardigan)
Glan-rhyd. *Pemb* 1F 43
(nr. Crymych)
Glan-rhyd. *Powy* 5A 46
Glanton. *Nmbd* 3E 121
Glanton Pyke. *Nmbd* 3E 121
Glanvilles Wootton. *Dors* 2B 14
Glan-y-don. *Flin* 3D 82
Glan-y-nant. *Powy* 2B 58
Glan-yr-afon. *Gwyn* 1C 70
Glan-yr-afon. *IOA* 2F 81
Glan-yr-afon. *Powy* 5C 70
Glan-y-wern. *Gwyn* 2F 69
Glapthorn. *Nptn* 1H 63
Glapwell. *Derbs* 4B 86
Glas Aird. *Arg* 4A 132
Glas-allt Shiel. *Abers* 5G 151
Glasbury. *Powy* 2E 47
Glaschoil. *Mor* 5E 159
Glascoed. *Den* 3B 82
Glascoed. *Mon* 5G 47
Glascote. *Staf* 5G 73
Glascwm. *Powy* 5D 58
Glasfryn. *Cnwy* 5B 82
Glasgow. *Glas* 3G 127
Glasgow Airport. *Ren* 3F 127
Glasgow Prestwick
International Airport.
S Ayr 2C 116
Glashvin. *High* 2D 154
Glasinfryn. *Gwyn* 4E 81
Glasnakille. *High* 2D 146
Glasnacardoch. *High* 4E 147
Glaspwll. *Cdgn* 1G 57
Glassburn. *High* 5F 157
Glassenbury. *Kent* 2B 28
Glasserton. *Dum* 5B 110
Glassford. *S Lan* 5A 128
Glassgreen. *Mor* 2G 159
Glasshouse. *Glos* 3C 48
Glasshouses. *N Yor* 3D 98
Glasson. *Cumb* 3D 112
Glasson. *Lanc* 4D 96
Glassonby. *Cumb* 1G 103
Glasterlaw. *Ang* 3E 145
Glaston. *Rut* 5F 75
Glastonbury. *Som* 3H 21
Glatton. *Cambs* 2A 64
Glazebrook. *Warr* 1A 84
Glazebury. *Warr* 1A 84
Glazeley. *Shrp* 2B 60
Gleadless. *S Yor* 2A 86
Gleadsmoss. *Ches* 4C 84
Gleann Dail bho Dheas.
W Isl 7C 170
Gleann Tholastaidh. *W Isl* 3H 171
Gleaston. *Cumb* 2B 96
Glecknabae. *Arg* 3B 126
Gledrid. *Shrp* 2E 71
Gleiniant. *Powy* 1B 58
Glemsford. *Suff* 1B 54
Glen. *Dum* 4C 110
Glenancross. *High* 4E 147
Glen Audlyn. *IOM* 2D 108
Glenbarr. *Arg* 2A 122
Glenbeg. *High* 2G 139
Glen Bernisdale. *High* 4D 154
Glenbervie. *Abers* 5E 153
Glenboig. *N Lan* 3A 128
Glenborrodale. *High* 2A 140
Glenbranter. *Arg* 4A 134
Glenbreck. *Bord* 2C 118
Glenbrein Lodge. *High* 2G 149
Glenbrittle. *High* 1C 146
Glenbuchat Lodge. *Abers* 2H 151
Glenbuck. *E Ayr* 2G 117
Glenburn. *Ren* 3F 127
Glencalvie Lodge. *High* 5B 164
Glencaple. *Dum* 3A 112
Glencarron Lodge. *High* 3C 156
Glencarse. *Per* 1D 136
Glencassley Castle. *High* 3B 164
Glencat. *Abers* 4C 152
Glencoe. *High* 3F 141
Glen Cottage. *High* 5E 147
Glencraig. *Fife* 4D 136
Glendale. *High* 4A 154
Glendevon. *Per* 3B 136
Glendoebeg. *High* 3G 149
Glendoick. *Per* 1E 136
Glendoune. *S Ayr* 5A 116
Glenduckie. *Fife* 2E 137
Gleneagles. *Per* 3B 136
Glenegedale. *Arg* 4B 124
Glenegedale Lots. *Arg* 4B 124
Glenelg. *High* 2G 147
Glenernie. *Mor* 4E 159
Glenesslin. *Dum* 1F 111
Glenfarg. *Per* 2D 136
Glenfarquhar Lodge. *Abers* 5E 152
Glenferness Mains. *High* 4D 158
Glenfeshie Lodge. *High* 4C 150
Glenfiddich Lodge. *Mor* 5H 159
Glenfield. *Leics* 5C 74
Glenfinnan. *High* 5B 148
Glenfintaig Lodge. *High* 5E 149
Glenfoot. *Per* 2D 136
Glenfyne Lodge. *Arg* 2B 134
Glengap. *Dum* 4D 110
Glengarnock. *N Ayr* 4E 126
Glengolly. *High* 2D 168
Glengorm Castle. *Arg* 3F 139
Glengrasco. *High* 4D 154
Glenhead Farm. *Ang* 2B 144
Glenholm. *Bord* 1D 118
Glen House. *Bord* 1E 119

Glenhurich. *High* 2C 140
Glenkerry. *Bord* 3E 119
Glenkiln. *Dum* 2F 111
Glenkindle. *Abers* 2B 152
Glenkinglass Lodge. *Arg* 5F 141
Glenkirk. *Bord* 2C 118
Glenlean. *Arg* 1B 126
Glenlee. *Dum* 1D 110
Glenleraig. *High* 5B 166
Glenlichorn. *Per* 2G 135
Glenlivet. *Mor* 1F 151
Glenlochar. *Dum* 3E 111
Glenlochsie Lodge. *Per* 1H 143
Glenluce. *Dum* 4G 109
Glenmarskie. *High* 3F 157
Glenmassan. *Arg* 1C 126
Glenmavis. *N Lan* 3A 128
Glenmaye. *IOM* 4B 108
Glenmazeran Lodge. *High* 1B 150
Glenmidge. *Dum* 1F 111
Glen Mona. *IOM* 3D 108
Glenmore. *High* 2G 139
(nr. Glenborrodale)
Glenmore. *High* 3D 151
(nr. Kingussie)
Glenmore. *High* 4D 154
(on Isle of Skye)
Glenmoy. *Ang* 2D 144
Glennoe. *Arg* 5E 141
Glen of Coachford. *Abers* 4B 160
Glenogil. *Ang* 2D 144
Glen Parva. *Leics* 1C 62
Glenprosen Village. *Ang* 2C 144
Glenree. *N Ayr* 3D 122
Glenridding. *Cumb* 3E 103
Glenrosa. *N Ayr* 2E 123
Glenrothes. *Fife* 3E 137
Glensanda. *High* 4C 140
Glensaugh. *Abers* 1F 145
Glenshero Lodge. *High* 4H 149
Glensluain. *Arg* 4H 133
Glenstockadale. *Dum* 3F 109
Glenstriven. *Arg* 2B 126
Glen Tanar House. *Abers* 4B 152
Glentham. *Linc* 1H 87
Glenton. *Abers* 1D 152
Glentress. *Bord* 1E 119
Glentromie Lodge. *High* 4B 150
Glentrool Lodge. *Dum* 1B 110
Glentrool Village. *Dum* 2A 110
Glentruim House. *High* 4A 150
Glentworth. *Linc* 2G 87
Glenuig. *High* 1A 140
Glen Village. *Falk* 2B 128
Glen Vine. *IOM* 4C 108
Glenwhilly. *Dum* 2G 109
Glenzierfoot. *Dum* 2E 113
Glespin. *S Lan* 2H 117
Gletness. *Shet* 6F 173
Glewstone. *Here* 3A 48
Glib Cheois. *W Isl* 5F 171
Glinton. *Pet* 5A 76
Glooston. *Leics* 1E 63
Glossop. *Derbs* 1E 85
Gloster Hill. *Nmbd* 4G 121
Gloucester. *Glos* 4D 48
Gloucestershire Airport. *Glos* 3D 49
Gloup. *Shet* 1G 173
Glusburn. *N Yor* 5C 98
Glutt Lodge. *High* 5B 168
Glutton Bridge. *Staf* 4E 85
Gluvian. *Corn* 2D 6
Glympton. *Oxon* 3C 50
Glyn. *Cnwy* 3A 82
Glynarthen. *Cdgn* 1D 44
Glynbrochan. *Powy* 2B 58
Glyn Ceiriog. *Wrex* 2E 70
Glyncoch. *Rhon* 2D 32
Glyncorrwg. *Neat* 2B 32
Glynde. *E Sus* 5F 27
Glyndebourne. *E Sus* 4F 27
Glyndyfrdwy. *Den* 1D 70
Glyn Ebwy. *Blae* 5E 47
Glynllan. *B'end* 3C 32
Glyn-neath. *Neat* 5B 46
Glynogwr. *B'end* 3C 32
Glyntaff. *Rhon* 3D 32
Glyntawe. *Powy* 4B 46
Glynteg. *Carm* 2D 44
Gnosall. *Staf* 3C 72
Gnosall Heath. *Staf* 3C 72
Goadby. *Leics* 1E 63
Goadby Marwood. *Leics* 3E 75
Goatacre. *Wilts* 4F 35
Goathill. *Dors* 1B 14
Goathland. *N Yor* 4F 107
Goathurst. *Som* 3F 21
Goathurst Common. *Kent* 5F 39
Goat Lees. *Kent* 1E 28
Gobernuisgach Lodge. *High* 4E 167
Gobernuisgeach. *High* 5B 168
Gobhaig. *W Isl* 7C 171
Gobowen. *Shrp* 2F 71
Godalming. *Surr* 1A 26
Goddard's Corner. *Suff* 4E 67
Goddard's Green. *Kent* 2C 28
(nr. Benenden)
Goddard's Green. *Kent* 2B 28
(nr. Cranbrook)
Goddards Green. *W Sus* 3D 27
Godford Cross. *Devn* 2E 13
Godleybrook. *Staf* 1D 73
Godmanchester. *Cambs* 3B 64
Godmanstone. *Dors* 3B 14
Godmersham. *Kent* 5E 41
Godolphin Cross. *Corn* 3D 4
Godre'r-graig. *Neat* 5A 46
Godshill. *Hants* 1G 15
Godshill. *IOW* 4D 16
Godstone. *Staf* 2E 73
Godstone. *Surr* 5E 39
Godwell. *Devn* 3C 8
Goetre. *Mon* 5G 47
Goff's Oak. *Herts* 5D 52
Gogar. *Edin* 2E 129
Goginan. *Cdgn* 2F 57
Golan. *Gwyn* 1E 69
Golant. *Corn* 3F 7
Golberdon. *Corn* 5D 10
Golborne. *G Man* 1A 84
Golcar. *W Yor* 3A 92
Goldcliff. *Newp* 3G 33
Golden Cross. *E Sus* 4G 27
Golden Green. *Kent* 1H 27
Golden Grove. *Carm* 4F 45
Golden Grove. *N Yor* 4F 107
Golden Hill. *Pemb* 2D 43
Goldenhill. *Stoke* 5C 84
Golden Pot. *Hants* 2F 25
Golden Valley. *Glos* 3E 49
Golders Green. *G Lon* 2D 38
Goldhanger. *Essx* 5C 54
Gold Hill. *Norf* 1E 65
Golding. *Shrp* 5H 71
Goldington. *Beds* 5H 63
Goldsborough. *N Yor* 4F 99
(nr. Harrogate)
Goldsborough. *N Yor* 3F 107
(nr. Whitby)
Goldsithney. *Corn* 3C 4
Goldstone. *Kent* 4G 41
Goldstone. *Shrp* 3B 72
Goldthorpe. *S Yor* 4E 93
Goldworthy. *Devn* 4D 19
Golfa. *Powy* 3D 70
Gollanfield. *High* 3C 158
Gollinglith Foot. *N Yor* 1D 98
Golsoncott. *Som* 3D 20
Golspie. *High* 4F 165
Gomeldon. *Wilts* 3G 23
Gomersal. *W Yor* 2C 92
Gometra House. *Arg* 4E 139
Gomshall. *Surr* 1B 26
Gonalston. *Notts* 1D 74
Gonerby Hill Foot. *Linc* 2G 75
Gonnabarn. *Corn* 3D 6
Good Easter. *Essx* 4G 53
Gooderstone. *Norf* 5G 77
Goodleigh. *Devn* 3G 19
Goodmanham. *E Yor* 5C 100
Goodmayes. *G Lon* 2F 39
Goodnestone. *Kent* 5G 41
(nr. Aylesham)
Goodnestone. *Kent* 4E 41
(nr. Faversham)
Goodrich. *Here* 4A 48
Goodrington. *Torb* 3E 9
Goodshaw. *Lanc* 2G 91
Goodshaw Fold. *Lanc* 2G 91
Goodstone. *Devn* 5A 12
Goodwick. *Pemb* 1D 42
Goodworth Clatford. *Hants* 2B 24
Goole. *E Yor* 2H 93
Goom's Hill. *Worc* 5E 61
Goonbell. *Corn* 4B 6
Goonhavern. *Corn* 3B 6
Goonvrea. *Corn* 4B 6
Goose Green. *Cumb* 1E 97
Goose Green. *S Glo* 3C 34
Gooseham. *Corn* 1C 10
Goosewell. *Plym* 3B 8
Goosey. *Oxon* 2B 36
Goosnargh. *Lanc* 1D 90
Goostrey. *Ches* 3B 84
Gorcott Hill. *Warw* 4E 61
Gordon. *Bord* 5C 130
Gordonbush. *High* 3F 165
Gordonstown. *Abers* 3C 160
(nr. Cornhill)
Gordonstown. *Abers* 5E 160
(nr. Fyvie)
Gorebridge. *Midl* 3G 129
Gorefield. *Cambs* 4D 76
Gores. *Wilts* 1G 23
Gorgie. *Edin* 2F 129
Goring. *Oxon* 3E 36
Goring-by-Sea. *W Sus* 5C 26
Goring Heath. *Oxon* 4E 37
Gorleston-on-Sea. *Norf* 5H 79
Gornalwood. *W Mid* 1D 60
Gorran Churchtown. *Corn* 4D 6
Gorran Haven. *Corn* 4E 6
Gorran High Lanes. *Corn* 4D 6
Gors. *Cdgn* 3F 57
Gorsedd. *Flin* 3D 82
Gorseinon. *Swan* 3E 31
Gorseness. *Orkn* 6D 172
Gorseybank. *Derbs* 5G 85
Gorsgoch. *Cdgn* 5D 57
Gorslas. *Carm* 4F 45
Gorsley. *Glos* 3B 48
Gorsley Common. *Here* 3B 48
Gorstan. *High* 2F 157
Gorstella. *Ches* 4F 83
Gorsty Common. *Here* 2H 47
Gorsty Hill. *Staf* 3E 73
Gortantaoid. *Arg* 2B 124
Gorteneorn. *High* 2A 140
Gortenfern. *High* 2A 140
Gorton. *G Man* 1C 84
Gosbeck. *Suff* 5D 66
Gosberton. *Linc* 2B 76
Gosberton Clough. *Linc* 3A 76
Goseley Dale. *Derbs* 3H 73
Gosfield. *Essx* 3A 54
Gosford. *Oxon* 4D 50
Gosforth. *Cumb* 4B 102
Gosforth. *Tyne* 3F 115
Gosmore. *Herts* 3B 52
Gospel End Village. *Staf* 1C 60
Gosport. *Hants* 2E 16
Gossabrough. *Shet* 3G 173
Gossington. *Glos* 5C 48
Gossops Green. *W Sus* 2D 26
Goswick. *Nmbd* 5G 131
Gotham. *Notts* 2C 74
Gotherington. *Glos* 3E 49
Gott. *Arg* 4B 138
Goudhurst. *Kent* 2B 28
Goulceby. *Linc* 3B 88
Gourdon. *Abers* 1H 145
Gourock. *Inv* 2D 126
Govan. *Glas* 3G 127
Govanhill. *Glas* 3G 127
Goverton. *Notts* 1E 74
Goveton. *Devn* 4D 8
Govilon. *Mon* 4F 47
Gowanhill. *Abers* 2H 161
Gowdall. *E Yor* 2G 93
Gowerton. *Swan* 3E 31
Gowkhall. *Fife* 1D 128
Gowthorpe. *E Yor* 4B 100
Goxhill. *E Yor* 5F 101
Goxhill. *N Lin* 2E 94
Goxhill Haven. *N Lin* 2E 94
Goytre. *Neat* 3A 32
Grabhair. *W Isl* 6F 171
Graby. *Linc* 3H 75
Graffham. *W Sus* 4A 26
Grafham. *Cambs* 4A 64
Grafham. *Surr* 1B 26
Grafton. *Here* 2H 47
Grafton. *N Yor* 3G 99
Grafton. *Oxon* 5A 50
Grafton. *Shrp* 4G 71
Grafton. *Worc* 2E 49
(nr. Evesham)
Grafton. *Worc* 4H 59
(nr. Leominster)
Grafton Flyford. *Worc* 5D 60
Grafton Regis. *Nptn* 1F 51
Grafton Underwood. *Nptn* 2G 63
Grafty Green. *Kent* 1C 28
Graianrhyd. *Den* 5E 82
Graig. *Carm* 5E 45
Graig. *Cnwy* 3H 81
Graig. *Den* 3C 82
Graig-fechan. *Den* 5D 82
Graig Penllyn. *V Glam* 4C 32
Grain. *Medw* 3C 40
Grainsby. *Linc* 1B 88
Grainthorpe. *Linc* 1C 88
Grainthorpe Fen. *Linc* 1C 88
Graiselound. *N Lin* 1E 87
Gramasdail. *W Isl* 3D 170
Grampound. *Corn* 4D 6
Grampound Road. *Corn* 3D 6
Granborough. *Buck* 3F 51
Granby. *Notts* 2E 75
Grandborough. *Warw* 4B 62
Grandpont. *Oxon* 5D 50
Grandtully. *Per* 3G 143
Grange. *Cumb* 3D 102
Grange. *E Ayr* 1D 116
Grange. *Here* 3G 59
Grange. *Mers* 2E 83
Grange. *Per* 1E 137
Grange Crossroads. *Mor* 3B 160
Grange Hill. *G Lon* 1F 39
Grangemill. *Derbs* 5G 85
Grange Moor. *W Yor* 3C 92
Grangemouth. *Falk* 1C 128
Grange of Lindores. *Fife* 2E 137
Grange-over-Sands. *Cumb* 2D 96
Grangepans. *Falk* 1D 128
Grange, The. *N Yor* 5C 106
Grangetown. *Card* 4E 33
Grangetown. *Red C* 2C 106
Grange Villa. *Dur* 4F 115
Granish. *High* 2C 150
Gransmoor. *E Yor* 4F 101
Granston. *Pemb* 1C 42
Grantchester. *Cambs* 5D 64
Grantham. *Linc* 2G 75
Grantley. *N Yor* 3E 99
Grantlodge. *Abers* 2E 152
Granton. *Edin* 2F 129
Grantown-on-Spey. *High* 1E 151
Grantshouse. *Bord* 3E 130
Grappenhall. *Warr* 2A 84
Grasby. *Linc* 4D 94
Grasmere. *Cumb* 4E 103
Grasscroft. *G Man* 4H 91
Grassendale. *Mers* 2F 83
Grassgarth. *Cumb* 5E 113
Grassholme. *Dur* 2C 104
Grassington. *N Yor* 3C 98
Grassmoor. *Derbs* 4B 86
Grassthorpe. *Notts* 4E 87
Grateley. *Hants* 2A 24
Gratton. *Devn* 1D 11
Gratton. *Staf* 5D 84
Gratwich. *Staf* 2E 73
Graveley. *Cambs* 4B 64
Graveley. *Herts* 3C 52
Gravelhill. *Shrp* 4G 71
Gravel Hole. *G Man* 4H 91
Gravelly Hill. *W Mid* 1F 61
Graven. *Shet* 4F 173
Graveney. *Kent* 4E 41
Gravesend. *Kent* 3H 39
Grayingham. *Linc* 1G 87
Grayrigg. *Cumb* 5G 103
Grays. *Thur* 3H 39
Grayshott. *Hants* 3G 25
Grayson Green. *Cumb* 2A 102
Grayswood. *Surr* 2A 26
Graythorp. *Hart* 2C 106
Grazeley. *Wok* 5E 37
Grealin. *High* 2E 155
Greasbrough. *S Yor* 1B 86
Greasby. *Mers* 2E 83
Great Abington. *Cambs* 1F 53
Great Addington. *Nptn* 3G 63
Great Alne. *Warw* 5F 61
Great Altcar. *Lanc* 4B 90
Great Amwell. *Herts* 4D 52
Great Asby. *Cumb* 3H 103
Great Ashfield. *Suff* 4B 66
Great Ayton. *N Yor* 3C 106
Great Baddow. *Essx* 5H 53
Great Bardfield. *Essx* 2G 53
Great Barford. *Beds* 5A 64
Great Barr. *W Mid* 1E 61
Great Barrington. *Glos* 4H 49
Great Barrow. *Ches* 4G 83
Great Barton. *Suff* 4A 66
Great Barugh. *N Yor* 2B 100
Great Bavington. *Nmbd* 1C 114
Great Bealings. *Suff* 1F 55
Great Bedwyn. *Wilts* 5A 36
Great Bentley. *Essx* 3E 54
Great Billing. *Nptn* 4F 63
Great Bircham. *Norf* 2G 77
Great Blakenham. *Suff* 5D 66
Great Blencow. *Cumb* 1F 103
Great Bolas. *Telf* 3A 72
Great Bookham. *Surr* 5C 38
Great Bosullow. *Corn* 3B 4
Great Bourton. *Oxon* 1C 50
Great Bowden. *Leics* 2E 63
Great Bradley. *Suff* 5F 65
Great Braxted. *Essx* 4B 54
Great Bricett. *Suff* 5C 66
Great Brickhill. *Buck* 2H 51
Great Bridgeford. *Staf* 3C 72
Great Brington. *Nptn* 4D 62
Great Bromley. *Essx* 3D 54
Great Broughton. *Cumb* 1B 102
Great Broughton. *N Yor* 4C 106
Great Budworth. *Ches* 3A 84
Great Burdon. *Darl* 3A 106
Great Burstead. *Essx* 1A 40
Great Busby. *N Yor* 4C 106
Great Canfield. *Essx* 4F 53
Great Carlton. *Linc* 2D 88
Great Casterton. *Rut* 5H 75
Great Chalfield. *Wilts* 5D 34
Great Chart. *Kent* 1D 28
Great Chatwell. *Staf* 4B 72
Great Chesterford. *Essx* 1F 53
Great Cheverell. *Wilts* 1E 23
Great Chilton. *Dur* 1F 105
Great Chishill. *Cambs* 2E 53
Great Clacton. *Essx* 4E 55
Great Cliff. *W Yor* 3D 92
Great Clifton. *Cumb* 2B 102
Great Coates. *NE Lin* 3F 95
Great Comberton. *Worc* 1E 49
Great Corby. *Cumb* 4F 113

Great Cornard—Gun Hill

Great Cornard. *Suff* 1B **54**
Great Cowden. *E Yor* 5G **101**
Great Coxwell. *Oxon* 2A **36**
Great Crakehall. *N Yor* 1E **99**
Great Cransley. *Nptn* 3F **63**
Great Cressingham. *Norf* 5H **77**
Great Crosby. *Mers* 1F **83**
Great Cubley. *Derbs* 2F **73**
Great Dalby. *Leics* 4E **75**
Great Doddington. *Nptn* 4F **63**
Great Doward. *Here* 4A **48**
Great Dunham. *Norf* 4A **78**
Great Dunmow. *Essx* 3G **53**
Great Durnford. *Wilts* 3G **23**
Great Easton. *Essx* 3G **53**
Great Easton. *Leics* 1F **63**
Great Eccleston. *Lanc* 5D **96**
Great Edstone. *N Yor* 1B **100**
Great Ellingham. *Norf* 1C **66**
Great Elm. *Som* 2C **22**
Great Eppleton. *Tyne* 5G **115**
Great Eversden. *Cambs* 5C **64**
Great Fencote. *N Yor* 5F **105**
Great Finborough. *Suff* 5C **66**
Greatford. *Linc* 4H **75**
Great Fransham. *Norf* 4A **78**
Great Gaddesden. *Herts* 4A **52**
Great Gate. *Staf* 1E **73**
Great Gidding. *Cambs* 2A **64**
Great Givendale. *E Yor* 4C **100**
Great Glemham. *Suff* 4F **67**
Great Glen. *Leics* 1D **62**
Great Gonerby. *Linc* 2G **75**
Great Gransden. *Cambs* 5B **64**
Great Green. *Norf* 2E **67**
Great Green. *Suff* 5B **66**
(nr. Lavenham)
Great Green. *Suff* 3D **66**
(nr. Palgrave)
Great Habton. *N Yor* 2B **100**
Great Hale. *Linc* 1A **76**
Great Hallingbury. *Essx* 4F **53**
Greatham. *Hants* 3F **25**
Greatham. *Hart* 2B **106**
Greatham. *W Sus* 4B **26**
Great Hampden. *Buck* 5G **51**
Great Harrowden. *Nptn* 3F **63**
Great Harwood. *Lanc* 1F **91**
Great Haseley. *Oxon* 5E **51**
Great Hatfield. *E Yor* 5F **101**
Great Haywood. *Staf* 3D **73**
Great Heath. *W Mid* 2H **61**
Great Heck. *N Yor* 2F **93**
Great Henny. *Essx* 2B **54**
Great Hinton. *Wilts* 1E **23**
Great Hockham. *Norf* 1B **66**
Great Holland. *Essx* 4F **55**
Great Horkesley. *Essx* 2C **54**
Great Hormead. *Herts* 2E **53**
Great Horton. *W Yor* 1B **92**
Great Horwood. *Buck* 2F **51**
Great Houghton. *Nptn* 5E **63**
Great Houghton. *S Yor* 4E **93**
Great Hucklow. *Derbs* 3F **85**
Great Kelk. *E Yor* 4F **101**
Great Kendale. *E Yor* 3E **101**
Great Kimble. *Buck* 5G **51**
Great Kingshill. *Buck* 2G **37**
Great Langdale. *Cumb* 4D **102**
Great Langton. *N Yor* 5F **105**
Great Leighs. *Essx* 4H **53**
Great Limber. *Linc* 4E **95**
Great Linford. *Mil* 1G **51**
Great Livermere. *Suff* 3A **66**
Great Longstone. *Derbs* 3G **85**
Great Lumley. *Dur* 5F **115**
Great Lyth. *Shrp* 5G **71**
Great Malvern. *Worc* 1C **48**
Great Maplestead. *Essx* 2B **54**
Great Marton. *Bkpl* 1B **90**
Great Massingham. *Norf* 3G **77**
Great Melton. *Norf* 5D **78**
Great Milton. *Oxon* 5E **51**
Great Missenden. *Buck* 5G **51**
Great Mitton. *Lanc* 1F **91**
Great Mongeham. *Kent* 5H **41**
Great Moulton. *Norf* 1D **66**
Great Munden. *Herts* 3D **52**
Great Musgrave. *Cumb* 3A **104**
Great Ness. *Shrp* 4F **71**
Great Notley. *Essx* 3H **53**
Great Oak. *Mon* 5G **47**
Great Oakley. *Essx* 3E **55**
Great Oakley. *Nptn* 2F **63**
Great Offley. *Herts* 3B **52**
Great Ormside. *Cumb* 3A **104**
Great Orton. *Cumb* 4E **113**
Great Ouseburn. *N Yor* 3G **99**
Great Oxendon. *Nptn* 2E **63**
Great Oxney Green. *Essx* 5G **53**
Great Parndon. *Essx* 5E **53**
Great Paxton. *Cambs* 4B **64**
Great Plumpton. *Lanc* 1B **90**
Great Plumstead. *Norf* 4F **79**
Great Ponton. *Linc* 2G **75**
Great Potheridge. *Devn* 1F **11**
Great Preston. *W Yor* 2E **93**
Great Raveley. *Cambs* 2B **64**
Great Rissington. *Glos* 4G **49**
Great Rollright. *Oxon* 2B **50**
Great Ryburgh. *Norf* 3B **78**
Great Ryle. *Nmbd* 3E **121**
Great Ryton. *Shrp* 5G **71**
Great Saling. *Essx* 3G **53**
Great Salkeld. *Cumb* 1G **103**
Great Sampford. *Essx* 2G **53**
Great Sankey. *Warr* 2H **83**
Great Saredon. *Staf* 5D **72**
Great Saxham. *Suff* 4G **65**
Great Shefford. *W Ber* 4B **36**
Great Shelford. *Cambs* 5D **64**
Great Shoddesden. *Hants* 2A **24**
Great Smeaton. *N Yor* 4A **106**
Great Snoring. *Norf* 2B **78**
Great Somerford. *Wilts* 3E **35**
Great Stainton. *Darl* 2A **106**
Great Stambridge. *Essx* 1C **40**
Great Staughton. *Cambs* 4A **64**
Great Steeping. *Linc* 4D **88**
Great Stonar. *Kent* 5H **41**
Greatstone-on-Sea. *Kent* 3E **29**
Great Strickland. *Cumb* 2G **103**
Great Stukeley. *Cambs* 3B **64**
Great Sturton. *Linc* 3B **88**
Great Sutton. *Ches* 3F **83**
Great Sutton. *Shrp* 2H **59**
Great Swinburne. *Nmbd* 2C **114**
Great Tew. *Oxon* 3B **50**
Great Tey. *Essx* 3B **54**
Great Thirkleby. *N Yor* 2G **99**
Great Thorness. *IOW* 3C **16**
Great Thurlow. *Suff* 5F **65**
Great Torr. *Devn* 4C **8**
Great Torrington. *Devn* 1E **11**
Great Tosson. *Nmbd* 4E **121**
Great Totham North. *Essx* 4B **54**
Great Totham South. *Essx* 4B **54**
Great Tows. *Linc* 1B **88**
Great Urswick. *Cumb* 2B **96**
Great Wakering. *Essx* 2D **40**
Great Waldingfield. *Suff* 1C **54**
Great Walsingham. *Norf* 2B **78**
Great Waltham. *Essx* 4G **53**
Great Warley. *Essx* 1G **39**
Great Washbourne. *Glos* 2E **49**
Great Wenham. *Suff* 2D **54**
Great Whelnetham. *Suff* 5A **66**
Great Whittington. *Nmbd* 2D **114**
Great Wigborough. *Essx* 4C **54**
Great Wilbraham. *Cambs* 5E **65**
Great Wilne. *Derbs* 2B **74**
Great Wishford. *Wilts* 3F **23**
Great Witchingham. *Norf* 3D **78**
Great Witcombe. *Glos* 4E **49**
Great Witley. *Worc* 4B **60**
Great Wolford. *Warw* 2H **49**
Greatworth. *Nptn* 1D **50**
Great Wratting. *Suff* 1G **53**
Great Wymondley. *Herts* 3C **52**
Great Wyrley. *Staf* 5D **73**
Great Wytheford. *Shrp* 4H **71**
Great Yarmouth. *Norf* 5H **79**
Great Yeldham. *Essx* 2A **54**
Grebby. *Linc* 4D **88**
Greeba Castle. *IOM* 3C **108**
Greenbank. *Shet* 1G **173**
Greenbottom. *Corn* 4B **6**
Greenburn. *W Lot* 3C **128**
Greencroft. *Dur* 4E **115**
Greencroft Park. *Dur* 5E **115**
Greendown. *Som* 1A **22**
Greendykes. *Nmbd* 2E **121**
Green End. *Beds* 1A **52**
Green End. *Herts* 2D **52**
(nr. Buntingford)
Green End. *Herts* 3D **52**
(nr. Stevenage)
Green End. *N Yor* 4F **107**
Green End. *Warw* 2G **61**
Greenfield. *Arg* 4B **134**
Greenfield. *Beds* 2A **52**
Greenfield. *Flin* 3D **82**
Greenfield. *G Man* 4H **91**
Greenfield. *Oxon* 2F **37**
Greenfoot. *N Lan* 3A **128**
Greenford. *G Lon* 2C **38**
Greengairs. *N Lan* 2A **128**
Greengate. *Norf* 4C **78**
Greengill. *Cumb* 1C **102**
Greenhalgh. *Lanc* 1C **90**
Greenham. *Dors* 2H **13**
Greenham. *Som* 4D **20**
Greenham. *W Ber* 5C **36**
Green Hammerton. *N Yor* 4G **99**
Greenhaugh. *Nmbd* 1A **114**
Greenhead. *Nmbd* 3H **113**
Green Heath. *Staf* 4D **73**
Greenhill. *Dum* 2C **112**
Greenhill. *Falk* 2B **128**
Greenhill. *Kent* 4F **41**
Greenhill. *S Yor* 2H **85**
Greenhill. *Worc* 3C **60**
Greenhills. *N Ayr* 4E **127**
Greenhithe. *Kent* 3G **39**
Greenholm. *E Ayr* 1E **117**
Greenhow Hill. *N Yor* 3D **98**
Greenigo. *Orkn* 7D **172**
Greenland. *High* 2E **169**
Greenland Mains. *High* 2E **169**
Greenlands. *Worc* 4E **61**
Green Lane. *Shrp* 3A **72**
Green Lane. *Warw* 4E **61**
Greenlaw. *Bord* 5D **130**
Greenlea. *Dum* 2B **112**
Greenloaning. *Per* 3H **135**
Greenmount. *G Man* 3F **91**
Greenock. *Inv* 2D **126**
Greenock Mains. *E Ayr* 2F **117**
Greenodd. *Cumb* 1C **96**
Green Ore. *Som* 1A **22**
Greenrow. *Cumb* 4C **112**
Greens. *Abers* 4F **161**
Greensgate. *Norf* 4D **78**
Greenside. *Tyne* 3E **115**
Greensidehill. *Nmbd* 3D **121**
Greens Norton. *Nptn* 1E **51**
Greenstead Green. *Essx* 3B **54**
Greensted Green. *Essx* 5F **53**
Green Street. *Herts* 1C **38**
Green Street. *Suff* 3D **66**
Green Street Green. *G Lon* 4F **39**
Green Street Green. *Kent* 3G **39**
Greenstreet Green. *Suff* 1D **54**
Green, The. *Cumb* 1A **96**
Green, The. *Wilts* 3D **22**
Green Tye. *Herts* 4E **53**
Greenway. *Pemb* 2E **43**
Greenway. *V Glam* 4D **32**
Greenwell. *Cumb* 4G **113**
Greenwich. *G Lon* 3E **39**
Greet. *Glos* 2F **49**
Greete. *Shrp* 3H **59**
Greetham. *Linc* 3C **88**
Greetham. *Rut* 4G **75**
Greetland. *W Yor* 2A **92**
Gregson Lane. *Lanc* 2D **90**
Grein. *W Isl* 8B **170**
Greinetobht. *W Isl* 1D **170**
Greinton. *Som* 3H **21**
Grenaby. *IOM* 4B **108**
Grendon. *Nptn* 4F **63**
Grendon. *Warw* 1G **61**
Grendon Common. *Warw* 1G **61**
Grendon Green. *Here* 5H **59**
Grendon Underwood. *Buck* 3E **51**
Grenofen. *Devn* 5E **11**
Grenoside. *S Yor* 1H **85**
Greosabhagh. *W Isl* 8D **171**
Gresford. *Wrex* 5F **83**
Gresham. *Norf* 2D **78**
Greshornish. *High* 3C **154**
Gressenhall. *Norf* 4B **78**
Gressingham. *Lanc* 2E **97**
Greta Bridge. *Dur* 3D **105**
Gretna. *Dum* 3E **112**
Gretna Green. *Dum* 3E **112**
Gretton. *Glos* 2F **49**
Gretton. *Nptn* 1G **63**
Gretton. *Shrp* 1H **59**
Grewelthorpe. *N Yor* 2E **99**
Greygarth. *N Yor* 2D **98**
Grey Green. *N Lin* 4A **94**
Greylake. *Som* 3G **21**
Greysouthen. *Cumb* 2B **102**
Greystoke. *Cumb* 1F **103**
Greystoke Gill. *Cumb* 2F **103**
Greystone. *Ang* 4E **145**
Greystones. *S Yor* 2H **85**
Greywell. *Hants* 1F **25**
Griais. *W Isl* 3G **171**
Grianan. *W Isl* 4G **171**
Gribthorpe. *E Yor* 1A **94**
Gribun. *Arg* 5F **139**
Griff. *Warw* 2A **62**
Griffithstown. *Torf* 2F **33**
Griffydam. *Leics* 4B **74**
Griggs Green. *Hants* 3G **25**
Grimbister. *Orkn* 6C **172**
Grimeford Village. *Lanc* 3E **90**
Grimethorpe. *S Yor* 4E **93**
Griminis. *W Isl* 3C **170**
(on Benbecula)
Griminis. *W Isl* 1C **170**
(on North Uist)
Grimister. *Shet* 2F **173**
Grimley. *Worc* 4C **60**
Grimoldby. *Linc* 2C **88**
Grimpo. *Shrp* 3F **71**
Grimsargh. *Lanc* 1D **90**
Grimsby. *NE Lin* 3F **95**
Grimscote. *Nptn* 5D **62**
Grimscott. *Corn* 2C **10**
Grimshaw. *Bkbn* 2F **91**
Grimshaw Green. *Lanc* 3C **90**
Grimsthorpe. *Linc* 3H **75**
Grimston. *E Yor* 1F **95**
Grimston. *Leics* 3D **74**
Grimston. *Norf* 3G **77**
Grimston. *York* 4A **100**
Grimstone. *Dors* 3B **14**
Grimstone End. *Suff* 4B **66**
Grinacombe Moor. *Devn* 3E **11**
Grindale. *E Yor* 2F **101**
Grindhill. *Devn* 3E **11**
Grindiscol. *Shet* 8F **173**
Grindle. *Shrp* 5B **72**
Grindleford. *Derbs* 3G **85**
Grindleton. *Lanc* 5G **97**
Grindley. *Staf* 3E **73**
Grindley Brook. *Shrp* 1H **71**
Grindlow. *Derbs* 3F **85**
Grindon. *Nmbd* 5F **131**
Grindon. *Staf* 5E **85**
Gringley on the Hill. *Notts* 1E **87**
Grinsdale. *Cumb* 4E **113**
Grinshill. *Shrp* 3H **71**
Grinton. *N Yor* 5D **104**
Griomsidar. *W Isl* 5G **171**
Grishipoll. *Arg* 3C **138**
Grisling Common. *E Sus* 3F **27**
Gristhorpe. *N Yor* 1E **101**
Griston. *Norf* 1B **66**
Gritley. *Orkn* 7E **172**
Grittenham. *Wilts* 3F **35**
Grittleton. *Wilts* 4D **34**
Grizebeck. *Cumb* 1B **96**
Grizedale. *Cumb* 5E **103**
Grobister. *Orkn* 5F **172**
Groby. *Leics* 5C **74**
Groes. *Cnwy* 4C **82**
Groes. *Neat* 3A **32**
Groes-faen. *Rhon* 3D **32**
Groesffordd. *Gwyn* 2B **68**
Groesffordd. *Powy* 3D **46**
Groeslon. *Gwyn* 5D **81**
Groes-lwyd. *Powy* 4E **70**
Groes-wen. *Cphy* 3E **33**
Grogport. *Arg* 5G **125**
Groigearraidh. *W Isl* 4C **170**
Gromford. *Suff* 5F **67**
Gronant. *Flin* 2C **82**
Groombridge. *E Sus* 2G **27**
Grosmont. *Mon* 3H **47**
Grosmont. *N Yor* 4F **107**
Groton. *Suff* 1C **54**
Grove. *Dors* 5C **14**
Grove. *Kent* 4G **41**
Grove. *Notts* 3E **87**
Grove. *Oxon* 2B **36**
Grovehill. *E Yor* 1D **94**
Grove Park. *G Lon* 3F **39**
Grovesend. *Swan* 5F **45**
Grove, The. *Dum* 2A **112**
Grove, The. *Worc* 1D **48**
Grub Street. *Staf* 3B **72**
Grudie. *High* 2F **157**
Gruids. *High* 3C **164**
Gruinard House. *High* 4D **162**
Gruinart. *Arg* 3A **124**
Grulinbeg. *Arg* 3A **124**
Gruline. *Arg* 4G **139**
Grummore. *High* 5G **167**
Grundisburgh. *Suff* 5E **66**
Gruting. *Shet* 7D **173**
Grutness. *Shet* 10F **173**
Gualachulain. *High* 4F **141**
Gualin House. *High* 3D **166**
Guardbridge. *Fife* 2G **137**
Guarlford. *Worc* 1D **48**
Guay. *Per* 4H **143**
Gubblecote. *Herts* 4H **51**
Guestling Green. *E Sus* 4C **28**
Guestling Thorn. *E Sus* 4C **28**
Guestwick. *Norf* 3C **78**
Guestwick Green. *Norf* 3C **78**
Guide. *Bkbn* 2F **91**
Guide Post. *Nmbd* 1F **115**
Guilden Down. *Shrp* 2F **59**
Guilden Morden. *Cambs* 1C **52**
Guilden Sutton. *Ches* 4G **83**
Guildford. *Surr* 1A **26**
Guildtown. *Per* 5A **144**
Guilsborough. *Nptn* 3D **62**
Guilsfield. *Powy* 4E **70**
Guineaford. *Devn* 3F **19**
Guisborough. *Red C* 3D **106**
Guiseley. *W Yor* 5D **98**
Guist. *Norf* 3B **78**
Guiting Power. *Glos* 3F **49**
Gulberwick. *Shet* 8F **173**
Gullane. *E Lot* 1A **130**
Gulling Green. *Suff* 5H **65**
Gulval. *Corn* 3B **4**
Gumfreston. *Pemb* 4F **43**
Gumley. *Leics* 1D **62**
Gunby. *E Yor* 1H **93**
Gunby. *Linc* 3G **75**
Gundleton. *Hants* 3E **24**
Gun Green. *Kent* 2B **28**
Gun Hill. *E Sus* 4G **27**

Gunn—Hardwick

Gunn. *Devn* 3G 19
Gunnerside. *N Yor* 5C 104
Gunnerton. *Nmbd* 2C 114
Gunness. *N Lin* 3B 94
Gunnislake. *Corn* 5E 11
Gunsgreenhill. *Bord* 3F 131
Gunstone. *Staf* 5C 72
Gunthorpe. *Norf* 2C 78
Gunthorpe. *N Lin* 1F 87
Gunthorpe. *Notts* 1D 74
Gunthorpe. *Pet* 5A 76
Gunville. *IOW* 4C 16
Gupworthy. *Som* 3C 20
Gurnard. *IOW* 3C 16
Gurney Slade. *Som* 2B 22
Gurnos. *Powy* 5A 46
Gussage All Saints. *Dors* 1F 15
Gussage St Andrew. *Dors* 1E 15
Gussage St Michael. *Dors* 1E 15
Guston. *Kent* 1H 29
Gutcher. *Shet* 2G 173
Guthram Gowt. *Linc* 3A 76
Guthrie. *Ang* 3E 145
Guyhirn. *Cambs* 5D 76
Guyhirn Gull. *Cambs* 5C 76
Guy's Head. *Linc* 3D 77
Guy's Marsh. *Dors* 4D 22
Guyzance. *Nmbd* 4G 121
Gwaelod-y-garth. *Card* 3E 32
Gwaenynog Bach. *Den* 4C 82
Gwaenysgor. *Flin* 2C 82
Gwalchmai. *IOA* 3C 80
Gwastad. *Pemb* 2E 43
Gwaun-Cae-Gurwen. *Neat* 4H 45
Gwaun-y-bara. *Cphy* 3E 33
Gwbert. *Cdgn* 1B 44
Gweek. *Corn* 4E 5
Gwehelog. *Mon* 5G 47
Gwenddwr. *Powy* 1D 46
Gwennap. *Corn* 4B 6
Gwenter. *Corn* 5E 5
Gwernaffield. *Flin* 4E 82
Gwernesney. *Mon* 5H 47
Gwernogle. *Carm* 2F 45
Gwern-y-go. *Powy* 1E 58
Gwernymynydd. *Flin* 4E 82
Gwersyllt. *Wrex* 5F 83
Gwespyr. *Flin* 2D 82
Gwinear. *Corn* 3C 4
Gwithian. *Corn* 2C 4
Gwredog. *IOA* 2D 80
Gwyddelwern. *Den* 1C 70
Gwyddgrug. *Carm* 2E 45
Gwynfryn. *Wrex* 5E 83
Gwystre. *Powy* 4C 58
Gwytherin. *Cnwy* 4A 82
Gyfelia. *Wrex* 1F 71
Gyffin. *Cnwy* 3G 81

H

Habberley. *Shrp* 5F 71
Habblesthorpe. *Notts* 2E 87
Habergham. *Lanc* 1G 91
Habin. *W Sus* 4G 25
Habrough. *NE Lin* 3E 95
Hacconby. *Linc* 3A 76
Haceby. *Linc* 2H 75
Hacheston. *Suff* 5F 67
Hackenthorpe. *S Yor* 2B 86
Hackford. *Norf* 5C 78
Hackforth. *N Yor* 5F 105
Hackleton. *Nptn* 5F 63
Hackness. *N Yor* 5G 107
Hackness. *Orkn* 8C 172
Hackney. *G Lon* 2E 39
Hackthorn. *Linc* 2G 87
Hackthorpe. *Cumb* 2G 103
Haclait. *W Isl* 4D 170
Hadden. *Bord* 1B 120
Haddenham. *Buck* 5F 51
Haddenham. *Cambs* 3D 64
Haddenham End. *Cambs* 3D 64
Haddington. *E Lot* 2B 130
Haddington. *Linc* 4G 87
Haddiscoe. *Norf* 1G 67
Haddo. *Abers* 5F 161
Haddon. *Cambs* 1A 64
Hademore. *Staf* 5F 73
Hadfield. *Derbs* 1E 85
Hadham Cross. *Herts* 4E 53
Hadham Ford. *Herts* 3E 53
Hadleigh. *Essx* 2C 40
Hadleigh. *Suff* 1D 54
Hadleigh Heath. *Suff* 1C 54
Hadley. *Telf* 4A 72
Hadley. *Worc* 4C 60
Hadley End. *Staf* 3F 73
Hadley Wood. *G Lon* 1D 38
Hadlow. *Kent* 1H 27
Hadlow Down. *E Sus* 3G 27
Hadnall. *Shrp* 3H 71
Hadstock. *Essx* 1F 53
Hadston. *Nmbd* 5G 121
Hady. *Derbs* 3A 86
Hadzor. *Worc* 4D 60
Haffenden Quarter. *Kent* 1C 28
Haggate. *Lanc* 1G 91
Haggbeck. *Cumb* 2F 113
Haggerston. *Nmbd* 5G 131
Haggrister. *Shet* 4E 173
Hagley. *Here* 1A 48
Hagley. *Worc* 2D 60
Hagnaby. *Linc* 4C 88
Hagworthingham. *Linc* 4C 88
Haigh. *G Man* 4E 90
Haigh Moor. *W Yor* 2C 92
Haighton Green. *Lanc* 1D 90
Haile. *Cumb* 4B 102
Hailes. *Glos* 2F 49
Hailey. *Herts* 4D 52
Hailey. *Oxon* 4B 50
Hailsham. *E Sus* 5G 27
Hail Weston. *Cambs* 4A 64
Hainault. *G Lon* 1F 39
Hainford. *Norf* 4E 78
Hainton. *Linc* 2A 88
Hainworth. *W Yor* 1A 92
Haisthorpe. *E Yor* 3F 101
Hakin. *Pemb* 4C 42
Halam. *Notts* 5D 86
Halbeath. *Fife* 1E 129
Halberton. *Devn* 1D 12
Halcro. *High* 2E 169
Hale. *Cumb* 2E 97
Hale. *G Man* 2B 84
Hale. *Hal* 2G 83
Hale. *Hants* 1G 15
Hale. *Surr* 2G 25
Hale Bank. *Hal* 2G 83
Halebarns. *G Man* 2B 84
Hales. *Norf* 1F 67
Hales. *Staf* 2B 72
Halesgate. *Linc* 3C 76
Hales Green. *Derbs* 1F 73
Halesowen. *W Mid* 2D 60
Hale Street. *Kent* 1A 28
Halesworth. *Suff* 3F 67
Halewood. *Mers* 2G 83
Halford. *Devn* 5B 12
Halford. *Shrp* 2G 59
Halford. *Warw* 1A 50
Halfpenny. *Cumb* 1E 97
Halfpenny Furze. *Carm* 3G 43
Halfpenny Green. *Shrp* 1C 60
Halfway. *Carm* 2G 45
Halfway. *Powy* 2B 46
Halfway. *S Yor* 2B 86
Halfway. *W Ber* 5C 36
Halfway House. *Shrp* 4F 71
Halfway Houses. *Kent* 3D 40
Halgabron. *Corn* 4A 10
Halifax. *W Yor* 2A 92
Halistra. *High* 3B 154
Halket. *E Ayr* 4F 127
Halkirk. *High* 3D 168
Halkyn. *Flin* 3E 82
Hall. *E Ren* 4F 127
Hallam Fields. *Derbs* 1B 74
Halland. *E Sus* 4G 27
Hallands, The. *N Lin* 2D 94
Hallaton. *Leics* 1E 63
Hallatrow. *Bath* 1B 22
Hallbank. *Cumb* 5H 103
Hallbankgate. *Cumb* 4G 113
Hall Dunnerdale. *Cumb* 5D 102
Hallen. *S Glo* 3A 34
Hall End. *Beds* 1A 52
Hallgarth. *Dur* 5G 115
Hall Green. *Ches* 5C 84
Hall Green. *Norf* 2D 66
Hall Green. *W Mid* 2F 61
Hall Green. *W Yor* 3D 92
Hall Green. *Wrex* 1G 71
Halliburton. *Bord* 5C 130
Hallin. *High* 3B 154
Halling. *Medw* 4B 40
Hallington. *Linc* 2C 88
Hallington. *Nmbd* 2C 114
Halloughton. *Notts* 5D 86
Hallow. *Worc* 5C 60
Hallow Heath. *Worc* 5C 60
Hallowsgate. *Ches* 4H 83
Hallsands. *Devn* 5E 9
Hall's Green. *Herts* 3C 52
Hallspill. *Devn* 4E 19
Hallthwaites. *Cumb* 1A 96
Hall Waberthwaite. *Cumb* 5C 102
Hallwood Green. *Glos* 2B 48
Hallworthy. *Corn* 4B 10
Hallyne. *Bord* 5E 129
Halmer End. *Staf* 1C 72
Halmond's Frome. *Here* 1B 48
Halmore. *Glos* 5B 48
Halnaker. *W Sus* 5A 26
Halsall. *Lanc* 3B 90
Halse. *Nptn* 1D 50
Halse. *Som* 4E 21
Halsetown. *Corn* 3C 4
Halsham. *E Yor* 2F 95
Halsinger. *Devn* 3F 19
Halstead. *Essx* 2B 54
Halstead. *Kent* 4F 39
Halstead. *Leics* 5E 75
Halstock. *Dors* 2A 14
Halstow. *Devn* 3B 12
Halsway. *Som* 3E 21
Haltcliff Bridge. *Cumb* 1E 103
Haltham. *Linc* 4B 88
Haltoft End. *Linc* 1C 76
Halton. *Buck* 5G 51
Halton. *Hal* 2H 83
Halton. *Lanc* 3E 97
Halton. *Nmbd* 3C 114
Halton. *W Yor* 1D 92
Halton. *Wrex* 2F 71
Halton East. *N Yor* 4C 98
Halton Fenside. *Linc* 4D 88
Halton Gill. *N Yor* 2A 98
Halton Holegate. *Linc* 4D 88
Halton Lea Gate. *Nmbd* 4H 113
Halton Moor. *W Yor* 1D 92
Halton Shields. *Nmbd* 3D 114
Halton West. *N Yor* 4H 97
Haltwhistle. *Nmbd* 3A 114
Halvergate. *Norf* 5G 79
Halwell. *Devn* 3D 9
Halwill. *Devn* 3E 11
Halwill Junction. *Devn* 3E 11
Ham. *Devn* 2F 13
Ham. *Glos* 2B 34
Ham. *G Lon* 3C 38
Ham. *High* 1E 169
Ham. *Kent* 5H 41
Ham. *Plym* 3A 8
Ham. *Shet* 8A 173
Ham. *Som* 1F 13
(nr. Ilminster)
Ham. *Som* 4F 21
(nr. Taunton)
Ham. *Wilts* 5B 36
Hambleden. *Buck* 3F 37
Hambledon. *Hants* 1E 17
Hambledon. *Surr* 2A 26
Hamble-le-Rice. *Hants* 2C 16
Hambleton. *Lanc* 5C 96
Hambleton. *N Yor* 1F 93
Hambridge. *Som* 4G 21
Hambrook. *S Glo* 4B 34
Hambrook. *W Sus* 2F 17
Ham Common. *Dors* 4D 22
Hameringham. *Linc* 4C 88
Hamerton. *Cambs* 3A 64
Ham Green. *Here* 1C 48
Ham Green. *Kent* 4C 40
Ham Green. *N Som* 4A 34
Ham Green. *Worc* 4E 61
Ham Hill. *Kent* 4A 40
Hamilton. *Leics* 5D 74
Hamilton. *S Lan* 4A 128
Hammer. *W Sus* 3G 25
Hammersmith. *G Lon* 3D 38
Hammerwich. *Staf* 5E 73
Hammerwood. *E Sus* 2F 27
Hammill. *Kent* 5G 41
Hammond Street. *Herts* 5D 52
Hammoon. *Dors* 1D 14
Hamnavoe. *Shet* 8E 173
(nr. Burland)
Hamnavoe. *Shet* 3F 173
(on Yell)
Hamp. *Som* 3G 21
Hampden Park. *E Sus* 5H 27
Hampen. *Glos* 3F 49
Hamperden End. *Essx* 2F 53
Hamperley. *Shrp* 2G 59
Hampnett. *Glos* 4F 49
Hampole. *S Yor* 3F 93
Hampreston. *Dors* 3F 15
Hampstead. *G Lon* 2D 38
Hampstead Norreys. *W Ber* 4D 36
Hampsthwaite. *N Yor* 4E 99
Hampton. *Devn* 3F 13
Hampton. *G Lon* 3C 38
Hampton. *Kent* 4F 41
Hampton. *Shrp* 2B 60
Hampton. *Swin* 2G 35
Hampton. *Worc* 1F 49
Hampton Bishop. *Here* 2A 48
Hampton Fields. *Glos* 2D 35
Hampton Hargate. *Pet* 1A 64
Hampton Heath. *Ches* 1H 71
Hampton in Arden. *W Mid* 2G 61
Hampton Loade. *Shrp* 2B 60
Hampton Lovett. *Worc* 4C 60
Hampton Lucy. *Warw* 5G 61
Hampton Magna. *Warw* 4G 61
Hampton on the Hill. *Warw* 4G 61
Hampton Poyle. *Oxon* 4D 50
Hampton Wick. *G Lon* 4C 38
Hamptworth. *Wilts* 1H 15
Hamrow. *Norf* 3B 78
Hamsey. *E Sus* 4F 27
Hamsey Green. *Surr* 5E 39
Hamstall Ridware. *Staf* 4F 73
Hamstead. *IOW* 3C 16
Hamstead. *W Mid* 1E 61
Hamstead Marshall. *W Ber* 5C 36
Hamsterley. *Dur* 4E 115
(nr. Consett)
Hamsterley. *Dur* 1E 105
(nr. Wolsingham)
Hamsterley Mill. *Dur* 4E 115
Hamstreet. *Kent* 2E 28
Ham Street. *Som* 3A 22
Hamworthy. *Pool* 3E 15
Hanbury. *Staf* 3F 73
Hanbury. *Worc* 4D 60
Hanbury Woodend. *Staf* 3F 73
Hanby. *Linc* 2H 75
Hanchurch. *Staf* 1C 72
Hand and Pen. *Devn* 3D 12
Handbridge. *Ches* 4G 83
Handcross. *W Sus* 3D 26
Handforth. *Ches* 2C 84
Handley. *Ches* 5G 83
Handley. *Derbs* 4A 86
Handsacre. *Staf* 4E 73
Handsworth. *S Yor* 2B 86
Handsworth. *W Mid* 1E 61
Handy Cross. *Buck* 2G 37
Hanford. *Dors* 1D 14
Hanford. *Stoke* 1C 72
Hangersley. *Hants* 2G 15
Hanging Houghton. *Nptn* 3E 63
Hanging Langford. *Wilts* 3F 23
Hangleton. *Brig* 5D 26
Hangleton. *W Sus* 5B 26
Hanham. *S Glo* 4B 34
Hanham Green. *S Glo* 4B 34
Hankelow. *Ches* 1A 72
Hankerton. *Wilts* 2E 35
Hankham. *E Sus* 5H 27
Hanley. *Stoke* 1C 72
Hanley Castle. *Worc* 1D 48
Hanley Childe. *Worc* 4A 60
Hanley Swan. *Worc* 1D 48
Hanley William. *Worc* 4A 60
Hanlith. *N Yor* 3B 98
Hanmer. *Wrex* 2G 71
Hannaborough. *Devn* 2F 11
Hannaford. *Devn* 4G 19
Hannah. *Linc* 3E 89
Hannington. *Hants* 1D 24
Hannington. *Nptn* 3F 63
Hannington. *Swin* 2G 35
Hannington Wick. *Swin* 2G 35
Hanscombe End. *Beds* 2B 52
Hanslope. *Mil* 1G 51
Hanthorpe. *Linc* 3H 75
Hanwell. *G Lon* 2C 38
Hanwell. *Oxon* 1C 50
Hanwood. *Shrp* 5G 71
Hanworth. *G Lon* 3C 38
Hanworth. *Norf* 2D 78
Happas. *Ang* 4D 144
Happendon. *S Lan* 1A 118
Happisburgh. *Norf* 2F 79
Happisburgh Common. *Norf* 3F 79
Hapsford. *Ches* 3G 83
Hapton. *Lanc* 1F 91
Hapton. *Norf* 1D 66
Harberton. *Devn* 3D 9
Harbertonford. *Devn* 3D 9
Harbledown. *Kent* 5F 41
Harborne. *W Mid* 2E 61
Harborough Magna. *Warw* 3B 62
Harbottle. *Nmbd* 4D 120
Harbourneford. *Devn* 2D 8
Harbours Hill. *Worc* 4D 60
Harbridge. *Hants* 1G 15
Harbury. *Warw* 4A 62
Harby. *Leics* 2E 75
Harby. *Notts* 3F 87
Harcombe. *Devn* 3E 13
Harcombe Bottom. *Devn* 3G 13
Harcourt. *Corn* 5C 6
Harden. *W Yor* 1A 92
Hardenhuish. *Wilts* 4E 35
Hardgate. *Abers* 3E 153
Hardgate. *Dum* 3F 111
Hardham. *W Sus* 4B 26
Hardingham. *Norf* 5C 78
Hardingstone. *Nptn* 5E 63
Hardings Wood. *Ches* 5C 84
Hardington. *Som* 1C 22
Hardington Mandeville. *Som* 1A 14
Hardington Marsh. *Som* 2A 14
Hardington Moor. *Som* 1A 14
Hardley. *Hants* 2C 16
Hardley Street. *Norf* 5F 79
Hardmead. *Mil* 1H 51
Hardraw. *N Yor* 5B 104
Hardstoft. *Derbs* 4B 86
Hardway. *Hants* 2E 16
Hardway. *Som* 3C 22
Hardwick. *Buck* 4G 51
Hardwick. *Cambs* 5C 64
Hardwick. *Norf* 2E 66

Hardwick. Nptn 4F 63
Hardwick. Oxon 3D 50
(nr. Bicester)
Hardwick. Oxon 5B 50
(nr. Witney)
Hardwick. Shrp 1F 59
Hardwick. S Yor 2B 86
Hardwick. Stoc T 2B 106
Hardwick. W Mid 1E 61
Hardwicke. Glos 3E 49
(nr. Cheltenham)
Hardwicke. Glos 4C 48
(nr. Gloucester)
Hardwicke. Here 1F 47
Hardwick Village. Notts 3D 86
Hardy's Green. Essx 3C 54
Hareby. Linc 4C 88
Hareden. Lanc 4F 97
Harefield. G Lon 1B 38
Hare Green. Essx 3D 54
Hare Hatch. Wok 4G 37
Harehill. Derbs 2F 73
Harehills. W Yor 1D 92
Harehope. Nmbd 2E 121
Harelaw. Dum 2F 113
Harelaw. Dur 4E 115
Hareplain. Kent 2C 28
Harescеugh. Cumb 5H 113
Harescombe. Glos 4D 48
Haresfield. Glos 4D 48
Haresfinch. Mers 1H 83
Hareshaw. N Lan 3B 128
Hare Street. Essx 5E 53
Hare Street. Herts 3D 53
Harewood. W Yor 5F 99
Harewood End. Here 3A 48
Harford. Devn 3C 8
Hargate. Norf 1D 66
Hargatewall. Derbs 3F 85
Hargrave. Ches 4G 83
Hargrave. Nptn 3H 63
Hargrave. Suff 5G 65
Harker. Cumb 3E 113
Harkstead. Suff 2E 55
Harlaston. Staf 4G 73
Harlaxton. Linc 2F 75
Harlech. Gwyn 2E 69
Harlequin. Notts 2D 74
Harlescott. Shrp 4H 71
Harleston. Devn 4D 9
Harleston. Norf 2E 67
Harleston. Suff 4C 66
Harlestone. Nptn 4E 62
Harley. Shrp 5H 71
Harley. S Yor 1A 86
Harling Road. Norf 2B 66
Harlington. Beds 2A 52
Harlington. G Lon 3B 38
Harlington. S Yor 4E 93
Harlosh. High 4B 154
Harlow. Essx 4E 53
Harlow Hill. Nmbd 3D 115
Harlsey Castle. N Yor 5B 106
Harlthorpe. E Yor 1H 93
Harlton. Cambs 5C 64
Harlyn. Corn 1C 6
Harman's Cross. Dors 4E 15
Harmby. N Yor 1D 98
Harmer Green. Herts 4C 52
Harmer Hill. Shrp 3G 71
Harmondsworth. G Lon 3B 38
Harmston. Linc 4G 87
Harnage. Shrp 5H 71
Harnham. Nmbd 1D 115
Harnhill. Glos 5F 49
Harold Hill. G Lon 1G 39
Haroldston West. Pemb 3C 42
Haroldswick. Shet 1H 173
Harold Wood. G Lon 1G 39
Harome. N Yor 1A 100
Harpenden. Herts 4B 52
Harpford. Devn 3D 12
Harpham. E Yor 3E 101
Harpley. Norf 3G 77
Harpley. Worc 4A 60
Harpole. Nptn 4D 62
Harpsdale. High 3D 168
Harpsden. Oxon 3F 37
Harpswell. Linc 2G 87
Harpurhey. G Man 4G 91
Harpur Hill. Derbs 3E 85
Harraby. Cumb 4F 113
Harracott. Devn 4F 19
Harrapool. High 1E 147
Harrietfield. Per 1B 136
Harrietsham. Kent 5C 40
Harrington. Cumb 2A 102
Harrington. Linc 3C 88
Harrington. Nptn 2E 63
Harringworth. Nptn 1G 63
Harriseahead. Staf 5C 84
Harriston. Cumb 5C 112
Harrogate. N Yor 4F 99
Harrold. Beds 5G 63
Harrop Dale. G Man 4A 92
Harrow. G Lon 2C 38
Harrowbarrow. Corn 2H 7
Harrowden. Beds 1A 52
Harrowgate Hill. Darl 3F 105
Harrow on the Hill. G Lon 2C 38
Harrow Weald. G Lon 1C 38
Harry Stoke. S Glo 4B 34
Harston. Cambs 5D 64
Harston. Leics 2F 75
Harswell. E Yor 5C 100
Hart. Hart 1B 106
Hartburn. Nmbd 1D 115
Hartburn. Stoc T 3B 106
Hartest. Suff 5H 65
Hartfield. E Sus 2F 27
Hartford. Cambs 3B 64
Hartford. Ches 3A 84
Hartford. Som 4C 20
Hartfordbridge. Hants 1F 25
Hartford End. Essx 4G 53
Harthill. Ches 5H 83
Harthill. N Lan 3C 128
Harthill. S Yor 2B 86
Hartington. Derbs 4F 85
Hartland. Devn 4C 18
Hartland Quay. Devn 4C 18
Hartle. Worc 3D 60
Hartlebury. Worc 3C 60
Hartlepool. Hart 1C 106
Hartley. Cumb 4A 104
Hartley. Kent 2B 28
(nr. Cranbrook)
Hartley. Kent 4H 39
(nr. Dartford)
Hartley. Nmbd 2G 115
Hartley Green. Staf 2D 73
Hartley Mauditt. Hants 3F 25
Hartley Wespall. Hants 1E 25
Hartley Wintney. Hants 1F 25
Hartlip. Kent 4C 40
Hartmount. High 1B 158
Hartoft End. N Yor 5E 107
Harton. N Yor 3B 100
Harton. Shrp 2G 59
Harton. Tyne 3G 115
Hartpury. Glos 3C 48
Hartshead. W Yor 2B 92
Hartshill. Warw 1H 61
Hartshorne. Derbs 3H 73
Hartsop. Cumb 3F 103
Hart Station. Hart 1B 106
Hartswell. Som 4D 20
Hartwell. Nptn 5E 63
Hartwood. Lanc 3D 90
Hartwood. N Lan 4B 128
Harvel. Kent 4A 40
Harvington. Worc 1F 49
(nr. Evesham)
Harvington. Worc 3C 60
(nr. Kidderminster)
Harwell. Oxon 3C 36
Harwich. Essx 2F 55
Harwood. Dur 1B 104
Harwood. G Man 3F 91
Harwood Dale. N Yor 5G 107
Harworth. Notts 1D 86
Hascombe. Surr 2A 26
Haselbech. Nptn 3E 62
Haselbury Plucknett. Som 1H 13
Haseley. Warw 4G 61
Haselor. Warw 5F 61
Hasfield. Glos 3D 48
Hasguard. Pemb 4C 42
Haskayne. Lanc 4B 90
Hasketon. Suff 5E 67
Hasland. Derbs 4A 86
Haslemere. Surr 2A 26
Haslingden. Lanc 2F 91
Haslingden Grane. Lanc 2F 91
Haslingfield. Cambs 5D 64
Haslington. Ches 5B 84
Hassall. Ches 5B 84
Hassall Green. Ches 5B 84
Hassell Street. Kent 1E 29
Hassendean. Bord 2H 119
Hassingham. Norf 5F 79
Hassness. Cumb 3C 102
Hassocks. W Sus 4E 27
Hassop. Derbs 3G 85
Haste Hill. Surr 2A 26
Haster. High 3F 169
Hasthorpe. Linc 4D 89
Hastigrow. High 2E 169
Hastingleigh. Kent 1E 29
Hastings. E Sus 5C 28
Hastingwood. Essx 5E 53
Hastoe. Herts 5H 51
Haston. Shrp 3H 71
Haswell. Dur 5G 115
Haswell Plough. Dur 5G 115
Hatch. Beds 1B 52
Hatch Beauchamp. Som 4G 21
Hatch End. G Lon 1C 38
Hatch Green. Som 1G 13
Hatching Green. Herts 4B 52
Hatchmere. Ches 3H 83
Hatch Warren. Hants 2E 24
Hatcliffe. NE Lin 4F 95
Hatfield. Here 5H 59
Hatfield. Herts 5C 52
Hatfield. S Yor 4G 93
Hatfield. Worc 5C 60
Hatfield Broad Oak. Essx 4F 53
Hatfield Heath. Essx 4F 53
Hatfield Hyde. Herts 4C 52
Hatfield Peverel. Essx 4A 54
Hatfield Woodhouse. S Yor 4G 93
Hatford. Oxon 2B 36
Hatherden. Hants 1B 24
Hatherleigh. Devn 2F 11
Hathern. Leics 3C 74
Hatherop. Glos 5G 49
Hathersage. Derbs 2G 85
Hathersage Booths. Derbs 2G 85
Hatherton. Ches 1A 72
Hatherton. Staf 4D 72
Hatley St George. Cambs 5B 64
Hatt. Corn 2H 7
Hattersley. G Man 1D 85
Hattingley. Hants 3E 25
Hatton. Abers 5H 161
Hatton. Derbs 2G 73
Hatton. G Lon 3B 38
Hatton. Linc 3A 88
Hatton. Shrp 1G 59
Hatton. Warr 2H 83
Hatton. Warw 4G 61
Hattoncrook. Abers 1F 153
Hatton Heath. Ches 4G 83
Hatton of Fintray. Abers 2F 153
Haugh. E Ayr 2D 117
Haugh. Linc 3D 88
Haugham. Linc 2C 88
Haugh Head. Nmbd 2E 121
Haughley. Suff 4C 66
Haughley Green. Suff 4C 66
Haugh of Ballechin. Per 3G 143
Haugh of Glass. Mor 5B 160
Haugh of Urr. Dum 3F 111
Haughton. Notts 3D 86
Haughton. Shrp 1A 60
(nr. Bridgnorth)
Haughton. Shrp 3F 71
(nr. Oswestry)
Haughton. Shrp 5B 72
(nr. Shifnal)
Haughton. Shrp 4H 71
(nr. Shrewsbury)
Haughton. Staf 3C 72
Haughton Green. G Man 1D 84
Haughton le Skerne. Darl 3A 106
Haughton Moss. Ches 5H 83
Haultwick. Herts 3D 52
Haunn. Arg 4E 139
Haunn. W Isl 7C 170
Haunton. Staf 4G 73
Hauxton. Cambs 5D 64
Havannah. Ches 4C 84
Havant. Hants 2F 17
Haven. Here 5G 59
Haven Bank. Linc 5B 88
Havenside. E Yor 2E 95
Havenstreet. IOW 3D 16
Haven, The. W Sus 2B 26
Havercroft. W Yor 3D 93
Haverfordwest. Pemb 3D 42
Haverhill. Suff 1G 53
Haverigg. Cumb 2A 96
Havering-atte-Bower. G Lon 1G 39
Havering's Grove. Essx 1A 40
Haversham. Mil 1G 51
Haverthwaite. Cumb 1C 96
Haverton Hill. Stoc T 2B 106
Havyatt. Som 3A 22
Hawarden. Flin 4F 83
Hawcoat. Cumb 2B 96
Hawcross. Glos 2C 48
Hawen. Cdgn 1D 44
Hawes. N Yor 1A 98
Hawes Green. Norf 1E 67
Hawick. Bord 3H 119
Hawkchurch. Devn 2G 13
Hawkedon. Suff 5G 65
Hawkenbury. Kent 1C 28
Hawkeridge. Wilts 1D 22
Hawkerland. Devn 4D 12
Hawkesbury. S Glo 3C 34
Hawkesbury Upton. S Glo 3C 34
Hawkes End. W Mid 2G 61
Hawk Green. G Man 2D 84
Hawkhurst. Kent 2B 28
Hawkhurst Common. E Sus 4G 27
Hawkinge. Kent 1G 29
Hawkley. Hants 4F 25
Hawkridge. Som 3B 20
Hawksdale. Cumb 5E 113
Hawkshaw. G Man 3F 91
Hawkshead. Cumb 5E 103
Hawkshead Hill. Cumb 5E 103
Hawkswick. N Yor 2B 98
Hawksworth. Notts 1E 75
Hawksworth. W Yor 5D 98
Hawkwell. Essx 1C 40
Hawley. Hants 1G 25
Hawley. Kent 3G 39
Hawling. Glos 3F 49
Hawnby. N Yor 1H 99
Haworth. W Yor 1A 92
Hawstead. Suff 5A 66
Hawthorn. Dur 5H 115
Hawthorn Hill. Brac 4G 37
Hawthorn Hill. Linc 5B 88
Hawthorpe. Linc 3H 75
Hawton. Notts 5E 87
Haxby. York 4A 100
Haxey. N Lin 1E 87
Haybridge. Shrp 3A 60
Haybridge. Som 2A 22
Haydock. Mers 1H 83
Haydon. Bath 1B 22
Haydon. Dors 1B 14
Haydon. Som 4F 21
Haydon Bridge. Nmbd 3B 114
Haydon Wick. Swin 3G 35
Haye. Corn 2H 7
Hayes. G Lon 4F 39
(nr. Bromley)
Hayes. G Lon 2B 38
(nr. Uxbridge)
Hayfield. Derbs 2E 85
Hay Green. Norf 4E 77
Hayhill. E Ayr 3D 116
Haylands. IOW 3D 16
Hayle. Corn 3C 4
Hayley Green. W Mid 2D 60
Hayling Island. Hants 3F 17
Hayne. Devn 2B 12
Haynes. Beds 1A 52
Haynes West End. Beds 1A 52
Hay-on-Wye. Powy 1F 47
Hayscastle. Pemb 2C 42
Hayscastle Cross. Pemb 2D 42
Haysden. Kent 1G 27
Hayshead. Ang 4F 145
Hay Street. Herts 3D 53
Hayton. Aber 3G 153
Hayton. Cumb 5C 112
(nr. Aspatria)
Hayton. Cumb 4G 113
(nr. Brampton)
Hayton. E Yor 5C 100
Hayton. Notts 2E 87
Hayton's Bent. Shrp 2H 59
Haytor Vale. Devn 5A 12
Haytown. Devn 1D 11
Haywards Heath. W Sus 3E 27
Haywood. S Lan 4C 128
Hazelbank. S Lan 5B 128
Hazelbury Bryan. Dors 2C 14
Hazeleigh. Essx 5B 54
Hazeley. Hants 1F 25
Hazel Grove. G Man 2D 84
Hazelhead. S Yor 4B 92
Hazelslade. Staf 4E 73
Hazel Street. Kent 2A 28
Hazelton Walls. Fife 1F 137
Hazelwood. Derbs 1H 73
Hazlemere. Buck 2G 37
Hazler. Shrp 1G 59
Hazlerigg. Tyne 2F 115
Hazles. Staf 1E 73
Hazleton. Glos 4F 49
Hazon. Nmbd 4F 121
Heacham. Norf 2F 77
Headbourne Worthy. Hants 3C 24
Headcorn. Kent 1C 28
Headingley. W Yor 1C 92
Headington. Oxon 5D 50
Headlam. Dur 3E 105
Headless Cross. Worc 4E 61
Headley. Hants 3G 25
(nr. Haslemere)
Headley. Hants 5D 36
(nr. Kingsclere)
Headley. Surr 5D 38
Headley Down. Hants 3G 25
Headley Heath. Worc 3E 61
Headley Park. Bris 5A 34
Head of Muir. Falk 1B 128
Headon. Notts 3E 87
Heads Nook. Cumb 4F 113
Heage. Derbs 5A 86
Healaugh. N Yor 5D 104
(nr. Grinton)
Healaugh. N Yor 5H 99
(nr. York)
Heald Green. G Man 2C 84
Heale. Devn 2G 19
Healey. G Man 3G 91
Healey. Nmbd 4D 114
Healey. N Yor 1D 98
Healeyfield. Dur 5D 114
Healey Hall. Nmbd 4D 114
Healing. NE Lin 3F 95
Heamoor. Corn 3B 4

Heanish. *Arg* 4B 138
Heanor. *Derbs* 1B 74
Heanton Punchardon. *Devn* 3F 19
Heapham. *Linc* 2F 87
Heartsease. *Powy* 4D 58
Heasley Mill. *Devn* 3H 19
Heaste. *High* 2E 147
Heath. *Derbs* 4B 86
Heath and Reach. *Beds* 3H 51
Heath Common. *W Sus* 4C 26
Heathcote. *Derbs* 4F 85
Heath Cross. *Devn* 3H 11
Heathencote. *Nptn* 1F 51
Heath End. *Derbs* 3A 74
Heath End. *Hants* 5D 36
Heath End. *W Mid* 5E 73
Heather. *Leics* 4A 74
Heatherfield. *High* 4D 155
Heatherton. *Derb* 2H 73
Heathfield. *Cumb* 5C 112
Heathfield. *Devn* 5B 12
Heathfield. *E Sus* 3G 27
Heathfield. *Ren* 3E 126
Heathfield. *Som* 4E 21
Heath Green. *Worc* 3E 61
Heathhall. *Dum* 2A 112
Heath Hayes. *Staf* 4E 73
Heath Hill. *Shrp* 4B 72
Heath House. *Som* 2H 21
Heathrow (London) Airport. *G Lon* 3B 38
Heathstock. *Devn* 2F 13
Heath, The. *Norf* 3E 79 (nr. Buxton)
Heath, The. *Norf* 3B 78 (nr. Fakenham)
Heath, The. *Norf* 3D 78 (nr. Hevingham)
Heath, The. *Staf* 2E 73
Heathton. *Shrp* 1C 60
Heathton. *Suff* 2E 55
Heathtop. *Derbs* 2F 73
Heath Town. *W Mid* 1D 60
Heatley. *G Man* 2B 84
Heatley. *Staf* 3E 73
Heaton. *Lanc* 3D 96
Heaton. *Staf* 4D 84
Heaton. *Tyne* 3F 115
Heaton. *W Yor* 1B 92
Heaton Moor. *G Man* 1C 84
Heaton's Bridge. *Lanc* 3C 90
Heaverham. *Kent* 5G 39
Heavitree. *Devn* 3C 12
Hebburn. *Tyne* 3G 115
Hebden. *N Yor* 3C 98
Hebden Bridge. *W Yor* 2H 91
Hebden Green. *Ches* 4A 84
Hebing End. *Herts* 3D 52
Hebron. *Carm* 2F 43
Hebron. *Nmbd* 1E 115
Heck. *Dum* 1B 112
Heckdyke. *Notts* 1E 87
Heckfield. *Hants* 5F 37
Heckfield Green. *Suff* 3D 66
Heckfordbridge. *Essx* 3C 54
Heckington. *Linc* 1A 76
Heckmondwike. *W Yor* 2C 92
Heddington. *Wilts* 5E 35
Heddon. *Devn* 4G 19
Heddon-on-the-Wall. *Nmbd* 3E 115
Hedenham. *Norf* 1F 67
Hedge End. *Hants* 1C 16
Hedgerley. *Buck* 2A 38
Hedging. *Som* 4G 21
Hedley on the Hill. *Nmbd* 4D 115
Hednesford. *Staf* 4E 73
Hedon. *E Yor* 2E 95
Hegdon Hill. *Here* 5H 59
Heighington. *Darl* 2F 105
Heighington. *Linc* 4H 87
Heightington. *Worc* 3B 60
Heights of Brae. *High* 2H 157
Heights of Fodderty. *High* 2H 157
Heights of Kinlochewe. *High* 2C 156
Heiton. *Bord* 1B 120
Hele. *Devn* 5H 11 (nr. Ashburton)
Hele. *Devn* 2C 12 (nr. Exeter)
Hele. *Devn* 3D 10 (nr. Holsworthy)
Hele. *Devn* 2F 19 (nr. Ilfracombe)
Hele. *Torb* 2F 9
Helensburgh. *Arg* 1D 126
Helford. *Corn* 4E 5
Helhoughton. *Norf* 3A 78
Helions Bumpstead. *Essx* 1G 53
Helland. *Corn* 5A 10
Helland. *Som* 4G 21
Hellandbridge. *Corn* 5A 10
Hellesdon. *Norf* 4E 78
Hellesveor. *Corn* 2C 4
Hellidon. *Nptn* 5C 62
Hellifield. *N Yor* 4A 98
Hellingly. *E Sus* 4G 27
Hellington. *Norf* 5F 79
Helmdon. *Nptn* 1D 50
Helmingham. *Suff* 5D 66
Helmington Row. *Dur* 1E 105
Helmsdale. *High* 2H 165
Helmshore. *Lanc* 2F 91
Helmsley. *N Yor* 1A 100
Helperby. *N Yor* 3G 99
Helperthorpe. *N Yor* 2D 100
Helpringham. *Linc* 1A 76
Helpston. *Pet* 5A 76
Helsby. *Ches* 3G 83
Helsey. *Linc* 3E 89
Helston. *Corn* 4D 4
Helstone. *Corn* 4A 10
Helton. *Cumb* 2G 103
Helwith. *N Yor* 4D 105
Helwith Bridge. *N Yor* 3H 97
Helygain. *Flin* 3E 82
Hemblington. *Norf* 4F 79
Hemel Hempstead. *Herts* 5A 52
Hemerdon. *Devn* 3B 8
Hemingbrough. *N Yor* 1G 93
Hemingby. *Linc* 3B 88
Hemingfield. *S Yor* 4D 93
Hemingford Abbots. *Cambs* 3B 64
Hemingford Grey. *Cambs* 3B 64
Hemingstone. *Suff* 5D 66
Hemington. *Leics* 3B 74
Hemington. *Nptn* 2H 63
Hemington. *Som* 1C 22
Hemley. *Suff* 1F 55
Hemlington. *Midd* 3B 106
Hempholme. *E Yor* 4E 101
Hempnall. *Norf* 1E 67
Hempnall Green. *Norf* 1E 67
Hempriggs. *High* 4F 169
Hemp's Green. *Essx* 3C 54
Hempstead. *Essx* 2G 53
Hempstead. *Medw* 4B 40
Hempstead. *Norf* 2D 78 (nr. Holt)
Hempstead. *Norf* 3G 79 (nr. Stalham)
Hempsted. *Glos* 4D 48
Hempton. *Norf* 3B 78
Hempton. *Oxon* 2C 50
Hemsby. *Norf* 4G 79
Hemswell. *Linc* 1G 87
Hemswell Cliff. *Linc* 2G 87
Hemsworth. *Dors* 2E 15
Hemsworth. *W Yor* 3E 93
Hem, The. *Shrp* 5B 72
Hemyock. *Devn* 1E 13
Henallt. *Carm* 3E 45
Henbury. *Bris* 4A 34
Henbury. *Ches* 3C 84
Hendomen. *Powy* 1E 58
Hendon. *G Lon* 2D 38
Hendon. *Tyne* 4H 115
Hendra. *Corn* 3D 6
Hendre. *B'end* 3C 32
Hendreforgan. *Rhon* 3C 32
Hendy. *Carm* 5F 45
Heneglwys. *IOA* 3D 80
Henfeddau Fawr. *Pemb* 1G 43
Henfield. *S Glo* 4B 34
Henfield. *W Sus* 4D 26
Henford. *Devn* 3D 10
Hengoed. *Cphy* 2E 33
Hengoed. *Shrp* 2E 71
Hengrave. *Suff* 4H 65
Henham. *Essx* 3F 53
Heniarth. *Powy* 5D 70
Henlade. *Som* 4F 21
Henley. *Dors* 2B 14
Henley. *Shrp* 2G 59 (nr. Church Stretton)
Henley. *Shrp* 3H 59 (nr. Ludlow)
Henley. *Som* 3H 21
Henley. *Suff* 5D 66
Henley. *W Sus* 4G 25
Henley-in-Arden. *Warw* 4F 61
Henley-on-Thames. *Oxon* 3F 37
Henley's Down. *E Sus* 4B 28
Henley Street. *Kent* 4A 40
Henllan. *Cdgn* 1D 44
Henllan. *Den* 4C 82
Henllan. *Mon* 3F 47
Henllan Amgoed. *Carm* 3F 43
Henllys. *Torf* 2F 33
Henlow. *Beds* 2B 52
Hennock. *Devn* 4B 12
Henny Street. *Essx* 2B 54
Henryd. *Cnwy* 3G 81
Henry's Moat. *Pemb* 2E 43
Hensall. *N Yor* 2F 93
Henshaw. *Nmbd* 3A 114
Hensingham. *Cumb* 3A 102
Henstead. *Suff* 2G 67
Hensting. *Hants* 4C 24
Henstridge. *Som* 1C 14
Henstridge Ash. *Som* 4C 22
Henstridge Bowden. *Som* 4B 22
Henstridge Marsh. *Som* 4C 22
Henton. *Oxon* 5F 51
Henton. *Som* 2H 21
Henwood. *Corn* 5C 10
Heogan. *Shet* 7F 173
Heol Senni. *Powy* 3C 46
Heol-y-Cyw. *B'end* 3C 32
Hepburn. *Nmbd* 2E 121
Hepple. *Nmbd* 4D 121
Hepscott. *Nmbd* 1F 115
Heptonstall. *W Yor* 2H 91
Hepworth. *Suff* 3B 66
Hepworth. *W Yor* 4B 92
Herbrandston. *Pemb* 4C 42
Hereford. *Here* 2A 48
Heribusta. *High* 1D 154
Heriot. *Bord* 4H 129
Hermiston. *Edin* 2E 129
Hermitage. *Dors* 2B 14
Hermitage. *Bord* 5H 119
Hermitage. *W Ber* 4D 36
Hermitage. *W Sus* 2F 17
Hermon. *Carm* 3G 45 (nr. Llandeilo)
Hermon. *Carm* 2D 44 (nr. Newcastle Emlyn)
Hermon. *IOA* 4C 80
Hermon. *Pemb* 1G 43
Herne. *Kent* 4F 41
Herne Bay. *Kent* 4F 41
Herne Common. *Kent* 4F 41
Herne Pound. *Kent* 5A 40
Herner. *Devn* 4F 19
Hernhill. *Kent* 4E 41
Herodsfoot. *Corn* 2G 7
Heronden. *Kent* 5G 41
Herongate. *Essx* 1H 39
Heronsford. *S Ayr* 1G 109
Heronsgate. *Herts* 1B 38
Heron's Ghyll. *E Sus* 3F 27
Herra. *Shet* 2H 173
Herriard. *Hants* 2E 25
Herringfleet. *Suff* 1G 67
Herringswell. *Suff* 4G 65
Herrington. *Tyne* 4G 115
Hersden. *Kent* 4G 41
Hersham. *Corn* 2C 10
Hersham. *Surr* 4C 38
Herstmonceux. *E Sus* 4H 27
Herston. *Dors* 5F 15
Herston. *Orkn* 8D 172
Hertford. *Herts* 4D 52
Hertford Heath. *Herts* 4D 52
Hertingfordbury. *Herts* 4D 52
Hesketh. *Lanc* 2C 90
Hesketh Bank. *Lanc* 2C 90
Hesketh Lane. *Lanc* 5F 97
Hesket Newmarket. *Cumb* 1E 103
Heskin Green. *Lanc* 3D 90
Hesleden. *Dur* 1B 106
Hesleyside. *Nmbd* 1B 114
Heslington. *York* 4A 100
Hessay. *York* 4H 99
Hessenford. *Corn* 3H 7
Hessett. *Suff* 4B 66
Hessilhead. *N Ayr* 4E 127
Hessle. *Hull* 2D 94
Hestaford. *Shet* 6D 173
Hest Bank. *Lanc* 3D 96
Hester's Way. *Glos* 3E 49
Heston. *G Lon* 3C 38
Hestwall. *Orkn* 6B 172
Heswall. *Mers* 2E 83
Hethe. *Oxon* 3D 50
Hethelpit Cross. *Glos* 3C 48
Hethersett. *Norf* 5D 78
Hethersgill. *Cumb* 3F 113
Hetherside. *Cumb* 3F 113
Hethpool. *Nmbd* 2C 120
Hett. *Dur* 1F 105
Hetton. *N Yor* 4B 98
Hetton-le-Hole. *Tyne* 5G 115
Hetton Steads. *Nmbd* 1E 121
Heugh. *Nmbd* 2D 115
Heugh-head. *Abers* 2A 152
Heveningham. *Suff* 3F 67
Hever. *Kent* 1F 27
Heversham. *Cumb* 1D 97
Hevingham. *Norf* 3D 78
Hewas Water. *Corn* 4D 6
Hewelsfield. *Glos* 5A 48
Hewish. *N Som* 5G 33
Hewish. *Som* 2H 13
Heworth. *York* 4A 100
Hexham. *Nmbd* 3C 114
Hextable. *Kent* 3G 39
Hexton. *Herts* 2B 52
Hexworthy. *Devn* 5G 11
Heybridge. *Essx* 1H 39 (nr. Brentwood)
Heybridge. *Essx* 5B 54 (nr. Maldon)
Heybridge Basin. *Essx* 5B 54
Heybrook Bay. *Devn* 4A 8
Heydon. *Cambs* 1E 53
Heydon. *Norf* 3D 78
Heydour. *Linc* 2H 75
Heylipol. *Arg* 4A 138
Heyop. *Powy* 3E 59
Heysham. *Lanc* 3D 96
Heyshott. *W Sus* 1G 17
Heytesbury. *Wilts* 2E 23
Heythrop. *Oxon* 3B 50
Heywood. *G Man* 3G 91
Heywood. *Wilts* 1D 22
Hibaldstow. *N Lin* 4C 94
Hickleton. *S Yor* 4E 93
Hickling. *Norf* 3G 79
Hickling. *Notts* 3D 74
Hickling Green. *Norf* 3G 79
Hickling Heath. *Norf* 3G 79
Hickstead. *W Sus* 3D 26
Hidcote Bartrim. *Glos* 1G 49
Hidcote Boyce. *Glos* 1G 49
Higford. *Shrp* 5B 72
High Ackworth. *W Yor* 3E 93
Higham. *Derbs* 5A 86
Higham. *Kent* 3B 40
Higham. *Lanc* 1G 91
Higham. *S Yor* 4D 92
Higham. *Suff* 2D 54 (nr. Ipswich)
Higham. *Suff* 4G 65 (nr. Newmarket)
Higham Dykes. *Nmbd* 2E 115
Higham Ferrers. *Nptn* 4G 63
Higham Gobion. *Beds* 2B 52
Higham on the Hill. *Leics* 1A 62
Highampton. *Devn* 2E 11
Higham Wood. *Kent* 1G 27
High Angerton. *Nmbd* 1D 115
High Auldgirth. *Dum* 1G 111
High Bankhill. *Cumb* 5G 113
High Banton. *N Lan* 1A 128
High Barnet. *G Lon* 1D 38
High Beech. *Essx* 1F 39
High Bentham. *N Yor* 3F 97
High Bickington. *Devn* 4G 19
High Biggins. *Cumb* 2F 97
High Birkwith. *N Yor* 2H 97
High Blantyre. *S Lan* 4H 127
High Bonnybridge. *Falk* 2B 128
High Borrans. *Cumb* 4F 103
High Bradfield. *S Yor* 1G 85
High Bray. *Devn* 3G 19
Highbridge. *Cumb* 5E 113
Highbridge. *High* 5D 148
Highbridge. *Som* 2G 21
Highbrook. *W Sus* 2E 27
High Brooms. *Kent* 1G 27
High Bullen. *Devn* 4F 19
Highburton. *W Yor* 3B 92
Highbury. *Som* 2B 22
High Buston. *Nmbd* 4G 121
High Callerton. *Nmbd* 2E 115
High Carlingill. *Cumb* 4H 103
High Catton. *E Yor* 4B 100
High Church. *Nmbd* 1E 115
Highclere. *Hants* 5C 36
Highcliffe. *Dors* 3H 15
High Cogges. *Oxon* 5B 50
High Common. *Norf* 5B 78
High Coniscliffe. *Darl* 3F 105
High Crosby. *Cumb* 4F 113
High Cross. *Hants* 4F 25
High Cross. *Herts* 4D 52
High Dougarie. *N Ayr* 2C 122
High Easter. *Essx* 4G 53
High Eggborough. *N Yor* 2F 93
High Ellington. *N Yor* 1D 98
Higher Alham. *Som* 2B 22
Higher Ansty. *Dors* 2C 14
Higher Ashton. *Devn* 4B 12
Higher Ballam. *Lanc* 1B 90
Higher Bartle. *Lanc* 1D 90
Higher Bockhampton. *Dors* 3C 14
Higher Bojewyan. *Corn* 3A 4
High Ercall. *Telf* 4H 71
Higher Cheriton. *Devn* 2E 12
Higher Clovelly. *Devn* 4D 18
Higher Dinting. *Derbs* 1E 85
Higher Dunstone. *Devn* 5H 11
Higher End. *G Man* 4D 90
Higher Gabwell. *Devn* 2F 9
Higher Halstock Leigh. *Dors* 2A 14
Higher Heysham. *Lanc* 3D 96
Higher Hurdsfield. *Ches* 3D 84
Higher Kingcombe. *Dors* 3A 14
Higher Kinnerton. *Flin* 4F 83
Higher Melcombe. *Dors* 2C 14
Higher Penwortham. *Lanc* 2D 90
Higher Porthpean. *Corn* 3E 7
Higher Poynton. *Ches* 2D 84
Higher Shotton. *Flin* 4F 83
Higher Shurlach. *Ches* 3A 84
Higher Tale. *Devn* 2D 12
Highertown. *Corn* 4C 6
Higher Town. *IOS* 1B 4
Higher Town. *Som* 2C 20

Higher Walton—Holme

Higher Walton. Lanc 2D 90
Higher Walton. Warr 2H 83
Higher Whatcombe. Dors 2D 14
Higher Wheelton. Lanc 2E 90
Higher Whiteleigh. Corn 3C 10
Higher Whitley. Ches 3A 84
Higher Wincham. Ches 3A 84
Higher Wraxall. Dors 2A 14
Higher Wych. Wrex 1G 71
High Etherley. Dur 2E 105
High Ferry. Linc 1C 76
Highfield. E Yor 1H 93
Highfield. N Ayr 4E 126
Highfield. Tyne 4E 115
Highfields. Cambs 5C 64
High Garrett. Essx 3A 54
Highgate. G Lon 2D 39
Highgate. N Ayr 4E 127
Highgate. Powy 1D 58
High Grange. Dur 1E 105
High Green. Cumb 4F 103
High Green. Norf 5D 78
High Green. Shrp 2B 60
High Green. S Yor 1H 85
High Green. W Yor 3B 92
High Green. Worc 1D 49
Highgreen Manor. Nmbd 5C 120
High Halden. Kent 2C 28
High Halstow. Medw 3B 40
High Ham. Som 3H 21
High Harrington. Cumb 2B 102
High Haswell. Dur 5G 115
High Hatton. Shrp 3A 72
High Hawkser. N Yor 4G 107
High Hesket. Cumb 5F 113
High Hesleden. Dur 1B 106
High Hoyland. S Yor 3C 92
High Hunsley. E Yor 1C 94
High Hurstwood. E Sus 3F 27
High Hutton. N Yor 3B 100
High Ireby. Cumb 1D 102
High Keil. Arg 5A 122
High Kelling. Norf 1D 78
High Kilburn. N Yor 2H 99
High Killerby. N Yor 1E 101
High Knipe. Cumb 3G 103
High Lands. Dur 2E 105
Highlands, The. Shrp 2A 60
Highlane. Ches 4C 84
Highlane. Derbs 2B 86
High Lane. G Man 2D 84
High Lane. Here 4A 60
High Laver. Essx 5F 53
Highlaws. Cumb 5C 112
Highleadon. Glos 3C 48
High Legh. Ches 2A 84
Highleigh. W Sus 3G 17
High Leven. Stoc T 3B 106
Highley. Shrp 2B 60
High Littleton. Bath 1B 22
High Longthwaite. Cumb 5D 112
High Lorton. Cumb 2C 102
High Marishes. N Yor 2C 100
High Marnham. Notts 3F 87
High Melton. S Yor 4F 93
High Mickley. Nmbd 3D 115
Highmoor. Cumb 5D 112
High Moor. Lanc 3D 90
Highmoor. Oxon 3F 37
Highmoor Hill. Mon 3H 33
High Mowthorpe. N Yor 3C 100
Highnam. Glos 4C 48
High Newport. Tyne 4G 115
High Newton. Cumb 1D 96
High Newton-by-the-Sea. Nmbd 2G 121
High Nibthwaite. Cumb 1B 96
High Offley. Staf 3B 72
High Ongar. Essx 5F 53
High Onn. Staf 4C 72
High Orchard. Glos 4D 48
High Park. Mers 3B 90
High Roding. Essx 4G 53
High Row. Cumb 1E 103
High Salvington. W Sus 5C 26
High Scales. Cumb 5C 112
High Shaw. N Yor 5B 104
High Shincliffe. Dur 5F 115
High Side. Cumb 1D 102
High Spen. Tyne 3E 115
Highsted. Kent 4D 40
High Stoop. Dur 5E 115
High Street. Corn 3D 6
High Street. Suff 5G 67
(nr. Aldeburgh)
High Street. Suff 2F 67
(nr. Bungay)
High Street. Suff 3G 67
(nr. Yoxford)
Highstreet Green. Essx 2A 54
High Street Green. Suff 5C 66
Highstreet Green. Surr 2A 26
Hightae. Dum 2B 112
High Throston. Hart 1B 106
Hightown. Ches 4C 84
Hightown. Mers 4A 90
High Town. Staf 4D 73
Hightown Green. Suff 5B 66
High Toynton. Linc 4B 88
High Trewhitt. Nmbd 4E 121
High Valleyfield. Fife 1D 128
Highway. Here 1H 47
Highweek. Devn 5B 12
High Westwood. Dur 4E 115
Highwood. Staf 2E 73
Highwood. Worc 4A 60
High Worsall. N Yor 4A 106
Highworth. Swin 2H 35
High Wray. Cumb 5E 103
High Wych. Herts 4E 53
High Wycombe. Buck 2G 37
Hilborough. Norf 5H 77
Hilcott. Wilts 1G 23
Hildenborough. Kent 1G 27
Hildersham. Cambs 1F 53
Hilderstone. Staf 2D 72
Hilderthorpe. E Yor 3F 101
Hilfield. Dors 2B 14
Hilgay. Norf 1F 65
Hill. S Glo 2B 34
Hill. Warw 4B 62
Hill. Worc 1E 49
Hillam. N Yor 2F 93
Hillbeck. Cumb 3A 104
Hillberry. IOM 4C 108
Hillborough. Kent 4G 41
Hillbourne. Pool 3F 15
Hillbrae. Abers 4D 160
(nr. Aberchirder)
Hillbrae. Abers 1E 153
(nr. Inverurie)
Hillbrae. Abers 5F 161
(nr. Methlick)
Hill Brow. Hants 4F 25
Hillbutts. Dors 2E 15
Hillclifflane. Derbs 1G 73
Hill Deverill. Wilts 2D 22
Hilldyke. Linc 1C 76
Hill End. Dur 1D 104
Hillend. Fife 1E 129
(nr. Inverkeithing)
Hill End. Fife 4C 136
(nr. Saline)
Hillend. N Lan 3B 128
Hill End. N Yor 4C 98
Hillend. Shrp 1C 60
Hillend. Swan 3D 30
Hillersland. Glos 4A 48
Hillerton. Devn 3H 11
Hillesden. Buck 3E 51
Hillesley. Glos 3C 34
Hillfarrance. Som 4E 21
Hill Furze. Worc 1E 49
Hill Gate. Here 3H 47
Hill Green. Essx 2E 53
Hillgreen. W Ber 4C 36
Hillhead. Abers 5C 160
Hill Head. Hants 2D 16
Hillhead. S Ayr 3D 116
Hillhead. Torb 3F 9
Hillhead of Auchentumb. Abers 3G 161
Hilliard's Cross. Staf 4F 73
Hilliclay. High 2D 168
Hillingdon. G Lon 2B 38
Hillington. Norf 3G 77
Hillington. Ren 3G 127
Hillmorton. Warw 3C 62
Hill of Beath. Fife 4D 136
Hill of Fearn. High 1C 158
Hill of Fiddes. Abers 1G 153
Hill of Keillor. Ang 4B 144
Hill of Overbrae. Abers 2F 161
Hill Ridware. Staf 4E 73
Hillsborough. S Yor 1H 85
Hillside. Abers 4G 153
Hillside. Ang 2G 145
Hillside. Devn 2D 8
Hillside. Hants 1F 25
Hillside. Mers 3B 90
Hillside. Orkn 5C 172
Hillside. Shet 5F 173
Hillside. Shrp 2A 60
Hill Side. W Yor 3B 92
Hillside. Worc 4B 60
Hillside of Prieston. Ang 5C 144
Hill Somersal. Derbs 2F 73
Hillstown. Derbs 4B 86
Hillstreet. Hants 1B 16
Hillswick. Shet 4D 173
Hill, The. Cumb 1A 96
Hill Top. Dur 2C 104
(nr. Barnard Castle)
Hill Top. Dur 5F 115
(nr. Durham)
Hill Top. Dur 4E 115
(nr. Stanley)
Hill Top. Hants 2C 16
Hill View. Dors 3E 15
Hill Wootton. Warw 4H 61
Hillyland. Per 1C 136
Hilmarton. Wilts 4F 35
Hilperton. Wilts 1D 22
Hilperton Marsh. Wilts 1D 22
Hilsea. Port 2E 17
Hilston. E Yor 1F 95
Hiltingbury. Hants 4C 24
Hilton. Cambs 4B 64
Hilton. Cumb 2A 104
Hilton. Derbs 2G 73
Hilton. Dors 2C 14
Hilton. Dur 2E 105
Hilton. High 5E 165
Hilton. Shrp 1B 60
Hilton. Staf 5E 73
Hilton. Stoc T 3B 106
Hilton of Cadboll. High 1C 158
Himbleton. Worc 5D 60
Himley. Staf 1C 60
Hincaster. Cumb 1E 97
Hinchcliffe Mill. W Yor 4B 92
Hinchwick. Glos 2G 49
Hinckley. Leics 1B 62
Hinderclay. Suff 3C 66
Hinderwell. N Yor 3E 107
Hindford. Shrp 2F 71
Hindhead. Surr 3G 25
Hindley. G Man 4E 90
Hindley. Nmbd 4D 114
Hindley Green. G Man 4E 91
Hindlip. Worc 5C 60
Hindolveston. Norf 3C 78
Hindon. Wilts 3E 23
Hindringham. Norf 2B 78
Hingham. Norf 5C 78
Hinksford. Staf 2C 60
Hinstock. Shrp 3A 72
Hintlesham. Suff 1D 54
Hinton. Hants 3H 15
Hinton. Here 2G 47
Hinton. Nptn 5C 62
Hinton. Shrp 5G 71
Hinton. S Glo 4C 34
Hinton Ampner. Hants 4D 24
Hinton Blewett. Bath 1A 22
Hinton Charterhouse. Bath 1C 22
Hinton-in-the-Hedges. Nptn 2D 50
Hinton Martell. Dors 2F 15
Hinton on the Green. Worc 1F 49
Hinton Parva. Swin 3H 35
Hinton St George. Som 1H 13
Hinton St Mary. Dors 1C 14
Hinton Waldrist. Oxon 2B 36
Hints. Shrp 3A 60
Hints. Staf 5F 73
Hinwick. Beds 4G 63
Hinxhill. Kent 1E 29
Hinxton. Cambs 1E 53
Hinxworth. Herts 1C 52
Hipley. Hants 1E 16
Hipperholme. W Yor 2B 92
Hipsburn. Nmbd 3G 121
Hipswell. N Yor 5E 105
Hiraeth. Carm 2F 43
Hirn. Abers 3E 153
Hirnant. Powy 3C 70
Hirst. N Lan 3B 128
Hirst. Nmbd 1F 115
Hirst Courtney. N Yor 2G 93
Hirwaen. Den 4D 82
Hirwaun. Rhon 5C 46
Hiscott. Devn 4F 19
Histon. Cambs 4D 64
Hitcham. Suff 5B 66
Hitchin. Herts 3B 52
Hittisleigh. Devn 3H 11
Hittisleigh Barton. Devn 3H 11
Hive. E Yor 1B 94
Hixon. Staf 3E 73
Hoaden. Kent 5G 41
Hoar Cross. Staf 3F 73
Hoarwithy. Here 3A 48
Hoath. Kent 4G 41
Hobarris. Shrp 3F 59
Hobbles Green. Suff 5G 65
Hobbs Cross. Essx 1F 39
Hobkirk. Bord 3H 119
Hobson. Dur 4E 115
Hoby. Leics 4D 74
Hockering. Norf 4C 78
Hockering Heath. Norf 4C 78
Hockerton. Notts 5E 86
Hockley. Essx 1C 40
Hockley. Staf 5G 73
Hockley. W Mid 3G 61
Hockley Heath. W Mid 3F 61
Hockliffe. Beds 3H 51
Hockwold cum Wilton. Norf 2G 65
Hockworthy. Devn 1D 12
Hoddesdon. Herts 5D 52
Hoddlesden. Bkbn 2F 91
Hoddomcross. Dum 2C 112
Hodgeston. Pemb 5E 43
Hodley. Powy 1D 58
Hodnet. Shrp 3A 72
Hodsoll Street. Kent 4H 39
Hodson. Swin 3G 35
Hodthorpe. Derbs 3C 86
Hoe. Norf 4B 78
Hoe Gate. Hants 1E 17
Hoe, The. Plym 3A 8
Hoff. Cumb 3H 103
Hoffleet Stow. Linc 2B 76
Hogaland. Shet 4E 173
Hogben's Hill. Kent 5E 41
Hoggard's Green. Suff 5A 66
Hoggeston. Buck 3G 51
Hoggrill's End. Warw 1G 61
Hogha Gearraidh. W Isl 1C 170
Hoghton. Lanc 2E 90
Hoghton Bottoms. Lanc 2E 91
Hognaston. Derbs 5G 85
Hogsthorpe. Linc 3E 89
Hogstock. Dors 2E 15
Holbeach. Linc 3C 76
Holbeach Bank. Linc 3C 76
Holbeach Clough. Linc 3C 76
Holbeach Drove. Linc 4C 76
Holbeach Hurn. Linc 3C 76
Holbeach St Johns. Linc 4C 76
Holbeach St Marks. Linc 2C 76
Holbeach St Matthew. Linc 2D 76
Holbeck. Notts 3C 86
Holbeck. W Yor 1C 92
Holberrow Green. Worc 5E 61
Holbeton. Devn 3C 8
Holborn. G Lon 2E 39
Holbrook. Derbs 1A 74
Holbrook. S Yor 2B 86
Holbrook. Suff 2E 55
Holburn. Nmbd 1E 121
Holbury. Hants 2C 16
Holcombe. Devn 5C 12
Holcombe. G Man 3F 91
Holcombe. Som 2B 22
Holcombe Brook. G Man 3F 91
Holcombe Rogus. Devn 1D 12
Holcot. Nptn 4E 63
Holden. Lanc 5G 97
Holdenby. Nptn 4D 62
Holder's Green. Essx 3G 53
Holdgate. Shrp 2H 59
Holdingham. Linc 1H 75
Holditch. Dors 2G 13
Holemoor. Devn 2E 11
Hole Street. W Sus 4C 26
Holford. Som 2E 21
Holker. Cumb 2C 96
Holkham. Norf 1A 78
Hollacombe. Devn 2D 11
Holland. Orkn 2D 172
Holland Fen. Linc 1B 76
Holland Lees. Lanc 4D 90
Holland-on-Sea. Essx 4F 55
Holland Park. W Mid 5E 73
Hollandstoun. Orkn 2G 172
Hollesley. Suff 1G 55
Hollinfare. Warr 1A 84
Hollingbourne. Kent 5C 40
Hollingbury. Brig 5E 27
Hollingdon. Buck 3G 51
Hollingrove. E Sus 3A 28
Hollington. Derbs 1G 73
Hollington. E Sus 4B 28
Hollington. Staf 2E 73
Hollington Grove. Derbs 2G 73
Hollingworth. G Man 1E 85
Hollins. Derbs 3H 85
Hollins. G Man 4G 91
(nr. Bury)
Hollins. G Man 4G 91
(nr. Middleton)
Hollinsclough. Staf 4E 85
Hollinswood. Telf 5A 72
Hollinthorpe. W Yor 1D 93
Hollinwood. G Man 4H 91
Hollinwood. Shrp 2H 71
Hollocombe. Devn 1G 11
Holloway. Derbs 5H 85
Hollow Court. Worc 5D 61
Hollowell. Nptn 3D 62
Hollow Meadows. S Yor 2G 85
Hollows. Dum 2E 113
Hollybush. Cphy 5E 47
Hollybush. E Ayr 3C 116
Hollybush. Worc 2C 48
Holly End. Norf 5D 77
Holly Hill. N Yor 4E 105
Hollyhurst. Ches 1H 71
Hollym. E Yor 2G 95
Hollywood. Staf 2D 72
Hollywood. Worc 3E 61
Holmacott. Devn 4F 19
Holmbridge. W Yor 4B 92
Holmbury St Mary. Surr 1C 26
Holmbush. Corn 3E 7
Holmcroft. Staf 3D 72
Holme. Cambs 2A 64
Holme. Cumb 2E 97
Holme. N Lin 4C 94

Holme. *N Yor* 1F **99**
Holme. *Notts* 5F **87**
Holme. *W Yor* 4B **92**
Holmebridge. *Dors* 4D **15**
Holme Chapel. *Lanc* 2G **91**
Holme Hale. *Norf* 5A **78**
Holme Lacy. *Here* 2A **48**
Holme Marsh. *Here* 5F **59**
Holmend. *Dum* 4C **118**
Holme next the Sea. *Norf* 1G **77**
Holme-on-Spalding-Moor. *E Yor* 1B **94**
Holme on the Wolds. *E Yor* 5D **100**
Holme Pierrepont. *Notts* 2D **74**
Holmer. *Here* 1A **48**
Holmer Green. *Buck* 1A **38**
Holmes. *Lanc* 3C **90**
Holme St Cuthbert. *Cumb* 5C **112**
Holmes Chapel. *Ches* 4B **84**
Holmesfield. *Derbs* 3H **85**
Holmeswood. *Lanc* 3C **90**
Holmewood. *Derbs* 4B **86**
Holmfirth. *W Yor* 4B **92**
Holmhead. *E Ayr* 2E **117**
Holmisdale. *High* 4A **154**
Holm of Drumlanrig. *Dum* 5H **117**
Holmpton. *E Yor* 2G **95**
Holmrook. *Cumb* 5B **102**
Holmsey Green. *Suff* 3F **65**
Holmside. *Dur* 5F **115**
Holmwrangle. *Cumb* 5G **113**
Holne. *Devn* 2D **8**
Holsworthy. *Devn* 2D **10**
Holsworthy Beacon. *Devn* 2D **10**
Holt. *Dors* 2F **15**
Holt. *Norf* 2C **78**
Holt. *Wilts* 5D **34**
Holt. *Worc* 4C **60**
Holt. *Wrex* 5G **83**
Holtby. *York* 4A **100**
Holt End. *Hants* 3E **25**
Holt End. *Worc* 4E **61**
Holt Fleet. *Worc* 4C **60**
Holt Green. *Lanc* 4B **90**
Holt Heath. *Dors* 2F **15**
Holt Heath. *Worc* 4C **60**
Holton. *Oxon* 5E **50**
Holton. *Som* 4B **22**
Holton. *Suff* 3F **67**
Holton cum Beckering. *Linc* 2A **88**
Holton Heath. *Dors* 3E **15**
Holton le Clay. *Linc* 4F **95**
Holton le Moor. *Linc* 1H **87**
Holton St Mary. *Suff* 2D **54**
Holt Pound. *Hants* 2G **25**
Holtsmere End. *Herts* 4A **52**
Holtye. *E Sus* 2F **27**
Holwell. *Dors* 1C **14**
Holwell. *Herts* 2B **52**
Holwell. *Leics* 3E **75**
Holwell. *Oxon* 5H **49**
Holwell. *Som* 2C **22**
Holwick. *Dur* 2C **104**
Holworth. *Dors* 4C **14**
Holybourne. *Hants* 2F **25**
Holy Cross. *Worc* 3D **60**
Holyfield. *Essx* 5D **53**
Holyhead. *IOA* 2B **80**
Holy Island. *Nmbd* 5H **131**
Holymoorside. *Derbs* 4H **85**
Holyport. *Wind* 4G **37**
Holystone. *Nmbd* 4D **120**
Holytown. *N Lan* 3A **128**
Holywell. *Cambs* 3C **64**
Holywell. *Corn* 3B **6**
Holywell. *Dors* 2A **14**
Holywell. *Flin* 3D **82**
Holywell. *Glos* 2C **34**
Holywell. *Nmbd* 2G **115**
Holywell. *Warw* 4F **61**
Holywell Green. *W Yor* 3A **92**
Holywell Lake. *Som* 4E **20**
Holywell Row. *Suff* 3G **65**
Holywood. *Dum* 1G **111**
Homer. *Shrp* 5A **72**
Homer Green. *Mers* 4B **90**
Homersfield. *Suff* 2E **67**
Hom Green. *Here* 3A **48**
Homington. *Wilts* 4G **23**
Honeyborough. *Pemb* 4D **42**
Honeybourne. *Worc* 1G **49**
Honeychurch. *Devn* 2G **11**
Honey Hill. *Kent* 4F **41**
Honey Street. *Wilts* 5G **35**
Honey Tye. *Suff* 2C **54**
Honeywick. *Beds* 3H **51**
Honiley. *Warw* 3G **61**
Honing. *Norf* 3F **79**
Honingham. *Norf* 4D **78**
Honington. *Linc* 1G **75**
Honington. *Suff* 3B **66**
Honington. *Warw* 1A **50**
Honiton. *Devn* 2E **13**
Honley. *W Yor* 3B **92**
Honnington. *Telf* 4B **72**
Hoo. *Suff* 5E **67**
Hoobrook. *Worc* 3C **60**
Hood Green. *S Yor* 4D **92**
Hooe. *E Sus* 5A **28**
Hooe. *Plym* 3B **8**
Hooe Common. *E Sus* 4A **28**
Hoohill. *Bkpl* 1B **90**
Hook. *Cambs* 1D **64**
Hook. *E Yor* 2A **94**
Hook. *G Lon* 4C **38**
Hook. *Hants* 1F **25** (nr. Basingstoke)
Hook. *Hants* 2D **16** (nr. Fareham)
Hook. *Pemb* 3D **43**
Hook. *Wilts* 3F **35**
Hook-a-Gate. *Shrp* 5G **71**
Hook Bank. *Worc* 1D **48**
Hooke. *Dors* 2A **14**
Hooker Gate. *Tyne* 4E **115**
Hookgate. *Staf* 2B **72**
Hook Green. *Kent* 2A **28** (nr. Lamberhurst)
Hook Green. *Kent* 3H **39** (nr. Longfield)
Hook Green. *Kent* 4H **39** (nr. Meopham)
Hook Norton. *Oxon* 2B **50**
Hook's Cross. *Herts* 3C **52**
Hook Street. *Glos* 2B **34**
Hookway. *Devn* 3B **12**
Hookwood. *Surr* 1D **26**
Hoole. *Ches* 4G **83**
Hooley. *Surr* 5D **39**
Hooley Bridge. *G Man* 3G **91**
Hooley Brow. *G Man* 3G **91**
Hoo St Werburgh. *Medw* 3B **40**
Hooton. *Ches* 3F **83**
Hooton Levitt. *S Yor* 1C **86**
Hooton Pagnell. *S Yor* 4E **93**
Hooton Roberts. *S Yor* 1B **86**
Hope. *Derbs* 2F **85**
Hope. *Flin* 5F **83**
Hope. *High* 2E **167**
Hope. *Powy* 5E **71**
Hope. *Shrp* 5F **71**
Hope. *Staf* 5F **85**
Hope Bagot. *Shrp* 3H **59**
Hope Bowdler. *Shrp* 1G **59**
Hopedale. *Staf* 5F **85**
Hope Green. *Ches* 2D **84**
Hopeman. *Mor* 2F **159**
Hope Mansell. *Here* 4B **48**
Hopesay. *Shrp* 2F **59**
Hope's Green. *Essx* 2B **40**
Hopetown. *W Yor* 2D **93**
Hope under Dinmore. *Here* 5H **59**
Hopley's Green. *Here* 5F **59**
Hopperton. *N Yor* 4G **99**
Hop Pole. *Linc* 4A **76**
Hopstone. *Shrp* 1B **60**
Hopton. *Derbs* 5G **85**
Hopton. *Powy* 1E **59**
Hopton. *Shrp* 3F **71** (nr. Oswestry)
Hopton. *Shrp* 3H **71** (nr. Wem)
Hopton. *Staf* 3D **72**
Hopton. *Suff* 3B **66**
Hopton Cangeford. *Shrp* 2H **59**
Hopton Castle. *Shrp* 3F **59**
Hoptonheath. *Shrp* 3F **59**
Hopton Heath. *Staf* 3D **72**
Hopton on Sea. *Norf* 5H **79**
Hopton Wafers. *Shrp* 3A **60**
Hopwas. *Staf* 5F **73**
Hopwood. *Worc* 3E **61**
Horam. *E Sus* 4G **27**
Horbling. *Linc* 2A **76**
Horbury. *W Yor* 3C **92**
Horcott. *Glos* 5G **49**
Horden. *Dur* 5H **115**
Horderley. *Shrp* 2G **59**
Hordle. *Hants* 3A **16**
Hordley. *Shrp* 2F **71**
Horeb. *Carm* 3F **45** (nr. Brechfa)
Horeb. *Carm* 5E **45** (nr. Llanelli)
Horeb. *Cdgn* 1D **45**
Horfield. *Bris* 4B **34**
Horgabost. *W Isl* 8C **171**
Horham. *Suff* 3E **66**
Horkesley Heath. *Essx* 3C **54**
Horkstow. *N Lin* 3C **94**
Horley. *Oxon* 1C **50**
Horley. *Surr* 1D **27**
Hornblotton Green. *Som* 3A **22**
Hornby. *Lanc* 3E **97**
Hornby. *N Yor* 4A **106** (nr. Appleton Wiske)
Hornby. *N Yor* 5F **105** (nr. Catterick Garrison)
Horncastle. *Linc* 4B **88**
Hornchurch. *G Lon* 2G **39**
Horncliffe. *Nmbd* 5F **131**
Horndean. *Hants* 1E **17**
Horndean. *Bord* 5E **131**
Horndon. *Devn* 4F **11**
Horndon on the Hill. *Thur* 2A **40**
Horne. *Surr* 1E **27**
Horner. *Som* 2C **20**
Horning. *Norf* 4F **79**
Horninghold. *Leics* 1F **63**
Horninglow. *Staf* 3G **73**
Horningsea. *Cambs* 4D **65**
Horningsham. *Wilts* 2D **22**
Horningtoft. *Norf* 3B **78**
Hornsby. *Cumb* 4G **113**
Hornsbygate. *Cumb* 4G **113**
Horns Corner. *Kent* 3B **28**
Horns Cross. *Devn* 4D **19**
Hornsea. *E Yor* 5G **101**
Hornsea Burton. *E Yor* 5G **101**
Hornsey. *G Lon* 2E **39**
Hornton. *Oxon* 1B **50**
Horpit. *Swin* 3H **35**
Horrabridge. *Devn* 2B **8**
Horringer. *Suff* 4H **65**
Horringford. *IOW* 4D **16**
Horrocks Fold. *G Man* 3F **91**
Horrocksford. *Lanc* 5G **97**
Horsbrugh Ford. *Bord* 1E **119**
Horsebridge. *Devn* 5E **11**
Horsebridge. *Hants* 3B **24**
Horse Bridge. *Staf* 5D **84**
Horsebrook. *Staf* 4C **72**
Horsecastle. *N Som* 5H **33**
Horsehay. *Telf* 5A **72**
Horseheath. *Cambs* 1G **53**
Horsehouse. *N Yor* 1C **98**
Horsell. *Surr* 5A **38**
Horseman's Green. *Wrex* 1G **71**
Horsenden. *Buck* 5F **51**
Horseway. *Cambs* 2D **64**
Horsey. *Norf* 3G **79**
Horsey. *Som* 3G **21**
Horsford. *Norf* 4D **78**
Horsforth. *W Yor* 1C **92**
Horsham. *W Sus* 2C **26**
Horsham. *Worc* 5B **60**
Horsham St Faith. *Norf* 4E **78**
Horsington. *Linc* 4A **88**
Horsington. *Som* 4C **22**
Horsley. *Derbs* 1A **74**
Horsley. *Glos* 2D **34**
Horsley. *Nmbd* 3D **115** (nr. Prudhoe)
Horsley. *Nmbd* 5C **120** (nr. Rochester)
Horsley Cross. *Essx* 3E **54**
Horsleycross Street. *Essx* 3E **54**
Horsleyhill. *Bord* 3H **119**
Horsleyhope. *Dur* 5D **114**
Horsley Woodhouse. *Derbs* 1A **74**
Horsmonden. *Kent* 1A **28**
Horspath. *Oxon* 5D **50**
Horstead. *Norf* 4E **79**
Horsted Keynes. *W Sus* 3E **27**
Horton. *Buck* 4H **51**
Horton. *Dors* 2F **15**
Horton. *Lanc* 4A **98**
Horton. *Nptn* 5F **63**
Horton. *Shrp* 2G **71**
Horton. *Som* 1G **13**
Horton. *S Glo* 3C **34**
Horton. *Staf* 5D **84**
Horton. *Swan* 4D **30**
Horton. *Wilts* 5F **35**
Horton. *Wind* 3B **38**
Horton Cross. *Som* 1G **13**
Horton-cum-Studley. *Oxon* 4D **50**
Horton Grange. *Nmbd* 2F **115**
Horton Green. *Ches* 1G **71**
Horton Heath. *Hants* 1C **16**
Horton in Ribblesdale. *N Yor* 2H **97**
Horton Kirby. *Kent* 4G **39**
Hortonwood. *Telf* 4A **72**
Horwich. *G Man* 3E **91**
Horwich End. *Derbs* 2E **85**
Horwood. *Devn* 4F **19**
Hoscar. *Lanc* 3C **90**
Hose. *Leics* 3E **75**
Hosh. *Per* 1A **136**
Hosta. *W Isl* 1C **170**
Hoswick. *Shet* 9F **173**
Hotham. *E Yor* 1B **94**
Hothfield. *Kent* 1D **28**
Hoton. *Leics* 3C **74**
Houbie. *Shet* 2H **173**
Hough. *Arg* 4A **138**
Hough. *Ches* 5B **84** (nr. Crewe)
Hough. *Ches* 3C **84** (nr. Wilmslow)
Hougham. *Linc* 1F **75**
Hough Green. *Hal* 2G **83**
Hough-on-the-Hill. *Linc* 1G **75**
Houghton. *Cambs* 3B **64**
Houghton. *Cumb* 4F **113**
Houghton. *Hants* 3B **24**
Houghton. *Nmbd* 3E **115**
Houghton. *Pemb* 4D **43**
Houghton. *W Sus* 4B **26**
Houghton Bank. *Darl* 2F **105**
Houghton Conquest. *Beds* 1A **52**
Houghton Green. *E Sus* 3D **28**
Houghton-le-Side. *Darl* 2F **105**
Houghton-le-Spring. *Tyne* 5G **115**
Houghton on the Hill. *Leics* 5D **74**
Houghton Regis. *Beds* 3A **52**
Houghton St Giles. *Norf* 2B **78**
Houlsyke. *N Yor* 4E **107**
Hound. *Hants* 2C **16**
Hound Green. *Hants* 1F **25**
Houndslow. *Bord* 5C **130**
Houndsmoor. *Som* 4E **21**
Houndwood. *Bord* 3E **131**
Hounsdown. *Hants* 1B **16**
Hounslow. *G Lon* 3C **38**
Housay. *Shet* 4H **173**
Househill. *High* 3C **158**
Housetter. *Shet* 3E **173**
Houss. *Shet* 8E **173**
Houston. *Ren* 3F **127**
Housty. *High* 5D **168**
Houton. *Orkn* 7C **172**
Hove. *Brig* 5D **27**
Hoveringham. *Notts* 1E **74**
Hoveton. *Norf* 4F **79**
Hovingham. *N Yor* 2A **100**
How. *Cumb* 4G **113**
How Caple. *Here* 2B **48**
Howden. *E Yor* 2H **93**
Howden-le-Wear. *Dur* 1E **105**
Howe. *High* 2F **169**
Howe. *Norf* 5E **79**
Howe. *N Yor* 1F **99**
Howe Green. *Essx* 5H **53** (nr. Chelmsford)
Howegreen. *Essx* 5B **54** (nr. Maldon)
Howe Green. *Warw* 2H **61**
Howell. *Linc* 1A **76**
How End. *Beds* 1A **52**
Howe of Teuchar. *Abers* 4E **161**
Howes. *Dum* 3C **112**
Howe Street. *Essx* 4G **53** (nr. Chelmsford)
Howe Street. *Essx* 2G **53** (nr. Finchingfield)
Howe, The. *Cumb* 1D **96**
Howe, The. *IOM* 5A **108**
Howey. *Powy* 5C **58**
Howgate. *Midl* 4F **129**
Howgill. *Lanc* 5H **97**
Howgill. *N Yor* 4C **98**
How Green. *Kent* 1F **27**
How Hill. *Norf* 4F **79**
Howick. *Nmbd* 3G **121**
Howle. *Telf* 3A **72**
Howle Hill. *Here* 3B **48**
Howleigh. *Som* 1F **13**
Howlett End. *Essx* 2F **53**
Howley. *Som* 2F **13**
Howley. *Warr* 2A **84**
Hownam. *Bord* 3B **120**
Howsham. *N Lin* 4D **94**
Howsham. *N Yor* 3B **100**
Howtel. *Nmbd* 1C **120**
Howt Green. *Kent* 4C **40**
Howton. *Here* 3H **47**
Howwood. *Ren* 3E **127**
Hoxne. *Suff* 3D **66**
Hoylake. *Mers* 2E **82**
Hoyland. *S Yor* 4D **92**
Hoylandswaine. *S Yor* 4C **92**
Hoyle. *W Sus* 4A **26**
Hubberholme. *N Yor* 2B **98**
Hubberston. *Pemb* 4C **42**
Hubbert's Bridge. *Linc* 1B **76**
Huby. *N Yor* 5E **99** (nr. Harrogate)
Huby. *N Yor* 3H **99** (nr. York)
Huccaby. *Devn* 5G **11**
Hucclecote. *Glos* 4D **48**
Hucking. *Kent* 5C **40**
Hucknall. *Notts* 1C **74**
Huddersfield. *W Yor* 3B **92**
Huddington. *Worc* 5D **60**
Huddlesford. *Staf* 5F **73**
Hudswell. *N Yor* 4E **105**
Huggate. *E Yor* 4C **100**
Hugglescote. *Leics* 4B **74**
Hughenden Valley. *Buck* 2G **37**
Hughley. *Shrp* 1H **59**
Hughton. *High* 4G **157**
Hugh Town. *IOS* 1B **4**
Hugus. *Corn* 4B **6**
Huish. *Wilts* 5G **35**
Huish Champflower. *Som* 4D **20**

Huish Episcopi. *Som* 4H 21
Huisinis. *W Isl* 6B 171
Hulcote. *Nptn* 5E 62
Hulcott. *Buck* 4G 51
Hulham. *Devn* 4D 12
Hull. *Hull* 2D 94
Hulland. *Derbs* 1G 73
Hulland Moss. *Derbs* 1G 73
Hulland Ward. *Derbs* 1G 73
Hullavington. *Wilts* 3D 35
Hullbridge. *Essx* 1C 40
Hulme. *G Man* 1C 84
Hulme. *Staf* 1D 72
Hulme End. *Staf* 5F 85
Hulme Walfield. *Ches* 4C 84
Hulverstone. *IOW* 4B 16
Hulver Street. *Suff* 2G 67
Humber. *Devn* 5C 12
Humber Bridge. *N Lin* 2D 94
Humber Court. *Here* 5H 59
Humberside International Airport. *N Lin* 3D 94
Humberston. *NE Lin* 4G 95
Humberstone. *Leic* 5D 74
Humbie. *E Lot* 3A 130
Humbleton. *E Yor* 1F 95
Humbleton. *Nmbd* 2D 121
Humby. *Linc* 2H 75
Hume. *Bord* 5D 130
Humshaugh. *Nmbd* 2C 114
Huna. *High* 1F 169
Huncoat. *Lanc* 1F 91
Huncote. *Leics* 1C 62
Hundall. *Derbs* 3A 86
Hunderthwaite. *Dur* 2C 104
Hundleby. *Linc* 4C 88
Hundle Houses. *Linc* 5B 88
Hundleton. *Pemb* 4D 42
Hundon. *Suff* 1H 53
Hundred Acres. *Hants* 1D 16
Hundred House. *Powy* 5D 58
Hundred, The. *Here* 4H 59
Hungarton. *Leics* 5D 74
Hungerford. *Hants* 1G 15
Hungerford. *Shrp* 2H 59
Hungerford. *Som* 2D 20
Hungerford. *W Ber* 5B 36
Hungerford Newtown. *W Ber* 4B 36
Hunger Hill. *G Man* 4E 91
Hungerton. *Linc* 2F 75
Hungladder. *High* 1C 154
Hungryhatton. *Shrp* 3A 72
Hunmanby. *N Yor* 2E 101
Hunmanby Sands. *N Yor* 2F 101
Hunningham. *Warw* 4A 62
Hunnington. *Worc* 2D 60
Hunny Hill. *IOW* 4C 16
Hunsdon. *Herts* 4E 53
Hunsingore. *N Yor* 4G 99
Hunslet. *W Yor* 1D 92
Hunslet Carr. *W Yor* 2D 92
Hunsonby. *Cumb* 1G 103
Hunspow. *High* 1E 169
Hunstanton. *Norf* 1F 77
Hunstanworth. *Dur* 5C 114
Hunston. *Suff* 4B 66
Hunston. *W Sus* 2G 17
Hunstrete. *Bath* 5B 34
Hunt End. *Worc* 4E 61
Hunterfield. *Midl* 3G 129
Hunters Forstal. *Kent* 4F 41
Hunter's Quay. *Arg* 2C 126
Huntham. *Som* 4G 21
Hunthill Lodge. *Ang* 1D 144
Huntingdon. *Cambs* 3B 64
Huntingfield. *Suff* 3F 67
Huntingford. *Wilts* 3D 22
Huntington. *Ches* 4G 83
Huntington. *E Lot* 2A 130
Huntington. *Here* 5E 59
Huntington. *Staf* 4D 72
Huntington. *Telf* 5A 72
Huntington. *York* 4A 100
Huntingtower. *Per* 1C 136
Huntley. *Glos* 4C 48
Huntley. *Staf* 1E 73
Huntly. *Abers* 4C 160
Huntlywood. *Bord* 5C 130
Hunton. *Hants* 3C 24
Hunton. *Kent* 1B 28
Hunton. *N Yor* 5E 105
Hunton Bridge. *Herts* 5A 52
Hunt's Corner. *Norf* 2C 66
Huntscott. *Som* 2C 20
Hunt's Cross. *Mers* 2G 83
Hunts Green. *Warw* 1F 61
Huntsham. *Devn* 4D 20
Huntshaw. *Devn* 4F 19
Huntspill. *Som* 2G 21
Huntstile. *Som* 3F 21
Huntstrete. *Bath* 5B 34
Huntworth. *Som* 3G 21
Hunwick. *Dur* 1E 105
Hunworth. *Norf* 2C 78
Hurcott. *Som* 1G 13 (nr. Ilminster)
Hurcott. *Som* 4A 22 (nr. Somerton)
Hurdcott. *Wilts* 3G 23
Hurdley. *Powy* 1E 59
Hurdsfield. *Ches* 3D 84
Hurlet. *Glas* 3G 127
Hurley. *Warw* 1G 61
Hurley. *Wind* 3G 37
Hurlford. *E Ayr* 1D 116
Hurlston Green. *Lanc* 3B 90
Hurn. *Dors* 3G 15
Hursey. *Dors* 2H 13
Hursley. *Hants* 4C 24
Hurst. *G Man* 4H 91
Hurst. *N Yor* 4D 104
Hurst. *Wok* 4F 37
Hurstbourne Priors. *Hants* 2C 24
Hurstbourne Tarrant. *Hants* 1B 24
Hurst Green. *Ches* 1H 71
Hurst Green. *E Sus* 3B 28
Hurst Green. *Essx* 4D 54
Hurst Green. *Lanc* 1E 91
Hurst Green. *Surr* 5E 39
Hurstley. *Here* 1G 47
Hurstpierpoint. *W Sus* 4D 27
Hurstway Common. *Here* 1F 47
Hurst Wickham. *W Sus* 4D 27
Hurstwood. *Lanc* 1G 91
Hurtmore. *Surr* 1A 26
Hurworth-on-Tees. *Darl* 3A 106
Hurworth Place. *Darl* 3F 105
Hury. *Dur* 3C 104
Husbands Bosworth. *Leics* 2D 62
Husborne Crawley. *Beds* 2H 51
Husthwaite. *N Yor* 2H 99
Hutcherleigh. *Devn* 3D 9
Hut Green. *N Yor* 2F 93
Huthwaite. *Notts* 5B 86
Huttoft. *Linc* 3E 89
Hutton. *Cumb* 2F 103
Hutton. *E Yor* 4E 101
Hutton. *Essx* 1H 39
Hutton. *Lanc* 2C 90
Hutton. *N Som* 1G 21
Hutton. *Bord* 4F 131
Hutton Bonville. *N Yor* 4A 106
Hutton Buscel. *N Yor* 1D 100
Hutton Conyers. *N Yor* 2F 99
Hutton Cranswick. *E Yor* 4E 101
Hutton End. *Cumb* 1F 103
Hutton Gate. *Red C* 3C 106
Hutton Henry. *Dur* 1B 106
Hutton-le-Hole. *N Yor* 1B 100
Hutton Magna. *Dur* 3E 105
Hutton Mulgrave. *N Yor* 4F 107
Hutton Roof. *Cumb* 2E 97 (nr. Kirkby Lonsdale)
Hutton Roof. *Cumb* 1E 103 (nr. Penrith)
Hutton Rudby. *N Yor* 4B 106
Huttons Ambo. *N Yor* 3B 100
Hutton Sessay. *N Yor* 2G 99
Hutton Village. *Red C* 3D 106
Hutton Wandesley. *N Yor* 4H 99
Huxham. *Devn* 3C 12
Huxham Green. *Som* 3A 22
Huxley. *Ches* 4H 83
Huyton. *Mers* 1G 83
Hwlffordd. *Pemb* 3D 42
Hycemoor. *Cumb* 1A 96
Hyde. *Glos* 5D 49 (nr. Stroud)
Hyde. *Glos* 3F 49 (nr. Winchcombe)
Hyde. *G Man* 1D 84
Hyde Heath. *Buck* 5H 51
Hyde Lea. *Staf* 3D 72
Hyde Park. *S Yor* 4F 93
Hydestile. *Surr* 1A 26
Hyndford Bridge. *S Lan* 5C 128
Hynish. *Arg* 5A 138
Hyssington. *Powy* 1F 59
Hythe. *Hants* 2C 16
Hythe. *Kent* 2F 29
Hythe End. *Wind* 3B 38
Hythie. *Abers* 3H 161
Hyton. *Cumb* 1A 96

I

Ianstown. *Mor* 2B 160
Iarsiadar. *W Isl* 4D 171
Ibberton. *Dors* 2C 14
Ible. *Derbs* 5G 85
Ibrox. *Glas* 3G 127
Ibsley. *Hants* 2G 15
Ibstock. *Leics* 4B 74
Ibstone. *Buck* 2F 37
Ibthorpe. *Hants* 1B 24
Iburndale. *N Yor* 4F 107
Ibworth. *Hants* 1D 24
Icelton. *N Som* 5G 33
Ichrachan. *Arg* 5E 141
Ickburgh. *Norf* 1H 65
Ickenham. *G Lon* 2B 38
Ickford. *Buck* 5E 51
Ickham. *Kent* 5G 41
Ickleford. *Herts* 2B 52
Icklesham. *E Sus* 4C 28
Ickleton. *Cambs* 1E 53
Icklingham. *Suff* 3G 65
Ickwell. *Beds* 1B 52
Icomb. *Glos* 3H 49
Idbury. *Oxon* 3H 49
Iddesleigh. *Devn* 2F 11
Ide. *Devn* 3B 12
Ideford. *Devn* 5B 12
Ide Hill. *Kent* 5F 39
Iden. *E Sus* 3D 28
Iden Green. *Kent* 2C 28 (nr. Benenden)
Iden Green. *Kent* 2B 28 (nr. Goudhurst)
Idle. *W Yor* 1B 92
Idless. *Corn* 4C 6
Idlicote. *Warw* 1A 50
Idmiston. *Wilts* 3G 23
Idole. *Carm* 4E 45
Idridgehay. *Derbs* 1G 73
Idrigill. *High* 2C 154
Idstone. *Oxon* 3A 36
Iffley. *Oxon* 5D 50
Ifield. *W Sus* 2D 26
Ifieldwood. *W Sus* 2D 26
Ifold. *W Sus* 2B 26
Iford. *E Sus* 5F 27
Ifton Heath. *Shrp* 2F 71
Ightfield. *Shrp* 2H 71
Ightham. *Kent* 5G 39
Iken. *Suff* 5G 67
Ilam. *Staf* 5F 85
Ilchester. *Som* 4A 22
Ilderton. *Nmbd* 2E 121
Ilford. *G Lon* 2F 39
Ilford. *Som* 1G 13
Ilfracombe. *Devn* 2F 19
Ilkeston. *Derbs* 1B 74
Ilketshall St Andrew. *Suff* 2F 67
Ilketshall St Lawrence. *Suff* 2F 67
Ilketshall St Margaret. *Suff* 2F 67
Ilkley. *W Yor* 5D 98
Illand. *Corn* 5C 10
Illey. *W Mid* 2D 61
Illidge Green. *Ches* 4B 84
Illington. *Norf* 2B 66
Illingworth. *W Yor* 2A 92
Illogan. *Corn* 4A 6
Illogan Highway. *Corn* 4A 6
Illston on the Hill. *Leics* 1E 62
Ilmer. *Buck* 5F 51
Ilmington. *Warw* 1H 49
Ilminster. *Som* 1G 13
Ilsington. *Devn* 5A 12
Ilsington. *Dors* 3C 14
Ilston. *Swan* 3E 31
Ilton. *N Yor* 2D 98
Ilton. *Som* 1G 13
Imachar. *N Ayr* 5G 125
Imber. *Wilts* 2E 23
Immingham. *NE Lin* 3E 95
Immingham Dock. *NE Lin* 3E 95
Impington. *Cambs* 4D 64
Ince. *Ches* 3G 83
Ince Blundell. *Mers* 4B 90
Ince-in-Makerfield. *G Man* 4D 90
Inchbae Lodge. *High* 2G 157
Inchbare. *Ang* 2F 145
Inchberry. *Mor* 3H 159
Inchbraoch. *Ang* 3G 145
Inchbrook. *Glos* 5D 48
Incheril. *High* 2C 156
Inchinnan. *Ren* 3F 127
Inchlaggan. *High* 3D 148
Inchmichael. *Per* 1E 137
Inchnadamph. *High* 1G 163
Inchree. *High* 2E 141
Inchture. *Per* 1E 137
Inchyra. *Per* 1D 136
Indian Queens. *Corn* 3D 6
Ingatestone. *Essx* 1H 39
Ingbirchworth. *S Yor* 4C 92
Ingestre. *Staf* 3D 73
Ingham. *Linc* 2G 87
Ingham. *Norf* 3F 79
Ingham. *Suff* 3A 66
Ingham Corner. *Norf* 3F 79
Ingleborough. *Norf* 4D 76
Ingleby. *Derbs* 3H 73
Ingleby Arncliffe. *N Yor* 4B 106
Ingleby Barwick. *Stoc T* 3B 106
Ingleby Greenhow. *N Yor* 4C 106
Ingleigh Green. *Devn* 2G 11
Inglemire. *Hull* 1D 94
Inglesbatch. *Bath* 5C 34
Ingleton. *Dur* 2E 105
Ingleton. *N Yor* 2F 97
Inglewhite. *Lanc* 5E 97
Ingoe. *Nmbd* 2D 114
Ingol. *Lanc* 1D 90
Ingoldisthorpe. *Norf* 2F 77
Ingoldmells. *Linc* 4E 89
Ingoldsby. *Linc* 2H 75
Ingon. *Warw* 5G 61
Ingram. *Nmbd* 3E 121
Ingrave. *Essx* 1H 39
Ingrow. *W Yor* 1A 92
Ings. *Cumb* 5F 103
Ingst. *S Glo* 3A 34
Ingthorpe. *Rut* 5G 75
Ingworth. *Norf* 3D 78
Inkberrow. *Worc* 5E 61
Inkford. *Worc* 3E 61
Inkpen. *W Ber* 5B 36
Inkstack. *High* 1E 169
Innellan. *Arg* 3C 126
Inner Hope. *Devn* 5C 8
Innerleith. *Fife* 2E 137
Innerleithen. *Bord* 1F 119
Innerleven. *Fife* 3F 137
Innermessan. *Dum* 3F 109
Innerwick. *E Lot* 2D 130
Innerwick. *Per* 4C 142
Innsworth. *Glos* 3D 48
Insch. *Abers* 1D 152
Insh. *High* 3C 150
Inshegra. *High* 3C 166
Inshore. *High* 1D 166
Inskip. *Lanc* 1C 90
Instow. *Devn* 3E 19
Intwood. *Norf* 5D 78
Inver. *Abers* 4G 151
Inver. *High* 5F 165
Inver. *Per* 4H 143
Inverailort. *High* 5F 147
Inveralligin. *High* 3H 155
Inverallochy. *Abers* 2H 161
Inveramsay. *Abers* 1E 153
Inveran. *High* 4C 164
Inveraray. *Arg* 3H 133
Inverarish. *High* 5E 155
Inverarity. *Ang* 4D 144
Inverarnan. *Arg* 2C 134
Inverarnie. *High* 5A 158
Inverbeg. *Arg* 4C 134
Inverbervie. *Abers* 1H 145
Inverboyndie. *Abers* 2D 160
Invercassley. *High* 3B 164
Invercharnan. *High* 4F 141
Inverchoran. *High* 3E 157
Invercreran. *Arg* 4E 141
Inverdruie. *High* 2D 150
Inverebrie. *Abers* 5G 161
Invereck. *Arg* 1C 126
Inveresk. *E Lot* 2G 129
Inveresragan. *Arg* 5D 141
Inverey. *Abers* 5E 151
Inverfarigaig. *High* 1H 149
Invergarry. *High* 3F 149
Invergeldie. *Per* 1G 135
Invergordon. *High* 2B 158
Invergowrie. *Per* 5C 144
Inverguseran. *High* 3F 147
Inverharroch. *Mor* 5A 160
Inverie. *High* 3F 147
Inverinan. *Arg* 2G 133
Inverinate. *High* 1B 148
Inverkeilor. *Ang* 4F 145
Inverkeithing. *Fife* 1E 129
Inverkeithny. *Abers* 4D 160
Inverkip. *Inv* 2D 126
Inverkirkaig. *High* 2E 163
Inverlael. *High* 5F 163
Inverliever Lodge. *Arg* 3F 133
Inverliver. *Arg* 5E 141
Inverloch. *High* 1F 141
Inverlochlarig. *Stir* 2D 134
Inverlussa. *Arg* 1E 125
Inver Mallie. *High* 5D 148
Invermarkie. *Abers* 5B 160
Invermoriston. *High* 2G 149
Invernaver. *High* 2H 167
Inverneil House. *Arg* 1G 125
Inverness. *High* 4A 158
Inverness Airport. *High* 3B 158
Invernettie. *Abers* 4H 161
Inverpolly Lodge. *High* 2E 163
Inverquhomery. *Abers* 4H 161
Inverroy. *High* 5E 149
Inversanda. *High* 3D 140
Invershiel. *High* 2B 148
Invershin. *High* 4C 164
Invershore. *High* 5E 169
Inversnaid. *Stir* 3C 134
Inverugie. *Abers* 4H 161
Inveruglas. *Arg* 3C 134
Inverurie. *Abers* 1E 153
Invervar. *Per* 4D 142
Inverythan. *Abers* 4E 161

Inwardleigh. *Devn* 3F **11**
Inworth. *Essx* 4B **54**
Iochdar. *W Isl* 4C **170**
Iping. *W Sus* 4G **25**
Ipplepen. *Devn* 2E **9**
Ipsden. *Oxon* 3E **37**
Ipstones. *Staf* 1E **73**
Ipswich. *Suff* 1E **55**
Irby. *Mers* 2E **83**
Irby in the Marsh. *Linc* 4D **88**
Irby upon Humber. *NE Lin* 4E **95**
Irchester. *Nptn* 4G **63**
Ireby. *Cumb* 1D **102**
Ireby. *Lanc* 2F **97**
Ireland. *Shet* 9E **173**
Ireleth. *Cumb* 2B **96**
Ireshopeburn. *Dur* 1B **104**
Ireton Wood. *Derbs* 1G **73**
Irlam. *G Man* 1B **84**
Irnham. *Linc* 3H **75**
Iron Acton. *S Glo* 3B **34**
Iron Bridge. *Cambs* 1D **65**
Ironbridge. *Telf* 5A **72**
Iron Cross. *Warw* 5E **61**
Ironville. *Derbs* 5B **86**
Irstead. *Norf* 3F **79**
Irthington. *Cumb* 3F **113**
Irthlingborough. *Nptn* 3G **63**
Irton. *N Yor* 1E **101**
Irvine. *N Ayr* 1C **116**
Irvine Mains. *N Ayr* 1C **116**
Isabella Pit. *Nmbd* 1G **115**
Isauld. *High* 2B **168**
Isbister. *Orkn* 6C **172**
Isbister. *Shet* 5G **173**
Isfield. *E Sus* 4F **27**
Isham. *Nptn* 3F **63**
Island Carr. *N Lin* 4C **94**
Islay Airport. *Arg* 4B **124**
Isle Abbotts. *Som* 4G **21**
Isle Brewers. *Som* 4G **21**
Isleham. *Cambs* 3F **65**
Isle of Man Airport. *IOM* 5B **108**
Isle of Thanet. *Kent* 4H **41**
Isle of Whithorn. *Dum* 5B **110**
Isleornsay. *High* 2F **147**
Isles of Scilly (St Mary's) Airport. *IOS* 1B **4**
Islesteps. *Dum* 2A **112**
Isleworth. *G Lon* 3C **38**
Isley Walton. *Leics* 3B **74**
Islibhig. *W Isl* 5B **171**
Islington. *G Lon* 2E **39**
Islington. *Telf* 3B **72**
Islip. *Nptn* 3G **63**
Islip. *Oxon* 4D **50**
Islwyn. *Cphy* 2F **33**
Istead Rise. *Kent* 4H **39**
Itchen. *Sotn* 1C **16**
Itchen Abbas. *Hants* 3D **24**
Itchen Stoke. *Hants* 3D **24**
Itchingfield. *W Sus* 3C **26**
Itchington. *S Glo* 3B **34**
Itlaw. *Abers* 3D **160**
Itteringham. *Norf* 2D **78**
Itteringham Common. *Norf* 3D **78**
Itton. *Devn* 3G **11**
Itton Common. *Mon* 2H **33**
Ivegill. *Cumb* 5F **113**
Ivelet. *N Yor* 5C **104**
Iverchaolain. *Arg* 2B **126**
Iver Heath. *Buck* 2B **38**
Iveston. *Dur* 4E **115**
Ivetsey Bank. *Staf* 4C **72**
Ivinghoe. *Buck* 4H **51**
Ivinghoe Aston. *Buck* 4H **51**
Ivington. *Here* 5G **59**
Ivington Green. *Here* 5G **59**
Ivybridge. *Devn* 3C **8**
Ivychurch. *Kent* 3E **29**
Ivy Hatch. *Kent* 5G **39**
Ivy Todd. *Norf* 5A **78**
Iwade. *Kent* 4D **40**
Iwerne Courtney. *Dors* 1D **14**
Iwerne Minster. *Dors* 1D **14**
Ixworth. *Suff* 3B **66**
Ixworth Thorpe. *Suff* 3B **66**

J

Jackfield. *Shrp* 5A **72**
Jack Hill. *N Yor* 4E **98**
Jacksdale. *Notts* 5B **86**
Jackton. *S Lan* 4G **127**
Jacobstow. *Corn* 3B **10**
Jacobstowe. *Devn* 2F **11**
Jacobswell. *Surr* 5A **38**
Jameston. *Pemb* 5E **43**
Jamestown. *Dum* 5F **119**
Jamestown. *Fife* 1E **129**
Jamestown. *High* 3G **157**
Jamestown. *W Dun* 1E **127**
Janetstown. *High* 2C **168** (nr. Thurso)
Janetstown. *High* 3F **169** (nr. Wick)
Jarrow. *Tyne* 3G **115**
Jarvis Brook. *E Sus* 3G **27**
Jasper's Green. *Essx* 3H **53**
Jaywick. *Essx* 4E **55**
Jedburgh. *Bord* 2A **120**
Jeffreyston. *Pemb* 4E **43**
Jemimaville. *High* 2B **158**
Jenkins Park. *High* 3F **149**
Jersey Marine. *Neat* 3G **31**
Jesmond. *Tyne* 3F **115**
Jevington. *E Sus* 5G **27**
Jingle Street. *Mon* 4H **47**
Jockey End. *Herts* 4A **52**
Jodrell Bank. *Ches* 3B **84**
Johnby. *Cumb* 1F **103**
John o' Gaunts. *W Yor* 2D **92**
John o' Groats. *High* 1F **169**
John's Cross. *E Sus* 3B **28**
Johnshaven. *Abers* 2G **145**
Johnson's Street. *Norf* 4F **79**
Johnston. *Pemb* 3D **42**
Johnstone. *Ren* 3F **127**
Johnstonebridge. *Dum* 5C **118**
Johnstown. *Carm* 4D **45**
Johnstown. *Wrex* 1F **71**
Joppa. *Edin* 2G **129**
Joppa. *S Ayr* 3D **116**
Jordan Green. *Norf* 3C **78**
Jordans. *Buck* 1A **38**
Jordanston. *Pemb* 1D **42**
Jump. *S Yor* 4D **93**
Jumpers Common. *Dors* 3G **15**
Juniper. *Nmbd* 4C **114**
Juniper Green. *Edin* 3E **129**
Jurby East. *IOM* 2C **108**
Jurby West. *IOM* 2C **108**
Jury's Gap. *E Sus* 4D **28**

K

Kaber. *Cumb* 3A **104**
Kaimend. *S Lan* 5C **128**
Kaimes. *Edin* 3F **129**
Kaimrig End. *Bord* 5D **129**
Kames. *Arg* 2A **126**
Kames. *E Ayr* 2F **117**
Kea. *Corn* 4C **6**
Keadby. *N Lin* 3B **94**
Keal Cotes. *Linc* 4C **88**
Kearsley. *G Man* 4F **91**
Kearsney. *Kent* 1G **29**
Kearstwick. *Cumb* 1F **97**
Kearton. *N Yor* 5C **104**
Kearvaig. *High* 1C **166**
Keasden. *N Yor* 3G **97**
Keason. *Corn* 2H **7**
Keckwick. *Hal* 2H **83**
Keddington. *Linc* 2C **88**
Keddington Corner. *Linc* 2C **88**
Kedington. *Suff* 1H **53**
Kedleston. *Derbs* 1H **73**
Kedlock Feus. *Fife* 2F **137**
Keelby. *Linc* 3E **95**
Keele. *Staf* 1C **72**
Keeley Green. *Beds* 1A **52**
Keeston. *Pemb* 3D **42**
Keevil. *Wilts* 1E **23**
Kegworth. *Leics* 3B **74**
Kehelland. *Corn* 2D **4**
Keig. *Abers* 2D **152**
Keighley. *W Yor* 5C **98**
Keilarsbrae. *Clac* 4A **136**
Keillmore. *Arg* 1E **125**
Keillor. *Per* 4B **144**
Keillour. *Per* 1B **136**
Keills. *Arg* 3C **124**
Keiloch. *Abers* 4F **151**
Keils. *Arg* 3D **124**
Keinton Mandeville. *Som* 3A **22**
Keir Mill. *Dum* 5A **118**
Keirsleywell Row. *Nmbd* 4A **114**
Keisby. *Linc* 3H **75**
Keisley. *Cumb* 2A **104**
Keiss. *High* 2F **169**
Keith. *Mor* 3B **160**
Keith Inch. *Abers* 4H **161**
Kelbrook. *Lanc* 5B **98**
Kelby. *Linc* 1H **75**
Keld. *Cumb* 3G **103**
Keld. *N Yor* 4B **104**
Keldholme. *N Yor* 1B **100**
Kelfield. *N Lin* 4B **94**
Kelfield. *N Yor* 1F **93**
Kelham. *Notts* 5E **87**
Kellacott. *Devn* 4E **11**
Kellan. *Arg* 4G **139**
Kellas. *Ang* 5D **144**
Kellas. *Mor* 3F **159**
Kellaton. *Devn* 5E **9**
Kelleth. *Cumb* 4H **103**
Kelling. *Norf* 1C **78**
Kellingley. *N Yor* 2F **93**
Kellington. *N Yor* 2F **93**
Kelloe. *Dur* 1A **106**
Kelloholm. *Dum* 3G **117**
Kells. *Cumb* 3A **102**
Kelly. *Devn* 4D **11**
Kelly Bray. *Corn* 5D **10**
Kelmarsh. *Nptn* 3E **63**
Kelmscott. *Oxon* 2A **36**
Kelsale. *Suff* 4F **67**
Kelsall. *Ches* 4H **83**
Kelshall. *Herts* 2D **52**
Kelsick. *Cumb* 4C **112**
Kelso. *Bord* 1B **120**
Kelstedge. *Derbs* 4H **85**
Kelstern. *Linc* 1B **88**
Kelsterton. *Flin* 3E **83**
Kelston. *Bath* 5C **34**
Keltneyburn. *Per* 4E **143**
Kelton. *Dum* 2A **112**
Kelton Hill. *Dum* 4E **111**
Kelty. *Fife* 4D **136**
Kelvedon. *Essx* 4B **54**
Kelvedon Hatch. *Essx* 1G **39**
Kelvinside. *Glas* 3G **127**
Kelynack. *Corn* 3A **4**
Kemback. *Fife* 2G **137**
Kemberton. *Shrp* 5B **72**
Kemble. *Glos* 2E **35**
Kemerton. *Worc* 2E **49**
Kemeys Commander. *Mon* 5G **47**
Kemnay. *Abers* 2E **153**
Kempley. *Glos* 3B **48**
Kempley Green. *Glos* 3B **48**
Kempsey. *Worc* 1D **48**
Kempsford. *Glos* 2G **35**
Kemps Green. *Warw* 3F **61**
Kempshott. *Hants* 1E **24**
Kempston. *Beds* 1A **52**
Kempston Hardwick. *Beds* 1A **52**
Kempton. *Shrp* 2F **59**
Kemp Town. *Brig* 5E **27**
Kemsing. *Kent* 5G **39**
Kemsley. *Kent* 4D **40**
Kenardington. *Kent* 2D **28**
Kenchester. *Here* 1H **47**
Kencot. *Oxon* 5A **50**
Kendal. *Cumb* 5G **103**
Kendleshire. *S Glo* 4B **34**
Kendray. *S Yor* 4D **92**
Kenfig. *B'end* 3B **32**
Kenfig Hill. *B'end* 3B **32**
Kengharair. *Arg* 4F **139**
Kenidjack. *Corn* 3A **4**
Kenilworth. *Warw* 3G **61**
Kenknock. *Stir* 5B **142**
Kenley. *G Lon* 5E **39**
Kenley. *Shrp* 5H **71**
Kenmore. *High* 3G **155**
Kenmore. *Per* 4E **143**
Kenn. *Devn* 4C **12**
Kenn. *N Som* 5H **33**
Kennacraig. *Arg* 3G **125**
Kenneggy Downs. *Corn* 4C **4**
Kennerleigh. *Devn* 2B **12**
Kennet. *Clac* 4B **136**
Kennethmont. *Abers* 1C **152**
Kennett. *Cambs* 4G **65**
Kennford. *Devn* 4C **12**
Kenninghall. *Norf* 2C **66**
Kennington. *Kent* 1E **29**
Kennington. *Oxon* 5D **50**
Kennoway. *Fife* 3F **137**
Kennyhill. *Suff* 3F **65**
Kennythorpe. *N Yor* 3B **100**
Kenovay. *Arg* 4A **138**
Kensaleyre. *High* 3D **154**
Kensington. *G Lon* 3D **38**
Kenstone. *Shrp* 3H **71**
Kensworth. *Beds* 4A **52**
Kensworth Common. *Beds* 4A **52**
Kentallen. *High* 3E **141**
Kentchurch. *Here* 3H **47**
Kentford. *Suff* 4G **65**
Kent International (Manston) Airport. *Kent* 4H **41**
Kentisbeare. *Devn* 2D **12**
Kentisbury. *Devn* 2G **19**
Kentisbury Ford. *Devn* 2G **19**
Kentmere. *Cumb* 4F **103**
Kenton. *Devn* 4C **12**
Kenton. *G Lon* 2C **38**
Kenton. *Suff* 4D **66**
Kenton Bankfoot. *Tyne* 3F **115**
Kentra. *High* 2A **140**
Kentrigg. *Cumb* 5G **103**
Kents Bank. *Cumb* 2C **96**
Kent's Green. *Glos* 3C **48**
Kent's Oak. *Hants* 4B **24**
Kent Street. *E Sus* 4B **28**
Kent Street. *Kent* 5A **40**
Kent Street. *W Sus* 3D **26**
Kenwick. *Shrp* 2G **71**
Kenwyn. *Corn* 4C **6**
Kenyon. *Warr* 1A **84**
Keoldale. *High* 2D **166**
Keppoch. *High* 1B **148**
Kepwick. *N Yor* 5B **106**
Keresley. *W Mid* 2H **61**
Keresley Newland. *Warw* 2H **61**
Keristal. *IOM* 4C **108**
Kerne Bridge. *Here* 4A **48**
Kerridge. *Ches* 3D **84**
Kerris. *Corn* 4B **4**
Kerrow. *High* 5F **157**
Kerry. *Powy* 2D **58**
Kerrycroy. *Arg* 3C **126**
Kerry's Gate. *Here* 2G **47**
Kersall. *Notts* 4E **86**
Kersbrook. *Devn* 4D **12**
Kerse. *Ren* 4E **127**
Kersey. *Suff* 1D **54**
Kershopefoot. *Cumb* 1F **113**
Kersoe. *Worc* 2E **49**
Kerswell. *Devn* 2D **12**
Kerswell Green. *Worc* 1D **48**
Kesgrave. *Suff* 1F **55**
Kessingland. *Suff* 2H **67**
Kessingland Beach. *Suff* 2H **67**
Kestle. *Corn* 4D **6**
Kestle Mill. *Corn* 3C **6**
Keston. *G Lon* 4F **39**
Keswick. *Cumb* 2D **102**
Keswick. *Norf* 2F **79** (nr. North Walsham)
Keswick. *Norf* 5E **78** (nr. Norwich)
Ketsby. *Linc* 3C **88**
Kettering. *Nptn* 3F **63**
Ketteringham. *Norf* 5D **78**
Kettins. *Per* 5B **144**
Kettlebaston. *Suff* 5B **66**
Kettlebridge. *Fife* 3F **137**
Kettlebrook. *Staf* 5G **73**
Kettleburgh. *Suff* 4E **67**
Kettleholm. *Dum* 2C **112**
Kettleness. *N Yor* 3F **107**
Kettleshulme. *Ches* 3D **85**
Kettlesing. *N Yor* 4E **99**
Kettlesing Bottom. *N Yor* 4E **99**
Kettlestone. *Norf* 2B **78**
Kettlethorpe. *Linc* 3F **87**
Kettletoft. *Orkn* 4F **172**
Kettlewell. *N Yor* 2B **98**
Ketton. *Rut* 5G **75**
Kew. *G Lon* 3C **38**
Kewaigue. *IOM* 4C **108**
Kewstoke. *N Som* 5G **33**
Kexbrough. *S Yor* 4D **92**
Kexby. *Linc* 2F **87**
Kexby. *York* 4B **100**
Keyford. *Som* 2C **22**
Key Green. *Ches* 4C **84**
Key Green. *N Yor* 4F **107**
Keyham. *Leics* 5D **74**
Keyhaven. *Hants* 3B **16**
Keyhead. *Abers* 3H **161**
Keyingham. *E Yor* 2F **95**
Keymer. *W Sus* 4E **27**
Keynsham. *Bath* 5B **34**
Keysoe. *Beds* 4H **63**
Keysoe Row. *Beds* 4H **63**
Key's Toft. *Linc* 5D **89**
Keyston. *Cambs* 3H **63**
Key Street. *Kent* 4C **40**
Keyworth. *Notts* 2D **74**
Kibblesworth. *Tyne* 4F **115**
Kibworth Beauchamp. *Leics* 1D **62**
Kibworth Harcourt. *Leics* 1D **62**
Kidbrooke. *G Lon* 3F **39**
Kidburngill. *Cumb* 2B **102**
Kiddemore Green. *Staf* 5C **72**
Kidderminster. *Worc* 3C **60**
Kiddington. *Oxon* 3C **50**
Kidd's Moor. *Norf* 5D **78**
Kidlington. *Oxon* 4C **50**
Kidmore End. *Oxon* 4E **37**
Kidnal. *Ches* 1G **71**
Kidsgrove. *Staf* 5C **84**
Kidstones. *N Yor* 1B **98**
Kidwelly. *Carm* 5E **45**
Kiel Crofts. *Arg* 5D **140**
Kielder. *Nmbd* 5A **120**
Kilbagie. *Fife* 4B **136**
Kilbarchan. *Ren* 3F **127**
Kilbeg. *High* 3E **147**
Kilberry. *Arg* 3F **125**
Kilbirnie. *N Ayr* 4E **126**
Kilbride. *Arg* 1F **133**
Kilbride. *High* 1D **147**
Kilbucho Place. *Bord* 1C **118**
Kilburn. *Derbs* 1A **74**
Kilburn. *G Lon* 2D **38**
Kilburn. *N Yor* 2H **99**
Kilby. *Leics* 1D **62**
Kilchattan. *Arg* 4A **132** (on Colonsay)
Kilchattan. *Arg* 4C **126** (on Isle of Bute)
Kilchattan Bay. *Arg* 4B **126**
Kilchenzie. *Arg* 3A **122**

Kilcheran. *Arg* 5C 140
Kilchiaran. *Arg* 3A 124
Kilchoan. *High* 4F 147
  (nr. Inverie)
Kilchoan. *High* 2F 139
  (nr. Tobermory)
Kilchoman. *Arg* 3A 124
Kilchrenan. *Arg* 1H 133
Kilconquhar. *Fife* 3G 137
Kilcot. *Glos* 3B 48
Kilcoy. *High* 3H 157
Kilcreggan. *Arg* 1D 126
Kildale. *N Yor* 4D 106
Kildary. *High* 1B 158
Kildermorie Lodge. *High* 1H 157
Kildonan. *Dum* 4F 109
Kildonan. *High* 1G 165
  (nr. Helmsdale)
Kildonan. *High* 3C 154
  (on Isle of Skye)
Kildonan. *N Ayr* 3E 123
Kildrummy. *Abers* 2B 152
Kildwick. *N Yor* 5C 98
Kilfillan. *Dum* 4H 109
Kilfinan. *Arg* 2H 125
Kilfinnan. *High* 4E 149
Kilgetty. *Pemb* 4F 43
Kilgour. *Fife* 3E 136
Kilgrammie. *S Ayr* 4B 116
Kilham. *E Yor* 3E 101
Kilham. *Nmbd* 1C 120
Kilkenneth. *Arg* 4A 138
Kilkhampton. *Corn* 1C 10
Killamarsh. *Derbs* 2B 86
Killandrist. *Arg* 4C 140
Killay. *Swan* 3F 31
Killean. *Arg* 5E 125
Killearn. *Stir* 1G 127
Killellan. *Arg* 4A 122
Killen. *High* 3A 158
Killerby. *Darl* 3E 105
Killichonan. *Per* 3C 142
Killiechronan. *Arg* 4G 139
Killiecrankie. *Per* 2G 143
Killilan. *High* 5B 156
Killimster. *High* 3F 169
Killin. *Stir* 5C 142
Killinghall. *N Yor* 4E 99
Killinghurst. *Surr* 2A 26
Killington. *Cumb* 1F 97
Killingworth. *Tyne* 2F 115
Killin Lodge. *High* 3H 149
Killinochonoch. *Arg* 4F 133
Killochyett. *Bord* 5A 130
Killundine. *High* 4G 139
Kilmacolm. *Inv* 3E 127
Kilmahog. *Stir* 3F 135
Kilmahumaig. *Arg* 4E 133
Kilmalieu. *High* 3C 140
Kilmaluag. *High* 1D 154
Kilmany. *Fife* 1F 137
Kilmarie. *High* 2D 146
Kilmarnock. *E Ayr* 1D 116
Kilmaron. *Fife* 2F 137
Kilmartin. *Arg* 4F 133
Kilmaurs. *E Ayr* 5F 127
Kilmelford. *Arg* 2F 133
Kilmeny. *Arg* 3B 124
Kilmersdon. *Som* 1B 22
Kilmeston. *Hants* 4D 24
Kilmichael Glassary. *Arg* 4F 133
Kilmichael of Inverlussa. *Arg* 1F 125
Kilmington. *Devn* 3F 13
Kilmington. *Wilts* 3C 22
Kilmoluag. *Arg* 4A 138
Kilmorack. *High* 4G 157
Kilmore. *Arg* 1F 133
Kilmore. *High* 3E 147
Kilmory. *Arg* 1G 125
Kilmory. *High* 3B 146
  (nr. Kilchoan)
Kilmory. *High* 3B 146
  (on Rùm)
Kilmory. *N Ayr* 3D 122

Kilmory Lodge. *Arg* 3E 132
Kilmote. *High* 2G 165
Kilmuir. *High* 4B 154
  (nr. Dunvegan)
Kilmuir. *High* 1B 158
  (nr. Invergordon)
Kilmuir. *High* 4A 158
  (nr. Inverness)
Kilmuir. *High* 1C 154
  (nr. Uig)
Kilmun. *Arg* 1C 126
Kilnave. *Arg* 2A 124
Kilncadzow. *S Lan* 5B 128
Kilndown. *Kent* 2B 28
Kiln Green. *Here* 4B 48
Kiln Green. *Wind* 4G 37
Kilnhill. *Cumb* 1D 102
Kilnhurst. *S Yor* 1B 86
Kilninian. *Arg* 4E 139
Kilninver. *Arg* 1F 133
Kiln Pit Hill. *Nmbd* 4D 114
Kilnsea. *E Yor* 3H 95
Kilnsey. *N Yor* 3B 98
Kilnwick. *E Yor* 5D 101
Kiloran. *Arg* 4A 132
Kilpatrick. *N Ayr* 3D 122
Kilpeck. *Here* 2H 47
Kilpin. *E Yor* 2A 94
Kilpin Pike. *E Yor* 2A 94
Kilrenny. *Fife* 3H 137
Kilsby. *Nptn* 3C 62
Kilspindie. *Per* 1E 136
Kilsyth. *N Lan* 2A 128
Kiltarlity. *High* 4H 157
Kilton. *Som* 2E 21
Kilton Thorpe. *Red C* 3D 107
Kilvaxter. *High* 2C 154
Kilve. *Som* 2E 21
Kilvington. *Notts* 1F 75
Kilwinning. *N Ayr* 5D 126
Kimberley. *Norf* 5C 78
Kimberley. *Notts* 1B 74
Kimblesworth. *Dur* 5F 115
Kimble Wick. *Buck* 5G 51
Kimbolton. *Cambs* 4H 63
Kimbolton. *Here* 4H 59
Kimcote. *Leics* 2C 62
Kimmeridge. *Dors* 5E 15
Kimmerston. *Nmbd* 1D 120
Kimpton. *Hants* 2A 24
Kimpton. *Herts* 4B 52
Kinbeachie. *High* 2A 158
Kinbrace. *High* 5A 168
Kinbuck. *Stir* 3G 135
Kincaple. *Fife* 2G 137
Kincardine. *Fife* 1C 128
Kincardine. *High* 5D 164
Kincardine Bridge. *Fife* 1C 128
Kincardine O'Neil. *Abers* 4C 152
Kinchrackine. *Arg* 1A 134
Kincorth. *Aber* 3G 153
Kincraig. *High* 3C 150
Kincraigie. *Per* 4G 143
Kindallachan. *Per* 3G 143
Kineton. *Glos* 3F 49
Kineton. *Warw* 5H 61
Kinfauns. *Per* 1D 136
Kingairloch. *High* 3C 140
Kingarth. *Arg* 4B 126
Kingcoed. *Mon* 5H 47
Kingerby. *Linc* 1H 87
Kingham. *Oxon* 3A 50
Kingholm Quay. *Dum* 2A 112
Kinghorn. *Fife* 1F 129
Kingie. *High* 3D 148
Kinglassie. *Fife* 4E 137
Kingledores. *Bord* 2D 118
Kingodie. *Per* 1F 137
King o' Muirs. *Clac* 4A 136
King's Acre. *Here* 1H 47
Kingsand. *Corn* 3A 8
Kingsash. *Buck* 5G 51
Kingsbarns. *Fife* 2H 137
Kingsbridge. *Devn* 4D 8

Kingsbridge. *Som* 3C 20
King's Bromley. *Staf* 4F 73
Kingsburgh. *High* 3C 154
Kingsbury. *G Lon* 2C 38
Kingsbury. *Warw* 1G 61
Kingsbury Episcopi. *Som* 4H 21
Kings Caple. *Here* 3A 48
Kingscavil. *W Lot* 2D 128
Kingsclere. *Hants* 1D 24
King's Cliffe. *Nptn* 1H 63
Kingscote. *Glos* 2D 34
Kingscott. *Devn* 1F 11
Kings Coughton. *Warw* 5E 61
Kingscross. *N Ayr* 3E 123
Kingsdon. *Som* 4A 22
Kingsdown. *Kent* 1H 29
Kingsdown. *Swin* 3G 35
Kingsdown. *Wilts* 5D 34
Kingseat. *Fife* 4D 136
Kingsey. *Buck* 5F 51
Kingsfold. *Lanc* 2D 90
Kingsfold. *W Sus* 2C 26
Kingsford. *E Ayr* 5F 127
Kingsford. *Worc* 2C 60
Kingsforth. *N Lin* 3D 94
Kingsgate. *Kent* 3H 41
King's Green. *Glos* 2C 48
Kingshall Street. *Suff* 4B 66
King's Heath. *W Mid* 2E 61
Kings Hill. *Kent* 5A 40
Kingsholm. *Glos* 4D 48
Kingshouse. *High* 3G 141
Kingshouse. *Stir* 1E 135
Kingskerswell. *Devn* 2E 9
Kingskettle. *Fife* 3F 137
Kingsland. *Here* 4G 59
Kingsland. *IOA* 2B 80
Kings Langley. *Herts* 5A 52
Kingsley. *Ches* 3H 83
Kingsley. *Hants* 3F 25
Kingsley. *Staf* 1E 73
Kingsley Green. *W Sus* 3G 25
Kingsley Holt. *Staf* 1E 73
King's Lynn. *Norf* 3F 77
King's Meaburn. *Cumb* 2H 103
Kings Moss. *Mers* 4D 90
Kingsmuir. *Ang* 4D 145
Kingsmuir. *Fife* 3H 137
Kings Muir. *Bord* 1E 119
King's Newnham. *Warw* 3B 62
Kingsnorth. *Kent* 2E 28
Kingsnorth. *Medw* 3C 40
King's Norton. *Leics* 5D 74
King's Norton. *W Mid* 3E 61
King's Nympton. *Devn* 1G 11
King's Pyon. *Here* 5G 59
Kings Ripton. *Cambs* 3B 64
King's Somborne. *Hants* 3B 24
King's Stag. *Dors* 1C 14
King's Stanley. *Glos* 5D 48
King's Sutton. *Nptn* 2C 50
Kingstanding. *W Mid* 1E 61
Kingsteignton. *Devn* 5B 12
Kingsteps. *High* 3D 158
King Sterndale. *Derbs* 3E 85
King's Thorn. *Here* 2A 48
Kingsthorpe. *Nptn* 4E 63
Kingston. *Cambs* 5C 64
Kingston. *Devn* 4C 8
Kingston. *Dors* 2C 14
  (nr. Sturminster Newton)
Kingston. *Dors* 5E 15
  (nr. Swanage)
Kingston. *E Lot* 1B 130
Kingston. *Hants* 2G 15
Kingston. *IOW* 4C 16
Kingston. *Kent* 5F 41
Kingston. *Mor* 2H 159
Kingston. *W Sus* 5B 26
Kingston Bagpuize. *Oxon* 2C 36
Kingston Blount. *Oxon* 2F 37
Kingston by Sea. *W Sus* 5D 26

Kingston Deverill. *Wilts* 3D 22
Kingstone. *Here* 2H 47
Kingstone. *Som* 1G 13
Kingstone. *Staf* 3E 73
Kingston Lisle. *Oxon* 3B 36
Kingston Maurward. *Dors* 3C 14
Kingston near Lewes. *E Sus* 5E 27
Kingston on Soar. *Notts* 3C 74
Kingston Russell. *Dors* 3A 14
Kingston St Mary. *Som* 4F 21
Kingston Seymour. *N Som* 5H 33
Kingston Stert. *Oxon* 5F 51
Kingston upon Hull. *Hull* 2D 94
Kingston upon Thames.
  G Lon 4C 38
King's Walden. *Herts* 3B 52
Kingswear. *Devn* 3E 9
Kingswells. *Aber* 3F 153
Kingswinford. *W Mid* 2C 60
Kingswood. *Buck* 4E 51
Kingswood. *Glos* 2C 34
Kingswood. *Here* 5E 59
Kingswood. *Kent* 5C 40
Kingswood. *Per* 5H 143
Kingswood. *Powy* 5E 70
Kingswood. *Som* 3E 21
Kingswood. *S Glo* 4B 34
Kingswood. *Surr* 5D 38
Kingswood. *Warw* 3F 61
Kingswood Common. *Staf* 5C 72
Kings Worthy. *Hants* 3C 24
Kingthorpe. *Linc* 3A 88
Kington. *Here* 5F 59
Kington. *S Glo* 2B 34
Kington. *Worc* 5D 61
Kington Langley. *Wilts* 4E 35
Kington Magna. *Dors* 4C 22
Kington St Michael. *Wilts* 4E 35
Kingussie. *High* 3B 150
Kingweston. *Som* 3A 22
Kinharrachie. *Abers* 5G 161
Kinhrive. *High* 1B 158
Kinkell Bridge. *Per* 2B 136
Kinknockie. *Abers* 4H 161
Kinkry Hill. *Cumb* 2G 113
Kinlet. *Shrp* 2B 60
Kinloch. *High* 5D 166
  (nr. Loch More)
Kinloch. *High* 3A 140
  (nr. Lochaline)
Kinloch. *High* 4C 146
  (on Rùm)
Kinloch. *Per* 4A 144
Kinlochard. *Stir* 3D 134
Kinlochbervie. *High* 3C 166
Kinlocheil. *High* 1D 141
Kinlochewe. *High* 2C 156
Kinloch Hourn. *High* 3B 148
Kinloch Laggan. *High* 5H 149
Kinlochleven. *High* 2F 141
Kinloch Lodge. *High* 3F 167
Kinlochmoidart. *High* 1B 140
Kinlochmore. *High* 2F 141
Kinloch Rannoch. *Per* 3D 142
Kinlochspelve. *Arg* 1D 132
Kinloid. *High* 5E 147
Kinloss. *Mor* 2E 159
Kinmel Bay. *Cnwy* 2B 82
Kinmuck. *Abers* 2F 153
Kinnadie. *Abers* 4G 161
Kinnaird. *Per* 1E 137
Kinneff. *Abers* 1H 145
Kinnelhead. *Dum* 4C 118
Kinnell. *Ang* 3F 145
Kinnerley. *Shrp* 3F 71
Kinnernie. *Abers* 2E 152
Kinnersley. *Here* 1G 47
Kinnersley. *Worc* 1D 48
Kinnerton. *Powy* 4E 59
Kinnerton. *Shrp* 1F 59
Kinnesswood. *Per* 3D 136
Kinninvie. *Dur* 2D 104
Kinnordy. *Ang* 3C 144
Kinoulton. *Notts* 2D 74

Kinross. *Per* 3D 136
Kinrossie. *Per* 5A 144
Kinsbourne Green. *Herts* 4B 52
Kinsey Heath. *Ches* 1A 72
Kinsham. *Here* 4F 59
Kinsham. *Worc* 2E 49
Kinsley. *W Yor* 3E 93
Kinson. *Bour* 3F 15
Kintbury. *W Ber* 5B 36
Kintessack. *Mor* 2E 159
Kintillo. *Per* 2D 136
Kinton. *Here* 3G 59
Kinton. *Shrp* 4F 71
Kintore. *Abers* 2E 153
Kintour. *Arg* 4C 124
Kintra. *Arg* 2B 132
Kintraw. *Arg* 3F 133
Kinveachy. *High* 2D 150
Kinver. *Staf* 2C 60
Kinwarton. *Warw* 5F 61
Kiplingcotes. *E Yor* 5D 100
Kippax. *W Yor* 1E 93
Kippen. *Stir* 4F 135
Kippford. *Dum* 4F 111
Kipping's Cross. *Kent* 1H 27
Kirbister. *Orkn* 7C 172
Kirby Bedon. *Norf* 5E 79
Kirby Bellars. *Leics* 4E 74
Kirby Cane. *Norf* 1F 67
Kirby Cross. *Essx* 3F 55
Kirby Fields. *Leics* 5C 74
Kirby Grindalythe. *N Yor* 3D 100
Kirby Hill. *N Yor* 4E 105
  (nr. Richmond)
Kirby Hill. *N Yor* 3F 99
  (nr. Ripon)
Kirby Knowle. *N Yor* 1G 99
Kirby-le-Soken. *Essx* 3F 55
Kirby Misperton. *N Yor* 2B 100
Kirby Muxloe. *Leics* 5C 74
Kirby Row. *Norf* 1F 67
Kirby Sigston. *N Yor* 5B 106
Kirby Underdale. *E Yor* 4C 100
Kirby Wiske. *N Yor* 1F 99
Kirdford. *W Sus* 3B 26
Kirk. *High* 3E 169
Kirkabister. *Shet* 6F 173
Kirkandrews. *Dum* 5D 110
Kirkandrews-on-Eden. *Cumb* 4E 113
Kirkapol. *Arg* 4B 138
Kirkbampton. *Cumb* 4E 112
Kirkbean. *Dum* 4A 112
Kirk Bramwith. *S Yor* 3G 93
Kirkbride. *Cumb* 4D 112
Kirkbridge. *N Yor* 5F 105
Kirkburn. *E Yor* 4D 101
Kirkburton. *W Yor* 3B 92
Kirkby. *Linc* 1H 87
Kirkby. *Mers* 1G 83
Kirkby. *N Yor* 4C 106
Kirkby Fenside. *Linc* 4C 88
Kirkby Fleetham. *N Yor* 5F 105
Kirkby Green. *Linc* 5H 87
Kirkby-in-Ashfield. *Notts* 5C 86
Kirkby Industrial Estate.
  Mers 1G 83
Kirkby-in-Furness. *Cumb* 1B 96
Kirkby la Thorpe. *Linc* 1A 76
Kirkby Lonsdale. *Cumb* 2F 97
Kirkby Malham. *N Yor* 3A 98
Kirkby Mallory. *Leics* 5B 74
Kirkby Malzeard. *N Yor* 2E 99
Kirkby Mills. *N Yor* 1B 100
Kirkbymoorside. *N Yor* 1A 100
Kirkby on Bain. *Linc* 4B 88
Kirkby Overblow. *N Yor* 5F 99
Kirkby Stephen. *Cumb* 4A 104
Kirkby Thore. *Cumb* 2H 103
Kirkby Underwood. *Linc* 3H 75
Kirkby Wharfe. *N Yor* 5H 99
Kirkcaldy. *Fife* 4E 137
Kirkcambeck. *Cumb* 3G 113
Kirkcolm. *Dum* 3F 109

Kirkconnel—Lane

Kirkconnel. *Dum* 3G 117
Kirkconnell. *Dum* 3A 112
Kirkcowan. *Dum* 3A 110
Kirkcudbright. *Dum* 4D 111
Kirkdale. *Mers* 1F 83
Kirk Deighton. *N Yor* 4F 99
Kirk Ella. *E Yor* 2D 94
Kirkfieldbank. *S Lan* 5B 128
Kirkforthar Feus. *Fife* 3E 137
Kirkgunzeon. *Dum* 3F 111
Kirk Hallam. *Derbs* 1B 74
Kirkham. *Lanc* 1C 90
Kirkham. *N Yor* 3B 100
Kirkhamgate. *W Yor* 2C 92
Kirk Hammerton. *N Yor* 4G 99
Kirkharle. *Nmbd* 1D 114
Kirkheaton. *Nmbd* 2D 114
Kirkheaton. *W Yor* 3B 92
Kirkhill. *Ang* 2F 145
Kirkhill. *High* 4H 157
Kirkhope. *S Lan* 4B 118
Kirkhouse. *Bord* 1F 119
Kirkibost. *High* 2D 146
Kirkinch. *Ang* 4C 144
Kirkinner. *Dum* 4B 110
Kirkintilloch. *E Dun* 2H 127
Kirk Ireton. *Derbs* 5G 85
Kirkland. *Cumb* 3B 102
(nr. Cleator Moor)
Kirkland. *Cumb* 1H 103
(nr. Penrith)
Kirkland. *Cumb* 5D 112
(nr. Wigton)
Kirkland. *Dum* 3G 117
(nr. Kirkconnel)
Kirkland. *Dum* 5H 117
(nr. Moniaive)
Kirkland Guards. *Cumb* 5C 112
Kirk Langley. *Derbs* 2G 73
Kirklauchline. *Dum* 4F 109
Kirkleatham. *Red C* 2C 106
Kirklevington. *Stoc T* 4B 106
Kirkley. *Suff* 1H 67
Kirklington. *N Yor* 1F 99
Kirklington. *Notts* 5D 86
Kirklinton. *Cumb* 3F 113
Kirkliston. *Edin* 2E 129
Kirkmabreck. *Dum* 4B 110
Kirkmaiden. *Dum* 5E 109
Kirk Merrington. *Dur* 1F 105
Kirk Michael. *IOM* 2C 108
Kirkmichael. *Per* 2H 143
Kirkmichael. *S Ayr* 4C 116
Kirkmuirhill. *S Lan* 5A 128
Kirknewton. *Nmbd* 1D 120
Kirknewton. *W Lot* 3E 129
Kirkney. *Abers* 5C 160
Kirk of Shotts. *N Lan* 3B 128
Kirkoswald. *Cumb* 5G 113
Kirkoswald. *S Ayr* 4B 116
Kirkpatrick. *Dum* 5B 118
Kirkpatrick Durham. *Dum* 2E 111
Kirkpatrick-Fleming. *Dum* 2D 112
Kirk Sandall. *S Yor* 4G 93
Kirksanton. *Cumb* 1A 96
Kirk Smeaton. *N Yor* 3F 93
Kirkstall. *W Yor* 1C 92
Kirkstile. *Dum* 5F 119
Kirkstyle. *High* 1F 169
Kirkthorpe. *W Yor* 2D 92
Kirkton. *Abers* 2D 152
(nr. Alford)
Kirkton. *Abers* 1D 152
(nr. Insch)
Kirkton. *Abers* 4F 161
(nr. Turriff)
Kirkton. *Ang* 5D 144
(nr. Dundee)
Kirkton. *Ang* 4D 144
(nr. Forfar)
Kirkton. *Ang* 5B 152
(nr. Tarfside)
Kirkton. *Dum* 1A 112
Kirkton. *Fife* 1F 137
Kirkton. *High* 4E 165
(nr. Golspie)
Kirkton. *High* 1G 147
(nr. Kyle of Lochalsh)
Kirkton. *High* 4B 156
(nr. Lochcarron)
Kirkton. *Bord* 3H 119
Kirkton. *S Lan* 2B 118
Kirktonhill. *W Dun* 2E 127
Kirkton Manor. *Bord* 1E 118
Kirkton of Airlie. *Ang* 3C 144
Kirkton of Auchterhouse.
Ang 5C 144
Kirkton of Bourtie. *Abers* 1F 153
Kirkton of Collace. *Per* 5A 144
Kirkton of Craig. *Ang* 3G 145
Kirkton of Culsalmond.
Abers 5D 160
Kirkton of Durris. *Abers* 4E 153
Kirkton of Glenbuchat.
Abers 2A 152
Kirkton of Glenisla. *Ang* 2B 144
Kirkton of Kingoldrum. *Ang* 3C 144
Kirkton of Largo. *Fife* 3G 137
Kirkton of Lethendy. *Per* 4A 144
Kirkton of Logie Buchan.
Abers 1G 153
Kirkton of Maryculter. *Abers* 4F 153
Kirkton of Menmuir. *Ang* 2E 145
Kirkton of Monikie. *Ang* 5E 145
Kirkton of Oyne. *Abers* 1D 152
Kirkton of Rayne. *Abers* 5D 160
Kirkton of Skene. *Abers* 3F 153
Kirktown. *Abers* 2G 161
(nr. Fraserburgh)
Kirktown. *Abers* 3H 161
(nr. Peterhead)
Kirktown of Alvah. *Abers* 2D 160
Kirktown of Auchterless.
Abers 4E 160
Kirktown of Deskford. *Mor* 2C 160
Kirktown of Fetteresso.
Abers 5F 153
Kirktown of Mortlach. *Mor* 5H 159
Kirktown of Slains. *Abers* 1H 153
Kirkurd. *Bord* 5E 129
Kirkwall. *Orkn* 6D 172
Kirkwall Airport. *Orkn* 7D 172
Kirkwhelpington. *Nmbd* 1C 114
Kirk Yetholm. *Bord* 2C 120
Kirmington. *N Lin* 3E 94
Kirmond le Mire. *Linc* 1A 88
Kirn. *Arg* 2C 126
Kirriemuir. *Ang* 3C 144
Kirstead Green. *Norf* 1E 67
Kirtlebridge. *Dum* 2D 112
Kirtleton. *Dum* 2D 112
Kirtling. *Cambs* 5F 65
Kirtling Green. *Cambs* 5F 65
Kirtlington. *Oxon* 4D 50
Kirtomy. *High* 2H 167
Kirton. *Linc* 2C 76
Kirton. *Notts* 4D 86
Kirton. *Suff* 2F 55
Kirton End. *Linc* 1B 76
Kirton Holme. *Linc* 1B 76
Kirton in Lindsey. *N Lin* 1G 87
Kishorn. *High* 4H 155
Kislingbury. *Nptn* 5D 62
Kite Hill. *IOW* 3D 16
Kites Hardwick. *Warw* 4B 62
Kittisford. *Som* 4D 20
Kittle. *Swan* 4E 31
Kittybrowster. *Aber* 3G 153
Kitwood. *Hants* 3E 25
Kivernoll. *Here* 2H 47
Kiveton Park. *S Yor* 2B 86
Knaith. *Linc* 2F 87
Knaith Park. *Linc* 2F 87
Knap Corner. *Dors* 4D 22
Knaphill. *Surr* 5A 38
Knapp. *Hants* 4C 24
Knapp. *Per* 5B 144
Knapp. *Som* 4G 21
Knapperfield. *High* 3E 169
Knapton. *Norf* 2F 79
Knapton. *York* 4H 99
Knapton Green. *Here* 5G 59
Knapwell. *Cambs* 4C 64
Knaresborough. *N Yor* 4F 99
Knarsdale. *Nmbd* 4H 113
Knatts Valley. *Kent* 4G 39
Knaven. *Abers* 4F 161
Knayton. *N Yor* 1G 99
Knebworth. *Herts* 3C 52
Knedlington. *E Yor* 2H 93
Kneesall. *Notts* 4E 86
Kneesworth. *Cambs* 1D 52
Kneeton. *Notts* 1E 74
Knelston. *Swan* 4D 30
Knenhall. *Staf* 2D 72
Knightacott. *Devn* 3G 19
Knightcote. *Warw* 5B 62
Knightcott. *N Som* 1G 21
Knightley. *Staf* 3C 72
Knightley Dale. *Staf* 3C 72
Knightlow Hill. *Warw* 3B 62
Knighton. *Devn* 4B 8
Knighton. *Dors* 1B 14
Knighton. *Leic* 5D 74
Knighton. *Powy* 3E 59
Knighton. *Som* 2E 21
Knighton. *Staf* 3B 72
Knighton. *Wilts* 4A 36
Knighton. *Worc* 5E 61
Knighton Common. *Worc* 3A 60
Knight's End. *Cambs* 1D 64
Knightswood. *Glas* 3G 127
Knightwick. *Worc* 5B 60
Knill. *Here* 4E 59
Knipton. *Leics* 2F 75
Knitsley. *Dur* 5E 115
Kniveton. *Derbs* 5G 85
Knock. *Arg* 5G 139
Knock. *Cumb* 2H 103
Knock. *Mor* 3C 160
Knockally. *High* 5D 168
Knockan. *Arg* 1B 132
Knockan. *High* 2G 163
Knockandhu. *Mor* 1G 151
Knockando. *Mor* 4F 159
Knockarthur. *High* 3E 165
Knockbain. *High* 3A 158
Knockbreck. *High* 2B 154
Knockdee. *High* 2D 168
Knockdolian. *S Ayr* 1G 109
Knockdon. *S Ayr* 3C 116
Knockdown. *Glos* 3D 34
Knockenbaird. *Abers* 1D 152
Knockenkelly. *N Ayr* 3E 123
Knockentiber. *E Ayr* 1C 116
Knockfarrel. *High* 3H 157
Knockglass. *High* 2C 168
Knockholt. *Kent* 5F 39
Knockholt Pound. *Kent* 5F 39
Knockie Lodge. *High* 2G 149
Knockin. *Shrp* 3F 71
Knockinlaw. *E Ayr* 1D 116
Knockinnon. *High* 5D 169
Knockrome. *Arg* 2D 124
Knocksharry. *IOM* 3B 108
Knockshinnoch. *E Ayr* 3D 116
Knockvennie. *Dum* 2E 111
Knockvologan. *Arg* 3B 132
Knodishall. *Suff* 4G 67
Knole. *Som* 4H 21
Knollbury. *Mon* 3H 33
Knolls Green. *Ches* 3C 84
Knolton. *Wrex* 2F 71
Knook. *Wilts* 2E 23
Knossington. *Leics* 5F 75
Knott. *High* 3C 154
Knott End-on-Sea. *Lanc* 5C 96
Knotting. *Beds* 4H 63
Knotting Green. *Beds* 4H 63
Knottingley. *W Yor* 2E 93
Knotts. *Cumb* 2F 103
Knotty Ash. *Mers* 1G 83
Knotty Green. *Buck* 1A 38
Knowbury. *Shrp* 3H 59
Knowe. *Dum* 2A 110
Knowefield. *Cumb* 4F 113
Knowehead. *Dum* 5F 117
Knowes. *E Lot* 2C 130
Knowesgate. *Nmbd* 1C 114
Knoweside. *S Ayr* 3B 116
Knowle. *Bris* 4A 34
Knowle. *Devn* 3E 19
(nr. Braunton)
Knowle. *Devn* 4D 12
(nr. Budleigh Salterton)
Knowle. *Devn* 2A 12
(nr. Crediton)
Knowle. *Shrp* 3H 59
Knowle. *W Mid* 3F 61
Knowle Green. *Lanc* 1E 91
Knowle St Giles. *Som* 1G 13
Knowles of Elrick. *Abers* 3D 160
Knowle Village. *Hants* 2D 16
Knowl Hill. *Wind* 4G 37
Knowlton. *Kent* 5G 41
Knowsley. *Mers* 1G 83
Knowstone. *Devn* 4B 20
Knucklas. *Powy* 3E 59
Knuston. *Nptn* 4G 63
Knutsford. *Ches* 3B 84
Knypersley. *Staf* 5C 84
Krumlin. *W Yor* 3A 92
Kuggar. *Corn* 5E 5
Kyleakin. *High* 1F 147
Kyle of Lochalsh. *High* 1F 147
Kylerhea. *High* 1F 147
Kylesku. *High* 5C 166
Kyles Lodge. *W Isl* 9B 171
Kylesmorar. *High* 4G 147
Kylestrome. *High* 5C 166
Kymin. *Mon* 4A 48
Kynaston. *Here* 2B 48
Kynaston. *Shrp* 3F 71
Kynnersley. *Telf* 4A 72
Kyre Green. *Worc* 4A 60
Kyre Park. *Worc* 4A 60
Kyrewood. *Worc* 4A 60
Kyrle. *Som* 4D 20

L

Labost. *W Isl* 3E 171
Lacasaidh. *W Isl* 5F 171
Lacasdail. *W Isl* 4G 171
Laceby. *NE Lin* 4F 95
Lacey Green. *Buck* 5G 51
Lach Dennis. *Ches* 3B 84
Lache. *Ches* 4F 83
Lackford. *Suff* 3G 65
Lacock. *Wilts* 5E 35
Ladbroke. *Warw* 5B 62
Laddingford. *Kent* 1A 28
Lade Bank. *Linc* 5C 88
Ladock. *Corn* 3C 6
Ladybank. *Fife* 2F 137
Ladycross. *Corn* 4D 10
Lady Green. *Mers* 4B 90
Lady Hall. *Cumb* 1A 96
Ladykirk. *Bord* 5E 131
Ladysford. *Abers* 2G 161
Ladywood. *W Mid* 2E 61
Ladywood. *Worc* 4C 60
Laga. *High* 2A 140
Lagavulin. *Arg* 5C 124
Lagg. *Arg* 2D 125
Lagg. *N Ayr* 3D 122
Laggan. *Arg* 4A 124
Laggan. *High* 4E 149
(nr. Fort Augustus)
Laggan. *High* 4A 150
(nr. Newtonmore)
Laggan. *Mor* 5H 159
Lagganlia. *High* 3C 150
Lagganulva. *Arg* 4F 139
Laglingarten. *Arg* 3A 134
Lagness. *W Sus* 2G 17
Laid. *High* 3E 166
Laide. *High* 4D 162
Laigh Fenwick. *E Ayr* 5F 127
Laindon. *Essx* 2A 40
Lairg. *High* 3C 164
Lairg Muir. *High* 3C 164
Laithes. *Cumb* 1F 103
Laithkirk. *Dur* 2C 104
Lake. *Devn* 3F 19
Lake. *IOW* 4D 16
Lake. *Wilts* 3G 23
Lakenham. *Norf* 5E 79
Lakenheath. *Suff* 2G 65
Lakesend. *Norf* 1E 65
Lakeside. *Cumb* 1C 96
Laleham. *Surr* 4B 38
Laleston. *B'end* 3B 32
Lamancha. *Bord* 4F 129
Lamarsh. *Essx* 2B 54
Lamas. *Norf* 3E 79
Lamb Corner. *Essx* 2D 54
Lambden. *Bord* 5D 130
Lamberhead Green. *G Man* 4D 90
Lamberhurst. *Kent* 2A 28
Lamberhurst Quarter. *Kent* 2A 28
Lamberton. *Bord* 4F 131
Lambeth. *G Lon* 3E 39
Lambfell Moar. *IOM* 3B 108
Lambhill. *Glas* 3G 127
Lambley. *Nmbd* 4H 113
Lambley. *Notts* 1D 74
Lambourn. *W Ber* 4B 36
Lambourne End. *Essx* 1F 39
Lambourn Woodlands. *W Ber* 4B 36
Lambrook. *Som* 4F 21
Lambs Green. *Dors* 3E 15
Lambs Green. *W Sus* 2D 26
Lambston. *Pemb* 3D 42
Lamellion. *Corn* 2G 7
Lamerton. *Devn* 5E 11
Lamesley. *Tyne* 4F 115
Laminess. *Orkn* 4F 172
Lamington. *High* 1B 158
Lamington. *S Lan* 1B 118
Lamlash. *N Ayr* 2E 123
Lamonby. *Cumb* 1F 103
Lamorick. *Corn* 2E 7
Lamorna. *Corn* 4B 4
Lamorran. *Corn* 4C 6
Lampeter. *Cdgn* 1F 45
Lampeter Velfrey. *Pemb* 3F 43
Lamphey. *Pemb* 4E 43
Lamplugh. *Cumb* 2B 102
Lamport. *Nptn* 3E 63
Lamyatt. *Som* 3B 22
Lana. *Devn* 3D 10
(nr. Ashwater)
Lana. *Devn* 2D 10
(nr. Holsworthy)
Lanark. *S Lan* 5B 128
Lanarth. *Corn* 4E 5
Lancaster. *Lanc* 3D 97
Lanchester. *Dur* 5E 115
Lancing. *W Sus* 5C 26
Landbeach. *Cambs* 4D 64
Landcross. *Devn* 4E 19
Landerberry. *Abers* 3E 153
Landford. *Wilts* 1A 16
Land Gate. *G Man* 4D 90
Landhallow. *High* 5D 169
Landimore. *Swan* 3D 30
Landkey. *Devn* 3F 19
Landkey Newland. *Devn* 3F 19
Landore. *Swan* 3F 31
Landport. *Port* 2E 17
Landrake. *Corn* 2H 7
Landscove. *Devn* 2D 9
Land's End (St Just) Airport.
Corn 4A 4
Landshipping. *Pemb* 3E 43
Landulph. *Corn* 2A 8
Landywood. *Staf* 5D 73
Lane. *Corn* 2C 6

Laneast. *Corn* . . . 4C **10**
Lane Bottom. *Lanc* . . . 1G **91**
Lane End. *Buck* . . . 2G **37**
Lane End. *Cumb* . . . 5C **102**
Lane End. *Hants* . . . 4D **24**
Lane End. *IOW* . . . 4E **17**
Lane End. *Wilts* . . . 2D **22**
Lane Ends. *Derbs* . . . 2G **73**
Lane Ends. *Dur* . . . 1E **105**
Lane Ends. *Lanc* . . . 4G **97**
Laneham. *Notts* . . . 3F **87**
Lanehead. *Dur* . . . 5B **114**
(nr. Cowshill)
Lane Head. *Dur* . . . 3E **105**
(nr. Hutton Magna)
Lane Head. *Dur* . . . 2D **105**
(nr. Woodland)
Lane Head. *G Man* . . . 1A **84**
Lanehead. *Nmbd* . . . 1A **114**
Lane Head. *W Yor* . . . 4B **92**
Lane Heads. *Lanc* . . . 1C **90**
Lanercost. *Cumb* . . . 3G **113**
Laneshaw Bridge. *Lanc* . . . 5B **98**
Laney Green. *Staf* . . . 5D **72**
Langais. *W Isl* . . . 2D **170**
Langal. *High* . . . 2B **140**
Langar. *Notts* . . . 2E **74**
Langbank. *Ren* . . . 2E **127**
Langbar. *N Yor* . . . 4C **98**
Langburnshiels. *Bord* . . . 4H **119**
Langcliffe. *N Yor* . . . 3H **97**
Langdale End. *N Yor* . . . 5G **107**
Langdon. *Corn* . . . 3C **10**
Langdon Beck. *Dur* . . . 1B **104**
Langdon Cross. *Corn* . . . 4D **10**
Langdon Hills. *Essx* . . . 2A **40**
Langdown. *Hants* . . . 2C **16**
Langdyke. *Fife* . . . 3F **137**
Langenhoe. *Essx* . . . 4D **54**
Langford. *Beds* . . . 1B **52**
Langford. *Devn* . . . 2D **12**
Langford. *Essx* . . . 5B **54**
Langford. *Notts* . . . 5F **87**
Langford. *Oxon* . . . 5H **49**
Langford Budville. *Som* . . . 4E **20**
Langham. *Dors* . . . 4C **22**
Langham. *Essx* . . . 2D **54**
Langham. *Norf* . . . 1C **78**
Langham. *Rut* . . . 4F **75**
Langham. *Suff* . . . 4B **66**
Langho. *Lanc* . . . 1F **91**
Langholm. *Dum* . . . 1E **113**
Langland. *Swan* . . . 4F **31**
Langleeford. *Nmbd* . . . 2D **120**
Langley. *Ches* . . . 3D **84**
Langley. *Derbs* . . . 1B **74**
Langley. *Essx* . . . 2E **53**
Langley. *Glos* . . . 3F **49**
Langley. *Hants* . . . 2C **16**
Langley. *Herts* . . . 3C **52**
Langley. *Kent* . . . 5C **40**
Langley. *Nmbd* . . . 3B **114**
Langley. *Slo* . . . 3B **38**
Langley. *Som* . . . 4D **20**
Langley. *Warw* . . . 4F **61**
Langley. *W Sus* . . . 4G **25**
Langley Burrell. *Wilts* . . . 4E **35**
Langleybury. *Herts* . . . 5A **52**
Langley Common. *Derbs* . . . 2G **73**
Langley Green. *Derbs* . . . 2G **73**
Langley Green. *Norf* . . . 5F **79**
Langley Green. *Warw* . . . 4F **61**
Langley Green. *W Sus* . . . 2D **26**
Langley Heath. *Kent* . . . 5C **40**
Langley Marsh. *Som* . . . 4D **20**
Langley Moor. *Dur* . . . 5F **115**
Langley Park. *Dur* . . . 5F **115**
Langley Street. *Norf* . . . 5F **79**
Langney. *E Sus* . . . 5H **27**
Langold. *Notts* . . . 2C **86**
Langore. *Corn* . . . 4D **10**
Langport. *Som* . . . 4H **21**
Langrick. *Linc* . . . 1B **76**
Langridge. *Bath* . . . 5C **34**
Langridgeford. *Devn* . . . 4F **19**
Langrigg. *Cumb* . . . 5C **112**
Langrish. *Hants* . . . 4F **25**
Langsett. *S Yor* . . . 4C **92**
Langshaw. *Bord* . . . 1H **119**
Langstone. *Hants* . . . 2F **17**
Langthorne. *N Yor* . . . 5F **105**
Langthorpe. *N Yor* . . . 3F **99**
Langthwaite. *N Yor* . . . 4D **104**
Langtoft. *E Yor* . . . 3E **101**
Langtoft. *Linc* . . . 4A **76**
Langton. *Dur* . . . 3E **105**
Langton. *Linc* . . . 4B **88**
(nr. Horncastle)
Langton. *Linc* . . . 3C **88**
(nr. Spilsby)
Langton. *N Yor* . . . 3B **100**
Langton by Wragby. *Linc* . . . 3A **88**
Langton Green. *Kent* . . . 2G **27**
Langton Herring. *Dors* . . . 4B **14**
Langton Long Blandford.
Dors . . . 2E **15**
Langton Matravers. *Dors* . . . 5F **15**
Langtree. *Devn* . . . 1E **11**
Langwathby. *Cumb* . . . 1G **103**
Langwith. *Derbs* . . . 4C **86**
Langworth. *Linc* . . . 3H **87**
Lanivet. *Corn* . . . 2E **7**
Lanjeth. *Corn* . . . 3D **6**
Lank. *Corn* . . . 5A **10**
Lanlivery. *Corn* . . . 3E **7**
Lanner. *Corn* . . . 5B **6**
Lanreath. *Corn* . . . 3F **7**
Lansallos. *Corn* . . . 3F **7**
Lansdown. *Bath* . . . 5C **34**
Lansdown. *Glos* . . . 3E **49**
Lanteglos Highway. *Corn* . . . 3F **7**
Lanton. *Nmbd* . . . 1D **120**
Lanton. *Bord* . . . 2A **120**
Lapford. *Devn* . . . 2H **11**
Laphroaig. *Arg* . . . 5B **124**
Lapley. *Staf* . . . 4C **72**
Lapworth. *Warw* . . . 3F **61**
Larachbeg. *High* . . . 4A **140**
Larbert. *Falk* . . . 1B **128**
Larden Green. *Ches* . . . 5H **83**
Larel. *High* . . . 3D **169**
Largie. *Abers* . . . 5D **160**
Largiemore. *Arg* . . . 1H **125**
Largoward. *Fife* . . . 3G **137**
Largs. *N Ayr* . . . 4D **126**
Largue. *Abers* . . . 4D **160**
Largybeg. *N Ayr* . . . 3E **123**
Largymeanoch. *N Ayr* . . . 3E **123**
Largymore. *N Ayr* . . . 3E **123**
Larkfield. *Inv* . . . 2D **126**
Larkfield. *Kent* . . . 5A **40**
Larkhall. *Bath* . . . 5C **34**
Larkhall. *S Lan* . . . 4A **128**
Larkhill. *Wilts* . . . 2G **23**
Larling. *Norf* . . . 2B **66**
Larport. *Here* . . . 2A **48**
Lartington. *Dur* . . . 3D **104**
Lary. *Abers* . . . 3H **151**
Lasham. *Hants* . . . 2E **25**
Lashenden. *Kent* . . . 1C **28**
Lassodie. *Fife* . . . 4D **136**
Lasswade. *Midl* . . . 3G **129**
Lastingham. *N Yor* . . . 5E **107**
Latchford. *Herts* . . . 3D **53**
Latchford. *Oxon* . . . 5E **51**
Latchingdon. *Essx* . . . 5B **54**
Latchley. *Corn* . . . 5E **11**
Latchmere Green. *Hants* . . . 5E **37**
Lathbury. *Mil* . . . 1G **51**
Latheron. *High* . . . 5D **169**
Latheronwheel. *High* . . . 5D **169**
Lathom. *Lanc* . . . 4C **90**
Lathones. *Fife* . . . 3G **137**
Latimer. *Buck* . . . 1B **38**
Latteridge. *S Glo* . . . 3B **34**
Lattiford. *Som* . . . 4B **22**
Latton. *Wilts* . . . 2F **35**
Laudale House. *High* . . . 3B **140**
Lauder. *Bord* . . . 5B **130**
Laugharne. *Carm* . . . 3H **43**
Laughterton. *Linc* . . . 3F **87**
Laughton. *E Sus* . . . 4G **27**
Laughton. *Leics* . . . 2D **62**
Laughton. *Linc* . . . 1F **87**
(nr. Gainsborough)
Laughton. *Linc* . . . 2H **75**
(nr. Grantham)
Laughton Common. *S Yor* . . . 2C **86**
Laughton en le Morthen.
S Yor . . . 2C **86**
Launcells. *Corn* . . . 2C **10**
Launceston. *Corn* . . . 4D **10**
Launcherley. *Som* . . . 2A **22**
Launton. *Oxon* . . . 3E **50**
Laurencekirk. *Abers* . . . 1G **145**
Laurieston. *Dum* . . . 3D **111**
Laurieston. *Falk* . . . 2C **128**
Lavendon. *Mil* . . . 5G **63**
Lavenham. *Suff* . . . 1C **54**
Laverhay. *Dum* . . . 5D **118**
Laversdale. *Cumb* . . . 3F **113**
Laverstock. *Wilts* . . . 3G **23**
Laverstoke. *Hants* . . . 2C **24**
Laverton. *Glos* . . . 2F **49**
Laverton. *N Yor* . . . 2E **99**
Laverton. *Som* . . . 1C **22**
Lavister. *Wrex* . . . 5F **83**
Law. *S Lan* . . . 4B **128**
Lawers. *Per* . . . 5D **142**
Lawford. *Essx* . . . 2D **54**
Lawhitton. *Corn* . . . 4D **10**
Lawkland. *N Yor* . . . 3G **97**
Lawnhead. *Staf* . . . 3C **72**
Lawrenny. *Pemb* . . . 4E **43**
Lawshall. *Suff* . . . 5A **66**
Lawton. *Here* . . . 5G **59**
Laxey. *IOM* . . . 3D **108**
Laxfield. *Suff* . . . 3E **67**
Laxfirth. *Shet* . . . 6F **173**
Laxo. *Shet* . . . 5F **173**
Laxton. *E Yor* . . . 2A **94**
Laxton. *Nptn* . . . 1G **63**
Laxton. *Notts* . . . 4E **86**
Laycock. *W Yor* . . . 5C **98**
Layer Breton. *Essx* . . . 4C **54**
Layer-de-la-Haye. *Essx* . . . 3C **54**
Layer Marney. *Essx* . . . 4C **54**
Layland's Green. *W Ber* . . . 5B **36**
Laymore. *Dors* . . . 2G **13**
Laysters Pole. *Here* . . . 4H **59**
Layter's Green. *Buck* . . . 1A **38**
Laytham. *E Yor* . . . 1H **93**
Lazenby. *Red C* . . . 3C **106**
Lazonby. *Cumb* . . . 1G **103**
Lea. *Derbs* . . . 5H **85**
Lea. *Here* . . . 3B **48**
Lea. *Linc* . . . 2F **87**
Lea. *Shrp* . . . 2F **59**
(nr. Bishop's Castle)
Lea. *Shrp* . . . 5G **71**
(nr. Shrewsbury)
Lea. *Wilts* . . . 3E **35**
Leabrooks. *Derbs* . . . 5B **86**
Leachd. *Arg* . . . 4H **133**
Leachkin. *High* . . . 4A **158**
Leachpool. *Pemb* . . . 3D **42**
Leadburn. *Midl* . . . 4F **129**
Leadenham. *Linc* . . . 5G **87**
Leaden Roding. *Essx* . . . 4F **53**
Leaderfoot. *Bord* . . . 1H **119**
Leadgate. *Cumb* . . . 5A **114**
Leadgate. *Dur* . . . 4E **115**
Leadgate. *Nmbd* . . . 4E **115**
Leadhills. *S Lan* . . . 3A **118**
Leadingcross Green. *Kent* . . . 5C **40**
Lea End. *Worc* . . . 3E **61**
Leafield. *Oxon* . . . 4B **50**
Leagrave. *Lutn* . . . 3A **52**
Lea Hall. *W Mid* . . . 2F **61**
Lea Heath. *Staf* . . . 3E **73**
Leake. *N Yor* . . . 5B **106**
Leake Common Side. *Linc* . . . 5C **88**
Leake Fold Hill. *Linc* . . . 5D **88**
Leake Hurn's End. *Linc* . . . 1D **76**
Lealholm. *N Yor* . . . 4E **107**
Lealt. *Arg* . . . 4D **132**
Lealt. *High* . . . 2E **155**
Leam. *Derbs* . . . 3G **85**
Lea Marston. *Warw* . . . 1G **61**
Leamington Hastings. *Warw* . . . 4B **62**
Leamington Spa, Royal.
Warw . . . 4H **61**
Leamonsley. *Staf* . . . 5F **73**
Leamside. *Dur* . . . 5G **115**
Leargybreck. *Arg* . . . 2D **124**
Lease Rigg. *N Yor* . . . 4F **107**
Leasgill. *Cumb* . . . 1D **97**
Leasingham. *Linc* . . . 1H **75**
Leasingthorne. *Dur* . . . 1F **105**
Leasowe. *Mers* . . . 1E **83**
Leatherhead. *Surr* . . . 5C **38**
Leathley. *N Yor* . . . 5E **99**
Leaths. *Dum* . . . 3E **111**
Leaton. *Shrp* . . . 4G **71**
Lea Town. *Lanc* . . . 1C **90**
Leaveland. *Kent* . . . 5E **40**
Leavenheath. *Suff* . . . 2C **54**
Leavening. *N Yor* . . . 3B **100**
Leaves Green. *G Lon* . . . 4F **39**
Lea Yeat. *Cumb* . . . 1G **97**
Leazes. *Dur* . . . 4E **115**
Lebberston. *N Yor* . . . 1E **101**
Lechlade on Thames. *Glos* . . . 2H **35**
Leck. *Lanc* . . . 2F **97**
Leckford. *Hants* . . . 3B **24**
Leckfurin. *High* . . . 3H **167**
Leckgruinart. *Arg* . . . 3A **124**
Leckhampstead. *Buck* . . . 2F **51**
Leckhampstead. *W Ber* . . . 4C **36**
Leckhampstead Street. *W Ber* . . . 4C **36**
Leckhampton. *Glos* . . . 4E **49**
Leckmelm. *High* . . . 4F **163**
Leckwith. *V Glam* . . . 4E **33**
Leconfield. *E Yor* . . . 5E **101**
Ledaig. *Arg* . . . 5D **140**
Ledburn. *Buck* . . . 3H **51**
Ledbury. *Here* . . . 2C **48**
Ledgemoor. *Here* . . . 5G **59**
Ledgowan. *High* . . . 3D **156**
Ledicot. *Here* . . . 4G **59**
Ledmore. *High* . . . 2G **163**
Lednabirichen. *High* . . . 4E **165**
Lednagullin. *High* . . . 2A **168**
Ledsham. *Ches* . . . 3F **83**
Ledsham. *W Yor* . . . 2E **93**
Ledston. *W Yor* . . . 2E **93**
Ledstone. *Devn* . . . 4D **8**
Ledwell. *Oxon* . . . 3C **50**
Lee. *Devn* . . . 2E **19**
(nr. Ilfracombe)
Lee. *Devn* . . . 4B **20**
(nr. South Molton)
Lee. *G Lon* . . . 3F **39**
Lee. *Hants* . . . 1B **16**
Lee. *Lanc* . . . 4E **97**
Lee. *Shrp* . . . 2G **71**
Leeans. *Shet* . . . 7E **173**
Leebotten. *Shet* . . . 9F **173**
Leebotwood. *Shrp* . . . 1G **59**
Lee Brockhurst. *Shrp* . . . 3H **71**
Leece. *Cumb* . . . 3B **96**
Leechpool. *Mon* . . . 3A **34**
Lee Clump. *Buck* . . . 5H **51**
Leeds. *Kent* . . . 5C **40**
Leeds. *W Yor* . . . 1C **92**
Leeds Bradford International Airport.
W Yor . . . 5E **98**
Leedstown. *Corn* . . . 3D **4**
Leegomery. *Telf* . . . 4A **72**
Lee Head. *Derbs* . . . 1E **85**
Leek. *Staf* . . . 5D **85**
Leekbrook. *Staf* . . . 5D **85**
Leek Wootton. *Warw* . . . 4G **61**
Lee Mill. *Devn* . . . 3B **8**
Leeming. *N Yor* . . . 1E **99**
Leeming Bar. *N Yor* . . . 5F **105**
Lee Moor. *Devn* . . . 2B **8**
Lee Moor. *W Yor* . . . 2D **92**
Lee-on-the-Solent. *Hants* . . . 2D **16**
Lees. *Derbs* . . . 2G **73**
Lees. *G Man* . . . 4H **91**
Lees. *W Yor* . . . 1A **92**
Lees, The. *Kent* . . . 5E **40**
Leeswood. *Flin* . . . 4E **83**
Lee, The. *Buck* . . . 5H **51**
Leetown. *Per* . . . 1E **136**
Leftwich. *Ches* . . . 3A **84**
Legbourne. *Linc* . . . 2C **88**
Legburthwaite. *Cumb* . . . 3E **102**
Legerwood. *Bord* . . . 5B **130**
Legsby. *Linc* . . . 2A **88**
Leicester. *Leic* . . . 5C **74**
Leicester Forest East. *Leics* . . . 5C **74**
Leigh. *Dors* . . . 2B **14**
Leigh. *G Man* . . . 4E **91**
Leigh. *Kent* . . . 1G **27**
Leigh. *Shrp* . . . 5F **71**
Leigh. *Surr* . . . 1D **26**
Leigh. *Wilts* . . . 2F **35**
Leigh. *Worc* . . . 5B **60**
Leigham. *Plym* . . . 3B **8**
Leigh Beck. *Essx* . . . 2C **40**
Leigh Common. *Som* . . . 4C **22**
Leigh Delamere. *Wilts* . . . 4D **35**
Leigh Green. *Kent* . . . 2D **28**
Leighland Chapel. *Som* . . . 3D **20**
Leigh-on-Sea. *S'end* . . . 2C **40**
Leigh Park. *Hants* . . . 2F **17**
Leigh Sinton. *Worc* . . . 5B **60**
Leighterton. *Glos* . . . 2D **34**
Leigh, The. *Glos* . . . 3D **48**
Leighton. *N Yor* . . . 2D **98**
Leighton. *Powy* . . . 5E **71**
Leighton. *Shrp* . . . 5A **72**
Leighton. *Som* . . . 2C **22**
Leighton Bromswold. *Cambs* . . . 3A **64**
Leighton Buzzard. *Beds* . . . 3H **51**
Leigh-upon-Mendip. *Som* . . . 2B **22**
Leinthall Earls. *Here* . . . 4G **59**
Leinthall Starkes. *Here* . . . 4G **59**
Leintwardine. *Here* . . . 3G **59**
Leire. *Leics* . . . 1C **62**
Leirinmore. *High* . . . 2E **166**
Leishmore. *High* . . . 4G **157**
Leiston. *Suff* . . . 4G **67**
Leitfie. *Per* . . . 4B **144**
Leith. *Edin* . . . 2F **129**
Leitholm. *Bord* . . . 5D **130**
Lelant. *Corn* . . . 3C **4**
Lelant Downs. *Corn* . . . 3C **4**
Lelley. *E Yor* . . . 1F **95**
Lem Hill. *Worc* . . . 3B **60**
Lemington. *Tyne* . . . 3E **115**
Lemmington Hall. *Nmbd* . . . 3F **121**
Lempitlaw. *Bord* . . . 1B **120**
Lemsford. *Herts* . . . 4C **52**
Lenacre. *Cumb* . . . 1F **97**
Lenchie. *Abers* . . . 5C **160**
Lenchwick. *Worc* . . . 1F **49**
Lendalfoot. *S Ayr* . . . 5A **116**
Lendrick. *Stir* . . . 3E **135**
Lenham. *Kent* . . . 5C **40**
Lenham Heath. *Kent* . . . 1D **28**
Lenimore. *N Ayr* . . . 5G **125**
Lennel. *Bord* . . . 5E **131**
Lennoxtown. *E Dun* . . . 2H **127**
Lenton. *Linc* . . . 2H **75**
Lentran. *High* . . . 4H **157**
Lenwade. *Norf* . . . 4C **78**
Lenzie. *E Dun* . . . 2H **127**
Leochel Cushnie. *Abers* . . . 2C **152**
Leominster. *Here* . . . 5G **59**
Leonard Stanley. *Glos* . . . 5D **48**
Lepe. *Hants* . . . 3C **16**
Lephenstrath. *Arg* . . . 5A **122**
Lephin. *High* . . . 4A **154**
Lephinchapel. *Arg* . . . 4G **133**
Lephinmore. *Arg* . . . 4G **133**
Leppington. *N Yor* . . . 3B **100**
Lepton. *W Yor* . . . 3C **92**

Lerryn. *Corn* 3F 7
Lerwick. *Shet* 7F 173
Lerwick (Tingwall) Airport. *Shet* 7F 173
Lesbury. *Nmbd* 3G 121
Leslie. *Abers* 1C 152
Leslie. *Fife* 3E 137
Lesmahagow. *S Lan* 1H 117
Lesnewth. *Corn* 3B 10
Lessingham. *Norf* 3F 79
Lessonhall. *Cumb* 4D 112
Leswalt. *Dum* 3F 109
Letchmore Heath. *Herts* 1C 38
Letchworth Garden City. *Herts* 2C 52
Letcombe Bassett. *Oxon* 3B 36
Letcombe Regis. *Oxon* 3B 36
Letham. *Ang* 4E 145
Letham. *Falk* 1B 128
Letham. *Fife* 2F 137
Lethanhill. *E Ayr* 3D 116
Lethenty. *Abers* 4F 161
Letheringham. *Suff* 5E 67
Letheringsett. *Norf* 2C 78
Lettaford. *Devn* 4H 11
Lettan. *Orkn* 3G 172
Letter. *Abers* 2E 153
Letterewe. *High* 1B 156
Letterfearn. *High* 1A 148
Lettermore. *Arg* 4F 139
Letters. *High* 5F 163
Letterston. *Pemb* 2D 42
Letton. *Here* 1G 47 (nr. Kington)
Letton. *Here* 3F 59 (nr. Leintwardine)
Letty Green. *Herts* 4C 52
Letwell. *S Yor* 2C 86
Leuchars. *Fife* 1G 137
Leumrabhagh. *W Isl* 6F 171
Leusdon. *Devn* 5H 11
Levedale. *Staf* 4C 72
Leven. *E Yor* 5F 101
Leven. *Fife* 3F 137
Levencorroch. *N Ayr* 3E 123
Levenhall. *E Lot* 2G 129
Levens. *Cumb* 1D 97
Levens Green. *Herts* 3D 52
Levenshulme. *G Man* 1C 84
Levenwick. *Shet* 9F 173
Leverburgh. *W Isl* 9C 171
Leverington. *Cambs* 4D 76
Leverton. *Linc* 1C 76
Leverton. *W Ber* 4B 36
Leverton Lucasgate. *Linc* 1D 76
Leverton Outgate. *Linc* 1D 76
Levington. *Suff* 2F 55
Levisham. *N Yor* 5F 107
Levishie. *High* 2G 149
Lew. *Oxon* 5B 50
Lewaigue. *IOM* 2D 108
Lewannick. *Corn* 4C 10
Lewdown. *Devn* 4E 11
Lewes. *E Sus* 4F 27
Leweston. *Pemb* 2D 42
Lewisham. *G Lon* 3E 39
Lewiston. *High* 1H 149
Lewistown. *B'end* 3C 32
Lewknor. *Oxon* 2F 37
Leworthy. *Devn* 3G 19 (nr. Barnstaple)
Leworthy. *Devn* 2D 10 (nr. Holsworthy)
Lewson Street. *Kent* 4D 40
Lewthorn Cross. *Devn* 5A 12
Lewtrenchard. *Devn* 4E 11
Ley. *Corn* 2F 7
Leybourne. *Kent* 5A 40
Leyburn. *N Yor* 5E 105
Leycett. *Staf* 1B 72
Leyfields. *Staf* 5G 73
Ley Green. *Herts* 3B 52
Ley Hill. *Buck* 5H 51
Leyland. *Lanc* 2D 90
Leylodge. *Abers* 2E 153
Leymoor. *W Yor* 3B 92
Leys. *Per* 5B 144
Leysdown-on-Sea. *Kent* 3E 41
Leysmill. *Ang* 4F 145
Leyton. *G Lon* 2E 39
Leytonstone. *G Lon* 2F 39
Lezant. *Corn* 5D 10
Leziate. *Norf* 4F 77
Lhanbryde. *Mor* 2G 159
Lhen, The. *IOM* 1C 108
Liatrie. *High* 5E 157
Libanus. *Powy* 3C 46
Libberton. *S Lan* 5C 128
Libbery. *Worc* 5D 60
Liberton. *Edin* 3F 129
Lichfield. *Staf* 5F 73
Lickey. *Worc* 3D 61
Lickey End. *Worc* 3D 61
Lickfold. *W Sus* 3A 26
Liddaton. *Devn* 4E 11
Liddington. *Swin* 3H 35
Lidgate. *Suff* 5G 65
Lidgett. *Notts* 4D 86
Lidham Hill. *E Sus* 4C 28
Lidlington. *Beds* 2H 51
Lidsey. *W Sus* 5A 26
Lidstone. *Oxon* 3B 50
Lienassie. *High* 1B 148
Liff. *Ang* 5C 144
Lifford. *W Mid* 2E 61
Lifton. *Devn* 4D 11
Liftondown. *Devn* 4D 10
Lighthorne. *Warw* 5H 61
Light Oaks. *Staf* 5D 84
Lightwater. *Surr* 4A 38
Lightwood. *Staf* 1E 73
Lightwood. *Stoke* 1D 72
Lightwood Green. *Ches* 1A 72
Lightwood Green. *Wrex* 1F 71
Lilbourne. *Nptn* 3C 62
Lilburn Tower. *Nmbd* 2E 121
Lillesdon. *Som* 4G 21
Lilleshall. *Telf* 4B 72
Lilley. *Herts* 3B 52
Lilliesleaf. *Bord* 2H 119
Lillingstone Dayrell. *Buck* 2F 51
Lillingstone Lovell. *Buck* 1F 51
Lillington. *Dors* 1B 14
Lilstock. *Som* 2E 21
Lilybank. *Inv* 2E 126
Lilyhurst. *Shrp* 4B 72
Limbrick. *Lanc* 3E 90
Limbury. *Lutn* 3A 52
Limekilnburn. *S Lan* 4A 128
Lime Kiln Nook. *Cumb* 5E 113
Limekilns. *Fife* 1D 129
Limerigg. *Falk* 2B 128
Limestone Brae. *Nmbd* 5A 114
Lime Street. *Worc* 2D 48
Limington. *Som* 4A 22
Limpenhoe. *Norf* 5F 79
Limpley Stoke. *Wilts* 5C 34
Limpsfield. *Surr* 5E 39
Linburn. *W Lot* 3E 129
Linby. *Notts* 5C 86
Linchmere. *W Sus* 3G 25
Lincluden. *Dum* 2A 112
Lincoln. *Linc* 3G 87
Lincomb. *Worc* 4C 60
Lindale. *Cumb* 1D 96
Lindal in Furness. *Cumb* 2B 96
Lindean. *Bord* 1G 119
Linden. *Glos* 4D 48
Lindfield. *W Sus* 3E 27
Lindford. *Hants* 3G 25
Lindores. *Fife* 2E 137
Lindridge. *Worc* 4A 60
Lindsell. *Essx* 3G 53
Lindsey. *Suff* 1C 54
Lindsey Tye. *Suff* 1C 54
Linford. *Hants* 2G 15
Linford. *Thur* 3A 40
Lingague. *IOM* 4B 108
Lingdale. *Red C* 3D 106
Lingen. *Here* 4F 59
Lingfield. *Surr* 1E 27
Lingoed. *Mon* 3G 47
Lingreabhagh. *W Isl* 9C 171
Ling, The. *Norf* 1F 67
Lingwood. *Norf* 5F 79
Lingyclose Head. *Cumb* 4E 113
Linicro. *High* 2C 154
Linkend. *Worc* 2D 48
Linkenholt. *Hants* 1B 24
Linkinhorne. *Corn* 5D 10
Linklater. *Orkn* 9D 172
Linktown. *Fife* 4E 137
Linkwood. *Mor* 2G 159
Linley. *Shrp* 1F 59 (nr. Bishop's Castle)
Linley. *Shrp* 1A 60 (nr. Bridgnorth)
Linley Green. *Here* 5A 60
Linlithgow. *W Lot* 2C 128
Linlithgow Bridge. *Falk* 2C 128
Linneraineach. *High* 3F 163
Linshiels. *Nmbd* 4C 120
Linsiadar. *W Isl* 4E 171
Linsidemore. *High* 4C 164
Linslade. *Beds* 3H 51
Linstead Parva. *Suff* 3F 67
Linstock. *Cumb* 4F 113
Linthwaite. *W Yor* 3B 92
Lintlaw. *Bord* 4E 131
Lintmill. *Mor* 2C 160
Linton. *Cambs* 1F 53
Linton. *Derbs* 4G 73
Linton. *Here* 3B 48
Linton. *Kent* 5B 40
Linton. *N Yor* 3B 98
Linton. *Bord* 2B 120
Linton. *W Yor* 5F 99
Linton Colliery. *Nmbd* 5G 121
Linton Hill. *Here* 3B 48
Linton-on-Ouse. *N Yor* 3G 99
Lintzford. *Tyne* 4E 115
Lintzgarth. *Dur* 5C 114
Linwood. *Hants* 2G 15
Linwood. *Linc* 2A 88
Linwood. *Ren* 3F 127
Lionacleit. *W Isl* 4C 170
Lionacuidhe. *W Isl* 4C 170
Lional. *W Isl* 1H 171
Liphook. *Hants* 3G 25
Lipley. *Shrp* 2B 72
Lipyeate. *Som* 1B 22
Liquo. *N Lan* 4B 128
Liscard. *Mers* 1F 83
Liscombe. *Som* 3B 20
Liskeard. *Corn* 2G 7
Lisle Court. *Hants* 3B 16
Liss. *Hants* 4F 25
Lissett. *E Yor* 4F 101
Liss Forest. *Hants* 4F 25
Lissington. *Linc* 2A 88
Liston. *Essx* 1B 54
Lisvane. *Card* 3E 33
Liswerry. *Newp* 3G 33
Litcham. *Norf* 4A 78
Litchard. *B'end* 3C 32
Litchborough. *Nptn* 5D 62
Litchfield. *Hants* 1C 24
Litherland. *Mers* 1F 83
Litlington. *Cambs* 1D 52
Litlington. *E Sus* 5G 27
Littemill. *Nmbd* 3G 121
Litterty. *Abers* 3E 161
Little Abington. *Cambs* 1F 53
Little Addington. *Nptn* 3G 63
Little Airmyn. *N Yor* 2H 93
Little Alne. *Warw* 4F 61
Little Ardo. *Abers* 5F 161
Little Asby. *Cumb* 4H 103
Little Aston. *Staf* 5E 73
Little Atherfield. *IOW* 4C 16
Little Ayton. *N Yor* 3C 106
Little Baddow. *Essx* 5A 54
Little Badminton. *S Glo* 3D 34
Little Ballinluig. *Per* 3G 143
Little Bampton. *Cumb* 4D 112
Little Bardfield. *Essx* 2G 53
Little Barford. *Beds* 5A 64
Little Barningham. *Norf* 2D 78
Little Barrington. *Glos* 4H 49
Little Barrow. *Ches* 4G 83
Little Barugh. *N Yor* 2B 100
Little Bavington. *Nmbd* 2C 114
Little Bealings. *Suff* 1F 55
Little Bedwyn. *Wilts* 5A 36
Little Bentley. *Essx* 3E 54
Little Berkhamsted. *Herts* 5C 52
Little Billing. *Nptn* 4F 63
Little Billington. *Beds* 3H 51
Little Birch. *Here* 2A 48
Little Bispham. *Bkpl* 5C 96
Little Blakenham. *Suff* 1E 54
Little Blencow. *Cumb* 1F 103
Little Bognor. *W Sus* 3B 26
Little Bolas. *Shrp* 3A 72
Little Bollington. *Ches* 2B 84
Little Bookham. *Surr* 5C 38
Littleborough. *Devn* 1B 12
Littleborough. *G Man* 3H 91
Littleborough. *Notts* 2F 87
Littlebourne. *Kent* 5G 41
Little Bourton. *Oxon* 1C 50
Little Bowden. *Leics* 2E 63
Little Bradley. *Suff* 5F 65
Little Brampton. *Shrp* 2F 59
Little Brechin. *Ang* 2E 145
Littlebredy. *Dors* 4A 14
Little Brickhill. *Mil* 2H 51
Little Bridgeford. *Staf* 3C 72
Little Brington. *Nptn* 4D 62
Little Bromley. *Essx* 3D 54
Little Broughton. *Cumb* 1B 102
Little Budworth. *Ches* 4H 83
Little Burstead. *Essx* 1A 40
Little Burton. *E Yor* 5F 101
Littlebury. *Essx* 2F 53
Littlebury Green. *Essx* 2E 53
Little Bytham. *Linc* 4H 75
Little Canfield. *Essx* 3F 53
Little Canford. *Dors* 3F 15
Little Carlton. *Linc* 2C 88
Little Carlton. *Notts* 5E 87
Little Casterton. *Rut* 5H 75
Little Catwick. *E Yor* 5F 101
Little Catworth. *Cambs* 3A 64
Little Cawthorpe. *Linc* 2C 88
Little Chalfont. *Buck* 1A 38
Little Chart. *Kent* 1D 28
Little Chesterford. *Essx* 1F 53
Little Cheverell. *Wilts* 1E 23
Little Chishill. *Cambs* 2E 53
Little Clacton. *Essx* 4E 55
Little Clanfield. *Oxon* 5A 50
Little Clifton. *Cumb* 2B 102
Little Coates. *NE Lin* 4F 95
Little Comberton. *Worc* 1E 49
Little Common. *E Sus* 5B 28
Little Compton. *Warw* 2A 50
Little Cornard. *Suff* 2B 54
Littlecote. *Buck* 3G 51
Littlecott. *Wilts* 1G 23
Little Cowarne. *Here* 5A 60
Little Coxwell. *Oxon* 2A 36
Little Crakehall. *N Yor* 5F 105
Little Crawley. *Mil* 1H 51
Little Creich. *High* 5D 164
Little Cressingham. *Norf* 5A 78
Little Crosby. *Mers* 4B 90
Little Crosthwaite. *Cumb* 2D 102
Little Cubley. *Derbs* 2F 73
Little Dalby. *Leics* 4E 75
Little Dawley. *Telf* 5A 72
Littledean. *Glos* 4B 48
Little Dens. *Abers* 4H 161
Little Dewchurch. *Here* 2A 48
Little Ditton. *Cambs* 5F 65
Little Down. *Hants* 1B 24
Little Downham. *Cambs* 2E 65
Little Drayton. *Shrp* 2A 72
Little Driffield. *E Yor* 4E 101
Little Dunham. *Norf* 4A 78
Little Dunkeld. *Per* 4H 143
Little Dunmow. *Essx* 3G 53
Little Easton. *Essx* 3G 53
Little Eaton. *Derbs* 1A 74
Little Eccleston. *Lanc* 5D 96
Little Ellingham. *Norf* 1C 66
Little Elm. *Som* 2C 22
Little End. *Essx* 5F 53
Little Everdon. *Nptn* 5C 62
Little Eversden. *Cambs* 5C 64
Little Faringdon. *Oxon* 5H 49
Little Fencote. *N Yor* 5F 105
Little Fenton. *N Yor* 1F 93
Littleferry. *High* 4F 165
Little Fransham. *Norf* 4B 78
Little Gaddesden. *Herts* 4H 51
Little Garway. *Here* 3H 47
Little Gidding. *Cambs* 2A 64
Little Glemham. *Suff* 5F 67
Little Glenshee. *Per* 5G 143
Little Gransden. *Cambs* 5B 64
Little Green. *Wrex* 1G 71
Little Grimsby. *Linc* 1C 88
Little Habton. *N Yor* 2B 100
Little Hadham. *Herts* 3E 53
Little Hale. *Linc* 1A 76
Little Hallingbury. *Essx* 4E 53
Littleham. *Devn* 4E 19 (nr. Bideford)
Littleham. *Devn* 4D 12 (nr. Exmouth)
Little Hampden. *Buck* 5G 51
Littlehampton. *W Sus* 5B 26
Little Haresfield. *Glos* 5D 48
Little Harrowden. *Nptn* 3F 63
Little Haseley. *Oxon* 5E 51
Little Hatfield. *E Yor* 5F 101
Little Hautbois. *Norf* 3E 79
Little Haven. *Pemb* 3C 42
Little Hay. *Staf* 5F 73
Little Hayfield. *Derbs* 2E 85
Little Haywood. *Staf* 3E 73
Little Heath. *W Mid* 2H 61
Little Heck. *N Yor* 2F 93
Littlehempston. *Devn* 2E 9
Little Herbert's. *Glos* 3E 49
Little Hereford. *Here* 4H 59
Little Horkesley. *Essx* 2C 54
Little Hormead. *Herts* 3E 53
Little Horsted. *E Sus* 4F 27
Little Horton. *W Yor* 1B 92
Little Horwood. *Buck* 2F 51
Little Houghton. *Nptn* 5F 63
Littlehoughton. *Nmbd* 3G 121
Little Houghton. *S Yor* 4E 93
Little Hucklow. *Derbs* 3F 85
Little Hulton. *G Man* 4F 91
Little Ingestre. *Staf* 3D 73
Little Irchester. *Nptn* 4G 63
Little Kelk. *E Yor* 3E 101
Little Kimble. *Buck* 5G 51
Little Kineton. *Warw* 5H 61
Little Kingshill. *Buck* 2G 37
Little Langdale. *Cumb* 4E 102
Little Langford. *Wilts* 3F 23
Little Laver. *Essx* 5F 53
Little Lawford. *Warw* 3B 62
Little Leigh. *Ches* 3A 84
Little Leighs. *Essx* 4H 53
Little Leven. *E Yor* 5E 101
Little Lever. *G Man* 4F 91
Little Linford. *Mil* 1G 51
Little London. *Buck* 4E 51
Little London. *E Sus* 4G 27
Little London. *Hants* 2B 24 (nr. Andover)
Little London. *Hants* 1E 24 (nr. Basingstoke)
Little London. *Linc* 3D 76 (nr. Long Sutton)

Little London. *Linc* 3B **76** (nr. Spalding)
Little London. *Norf* 2E **79** (nr. North Walsham)
Little London. *Norf* 1G **65** (nr. Northwold)
Little London. *Norf* 2D **78** (nr. Saxthorpe)
Little London. *Norf* 1F **65** (nr. Southery)
Little London. *Powy* 2C **58**
Little Longstone. *Derbs* 3F **85**
Little Malvern. *Worc* 1C **48**
Little Maplestead. *Essx* 2B **54**
Little Marcle. *Here* 2B **48**
Little Marlow. *Buck* 3G **37**
Little Massingham. *Norf* 3G **77**
Little Melton. *Norf* 5D **78**
Littlemill. *Abers* 4H **151**
Littlemill. *E Ayr* 3D **116**
Littlemill. *High* 4D **158**
Little Mill. *Mon* 5G **47**
Little Milton. *Oxon* 5E **50**
Little Missenden. *Buck* 1A **38**
Littlemoor. *Derbs* 4A **86**
Littlemoor. *Dors* 4B **14**
Littlemore. *Oxon* 5D **50**
Little Mountain. *Flin* 4E **83**
Little Musgrave. *Cumb* 3A **104**
Little Ness. *Shrp* 4G **71**
Little Neston. *Ches* 3F **83**
Little Newcastle. *Pemb* 2D **43**
Little Newsham. *Dur* 3E **105**
Little Oakley. *Essx* 3F **55**
Little Oakley. *Nptn* 2F **63**
Little Onn. *Staf* 4C **72**
Little Ormside. *Cumb* 3A **104**
Little Orton. *Cumb* 4E **113**
Little Orton. *Leics* 5H **73**
Little Ouse. *Norf* 2F **65**
Little Ouseburn. *N Yor* 3G **99**
Littleover. *Derb* 2H **73**
Little Packington. *Warw* 2G **61**
Little Paxton. *Cambs* 4A **64**
Little Petherick. *Corn* 1D **6**
Little Plumpton. *Lanc* 1B **90**
Little Plumstead. *Norf* 4F **79**
Little Ponton. *Linc* 2G **75**
Littleport. *Cambs* 2E **65**
Little Posbrook. *Hants* 2D **16**
Little Potheridge. *Devn* 1F **11**
Little Preston. *Nptn* 5C **62**
Little Raveley. *Cambs* 3B **64**
Little Reynoldston. *Swan* 4D **31**
Little Ribston. *N Yor* 4F **99**
Little Rissington. *Glos* 4G **49**
Little Rogart. *High* 3E **165**
Little Rollright. *Oxon* 2A **50**
Little Ryburgh. *Norf* 3B **78**
Little Ryle. *Nmbd* 3E **121**
Little Ryton. *Shrp* 5G **71**
Little Salkeld. *Cumb* 1G **103**
Little Sampford. *Essx* 2G **53**
Little Sandhurst. *Brac* 5G **37**
Little Saredon. *Staf* 5D **72**
Little Saxham. *Suff* 4G **65**
Little Scatwell. *High* 3F **157**
Little Shelford. *Cambs* 5D **64**
Little Shoddesden. *Hants* 2A **24**
Little Singleton. *Lanc* 1B **90**
Little Smeaton. *N Yor* 3F **93**
Little Snoring. *Norf* 2B **78**
Little Sodbury. *S Glo* 3C **34**
Little Somborne. *Hants* 3B **24**
Little Somerford. *Wilts* 3E **35**
Little Soudley. *Shrp* 3B **72**
Little Stainforth. *N Yor* 3H **97**
Little Stainton. *Darl* 2A **106**
Little Stanney. *Ches* 3G **83**
Little Staughton. *Beds* 4A **64**
Little Steeping. *Linc* 4D **88**
Littlester. *Shet* 3G **173**
Little Stoke. *Staf* 2D **72**
Littlestone-on-Sea. *Kent* 3E **29**
Little Stonham. *Suff* 4D **66**
Little Street. *Cambs* 2E **65**
Little Stretton. *Leics* 5D **74**
Little Stretton. *Shrp* 1G **59**
Little Strickland. *Cumb* 3G **103**
Little Stukeley. *Cambs* 3B **64**
Little Sugnall. *Staf* 2C **72**
Little Sutton. *Ches* 3F **83**
Little Sutton. *Linc* 3D **76**
Little Swinburne. *Nmbd* 2C **114**
Little Tew. *Oxon* 3B **50**
Little Tey. *Essx* 3B **54**
Little Thetford. *Cambs* 3E **65**
Little Thirkleby. *N Yor* 2G **99**
Little Thornton. *Lanc* 5C **96**
Littlethorpe. *Leics* 1C **62**
Littlethorpe. *N Yor* 3F **99**
Little Thorpe. *W Yor* 2B **92**
Little Thurlow. *Suff* 5F **65**
Little Thurrock. *Thur* 3H **39**
Littleton. *Ches* 4G **83**
Littleton. *Hants* 3C **24**
Littleton. *Som* 3H **21**
Littleton. *Surr* 1A **26** (nr. Guildford)
Littleton. *Surr* 4B **38** (nr. Staines)
Littleton Drew. *Wilts* 3D **34**
Littleton Pannell. *Wilts* 1E **23**
Littleton-upon-Severn. *S Glo* 3A **34**
Little Torboll. *High* 4E **165**
Little Torrington. *Devn* 1E **11**
Little Totham. *Essx* 4B **54**
Little Town. *Cumb* 3D **102**
Littletown. *Dur* 5G **115**
Littletown. *High* 5E **165**
Little Town. *Lanc* 1E **91**
Little Twycross. *Leics* 5H **73**
Little Urswick. *Cumb* 2B **96**
Little Wakering. *Essx* 2D **40**
Little Walden. *Essx* 1F **53**
Little Waldingfield. *Suff* 1C **54**
Little Walsingham. *Norf* 2B **78**
Little Waltham. *Essx* 4H **53**
Little Warley. *Essx* 1H **39**
Little Washbourne. *Glos* 2E **49**
Little Weighton. *E Yor* 1C **94**
Little Wenham. *Suff* 2D **54**
Little Wenlock. *Telf* 5A **72**
Little Whelnetham. *Suff* 5A **66**
Little Whittingham Green. *Suff* 3E **67**
Littlewick Green. *Wind* 4G **37**
Little Wilbraham. *Cambs* 5E **65**
Littlewindsor. *Dors* 2H **13**
Little Wisbeach. *Linc* 2A **76**
Little Witcombe. *Glos* 4E **49**
Little Witley. *Worc* 4B **60**
Little Wittenham. *Oxon* 2D **36**
Little Wolford. *Warw* 2A **50**
Littleworth. *Beds* 1A **52**
Littleworth. *Glos* 2G **49**
Littleworth. *Oxon* 2B **36**
Littleworth. *Staf* 4E **73** (nr. Cannock)
Littleworth. *Staf* 3B **72** (nr. Eccleshall)
Littleworth. *Staf* 3D **72** (nr. Stafford)
Littleworth. *W Sus* 3C **26**
Littleworth. *Worc* 4D **61** (nr. Redditch)
Littleworth. *Worc* 1D **49** (nr. Worcester)
Little Wratting. *Suff* 1G **53**
Little Wymington. *Nptn* 4G **63**
Little Wymondley. *Herts* 3C **52**
Little Wyrley. *Staf* 5E **73**
Little Yeldham. *Essx* 2A **54**
Littley Green. *Essx* 4G **53**
Litton. *Derbs* 3F **85**
Litton. *N Yor* 2B **98**
Litton. *Som* 1A **22**
Litton Cheney. *Dors* 3A **14**
Liurbost. *W Isl* 5F **171**
Liverpool. *Mers* 1F **83**
Liverpool John Lennon Airport. *Mers* 2G **83**
Liversedge. *W Yor* 2B **92**
Liverton. *Devn* 5B **12**
Liverton. *Red C* 3E **107**
Liverton Mines. *Red C* 3E **107**
Livingston. *W Lot* 3D **128**
Livingston Village. *W Lot* 3D **128**
Lixwm. *Flin* 3D **82**
Lizard. *Corn* 5E **5**
Llaingoch. *IOA* 2B **80**
Llaithddu. *Powy* 2C **58**
Llampha. *V Glam* 4C **32**
Llan. *Powy* 5A **70**
Llanaber. *Gwyn* 4F **69**
Llanaelhaearn. *Gwyn* 1C **68**
Llanaeron. *Cdgn* 4D **57**
Llanafan. *Cdgn* 3F **57**
Llanafan-fawr. *Powy* 5B **58**
Llanafan-fechan. *Powy* 5B **58**
Llanallgo. *IOA* 2D **81**
Llanandras. *Powy* 4F **59**
Llananno. *Powy* 3C **58**
Llanarmon. *Gwyn* 2D **68**
Llanarmon Dyffryn Ceiriog. *Wrex* 2D **70**
Llanarmon-yn-Ial. *Den* 5D **82**
Llanarth. *Cdgn* 5D **56**
Llanarth. *Mon* 4G **47**
Llanarthne. *Carm* 3F **45**
Llanasa. *Flin* 2D **82**
Llanbabo. *IOA* 2C **80**
Llanbadarn Fawr. *Cdgn* 2F **57**
Llanbadarn Fynydd. *Powy* 3C **58**
Llanbadarn-y-garreg. *Powy* 1E **46**
Llanbadoc. *Mon* 5G **47**
Llanbadrig. *IOA* 1C **80**
Llanbeder. *Newp* 2G **33**
Llanbedr. *Gwyn* 3E **69**
Llanbedr. *Powy* 3F **47** (nr. Crickhowell)
Llanbedr. *Powy* 1E **47** (nr. Hay-on-Wye)
Llanbedr-Dyffryn-Clwyd. *Den* 5D **82**
Llanbedrgoch. *IOA* 2E **81**
Llanbedrog. *Gwyn* 2C **68**
Llanbedr Pont Steffan. *Cdgn* 1F **45**
Llanbedr-y-cennin. *Cnwy* 4G **81**
Llanberis. *Gwyn* 4E **81**
Llanbethery. *V Glam* 5D **32**
Llanbister. *Powy* 3D **58**
Llanblethian. *V Glam* 4C **32**
Llanboidy. *Carm* 2G **43**
Llanbradach. *Cphy* 2E **33**
Llanbrynmair. *Powy* 5A **70**
Llanbydderi. *V Glam* 5D **32**
Llancadle. *V Glam* 5D **32**
Llancarfan. *V Glam* 4D **32**
Llancatal. *V Glam* 5D **32**
Llancayo. *Mon* 5G **47**
Llancloudy. *Here* 3H **47**
Llancoch. *Powy* 3E **58**
Llancynfelyn. *Cdgn* 1F **57**
Llandaff. *Card* 4E **33**
Llandanwg. *Gwyn* 3E **69**
Llandarcy. *Neat* 3G **31**
Llandawke. *Carm* 3G **43**
Llanddaniel-Fab. *IOA* 3D **81**
Llanddarog. *Carm* 4F **45**
Llanddeiniol. *Cdgn* 3E **57**
Llanddeiniolen. *Gwyn* 4E **81**
Llandderfel. *Gwyn* 2B **70**
Llanddeusant. *Carm* 3A **46**
Llanddeusant. *IOA* 2C **80**
Llanddew. *Powy* 2D **46**
Llanddewi. *Swan* 4D **30**
Llanddewi Brefi. *Cdgn* 5F **57**
Llanddewi'r Cwm. *Powy* 1D **46**
Llanddewi Rhydderch. *Mon* 4G **47**
Llanddewi Velfrey. *Pemb* 3F **43**
Llanddewi Ystradenni. *Powy* 4D **58**
Llanddoged. *Cnwy* 4H **81**
Llanddona. *IOA* 3E **81**
Llanddowror. *Carm* 3G **43**
Llanddulas. *Cnwy* 3B **82**
Llanddwywe. *Gwyn* 3E **69**
Llanddyfnan. *IOA* 3E **81**
Llandecwyn. *Gwyn* 2F **69**
Llandefaelog Fach. *Powy* 2D **46**
Llandefaelog-tre'r-graig. *Powy* 2E **47**
Llandefalle. *Powy* 2E **46**
Llandegai. *Gwyn* 3E **81**
Llandegfan. *IOA* 3E **81**
Llandegla. *Den* 5D **82**
Llandegley. *Powy* 4D **58**
Llandegveth. *Mon* 2G **33**
Llandeilo. *Carm* 3G **45**
Llandeilo Graban. *Powy* 1D **46**
Llandeilo'r Fan. *Powy* 2B **46**
Llandeloy. *Pemb* 2C **42**
Llandenny. *Mon* 5H **47**
Llandevaud. *Newp* 2H **33**
Llandevenny. *Mon* 3G **33**
Llandilo. *Pemb* 2F **43**
Llandinabo. *Here* 3A **48**
Llandinam. *Powy* 2C **58**
Llandissilio. *Pemb* 2F **43**
Llandogo. *Mon* 5A **48**
Llandough. *V Glam* 4C **32** (nr. Cowbridge)
Llandough. *V Glam* 4E **33** (nr. Penarth)
Llandovery. *Carm* 2A **46**
Llandow. *V Glam* 4C **32**
Llandre. *Cdgn* 2F **57**
Llandrillo. *Den* 2C **70**
Llandrillo-yn-Rhos. *Cnwy* 2H **81**
Llandrindod. *Powy* 4C **58**
Llandrindod Wells. *Powy* 4C **58**
Llandrinio. *Powy* 4E **71**
Llandsadwrn. *Carm* 2G **45**
Llandudno. *Cnwy* 2G **81**
Llandudno Junction. *Cnwy* 3G **81**
Llandudoch. *Pemb* 1B **44**
Llandw. *V Glam* 4C **32**
Llandwrog. *Gwyn* 5D **80**
Llandybie. *Carm* 4G **45**
Llandyfaelog. *Carm* 4E **45**
Llandyfan. *Carm* 4G **45**
Llandyfriog. *Cdgn* 1D **44**
Llandyfrydog. *IOA* 2D **80**
Llandygwydd. *Cdgn* 1C **44**
Llandynan. *Den* 1D **70**
Llandyrnog. *Den* 4D **82**
Llandysilio. *Powy* 4E **71**
Llandyssil. *Powy* 1D **58**
Llandysul. *Cdgn* 1E **45**
Llanedeyrn. *Card* 3F **33**
Llaneglwys. *Powy* 2D **46**
Llanegryn. *Gwyn* 5F **69**
Llanegwad. *Carm* 3F **45**
Llaneilian. *IOA* 1D **80**
Llanelian-yn-Rhos. *Cnwy* 3A **82**
Llanelidan. *Den* 5D **82**
Llanelieu. *Powy* 2E **47**
Llanellen. *Mon* 4G **47**
Llanelli. *Carm* 3E **31**
Llanelltyd. *Gwyn* 4G **69**
Llanelly. *Mon* 4F **47**
Llanelly Hill. *Mon* 4F **47**
Llanelwedd. *Powy* 5C **58**
Llanelwy. *Den* 3C **82**
Llanenddwyn. *Gwyn* 3E **69**
Llanengan. *Gwyn* 3B **68**
Llanerch. *Powy* 1F **59**
Llanerchymedd. *IOA* 2D **80**
Llanerfyl. *Powy* 5C **70**
Llaneuddog. *IOA* 2D **80**
Llanfachraeth. *IOA* 2C **80**
Llanfaelog. *IOA* 3C **80**
Llanfaelrhys. *Gwyn* 3B **68**
Llanfaenor. *Mon* 4H **47**
Llanfaes. *IOA* 3F **81**
Llanfaes. *Powy* 3D **46**
Llanfaethlu. *IOA* 2C **80**
Llanfaglan. *Gwyn* 4D **80**
Llanfair. *Gwyn* 3E **69**
Llanfair. *Here* 1F **47**
Llanfair Caereinion. *Powy* 5D **70**
Llanfair Clydogau. *Cdgn* 5F **57**
Llanfair Dyffryn Clwyd. *Den* 5D **82**
Llanfairfechan. *Cnwy* 3F **81**
Llanfair-Nant-Gwyn. *Pemb* 1F **43**
Llanfair Pwllgwyngyll. *IOA* 3E **81**
Llanfair Talhaiarn. *Cnwy* 3B **82**
Llanfair Waterdine. *Shrp* 3E **59**
Llanfair-ym-Muallt. *Powy* 5C **58**
Llanfairyneubwll. *IOA* 3C **80**
Llanfairynghornwy. *IOA* 1C **80**
Llanfallteg. *Carm* 3F **43**
Llanfallteg West. *Carm* 3F **43**
Llanfaredd. *Powy* 5C **58**
Llanfarian. *Cdgn* 3E **57**
Llanfechain. *Powy* 3D **70**
Llanfechell. *IOA* 1C **80**
Llanfechreth. *Gwyn* 3G **69**
Llanfendigaid. *Gwyn* 5E **69**
Llanferres. *Den* 4D **82**
Llan Ffestiniog. *Gwyn* 1G **69**
Llanfflewyn. *IOA* 2C **80**
Llanfihangel Glyn Myfyr. *Cnwy* 1B **70**
Llanfihangel Nant Bran. *Powy* 2C **46**
Llanfihangel-Nant-Melan. *Powy* 5D **58**
Llanfihangel Rhydithon. *Powy* 4D **58**
Llanfihangel Rogiet. *Mon* 3H **33**
Llanfihangel Tal-y-llyn. *Powy* 3E **46**
Llanfihangel-uwch-Gwili. *Carm* 3E **45**
Llanfihangel-yng-Ngwynfa. *Powy* 4C **70**
Llanfihangel yn Nhowyn. *IOA* 3C **80**
Llanfihangel-y-pennant. *Gwyn* 1E **69** (nr. Golan)
Llanfihangel-y-pennant. *Gwyn* 5F **69** (nr. Tywyn)
Llanfilo. *Powy* 2E **46**
Llanfinhangel-ar-Arth. *Carm* 2E **45**
Llanfinhangel-y-Creuddyn. *Cdgn* 3F **57**
Llanfinhangel-y-traethau. *Gwyn* 2E **69**
Llanfleiddan. *V Glam* 4C **32**
Llanfoist. *Mon* 4F **47**
Llanfor. *Gwyn* 2B **70**
Llanfrechfa. *Torf* 2G **33**
Llanfrothen. *Gwyn* 1F **69**
Llanfrynach. *Powy* 3D **46**
Llanfwrog. *Den* 5D **82**
Llanfwrog. *IOA* 2C **80**
Llanfyllin. *Powy* 4D **70**
Llanfynydd. *Carm* 3F **45**
Llanfynydd. *Flin* 5E **83**
Llanfyrnach. *Pemb* 1G **43**
Llangadfan. *Powy* 4C **70**
Llangadog. *Carm* 3H **45** (nr. Llandovery)
Llangadog. *Carm* 5E **45** (nr. Llanelli)
Llangadwaladr. *IOA* 4C **80**
Llangadwaladr. *Powy* 2D **70**
Llangaffo. *IOA* 4D **80**
Llangain. *Carm* 4D **45**
Llangammarch Wells. *Powy* 1C **46**
Llangan. *V Glam* 4C **32**
Llangarron. *Here* 3A **48**
Llangasty-Talyllyn. *Powy* 3E **47**
Llangathen. *Carm* 3F **45**
Llangattock. *Powy* 4F **47**
Llangattock Lingoed. *Mon* 3G **47**
Llangattock-Vibon-Avel. *Mon* 4H **47**
Llangedwyn. *Powy* 3D **70**
Llangefni. *IOA* 3D **80**
Llangeinor. *B'end* 3C **32**
Llangeitho. *Cdgn* 5F **57**
Llangeler. *Carm* 2D **44**
Llangelynin. *Gwyn* 5E **69**

Llangendeirne. *Carm* 4E 45
Llangennech. *Carm* 5F 45
Llangennith. *Swan* 3D 30
Llangenny. *Powy* 4F 47
Llangernyw. *Cnwy* 4A 82
Llangian. *Gwyn* 3B 68
Llangiwg. *Neat* 5H 45
Llangloffan. *Pemb* 1D 42
Llanglydwen. *Carm* 2F 43
Llangoed. *IOA* 3F 81
Llangoedmor. *Cdgn* 1B 44
Llangollen. *Den* 1E 70
Llangolman. *Pemb* 2F 43
Llangorse. *Powy* 3E 47
Llangorwen. *Cdgn* 2F 57
Llangovan. *Mon* 5H 47
Llangower. *Gwyn* 2B 70
Llangranog. *Cdgn* 5C 56
Llangristiolus. *IOA* 3D 80
Llangrove. *Here* 4A 48
Llangua. *Mon* 3G 47
Llangunllo. *Powy* 3E 58
Llangunnor. *Carm* 3E 45
Llangurig. *Powy* 3B 58
Llangwm. *Cnwy* 1B 70
Llangwm. *Mon* 5H 47
Llangwm. *Pemb* 4D 43
Llangwm-isaf. *Mon* 5H 47
Llangwnnadl. *Gwyn* 2B 68
Llangwyfan. *Den* 4D 82
Llangwyfan-isaf. *IOA* 4C 80
Llangwyllog. *IOA* 3D 80
Llangwyryfon. *Cdgn* 3E 57
Llangybi. *Cdgn* 5F 57
Llangybi. *Gwyn* 1D 68
Llangybi. *Mon* 2G 33
Llangyfelach. *Swan* 3F 31
Llangynhafal. *Den* 4D 82
Llangynidr. *Powy* 4E 47
Llangynin. *Carm* 3G 43
Llangynog. *Carm* 3H 43
Llangynog. *Powy* 3C 70
Llangynwyd. *B'end* 3B 32
Llanhamlach. *Powy* 3D 46
Llanharan. *Rhon* 3D 32
Llanharry. *Rhon* 3D 32
Llanhennock. *Mon* 2G 33
Llanhilleth. *Blae* 5F 47
Llanidloes. *Powy* 2B 58
Llaniestyn. *Gwyn* 2B 68
Llanigon. *Powy* 1F 47
Llanilar. *Cdgn* 3F 57
Llanilid. *Rhon* 3C 32
Llanilltud Fawr. *V Glam* 5C 32
Llanishen. *Card* 3E 33
Llanishen. *Mon* 5H 47
Llanllawddog. *Carm* 3E 45
Llanllechid. *Gwyn* 4F 81
Llanllowell. *Mon* 2G 33
Llanllugan. *Powy* 5C 70
Llanllwch. *Carm* 4D 45
Llanllwchaiarn. *Powy* 1D 58
Llanllwni. *Carm* 2E 45
Llanllyfni. *Gwyn* 5D 80
Llanmadoc. *Swan* 3D 30
Llanmaes. *V Glam* 5C 32
Llanmartin. *Newp* 3G 33
Llanmerwig. *Powy* 1D 58
Llanmihangel. *V Glam* 4C 32
Llan-mill. *Pemb* 3F 43
Llanmiloe. *Carm* 4G 43
Llanmorlais. *Swan* 3E 31
Llannefydd. *Cnwy* 3B 82
Llannon. *Carm* 5F 45
Llan-non. *Cdgn* 4E 57
Llannor. *Gwyn* 2C 68
Llanpumsaint. *Carm* 3E 45
Llanrhaeadr. *Den* 4C 82
Llanrhaeadr-ym-Mochnant. *Powy* 3D 70
Llanrhidian. *Swan* 3D 31
Llanrhos. *Cnwy* 2G 81
Llanrhyddlad. *IOA* 2C 80
Llanrhystud. *Cdgn* 4E 57
Llanrian. *Pemb* 1C 42
Llanrothal. *Here* 4H 47
Llanrug. *Gwyn* 4E 81
Llanrumney. *Card* 3F 33
Llanrwst. *Cnwy* 4G 81
Llansadurnen. *Carm* 3G 43
Llansadwrn. *IOA* 3E 81
Llansaint. *Carm* 5D 45
Llansamlet. *Swan* 3F 31
Llansanffraid Glan Conwy. *Cnwy* 3H 81
Llansannan. *Cnwy* 4B 82
Llansannor. *V Glam* 4C 32
Llansantffraed. *Cdgn* 4E 57
Llansantffraed. *Powy* 3E 46
Llansantffraed Cwmdeuddwr. *Powy* 4B 58
Llansantffraed in Elwel. *Powy* 5C 58
Llansantffraid-ym-Mechain. *Powy* 3E 70
Llansawel. *Carm* 2G 45
Llansawel. *Neat* 3G 31
Llansilin. *Powy* 3E 70
Llansoy. *Mon* 5H 47
Llanspyddid. *Powy* 3D 46
Llanstadwell. *Pemb* 4D 42
Llansteffan. *Carm* 3H 43
Llanstephan. *Powy* 1E 46
Llantarnam. *Torf* 2F 33
Llanteg. *Pemb* 3F 43
Llanthony. *Mon* 3F 47
Llantilio Crossenny. *Mon* 4G 47
Llantilio Pertholey. *Mon* 4G 47
Llantood. *Pemb* 1B 44
Llantrisant. *Mon* 2G 33
Llantrisant. *Rhon* 3D 32
Llantrithyd. *V Glam* 4D 32
Llantwit Fardre. *Rhon* 3D 32
Llantwit Major. *V Glam* 5C 32
Llanuwchllyn. *Gwyn* 2A 70
Llanvaches. *Newp* 2H 33
Llanvair Discoed. *Mon* 2H 33
Llanvapley. *Mon* 4G 47
Llanvetherine. *Mon* 4G 47
Llanveynoe. *Here* 2G 47
Llanvihangel Crucorney. *Mon* 3G 47
Llanvihangel Gobion. *Mon* 5G 47
Llanvihangel Ystern-Llewern. *Mon* 4H 47
Llanwarne. *Here* 3A 48
Llanwddyn. *Powy* 4C 70
Llanwenarth. *Mon* 4F 47
Llanwenog. *Cdgn* 1E 45
Llanwern. *Newp* 3G 33
Llanwinio. *Carm* 2G 43
Llanwnda. *Gwyn* 5D 81
Llanwnda. *Pemb* 1D 42
Llanwnnen. *Cdgn* 1F 45
Llanwnog. *Powy* 1C 58
Llanwrda. *Carm* 2H 45
Llanwrin. *Powy* 5G 69
Llanwrthwl. *Powy* 4B 58
Llanwrtud. *Powy* 1B 46
Llanwrtyd. *Powy* 1B 46
Llanwrtyd Wells. *Powy* 1B 46
Llanwyddelan. *Powy* 5C 70
Llanyblodwel. *Shrp* 3E 71
Llanybri. *Carm* 3H 43
Llanybydder. *Carm* 1F 45
Llanycefn. *Pemb* 2E 43
Llanychaer. *Pemb* 1D 43
Llanycil. *Gwyn* 2B 70
Llanymawddwy. *Gwyn* 4B 70
Llanymddyfri. *Carm* 2A 46
Llanymynech. *Shrp* 3E 71
Llanynghenedl. *IOA* 2C 80
Llanynys. *Den* 4D 82
Llan-y-pwll. *Wrex* 5F 83
Llanyrafon. *Torf* 2G 33
Llanyre. *Powy* 4C 58
Llanystumdwy. *Gwyn* 2D 68
Llanywern. *Powy* 3E 46
Llawhaden. *Pemb* 3E 43
Llawndy. *Flin* 2D 82
Llawnt. *Shrp* 2E 71
Llawr Dref. *Gwyn* 3B 68
Llawryglyn. *Powy* 1B 58
Llay. *Wrex* 5F 83
Llechfaen. *Powy* 3D 46
Llechryd. *Cphy* 5E 46
Llechryd. *Cdgn* 1C 44
Llechrydau. *Wrex* 2E 71
Lledrod. *Cdgn* 3F 57
Llethrid. *Swan* 3E 31
Llidiad-Nenog. *Carm* 2F 45
Llidiardau. *Gwyn* 2A 70
Llidiart y Parc. *Den* 1D 70
Llithfaen. *Gwyn* 1C 68
Lloc. *Flin* 3D 82
Llong. *Flin* 4E 83
Llowes. *Powy* 1E 47
Lloyney. *Powy* 3E 59
Llundain-fach. *Cdgn* 5E 57
Llwydcoed. *Rhon* 5C 46
Llwyncelyn. *Cdgn* 5D 56
Llwyncelyn. *Swan* 5G 45
Llwyndaffydd. *Cdgn* 5C 56
Llwynderw. *Powy* 5E 70
Llwyn-du. *Mon* 4F 47
Llwyngwril. *Gwyn* 5E 69
Llwynhendy. *Carm* 3E 31
Llwynmawr. *Wrex* 2E 71
Llwyn-on Village. *Mer T* 4D 46
Llwyn-teg. *Carm* 5F 45
Llwyn-y-brain. *Carm* 3F 43
Llwynygog. *Powy* 1A 58
Llwyn-y-groes. *Cdgn* 5E 57
Llwynypia. *Rhon* 2C 32
Llynclys. *Shrp* 3E 71
Llynfaes. *IOA* 3D 80
Llysfaen. *Cnwy* 3A 82
Llyswen. *Powy* 2E 47
Llysworney. *V Glam* 4C 32
Llys-y-fran. *Pemb* 2E 43
Llywel. *Powy* 2B 46
Llywernog. *Cdgn* 2G 57
Loan. *Falk* 2C 128
Loanend. *Nmbd* 4F 131
Loanhead. *Midl* 3F 129
Loaningfoot. *Dum* 4A 112
Loanreoch. *High* 1A 158
Loans. *S Ayr* 1C 116
Loansdean. *Nmbd* 1F 115
Lobb. *Devn* 3E 19
Lobhillcross. *Devn* 4E 11
Lochaber. *Mor* 3E 159
Loch a Charnain. *W Isl* 4D 170
Lochailort. *High* 5F 147
Lochaline. *High* 4A 140
Lochans. *Dum* 4F 109
Locharbriggs. *Dum* 1A 112
Lochardil. *High* 4A 158
Lochassynt Lodge. *High* 1F 163
Lochavich. *Arg* 2G 133
Lochawe. *Arg* 1A 134
Loch Baghasdail. *W Isl* 7C 170
Lochboisdale. *W Isl* 7C 170
Lochbuie. *Arg* 1D 132
Lochcarron. *High* 5A 156
Loch Choire Lodge. *High* 5G 167
Lochdochart House. *Stir* 1D 134
Lochdon. *Arg* 5B 140
Lochearnhead. *Stir* 1E 135
Lochee. *D'dee* 5C 144
Lochend. *High* 5H 157
(nr. Inverness)
Lochend. *High* 2E 169
(nr. Thurso)
Locherben. *Dum* 5B 118
Loch Euphort. *W Isl* 2D 170
Lochfoot. *Dum* 2F 111
Lochgair. *Arg* 4G 133
Lochgarthside. *High* 2H 149
Lochgelly. *Fife* 4D 136
Lochgilphead. *Arg* 1G 125
Lochgoilhead. *Arg* 3A 134
Loch Head. *Dum* 5A 110
Lochhill. *Mor* 2G 159
Lochindorb Lodge. *High* 5D 158
Lochinver. *High* 1E 163
Lochlane. *Per* 1H 135
Loch Loyal Lodge. *High* 4G 167
Lochluichart. *High* 2F 157
Lochmaben. *Dum* 1B 112
Lochmaddy. *W Isl* 2E 170
Loch nam Madadh. *W Isl* 2E 170
Lochore. *Fife* 4D 136
Lochportain. *W Isl* 1E 170
Lochranza. *N Ayr* 4H 125
Loch Sgioport. *W Isl* 5D 170
Lochside. *Abers* 2G 145
Lochside. *High* 5A 168
(nr. Achentoul)
Lochside. *High* 3C 158
(nr. Nairn)
Lochslin. *High* 5F 165
Lochstack Lodge. *High* 4C 166
Lochton. *Abers* 4E 153
Lochty. *Fife* 3H 137
Lochuisge. *High* 3B 140
Lochussie. *High* 3G 157
Lochwinnoch. *Ren* 4E 127
Lochyside. *High* 1F 141
Lockengate. *Corn* 2E 7
Lockerbie. *Dum* 1C 112
Lockeridge. *Wilts* 5G 35
Lockerley. *Hants* 4A 24
Lockhills. *Cumb* 5G 113
Locking. *N Som* 1G 21
Lockington. *E Yor* 5D 101
Lockington. *Leics* 3B 74
Lockleywood. *Shrp* 3A 72
Locksgreen. *IOW* 3C 16
Locks Heath. *Hants* 2D 16
Lockton. *N Yor* 5F 107
Loddington. *Leics* 5E 75
Loddington. *Nptn* 3F 63
Loddiswell. *Devn* 4D 8
Loddon. *Norf* 1F 67
Lode. *Cambs* 4E 65
Loders. *Dors* 3H 13
Lodsworth. *W Sus* 3A 26
Lofthouse. *N Yor* 2D 98
Lofthouse. *W Yor* 2D 92
Lofthouse Gate. *W Yor* 2D 92
Loftus. *Red C* 3E 107
Logan. *E Ayr* 2E 117
Loganlea. *W Lot* 3C 128
Logaston. *Here* 5F 59
Loggerheads. *Staf* 2B 72
Loggie. *High* 4F 163
Logie. *Ang* 2F 145
Logie. *Fife* 1G 137
Logie. *Mor* 3E 159
Logie Coldstone. *Abers* 3B 152
Logie Pert. *Ang* 2F 145
Logierait. *Per* 3G 143
Login. *Carm* 2F 43
Lolworth. *Cambs* 4C 64
Lonbain. *High* 3F 155
Londesborough. *E Yor* 5C 100
London. *G Lon* 2E 39
London Apprentice. *Corn* 3E 6
London Ashford (Lydd) Airport. *Kent* 3E 29
London Biggin Hill Airport. *G Lon* 4F 39
London City Airport. *G Lon* 2F 39
London Colney. *Herts* 5B 52
Londonderry. *N Yor* 1F 99
London Gatwick Airport. *W Sus* 1D 27
London Heathrow Airport. *G Lon* 3B 38
London Luton Airport. *Lutn* 3B 52
London Southend Airport. *Essx* 2C 40
London Stansted Airport. *Essx* 3F 53
Londonthorpe. *Linc* 2G 75
Londubh. *High* 5C 162
Lone. *High* 4D 166
Lonemore. *High* 5E 165
(nr. Dornoch)
Lonemore. *High* 1G 155
(nr. Gairloch)
Long Ashton. *N Som* 4A 34
Long Bank. *Worc* 3B 60
Longbar. *N Ayr* 4E 127
Long Bennington. *Linc* 1F 75
Longbenton. *Tyne* 3F 115
Longborough. *Glos* 3G 49
Long Bredy. *Dors* 3A 14
Longbridge. *Warw* 4G 61
Longbridge. *W Mid* 3E 61
Longbridge Deverill. *Wilts* 2D 22
Long Buckby. *Nptn* 4D 62
Long Buckby Wharf. *Nptn* 4D 62
Longburgh. *Cumb* 4E 112
Longburton. *Dors* 1B 14
Long Clawson. *Leics* 3E 74
Longcliffe. *Derbs* 5G 85
Long Common. *Hants* 1D 16
Long Compton. *Staf* 3C 72
Long Compton. *Warw* 2A 50
Longcot. *Oxon* 2A 36
Long Crendon. *Buck* 5E 51
Long Crichel. *Dors* 1E 15
Longcroft. *Cumb* 4D 112
Longcroft. *Falk* 2A 128
Longcross. *Surr* 4A 38
Longdale. *Cumb* 4H 103
Longdales. *Cumb* 5G 113
Longden. *Shrp* 5G 71
Longden Common. *Shrp* 5G 71
Long Ditton. *Surr* 4C 38
Longdon. *Staf* 4E 73
Longdon. *Worc* 2D 48
Longdon Green. *Staf* 4E 73
Longdon on Tern. *Telf* 4A 72
Longdown. *Devn* 3B 12
Longdowns. *Corn* 5B 6
Long Drax. *N Yor* 2G 93
Long Duckmanton. *Derbs* 3B 86
Long Eaton. *Derbs* 2B 74
Longfield. *Kent* 4H 39
Longfield Hill. *Kent* 4H 39
Longford. *Derbs* 2G 73
Longford. *Glos* 3D 48
Longford. *G Lon* 3B 38
Longford. *Shrp* 2A 72
Longford. *Telf* 4B 72
Longford. *W Mid* 2H 61
Longforgan. *Per* 1F 137
Longformacus. *Bord* 4C 130
Longframlington. *Nmbd* 4F 121
Long Gardens. *Essx* 2B 54
Long Green. *Ches* 3G 83
Long Green. *Worc* 2D 48
Longham. *Dors* 3F 15
Longham. *Norf* 4B 78
Long Hanborough. *Oxon* 4C 50
Longhedge. *Wilts* 2D 22
Longhill. *Abers* 3H 161
Longhirst. *Nmbd* 1F 115
Longhope. *Glos* 4B 48
Longhope. *Orkn* 8C 172
Longhorsley. *Nmbd* 5F 121
Longhoughton. *Nmbd* 3G 121
Long Itchington. *Warw* 4B 62
Longlands. *Cumb* 1D 102
Longlane. *Derbs* 2G 73
Long Lane. *Telf* 4A 72
Longlane. *W Ber* 4C 36
Long Lawford. *Warw* 3B 62
Long Lease. *N Yor* 4G 107
Longley Green. *Worc* 5B 60
Long Load. *Som* 4H 21
Longmanhill. *Abers* 2E 161
Long Marston. *Herts* 4G 51
Long Marston. *N Yor* 4H 99
Long Marston. *Warw* 1G 49
Long Marton. *Cumb* 2H 103
Long Meadow. *Cambs* 4E 65
Long Meadowend. *Shrp* 2G 59

Long Melford. *Suff* 1B **54**
Longmoor Camp. *Hants* 3F **25**
Longmorn. *Mor* 3G **159**
Longmoss. *Ches* 3C **84**
Long Newnton. *Glos* 2E **35**
Longnewton. *Bord* 2H **119**
Long Newton. *Stoc T* 3A **106**
Longney. *Glos* 4C **48**
Longniddry. *E Lot* 2H **129**
Longnor. *Shrp* 5G **71**
Longnor. *Staf* 4E **85**
(nr. Leek)
Longnor. *Staf* 4C **72**
(nr. Stafford)
Longparish. *Hants* 2C **24**
Longpark. *Cumb* 3F **113**
Long Preston. *N Yor* 4H **97**
Longridge. *Lanc* 1E **90**
Longridge. *Staf* 4D **72**
Longridge. *W Lot* 3C **128**
Longriggend. *N Lan* 2B **128**
Long Riston. *E Yor* 5F **101**
Long Rock. *Corn* 3C **4**
Longsdon. *Staf* 5D **84**
Longshaw. *G Man* 4D **90**
Longshaw. *Staf* 1E **73**
Longside. *Abers* 4H **161**
Longslow. *Shrp* 2A **72**
Longstanton. *Cambs* 4C **64**
Longstock. *Hants* 3B **24**
Longstowe. *Cambs* 5C **64**
Long Stratton. *Norf* 1D **66**
Long Street. *Mil* 1F **51**
Longstreet. *Wilts* 1G **23**
Long Sutton. *Hants* 2F **25**
Long Sutton. *Linc* 3D **76**
Long Sutton. *Som* 4H **21**
Longthorpe. *Pet* 1A **64**
Long Thurlow. *Suff* 4C **66**
Longthwaite. *Cumb* 2F **103**
Longton. *Lanc* 2C **90**
Longton. *Stoke* 1D **72**
Longtown. *Cumb* 3E **113**
Longtown. *Here* 3G **47**
Longville in the Dale. *Shrp* 1H **59**
Long Whatton. *Leics* 3B **74**
Longwick. *Buck* 5F **51**
Long Wittenham. *Oxon* 2D **36**
Longwitton. *Nmbd* 1D **115**
Longworth. *Oxon* 2B **36**
Longyester. *E Lot* 3B **130**
Lonmore. *High* 4B **154**
Looe. *Corn* 3G **7**
Loose. *Kent* 5B **40**
Loosegate. *Linc* 3C **76**
Loosley Row. *Buck* 5G **51**
Lopcombe Corner. *Wilts* 3A **24**
Lopen. *Som* 1H **13**
Loppington. *Shrp* 3G **71**
Lorbottle. *Nmbd* 4E **121**
Lorbottle Hall. *Nmbd* 4E **121**
Lordington. *W Sus* 2F **17**
Loscoe. *Derbs* 1B **74**
Loscombe. *Dors* 3A **14**
Losgaintir. *W Isl* 8C **171**
Lossiemouth. *Mor* 2G **159**
Lossit. *Arg* 4A **124**
Lostock Gralam. *Ches* 3A **84**
Lostock Green. *Ches* 3A **84**
Lostock Hall. *Lanc* 2D **90**
Lostock Junction. *G Man* 4E **91**
Lostwithiel. *Corn* 3F **7**
Lothbeg. *High* 2G **165**
Lothersdale. *N Yor* 5B **98**
Lothianbridge. *Midl* 3G **129**
Lothianburn. *Edin* 3F **129**
Lothmore. *High* 2G **165**
Lottisham. *Som* 3A **22**
Loudwater. *Buck* 1A **38**
Loughborough. *Leics* 4C **74**
Loughor. *Swan* 3E **31**
Loughton. *Essx* 1F **39**
Loughton. *Mil* 2G **51**
Loughton. *Shrp* 2A **60**
Lound. *Linc* 4H **75**
Lound. *Notts* 2D **86**
Lound. *Suff* 1H **67**
Lount. *Leics* 4A **74**
Louth. *Linc* 2C **88**
Love Clough. *Lanc* 2G **91**
Lovedean. *Hants* 1E **17**
Lover. *Wilts* 4H **23**
Loversall. *S Yor* 1C **86**
Loves Green. *Essx* 5G **53**
Loveston. *Pemb* 4E **43**
Lovington. *Som* 3A **22**
Low Ackworth. *W Yor* 3E **93**
Low Angerton. *Nmbd* 1D **115**
Low Ardwell. *Dum* 5F **109**
Low Ballochdoan. *S Ayr* 2F **109**
Lowbands. *Glos* 2C **48**
Low Barlings. *Linc* 3H **87**
Low Bell End. *N Yor* 5E **107**
Low Bentham. *N Yor* 3F **97**
Low Borrowbridge. *Cumb* 4H **103**
Low Bradfield. *S Yor* 1G **85**
Low Bradley. *N Yor* 5C **98**
Low Braithwaite. *Cumb* 5F **113**
Low Brunton. *Nmbd* 2C **114**
Low Burnham. *N Lin* 4A **94**
Lowca. *Cumb* 2A **102**
Low Catton. *E Yor* 4B **100**
Low Coniscliffe. *Darl* 3F **105**
Low Coylton. *S Ayr* 3D **116**
Low Crosby. *Cumb* 4F **113**
Low Dalby. *N Yor* 1C **100**
Lowdham. *Notts* 1D **74**
Low Dinsdale. *Darl* 3A **106**
Lowe. *Shrp* 2G **71**
Low Ellington. *N Yor* 1E **98**
Lower Amble. *Corn* 1D **6**
Lower Ansty. *Dors* 2C **14**
Lower Arboll. *High* 5F **165**
Lower Arncott. *Oxon* 4E **50**
Lower Ashton. *Devn* 4B **12**
Lower Assendon. *Oxon* 3F **37**
Lower Auchenreath. *Mor* 2A **160**
Lower Badcall. *High* 4B **166**
Lower Ballam. *Lanc* 1B **90**
Lower Basildon. *W Ber* 4E **36**
Lower Beeding. *W Sus* 3D **26**
Lower Benefield. *Nptn* 2G **63**
Lower Bentley. *Worc* 4D **61**
Lower Beobridge. *Shrp* 1B **60**
Lower Bockhampton. *Dors* 3C **14**
Lower Boddington. *Nptn* 5B **62**
Lower Bordean. *Hants* 4E **25**
Lower Brailes. *Warw* 2B **50**
Lower Breakish. *High* 1E **147**
Lower Broadheath. *Worc* 5C **60**
Lower Brynamman. *Neat* 4H **45**
Lower Bullingham. *Here* 2A **48**
Lower Bullington. *Hants* 2C **24**
Lower Burgate. *Hants* 1G **15**
Lower Cam. *Glos* 5C **48**
Lower Catesby. *Nptn* 5C **62**
Lower Chapel. *Powy* 2D **46**
Lower Cheriton. *Devn* 2E **12**
Lower Chicksgrove. *Wilts* 3E **23**
Lower Chute. *Wilts* 1B **24**
Lower Clopton. *Warw* 5F **61**
Lower Common. *Hants* 2E **25**
Lower Cumberworth. *W Yor* . . . 4C **92**
Lower Darwen. *Bkbn* 2E **91**
Lower Dean. *Beds* 4H **63**
Lower Dean. *Devn* 2D **8**
Lower Diabaig. *High* 2G **155**
Lower Dicker. *E Sus* 4G **27**
Lower Dounreay. *High* 2B **168**
Lower Down. *Shrp* 2F **59**
Lower Dunsforth. *N Yor* 3G **99**
Lower East Carleton. *Norf* 5D **78**
Lower Egleton. *Here* 1B **48**
Lower Ellastone. *Derbs* 1F **73**
Lower End. *Nptn* 4F **63**
Lower Everleigh. *Wilts* 1G **23**
Lower Eype. *Dors* 3H **13**
Lower Failand. *N Som* 4A **34**
Lower Faintree. *Shrp* 2A **60**
Lower Farringdon. *Hants* 3F **25**
Lower Foxdale. *IOM* 4B **108**
Lower Frankton. *Shrp* 2F **71**
Lower Froyle. *Hants* 2F **25**
Lower Gabwell. *Devn* 2F **9**
Lower Gledfield. *High* 4C **164**
Lower Godney. *Som* 2H **21**
Lower Gravenhurst. *Beds* 2B **52**
Lower Green. *Essx* 2E **53**
Lower Green. *Norf* 2B **78**
Lower Green. *Staf* 5D **72**
Lower Green. *W Ber* 5B **36**
Lower Halstow. *Kent* 4C **40**
Lower Hardres. *Kent* 5F **41**
Lower Hardwick. *Here* 5G **59**
Lower Hartshay. *Derbs* 5A **86**
Lower Hawthwaite. *Cumb* 1B **96**
Lower Hayton. *Shrp* 2H **59**
Lower Hergest. *Here* 5E **59**
Lower Heyford. *Oxon* 3C **50**
Lower Heysham. *Lanc* 3D **96**
Lower Higham. *Kent* 3B **40**
Lower Holbrook. *Suff* 2E **55**
Lower Hordley. *Shrp* 3F **71**
Lower Horncroft. *W Sus* 4B **26**
Lower Horsebridge. *E Sus* 4G **27**
Lower Kilcott. *Glos* 3C **34**
Lower Killeyan. *Arg* 5A **124**
Lower Kingcombe. *Dors* 3A **14**
Lower Kingswood. *Surr* 5D **38**
Lower Kinnerton. *Ches* 4F **83**
Lower Langford. *N Som* 5H **33**
Lower Largo. *Fife* 3G **137**
Lower Layham. *Suff* 1D **54**
Lower Ledwyche. *Shrp* 3H **59**
Lower Leigh. *Staf* 2E **73**
Lower Lemington. *Glos* 2H **49**
Lower Lenie. *High* 1H **149**
Lower Ley. *Glos* 4C **48**
Lower Llanfadog. *Powy* 4B **58**
Lower Lode. *Glos* 2D **49**
Lower Loxhore. *Devn* 3G **19**
Lower Loxley. *Staf* 2E **73**
Lower Lydbrook. *Glos* 4A **48**
Lower Lye. *Here* 4G **59**
Lower Machen. *Newp* 3F **33**
Lower Maes-coed. *Here* 2G **47**
Lower Meend. *Glos* 5A **48**
Lower Milovaig. *High* 3A **154**
Lower Moor. *Worc* 1E **49**
Lower Morton. *S Glo* 2B **34**
Lower Mountain. *Flin* 5F **83**
Lower Nazeing. *Essx* 5D **53**
Lower Nyland. *Dors* 4C **22**
Lower Oakfield. *Fife* 4D **136**
Lower Oddington. *Glos* 3H **49**
Lower Ollach. *High* 5E **155**
Lower Penarth. *V Glam* 5E **33**
Lower Penn. *Staf* 1C **60**
Lower Pennington. *Hants* 3B **16**
Lower Peover. *Ches* 3B **84**
Lower Pitkerrie. *High* 1C **158**
Lower Place. *G Man* 3H **91**
Lower Quinton. *Warw* 1G **49**
Lower Rainham. *Medw* 4C **40**
Lower Raydon. *Suff* 2D **54**
Lower Seagry. *Wilts* 3E **35**
Lower Shelton. *Beds* 1H **51**
Lower Shiplake. *Oxon* 4F **37**
Lower Shuckburgh. *Warw* 4B **62**
Lower Sketty. *Swan* 3F **31**
Lower Slaughter. *Glos* 3G **49**
Lower Soudley. *Glos* 4B **48**
Lower Stanton St Quintin.
Wilts 3E **35**
Lower Stoke. *Medw* 3C **40**
Lower Stonnall. *Staf* 5E **73**
Lower Stow Bedon. *Norf* 1B **66**
Lower Street. *Norf* 2E **79**
Lower Strensham. *Worc* 1E **49**
Lower Sundon. *Beds* 3A **52**
Lower Swanwick. *Hants* 2C **16**
Lower Swell. *Glos* 3G **49**
Lower Tale. *Devn* 2D **12**
Lower Tean. *Staf* 2E **73**
Lower Thurlton. *Norf* 1G **67**
Lower Thurnham. *Lanc* 4D **96**
Lower Thurvaston. *Derbs* 2G **73**
Lowertown. *Corn* 4D **4**
Lower Town. *Devn* 5H **11**
Lower Town. *Here* 1B **48**
Lower Town. *IOS* 1B **4**
Lower Town. *Pemb* 1D **42**
Lower Tysoe. *Warw* 1B **50**
Lower Upham. *Hants* 1D **16**
Lower Upnor. *Medw* 3B **40**
Lower Vexford. *Som* 3E **20**
Lower Walton. *Warr* 2A **84**
Lower Wear. *Devn* 4C **12**
Lower Weare. *Som* 1H **21**
Lower Welson. *Here* 5E **59**
Lower Whatcombe. *Dors* 2D **14**
Lower Whitley. *Ches* 3A **84**
Lower Wield. *Hants* 2E **25**
Lower Winchendon. *Buck* 4F **51**
Lower Withington. *Ches* 4C **84**
Lower Woodend. *Buck* 3G **37**
Lower Woodford. *Wilts* 3G **23**
Lower Wraxall. *Dors* 2A **14**
Lower Wych. *Ches* 1G **71**
Lower Wyche. *Worc* 1C **48**
Lowesby. *Leics* 5E **74**
Lowestoft. *Suff* 1H **67**
Loweswater. *Cumb* 2C **102**
Low Etherley. *Dur* 2E **105**
Lowfield Heath. *W Sus* 1D **26**
Lowford. *Hants* 1C **16**
Low Fulney. *Linc* 3B **76**
Low Gate. *Nmbd* 3C **114**
Lowgill. *Cumb* 5H **103**
Lowgill. *Lanc* 3F **97**
Low Grantley. *N Yor* 2E **99**
Low Green. *N Yor* 4E **98**
Low Habberley. *Worc* 3C **60**
Low Ham. *Som* 4H **21**
Low Hameringham. *Linc* 4C **88**
Low Hawkser. *N Yor* 4G **107**
Low Hesket. *Cumb* 5F **113**
Low Hesleyhurst. *Nmbd* 5E **121**
Lowick. *Cumb* 1B **96**
Lowick. *Nptn* 2G **63**
Lowick. *Nmbd* 1E **121**
Lowick Bridge. *Cumb* 1B **96**
Lowick Green. *Cumb* 1B **96**
Low Knipe. *Cumb* 2G **103**
Low Leighton. *Derbs* 2E **85**
Low Lorton. *Cumb* 2C **102**
Low Marishes. *N Yor* 2C **100**
Low Marnham. *Notts* 4F **87**
Low Mill. *N Yor* 5D **106**
Low Moor. *Lanc* 5G **97**
Low Moor. *W Yor* 2B **92**
Low Moorsley. *Tyne* 5G **115**
Low Newton-by-the-Sea.
Nmbd 2G **121**
Lownie Moor. *Ang* 4D **145**
Lowood. *Bord* 1H **119**
Low Row. *Cumb* 3G **113**
(nr. Brampton)
Low Row. *Cumb* 5C **112**
(nr. Wigton)
Low Row. *N Yor* 5C **104**
Lowsonford. *Warw* 4F **61**
Low Street. *Norf* 5C **78**
Lowther. *Cumb* 2G **103**
Lowthorpe. *E Yor* 3E **101**
Lowton. *Devn* 2G **11**
Lowton. *G Man* 1A **84**
Lowton. *Som* 1E **13**
Lowton Common. *G Man* 1A **84**
Low Torry. *Fife* 1D **128**
Low Toynton. *Linc* 3B **88**
Low Valleyfield. *Fife* 1C **128**
Low Westwood. *Dur* 4E **115**
Low Whinnow. *Cumb* 4E **112**
Low Wood. *Cumb* 1C **96**
Low Worsall. *N Yor* 4A **106**
Low Wray. *Cumb* 4E **103**
Loxbeare. *Devn* 1C **12**
Loxhill. *Surr* 2B **26**
Loxhore. *Devn* 3G **19**
Loxley. *S Yor* 2H **85**
Loxley. *Warw* 5G **61**
Loxley Green. *Staf* 2E **73**
Loxton. *N Som* 1G **21**
Loxwood. *W Sus* 2B **26**
Lubcroy. *High* 3A **164**
Lubenham. *Leics* 2E **62**
Lubinvullin. *High* 2F **167**
Luccombe. *Som* 2C **20**
Luccombe Village. *IOW* 4D **16**
Lucker. *Nmbd* 1F **121**
Luckett. *Corn* 5D **11**
Luckington. *Wilts* 3D **34**
Lucklawhill. *Fife* 1G **137**
Luckwell Bridge. *Som* 3C **20**
Lucton. *Here* 4G **59**
Ludag. *W Isl* 7C **170**
Ludborough. *Linc* 1B **88**
Ludchurch. *Pemb* 3F **43**
Luddenden. *W Yor* 2A **92**
Luddenden Foot. *W Yor* 2A **92**
Luddenham. *Kent* 4D **40**
Ludderburn. *Cumb* 5F **103**
Luddesdown. *Kent* 4A **40**
Luddington. *N Lin* 3B **94**
Luddington. *Warw* 5F **61**
Luddington in the Brook.
Nptn 2A **64**
Ludford. *Linc* 2A **88**
Ludford. *Shrp* 3H **59**
Ludgershall. *Buck* 4E **51**
Ludgershall. *Wilts* 1A **24**
Ludgvan. *Corn* 3C **4**
Ludham. *Norf* 4F **79**
Ludlow. *Shrp* 3H **59**
Ludstone. *Shrp* 1C **60**
Ludwell. *Wilts* 4E **23**
Ludworth. *Dur* 5G **115**
Luffenhall. *Herts* 3C **52**
Luffincot. *Devn* 3D **10**
Lugar. *E Ayr* 2E **117**
Luggate Burn. *E Lot* 2C **130**
Lugg Green. *Here* 4G **59**
Luggiebank. *N Lan* 2A **128**
Lugton. *E Ayr* 4F **127**
Lugwardine. *Here* 1A **48**
Luib. *High* 1D **146**
Luib. *Stir* 1D **135**
Lulham. *Here* 1H **47**
Lullington. *Derbs* 4G **73**
Lullington. *Som* 1C **22**
Lulsgate Bottom. *N Som* 5A **34**
Lulsley. *Worc* 5B **60**
Lulworth Camp. *Dors* 4D **14**
Lumb. *Lanc* 2G **91**
Lumb. *W Yor* 2A **92**
Lumby. *N Yor* 1E **93**
Lumphanan. *Abers* 3C **152**
Lumphinnans. *Fife* 4D **136**
Lumsdaine. *Bord* 3E **131**
Lumsden. *Abers* 1B **152**
Lunan. *Ang* 3F **145**
Lunanhead. *Ang* 3D **145**
Luncarty. *Per* 1C **136**
Lund. *E Yor* 5D **100**
Lund. *N Yor* 1G **93**
Lundie. *Ang* 5B **144**
Lundin Links. *Fife* 3G **137**
Lundy Green. *Norf* 1E **67**
Lunna. *Shet* 5F **173**
Lunning. *Shet* 5G **173**
Lunnon. *Swan* 4E **31**
Lunsford. *Kent* 5B **40**
Lunsford's Cross. *E Sus* 4B **28**
Lunt. *Mers* 4B **90**
Luppitt. *Devn* 2E **13**
Lupridge. *Devn* 3D **8**
Lupset. *W Yor* 3D **92**
Lupton. *Cumb* 1E **97**
Lurgashall. *W Sus* 3A **26**

Lurley. *Devn* 1C **12**
Lusby. *Linc* 4C **88**
Luscombe. *Devn* 3D **9**
Luson. *Devn* 4C **8**
Luss. *Arg* 4C **134**
Lussagiven. *Arg* 1E **125**
Lusta. *High* 3B **154**
Lustleigh. *Devn* 4A **12**
Luston. *Here* 4G **59**
Luthermuir. *Abers* 2F **145**
Luthrie. *Fife* 2F **137**
Lutley. *Staf* 2C **60**
Luton. *Devn* 2D **12**
(nr. Honiton)
Luton. *Devn* 5C **12**
(nr. Teignmouth)
Luton. *Lutn* 3A **52**
Luton (London) Airport. *Lutn* 3B **52**
Lutterworth. *Leics* 2C **62**
Lutton. *Devn* 3B **8**
(nr. Ivybridge)
Lutton. *Devn* 2C **8**
(nr. South Brent)
Lutton. *Linc* 3D **76**
Lutton. *Nptn* 2A **64**
Lutton Gowts. *Linc* 3D **76**
Lutworthy. *Devn* 1A **12**
Luxborough. *Som* 3C **20**
Luxley. *Glos* 3B **48**
Luxulyan. *Corn* 3E **7**
Lybster. *High* 5E **169**
Lydbury North. *Shrp* 2F **59**
Lydcott. *Devn* 3G **19**
Lydd. *Kent* 3E **29**
Lydden. *Kent* 1G **29**
(nr. Dover)
Lydden. *Kent* 4H **41**
(nr. Margate)
Lyddington. *Rut* 1F **63**
Lydd (London Ashford) Airport.
Kent 3E **29**
Lydd-on-Sea. *Kent* 4E **29**
Lydeard St Lawrence. *Som* 3E **21**
Lyde Green. *Hants* 1F **25**
Lydford. *Devn* 4F **11**
Lydford Fair Place. *Som* 3A **22**
Lydgate. *G Man* 4H **91**
Lydgate. *W Yor* 2H **91**
Lydham. *Shrp* 1F **59**
Lydiard Millicent. *Wilts* 3F **35**
Lydiate. *Mers* 4B **90**
Lydiate Ash. *Worc* 3D **61**
Lydlinch. *Dors* 1C **14**
Lydney. *Glos* 5B **48**
Lydstep. *Pemb* 5E **43**
Lye. *W Mid* 2D **60**
Lye Green. *Buck* 5H **51**
Lye Green. *E Sus* 2G **27**
Lye Head. *Worc* 3B **60**
Lye, The. *Shrp* 1A **60**
Lyford. *Oxon* 2B **36**
Lyham. *Nmbd* 1E **121**
Lylestone. *N Ayr* 5E **127**
Lymbridge Green. *Kent* 1F **29**
Lyme Regis. *Dors* 3G **13**
Lyminge. *Kent* 1F **29**
Lymington. *Hants* 3B **16**
Lyminster. *W Sus* 5B **26**
Lymm. *Warr* 2A **84**
Lymore. *Hants* 3A **16**
Lympne. *Kent* 2F **29**
Lympsham. *Som* 1G **21**
Lympstone. *Devn* 4C **12**
Lynaberack Lodge. *High* 4B **150**
Lynbridge. *Devn* 2H **19**
Lynch. *Som* 2C **20**
Lynchat. *High* 3B **150**
Lynch Green. *Norf* 5D **78**
Lyndhurst. *Hants* 2B **16**
Lyndon. *Rut* 5G **75**
Lyne. *Bord* 5F **129**
Lyne. *Surr* 4B **38**
Lyneal. *Shrp* 2G **71**
Lyne Down. *Here* 2B **48**
Lyneham. *Oxon* 3A **50**
Lyneham. *Wilts* 4F **35**
Lyneholmeford. *Cumb* 2G **113**
Lynemouth. *Nmbd* 5G **121**
Lyne of Gorthleck. *High* 1H **149**
Lyne of Skene. *Abers* 2E **153**
Lynesack. *Dur* 2D **105**
Lyness. *Orkn* 8C **172**
Lyng. *Norf* 4C **78**
Lyng. *Som* 4G **21**
Lyngate. *Norf* 2E **79**
(nr. North Walsham)
Lyngate. *Norf* 3F **79**
(nr. Worstead)
Lynmouth. *Devn* 2H **19**
Lynn. *Staf* 5E **73**
Lynn. *Telf* 4B **72**
Lynsted. *Kent* 4D **40**
Lynstone. *Corn* 2C **10**
Lynton. *Devn* 2H **19**
Lynwilg. *High* 2C **150**
Lyon's Gate. *Dors* 2B **14**
Lyonshall. *Here* 5F **59**
Lytchett Matravers. *Dors* 3E **15**
Lytchett Minster. *Dors* 3E **15**
Lyth. *High* 2E **169**
Lytham. *Lanc* 2B **90**
Lytham St Anne's. *Lanc* 2B **90**
Lythe. *N Yor* 3F **107**
Lythes. *Orkn* 9D **172**
Lythmore. *High* 2C **168**

M

Mabe Burnthouse. *Corn* 5B **6**
Mabie. *Dum* 2A **112**
Mablethorpe. *Linc* 2E **89**
Macbiehill. *Bord* 4E **129**
Macclesfield. *Ches* 3D **84**
Macclesfield Forest. *Ches* 3D **85**
Macduff. *Abers* 2E **160**
Machan. *S Lan* 4A **128**
Macharioch. *Arg* 5B **122**
Machen. *Cphy* 3F **33**
Machrie. *N Ayr* 2C **122**
Machrihanish. *Arg* 3A **122**
Machroes. *Gwyn* 3C **68**
Machynlleth. *Powy* 5G **69**
Mackerye End. *Herts* 4B **52**
Mackworth. *Derb* 2H **73**
Macmerry. *E Lot* 2H **129**
Maddaford. *Devn* 3F **11**
Madderty. *Per* 1B **136**
Maddington. *Wilts* 2F **23**
Maddiston. *Falk* 2C **128**
Madehurst. *W Sus* 4A **26**
Madeley. *Staf* 1B **72**
Madeley. *Telf* 5A **72**
Madeley Heath. *Staf* 1B **72**
Madeley Heath. *Worc* 3D **60**
Madford. *Devn* 1E **13**
Madingley. *Cambs* 4C **64**
Madley. *Here* 2H **47**
Madresfield. *Worc* 1D **48**
Madron. *Corn* 3B **4**
Maenaddwyn. *IOA* 2D **80**
Maenclochog. *Pemb* 2E **43**
Maendy. *V Glam* 4D **32**
Maenporth. *Corn* 4E **5**
Maentwrog. *Gwyn* 1F **69**
Maen-y-groes. *Cdgn* 5C **56**
Maer. *Staf* 2B **72**
Maerdy. *Carm* 3G **45**
Maerdy. *Cnwy* 1C **70**
Maerdy. *Rhon* 2C **32**
Maesbrook. *Shrp* 3F **71**
Maesbury. *Shrp* 3F **71**
Maesbury Marsh. *Shrp* 3F **71**
Maes-glas. *Flin* 3D **82**
Maesgwyn-Isaf. *Powy* 4D **70**
Maeshafn. *Den* 4E **82**
Maes Llyn. *Cdgn* 1D **44**
Maesmynis. *Powy* 1D **46**
Maesteg. *B'end* 2B **32**
Maestir. *Cdgn* 1F **45**
Maesybont. *Carm* 4F **45**
Maesycrugiau. *Carm* 1E **45**
Maesycwmmer. *Cphy* 2E **33**
Maesyrhandir. *Powy* 1C **58**
Magdalen Laver. *Essx* 5F **53**
Maggieknockater. *Mor* 4H **159**
Magham Down. *E Sus* 4H **27**
Maghull. *Mers* 4B **90**
Magna Park. *Leics* 2C **62**
Magor. *Mon* 3H **33**
Magpie Green. *Suff* 3C **66**
Magwyr. *Mon* 3H **33**
Maidenbower. *W Sus* 2D **27**
Maiden Bradley. *Wilts* 3D **22**
Maidencombe. *Torb* 2F **9**
Maidenhayne. *Devn* 3F **13**
Maidenhead. *Wind* 3G **37**
Maiden Law. *Dur* 5E **115**
Maiden Newton. *Dors* 3A **14**
Maidens. *S Ayr* 4B **116**
Maiden's Green. *Brac* 4G **37**
Maidensgrove. *Oxon* 3F **37**
Maidenwell. *Corn* 5B **10**
Maidenwell. *Linc* 3C **88**
Maiden Wells. *Pemb* 5D **42**
Maidford. *Nptn* 5D **62**
Maids Moreton. *Buck* 2F **51**
Maidstone. *Kent* 5B **40**
Maidwell. *Nptn* 3E **63**
Mail. *Shet* 9F **173**
Maindee. *Newp* 3G **33**
Mainsforth. *Dur* 1A **106**
Mains of Auchindachy. *Mor* 4B **160**
Mains of Auchnagatt. *Abers* 4G **161**
Mains of Drum. *Abers* 4F **153**
Mains of Edingight. *Mor* 3C **160**
Mainsriddle. *Dum* 4G **111**
Mainstone. *Shrp* 2E **59**
Maisemore. *Glos* 3D **48**
Major's Green. *Worc* 3F **61**
Makeney. *Derbs* 1A **74**
Makerstoun. *Bord* 1A **120**
Malacleit. *W Isl* 1C **170**
Malborough. *Devn* 5D **8**
Malcoff. *Derbs* 2E **85**
Malcolmburn. *Mor* 3A **160**
Malden Rushett. *G Lon* 4C **38**
Maldon. *Essx* 5B **54**
Malham. *N Yor* 3B **98**
Maligar. *High* 2D **155**
Malinslee. *Telf* 5A **72**
Mallaig. *High* 4E **147**
Mallaig Bheag. *High* 4E **147**
Malleny Mills. *Edin* 3E **129**
Mallows Green. *Essx* 3E **53**
Malltraeth. *IOA* 4D **80**
Mallwyd. *Gwyn* 4A **70**
Malmesbury. *Wilts* 3E **35**
Malmsmead. *Devn* 2A **20**
Malpas. *Ches* 1G **71**
Malpas. *Corn* 4C **6**
Malpas. *Newp* 2F **33**
Malswick. *Glos* 3C **48**
Maltby. *S Yor* 1C **86**
Maltby. *Stoc T* 3B **106**
Maltby le Marsh. *Linc* 2D **88**
Malt Lane. *Arg* 3H **133**
Maltman's Hill. *Kent* 1D **28**
Malton. *N Yor* 2B **100**
Malvern Link. *Worc* 1C **48**
Malvern Wells. *Worc* 1C **48**
Mamble. *Worc* 3A **60**
Mamhilad. *Mon* 5G **47**
Manaccan. *Corn* 4E **5**
Manafon. *Powy* 5D **70**
Manaton. *Devn* 4A **12**
Manby. *Linc* 2C **88**
Mancetter. *Warw* 1H **61**
Manchester. *G Man* 1C **84**
Manchester International Airport.
G Man 2C **84**
Mancot. *Flin* 4F **83**
Manea. *Cambs* 2D **65**
Maney. *W Mid* 1F **61**
Manfield. *N Yor* 3F **105**
Mangotsfield. *S Glo* 4B **34**
Mangurstadh. *W Isl* 4C **171**
Mankinholes. *W Yor* 2H **91**
Manley. *Ches* 3H **83**
Manley. *Devn* 1C **12**
Manmoel. *Cphy* 5E **47**
Mannal. *Arg* 4A **138**
Mannerston. *Falk* 2D **128**
Manningford Bohune. *Wilts* 1G **23**
Manningford Bruce. *Wilts* 1G **23**
Manningham. *W Yor* 1B **92**
Mannings Heath. *W Sus* 3D **26**
Mannington. *Dors* 2F **15**
Manningtree. *Essx* 2E **54**
Mannofield. *Aber* 3G **153**
Manorbier. *Pemb* 5E **43**
Manorbier Newton. *Pemb* 5E **43**
Manorowen. *Pemb* 1D **42**
Manor Park. *G Lon* 2F **39**
Mansell Gamage. *Here* 1G **47**
Mansell Lacy. *Here* 1H **47**
Mansergh. *Cumb* 1F **97**
Mansewood. *Glas* 3G **127**
Mansfield. *E Ayr* 3F **117**
Mansfield. *Notts* 4C **86**
Mansfield Woodhouse.
Notts 4C **86**
Mansriggs. *Cumb* 1B **96**
Manston. *Dors* 1D **14**
Manston. *Kent* 4H **41**
Manston. *W Yor* 1D **92**
Manswood. *Dors* 2E **15**
Manthorpe. *Linc* 4H **75**
(nr. Bourne)
Manthorpe. *Linc* 2G **75**
(nr. Grantham)
Manton. *N Lin* 4C **94**
Manton. *Notts* 3C **86**
Manton. *Rut* 5F **75**
Manton. *Wilts* 5G **35**
Manuden. *Essx* 3E **53**
Maperton. *Som* 4B **22**
Maplebeck. *Notts* 4E **86**
Maple Cross. *Herts* 1B **38**
Mapledurham. *Oxon* 4E **37**
Mapledurwell. *Hants* 1E **25**
Maplehurst. *W Sus* 3C **26**
Maplescombe. *Kent* 4G **39**
Mapleton. *Derbs* 1F **73**
Mapperley. *Derbs* 1B **74**
Mapperley. *Notts* 1C **74**
Mapperley Park. *Notts* 1C **74**
Mapperton. *Dors* 3A **14**
(nr. Beaminster)
Mapperton. *Dors* 3E **15**
(nr. Poole)
Mappleborough Green.
Warw 4E **61**
Mappleton. *E Yor* 5G **101**
Mapplewell. *S Yor* 4D **92**
Mappowder. *Dors* 2C **14**
Maraig. *W Isl* 7E **171**
Marazion. *Corn* 3C **4**
Marbhig. *W Isl* 6G **171**
Marbury. *Ches* 1H **71**
March. *Cambs* 1D **64**
Marcham. *Oxon* 2C **36**
Marchamley. *Shrp* 3H **71**
Marchington. *Staf* 2F **73**
Marchington Woodlands.
Staf 3F **73**
Marchwiel. *Wrex* 1F **71**
Marchwood. *Hants* 1B **16**
Marcross. *V Glam* 5C **32**
Marden. *Here* 1A **48**
Marden. *Kent* 1B **28**
Marden. *Wilts* 1F **23**
Marden Beech. *Kent* 1B **28**
Marden Thorn. *Kent* 1B **28**
Mardu. *Shrp* 2E **59**
Mardy. *Mon* 4G **47**
Marefield. *Leics* 5E **75**
Mareham le Fen. *Linc* 4B **88**
Mareham on the Hill. *Linc* 4B **88**
Marehay. *Derbs* 1A **74**
Marehill. *W Sus* 4B **26**
Maresfield. *E Sus* 3F **27**
Marfleet. *Hull* 2E **95**
Marford. *Wrex* 5F **83**
Margam. *Neat* 3A **32**
Margaret Marsh. *Dors* 1D **14**
Margaret Roding. *Essx* 4F **53**
Margaretting. *Essx* 5G **53**
Margaretting Tye. *Essx* 5G **53**
Margate. *Kent* 3H **41**
Margery. *Surr* 5D **38**
Margnaheglish. *N Ayr* 2E **123**
Marham. *Norf* 5G **77**
Marhamchurch. *Corn* 2C **10**
Marholm. *Pet* 5A **76**
Marian Cwm. *Den* 3C **82**
Mariandyrys. *IOA* 2F **81**
Marian-glas. *IOA* 2E **81**
Mariansleigh. *Devn* 4H **19**
Marian-y-de. *Gwyn* 2C **68**
Marine Town. *Kent* 3D **40**
Marion-y-mor. *Gwyn* 2C **68**
Marishader. *High* 2D **155**
Marjoriebanks. *Dum* 1B **112**
Mark. *Dum* 4G **109**
Mark. *Som* 2G **21**
Markbeech. *Kent* 1F **27**
Markby. *Linc* 3D **89**
Mark Causeway. *Som* 2G **21**
Mark Cross. *E Sus* 2G **27**
Markeaton. *Derb* 2H **73**
Market Bosworth. *Leics* 5B **74**
Market Deeping. *Linc* 4A **76**
Market Drayton. *Shrp* 2A **72**
Market End. *Warw* 2H **61**
Market Harborough. *Leics* 2E **63**
Markethill. *Per* 5B **144**
Market Lavington. *Wilts* 1F **23**
Market Overton. *Rut* 4F **75**
Market Rasen. *Linc* 2A **88**
Market Stainton. *Linc* 2B **88**
Market Warsop. *Notts* 4C **86**
Market Weighton. *E Yor* 5C **100**
Market Weston. *Suff* 3B **66**
Markfield. *Leics* 4B **74**
Markham. *Cphy* 5E **47**
Markinch. *Fife* 3E **137**
Markington. *N Yor* 3E **99**
Marksbury. *Bath* 5B **34**
Mark's Corner. *IOW* 3C **16**
Marks Tey. *Essx* 3C **54**
Markwell. *Corn* 3H **7**
Markyate. *Herts* 4A **52**
Marlborough. *Wilts* 5G **35**
Marlcliff. *Warw* 5E **61**
Marldon. *Devn* 2E **9**
Marle Green. *E Sus* 4G **27**
Marlesford. *Suff* 5F **67**
Marley Green. *Ches* 1H **71**
Marley Hill. *Tyne* 4F **115**
Marlingford. *Norf* 5D **78**
Marloes. *Pemb* 4B **42**
Marlow. *Buck* 3G **37**
Marlow. *Here* 3G **59**
Marlow Bottom. *Buck* 3G **37**
Marlpit Hill. *Kent* 1F **27**
Marlpits. *E Sus* 3F **27**
Marlpool. *Derbs* 1B **74**
Marnhull. *Dors* 1C **14**
Marnoch. *Abers* 3C **160**
Marnock. *N Lan* 3A **128**
Marple. *G Man* 2D **84**
Marr. *S Yor* 4F **93**
Marrel. *High* 2H **165**
Marrick. *N Yor* 5D **105**
Marros. *Carm* 4G **43**
Marsden. *Tyne* 3G **115**
Marsden. *W Yor* 3A **92**
Marsett. *N Yor* 1B **98**
Marsh. *Buck* 5G **51**

Marsh—Micheldever Station

Marsh. *Devn* 1F **13**
Marshall Meadows. *Nmbd* 4F **131**
Marshalsea. *Dors* 2G **13**
Marshalswick. *Herts* 5B **52**
Marsham. *Norf* 3D **78**
Marshaw. *Lanc* 4E **97**
Marsh Baldon. *Oxon* 2D **36**
Marsh Benham. *W Ber* 5C **36**
Marshborough. *Kent* 5H **41**
Marshbrook. *Shrp* 2G **59**
Marshchapel. *Linc* 1C **88**
Marshfield. *Newp* 3F **33**
Marshfield. *S Glo* 4C **34**
Marshgate. *Corn* 3B **10**
Marsh Gibbon. *Buck* 3E **51**
Marsh Green. *Devn* 3D **12**
Marsh Green. *Kent* 1F **27**
Marsh Green. *Staf* 5C **84**
Marsh Green. *Telf* 4A **72**
Marsh Lane. *Derbs* 3B **86**
Marshside. *Kent* 4G **41**
Marshside. *Mers* 3B **90**
Marsh Side. *Norf* 1G **77**
Marsh Street. *Som* 2C **20**
Marsh, The. *Powy* 1F **59**
Marsh, The. *Shrp* 3A **72**
Marshwood. *Dors* 3G **13**
Marske. *N Yor* 4E **105**
Marske-by-the-Sea. *Red C* 2D **106**
Marston. *Ches* 3A **84**
Marston. *Here* 5F **59**
Marston. *Linc* 1F **75**
Marston. *Oxon* 5D **50**
Marston. *Staf* 3D **72**
(nr. Stafford)
Marston. *Staf* 4C **72**
(nr. Wheaton Aston)
Marston. *Warw* 1G **61**
Marston. *Wilts* 1E **23**
Marston Doles. *Warw* 5B **62**
Marston Green. *W Mid* 2F **61**
Marston Hill. *Glos* 2G **35**
Marston Jabbett. *Warw* 2A **62**
Marston Magna. *Som* 4A **22**
Marston Meysey. *Wilts* 2G **35**
Marston Montgomery.
Derbs 2F **73**
Marston Moretaine. *Beds* 1H **51**
Marston on Dove. *Derbs* 3G **73**
Marston St Lawrence.
Nptn 1D **50**
Marston Stannett. *Here* 5H **59**
Marston Trussell. *Nptn* 2D **62**
Marstow. *Here* 4A **48**
Marsworth. *Buck* 4H **51**
Marten. *Wilts* 5A **36**
Marthall. *Ches* 3C **84**
Martham. *Norf* 4G **79**
Marthwaite. *Cumb* 5H **103**
Martin. *Hants* 1F **15**
Martin. *Kent* 1H **29**
Martin. *Linc* 4B **88**
(nr. Horncastle)
Martin. *Linc* 5A **88**
(nr. Metheringham)
Martindale. *Cumb* 3F **103**
Martin Dales. *Linc* 4A **88**
Martin Drove End. *Hants* 4F **23**
Martinhoe. *Devn* 2G **19**
Martinhoe Cross. *Devn* 2G **19**
Martin Hussingtree. *Worc* 4C **60**
Martin Mill. *Kent* 1H **29**
Martinscroft. *Warr* 2A **84**
Martin's Moss. *Ches* 4C **84**
Martinstown. *Dors* 4B **14**
Martlesham. *Suff* 1F **55**
Martlesham Heath. *Suff* 1F **55**
Martletwy. *Pemb* 3E **43**
Martley. *Worc* 5B **60**
Martock. *Som* 1H **13**
Marton. *Ches* 4C **84**
Marton. *Cumb* 2B **96**
Marton. *E Yor* 3G **101**
(nr. Bridlington)
Marton. *E Yor* 1E **95**
(nr. Hull)
Marton. *Linc* 2F **87**
Marton. *Midd* 3C **106**
Marton. *N Yor* 3G **99**
(nr. Boroughbridge)
Marton. *N Yor* 1B **100**
(nr. Pickering)
Marton. *Shrp* 3G **71**
(nr. Myddle)
Marton. *Shrp* 5E **71**
(nr. Worthen)
Marton. *Warw* 4B **62**
Marton Abbey. *N Yor* 3H **99**
Marton-le-Moor. *N Yor* 2F **99**
Martyr's Green. *Surr* 5B **38**
Martyr Worthy. *Hants* 3D **24**
Marwood. *Devn* 3F **19**
Marybank. *High* 3G **157**
(nr. Dingwall)
Marybank. *High* 1B **158**
(nr. Invergordon)
Maryburgh. *High* 3H **157**
Maryfield. *Corn* 3A **8**
Maryhill. *Glas* 3G **127**
Marykirk. *Abers* 2F **145**
Marylebone. *G Lon* 2D **39**
Marylebone. *G Man* 4D **90**
Marypark. *Mor* 5F **159**
Maryport. *Cumb* 1B **102**
Maryport. *Dum* 5E **109**
Marystow. *Devn* 4E **11**
Mary Tavy. *Devn* 5F **11**
Maryton. *Ang* 3C **144**
(nr. Kirriemuir)
Maryton. *Ang* 3F **145**
(nr. Montrose)
Marywell. *Abers* 4C **152**
Marywell. *Ang* 4F **145**
Masham. *N Yor* 1E **98**
Mashbury. *Essx* 4G **53**
Masongill. *N Yor* 2F **97**
Masons Lodge. *Abers* 3F **153**
Mastin Moor. *Derbs* 3B **86**
Mastrick. *Aber* 3G **153**
Matching. *Essx* 4F **53**
Matching Green. *Essx* 4F **53**
Matching Tye. *Essx* 4F **53**
Matfen. *Nmbd* 2D **114**
Matfield. *Kent* 1A **28**
Mathern. *Mon* 2A **34**
Mathon. *Here* 1C **48**
Mathry. *Pemb* 1C **42**
Matlaske. *Norf* 2D **78**
Matlock. *Derbs* 4G **85**
Matlock Bath. *Derbs* 5G **85**
Matterdale End. *Cumb* 2E **103**
Mattersey. *Notts* 2D **86**
Mattersey Thorpe. *Notts* 2D **86**
Mattingley. *Hants* 1F **25**
Mattishall. *Norf* 4C **78**
Mattishall Burgh. *Norf* 4C **78**
Mauchline. *E Ayr* 2D **117**
Maud. *Abers* 4G **161**
Maudlin. *Corn* 2E **7**
Maugersbury. *Glos* 3G **49**
Maughold. *IOM* 2D **108**
Maulden. *Beds* 2A **52**
Maulds Meaburn. *Cumb* 3H **103**
Maunby. *N Yor* 1F **99**
Maund Bryan. *Here* 5H **59**
Mautby. *Norf* 4G **79**
Mavesyn Ridware. *Staf* 4E **73**
Mavis Enderby. *Linc* 4C **88**
Mawbray. *Cumb* 5B **112**
Mawdesley. *Lanc* 3C **90**
Mawdlam. *B'end* 3B **32**
Mawgan. *Corn* 4E **5**
Mawgan Porth. *Corn* 2C **6**
Maw Green. *Ches* 5B **84**
Mawla. *Corn* 4B **6**
Mawnan. *Corn* 4E **5**
Mawnan Smith. *Corn* 4E **5**
Mawthorpe. *Linc* 3D **88**
Maxey. *Pet* 5A **76**
Maxstoke. *Warw* 2G **61**
Maxton. *Kent* 1G **29**
Maxton. *Bord* 1A **120**
Maxwellheugh. *Bord* 1B **120**
Maxwelltown. *Dum* 2A **112**
Maxworthy. *Corn* 3C **10**
Mayals. *Swan* 4F **31**
Maybole. *S Ayr* 4C **116**
Maybush. *Sotn* 1B **16**
Mayes Green. *Surr* 2C **26**
Mayfield. *E Sus* 3G **27**
Mayfield. *Midl* 3G **129**
Mayfield. *Per* 1C **136**
Mayfield. *Staf* 1F **73**
Mayford. *Surr* 5A **38**
Mayhill. *Swan* 3F **31**
Mayland. *Essx* 5C **54**
Maylandsea. *Essx* 5C **54**
Maynard's Green. *E Sus* 4G **27**
Maypole. *IOS* 1B **4**
Maypole. *Kent* 4G **41**
Maypole. *Mon* 4H **47**
Maypole Green. *Norf* 1G **67**
Maypole Green. *Suff* 5B **66**
Mayshill. *S Glo* 3B **34**
Maywick. *Shet* 9E **173**
Mead. *Devn* 1C **10**
Meadgate. *Bath* 1B **22**
Meadle. *Buck* 5G **51**
Meadowbank. *Ches* 4A **84**
Meadowfield. *Dur* 1F **105**
Meadow Green. *Here* 5B **60**
Meadowmill. *E Lot* 2H **129**
Meadows. *Nott* 2C **74**
Meadowtown. *Shrp* 5F **71**
Meadwell. *Devn* 4E **11**
Mealabost. *W Isl* 2G **171**
(nr. Borgh)
Mealabost. *W Isl* 4G **171**
(nr. Stornoway)
Meal Bank. *Cumb* 5G **103**
Mealrigg. *Cumb* 5C **112**
Mealsgate. *Cumb* 5D **112**
Meanwood. *W Yor* 1C **92**
Mearbeck. *N Yor* 3H **97**
Meare. *Som* 2H **21**
Meare Green. *Som* 4F **21**
(nr. Curry Mallet)
Meare Green. *Som* 4G **21**
(nr. Stoke St Gregory)
Mears Ashby. *Nptn* 4F **63**
Measham. *Leics* 4H **73**
Meath Green. *Surr* 1D **27**
Meathop. *Cumb* 1D **96**
Meaux. *E Yor* 1D **94**
Meavy. *Devn* 2B **8**
Medbourne. *Leics* 1E **63**
Medburn. *Nmbd* 2E **115**
Meddon. *Devn* 1C **10**
Meden Vale. *Notts* 4C **86**
Medlam. *Linc* 5C **88**
Medlicott. *Shrp* 1G **59**
Medmenham. *Buck* 3G **37**
Medomsley. *Dur* 4E **115**
Medstead. *Hants* 3E **25**
Medway Towns. *Medw* 4B **40**
Meerbrook. *Staf* 4D **85**
Meer End. *W Mid* 3G **61**
Meers Bridge. *Linc* 2D **89**
Meesden. *Herts* 2E **53**
Meeson. *Telf* 3A **72**
Meeth. *Devn* 2F **11**
Meeting Green. *Suff* 5G **65**
Meidrim. *Carm* 2G **43**
Meifod. *Powy* 4D **70**
Meigle. *Per* 4B **144**
Meikle Earnock. *S Lan* 4A **128**
Meikle Kilchattan Butts.
Arg 4B **126**
Meikleour. *Per* 5A **144**
Meikle Tarty. *Abers* 1G **153**
Meikle Wartle. *Abers* 5E **160**
Meinciau. *Carm* 4E **45**
Meir. *Stoke* 1D **72**
Meir Heath. *Staf* 1D **72**
Melbourn. *Cambs* 1D **53**
Melbourne. *Derbs* 3A **74**
Melbourne. *E Yor* 5B **100**
Melbury Abbas. *Dors* 4D **23**
Melbury Bubb. *Dors* 2A **14**
Melbury Osmond. *Dors* 2A **14**
Melbury Sampford. *Dors* 2A **14**
Melby. *Shet* 6C **173**
Melchbourne. *Beds* 4H **63**
Melcombe Bingham. *Dors* 2C **14**
Melcombe Regis. *Dors* 4B **14**
Meldon. *Devn* 3F **11**
Meldon. *Nmbd* 1E **115**
Meldreth. *Cambs* 1D **53**
Melfort. *Arg* 2F **133**
Melgarve. *High* 4G **149**
Meliden. *Den* 2C **82**
Melinbyrhedyn. *Powy* 1H **57**
Melincourt. *Neat* 5B **46**
Melin-y-coed. *Cnwy* 4H **81**
Melin-y-ddol. *Powy* 5C **70**
Melin-y-wig. *Den* 1C **70**
Melkington. *Nmbd* 5E **131**
Melkinthorpe. *Cumb* 2G **103**
Melkridge. *Nmbd* 3A **114**
Melksham. *Wilts* 5E **35**
Mellangaun. *High* 5C **162**
Melldalloch. *Arg* 2H **125**
Mellguards. *Cumb* 5F **113**
Melling. *Lanc* 2E **97**
Melling. *Mers* 4B **90**
Melling Mount. *Mers* 4C **90**
Mellis. *Suff* 3C **66**
Mellon Charles. *High* 4C **162**
Mellon Udrigle. *High* 4C **162**
Mellor. *G Man* 2D **85**
Mellor. *Lanc* 1E **91**
Mellor Brook. *Lanc* 1E **91**
Mells. *Som* 2C **22**
Melmerby. *Cumb* 1H **103**
Melmerby. *N Yor* 1C **98**
(nr. Middleham)
Melmerby. *N Yor* 2F **99**
(nr. Ripon)
Melplash. *Dors* 3H **13**
Melrose. *Bord* 1H **119**
Melsonby. *N Yor* 4E **105**
Meltham. *W Yor* 3A **92**
Meltham Mills. *W Yor* 3B **92**
Melton. *E Yor* 2C **94**
Melton. *Suff* 5E **67**
Meltonby. *E Yor* 4B **100**
Melton Constable. *Norf* 2C **78**
Melton Mowbray. *Leics* 4E **75**
Melton Ross. *N Lin* 3D **94**
Melvaig. *High* 5B **162**
Melverley. *Shrp* 4F **71**
Melverley Green. *Shrp* 4F **71**
Melvich. *High* 2A **168**
Membury. *Devn* 2F **13**
Memsie. *Abers* 2G **161**
Memus. *Ang* 3D **144**
Menabilly. *Corn* 3E **7**
Menai Bridge. *IOA* 3E **81**
Mendham. *Suff* 2E **67**
Mendlesham. *Suff* 4D **66**
Mendlesham Green. *Suff* 4C **66**
Menethorpe. *N Yor* 3B **100**
Menheniot. *Corn* 2G **7**
Menithwood. *Worc* 4B **60**
Menna. *Corn* 3D **6**
Mennock. *Dum* 4H **117**
Menston. *W Yor* 5D **98**
Menstrie. *Clac* 4H **135**
Menthorpe. *N Yor* 1H **93**
Mentmore. *Buck* 4H **51**
Meole Brace. *Shrp* 4G **71**
Meols. *Mers* 2E **83**
Meon. *Hants* 2D **16**
Meonstoke. *Hants* 4E **24**
Meopham. *Kent* 4H **39**
Meopham Green. *Kent* 4H **39**
Meopham Station. *Kent* 4H **39**
Mepal. *Cambs* 2D **64**
Meppershall. *Beds* 2B **52**
Merbach. *Here* 1G **47**
Mercaston. *Derbs* 1G **73**
Merchiston. *Edin* 2F **129**
Mere. *Ches* 2B **84**
Mere. *Wilts* 3D **22**
Mere Brow. *Lanc* 3C **90**
Mereclough. *Lanc* 1G **91**
Mere Green. *W Mid* 1F **61**
Mere Green. *Worc* 4D **60**
Mere Heath. *Ches* 3A **84**
Mereside. *Bkpl* 1B **90**
Meretown. *Staf* 3B **72**
Mereworth. *Kent* 5A **40**
Meriden. *W Mid* 2G **61**
Merkadale. *High* 5C **154**
Merkland. *S Ayr* 5B **116**
Merkland Lodge. *High* 1A **164**
Merley. *Pool* 3F **15**
Merlin's Bridge. *Pemb* 3D **42**
Merridge. *Som* 3F **21**
Merrington. *Shrp* 3G **71**
Merrion. *Pemb* 5D **42**
Merriott. *Som* 1H **13**
Merrivale. *Devn* 5F **11**
Merrow. *Surr* 5B **38**
Merrybent. *Darl* 3F **105**
Merry Lees. *Leics* 5B **74**
Merrymeet. *Corn* 2G **7**
Mersham. *Kent* 2E **29**
Merstham. *Surr* 5D **39**
Merston. *W Sus* 2G **17**
Merstone. *IOW* 4D **16**
Merther. *Corn* 4C **6**
Merthyr. *Carm* 3D **44**
Merthyr Cynog. *Powy* 2C **46**
Merthyr Dyfan. *V Glam* 4E **32**
Merthyr Mawr. *B'end* 4B **32**
Merthyr Tudful. *Mer T* 5D **46**
Merthyr Tydfil. *Mer T* 5D **46**
Merthyr Vale. *Mer T* 5D **46**
Merton. *Devn* 1F **11**
Merton. *G Lon* 4D **38**
Merton. *Norf* 1B **66**
Merton. *Oxon* 4D **50**
Meshaw. *Devn* 1A **12**
Messing. *Essx* 4B **54**
Messingham. *N Lin* 4B **94**
Metcombe. *Devn* 3D **12**
Metfield. *Suff* 2E **67**
Metherell. *Corn* 2A **8**
Metheringham. *Linc* 4H **87**
Methil. *Fife* 4F **137**
Methilhill. *Fife* 4F **137**
Methley. *W Yor* 2D **93**
Methley Junction. *W Yor* 2D **93**
Methlick. *Abers* 5F **161**
Methven. *Per* 1C **136**
Methwold. *Norf* 1G **65**
Methwold Hythe. *Norf* 1G **65**
Mettingham. *Suff* 1F **67**
Metton. *Norf* 2D **78**
Mevagissey. *Corn* 4E **6**
Mexborough. *S Yor* 4E **93**
Mey. *High* 1E **169**
Meysey Hampton. *Glos* 2G **35**
Miabhag. *W Isl* 8D **171**
Miabhaig. *W Isl* 7C **171**
(nr. Cliasmol)
Miabhaig. *W Isl* 4C **171**
(nr. Timsgearraidh)
Mial. *High* 1G **155**
Michaelchurch. *Here* 3A **48**
Michaelchurch Escley. *Here* 2G **47**
Michaelchurch-on-Arrow.
Powy 5E **59**
Michaelcombe. *Devn* 2C **8**
Michaelston-le-Pit. *V Glam* 4E **33**
Michaelston-y-Vedw. *Newp* 3F **33**
Michaelstow. *Corn* 5A **10**
Micheldever. *Hants* 3D **24**
Micheldever Station. *Hants* 2D **24**

Michelmersh—Mitchel Troy

Michelmersh. Hants 4B 24
Mickfield. Suff 4D 66
Micklebring. S Yor 1C 86
Mickleby. N Yor 3F 107
Micklefield. W Yor 1E 93
Micklefield Green. Herts 1B 38
Mickleham. Surr 5C 38
Mickleover. Derb 2H 73
Micklethwaite. Cumb 4D 112
Micklethwaite. W Yor 5D 98
Mickleton. Dur 2C 104
Mickleton. Glos 1G 49
Mickletown. W Yor 2D 93
Mickle Trafford. Ches 4G 83
Mickley. N Yor 2E 99
Mickley Green. Suff 5H 65
Mickley Square. Nmbd 3D 115
Mid Ardlaw. Abers 2G 161
Midbea. Orkn 3D 172
Mid Beltie. Abers 3D 152
Mid Calder. W Lot 3D 129
Mid Clyth. High 5E 169
Middle Assendon. Oxon 3F 37
Middle Aston. Oxon 3C 50
Middle Barton. Oxon 3C 50
Middlebie. Dum 2D 112
Middle Chinnock. Som 1H 13
Middle Claydon. Buck 3F 51
Middlecliff. S Yor 4E 93
Middlecott. Devn 4H 11
Middle Drums. Ang 3E 145
Middle Duntisbourne. Glos 5E 49
Middle Essie. Abers 3H 161
Middleforth Green. Lanc 2D 90
Middleham. N Yor 1D 98
Middle Handley. Derbs 3B 86
Middle Harling. Norf 2B 66
Middlehope. Shrp 2G 59
Middle Littleton. Worc 1F 49
Middle Maes-coed. Here 2G 47
Middlemarsh. Dors 2B 14
Middle Marwood. Devn 3F 19
Middle Mayfield. Staf 1F 73
Middlemoor. Devn 5E 11
Middlemuir. Abers 4F 161 (nr. New Deer)
Middlemuir. Abers 3G 161 (nr. Strichen)
Middle Rainton. Tyne 5G 115
Middle Rasen. Linc 2H 87
Middlesbrough. Midd 3B 106
Middlesceugh. Cumb 5E 113
Middleshaw. Cumb 1E 97
Middlesmoor. N Yor 2C 98
Middles, The. Dur 4F 115
Middlestone. Dur 1F 105
Middlestone Moor. Dur 1F 105
Middle Stoughton. Som 2H 21
Middlestown. W Yor 3C 92
Middle Street. Glos 5C 48
Middle Taphouse. Corn 2F 7
Middleton. Ang 4E 145
Middleton. Arg 4A 138
Middleton. Cumb 1F 97
Middleton. Derbs 4F 85 (nr. Bakewell)
Middleton. Derbs 5G 85 (nr. Wirksworth)
Middleton. Essx 2B 54
Middleton. G Man 4G 91
Middleton. Hants 2C 24
Middleton. Hart 1C 106
Middleton. Here 4H 59
Middleton. IOW 4B 16
Middleton. Lanc 4D 96
Middleton. Midl 4G 129
Middleton. Norf 4F 77
Middleton. Nptn 1F 63
Middleton. Nmbd 1F 121 (nr. Belford)
Middleton. Nmbd 1D 114 (nr. Morpeth)
Middleton. N Yor 5D 98 (nr. Ilkley)
Middleton. N Yor 1B 100 (nr. Pickering)
Middleton. Per 3D 136
Middleton. Shrp 3H 59 (nr. Ludlow)
Middleton. Shrp 3F 71 (nr. Oswestry)
Middleton. Suff 4G 67
Middleton. Swan 4D 30
Middleton. Warw 1F 61
Middleton. W Yor 2D 92
Middleton Cheney. Nptn 1D 50
Middleton Green. Staf 2D 73
Middleton Hall. Nmbd 2D 121
Middleton-in-Teesdale. Dur 2C 104
Middleton One Row. Darl 3A 106
Middleton-on-Leven. N Yor 4B 106
Middleton-on-Sea. W Sus 5A 26
Middleton on the Hill. Here 4H 59
Middleton-on-the-Wolds. E Yor 5D 100
Middleton Priors. Shrp 1A 60
Middleton Quernhow. N Yor 2F 99
Middleton St George. Darl 3A 106
Middleton Scriven. Shrp 2A 60
Middleton Stoney. Oxon 3D 50
Middleton Tyas. N Yor 4F 105
Middletown. Cumb 4A 102
Middle Town. IOS 1B 4
Middletown. Powy 4F 71
Middle Tysoe. Warw 1B 50
Middle Wallop. Hants 3A 24
Middlewich. Ches 4B 84
Middle Winterslow. Wilts 3H 23
Middlewood. Corn 5C 10
Middlewood. S Yor 1H 85
Middle Woodford. Wilts 3G 23
Middlewood Green. Suff 4C 66
Middleyard. Glos 5D 48
Middlezoy. Som 3G 21
Middridge. Dur 2F 105
Midfield. High 2F 167
Midford. Bath 5C 34
Mid Garrary. Dum 2C 110
Midge Hall. Lanc 2D 90
Midgeholme. Cumb 4H 113
Midgham. W Ber 5D 36
Midgley. W Yor 2A 92 (nr. Halifax)
Midgley. W Yor 3C 92 (nr. Horbury)
Midhopestones. S Yor 1G 85
Midhurst. W Sus 4G 25
Mid Kirkton. N Ayr 4C 126
Mid Lambrook. Som 1H 13
Midland. Orkn 7C 172
Mid Lavant. W Sus 2G 17
Midlem. Bord 2H 119
Midney. Som 4A 22
Midsomer Norton. Bath 1B 22
Midton. Inv 2D 126
Midtown. High 5C 162 (nr. Poolewe)
Midtown. High 2F 167 (nr. Tongue)
Midville. Linc 5C 88
Midway. Derbs 3H 73
Mid Yell. Shet 2G 173
Migdale. High 4D 164
Migvie. Abers 3B 152
Milborne Port. Som 1B 14
Milborne St Andrew. Dors 3D 14
Milborne Wick. Som 4B 22
Milbourne. Nmbd 2E 115
Milbourne. Wilts 3E 35
Milburn. Cumb 2H 103
Milbury Heath. S Glo 2B 34
Milby. N Yor 3G 99
Milcombe. Oxon 2C 50
Milden. Suff 1C 54
Mildenhall. Suff 3G 65
Mildenhall. Wilts 5H 35
Milebrook. Powy 3F 59
Milebush. Kent 1B 28
Mile End. Cambs 2F 65
Mile End. Essx 3C 54
Mileham. Norf 4B 78
Mile Oak. Brig 5D 26
Miles Green. Staf 5C 84
Miles Hope. Here 4H 59
Milesmark. Fife 1D 128
Mile Town. Kent 3D 40
Milfield. Nmbd 1D 120
Milford. Derbs 1A 74
Milford. Devn 4C 18
Milford. Powy 1C 58
Milford. Staf 3D 72
Milford. Surr 1A 26
Milford Haven. Pemb 4D 42
Milford on Sea. Hants 3A 16
Milkwall. Glos 5A 48
Milkwell. Wilts 4E 23
Milland. W Sus 4G 25
Millbank. High 2D 168
Mill Bank. W Yor 2A 92
Millbeck. Cumb 2D 102
Millbounds. Orkn 4E 172
Millbreck. Abers 4H 161
Millbridge. Surr 2G 25
Millbrook. Beds 2A 52
Millbrook. Corn 3A 8
Millbrook. G Man 1D 85
Millbrook. Sotn 1B 16
Mill Common. Suff 2G 67
Mill Corner. E Sus 3C 28
Milldale. Staf 5F 85
Millden Lodge. Ang 1E 145
Milldens. Ang 3E 145
Millearn. Per 2B 136
Mill End. Buck 3F 37
Mill End. Cambs 5F 65
Millend. Glos 2C 34 (nr. Dursley)
Mill End. Glos 4G 49 (nr. Northleach)
Mill End. Herts 2D 52
Millerhill. Midl 3G 129
Miller's Dale. Derbs 3F 85
Millers Green. Derbs 5G 85
Millerston. N Lan 3H 127
Millfield. Abers 4B 152
Millfield. Pet 1A 64
Millgate. Lanc 3G 91
Mill Green. Essx 5G 53
Mill Green. Norf 2D 66
Mill Green. Shrp 3A 72
Mill Green. Staf 3E 73
Mill Green. Suff 1C 54
Millhalf. Here 1F 47
Millhall. E Ren 4G 127
Millhayes. Devn 2F 13 (nr. Honiton)
Millhayes. Devn 1E 13 (nr. Wellington)
Millhead. Lanc 2D 97
Millheugh. S Lan 4A 128
Mill Hill. Bkbn 2E 91
Mill Hill. G Lon 1D 38
Millholme. Cumb 5G 103
Millhouse. Arg 2A 126
Millhousebridge. Dum 1C 112
Millhouses. S Yor 2H 85
Millikenpark. Ren 3F 127
Millington. E Yor 4C 100
Millington Green. Derbs 1G 73
Mill Knowe. Arg 3B 122
Mill Lane. Hants 1F 25
Millmeece. Staf 2C 72
Mill of Craigievar. Abers 2C 152
Mill of Fintray. Abers 2F 153
Mill of Haldane. W Dun 1F 127
Millom. Cumb 1A 96
Millow. Beds 1C 52
Millpool. Corn 5B 10
Millport. N Ayr 4C 126
Mill Side. Cumb 1D 96
Mill Street. Norf 4C 78 (nr. Lyng)
Mill Street. Norf 4C 78 (nr. Swanton Morley)
Mill Street. Suff 3C 66
Millthorpe. Derbs 3H 85
Millthorpe. Linc 2A 76
Millthrop. Cumb 5H 103
Milltimber. Aber 3F 153
Milltown. Abers 3G 151 (nr. Corgarff)
Milltown. Abers 2B 152 (nr. Lumsden)
Milltown. Corn 3F 7
Milltown. Derbs 4A 86
Milltown. Devn 3F 19
Milltown. Dum 2E 113
Milltown. Mor 4C 160
Milltown of Aberdalgie. Per 1C 136
Milltown of Auchindoun. Mor 4A 160
Milltown of Campfield. Abers 3D 152
Milltown of Edinville. Mor 4G 159
Milltown of Towie. Abers 2B 152
Milnacraig. Ang 3B 144
Milnathort. Per 3D 136
Milngavie. E Dun 2G 127
Milnholm. Stir 1A 128
Milnrow. G Man 3H 91
Milnthorpe. Cumb 1D 97
Milnthorpe. W Yor 3D 92
Milson. Shrp 3A 60
Milstead. Kent 5D 40
Milston. Wilts 2G 23
Milthorpe. Nptn 1D 50
Milton. Ang 4C 144
Milton. Cambs 4D 65
Milton. Cumb 3G 113
Milton. Derbs 3H 73
Milton. Dum 2F 111 (nr. Crocketford)
Milton. Dum 4H 109 (nr. Glenluce)
Milton. E Ayr 2D 116
Milton. Glas 2G 127
Milton. High 3F 157 (nr. Achnasheen)
Milton. High 4G 155 (nr. Applecross)
Milton. High 5G 157 (nr. Drumnadrochit)
Milton. High 1B 158 (nr. Invergordon)
Milton. High 4H 157 (nr. Inverness)
Milton. High 3F 169 (nr. Wick)
Milton. Mor 2C 160 (nr. Cullen)
Milton. Mor 2F 151 (nr. Tomintoul)
Milton. N Som 5G 33
Milton. Notts 3E 86
Milton. Oxon 2C 50 (nr. Banbury)
Milton. Oxon 2C 36 (nr. Didcot)
Milton. Pemb 4E 43
Milton. Port 3E 17
Milton. Som 4H 21
Milton. Stir 3E 135 (nr. Aberfoyle)
Milton. Stir 4D 134 (nr. Drymen)
Milton. Stoke 5D 84
Milton. W Dun 2F 127
Milton Abbas. Dors 2D 14
Milton Abbot. Devn 5E 11
Milton Auchlossan. Abers 3C 152
Milton Bridge. Midl 3F 129
Milton Bryan. Beds 2H 51
Milton Clevedon. Som 3B 22
Milton Coldwells. Abers 5G 161
Milton Combe. Devn 2A 8
Milton Common. Oxon 5E 51
Milton Damerel. Devn 1D 11
Miltonduff. Mor 2F 159
Milton End. Glos 5G 49
Milton Ernest. Beds 5H 63
Milton Green. Ches 5G 83
Milton Hill. Devn 5C 12
Milton Hill. Oxon 2C 36
Milton Keynes. Mil 2G 51
Milton Keynes Village. Mil 2G 51
Milton Lilbourne. Wilts 5G 35
Milton Malsor. Nptn 5E 63
Milton Morenish. Per 5D 142
Milton of Auchinhove. Abers 3C 152
Milton of Balgonie. Fife 3F 137
Milton of Barras. Abers 1H 145
Milton of Campsie. E Dun 2H 127
Milton of Cultoquhey. Per 1A 136
Milton of Cushnie. Abers 2C 152
Milton of Finavon. Ang 3D 145
Milton of Gollanfield. High 3B 158
Milton of Lesmore. Abers 1B 152
Milton of Tullich. Abers 4A 152
Milton on Stour. Dors 4C 22
Milton Regis. Kent 4C 40
Milton Street. E Sus 5G 27
Milton-under-Wychwood. Oxon 4A 50
Milverton. Som 4E 20
Milverton. Warw 4H 61
Milwich. Staf 2D 72
Mimbridge. Surr 4A 38
Minard. Arg 4G 133
Minchington. Dors 1E 15
Minchinhampton. Glos 5D 49
Mindrum. Nmbd 1C 120
Minehead. Som 2C 20
Minera. Wrex 5E 83
Minety. Wilts 2F 35
Minffordd. Gwyn 2E 69
Mingarrypark. High 2A 140
Mingary. High 2G 139
Mingearraidh. W Isl 6C 170
Miningsby. Linc 4C 88
Minions. Corn 5C 10
Minishant. S Ayr 3C 116
Minllyn. Gwyn 4A 70
Minnigaff. Dum 3B 110
Minorca. IOM 3D 108
Minskip. N Yor 3F 99
Minstead. Hants 1A 16
Minsted. W Sus 4G 25
Minster. Kent 4H 41 (nr. Ramsgate)
Minster. Kent 3D 40 (nr. Sheerness)
Minsteracres. Nmbd 4D 114
Minsterley. Shrp 5F 71
Minster Lovell. Oxon 4B 50
Minsterworth. Glos 4C 48
Minterne Magna. Dors 2B 14
Minterne Parva. Dors 2B 14
Minting. Linc 3A 88
Mintlaw. Abers 4H 161
Minto. Bord 2H 119
Minton. Shrp 1G 59
Minwear. Pemb 3E 43
Minworth. W Mid 1F 61
Miodar. Arg 4B 138
Mirehouse. Cumb 3A 102
Mireland. High 2F 169
Mirfield. W Yor 3C 92
Miserden. Glos 5E 49
Miskin. Rhon 3D 32
Misson. Notts 1D 86
Misterton. Leics 2C 62
Misterton. Notts 1E 87
Misterton. Som 2H 13
Mistley. Essx 2E 54
Mistley Heath. Essx 2E 55
Mitcham. G Lon 4D 39
Mitcheldean. Glos 4B 48
Mitchell. Corn 3C 6
Mitchel Troy. Mon 4H 47

Mitcheltroy Common—Muirshearlich

Mitcheltroy Common. Mon 5H 47
Mitford. Nmbd 1E 115
Mithian. Corn 3B 6
Mitton. Staf 4C 72
Mixbury. Oxon 2E 50
Mixenden. W Yor 2A 92
Mixon. Staf 5E 85
Moat. Cumb 2F 113
Moats Tye. Suff 5C 66
Mobberley. Ches 3B 84
Mobberley. Staf 1E 73
Moccas. Here 1G 47
Mochdre. Cnwy 3H 81
Mochdre. Powy 2C 58
Mochrum. Dum 5A 110
Mockbeggar. Hants 2G 15
Mockerkin. Cumb 2B 102
Modbury. Devn 3C 8
Moddershall. Staf 2D 72
Modsarie. High 2G 167
Moelfre. Cnwy 3B 82
Moelfre. IOA 2E 81
Moelfre. Powy 3D 70
Moffat. Dum 4C 118
Moggerhanger. Beds 1B 52
Mogworthy. Devn 1B 12
Moira. Leics 4H 73
Molash. Kent 5E 41
Mol-chlach. High 2C 146
Mold. Flin 4E 83
Molehill Green. Essx 3F 53
Molescroft. E Yor 5E 101
Molesden. Nmbd 1E 115
Molesworth. Cambs 3H 63
Moll. High 5E 155
Molland. Devn 4B 20
Mollington. Ches 3F 83
Mollington. Oxon 1C 50
Mollinsburn. N Lan 2A 128
Monachty. Cdgn 4E 57
Monachyle. Stir 2D 134
Monar Lodge. High 4E 156
Monaughty. Powy 4E 59
Monewden. Suff 5E 67
Moneydie. Per 1C 136
Moneyrow Green. Wind 4G 37
Moniaive. Dum 5G 117
Monifieth. Ang 5E 145
Monikie. Ang 5E 145
Monimail. Fife 2E 137
Monington. Pemb 1B 44
Monk Bretton. S Yor 4D 92
Monken Hadley. G Lon 1D 38
Monk Fryston. N Yor 2F 93
Monk Hesleden. Dur 1B 106
Monkhide. Here 1B 48
Monkhill. Cumb 4E 113
Monkhopton. Shrp 1A 60
Monkland. Here 5G 59
Monkleigh. Devn 4E 19
Monknash. V Glam 4C 32
Monkokehampton. Devn 2F 11
Monkseaton. Tyne 2G 115
Monks Eleigh. Suff 1C 54
Monk's Gate. W Sus 3D 26
Monk's Heath. Ches 3C 84
Monk Sherborne. Hants 1E 24
Monkshill. Abers 4E 161
Monksilver. Som 3D 20
Monks Kirby. Warw 2B 62
Monk Soham. Suff 4E 66
Monk Soham Green. Suff 4E 66
Monkspath. W Mid 3F 61
Monks Risborough. Buck 5G 51
Monksthorpe. Linc 4D 88
Monk Street. Essx 3G 53
Monkswood. Mon 5G 47
Monkton. Devn 2E 13
Monkton. Kent 4G 41
Monkton. Pemb 4D 42
Monkton. S Ayr 2C 116
Monkton Combe. Bath 5C 34
Monkton Deverill. Wilts 3D 22
Monkton Farleigh. Wilts 5D 34
Monkton Heathfield. Som 4F 21
Monktonhill. S Ayr 2C 116
Monkton Up Wimborne. Dors 1F 15
Monkton Wyld. Dors 3G 13
Monkwearmouth. Tyne 4H 115
Monkwood. Dors 3H 13
Monkwood. Hants 3E 25
Monmarsh. Here 1A 48
Monmouth. Mon 4A 48
Monnington on Wye. Here 1G 47
Monreith. Dum 5A 110
Montacute. Som 1H 13
Montford. Arg 3C 126
Montford. Shrp 4G 71
Montford Bridge. Shrp 4G 71
Montgarrie. Abers 2C 152
Montgarswood. E Ayr 2E 117
Montgomery. Powy 1E 58
Montgreenan. N Ayr 5E 127
Montrave. Fife 3F 137
Montrose. Ang 3G 145
Monxton. Hants 2B 24
Monyash. Derbs 4F 85
Monymusk. Abers 2D 152
Monzie. Per 1A 136
Moodiesburn. N Lan 2H 127
Moon's Green. Kent 3C 28
Moonzie. Fife 2F 137
Moor Allerton. W Yor 1C 92
Moorbath. Dors 3H 13
Moorby. Linc 4B 88
Moorcot. Here 5F 59
Moor Crichel. Dors 2E 15
Moor Cross. Devn 3C 8
Moordown. Bour 3F 15
Moore. Hal 2H 83
Moorend. Dum 2D 112
Moor End. E Yor 1B 94
Moorend. Glos 5C 48 (nr. Dursley)
Moorend. Glos 4D 48 (nr. Gloucester)
Moorends. S Yor 3G 93
Moorgate. S Yor 1B 86
Moorgreen. Hants 1C 16
Moorgreen. Notts 1B 74
Moor Green. Wilts 5D 34
Moorhaigh. Notts 4C 86
Moorhall. Derbs 3H 85
Moorhampton. Here 1G 47
Moorhouse. Cumb 4E 113 (nr. Carlisle)
Moorhouse. Cumb 4D 112 (nr. Wigton)
Moorhouse. Notts 4E 87
Moorhouse. Surr 5F 39
Moorhouses. Linc 5B 88
Moorland. Som 3G 21
Moorlinch. Som 3H 21
Moor Monkton. N Yor 4H 99
Moor of Granary. Mor 3E 159
Moor Row. Cumb 3B 102 (nr. Whitehaven)
Moor Row. Cumb 5D 112 (nr. Wigton)
Moorsholm. Red C 3D 107
Moorside. Dors 1C 14
Moorside. G Man 4H 91
Moor, The. Kent 3B 28
Moortown. Devn 3D 10
Moortown. Hants 2G 15
Moortown. IOW 4C 16
Moortown. Linc 1H 87
Moortown. Telf 4A 72
Moortown. W Yor 1D 92
Morangie. High 5E 165
Morar. High 4E 147
Morborne. Cambs 1A 64
Morchard Bishop. Devn 2A 12
Morcombelake. Dors 3H 13
Morcott. Rut 5G 75
Morda. Shrp 3E 71
Morden. G Lon 4D 38
Mordiford. Here 2A 48
Mordon. Dur 2A 106
More. Shrp 1F 59
Morebath. Devn 4C 20
Morebattle. Bord 2B 120
Morecambe. Lanc 3D 96
Morefield. High 4F 163
Morehouse, The. Shrp 1H 59
Moreleigh. Devn 3D 8
Morely St Botolph. Norf 1C 66
Morenish. Per 5C 142
Moresby Parks. Cumb 3A 102
Morestead. Hants 4D 24
Moreton. Dors 4D 14
Moreton. Essx 5F 53
Moreton. Here 4H 59
Moreton. Mers 1E 83
Moreton. Oxon 5E 51
Moreton. Staf 4B 72
Moreton Corbet. Shrp 3H 71
Moretonhampstead. Devn 4A 12
Moreton-in-Marsh. Glos 2H 49
Moreton Jeffries. Here 1B 48
Moreton Morrell. Warw 5H 61
Moreton on Lugg. Here 1A 48
Moreton Pinkney. Nptn 1D 50
Moreton Say. Shrp 2A 72
Moreton Valence. Glos 5C 48
Morfa. Cdgn 5C 56
Morfa Bach. Carm 4D 44
Morfa Bychan. Gwyn 2E 69
Morfa Glas. Neat 5B 46
Morfa Nefyn. Gwyn 1B 68
Morganstown. Card 3E 33
Morgan's Vale. Wilts 4G 23
Morham. E Lot 2B 130
Moriah. Cdgn 3F 57
Morland. Cumb 2G 103
Morley. Ches 2C 84
Morley. Derbs 1A 74
Morley. Dur 2E 105
Morley. W Yor 2C 92
Morningside. Edin 2F 129
Morningside. N Lan 4B 128
Morningthorpe. Norf 1E 66
Morpeth. Nmbd 1F 115
Morrey. Staf 4F 73
Morridge Side. Staf 5E 85
Morridge Top. Staf 4E 85
Morrington. Dum 1F 111
Morris Green. Essx 2H 53
Morriston. Swan 3F 31
Morston. Norf 1C 78
Mortehoe. Devn 2E 19
Morthen. S Yor 2B 86
Mortimer Common. W Ber 5E 37
Mortimer's Cross. Here 4G 59
Mortimer West End. Hants 5E 37
Mortomley. S Yor 1H 85
Morton. Cumb 1F 103 (nr. Calthwaite)
Morton. Cumb 4E 113 (nr. Carlisle)
Morton. Derbs 4B 86
Morton. Linc 3H 75 (nr. Bourne)
Morton. Linc 1F 87 (nr. Gainsborough)
Morton. Linc 4F 87 (nr. Lincoln)
Morton. Norf 4D 78
Morton. Notts 5E 87
Morton. Shrp 3E 71
Morton. S Glo 2B 34
Morton Bagot. Warw 4F 61
Morton Mill. Shrp 3H 71
Morton-on-Swale. N Yor 5A 106
Morton Tinmouth. Dur 2E 105
Morvah. Corn 3B 4
Morval. Corn 3G 7
Morvich. High 3E 165 (nr. Golspie)
Morvich. High 1B 148 (nr. Shiel Bridge)
Morvil. Pemb 1E 43
Morville. Shrp 1A 60
Morwenstow. Corn 1C 10
Morwick Hall. Nmbd 4G 121
Mosborough. S Yor 2B 86
Moscow. E Ayr 5F 127
Mose. Shrp 1B 60
Mosedale. Cumb 1E 103
Moseley. W Mid 2E 61 (nr. Birmingham)
Moseley. W Mid 5D 72 (nr. Wolverhampton)
Moseley. Worc 5C 60
Moss. Arg 4A 138
Moss. High 2A 140
Moss. S Yor 3F 93
Moss. Wrex 5F 83
Mossatt. Abers 2B 152
Moss Bank. Mers 1H 83
Mossbank. Shet 4F 173
Mossblown. S Ayr 2D 116
Mossbrow. G Man 2B 84
Mossburnford. Bord 3A 120
Mossdale. Dum 2D 110
Mossedge. Cumb 3F 113
Mossend. N Lan 3A 128
Mossgate. Staf 2D 72
Moss Lane. Ches 3D 84
Mossley. Ches 4C 84
Mossley. G Man 4H 91
Mossley Hill. Mers 2F 83
Moss of Barmuckity. Mor 2G 159
Mosspark. Glas 3G 127
Mosspaul. Bord 5G 119
Moss Side. Cumb 4C 112
Moss Side. G Man 1C 84
Moss-side. High 3C 158
Moss Side. Lanc 1B 90 (nr. Blackpool)
Moss Side. Lanc 2D 90 (nr. Preston)
Moss Side. Mers 4B 90
Moss-side of Cairness. Abers 2H 161
Mosstodloch. Mor 3H 159
Mosswood. Nmbd 4D 114
Mossy Lea. Lanc 3D 90
Mosterton. Dors 2H 13
Moston. Shrp 3H 71
Moston Green. Ches 4B 84
Mostyn. Flin 2D 82
Mostyn Quay. Flin 2D 82
Motcombe. Dors 4D 22
Mothecombe. Devn 4C 8
Motherby. Cumb 2F 103
Motherwell. N Lan 4A 128
Mottingham. G Lon 3F 39
Mottisfont. Hants 4B 24
Mottistone. IOW 4C 16
Mottram in Longdendale. G Man 1D 85
Mottram St Andrew. Ches 3C 84
Mott's Mill. E Sus 2G 27
Mouldsworth. Ches 3H 83
Moulin. Per 3G 143
Moulsecoomb. Brig 5E 27
Moulsford. Oxon 3D 36
Moulsoe. Mil 1H 51
Moulton. Ches 4A 84
Moulton. Linc 3C 76
Moulton. Nptn 4E 63
Moulton. N Yor 4F 105
Moulton. Suff 4F 65
Moulton. V Glam 4D 32
Moulton Chapel. Linc 4B 76
Moulton Eugate. Linc 4B 76
Moulton St Mary. Norf 5F 79
Moulton Seas End. Linc 3C 76
Mount. Corn 2F 7 (nr. Bodmin)
Mount. Corn 3B 6 (nr. Newquay)
Mountain Ash. Rhon 2D 32
Mountain Cross. Bord 5E 129
Mountain Street. Kent 5E 41
Mountain Water. Pemb 2D 42
Mount Ambrose. Corn 4B 6
Mountbenger. Bord 2F 119
Mountblow. W Dun 2F 127
Mount Bures. Essx 2C 54
Mountfield. E Sus 3B 28
Mountgerald. High 2H 157
Mount Hawke. Corn 4B 6
Mount High. High 2A 158
Mountjoy. Corn 2C 6
Mount Lothian. Midl 4F 129
Mountnessing. Essx 1H 39
Mounton. Mon 2A 34
Mount Pleasant. Buck 2E 51
Mount Pleasant. Ches 5C 84
Mount Pleasant. Derbs 1H 73 (nr. Derby)
Mount Pleasant. Derbs 4G 73 (nr. Swadlincote)
Mount Pleasant. E Sus 4F 27
Mount Pleasant. Fife 2E 137
Mount Pleasant. Hants 3A 16
Mount Pleasant. Norf 1B 66
Mountsorrel. Leics 4C 74
Mount Stuart. Arg 4C 126
Mousehole. Corn 4B 4
Mouswald. Dum 2B 112
Mow Cop. Ches 5C 84
Mowden. Darl 3F 105
Mowhaugh. Bord 2C 120
Mowmacre Hill. Leic 5C 74
Mowsley. Leics 2D 62
Moy. High 5B 158
Moylgrove. Pemb 1B 44
Moy Lodge. High 5G 149
Muasdale. Arg 5E 125
Muchalls. Abers 4G 153
Much Birch. Here 2A 48
Much Cowarne. Here 1B 48
Much Dewchurch. Here 2H 47
Muchelney. Som 4H 21
Muchelney Ham. Som 4H 21
Much Hadham. Herts 4E 53
Much Hoole. Lanc 2C 90
Muchlarnick. Corn 3G 7
Much Marcle. Here 2B 48
Muchrachd. High 5E 157
Much Wenlock. Shrp 1A 60
Mucking. Thur 2A 40
Muckleford. Dors 3B 14
Mucklestone. Staf 2B 72
Muckleton. Norf 2H 77
Muckleton. Shrp 3H 71
Muckley. Shrp 1A 60
Muckley Corner. Staf 5E 73
Muckton. Linc 2C 88
Mudale. High 5F 167
Muddiford. Devn 3F 19
Mudeford. Dors 3G 15
Mudford. Som 1A 14
Mudgley. Som 2H 21
Mugdock. Stir 2G 127
Mugeary. High 5D 154
Mugginton. Derbs 1G 73
Muggintonlane End. Derbs 1G 73
Muggleswick. Dur 4D 114
Mugswell. Surr 5D 38
Muie. High 3D 164
Muirden. Abers 3E 160
Muirdrum. Ang 5E 145
Muiredge. Per 1E 137
Muirend. Glas 3G 127
Muirhead. Ang 5C 144
Muirhead. Fife 3E 137
Muirhead. N Lan 3H 127
Muirhouses. Falk 1D 128
Muirkirk. E Ayr 2F 117
Muir of Alford. Abers 2C 152
Muir of Fairburn. High 3G 157
Muir of Fowlis. Abers 2C 152
Muir of Miltonduff. Mor 3F 159
Muir of Ord. High 3H 157
Muir of Tarradale. High 3H 157
Muirshearlich. High 5D 148

Muirtack. *Abers* 5G **161**
Muirton. *High* 2B **158**
Muirton. *Per* 1D **136**
Muirton of Ardblair. *Per* 4A **144**
Muirtown. *Per* 2B **136**
Muiryfold. *Abers* 3E **161**
Muker. *N Yor* 5C **104**
Mulbarton. *Norf* 5D **78**
Mulben. *Mor* 3A **160**
Mulindry. *Arg* 4B **124**
Mullach Charlabhaigh. *W Isl* 3E **171**
Mullacott. *Devn* 2F **19**
Mullion. *Corn* 5D **5**
Mullion Cove. *Corn* 5D **4**
Mumbles, The. *Swan* 4F **31**
Mumby. *Linc* 3E **89**
Munderfield Row. *Here* 5A **60**
Munderfield Stocks. *Here* 5A **60**
Mundesley. *Norf* 2F **79**
Mundford. *Norf* 1H **65**
Mundham. *Norf* 1F **67**
Mundon. *Essx* 5B **54**
Munerigie. *High* 3E **149**
Muness. *Shet* 1H **173**
Mungasdale. *High* 4D **162**
Mungrisdale. *Cumb* 1E **103**
Munlochy. *High* 3A **158**
Munsley. *Here* 1B **48**
Munslow. *Shrp* 2H **59**
Murchington. *Devn* 4G **11**
Murcot. *Worc* 1F **49**
Murcott. *Oxon* 4D **50**
Murdishaw. *Hal* 2H **83**
Murieston. *W Lot* 3D **128**
Murkle. *High* 2D **168**
Murlaggan. *High* 4C **148**
Murra. *Orkn* 7B **172**
Murrayfield. *Edin* 2F **129**
Murray, The. *S Lan* 4H **127**
Murrell Green. *Hants* 1F **25**
Murroes. *Ang* 5D **144**
Murrow. *Cambs* 5C **76**
Mursley. *Buck* 3G **51**
Murthly. *Per* 5H **143**
Murton. *Cumb* 2A **104**
Murton. *Dur* 5G **115**
Murton. *Nmbd* 5F **131**
Murton. *Swan* 4E **31**
Murton. *York* 4A **100**
Musbury. *Devn* 3F **13**
Muscoates. *N Yor* 1A **100**
Muscott. *Nptn* 4D **62**
Musselburgh. *E Lot* 2G **129**
Muston. *Leics* 2F **75**
Muston. *N Yor* 2E **101**
Mustow Green. *Worc* 3C **60**
Muswell Hill. *G Lon* 2D **39**
Mutehill. *Dum* 5D **111**
Mutford. *Suff* 2G **67**
Muthill. *Per* 2A **136**
Mutterton. *Devn* 2D **12**
Muxton. *Telf* 4B **72**
Mwmbwls. *Swan* 4F **31**
Mybster. *High* 3D **168**
Myddfai. *Carm* 2A **46**
Myddle. *Shrp* 3G **71**
Mydroilyn. *Cdgn* 5D **56**
Myerscough. *Lanc* 1C **90**
Mylor Bridge. *Corn* 5C **6**
Mylor Churchtown. *Corn* 5C **6**
Mynachlog-ddu. *Pemb* 1F **43**
Mynydd-bach. *Mon* 2H **33**
Mynydd Isa. *Flin* 4E **83**
Mynyddislwyn. *Cphy* 2E **33**
Mynydd Llandegai. *Gwyn* 4F **81**
Mynydd Mechell. *IOA* 1C **80**
Mynydd-y-briw. *Powy* 3D **70**
Mynyddygarreg. *Carm* 5E **45**
Mynytho. *Gwyn* 2C **68**
Myrebird. *Abers* 4E **153**
Myrelandhorn. *High* 3E **169**
Mytchett. *Surr* 1G **25**
Mythe, The. *Glos* 2D **49**
Mytholmroyd. *W Yor* 2A **92**
Myton-on-Swale. *N Yor* 3G **99**
Mytton. *Shrp* 4G **71**

N

Naast. *High* 5C **162**
Na Buirgh. *W Isl* 8C **171**
Naburn. *York* 5H **99**
Nab Wood. *W Yor* 1B **92**
Nackington. *Kent* 5F **41**
Nacton. *Suff* 1F **55**
Nafferton. *E Yor* 4E **101**
Na Gearrannan. *W Isl* 3D **171**
Nailbridge. *Glos* 4B **48**
Nailsbourne. *Som* 4F **21**
Nailsea. *N Som* 4H **33**
Nailstone. *Leics* 5B **74**
Nailsworth. *Glos* 2D **34**
Nairn. *High* 3C **158**
Nalderswood. *Surr* 1D **26**
Nancegollan. *Corn* 3D **4**
Nancekuke. *Corn* 4A **6**
Nancledra. *Corn* 3B **4**
Nangreaves. *Lanc* 3G **91**
Nanhyfer. *Pemb* 1E **43**
Nannerch. *Flin* 4D **82**
Nanpantan. *Leics* 4C **74**
Nanpean. *Corn* 3D **6**
Nanstallon. *Corn* 2E **7**
Nant-ddu. *Powy* 4D **46**
Nanternis. *Cdgn* 5C **56**
Nantgaredig. *Carm* 3E **45**
Nantgarw. *Rhon* 3E **33**
Nant Glas. *Powy* 4B **58**
Nantglyn. *Den* 4C **82**
Nantgwyn. *Powy* 3B **58**
Nantlle. *Gwyn* 5E **81**
Nantmawr. *Shrp* 3E **71**
Nantmel. *Powy* 4C **58**
Nantmor. *Gwyn* 1F **69**
Nant Peris. *Gwyn* 5F **81**
Nantwich. *Ches* 5A **84**
Nant-y-bai. *Carm* 1A **46**
Nant-y-bwch. *Blae* 4E **47**
Nant-y-Derry. *Mon* 5G **47**
Nant-y-dugoed. *Powy* 4B **70**
Nant-y-felin. *Cnwy* 3F **81**
Nantyffyllon. *B'end* 2B **32**
Nantyglo. *Blae* 4E **47**
Nant-y-meichiaid. *Powy* 4D **70**
Nant-y-moel. *B'end* 2C **32**
Nant-y-Pandy. *Cnwy* 3F **81**
Naphill. *Buck* 2G **37**
Nappa. *Lanc* 4A **98**
Napton on the Hill. *Warw* 4B **62**
Narberth. *Pemb* 3F **43**
Narberth Bridge. *Pemb* 3F **43**
Narborough. *Leics* 1C **62**
Narborough. *Norf* 4G **77**
Narkurs. *Corn* 3H **7**
Narth, The. *Mon* 5A **48**
Narthwaite. *Cumb* 5A **104**
Nasareth. *Gwyn* 1D **68**
Naseby. *Nptn* 3D **62**
Nash. *Buck* 2F **51**
Nash. *Here* 4F **59**
Nash. *Kent* 5G **41**
Nash. *Newp* 3G **33**
Nash. *Shrp* 3A **60**
Nash Lee. *Buck* 5G **51**
Nassington. *Nptn* 1H **63**
Nasty. *Herts* 3D **52**
Natcott. *Devn* 4C **18**
Nateby. *Cumb* 4A **104**
Nateby. *Lanc* 5D **96**
Nately Scures. *Hants* 1F **25**
Natland. *Cumb* 1E **97**
Naughton. *Suff* 1D **54**
Naunton. *Glos* 3G **49**
Naunton. *Worc* 2D **49**
Naunton Beauchamp. *Worc* 5D **60**
Navenby. *Linc* 5G **87**
Navestock Heath. *Essx* 1G **39**
Navestock Side. *Essx* 1G **39**
Navidale. *High* 2H **165**
Nawton. *N Yor* 1A **100**
Nayland. *Suff* 2C **54**
Nazeing. *Essx* 5E **53**
Neacroft. *Hants* 3G **15**
Neal's Green. *W Mid* 2H **61**
Neap House. *N Lin* 3B **94**
Near Sawrey. *Cumb* 5E **103**
Neasden. *G Lon* 2D **38**
Neasham. *Darl* 3A **106**
Neath. *Neat* 2A **32**
Neath Abbey. *Neat* 3G **31**
Neatishead. *Norf* 3F **79**
Neaton. *Norf* 5B **78**
Nebo. *Cdgn* 4E **57**
Nebo. *Cnwy* 5H **81**
Nebo. *Gwyn* 5D **81**
Nebo. *IOA* 1D **80**
Necton. *Norf* 5A **78**
Nedd. *High* 5B **166**
Nedderton. *Nmbd* 1F **115**
Nedging. *Suff* 1D **54**
Nedging Tye. *Suff* 1D **54**
Needham. *Norf* 2E **67**
Needham Market. *Suff* 5C **66**
Needham Street. *Suff* 4G **65**
Needingworth. *Cambs* 3C **64**
Needwood. *Staf* 3F **73**
Neen Savage. *Shrp* 3A **60**
Neen Sollars. *Shrp* 3A **60**
Neenton. *Shrp* 2A **60**
Nefyn. *Gwyn* 1C **68**
Neilston. *E Ren* 4F **127**
Neithrop. *Oxon* 1C **50**
Nelly Andrews Green. *Powy* 5E **71**
Nelson. *Cphy* 2E **32**
Nelson. *Lanc* 1G **91**
Nelson Village. *Nmbd* 2F **115**
Nemphlar. *S Lan* 5B **128**
Nempnett Thrubwell. *Bath* 5A **34**
Nene Terrace. *Linc* 5B **76**
Nenthall. *Cumb* 5A **114**
Nenthead. *Cumb* 5A **114**
Nenthorn. *Bord* 1A **120**
Nercwys. *Flin* 4E **83**
Neribus. *Arg* 4A **124**
Nerston. *S Lan* 4H **127**
Nesbit. *Nmbd* 1D **121**
Nesfield. *N Yor* 5C **98**
Ness. *Ches* 3F **83**
Nesscliffe. *Shrp* 4F **71**
Neston. *Ches* 3E **83**
Neston. *Wilts* 5D **34**
Netchwood. *Shrp* 1A **60**
Nethanfoot. *S Lan* 5B **128**
Nether Alderley. *Ches* 3C **84**
Netheravon. *Wilts* 2G **23**
Nether Blainslie. *Bord* 5B **130**
Netherbrae. *Abers* 3E **161**
Netherbrough. *Orkn* 6C **172**
Nether Broughton. *Leics* 3D **74**
Netherburn. *S Lan* 5B **128**
Nether Burrow. *Lanc* 2F **97**
Netherbury. *Dors* 3H **13**
Netherby. *Cumb* 2E **113**
Nether Careston. *Ang* 3E **145**
Nether Cerne. *Dors* 3B **14**
Nether Compton. *Dors* 1A **14**
Nethercote. *Glos* 3G **49**
Nethercote. *Warw* 4C **62**
Nethercott. *Devn* 3E **19**
Nethercott. *Oxon* 3C **50**
Nether Dallachy. *Mor* 2A **160**
Nether Durdie. *Per* 1E **136**
Nether End. *Derbs* 3G **85**
Netherend. *Glos* 5A **48**
Nether Exe. *Devn* 2C **12**
Netherfield. *E Sus* 4B **28**
Netherfield. *Notts* 1D **74**
Nethergate. *Norf* 3C **78**
Netherhampton. *Wilts* 4G **23**
Nether Handley. *Derbs* 3B **86**
Nether Haugh. *S Yor* 1B **86**
Nether Heage. *Derbs* 5A **86**
Nether Heyford. *Nptn* 5D **62**
Netherhouses. *Cumb* 1B **96**
Nether Howcleugh. *Dum* 3C **118**
Nether Kellet. *Lanc* 3E **97**
Nether Kinmundy. *Abers* 4H **161**
Netherland Green. *Staf* 2F **73**
Nether Langwith. *Notts* 3C **86**
Netherlaw. *Dum* 5E **111**
Netherley. *Abers* 4F **153**
Nethermill. *Dum* 1B **112**
Nethermills. *Mor* 3C **160**
Nether Moor. *Derbs* 4A **86**
Nether Padley. *Derbs* 3G **85**
Netherplace. *E Ren* 4G **127**
Nether Poppleton. *York* 4H **99**
Netherseal. *Derbs* 4G **73**
Nether Silton. *N Yor* 5B **106**
Nether Stowey. *Som* 3E **21**
Nether Street. *Essx* 4F **53**
Netherstreet. *Wilts* 5E **35**
Netherthird. *E Ayr* 3E **117**
Netherthong. *W Yor* 4B **92**
Netherton. *Ang* 3E **145**
Netherton. *Cumb* 1B **102**
Netherton. *Devn* 5B **12**
Netherton. *Hants* 1B **24**
Netherton. *Here* 3A **48**
Netherton. *Mers* 1F **83**
Netherton. *N Lan* 4A **128**
Netherton. *Nmbd* 4D **121**
Netherton. *Per* 3A **144**
Netherton. *Shrp* 2B **60**
Netherton. *Stir* 2G **127**
Netherton. *W Mid* 2D **60**
Netherton. *W Yor* 3C **92** (nr. Horbury)
Netherton. *W Yor* 3B **92** (nr. Huddersfield)
Netherton. *Worc* 1E **49**
Nethertown. *Cumb* 4A **102**
Nethertown. *High* 1F **169**
Nethertown. *Staf* 4F **73**
Nether Urquhart. *Fife* 3D **136**
Nether Wallop. *Hants* 3B **24**
Nether Wasdale. *Cumb* 4C **102**
Nether Welton. *Cumb* 5E **113**
Nether Westcote. *Glos* 3H **49**
Nether Whitacre. *Warw* 1G **61**
Netherwhitton. *Nmbd* 5F **121**
Nether Worton. *Oxon* 2C **50**
Nethy Bridge. *High* 1E **151**
Netley. *Hants* 2C **16**
Netley. *Shrp* 5G **71**
Netley Marsh. *Hants* 1B **16**
Nettlebed. *Oxon* 3F **37**
Nettlebridge. *Som* 2B **22**
Nettlecombe. *Dors* 3A **14**
Nettlecombe. *IOW* 5D **16**
Nettleden. *Herts* 4A **52**
Nettleham. *Linc* 3H **87**
Nettlestead. *Kent* 5A **40**
Nettlestead Green. *Kent* 5A **40**
Nettlestone. *IOW* 3E **16**
Nettlesworth. *Dur* 5F **115**
Nettleton. *Linc* 4E **94**
Nettleton. *Wilts* 4D **34**
Netton. *Devn* 4B **8**
Netton. *Wilts* 3G **23**
Neuadd. *Carm* 3H **45**
Neuadd. *Powy* 5C **70**
Neuk, The. *Abers* 4E **153**
Nevendon. *Essx* 1B **40**
Nevern. *Pemb* 1A **44**
New Abbey. *Dum* 3A **112**
New Aberdour. *Abers* 2F **161**
New Addington. *G Lon* 4E **39**
Newall. *W Yor* 5D **98**
New Alresford. *Hants* 3D **24**
New Alyth. *Per* 4B **144**
Newark. *Orkn* 3G **172**
Newark. *Pet* 5B **76**
Newark-on-Trent. *Notts* 5E **87**
New Arley. *Warw* 2G **61**
Newarthill. *N Lan* 4A **128**
New Ash Green. *Kent* 4H **39**
New Balderton. *Notts* 5F **87**
New Barn. *Kent* 4H **39**
New Barnetby. *N Lin* 3D **94**
Newbattle. *Midl* 3G **129**
New Bewick. *Nmbd* 2E **121**
Newbiggin. *Cumb* 2H **103** (nr. Appleby)
Newbiggin. *Cumb* 3B **96** (nr. Barrow-in-Furness)
Newbiggin. *Cumb* 5G **113** (nr. Cumrew)
Newbiggin. *Cumb* 2F **103** (nr. Penrith)
Newbiggin. *Cumb* 5B **102** (nr. Seascale)
Newbiggin. *Dur* 5E **115** (nr. Consett)
Newbiggin. *Dur* 2C **104** (nr. Holwick)
Newbiggin. *Nmbd* 5C **114**
Newbiggin. *N Yor* 5C **104** (nr. Askrigg)
Newbiggin. *N Yor* 1F **101** (nr. Filey)
Newbiggin. *N Yor* 1B **98** (nr. Thoralby)
Newbiggin-by-the-Sea. *Nmbd* 1G **115**
Newbigging. *Ang* 5D **145** (nr. Monikie)
Newbigging. *Ang* 4B **144** (nr. Newtyle)
Newbigging. *Ang* 5D **144** (nr. Tealing)
Newbigging. *Edin* 2E **129**
Newbigging. *S Lan* 5D **128**
Newbiggin-on-Lune. *Cumb* 4A **104**
Newbold. *Derbs* 3A **86**
Newbold. *Leics* 4B **74**
Newbold on Avon. *Warw* 3B **62**
Newbold on Stour. *Warw* 1H **49**
Newbold Pacey. *Warw* 5G **61**
Newbold Verdon. *Leics* 5B **74**
New Bolingbroke. *Linc* 5C **88**
Newborough. *IOA* 4D **80**
Newborough. *Pet* 5B **76**
Newborough. *Staf* 3F **73**
Newbottle. *Nptn* 2D **50**
Newbottle. *Tyne* 4G **115**
New Boultham. *Linc* 3G **87**
Newbourne. *Suff* 1F **55**
New Brancepeth. *Dur* 5F **115**
Newbridge. *Cphy* 2F **33**
Newbridge. *Cdgn* 5E **57**
Newbridge. *Corn* 3B **4**
New Bridge. *Dum* 2G **111**
Newbridge. *Edin* 2E **129**
Newbridge. *Hants* 1A **16**
Newbridge. *IOW* 4C **16**
Newbridge. *N Yor* 1C **100**
Newbridge. *Pemb* 1D **42**
Newbridge. *Wrex* 1E **71**
Newbridge Green. *Worc* 2D **48**
Newbridge-on-Usk. *Mon* 2G **33**
Newbridge on Wye. *Powy* 5C **58**
New Brighton. *Flin* 4E **83**
New Brighton. *Hants* 2F **17**
New Brighton. *Mers* 1F **83**
New Brinsley. *Notts* 5B **86**
Newbrough. *Nmbd* 3B **114**
New Broughton. *Wrex* 5F **83**
New Buckenham. *Norf* 1C **66**
Newbuildings. *Devn* 2A **12**
Newburgh. *Abers* 1G **153**
Newburgh. *Fife* 2E **137**
Newburgh. *Lanc* 3C **90**
Newburn. *Tyne* 3E **115**
Newbury. *W Ber* 5C **36**
Newbury. *Wilts* 2D **22**
Newby. *Cumb* 2G **103**
Newby. *N Yor* 2G **97** (nr. Ingleton)

Newby—Newtown-in-St Martin

Newby. *N Yor* 1E **101**
(nr. Scarborough)
Newby. *N Yor* 3C **106**
(nr. Stokesley)
Newby Bridge. *Cumb* 1C **96**
Newby Cote. *N Yor* 2G **97**
Newby East. *Cumb* 4F **113**
Newby Head. *Cumb* 2G **103**
New Byth. *Abers* 3F **161**
Newby West. *Cumb* 4E **113**
Newby Wiske. *N Yor* 1F **99**
Newcastle. *B'end* 3B **32**
Newcastle. *Mon* 4H **47**
Newcastle. *Shrp* 2E **59**
Newcastle Emlyn. *Carm* 1D **44**
Newcastle International Airport.
Tyne 2E **115**
Newcastleton. *Bord* 1F **113**
Newcastle-under-Lyme. *Staf* 1C **72**
Newcastle upon Tyne. *Tyne* 3F **115**
Newchapel. *Pemb* 1G **43**
Newchapel. *Powy* 2B **58**
Newchapel. *Staf* 5C **84**
Newchapel. *Surr* 1E **27**
New Cheriton. *Hants* 4D **24**
Newchurch. *Carm* 3D **45**
Newchurch. *Here* 5F **59**
Newchurch. *IOW* 4D **16**
Newchurch. *Kent* 2E **29**
Newchurch. *Lanc* 1G **91**
(nr. Nelson)
Newchurch. *Lanc* 2G **91**
(nr. Rawtenstall)
Newchurch. *Mon* 2H **33**
Newchurch. *Powy* 5E **58**
Newchurch. *Staf* 3F **73**
New Costessey. *Norf* 4D **78**
Newcott. *Devn* 2F **13**
New Cowper. *Cumb* 5C **112**
Newcraighall. *Edin* 2G **129**
New Crofton. *W Yor* 3D **93**
New Cross. *Cdgn* 3F **57**
New Cumnock. *E Ayr* 3F **117**
New Deer. *Abers* 4F **161**
New Denham. *Buck* 2B **38**
Newdigate. *Surr* 1C **26**
New Duston. *Nptn* 4E **62**
New Earswick. *York* 4A **100**
New Edlington. *S Yor* 1C **86**
New Elgin. *Mor* 2G **159**
New Ellerby. *E Yor* 1E **95**
Newell Green. *Brac* 4G **37**
New Eltham. *G Lon* 3F **39**
New End. *Warw* 4F **61**
New End. *Worc* 5E **61**
Newenden. *Kent* 3C **28**
New England. *Essx* 1H **53**
New England. *Pet* 5A **76**
Newent. *Glos* 3C **48**
New Ferry. *Mers* 2F **83**
Newfield. *Dur* 4F **115**
(nr. Chester-le-Street)
Newfield. *Dur* 1F **105**
(nr. Willington)
Newfound. *Hants* 1D **24**
New Fryston. *W Yor* 2E **93**
New Galloway. *Dum* 2D **110**
Newgate. *Norf* 1C **78**
Newgate. *Pemb* 2C **42**
Newgate Street. *Herts* 5D **52**
New Greens. *Herts* 5B **52**
New Grimsby. *IOS* 1A **4**
New Hainford. *Norf* 4E **78**
Newhall. *Ches* 1A **72**
Newhall. *Staf* 3G **73**
Newham. *Nmbd* 2F **121**
New Hartley. *Nmbd* 2G **115**
Newhaven. *Derbs* 4F **85**
Newhaven. *E Sus* 5F **27**
Newhaven. *Edin* 2F **129**
New Haw. *Surr* 4B **38**
New Hedges. *Pemb* 4F **43**
New Herrington. *Tyne* 4G **115**
Newhey. *G Man* 3H **91**
New Holkham. *Norf* 2A **78**
New Holland. *N Lin* 2D **94**
Newholm. *N Yor* 3F **107**
New Houghton. *Derbs* 4C **86**
New Houghton. *Norf* 3G **77**
Newhouse. *N Lan* 3A **128**
New Houses. *N Yor* 2H **97**
New Hutton. *Cumb* 5G **103**
New Hythe. *Kent* 5B **40**
Newick. *E Sus* 3F **27**
Newington. *Edin* 2F **129**
Newington. *Kent* 2F **29**
(nr. Folkestone)
Newington. *Kent* 4C **40**
(nr. Sittingbourne)
Newington. *Notts* 1D **86**
Newington. *Oxon* 2E **36**
Newington Bagpath. *Glos* 2D **34**
New Inn. *Carm* 2E **45**
New Inn. *Mon* 5H **47**
New Inn. *N Yor* 2H **97**
New Inn. *Torf* 5G **47**
New Invention. *Shrp* 3E **59**
New Kelso. *High* 4B **156**
New Lanark. *S Lan* 5B **128**
Newland. *Glos* 5A **48**
Newland. *Hull* 1D **94**
Newland. *N Yor* 2G **93**
Newland. *Som* 3B **20**
Newland. *Worc* 1C **48**
Newlandrig. *Midl* 3G **129**
Newlands. *Cumb* 1E **103**
Newlands. *Essx* 2C **40**
Newlands. *High* 4B **158**
Newlands. *Nmbd* 4D **115**
Newlands. *Notts* 4C **86**
Newlands. *Staf* 3E **73**
Newlands of Geise. *High* 2C **168**
Newlands of Tynet. *Mor* 2A **160**
Newlands Park. *IOA* 2B **80**
New Lane. *Lanc* 3C **90**
New Lane End. *Warr* 1A **84**
New Langholm. *Dum* 1E **113**
New Leake. *Linc* 5D **88**
New Leeds. *Abers* 3G **161**
New Lenton. *Nott* 2C **74**
New Longton. *Lanc* 2D **90**
Newlot. *Orkn* 6E **172**
New Luce. *Dum* 3G **109**
Newlyn. *Corn* 4B **4**
Newmachar. *Abers* 2F **153**
Newmains. *N Lan* 4B **128**
New Mains of Ury. *Abers* 5F **153**
New Malden. *G Lon* 4D **38**
Newman's Green. *Suff* 1B **54**
Newmarket. *Suff* 4F **65**
Newmarket. *W Isl* 4G **171**
New Marske. *Red C* 2D **106**
New Marton. *Shrp* 2F **71**
New Micklefield. *W Yor* 1E **93**
New Mill. *Abers* 4E **160**
New Mill. *Corn* 3B **4**
New Mill. *Herts* 4H **51**
Newmill. *Mor* 3B **160**
Newmill. *Bord* 3G **119**
New Mill. *W Yor* 4B **92**
New Mill. *Wilts* 5G **35**
Newmillerdam. *W Yor* 3D **92**
New Mills. *Corn* 3C **6**
New Mills. *Derbs* 2E **85**
Newmills. *Fife* 1D **128**
Newmills. *High* 2A **158**
New Mills. *Mon* 5A **48**
New Mills. *Powy* 5C **70**
Newmiln. *Per* 5A **144**
Newmilns. *E Ayr* 1E **117**
New Milton. *Hants* 3H **15**
New Mistley. *Essx* 2E **54**
New Moat. *Pemb* 2E **43**
Newmore. *High* 3H **157**
(nr. Dingwall)
Newmore. *High* 1A **158**
(nr. Invergordon)
Newnham. *Cambs* 5D **64**
Newnham. *Glos* 4B **48**
Newnham. *Hants* 1F **25**
Newnham. *Herts* 2C **52**
Newnham. *Kent* 5D **40**
Newnham. *Nptn* 5C **62**
Newnham. *Warw* 4F **61**
Newnham Bridge. *Worc* 4A **60**
New Ollerton. *Notts* 4D **86**
New Oscott. *W Mid* 1F **61**
Newpark. *Fife* 2G **137**
New Park. *N Yor* 4E **99**
New Pitsligo. *Abers* 3F **161**
New Polzeath. *Corn* 1D **6**
Newport. *Corn* 4D **10**
Newport. *Devn* 3F **19**
Newport. *E Yor* 1B **94**
Newport. *Essx* 2F **53**
Newport. *Glos* 2B **34**
Newport. *High* 1H **165**
Newport. *IOW* 4D **16**
Newport. *Newp* 3G **33**
Newport. *Norf* 4H **79**
Newport. *Pemb* 1E **43**
Newport. *Som* 4G **21**
Newport. *Telf* 4B **72**
Newport-on-Tay. *Fife* 1G **137**
Newport Pagnell. *Mil* 1G **51**
Newpound Common. *W Sus* 3B **26**
New Prestwick. *S Ayr* 2C **116**
New Quay. *Cdgn* 5C **56**
Newquay. *Corn* 2C **6**
Newquay Airport. *Corn* 2C **6**
New Rackheath. *Norf* 4E **79**
New Radnor. *Powy* 4E **58**
New Rent. *Cumb* 1F **103**
New Ridley. *Nmbd* 4D **114**
New Romney. *Kent* 3E **29**
New Rossington. *S Yor* 1D **86**
New Row. *Cdgn* 3G **57**
New Row. *Lanc* 1E **91**
New Row. *N Yor* 3D **106**
New Sauchie. *Clac* 4A **136**
Newsbank. *Ches* 4C **84**
Newseat. *Abers* 5E **160**
Newsham. *Lanc* 1D **90**
Newsham. *Nmbd* 2G **115**
Newsham. *N Yor* 3E **105**
(nr. Richmond)
Newsham. *N Yor* 1F **99**
(nr. Thirsk)
New Sharlston. *W Yor* 3D **93**
Newsholme. *E Yor* 2H **93**
Newsholme. *Lanc* 4H **97**
New Shoreston. *Nmbd* 1F **121**
New Springs. *G Man* 4D **90**
Newstead. *Notts* 5C **86**
Newstead. *Bord* 1H **119**
New Stevenston. *N Lan* 4A **128**
New Street. *Here* 5F **59**
Newstreet Lane. *Shrp* 2A **72**
New Swanage. *Dors* 4F **15**
New Swannington. *Leics* 4B **74**
Newthorpe. *N Yor* 1E **93**
Newthorpe. *Notts* 1B **74**
Newton. *Arg* 4H **133**
Newton. *B'end* 4B **32**
Newton. *Cambs* 1E **53**
(nr. Cambridge)
Newton. *Cambs* 4D **76**
(nr. Wisbech)
Newton. *Ches* 4G **83**
(nr. Chester)
Newton. *Ches* 5H **83**
(nr. Tattenhall)
Newton. *Cumb* 2B **96**
Newton. *Derbs* 5B **86**
Newton. *Dors* 1C **14**
Newton. *Dum* 2D **112**
(nr. Annan)
Newton. *Dum* 5D **118**
(nr. Moffat)
Newton. *G Man* 1D **84**
Newton. *Here* 2G **47**
(nr. Ewyas Harold)
Newton. *Here* 5H **59**
(nr. Leominster)
Newton. *High* 2B **158**
(nr. Cromarty)
Newton. *High* 4B **158**
(nr. Inverness)
Newton. *High* 5C **166**
(nr. Kylestrome)
Newton. *High* 4F **169**
(nr. Wick)
Newton. *Lanc* 2E **97**
(nr. Carnforth)
Newton. *Lanc* 4F **97**
(nr. Clitheroe)
Newton. *Lanc* 1C **90**
(nr. Kirkham)
Newton. *Linc* 2H **75**
Newton. *Mers* 2E **83**
Newton. *Mor* 2F **159**
Newton. *Norf* 4H **77**
Newton. *Nptn* 2F **63**
Newton. *Nmbd* 3D **114**
Newton. *Notts* 1D **74**
Newton. *Bord* 2A **120**
Newton. *Shrp* 1B **60**
(nr. Bridgnorth)
Newton. *Shrp* 2G **71**
(nr. Wem)
Newton. *Som* 3E **20**
Newton. *S Lan* 3H **127**
(nr. Glasgow)
Newton. *S Lan* 1B **118**
(nr. Lanark)
Newton. *Staf* 3E **73**
Newton. *Suff* 1C **54**
Newton. *Swan* 4F **31**
Newton. *Warw* 3C **62**
Newton. *W Lot* 2D **129**
Newton. *Wilts* 4H **23**
Newton Abbot. *Devn* 5B **12**
Newtonairds. *Dum* 1F **111**
Newton Arlosh. *Cumb* 4D **112**
Newton Aycliffe. *Dur* 2F **105**
Newton Bewley. *Hart* 2B **106**
Newton Blossomville. *Mil* 5G **63**
Newton Bromswold. *Nptn* 4G **63**
Newton Burgoland. *Leics* 5A **74**
Newton by Toft. *Linc* 2H **87**
Newton Ferrers. *Devn* 4B **8**
Newton Flotman. *Norf* 1E **66**
Newtongrange. *Midl* 3G **129**
Newton Green. *Mon* 2A **34**
Newton Hall. *Dur* 5F **115**
Newton Hall. *Nmbd* 3D **114**
Newton Harcourt. *Leics* 1D **62**
Newton Heath. *G Man* 4G **91**
Newtonhill. *Abers* 4G **153**
Newtonhill. *High* 4H **157**
Newton Hill. *W Yor* 2D **92**
Newton Ketton. *Darl* 2A **106**
Newton Kyme. *N Yor* 5G **99**
Newton-le-Willows. *Mers* 1H **83**
Newton-le-Willows. *N Yor* 1E **98**
Newton Longville. *Buck* 2G **51**
Newton Mearns. *E Ren* 4G **127**
Newtonmore. *High* 4B **150**
Newton Morrell. *N Yor* 4F **105**
Newton Mulgrave. *N Yor* 3E **107**
Newton of Ardtoe. *High* 1A **140**
Newton of Balcanquhal.
Per 2D **136**
Newton of Beltrees. *Ren* 4E **127**
Newton of Falkland. *Fife* 3E **137**
Newton of Mountblairy.
Abers 3E **160**
Newton of Pitcairns. *Per* 2C **136**
Newton-on-Ouse. *N Yor* 4H **99**
Newton-on-Rawcliffe. *N Yor* 5F **107**
Newton on the Hill. *Shrp* 3G **71**
Newton-on-the-Moor.
Nmbd 4F **121**
Newton on Trent. *Linc* 3F **87**
Newton Poppleford. *Devn* 4D **12**
Newton Purcell. *Oxon* 2E **51**
Newton Regis. *Warw* 5G **73**
Newton Reigny. *Cumb* 1F **103**
Newton Rigg. *Cumb* 1F **103**
Newton St Cyres. *Devn* 3B **12**
Newton St Faith. *Norf* 4E **78**
Newton St Loe. *Bath* 5C **34**
Newton St Petrock. *Devn* 1E **11**
Newton Solney. *Derbs* 3G **73**
Newton Stacey. *Hants* 2C **24**
Newton Stewart. *Dum* 3B **110**
Newton Toney. *Wilts* 2H **23**
Newton Tony. *Wilts* 2H **23**
Newton Tracey. *Devn* 4F **19**
Newton under Roseberry.
Red C 3C **106**
Newton Unthank. *Leics* 5B **74**
Newton upon Ayr. *S Ayr* 2C **116**
Newton upon Derwent.
E Yor 5B **100**
Newton Valence. *Hants* 3F **25**
Newton-with-Scales. *Lanc* 1B **90**
Newtown. *Abers* 2E **160**
Newtown. *Cambs* 4H **63**
Newtown. *Ches* 1A **72**
Newtown. *Corn* 5C **10**
Newtown. *Cumb* 5B **112**
(nr. Aspatria)
Newtown. *Cumb* 3G **113**
(nr. Brampton)
Newtown. *Cumb* 2G **103**
(nr. Penrith)
Newtown. *Derbs* 2D **85**
Newtown. *Devn* 4A **20**
Newtown. *Dors* 2H **13**
(nr. Beaminster)
New Town. *Dors* 1E **15**
(nr. Sixpenny Handley)
New Town. *E Lot* 2H **129**
Newtown. *Falk* 1C **128**
Newtown. *Glos* 5B **48**
(nr. Lydney)
Newtown. *Glos* 2E **49**
(nr. Tewkesbury)
Newtown. *Hants* 1D **16**
(nr. Bishop's Waltham)
Newtown. *Hants* 1A **16**
(nr. Lyndhurst)
Newtown. *Hants* 5C **36**
(nr. Newbury)
Newtown. *Hants* 4B **24**
(nr. Romsey)
Newtown. *Hants* 2C **16**
(nr. Warsash)
Newtown. *Hants* 1E **16**
(nr. Wickham)
Newtown. *Here* 2B **48**
(nr. Ledbury)
Newtown. *Here* 2A **48**
(nr. Little Dewchurch)
Newtown. *Here* 1B **48**
(nr. Stretton Grandison)
Newtown. *High* 3F **149**
Newtown. *IOM* 4C **108**
Newtown. *IOW* 3C **16**
Newtown. *Lanc* 3D **90**
New Town. *Lutn* 3A **52**
Newtown. *Nmbd* 4E **121**
(nr. Rothbury)
Newtown. *Nmbd* 2E **121**
(nr. Wooler)
Newtown. *Pool* 3F **15**
Newtown. *Powy* 1D **58**
Newtown. *Rhon* 2D **32**
Newtown. *Shrp* 2G **71**
Newtown. *Som* 1F **13**
Newtown. *Staf* 4D **84**
(nr. Biddulph)
Newtown. *Staf* 5D **73**
(nr. Cannock)
Newtown. *Staf* 4E **85**
(nr. Longnor)
New Town. *W Yor* 2E **93**
Newtown. *Wilts* 4E **23**
Newtown-in-St Martin. *Corn* 4E **5**

Newtown Linford—Norton Hawkfield

Newtown Linford. *Leics* 4C 74
Newtown St Boswells. *Bord* 1H 119
New Tredegar. *Cphy* 5E 47
Newtyle. *Ang* 4B 144
New Village. *E Yor* 1D 94
New Village. *S Yor* 4F 93
New Walsoken. *Cambs* 5D 76
New Waltham. *NE Lin* 4F 95
New Wimpole. *Cambs* 1D 52
New Winton. *E Lot* 2H 129
New World. *Cambs* 1C 64
New Yatt. *Oxon* 4B 50
Newyears Green. *G Lon* 2B 38
New York. *Linc* 5B 88
New York. *Tyne* 2G 115
Nextend. *Here* 5F 59
Neyland. *Pemb* 4D 42
Nib Heath. *Shrp* 4G 71
Nicholashayne. *Devn* 1E 12
Nicholaston. *Swan* 4E 31
Nidd. *N Yor* 3F 99
Niddrie. *Edin* 2F 129
Niddry. *Edin* 2D 129
Nigg. *Aber* 3G 153
Nigg. *High* 1C 158
Nigg Ferry. *High* 2B 158
Nightcott. *Som* 4B 20
Nine Ashes. *Essx* 5F 53
Ninebanks. *Nmbd* 4A 114
Nine Elms. *Swin* 3G 35
Ninemile Bar. *Dum* 2F 111
Nine Mile Burn. *Midl* 4E 129
Ninfield. *E Sus* 4B 28
Ningwood. *IOW* 4C 16
Nisbet. *Bord* 2A 120
Nisbet Hill. *Bord* 4D 130
Niton. *IOW* 5D 16
Nitshill. *E Ren* 4G 127
Niwbwrch. *IOA* 4D 80
Noak Hill. *G Lon* 1G 39
Nobold. *Shrp* 4G 71
Nobottle. *Nptn* 4D 62
Nocton. *Linc* 4H 87
Nogdam End. *Norf* 5F 79
Noke. *Oxon* 4D 50
Nolton. *Pemb* 3C 42
Nolton Haven. *Pemb* 3C 42
No Man's Heath. *Ches* 1H 71
No Man's Heath. *Warw* 5G 73
Nomansland. *Devn* 1B 12
Nomansland. *Wilts* 1A 16
Noneley. *Shrp* 3G 71
Nonikiln. *High* 1A 158
Nonington. *Kent* 5G 41
Nook. *Cumb* 2F 113
(nr. Longtown)
Nook. *Cumb* 1E 97
(nr. Milnthorpe)
Noranside. *Ang* 2D 144
Norbreck. *Bkpl* 5C 96
Norbridge. *Here* 1C 48
Norbury. *Ches* 1H 71
Norbury. *Derbs* 1F 73
Norbury. *Shrp* 1F 59
Norbury. *Staf* 3B 72
Norby. *N Yor* 1G 99
Norby. *Shet* 6C 173
Norcross. *Lanc* 5C 96
Nordelph. *Norf* 5E 77
Norden. *G Man* 3G 91
Nordley. *Shrp* 1A 60
Norham. *Nmbd* 5F 131
Norland Town. *W Yor* 2A 92
Norley. *Ches* 3H 83
Norleywood. *Hants* 3B 16
Normanby. *N Lin* 3B 94
Normanby. *N Yor* 1B 100
Normanby. *Red C* 3C 106
Normanby-by-Spital. *Linc* 2H 87
Normanby le Wold. *Linc* 1A 88
Norman Cross. *Cambs* 1A 64
Normandy. *Surr* 5A 38
Norman's Bay. *E Sus* 5A 28
Norman's Green. *Devn* 2D 12
Normanton. *Derb* 2H 73
Normanton. *Leics* 1F 75
Normanton. *Linc* 1G 75
Normanton. *Notts* 5E 86
Normanton. *W Yor* 2D 93
Normanton le Heath. *Leics* 4A 74
Normanton on Soar. *Notts* 3C 74
Normanton-on-the-Wolds. *Notts* 2D 74
Normanton on Trent. *Notts* 4E 87
Normoss. *Lanc* 1B 90
Norrington Common. *Wilts* 5D 35
Norris Green. *Mers* 1F 83
Norris Hill. *Leics* 4H 73
Norristhorpe. *W Yor* 2C 92
North Acre. *Norf* 1B 66
Northall. *Buck* 3H 51
Northallerton. *N Yor* 5A 106
Northam. *Devn* 4E 19
Northam. *Sotn* 1C 16
Northampton. *Nptn* 4E 63
North Anston. *S Yor* 2C 86
North Ascot. *Brac* 4A 38
North Aston. *Oxon* 3C 50
Northaw. *Herts* 5C 52
Northay. *Som* 1F 13
North Baddesley. *Hants* 4B 24
North Balfern. *Dum* 4B 110
North Ballachulish. *High* 2E 141
North Barrow. *Som* 4B 22
North Barsham. *Norf* 2B 78
Northbeck. *Linc* 1H 75
North Benfleet. *Essx* 2B 40
North Bersted. *W Sus* 5A 26
North Berwick. *E Lot* 1B 130
North Bitchburn. *Dur* 1E 105
North Blyth. *Nmbd* 1G 115
North Boarhunt. *Hants* 1E 16
North Bockhampton. *Dors* 3G 15
Northborough. *Pet* 5A 76
Northbourne. *Kent* 5H 41
Northbourne. *Oxon* 3D 36
North Bovey. *Devn* 4H 11
North Bowood. *Dors* 3H 13
North Bradley. *Wilts* 1D 22
North Brentor. *Devn* 4E 11
North Brewham. *Som* 3C 22
Northbrook. *Oxon* 3C 50
North Brook End. *Cambs* 1C 52
North Broomhill. *Nmbd* 4G 121
North Buckland. *Devn* 2E 19
North Burlingham. *Norf* 4F 79
North Cadbury. *Som* 4B 22
North Carlton. *Linc* 3G 87
North Cave. *E Yor* 1B 94
North Cerney. *Glos* 5F 49
North Chailey. *E Sus* 3E 27
Northchapel. *W Sus* 3A 26
North Charford. *Hants* 1G 15
North Charlton. *Nmbd* 2F 121
North Cheriton. *Som* 4B 22
North Chideock. *Dors* 3H 13
Northchurch. *Herts* 5H 51
North Cliffe. *E Yor* 1B 94
North Clifton. *Notts* 3F 87
North Close. *Dur* 1F 105
North Cockerington. *Linc* 1C 88
North Coker. *Som* 1A 14
North Collafirth. *Shet* 3E 173
North Common. *E Sus* 3E 27
North Commonty. *Abers* 4F 161
North Coombe. *Devn* 1B 12
North Corbelly. *Dum* 3A 112
North Cornelly. *B'end* 3B 32
North Cotes. *Linc* 4G 95
Northcott. *Devn* 3D 10
Northcourt. *Oxon* 2D 36
North Cove. *Suff* 2G 67
North Cowton. *N Yor* 4F 105
North Craigo. *Ang* 2F 145
North Crawley. *Mil* 1H 51
North Cray. *G Lon* 3F 39
North Creake. *Norf* 2A 78
North Curry. *Som* 4G 21
North Dalton. *E Yor* 4D 100
North Deighton. *N Yor* 4F 99
North Dronley. *Ang* 5C 144
North Duffield. *N Yor* 1G 93
Northedge. *Derbs* 4A 86
North Elkington. *Linc* 1B 88
North Elmham. *Norf* 3B 78
North Elmsall. *W Yor* 3E 93
Northend. *Buck* 2F 37
North End. *E Yor* 1F 95
North End. *Essx* 4G 53
(nr. Great Dunmow)
North End. *Essx* 2A 54
(nr. Great Yeldham)
North End. *Hants* 5C 36
North End. *Leics* 4C 74
North End. *Linc* 1B 76
North End. *Norf* 1B 66
North End. *N Som* 5H 33
North End. *Port* 2E 17
Northend. *Warw* 5A 62
North End. *W Sus* 5C 26
North End. *Wilts* 2F 35
North Erradale. *High* 5B 162
North Evington. *Leic* 5D 74
North Fambridge. *Essx* 1C 40
North Fearns. *High* 5E 155
North Featherstone. *W Yor* 2E 93
North Feorline. *N Ayr* 3D 122
North Ferriby. *E Yor* 2C 94
Northfield. *Aber* 3F 153
Northfield. *Hull* 2D 94
Northfield. *Som* 3F 21
Northfield. *W Mid* 3E 61
Northfleet. *Kent* 3H 39
North Frodingham. *E Yor* 4F 101
Northgate. *Linc* 3A 76
North Gluss. *Shet* 4E 173
North Gorley. *Hants* 1G 15
North Green. *Norf* 2E 66
North Green. *Suff* 4F 67
(nr. Framlingham)
North Green. *Suff* 3F 67
(nr. Halesworth)
North Green. *Suff* 4F 67
(nr. Saxmundham)
North Greetwell. *Linc* 3H 87
North Grimston. *N Yor* 3C 100
North Halling. *Medw* 4B 40
North Hayling. *Hants* 2F 17
North Hazelrigg. *Nmbd* 1E 121
North Heasley. *Devn* 3H 19
North Heath. *W Sus* 3B 26
North Hill. *Corn* 5C 10
North Hinksey Village. *Oxon* 5C 50
North Holmwood. *Surr* 1C 26
North Huish. *Devn* 3D 8
North Hykeham. *Linc* 4G 87
Northiam. *E Sus* 3C 28
Northill. *Beds* 1B 52
Northington. *Hants* 3D 24
North Kelsey. *Linc* 4D 94
North Kelsey Moor. *Linc* 4D 94
North Kessock. *High* 4A 158
North Killingholme. *N Lin* 3E 95
North Kilvington. *N Yor* 1G 99
North Kilworth. *Leics* 2D 62
North Kyme. *Linc* 5A 88
North Lancing. *W Sus* 5C 26
Northlands. *Linc* 5C 88
Northleach. *Glos* 4G 49
North Lee. *Buck* 5G 51
North Lees. *N Yor* 2E 99
Northleigh. *Devn* 3G 19
(nr. Barnstaple)
Northleigh. *Devn* 3E 13
(nr. Honiton)
North Leigh. *Kent* 1F 29
North Leigh. *Oxon* 4B 50
North Leverton. *Notts* 2E 87
Northlew. *Devn* 3F 11
North Littleton. *Worc* 1F 49
North Lopham. *Norf* 2C 66
North Luffenham. *Rut* 5G 75
North Marden. *W Sus* 1G 17
North Marston. *Buck* 3F 51
North Middleton. *Midl* 4G 129
North Middleton. *Nmbd* 2E 121
North Molton. *Devn* 4H 19
North Moor. *N Yor* 1D 100
Northmoor. *Oxon* 5C 50
Northmoor Green. *Som* 3G 21
North Moreton. *Oxon* 3D 36
Northmuir. *Ang* 3C 144
North Mundham. *W Sus* 2G 17
North Murie. *Per* 1E 137
North Muskham. *Notts* 5E 87
North Ness. *Orkn* 8C 172
North Newbald. *E Yor* 1C 94
North Newington. *Oxon* 2C 50
North Newnton. *Wilts* 1G 23
North Newton. *Som* 3F 21
Northney. *Hants* 2F 17
North Nibley. *Glos* 2C 34
North Oakley. *Hants* 1D 24
North Ockendon. *G Lon* 2G 39
Northolt. *G Lon* 2C 38
Northop. *Flin* 4E 83
Northop Hall. *Flin* 4E 83
North Ormesby. *Midd* 3C 106
North Ormsby. *Linc* 1B 88
Northorpe. *Linc* 4H 75
(nr. Bourne)
Northorpe. *Linc* 2B 76
(nr. Donington)
Northorpe. *Linc* 1F 87
(nr. Gainsborough)
North Otterington. *N Yor* 1F 99
Northover. *Som* 3H 21
(nr. Glastonbury)
Northover. *Som* 4A 22
(nr. Yeovil)
North Owersby. *Linc* 1H 87
Northowram. *W Yor* 2B 92
North Perrott. *Som* 2H 13
North Petherton. *Som* 3F 21
North Petherwin. *Corn* 4C 10
North Pickenham. *Norf* 5A 78
North Piddle. *Worc* 5D 60
North Poorton. *Dors* 3A 14
North Port. *Arg* 1H 133
Northport. *Dors* 4E 15
North Queensferry. *Fife* 1E 129
North Radworthy. *Devn* 3A 20
North Rauceby. *Linc* 1H 75
Northrepps. *Norf* 2E 79
North Rigton. *N Yor* 5E 99
North Rode. *Ches* 4C 84
North Roe. *Shet* 3E 173
North Ronaldsay Airport. *Orkn* 2G 172
North Row. *Cumb* 1D 102
North Runcton. *Norf* 4F 77
North Sannox. *N Ayr* 5B 126
North Scale. *Cumb* 3A 96
North Scarle. *Linc* 4F 87
North Seaton. *Nmbd* 1F 115
North Seaton Colliery. *Nmbd* 1F 115
North Sheen. *G Lon* 3C 38
North Shian. *Arg* 4D 140
North Shields. *Tyne* 3G 115
North Shoebury. *S'end* 2D 40
North Shore. *Bkpl* 1B 90
North Side. *Cumb* 2B 102
North Skelton. *Red C* 3D 106
North Somercotes. *Linc* 1D 88
North Stainley. *N Yor* 2E 99
North Stainmore. *Cumb* 3B 104
North Stifford. *Thur* 2H 39
North Stoke. *Bath* 5C 34
North Stoke. *Oxon* 3E 36
North Stoke. *W Sus* 4B 26
Northstowe. *Cambs* 4D 64
North Street. *Hants* 3E 25
North Street. *Kent* 5E 40
North Street. *Medw* 3C 40
North Street. *W Ber* 4E 37
North Sunderland. *Nmbd* 1G 121
North Tamerton. *Corn* 3D 10
North Tawton. *Devn* 2G 11
North Thoresby. *Linc* 1B 88
North Town. *Devn* 2F 11
North Tuddenham. *Norf* 4C 78
North Walbottle. *Tyne* 3E 115
North Walsham. *Norf* 2E 79
North Waltham. *Hants* 2D 24
North Warnborough. *Hants* 1F 25
North Water Bridge. *Ang* 2F 145
North Watten. *High* 3E 169
Northway. *Glos* 2E 49
Northway. *Swan* 4E 31
North Weald Bassett. *Essx* 5F 53
North Weston. *N Som* 4H 33
North Weston. *Oxon* 5E 51
North Wheatley. *Notts* 2E 87
North Whilborough. *Devn* 2E 9
Northwich. *Ches* 3A 84
North Wick. *Bath* 5A 34
Northwick. *Som* 2G 21
Northwick. *S Glo* 3A 34
North Widcombe. *Bath* 1A 22
North Willingham. *Linc* 2A 88
North Wingfield. *Derbs* 4B 86
North Witham. *Linc* 3G 75
Northwold. *Norf* 1G 65
Northwood. *Derbs* 4G 85
Northwood. *G Lon* 1B 38
Northwood. *IOW* 3C 16
Northwood. *Kent* 4H 41
Northwood. *Shrp* 2G 71
Northwood. *Stoke* 1C 72
Northwood Green. *Glos* 4C 48
North Wootton. *Dors* 1B 14
North Wootton. *Norf* 3F 77
North Wootton. *Som* 2A 22
North Wraxall. *Wilts* 4D 34
North Wroughton. *Swin* 3G 35
North Yardhope. *Nmbd* 4D 120
Norton. *Devn* 3E 9
Norton. *Glos* 3D 48
Norton. *Hal* 2H 83
Norton. *Herts* 2C 52
Norton. *IOW* 4B 16
Norton. *Mon* 3H 47
Norton. *Nptn* 4D 62
Norton. *Notts* 3C 86
Norton. *Powy* 4F 59
Norton. *Shrp* 2G 59
(nr. Ludlow)
Norton. *Shrp* 5B 72
(nr. Madeley)
Norton. *Shrp* 5H 71
(nr. Shrewsbury)
Norton. *S Yor* 3F 93
(nr. Askern)
Norton. *S Yor* 2A 86
(nr. Sheffield)
Norton. *Stoc T* 2B 106
Norton. *Suff* 4B 66
Norton. *Swan* 4F 31
Norton. *W Sus* 5A 26
(nr. Arundel)
Norton. *W Sus* 3G 17
(nr. Selsey)
Norton. *Wilts* 3D 35
Norton. *Worc* 1F 49
(nr. Evesham)
Norton. *Worc* 5C 60
(nr. Worcester)
Norton Bavant. *Wilts* 2E 23
Norton Bridge. *Staf* 2C 72
Norton Canes. *Staf* 5E 73
Norton Canon. *Here* 1G 47
Norton Corner. *Norf* 3C 78
Norton Disney. *Linc* 5F 87
Norton East. *Staf* 5E 73
Norton Ferris. *Wilts* 3C 22
Norton Fitzwarren. *Som* 4F 21
Norton Green. *IOW* 4B 16
Norton Green. *Stoke* 5D 84
Norton Hawkfield. *Bath* 5A 34

Norton Heath—Osbaston

Norton Heath. *Essx* 5G **53**
Norton in Hales. *Shrp* 2B **72**
Norton in the Moors. *Stoke* 5C **84**
Norton-Juxta-Twycross. *Leics* 5H **73**
Norton-le-Clay. *N Yor* 2G **99**
Norton Lindsey. *Warw* 4G **61**
Norton Little Green. *Suff* 4B **66**
Norton Malreward. *Bath* 5B **34**
Norton Mandeville. *Essx* 5F **53**
Norton-on-Derwent. *N Yor* 2B **100**
Norton St Philip. *Som* 1C **22**
Norton Subcourse. *Norf* 1G **67**
Norton sub Hamdon. *Som* 1H **13**
Norton Woodseats. *S Yor* 2A **86**
Norwell. *Notts* 4E **87**
Norwell Woodhouse. *Notts* 4E **87**
Norwich. *Norf* 5E **79**
Norwich International Airport. *Norf* 4E **79**
Norwick. *Shet* 1H **173**
Norwood. *Derbs* 2B **86**
Norwood Green. *W Yor* 2B **92**
Norwood Hill. *Surr* 1D **26**
Norwood Park. *Som* 3A **22**
Norwoodside. *Cambs* 1D **64**
Noseley. *Leics* 1E **63**
Noss Mayo. *Devn* 4B **8**
Nosterfield. *N Yor* 1E **99**
Nostie. *High* 1A **148**
Notgrove. *Glos* 3G **49**
Nottage. *B'end* 4B **32**
Nottingham. *Nott* 1C **74**
Nottingham East Midlands International Airport. *Leics* 3B **74**
Nottington. *Dors* 4B **14**
Notton. *Dors* 3B **14**
Notton. *W Yor* 3D **92**
Notton. *Wilts* 5E **35**
Nounsley. *Essx* 4A **54**
Noutard's Green. *Worc* 4B **60**
Nox. *Shrp* 4G **71**
Noyadd Trefawr. *Cdgn* 1C **44**
Nuffield. *Oxon* 3E **37**
Nunburnholme. *E Yor* 5C **100**
Nuncargate. *Notts* 5B **86**
Nunclose. *Cumb* 5F **113**
Nuneaton. *Warw* 1A **62**
Nuneham Courtenay. *Oxon* 2D **36**
Nun Monkton. *N Yor* 4H **99**
Nunnerie. *S Lan* 3B **118**
Nunney. *Som* 2C **22**
Nunnington. *N Yor* 2A **100**
Nunnykirk. *Nmbd* 5E **121**
Nunsthorpe. *NE Lin* 4F **95**
Nunthorpe. *Red C* 3C **106**
Nunthorpe. *York* 5H **99**
Nunton. *Wilts* 4G **23**
Nunwick. *Nmbd* 2B **114**
Nunwick. *N Yor* 2F **99**
Nupend. *Glos* 5C **48**
Nursling. *Hants* 1B **16**
Nursted. *W Sus* 4F **25**
Nursteed. *Wilts* 5F **35**
Nurston. *V Glam* 5D **32**
Nutbourne. *W Sus* 2F **17** (nr. Chichester)
Nutbourne. *W Sus* 4B **26** (nr. Pulborough)
Nutfield. *Surr* 5E **39**
Nuthall. *Notts* 1C **74**
Nuthampstead. *Herts* 2E **53**
Nuthurst. *Warw* 3F **61**
Nuthurst. *W Sus* 3C **26**
Nutley. *E Sus* 3F **27**
Nuttall. *G Man* 3F **91**
Nutwell. *S Yor* 4G **93**
Nybster. *High* 2F **169**
Nyetimber. *W Sus* 3G **17**
Nyewood. *W Sus* 4G **25**
Nymet Rowland. *Devn* 2H **11**
Nymet Tracey. *Devn* 2H **11**
Nympsfield. *Glos* 5D **48**
Nynehead. *Som* 4E **21**
Nyton. *W Sus* 5A **26**

O

Oadby. *Leics* 5D **74**
Oad Street. *Kent* 4C **40**
Oakamoor. *Staf* 1E **73**
Oakbank. *Arg* 5B **140**
Oakbank. *W Lot* 3D **129**
Oakdale. *Cphy* 2E **33**
Oakdale. *Pool* 3F **15**
Oake. *Som* 4E **21**
Oaken. *Staf* 5C **72**
Oakenclough. *Lanc* 5E **97**
Oakengates. *Telf* 4B **72**
Oakenholt. *Flin* 3E **83**
Oakenshaw. *Dur* 1F **105**
Oakenshaw. *W Yor* 2B **92**
Oakerthorpe. *Derbs* 5A **86**
Oakford. *Cdgn* 5D **56**
Oakford. *Devn* 4C **20**
Oakfordbridge. *Devn* 4C **20**
Oakgrove. *Ches* 4D **84**
Oakham. *Rut* 5F **75**
Oakhanger. *Ches* 5B **84**
Oakhanger. *Hants* 3F **25**
Oakhill. *Som* 2B **22**
Oakington. *Cambs* 4D **64**
Oaklands. *Powy* 5C **58**
Oakle Street. *Glos* 4C **48**
Oakley. *Beds* 5H **63**
Oakley. *Buck* 4E **51**
Oakley. *Fife* 1D **128**
Oakley. *Hants* 1D **24**
Oakley. *Suff* 3D **66**
Oakley Green. *Wind* 3A **38**
Oakley Park. *Powy* 2B **58**
Oakmere. *Ches* 4H **83**
Oakridge. *Glos* 5E **49**
Oaks. *Shrp* 5G **71**
Oaksey. *Wilts* 2E **35**
Oaks Green. *Derbs* 2F **73**
Oakshaw Ford. *Cumb* 2G **113**
Oakshott. *Hants* 4F **25**
Oakthorpe. *Leics* 4H **73**
Oak Tree. *Darl* 3A **106**
Oakwood. *Derb* 2A **74**
Oakwood. *W Yor* 1D **92**
Oakwoodhill. *Surr* 2C **26**
Oakworth. *W Yor* 1A **92**
Oape. *High* 3B **164**
Oare. *Kent* 4E **40**
Oare. *Som* 2B **20**
Oare. *W Ber* 4D **36**
Oare. *Wilts* 5G **35**
Oareford. *Som* 2B **20**
Oasby. *Linc* 2H **75**
Oath. *Som* 4G **21**
Oathlaw. *Ang* 3D **145**
Oatlands. *N Yor* 4F **99**
Oban. *Arg* 1F **133**
Oban. *W Isl* 7D **171**
Oborne. *Dors* 1B **14**
Obsdale. *High* 2A **158**
Obthorpe. *Linc* 4H **75**
Occlestone Green. *Ches* 4A **84**
Occold. *Suff* 3D **66**
Ochiltree. *E Ayr* 2E **117**
Ochtermuthill. *Per* 2H **135**
Ochtertyre. *Per* 1H **135**
Ockbrook. *Derbs* 2B **74**
Ockeridge. *Worc* 4B **60**
Ockham. *Surr* 5B **38**
Ockle. *High* 1G **139**
Ockley. *Surr* 1C **26**
Ocle Pychard. *Here* 1A **48**
Octofad. *Arg* 4A **124**
Octomore. *Arg* 4A **124**
Octon. *E Yor* 3E **101**
Odcombe. *Som* 1A **14**
Odd Down. *Bath* 5C **34**
Oddingley. *Worc* 5D **60**
Oddington. *Oxon* 4D **50**
Oddsta. *Shet* 2G **173**
Odell. *Beds* 5G **63**
Odiham. *Hants* 1F **25**
Odsey. *Cambs* 2C **52**
Odstock. *Wilts* 4G **23**
Odstone. *Leics* 5A **74**
Offchurch. *Warw* 4A **62**
Offenham. *Worc* 1F **49**
Offenham Cross. *Worc* 1F **49**
Offerton. *G Man* 2D **84**
Offerton. *Tyne* 4G **115**
Offham. *E Sus* 4F **27**
Offham. *Kent* 5A **40**
Offham. *W Sus* 5B **26**
Offleyhay. *Staf* 3C **72**
Offley Hoo. *Herts* 3B **52**
Offleymarsh. *Staf* 3B **72**
Offord Cluny. *Cambs* 4B **64**
Offord D'Arcy. *Cambs* 4B **64**
Offton. *Suff* 1D **54**
Offwell. *Devn* 3E **13**
Ogbourne Maizey. *Wilts* 4G **35**
Ogbourne St Andrew. *Wilts* 4G **35**
Ogbourne St George. *Wilts* 4H **35**
Ogden. *G Man* 3H **91**
Ogle. *Nmbd* 2E **115**
Ogmore. *V Glam* 4B **32**
Ogmore-by-Sea. *V Glam* 4B **32**
Ogmore Vale. *B'end* 2C **32**
Okeford Fitzpaine. *Dors* 1D **14**
Okehampton. *Devn* 3F **11**
Okehampton Camp. *Devn* 3F **11**
Okus. *Swin* 3G **35**
Old. *Nptn* 3E **63**
Old Aberdeen. *Aber* 3G **153**
Old Alresford. *Hants* 3D **24**
Oldany. *High* 5B **166**
Old Arley. *Warw* 1G **61**
Old Basford. *Nott* 1C **74**
Old Basing. *Hants* 1E **25**
Oldberrow. *Warw* 4F **61**
Old Bewick. *Nmbd* 2E **121**
Old Bexley. *G Lon* 3F **39**
Old Blair. *Per* 2F **143**
Old Bolingbroke. *Linc* 4C **88**
Oldborough. *Devn* 2A **12**
Old Brampton. *Derbs* 3H **85**
Old Bridge of Tilt. *Per* 2F **143**
Old Bridge of Urr. *Dum* 3E **111**
Old Buckenham. *Norf* 1C **66**
Old Burghclere. *Hants* 1C **24**
Oldbury. *Shrp* 1B **60**
Oldbury. *Warw* 1H **61**
Oldbury. *W Mid* 2D **61**
Oldbury-on-Severn. *S Glo* 2B **34**
Oldbury on the Hill. *Glos* 3D **34**
Old Byland. *N Yor* 1H **99**
Old Cassop. *Dur* 1A **106**
Oldcastle. *Mon* 3G **47**
Oldcastle Heath. *Ches* 1G **71**
Old Clee. *NE Lin* 4F **95**
Old Cleeve. *Som* 2D **20**
Old Clipstone. *Notts* 4D **86**
Old Colwyn. *Cnwy* 3A **82**
Oldcotes. *Notts* 2C **86**
Old Coulsdon. *G Lon* 5E **39**
Old Dailly. *S Ayr* 5B **116**
Old Dalby. *Leics* 3D **74**
Old Dam. *Derbs* 3F **85**
Old Deer. *Abers* 4G **161**
Old Dilton. *Wilts* 2D **22**
Old Down. *S Glo* 3B **34**
Oldeamere. *Cambs* 1C **64**
Old Edlington. *S Yor* 1C **86**
Old Eldon. *Dur* 2F **105**
Old Ellerby. *E Yor* 1E **95**
Old Fallings. *W Mid* 5D **72**
Oldfallow. *Staf* 4D **72**
Old Felixstowe. *Suff* 2G **55**
Oldfield. *Shrp* 2A **60**
Oldfield. *Worc* 4C **60**
Old Fletton. *Pet* 1A **64**
Oldford. *Som* 1C **22**
Old Forge. *Here* 4A **48**
Old Glossop. *Derbs* 1E **85**
Old Goole. *E Yor* 2H **93**
Old Gore. *Here* 3B **48**
Old Graitney. *Dum* 3E **112**
Old Grimsbury. *Oxon* 1C **50**
Old Grimsby. *IOS* 1A **4**
Old Hall. *E Yor* 3F **95**
Oldhall. *High* 3E **169**
Old Hall Street. *Norf* 2F **79**
Oldham. *G Man* 4H **91**
Oldhamstocks. *E Lot* 2D **130**
Old Heathfield. *E Sus* 3G **27**
Old Hill. *W Mid* 2D **60**
Old Hunstanton. *Norf* 1F **77**
Old Hurst. *Cambs* 3B **64**
Old Hutton. *Cumb* 1E **97**
Old Kea. *Corn* 4C **6**
Old Kilpatrick. *W Dun* 2F **127**
Old Kinnernie. *Abers* 3E **152**
Old Knebworth. *Herts* 3C **52**
Oldland. *S Glo* 4B **34**
Old Laxey. *IOM* 3D **108**
Old Leake. *Linc* 5D **88**
Old Lenton. *Nott* 2C **74**
Old Llanberis. *Gwyn* 5F **81**
Old Malton. *N Yor* 2B **100**
Oldmeldrum. *Abers* 1F **153**
Old Micklefield. *W Yor* 1E **93**
Oldmill. *Corn* 5D **10**
Oldmixon. *N Som* 1G **21**
Old Monkland. *N Lan* 3A **128**
Old Newton. *Suff* 4C **66**
Old Park. *Telf* 5A **72**
Old Pentland. *Midl* 3F **129**
Old Philpstoun. *W Lot* 2D **128**
Old Quarrington. *Dur* 1A **106**
Old Radnor. *Powy* 5E **59**
Old Rayne. *Abers* 1D **152**
Oldridge. *Devn* 3B **12**
Old Romney. *Kent* 3E **29**
Old Scone. *Per* 1D **136**
Oldshore Beg. *High* 3B **166**
Oldshoremore. *High* 3C **166**
Old Snydale. *W Yor* 2E **93**
Old Sodbury. *S Glo* 3C **34**
Old Somerby. *Linc* 2G **75**
Old Spital. *Dur* 3C **104**
Oldstead. *N Yor* 1H **99**
Old Stratford. *Nptn* 1F **51**
Old Swan. *Mers* 1F **83**
Old Swarland. *Nmbd* 4F **121**
Old Tebay. *Cumb* 4H **103**
Old Town. *Cumb* 5F **113**
Old Town. *E Sus* 5G **27**
Oldtown. *High* 5C **164**
Old Town. *IOS* 1B **4**
Old Town. *Nmbd* 5C **120**
Oldtown of Ord. *Abers* 3D **160**
Old Trafford. *G Man* 1C **84**
Old Tupton. *Derbs* 4A **86**
Oldwall. *Cumb* 3F **113**
Oldwalls. *Swan* 3D **31**
Old Warden. *Beds* 1B **52**
Oldways End. *Som* 4B **20**
Old Westhall. *Abers* 1D **152**
Old Weston. *Cambs* 3H **63**
Oldwhat. *Abers* 3F **161**
Old Windsor. *Wind* 3A **38**
Old Wives Lees. *Kent* 5E **41**
Old Woking. *Surr* 5B **38**
Oldwood Common. *Worc* 4H **59**
Old Woodstock. *Oxon* 4C **50**
Olgrinmore. *High* 3C **168**
Oliver's Battery. *Hants* 4C **24**
Ollaberry. *Shet* 3E **173**
Ollerton. *Ches* 3B **84**
Ollerton. *Notts* 4D **86**
Ollerton. *Shrp* 3A **72**
Olmarch. *Cdgn* 5F **57**
Olmstead Green. *Cambs* 1G **53**
Olney. *Mil* 5F **63**
Olrig. *High* 2D **169**
Olton. *W Mid* 2F **61**
Olveston. *S Glo* 3B **34**
Ombersley. *Worc* 4C **60**
Ompton. *Notts* 4D **86**
Omunsgarth. *Shet* 7E **173**
Onchan. *IOM* 4D **108**
Onecote. *Staf* 5E **85**
Onehouse. *Suff* 5C **66**
Onen. *Mon* 4H **47**
Ongar Hill. *Norf* 3E **77**
Ongar Street. *Here* 4F **59**
Onibury. *Shrp* 3G **59**
Onich. *High* 2E **141**
Onllwyn. *Neat* 4B **46**
Onneley. *Shrp* 1B **72**
Onslow Green. *Essx* 4G **53**
Onslow Village. *Surr* 1A **26**
Onthank. *E Ayr* 1D **116**
Openwoodgate. *Derbs* 1A **74**
Opinan. *High* 1G **155** (nr. Gairloch)
Opinan. *High* 4C **162** (nr. Laide)
Orasaigh. *W Isl* 6F **171**
Orbost. *High* 4B **154**
Orby. *Linc* 4D **89**
Orchard Hill. *Devn* 4E **19**
Orchard Portman. *Som* 4F **21**
Orcheston. *Wilts* 2F **23**
Orcop. *Here* 3H **47**
Orcop Hill. *Here* 3H **47**
Ord. *High* 2E **147**
Ordhead. *Abers* 2D **152**
Ordie. *Abers* 3B **152**
Ordiquish. *Mor* 3H **159**
Ordley. *Nmbd* 4C **114**
Ordsall. *Notts* 3E **86**
Ore. *E Sus* 4C **28**
Oreham Common. *W Sus* 4D **26**
Oreton. *Shrp* 2A **60**
Orford. *Linc* 1B **88**
Orford. *Suff* 1H **55**
Orford. *Warr* 1A **84**
Organford. *Dors* 3E **15**
Orgil. *Orkn* 7B **172**
Orgreave. *Staf* 4F **73**
Oridge Street. *Glos* 3C **48**
Orlestone. *Kent* 2D **28**
Orleton. *Here* 4G **59**
Orleton. *Worc* 4A **60**
Orleton Common. *Here* 4G **59**
Orlingbury. *Nptn* 3F **63**
Ormacleit. *W Isl* 5C **170**
Ormathwaite. *Cumb* 2D **102**
Ormesby. *Midd* 3C **106**
Ormesby St Margaret. *Norf* 4G **79**
Ormesby St Michael. *Norf* 4G **79**
Ormiscaig. *High* 4C **162**
Ormiston. *E Lot* 3H **129**
Ormsaigbeg. *High* 2F **139**
Ormsaigmore. *High* 2F **139**
Ormsary. *Arg* 2F **125**
Ormsgill. *Cumb* 2A **96**
Ormskirk. *Lanc* 4C **90**
Orphir. *Orkn* 7C **172**
Orpington. *G Lon* 4F **39**
Orrell. *Lanc* 4D **90**
Orrell. *Mers* 1F **83**
Orrisdale. *IOM* 2C **108**
Orsett. *Thur* 2H **39**
Orslow. *Staf* 4C **72**
Orston. *Notts* 1E **75**
Orthwaite. *Cumb* 1D **102**
Orton. *Cumb* 4H **103**
Orton. *Mor* 3H **159**
Orton. *Nptn* 3F **63**
Orton. *Staf* 1C **60**
Orton Longueville. *Pet* 1A **64**
Orton-on-the-Hill. *Leics* 5H **73**
Orton Waterville. *Pet* 1A **64**
Orton Wistow. *Pet* 1A **64**
Orwell. *Cambs* 5C **64**
Osbaldeston. *Lanc* 1E **91**
Osbaldwick. *York* 4A **100**
Osbaston. *Leics* 5B **74**

Osbaston. Shrp 3F 71
Osbournby. Linc 2H 75
Osclay. High 5E 169
Oscroft. Ches 4H 83
Ose. High 4C 154
Osgathorpe. Leics 4B 74
Osgodby. Linc 1H 87
Osgodby. N Yor 1E 101 (nr. Scarborough)
Osgodby. N Yor 1G 93 (nr. Selby)
Oskaig. High 5E 155
Oskamull. Arg 4F 139
Osleston. Derbs 2G 73
Osmaston. Derb 2A 74
Osmaston. Derbs 1G 73
Osmington. Dors 4C 14
Osmington Mills. Dors 4C 14
Osmondthorpe. W Yor 1D 92
Osmotherley. N Yor 5B 106
Osnaburgh. Fife 2G 137
Ospisdale. High 5E 164
Ospringe. Kent 4E 40
Ossett. W Yor 2C 92
Ossington. Notts 4E 87
Ostend. Essx 1D 40
Ostend. Norf 2F 79
Osterley. G Lon 3C 38
Oswaldkirk. N Yor 2A 100
Oswaldtwistle. Lanc 2F 91
Oswestry. Shrp 3E 71
Otby. Linc 1A 88
Otford. Kent 5G 39
Otham. Kent 5B 40
Otherton. Staf 4D 72
Othery. Som 3G 21
Otley. Suff 5E 66
Otley. W Yor 5E 98
Otterbourne. Hants 4C 24
Otterburn. Nmbd 5C 120
Otterburn. N Yor 4A 98
Otterburn Camp. Nmbd 5C 120
Otterburn Hall. Nmbd 5C 120
Otter Ferry. Arg 1H 125
Otterford. Som 1F 13
Otterham. Corn 3B 10
Otterhampton. Som 2F 21
Otterham Quay. Kent 4C 40
Ottershaw. Surr 4B 38
Otterspool. Mers 2F 83
Otterswick. Shet 3G 173
Otterton. Devn 4D 12
Otterwood. Hants 2C 16
Ottery St Mary. Devn 3E 12
Ottinge. Kent 1F 29
Ottringham. E Yor 2F 95
Oughterby. Cumb 4D 112
Oughtershaw. N Yor 1A 98
Oughterside. Cumb 5C 112
Oughtibridge. S Yor 1H 85
Oughtrington. Warr 2A 84
Oulston. N Yor 2H 99
Oulton. Cumb 4D 112
Oulton. Norf 3D 78
Oulton. Staf 3B 72 (nr. Gnosall Heath)
Oulton. Staf 2D 72 (nr. Stone)
Oulton. Suff 1H 67
Oulton. W Yor 2D 92
Oulton Broad. Suff 1H 67
Oulton Street. Norf 3D 78
Oundle. Nptn 2H 63
Ousby. Cumb 1H 103
Ousdale. High 1H 165
Ousden. Suff 5G 65
Ousefleet. E Yor 2B 94
Ouston. Dur 4F 115
Ouston. Nmbd 4A 114 (nr. Bearsbridge)
Ouston. Nmbd 2D 114 (nr. Stamfordham)
Outer Hope. Devn 4C 8
Outertown. Orkn 6B 172
Outgate. Cumb 5E 103
Outhgill. Cumb 4A 104
Outlands. Staf 2B 72
Outlane. W Yor 3A 92
Out Newton. E Yor 2G 95
Out Rawcliffe. Lanc 5D 96
Outwell. Norf 5E 77
Outwick. Hants 1G 15
Outwood. Surr 1E 27
Outwood. W Yor 2D 92
Outwood. Worc 3D 60
Outwoods. Leics 4B 74
Outwoods. Staf 4B 72
Ouzlewell Green. W Yor 2D 92
Ovenden. W Yor 2A 92
Over. Cambs 3C 64
Over. Ches 4A 84
Over. Glos 4D 48
Over. S Glo 3A 34
Overbister. Orkn 3F 172
Over Burrows. Derbs 2G 73
Overbury. Worc 2E 49
Overcombe. Dors 4B 14
Over Compton. Dors 1A 14
Over End. Cambs 1H 63
Over Finlarg. Ang 4D 144
Overgreen. Derbs 3H 85
Over Green. W Mid 1F 61
Over Haddon. Derbs 4G 85
Over Hulton. G Man 4E 91
Over Kellet. Lanc 2E 97
Over Kiddington. Oxon 3C 50
Overleigh. Som 3H 21
Overley. Staf 4F 73
Over Monnow. Mon 4A 48
Over Norton. Oxon 3B 50
Over Peover. Ches 3B 84
Overpool. Ches 3F 83
Overscaig. High 1B 164
Overseal. Derbs 4G 73
Over Silton. N Yor 5B 106
Oversland. Kent 5E 41
Overstone. Nptn 4F 63
Over Stowey. Som 3E 21
Overstrand. Norf 1E 79
Over Stratton. Som 1H 13
Over Street. Wilts 3F 23
Overthorpe. Nptn 1C 50
Overton. Aber 2F 153
Overton. Ches 3H 83
Overton. Hants 2D 24
Overton. High 5E 169
Overton. Lanc 4D 96
Overton. N Yor 4H 99
Overton. Shrp 2A 60 (nr. Bridgnorth)
Overton. Shrp 3H 59 (nr. Ludlow)
Overton. Swan 4D 30
Overton. W Yor 3C 92
Overton. Wrex 1F 71
Overtown. N Lan 4B 128
Overtown. Swin 4G 35
Over Wallop. Hants 3A 24
Over Whitacre. Warw 1G 61
Over Worton. Oxon 3C 50
Oving. Buck 3F 51
Oving. W Sus 5A 26
Ovingdean. Brig 5E 27
Ovingham. Nmbd 3D 115
Ovington. Dur 3E 105
Ovington. Essx 1A 54
Ovington. Hants 3D 24
Ovington. Norf 5B 78
Ovington. Nmbd 3D 114
Owen's Bank. Staf 3G 73
Ower. Hants 2C 16 (nr. Holbury)
Ower. Hants 1B 16 (nr. Totton)
Owermoigne. Dors 4C 14
Owlbury. Shrp 1F 59
Owler Bar. Derbs 3G 85
Owlerton. S Yor 2H 85
Owlswick. Buck 5F 51
Owmby. Linc 4D 94
Owmby-by-Spital. Linc 2H 87
Ownham. W Ber 4C 36
Owrytn. Wrex 1F 71
Owslebury. Hants 4D 24
Owston. Leics 5E 75
Owston. S Yor 3F 93
Owston Ferry. N Lin 4B 94
Owstwick. E Yor 1F 95
Owthorne. E Yor 2G 95
Owthorpe. Notts 2D 74
Owton Manor. Hart 2B 106
Oxborough. Norf 5G 77
Oxbridge. Dors 3H 13
Oxcombe. Linc 3C 88
Oxen End. Essx 3G 53
Oxenhall. Glos 3C 48
Oxenholme. Cumb 5G 103
Oxenhope. W Yor 1A 92
Oxen Park. Cumb 1C 96
Oxenpill. Som 2H 21
Oxenton. Glos 2E 49
Oxenwood. Wilts 1B 24
Oxford. Oxon 5D 50
Oxgangs. Edin 3F 129
Oxhey. Herts 1C 38
Oxhill. Warw 1B 50
Oxley. W Mid 5C 72
Oxley Green. Essx 4C 54
Oxley's Green. E Sus 3A 28
Oxlode. Cambs 2D 65
Oxnam. Bord 3B 120
Oxshott. Surr 4C 38
Oxspring. S Yor 4C 92
Oxted. Surr 5E 39
Oxton. Mers 2E 83
Oxton. N Yor 5H 99
Oxton. Notts 5D 86
Oxton. Bord 4A 130
Oxwich. Swan 4D 31
Oxwich Green. Swan 4D 31
Oxwick. Norf 3B 78
Oykel Bridge. High 3A 164
Oyne. Abers 1D 152
Oystermouth. Swan 4F 31
Ozleworth. Glos 2C 34

P

Pabail Iarach. W Isl 4H 171
Pabail Uarach. W Isl 4H 171
Pachesham. Surr 5C 38
Packers Hill. Dors 1C 14
Packington. Leics 4A 74
Packmoor. Stoke 5C 84
Packmores. Warw 4G 61
Packwood. W Mid 3F 61
Packwood Gullett. W Mid 3F 61
Padanaram. Ang 3D 144
Padbury. Buck 2F 51
Paddington. G Lon 2D 38
Paddington. Warr 2A 84
Paddlesworth. Kent 2F 29
Paddock. Kent 5D 40
Paddockhole. Dum 1D 112
Paddock Wood. Kent 1A 28
Paddolgreen. Shrp 2H 71
Padeswood. Flin 4E 83
Padiham. Lanc 1F 91
Padside. N Yor 4D 98
Padson. Devn 3F 11
Padstow. Corn 1D 6
Padworth. W Ber 5E 36
Page Bank. Dur 1F 105
Pagham. W Sus 3G 17
Paglesham Churchend. Essx 1D 40
Paglesham Eastend. Essx 1D 40
Paibeil. W Isl 2C 170 (on North Uist)
Paibeil. W Isl 8C 171 (on Taransay)
Paignton. Torb 2E 9
Pailton. Warw 2B 62
Paine's Corner. E Sus 3H 27
Painleyhill. Staf 2E 73
Painscastle. Powy 1E 47
Painshawfield. Nmbd 3D 114
Painsthorpe. E Yor 4C 100
Painswick. Glos 5D 48
Painter's Forstal. Kent 5D 40
Painthorpe. W Yor 3D 92
Pairc Shiaboist. W Isl 3E 171
Paisley. Ren 3F 127
Pakefield. Suff 1H 67
Pakenham. Suff 4B 66
Pale. Gwyn 2B 70
Palehouse Common. E Sus 4F 27
Palestine. Hants 2A 24
Paley Street. Wind 4G 37
Palgowan. Dum 1A 110
Palgrave. Suff 3D 66
Pallington. Dors 3C 14
Palmarsh. Kent 2F 29
Palmer Moor. Derbs 2F 73
Palmers Cross. W Mid 5C 72
Palmerstown. V Glam 5E 33
Palnackie. Dum 4F 111
Palnure. Dum 3B 110
Palterton. Derbs 4B 86
Pamber End. Hants 1E 24
Pamber Green. Hants 1E 24
Pamber Heath. Hants 5E 36
Pamington. Glos 2E 49
Pamphill. Dors 2E 15
Pampisford. Cambs 1E 53
Panborough. Som 2H 21
Panbride. Ang 5E 145
Pancakehill. Glos 4F 49
Pancrasweek. Devn 2C 10
Pandy. Gwyn 3A 70 (nr. Bala)
Pandy. Gwyn 5F 69 (nr. Tywyn)
Pandy. Mon 3G 47
Pandy. Powy 5B 70
Pandy. Wrex 2D 70
Pandy Tudur. Cnwy 4A 82
Panfield. Essx 3H 53
Pangbourne. W Ber 4E 37
Pannal. N Yor 4F 99
Pannal Ash. N Yor 4E 99
Pannanich. Abers 4A 152
Pant. Shrp 3E 71
Pant. Wrex 1F 71
Pantasaph. Flin 3D 82
Pant Glas. Gwyn 1D 68
Pant-glas. Shrp 2E 71
Pantgwyn. Carm 3F 45
Pantgwyn. Cdgn 1C 44
Pant-lasau. Swan 3F 31
Panton. Linc 3A 88
Pant-pastynog. Den 4C 82
Pantperthog. Gwyn 5G 69
Pant-teg. Carm 3E 45
Pant-y-Caws. Carm 2F 43
Pant-y-dwr. Powy 3B 58
Pant-y-ffridd. Powy 5D 70
Pantyffynnon. Carm 4G 45
Pantygasseg. Torf 5F 47
Pant-y-llyn. Carm 4G 45
Pant-yr-awel. B'end 3C 32
Pant y Wacco. Flin 3D 82
Panxworth. Norf 4F 79
Papa Stour Airport. Shet 6C 173
Papa Westray Airport. Orkn 2D 172
Papcastle. Cumb 1C 102
Papigoe. High 3F 169
Papil. Shet 8E 173
Papple. E Lot 2B 130
Papplewick. Notts 5C 86
Papworth Everard. Cambs 4B 64
Papworth St Agnes. Cambs 4B 64
Par. Corn 3E 7
Paramour Street. Kent 4G 41
Parbold. Lanc 3C 90
Parbrook. Som 3A 22
Parbrook. W Sus 3B 26
Parc. Gwyn 2A 70
Parcllyn. Cdgn 5B 56
Parc-Seymour. Newp 2H 33
Pardown. Hants 2D 24
Pardshaw. Cumb 2B 102
Parham. Suff 4F 67
Park. Abers 4E 153
Park. Arg 4D 140
Park. Dum 5B 118
Park Bottom. Corn 4A 6
Parkburn. Abers 5E 161
Park Corner. E Sus 2G 27
Park Corner. Oxon 3E 37
Parkend. Glos 5B 48
Park End. Nmbd 2B 114
Parkeston. Essx 2F 55
Parkfield. Corn 2H 7
Parkgate. Ches 3E 83
Parkgate. Cumb 5D 112
Parkgate. Dum 1B 112
Park Gate. Hants 2D 16
Parkgate. Surr 1D 26
Park Gate. Worc 3D 60
Parkhall. W Dun 2F 127
Parkham. Devn 4D 19
Parkham Ash. Devn 4D 18
Parkhead. Cumb 5E 113
Parkhead. Glas 3H 127
Park Hill. Mers 4C 90
Parkhouse. Mon 5H 47
Parkhurst. IOW 3C 16
Park Lane. G Man 4F 91
Park Lane. Staf 5C 72
Parkmill. Swan 4E 31
Park Mill. W Yor 3C 92
Parkneuk. Abers 1G 145
Parkside. N Lan 4B 128
Parkstone. Pool 3F 15
Park Street. Herts 5B 52
Park Street. W Sus 2C 26
Park Town. Oxon 5D 50
Park Village. Nmbd 3H 113
Parkway. Here 2C 48
Parley Cross. Dors 3F 15
Parmoor. Buck 3F 37
Parr. Mers 1H 83
Parracombe. Devn 2G 19
Parrog. Pemb 1E 43
Parsonage Green. Essx 4H 53
Parsonby. Cumb 1C 102
Parson Cross. S Yor 1A 86
Parson Drove. Cambs 5C 76
Partick. Glas 3G 127
Partington. G Man 1B 84
Partney. Linc 4D 88
Parton. Cumb 2A 102 (nr. Whitehaven)
Parton. Cumb 4D 112 (nr. Wigton)
Parton. Dum 2D 111
Partridge Green. W Sus 4C 26
Parwich. Derbs 5F 85
Passenham. Nptn 2F 51
Passfield. Hants 3G 25
Passingford Bridge. Essx 1G 39
Paston. Norf 2F 79
Pasturefields. Staf 3D 73
Patchacott. Devn 3E 11
Patcham. Brig 5E 27
Patchetts Green. Herts 1C 38
Patching. W Sus 5B 26
Patchole. Devn 2G 19
Patchway. S Glo 3B 34
Pateley Bridge. N Yor 3D 98
Pathe. Som 3G 21
Pathfinder Village. Devn 3B 12
Pathhead. Abers 2G 145
Pathhead. E Ayr 3F 117
Pathhead. Fife 4E 137
Pathhead. Midl 3G 129
Pathlow. Warw 5F 61
Path of Condie. Per 2C 136
Pathstruie. Per 2C 136

Patmore Heath. *Herts* 3E **53**
Patna. *E Ayr* 3D **116**
Patney. *Wilts* 1F **23**
Patrick. *IOM* 3B **108**
Patrick Brompton. *N Yor* 5F **105**
Patrington. *E Yor* 2G **95**
Patrington Haven. *E Yor* 2G **95**
Patrixbourne. *Kent* 5F **41**
Patterdale. *Cumb* 3E **103**
Pattiesmuir. *Fife* 1D **129**
Pattingham. *Staf* 1C **60**
Pattishall. *Nptn* 5D **62**
Pattiswick. *Essx* 3B **54**
Patton Bridge. *Cumb* 5G **103**
Paul. *Corn* 4B **4**
Paulerspury. *Nptn* 1F **51**
Paull. *E Yor* 2E **95**
Paulton. *Bath* 1B **22**
Pauperhaugh. *Nmbd* 5F **121**
Pave Lane. *Telf* 4B **72**
Pavenham. *Beds* 5G **63**
Pawlett. *Som* 2G **21**
Pawston. *Nmbd* 1C **120**
Paxford. *Glos* 2G **49**
Paxton. *Bord* 4F **131**
Payhembury. *Devn* 2D **12**
Paythorne. *Lanc* 4H **97**
Peacehaven. *E Sus* 5F **27**
Peak Dale. *Derbs* 3E **85**
Peak Forest. *Derbs* 3F **85**
Peak Hill. *Linc* 4B **76**
Peakirk. *Pet* 5A **76**
Peanmeanach. *High* 5F **147**
Pearsie. *Ang* 3C **144**
Peasedown St John. *Bath* 1C **22**
Peaseland Green. *Norf* 4C **78**
Peasemore. *W Ber* 4C **36**
Peasenhall. *Suff* 4F **67**
Pease Pottage. *W Sus* 2D **26**
Peaslake. *Surr* 1B **26**
Peasley Cross. *Mers* 1H **83**
Peasmarsh. *E Sus* 3C **28**
Peasmarsh. *Surr* 1A **26**
Peaston. *E Lot* 3H **129**
Peastonbank. *E Lot* 3H **129**
Peathill. *Abers* 2G **161**
Peat Inn. *Fife* 3G **137**
Peatling Magna. *Leics* 1C **62**
Peatling Parva. *Leics* 2C **62**
Peaton. *Arg* 1D **126**
Peaton. *Shrp* 2H **59**
Peats Corner. *Suff* 4D **66**
Pebmarsh. *Essx* 2B **54**
Pebworth. *Worc* 1G **49**
Pecket Well. *W Yor* 2H **91**
Peckforton. *Ches* 5H **83**
Peckham Bush. *Kent* 5A **40**
Peckleton. *Leics* 5B **74**
Pedair-ffordd. *Powy* 3D **70**
Pedlinge. *Kent* 2F **29**
Pedmore. *W Mid* 2D **60**
Pedwell. *Som* 3H **21**
Peebles. *Bord* 5F **129**
Peel. *IOM* 3B **108**
Peel. *Bord* 1G **119**
Peel Common. *Hants* 2D **16**
Peening Quarter. *Kent* 3C **28**
Peggs Green. *Leics* 4B **74**
Pegsdon. *Beds* 2B **52**
Pegswood. *Nmbd* 1F **115**
Peinchorran. *High* 5E **155**
Peinlich. *High* 3D **154**
Pelaw. *Tyne* 3G **115**
Pelcomb Bridge. *Pemb* 3D **42**
Pelcomb Cross. *Pemb* 3D **42**
Peldon. *Essx* 4C **54**
Pelsall. *W Mid* 5E **73**
Pelton. *Dur* 4F **115**
Pelutho. *Cumb* 5C **112**
Pelynt. *Corn* 3G **7**
Pemberton. *Carm* 5F **45**
Pembrey. *Carm* 5E **45**
Pembridge. *Here* 5F **59**
Pembroke. *Pemb* 4D **43**
Pembroke Dock. *Pemb* 4D **42**
Pembroke Ferry. *Pemb* 4D **43**
Pembury. *Kent* 1H **27**
Penallt. *Mon* 4A **48**
Penally. *Pemb* 5F **43**
Penalt. *Here* 3A **48**
Penalum. *Pemb* 5F **43**
Penare. *Corn* 4D **6**
Penarth. *V Glam* 4E **33**
Penbeagle. *Corn* 3C **4**
Penberth. *Corn* 4B **4**
Pen-bont Rhydybeddau. *Cdgn* 2F **57**
Penbryn. *Cdgn* 5B **56**
Pencader. *Carm* 2E **45**
Pen-cae. *Cdgn* 5D **56**
Pencaenewydd. *Gwyn* 1D **68**
Pencaerau. *Neat* 3G **31**
Pencaitland. *E Lot* 3H **129**
Pencarnisiog. *IOA* 3C **80**
Pencarreg. *Carm* 1F **45**
Pencarrow. *Corn* 4B **10**
Pencelli. *Powy* 3D **46**
Pen-clawdd. *Swan* 3E **31**
Pencoed. *B'end* 3C **32**
Pencombe. *Here* 5H **59**
Pencraig. *Here* 3A **48**
Pencraig. *Powy* 3C **70**
Pendeen. *Corn* 3A **4**
Pendeford. *W Mid* 5D **72**
Penderyn. *Rhon* 5C **46**
Pendine. *Carm* 4G **43**
Pendlebury. *G Man* 4F **91**
Pendleton. *G Man* 1C **84**
Pendleton. *Lanc* 1F **91**
Pendock. *Worc* 2C **48**
Pendoggett. *Corn* 5A **10**
Pendomer. *Som* 1A **14**
Pendoylan. *V Glam* 4D **32**
Pendre. *B'end* 3C **32**
Penegoes. *Powy* 5G **69**
Penelewey. *Corn* 4C **6**
Penffordd. *Pemb* 2E **43**
Penffordd-Lâs. *Powy* 1A **58**
Penfro. *Pemb* 4D **43**
Pengam. *Cphy* 2E **33**
Pengam. *Card* 4F **33**
Penge. *G Lon* 3E **39**
Pengelly. *Corn* 4A **10**
Pengenffordd. *Powy* 2E **47**
Pengorffwysfa. *IOA* 1D **80**
Pengover Green. *Corn* 2G **7**
Pengwern. *Den* 3C **82**
Penhale. *Corn* 5D **5**
(nr. Mullion)
Penhale. *Corn* 3D **6**
(nr. St Austell)
Penhale Camp. *Corn* 3B **6**
Penhallow. *Corn* 3B **6**
Penhalvean. *Corn* 5B **6**
Penhelig. *Gwyn* 1F **57**
Penhill. *Swin* 3G **35**
Penhow. *Newp* 2H **33**
Penhurst. *E Sus* 4A **28**
Peniarth. *Gwyn* 5F **69**
Penicuik. *Midl* 3F **129**
Peniel. *Carm* 3E **45**
Penifiler. *High* 4D **155**
Peninver. *Arg* 3B **122**
Penisa'r Waun. *Gwyn* 4E **81**
Penistone. *S Yor* 4C **92**
Penketh. *Warr* 2H **83**
Penkill. *S Ayr* 5B **116**
Penkridge. *Staf* 4D **72**
Penley. *Wrex* 2G **71**
Penllech. *Gwyn* 2B **68**
Penllergaer. *Swan* 3F **31**
Pen-llyn. *IOA* 2C **80**
Penmachno. *Cnwy* 5G **81**
Penmaen. *Swan* 4E **31**
Penmaenmawr. *Cnwy* 3G **81**
Penmaenpool. *Gwyn* 4F **69**
Penmaen Rhos. *Cnwy* 3A **82**
Pen-marc. *V Glam* 5D **32**
Penmark. *V Glam* 5D **32**
Penmarth. *Corn* 5B **6**
Penmon. *IOA* 2F **81**
Penmorfa. *Gwyn* 1E **69**
Penmynydd. *IOA* 3E **81**
Penn. *Buck* 1A **38**
Penn. *Dors* 3G **13**
Penn. *W Mid* 1C **60**
Pennal. *Gwyn* 5G **69**
Pennan. *Abers* 2F **161**
Pennant. *Cdgn* 4E **57**
Pennant. *Den* 2C **70**
Pennant. *Gwyn* 3B **70**
Pennant. *Powy* 1A **58**
Pennant Melangell. *Powy* 3C **70**
Pennar. *Pemb* 4D **42**
Pennard. *Swan* 4E **31**
Pennerley. *Shrp* 1F **59**
Pennington. *Cumb* 2B **96**
Pennington. *G Man* 1A **84**
Pennington. *Hants* 3B **16**
Pennorth. *Powy* 3E **46**
Penn Street. *Buck* 1A **38**
Pennsylvania. *Devn* 3C **12**
Pennsylvania. *S Glo* 4C **34**
Penny Bridge. *Cumb* 1C **96**
Pennycross. *Plym* 3A **8**
Pennygate. *Norf* 3F **79**
Pennyghael. *Arg* 1C **132**
Penny Hill. *Linc* 3C **76**
Pennylands. *Lanc* 4C **90**
Pennymoor. *Devn* 1B **12**
Pennyvenie. *E Ayr* 4D **117**
Pennywell. *Tyne* 4G **115**
Penparc. *Cdgn* 1C **44**
Penparcau. *Cdgn* 2E **57**
Penpedairheol. *Cphy* 2E **33**
Penperlleni. *Mon* 5G **47**
Penpillick. *Corn* 3E **7**
Penpol. *Corn* 5C **6**
Penpoll. *Corn* 3F **7**
Penponds. *Corn* 3D **4**
Penpont. *Corn* 5A **10**
Penpont. *Dum* 5H **117**
Penpont. *Powy* 3C **46**
Penprysg. *B'end* 3C **32**
Penquit. *Devn* 3C **8**
Penrherber. *Carm* 1G **43**
Penrhiw. *Pemb* 1C **44**
Penrhiwceiber. *Rhon* 2D **32**
Pen Rhiwfawr. *Neat* 4H **45**
Penrhiw-llan. *Cdgn* 1D **44**
Penrhiw-pal. *Cdgn* 1D **44**
Penrhos. *Gwyn* 2C **68**
Penrhos. *Here* 5F **59**
Penrhos. *IOA* 2B **80**
Penrhos. *Mon* 4H **47**
Penrhos. *Powy* 4A **46**
Penrhos Garnedd. *Gwyn* 3E **81**
Penrhyn. *IOA* 1C **80**
Penrhyn Bay. *Cnwy* 2H **81**
Penrhyn-coch. *Cdgn* 2F **57**
Penrhyndeudraeth. *Gwyn* 2F **69**
Penrhyn Side. *Cnwy* 2H **81**
Penrice. *Swan* 4D **31**
Penrith. *Cumb* 2G **103**
Penrose. *Corn* 1C **6**
Penruddock. *Cumb* 2F **103**
Penryn. *Corn* 5B **6**
Pensarn. *Carm* 4E **45**
Pen-sarn. *Gwyn* 3E **69**
Pensax. *Worc* 4B **60**
Pensby. *Mers* 2E **83**
Penselwood. *Som* 3C **22**
Pensford. *Bath* 5B **34**
Pensham. *Worc* 1E **49**
Penshaw. *Tyne* 4G **115**
Penshurst. *Kent* 1G **27**
Pensilva. *Corn* 2G **7**
Pensnett. *W Mid* 2D **60**
Penston. *E Lot* 2H **129**
Penstone. *Devn* 2A **12**
Pente-tafarn-y-fedw. *Cnwy* 4H **81**
Pentewan. *Corn* 4E **6**
Pentir. *Gwyn* 4E **81**
Pentire. *Corn* 2B **6**
Pentlepoir. *Pemb* 4F **43**
Pentlow. *Essx* 1B **54**
Pentney. *Norf* 4G **77**
Penton Mewsey. *Hants* 2B **24**
Pentraeth. *IOA* 3E **81**
Pentre. *Powy* 1E **59**
(nr. Church Stoke)
Pentre. *Powy* 2D **58**
(nr. Kerry)
Pentre. *Powy* 2C **58**
(nr. Mochdre)
Pentre. *Rhon* 2C **32**
Pentre. *Shrp* 4F **71**
Pentre. *Wrex* 2D **70**
(nr. Llanfyllin)
Pentre. *Wrex* 1E **71**
(nr. Rhosllanerchrugog)
Pentrebach. *Carm* 2B **46**
Pentre-bach. *Cdgn* 1F **45**
Pentrebach. *Mer T* 5D **46**
Pentre-bach. *Powy* 2C **46**
Pentrebach. *Swan* 5G **45**
Pentre Berw. *IOA* 3D **80**
Pentre-bont. *Cnwy* 5G **81**
Pentrecagal. *Carm* 1D **44**
Pentre-celyn. *Den* 5D **82**
Pentre-clawdd. *Shrp* 2E **71**
Pentreclwydau. *Neat* 5B **46**
Pentre-cwrt. *Carm* 2D **45**
Pentre Dolau Honddu. *Powy* 1C **46**
Pentre-du. *Cnwy* 5G **81**
Pentre-dwr. *Swan* 3F **31**
Pentrefelin. *Carm* 3F **45**
Pentrefelin. *Cdgn* 1G **45**
Pentrefelin. *Cnwy* 3H **81**
Pentrefelin. *Gwyn* 2E **69**
Pentrefoelas. *Cnwy* 5A **82**
Pentre Galar. *Pemb* 1F **43**
Pentregat. *Cdgn* 5C **56**
Pentre Gwenlais. *Carm* 4G **45**
Pentre Gwynfryn. *Gwyn* 3E **69**
Pentre Halkyn. *Flin* 3E **82**
Pentre Hodre. *Shrp* 3F **59**
Pentre-Llanrhaeadr. *Den* 4C **82**
Pentre Llifior. *Powy* 1D **58**
Pentrellwyn. *IOA* 2E **81**
Pentre-llwyn-llwyd. *Powy* 5B **58**
Pentre-llyn-cymmer. *Cnwy* 5B **82**
Pentre Meyrick. *V Glam* 4C **32**
Pentre-piod. *Gwyn* 2A **70**
Pentre-poeth. *Newp* 3F **33**
Pentre'r Beirdd. *Powy* 4D **70**
Pentre'r-felin. *Powy* 2C **46**
Pentre-ty-gwyn. *Carm* 2B **46**
Pentre-uchaf. *Gwyn* 2C **68**
Pentrich. *Derbs* 5A **86**
Pentridge. *Dors* 1F **15**
Pen-twyn. *Cphy* 5F **47**
(nr. Oakdale)
Pentwyn. *Cphy* 5E **46**
(nr. Rhymney)
Pentwyn. *Card* 3F **33**
Pentyrch. *Card* 3E **32**
Pentywyn. *Carm* 4G **43**
Penuwch. *Cdgn* 4E **57**
Penwithick. *Corn* 3E **7**
Penwyllt. *Powy* 4B **46**
Penybanc. *Carm* 4G **45**
(nr. Ammanford)
Pen-y-banc. *Carm* 3G **45**
(nr. Llandeilo)
Pen-y-bont. *Carm* 2H **43**
Penybont. *Powy* 4D **58**
(nr. Llandrindod Wells)
Pen-y-bont. *Powy* 3E **70**
(nr. Llanfyllin)
Pen-y-Bont Ar Ogwr. *B'end* 3C **32**
Penybontfawr. *Powy* 3C **70**
Penybryn. *Cphy* 2E **33**
Pen-y-bryn. *Pemb* 1B **44**
Pen-y-bryn. *Wrex* 1E **71**
Pen-y-cae. *Powy* 4B **46**
Penycae. *Wrex* 1E **71**
Pen-y-cae-mawr. *Mon* 2H **33**
Penycaerau. *Gwyn* 3A **68**
Pen-y-cefn. *Flin* 3D **82**
Pen-y-clawdd. *Mon* 5H **47**
Pen-y-coedcae. *Rhon* 3D **32**
Penycwm. *Pemb* 2C **42**
Pen-y-Darren. *Mer T* 5D **46**
Pen-y-fai. *B'end* 3B **32**
Penyffordd. *Flin* 4F **83**
(nr. Mold)
Pen-y-ffordd. *Flin* 2D **82**
(nr. Prestatyn)
Penyffridd. *Gwyn* 5E **81**
Pen-y-garn. *Cdgn* 2F **57**
Pen-y-garnedd. *IOA* 3E **81**
Penygarnedd. *Powy* 3D **70**
Pen-y-graig. *Gwyn* 2B **68**
Penygraig. *Rhon* 2C **32**
Penygraigwen. *IOA* 2D **80**
Pen-y-groes. *Carm* 4F **45**
Penygroes. *Gwyn* 5D **80**
Penygroes. *Pemb* 1F **43**
Penymynydd. *Flin* 4F **83**
Penyrheol. *Cphy* 3E **33**
Pen-yr-heol. *Mon* 4H **47**
Penyrheol. *Swan* 3E **31**
Pen-yr-Heolgerrig. *Mer T* 5D **46**
Penysarn. *IOA* 1D **80**
Pen-y-stryt. *Den* 5E **82**
Penywaun. *Rhon* 5C **46**
Penzance. *Corn* 3B **4**
Peopleton. *Worc* 5D **60**
Peover Heath. *Ches* 3B **84**
Peper Harow. *Surr* 1A **26**
Peplow. *Shrp* 3A **72**
Pepper Arden. *N Yor* 4F **105**
Perceton. *N Ayr* 5E **127**
Percyhorner. *Abers* 2G **161**
Perham Down. *Wilts* 2A **24**
Periton. *Som* 2C **20**
Perkinsville. *Dur* 4F **115**
Perlethorpe. *Notts* 3D **86**
Perranarworthal. *Corn* 5B **6**
Perranporth. *Corn* 3B **6**
Perranuthnoe. *Corn* 4C **4**
Perranwell. *Corn* 5B **6**
Perranzabuloe. *Corn* 3B **6**
Perrott's Brook. *Glos* 5F **49**
Perry. *W Mid* 1E **61**
Perry Barr. *W Mid* 1E **61**
Perry Crofts. *Staf* 5G **73**
Perry Green. *Essx* 3B **54**
Perry Green. *Herts* 4E **53**
Perry Green. *Wilts* 3E **35**
Perry Street. *Kent* 3H **39**
Perry Street. *Som* 2G **13**
Perrywood. *Kent* 5E **41**
Pershall. *Staf* 2C **72**
Pershore. *Worc* 1E **49**
Pertenhall. *Beds* 4H **63**
Perth. *Per* 1D **136**
Perthy. *Shrp* 2F **71**
Perton. *Staf* 1C **60**
Pertwood. *Wilts* 3D **23**
Peterborough. *Pet* 1A **64**
Peterburn. *High* 5B **162**
Peterchurch. *Here* 2G **47**
Peterculter. *Aber* 3F **153**
Peterhead. *Abers* 4H **161**
Peterlee. *Dur* 5H **115**
Petersfield. *Hants* 4F **25**
Petersfinger. *Wilts* 4G **23**
Peter's Green. *Herts* 4B **52**
Peters Marland. *Devn* 1E **11**
Peterstone Wentlooge. *Newp* 3F **33**
Peterston-super-Ely. *V Glam* 4D **32**
Peterstow. *Here* 3A **48**
Peter Tavy. *Devn* 5F **11**
Petham. *Kent* 5F **41**
Petherwin Gate. *Corn* 4C **10**
Petrockstowe. *Devn* 2F **11**
Petsoe End. *Mil* 1G **51**
Pett. *E Sus* 4C **28**
Pettaugh. *Suff* 5D **66**

Pett Bottom. *Kent* 5F **41**
Petteridge. *Kent* 1A **28**
Petteril Green. *Cumb* 5F **113**
Pettinain. *S Lan* 5C **128**
Pettistree. *Suff* 5E **67**
Petton. *Devn* 4D **20**
Petton. *Shrp* 3G **71**
Petts Wood. *G Lon* 4F **39**
Pettycur. *Fife* 1F **129**
Pettywell. *Norf* 3C **78**
Petworth. *W Sus* 3A **26**
Pevensey. *E Sus* 5A **28**
Pevensey Bay. *E Sus* 5A **28**
Pewsey. *Wilts* 5G **35**
Pheasants Hill. *Buck* 3F **37**
Philadelphia. *Tyne* 4G **115**
Philham. *Devn* 4C **18**
Philiphaugh. *Bord* 2G **119**
Phillack. *Corn* 3C **4**
Philleigh. *Corn* 5C **6**
Philpstoun. *W Lot* 2D **128**
Phocle Green. *Here* 3B **48**
Phoenix Green. *Hants* 1F **25**
Pibsbury. *Som* 4H **21**
Pibwrlwyd. *Carm* 4E **45**
Pica. *Cumb* 2B **102**
Piccadilly. *Warw* 1G **61**
Piccadilly Corner. *Norf* 2E **67**
Piccotts End. *Herts* 5A **52**
Pickering. *N Yor* 1B **100**
Picket Piece. *Hants* 2B **24**
Picket Post. *Hants* 2G **15**
Pickford. *W Mid* 2G **61**
Pickhill. *N Yor* 1F **99**
Picklenash. *Glos* 3C **48**
Picklescott. *Shrp* 1G **59**
Pickletillem. *Fife* 1G **137**
Pickmere. *Ches* 3A **84**
Pickstock. *Telf* 3B **72**
Pickwell. *Devn* 2E **19**
Pickwell. *Leics* 4E **75**
Pickworth. *Linc* 2H **75**
Pickworth. *Rut* 4G **75**
Picton. *Ches* 3G **83**
Picton. *Flin* 2D **82**
Picton. *N Yor* 4B **106**
Piddinghoe. *E Sus* 5F **27**
Piddington. *Buck* 2G **37**
Piddington. *Nptn* 5F **63**
Piddington. *Oxon* 4E **51**
Piddlehinton. *Dors* 3C **14**
Piddletrenthide. *Dors* 2C **14**
Pidley. *Cambs* 3C **64**
Pidney. *Dors* 2C **14**
Pie Corner. *Here* 4A **60**
Piercebridge. *Darl* 3F **105**
Pierowall. *Orkn* 3D **172**
Pigdon. *Nmbd* 1E **115**
Pightley. *Som* 3F **21**
Pikehall. *Derbs* 5F **85**
Pikeshill. *Hants* 2A **16**
Pilford. *Dors* 2F **15**
Pilgrims Hatch. *Essx* 1G **39**
Pilham. *Linc* 1F **87**
Pill. *N Som* 4A **34**
Pillaton. *Corn* 2H **7**
Pillaton. *Staf* 4D **72**
Pillerton Hersey. *Warw* 1A **50**
Pillerton Priors. *Warw* 1A **50**
Pilleth. *Powy* 4E **59**
Pilley. *Hants* 3B **16**
Pilley. *S Yor* 4D **92**
Pillgwenlly. *Newp* 3G **33**
Pilling. *Lanc* 5D **96**
Pilling Lane. *Lanc* 5C **96**
Pillowell. *Glos* 5B **48**
Pill, The. *Mon* 3H **33**
Pillwell. *Dors* 1C **14**
Pilning. *S Glo* 3A **34**
Pilsbury. *Derbs* 4F **85**
Pilsdon. *Dors* 3H **13**
Pilsgate. *Pet* 5H **75**
Pilsley. *Derbs* 3G **85**
(nr. Bakewell)
Pilsley. *Derbs* 4B **86**
(nr. Clay Cross)
Pilson Green. *Norf* 4F **79**
Piltdown. *E Sus* 3F **27**
Pilton. *Edin* 2F **129**
Pilton. *Nptn* 2H **63**
Pilton. *Rut* 5G **75**
Pilton. *Som* 2A **22**
Pilton Green. *Swan* 4D **30**
Pimperne. *Dors* 2E **15**
Pinchbeck. *Linc* 3B **76**
Pinchbeck Bars. *Linc* 3A **76**
Pinchbeck West. *Linc* 3B **76**
Pinfold. *Lanc* 3B **90**
Pinford End. *Suff* 5H **65**
Pinged. *Carm* 5E **45**
Pinhoe. *Devn* 3C **12**
Pinkerton. *E Lot* 2D **130**
Pinkneys Green. *Wind* 3G **37**
Pinley. *W Mid* 3A **62**
Pinley Green. *Warw* 4G **61**
Pin Mill. *Suff* 2F **55**
Pinmore. *S Ayr* 5B **116**
Pinner. *G Lon* 2C **38**
Pins Green. *Worc* 1C **48**
Pinsley Green. *Ches* 1H **71**
Pinvin. *Worc* 1E **49**
Pinwherry. *S Ayr* 1G **109**
Pinxton. *Derbs* 5B **86**
Pipe and Lyde. *Here* 1A **48**
Pipe Aston. *Here* 3G **59**
Pipe Gate. *Shrp* 1B **72**
Pipehill. *Staf* 5E **73**
Piperhill. *High* 3C **158**
Pipe Ridware. *Staf* 4E **73**
Pipers Pool. *Corn* 4C **10**
Pipewell. *Nptn* 2F **63**
Pippacott. *Devn* 3F **19**
Pipton. *Powy* 2E **47**
Pirbright. *Surr* 5A **38**
Pirnmill. *N Ayr* 5G **125**
Pirton. *Herts* 2B **52**
Pirton. *Worc* 1D **49**
Pisgah. *Stir* 3G **135**
Pishill. *Oxon* 3F **37**
Pistyll. *Gwyn* 1C **68**
Pitagowan. *Per* 2F **143**
Pitcairn. *Per* 3F **143**
Pitcairngreen. *Per* 1C **136**
Pitcalnie. *High* 1C **158**
Pitcaple. *Abers* 1E **152**
Pitchcombe. *Glos* 5D **48**
Pitchcott. *Buck* 3F **51**
Pitchford. *Shrp* 5H **71**
Pitch Green. *Buck* 5F **51**
Pitch Place. *Surr* 5A **38**
Pitcombe. *Som* 3B **22**
Pitcox. *E Lot* 2C **130**
Pitcur. *Per* 5B **144**
Pitfichie. *Abers* 2D **152**
Pitgrudy. *High* 4E **165**
Pitkennedy. *Ang* 3E **145**
Pitlessie. *Fife* 3F **137**
Pitlochry. *Per* 3G **143**
Pitmachie. *Abers* 1D **152**
Pitmaduthy. *High* 1B **158**
Pitmedden. *Abers* 1F **153**
Pitminster. *Som* 1F **13**
Pitnacree. *Per* 3G **143**
Pitney. *Som* 4H **21**
Pitroddie. *Per* 1E **136**
Pitscottie. *Fife* 2G **137**
Pitsea. *Essx* 2B **40**
Pitsford. *Nptn* 4E **63**
Pitsford Hill. *Som* 3E **20**
Pitsmoor. *S Yor* 2A **86**
Pitstone. *Buck* 4H **51**
Pitt. *Hants* 4C **24**
Pitt Court. *Glos* 2C **34**
Pittentrail. *High* 3E **164**
Pittenweem. *Fife* 3H **137**
Pittington. *Dur* 5G **115**
Pitton. *Swan* 4D **30**
Pitton. *Wilts* 3H **23**
Pittswood. *Kent* 1H **27**
Pittulie. *Abers* 2G **161**
Pittville. *Glos* 3E **49**
Pitversie. *Per* 2D **136**
Pityme. *Corn* 1D **6**
Pity Me. *Dur* 5F **115**
Pixey Green. *Suff* 3E **67**
Pixley. *Here* 2B **48**
Place Newton. *N Yor* 2C **100**
Plaidy. *Abers* 3E **161**
Plaidy. *Corn* 3G **7**
Plain Dealings. *Pemb* 3E **43**
Plains. *N Lan* 3A **128**
Plainsfield. *Som* 3E **21**
Plaish. *Shrp* 1H **59**
Plaistow. *Here* 2B **48**
Plaistow. *W Sus* 2B **26**
Plaitford. *Wilts* 1A **16**
Plas Llwyd. *Cnwy* 3B **82**
Plastow Green. *Hants* 5D **36**
Plas yn Cefn. *Den* 3C **82**
Platt. *Kent* 5H **39**
Platt Bridge. *G Man* 4E **90**
Platt Lane. *Shrp* 2H **71**
Platts Common. *S Yor* 4D **92**
Platt's Heath. *Kent* 5C **40**
Platt, The. *E Sus* 2G **27**
Plawsworth. *Dur* 5F **115**
Plaxtol. *Kent* 5H **39**
Playden. *E Sus* 3D **28**
Playford. *Suff* 1F **55**
Play Hatch. *Oxon* 4F **37**
Playing Place. *Corn* 4C **6**
Playley Green. *Glos* 2C **48**
Plealey. *Shrp* 5G **71**
Plean. *Stir* 1B **128**
Pleasington. *Bkbn* 2E **91**
Pleasley. *Derbs* 4C **86**
Pledgdon Green. *Essx* 3F **53**
Plenmeller. *Nmbd* 3A **114**
Pleshey. *Essx* 4G **53**
Plockton. *High* 5H **155**
Plocrapol. *W Isl* 8D **171**
Ploughfield. *Here* 1G **47**
Plowden. *Shrp* 2F **59**
Ploxgreen. *Shrp* 5F **71**
Pluckley. *Kent* 1D **28**
Plumbland. *Cumb* 1C **102**
Plumgarths. *Cumb* 5F **103**
Plumley. *Ches* 3B **84**
Plummers Plain. *W Sus* 3D **26**
Plumpton. *Cumb* 1F **103**
Plumpton. *E Sus* 4E **27**
Plumpton. *Nptn* 1D **50**
Plumptonfoot. *Cumb* 1F **103**
Plumpton Green. *E Sus* 4E **27**
Plumpton Head. *Cumb* 1G **103**
Plumstead. *G Lon* 3F **39**
Plumstead. *Norf* 2D **78**
Plumtree. *Notts* 2D **74**
Plumtree Park. *Notts* 2D **74**
Plungar. *Leics* 2E **75**
Plush. *Dors* 2C **14**
Plushabridge. *Corn* 5D **10**
Plwmp. *Cdgn* 5C **56**
Plymouth. *Plym* 3A **8**
Plymouth City Airport. *Plym* 3B **8**
Plympton. *Plym* 3B **8**
Plymstock. *Plym* 3B **8**
Plymtree. *Devn* 2D **12**
Pockley. *N Yor* 1A **100**
Pocklington. *E Yor* 5C **100**
Pode Hole. *Linc* 3B **76**
Podimore. *Som* 4A **22**
Podington. *Beds* 4G **63**
Podmore. *Staf* 2B **72**
Poffley End. *Oxon* 4B **50**
Point Clear. *Essx* 4D **54**
Pointon. *Linc* 2A **76**
Pokesdown. *Bour* 3G **15**
Polbae. *Dum* 2H **109**
Polbain. *High* 3E **163**
Polbathic. *Corn* 3H **7**
Polbeth. *W Lot* 3D **128**
Polbrock. *Corn* 2E **6**
Polchar. *High* 3C **150**
Polebrook. *Nptn* 2H **63**
Pole Elm. *Worc* 1D **48**
Polegate. *E Sus* 5G **27**
Pole Moor. *W Yor* 3A **92**
Poles. *High* 4E **165**
Polesworth. *Warw* 5G **73**
Polglass. *High* 3E **163**
Polgooth. *Corn* 3D **6**
Poling. *W Sus* 5B **26**
Poling Corner. *W Sus* 5B **26**
Polio. *High* 1B **158**
Polkerris. *Corn* 3E **7**
Polla. *High* 3D **166**
Pollard Street. *Norf* 2F **79**
Pollicott. *Buck* 4F **51**
Pollington. *E Yor* 3G **93**
Polloch. *High* 2B **140**
Pollok. *Glas* 3G **127**
Pollokshaws. *Glas* 3G **127**
Pollokshields. *Glas* 3G **127**
Polmaily. *High* 5G **157**
Polmassick. *Corn* 4D **6**
Polmont. *Falk* 2C **128**
Polnessan. *E Ayr* 3D **116**
Polnish. *High* 5F **147**
Polperro. *Corn* 3G **7**
Polruan. *Corn* 3F **7**
Polscoe. *Corn* 2F **7**
Polsham. *Som* 2A **22**
Polskeoch. *Dum* 4F **117**
Polstead. *Suff* 2C **54**
Polstead Heath. *Suff* 1C **54**
Poltescoe. *Corn* 5E **5**
Poltimore. *Devn* 3C **12**
Polton. *Midl* 3G **129**
Polwarth. *Bord* 4D **130**
Polyphant. *Corn* 4C **10**
Polzeath. *Corn* 1D **6**
Ponde. *Powy* 2E **46**
Pondersbridge. *Cambs* 1B **64**
Ponders End. *G Lon* 1E **39**
Pond Street. *Essx* 2E **53**
Pondtail. *Hants* 1G **25**
Ponsanooth. *Corn* 5B **6**
Ponsongath. *Corn* 5E **5**
Ponsworthy. *Devn* 5H **11**
Pontamman. *Carm* 4G **45**
Pontantwn. *Carm* 4E **45**
Pontardawe. *Neat* 5H **45**
Pontarddulais. *Swan* 5F **45**
Pontarfynach. *Cdgn* 3G **57**
Pont-ar-gothi. *Carm* 3F **45**
Pont ar Hydfer. *Powy* 3B **46**
Pontarllechau. *Carm* 3H **45**
Pontarsais. *Carm* 3E **45**
Pontblyddyn. *Flin* 4E **83**
Pontbren Llwyd. *Rhon* 5C **46**
Pont Cyfyng. *Cnwy* 5G **81**
Pontdolgoch. *Powy* 1C **58**
Pontefract. *W Yor* 2E **93**
Ponteland. *Nmbd* 2E **115**
Ponterwyd. *Cdgn* 2G **57**
Pontesbury. *Shrp* 5G **71**
Pontesford. *Shrp* 5G **71**
Pontfadog. *Wrex* 2E **71**
Pontfaen. *Pemb* 1E **43**
Pont-faen. *Powy* 2C **46**
Pont-Faen. *Shrp* 2E **71**
Pontgarreg. *Cdgn* 5C **56**
Pont-Henri. *Carm* 5E **45**
Ponthir. *Torf* 2G **33**
Ponthirwaun. *Cdgn* 1C **44**
Pont-iets. *Carm* 5E **45**
Pontllanfraith. *Cphy* 2E **33**
Pontlliw. *Swan* 5G **45**
Pont Llogel. *Powy* 4C **70**
Pontllyfni. *Gwyn* 5D **80**
Pontlottyn. *Cphy* 5E **46**
Pontneddfechan. *Neat* 5C **46**
Pont-newydd. *Carm* 5E **45**
Pont-newydd. *Flin* 4D **82**
Pontnewydd. *Torf* 2F **33**
Pont Pen-y-benglog. *Gwyn* 4F **81**
Pontrhydfendigaid. *Cdgn* 4G **57**
Pont Rhyd-y-cyff. *B'end* 3B **32**
Pontrhydyfen. *Neat* 2A **32**
Pont-rhyd-y-groes. *Cdgn* 3G **57**
Pontrhydyrun. *Torf* 2F **33**
Pont Rhythallt. *Gwyn* 4E **81**
Pontrilas. *Here* 3G **47**
Pontrilas Road. *Here* 3G **47**
Pontrobert. *Powy* 4D **70**
Pont-rug. *Gwyn* 4E **81**
Ponts Green. *E Sus* 4A **28**
Pontshill. *Here* 3B **48**
Pont-Sian. *Cdgn* 1E **45**
Pontsticill. *Mer T* 4D **46**
Pont-Walby. *Neat* 5B **46**
Pontwelly. *Carm* 2E **45**
Pontwgan. *Cnwy* 3G **81**
Pontyates. *Carm* 5E **45**
Pontyberem. *Carm* 4F **45**
Pontybodkin. *Flin* 5E **83**
Pontyclun. *Rhon* 3D **32**
Pontycymer. *B'end* 2C **32**
Pontyglazier. *Pemb* 1F **43**
Pontygwaith. *Rhon* 2D **32**
Pont-y-pant. *Cnwy* 5G **81**
Pontypool. *Torf* 2G **33**
Pontypridd. *Rhon* 2D **32**
Pontypwl. *Torf* 2G **33**
Pontywaun. *Cphy* 2F **33**
Pooksgreen. *Hants* 1B **16**
Pool. *Corn* 4A **6**
Pool. *W Yor* 5E **99**
Poole. *N Yor* 2E **93**
Poole. *Pool* 3F **15**
Poole Green. *Ches* 5A **84**
Poole Keynes. *Glos* 2E **35**
Poolend. *Staf* 5D **84**
Poolewe. *High* 5C **162**
Pooley Bridge. *Cumb* 2F **103**
Poolfold. *Staf* 5C **84**
Pool Head. *Here* 5H **59**
Pool Hey. *Lanc* 3B **90**
Poolhill. *Glos* 3C **48**
Poolmill. *Here* 3A **48**
Pool o' Muckhart. *Clac* 3C **136**
Pool Quay. *Powy* 4E **71**
Poolsbrook. *Derbs* 3B **86**
Pool Street. *Essx* 2A **54**
Pootings. *Kent* 1F **27**
Pope Hill. *Pemb* 3D **42**
Pope's Hill. *Glos* 4B **48**
Popeswood. *Brac* 5G **37**
Popham. *Hants* 2D **24**
Poplar. *G Lon* 2E **39**
Popley. *Hants* 1E **25**
Porchfield. *IOW* 3C **16**
Porin. *High* 3F **157**
Poringland. *Norf* 5E **79**
Porkellis. *Corn* 5A **6**
Porlock. *Som* 2B **20**
Porlock Weir. *Som* 2B **20**
Portachoillan. *Arg* 4F **125**
Port Adhair Bheinn na Faoghla. *W Isl* 3C **170**
Port Ann. *Arg* 1H **125**
Port Appin. *Arg* 4D **140**
Port Asgaig. *Arg* 3C **124**
Port Askaig. *Arg* 3C **124**
Portavadie. *Arg* 3H **125**
Port Bannatyne. *Arg* 3B **126**
Portbury. *N Som* 4A **34**
Port Carlisle. *Cumb* 3D **112**
Port Charlotte. *Arg* 4A **124**
Portchester. *Hants* 2E **16**
Port Clarence. *Stoc T* 2B **106**
Port Dinorwig. *Gwyn* 4E **81**
Port Driseach. *Arg* 2A **126**
Port Dundas. *Glas* 3H **127**
Port Ellen. *Arg* 5B **124**
Port Elphinstone. *Abers* 1E **153**
Portencalzie. *Dum* 2F **109**
Portencross. *N Ayr* 5C **126**
Port Erin. *IOM* 5A **108**

Port Erroll. *Abers* 5H **161**
Porter's Fen Corner. *Norf* 5E **77**
Portesham. *Dors* 4B **14**
Portessie. *Mor* 2B **160**
Port e Vullen. *IOM* 2D **108**
Port-Eynon. *Swan* 4D **30**
Portfield Gate. *Pemb* 3D **42**
Portgate. *Devn* 4E **11**
Port Gaverne. *Corn* 4A **10**
Port Glasgow. *Inv* 2E **127**
Portgordon. *Mor* 2A **160**
Portgower. *High* 2H **165**
Porth. *Corn* 2C **6**
Porth. *Rhon* 2D **32**
Porthaethwy. *IOA* 3E **81**
Porthallow. *Corn* 3G **7** (nr. Looe)
Porthallow. *Corn* 4E **5** (nr. St Keverne)
Porthalong. *High* 5C **154**
Porthcawl. *B'end* 4B **32**
Porthceri. *V Glam* 5D **32**
Porthcothan. *Corn* 1C **6**
Porthcurno. *Corn* 4A **4**
Port Henderson. *High* 1G **155**
Porthgain. *Pemb* 1C **42**
Porthgwarra. *Corn* 4A **4**
Porthill. *Shrp* 4G **71**
Porthkerry. *V Glam* 5D **32**
Porthleven. *Corn* 4D **4**
Porthllechog. *IOA* 1D **80**
Porth Llechog. *IOA* 1D **80**
Porthmadog. *Gwyn* 2E **69**
Porthmeirion. *Gwyn* 2E **69**
Porthmeor. *Corn* 3B **4**
Porth Navas. *Corn* 4E **5**
Portholland. *Corn* 4D **6**
Porthoustock. *Corn* 4F **5**
Porthtowan. *Corn* 4A **6**
Porth Tywyn. *Carm* 5E **45**
Porth-y-felin. *IOA* 2B **80**
Porthyrhyd. *Carm* 4F **45** (nr. Carmarthen)
Porthyrhyd. *Carm* 2H **45** (nr. Llandovery)
Porth-y-waen. *Shrp* 3E **71**
Portincaple. *Arg* 4B **134**
Portington. *E Yor* 1A **94**
Portinnisherrich. *Arg* 2G **133**
Portinscale. *Cumb* 2D **102**
Port Isaac. *Corn* 1D **6**
Portishead. *N Som* 4H **33**
Portknockie. *Mor* 2B **160**
Port Lamont. *Arg* 2B **126**
Portlethen. *Abers* 4G **153**
Portlethen Village. *Abers* 4G **153**
Portling. *Dum* 4F **111**
Port Lion. *Pemb* 4D **43**
Portloe. *Corn* 5D **6**
Port Logan. *Dum* 5F **109**
Portmahomack. *High* 5G **165**
Port Mead. *Swan* 3F **31**
Portmellon. *Corn* 4E **6**
Port Mholair. *W Isl* 4H **171**
Port Mor. *High* 1F **139**
Portmore. *Hants* 3B **16**
Port Mulgrave. *N Yor* 3E **107**
Portnacroish. *Arg* 4D **140**
Portnahaven. *Arg* 4A **124**
Portnalong. *High* 5C **154**
Portnaluchaig. *High* 5E **147**
Portnancon. *High* 2E **167**
Port Nan Giuran. *W Isl* 4H **171**
Port nan Long. *W Isl* 1D **170**
Port Nis. *W Isl* 1H **171**
Portobello. *Edin* 2G **129**
Portobello. *W Yor* 3D **92**
Port of Menteith. *Stir* 3E **135**
Porton. *Wilts* 3G **23**
Portormin. *High* 5D **168**
Portpatrick. *Dum* 4F **109**
Port Quin. *Corn* 1D **6**
Port Ramsay. *Arg* 4C **140**
Portreath. *Corn* 4A **6**
Portree. *High* 4D **155**
Port St Mary. *IOM* 5B **108**
Portscatho. *Corn* 5C **6**
Portsea. *Port* 2E **17**
Portskerra. *High* 2A **168**
Portskewett. *Mon* 3A **34**
Portslade-by-Sea. *Brig* 5D **26**
Portsmouth. *Port* 3E **17**
Portsmouth. *W Yor* 2H **91**
Port Soderick. *IOM* 4C **108**
Port Solent. *Port* 2E **17**
Portsonachan. *Arg* 1H **133**
Portsoy. *Abers* 2C **160**
Port Sunlight. *Mers* 2F **83**
Portswood. *Sotn* 1C **16**
Port Talbot. *Neat* 4G **31**
Porttannachy. *Mor* 2A **160**
Port Tennant. *Swan* 3F **31**
Portuairk. *High* 2F **139**
Portway. *Here* 1H **47**
Portway. *Worc* 3E **61**
Port Wemyss. *Arg* 4A **124**
Port William. *Dum* 5A **110**
Portwrinkle. *Corn* 3H **7**
Poslingford. *Suff* 1A **54**
Postbridge. *Devn* 5G **11**
Postcombe. *Oxon* 2F **37**
Post Green. *Dors* 3E **15**
Posthill. *Staf* 5G **73**
Postling. *Kent* 2F **29**
Postlip. *Glos* 3F **49**
Post-Mawr. *Cdgn* 5D **56**
Postwick. *Norf* 5E **79**
Potarch. *Abers* 4D **152**
Potsgrove. *Beds* 3H **51**
Potten End. *Herts* 5A **52**
Potter Brompton. *N Yor* 2D **101**
Pottergate Street. *Norf* 1D **66**
Potterhanworth. *Linc* 4H **87**
Potterhanworth Booths. *Linc* 4H **87**
Potter Heigham. *Norf* 4G **79**
Potter Hill. *Leics* 3E **75**
Potteries, The. *Stoke* 1C **72**
Potterne. *Wilts* 1E **23**
Potterne Wick. *Wilts* 1E **23**
Potternewton. *W Yor* 1D **92**
Potters Bar. *Herts* 5C **52**
Potters Brook. *Lanc* 4D **97**
Potter's Cross. *Staf* 2C **60**
Potters Crouch. *Herts* 5B **52**
Potter Somersal. *Derbs* 2F **73**
Potterspury. *Nptn* 1F **51**
Potter Street. *Essx* 5E **53**
Potterton. *Abers* 2G **153**
Potthorpe. *Norf* 3B **78**
Pottle Street. *Wilts* 2D **22**
Potto. *N Yor* 4B **106**
Potton. *Beds* 1C **52**
Pott Row. *Norf* 3G **77**
Pott Shrigley. *Ches* 3D **84**
Poughill. *Corn* 2C **10**
Poughill. *Devn* 2B **12**
Poulner. *Hants* 2G **15**
Poulshot. *Wilts* 1E **23**
Poulton. *Glos* 5G **49**
Poulton-le-Fylde. *Lanc* 1B **90**
Pound Bank. *Worc* 3B **60**
Poundbury. *Dors* 3B **14**
Poundfield. *E Sus* 2G **27**
Poundgate. *E Sus* 3F **27**
Pound Green. *E Sus* 3G **27**
Pound Hill. *W Sus* 2D **27**
Poundland. *S Ayr* 1G **109**
Poundon. *Buck* 3E **51**
Poundsgate. *Devn* 5H **11**
Poundstock. *Corn* 3C **10**
Pound Street. *Hants* 5C **36**
Pounsley. *E Sus* 3G **27**
Powburn. *Nmbd* 3E **121**
Powderham. *Devn* 4C **12**
Powerstock. *Dors* 3A **14**
Powfoot. *Dum* 3C **112**
Powick. *Worc* 5C **60**
Powmill. *Per* 4C **136**
Poxwell. *Dors* 4C **14**
Poyle. *Slo* 3B **38**
Poynings. *W Sus* 4D **26**
Poyntington. *Dors* 4B **22**
Poynton. *Ches* 2D **84**
Poynton. *Telf* 4H **71**
Poynton Green. *Telf* 4H **71**
Poys Street. *Suff* 3F **67**
Poystreet Green. *Suff* 5B **66**
Praa Sands. *Corn* 4C **4**
Pratt's Bottom. *G Lon* 4F **39**
Praze-an-Beeble. *Corn* 3D **4**
Prees. *Shrp* 2H **71**
Preesall. *Lanc* 5C **96**
Preesall Park. *Lanc* 5C **96**
Prees Green. *Shrp* 2H **71**
Prees Higher Heath. *Shrp* 2H **71**
Prendergast. *Pemb* 3D **42**
Prendwick. *Nmbd* 3E **121**
Pren-gwyn. *Cdgn* 1E **45**
Prenteg. *Gwyn* 1E **69**
Prenton. *Mers* 2F **83**
Prescot. *Mers* 1G **83**
Prescott. *Devn* 1D **12**
Prescott. *Shrp* 3G **71**
Preshute. *Wilts* 5G **35**
Pressen. *Nmbd* 1C **120**
Prestatyn. *Den* 2C **82**
Prestbury. *Ches* 3D **84**
Prestbury. *Glos* 3E **49**
Presteigne. *Powy* 4F **59**
Presthope. *Shrp* 1H **59**
Prestleigh. *Som* 2B **22**
Preston. *Brig* 5E **27**
Preston. *Devn* 5B **12**
Preston. *Dors* 4C **14**
Preston. *E Lot* 2B **130** (nr. East Linton)
Preston. *E Lot* 2G **129** (nr. Prestonpans)
Preston. *E Yor* 1E **95**
Preston. *Glos* 5F **49**
Preston. *Herts* 3B **52**
Preston. *Kent* 4G **41** (nr. Canterbury)
Preston. *Kent* 4E **40** (nr. Faversham)
Preston. *Lanc* 2D **90**
Preston. *Nmbd* 2F **121**
Preston. *Rut* 5F **75**
Preston. *Bord* 4D **130**
Preston. *Shrp* 4H **71**
Preston. *Suff* 5B **66**
Preston. *Wilts* 4A **36** (nr. Aldbourne)
Preston. *Wilts* 4F **35** (nr. Lyneham)
Preston Bagot. *Warw* 4F **61**
Preston Bissett. *Buck* 3E **51**
Preston Bowyer. *Som* 4E **21**
Preston Brockhurst. *Shrp* 3H **71**
Preston Brook. *Hal* 3H **83**
Preston Candover. *Hants* 2E **24**
Preston Capes. *Nptn* 5C **62**
Preston Cross. *Glos* 2B **48**
Preston Gubbals. *Shrp* 4G **71**
Preston-le-Skerne. *Dur* 2A **106**
Preston Marsh. *Here* 1A **48**
Prestonmill. *Dum* 4A **112**
Preston on Stour. *Warw* 5G **61**
Preston on the Hill. *Hal* 2H **83**
Preston on Wye. *Here* 1G **47**
Prestonpans. *E Lot* 2G **129**
Preston Plucknett. *Som* 1A **14**
Preston-under-Scar. *N Yor* 5D **104**
Preston upon the Weald Moors. *Telf* 4A **72**
Preston Wynne. *Here* 1A **48**
Prestwich. *G Man* 4G **91**
Prestwick. *Nmbd* 2E **115**
Prestwick. *S Ayr* 2C **116**
Prestwold. *Leics* 3C **74**
Prestwood. *Buck* 5G **51**
Prestwood. *Staf* 1E **73**
Price Town. *B'end* 2C **32**
Prickwillow. *Cambs* 2E **65**
Priddy. *Som* 1A **22**
Priestcliffe. *Derbs* 3F **85**
Priesthill. *Glas* 3G **127**
Priest Hutton. *Lanc* 2E **97**
Priestland. *E Ayr* 1E **117**
Priest Weston. *Shrp* 1E **59**
Priestwood. *Brac* 4G **37**
Priestwood. *Kent* 4A **40**
Primethorpe. *Leics* 1C **62**
Primrose Green. *Norf* 4C **78**
Primrose Hill. *Derbs* 5B **86**
Primrose Hill. *Glos* 5B **48**
Primrose Hill. *Lanc* 4B **90**
Primrose Valley. *N Yor* 2F **101**
Primsidemill. *Bord* 2C **120**
Princes Gate. *Pemb* 3F **43**
Princes Risborough. *Buck* 5G **51**
Princethorpe. *Warw* 3B **62**
Princetown. *Devn* 5F **11**
Prinsted. *W Sus* 2F **17**
Prion. *Den* 4C **82**
Prior Muir. *Fife* 2H **137**
Prior's Frome. *Here* 2A **48**
Priors Halton. *Shrp* 3G **59**
Priors Hardwick. *Warw* 5B **62**
Priorslee. *Telf* 4B **72**
Priors Marston. *Warw* 5B **62**
Prior's Norton. *Glos* 3D **48**
Priory, The. *W Ber* 5B **36**
Priory Wood. *Here* 1F **47**
Priston. *Bath* 5B **34**
Pristow Green. *Norf* 2D **66**
Prittlewell. *S'end* 2C **40**
Privett. *Hants* 4E **25**
Prixford. *Devn* 3F **19**
Probus. *Corn* 4D **6**
Prospect. *Cumb* 5C **112**
Provanmill. *Glas* 3H **127**
Prudhoe. *Nmbd* 3D **115**
Publow. *Bath* 5B **34**
Puckeridge. *Herts* 3D **53**
Puckington. *Som* 1G **13**
Pucklechurch. *S Glo* 4B **34**
Puckrup. *Glos* 2D **49**
Puddinglake. *Ches* 4B **84**
Puddington. *Ches* 3F **83**
Puddington. *Devn* 1B **12**
Puddlebrook. *Glos* 4B **48**
Puddledock. *Norf* 1C **66**
Puddletown. *Dors* 3C **14**
Pudleston. *Here* 5H **59**
Pudsey. *W Yor* 1C **92**
Pulborough. *W Sus* 4B **26**
Puleston. *Telf* 3B **72**
Pulford. *Ches* 5F **83**
Pulham. *Dors* 2C **14**
Pulham Market. *Norf* 2D **66**
Pulham St Mary. *Norf* 2E **66**
Pulley. *Shrp* 5G **71**
Pulloxhill. *Beds* 2A **52**
Pulpit Hill. *Arg* 1F **133**
Pulverbatch. *Shrp* 5G **71**
Pumpherston. *W Lot* 3D **128**
Pumsaint. *Carm* 1G **45**
Puncheston. *Pemb* 2E **43**
Puncknowle. *Dors* 4A **14**
Punnett's Town. *E Sus* 3H **27**
Purbrook. *Hants* 2E **17**
Purfleet. *Thur* 3G **39**
Puriton. *Som* 2G **21**
Purleigh. *Essx* 5B **54**
Purley. *G Lon* 4E **39**
Purley on Thames. *W Ber* 4E **37**
Purlogue. *Shrp* 3E **59**
Purl's Bridge. *Cambs* 2D **65**
Purse Caundle. *Dors* 1B **14**
Purslow. *Shrp* 2F **59**
Purston Jaglin. *W Yor* 3E **93**
Purtington. *Som* 2G **13**
Purton. *Glos* 5B **48** (nr. Lydney)
Purton. *Glos* 5B **48** (nr. Sharpness)
Purton. *Wilts* 3F **35**
Purton Stoke. *Wilts* 2F **35**
Pury End. *Nptn* 1F **51**
Pusey. *Oxon* 2B **36**
Putley. *Here* 2B **48**
Putney. *G Lon* 3D **38**
Putsborough. *Devn* 2E **19**
Puttenham. *Herts* 4G **51**
Puttenham. *Surr* 1A **26**
Puttock End. *Essx* 1B **54**
Puttock's End. *Essx* 4F **53**
Puxey. *Dors* 1C **14**
Puxton. *N Som* 5H **33**
Pwll. *Carm* 5E **45**
Pwll. *Powy* 5D **70**
Pwllcrochan. *Pemb* 4D **42**
Pwll-glas. *Den* 5D **82**
Pwllgloyw. *Powy* 2D **46**
Pwllheli. *Gwyn* 2C **68**
Pwllmeyric. *Mon* 2A **34**
Pwlltrap. *Carm* 3G **43**
Pwll-y-glaw. *Neat* 2A **32**
Pyecombe. *W Sus* 4D **27**
Pye Corner. *Herts* 4E **53**
Pye Corner. *Newp* 3G **33**
Pye Green. *Staf* 4D **73**
Pyewipe. *NE Lin* 3F **95**
Pyle. *B'end* 3B **32**
Pyle. *IOW* 5C **16**
Pylle. *Som* 3B **22**
Pymore. *Cambs* 2D **65**
Pymore. *Dors* 3H **13**
Pyrford. *Surr* 5B **38**
Pyrton. *Oxon* 2E **37**
Pytchley. *Nptn* 3F **63**
Pyworthy. *Devn* 2D **10**

Q

Quabbs. *Shrp* 2E **58**
Quadring. *Linc* 2B **76**
Quadring Eaudike. *Linc* 2B **76**
Quainton. *Buck* 3F **51**
Quaking Houses. *Dur* 4E **115**
Quarley. *Hants* 2A **24**
Quarndon. *Derbs* 1H **73**
Quarndon Common. *Derbs* 1H **73**
Quarrendon. *Buck* 4G **51**
Quarrier's Village. *Inv* 3E **127**
Quarrington. *Linc* 1H **75**
Quarrington Hill. *Dur* 1A **106**
Quarrybank. *Ches* 4H **83**
Quarry Bank. *W Mid* 2D **60**
Quarry, The. *Glos* 2C **34**
Quarrywood. *Mor* 2F **159**
Quartalehouse. *Abers* 4G **161**
Quarter. *N Ayr* 3C **126**
Quarter. *S Lan* 4A **128**
Quatford. *Shrp* 1B **60**
Quatt. *Shrp* 2B **60**
Quebec. *Dur* 5E **115**
Quedgeley. *Glos* 4D **48**
Queen Adelaide. *Cambs* 2E **65**
Queenborough. *Kent* 3D **40**
Queen Camel. *Som* 4A **22**
Queen Charlton. *Bath* 5B **34**
Queen Dart. *Devn* 1B **12**
Queenhill. *Worc* 2D **48**
Queen Oak. *Dors* 3C **22**
Queensbury. *W Yor* 2B **92**
Queensferry. *Flin* 4F **83**
Queenstown. *Bkpl* 1B **90**
Queen Street. *Kent* 1A **28**
Queenzieburn. *N Lan* 2H **127**
Quemerford. *Wilts* 5F **35**
Quendale. *Shet* 10E **173**
Quendon. *Essx* 2F **53**
Queniborough. *Leics* 4D **74**
Quenington. *Glos* 5G **49**
Quernmore. *Lanc* 3E **97**
Quethiock. *Corn* 2H **7**

Quick's Green—Rhoslefain

Quick's Green. *W Ber* 4D **36**
Quidenham. *Norf* 2C **66**
Quidhampton. *Hants* 1D **24**
Quidhampton. *Wilts* 3G **23**
Quilquox. *Abers* 5G **161**
Quina Brook. *Shrp* 2H **71**
Quine's Hill. *IOM* 4C **108**
Quinton. *Nptn* 5E **63**
Quinton. *W Mid* 2D **61**
Quintrell Downs. *Corn* 2C **6**
Quixhill. *Staf* 1F **73**
Quoditch. *Devn* 3E **11**
Quorn. *Leics* 4C **74**
Quorndon. *Leics* 4C **74**
Quothquan. *S Lan* 1B **118**
Quoyloo. *Orkn* 5B **172**
Quoyness. *Orkn* 7B **172**

R

Rableyheath. *Herts* 4C **52**
Raby. *Cumb* 4C **112**
Raby. *Mers* 3F **83**
Rachan Mill. *Bord* 1D **118**
Rachub. *Gwyn* 4F **81**
Rackenford. *Devn* 1B **12**
Rackham. *W Sus* 4B **26**
Rackheath. *Norf* 4E **79**
Racks. *Dum* 2B **112**
Rackwick. *Orkn* 8A **172** (on Hoy)
Rackwick. *Orkn* 3D **172** (on Westray)
Radbourne. *Derbs* 2G **73**
Radcliffe. *G Man* 4F **91**
Radcliffe. *Nmbd* 4G **121**
Radcliffe on Trent. *Notts* 2D **74**
Radclive. *Buck* 2E **51**
Radernie. *Fife* 2G **137**
Radfall. *Kent* 4F **41**
Radford. *Bath* 1B **22**
Radford. *Nott* 1C **74**
Radford. *W Mid* 2H **61**
Radford. *Worc* 5E **61**
Radford Semele. *Warw* 4H **61**
Radipole. *Dors* 4B **14**
Radlett. *Herts* 1C **38**
Radley. *Oxon* 2D **36**
Radnage. *Buck* 2F **37**
Radstock. *Bath* 1B **22**
Radstone. *Nptn* 1D **50**
Radway. *Warw* 1B **50**
Radway Green. *Ches* 5B **84**
Radwell. *Beds* 5H **63**
Radwell. *Herts* 2C **52**
Radwinter. *Essx* 2G **53**
Radyr. *Card* 3E **33**
Rafford. *Mor* 3E **159**
Ragdale. *Leics* 4D **74**
Ragdon. *Shrp* 1G **59**
Ragged Appleshaw. *Hants* 2B **24**
Raggra. *High* 4F **169**
Raglan. *Mon* 5H **47**
Ragnall. *Notts* 3F **87**
Raigbeg. *High* 1C **150**
Rainford. *Mers* 4C **90**
Rainford Junction. *Mers* 4C **90**
Rainham. *G Lon* 2G **39**
Rainham. *Medw* 4C **40**
Rainhill. *Mers* 1G **83**
Rainow. *Ches* 3D **84**
Rainton. *N Yor* 2F **99**
Rainworth. *Notts* 5C **86**
Raisbeck. *Cumb* 4H **103**
Raise. *Cumb* 5A **114**
Rait. *Per* 1E **137**
Raithby. *Linc* 2C **88** (nr. Louth)
Raithby. *Linc* 4C **88** (nr. Spilsby)
Raithwaite. *N Yor* 3F **107**
Rake. *W Sus* 4G **25**
Rake End. *Staf* 4E **73**
Rakeway. *Staf* 1E **73**
Rakewood. *G Man* 3H **91**
Ralia. *High* 4B **150**
Ram Alley. *Wilts* 5H **35**
Ramasaig. *High* 4A **154**
Rame. *Corn* 4A **8** (nr. Millbrook)
Rame. *Corn* 5B **6** (nr. Penryn)
Ram Lane. *Kent* 1D **28**
Ramnageo. *Shet* 1H **173**
Rampisham. *Dors* 2A **14**
Rampside. *Cumb* 3B **96**
Rampton. *Cambs* 4D **64**
Rampton. *Notts* 3E **87**
Ramsbottom. *G Man* 3F **91**
Ramsburn. *Mor* 3C **160**
Ramsbury. *Wilts* 4A **36**
Ramscraigs. *High* 1H **165**
Ramsdean. *Hants* 4F **25**
Ramsdell. *Hants* 1D **24**
Ramsden. *Oxon* 4B **50**
Ramsden. *Worc* 1E **49**
Ramsden Bellhouse. *Essx* 1B **40**
Ramsden Heath. *Essx* 1B **40**
Ramsey. *Cambs* 2B **64**
Ramsey. *Essx* 2F **55**
Ramsey. *IOM* 2D **108**
Ramsey Forty Foot. *Cambs* 2C **64**
Ramsey Heights. *Cambs* 2B **64**
Ramsey Island. *Essx* 5C **54**
Ramsey Mereside. *Cambs* 2B **64**
Ramsey St Mary's. *Cambs* 2B **64**
Ramsgate. *Kent* 4H **41**
Ramsgill. *N Yor* 2D **98**
Ramshaw. *Dur* 5C **114**
Ramshorn. *Staf* 1E **73**
Ramsley. *Devn* 3G **11**
Ramsnest Common. *Surr* 2A **26**
Ramstone. *Abers* 2D **152**
Ranais. *W Isl* 5G **171**
Ranby. *Linc* 3B **88**
Ranby. *Notts* 2D **86**
Rand. *Linc* 3A **88**
Randwick. *Glos* 5D **48**
Ranfurly. *Ren* 3E **127**
Rangag. *High* 4D **168**
Rangemore. *Staf* 3F **73**
Rangeworthy. *S Glo* 3B **34**
Rankinston. *E Ayr* 3D **116**
Rank's Green. *Essx* 4H **53**
Ranmore Common. *Surr* 5C **38**
Rannoch School. *Per* 3C **142**
Rannoch Station. *Per* 3B **142**
Ranochan. *High* 5G **147**
Ranskill. *Notts* 2D **86**
Ranton. *Staf* 3C **72**
Ranton Green. *Staf* 3C **72**
Ranworth. *Norf* 4F **79**
Raploch. *Stir* 4G **135**
Rapness. *Orkn* 3E **172**
Rapps. *Som* 1G **13**
Rascal Moor. *E Yor* 1B **94**
Rascarrel. *Dum* 5E **111**
Rashfield. *Arg* 1C **126**
Rashwood. *Worc* 4D **60**
Raskelf. *N Yor* 2G **99**
Rassau. *Blae* 4E **47**
Rastrick. *W Yor* 2B **92**
Ratagan. *High* 2B **148**
Ratby. *Leics* 5C **74**
Ratcliffe Culey. *Leics* 1H **61**
Ratcliffe on Soar. *Notts* 3B **74**
Ratcliffe on the Wreake. *Leics* 4D **74**
Rathen. *Abers* 2H **161**
Rathillet. *Fife* 1F **137**
Rathmell. *N Yor* 4H **97**
Ratho. *Edin* 2E **129**
Ratho Station. *Edin* 2E **129**
Rathven. *Mor* 2B **160**
Ratley. *Hants* 4B **24**
Ratley. *Warw* 1B **50**
Ratlinghope. *Shrp* 1G **59**
Rattar. *High* 1E **169**
Ratten Row. *Cumb* 5E **113**
Ratten Row. *Lanc* 5D **96**
Rattery. *Devn* 2D **8**
Rattlesden. *Suff* 5B **66**
Ratton Village. *E Sus* 5G **27**
Rattray. *Abers* 3H **161**
Rattray. *Per* 4A **144**
Raughton. *Cumb* 5E **113**
Raughton Head. *Cumb* 5E **113**
Raunds. *Nptn* 3G **63**
Ravenfield. *S Yor* 1B **86**
Ravenglass. *Cumb* 5B **102**
Ravenhills Green. *Worc* 5B **60**
Raveningham. *Norf* 1F **67**
Ravenscar. *N Yor* 4G **107**
Ravensdale. *IOM* 2C **108**
Ravensden. *Beds* 5H **63**
Ravenseat. *N Yor* 4B **104**
Ravenshead. *Notts* 5C **86**
Ravensmoor. *Ches* 5A **84**
Ravensthorpe. *Nptn* 3D **62**
Ravensthorpe. *W Yor* 2C **92**
Ravenstone. *Leics* 4B **74**
Ravenstone. *Mil* 5F **63**
Ravenstonedale. *Cumb* 4A **104**
Ravenstown. *Cumb* 2C **96**
Ravenstruther. *S Lan* 5C **128**
Ravensworth. *N Yor* 4E **105**
Raw. *N Yor* 4G **107**
Rawcliffe. *E Yor* 2G **93**
Rawcliffe. *York* 4H **99**
Rawcliffe Bridge. *E Yor* 2G **93**
Rawdon. *W Yor* 1C **92**
Rawgreen. *Nmbd* 4C **114**
Rawmarsh. *S Yor* 1B **86**
Rawnsley. *Staf* 4E **73**
Rawreth. *Essx* 1B **40**
Rawridge. *Devn* 2F **13**
Rawson Green. *Derbs* 1A **74**
Rawtenstall. *Lanc* 2F **91**
Raydon. *Suff* 2D **54**
Raylees. *Nmbd* 5D **120**
Rayleigh. *Essx* 1C **40**
Raymond's Hill. *Devn* 3G **13**
Rayne. *Essx* 3H **53**
Rayners Lane. *G Lon* 2C **38**
Reach. *Cambs* 4E **65**
Read. *Lanc* 1F **91**
Reading. *Read* 4F **37**
Reading Green. *Suff* 3D **66**
Reading Street. *Kent* 2D **28**
Readymoney. *Corn* 3F **7**
Reagill. *Cumb* 3H **103**
Rea Hill. *Torb* 3F **9**
Rearquhar. *High* 4E **165**
Rearsby. *Leics* 4D **74**
Reasby. *Linc* 3H **87**
Rease Heath. *Ches* 5A **84**
Reaster. *High* 2E **169**
Reawick. *Shet* 7E **173**
Reay. *High* 2B **168**
Rechullin. *High* 3A **156**
Reculver. *Kent* 4G **41**
Redberth. *Pemb* 4E **43**
Redbourn. *Herts* 4B **52**
Redbourne. *N Lin* 4C **94**
Redbrook. *Glos* 4A **48**
Redbrook. *Wrex* 1H **71**
Redburn. *High* 4D **158**
Redburn. *Nmbd* 3A **114**
Redcar. *Red C* 2D **106**
Redcastle. *High* 4H **157**
Redcliff Bay. *N Som* 4H **33**
Red Dial. *Cumb* 5D **112**
Redding. *Falk* 2C **128**
Reddingmuirhead. *Falk* 2C **128**
Reddings, The. *Glos* 3E **49**
Reddish. *G Man* 1C **84**
Redditch. *Worc* 4E **61**
Rede. *Suff* 5H **65**
Redenhall. *Norf* 2E **67**
Redesdale Camp. *Nmbd* 5C **120**
Redesmouth. *Nmbd* 1B **114**
Redford. *Ang* 4E **145**
Redford. *Dur* 1D **105**
Redford. *W Sus* 4G **25**
Redfordgreen. *Bord* 3F **119**
Redgate. *Corn* 2G **7**
Redgrave. *Suff* 3C **66**
Redhill. *Abers* 3E **153**
Redhill. *Herts* 2C **52**
Redhill. *N Som* 5H **33**
Redhill. *Shrp* 4B **72**
Redhill. *Surr* 5D **39**
Red Hill. *Warw* 5F **61**
Red Hill. *W Yor* 2E **93**
Redhouses. *Arg* 3B **124**
Redisham. *Suff* 2G **67**
Redland. *Bris* 4A **34**
Redland. *Orkn* 5C **172**
Redlingfield. *Suff* 3D **66**
Red Lodge. *Suff* 3F **65**
Redlynch. *Som* 3C **22**
Redlynch. *Wilts* 4H **23**
Redmain. *Cumb* 1C **102**
Redmarley. *Worc* 4B **60**
Redmarley D'Abitot. *Glos* 2C **48**
Redmarshall. *Stoc T* 2A **106**
Redmile. *Leics* 2E **75**
Redmire. *N Yor* 5D **104**
Rednal. *Shrp* 3F **71**
Redpath. *Bord* 1H **119**
Redpoint. *High* 2G **155**
Red Post. *Corn* 2C **10**
Red Rock. *G Man* 4D **90**
Red Roses. *Carm* 3G **43**
Red Row. *Nmbd* 5G **121**
Redruth. *Corn* 4B **6**
Red Street. *Staf* 5C **84**
Redvales. *G Man* 4F **91**
Red Wharf Bay. *IOA* 2E **81**
Redwick. *Newp* 3H **33**
Redwick. *S Glo* 3A **34**
Redworth. *Darl* 2F **105**
Reed. *Herts* 2D **52**
Reed End. *Herts* 2D **52**
Reedham. *Linc* 5B **88**
Reedham. *Norf* 5G **79**
Reedness. *E Yor* 2B **94**
Reeds Beck. *Linc* 4B **88**
Reemshill. *Abers* 4E **161**
Reepham. *Linc* 3H **87**
Reepham. *Norf* 3C **78**
Reeth. *N Yor* 5D **104**
Regaby. *IOM* 2D **108**
Regil. *N Som* 5A **34**
Regoul. *High* 3C **158**
Reiff. *High* 2D **162**
Reigate. *Surr* 5D **38**
Reighton. *N Yor* 2F **101**
Reilth. *Shrp* 2E **59**
Reinigeadal. *W Isl* 7E **171**
Reisque. *Abers* 1F **153**
Reiss. *High* 3F **169**
Rejerrah. *Corn* 3B **6**
Releath. *Corn* 5A **6**
Relubbus. *Corn* 3C **4**
Relugas. *Mor* 4D **159**
Remenham. *Wok* 3F **37**
Remenham Hill. *Wok* 3F **37**
Rempstone. *Notts* 3C **74**
Rendcomb. *Glos* 5F **49**
Rendham. *Suff* 4F **67**
Rendlesham. *Suff* 5F **67**
Renfrew. *Ren* 3G **127**
Renhold. *Beds* 5H **63**
Renishaw. *Derbs* 3B **86**
Rennington. *Nmbd* 3G **121**
Renton. *W Dun* 2E **127**
Renwick. *Cumb* 5G **113**
Repps. *Norf* 4G **79**
Repton. *Derbs* 3H **73**
Resaurie. *High* 4B **158**
Rescassa. *Corn* 4D **6**
Rescobie. *Ang* 3E **145**
Rescorla. *Corn* 3E **7** (nr. Rosevean)
Rescorla. *Corn* 4D **6** (nr. St Ewe)
Resipole. *High* 2B **140**
Resolfen. *Neat* 5B **46**
Resolis. *High* 2A **158**
Resolven. *Neat* 5B **46**
Rest and be thankful. *Arg* 3B **134**
Reston. *Bord* 3E **131**
Restrop. *Wilts* 3F **35**
Retford. *Notts* 2E **86**
Retire. *Corn* 2E **6**
Rettendon. *Essx* 1B **40**
Retyn. *Corn* 3C **6**
Revesby. *Linc* 4C **88**
Rew. *Devn* 5D **8**
Rewe. *Devn* 3C **12**
Rew Street. *IOW* 3C **16**
Rexon. *Devn* 4E **11**
Reybridge. *Wilts* 5E **35**
Reydon. *Suff* 3H **67**
Reymerston. *Norf* 5C **78**
Reynalton. *Pemb* 4E **43**
Reynoldston. *Swan* 4D **31**
Rezare. *Corn* 5D **10**
Rhadyr. *Mon* 5G **47**
Rhaeadr Gwy. *Powy* 4B **58**
Rhandirmwyn. *Carm* 1A **46**
Rhayader. *Powy* 4B **58**
Rheindown. *High* 4H **157**
Rhemore. *High* 3G **139**
Rhenetra. *High* 3D **154**
Rhewl. *Den* 1D **70** (nr. Llangollen)
Rhewl. *Den* 4D **82** (nr. Ruthin)
Rhewl. *Shrp* 2F **71**
Rhewl-Mostyn. *Flin* 3D **82**
Rhian. *High* 2C **164**
Rhian Breck. *High* 3C **164**
Rhicarn. *High* 1E **163**
Rhiconich. *High* 3C **166**
Rhicullen. *High* 1A **158**
Rhidorroch. *High* 4F **163**
Rhifail. *High* 4H **167**
Rhigos. *Rhon* 5C **46**
Rhilochan. *High* 3E **165**
Rhiroy. *High* 5F **163**
Rhitongue. *High* 3G **167**
Rhiw. *Gwyn* 3B **68**
Rhiwabon. *Wrex* 1F **71**
Rhiwbina. *Card* 3E **33**
Rhiwbryfdir. *Gwyn* 1F **69**
Rhiwderin. *Newp* 3F **33**
Rhiwlas. *Gwyn* 2B **70** (nr. Bala)
Rhiwlas. *Gwyn* 4E **81** (nr. Bangor)
Rhiwlas. *Powy* 2D **70**
Rhodes. *G Man* 4G **91**
Rhodesia. *Notts* 2C **86**
Rhodes Minnis. *Kent* 1F **29**
Rhodiad-y-Brenin. *Pemb* 2B **42**
Rhondda. *Rhon* 2C **32**
Rhonehouse. *Dum* 4E **111**
Rhoose. *V Glam* 5D **32**
Rhos. *Carm* 2D **45**
Rhos. *Neat* 5H **45**
Rhosaman. *Carm* 4H **45**
Rhoscefnhir. *IOA* 3E **81**
Rhoscolyn. *IOA* 3B **80**
Rhos Common. *Powy* 4E **71**
Rhoscrowther. *Pemb* 4D **42**
Rhos-ddu. *Gwyn* 2B **68**
Rhosdylluan. *Gwyn* 3A **70**
Rhosesmor. *Flin* 4E **82**
Rhos-fawr. *Gwyn* 2C **68**
Rhosgadfan. *Gwyn* 5E **81**
Rhosgoch. *IOA* 2D **80**
Rhosgoch. *Powy* 1E **47**
Rhos Haminiog. *Cdgn* 4E **57**
Rhos-hill. *Pemb* 1B **44**
Rhoshirwaun. *Gwyn* 3A **68**
Rhoslan. *Gwyn* 1D **69**
Rhoslefain. *Gwyn* 5E **69**

Rhosllanerchrugog. *Wrex* 1E **71**
Rhos Lligwy. *IOA* 2D **81**
Rhosmaen. *Carm* 3G **45**
Rhosmeirch. *IOA* 3D **80**
Rhosneigr. *IOA* 3C **80**
Rhos-on-Sea. *Cnwy* 2H **81**
Rhossili. *Swan* 4D **30**
Rhosson. *Pemb* 2B **42**
Rhos, The. *Pemb* 3E **43**
Rhostrenwfa. *IOA* 3D **80**
Rhostryfan. *Gwyn* 5D **81**
Rhostyllen. *Wrex* 1F **71**
Rhoswiel. *Shrp* 2E **71**
Rhosybol. *IOA* 2D **80**
Rhos-y-brithdir. *Powy* 3D **70**
Rhos-y-garth. *Cdgn* 3F **57**
Rhos-y-gwaliau. *Gwyn* 2B **70**
Rhos-y-llan. *Gwyn* 2B **68**
Rhos-y-meirch. *Powy* 4E **59**
Rhu. *Arg* 1D **126**
Rhuallt. *Den* 3C **82**
Rhubadach. *Arg* 2B **126**
Rhubha Stoer. *High* 1E **163**
Rhuddall Heath. *Ches* 4H **83**
Rhuddlan. *Cdgn* 1E **45**
Rhuddlan. *Den* 3C **82**
Rhue. *High* 4E **163**
Rhulen. *Powy* 1E **47**
Rhunahaorine. *Arg* 5F **125**
Rhuthun. *Den* 5D **82**
Rhuvoult. *High* 3C **166**
Rhyd. *Gwyn* 1F **69**
Rhydaman. *Carm* 4G **45**
Rhydargaeau. *Carm* 3E **45**
Rhydcymerau. *Carm* 2F **45**
Rhydd. *Worc* 1D **48**
Rhyd-Ddu. *Gwyn* 5E **81**
Rhydding. *Neat* 3G **31**
Rhydfudr. *Cdgn* 4E **57**
Rhydlanfair. *Cnwy* 5H **81**
Rhydlewis. *Cdgn* 1D **44**
Rhydlios. *Gwyn* 2A **68**
Rhydlydan. *Cnwy* 5A **82**
Rhyd-meirionydd. *Cdgn* 2F **57**
Rhydowen. *Cdgn* 1E **45**
Rhyd-Rosser. *Cdgn* 4E **57**
Rhydspence. *Powy* 1F **47**
Rhydtalog. *Flin* 5E **83**
Rhyd-uchaf. *Gwyn* 2B **70**
Rhydwyn. *IOA* 2C **80**
Rhyd-y-clafdy. *Gwyn* 2C **68**
Rhydycroesau. *Shrp* 2E **71**
Rhydyfelin. *Cdgn* 3E **57**
Rhydyfelin. *Rhon* 3E **32**
Rhyd-y-foel. *Cnwy* 3B **82**
Rhyd-y-fro. *Neat* 5H **45**
Rhydymain. *Gwyn* 3H **69**
Rhyd-y-meirch. *Mon* 5G **47**
Rhyd-y-meudwy. *Den* 5D **82**
Rhydymwyn. *Flin* 4E **82**
Rhyd-yr-onen. *Gwyn* 5F **69**
Rhyd-y-sarn. *Gwyn* 1F **69**
Rhyl. *Den* 2C **82**
Rhymney. *Cphy* 5E **46**
Rhymni. *Cphy* 5E **46**
Rhynd. *Per* 1D **136**
Rhynie. *Abers* 1B **152**
Ribbesford. *Worc* 3B **60**
Ribbleton. *Lanc* 1D **90**
Ribby. *Lanc* 1C **90**
Ribchester. *Lanc* 1E **91**
Riber. *Derbs* 5H **85**
Ribigill. *High* 3F **167**
Riby. *Linc* 4E **95**
Riccall. *N Yor* 1G **93**
Riccarton. *E Ayr* 1D **116**
Richards Castle. *Here* 4G **59**
Richborough Port. *Kent* 4H **41**
Richings Park. *Buck* 3B **38**
Richmond. *G Lon* 3C **38**
Richmond. *N Yor* 4E **105**
Rickarton. *Abers* 5F **153**
Rickerby. *Cumb* 4F **113**
Rickerscote. *Staf* 3D **72**
Rickford. *N Som* 1H **21**
Rickham. *Devn* 5D **8**
Rickinghall. *Suff* 3C **66**
Rickleton. *Tyne* 4F **115**
Rickling. *Essx* 2E **53**
Rickling Green. *Essx* 3F **53**
Rickmansworth. *Herts* 1B **38**
Riddings. *Derbs* 5B **86**
Riddlecombe. *Devn* 1G **11**
Riddlesden. *W Yor* 5C **98**
Ridge. *Dors* 4E **15**
Ridge. *Herts* 5C **52**
Ridge. *Wilts* 3E **23**
Ridgebourne. *Powy* 4C **58**
Ridge Lane. *Warw* 1G **61**
Ridgeway. *Derbs* 5A **86**
(nr. Alfreton)
Ridgeway. *Derbs* 2B **86**
(nr. Sheffield)
Ridgeway. *Staf* 5C **84**
Ridgeway Cross. *Here* 1C **48**
Ridgeway Moor. *Derbs* 2B **86**
Ridgewell. *Essx* 1H **53**
Ridgewood. *E Sus* 3F **27**
Ridgmont. *Beds* 2H **51**
Ridgwardine. *Shrp* 2A **72**
Riding Mill. *Nmbd* 3D **114**
Ridley. *Kent* 4H **39**
Ridley. *Nmbd* 3A **114**
Ridlington. *Norf* 2F **79**
Ridlington. *Rut* 5F **75**
Ridsdale. *Nmbd* 1C **114**
Riemore Lodge. *Per* 4H **143**
Rievaulx. *N Yor* 1H **99**
Rift House. *Hart* 1B **106**
Rigg. *Dum* 3D **112**
Riggend. *N Lan* 2A **128**
Rigmaden Park. *Cumb* 1F **97**
Rigsby. *Linc* 3D **88**
Rigside. *S Lan* 1A **118**
Riley Green. *Lanc* 2E **90**
Rileyhill. *Staf* 4F **73**
Rilla Mill. *Corn* 5C **10**
Rillington. *N Yor* 2C **100**
Rimington. *Lanc* 5H **97**
Rimpton. *Som* 4B **22**
Rimsdale. *High* 4H **167**
Rimswell. *E Yor* 2G **95**
Ringasta. *Shet* 10E **173**
Ringford. *Dum* 4D **111**
Ringing Hill. *Leics* 4B **74**
Ringinglow. *S Yor* 2G **85**
Ringland. *Norf* 4D **78**
Ringlestone. *Kent* 5C **40**
Ringmer. *E Sus* 4F **27**
Ringmore. *Devn* 4C **8**
(nr. Kingsbridge)
Ringmore. *Devn* 5C **12**
(nr. Teignmouth)
Ring o' Bells. *Lanc* 3C **90**
Ring's End. *Cambs* 5C **76**
Ringsfield. *Suff* 2G **67**
Ringsfield Corner. *Suff* 2G **67**
Ringshall. *Buck* 4H **51**
Ringshall. *Suff* 5C **66**
Ringshall Stocks. *Suff* 5C **66**
Ringstead. *Norf* 1G **77**
Ringstead. *Nptn* 3G **63**
Ringwood. *Hants* 2G **15**
Ringwould. *Kent* 1H **29**
Rinmore. *Abers* 2B **152**
Rinnigill. *Orkn* 8C **172**
Rinsey. *Corn* 4C **4**
Riof. *W Isl* 4D **171**
Ripe. *E Sus* 4G **27**
Ripley. *Derbs* 1B **74**
Ripley. *Hants* 3G **15**
Ripley. *N Yor* 3E **99**
Ripley. *Surr* 5B **38**
Riplingham. *E Yor* 1C **94**
Riplington. *Hants* 4E **25**
Ripon. *N Yor* 2F **99**
Rippingale. *Linc* 3H **75**
Ripple. *Kent* 1H **29**
Ripple. *Worc* 2D **48**
Ripponden. *W Yor* 3A **92**
Rireavach. *High* 4E **163**
Risabus. *Arg* 5B **124**
Risbury. *Here* 5H **59**
Risby. *E Yor* 1D **94**
Risby. *N Lin* 3C **94**
Risby. *Suff* 4G **65**
Risca. *Cphy* 2F **33**
Rise. *E Yor* 5F **101**
Riseden. *E Sus* 2H **27**
Riseden. *Kent* 2B **28**
Rise End. *Derbs* 5G **85**
Risegate. *Linc* 2B **76**
Riseholme. *Linc* 3G **87**
Riseley. *Beds* 4H **63**
Riseley. *Wok* 5F **37**
Rishangles. *Suff* 4D **66**
Rishton. *Lanc* 1F **91**
Rishworth. *W Yor* 3A **92**
Risley. *Derbs* 2B **74**
Risley. *Warr* 1A **84**
Risplith. *N Yor* 3E **99**
Rispond. *High* 2E **167**
Rivar. *Wilts* 5B **36**
Rivenhall. *Essx* 4B **54**
Rivenhall End. *Essx* 4B **54**
River. *Kent* 1G **29**
River. *W Sus* 3A **26**
River Bank. *Cambs* 4E **65**
Riverhead. *Kent* 5G **39**
Rivington. *Lanc* 3E **91**
Roach Bridge. *Lanc* 2D **90**
Roachill. *Devn* 4B **20**
Roade. *Nptn* 5E **63**
Road Green. *Norf* 1E **67**
Roadhead. *Cumb* 2G **113**
Roadmeetings. *S Lan* 5B **128**
Roadside. *High* 2D **168**
Roadside of Catterline.
Abers 1H **145**
Roadside of Kinneff. *Abers* 1H **145**
Roadwater. *Som* 3D **20**
Road Weedon. *Nptn* 5D **62**
Roag. *High* 4B **154**
Roa Island. *Cumb* 3B **96**
Roath. *Card* 4E **33**
Roberton. *Bord* 3G **119**
Roberton. *S Lan* 2B **118**
Robertsbridge. *E Sus* 3B **28**
Robertstown. *Mor* 4G **159**
Robertstown. *Rhon* 5C **46**
Roberttown. *W Yor* 2B **92**
Robeston Back. *Pemb* 3E **43**
Robeston Wathen. *Pemb* 3E **43**
Robeston West. *Pemb* 4C **42**
Robin Hood. *Lanc* 3D **90**
Robin Hood. *W Yor* 2D **92**
Robin Hood Airport Doncaster
Sheffield. *S Yor* 1D **86**
Robinhood End. *Essx* 2H **53**
Robin Hood's Bay. *N Yor* 4G **107**
Roborough. *Devn* 1F **11**
(nr. Great Torrington)
Roborough. *Devn* 2B **8**
(nr. Plymouth)
Rob Roy's House. *Arg* 2A **134**
Roby Mill. *Lanc* 4D **90**
Rocester. *Staf* 2F **73**
Roch. *Pemb* 2C **42**
Rochdale. *G Man* 3G **91**
Roche. *Corn* 2D **6**
Rochester. *Medw* 4B **40**
Rochester. *Nmbd* 5C **120**
Rochford. *Essx* 1C **40**
Rock. *Corn* 1D **6**
Rock. *Nmbd* 2G **121**
Rock. *W Sus* 4C **26**
Rock. *Worc* 3B **60**
Rockbeare. *Devn* 3D **12**
Rockbourne. *Hants* 1G **15**
Rockcliffe. *Cumb* 3E **113**
Rockcliffe. *Dum* 4F **111**
Rockcliffe Cross. *Cumb* 3E **113**
Rock Ferry. *Mers* 2F **83**
Rockfield. *High* 5G **165**
Rockfield. *Mon* 4H **47**
Rockford. *Hants* 2G **15**
Rockgreen. *Shrp* 3H **59**
Rockhampton. *S Glo* 2B **34**
Rockhead. *Corn* 4A **10**
Rockingham. *Nptn* 1F **63**
Rockland All Saints. *Norf* 1B **66**
Rockland St Mary. *Norf* 5F **79**
Rockland St Peter. *Norf* 1B **66**
Rockley. *Wilts* 4G **35**
Rockwell End. *Buck* 3F **37**
Rockwell Green. *Som* 1E **13**
Rodborough. *Glos* 5D **48**
Rodbourne. *Wilts* 3E **35**
Rodd. *Here* 4F **59**
Roddam. *Nmbd* 2E **121**
Rodden. *Dors* 4B **14**
Roddenloft. *E Ayr* 2D **117**
Roddymoor. *Dur* 1E **105**
Rode. *Som* 1D **22**
Rodeheath. *Ches* 4C **84**
Rode Heath. *Ches* 5C **84**
Roden. *Telf* 4H **71**
Rodhuish. *Som* 3D **20**
Rodington. *Telf* 4H **71**
Rodington Heath. *Telf* 4H **71**
Rodley. *Glos* 4C **48**
Rodmarton. *Glos* 2E **35**
Rodmell. *E Sus* 5F **27**
Rodmersham. *Kent* 4D **40**
Rodmersham Green. *Kent* 4D **40**
Rodney Stoke. *Som* 2H **21**
Rodsley. *Derbs* 1G **73**
Rodway. *Som* 2F **21**
Rodway. *Telf* 4A **72**
Rodwell. *Dors* 5B **14**
Roecliffe. *N Yor* 3F **99**
Roe Green. *Herts* 2D **52**
Roehampton. *G Lon* 3D **38**
Roffey. *W Sus* 2C **26**
Rogart. *High* 3E **165**
Rogate. *W Sus* 4G **25**
Roger Ground. *Cumb* 5E **103**
Rogerstone. *Newp* 3F **33**
Roghadal. *W Isl* 9C **171**
Rogiet. *Mon* 3H **33**
Rogue's Alley. *Cambs* 5C **76**
Roke. *Oxon* 2E **37**
Rokemarsh. *Oxon* 2E **36**
Roker. *Tyne* 4H **115**
Rollesby. *Norf* 4G **79**
Rolleston. *Leics* 5E **75**
Rolleston. *Notts* 5E **87**
Rolleston on Dove. *Staf* 3G **73**
Rolston. *E Yor* 5G **101**
Rolvenden. *Kent* 2C **28**
Rolvenden Layne. *Kent* 2C **28**
Romaldkirk. *Dur* 2C **104**
Roman Bank. *Shrp* 1H **59**
Romanby. *N Yor* 5A **106**
Roman Camp. *W Lot* 2D **129**
Romannobridge. *Bord* 5E **129**
Romansleigh. *Devn* 4H **19**
Romers Common. *Worc* 4H **59**
Romesdal. *High* 3D **154**
Romford. *Dors* 2F **15**
Romford. *G Lon* 2G **39**
Romiley. *G Man* 1D **84**
Romsey. *Hants* 4B **24**
Romsley. *Shrp* 2B **60**
Romsley. *Worc* 3D **60**
Ronague. *IOM* 4B **108**
Rookby. *Cumb* 3B **104**
Rookhope. *Dur* 5C **114**
Rooking. *Cumb* 3F **103**
Rookley. *IOW* 4D **16**
Rooks Bridge. *Som* 1G **21**
Rooksey Green. *Suff* 5B **66**
Rooks Nest. *Som* 3D **20**
Rookwood. *W Sus* 3F **17**
Roos. *E Yor* 1F **95**
Roosebeck. *Cumb* 3B **96**
Roosecote. *Cumb* 3B **96**
Rootfield. *High* 3H **157**
Rootham's Green. *Beds* 5A **64**
Rootpark. *S Lan* 4C **128**
Ropley. *Hants* 3E **25**
Ropley Dean. *Hants* 3E **25**
Ropsley. *Linc* 2G **75**
Rora. *Abers* 3H **161**
Rorandle. *Abers* 2D **152**
Rorrington. *Shrp* 5F **71**
Rose. *Corn* 3B **6**
Roseacre. *Lanc* 1C **90**
Rose Ash. *Devn* 4A **20**
Rosebank. *S Lan* 5B **128**
Rosebush. *Pemb* 2E **43**
Rosedale Abbey. *N Yor* 5E **107**
Roseden. *Nmbd* 2E **121**
Rose Green. *Essx* 3B **54**
Rose Green. *Suff* 1C **54**
Rosehall. *High* 3B **164**
Rosehearty. *Abers* 2G **161**
Rose Hill. *E Sus* 4F **27**
Rose Hill. *Lanc* 1G **91**
Rosehill. *Shrp* 2A **72**
(nr. Market Drayton)
Rosehill. *Shrp* 4G **71**
(nr. Shrewsbury)
Roseisle. *Mor* 2F **159**
Rosemarket. *Pemb* 4D **42**
Rosemarkie. *High* 3B **158**
Rosemary Lane. *Devn* 1E **13**
Rosemount. *Per* 4A **144**
Rosenannon. *Corn* 2D **6**
Roser's Cross. *E Sus* 3G **27**
Rosevean. *Corn* 3E **6**
Rosewell. *Midl* 3F **129**
Roseworth. *Stoc T* 2B **106**
Roseworthy. *Corn* 3D **4**
Rosgill. *Cumb* 3G **103**
Roshven. *High* 1B **140**
Roskhill. *High* 4B **154**
Roskorwell. *Corn* 4E **5**
Rosley. *Cumb* 5E **112**
Roslin. *Midl* 3F **129**
Rosliston. *Derbs* 4G **73**
Rosneath. *Arg* 1D **126**
Ross. *Dum* 5D **110**
Ross. *Nmbd* 1F **121**
Ross. *Per* 1G **135**
Ross. *Bord* 3F **131**
Rossendale. *Lanc* 2F **91**
Rossett. *Wrex* 5F **83**
Rossington. *S Yor* 1D **86**
Rosskeen. *High* 2A **158**
Rossland. *Ren* 2F **127**
Ross-on-Wye. *Here* 3B **48**
Roster. *High* 4E **169**
Rostherne. *Ches* 2B **84**
Rostholme. *S Yor* 4F **93**
Rosthwaite. *Cumb* 3D **102**
Roston. *Derbs* 1F **73**
Rosudgeon. *Corn* 4C **4**
Rosyth. *Fife* 1E **129**
Rothbury. *Nmbd* 4E **121**
Rotherby. *Leics* 4D **74**
Rotherfield. *E Sus* 3G **27**
Rotherfield Greys. *Oxon* 3F **37**
Rotherfield Peppard. *Oxon* 3F **37**
Rotherham. *S Yor* 1B **86**
Rothersthorpe. *Nptn* 5E **62**
Rotherwick. *Hants* 1F **25**
Rothes. *Mor* 4G **159**
Rothesay. *Arg* 3B **126**
Rothienorman. *Abers* 5E **160**
Rothiesholm. *Orkn* 5F **172**
Rothley. *Leics* 4C **74**
Rothley. *Nmbd* 1D **114**
Rothwell. *Linc* 1A **88**
Rothwell. *Nptn* 2F **63**
Rothwell. *W Yor* 2D **92**
Rothwell Haigh. *W Yor* 2D **92**
Rotsea. *E Yor* 4E **101**
Rottal. *Ang* 2C **144**
Rotten End. *Suff* 4F **67**

Rotten Row—St Mark's

Rotten Row. *Norf* 4C **78**
Rotten Row. *W Ber* 4D **36**
Rotten Row. *W Mid* 3F **61**
Rottingdean. *Brig* 5E **27**
Rottington. *Cumb* 3A **102**
Roud. *IOW* 4D **16**
Rougham. *Norf* 3H **77**
Rougham. *Suff* 4B **66**
Rough Close. *Staf* 2D **72**
Rough Common. *Kent* 5F **41**
Roughcote. *Staf* 1D **72**
Rough Haugh. *High* 4H **167**
Rough Hay. *Staf* 3G **73**
Roughlee. *Lanc* 5H **97**
Roughley. *W Mid* 1F **61**
Roughsike. *Cumb* 2G **113**
Roughton. *Linc* 4B **88**
Roughton. *Norf* 2E **78**
Roughton. *Shrp* 1B **60**
Roundbush Green. *Essx* 4F **53**
Roundham. *Som* 2H **13**
Roundhay. *W Yor* 1D **92**
Round Hill. *Torb* 2F **9**
Roundhurst Common. *W Sus* 2A **26**
Round Oak. *Shrp* 2F **59**
Roundstreet Common. *W Sus* 3B **26**
Roundthwaite. *Cumb* 4H **103**
Roundway. *Wilts* 5F **35**
Roundyhill. *Ang* 3C **144**
Rousdon. *Devn* 3F **13**
Rousham. *Oxon* 3C **50**
Rous Lench. *Worc* 5E **61**
Routh. *E Yor* 5E **101**
Rout's Green. *Buck* 2F **37**
Row. *Corn* 5A **10**
Row. *Cumb* 1D **96** (nr. Kendal)
Row. *Cumb* 1H **103** (nr. Penrith)
Rowanburn. *Dum* 2F **113**
Rowanhill. *Abers* 3H **161**
Rowardennan. *Stir* 4C **134**
Rowarth. *Derbs* 2E **85**
Row Ash. *Hants* 1D **16**
Rowberrow. *Som* 1H **21**
Rowde. *Wilts* 5E **35**
Rowden. *Devn* 3G **11**
Rowden Hill. *Wilts* 4E **35**
Rowen. *Cnwy* 3G **81**
Rowfoot. *Nmbd* 3H **113**
Row Green. *Essx* 3H **53**
Row Heath. *Essx* 4E **55**
Rowhedge. *Essx* 3D **54**
Rowhook. *W Sus* 2C **26**
Rowington. *Warw* 4G **61**
Rowland. *Derbs* 3G **85**
Rowland's Castle. *Hants* 1F **17**
Rowlands Gill. *Tyne* 4E **115**
Rowledge. *Surr* 2G **25**
Rowley. *Dur* 5D **115**
Rowley. *E Yor* 1C **94**
Rowley. *Shrp* 5F **71**
Rowley. *Staf* 3F **73**
Rowley Hill. *W Yor* 3B **92**
Rowley Regis. *W Mid* 2D **60**
Rowlstone. *Here* 3G **47**
Rowly. *Surr* 1B **26**
Rowner. *Hants* 2D **16**
Rowney Green. *Worc* 3E **61**
Rownhams. *Hants* 1B **16**
Rowrah. *Cumb* 3B **102**
Rowsham. *Buck* 4G **51**
Rowsley. *Derbs* 4G **85**
Rowstock. *Oxon* 3C **36**
Rowston. *Linc* 5H **87**
Row, The. *Lanc* 2D **96**
Rowthorne. *Derbs* 4B **86**
Rowton. *Ches* 4G **83**
Rowton. *Shrp* 2G **59** (nr. Ludlow)
Rowton. *Shrp* 4F **71** (nr. Shrewsbury)
Rowton. *Telf* 4A **72**
Row Town. *Surr* 4B **38**
Roxburgh. *Bord* 1B **120**
Roxby. *N Lin* 3C **94**
Roxby. *N Yor* 3E **107**
Roxton. *Beds* 5A **64**
Roxwell. *Essx* 5G **53**
Royal Leamington Spa. *Warw* 4H **61**
Royal Oak. *Darl* 2F **105**
Royal Oak. *Lanc* 4C **90**
Royal Oak. *N Yor* 2F **101**
Royal's Green. *Ches* 1A **72**
Royal Tunbridge Wells. *Kent* 2G **27**
Roybridge. *High* 5E **149**
Roydon. *Essx* 4E **53**
Roydon. *Norf* 2C **66** (nr. Diss)
Roydon. *Norf* 3G **77** (nr. King's Lynn)
Roydon Hamlet. *Essx* 5E **53**
Royston. *Herts* 1D **52**
Royston. *S Yor* 3D **92**
Royston Water. *Som* 1F **13**
Royton. *G Man* 4H **91**
Ruabon. *Wrex* 1F **71**
Ruaig. *Arg* 4B **138**
Ruan High Lanes. *Corn* 5D **6**
Ruan Lanihorne. *Corn* 4C **6**
Ruan Major. *Corn* 5E **5**
Ruan Minor. *Corn* 5E **5**
Ruarach. *High* 1B **148**
Ruardean. *Glos* 4B **48**
Ruardean Hill. *Glos* 4B **48**
Ruardean Woodside. *Glos* 4B **48**
Rubery. *W Mid* 3D **61**
Ruchazie. *Glas* 3H **127**
Ruckcroft. *Cumb* 5G **113**
Ruckinge. *Kent* 2E **29**
Ruckland. *Linc* 3C **88**
Rucklers Lane. *Herts* 5A **52**
Ruckley. *Shrp* 5H **71**
Rudbaxton. *Pemb* 2D **42**
Rudby. *N Yor* 4B **106**
Ruddington. *Notts* 2C **74**
Rudford. *Glos* 3C **48**
Rudge. *Shrp* 1C **60**
Rudge. *Wilts* 1D **22**
Rudge Heath. *Shrp* 1B **60**
Rudgeway. *S Glo* 3B **34**
Rudgwick. *W Sus* 2B **26**
Rudhall. *Here* 3B **48**
Rudheath. *Ches* 3A **84**
Rudheath Woods. *Ches* 3B **84**
Rudley Green. *Essx* 5B **54**
Rudloe. *Wilts* 4D **34**
Rudry. *Cphy* 3E **33**
Rudston. *E Yor* 3E **101**
Rudyard. *Staf* 5D **84**
Rufford. *Lanc* 3C **90**
Rufforth. *York* 4H **99**
Rugby. *Warw* 3C **62**
Rugeley. *Staf* 4E **73**
Ruglen. *S Ayr* 4B **116**
Ruilick. *High* 4H **157**
Ruisaurie. *High* 4G **157**
Ruishton. *Som* 4F **21**
Ruisigearraidh. *W Isl* 1E **170**
Ruislip. *G Lon* 2B **38**
Ruislip Common. *G Lon* 2B **38**
Rumbling Bridge. *Per* 4C **136**
Rumburgh. *Suff* 2F **67**
Rumford. *Corn* 1C **6**
Rumford. *Falk* 2C **128**
Rumney. *Card* 4F **33**
Rumwell. *Som* 4E **21**
Runcorn. *Hal* 2H **83**
Runcton. *W Sus* 2G **17**
Runcton Holme. *Norf* 5F **77**
Rundlestone. *Devn* 5F **11**
Runfold. *Surr* 2G **25**
Runhall. *Norf* 5C **78**
Runham. *Norf* 4G **79**
Runnington. *Som* 4E **20**
Runshaw Moor. *Lanc* 3D **90**
Runswick. *N Yor* 3F **107**
Runtaleave. *Ang* 2B **144**
Runwell. *Essx* 1B **40**
Ruscombe. *Wok* 4F **37**
Rushall. *Here* 2B **48**
Rushall. *Norf* 2D **66**
Rushall. *W Mid* 5E **73**
Rushall. *Wilts* 1G **23**
Rushbrooke. *Suff* 4A **66**
Rushbury. *Shrp* 1H **59**
Rushden. *Herts* 2D **52**
Rushden. *Nptn* 4G **63**
Rushenden. *Kent* 3D **40**
Rushford. *Devn* 5E **11**
Rushford. *Suff* 2B **66**
Rush Green. *Herts* 3C **52**
Rushlake Green. *E Sus* 4H **27**
Rushmere. *Suff* 2G **67**
Rushmere St Andrew. *Suff* 1E **55**
Rushmoor. *Surr* 2G **25**
Rushock. *Worc* 3C **60**
Rusholme. *G Man* 1C **84**
Rushton. *Ches* 4H **83**
Rushton. *Nptn* 2F **63**
Rushton. *Shrp* 5A **72**
Rushton Spencer. *Staf* 4D **84**
Rushwick. *Worc* 5C **60**
Rushyford. *Dur* 2F **105**
Ruskie. *Stir* 3F **135**
Ruskington. *Linc* 5H **87**
Rusland. *Cumb* 1C **96**
Rusper. *W Sus* 2D **26**
Ruspidge. *Glos* 4B **48**
Russell's Water. *Oxon* 3F **37**
Russel's Green. *Suff* 3E **67**
Russ Hill. *Surr* 1D **26**
Russland. *Orkn* 6C **172**
Rusthall. *Kent* 2G **27**
Rustington. *W Sus* 5B **26**
Ruston. *N Yor* 1D **100**
Ruston Parva. *E Yor* 3E **101**
Ruswarp. *N Yor* 4F **107**
Rutherglen. *S Lan* 3H **127**
Ruthernbridge. *Corn* 2E **6**
Ruthin. *Den* 5D **82**
Ruthin. *V Glam* 4C **32**
Ruthrieston. *Aber* 3G **153**
Ruthven. *Abers* 4C **160**
Ruthven. *Ang* 4B **144**
Ruthven. *High* 5C **158** (nr. Inverness)
Ruthven. *High* 4B **150** (nr. Kingussie)
Ruthvoes. *Corn* 2D **6**
Ruthwaite. *Cumb* 1D **102**
Ruthwell. *Dum* 3C **112**
Ruxton Green. *Here* 4A **48**
Ruyton-XI-Towns. *Shrp* 3F **71**
Ryal. *Nmbd* 2D **114**
Ryall. *Dors* 3H **13**
Ryall. *Worc* 1D **48**
Ryarsh. *Kent* 5A **40**
Rychraggan. *High* 5G **157**
Rydal. *Cumb* 4E **103**
Ryde. *IOW* 3D **16**
Rye. *E Sus* 3D **28**
Ryecroft Gate. *Staf* 4D **84**
Ryeford. *Here* 3B **48**
Rye Foreign. *E Sus* 3D **28**
Rye Harbour. *E Sus* 4D **28**
Ryehill. *E Yor* 2F **95**
Rye Street. *Worc* 2C **48**
Ryhall. *Rut* 4H **75**
Ryhill. *W Yor* 3D **93**
Ryhope. *Tyne* 4H **115**
Ryhope Colliery. *Tyne* 4H **115**
Rylands. *Notts* 2C **74**
Rylstone. *N Yor* 4B **98**
Ryme Intrinseca. *Dors* 1A **14**
Ryther. *N Yor* 1F **93**
Ryton. *Glos* 2C **48**
Ryton. *N Yor* 2B **100**
Ryton. *Shrp* 5B **72**
Ryton. *Tyne* 3E **115**
Ryton. *Warw* 2A **62**
Ryton-on-Dunsmore. *Warw* 3A **62**
Ryton Woodside. *Tyne* 3E **115**

S

Saasaig. *High* 3E **147**
Sabden. *Lanc* 1F **91**
Sacombe. *Herts* 4D **52**
Sacriston. *Dur* 5F **115**
Sadberge. *Darl* 3A **106**
Saddell. *Arg* 2B **122**
Saddington. *Leics* 1D **62**
Saddle Bow. *Norf* 4F **77**
Saddlescombe. *W Sus* 4D **26**
Saddleworth. *G Man* 4H **91**
Sadgill. *Cumb* 4F **103**
Saffron Walden. *Essx* 2F **53**
Sageston. *Pemb* 4E **43**
Saham Hills. *Norf* 5B **78**
Saham Toney. *Norf* 5A **78**
Saighdinis. *W Isl* 2D **170**
Saighton. *Ches* 4G **83**
Sain Dunwyd. *V Glam* 5C **32**
Sain Hilari. *V Glam* 4D **32**
St Abbs. *Bord* 3F **131**
St Agnes. *Corn* 3B **6**
St Albans. *Herts* 5B **52**
St Allen. *Corn* 3C **6**
St Andrews. *Fife* 2H **137**
St Andrews Major. *V Glam* 4E **33**
St Anne's. *Lanc* 2B **90**
St Ann's. *Dum* 5C **118**
St Ann's Chapel. *Corn* 5E **11**
St Ann's Chapel. *Devn* 4C **8**
St Anthony. *Corn* 5C **6**
St Anthony-in-Meneage. *Corn* 4E **5**
St Arvans. *Mon* 2A **34**
St Asaph. *Den* 3C **82**
St Athan. *V Glam* 5D **32**
Sain Tathan. *V Glam* 5D **32**
St Austell. *Corn* 3E **6**
St Bartholomew's Hill. *Wilts* 4E **23**
St Bees. *Cumb* 3A **102**
St Blazey. *Corn* 3E **7**
St Blazey Gate. *Corn* 3E **7**
St Boswells. *Bord* 1A **120**
St Breock. *Corn* 1D **6**
St Breward. *Corn* 5A **10**
St Briavels. *Glos* 5A **48**
St Brides. *Pemb* 3B **42**
St Bride's Major. *V Glam* 4B **32**
St Bride's Netherwent. *Mon* 3H **33**
St Bride's-super-Ely. *V Glam* 4D **32**
St Brides Wentlooge. *Newp* 3F **33**
St Budeaux. *Plym* 3A **8**
Saintbury. *Glos* 2G **49**
St Buryan. *Corn* 4B **4**
St Catherine. *Bath* 4C **34**
St Catherines. *Arg* 3A **134**
St Clears. *Carm* 3G **43**
St Cleer. *Corn* 2G **7**
St Clement. *Corn* 4C **6**
St Clether. *Corn* 4C **10**
St Colmac. *Arg* 3B **126**
St Columb Major. *Corn* 2D **6**
St Columb Minor. *Corn* 2C **6**
St Columb Road. *Corn* 3D **6**
St Combs. *Abers* 2H **161**
St Cross. *Hants* 4C **24**
St Cross South Elmham. *Suff* 2E **67**
St Cyrus. *Abers* 2G **145**
St David's. *Pemb* 2B **42**
St David's. *Per* 1B **136**
St Day. *Corn* 4B **6**
St Dennis. *Corn* 3D **6**
St Dogmaels. *Pemb* 1B **44**
St Dominick. *Corn* 2H **7**
St Donat's. *V Glam* 5C **32**
St Edith's Marsh. *Wilts* 5E **35**
St Endellion. *Corn* 1D **6**
St Enoder. *Corn* 3C **6**
St Erme. *Corn* 4C **6**
St Erney. *Corn* 3H **7**
St Erth. *Corn* 3C **4**
St Erth Praze. *Corn* 3C **4**
St Ervan. *Corn* 1C **6**
St Eval. *Corn* 2C **6**
St Ewe. *Corn* 4D **6**
St Fagans. *Card* 4E **32**
St Fergus. *Abers* 3H **161**
St Fillans. *Per* 1F **135**
St Florence. *Pemb* 4E **43**
St Gennys. *Corn* 3B **10**
St George. *Cnwy* 3B **82**
St George's. *N Som* 5G **33**
St Georges. *V Glam* 4D **32**
St Germans. *Corn* 3H **7**
St Gile's Hill. *Hants* 4C **24**
St Giles in the Wood. *Devn* 1F **11**
St Giles on the Heath. *Devn* 3D **10**
St Gluvias. *Corn* 5B **6**
St Harmon. *Powy* 3B **58**
St Helena. *Warw* 5G **73**
St Helen Auckland. *Dur* 2E **105**
St Helens. *Cumb* 1B **102**
St Helens. *E Sus* 4C **28**
St Helens. *IOW* 4E **17**
St Helens. *Mers* 1G **83**
St Hilary. *Corn* 3C **4**
St Hilary. *V Glam* 4D **32**
Saint Hill. *Devn* 2D **12**
Saint Hill. *W Sus* 2E **27**
St Illtyd. *Blae* 5F **47**
St Ippolyts. *Herts* 3B **52**
St Ishmael. *Carm* 5D **44**
St Ishmael's. *Pemb* 4C **42**
St Issey. *Corn* 1D **6**
St Ive. *Corn* 2H **7**
St Ives. *Cambs* 3C **64**
St Ives. *Corn* 2C **4**
St Ives. *Dors* 2G **15**
St James End. *Nptn* 4E **63**
St James South Elmham. *Suff* 2F **67**
St Jidgey. *Corn* 2D **6**
St John. *Corn* 3A **8**
St John's. *IOM* 3B **108**
St Johns. *Worc* 5C **60**
St John's Chapel. *Devn* 4F **19**
St John's Chapel. *Dur* 1B **104**
St John's Fen End. *Norf* 4E **77**
St John's Hall. *Dur* 1D **104**
St John's Town of Dalry. *Dum* 1D **110**
St Judes. *IOM* 2C **108**
St Just. *Corn* 5C **6** (nr. Falmouth)
St Just. *Corn* 3A **4** (nr. Penzance)
St Just in Roseland. *Corn* 5C **6**
St Katherines. *Abers* 5E **161**
St Keverne. *Corn* 4E **5**
St Kew. *Corn* 5A **10**
St Kew Highway. *Corn* 5A **10**
St Keyne. *Corn* 2G **7**
St Lawrence. *Corn* 2E **7**
St Lawrence. *Essx* 5C **54**
St Lawrence. *IOW* 5D **16**
St Leonards. *Buck* 5H **51**
St Leonards. *Dors* 2G **15**
St Leonards. *E Sus* 5B **28**
St Levan. *Corn* 4A **4**
St Lythans. *V Glam* 4E **32**
St Mabyn. *Corn* 5A **10**
St Madoes. *Per* 1D **136**
St Margarets. *Here* 2G **47**
St Margaret's. *Herts* 4A **52** (nr. Hemel Hempstead)
St Margarets. *Herts* 4D **53** (nr. Hoddesdon)
St Margaret's. *Wilts* 5G **35**
St Margaret's at Cliffe. *Kent* 1H **29**
St Margaret's Hope. *Orkn* 8D **172**
St Margaret South Elmham. *Suff* 2F **67**
St Mark's. *IOM* 4B **108**

St Martin. *Corn* 4E **5**
(nr. Helston)
St Martin. *Corn* 3G **7**
(nr. Looe)
St Martins. *Per* 5A **144**
St Martin's. *Shrp* 2F **71**
St Mary Bourne. *Hants* 1C **24**
St Marychurch. *Torb* 2F **9**
St Mary Church. *V Glam* 4D **32**
St Mary Cray. *G Lon* 4F **39**
St Mary Hill. *V Glam* 4C **32**
St Mary Hoo. *Medw* 3C **40**
St Mary in the Marsh. *Kent* 3E **29**
St Mary's. *Orkn* 7D **172**
St Mary's Bay. *Kent* 3E **29**
St Maughan's Green. *Mon* 4H **47**
St Mawes. *Corn* 5C **6**
St Mawgan. *Corn* 2C **6**
St Mellion. *Corn* 2H **7**
St Mellons. *Card* 3F **33**
St Merryn. *Corn* 1C **6**
St Mewan. *Corn* 3D **6**
St Michael Caerhays. *Corn* 4D **6**
St Michael Penkevil. *Corn* 4C **6**
St Michaels. *Kent* 2C **28**
St Michaels. *Torb* 3E **9**
St Michaels. *Worc* 4H **59**
St Michael's on Wyre. *Lanc* 5D **96**
St Michael South Elmham. *Suff* 2F **67**
St Minver. *Corn* 1D **6**
St Monans. *Fife* 3H **137**
St Neot. *Corn* 2F **7**
St Neots. *Cambs* 4A **64**
St Newlyn East. *Corn* 3C **6**
St Nicholas. *Pemb* 1D **42**
St Nicholas. *V Glam* 4D **32**
St Nicholas at Wade. *Kent* 4G **41**
St Nicholas South Elmham. *Suff* 2F **67**
St Ninians. *Stir* 4H **135**
St Olaves. *Norf* 1G **67**
St Osyth. *Essx* 4E **54**
St Osyth Heath. *Essx* 4E **55**
St Owen's Cross. *Here* 3A **48**
St Paul's Cray. *G Lon* 4F **39**
St Paul's Walden. *Herts* 3B **52**
St Peter's. *Kent* 4H **41**
St Peter The Great. *Worc* 5C **60**
St Petrox. *Pemb* 5D **42**
St Pinnock. *Corn* 2G **7**
St Quivox. *S Ayr* 2C **116**
St Ruan. *Corn* 5E **5**
St Stephen. *Corn* 3D **6**
St Stephens. *Corn* 4D **10**
(nr. Launceston)
St Stephens. *Corn* 3A **8**
(nr. Saltash)
St Teath. *Corn* 4A **10**
St Thomas. *Devn* 3C **12**
St Thomas. *Swan* 3F **31**
St Tudy. *Corn* 5A **10**
St Twynnells. *Pemb* 5D **42**
St Veep. *Corn* 3F **7**
St Vigeans. *Ang* 4F **145**
St Wenn. *Corn* 2D **6**
St Weonards. *Here* 3H **47**
St Winnolls. *Corn* 3H **7**
St Winnow. *Corn* 3F **7**
Salcombe. *Devn* 5D **8**
Salcombe Regis. *Devn* 4E **13**
Salcott. *Essx* 4C **54**
Sale. *G Man* 1B **84**
Saleby. *Linc* 3D **88**
Sale Green. *Worc* 5D **60**
Salehurst. *E Sus* 3B **28**
Salem. *Carm* 3G **45**
Salem. *Cdgn* 2F **57**
Salem. *Gwyn* 5E **81**
Salen. *Arg* 4G **139**
Salen. *High* 2A **140**
Salesbury. *Lanc* 1E **91**
Saleway. *Worc* 5D **60**
Salford. *Beds* 2H **51**
Salford. *G Man* 1C **84**
Salford. *Oxon* 3A **50**
Salford Priors. *Warw* 5E **61**
Salfords. *Surr* 1D **27**
Salhouse. *Norf* 4F **79**
Saligo. *Arg* 3A **124**
Saline. *Fife* 4C **136**
Salisbury. *Wilts* 3G **23**
Salkeld Dykes. *Cumb* 1G **103**
Sallachan. *High* 2D **141**
Sallachy. *High* 3C **164**
(nr. Lairg)
Sallachy. *High* 5B **156**
(nr. Stromeferry)
Salle. *Norf* 3D **78**
Salmonby. *Linc* 3C **88**
Salmond's Muir. *Ang* 5E **145**
Salperton. *Glos* 3F **49**
Salph End. *Beds* 5H **63**
Salsburgh. *N Lan* 3B **128**
Salt. *Staf* 3D **72**
Salta. *Cumb* 5B **112**
Saltaire. *W Yor* 1B **92**
Saltash. *Corn* 3A **8**
Saltburn. *High* 2B **158**
Saltburn-by-the-Sea. *Red C* 2D **106**
Saltby. *Leics* 3F **75**
Saltcoats. *Cumb* 5B **102**
Saltcoats. *N Ayr* 5D **126**
Saltdean. *Brig* 5E **27**
Salt End. *E Yor* 2E **95**
Salter. *Lanc* 3F **97**
Salterforth. *Lanc* 5A **98**
Salters Lode. *Norf* 5E **77**
Salterswall. *Ches* 4A **84**
Salterton. *Wilts* 3G **23**
Saltfleet. *Linc* 1D **88**
Saltfleetby All Saints. *Linc* 1D **88**
Saltfleetby St Clements. *Linc* 1D **88**
Saltfleetby St Peter. *Linc* 2D **88**
Saltford. *Bath* 5B **34**
Salthouse. *Norf* 1C **78**
Saltmarshe. *E Yor* 2A **94**
Saltmead. *Card* 4E **33**
Saltney. *Flin* 4F **83**
Salton. *N Yor* 2B **100**
Saltrens. *Devn* 4E **19**
Saltwick. *Nmbd* 2E **115**
Saltwood. *Kent* 2F **29**
Salum. *Arg* 4B **138**
Salwarpe. *Worc* 4C **60**
Salwayash. *Dors* 3H **13**
Samalaman. *High* 1A **140**
Sambourne. *Warw* 4E **61**
Sambourne. *Wilts* 2D **22**
Sambrook. *Telf* 3B **72**
Samhia. *W Isl* 2C **170**
Samlesbury. *Lanc* 1D **90**
Samlesbury Bottoms. *Lanc* 2E **90**
Sampford Arundel. *Som* 1E **12**
Sampford Brett. *Som* 2D **20**
Sampford Courtenay. *Devn* 2G **11**
Sampford Peverell. *Devn* 1D **12**
Sampford Spiney. *Devn* 5F **11**
Samsonlane. *Orkn* 5F **172**
Samuelston. *E Lot* 2A **130**
Sanaigmore. *Arg* 2A **124**
Sancreed. *Corn* 4B **4**
Sancton. *E Yor* 1C **94**
Sand. *High* 4D **162**
Sand. *Som* 2H **21**
Sandaig. *Arg* 4A **138**
Sandaig. *High* 3F **147**
Sandale. *Cumb* 5D **112**
Sandal Magna. *W Yor* 3D **92**
Sandavore. *High* 5C **146**
Sanday Airport. *Orkn* 3F **172**
Sandbach. *Ches* 4B **84**
Sandbank. *Arg* 1C **126**
Sandbanks. *Pool* 4F **15**
Sandend. *Abers* 2C **160**
Sanderstead. *G Lon* 4E **39**
Sandfields. *Neat* 3G **31**
Sandford. *Cumb* 3A **104**
Sandford. *Devn* 2B **12**
Sandford. *Dors* 4E **15**
Sandford. *Hants* 2G **15**
Sandford. *IOW* 4D **16**
Sandford. *N Som* 1H **21**
Sandford. *Shrp* 3F **71**
(nr. Oswestry)
Sandford. *Shrp* 2H **71**
(nr. Whitchurch)
Sandford. *S Lan* 5A **128**
Sandfordhill. *Abers* 4H **161**
Sandford-on-Thames. *Oxon* 5D **50**
Sandford Orcas. *Dors* 4B **22**
Sandford St Martin. *Oxon* 3C **50**
Sandgate. *Kent* 2F **29**
Sandgreen. *Dum* 4C **110**
Sandhaven. *Abers* 2G **161**
Sandhead. *Dum* 4F **109**
Sandhill. *Cambs* 2E **65**
Sandhills. *Dors* 1B **14**
Sandhills. *Surr* 2A **26**
Sandhoe. *Nmbd* 3C **114**
Sand Hole. *E Yor* 1B **94**
Sandholme. *E Yor* 1B **94**
Sandholme. *Linc* 2C **76**
Sandhurst. *Brac* 5G **37**
Sandhurst. *Glos* 3D **48**
Sandhurst. *Kent* 3B **28**
Sandhurst Cross. *Kent* 3B **28**
Sandhutton. *N Yor* 1F **99**
(nr. Thirsk)
Sand Hutton. *N Yor* 4A **100**
(nr. York)
Sandiacre. *Derbs* 2B **74**
Sandilands. *Linc* 2E **89**
Sandiway. *Ches* 3A **84**
Sandleheath. *Hants* 1G **15**
Sandling. *Kent* 5B **40**
Sandlow Green. *Ches* 4B **84**
Sandness. *Shet* 6C **173**
Sandon. *Essx* 5H **53**
Sandon. *Herts* 2D **52**
Sandon. *Staf* 3D **72**
Sandonbank. *Staf* 3D **72**
Sandown. *IOW* 4D **16**
Sandplace. *Corn* 3G **7**
Sandridge. *Herts* 4B **52**
Sandridge. *Wilts* 5E **35**
Sandringham. *Norf* 3F **77**
Sandsend. *N Yor* 3F **107**
Sandside. *Cumb* 2C **96**
Sands, The. *Surr* 2G **25**
Sandtoft. *N Lin* 4H **93**
Sandway. *Kent* 5C **40**
Sandwich. *Kent* 5H **41**
Sandwick. *Cumb* 3F **103**
Sandwick. *Orkn* 6B **172**
Sandwick. *Shet* 9F **173**
Sandwith. *Cumb* 3A **102**
Sandy. *Beds* 1B **52**
Sandy. *Carm* 5E **45**
Sandy Bank. *Linc* 5B **88**
Sandycroft. *Flin* 4F **83**
Sandy Cross. *Here* 5A **60**
Sandygate. *Devn* 5B **12**
Sandygate. *IOM* 2C **108**
Sandy Haven. *Pemb* 4C **42**
Sandyhills. *Dum* 4F **111**
Sandylands. *Lanc* 3D **96**
Sandylane. *Swan* 4E **31**
Sandy Lane. *Wilts* 5E **35**
Sandy Park. *Devn* 4H **11**
Sandystones. *Bord* 2H **119**
Sandyway. *Here* 3H **47**
Sangobeg. *High* 2E **167**
Sangomore. *High* 2E **166**
Sankyn's Green. *Worc* 4B **60**
Sanna. *High* 2F **139**
Sanndabhaig. *W Isl* 4G **171**
(on Isle of Lewis)
Sanndabhaig. *W Isl* 4D **170**
(on South Uist)
Sannox. *N Ayr* 5B **126**
Sanquhar. *Dum* 3G **117**
Santon. *Cumb* 4B **102**
Santon Bridge. *Cumb* 4C **102**
Santon Downham. *Suff* 2H **65**
Sapcote. *Leics* 1B **62**
Sapey Common. *Here* 4B **60**
Sapiston. *Suff* 3B **66**
Sapley. *Cambs* 3B **64**
Sapperton. *Derbs* 2F **73**
Sapperton. *Glos* 5E **49**
Sapperton. *Linc* 2H **75**
Saracen's Head. *Linc* 3C **76**
Sarclet. *High* 4F **169**
Sardis. *Carm* 5F **45**
Sardis. *Pemb* 4D **42**
(nr. Milford Haven)
Sardis. *Pemb* 4F **43**
(nr. Tenby)
Sarisbury. *Hants* 2D **16**
Sarn. *B'end* 3C **32**
Sarn. *Powy* 1E **58**
Sarnau. *Carm* 3E **45**
Sarnau. *Cdgn* 5C **56**
Sarnau. *Gwyn* 2B **70**
Sarnau. *Powy* 2D **46**
(nr. Brecon)
Sarnau. *Powy* 4E **71**
(nr. Welshpool)
Sarn Bach. *Gwyn* 3C **68**
Sarnesfield. *Here* 5F **59**
Sarn Meyllteyrn. *Gwyn* 2B **68**
Saron. *Carm* 4G **45**
(nr. Ammanford)
Saron. *Carm* 2D **45**
(nr. Newcastle Emlyn)
Saron. *Gwyn* 4E **81**
(nr. Bethel)
Saron. *Gwyn* 5D **80**
(nr. Bontnewydd)
Sarratt. *Herts* 1B **38**
Sarre. *Kent* 4G **41**
Sarsden. *Oxon* 3A **50**
Satley. *Dur* 5E **115**
Satron. *N Yor* 5C **104**
Satterleigh. *Devn* 4G **19**
Satterthwaite. *Cumb* 5E **103**
Satwell. *Oxon* 3F **37**
Sauchen. *Abers* 2D **152**
Saucher. *Per* 5A **144**
Saughall. *Ches* 4F **83**
Saughtree. *Bord* 5H **119**
Saul. *Glos* 5C **48**
Saundby. *Notts* 2E **87**
Saundersfoot. *Pemb* 4F **43**
Saunderton. *Buck* 5F **51**
Saunderton Lee. *Buck* 2G **37**
Saunton. *Devn* 3E **19**
Sausthorpe. *Linc* 4C **88**
Saval. *High* 3C **164**
Saverley Green. *Staf* 2D **72**
Sawbridge. *Warw* 4C **62**
Sawbridgeworth. *Herts* 4E **53**
Sawdon. *N Yor* 1D **100**
Sawley. *Derbs* 2B **74**
Sawley. *Lanc* 5G **97**
Sawley. *N Yor* 3E **99**
Sawston. *Cambs* 1E **53**
Sawtry. *Cambs* 2A **64**
Saxby. *Leics* 3F **75**
Saxby. *Linc* 2H **87**
Saxby All Saints. *N Lin* 3C **94**
Saxelby. *Leics* 3D **74**
Saxham Street. *Suff* 4C **66**
Saxilby. *Linc* 3F **87**
Saxlingham. *Norf* 2C **78**
Saxlingham Green. *Norf* 1E **67**
Saxlingham Nethergate. *Norf* 1E **67**
Saxlingham Thorpe. *Norf* 1E **66**
Saxmundham. *Suff* 4F **67**
Saxondale. *Notts* 1D **74**
Saxon Street. *Cambs* 5F **65**
Saxtead. *Suff* 4E **67**
Saxtead Green. *Suff* 4E **67**
Saxthorpe. *Norf* 2D **78**
Saxton. *N Yor* 1E **93**
Sayers Common. *W Sus* 4D **26**
Scackleton. *N Yor* 2A **100**
Scadabhagh. *W Isl* 8D **171**
Scaftworth. *Notts* 1D **86**
Scagglethorpe. *N Yor* 2C **100**
Scaitcliffe. *Lanc* 2F **91**
Scaladal. *W Isl* 6D **171**
Scalasaig. *Arg* 4A **132**
Scalby. *E Yor* 2B **94**
Scalby. *N Yor* 5H **107**
Scalby Mills. *N Yor* 5H **107**
Scaldwell. *Nptn* 3E **63**
Scaleby. *Cumb* 3F **113**
Scaleby Hill. *Cumb* 3F **113**
Scale Houses. *Cumb* 5G **113**
Scales. *Cumb* 2B **96**
(nr. Barrow-in-Furness)
Scales. *Cumb* 2E **103**
(nr. Keswick)
Scalford. *Leics* 3E **75**
Scaling. *Red C* 3E **107**
Scaling Dam. *Red C* 3E **107**
Scalloway. *Shet* 8E **173**
Scalpaigh. *W Isl* 8E **171**
Scalpay House. *High* 1E **147**
Scamblesby. *Linc* 3B **88**
Scamodale. *High* 1C **140**
Scampston. *N Yor* 2C **100**
Scampton. *Linc* 3G **87**
Scaniport. *High* 5A **158**
Scapa. *Orkn* 7D **172**
Scapegoat Hill. *W Yor* 3A **92**
Scar. *Orkn* 3F **172**
Scarasta. *W Isl* 8C **171**
Scarborough. *N Yor* 1E **101**
Scarcliffe. *Derbs* 4B **86**
Scarcroft. *W Yor* 5F **99**
Scardroy. *High* 3E **156**
Scarfskerry. *High* 1E **169**
Scargill. *Dur* 3D **104**
Scarinish. *Arg* 4B **138**
Scarisbrick. *Lanc* 3B **90**
Scarning. *Norf* 4B **78**
Scarrington. *Notts* 1E **75**
Scarth Hill. *Lanc* 4C **90**
Scartho. *NE Lin* 4F **95**
Scarvister. *Shet* 7E **173**
Scatwell. *High* 3F **157**
Scaur. *Dum* 4F **111**
Scawby. *N Lin* 4C **94**
Scawby Brook. *N Lin* 4C **94**
Scawsby. *S Yor* 4F **93**
Scawton. *N Yor* 1H **99**
Scayne's Hill. *W Sus* 3E **27**
Scethrog. *Powy* 3E **46**
Scholar Green. *Ches* 5C **84**
Scholes. *G Man* 4D **90**
Scholes. *W Yor* 2B **92**
(nr. Bradford)
Scholes. *W Yor* 4B **92**
(nr. Holmfirth)
Scholes. *W Yor* 1D **93**
(nr. Leeds)
Scholey Hill. *W Yor* 2D **93**
School Aycliffe. *Dur* 2F **105**
School Green. *Ches* 4A **84**
School Green. *Essx* 2H **53**
Scissett. *W Yor* 3C **92**
Scleddau. *Pemb* 1D **42**
Scofton. *Notts* 2D **86**
Scole. *Norf* 3D **66**
Scolton. *Pemb* 2D **43**
Scone. *Per* 1D **136**
Sconser. *High* 5E **155**
Scoonie. *Fife* 3F **137**
Scopwick. *Linc* 5H **87**
Scoraig. *High* 4E **163**
Scorborough. *E Yor* 5E **101**
Scorrier. *Corn* 4B **6**
Scorriton. *Devn* 2D **8**
Scorton. *Lanc* 5E **97**
Scorton. *N Yor* 4F **105**
Sco Ruston. *Norf* 3E **79**
Scotby. *Cumb* 4F **113**

Scotch Corner—Shilbottle Grange

Scotch Corner. N Yor 4F 105
Scotforth. Lanc 3D 97
Scot Hay. Staf 1C 72
Scothern. Linc 3H 87
Scotland End. Oxon 2B 50
Scotlandwell. Per 3D 136
Scot Lane End. G Man 4E 91
Scotsburn. High 1B 158
Scotsburn. Mor 2G 159
Scotsdike. Cumb 2E 113
Scots Gap. Nmbd 1D 114
Scotstoun. Glas 3G 127
Scotstown. High 2C 140
Scotswood. Tyne 3F 115
Scottas. High 3F 147
Scotter. Linc 4B 94
Scotterthorpe. Linc 4B 94
Scottlethorpe. Linc 3H 75
Scotton. Linc 1F 87
Scotton. N Yor 5E 105
(nr. Catterick Garrison)
Scotton. N Yor 4F 99
(nr. Harrogate)
Scottow. Norf 3E 79
Scoulton. Norf 5B 78
Scounslow Green. Staf 3E 73
Scourie. High 4B 166
Scourie More. High 4B 166
Scousburgh. Shet 10E 173
Scout Green. Cumb 4G 103
Scouthead. G Man 4H 91
Scrabster. High 1C 168
Scrafield. Linc 4C 88
Scrainwood. Nmbd 4D 121
Scrane End. Linc 1C 76
Scraptoft. Leic 5D 74
Scratby. Norf 4H 79
Scrayingham. N Yor 3B 100
Scredington. Linc 1H 75
Scremby. Linc 4D 88
Scremerston. Nmbd 5G 131
Screveton. Notts 1E 75
Scrivelsby. Linc 4B 88
Scriven. N Yor 4F 99
Scronkey. Lanc 5D 96
Scrooby. Notts 1D 86
Scropton. Derbs 2F 73
Scrub Hill. Linc 5B 88
Scruton. N Yor 5F 105
Scuggate. Cumb 2F 113
Sculcoates. Hull 1D 94
Sculthorpe. Norf 2A 78
Scunthorpe. N Lin 3B 94
Scurlage. Swan 4D 30
Sea. Som 1G 13
Seaborough. Dors 2H 13
Seabridge. Staf 1C 72
Seabrook. Kent 2F 29
Seaburn. Tyne 3H 115
Seacombe. Mers 1F 83
Seacroft. Linc 4E 89
Seacroft. W Yor 1D 92
Seadyke. Linc 2C 76
Seafield. High 5G 165
Seafield. Midl 3F 129
Seafield. S Ayr 2C 116
Seafield. W Lot 3D 128
Seaford. E Sus 5F 27
Seaforth. Mers 1F 83
Seagrave. Leics 4D 74
Seaham. Dur 5H 115
Seahouses. Nmbd 1G 121
Seal. Kent 5G 39
Sealand. Flin 4F 83
Seale. Surr 2G 25
Seamer. N Yor 1E 101
(nr. Scarborough)
Seamer. N Yor 3B 106
(nr. Stokesley)
Seamill. N Ayr 5C 126
Sea Mills. Bris 4A 34
Sea Palling. Norf 3G 79
Searby. Linc 4D 94
Seasalter. Kent 4E 41
Seascale. Cumb 4B 102
Seaside. Per 1E 137
Seater. High 1F 169
Seathorne. Linc 4E 89
Seathwaite. Cumb 3D 102
(nr. Buttermere)
Seathwaite. Cumb 5D 102
(nr. Ulpha)
Seatle. Cumb 1C 96
Seatoller. Cumb 3D 102
Seaton. Corn 3H 7
Seaton. Cumb 1B 102
Seaton. Devn 3F 13
Seaton. Dur 4G 115
Seaton. E Yor 5F 101
Seaton. Nmbd 2G 115
Seaton. Rut 1G 63
Seaton Burn. Tyne 2F 115
Seaton Carew. Hart 2C 106
Seaton Delaval. Nmbd 2G 115
Seaton Junction. Devn 3F 13
Seaton Ross. E Yor 5B 100
Seaton Sluice. Nmbd 2G 115
Seatown. Abers 2C 160
Seatown. Dors 3H 13
Seatown. Mor 2C 160
(nr. Cullen)
Seatown. Mor 1G 159
(nr. Lossiemouth)
Seave Green. N Yor 4C 106
Seaview. IOW 3E 17
Seaville. Cumb 4C 112
Seavington St Mary. Som 1H 13
Seavington St Michael. Som 1H 13
Seawick. Essx 4E 55
Sebastopol. Torf 2F 33
Sebergham. Cumb 5E 113
Seckington. Warw 5G 73
Second Coast. High 4D 162
Sedbergh. Cumb 5H 103
Sedbury. Glos 2A 34
Sedbusk. N Yor 5B 104
Sedgeberrow. Worc 2F 49
Sedgebrook. Linc 2F 75
Sedgefield. Dur 2A 106
Sedgeford. Norf 2G 77
Sedgehill. Wilts 4D 22
Sedgley. W Mid 1D 60
Sedgwick. Cumb 1E 97
Sedlescombe. E Sus 4B 28
Seend. Wilts 5E 35
Seend Cleeve. Wilts 5E 35
Seer Green. Buck 1A 38
Seething. Norf 1F 67
Sefton. Mers 4B 90
Sefton Park. Mers 2F 83
Seggat. Abers 4E 161
Seghill. Nmbd 2F 115
Seifton. Shrp 2G 59
Seighford. Staf 3C 72
Seilebost. W Isl 8C 171
Seisdon. Staf 1C 60
Seisiadar. W Isl 4H 171
Selattyn. Shrp 2E 71
Selborne. Hants 3F 25
Selby. N Yor 1G 93
Selham. W Sus 3A 26
Selkirk. Bord 2G 119
Sellack. Here 3A 48
Sellafirth. Shet 2G 173
Sellindge. Kent 2F 29
Selling. Kent 5E 41
Sells Green. Wilts 5E 35
Selly Oak. W Mid 2E 61
Selmeston. E Sus 5G 27
Selsdon. G Lon 4E 39
Selsey. W Sus 3G 17
Selsfield Common. W Sus 2E 27
Selside. Cumb 5G 103
Selside. N Yor 2G 97
Selsley. Glos 5D 48
Selsted. Kent 1G 29
Selston. Notts 5B 86
Selworthy. Som 2C 20
Semer. Suff 1D 54
Semington. Wilts 5D 35
Semley. Wilts 4D 23
Send. Surr 5B 38
Send Marsh. Surr 5B 38
Senghenydd. Cphy 2E 32
Sennen. Corn 4A 4
Sennen Cove. Corn 4A 4
Sennicotts. W Sus 2G 17
Sennybridge. Powy 3C 46
Serlby. Notts 2D 86
Sessay. N Yor 2G 99
Setchey. Norf 4F 77
Setley. Hants 2B 16
Setter. Shet 3F 173
Settiscarth. Orkn 6C 172
Settle. N Yor 3H 97
Settrington. N Yor 2C 100
Seven Ash. Som 3E 21
Sevenhampton. Glos 3F 49
Sevenhampton. Swin 2H 35
Sevenoaks. Kent 5G 39
Sevenoaks Weald. Kent 5G 39
Seven Sisters. Neat 5B 46
Seven Springs. Glos 4E 49
Severn Beach. S Glo 3A 34
Severn Stoke. Worc 1D 48
Sevington. Kent 1E 29
Sewards End. Essx 2F 53
Sewardstone. Essx 1E 39
Sewell. Beds 3H 51
Sewerby. E Yor 3G 101
Seworgan. Corn 5B 6
Sewstern. Leics 3F 75
Sgallairidh. W Isl 9B 170
Sgarasta Mhor. W Isl 8C 171
Sgiogarstaigh. W Isl 1H 171
Sgreadan. Arg 4A 132
Shabbington. Buck 5E 51
Shackerley. Shrp 5C 72
Shackerstone. Leics 5A 74
Shackleford. Surr 1A 26
Shadforth. Dur 5G 115
Shadingfield. Suff 2G 67
Shadoxhurst. Kent 2D 28
Shadsworth. Bkbn 2E 91
Shadwell. Norf 2B 66
Shadwell. W Yor 1D 92
Shaftesbury. Dors 4D 22
Shafton. S Yor 3D 93
Shafton Two Gates. S Yor 3D 93
Shaggs. Dors 4D 14
Shakesfield. Glos 2B 48
Shalbourne. Wilts 5B 36
Shalcombe. IOW 4B 16
Shalden. Hants 2E 25
Shaldon. Devn 5C 12
Shalfleet. IOW 4C 16
Shalford. Essx 3H 53
Shalford. Surr 1B 26
Shalford Green. Essx 3H 53
Shallowford. Devn 2H 19
Shallowford. Staf 3C 72
Shalmsford Street. Kent 5E 41
Shalstone. Buck 2E 51
Shamley Green. Surr 1B 26
Shandon. Arg 1D 126
Shandwick. High 1C 158
Shangton. Leics 1E 62
Shankhouse. Nmbd 2F 115
Shanklin. IOW 4D 16
Shannochie. N Ayr 3D 122
Shap. Cumb 3G 103
Shapwick. Dors 2E 15
Shapwick. Som 3H 21
Sharcott. Wilts 1G 23
Shardlow. Derbs 2B 74
Shareshill. Staf 5D 72
Sharlston. W Yor 3D 93
Sharlston Common. W Yor 3D 93
Sharnal Street. Medw 3B 40
Sharnbrook. Beds 5G 63
Sharneyford. Lanc 2G 91
Sharnford. Leics 1B 62
Sharnhill Green. Dors 2C 14
Sharow. N Yor 2F 99
Sharpe Green. Lanc 1D 90
Sharpenhoe. Beds 2A 52
Sharperton. Nmbd 4D 120
Sharpness. Glos 5B 48
Sharp Street. Norf 3F 79
Sharpthorne. W Sus 2E 27
Sharrington. Norf 2C 78
Shatterford. Worc 2B 60
Shatton. Derbs 2G 85
Shaugh Prior. Devn 2B 8
Shavington. Ches 5B 84
Shaw. G Man 4H 91
Shaw. W Ber 5C 36
Shaw. Wilts 5D 35
Shawbirch. Telf 4A 72
Shawbury. Shrp 3H 71
Shawdon Hall. Nmbd 3E 121
Shawell. Leics 2C 62
Shawford. Hants 4C 24
Shawforth. Lanc 2G 91
Shaw Green. Lanc 3D 90
Shawhead. Dum 2F 111
Shaw Mills. N Yor 3E 99
Shawwood. E Ayr 2E 117
Shearington. Dum 3B 112
Shearsby. Leics 1D 62
Shearston. Som 3F 21
Shebbear. Devn 2E 11
Shebdon. Staf 3B 72
Shebster. High 2C 168
Sheddocksley. Aber 3F 153
Shedfield. Hants 1D 16
Shedog. N Ayr 2D 122
Sheen. Staf 4F 85
Sheepbridge. Derbs 3A 86
Sheep Hill. Tyne 4E 115
Sheepscar. W Yor 1D 92
Sheepscombe. Glos 4D 49
Sheepstor. Devn 2B 8
Sheepwash. Devn 2E 11
Sheepwash. Nmbd 1F 115
Sheepway. N Som 4H 33
Sheepy Magna. Leics 5H 73
Sheepy Parva. Leics 5H 73
Sheering. Essx 4F 53
Sheerness. Kent 3D 40
Sheerwater. Surr 4B 38
Sheet. Hants 4F 25
Sheffield. S Yor 2H 85
Sheffield Bottom. W Ber 5E 37
Sheffield City Airport. S Yor 2B 86
Sheffield Green. E Sus 3F 27
Shefford. Beds 2B 52
Shefford Woodlands. W Ber 4B 36
Sheigra. High 2B 166
Sheinton. Shrp 5A 72
Shelderton. Shrp 3G 59
Sheldon. Derbs 4F 85
Sheldon. Devn 2E 12
Sheldon. W Mid 2F 61
Sheldwich. Kent 5E 40
Sheldwich Lees. Kent 5E 40
Shelf. W Yor 2B 92
Shelfanger. Norf 2D 66
Shelfield. Warw 4F 61
Shelfield. W Mid 5E 73
Shelford. Notts 1D 74
Shelford. Warw 2B 62
Shell. Worc 5D 60
Shelley. Suff 2D 54
Shelley. W Yor 3C 92
Shell Green. Hal 2H 83
Shellingford. Oxon 2B 36
Shellow Bowells. Essx 5G 53
Shelsley Beauchamp. Worc 4B 60
Shelsley Walsh. Worc 4B 60
Shelthorpe. Leics 4C 74
Shelton. Beds 4H 63
Shelton. Norf 1E 67
Shelton. Notts 1E 75
Shelton. Shrp 4G 71
Shelton Green. Norf 1E 67
Shelton Lock. Derb 2A 74
Shelve. Shrp 1F 59
Shelwick. Here 1A 48
Shelwick Green. Here 1A 48
Shenfield. Essx 1H 39
Shenington. Oxon 1B 50
Shenley. Herts 5B 52
Shenley Brook End. Mil 2G 51
Shenleybury. Herts 5B 52
Shenley Church End. Mil 2G 51
Shenmore. Here 2G 47
Shennanton. Dum 3A 110
Shenstone. Staf 5F 73
Shenstone. Worc 3C 60
Shenstone Woodend. Staf 5F 73
Shenton. Leics 5A 74
Shenval. Mor 1G 151
Shepeau Stow. Linc 4C 76
Shephall. Herts 3C 52
Shepherd's Bush. G Lon 2D 38
Shepherds Gate. Norf 4E 77
Shepherd's Green. Oxon 3F 37
Shepherd's Port. Norf 2F 77
Shepherdswell. Kent 1G 29
Shepley. W Yor 4B 92
Sheppardstown. High 4D 169
Shepperdine. S Glo 2B 34
Shepperton. Surr 4B 38
Shepreth. Cambs 1D 53
Shepshed. Leics 4B 74
Shepton Beauchamp. Som 1H 13
Shepton Mallet. Som 2B 22
Shepton Montague. Som 3B 22
Shepway. Kent 5B 40
Sheraton. Dur 1B 106
Sherborne. Bath 1A 22
Sherborne. Dors 1B 14
Sherborne. Glos 4G 49
Sherborne Causeway. Dors 4D 22
Sherborne St John. Hants 1E 24
Sherbourne. Warw 4G 61
Sherburn. Dur 5G 115
Sherburn. N Yor 2D 100
Sherburn Hill. Dur 5G 115
Sherburn in Elmet. N Yor 1E 93
Shere. Surr 1B 26
Shereford. Norf 3A 78
Sherfield English. Hants 4A 24
Sherfield on Loddon. Hants 1E 25
Sherford. Devn 4D 9
Sherford. Dors 3E 15
Sheriffhales. Shrp 4B 72
Sheriff Hutton. N Yor 3A 100
Sheriffston. Mor 2G 159
Sheringham. Norf 1D 78
Sherington. Mil 1G 51
Shermanbury. W Sus 4D 26
Shernal Green. Worc 4D 60
Shernborne. Norf 2G 77
Sherrington. Wilts 3E 23
Sherston. Wilts 3D 34
Sherwood. Nott 1C 74
Sherwood Green. Devn 4F 19
Shettleston. Glas 3H 127
Shevington. G Man 4D 90
Shevington Moor. G Man 3D 90
Shevington Vale. G Man 4D 90
Sheviock. Corn 3H 7
Shide. IOW 4D 16
Shiel Bridge. High 2B 148
Shieldaig. High 1H 155
(nr. Charlestown)
Shieldaig. High 3H 155
(nr. Torridon)
Shieldhill. Dum 1B 112
Shieldhill. Falk 2B 128
Shieldhill. S Lan 5D 128
Shieldmuir. N Lan 4A 128
Shielfoot. High 2A 140
Shielhill. Abers 3H 161
Shielhill. Ang 3D 144
Shifnal. Shrp 5B 72
Shilbottle. Nmbd 4F 121
Shilbottle Grange. Nmbd 4G 121

Shildon. Dur 2F 105
Shillford. E Ren 4F 127
Shillingford. Devn 4C 20
Shillingford. Oxon 2D 36
Shillingford St George. Devn 4C 12
Shillingstone. Dors 1D 14
Shillington. Beds 2B 52
Shillmoor. Nmbd 4C 120
Shilton. Oxon 5A 50
Shilton. Warw 2B 62
Shilvinghampton. Dors 4B 14
Shilvington. Nmbd 1E 115
Shimpling. Norf 2D 66
Shimpling. Suff 5A 66
Shimpling Street. Suff 5A 66
Shincliffe. Dur 5F 115
Shiney Row. Tyne 4G 115
Shinfield. Wok 5F 37
Shingay. Cambs 1D 52
Shingham. Norf 5G 77
Shingle Street. Suff 1G 55
Shinner's Bridge. Devn 2D 9
Shinness. High 2C 164
Shipbourne. Kent 5G 39
Shipdham. Norf 5B 78
Shipham. Som 1H 21
Shiphay. Torb 2E 9
Shiplake. Oxon 4F 37
Shipley. Derbs 1B 74
Shipley. Nmbd 3F 121
Shipley. Shrp 1C 60
Shipley. W Sus 3C 26
Shipley. W Yor 1B 92
Shipley Bridge. Surr 1E 27
Shipmeadow. Suff 1F 67
Shippon. Oxon 2C 36
Shipston-on-Stour. Warw 1A 50
Shipton. Buck 3F 51
Shipton. Glos 4F 49
Shipton. N Yor 4H 99
Shipton. Shrp 1H 59
Shipton Bellinger. Hants 2H 23
Shipton Gorge. Dors 3H 13
Shipton Green. W Sus 3G 17
Shipton Moyne. Glos 3D 35
Shipton-on-Cherwell. Oxon 4C 50
Shiptonthorpe. E Yor 5C 100
Shipton-under-Wychwood.
   Oxon 4A 50
Shirburn. Oxon 2E 37
Shirdley Hill. Lanc 3B 90
Shire. Cumb 1H 103
Shirebrook. Derbs 4C 86
Shiregreen. S Yor 1A 86
Shirehampton. Bris 4A 34
Shiremoor. Tyne 2G 115
Shirenewton. Mon 2H 33
Shireoaks. Notts 2C 86
Shires Mill. Fife 1C 128
Shirkoak. Kent 2D 28
Shirland. Derbs 5A 86
Shirley. Derbs 1G 73
Shirley. Sotn 1C 16
Shirley. W Mid 3F 61
Shirleywich. Staf 3D 73
Shirl Heath. Here 5G 59
Shirrell Heath. Hants 1D 16
Shirwell. Devn 3F 19
Shiskine. N Ayr 3D 122
Shobdon. Here 4F 59
Shobnall. Staf 3G 73
Shobrooke. Devn 2B 12
Shoby. Leics 3D 74
Shocklach. Ches 1G 71
Shoeburyness. S'end 2D 40
Sholden. Kent 5H 41
Sholing. Sotn 1C 16
Sholver. G Man 4H 91
Shoot Hill. Shrp 4G 71
Shop. Corn 1C 10
   (nr. Bude)
Shop. Corn 1C 6
   (nr. Padstow)
Shop. Devn 1D 11

Shopford. Cumb 2G 113
Shop Street. Suff 4E 66
Shoreditch. G Lon 2E 39
Shoreditch. Som 4F 21
Shoreham. Kent 4G 39
Shoreham Airport. W Sus 5D 26
Shoreham-by-Sea. W Sus 5D 26
Shoresdean. Nmbd 5F 131
Shoreswood. Nmbd 5F 131
Shore, The. Fife 2E 137
Shorncote. Glos 2F 35
Shorne. Kent 3A 40
Shorne Ridgeway. Kent 3A 40
Shortacombe. Devn 4F 11
Shortbridge. E Sus 3F 27
Shortgate. E Sus 4F 27
Short Green. Norf 2C 66
Shorthampton. Oxon 3B 50
Short Heath. Leics 4H 73
Short Heath. W Mid 1E 61
   (nr. Erdington)
Short Heath. W Mid 5D 73
   (nr. Wednesfield)
Shortlanesend. Corn 4C 6
Shorton. Torb 2E 9
Shortstown. Beds 1A 52
Shortwood. S Glo 4B 34
Shorwell. IOW 4C 16
Shoscombe. Bath 1C 22
Shotesham. Norf 1E 67
Shotgate. Essx 1B 40
Shotley. Suff 2F 55
Shotley Bridge. Dur 4D 115
Shotleyfield. Nmbd 4D 114
Shotley Gate. Suff 2F 55
Shottenden. Kent 5E 41
Shottermill. Surr 3G 25
Shottery. Warw 5F 61
Shotteswell. Warw 1C 50
Shottisham. Suff 1G 55
Shottle. Derbs 1H 73
Shotton. Dur 1B 106
   (nr. Peterlee)
Shotton. Dur 2A 106
   (nr. Sedgefield)
Shotton. Flin 4E 83
Shotton. Nmbd 1C 120
   (nr. Morpeth)
Shotton. Nmbd 1C 120
   (nr. Town Yetholm)
Shotton Colliery. Dur 5G 115
Shotts. N Lan 3B 128
Shotwick. Ches 3F 83
Shouldham. Norf 5F 77
Shouldham Thorpe. Norf 5F 77
Shoulton. Worc 5C 60
Shrawardine. Shrp 4F 71
Shrawley. Worc 4C 60
Shreding Green. Buck 2B 38
Shrewley. Warw 4G 61
Shrewsbury. Shrp 4G 71
Shrewton. Wilts 2F 23
Shripney. W Sus 5A 26
Shrivenham. Oxon 3H 35
Shropham. Norf 1B 66
Shroton. Dors 1D 14
Shrub End. Essx 3C 54
Shucknall. Here 1A 48
Shudy Camps. Cambs 1G 53
Shulishadermor. High 4D 155
Shulista. High 1D 154
Shurdington. Glos 4E 49
Shurlock Row. Wind 4G 37
Shurrery. High 3C 168
Shurton. Som 2F 21
Shustoke. Warw 1G 61
Shute. Devn 3E 13
   (nr. Axminster)
Shute. Devn 2B 12
   (nr. Crediton)
Shutford. Oxon 1B 50
Shut Heath. Staf 3C 72
Shuthonger. Glos 2D 49
Shutlanehead. Staf 1C 72

Shutlanger. Nptn 1F 51
Shutt Green. Staf 5C 72
Shuttington. Warw 5G 73
Shuttlewood. Derbs 3B 86
Shuttleworth. G Man 3G 91
Siabost. W Isl 3E 171
Siabost bho Dheas. W Isl 3E 171
Siabost bho Thuath. W Isl 3E 171
Siadar. W Isl 2F 171
Sibbaldbie. Dum 1C 112
Sibbertoft. Nptn 2D 62
Sibdon Carwood. Shrp 2G 59
Sibertswold. Kent 1G 29
Sibford Ferris. Oxon 2B 50
Sibford Gower. Oxon 2B 50
Sible Hedingham. Essx 2A 54
Sibsey. Linc 5C 88
Sibsey Fen Side. Linc 5C 88
Sibson. Cambs 1H 63
Sibson. Leics 5A 74
Sibster. High 3F 169
Sibthorpe. Notts 1E 75
Sibton. Suff 4F 67
Sicklesmere. Suff 4A 66
Sicklinghall. N Yor 5F 99
Sid. Devn 4E 13
Sidbury. Devn 3E 13
Sidbury. Shrp 2A 60
Sidcot. N Som 1H 21
Sidcup. G Lon 3F 39
Siddick. Cumb 1B 102
Siddington. Ches 3C 84
Siddington. Glos 2F 35
Side of the Moor. G Man 3F 91
Sidestrand. Norf 2E 79
Sidford. Devn 3E 13
Sidlesham. W Sus 3G 17
Sidley. E Sus 5B 28
Sidlowbridge. Surr 1D 26
Sidmouth. Devn 4E 13
Sigford. Devn 5A 12
Sigglesthorne. E Yor 5F 101
Sighthill. Edin 2E 129
Sigingstone. V Glam 4C 32
Signet. Oxon 4H 49
Silchester. Hants 5E 37
Sileby. Leics 4D 74
Silecroft. Cumb 1A 96
Silfield. Norf 1D 66
Silian. Cdgn 5E 57
Silkstone. S Yor 4C 92
Silkstone Common. S Yor 4C 92
Silksworth. Tyne 4G 115
Silk Willoughby. Linc 1H 75
Silloth. Cumb 4C 112
Sills. Nmbd 4C 120
Sillyearn. Mor 3C 160
Silpho. N Yor 5G 107
Silsden. W Yor 5C 98
Silsoe. Beds 2A 52
Silverbank. Abers 4E 152
Silverburn. Midl 3F 129
Silverdale. Lanc 2D 96
Silverdale. Staf 1C 72
Silverdale Green. Lanc 2D 96
Silver End. Essx 4B 54
Silver End. W Mid 2D 60
Silvergate. Norf 3D 78
Silverhillocks. Abers 2E 161
Silverley's Green. Suff 3E 67
Silverstone. Nptn 1E 51
Silverton. Devn 2C 12
Silverton. W Dun 2F 127
Silvington. Shrp 3A 60
Simm's Cross. Hal 2H 83
Simm's Lane End. Mers 1H 83
Simonburn. Nmbd 2B 114
Simonsbath. Som 3A 20
Simonstone. Lanc 1F 91
Simprim. Bord 5E 131
Simpson. Pemb 3C 42
Simpson Cross. Pemb 3C 42
Sinclairston. E Ayr 3D 116
Sinclairtown. Fife 4E 137

Sinderby. N Yor 1F 99
Sinderhope. Nmbd 4B 114
Sindlesham. Wok 5F 37
Sinfin. Derb 2A 74
Singleborough. Buck 2F 51
Singleton. Kent 1D 28
Singleton. Lanc 1B 90
Singleton. W Sus 1G 17
Singlewell. Kent 3A 40
Sinkhurst Green. Kent 1C 28
Sinnahard. Abers 2B 152
Sinnington. N Yor 1B 100
Sinton Green. Worc 4C 60
Sipson. G Lon 3B 38
Sirhowy. Blae 4E 47
Sisland. Norf 1F 67
Sissinghurst. Kent 2B 28
Siston. S Glo 4B 34
Sithney. Corn 4D 4
Sittingbourne. Kent 4D 40
Six Ashes. Staf 2B 60
Six Bells. Blae 5F 47
Six Hills. Leics 3D 74
Sixhills. Linc 2A 88
Six Mile Bottom. Cambs 5E 65
Sixpenny Handley. Dors 1E 15
Sizewell. Suff 4G 67
Skaill. High 4H 167
Skaills. Orkn 7E 172
Skares. E Ayr 3E 117
Skateraw. E Lot 2D 130
Skaw. Shet 5G 173
Skeabost. High 4D 154
Skeeby. N Yor 4E 105
Skeffington. Leics 5E 75
Skeffling. E Yor 3G 95
Skegby. Notts 4B 86
   (nr. Mansfield)
Skegby. Notts 3E 87
   (nr. Tuxford)
Skegness. Linc 4E 89
Skelberry. Shet 10E 173
   (nr. Boddam)
Skelberry. Shet 3E 173
   (nr. Housetter)
Skelbo. High 4E 165
Skelbo Street. High 4E 165
Skelbrooke. S Yor 3F 93
Skeldyke. Linc 2C 76
Skelfhill. Bord 4G 119
Skellingthorpe. Linc 3G 87
Skellister. Shet 6F 173
Skellorn Green. Ches 2D 84
Skellow. S Yor 3F 93
Skelmanthorpe. W Yor 3C 92
Skelmersdale. Lanc 4C 90
Skelmorlie. N Ayr 3C 126
Skelpick. High 3H 167
Skelton. Cumb 1F 103
Skelton. E Yor 2A 94
Skelton. N Yor 4D 105
   (nr. Richmond)
Skelton. N Yor 1F 99
   (nr. Ripon)
Skelton. Red C 3D 106
Skelton. York 4H 99
Skelton Green. Red C 3D 106
Skelwick. Orkn 3D 172
Skelwith Bridge. Cumb 4E 103
Skendleby. Linc 4D 88
Skendleby Psalter. Linc 3D 88
Skenfrith. Mon 3H 47
Skerne. E Yor 4E 101
Skeroblingarry. Arg 3B 122
Skerray. High 2G 167
Skerricha. High 3C 166
Skerries Airport. Shet 4H 173
Skerton. Lanc 3D 96
Sketchley. Leics 1B 62
Sketty. Swan 3F 31
Skewen. Neat 3G 31
Skewsby. N Yor 2A 100
Skeyton. Norf 3E 79
Skeyton Corner. Norf 3E 79
Skiall. High 2C 168

Skidbrooke. Linc 1D 88
Skidbrooke North End. Linc 1D 88
Skidby. E Yor 1D 94
Skilgate. Som 4C 20
Skillington. Linc 3F 75
Skinburness. Cumb 4C 112
Skinflats. Falk 1C 128
Skinidin. High 4B 154
Skinnet. High 2F 167
Skinningrove. Red C 2E 107
Skipness. Arg 4G 125
Skippool. Lanc 5C 96
Skiprigg. Cumb 5E 113
Skipsea. E Yor 4F 101
Skipsea Brough. E Yor 4F 101
Skipton. N Yor 4B 98
Skipton-on-Swale. N Yor 2F 99
Skipwith. N Yor 1G 93
Skirbeck. Linc 1C 76
Skirbeck Quarter. Linc 1C 76
Skirlaugh. E Yor 1E 95
Skirling. Bord 1C 118
Skirmett. Buck 2F 37
Skirpenbeck. E Yor 4B 100
Skirwith. Cumb 1H 103
Skirwith. N Yor 2G 97
Skirza. High 2F 169
Skitby. Cumb 3F 113
Skitham. Lanc 5D 96
Skittle Green. Buck 5F 51
Skulamus. High 1E 147
Skullomie. High 2G 167
Skyborry Green. Shrp 3E 59
Skye Green. Essx 3B 54
Skye of Curr. High 1D 151
Slack. W Yor 2H 91
Slack. Derbs 2E 85
Slack Head. Cumb 2D 97
Slackhall. Derbs 2E 85
Slackhead. Mor 2B 160
Slackholme End. Linc 3E 89
Slacks of Cairnbanno. Abers 4F 161
Slack, The. Dur 2E 105
Slad. Glos 5D 48
Slade. Devn 2F 19
Slade. Swan 4D 31
Slade End. Oxon 2D 36
Slade Field. Cambs 2C 64
Slade Green. G Lon 3G 39
Slade Heath. Staf 5D 72
Slade Hooton. S Yor 2C 86
Sladesbridge. Corn 5A 10
Slade, The. W Ber 5D 36
Slaggyford. Nmbd 4H 113
Slaidburn. Lanc 4G 97
Slaid Hill. W Yor 5F 99
Slaithwaite. W Yor 3A 92
Slaley. Derbs 5G 85
Slaley. Nmbd 4C 114
Slamannan. Falk 2B 128
Slapton. Buck 3H 51
Slapton. Devn 4E 9
Slapton. Nptn 1E 51
Slattock. G Man 4G 91
Slaugham. W Sus 3D 26
Slaughterbridge. Corn 4B 10
Slaughterford. Wilts 4D 34
Slawston. Leics 1E 63
Sleaford. Hants 3G 25
Sleaford. Linc 1H 75
Sleagill. Cumb 3G 103
Sleap. Shrp 3G 71
Sledmere. E Yor 3D 100
Sleightholme. Dur 3C 104
Sleights. N Yor 4F 107
Slepe. Dors 3E 15
Slickly. High 2E 169
Sliddery. N Ayr 3D 122
Sligachan. High 1C 146
Slimbridge. Glos 5C 48
Slindon. Staf 2C 72
Slindon. W Sus 5A 26
Slinfold. W Sus 2C 26
Slingsby. N Yor 2A 100
Slip End. Beds 4A 52

Slipton. *Nptn* 3G 63
Slitting Mill. *Staf* 4E 73
Slochd. *High* 1C 150
Slockavullin. *Arg* 4F 133
Sloley. *Norf* 3E 79
Sloncombe. *Devn* 4H 11
Sloothby. *Linc* 3D 89
Slough. *Slo* 2A 38
Slough Green. *Som* 4F 21
Slough Green. *W Sus* 3D 27
Sluggan. *High* 1C 150
Slyne. *Lanc* 3D 97
Smailholm. *Bord* 1A 120
Smallbridge. *G Man* 3H 91
Smallbrook. *Devn* 3B 12
Smallburgh. *Norf* 3F 79
Smallburn. *E Ayr* 2F 117
Smalldale. *Derbs* 3E 85
Small Dole. *W Sus* 4D 26
Smalley. *Derbs* 1B 74
Smallfield. *Surr* 1E 27
Small Heath. *W Mid* 2E 61
Smallholm. *Dum* 2C 112
Small Hythe. *Kent* 2C 28
Smallrice. *Staf* 2D 72
Smallridge. *Devn* 2G 13
Smallwood Hey. *Lanc* 5C 96
Smallworth. *Norf* 2C 66
Smannell. *Hants* 2B 24
Smardale. *Cumb* 4A 104
Smarden. *Kent* 1C 28
Smarden Bell. *Kent* 1C 28
Smart's Hill. *Kent* 1G 27
Smeatharpe. *Devn* 1F 13
Smeeth. *Kent* 2E 29
Smeeth, The. *Norf* 4E 77
Smeeton Westerby. *Leics* 1D 62
Smeircleit. *W Isl* 7C 170
Smerral. *High* 5D 168
Smestow. *Staf* 1C 60
Smethwick. *W Mid* 2E 61
Smirisary. *High* 1A 140
Smisby. *Derbs* 4H 73
Smitham Hill. *Bath* 1A 22
Smith End Green. *Worc* 5B 60
Smithfield. *Cumb* 3F 113
Smith Green. *Lanc* 4D 97
Smithies, The. *Shrp* 1A 60
Smithincott. *Devn* 1D 12
Smith's Green. *Essx* 3F 53
Smithstown. *High* 1G 155
Smithton. *High* 4B 158
Smithwood Green. *Suff* 5B 66
Smithy Bridge. *G Man* 3H 91
Smithy Green. *Ches* 3B 84
Smithy Lane Ends. *Lanc* 3C 90
Smockington. *Warw* 2B 62
Smyth's Green. *Essx* 4C 54
Snaigow House. *Per* 4H 143
Snailbeach. *Shrp* 5F 71
Snailwell. *Cambs* 4F 65
Snainton. *N Yor* 1D 100
Snaith. *E Yor* 2G 93
Snape. *N Yor* 1E 99
Snape. *Suff* 5F 67
Snape Green. *Lanc* 3B 90
Snarestone. *Leics* 5H 73
Snarford. *Linc* 2H 87
Snargate. *Kent* 3D 28
Snave. *Kent* 3E 28
Sneachill. *Worc* 5D 60
Snead. *Powy* 1F 59
Snead Common. *Worc* 4B 60
Sneaton. *N Yor* 4F 107
Sneatonthorpe. *N Yor* 4G 107
Snelland. *Linc* 2H 87
Snelston. *Derbs* 1F 73
Snetterton. *Norf* 1B 66
Snettisham. *Norf* 2F 77
Snibston. *Leics* 4B 74
Sniseabhal. *W Isl* 5C 170
Snitter. *Nmbd* 4E 121
Snitterby. *Linc* 1G 87
Snitterfield. *Warw* 5G 61
Snitton. *Shrp* 3H 59
Snodhill. *Here* 1G 47
Snodland. *Kent* 4A 40
Snods Edge. *Nmbd* 4D 114
Snowshill. *Glos* 2F 49
Snow Street. *Norf* 2C 66
Snydale. *W Yor* 3E 93
Soake. *Hants* 1E 17
Soar. *Carm* 3G 45
Soar. *Gwyn* 2F 69
Soar. *IOA* 3C 80
Soar. *Powy* 2C 46
Soberton. *Hants* 1E 16
Soberton Heath. *Hants* 1E 16
Sockbridge. *Cumb* 2G 103
Sockburn. *Darl* 4A 106
Sodom. *Den* 3C 82
Soham. *Cambs* 3E 65
Soham Cotes. *Cambs* 3E 65
Solas. *W Isl* 1D 170
Soldon Cross. *Devn* 1D 10
Soldridge. *Hants* 3E 25
Solent Breezes. *Hants* 2D 16
Sole Street. *Kent* 4A 40
(nr. Meopham)
Sole Street. *Kent* 1E 29
(nr. Waltham)
Solihull. *W Mid* 3F 61
Sollers Dilwyn. *Here* 5G 59
Sollers Hope. *Here* 2B 48
Sollom. *Lanc* 3C 90
Solva. *Pemb* 2B 42
Somerby. *Leics* 4E 75
Somerby. *Linc* 4D 94
Somercotes. *Derbs* 5B 86
Somerford. *Dors* 3G 15
Somerford. *Staf* 5C 72
Somerford Keynes. *Glos* 2F 35
Somerley. *W Sus* 3G 17
Somerleyton. *Suff* 1G 67
Somersal Herbert. *Derbs* 2F 73
Somersby. *Linc* 3C 88
Somersham. *Cambs* 3C 64
Somersham. *Suff* 1D 54
Somerton. *Oxon* 3C 50
Somerton. *Som* 4H 21
Somerton. *Suff* 5H 65
Sompting. *W Sus* 5C 26
Sonning. *Wok* 4F 37
Sonning Common. *Oxon* 3F 37
Sookholme. *Notts* 4C 86
Sopley. *Hants* 3G 15
Sopworth. *Wilts* 3D 34
Sorbie. *Dum* 5B 110
Sordale. *High* 2D 168
Sorisdale. *Arg* 2D 138
Sorn. *E Ayr* 2E 117
Sornhill. *E Ayr* 1E 117
Sortat. *High* 2E 169
Sotby. *Linc* 3B 88
Sots Hole. *Linc* 4A 88
Sotterley. *Suff* 2G 67
Soudley. *Shrp* 1G 59
(nr. Church Stretton)
Soudley. *Shrp* 3B 72
(nr. Market Drayton)
Soughton. *Flin* 4E 83
Soulbury. *Buck* 3G 51
Soulby. *Cumb* 3A 104
(nr. Appleby)
Soulby. *Cumb* 2F 103
(nr. Penrith)
Souldern. *Oxon* 2D 50
Souldrop. *Beds* 4G 63
Sound. *Shet* 7F 173
Soundwell. *Bris* 4B 34
Sourhope. *Bord* 2C 120
Sourin. *Orkn* 4D 172
Sourton. *Devn* 3F 11
Soutergate. *Cumb* 1B 96
South Acre. *Norf* 4H 77
Southall. *G Lon* 3C 38
South Allington. *Devn* 5D 9
South Alloa. *Falk* 4A 136
Southam. *Glos* 3E 49
Southam. *Warw* 4B 62
South Ambersham. *W Sus* 3A 26
Southampton. *Sotn* 1C 16
Southampton International Airport.
Hants 1C 16
Southannan. *N Ayr* 4D 126
South Anston. *S Yor* 2C 86
South Ascot. *Wind* 4A 38
South Baddesley. *Hants* 3B 16
South Balfern. *Dum* 4B 110
South Ballachulish. *High* 3E 141
South Bank. *Red C* 2C 106
South Barrow. *Som* 4B 22
South Benfleet. *Essx* 2B 40
South Bents. *Tyne* 3H 115
South Bersted. *W Sus* 5A 26
Southborough. *Kent* 1G 27
Southbourne. *Bour* 3G 15
Southbourne. *W Sus* 2F 17
South Bowood. *Dors* 3H 13
South Brent. *Devn* 2D 8
South Brewham. *Som* 3C 22
South Broomage. *Falk* 1B 128
South Broomhill. *Nmbd* 4G 121
Southburgh. *Norf* 5B 78
South Burlingham. *Norf* 5F 79
Southburn. *E Yor* 4D 101
South Cadbury. *Som* 4B 22
South Carlton. *Linc* 3G 87
South Cave. *E Yor* 1C 94
South Cerney. *Glos* 2F 35
South Chard. *Som* 2G 13
South Charlton. *Nmbd* 2F 121
South Cheriton. *Som* 4B 22
South Church. *Dur* 2F 105
Southchurch. *S'end* 2D 40
South Cleatlam. *Dur* 3E 105
South Cliffe. *E Yor* 1B 94
South Clifton. *Notts* 3F 87
South Clunes. *High* 4H 157
South Cockerington. *Linc* 2C 88
South Common. *E Sus* 4E 27
South Cornelly. *B'end* 3B 32
Southcott. *Devn* 1E 11
(nr. Great Torrington)
Southcott. *Devn* 3F 11
(nr. Okehampton)
Southcott. *Wilts* 1G 23
Southcourt. *Buck* 4G 51
South Cove. *Suff* 2G 67
South Creagan. *Arg* 4D 141
South Creake. *Norf* 2A 78
South Crosland. *W Yor* 3B 92
South Croxton. *Leics* 4D 74
South Dalton. *E Yor* 5D 100
South Darenth. *Kent* 4G 39
Southdean. *Bord* 4A 120
Southdown. *Bath* 5C 34
South Duffield. *N Yor* 1G 93
Southease. *E Sus* 5F 27
South Elkington. *Linc* 2B 88
South Elmsall. *W Yor* 3E 93
Southend. *Arg* 5A 122
South End. *Cumb* 3B 96
Southend. *Glos* 2C 34
South End. *N Lin* 2E 94
South End. *W Ber* 4D 36
Southend (London) Airport.
Essx 2C 40
Southend-on-Sea. *S'end* 2C 40
Southerfield. *Cumb* 5C 112
Southerly. *Devn* 4F 11
Southernden. *Kent* 1C 28
Southerndown. *V Glam* 4B 32
Southerness. *Dum* 4A 112
South Erradale. *High* 1G 155
Southerton. *Devn* 3D 12
Southery. *Norf* 1F 65
Southey Green. *Essx* 2A 54
South Fambridge. *Essx* 1C 40
South Fawley. *W Ber* 3B 36
South Feorline. *N Ayr* 3D 122
South Ferriby. *N Lin* 2C 94
South Field. *E Yor* 2D 94
Southfleet. *Kent* 3H 39
South Garvan. *High* 1D 141
Southgate. *Cdgn* 2E 57
Southgate. *G Lon* 1E 39
Southgate. *Norf* 3D 78
(nr. Aylsham)
Southgate. *Norf* 2A 78
(nr. Fakenham)
Southgate. *Swan* 4E 31
South Godstone. *Surr* 1E 27
South Gorley. *Hants* 1G 15
South Green. *Essx* 1A 40
(nr. Billericay)
South Green. *Essx* 4D 54
(nr. Colchester)
South Green. *Kent* 4C 40
South Hanningfield. *Essx* 1B 40
South Harting. *W Sus* 1F 17
South Hayling. *Hants* 3F 17
South Hazelrigg. *Nmbd* 1E 121
South Heath. *Buck* 5H 51
South Heath. *Essx* 4E 54
South Heighton. *E Sus* 5F 27
South Hetton. *Dur* 5G 115
South Hiendley. *W Yor* 3D 93
South Hill. *Corn* 5D 10
South Hill. *Som* 4H 21
South Hinksey. *Oxon* 5D 50
South Hole. *Devn* 4C 18
South Holme. *N Yor* 2B 100
South Holmwood. *Surr* 1C 26
South Hornchurch. *G Lon* 2G 39
South Huish. *Devn* 4C 8
South Hykeham. *Linc* 4G 87
South Hylton. *Tyne* 4G 115
Southill. *Beds* 1B 52
Southington. *Hants* 2D 24
South Kelsey. *Linc* 1H 87
South Kessock. *High* 4A 158
South Killingholme. *N Lin* 3E 95
South Kilvington. *N Yor* 1G 99
South Kilworth. *Leics* 2D 62
South Kirkby. *W Yor* 3E 93
South Kirton. *Abers* 3E 153
South Knighton. *Devn* 5B 12
South Kyme. *Linc* 1A 76
South Lancing. *W Sus* 5C 26
South Ledaig. *Arg* 5D 140
Southleigh. *Devn* 3F 13
South Leigh. *Oxon* 5B 50
South Leverton. *Notts* 2E 87
South Littleton. *Worc* 1F 49
South Lopham. *Norf* 2C 66
South Luffenham. *Rut* 5G 75
South Malling. *E Sus* 4F 27
South Marston. *Swin* 3G 35
South Middleton. *Nmbd* 2E 121
South Milford. *N Yor* 1E 93
South Milton. *Devn* 4D 8
South Mimms. *Herts* 5C 52
Southminster. *Essx* 1D 40
South Molton. *Devn* 4H 19
South Moor. *Dur* 4E 115
Southmoor. *Oxon* 2B 36
South Moreton. *Oxon* 3D 36
South Mundham. *W Sus* 2G 17
South Muskham. *Notts* 5E 87
South Newbald. *E Yor* 1C 94
South Newington. *Oxon* 2C 50
South Newsham. *Nmbd* 2G 115
South Newton. *N Ayr* 4H 125
South Newton. *Wilts* 3F 23
South Normanton. *Derbs* 5B 86
South Norwood. *G Lon* 4E 39
South Nutfield. *Surr* 1E 27
South Ockendon. *Thur* 2G 39
Southoe. *Cambs* 4A 64
Southolt. *Suff* 4D 66
South Ormsby. *Linc* 3C 88
Southorpe. *Pet* 5H 75
South Otterington. *N Yor* 1F 99
South Owersby. *Linc* 1H 87
Southowram. *W Yor* 2B 92
South Oxhey. *Herts* 1C 38
South Perrott. *Dors* 2H 13
South Petherton. *Som* 1H 13
South Petherwin. *Corn* 4D 10
South Pickenham. *Norf* 5A 78
South Pool. *Devn* 4D 9
South Poorton. *Dors* 3A 14
South Port. *Arg* 1H 133
Southport. *Mers* 3B 90
South Queensferry. *Edin* 2E 129
South Radworthy. *Devn* 3A 20
South Rauceby. *Linc* 1H 75
South Raynham. *Norf* 3A 78
Southrepps. *Norf* 2E 79
South Reston. *Linc* 2D 88
Southrey. *Linc* 4A 88
Southrop. *Glos* 5G 49
Southrope. *Hants* 2E 25
South Runcton. *Norf* 5F 77
South Scarle. *Notts* 4F 87
Southsea. *Port* 3E 17
South Shields. *Tyne* 3G 115
South Shore. *Bkpl* 1B 90
Southside. *Orkn* 5E 172
South Somercotes. *Linc* 1D 88
South Stainley. *N Yor* 3F 99
South Stainmore. *Cumb* 3B 104
South Stifford. *Thur* 3G 39
Southstoke. *Bath* 5C 34
South Stoke. *Oxon* 3D 36
South Stoke. *W Sus* 4B 26
South Street. *E Sus* 4E 27
South Street. *Kent* 5E 41
(nr. Faversham)
South Street. *Kent* 4F 41
(nr. Whitstable)
South Tawton. *Devn* 3G 11
South Thoresby. *Linc* 3D 88
South Tidworth. *Wilts* 2H 23
South Town. *Devn* 4C 12
South Town. *Hants* 3E 25
Southtown. *Norf* 5H 79
Southtown. *Orkn* 8D 172
Southwaite. *Cumb* 5F 113
South Walsham. *Norf* 4F 79
South Warnborough. *Hants* 2F 25
Southwater. *W Sus* 3C 26
Southwater Street. *W Sus* 3C 26
Southway. *Som* 2A 22
South Weald. *Essx* 1G 39
South Weirs. *Hants* 2A 16
Southwell. *Dors* 5B 14
Southwell. *Notts* 5D 86
South Weston. *Oxon* 2F 37
South Wheatley. *Corn* 3C 10
South Wheatley. *Notts* 2E 87
Southwick. *Hants* 2E 17
Southwick. *Nptn* 1H 63
Southwick. *Tyne* 4G 115
Southwick. *W Sus* 5D 26
Southwick. *Wilts* 1D 22
South Widcombe. *Bath* 1A 22
South Wigston. *Leics* 1C 62
South Willingham. *Linc* 2A 88
South Wingfield. *Derbs* 5A 86
South Witham. *Linc* 4G 75
Southwold. *Suff* 3H 67
South Wonston. *Hants* 3C 24
Southwood. *Norf* 5F 79
Southwood. *Som* 3A 22
South Woodham Ferrers.
Essx 1C 40
South Wootton. *Norf* 3F 77
South Wraxall. *Wilts* 5D 34
South Zeal. *Devn* 3G 11
Soval Lodge. *W Isl* 5F 171
Sowerby. *N Yor* 1G 99
Sowerby. *W Yor* 2A 92
Sowerby Bridge. *W Yor* 2A 92
Sowerby Row. *Cumb* 5E 113
Sower Carr. *Lanc* 5C 96
Sowley Green. *Suff* 5G 65
Sowood. *W Yor* 3A 92
Sowton. *Devn* 3C 12

Soyal—Stewarton

Soyal. *High* 4C 164
Soyland Town. *W Yor* 2A 92
Spacey Houses. *N Yor* 4F 99
Spa Common. *Norf* 2E 79
Spalding. *Linc* 3B 76
Spaldington. *E Yor* 1A 94
Spaldwick. *Cambs* 3A 64
Spalford. *Notts* 4F 87
Spanby. *Linc* 2H 75
Sparham. *Norf* 4C 78
Sparhamhill. *Norf* 4C 78
Spark Bridge. *Cumb* 1C 96
Sparket. *Cumb* 2F 103
Sparkford. *Som* 4B 22
Sparkwell. *Devn* 3B 8
Sparrow Green. *Norf* 4B 78
Sparrowpit. *Derbs* 2E 85
Sparrow's Green. *E Sus* 2H 27
Sparsholt. *Hants* 3C 24
Sparsholt. *Oxon* 3B 36
Spartylea. *Nmbd* 5B 114
Spath. *Staf* 2E 73
Spaunton. *N Yor* 1B 100
Spaxton. *Som* 3F 21
Spean Bridge. *High* 5E 149
Spear Hill. *W Sus* 4C 26
Speen. *Buck* 2G 37
Speen. *W Ber* 5C 36
Speeton. *N Yor* 2F 101
Speke. *Mers* 2G 83
Speldhurst. *Kent* 1G 27
Spellbrook. *Herts* 4E 53
Spelsbury. *Oxon* 3B 50
Spencers Wood. *Wok* 5F 37
Spennithorne. *N Yor* 1D 98
Spennymoor. *Dur* 1F 105
Spernall. *Warw* 4E 61
Spetchley. *Worc* 5C 60
Spetisbury. *Dors* 2E 15
Spexhall. *Suff* 2F 67
Speybank. *High* 3C 150
Spey Bay. *Mor* 2A 160
Speybridge. *High* 1E 151
Speyview. *Mor* 4G 159
Spilsby. *Linc* 4C 88
Spindlestone. *Nmbd* 1F 121
Spinkhill. *Derbs* 3B 86
Spinney Hills. *Leic* 5D 74
Spinningdale. *High* 5D 164
Spital. *Mers* 2F 83
Spitalhill. *Derbs* 1F 73
Spital in the Street. *Linc* 1G 87
Spithurst. *E Sus* 4F 27
Spittal. *Dum* 4A 110
Spittal. *E Lot* 2A 130
Spittal. *High* 3D 168
Spittal. *Nmbd* 4G 131
Spittal. *Pemb* 2D 43
Spittalfield. *Per* 4A 144
Spittal of Glenmuick. *Abers* 5H 151
Spittal of Glenshee. *Per* 1A 144
Spittal-on-Rule. *Bord* 3H 119
Spixworth. *Norf* 4E 79
Splatt. *Corn* 4C 10
Spofforth. *N Yor* 4F 99
Spondon. *Derb* 2B 74
Spon End. *W Mid* 3H 61
Spooner Row. *Norf* 1C 66
Sporle. *Norf* 4H 77
Spott. *E Lot* 2C 130
Spratton. *Nptn* 3E 62
Spreakley. *Surr* 2G 25
Spreyton. *Devn* 3H 11
Spridlington. *Linc* 2H 87
Springburn. *Glas* 3H 127
Springfield. *Dum* 3E 113
Springfield. *Fife* 2F 137
Springfield. *High* 2A 158
Springfield. *W Mid* 2E 61
Springhill. *Staf* 5D 73
Springholm. *Dum* 2F 111
Springside. *N Ayr* 1C 116
Springthorpe. *Linc* 2F 87
Spring Vale. *IOW* 3E 16
Spring Valley. *IOM* 4C 108
Springwell. *Tyne* 4F 115
Sproatley. *E Yor* 1E 95
Sproston Green. *Ches* 4B 84
Sprotbrough. *S Yor* 4F 93
Sproughton. *Suff* 1E 55
Sprouston. *Bord* 1B 120
Sprowston. *Norf* 4E 79
Sproxton. *Leics* 3F 75
Sproxton. *N Yor* 1A 100
Sprunston. *Cumb* 5E 113
Spurstow. *Ches* 5H 83
Squires Gate. *Bkpl* 1B 90
Sraid Ruadh. *Arg* 4A 138
Srannda. *W Isl* 9C 171
Sronphadruig Lodge. *Per* 1E 142
Sruth Mor. *W Isl* 2E 170
Stableford. *Shrp* 1B 60
Stackhouse. *N Yor* 3H 97
Stackpole. *Pemb* 5D 43
Stackpole Elidor. *Pemb* 5D 43
Stacksford. *Norf* 1C 66
Stacksteads. *Lanc* 2G 91
Staddiscombe. *Plym* 3B 8
Staddlethorpe. *E Yor* 2B 94
Staddon. *Devn* 2D 10
Staden. *Derbs* 3E 85
Stadhampton. *Oxon* 2E 36
Stadhlaigearraidh. *W Isl* 5C 170
Staffield. *Cumb* 5G 113
Staffin. *High* 2D 155
Stafford. *Staf* 3D 72
Stafford Park. *Telf* 5B 72
Stagden Cross. *Essx* 4G 53
Stagsden. *Beds* 1H 51
Stag's Head. *Devn* 4G 19
Stainburn. *Cumb* 2B 102
Stainburn. *N Yor* 5E 99
Stainby. *Linc* 3G 75
Staincliffe. *W Yor* 2C 92
Staincross. *S Yor* 3D 92
Staindrop. *Dur* 2E 105
Staines. *Surr* 3B 38
Stainfield. *Linc* 3H 75 (nr. Bourne)
Stainfield. *Linc* 3A 88 (nr. Lincoln)
Stainforth. *N Yor* 3H 97
Stainforth. *S Yor* 3G 93
Staining. *Lanc* 1B 90
Stainland. *W Yor* 3A 92
Stainsacre. *N Yor* 4G 107
Stainton. *Cumb* 4E 113 (nr. Carlisle)
Stainton. *Cumb* 1E 97 (nr. Kendal)
Stainton. *Cumb* 2F 103 (nr. Penrith)
Stainton. *Dur* 3D 104
Stainton. *Midd* 3B 106
Stainton. *N Yor* 5E 105
Stainton. *S Yor* 1C 86
Stainton by Langworth. *Linc* 3H 87
Staintondale. *N Yor* 5G 107
Stainton le Vale. *Linc* 1A 88
Stainton with Adgarley. *Cumb* 2B 96
Stair. *Cumb* 2D 102
Stair. *E Ayr* 2D 116
Staithes. *N Yor* 3E 107
Stakeford. *Nmbd* 1F 115
Stake Pool. *Lanc* 5D 96
Stakes. *Hants* 2E 17
Stalbridge. *Dors* 1C 14
Stalbridge Weston. *Dors* 1C 14
Stalham. *Norf* 3F 79
Stalham Green. *Norf* 3F 79
Stalisfield Green. *Kent* 5D 40
Stallen. *Dors* 1B 14
Stallingborough. *NE Lin* 3F 95
Stalling Busk. *N Yor* 1B 98
Stallington. *Staf* 2D 72
Stalmine. *Lanc* 5C 96
Stalybridge. *G Man* 1D 84
Stambourne. *Essx* 2H 53
Stamford. *Linc* 5H 75
Stamford. *Nmbd* 3G 121
Stamford Bridge. *Ches* 4G 83
Stamford Bridge. *E Yor* 4B 100
Stamfordham. *Nmbd* 2D 115
Stamperland. *E Ren* 4G 127
Stanah. *Lanc* 5C 96
Stanborough. *Herts* 4C 52
Stanbridge. *Beds* 3H 51
Stanbridge. *Dors* 2F 15
Stanbury. *W Yor* 1A 92
Stand. *N Lan* 3A 128
Standburn. *Falk* 2C 128
Standeford. *Staf* 5D 72
Standen. *Kent* 1C 28
Standen Street. *Kent* 2C 28
Standerwick. *Som* 1D 22
Standford. *Hants* 3G 25
Standford Bridge. *Telf* 3B 72
Standingstone. *Cumb* 5D 112
Standish. *Glos* 5D 48
Standish. *G Man* 3D 90
Standish Lower Ground. *G Man* 4D 90
Standlake. *Oxon* 5C 50
Standon. *Hants* 4C 24
Standon. *Herts* 3D 53
Standon. *Staf* 2C 72
Standon Green End. *Herts* 4D 52
Standwell Green. *Suff* 3D 66
Stane. *N Lan* 4B 128
Stanecastle. *N Ayr* 1C 116
Stanfield. *Norf* 3B 78
Stanford. *Beds* 1B 52
Stanford. *Kent* 2F 29
Stanford Bishop. *Here* 5A 60
Stanford Bridge. *Worc* 4B 60
Stanford Dingley. *W Ber* 4D 36
Stanford in the Vale. *Oxon* 2B 36
Stanford-le-Hope. *Thur* 2A 40
Stanford on Avon. *Nptn* 3C 62
Stanford on Soar. *Notts* 3C 74
Stanford on Teme. *Worc* 4B 60
Stanford Rivers. *Essx* 5F 53
Stanfree. *Derbs* 3B 86
Stanghow. *Red C* 3D 107
Stanground. *Pet* 1B 64
Stanhoe. *Norf* 2H 77
Stanhope. *Dur* 1C 104
Stanhope. *Bord* 1D 118
Stanion. *Nptn* 2G 63
Stanley. *Derbs* 1B 74
Stanley. *Dur* 4E 115
Stanley. *Per* 5A 144
Stanley. *Shrp* 2B 60
Stanley. *Staf* 5D 84
Stanley. *W Yor* 2D 92
Stanley Common. *Derbs* 1B 74
Stanley Crook. *Dur* 1E 105
Stanley Hill. *Here* 1B 48
Stanlow. *Ches* 3G 83
Stanmer. *Brig* 5E 27
Stanmore. *G Lon* 1C 38
Stanmore. *Hants* 4C 24
Stanmore. *W Ber* 4C 36
Stannersburn. *Nmbd* 1A 114
Stanningfield. *Suff* 5A 66
Stannington. *Nmbd* 2F 115
Stannington. *S Yor* 2H 85
Stansbatch. *Here* 4F 59
Stansfield. *Suff* 5G 65
Stanshope. *Staf* 5F 85
Stanstead. *Suff* 1B 54
Stanstead Abbotts. *Herts* 4D 53
Stansted. *Kent* 4H 39
Stansted (London) Airport. *Essx* 3F 53
Stansted Mountfitchet. *Essx* 3F 53
Stanthorne. *Ches* 4A 84
Stanton. *Derbs* 4G 73
Stanton. *Glos* 2F 49
Stanton. *Nmbd* 5F 121
Stanton. *Staf* 1F 73
Stanton. *Suff* 3B 66
Stanton by Bridge. *Derbs* 3A 74
Stanton by Dale. *Derbs* 2B 74
Stanton Chare. *Suff* 3B 66
Stanton Drew. *Bath* 5A 34
Stanton Fitzwarren. *Swin* 2G 35
Stanton Harcourt. *Oxon* 5C 50
Stanton Hill. *Notts* 4B 86
Stanton in Peak. *Derbs* 4G 85
Stanton Lacy. *Shrp* 3G 59
Stanton Long. *Shrp* 1H 59
Stanton-on-the-Wolds. *Notts* 2D 74
Stanton Prior. *Bath* 5B 34
Stanton St Bernard. *Wilts* 5F 35
Stanton St John. *Oxon* 5D 50
Stanton St Quintin. *Wilts* 4E 35
Stanton Street. *Suff* 4B 66
Stanton under Bardon. *Leics* 4B 74
Stanton upon Hine Heath. *Shrp* 3H 71
Stanton Wick. *Bath* 5B 34
Stanwardine in the Fields. *Shrp* 3G 71
Stanwardine in the Wood. *Shrp* 3G 71
Stanway. *Essx* 3C 54
Stanway. *Glos* 2F 49
Stanwell. *Surr* 3B 38
Stanwell Moor. *Surr* 3B 38
Stanwick. *Nptn* 3G 63
Staoinebrig. *W Isl* 5C 170
Stape. *N Yor* 5E 107
Stapehill. *Dors* 2F 15
Stapeley. *Ches* 1A 72
Stapenhill. *Staf* 3G 73
Staple. *Kent* 5G 41
Staple Cross. *Devn* 4D 20
Staplecross. *E Sus* 3B 28
Staplefield. *W Sus* 3D 27
Staple Fitzpaine. *Som* 1F 13
Stapleford. *Cambs* 5D 64
Stapleford. *Derbs* 2B 74
Stapleford. *Herts* 4D 52
Stapleford. *Leics* 4F 75
Stapleford. *Linc* 5F 87
Stapleford. *Wilts* 3F 23
Stapleford Abbotts. *Essx* 1G 39
Stapleford Tawney. *Essx* 1G 39
Staplegrove. *Som* 4F 21
Staplehay. *Som* 4F 21
Staple Hill. *S Glo* 4B 34
Staplehurst. *Kent* 1B 28
Staplers. *IOW* 4D 16
Stapleton. *Bris* 4B 34
Stapleton. *Cumb* 2G 113
Stapleton. *Here* 4F 59
Stapleton. *Leics* 1B 62
Stapleton. *N Yor* 3F 105
Stapleton. *Shrp* 5G 71
Stapleton. *Som* 4H 21
Stapley. *Som* 1E 13
Staploe. *Beds* 4A 64
Staplow. *Here* 1B 48
Star. *Fife* 3F 137
Star. *Pemb* 1G 43
Starbeck. *N Yor* 4F 99
Starbotton. *N Yor* 2B 98
Starcross. *Devn* 4C 12
Stareton. *Warw* 3H 61
Starkholmes. *Derbs* 5H 85
Starling. *G Man* 3F 91
Starling's Green. *Essx* 2E 53
Starston. *Norf* 2E 67
Start. *Devn* 4E 9
Startforth. *Dur* 3D 104
Start Hill. *Essx* 3F 53
Startley. *Wilts* 3E 35
Stathe. *Som* 4G 21
Stathern. *Leics* 2E 75
Station Town. *Dur* 1B 106
Staughton Green. *Cambs* 4A 64
Staughton Highway. *Cambs* 4A 64
Staunton. *Glos* 3C 48 (nr. Cheltenham)
Staunton. *Glos* 4A 48 (nr. Monmouth)
Staunton in the Vale. *Notts* 1F 75
Staunton on Arrow. *Here* 4F 59
Staunton on Wye. *Here* 1G 47
Staveley. *Cumb* 5F 103
Staveley. *Derbs* 3B 86
Staveley. *N Yor* 3F 99
Staveley-in-Cartmel. *Cumb* 1C 96
Staverton. *Devn* 2D 9
Staverton. *Glos* 3D 49
Staverton. *Nptn* 4C 62
Staverton. *Wilts* 5D 34
Stawell. *Som* 3G 21
Stawley. *Som* 4D 20
Staxigoe. *High* 3F 169
Staxton. *N Yor* 2E 101
Staylittle. *Powy* 1A 58
Staynall. *Lanc* 5C 96
Staythorpe. *Notts* 5E 87
Stean. *N Yor* 2C 98
Stearsby. *N Yor* 2A 100
Steart. *Som* 2F 21
Stebbing. *Essx* 3G 53
Stebbing Green. *Essx* 3G 53
Stedham. *W Sus* 4G 25
Steel. *Nmbd* 4C 114
Steel Cross. *E Sus* 2G 27
Steelend. *Fife* 4C 136
Steele Road. *Bord* 5H 119
Steel Heath. *Shrp* 2H 71
Steen's Bridge. *Here* 5H 59
Steep. *Hants* 4F 25
Steep Lane. *W Yor* 2A 92
Steeple. *Dors* 4E 15
Steeple. *Essx* 5C 54
Steeple Ashton. *Wilts* 1E 23
Steeple Aston. *Oxon* 3C 50
Steeple Barton. *Oxon* 3C 50
Steeple Bumpstead. *Essx* 1G 53
Steeple Claydon. *Buck* 3E 51
Steeple Gidding. *Cambs* 2A 64
Steeple Langford. *Wilts* 3F 23
Steeple Morden. *Cambs* 1C 52
Steeton. *W Yor* 5C 98
Stein. *High* 3B 154
Steinmanhill. *Abers* 4E 161
Stelling Minnis. *Kent* 1F 29
Stembridge. *Som* 4H 21
Stemster. *High* 2D 169 (nr. Halkirk)
Stemster. *High* 2C 168 (nr. Westfield)
Stenalees. *Corn* 3E 6
Stenhill. *Devn* 1D 12
Stenhouse. *Edin* 2F 129
Stenhousemuir. *Falk* 1B 128
Stenigot. *Linc* 2B 88
Stenscholl. *High* 2D 155
Stenso. *Orkn* 5C 172
Stenson. *Derbs* 3H 73
Stenson Fields. *Derbs* 2H 73
Stenton. *E Lot* 2C 130
Stenwith. *Linc* 2F 75
Steòrnabhagh. *W Isl* 4G 171
Stepaside. *Pemb* 4F 43
Stepford. *Dum* 1F 111
Stepney. *G Lon* 2E 39
Steppingley. *Beds* 2A 52
Stepps. *N Lan* 3H 127
Sterndale Moor. *Derbs* 4F 85
Sternfield. *Suff* 4F 67
Stert. *Wilts* 1F 23
Stetchworth. *Cambs* 5F 65
Stevenage. *Herts* 3C 52
Stevenston. *N Ayr* 5D 126
Steventon. *Hants* 2D 24
Steventon. *Oxon* 2C 36
Stevington. *Beds* 5G 63
Stevington End. *Cambs* 1G 53
Stewartby. *Beds* 1A 52
Stewarton. *Arg* 4A 122

Stewarton. *E Ayr* 5F 127
Stewkley. *Buck* 3G 51
Stewkley Dean. *Buck* 3G 51
Stewley. *Som* 1G 13
Stewton. *Linc* 2C 88
Steyning. *W Sus* 4C 26
Steynton. *Pemb* 4D 42
Stibb. *Corn* 1C 10
Stibbard. *Norf* 3B 78
Stibb Cross. *Devn* 1E 11
Stibb Green. *Wilts* 5H 35
Stibbington. *Cambs* 1H 63
Stichill. *Bord* 1B 120
Sticker. *Corn* 3D 6
Stickford. *Linc* 4C 88
Sticklepath. *Devn* 3G 11
Sticklinch. *Som* 3A 22
Stickling Green. *Essx* 2E 53
Stickney. *Linc* 5C 88
Stiffkey. *Norf* 1B 78
Stifford's Bridge. *Here* 1C 48
Stileway. *Som* 2H 21
Stillingfleet. *N Yor* 5H 99
Stillington. *N Yor* 3H 99
Stillington. *Stoc T* 2A 106
Stilton. *Cambs* 2A 64
Stinchcombe. *Glos* 2C 34
Stinsford. *Dors* 3C 14
Stiperstones. *Shrp* 5F 71
Stirchley. *Telf* 5B 72
Stirchley. *W Mid* 2E 61
Stirling. *Abers* 4H 161
Stirling. *Stir* 4G 135
Stirton. *N Yor* 4B 98
Stisted. *Essx* 3A 54
Stitchcombe. *Wilts* 5H 35
Stithians. *Corn* 5B 6
Stittenham. *High* 1A 158
Stivichall. *W Mid* 3H 61
Stixwould. *Linc* 4A 88
Stoak. *Ches* 3G 83
Stobo. *Bord* 1D 118
Stobo Castle. *Bord* 1D 118
Stoborough. *Dors* 4E 15
Stoborough Green. *Dors* 4E 15
Stobs Castle. *Bord* 4H 119
Stobswood. *Nmbd* 5G 121
Stock. *Essx* 1A 40
Stockbridge. *Hants* 3B 24
Stockbridge. *W Yor* 5C 98
Stockbury. *Kent* 4C 40
Stockcross. *W Ber* 5C 36
Stockdalewath. *Cumb* 5E 113
Stocker's Head. *Kent* 5D 40
Stockerston. *Leics* 1F 63
Stock Green. *Worc* 5D 61
Stocking. *Here* 2B 48
Stockingford. *Warw* 1H 61
Stocking Green. *Essx* 2F 53
Stocking Pelham. *Herts* 3E 53
Stockland. *Devn* 2F 13
Stockland Bristol. *Som* 2F 21
Stockleigh English. *Devn* 2B 12
Stockleigh Pomeroy. *Devn* 2B 12
Stockley. *Wilts* 5F 35
Stocklinch. *Som* 1G 13
Stockport. *G Man* 2D 84
Stocksbridge. *S Yor* 1G 85
Stocksfield. *Nmbd* 3D 114
Stocks, The. *Kent* 3D 28
Stockstreet. *Essx* 3B 54
Stockton. *Here* 4H 59
Stockton. *Norf* 1F 67
Stockton. *Shrp* 1B 60
(nr. Bridgnorth)
Stockton. *Shrp* 5E 71
(nr. Chirbury)
Stockton. *Telf* 4B 72
Stockton. *Warw* 4B 62
Stockton. *Wilts* 3E 23
Stockton Brook. *Staf* 5D 84
Stockton Cross. *Here* 4H 59
Stockton Heath. *Warr* 2A 84
Stockton-on-Tees. *Stoc T* 3B 106
Stockton on Teme. *Worc* 4B 60
Stockton-on-the-Forest. *York* 4A 100
Stockwell Heath. *Staf* 3E 73
Stockwood. *Bris* 5B 34
Stock Wood. *Worc* 5E 61
Stodmarsh. *Kent* 4G 41
Stody. *Norf* 2C 78
Stoer. *High* 1E 163
Stoford. *Som* 1A 14
Stoford. *Wilts* 3F 23
Stogumber. *Som* 3D 20
Stogursey. *Som* 2F 21
Stoke. *Devn* 4C 18
Stoke. *Hants* 1C 24
(nr. Andover)
Stoke. *Hants* 2F 17
(nr. South Hayling)
Stoke. *Medw* 3C 40
Stoke. *W Mid* 3A 62
Stoke Abbott. *Dors* 2H 13
Stoke Albany. *Nptn* 2F 63
Stoke Ash. *Suff* 3D 66
Stoke Bardolph. *Notts* 1D 74
Stoke Bliss. *Worc* 4A 60
Stoke Bruerne. *Nptn* 1F 51
Stoke by Clare. *Suff* 1H 53
Stoke-by-Nayland. *Suff* 2C 54
Stoke Canon. *Devn* 3C 12
Stoke Charity. *Hants* 3C 24
Stoke Climsland. *Corn* 5D 10
Stoke Cross. *Here* 5A 60
Stoke D'Abernon. *Surr* 5C 38
Stoke Doyle. *Nptn* 2H 63
Stoke Dry. *Rut* 1F 63
Stoke Edith. *Here* 1B 48
Stoke Farthing. *Wilts* 4F 23
Stoke Ferry. *Norf* 1G 65
Stoke Fleming. *Devn* 4E 9
Stokeford. *Dors* 4D 14
Stoke Gabriel. *Devn* 3E 9
Stoke Gifford. *S Glo* 4B 34
Stoke Golding. *Leics* 1A 62
Stoke Goldington. *Mil* 1G 51
Stokeham. *Notts* 3E 87
Stoke Hammond. *Buck* 3G 51
Stoke Heath. *Shrp* 3A 72
Stoke Holy Cross. *Norf* 5E 79
Stokeinteignhead. *Devn* 5C 12
Stoke Lacy. *Here* 1B 48
Stoke Lyne. *Oxon* 3D 50
Stoke Mandeville. *Buck* 4G 51
Stokenchurch. *Buck* 2F 37
Stoke Newington. *G Lon* 2E 39
Stokenham. *Devn* 4E 9
Stoke on Tern. *Shrp* 3A 72
Stoke-on-Trent. *Stoke* 1C 72
Stoke Orchard. *Glos* 3E 49
Stoke Pero. *Som* 2B 20
Stoke Poges. *Buck* 2A 38
Stoke Prior. *Here* 5H 59
Stoke Prior. *Worc* 4D 60
Stoke Rivers. *Devn* 3G 19
Stoke Rochford. *Linc* 3G 75
Stoke Row. *Oxon* 3E 37
Stoke St Gregory. *Som* 4G 21
Stoke St Mary. *Som* 4F 21
Stoke St Michael. *Som* 2B 22
Stoke St Milborough. *Shrp* 2H 59
Stokesay. *Shrp* 2G 59
Stokesby. *Norf* 4G 79
Stokesley. *N Yor* 4C 106
Stoke sub Hamdon. *Som* 1H 13
Stoke Talmage. *Oxon* 2E 37
Stoke Trister. *Som* 4C 22
Stoke-upon-Trent. *Stoke* 1C 72
Stoke Wake. *Dors* 2C 14
Stolford. *Som* 2F 21
Stondon Massey. *Essx* 5F 53
Stone. *Buck* 4F 51
Stone. *Glos* 2B 34
Stone. *Kent* 3G 39
Stone. *Som* 3A 22
Stone. *Staf* 2D 72
Stone. *Worc* 3C 60
Stonea. *Cambs* 1D 64
Stoneacton. *Shrp* 1H 59
Stone Allerton. *Som* 1H 21
Ston Easton. *Som* 1B 22
Stonebridge. *N Som* 1G 21
Stonebridge. *Som* 2C 22
Stonebridge. *Surr* 1C 26
Stone Bridge Corner. *Pet* 5B 76
Stonebroom. *Derbs* 5B 86
Stonebyres. *S Lan* 5B 128
Stone Chair. *W Yor* 2B 92
Stone Cross. *E Sus* 5H 27
Stone Cross. *Kent* 2G 27
Stone-edge-Batch. *N Som* 4H 33
Stoneferry. *Hull* 1D 94
Stonefield. *Arg* 5D 140
Stonefield. *S Lan* 4H 127
Stonegate. *E Sus* 3A 28
Stonegate. *N Yor* 4E 107
Stonegrave. *N Yor* 2A 100
Stonehall. *Worc* 1D 49
Stonehaugh. *Nmbd* 2A 114
Stonehaven. *Abers* 5F 153
Stone Heath. *Staf* 2D 72
Stone Hill. *Kent* 2E 29
Stone House. *Cumb* 1G 97
Stonehouse. *Glos* 5D 48
Stonehouse. *Nmbd* 4H 113
Stonehouse. *S Lan* 5A 128
Stone in Oxney. *Kent* 3D 28
Stoneleigh. *Warw* 3H 61
Stoneley Green. *Ches* 5A 84
Stonely. *Cambs* 4A 64
Stonepits. *Worc* 5E 61
Stoner Hill. *Hants* 4F 25
Stonesby. *Leics* 3F 75
Stonesfield. *Oxon* 4B 50
Stones Green. *Essx* 3E 55
Stone Street. *Kent* 5G 39
Stone Street. *Suff* 2C 54
(nr. Boxford)
Stone Street. *Suff* 2F 67
(nr. Halesworth)
Stonethwaite. *Cumb* 3D 102
Stoneyburn. *W Lot* 3C 128
Stoney Cross. *Hants* 1A 16
Stoneyford. *Devn* 2D 12
Stoneygate. *Leic* 5D 74
Stoneyhills. *Essx* 1D 40
Stoneykirk. *Dum* 4F 109
Stoney Middleton. *Derbs* 3G 85
Stoney Stanton. *Leics* 1B 62
Stoney Stoke. *Som* 3C 22
Stoney Stratton. *Som* 3B 22
Stoney Stretton. *Shrp* 5F 71
Stoneywood. *Aber* 2F 153
Stonham Aspal. *Suff* 5D 66
Stonnall. *Staf* 5E 73
Stonor. *Oxon* 3F 37
Stonton Wyville. *Leics* 1E 63
Stonybreck. *Shet* 1B 172
Stony Cross. *Devn* 4F 19
Stony Cross. *Here* 1C 48
(nr. Great Malvern)
Stony Cross. *Here* 4H 59
(nr. Leominster)
Stony Houghton. *Derbs* 4B 86
Stony Stratford. *Mil* 1F 51
Stoodleigh. *Devn* 3G 19
(nr. Barnstaple)
Stoodleigh. *Devn* 1C 12
(nr. Tiverton)
Stopham. *W Sus* 4B 26
Stopsley. *Lutn* 3B 52
Stoptide. *Corn* 1D 6
Storeton. *Mers* 2F 83
Stormontfield. *Per* 1D 136
Stornoway. *W Isl* 4G 171
Stornoway Airport. *W Isl* 4G 171
Storridge. *Here* 1C 48
Storrington. *W Sus* 4B 26
Storrs. *Cumb* 5E 103
Storth. *Cumb* 1D 97
Storwood. *E Yor* 5B 100
Stotfield. *Mor* 1G 159
Stotfold. *Beds* 2C 52
Stottesdon. *Shrp* 2A 60
Stoughton. *Leics* 5D 74
Stoughton. *Surr* 5A 38
Stoughton. *W Sus* 1G 17
Stoul. *High* 4F 147
Stoulton. *Worc* 1E 49
Stourbridge. *W Mid* 2C 60
Stourpaine. *Dors* 2D 14
Stourport-on-Severn. *Worc* 3C 60
Stour Provost. *Dors* 4C 22
Stour Row. *Dors* 4D 22
Stourton. *Staf* 2C 60
Stourton. *Warw* 2A 50
Stourton. *W Yor* 1D 92
Stourton. *Wilts* 3C 22
Stourton Caundle. *Dors* 1C 14
Stoven. *Suff* 2G 67
Stow. *Linc* 2H 75
(nr. Billingborough)
Stow. *Linc* 2F 87
(nr. Gainsborough)
Stow. *Bord* 5A 130
Stow Bardolph. *Norf* 5F 77
Stow Bedon. *Norf* 1B 66
Stowbridge. *Norf* 5F 77
Stow cum Quy. *Cambs* 4E 65
Stowe. *Glos* 5A 48
Stowe. *Shrp* 3F 59
Stowe. *Staf* 4F 73
Stowe-by-Chartley. *Staf* 3E 73
Stowell. *Som* 4B 22
Stowey. *Bath* 1A 22
Stowford. *Devn* 4D 12
(nr. Exmouth)
Stowford. *Devn* 4E 11
(nr. Tavistock)
Stowlangtoft. *Suff* 4B 66
Stow Longa. *Cambs* 3A 64
Stow Maries. *Essx* 1C 40
Stowmarket. *Suff* 5C 66
Stow-on-the-Wold. *Glos* 3G 49
Stowting. *Kent* 1F 29
Stowupland. *Suff* 5C 66
Straad. *Arg* 3B 126
Strachan. *Abers* 4D 152
Stradbroke. *Suff* 3E 67
Stradbrook. *Wilts* 1E 23
Stradishall. *Suff* 5G 65
Stradsett. *Norf* 5F 77
Stragglethorpe. *Linc* 5G 87
Stragglethorpe. *Notts* 2D 74
Straid. *S Ayr* 5A 116
Straight Soley. *Wilts* 4B 36
Straiton. *Edin* 3F 129
Straiton. *S Ayr* 4C 116
Straloch. *Per* 2H 143
Stramshall. *Staf* 2E 73
Strang. *IOM* 4C 108
Strangford. *Here* 3A 48
Stranraer. *Dum* 3F 109
Strata Florida. *Cdgn* 4G 57
Stratfield Mortimer. *W Ber* 5E 37
Stratfield Saye. *Hants* 5E 37
Stratfield Turgis. *Hants* 1E 25
Stratford. *Glos* 2D 49
Stratford. *G Lon* 2E 39
Stratford St Andrew. *Suff* 4F 67
Stratford St Mary. *Suff* 2D 54
Stratford sub Castle. *Wilts* 3G 23
Stratford Tony. *Wilts* 4F 23
Stratford-upon-Avon. *Warw* 5G 61
Strath. *High* 1G 155
(nr. Gairloch)
Strath. *High* 3E 169
(nr. Wick)
Strathan. *High* 4B 148
(nr. Fort William)
Strathan. *High* 1E 163
(nr. Lochinver)
Strathan. *High* 2F 167
(nr. Tongue)
Strathan Skerray. *High* 2G 167
Strathaven. *S Lan* 5A 128
Strathblane. *Stir* 2G 127
Strathcanaird. *High* 3F 163
Strathcarron. *High* 4B 156
Strathcoil. *Arg* 5A 140
Strathdon. *Abers* 2A 152
Strathkinness. *Fife* 2G 137
Strathmashie House. *High* 4H 149
Strathmiglo. *Fife* 2E 136
Strathmore Lodge. *High* 4D 168
Strathpeffer. *High* 3G 157
Strathrannoch. *High* 1F 157
Strathtay. *Per* 3G 143
Strathvaich Lodge. *High* 1F 157
Strathwhillan. *N Ayr* 2E 123
Strathy. *High* 1A 158
(nr. Invergordon)
Strathy. *High* 2A 168
(nr. Melvich)
Strathyre. *Stir* 2E 135
Stratton. *Corn* 2C 10
Stratton. *Dors* 3B 14
Stratton. *Glos* 5F 49
Stratton Audley. *Oxon* 3E 50
Stratton-on-the-Fosse. *Som* 1B 22
Stratton St Margaret. *Swin* 3G 35
Stratton St Michael. *Norf* 1E 66
Stratton Strawless. *Norf* 3E 78
Stravithie. *Fife* 2H 137
Stream. *Som* 3D 20
Streat. *E Sus* 4E 27
Streatham. *G Lon* 3D 39
Streatley. *Beds* 3A 52
Streatley. *W Ber* 3D 36
Street. *Corn* 3C 10
Street. *Lanc* 4E 97
Street. *N Yor* 4E 107
Street. *Som* 2G 13
(nr. Chard)
Street. *Som* 3H 21
(nr. Glastonbury)
Street Dinas. *Shrp* 2F 71
Street End. *Kent* 5F 41
Street End. *W Sus* 3G 17
Street Gate. *Tyne* 4F 115
Streethay. *Staf* 4F 73
Streethouse. *W Yor* 3D 93
Streetlam. *N Yor* 5A 106
Street Lane. *Derbs* 1A 74
Streetly. *W Mid* 1E 61
Streetly End. *Cambs* 1G 53
Street on the Fosse. *Som* 3B 22
Strefford. *Shrp* 2G 59
Strelley. *Notts* 1C 74
Strensall. *York* 3A 100
Strensall Camp. *York* 4A 100
Stretcholt. *Som* 2F 21
Strete. *Devn* 4E 9
Stretford. *G Man* 1C 84
Stretford. *Here* 5H 59
Strethall. *Essx* 2E 53
Stretham. *Cambs* 3E 65
Stretton. *Ches* 5G 83
Stretton. *Derbs* 4A 86
Stretton. *Rut* 4G 75
Stretton. *Staf* 4C 72
(nr. Brewood)
Stretton. *Staf* 3G 73
(nr. Burton upon Trent)
Stretton. *Warr* 2A 84
Stretton en le Field. *Leics* 4H 73
Stretton Grandison. *Here* 1B 48
Stretton Heath. *Shrp* 4F 71
Stretton-on-Dunsmore. *Warw* 3B 62
Stretton-on-Fosse. *Warw* 2H 49
Stretton Sugwas. *Here* 1H 47
Stretton under Fosse. *Warw* 2B 62
Stretton Westwood. *Shrp* 1H 59
Strichen. *Abers* 3G 161
Strines. *G Man* 2D 84
Stringston. *Som* 2E 21
Strixton. *Nptn* 4G 63
Stroanfreggan. *Dum* 5F 117

Stroat. *Glos* 2A 34
Stromeferry. *High* 5A 156
Stromemore. *High* 5A 156
Stromness. *Orkn* 7B 172
Stronachie. *Per* 3C 136
Stronachlachar. *Stir* 2D 134
Stronchreggan. *High* 1E 141
Strone. *Arg* 1C 126
Strone. *High* 1H 149
(nr. Drumnadrochit)
Strone. *High* 3B 150
(nr. Kingussie)
Stronenaba. *High* 5E 148
Stronmilchan. *Arg* 1A 134
Stronsay Airport. *Orkn* 5F 172
Strontian. *High* 2C 140
Strood. *Kent* 2C 28
Strood. *Medw* 4B 40
Strood Green. *Surr* 1D 26
Strood Green. *W Sus* 3B 26
(nr. Billingshurst)
Strood Green. *W Sus* 2C 26
(nr. Horsham)
Strothers Dale. *Nmbd* 4C 114
Stroud. *Glos* 5D 48
Stroud. *Hants* 4F 25
Stroud Green. *Essx* 1C 40
Stroxton. *Linc* 2G 75
Struan. *High* 5C 154
Struan. *Per* 2F 143
Struanmore. *High* 5C 154
Strubby. *Linc* 2D 88
Strugg's Hill. *Linc* 2B 76
Strumpshaw. *Norf* 5F 79
Strutherhill. *S Lan* 4A 128
Struy. *High* 5F 157
Stryd. *IOA* 2B 80
Stryt-issa. *Wrex* 1E 71
Stuartfield. *Abers* 4G 161
Stubbington. *Hants* 2D 16
Stubbins. *Lanc* 3F 91
Stubble Green. *Cumb* 5B 102
Stubb's Cross. *Kent* 2D 28
Stubbs Green. *Norf* 1F 67
Stubhampton. *Dors* 1E 15
Stubton. *Linc* 1F 75
Stubwood. *Staf* 2E 73
Stuckton. *Hants* 1G 15
Studham. *Beds* 4A 52
Studland. *Dors* 4F 15
Studley. *Warw* 4E 61
Studley. *Wilts* 4E 35
Studley Roger. *N Yor* 3E 99
Stuntney. *Cambs* 3E 65
Stunts Green. *E Sus* 4H 27
Sturbridge. *Staf* 2C 72
Sturgate. *Linc* 2F 87
Sturmer. *Essx* 1G 53
Sturminster Marshall. *Dors* 2E 15
Sturminster Newton. *Dors* 1C 14
Sturry. *Kent* 4F 41
Sturton. *N Lin* 4C 94
Sturton by Stow. *Linc* 2F 87
Sturton le Steeple. *Notts* 2E 87
Stuston. *Suff* 3D 66
Stutton. *N Yor* 5G 99
Stutton. *Suff* 2E 55
Styal. *Ches* 2C 84
Stydd. *Lanc* 1E 91
Styrrup. *Notts* 1D 86
Suainebost. *W Isl* 1H 171
Suardail. *W Isl* 4G 171
Succoth. *Abers* 5B 160
Succoth. *Arg* 3B 134
Suckley. *Worc* 5B 60
Suckley Knowl. *Worc* 5B 60
Sudborough. *Nptn* 2G 63
Sudbourne. *Suff* 5G 67
Sudbrook. *Linc* 1G 75
Sudbrook. *Mon* 3A 34
Sudbrooke. *Linc* 3H 87
Sudbury. *Derbs* 2F 73
Sudbury. *Suff* 1B 54
Sudgrove. *Glos* 5E 49
Suffield. *Norf* 2E 79
Suffield. *N Yor* 5G 107
Sugnall. *Staf* 2B 72
Sugwas Pool. *Here* 1H 47
Suisnish. *High* 5E 155
Sulaisiadar. *W Isl* 4H 171
Sulby. *IOM* 2C 108
Sulgrave. *Nptn* 1D 50
Sulham. *W Ber* 4E 37
Sulhamstead. *W Ber* 5E 37
Sullington. *W Sus* 4B 26
Sullom. *Shet* 4E 173
Sully. *V Glam* 5E 33
Sumburgh. *Shet* 10F 173
Sumburgh Airport. *Shet* 10E 173
Summer Bridge. *N Yor* 3E 98
Summercourt. *Corn* 3C 6
Summerfield. *Norf* 2G 77
Summergangs. *Hull* 1E 95
Summerhill. *Aber* 3G 153
Summerhill. *Pemb* 4F 43
Summer Hill. *W Mid* 1D 60
Summerhouse. *Darl* 3F 105
Summersdale. *W Sus* 2G 17
Summerseat. *G Man* 3F 91
Summit. *G Man* 3H 91
Sunbury. *Surr* 4C 38
Sunderland. *Cumb* 1C 102
Sunderland. *Lanc* 4D 96
Sunderland. *Tyne* 4G 115
Sunderland Bridge. *Dur* 1F 105
Sundon Park. *Lutn* 3A 52
Sundridge. *Kent* 5F 39
Sunk Island. *E Yor* 3F 95
Sunningdale. *Wind* 4A 38
Sunninghill. *Wind* 4A 38
Sunningwell. *Oxon* 5C 50
Sunniside. *Dur* 1E 105
Sunniside. *Tyne* 4F 115
Sunny Bank. *Cumb* 5D 102
Sunny Hill. *Derb* 2H 73
Sunnyhurst. *Bkbn* 2E 91
Sunnylaw. *Stir* 4G 135
Sunnymead. *Oxon* 5D 50
Sunnyside. *S Yor* 1B 86
Sunnyside. *W Sus* 2E 27
Sunton. *Wilts* 1H 23
Surbiton. *G Lon* 4C 38
Surby. *IOM* 4B 108
Surfleet. *Linc* 3B 76
Surfleet Seas End. *Linc* 3B 76
Surlingham. *Norf* 5F 79
Surrex. *Essx* 3B 54
Sustead. *Norf* 2D 78
Susworth. *Linc* 4B 94
Sutcombe. *Devn* 1D 10
Suton. *Norf* 1C 66
Sutors of Cromarty. *High* 2C 158
Sutterby. *Linc* 3C 88
Sutterton. *Linc* 2B 76
Sutterton Dowdyke. *Linc* 2B 76
Sutton. *Beds* 1C 52
Sutton. *Buck* 3B 38
Sutton. *Cambs* 3D 64
Sutton. *E Sus* 5F 27
Sutton. *G Lon* 4D 38
Sutton. *Kent* 1H 29
Sutton. *Norf* 3F 79
Sutton. *Notts* 2E 75
Sutton. *Oxon* 5C 50
Sutton. *Pemb* 3D 42
Sutton. *Pet* 1H 63
Sutton. *Shrp* 2B 60
(nr. Bridgnorth)
Sutton. *Shrp* 2A 72
(nr. Market Drayton)
Sutton. *Shrp* 3F 71
(nr. Oswestry)
Sutton. *Shrp* 4H 71
(nr. Shrewsbury)
Sutton. *Som* 3B 22
Sutton. *S Yor* 3F 93
Sutton. *Staf* 3B 72
Sutton. *Suff* 1G 55
Sutton. *W Sus* 4A 26
Sutton. *Worc* 4A 60
Sutton Abinger. *Surr* 1C 26
Sutton at Hone. *Kent* 4G 39
Sutton Bassett. *Nptn* 1E 63
Sutton Benger. *Wilts* 4E 35
Sutton Bingham. *Som* 1A 14
Sutton Bonington. *Notts* 3C 74
Sutton Bridge. *Linc* 3D 76
Sutton Cheney. *Leics* 5B 74
Sutton Coldfield. *W Mid* 1F 61
Sutton Corner. *Linc* 3D 76
Sutton Courtenay. *Oxon* 2D 36
Sutton Crosses. *Linc* 3D 76
Sutton cum Lound. *Notts* 2D 86
Sutton Gault. *Cambs* 3D 64
Sutton Grange. *N Yor* 2E 99
Sutton Green. *Surr* 5B 38
Sutton Howgrave. *N Yor* 2F 99
Sutton in Ashfield. *Notts* 5B 86
Sutton-in-Craven. *N Yor* 5C 98
Sutton Ings. *Hull* 1E 94
Sutton in the Elms. *Leics* 1C 62
Sutton Lane Ends. *Ches* 3D 84
Sutton Leach. *Mers* 1H 83
Sutton Maddock. *Shrp* 5B 72
Sutton Mallet. *Som* 3G 21
Sutton Mandeville. *Wilts* 4E 23
Sutton Montis. *Som* 4B 22
Sutton-on-Hull. *Hull* 1E 94
Sutton on Sea. *Linc* 2E 89
Sutton-on-the-Forest. *N Yor* 3H 99
Sutton on the Hill. *Derbs* 2G 73
Sutton on Trent. *Notts* 4E 87
Sutton Poyntz. *Dors* 4C 14
Sutton St Edmund. *Linc* 4C 76
Sutton St Edmund's Common. *Linc* 5C 76
Sutton St James. *Linc* 4C 76
Sutton St Michael. *Here* 1A 48
Sutton St Nicholas. *Here* 1A 48
Sutton Scarsdale. *Derbs* 4B 86
Sutton Scotney. *Hants* 3C 24
Sutton-under-Brailes. *Warw* 2B 50
Sutton-under-Whitestonecliffe. *N Yor* 1G 99
Sutton upon Derwent. *E Yor* 5B 100
Sutton Valence. *Kent* 1C 28
Sutton Veny. *Wilts* 2E 23
Sutton Waldron. *Dors* 1D 14
Sutton Weaver. *Ches* 3H 83
Swaby. *Linc* 3C 88
Swadlincote. *Derbs* 4G 73
Swaffham. *Norf* 5H 77
Swaffham Bulbeck. *Cambs* 4E 65
Swaffham Prior. *Cambs* 4E 65
Swafield. *Norf* 2E 79
Swainby. *N Yor* 4B 106
Swainshill. *Here* 1H 47
Swainsthorpe. *Norf* 5E 78
Swainswick. *Bath* 5C 34
Swalcliffe. *Oxon* 2B 50
Swalecliffe. *Kent* 4F 41
Swallow. *Linc* 4E 95
Swallow Beck. *Linc* 4G 87
Swallowcliffe. *Wilts* 4E 23
Swallowfield. *Wok* 5F 37
Swallownest. *S Yor* 2B 86
Swampton. *Hants* 1C 24
Swanage. *Dors* 5F 15
Swanbourne. *Buck* 3G 51
Swanbridge. *V Glam* 5E 33
Swan Green. *Ches* 3B 84
Swanland. *E Yor* 2C 94
Swanley. *Kent* 4G 39
Swanmore. *Hants* 1D 16
Swannington. *Leics* 4B 74
Swannington. *Norf* 4D 78
Swanpool. *Linc* 3G 87
Swanscombe. *Kent* 3G 39
Swansea. *Swan* 3F 31
Swansea Airport. *Swan* 3E 31
Swansmoor. *Staf* 3E 73
Swan Street. *Essx* 3B 54
Swanton Abbot. *Norf* 3E 79
Swanton Morley. *Norf* 4C 78
Swanton Novers. *Norf* 2C 78
Swanton Street. *Kent* 5C 40
Swanwick. *Derbs* 5B 86
Swanwick. *Hants* 2D 16
Swanwick Green. *Ches* 1H 71
Swarby. *Linc* 1H 75
Swardeston. *Norf* 5E 78
Swarkestone. *Derbs* 3A 74
Swarland. *Nmbd* 4F 121
Swarraton. *Hants* 3D 24
Swartha. *W Yor* 5C 98
Swarthmoor. *Cumb* 2B 96
Swaton. *Linc* 2A 76
Swavesey. *Cambs* 4C 64
Sway. *Hants* 3A 16
Swayfield. *Linc* 3G 75
Swaythling. *Sotn* 1C 16
Sweet Green. *Worc* 4A 60
Sweetham. *Devn* 3B 12
Sweetholme. *Cumb* 3G 103
Sweets. *Corn* 3B 10
Sweetshouse. *Corn* 2E 7
Swefling. *Suff* 4F 67
Swell. *Som* 4G 21
Swepstone. *Leics* 4A 74
Swerford. *Oxon* 2B 50
Swettenham. *Ches* 4C 84
Swetton. *N Yor* 2D 98
Swffryd. *Cphy* 2F 33
Swiftsden. *E Sus* 3B 28
Swilland. *Suff* 5D 66
Swillington. *W Yor* 1D 93
Swimbridge. *Devn* 4G 19
Swimbridge Newland. *Devn* 3G 19
Swinbrook. *Oxon* 4A 50
Swincliffe. *N Yor* 4E 99
Swincliffe. *W Yor* 2C 92
Swinderby. *Linc* 4F 87
Swindon. *Glos* 3E 49
Swindon. *Nmbd* 5D 121
Swindon. *Staf* 1C 60
Swindon. *Swin* 3G 35
Swine. *E Yor* 1E 95
Swinefleet. *E Yor* 2A 94
Swineford. *S Glo* 5B 34
Swineshead. *Beds* 4H 63
Swineshead. *Linc* 1B 76
Swineshead Bridge. *Linc* 1B 76
Swiney. *High* 5E 169
Swinford. *Leics* 3C 62
Swinford. *Oxon* 5C 50
Swingate. *Notts* 1C 74
Swingbrow. *Cambs* 2C 64
Swingfield Minnis. *Kent* 1G 29
Swingfield Street. *Kent* 1G 29
Swingleton Green. *Suff* 1C 54
Swinhill. *S Lan* 5A 128
Swinhoe. *Nmbd* 2G 121
Swinhope. *Linc* 1B 88
Swinithwaite. *N Yor* 1C 98
Swinmore Common. *Here* 1B 48
Swinscoe. *Staf* 1F 73
Swinside Hall. *Bord* 3B 120
Swinstead. *Linc* 3H 75
Swinton. *G Man* 4F 91
Swinton. *N Yor* 2B 100
(nr. Malton)
Swinton. *N Yor* 2E 98
(nr. Masham)
Swinton. *Bord* 5E 131
Swinton. *S Yor* 1B 86
Swithland. *Leics* 4C 74
Swordale. *High* 2H 157
Swordly. *High* 2H 167
Sworton Heath. *Ches* 2A 84
Swyddffynnon. *Cdgn* 4F 57
Swyffrd. *Cphy* 2F 33
Swynnerton. *Staf* 2C 72
Swyre. *Dors* 4A 14
Sycharth. *Powy* 3E 70
Sychdyn. *Flin* 4E 83
Sychnant. *Powy* 3B 58
Sychtyn. *Powy* 5B 70
Syde. *Glos* 4E 49
Sydenham. *G Lon* 3E 39
Sydenham. *Oxon* 5F 51
Sydenham. *Som* 3G 21
Sydenham Damerel. *Devn* 5E 11
Syderstone. *Norf* 2H 77
Sydling St Nicholas. *Dors* 3B 14
Sydmonton. *Hants* 1C 24
Sydney. *Ches* 5B 84
Syerston. *Notts* 1E 75
Syke. *G Man* 3G 91
Sykehouse. *S Yor* 3G 93
Sykes. *Lanc* 4F 97
Syleham. *Suff* 3E 66
Sylen. *Carm* 5F 45
Sylfaen. *Powy* 5D 70
Symbister. *Shet* 5G 173
Symington. *S Ayr* 1C 116
Symington. *S Lan* 1B 118
Symondsbury. *Dors* 3H 13
Symonds Yat. *Here* 4A 48
Synod Inn. *Cdgn* 5D 56
Syre. *High* 4G 167
Syreford. *Glos* 3F 49
Syresham. *Nptn* 1E 51
Syston. *Leics* 4D 74
Syston. *Linc* 1G 75
Sytchampton. *Worc* 4C 60
Sywell. *Nptn* 4F 63

T

Tabost. *W Isl* 6F 171
(nr. Cearsiadar)
Tabost. *W Isl* 1H 171
(nr. Suainebost)
Tachbrook Mallory. *Warw* 4H 61
Tackley. *Oxon* 3C 50
Tacleit. *W Isl* 4D 171
Tacolneston. *Norf* 1D 66
Tadcaster. *N Yor* 5G 99
Taddington. *Derbs* 3F 85
Taddington. *Glos* 2F 49
Taddiport. *Devn* 1E 11
Tadley. *Hants* 5E 36
Tadlow. *Cambs* 1C 52
Tadmarton. *Oxon* 2B 50
Tadwick. *Bath* 4C 34
Tadworth. *Surr* 5D 38
Tafarnaubach. *Blae* 4E 46
Tafarn-y-bwlch. *Pemb* 1E 43
Tafarn-y-Gelyn. *Den* 4D 82
Taff's Well. *Rhon* 3E 33
Tafolwern. *Powy* 5A 70
Taibach. *Neat* 3A 32
Tai-bach. *Powy* 3D 70
Taigh a Ghearraidh. *W Isl* 1C 170
Tain. *High* 5E 165
(nr. Invergordon)
Tain. *High* 2E 169
(nr. Thurso)
Tai-Nant. *Wrex* 1E 71
Tai'n Lon. *Gwyn* 5D 80
Tairbeart. *W Isl* 8D 171
Tairgwaith. *Neat* 4H 45
Takeley. *Essx* 3F 53
Takeley Street. *Essx* 3F 53
Talachddu. *Powy* 2D 46
Talacre. *Flin* 2D 82
Talardd. *Gwyn* 3A 70
Talaton. *Devn* 3D 12
Talbenny. *Pemb* 3C 42
Talbot Green. *Rhon* 3D 32
Taleford. *Devn* 3D 12
Talerddig. *Powy* 5B 70
Talgarreg. *Cdgn* 5D 56
Talgarth. *Powy* 2E 47
Talisker. *High* 5C 154
Talke. *Staf* 5C 84
Talkin. *Cumb* 4G 113

Talladale. High 1B 156
Talla Linnfoots. Bord 2D 118
Tallaminnock. S Ayr 5D 116
Tallarn Green. Wrex 1G 71
Tallentire. Cumb 1C 102
Talley. Carm 2G 45
Tallington. Linc 5H 75
Talmine. High 2F 167
Talog. Carm 2H 43
Talsarn. Carm 3A 46
Talsarn. Cdgn 5E 57
Talsarnau. Gwyn 2F 69
Talskiddy. Corn 2D 6
Talwrn. IOA 3D 81
Talwrn. Wrex 1E 71
Tal-y-bont. Cdgn 2F 57
Tal-y-Bont. Cnwy 4G 81
Tal-y-bont. Gwyn 3F 81
(nr. Bangor)
Tal-y-bont. Gwyn 3E 69
(nr. Barmouth)
Talybont-on-Usk. Powy 3E 46
Tal-y-cafn. Cnwy 3G 81
Tal-y-coed. Mon 4H 47
Tal-y-llyn. Gwyn 5G 69
Talyllyn. Powy 3E 46
Talysarn. Gwyn 5D 81
Tal-y-waenydd. Gwyn 1F 69
Talywain. Torf 5F 47
Talywern. Powy 5H 69
Tamerton Foliot. Plym 2A 8
Tamworth. Staf 5G 73
Tamworth Green. Linc 1C 76
Tandlehill. Ren 3F 127
Tandridge. Surr 5E 39
Tanerdy. Carm 3E 45
Tanfield. Dur 4E 115
Tanfield Lea. Dur 4E 115
Tangasdale. W Isl 8B 170
Tang Hall. York 4A 100
Tangiers. Pemb 3D 42
Tangley. Hants 1B 24
Tangmere. W Sus 5A 26
Tangwick. Shet 4D 173
Tankerness. Orkn 7E 172
Tankersley. S Yor 1H 85
Tankerton. Kent 4F 41
Tan-lan. Cnwy 4G 81
Tan-lan. Gwyn 1F 69
Tannach. High 4F 169
Tannadice. Ang 3D 145
Tanners Green. Worc 3E 61
Tannington. Suff 4E 67
Tannochside. N Lan 3A 128
Tan Office Green. Suff 5G 65
Tansley. Derbs 5H 85
Tansley Knoll. Derbs 4H 85
Tansor. Nptn 1H 63
Tantobie. Dur 4E 115
Tanton. N Yor 3C 106
Tanvats. Linc 4A 88
Tanworth-in-Arden. Warw 3F 61
Tan-y-bwlch. Gwyn 1F 69
Tan-y-fron. Cnwy 4B 82
Tanyfron. Wrex 5E 83
Tan-y-goes. Cdgn 1C 44
Tanygrisiau. Gwyn 1F 69
Tan-y-pistyll. Powy 3C 70
Tan-yr-allt. Den 2C 82
Taobh a Chaolais. W Isl 7C 170
Taobh a Deas Loch Aineort. W Isl 6C 170
Taobh a Ghlinne. W Isl 6F 171
Taobh a Tuath Loch Aineort. W Isl 6C 170
Taobh Tuath. W Isl 9B 171
Taplow. Buck 2A 38
Tapton. Derbs 3A 86
Tarbert. Arg 1E 125
(on Jura)
Tarbert. Arg 3G 125
(on Kintyre)
Tarbert. W Isl 8D 171
Tarbet. Arg 3C 134
Tarbet. High 4F 147
(nr. Mallaig)
Tarbet. High 4B 166
(nr. Scourie)
Tarbock Green. Mers 2G 83
Tarbolton. S Ayr 2D 116
Tarbrax. S Lan 4D 128
Tardebigge. Worc 4E 61
Tarfside. Ang 1D 145
Tarland. Abers 3B 152
Tarleton. Lanc 2C 90
Tarlogie. High 5E 165
Tarlscough. Lanc 3C 90
Tarlton. Glos 2E 35
Tarnbrook. Lanc 4E 97
Tarnock. Som 1G 21
Tarns. Cumb 5C 112
Tarporley. Ches 4H 83
Tarpots. Essx 2B 40
Tarr. Som 3E 20
Tarrant Crawford. Dors 2E 15
Tarrant Gunville. Dors 1E 15
Tarrant Hinton. Dors 1E 15
Tarrant Keyneston. Dors 2E 15
Tarrant Launceston. Dors 2E 15
Tarrant Monkton. Dors 2E 15
Tarrant Rawston. Dors 2E 15
Tarrant Rushton. Dors 2E 15
Tarrel. High 5F 165
Tarring Neville. E Sus 5F 27
Tarrington. Here 1B 48
Tarsappie. Per 1D 136
Tarskavaig. High 3D 147
Tarves. Abers 5F 161
Tarvie. High 3G 157
Tarvin. Ches 4G 83
Tasburgh. Norf 1E 66
Tasley. Shrp 1A 60
Taston. Oxon 3B 50
Tatenhill. Staf 3G 73
Tathall End. Mil 1G 51
Tatham. Lanc 3F 97
Tathwell. Linc 2C 88
Tatling End. Buck 2B 38
Tatsfield. Surr 5F 39
Tattenhall. Ches 5G 83
Tatterford. Norf 3A 78
Tattersett. Norf 2H 77
Tattershall. Linc 5B 88
Tattershall Bridge. Linc 5A 88
Tattershall Thorpe. Linc 5B 88
Tattingstone. Suff 2E 55
Tattingstone White Horse. Suff 2E 55
Tattle Bank. Warw 4F 61
Tatworth. Som 2G 13
Taunton. Som 4F 21
Taverham. Norf 4D 78
Taverners Green. Essx 4F 53
Tavernspite. Pemb 3F 43
Tavistock. Devn 5E 11
Tavool House. Arg 1B 132
Taw Green. Devn 3G 11
Tawstock. Devn 4F 19
Taxal. Derbs 2E 85
Tayinloan. Arg 5E 125
Taynish. Arg 1F 125
Taynton. Glos 3C 48
Taynton. Oxon 4H 49
Taynuilt. Arg 5E 141
Tayport. Fife 1G 137
Tay Road Bridge. Fife 1G 137
Tayvallich. Arg 1F 125
Tealby. Linc 1A 88
Tealing. Ang 5D 144
Teams. Tyne 3F 115
Teangue. High 3E 147
Tebay. Cumb 4H 103
Tebworth. Beds 3H 51
Tedburn St Mary. Devn 3B 12
Teddington. Glos 2E 49
Teddington. G Lon 3C 38
Tedsmore. Shrp 3F 71
Tedstone Delamere. Here 5A 60
Tedstone Wafer. Here 5A 60
Teesport. Red C 2C 106
Teesside. Stoc T 2C 106
Teeton. Nptn 3D 62
Teffont Evias. Wilts 3E 23
Teffont Magna. Wilts 3E 23
Tegryn. Pemb 1G 43
Teigh. Rut 4F 75
Teigncombe. Devn 4G 11
Teigngrace. Devn 5B 12
Teignmouth. Devn 5C 12
Telford. Telf 4A 72
Telham. E Sus 4B 28
Tellisford. Som 1D 22
Telscombe. E Sus 5F 27
Telscombe Cliffs. E Sus 5E 27
Tempar. Per 3D 142
Templand. Dum 1B 112
Temple. Corn 5B 10
Temple. Glas 3G 127
Temple. Midl 4G 129
Temple Balsall. W Mid 3G 61
Temple Bar. Carm 4F 45
Temple Bar. Cdgn 5E 57
Temple Cloud. Bath 1B 22
Templecombe. Som 4C 22
Temple Ewell. Kent 1G 29
Temple Grafton. Warw 5F 61
Temple Guiting. Glos 3F 49
Templehall. Fife 4E 137
Temple Hirst. N Yor 2G 93
Temple Normanton. Derbs 4B 86
Temple Sowerby. Cumb 2H 103
Templeton. Devn 1B 12
Templeton. Pemb 3F 43
Templeton. W Ber 5B 36
Templetown. Dur 5E 115
Tempsford. Beds 5A 64
Tenandry. Per 2G 143
Tenbury Wells. Worc 4H 59
Tenby. Pemb 4F 43
Tendring. Essx 3E 55
Tendring Green. Essx 3E 55
Tenga. Arg 4G 139
Ten Mile Bank. Norf 1F 65
Tenterden. Kent 2C 28
Terfyn. Cnwy 3B 82
Terling. Essx 4A 54
Ternhill. Shrp 2A 72
Terregles. Dum 2G 111
Terrick. Buck 5G 51
Terrington. N Yor 2A 100
Terrington St Clement. Norf 3E 77
Terrington St John. Norf 4E 77
Terry's Green. Warw 3F 61
Teston. Kent 5B 40
Testwood. Hants 1B 16
Tetbury. Glos 2D 35
Tetbury Upton. Glos 2D 35
Tetchill. Shrp 2F 71
Tetcott. Devn 3D 10
Tetford. Linc 3C 88
Tetney. Linc 4G 95
Tetney Lock. Linc 4G 95
Tetsworth. Oxon 5E 51
Tettenhall. W Mid 1C 60
Teversal. Notts 4B 86
Teversham. Cambs 5D 65
Teviothead. Bord 4G 119
Tewel. Abers 5F 153
Tewin. Herts 4C 52
Tewkesbury. Glos 2D 49
Teynham. Kent 4D 40
Teynham Street. Kent 4D 40
Thackthwaite. Cumb 2F 103
Thakeham. W Sus 4C 26
Thame. Oxon 5F 51
Thames Ditton. Surr 4C 38
Thames Haven. Thur 2B 40
Thamesmead. G Lon 2F 39
Thamesport. Medw 3C 40
Thanington Without. Kent 5F 41
Thankerton. S Lan 1B 118
Tharston. Norf 1D 66
Thatcham. W Ber 5D 36
Thatto Heath. Mers 1H 83
Thaxted. Essx 2G 53
Theakston. N Yor 1F 99
Thealby. N Lin 3B 94
Theale. Som 2H 21
Theale. W Ber 4E 37
Thearne. E Yor 1D 94
Theberton. Suff 4G 67
Theddingworth. Leics 2D 62
Theddlethorpe All Saints. Linc 2D 88
Theddlethorpe St Helen. Linc 2D 89
Thelbridge Barton. Devn 1A 12
Thelnetham. Suff 3C 66
Thelveton. Norf 2D 66
Thelwall. Warr 2A 84
Themelthorpe. Norf 3C 78
Thenford. Nptn 1D 50
Therfield. Herts 2D 52
Thetford. Linc 4A 76
Thetford. Norf 2A 66
Thethwaite. Cumb 5E 113
Theydon Bois. Essx 1F 39
Thick Hollins. W Yor 3B 92
Thickwood. Wilts 4D 34
Thimbleby. Linc 3B 88
Thimbleby. N Yor 5B 106
Thingwall. Mers 2E 83
Thirlby. N Yor 1G 99
Thirlestane. Bord 5B 130
Thirn. N Yor 1E 98
Thirsk. N Yor 1G 99
Thirtleby. E Yor 1E 95
Thistleton. Lanc 1C 90
Thistleton. Rut 4G 75
Thistley Green. Suff 3F 65
Thixendale. N Yor 3C 100
Thockrington. Nmbd 2C 114
Tholomas Drove. Cambs 5D 76
Tholthorpe. N Yor 3G 99
Thomas Chapel. Pemb 4F 43
Thomas Close. Cumb 5F 113
Thomastown. Abers 4E 160
Thomastown. Rhon 3D 32
Thompson. Norf 1B 66
Thomshill. Mor 3G 159
Thong. Kent 3A 40
Thongsbridge. W Yor 4B 92
Thoralby. N Yor 1C 98
Thoresby. Notts 3D 86
Thoresway. Linc 1A 88
Thorganby. Linc 1B 88
Thorganby. N Yor 5A 100
Thorgill. N Yor 5E 107
Thorington. Suff 3G 67
Thorington Street. Suff 2D 54
Thorlby. N Yor 4B 98
Thorley. Herts 4E 53
Thorley Street. Herts 4E 53
Thorley Street. IOW 4B 16
Thormanby. N Yor 2G 99
Thorn. Powy 4E 59
Thornaby-on-Tees. Stoc T 3B 106
Thornage. Norf 2C 78
Thornborough. Buck 2F 51
Thornborough. N Yor 2E 99
Thornbury. Devn 2E 11
Thornbury. Here 5A 60
Thornbury. S Glo 3B 34
Thornby. Cumb 4D 112
Thornby. Nptn 3D 62
Thorncliffe. Staf 5E 85
Thorncombe. Dors 2G 13
Thorncombe Street. Surr 1A 26
Thorncote Green. Beds 1B 52
Thorndon. Suff 4D 66
Thorndon Cross. Devn 3F 11
Thorne. S Yor 3G 93
Thornehillhead. Devn 1E 11
Thorner. W Yor 5F 99
Thorne St Margaret. Som 4D 20
Thorney. Notts 3F 87
Thorney. Pet 5B 76
Thorney. Som 4H 21
Thorney Hill. Hants 3G 15
Thorney Toll. Cambs 5C 76
Thornfalcon. Som 4F 21
Thornford. Dors 1B 14
Thorngrafton. Nmbd 3A 114
Thorngrove. Som 3G 21
Thorngumbald. E Yor 2F 95
Thornham. Norf 1G 77
Thornham Magna. Suff 3D 66
Thornham Parva. Suff 3D 66
Thornhaugh. Pet 5H 75
Thornhill. Cphy 3E 33
Thornhill. Cumb 4B 102
Thornhill. Derbs 2G 85
Thornhill. Dum 5A 118
Thornhill. Sotn 1C 16
Thornhill. Stir 4F 135
Thornhill. W Yor 3C 92
Thornhill Lees. W Yor 3C 92
Thornhills. W Yor 2B 92
Thornholme. E Yor 3F 101
Thornicombe. Dors 2D 14
Thornington. Nmbd 1C 120
Thornley. Dur 1A 106
(nr. Durham)
Thornley. Dur 1E 105
(nr. Tow Law)
Thornley Gate. Nmbd 4B 114
Thornliebank. E Ren 4G 127
Thornroan. Abers 5F 161
Thorns. Suff 5G 65
Thornsett. Derbs 2E 85
Thornthwaite. Cumb 2D 102
Thornthwaite. N Yor 4D 98
Thornton. Ang 4C 144
Thornton. Buck 2F 51
Thornton. E Yor 5B 100
Thornton. Fife 4E 137
Thornton. Lanc 5C 96
Thornton. Leics 5B 74
Thornton. Linc 4B 88
Thornton. Mers 4B 90
Thornton. Midd 3B 106
Thornton. Nmbd 5F 131
Thornton. Pemb 4D 42
Thornton. W Yor 1A 92
Thornton Curtis. N Lin 3D 94
Thorntonhall. S Lan 4G 127
Thornton Heath. G Lon 4E 39
Thornton Hough. Mers 2F 83
Thornton in Craven. N Yor 5B 98
Thornton in Lonsdale. N Yor 2F 97
Thornton-le-Beans. N Yor 5A 106
Thornton-le-Clay. N Yor 3A 100
Thornton-le-Dale. N Yor 1C 100
Thornton le Moor. Linc 1H 87
Thornton-le-Moor. N Yor 1F 99
Thornton-le-Moors. Ches 3G 83
Thornton-le-Street. N Yor 1G 99
Thorntonloch. E Lot 2D 130
Thornton Rust. N Yor 1B 98
Thornton Steward. N Yor 1D 98
Thornton Watlass. N Yor 1E 99
Thornwood Common. Essx 5E 53
Thornythwaite. Cumb 2E 103
Thoroton. Notts 1E 75
Thorp Arch. W Yor 5G 99
Thorpe. Derbs 5F 85
Thorpe. E Yor 5D 101
Thorpe. Linc 2D 89
Thorpe. Norf 1G 67
Thorpe. N Yor 3C 98
Thorpe. Notts 1E 75
Thorpe. Surr 4B 38
Thorpe Abbotts. Norf 3D 66
Thorpe Acre. Leics 3C 74
Thorpe Arnold. Leics 3E 75
Thorpe Audlin. W Yor 3E 93
Thorpe Bassett. N Yor 2C 100
Thorpe Bay. S'end 2D 40
Thorpe by Water. Rut 1F 63
Thorpe Common. S Yor 1A 86
Thorpe Common. Suff 2F 55

Thorpe Constantine—Torryburn

Thorpe Constantine. *Staf* 5G **73**
Thorpe End. *Norf* 4E **79**
Thorpe Fendike. *Linc* 4D **88**
Thorpe Green. *Essx* 3E **55**
Thorpe Green. *Suff* 5B **66**
Thorpe Hall. *N Yor* 2H **99**
Thorpe Hamlet. *Norf* 5E **79**
Thorpe Hesley. *S Yor* 1A **86**
Thorpe in Balne. *S Yor* 3F **93**
Thorpe in the Fallows. *Linc* 2G **87**
Thorpe Langton. *Leics* 1E **63**
Thorpe Larches. *Dur* 2A **106**
Thorpe Latimer. *Linc* 1A **76**
Thorpe-le-Soken. *Essx* 3E **55**
Thorpe le Street. *E Yor* 5C **100**
Thorpe Malsor. *Nptn* 3F **63**
Thorpe Mandeville. *Nptn* 1D **50**
Thorpe Market. *Norf* 2E **79**
Thorpe Marriott. *Norf* 4D **78**
Thorpe Morieux. *Suff* 5B **66**
Thorpeness. *Suff* 4G **67**
Thorpe on the Hill. *Linc* 4G **87**
Thorpe on the Hill. *W Yor* 2D **92**
Thorpe St Andrew. *Norf* 5E **79**
Thorpe St Peter. *Linc* 4D **89**
Thorpe Salvin. *S Yor* 2C **86**
Thorpe Satchville. *Leics* 4E **75**
Thorpe Thewles. *Stoc T* 2B **106**
Thorpe Tilney. *Linc* 5A **88**
Thorpe Underwood. *N Yor* 4G **99**
Thorpe Waterville. *Nptn* 2H **63**
Thorpe Willoughby. *N Yor* 1F **93**
Thorpland. *Norf* 5F **77**
Thorrington. *Essx* 3D **54**
Thorverton. *Devn* 2C **12**
Thrandeston. *Suff* 3D **66**
Thrapston. *Nptn* 3G **63**
Thrashbush. *N Lan* 3A **128**
Threapland. *Cumb* 1C **102**
Threapland. *N Yor* 3B **98**
Threapwood. *Ches* 1G **71**
Threapwood. *Staf* 1E **73**
Three Ashes. *Here* 3A **48**
Three Bridges. *Linc* 2D **88**
Three Bridges. *W Sus* 2D **27**
Three Burrows. *Corn* 4B **6**
Three Chimneys. *Kent* 2C **28**
Three Cocks. *Powy* 2E **47**
Three Crosses. *Swan* 3E **31**
Three Cups Corner. *E Sus* 3H **27**
Three Holes. *Norf* 5E **77**
Threekingham. *Linc* 2H **75**
Three Leg Cross. *E Sus* 2A **28**
Three Legged Cross. *Dors* 2F **15**
Three Mile Cross. *Wok* 5F **37**
Threemilestone. *Corn* 4B **6**
Three Oaks. *E Sus* 4C **28**
Threlkeld. *Cumb* 2E **102**
Threshfield. *N Yor* 3B **98**
Thrigby. *Norf* 4G **79**
Thringarth. *Dur* 2C **104**
Thringstone. *Leics* 4B **74**
Thrintoft. *N Yor* 5A **106**
Thriplow. *Cambs* 1E **53**
Throckenholt. *Linc* 5C **76**
Throcking. *Herts* 2D **52**
Throckley. *Tyne* 3E **115**
Throckmorton. *Worc* 1E **49**
Throop. *Bour* 3G **15**
Throphill. *Nmbd* 1E **115**
Thropton. *Nmbd* 4E **121**
Throsk. *Stir* 4A **136**
Througham. *Glos* 5E **49**
Throughgate. *Dum* 1F **111**
Throwleigh. *Devn* 3G **11**
Throwley. *Kent* 5D **40**
Throwley Forstal. *Kent* 5D **40**
Throxenby. *N Yor* 1E **101**
Thrumpton. *Notts* 2C **74**
Thrumster. *High* 4F **169**
Thrunton. *Nmbd* 3E **121**
Thrupp. *Glos* 5D **48**
Thrupp. *Oxon* 4C **50**
Thrushelton. *Devn* 4E **11**
Thrushgill. *Lanc* 3F **97**
Thrussington. *Leics* 4D **74**
Thruxton. *Hants* 2A **24**
Thruxton. *Here* 2H **47**
Thrybergh. *S Yor* 1B **86**
Thulston. *Derbs* 2B **74**
Thundergay. *N Ayr* 5G **125**
Thundersley. *Essx* 2B **40**
Thundridge. *Herts* 4D **52**
Thurcaston. *Leics* 4C **74**
Thurcroft. *S Yor* 2B **86**
Thurdon. *Corn* 1C **10**
Thurgarton. *Norf* 2D **78**
Thurgarton. *Notts* 1D **74**
Thurgoland. *S Yor* 4C **92**
Thurlaston. *Leics* 1C **62**
Thurlaston. *Warw* 3B **62**
Thurlby. *Linc* 3D **89**
(nr. Alford)
Thurlby. *Linc* 4A **76**
(nr. Baston)
Thurlby. *Linc* 4G **87**
(nr. Lincoln)
Thurleigh. *Beds* 5H **63**
Thurlestone. *Devn* 4C **8**
Thurloxton. *Som* 3F **21**
Thurlstone. *S Yor* 4C **92**
Thurlton. *Norf* 1G **67**
Thurmaston. *Leics* 5D **74**
Thurnby. *Leics* 5D **74**
Thurne. *Norf* 4G **79**
Thurnham. *Kent* 5C **40**
Thurning. *Norf* 3C **78**
Thurning. *Nptn* 2H **63**
Thurnscoe. *S Yor* 4E **93**
Thursby. *Cumb* 4E **113**
Thursford. *Norf* 2B **78**
Thursford Green. *Norf* 2B **78**
Thursley. *Surr* 2A **26**
Thurso. *High* 2D **168**
Thurso East. *High* 2D **168**
Thurstaston. *Mers* 2E **83**
Thurston. *Suff* 4B **66**
Thurston End. *Suff* 5G **65**
Thurstonfield. *Cumb* 4E **112**
Thurstonland. *W Yor* 3B **92**
Thurton. *Norf* 5F **79**
Thurvaston. *Derbs* 2F **73**
(nr. Ashbourne)
Thurvaston. *Derbs* 2G **73**
(nr. Derby)
Thuxton. *Norf* 5C **78**
Thwaite. *Dur* 3D **104**
Thwaite. *N Yor* 5B **104**
Thwaite. *Suff* 4D **66**
Thwaite Head. *Cumb* 5E **103**
Thwaites. *W Yor* 5C **98**
Thwaite St Mary. *Norf* 1F **67**
Thwing. *E Yor* 2E **101**
Tibbermore. *Per* 1C **136**
Tibberton. *Glos* 3C **48**
Tibberton. *Telf* 3A **72**
Tibberton. *Worc* 5D **60**
Tibenham. *Norf* 2D **66**
Tibshelf. *Derbs* 4B **86**
Tibthorpe. *E Yor* 4D **100**
Ticehurst. *E Sus* 2A **28**
Tichborne. *Hants* 3D **24**
Tickencote. *Rut* 5G **75**
Tickenham. *N Som* 4H **33**
Tickhill. *S Yor* 1C **86**
Ticklerton. *Shrp* 1G **59**
Ticknall. *Derbs* 3H **73**
Tickton. *E Yor* 5E **101**
Tidbury Green. *W Mid* 3F **61**
Tidcombe. *Wilts* 1A **24**
Tiddington. *Oxon* 5E **51**
Tiddington. *Warw* 5G **61**
Tiddleywink. *Wilts* 4D **34**
Tidebrook. *E Sus* 3H **27**
Tideford. *Corn* 3H **7**
Tideford Cross. *Corn* 2H **7**
Tidenham. *Glos* 2A **34**
Tideswell. *Derbs* 3F **85**
Tidmarsh. *W Ber* 4E **37**
Tidmington. *Warw* 2A **50**
Tidpit. *Hants* 1F **15**
Tidworth. *Wilts* 2H **23**
Tidworth Camp. *Wilts* 2H **23**
Tiers Cross. *Pemb* 3D **42**
Tiffield. *Nptn* 5D **62**
Tifty. *Abers* 4E **161**
Tigerton. *Ang* 2E **145**
Tighnabruaich. *Arg* 2A **126**
Tigley. *Devn* 2D **8**
Tilbrook. *Cambs* 4H **63**
Tilbury. *Thur* 3H **39**
Tilbury Green. *Essx* 1H **53**
Tilbury Juxta Clare. *Essx* 1A **54**
Tile Cross. *W Mid* 2F **61**
Tile Hill. *W Mid* 3G **61**
Tilehurst. *Read* 4E **37**
Tilford. *Surr* 2G **25**
Tilgate Forest Row. *W Sus* 2D **26**
Tillathrowie. *Abers* 5B **160**
Tillers Green. *Glos* 2B **48**
Tillery. *Abers* 1G **153**
Tilley. *Shrp* 3H **71**
Tillicoultry. *Clac* 4B **136**
Tillingham. *Essx* 5C **54**
Tillington. *Here* 1H **47**
Tillington. *W Sus* 3A **26**
Tillington Common. *Here* 1H **47**
Tillybirloch. *Abers* 3D **152**
Tillyfourie. *Abers* 2D **152**
Tilmanstone. *Kent* 5H **41**
Tilney All Saints. *Norf* 4E **77**
Tilney Fen Side. *Norf* 4E **77**
Tilney High End. *Norf* 4E **77**
Tilney St Lawrence. *Norf* 4E **77**
Tilshead. *Wilts* 2F **23**
Tilstock. *Shrp* 2H **71**
Tilston. *Ches* 5G **83**
Tilstone Fearnall. *Ches* 4H **83**
Tilsworth. *Beds* 3H **51**
Tilton on the Hill. *Leics* 5E **75**
Tiltups End. *Glos* 2D **34**
Timberland. *Linc* 5A **88**
Timbersbrook. *Ches* 4C **84**
Timberscombe. *Som* 2C **20**
Timble. *N Yor* 4D **98**
Timperley. *G Man* 2B **84**
Timsbury. *Bath* 1B **22**
Timsbury. *Hants* 4B **24**
Timsgearraidh. *W Isl* 4C **171**
Timworth Green. *Suff* 4A **66**
Tincleton. *Dors* 3C **14**
Tindale. *Cumb* 4H **113**
Tindale Crescent. *Dur* 2F **105**
Tingewick. *Buck* 2E **51**
Tingley. *W Yor* 2C **92**
Tingrith. *Beds* 2A **52**
Tingwall. *Orkn* 5D **172**
Tinhay. *Devn* 4D **11**
Tinshill. *W Yor* 1C **92**
Tinsley. *S Yor* 1B **86**
Tinsley Green. *W Sus* 2D **27**
Tintagel. *Corn* 4A **10**
Tintern Parva. *Mon* 5A **48**
Tintinhull. *Som* 1A **14**
Tintwistle. *Derbs* 1E **85**
Tinwald. *Dum* 1B **112**
Tinwell. *Rut* 5H **75**
Tippacott. *Devn* 2A **20**
Tipperty. *Abers* 1G **153**
Tips End. *Cambs* 1E **65**
Tiptoe. *Hants* 3A **16**
Tipton. *W Mid* 1D **60**
Tipton St John. *Devn* 3D **12**
Tiptree. *Essx* 4B **54**
Tiptree Heath. *Essx* 4B **54**
Tirabad. *Powy* 1B **46**
Tircoed. *Swan* 5G **45**
Tiree Airport. *Arg* 4B **138**
Tirinie. *Per* 2F **143**
Tirley. *Glos* 3D **48**
Tirnewydd. *Flin* 3D **82**
Tiroran. *Arg* 1B **132**
Tirphil. *Cphy* 5E **47**
Tirril. *Cumb* 2G **103**
Tirryside. *High* 2C **164**
Tir-y-dail. *Carm* 4G **45**
Tisbury. *Wilts* 4E **23**
Tisman's Common. *W Sus* 2B **26**
Tissington. *Derbs* 5F **85**
Titchberry. *Devn* 4C **18**
Titchfield. *Hants* 2D **16**
Titchmarsh. *Nptn* 3H **63**
Titchwell. *Norf* 1G **77**
Tithby. *Notts* 2D **74**
Titley. *Here* 5F **59**
Titlington. *Nmbd* 3F **121**
Titsey. *Surr* 5F **39**
Titson. *Corn* 2C **10**
Tittensor. *Staf* 2C **72**
Tittleshall. *Norf* 3A **78**
Titton. *Worc* 4C **60**
Tiverton. *Ches* 4H **83**
Tiverton. *Devn* 1C **12**
Tivetshall St Margaret. *Norf* 2D **66**
Tivetshall St Mary. *Norf* 2D **66**
Tivington. *Som* 2C **20**
Tixall. *Staf* 3D **73**
Tixover. *Rut* 5G **75**
Toab. *Orkn* 7E **172**
Toab. *Shet* 10E **173**
Toadmoor. *Derbs* 5H **85**
Tobermory. *Arg* 3G **139**
Toberonochy. *Arg* 3E **133**
Tobha-Beag. *W Isl* 1E **170**
Tobha Beag. *W Isl* 5C **170**
Tobha Mor. *W Isl* 5C **170**
Tobson. *W Isl* 4D **171**
Tocher. *Abers* 5D **160**
Tockenham. *Wilts* 4F **35**
Tockenham Wick. *Wilts* 3F **35**
Tockholes. *Bkbn* 2E **91**
Tockington. *S Glo* 3B **34**
Tockwith. *N Yor* 4G **99**
Todber. *Dors* 4D **22**
Todding. *Here* 3G **59**
Toddington. *Beds* 3A **52**
Toddington. *Glos* 2F **49**
Todenham. *Glos* 2H **49**
Todhills. *Cumb* 3E **113**
Todmorden. *W Yor* 2H **91**
Todwick. *S Yor* 2B **86**
Toft. *Cambs* 5C **64**
Toft. *Linc* 4H **75**
Toft Hill. *Dur* 2E **105**
Toft Monks. *Norf* 1G **67**
Toft next Newton. *Linc* 2H **87**
Toftrees. *Norf* 3A **78**
Tofts. *High* 2F **169**
Toftwood. *Norf* 4B **78**
Togston. *Nmbd* 4G **121**
Tokavaig. *High* 2E **147**
Tokers Green. *Oxon* 4F **37**
Tolastadh a Chaolais. *W Isl* 4D **171**
Tolladine. *Worc* 5C **60**
Tolland. *Som* 3E **20**
Tollard Farnham. *Dors* 1E **15**
Tollard Royal. *Wilts* 1E **15**
Toll Bar. *S Yor* 4F **93**
Toller Fratrum. *Dors* 3A **14**
Toller Porcorum. *Dors* 3A **14**
Tollerton. *N Yor* 3H **99**
Tollerton. *Notts* 2D **74**
Toller Whelme. *Dors* 2A **14**
Tollesbury. *Essx* 4C **54**
Tolleshunt D'Arcy. *Essx* 4C **54**
Tolleshunt Knights. *Essx* 4C **54**
Tolleshunt Major. *Essx* 4C **54**
Tollie. *High* 3H **157**
Tollie Farm. *High* 1A **156**
Tolm. *W Isl* 4G **171**
Tolpuddle. *Dors* 3C **14**
Tolstadh bho Thuath. *W Isl* 3H **171**
Tolworth. *G Lon* 4C **38**
Tomachlaggan. *Mor* 1F **151**
Tomaknock. *Per* 1A **136**
Tomatin. *High* 1C **150**
Tombuidhe. *Arg* 3H **133**
Tomdoun. *High* 3D **148**
Tomich. *High* 1F **149**
(nr. Cannich)
Tomich. *High* 1B **158**
(nr. Invergordon)
Tomich. *High* 3D **164**
(nr. Lairg)
Tomintoul. *Mor* 2F **151**
Tomnavoulin. *Mor* 1G **151**
Tomsleibhe. *Arg* 5A **140**
Ton. *Mon* 2G **33**
Tonbridge. *Kent* 1G **27**
Tondu. *B'end* 3B **32**
Tonedale. *Som* 4E **21**
Tonfanau. *Gwyn* 5E **69**
Tong. *Shrp* 5B **72**
Tonge. *Leics* 3B **74**
Tong Forge. *Shrp* 5B **72**
Tongham. *Surr* 2G **25**
Tongland. *Dum* 4D **111**
Tong Norton. *Shrp* 5B **72**
Tongue. *High* 3F **167**
Tongwynlais. *Card* 3E **33**
Tonmawr. *Neat* 2B **32**
Tonna. *Neat* 2A **32**
Tonnau. *Neat* 2A **32**
Ton-Pentre. *Rhon* 2C **32**
Tonwell. *Herts* 4D **52**
Tonypandy. *Rhon* 2C **32**
Tonyrefail. *Rhon* 3D **32**
Toot Baldon. *Oxon* 5D **50**
Toot Hill. *Essx* 5F **53**
Toot Hill. *Hants* 1B **16**
Topcliffe. *N Yor* 2G **99**
Topcliffe. *W Yor* 2C **92**
Topcroft. *Norf* 1E **67**
Topcroft Street. *Norf* 1E **67**
Toppesfield. *Essx* 2H **53**
Toppings. *G Man* 3F **91**
Toprow. *Norf* 1D **66**
Topsham. *Devn* 4C **12**
Torbay. *Torb* 2F **9**
Torbeg. *N Ayr* 3C **122**
Torbothie. *N Lan* 3B **128**
Torbryan. *Devn* 2E **9**
Torcross. *Devn* 4E **9**
Tore. *High* 3A **158**
Torgyle. *High* 2F **149**
Torinturk. *Arg* 3G **125**
Torksey. *Linc* 3F **87**
Torlum. *W Isl* 3C **170**
Torlundy. *High* 1F **141**
Tormarton. *S Glo* 4C **34**
Tormitchell. *S Ayr* 5B **116**
Tormore. *High* 3E **147**
Tormore. *N Ayr* 2C **122**
Tornagrain. *High* 4B **158**
Tornaveen. *Abers* 3D **152**
Torness. *High* 1H **149**
Toronto. *Dur* 1E **105**
Torpenhow. *Cumb* 1D **102**
Torphichen. *W Lot* 2C **128**
Torphins. *Abers* 3D **152**
Torpoint. *Corn* 3A **8**
Torquay. *Torb* 2F **9**
Torr. *Devn* 3B **8**
Torra. *Arg* 4B **124**
Torran. *High* 4E **155**
Torrance. *E Dun* 2H **127**
Torrans. *Arg* 1B **132**
Torranyard. *E Ayr* 5E **127**
Torre. *Torb* 2E **9**
Torridon. *High* 3B **156**
Torrin. *High* 1D **147**
Torrisdale. *Arg* 2B **122**
Torrisdale. *High* 2G **167**
Torrish. *High* 2G **165**
Torrisholme. *Lanc* 3D **96**
Torroble. *High* 3C **164**
Torroy. *High* 4C **164**
Tor Royal. *Devn* 5G **11**
Torry. *Aber* 3G **153**
Torryburn. *Fife* 1D **128**

Torthorwald. *Dum* 2B **112**
Tortington. *W Sus* 5B **26**
Tortworth. *S Glo* 2C **34**
Torvaig. *High* 4D **155**
Torver. *Cumb* 5D **102**
Torwood. *Falk* 1B **128**
Torworth. *Notts* 2D **86**
Toscaig. *High* 5G **155**
Toseland. *Cambs* 4B **64**
Tosside. *Lanc* 4G **97**
Tostock. *Suff* 4B **66**
Totaig. *High* 3B **154**
Totardor. *High* 5C **154**
Tote. *High* 4D **154**
Totegan. *High* 2A **168**
Tothill. *Linc* 2D **88**
Totland. *IOW* 4B **16**
Totley. *S Yor* 3H **85**
Totnell. *Dors* 2B **14**
Totnes. *Devn* 2E **9**
Toton. *Derbs* 2B **74**
Totronald. *Arg* 3C **138**
Totscore. *High* 2C **154**
Tottenham. *G Lon* 1E **39**
Tottenhill. *Norf* 4F **77**
Tottenhill Row. *Norf* 4F **77**
Totteridge. *G Lon* 1D **38**
Totternhoe. *Beds* 3H **51**
Tottington. *G Man* 3F **91**
Totton. *Hants* 1B **16**
Touchen-end. *Wind* 4G **37**
Touches. *Som* 2G **13**
Toulvaddie. *High* 5F **165**
Towans, The. *Corn* 3C **4**
Toward. *Arg* 3C **126**
Towcester. *Nptn* 1E **51**
Towednack. *Corn* 3B **4**
Tower End. *Norf* 4F **77**
Towerhill. *Devn* 3D **10**
Tower Hill. *Mers* 4C **90**
Tower Hill. *W Sus* 3C **26**
Towersey. *Oxon* 5F **51**
Towie. *Abers* 2B **152**
Towiemore. *Mor* 4A **160**
Tow Law. *Dur* 1E **105**
Town End. *Cambs* 1D **64**
Town End. *Cumb* 4F **103**
(nr. Ambleside)
Town End. *Cumb* 2H **103**
(nr. Kirkby Thore)
Town End. *Cumb* 1D **96**
(nr. Lindale)
Town End. *Cumb* 1C **96**
(nr. Newby Bridge)
Town End. *Mers* 2G **83**
Townend. *W Dun* 2F **127**
Townfield. *Dur* 5C **114**
Towngate. *Cumb* 5G **113**
Towngate. *Linc* 4A **76**
Town Green. *Lanc* 4B **90**
Town Head. *Cumb* 4E **103**
(nr. Grasmere)
Town Head. *Cumb* 3H **103**
(nr. Great Asby)
Townhead. *Cumb* 1G **103**
(nr. Lazonby)
Townhead. *Cumb* 1B **102**
(nr. Maryport)
Townhead. *Cumb* 1H **103**
(nr. Ousby)
Townhead. *Dum* 5D **111**
Townhead of Greenlaw. *Dum* 3E **111**
Townhill. *Fife* 1E **129**
Townhill. *Swan* 3F **31**
Town Kelloe. *Dur* 1A **106**
Town Littleworth. *E Sus* 4F **27**
Town Row. *E Sus* 2G **27**
Towns End. *Hants* 1D **24**
Townsend. *Herts* 5B **52**
Townshend. *Corn* 3C **4**
Town Street. *Suff* 2G **65**
Town, The. *IOS* 1A **4**
Town Yetholm. *Bord* 2C **120**
Towthorpe. *E Yor* 3C **100**
Towthorpe. *York* 4A **100**
Towton. *N Yor* 1E **93**
Towyn. *Cnwy* 3B **82**
Toxteth. *Mers* 2F **83**
Toynton All Saints. *Linc* 4C **88**
Toynton Fen Side. *Linc* 4C **88**
Toynton St Peter. *Linc* 4D **88**
Toy's Hill. *Kent* 5F **39**
Trabboch. *E Ayr* 2D **116**
Traboe. *Corn* 4E **5**
Tradespark. *High* 3C **158**
Trafford Park. *G Man* 1B **84**
Trallong. *Powy* 3C **46**
Tranent. *E Lot* 2H **129**
Tranmere. *Mers* 2F **83**
Trantlebeg. *High* 3A **168**
Trantlemore. *High* 3A **168**
Tranwell. *Nmbd* 1E **115**
Trapp. *Carm* 4G **45**
Traquair. *Bord* 1F **119**
Trash Green. *W Ber* 5E **37**
Trawden. *Lanc* 1H **91**
Trawscoed. *Powy* 2D **46**
Trawsfynydd. *Gwyn* 2G **69**
Trawsgoed. *Cdgn* 3F **57**
Treaddow. *Here* 3A **48**
Trealaw. *Rhon* 2D **32**
Treales. *Lanc* 1C **90**
Trearddur. *IOA* 3B **80**
Treaslane. *High* 3C **154**
Treator. *Corn* 1D **6**
Trebanog. *Rhon* 2D **32**
Trebanos. *Neat* 5H **45**
Trebarber. *Corn* 2C **6**
Trebartha. *Corn* 5C **10**
Trebarwith. *Corn* 4A **10**
Trebetherick. *Corn* 1D **6**
Treborough. *Som* 3D **20**
Trebudannon. *Corn* 2C **6**
Trebullett. *Corn* 5D **10**
Treburley. *Corn* 5D **10**
Treburrick. *Corn* 1C **6**
Trebyan. *Corn* 2E **7**
Trecastle. *Powy* 3B **46**
Trecenydd. *Cphy* 3E **33**
Trecott. *Devn* 2G **11**
Trecwn. *Pemb* 1D **42**
Trecynon. *Rhon* 5C **46**
Tredaule. *Corn* 4C **10**
Tredavoe. *Corn* 4B **4**
Tredegar. *Blae* 5E **47**
Trederwen. *Powy* 4E **71**
Tredington. *Glos* 3E **49**
Tredington. *Warw* 1A **50**
Tredinnick. *Corn* 2F **7**
(nr. Bodmin)
Tredinnick. *Corn* 3G **7**
(nr. Looe)
Tredinnick. *Corn* 1D **6**
(nr. Padstow)
Tredogan. *V Glam* 5D **32**
Tredomen. *Powy* 2E **46**
Tredunnock. *Mon* 2G **33**
Tredustan. *Powy* 2E **47**
Treen. *Corn* 4A **4**
(nr. Land's End)
Treen. *Corn* 3B **4**
(nr. St Ives)
Treeton. *S Yor* 2B **86**
Trefaldwyn. *Powy* 1E **58**
Trefasser. *Pemb* 1C **42**
Trefdraeth. *IOA* 3D **80**
Trefdraeth. *Pemb* 1E **43**
Trefecca. *Powy* 2E **47**
Trefechan. *Mer T* 5D **46**
Trefeglwys. *Powy* 1B **58**
Trefeitha. *Powy* 2E **46**
Trefenter. *Cdgn* 4F **57**
Treffgarne. *Pemb* 2D **42**
Treffynnon. *Flin* 3D **82**
Treffynnon. *Pemb* 2C **42**
Trefil. *Blae* 4E **46**
Trefilan. *Cdgn* 5E **57**
Trefin. *Pemb* 1C **42**
Treflach. *Shrp* 3E **71**
Trefnant. *Den* 3C **82**
Trefonen. *Shrp* 3E **71**
Trefor. *Gwyn* 1C **68**
Trefor. *IOA* 3C **80**
Treforest. *Rhon* 3D **32**
Trefrew. *Corn* 4B **10**
Trefriw. *Cnwy* 4G **81**
Tref-y-Clawdd. *Powy* 3E **59**
Trefynwy. *Mon* 4A **48**
Tregada. *Corn* 4D **10**
Tregadillett. *Corn* 4D **10**
Tregare. *Mon* 4H **47**
Tregarne. *Corn* 4E **5**
Tregaron. *Cdgn* 5F **57**
Tregarth. *Gwyn* 4F **81**
Tregear. *Corn* 3C **6**
Tregeare. *Corn* 4C **10**
Tregeiriog. *Wrex* 2D **70**
Tregele. *IOA* 1C **80**
Tregeseal. *Corn* 3A **4**
Tregiskey. *Corn* 4E **6**
Tregole. *Corn* 3B **10**
Tregolwyn. *V Glam* 4C **32**
Tregonetha. *Corn* 2D **6**
Tregonhawke. *Corn* 3A **8**
Tregony. *Corn* 4D **6**
Tregoodwell. *Corn* 4B **10**
Tregorrick. *Corn* 3E **6**
Tregoss. *Corn* 2D **6**
Tregowris. *Corn* 4E **5**
Tregoyd. *Powy* 2E **47**
Tregrehan Mills. *Corn* 3E **7**
Tre-groes. *Cdgn* 1E **45**
Tregullon. *Corn* 2E **7**
Tregurrian. *Corn* 2C **6**
Tregynon. *Powy* 1C **58**
Trehafod. *Rhon* 2D **32**
Trehan. *Corn* 3A **8**
Treharris. *Mer T* 2E **32**
Treherbert. *Rhon* 2C **32**
Trehunist. *Corn* 2H **7**
Trekenner. *Corn* 5D **10**
Trekenning. *Corn* 2D **6**
Treknow. *Corn* 4A **10**
Trelales. *B'end* 3B **32**
Trelan. *Corn* 5E **5**
Trelash. *Corn* 3B **10**
Trelassick. *Corn* 3C **6**
Trelawnyd. *Flin* 3C **82**
Trelech. *Carm* 1G **43**
Treleddyd-fawr. *Pemb* 2B **42**
Trelewis. *Mer T* 2E **32**
Treligga. *Corn* 4A **10**
Trelights. *Corn* 1D **6**
Trelill. *Corn* 5A **10**
Trelissick. *Corn* 5C **6**
Trelleck. *Mon* 5A **48**
Trelleck Grange. *Mon* 5H **47**
Trelogan. *Flin* 2D **82**
Trelystan. *Powy* 5E **71**
Tremadog. *Gwyn* 1E **69**
Tremail. *Corn* 4B **10**
Tremain. *Cdgn* 1C **44**
Tremaine. *Corn* 4C **10**
Tremar. *Corn* 2G **7**
Trematon. *Corn* 3H **7**
Tremeirchion. *Den* 3C **82**
Tremore. *Corn* 2E **6**
Tremorfa. *Card* 4F **33**
Trenance. *Corn* 5D **4**
(nr. Helston)
Trenance. *Corn* 2C **6**
(nr. Newquay)
Trenance. *Corn* 1D **6**
(nr. Padstow)
Trenarren. *Corn* 4E **7**
Trench. *Telf* 4A **72**
Trencreek. *Corn* 2C **6**
Trendeal. *Corn* 3C **6**
Trenear. *Corn* 5A **6**
Treneglos. *Corn* 4C **10**
Trenewan. *Corn* 3F **7**
Trengune. *Corn* 3B **10**
Trent. *Dors* 1A **14**
Trentham. *Stoke* 1C **72**
Trentishoe. *Devn* 2G **19**
Trentlock. *Derbs* 2B **74**
Treoes. *V Glam* 4C **32**
Treorchy. *Rhon* 2C **32**
Treorci. *Rhon* 2C **32**
Tre'r-ddol. *Cdgn* 1F **57**
Tre'r llai. *Powy* 5E **71**
Trerulefoot. *Corn* 3H **7**
Tresaith. *Cdgn* 5B **56**
Trescott. *Staf* 1C **60**
Trescowe. *Corn* 3C **4**
Tresham. *Glos* 2C **34**
Tresigin. *V Glam* 4C **32**
Tresillian. *Corn* 4C **6**
Tresimwn. *V Glam* 4D **32**
Tresinney. *Corn* 4B **10**
Treskillard. *Corn* 5A **6**
Treskinnick Cross. *Corn* 3C **10**
Tresmeer. *Corn* 4C **10**
Tresparrett. *Corn* 3B **10**
Tresparrett Posts. *Corn* 3B **10**
Tressady. *High* 3D **164**
Tressait. *Per* 2F **143**
Tresta. *Shet* 6E **173**
Treswell. *Notts* 3E **87**
Treswithian. *Corn* 3D **4**
Tre Taliesin. *Cdgn* 1F **57**
Trethomas. *Cphy* 3E **33**
Trethosa. *Corn* 3D **6**
Trethurgy. *Corn* 3E **7**
Tretio. *Pemb* 2B **42**
Tretire. *Here* 3A **48**
Tretower. *Powy* 3E **47**
Treuddyn. *Flin* 5E **83**
Trevadlock. *Corn* 5C **10**
Trevalga. *Corn* 3A **10**
Trevalyn. *Wrex* 5F **83**
Trevance. *Corn* 1D **6**
Trevanger. *Corn* 1D **6**
Trevanson. *Corn* 1D **6**
Trevarrack. *Corn* 3B **4**
Trevarren. *Corn* 2D **6**
Trevarrian. *Corn* 2C **6**
Trevarrick. *Corn* 4D **6**
Tre-vaughan. *Carm* 3E **45**
(nr. Carmarthen)
Trevaughan. *Carm* 3F **43**
(nr. Whitland)
Treveighan. *Corn* 5A **10**
Trevellas. *Corn* 3B **6**
Trevelmond. *Corn* 2G **7**
Treverva. *Corn* 5B **6**
Trevescan. *Corn* 4A **4**
Trevethin. *Torf* 5F **47**
Trevia. *Corn* 4A **10**
Trevigro. *Corn* 2H **7**
Trevilley. *Corn* 4A **4**
Treviscoe. *Corn* 3D **6**
Trevivian. *Corn* 4B **10**
Trevone. *Corn* 1C **6**
Trevor. *Wrex* 1E **71**
Trevor Uchaf. *Den* 1E **71**
Trew. *Corn* 4D **4**
Trewalder. *Corn* 4A **10**
Trewarlett. *Corn* 4D **10**
Trewarmett. *Corn* 4A **10**
Trewassa. *Corn* 4B **10**
Treween. *Corn* 4C **10**
Trewellard. *Corn* 3A **4**
Trewen. *Corn* 4C **10**
Trewennack. *Corn* 4D **5**
Trewern. *Powy* 4E **71**
Trewetha. *Corn* 5A **10**
Trewidland. *Corn* 2G **7**
Trewint. *Corn* 3B **10**
Trewithian. *Corn* 5C **6**
Trewoofe. *Corn* 4B **4**
Trewoon. *Corn* 3D **6**
Treworthal. *Corn* 5C **6**
Trewyddel. *Pemb* 1B **44**
Treyarnon. *Corn* 1C **6**
Treyford. *W Sus* 1G **17**
Triangle. *Staf* 5E **73**
Triangle. *W Yor* 2A **92**
Trickett's Cross. *Dors* 2F **15**
Trimdon. *Dur* 1A **106**
Trimdon Colliery. *Dur* 1A **106**
Trimdon Grange. *Dur* 1A **106**
Trimingham. *Norf* 2E **79**
Trimley Lower Street. *Suff* 2F **55**
Trimley St Martin. *Suff* 2F **55**
Trimley St Mary. *Suff* 2F **55**
Trimpley. *Worc* 3B **60**
Trimsaran. *Carm* 5E **45**
Trimstone. *Devn* 2F **19**
Trinafour. *Per* 2E **142**
Trinant. *Cphy* 2F **33**
Tring. *Herts* 4H **51**
Trinity. *Ang* 2F **145**
Trinity. *Edin* 2F **129**
Trisant. *Cdgn* 3G **57**
Trislaig. *High* 1E **141**
Trispen. *Corn* 3C **6**
Tritlington. *Nmbd* 5G **121**
Trochry. *Per* 4G **143**
Troedrhiwdalar. *Powy* 5B **58**
Troedrhiwfuwch. *Cphy* 5E **47**
Troedrhiwgwair. *Blae* 5E **47**
Troedyraur. *Cdgn* 1D **44**
Troedyrhiw. *Mer T* 5D **46**
Trondavoe. *Shet* 4E **173**
Troon. *Corn* 5A **6**
Troon. *S Ayr* 1C **116**
Troqueer. *Dum* 2A **112**
Troston. *Suff* 3A **66**
Trottiscliffe. *Kent* 4H **39**
Trotton. *W Sus* 4G **25**
Troutbeck. *Cumb* 4F **103**
(nr. Ambleside)
Troutbeck. *Cumb* 2E **103**
(nr. Penrith)
Troutbeck Bridge. *Cumb* 4F **103**
Troway. *Derbs* 3A **86**
Trowbridge. *Wilts* 1D **22**
Trowell. *Notts* 2B **74**
Trowle Common. *Wilts* 1D **22**
Trowley Bottom. *Herts* 4A **52**
Trowse Newton. *Norf* 5E **79**
Trudoxhill. *Som* 2C **22**
Trull. *Som* 4F **21**
Trumaisgearraidh. *W Isl* 1D **170**
Trumpan. *High* 2B **154**
Trumpet. *Here* 2B **48**
Trumpington. *Cambs* 5D **64**
Trumps Green. *Surr* 4A **38**
Trunch. *Norf* 2E **79**
Trunnah. *Lanc* 5C **96**
Truro. *Corn* 4C **6**
Trusham. *Devn* 4B **12**
Trusley. *Derbs* 2G **73**
Trusthorpe. *Linc* 2E **89**
Tryfil. *IOA* 2D **80**
Trysull. *Staf* 1C **60**
Tubney. *Oxon* 2C **36**
Tuckenhay. *Devn* 3E **9**
Tuckhill. *Staf* 2B **60**
Tuckingmill. *Corn* 4A **6**
Tuckton. *Bour* 3G **15**
Tuddenham. *Suff* 1E **55**
(nr. Ipswich)
Tuddenham. *Suff* 3G **65**
(nr. Mildenhall)
Tudeley. *Kent* 1H **27**
Tudhoe. *Dur* 1F **105**
Tudhoe Grange. *Dur* 1F **105**
Tudorville. *Here* 3A **48**
Tudweiliog. *Gwyn* 2B **68**
Tuesley. *Surr* 1A **26**
Tufton. *Hants* 2C **24**
Tufton. *Pemb* 2E **43**
Tugby. *Leics* 5E **75**
Tugford. *Shrp* 2H **59**
Tughall. *Nmbd* 2G **121**
Tulchan. *Per* 1B **136**
Tullibardine. *Per* 2B **136**
Tullibody. *Clac* 4A **136**

Tullich. *Arg* 2H **133**
Tullich. *High* 4B **156**
(nr. Lochcarron)
Tullich. *High* 1C **158**
(nr. Tain)
Tullich. *Mor* 4H **159**
Tullich Muir. *High* 1B **158**
Tulliemet. *Per* 3G **143**
Tulloch. *Abers* 5F **161**
Tulloch. *High* 4D **164**
(nr. Bonar Bridge)
Tulloch. *High* 5F **149**
(nr. Fort William)
Tulloch. *High* 2D **151**
(nr. Grantown-on-Spey)
Tulloch. *Per* 1C **136**
Tullochgorm. *Arg* 4G **133**
Tullybeagles Lodge. *Per* 5H **143**
Tullymurdoch. *Per* 3A **144**
Tullynessle. *Abers* 2C **152**
Tumble. *Carm* 4F **45**
Tumbler's Green. *Essx* 3B **54**
Tumby. *Linc* 4B **88**
Tumby Woodside. *Linc* 5B **88**
Tummel Bridge. *Per* 3E **143**
Tunbridge Wells, Royal. *Kent* 2G **27**
Tunga. *W Isl* 4G **171**
Tungate. *Norf* 3E **79**
Tunley. *Bath* 1B **22**
Tunstall. *E Yor* 1G **95**
Tunstall. *Kent* 4C **40**
Tunstall. *Lanc* 2F **97**
Tunstall. *Norf* 5G **79**
Tunstall. *N Yor* 5F **105**
Tunstall. *Staf* 3B **72**
Tunstall. *Stoke* 5C **84**
Tunstall. *Suff* 5F **67**
Tunstall. *Tyne* 4G **115**
Tunstead. *Derbs* 3F **85**
Tunstead. *Norf* 3E **79**
Tunstead Milton. *Derbs* 2E **85**
Tunworth. *Hants* 2E **25**
Tupsley. *Here* 1A **48**
Tupton. *Derbs* 4A **86**
Turfholm. *S Lan* 1H **117**
Turfmoor. *Devn* 2F **13**
Turgis Green. *Hants* 1E **25**
Turkdean. *Glos* 4G **49**
Turkey Island. *Hants* 1D **16**
Tur Langton. *Leics* 1E **62**
Turleigh. *Wilts* 5D **34**
Turlin Moor. *Pool* 3E **15**
Turnant. *Here* 3G **47**
Turnastone. *Here* 2G **47**
Turnberry. *S Ayr* 4B **116**
Turnchapel. *Plym* 3A **8**
Turnditch. *Derbs* 1G **73**
Turners Hill. *W Sus* 2E **27**
Turners Puddle. *Dors* 3D **14**
Turnford. *Herts* 5D **52**
Turnhouse. *Edin* 2E **129**
Turnworth. *Dors* 2D **14**
Turriff. *Abers* 4E **161**
Tursdale. *Dur* 1A **106**
Turton Bottoms. *Bkbn* 3F **91**
Turtory. *Mor* 4C **160**
Turves Green. *W Mid* 3E **61**
Turvey. *Beds* 5G **63**
Turville. *Buck* 2F **37**
Turville Heath. *Buck* 2F **37**
Turweston. *Buck* 2E **50**
Tushielaw. *Bord* 3F **119**
Tutbury. *Staf* 3G **73**
Tutnall. *Worc* 3D **61**
Tutsbill. *Glos* 2A **34**
Tuttington. *Norf* 3E **79**
Tutts Clump. *W Ber* 4D **36**
Tutwell. *Corn* 5D **11**
Tuxford. *Notts* 3E **87**
Twatt. *Orkn* 5B **172**
Twatt. *Shet* 6E **173**
Twechar. *E Dun* 2A **128**
Tweedale. *Telf* 5B **72**
Tweedmouth. *Nmbd* 4F **131**
Tweedsmuir. *Bord* 2C **118**
Twelveheads. *Corn* 4B **6**
Twemlow Green. *Ches* 4B **84**
Twenty. *Linc* 3A **76**
Twerton. *Bath* 5C **34**
Twickenham. *G Lon* 3C **38**
Twigworth. *Glos* 3D **48**
Twineham. *W Sus* 3D **26**
Twinhoe. *Bath* 1C **22**
Twinstead. *Essx* 2B **54**
Twinstead Green. *Essx* 2B **54**
Twiss Green. *Warr* 1A **84**
Twiston. *Lanc* 5H **97**
Twitchen. *Devn* 3A **20**
Twitchen. *Shrp* 3F **59**
Two Bridges. *Devn* 5G **11**
Two Bridges. *Glos* 5B **48**
Two Dales. *Derbs* 4G **85**
Two Gates. *Staf* 5G **73**
Two Mile Oak Cross. *Devn* 2E **9**
Twycross. *Leics* 5H **73**
Twyford. *Buck* 3E **51**
Twyford. *Derbs* 3H **73**
Twyford. *Dors* 1D **14**
Twyford. *Hants* 4C **24**
Twyford. *Leics* 4E **75**
Twyford. *Norf* 3C **78**
Twyford. *Wok* 4F **37**
Twyford Common. *Here* 2A **48**
Twyncarno. *Cphy* 5E **46**
Twynholm. *Dum* 4D **110**
Twyning. *Glos* 2D **49**
Twyning Green. *Glos* 2E **49**
Twynllanan. *Carm* 3A **46**
Twynmynydd. *Carm* 4G **45**
Twyn-y-Sheriff. *Mon* 5H **47**
Twywell. *Nptn* 3G **63**
Tyberton. *Here* 2G **47**
Tyburn. *W Mid* 1F **61**
Tyby. *Norf* 3C **78**
Tycroes. *Carm* 4G **45**
Tycrwyn. *Powy* 4D **70**
Tyddewi. *Pemb* 2B **42**
Tydd Gote. *Linc* 4D **76**
Tydd St Giles. *Cambs* 4D **76**
Tydd St Mary. *Linc* 4D **76**
Tye. *Hants* 2F **17**
Tye Green. *Essx* 3F **53**
(nr. Bishop's Stortford)
Tye Green. *Essx* 3A **54**
(nr. Braintree)
Tye Green. *Essx* 2F **53**
(nr. Saffron Walden)
Tyersal. *W Yor* 1B **92**
Ty Issa. *Powy* 3D **70**
Tyldesley. *G Man* 4E **91**
Tyle. *Carm* 3G **45**
Tyler Hill. *Kent* 4F **41**
Tylers Green. *Buck* 2G **37**
Tyler's Green. *Essx* 5F **53**
Tylorstown. *Rhon* 2D **32**
Tylwch. *Powy* 2B **58**
Ty-nant. *Cnwy* 1B **70**
Tyndrum. *Stir* 5H **141**
Tyneham. *Dors* 4D **15**
Tynehead. *Midl* 4G **129**
Tynemouth. *Tyne* 3G **115**
Tyneside. *Tyne* 3F **115**
Tyne Tunnel. *Tyne* 3G **115**
Tynewydd. *Rhon* 2C **32**
Tyninghame. *E Lot* 2C **130**
Tynron. *Dum* 5H **117**
Ty'n-y-bryn. *Rhon* 3D **32**
Tyn-y-celyn. *Wrex* 2D **70**
Tyn-y-cwm. *Swan* 5G **45**
Tyn-y-ffridd. *Powy* 2D **70**
Tynygongl. *IOA* 2E **81**
Tynygraig. *Cdgn* 4F **57**
Tyn-y-groes. *Cnwy* 3G **81**
Ty'n-yr-eithin. *Cdgn* 4F **57**
Tyn-y-rhyd. *Powy* 4C **70**
Tyn-y-wern. *Powy* 3C **70**
Tyrie. *Abers* 2G **161**
Tyringham. *Mil* 1G **51**
Tythecott. *Devn* 1E **11**
Tythegston. *B'end* 4B **32**
Tytherington. *Ches* 3D **84**
Tytherington. *Som* 2C **22**
Tytherington. *S Glo* 3B **34**
Tytherington. *Wilts* 2E **23**
Tytherleigh. *Devn* 2G **13**
Tywardreath. *Corn* 3E **7**
Tywardreath Highway. *Corn* 3E **7**
Tywyn. *Cnwy* 3G **81**
Tywyn. *Gwyn* 5E **69**

U

Uags. *High* 5G **155**
Ubbeston Green. *Suff* 3F **67**
Ubley. *Bath* 1A **22**
Uckerby. *N Yor* 4F **105**
Uckfield. *E Sus* 3F **27**
Uckinghall. *Worc* 2D **48**
Uckington. *Glos* 3E **49**
Uckington. *Shrp* 5H **71**
Uddingston. *S Lan* 3H **127**
Uddington. *S Lan* 1A **118**
Udimore. *E Sus* 4C **28**
Udny Green. *Abers* 1F **153**
Udny Station. *Abers* 1G **153**
Udston. *S Lan* 4A **128**
Udstonhead. *S Lan* 5A **128**
Uffcott. *Wilts* 4G **35**
Uffculme. *Devn* 1D **12**
Uffington. *Linc* 5H **75**
Uffington. *Oxon* 3B **36**
Uffington. *Shrp* 4H **71**
Ufford. *Pet* 5H **75**
Ufford. *Suff* 5E **67**
Ufton. *Warw* 4A **62**
Ufton Nervet. *W Ber* 5E **37**
Ugadale. *Arg* 3B **122**
Ugborough. *Devn* 3C **8**
Ugford. *Wilts* 3F **23**
Uggeshall. *Suff* 2G **67**
Ugglebarnby. *N Yor* 4F **107**
Ugley. *Essx* 3F **53**
Ugley Green. *Essx* 3F **53**
Ugthorpe. *N Yor* 3E **107**
Uidh. *W Isl* 9B **170**
Uig. *Arg* 3C **138**
Uig. *High* 2C **154**
(nr. Balgown)
Uig. *High* 3A **154**
(nr. Dunvegan)
Uigshader. *High* 4D **154**
Uisken. *Arg* 2A **132**
Ulbster. *High* 4F **169**
Ulcat Row. *Cumb* 2F **103**
Ulceby. *Linc* 3D **88**
Ulceby. *N Lin* 3E **94**
Ulceby Skitter. *N Lin* 3E **94**
Ulcombe. *Kent* 1C **28**
Uldale. *Cumb* 1D **102**
Uley. *Glos* 2C **34**
Ulgham. *Nmbd* 5G **121**
Ullapool. *High* 4F **163**
Ullenhall. *Warw* 4F **61**
Ulleskelf. *N Yor* 1F **93**
Ullesthorpe. *Leics* 2C **62**
Ulley. *S Yor* 2B **86**
Ullingswick. *Here* 1A **48**
Ullinish. *High* 5C **154**
Ullock. *Cumb* 2B **102**
Ulpha. *Cumb* 5C **102**
Ulrome. *E Yor* 4F **101**
Ulsta. *Shet* 3F **173**
Ulting. *Essx* 5B **54**
Ulva House. *Arg* 5F **139**
Ulverston. *Cumb* 2B **96**
Ulwell. *Dors* 4F **15**
Umberleigh. *Devn* 4G **19**
Unapool. *High* 5C **166**
Underbarrow. *Cumb* 5F **103**
Undercliffe. *W Yor* 1B **92**
Underdale. *Shrp* 4H **71**
Underriver. *Kent* 5G **39**
Under Tofts. *S Yor* 2H **85**
Underton. *Shrp* 1A **60**
Underwood. *Notts* 5B **86**
Underwood. *Plym* 3B **8**
Undley. *Suff* 2F **65**
Undy. *Mon* 3H **33**
Union Mills. *IOM* 4C **108**
Union Street. *E Sus* 2B **28**
Unstone. *Derbs* 3A **86**
Unstone Green. *Derbs* 3A **86**
Unthank. *Cumb* 5E **113**
(nr. Carlisle)
Unthank. *Cumb* 5H **113**
(nr. Gamblesby)
Unthank. *Cumb* 1F **103**
(nr. Penrith)
Unthank End. *Cumb* 1F **103**
Upavon. *Wilts* 1G **23**
Up Cerne. *Dors* 2B **14**
Upchurch. *Kent* 4C **40**
Upcott. *Devn* 2F **11**
Upcott. *Here* 5F **59**
Upend. *Cambs* 5G **65**
Up Exe. *Devn* 2C **12**
Upgate. *Norf* 4D **78**
Upgate Street. *Norf* 1C **66**
Uphall. *Dors* 2A **14**
Uphall. *W Lot* 2D **128**
Uphall Station. *W Lot* 2D **128**
Upham. *Devn* 2B **12**
Upham. *Hants* 4D **24**
Uphampton. *Here* 4F **59**
Uphampton. *Worc* 4C **60**
Up Hatherley. *Glos* 3E **49**
Uphill. *N Som* 1G **21**
Up Holland. *Lanc* 4D **90**
Uplawmoor. *E Ren* 4F **127**
Upleadon. *Glos* 3C **48**
Upleatham. *Red C* 3D **106**
Uplees. *Kent* 4D **40**
Uploders. *Dors* 3A **14**
Uplowman. *Devn* 1D **12**
Uplyme. *Devn* 3G **13**
Up Marden. *W Sus* 1F **17**
Upminster. *G Lon* 2G **39**
Up Nately. *Hants* 1E **25**
Upottery. *Devn* 2F **13**
Uppat. *High* 3F **165**
Upper Affcot. *Shrp* 2G **59**
Upper Arley. *Worc* 2B **60**
Upper Armley. *W Yor* 1C **92**
Upper Arncott. *Oxon* 4E **50**
Upper Astrop. *Nptn* 2D **50**
Upper Badcall. *High* 4B **166**
Upper Bangor. *Gwyn* 3E **81**
Upper Basildon. *W Ber* 4D **36**
Upper Batley. *W Yor* 2C **92**
Upper Beeding. *W Sus* 4C **26**
Upper Benefield. *Nptn* 2G **63**
Upper Bentley. *Worc* 4D **61**
Upper Bighouse. *High* 3A **168**
Upper Boddam. *Abers* 5D **160**
Upper Boddington. *Nptn* 5B **62**
Upper Bogside. *Mor* 3G **159**
Upper Booth. *Derbs* 2F **85**
Upper Borth. *Cdgn* 2F **57**
Upper Boyndlie. *Abers* 2G **161**
Upper Brailes. *Warw* 2B **50**
Upper Breakish. *High* 1E **147**
Upper Breinton. *Here* 1H **47**
Upper Broadheath. *Worc* 5C **60**
Upper Broughton. *Notts* 3D **74**
Upper Brynamman. *Carm* 4H **45**
Upper Bucklebury. *W Ber* 5D **36**
Upper Bullington. *Hants* 2C **24**
Upper Burgate. *Hants* 1G **15**
Upper Caldecote. *Beds* 1B **52**
Upper Canterton. *Hants* 1A **16**
Upper Catesby. *Nptn* 5C **62**
Upper Chapel. *Powy* 1D **46**
Upper Cheddon. *Som* 4F **21**
Upper Chicksgrove. *Wilts* 4E **23**
Upper Church Village. *Rhon* 3D **32**
Upper Chute. *Wilts* 1A **24**
Upper Clatford. *Hants* 2B **24**
Upper Coberley. *Glos* 4E **49**
Upper Coedcae. *Torf* 5F **47**
Upper Cokeham. *W Sus* 5C **26**
Upper Common. *Hants* 2E **25**
Upper Cound. *Shrp* 5H **71**
Upper Cudworth. *S Yor* 4D **93**
Upper Cumberworth. *W Yor* 4C **92**
Upper Cuttlehill. *Abers* 4B **160**
Upper Cwmbran. *Torf* 2F **33**
Upper Dallachy. *Mor* 2A **160**
Upper Dean. *Beds* 4H **63**
Upper Dean. *Devn* 2D **8**
Upper Denby. *W Yor* 4C **92**
Upper Derraid. *High* 5E **159**
Upper Diabaig. *High* 2H **155**
Upper Dicker. *E Sus* 5G **27**
Upper Dinchope. *Shrp* 2G **59**
Upper Dochcarty. *High* 2H **157**
Upper Dounreay. *High* 2B **168**
Upper Dovercourt. *Essx* 2F **55**
Upper Dunsforth. *N Yor* 3G **99**
Upper Dunsley. *Herts* 4H **51**
Upper Eastern Green. *W Mid* 2G **61**
Upper Elkstone. *Staf* 5E **85**
Upper Ellastone. *Staf* 1F **73**
Upper End. *Derbs* 3E **85**
Upper Enham. *Hants* 2B **24**
Upper Farringdon. *Hants* 3F **25**
Upper Framilode. *Glos* 4C **48**
Upper Froyle. *Hants* 2F **25**
Upper Gills. *High* 1F **169**
Upper Glenfintaig. *High* 5E **149**
Upper Godney. *Som* 2H **21**
Upper Gravenhurst. *Beds* 2B **52**
Upper Green. *Essx* 2E **53**
Upper Green. *W Ber* 5B **36**
Upper Green. *W Yor* 2C **92**
Upper Grove Common. *Here* 3A **48**
Upper Hackney. *Derbs* 4G **85**
Upper Hale. *Surr* 2G **25**
Upper Halliford. *Surr* 4B **38**
Upper Halling. *Medw* 4A **40**
Upper Hambleton. *Rut* 5G **75**
Upper Hardres Court. *Kent* 5F **41**
Upper Hardwick. *Here* 5G **59**
Upper Hartfield. *E Sus* 2F **27**
Upper Haugh. *S Yor* 1B **86**
Upper Hayton. *Shrp* 2H **59**
Upper Heath. *Shrp* 2H **59**
Upper Hellesdon. *Norf* 4E **79**
Upper Helmsley. *N Yor* 4A **100**
Upper Hengoed. *Shrp* 2E **71**
Upper Hergest. *Here* 5E **59**
Upper Heyford. *Nptn* 5D **62**
Upper Heyford. *Oxon* 3C **50**
Upper Hill. *Here* 5G **59**
Upper Hindhope. *Bord* 4B **120**
Upper Hopton. *W Yor* 3B **92**
Upper Horsebridge. *E Sus* 4G **27**
Upper Howsell. *Worc* 1C **48**
Upper Hulme. *Staf* 4E **85**
Upper Inglesham. *Swin* 2H **35**
Upper Kilcott. *Glos* 3C **34**
Upper Killay. *Swan* 3E **31**
Upper Kirkton. *Abers* 5E **161**
Upper Kirkton. *N Ayr* 4C **126**
Upper Knockando. *Mor* 4F **159**
Upper Knockchoilum. *High* 2G **149**
Upper Lambourn. *W Ber* 3B **36**
Upper Langford. *N Som* 1H **21**
Upper Langwith. *Derbs* 4C **86**
Upper Largo. *Fife* 3G **137**
Upper Latheron. *High* 5D **169**
Upper Layham. *Suff* 1D **54**
Upper Leigh. *Staf* 2E **73**
Upper Lenie. *High* 1H **149**
Upper Lochton. *Abers* 4E **152**
Upper Longdon. *Staf* 4E **73**
Upper Longwood. *Shrp* 5A **72**
Upper Lybster. *High* 5E **169**
Upper Lydbrook. *Glos* 4B **48**

Upper Lye. *Here* 4F **59**
Upper Maes-coed. *Here* 2G **47**
Upper Midway. *Derbs* 3G **73**
Uppermill. *G Man* 4H **91**
Upper Millichope. *Shrp* 2H **59**
Upper Milovaig. *High* 4A **154**
Upper Minety. *Wilts* 2F **35**
Upper Mitton. *Worc* 3C **60**
Upper Nash. *Pemb* 4E **43**
Upper Netchwood. *Shrp* 1A **60**
Upper Nobut. *Staf* 2E **73**
Upper North Dean. *Buck* 2G **37**
Upper Norwood. *W Sus* 4A **26**
Upper Nyland. *Dors* 4C **22**
Upper Oddington. *Glos* 3H **49**
Upper Ollach. *High* 5E **155**
Upper Outwoods. *Staf* 3G **73**
Upper Padley. *Derbs* 3G **85**
Upper Pennington. *Hants* 3B **16**
Upper Poppleton. *York* 4H **99**
Upper Quinton. *Warw* 1G **49**
Upper Rochford. *Worc* 4A **60**
Upper Rusko. *Dum* 3C **110**
Upper Sandaig. *High* 2F **147**
Upper Sanday. *Orkn* 7E **172**
Upper Sapey. *Here* 4A **60**
Upper Seagry. *Wilts* 3E **35**
Upper Shelton. *Beds* 1H **51**
Upper Sheringham. *Norf* 1D **78**
Upper Skelmorlie. *N Ayr* 3C **126**
Upper Slaughter. *Glos* 3G **49**
Upper Sonachan. *Arg* 1H **133**
Upper Soudley. *Glos* 4B **48**
Upper Staploe. *Beds* 5A **64**
Upper Stoke. *Norf* 5E **79**
Upper Stondon. *Beds* 2B **52**
Upper Stowe. *Nptn* 5D **62**
Upper Street. *Hants* 1G **15**
Upper Street. *Norf* 4F **79**
(nr. Horning)
Upper Street. *Norf* 4F **79**
(nr. Hoveton)
Upper Street. *Suff* 2E **55**
Upper Strensham. *Worc* 2E **49**
Upper Studley. *Wilts* 1D **22**
Upper Sundon. *Beds* 3A **52**
Upper Swell. *Glos* 3G **49**
Upper Tankersley. *S Yor* 1H **85**
Upper Tean. *Staf* 2E **73**
Upperthong. *W Yor* 4B **92**
Upperthorpe. *N Lin* 4A **94**
Upper Thurnham. *Lanc* 4D **96**
Upper Tillyrie. *Per* 3D **136**
Upperton. *W Sus* 3A **26**
Upper Tooting. *G Lon* 3D **38**
Uppertown. *Derbs* 4H **85**
(nr. Ashover)
Upper Town. *Derbs* 5G **85**
(nr. Bonsall)
Upper Town. *Derbs* 5G **85**
(nr. Hognaston)
Upper Town. *Here* 1A **48**
Uppertown. *High* 1F **169**
Upper Town. *N Som* 5A **34**
Uppertown. *Nmbd* 2B **114**
Uppertown. *Orkn* 8D **172**
Upper Tysoe. *Warw* 1B **50**
Upper Upham. *Wilts* 4H **35**
Upper Upnor. *Medw* 3B **40**
Upper Urquhart. *Fife* 3D **136**
Upper Wardington. *Oxon* 1C **50**
Upper Weald. *Mil* 2G **51**
Upper Weedon. *Nptn* 5D **62**
Upper Wellingham. *E Sus* 4F **27**
Upper Whiston. *S Yor* 2B **86**
Upper Wield. *Hants* 3E **25**
Upper Winchendon. *Buck* 4F **51**
Upperwood. *Derbs* 5G **85**
Upper Woodford. *Wilts* 3G **23**
Upper Wootton. *Hants* 1D **24**
Upper Wraxall. *Wilts* 4D **34**
Upper Wyche. *Here* 1C **48**
Uppincott. *Devn* 2B **12**
Uppingham. *Rut* 1F **63**
Uppington. *Shrp* 5H **71**
Upsall. *N Yor* 1G **99**
Upsettlington. *Bord* 5E **131**
Upshire. *Essx* 5E **53**
Up Somborne. *Hants* 3B **24**
Upstreet. *Kent* 4G **41**
Up Sydling. *Dors* 2B **14**
Upthorpe. *Suff* 3B **66**
Upton. *Buck* 4F **51**
Upton. *Cambs* 3A **64**
Upton. *Ches* 4G **83**
Upton. *Corn* 2C **10**
(nr. Bude)
Upton. *Corn* 5C **10**
(nr. Liskeard)
Upton. *Cumb* 1E **102**
Upton. *Devn* 2D **12**
(nr. Honiton)
Upton. *Devn* 4D **8**
(nr. Kingsbridge)
Upton. *Dors* 3E **15**
(nr. Poole)
Upton. *Dors* 4C **14**
(nr. Weymouth)
Upton. *E Yor* 4F **101**
Upton. *Hants* 1B **24**
(nr. Andover)
Upton. *Hants* 1B **16**
(nr. Southampton)
Upton. *IOW* 3D **16**
Upton. *Leics* 1A **62**
Upton. *Linc* 2F **87**
Upton. *Mers* 2E **83**
Upton. *Norf* 4F **79**
Upton. *Nptn* 4E **62**
Upton. *Notts* 3E **87**
(nr. Retford)
Upton. *Notts* 5E **87**
(nr. Southwell)
Upton. *Oxon* 3D **36**
Upton. *Pemb* 4E **43**
Upton. *Pet* 5A **76**
Upton. *Slo* 3A **38**
Upton. *Som* 4H **21**
(nr. Somerton)
Upton. *Som* 4C **20**
(nr. Wiveliscombe)
Upton. *Warw* 5F **61**
Upton. *W Yor* 3E **93**
Upton. *Wilts* 3D **22**
Upton Bishop. *Here* 3B **48**
Upton Cheyney. *S Glo* 5B **34**
Upton Cressett. *Shrp* 1A **60**
Upton Crews. *Here* 3B **48**
Upton Cross. *Corn* 5C **10**
Upton End. *Beds* 2B **52**
Upton Grey. *Hants* 2E **25**
Upton Heath. *Ches* 4G **83**
Upton Hellions. *Devn* 2B **12**
Upton Lovell. *Wilts* 2E **23**
Upton Magna. *Shrp* 4H **71**
Upton Noble. *Som* 3C **22**
Upton Pyne. *Devn* 3C **12**
Upton St Leonards. *Glos* 4D **48**
Upton Scudamore. *Wilts* 2D **22**
Upton Snodsbury. *Worc* 5D **60**
Upton upon Severn. *Worc* 1D **48**
Upton Warren. *Worc* 4D **60**
Upwaltham. *W Sus* 4A **26**
Upware. *Cambs* 3E **65**
Upwell. *Cambs* 5D **77**
Upwey. *Dors* 4B **14**
Upwick Green. *Herts* 3E **53**
Upwood. *Cambs* 2B **64**
Urafirth. *Shet* 4E **173**
Uragaig. *Arg* 4A **132**
Urchany. *High* 4C **158**
Urchfont. *Wilts* 1F **23**
Urdimarsh. *Here* 1A **48**
Ure. *Shet* 4D **173**
Ure Bank. *N Yor* 2F **99**
Urgha. *W Isl* 8D **171**
Urlay Nook. *Stoc T* 3B **106**
Urmston. *G Man* 1B **84**
Urquhart. *Mor* 2G **159**
Urra. *N Yor* 4C **106**
Urray. *High* 3H **157**
Usan. *Ang* 3G **145**
Ushaw Moor. *Dur* 5F **115**
Usk. *Mon* 5G **47**
Usselby. *Linc* 1H **87**
Usworth. *Tyne* 4G **115**
Uton. *Devn* 3B **12**
Utterby. *Linc* 1C **88**
Uttoxeter. *Staf* 2E **73**
Uwchmynydd. *Gwyn* 3A **68**
Uxbridge. *G Lon* 2B **38**
Uyeasound. *Shet* 1G **173**
Uzmaston. *Pemb* 3D **42**

V

Valley. *IOA* 3B **80**
Valley End. *Surr* 4A **38**
Valley Truckle. *Corn* 4B **10**
Valtos. *High* 2E **155**
Van. *Powy* 2B **58**
Vange. *Essx* 2B **40**
Varteg. *Torf* 5F **47**
Vatten. *High* 4B **154**
Vaul. *Arg* 4B **138**
Vauld,The. *Here* 1A **48**
Vaynol. *Gwyn* 3E **81**
Vaynor. *Mer T* 4D **46**
Veensgarth. *Shet* 7F **173**
Velindre. *Powy* 2E **47**
Vellow. *Som* 3D **20**
Velly. *Devn* 4C **18**
Venhay. *Devn* 1A **12**
Venn. *Devn* 4D **8**
Venngreen. *Devn* 1D **11**
Vennington. *Shrp* 5F **71**
Venn Ottery. *Devn* 3D **12**
Venn's Green. *Here* 1A **48**
Venny Tedburn. *Devn* 3B **12**
Venterdon. *Corn* 5D **10**
Ventnor. *IOW* 5D **16**
Vernham Dean. *Hants* 1B **24**
Vernham Street. *Hants* 1B **24**
Vernolds Common. *Shrp* 2G **59**
Verwood. *Dors* 2F **15**
Veryan. *Corn* 5D **6**
Veryan Green. *Corn* 4D **6**
Vicarage. *Devn* 4F **13**
Vickerstown. *Cumb* 3A **96**
Victoria. *Corn* 2D **6**
Vidlin. *Shet* 5F **173**
Viewpark. *N Lan* 3A **128**
Vigo. *W Mid* 5E **73**
Vigo Village. *Kent* 4H **39**
Village Bay. *High* 3B **154**
Vinehall Street. *E Sus* 3B **28**
Vine's Cross. *E Sus* 4G **27**
Viney Hill. *Glos* 5B **48**
Virginia Water. *Surr* 4A **38**
Virginstow. *Devn* 3D **11**
Vobster. *Som* 2C **22**
Voe. *Shet* 5F **173**
Vole. *Som* 2G **21**
Vowchurch. *Here* 2G **47**
Vulcan Village. *Warr* 1H **83**

W

Wackerfield. *Dur* 2E **105**
Wacton. *Norf* 1D **66**
Wadborough. *Worc* 1E **49**
Waddesdon. *Buck* 4F **51**
Waddeton. *Devn* 3E **9**
Waddicar. *Mers* 1F **83**
Waddingham. *Linc* 1G **87**
Waddington. *Lanc* 5G **97**
Waddington. *Linc* 4G **87**
Waddon. *Devn* 5B **12**
Wadebridge. *Corn* 1D **6**
Wadeford. *Som* 1G **13**
Wadenhoe. *Nptn* 2H **63**
Wadesmill. *Herts* 4D **52**
Wadhurst. *E Sus* 2H **27**
Wadshelf. *Derbs* 3H **85**
Wadsley. *S Yor* 1H **85**
Wadsley Bridge. *S Yor* 1H **85**
Wadswick. *Wilts* 5D **34**
Wadwick. *Hants* 1C **24**
Wadworth. *S Yor* 1C **86**
Waen. *Den* 4C **82**
(nr. Bodfari)
Waen. *Den* 4D **82**
(nr. Llandyrnog)
Waen. *Den* 4B **82**
(nr. Nantglyn)
Waen. *Powy* 1B **58**
Waen Fach. *Powy* 4E **70**
Waen Goleugoed. *Den* 3C **82**
Wag. *High* 1H **165**
Wainfleet All Saints. *Linc* 5D **89**
Wainfleet Bank. *Linc* 5D **88**
Wainfleet St Mary. *Linc* 5D **89**
Wainhouse Corner. *Corn* 3B **10**
Wainscott. *Medw* 3B **40**
Wainstalls. *W Yor* 2A **92**
Waitby. *Cumb* 4A **104**
Waithe. *Linc* 4F **95**
Wakefield. *W Yor* 2D **92**
Wakerley. *Nptn* 1G **63**
Wakes Colne. *Essx* 3B **54**
Walberswick. *Suff* 3G **67**
Walberton. *W Sus* 5A **26**
Walbottle. *Tyne* 3E **115**
Walby. *Cumb* 3F **113**
Walcombe. *Som* 2A **22**
Walcot. *Linc* 2H **75**
Walcot. *N Lin* 2B **94**
Walcot. *Swin* 3G **35**
Walcot. *Telf* 4H **71**
Walcot. *Warw* 5F **61**
Walcote. *Leics* 2C **62**
Walcot Green. *Norf* 2D **66**
Walcott. *Linc* 5A **88**
Walcott. *Norf* 2F **79**
Walden. *N Yor* 1C **98**
Walden Head. *N Yor* 1B **98**
Walden Stubbs. *N Yor* 3F **93**
Walderslade. *Medw* 4B **40**
Walderton. *W Sus* 1F **17**
Walditch. *Dors* 3H **13**
Waldley. *Derbs* 2F **73**
Waldridge. *Dur* 4F **115**
Waldringfield. *Suff* 1F **55**
Waldron. *E Sus* 4G **27**
Wales. *S Yor* 2B **86**
Walesby. *Linc* 1A **88**
Walesby. *Notts* 3D **86**
Walford. *Here* 3F **59**
(nr. Leintwardine)
Walford. *Here* 3A **48**
(nr. Ross-on-Wye)
Walford. *Shrp* 3G **71**
Walford. *Staf* 2C **72**
Walford Heath. *Shrp* 4G **71**
Walgherton. *Ches* 1A **72**
Walgrave. *Nptn* 3F **63**
Walhampton. *Hants* 3B **16**
Walkden. *G Man* 4F **91**
Walker. *Tyne* 3F **115**
Walkerburn. *Bord* 1F **119**
Walker Fold. *Lanc* 5F **97**
Walkeringham. *Notts* 1E **87**
Walkerith. *Linc* 1E **87**
Walkern. *Herts* 3C **52**
Walker's Green. *Here* 1A **48**
Walkerton. *Fife* 3E **137**
Walkerville. *N Yor* 5F **105**
Walkford. *Dors* 3H **15**
Walkhampton. *Devn* 2B **8**
Walkington. *E Yor* 1C **94**
Walkley. *S Yor* 2H **85**
Walk Mill. *Lanc* 1G **91**
Wall. *Corn* 3D **4**
Wall. *Nmbd* 3C **114**
Wall. *Staf* 5F **73**
Wallaceton. *Dum* 1F **111**
Wallacetown. *S Ayr* 2C **116**
(nr. Ayr)
Wallacetown. *S Ayr* 4B **116**
(nr. Dailly)
Wallands Park. *E Sus* 4F **27**
Wallasey. *Mers* 1F **83**
Wallaston Green. *Pemb* 4D **42**
Wallbrook. *W Mid* 1D **60**
Wallcrouch. *E Sus* 2A **28**
Wall End. *Cumb* 1B **96**
Wallend. *Medw* 3C **40**
Wall Heath. *W Mid* 2C **60**
Wallingford. *Oxon* 3E **36**
Wallington. *G Lon* 4D **39**
Wallington. *Hants* 2D **16**
Wallington. *Herts* 2C **52**
Wallis. *Pemb* 2E **43**
Wallisdown. *Pool* 3F **15**
Walliswood. *Surr* 2C **26**
Wall Nook. *Dur* 5F **115**
Walls. *Shet* 7D **173**
Wallsend. *Tyne* 3G **115**
Wallsworth. *Glos* 3D **48**
Wall under Heywood. *Shrp* 1H **59**
Wallyford. *E Lot* 2G **129**
Walmer. *Kent* 5H **41**
Walmer Bridge. *Lanc* 2C **90**
Walmersley. *G Man* 3G **91**
Walmley. *W Mid* 1F **61**
Walnut Grove. *Per* 1D **136**
Walpole. *Suff* 3F **67**
Walpole Cross Keys. *Norf* 4E **77**
Walpole Gate. *Norf* 4E **77**
Walpole Highway. *Norf* 4E **77**
Walpolelane. *Suff* 3F **67**
Walpole Marsh. *Norf* 4D **77**
Walpole St Andrew. *Norf* 4E **77**
Walpole St Peter. *Norf* 4E **77**
Walsall. *W Mid* 1E **61**
Walsall Wood. *W Mid* 5E **73**
Walsden. *W Yor* 2H **91**
Walsgrave on Sowe. *W Mid* 2A **62**
Walsham le Willows. *Suff* 3C **66**
Walshaw. *G Man* 3F **91**
Walshford. *N Yor* 4G **99**
Walsoken. *Cambs* 4D **76**
Walston. *S Lan* 5D **128**
Walsworth. *Herts* 2B **52**
Walter's Ash. *Buck* 2G **37**
Walterston. *V Glam* 4D **32**
Walterstone. *Here* 3G **47**
Waltham. *Kent* 1F **29**
Waltham. *NE Lin* 4F **95**
Waltham Abbey. *Essx* 5D **53**
Waltham Chase. *Hants* 1D **16**
Waltham Cross. *Herts* 5D **52**
Waltham on the Wolds. *Leics* 3F **75**
Waltham St Lawrence. *Wind* 4G **37**
Waltham's Cross. *Essx* 2G **53**
Walthamstow. *G Lon* 2E **39**
Walton. *Cumb* 3G **113**
Walton. *Derbs* 4A **86**
Walton. *Leics* 2C **62**
Walton. *Mers* 1F **83**
Walton. *Mil* 2G **51**
Walton. *Pet* 5A **76**
Walton. *Powy* 5E **59**
Walton. *Som* 3H **21**
Walton. *Staf* 3C **72**
(nr. Eccleshall)
Walton. *Staf* 2C **72**
(nr. Stone)
Walton. *Suff* 2F **55**
Walton. *Telf* 4H **71**
Walton. *Warw* 5G **61**
Walton. *W Yor* 3D **92**
(nr. Wakefield)
Walton. *W Yor* 5G **99**
(nr. Wetherby)
Walton Cardiff. *Glos* 2E **49**
Walton East. *Pemb* 2E **43**
Walton Elm. *Dors* 1C **14**

Walton Highway. *Norf* 4D **77**
Walton-in-Gordano. *N Som* 4H **33**
Walton-le-Dale. *Lanc* 2D **90**
Walton-on-Thames. *Surr* 4C **38**
Walton-on-the-Hill. *Staf* 3D **72**
Walton on the Hill. *Surr* 5D **38**
Walton-on-the-Naze. *Essx* 3F **55**
Walton on the Wolds. *Leics* 4C **74**
Walton-on-Trent. *Derbs* 4G **73**
Walton West. *Pemb* 3C **42**
Walwick. *Nmbd* 2C **114**
Walworth. *Darl* 3F **105**
Walworth Gate. *Darl* 2F **105**
Walwyn's Castle. *Pemb* 3C **42**
Wambrook. *Som* 2F **13**
Wampool. *Cumb* 4D **112**
Wanborough. *Surr* 1A **26**
Wanborough. *Swin* 3H **35**
Wandel. *S Lan* 2B **118**
Wandsworth. *G Lon* 3D **38**
Wangford. *Suff* 2G **65**
(nr. Lakenheath)
Wangford. *Suff* 3G **67**
(nr. Southwold)
Wanlip. *Leics* 4D **74**
Wanlockhead. *Dum* 3A **118**
Wannock. *E Sus* 5G **27**
Wansford. *E Yor* 4E **101**
Wansford. *Pet* 1H **63**
Wanshurst Green. *Kent* 1B **28**
Wanstead. *G Lon* 2F **39**
Wanstrow. *Som* 2C **22**
Wanswell. *Glos* 5B **48**
Wantage. *Oxon* 3C **36**
Wapley. *S Glo* 4C **34**
Wappenbury. *Warw* 4A **62**
Wappenham. *Nptn* 1E **51**
Warbleton. *E Sus* 4H **27**
Warblington. *Hants* 2F **17**
Warborough. *Devn* 3F **9**
Warborough. *Oxon* 2D **36**
Warboys. *Cambs* 2C **64**
Warbreck. *Bkpl* 1B **90**
Warbstow. *Corn* 3C **10**
Warburton. *G Man* 2A **84**
Warcop. *Cumb* 3A **104**
Warden. *Kent* 3E **40**
Warden. *Nmbd* 3C **114**
Ward End. *W Mid* 2F **61**
Ward Green. *Suff* 4C **66**
Ward Green Cross. *Lanc* 1E **91**
Wardhedges. *Beds* 2A **52**
Wardhouse. *Abers* 5C **160**
Wardington. *Oxon* 1C **50**
Wardle. *Ches* 5A **84**
Wardle. *G Man* 3H **91**
Wardley. *Rut* 5F **75**
Wardley. *W Sus* 4G **25**
Wardlow. *Derbs* 3F **85**
Wardsend. *Ches* 2D **84**
Wardy Hill. *Cambs* 2D **64**
Ware. *Herts* 4D **52**
Ware. *Kent* 4G **41**
Wareham. *Dors* 4E **15**
Warehorne. *Kent* 2D **28**
Warenford. *Nmbd* 2F **121**
Waren Mill. *Nmbd* 1F **121**
Warenton. *Nmbd* 1F **121**
Wareside. *Herts* 4D **53**
Waresley. *Cambs* 5B **64**
Waresley. *Worc* 4C **60**
Warfield. *Brac* 4G **37**
Warfleet. *Devn* 3E **9**
Wargate. *Linc* 2B **76**
Wargrave. *Wok* 4F **37**
Warham. *Norf* 1B **78**
Wark. *Nmbd* 1C **120**
(nr. Coldstream)
Wark. *Nmbd* 2B **114**
(nr. Hexham)
Warkleigh. *Devn* 4G **19**
Warkton. *Nptn* 3F **63**
Warkworth. *Nptn* 1C **50**
Warkworth. *Nmbd* 4G **121**
Warlaby. *N Yor* 5A **106**
Warland. *W Yor* 2H **91**
Warleggan. *Corn* 2F **7**
Warlingham. *Surr* 5E **39**
Warmanbie. *Dum* 3C **112**
Warmfield. *W Yor* 2D **93**
Warmingham. *Ches* 4B **84**
Warminghurst. *W Sus* 4C **26**
Warmington. *Nptn* 1H **63**
Warmington. *Warw* 1C **50**
Warminster. *Wilts* 2D **23**
Warmley. *S Glo* 4B **34**
Warmsworth. *S Yor* 4F **93**
Warmwell. *Dors* 4C **14**
Warndon. *Worc* 5C **60**
Warners End. *Herts* 5A **52**
Warnford. *Hants* 4E **24**
Warnham. *W Sus* 2C **26**
Warningcamp. *W Sus* 5B **26**
Warninglid. *W Sus* 3D **26**
Warren. *Ches* 3C **84**
Warren. *Pemb* 5D **42**
Warrenby. *Red C* 2C **106**
Warren Corner. *Hants* 2G **25**
(nr. Aldershot)
Warren Corner. *Hants* 4F **25**
(nr. Petersfield)
Warren Row. *Wind* 3G **37**
Warren Street. *Kent* 5D **40**
Warrington. *Mil* 5F **63**
Warrington. *Warr* 2A **84**
Warsash. *Hants* 2C **16**
Warse. *High* 1F **169**
Warslow. *Staf* 5E **85**
Warsop Vale. *Notts* 4C **86**
Warter. *E Yor* 4C **100**
Warthermarske. *N Yor* 2E **98**
Warthill. *N Yor* 4A **100**
Wartling. *E Sus* 5A **28**
Wartnaby. *Leics* 3E **74**
Warton. *Lanc* 2D **97**
(nr. Carnforth)
Warton. *Lanc* 2C **90**
(nr. Freckleton)
Warton. *Nmbd* 4E **121**
Warton. *Warw* 5G **73**
Warwick. *Cumb* 4F **113**
Warwick. *Warw* 4G **61**
Warwick Bridge. *Cumb* 4F **113**
Warwick Wold. *Surr* 5E **39**
Wasbister. *Orkn* 4C **172**
Wasdale Head. *Cumb* 4C **102**
Wash. *Derbs* 2E **85**
Washaway. *Corn* 2E **7**
Washbourne. *Devn* 3E **9**
Washbrook. *Suff* 1E **54**
Wash Common. *W Ber* 5C **36**
Washerwall. *Staf* 1D **72**
Washfield. *Devn* 1C **12**
Washfold. *N Yor* 4D **104**
Washford. *Som* 2D **20**
Washford Pyne. *Devn* 1B **12**
Washingborough. *Linc* 3H **87**
Washington. *Tyne* 4G **115**
Washington. *W Sus* 4C **26**
Washington Village. *Tyne* 4G **115**
Waskerley. *Dur* 5D **114**
Wasperton. *Warw* 5G **61**
Wasp Green. *Surr* 1E **27**
Wasps Nest. *Linc* 4H **87**
Wass. *N Yor* 2H **99**
Watchet. *Som* 2D **20**
Watchfield. *Oxon* 2H **35**
Watchgate. *Cumb* 5G **103**
Watchhill. *Cumb* 5C **112**
Watcombe. *Torb* 2F **9**
Watendlath. *Cumb* 3D **102**
Water. *Devn* 4A **12**
Water. *Lanc* 2G **91**
Waterbeach. *Cambs* 4D **65**
Waterbeach. *W Sus* 2G **17**
Waterbeck. *Dum* 2D **112**
Waterden. *Norf* 2A **78**
Waterditch. *Hants* 3G **15**
Water End. *Beds* 2A **52**
Water End. *E Yor* 1A **94**
Water End. *Herts* 5C **52**
(nr. Hatfield)
Water End. *Herts* 4A **52**
(nr. Hemel Hempstead)
Waterfall. *Staf* 5E **85**
Waterfoot. *E Ren* 4G **127**
Waterfoot. *Lanc* 2G **91**
Waterford. *Herts* 4D **52**
Water Fryston. *W Yor* 2E **93**
Waterhead. *Cumb* 4E **103**
Waterhead. *E Ayr* 3E **117**
Waterhead. *S Ayr* 5C **116**
Waterheads. *Bord* 4F **129**
Waterhouses. *Dur* 5E **115**
Waterhouses. *Staf* 5E **85**
Wateringbury. *Kent* 5A **40**
Waterlane. *Glos* 5E **49**
Waterlip. *Som* 2B **22**
Waterloo. *Cphy* 3E **33**
Waterloo. *Corn* 5B **10**
Waterloo. *Derbs* 4B **86**
Waterloo. *Here* 1G **47**
Waterloo. *High* 1E **147**
Waterloo. *Mers* 1F **83**
Waterloo. *Norf* 4E **78**
Waterloo. *N Lan* 4B **128**
Waterloo. *Pemb* 4D **42**
Waterloo. *Per* 5H **143**
Waterloo. *Pool* 3F **15**
Waterloo. *Shrp* 2G **71**
Waterlooville. *Hants* 2E **17**
Watermillock. *Cumb* 2F **103**
Water Newton. *Cambs* 1A **64**
Water Orton. *Warw* 1F **61**
Waterperry. *Oxon* 5E **51**
Waterrow. *Som* 4D **20**
Watersfield. *W Sus* 4B **26**
Waterside. *Buck* 5H **51**
Waterside. *Cambs* 3F **65**
Waterside. *Cumb* 5D **112**
Waterside. *E Ayr* 4D **116**
(nr. Ayr)
Waterside. *E Ayr* 5F **127**
(nr. Kilmarnock)
Waterside. *E Dun* 2H **127**
Waterstein. *High* 4A **154**
Waterstock. *Oxon* 5E **51**
Waterston. *Pemb* 4D **42**
Water Stratford. *Buck* 2E **51**
Waters Upton. *Telf* 4A **72**
Water Yeat. *Cumb* 1B **96**
Watford. *Herts* 1B **38**
Watford. *Nptn* 4D **62**
Wath. *Cumb* 4H **103**
Wath. *N Yor* 3D **98**
(nr. Pateley Bridge)
Wath. *N Yor* 2F **99**
(nr. Ripon)
Wath Brow. *Cumb* 3B **102**
Wath upon Dearne. *S Yor* 1B **86**
Watlington. *Norf* 4F **77**
Watlington. *Oxon* 2E **37**
Watten. *High* 3E **169**
Wattisfield. *Suff* 3C **66**
Wattisham. *Suff* 5C **66**
Wattlesborough Heath.
Shrp 4F **71**
Watton. *Dors* 3H **13**
Watton. *E Yor* 4E **101**
Watton. *Norf* 5B **78**
Watton at Stone. *Herts* 4C **52**
Wattston. *N Lan* 2A **128**
Wattstown. *Rhon* 2D **32**
Wattsville. *Cphy* 2F **33**
Wauldby. *E Yor* 2C **94**
Waulkmill. *Abers* 4D **152**
Waun. *Powy* 4E **71**
Waunarlwydd. *Swan* 3F **31**
Waun Fawr. *Cdgn* 2F **57**
Waunfawr. *Gwyn* 5E **81**
Waungilwen. *Carm* 1H **43**
Waunlwyd. *Blae* 5E **47**
Waun-y-Clyn. *Carm* 5E **45**
Wavendon. *Mil* 2H **51**
Waverbridge. *Cumb* 5D **112**
Waverley. *Surr* 2G **25**
Waverton. *Ches* 4G **83**
Waverton. *Cumb* 5D **112**
Wavertree. *Mers* 2F **83**
Wawne. *E Yor* 1D **94**
Waxham. *Norf* 3G **79**
Waxholme. *E Yor* 2G **95**
Wayford. *Som* 2H **13**
Way Head. *Cambs* 2D **65**
Waytown. *Dors* 3H **13**
Way Village. *Devn* 1B **12**
Wdig. *Pemb* 1D **42**
Wealdstone. *G Lon* 2C **38**
Weardley. *W Yor* 5E **99**
Weare. *Som* 1H **21**
Weare Giffard. *Devn* 4E **19**
Wearhead. *Dur* 1B **104**
Wearne. *Som* 4H **21**
Weasdale. *Cumb* 4H **103**
Weasenham All Saints. *Norf* 3H **77**
Weasenham St Peter. *Norf* 3A **78**
Weaverham. *Ches* 3A **84**
Weaverthorpe. *N Yor* 2D **100**
Webheath. *Worc* 4E **61**
Webton. *Here* 2H **47**
Wedderlairs. *Abers* 5F **161**
Weddington. *Warw* 1A **62**
Wedhampton. *Wilts* 1F **23**
Wedmore. *Som* 2H **21**
Wednesbury. *W Mid* 1D **61**
Wednesfield. *W Mid* 5D **72**
Weecar. *Notts* 4F **87**
Weedon. *Buck* 4G **51**
Weedon Bec. *Nptn* 5D **62**
Weedon Lois. *Nptn* 1E **50**
Weeford. *Staf* 5F **73**
Week. *Devn* 4F **19**
(nr. Barnstaple)
Week. *Devn* 2G **11**
(nr. Okehampton)
Week. *Devn* 1H **11**
(nr. South Molton)
Week. *Devn* 2D **9**
(nr. Totnes)
Week. *Som* 3C **20**
Weeke. *Devn* 2A **12**
Weeke. *Hants* 3C **24**
Week Green. *Corn* 3C **10**
Weekley. *Nptn* 2F **63**
Week St Mary. *Corn* 3C **10**
Weel. *E Yor* 1D **94**
Weeley. *Essx* 3E **55**
Weeley Heath. *Essx* 3E **55**
Weem. *Per* 4F **143**
Weeping Cross. *Staf* 3D **72**
Weethly. *Warw* 5E **61**
Weeting. *Norf* 2G **65**
Weeton. *E Yor* 2G **95**
Weeton. *Lanc* 1B **90**
Weeton. *N Yor* 5E **99**
Weetwood Hall. *Nmbd* 2E **121**
Weir. *Lanc* 2G **91**
Welborne. *Norf* 4C **78**
Welbourn. *Linc* 5G **87**
Welburn. *N Yor* 1A **100**
(nr. Kirkbymoorside)
Welburn. *N Yor* 3B **100**
(nr. Malton)
Welbury. *N Yor* 4A **106**
Welby. *Linc* 2G **75**
Welches Dam. *Cambs* 2D **64**
Welcombe. *Devn* 1C **10**
Weld Bank. *Lanc* 3D **90**
Weldon. *Nptn* 2G **63**
Weldon. *Nmbd* 5F **121**
Welford. *Nptn* 2D **62**
Welford. *W Ber* 4C **36**
Welford-on-Avon. *Warw* 5F **61**
Welham. *Leics* 1E **63**
Welham. *Notts* 2E **87**
Welham Green. *Herts* 5C **52**
Well. *Hants* 2F **25**
Well. *Linc* 3D **88**
Well. *N Yor* 1E **99**
Welland. *Worc* 1C **48**
Wellbank. *Ang* 5D **144**
Well Bottom. *Dors* 1E **15**
Welldale. *Dum* 3C **112**
Wellesbourne. *Warw* 5G **61**
Well Hill. *Kent* 4F **39**
Wellhouse. *W Ber* 4D **36**
Welling. *G Lon* 3F **39**
Wellingborough. *Nptn* 4F **63**
Wellingham. *Norf* 3A **78**
Wellingore. *Linc* 5G **87**
Wellington. *Cumb* 4B **102**
Wellington. *Here* 1H **47**
Wellington. *Som* 4E **21**
Wellington. *Telf* 4A **72**
Wellington Heath. *Here* 1C **48**
Wellow. *Bath* 1C **22**
Wellow. *IOW* 4B **16**
Wellow. *Notts* 4D **86**
Wellpond Green. *Herts* 3E **53**
Wells. *Som* 2A **22**
Wellsborough. *Leics* 5A **74**
Wells Green. *Ches* 5A **84**
Wells-next-the-Sea. *Norf* 1B **78**
Wells of Ythan. *Abers* 5D **160**
Wellswood. *Torb* 2F **9**
Wellwood. *Fife* 1D **129**
Welney. *Norf* 1E **65**
Welsford. *Devn* 4C **18**
Welshampton. *Shrp* 2G **71**
Welsh End. *Shrp* 2H **71**
Welsh Frankton. *Shrp* 2F **71**
Welsh Hook. *Pemb* 2D **42**
Welsh Newton. *Here* 4H **47**
Welsh Newton Common.
Here 4A **48**
Welshpool. *Powy* 5E **70**
Welsh St Donats. *V Glam* 4D **32**
Welton. *Bath* 1B **22**
Welton. *Cumb* 5E **113**
Welton. *E Yor* 2C **94**
Welton. *Linc* 2H **87**
Welton. *Nptn* 4C **62**
Welton Hill. *Linc* 2H **87**
Welton le Marsh. *Linc* 4D **88**
Welton le Wold. *Linc* 2B **88**
Welwick. *E Yor* 2G **95**
Welwyn. *Herts* 4C **52**
Welwyn Garden City. *Herts* . . . 4C **52**
Wem. *Shrp* 3H **71**
Wembdon. *Som* 3F **21**
Wembley. *G Lon* 2C **38**
Wembury. *Devn* 4B **8**
Wembworthy. *Devn* 2G **11**
Wemyss Bay. *Inv* 2C **126**
Wenallt. *Cdgn* 3F **57**
Wenallt. *Gwyn* 1B **70**
Wendens Ambo. *Essx* 2F **53**
Wending. *Norf* 4B **78**
Wendlebury. *Oxon* 4D **50**
Wendover. *Buck* 5G **51**
Wendron. *Corn* 5A **6**
Wendy. *Cambs* 1D **52**
Wenhaston. *Suff* 3G **67**
Wennington. *Cambs* 3B **64**
Wennington. *G Lon* 2G **39**
Wennington. *Lanc* 2F **97**
Wensley. *Derbs* 4G **85**
Wensley. *N Yor* 1C **98**
Wentbridge. *W Yor* 3E **93**
Wentfordbridge. *Corn* 5A **10**
Wentnor. *Shrp* 1F **59**
Wentworth. *Cambs* 3D **65**
Wentworth. *S Yor* 1A **86**
Wenvoe. *V Glam* 4E **32**
Weobley. *Here* 5G **59**
Weobley Marsh. *Here* 5G **59**
Wepham. *W Sus* 5B **26**
Wereham. *Norf* 5F **77**
Wergs. *W Mid* 5C **72**
Wern. *Gwyn* 1E **69**

Wern. *Powy* 4E **46** (nr. Brecon)
Wern. *Powy* 4E **71** (nr. Guilsfield)
Wern. *Powy* 4B **70** (nr. Llangadfan)
Wern. *Powy* 3E **71** (nr. Llanymynech)
Wernffrwd. *Swan* 3E **31**
Wernyrheolydd. *Mon* 4G **47**
Werrington. *Corn* 4D **10**
Werrington. *Pet* 5A **76**
Werrington. *Staf* 1D **72**
Wervin. *Ches* 3G **83**
Wesham. *Lanc* 1C **90**
Wessington. *Derbs* 5A **86**
West Aberthaw. *V Glam* 5D **32**
West Acre. *Norf* 4G **77**
West Allerdean. *Nmbd* 5F **131**
West Alvington. *Devn* 4D **8**
West Amesbury. *Wilts* 2G **23**
West Anstey. *Devn* 4B **20**
West Appleton. *N Yor* 5F **105**
West Arthurlie. *E Ren* 4F **127**
West Ashby. *Linc* 3B **88**
West Ashling. *W Sus* 2G **17**
West Ashton. *Wilts* 1D **23**
West Auckland. *Dur* 2E **105**
West Ayton. *N Yor* 1D **101**
West Bagborough. *Som* 3E **21**
West Bank. *Hal* 2H **83**
West Barkwith. *Linc* 2A **88**
West Barnby. *N Yor* 3F **107**
West Barns. *E Lot* 2C **130**
West Barsham. *Norf* 2B **78**
West Bay. *Dors* 3H **13**
West Beckham. *Norf* 2D **78**
West Bennan. *N Ayr* 3D **123**
Westbere. *Kent* 4F **41**
West Bergholt. *Essx* 3C **54**
West Bexington. *Dors* 4A **14**
West Bilney. *Norf* 4G **77**
West Blackdene. *Dur* 1B **104**
West Blatchington. *Brig* 5D **27**
Westborough. *Linc* 1F **75**
Westbourne. *Bour* 3F **15**
Westbourne. *W Sus* 2F **17**
West Bowling. *W Yor* 1B **92**
West Brabourne. *Kent* 1E **29**
West Bradford. *Lanc* 5G **97**
West Bradley. *Som* 3A **22**
West Bretton. *W Yor* 3C **92**
West Bridgford. *Notts* 2C **74**
West Briggs. *Norf* 4F **77**
West Bromwich. *W Mid* 1D **61**
Westbrook. *Here* 1F **47**
Westbrook. *Kent* 3H **41**
Westbrook. *Wilts* 5E **35**
West Buckland. *Devn* 3G **19**
West Buckland. *Som* 4E **21**
West Burnside. *Abers* 1G **145**
West Burrafirth. *Shet* 6D **173**
West Burton. *N Yor* 1C **98**
West Burton. *W Sus* 4B **26**
Westbury. *Buck* 2E **50**
Westbury. *Shrp* 5F **71**
Westbury. *Wilts* 1D **22**
Westbury Leigh. *Wilts* 2D **22**
Westbury-on-Severn. *Glos* 4C **48**
Westbury on Trym. *Bris* 4A **34**
Westbury-sub-Mendip. *Som* 2A **22**
West Butsfield. *Dur* 5E **115**
West Butterwick. *N Lin* 4B **94**
Westby. *Linc* 3G **75**
West Byfleet. *Surr* 4B **38**
West Caister. *Norf* 4H **79**
West Calder. *W Lot* 3D **128**
West Camel. *Som* 4A **22**
West Carr. *N Lin* 4H **93**
West Chaldon. *Dors* 4C **14**
West Challow. *Oxon* 3B **36**
West Charleton. *Devn* 4D **8**
West Chelborough. *Dors* 2A **14**
West Chevington. *Nmbd* 5G **121**
West Chiltington. *W Sus* 4B **26**
West Chiltington Common. *W Sus* 4B **26**
West Chinnock. *Som* 1H **13**
West Chisenbury. *Wilts* 1G **23**
West Clandon. *Surr* 5B **38**
West Cliffe. *Kent* 1H **29**
Westcliffe-on-Sea. *S'end* 2C **40**
West Clyne. *High* 3F **165**
West Coker. *Som* 1A **14**
Westcombe. *Som* 3B **22** (nr. Evercreech)
Westcombe. *Som* 4H **21** (nr. Somerton)
West Compton. *Dors* 3A **14**
West Compton. *Som* 2A **22**
West Cornforth. *Dur* 1A **106**
Westcot. *Oxon* 3B **36**
Westcott. *Buck* 4F **51**
Westcott. *Devn* 2D **12**
Westcott. *Surr* 1C **26**
Westcott Barton. *Oxon* 3C **50**
West Cowick. *E Yor* 2G **93**
West Cranmore. *Som* 2B **22**
West Croftmore. *High* 2D **150**
West Cross. *Swan* 4F **31**
West Cullerlie. *Abers* 3E **153**
West Culvennan. *Dum* 3H **109**
West Curry. *Corn* 3C **10**
West Curthwaite. *Cumb* 5E **113**
Westdean. *E Sus* 5G **27**
West Dean. *W Sus* 1G **17**
West Dean. *Wilts* 4A **24**
West Deeping. *Linc* 5A **76**
West Derby. *Mers* 1F **83**
West Dereham. *Norf* 5F **77**
West Down. *Devn* 2F **19**
Westdowns. *Corn* 4A **10**
West Drayton. *G Lon* 3B **38**
West Drayton. *Notts* 3E **86**
West Dunnet. *High* 1E **169**
West Ella. *E Yor* 2D **94**
West End. *Beds* 5G **63**
West End. *Cambs* 1D **64**
West End. *Dors* 2E **15**
West End. *E Yor* 3E **101** (nr. Kilham)
West End. *E Yor* 1E **95** (nr. Preston)
West End. *E Yor* 1C **94** (nr. South Cove)
West End. *E Yor* 4F **101** (nr. Ulrome)
West End. *G Lon* 2D **39**
West End. *Hants* 1C **16**
West End. *Herts* 5C **52**
West End. *Kent* 4F **41**
West End. *Linc* 1C **76**
West End. *Norf* 4G **79**
West End. *N Som* 5H **33**
West End. *N Yor* 4D **98**
West End. *S Glo* 3C **34**
West End. *S Lan* 5C **128**
West End. *Surr* 4A **38**
West End. *Wilts* 4E **23**
West End. *Wind* 4G **37**
West End. *Worc* 2F **49**
West End Green. *Hants* 5E **37**
Westenhanger. *Kent* 2F **29**
Wester Aberchalder. *High* 2H **149**
Wester Balgedie. *Per* 3D **136**
Wester Brae. *High* 2A **158**
Wester Culbeuchly. *Abers* 2D **160**
Westerdale. *High* 3D **168**
Westerdale. *N Yor* 4D **106**
Wester Dechmont. *W Lot* 2D **128**
Wester Fearn. *High* 5D **164**
Westerfield. *Suff* 1E **55**
Wester Galcantray. *High* 4C **158**
Westergate. *W Sus* 5A **26**
Wester Gruinards. *High* 4C **164**
Westerham. *Kent* 5F **39**
Westerleigh. *S Glo* 4B **34**
Westerloch. *High* 3F **169**
Wester Mandally. *High* 3E **149**
Wester Rarichie. *High* 1C **158**
Wester Shian. *Per* 5F **143**
Westerton. *Ang* 3F **145**
Westerton. *Dur* 1F **105**
Westerton. *W Sus* 2G **17**
Westerwick. *Shet* 7D **173**
West Farleigh. *Kent* 5B **40**
West Farndon. *Nptn* 5C **62**
West Felton. *Shrp* 3F **71**
Westfield. *Cumb* 2A **102**
Westfield. *E Sus* 4C **28**
Westfield. *High* 2C **168**
Westfield. *Norf* 5B **78**
Westfield. *N Lan* 2A **128**
Westfield. *W Lot* 2C **128**
Westfields. *Dors* 2C **14**
Westfields of Rattray. *Per* 4A **144**
West Firle. *E Sus* 5F **27**
West Fleetham. *Nmbd* 2F **121**
West Garforth. *W Yor* 1D **93**
Westgate. *Dur* 1C **104**
Westgate. *Norf* 1B **78**
Westgate. *N Lin* 4A **94**
Westgate on Sea. *Kent* 3H **41**
West Ginge. *Oxon* 3C **36**
West Grafton. *Wilts* 5H **35**
West Green. *Hants* 1F **25**
West Grimstead. *Wilts* 4H **23**
West Grinstead. *W Sus* 3C **26**
West Haddlesey. *N Yor* 2F **93**
West Haddon. *Nptn* 3D **62**
West Hagbourne. *Oxon* 3D **36**
West Hagley. *Worc* 2C **60**
West Hall. *Cumb* 3G **113**
Westhall. *Suff* 2G **67**
West Hallam. *Derbs* 1B **74**
Westhall Terrace. *Ang* 5D **144**
West Halton. *N Lin* 2C **94**
Westham. *Dors* 5B **14**
Westham. *E Sus* 5H **27**
West Ham. *G Lon* 2E **39**
Westham. *Som* 2H **21**
Westhampnett. *W Sus* 2G **17**
West Handley. *Derbs* 3A **86**
West Hanney. *Oxon* 2C **36**
West Hanningfield. *Essx* 1B **40**
West Hardwick. *W Yor* 3E **93**
West Harnham. *Wilts* 4G **23**
West Harptree. *Bath* 1A **22**
West Harting. *W Sus* 4F **25**
West Harton. *Tyne* 3G **115**
West Hatch. *Som* 4F **21**
Westhay. *Som* 2H **21**
Westhead. *Lanc* 4C **90**
West Head. *Norf* 5E **77**
West Heath. *Hants* 1D **24** (nr. Basingstoke)
West Heath. *Hants* 1G **25** (nr. Farnborough)
West Helmsdale. *High* 2H **165**
West Hendred. *Oxon* 3C **36**
West Heslerton. *N Yor* 2D **100**
West Hewish. *N Som* 5G **33**
Westhide. *Here* 1A **48**
Westhill. *Abers* 3F **153**
West Hill. *Devn* 3D **12**
West Hill. *E Yor* 3F **101**
Westhill. *High* 4B **158**
West Hill. *N Som* 4H **33**
West Hill. *W Sus* 2E **27**
West Hoathly. *W Sus* 2E **27**
West Holme. *Dors* 4D **15**
Westhope. *Here* 5G **59**
Westhope. *Shrp* 2G **59**
West Horndon. *Essx* 2H **39**
Westhorp. *Nptn* 5C **62**
Westhorpe. *Linc* 2B **76**
Westhorpe. *Suff* 4C **66**
West Horrington. *Som* 2A **22**
West Horsley. *Surr* 5B **38**
West Horton. *Nmbd* 1E **121**
West Hougham. *Kent* 1G **29**
Westhoughton. *G Man* 4E **91**
Westhouse. *N Yor* 2F **97**
West Howe. *Bour* 3F **15**
Westhumble. *Surr* 5C **38**
West Huntspill. *Som* 2G **21**
West Hyde. *Herts* 1B **38**
West Hynish. *Arg* 5A **138**
West Hythe. *Kent* 2F **29**
West Ilsley. *W Ber* 3C **36**
West Itchenor. *W Sus* 2G **17**
West Keal. *Linc* 4C **88**
West Kennett. *Wilts* 5G **35**
West Kilbride. *N Ayr* 5D **126**
West Kingsdown. *Kent* 4G **39**
West Kington. *Wilts* 4D **34**
West Kirby. *Mers* 2E **82**
West Knapton. *N Yor* 2C **100**
West Knighton. *Dors* 4C **14**
West Knoyle. *Wilts* 3D **22**
Westlake. *Devn* 3C **8**
West Lambrook. *Som* 1H **13**
West Langdon. *Kent* 1H **29**
West Langwell. *High* 3D **164**
West Lavington. *W Sus* 4G **25**
West Lavington. *Wilts* 1F **23**
West Layton. *N Yor* 4E **105**
West Leake. *Notts* 3C **74**
West Learmouth. *Nmbd* 1C **120**
Westleigh. *Devn* 4E **19** (nr. Bideford)
Westleigh. *Devn* 1D **12** (nr. Tiverton)
West Leigh. *Devn* 2G **11** (nr. Winkleigh)
Westleigh. *G Man* 4E **91**
West Leith. *Buck* 4H **51**
Westleton. *Suff* 4G **67**
West Lexham. *Norf* 4H **77**
Westley. *Shrp* 5F **71**
Westley. *Suff* 4H **65**
Westley Waterless. *Cambs* 5F **65**
West Lilling. *N Yor* 3A **100**
West Lingo. *Fife* 3G **137**
Westlington. *Buck* 4F **51**
Westlinton. *Cumb* 3E **113**
West Linton. *Bord* 4E **129**
West Littleton. *S Glo* 4C **34**
West Looe. *Corn* 3G **7**
West Lulworth. *Dors* 4D **14**
West Lutton. *N Yor* 3D **100**
West Lydford. *Som* 3A **22**
West Lynn. *Norf* 4F **77**
West Mains. *Per* 2B **136**
West Malling. *Kent* 5A **40**
West Malvern. *Worc* 1C **48**
Westmancote. *Worc* 2E **49**
West Marden. *W Sus* 1F **17**
West Markham. *Notts* 3E **86**
Westmarsh. *Kent* 4G **41**
West Marsh. *NE Lin* 4F **95**
West Marton. *N Yor* 4A **98**
West Meon. *Hants* 4E **25**
West Mersea. *Essx* 4D **54**
Westmeston. *E Sus* 4E **27**
Westmill. *Herts* 3D **52** (nr. Buntingford)
Westmill. *Herts* 2B **52** (nr. Hitchin)
West Milton. *Dors* 3A **14**
Westminster. *G Lon* 3D **39**
West Molesey. *Surr* 4C **38**
West Monkton. *Som* 4F **21**
Westmoor End. *Cumb* 1B **102**
West Moors. *Dors* 2F **15**
West Morden. *Dors* 3E **15**
West Muir. *Ang* 2E **145** (nr. Brechin)
Westmuir. *Ang* 3C **144** (nr. Forfar)
West Murkle. *High* 2D **168**
West Ness. *N Yor* 2A **100**
Westnewton. *Cumb* 5C **112**
West Newton. *E Yor* 1E **95**
West Newton. *Norf* 3F **77**
Westnewton. *Nmbd* 1D **120**
West Norwood. *G Lon* 3E **39**
Westoe. *Tyne* 3G **115**
West Ogwell. *Devn* 2E **9**
Weston. *Bath* 5C **34**
Weston. *Ches* 5B **84** (nr. Crewe)
Weston. *Ches* 3D **84** (nr. Macclesfield)
Weston. *Devn* 4E **13**
Weston. *Dors* 5B **14** (nr. Weymouth)
Weston. *Dors* 2A **14** (nr. Yeovil)
Weston. *Hal* 2H **83**
Weston. *Hants* 4F **25**
Weston. *Here* 5F **59**
Weston. *Herts* 2C **52**
Weston. *Linc* 3B **76**
Weston. *Nptn* 1D **50**
Weston. *Notts* 4E **87**
Weston. *Shrp* 1H **59** (nr. Bridgnorth)
Weston. *Shrp* 3F **59** (nr. Knighton)
Weston. *Shrp* 3H **71** (nr. Wem)
Weston. *S Lan* 5D **128**
Weston. *Staf* 3D **73**
Weston. *Suff* 2G **67**
Weston. *W Ber* 4B **36**
Weston Bampfylde. *Som* 4B **22**
Weston Beggard. *Here* 1A **48**
Westonbirt. *Glos* 3D **34**
Weston by Welland. *Nptn* 1E **63**
Weston Colville. *Cambs* 5F **65**
Westoncommon. *Shrp* 3G **71**
Weston Coyney. *Stoke* 1D **72**
Weston Ditch. *Suff* 3F **65**
Weston Favell. *Nptn* 4E **63**
Weston Green. *Cambs* 5F **65**
Weston Green. *Norf* 4D **78**
Weston Heath. *Shrp* 4B **72**
Weston Hills. *Linc* 4B **76**
Weston in Arden. *Warw* 2A **62**
Westoning. *Beds* 2A **52**
Weston-in-Gordano. *N Som* 4H **33**
Weston Jones. *Staf* 3B **72**
Weston Longville. *Norf* 4D **78**
Weston Lullingfields. *Shrp* 3G **71**
Weston-on-Avon. *Warw* 5F **61**
Weston-on-the-Green. *Oxon* 4D **50**
Weston-on-Trent. *Derbs* 3B **74**
Weston Patrick. *Hants* 2E **25**
Weston Rhyn. *Shrp* 2E **71**
Weston Subedge. *Glos* 1G **49**
Weston-super-Mare. *N Som* 5G **33**
Weston Town. *Som* 2C **22**
Weston Turville. *Buck* 4G **51**
Weston under Lizard. *Staf* 4C **72**
Weston under Penyard. *Here* 3B **48**
Weston under Wetherley. *Warw* 4A **62**
Weston Underwood. *Derbs* 1G **73**
Weston Underwood. *Mil* 5F **63**
Westonzoyland. *Som* 3G **21**
West Orchard. *Dors* 1D **14**
West Overton. *Wilts* 5G **35**
Westow. *N Yor* 3B **100**
Westown. *Per* 1E **137**
West Panson. *Devn* 3D **10**
West Park. *Hart* 1B **106**
West Parley. *Dors* 3F **15**
West Peckham. *Kent* 5H **39**
West Pelton. *Dur* 4F **115**
West Pennard. *Som* 3A **22**
West Pentire. *Corn* 2B **6**
West Perry. *Cambs* 4A **64**
West Pitcorthie. *Fife* 3H **137**
West Plean. *Stir* 1B **128**
West Poringland. *Norf* 5E **79**
West Porlock. *Som* 2B **20**
Westport. *Som* 1G **13**
West Putford. *Devn* 1D **10**

West Quantoxhead. *Som* 2E 20
Westra. *V Glam* 4E 33
West Rainton. *Dur* 5G 115
West Rasen. *Linc* 2H 87
West Ravendale. *NE Lin* 1B 88
Westray Airport. *Orkn* 2D 172
West Raynham. *Norf* 3A 78
Westrigg. *W Lot* 3C 128
West Rounton. *N Yor* 4B 106
West Row. *Suff* 3F 65
West Rudham. *Norf* 3H 77
West Runton. *Norf* 1D 78
Westruther. *Bord* 4C 130
Westry. *Cambs* 1C 64
West Saltoun. *E Lot* 3A 130
West Sandford. *Devn* 2B 12
West Sandwick. *Shet* 3F 173
West Scrafton. *N Yor* 1C 98
Westside. *Orkn* 5C 172
West Sleekburn. *Nmbd* 1F 115
West Somerton. *Norf* 4G 79
West Stafford. *Dors* 4C 14
West Stockwith. *Notts* 1E 87
West Stoke. *W Sus* 2G 17
West Stonesdale. *N Yor* 4B 104
West Stoughton. *Som* 2H 21
West Stour. *Dors* 4C 22
West Stourmouth. *Kent* 4G 41
West Stow. *Suff* 3H 65
West Stowell. *Wilts* 5G 35
West Strathan. *High* 2F 167
West Stratton. *Hants* 2D 24
West Street. *Kent* 5D 40
West Tanfield. *N Yor* 2E 99
West Taphouse. *Corn* 2F 7
West Tarbert. *Arg* 3G 125
West Thirston. *Nmbd* 4F 121
West Thorney. *W Sus* 2F 17
West Thurrock. *Thur* 3G 39
West Tilbury. *Thur* 3A 40
West Tisted. *Hants* 4E 25
West Tofts. *Norf* 1H 65
West Torrington. *Linc* 2A 88
West Town. *Bath* 5A 34
West Town. *Hants* 3F 17
West Town. *N Som* 5H 33
West Tytherley. *Hants* 4A 24
West Tytherton. *Wilts* 4E 35
West View. *Hart* 1C 106
Westville. *Notts* 1C 74
West Walton. *Norf* 4D 76
Westward. *Cumb* 5D 112
Westward Ho!. *Devn* 4E 19
Westwell. *Kent* 1D 28
Westwell. *Oxon* 5H 49
Westwell Leacon. *Kent* 1D 28
West Wellow. *Hants* 1A 16
West Wemyss. *Fife* 4F 137
Westwick. *Cambs* 4D 64
Westwick. *Dur* 3D 104
Westwick. *Norf* 3E 79
West Wick. *N Som* 5G 33
West Wickham. *Cambs* 1G 53
West Wickham. *G Lon* 4E 39
West Williamston. *Pemb* 4E 43
West Willoughby. *Linc* 1G 75
West Winch. *Norf* 4F 77
West Winterslow. *Wilts* 3H 23
West Wittering. *W Sus* 3F 17
West Witton. *N Yor* 1C 98
Westwood. *Devn* 3D 12
Westwood. *Kent* 4H 41
Westwood. *Pet* 1A 64
Westwood. *S Lan* 4H 127
Westwood. *Wilts* 1D 22
West Woodburn. *Nmbd* 1B 114
West Woodhay. *W Ber* 5B 36
West Woodlands. *Som* 2C 22
West Woodside. *Cumb* 5E 112
Westwoodside. *N Lin* 4H 93
West Worldham. *Hants* 3F 25
West Worlington. *Devn* 1A 12
West Worthing. *W Sus* 5C 26
West Wratting. *Cambs* 5F 65
West Wycombe. *Buck* 2G 37
West Wylam. *Nmbd* 3E 115
West Yatton. *Wilts* 4D 34
West Yell. *Shet* 3F 173
West Youlstone. *Corn* 1C 10
Wetheral. *Cumb* 4F 113
Wetherby. *W Yor* 5G 99
Wetherden. *Suff* 4C 66
Wetheringsett. *Suff* 4D 66
Wethersfield. *Essx* 2H 53
Wethersta. *Shet* 5E 173
Wetherup Street. *Suff* 4D 66
Wetley Rocks. *Staf* 1D 72
Wettenhall. *Ches* 4A 84
Wetton. *Staf* 5F 85
Wetwang. *E Yor* 4D 100
Wetwood. *Staf* 2B 72
Wexcombe. *Wilts* 1A 24
Wexham Street. *Buck* 2A 38
Weybourne. *Norf* 1D 78
Weybourne. *Surr* 2G 25
Weybread. *Suff* 2E 67
Weybridge. *Surr* 4B 38
Weycroft. *Devn* 3G 13
Weydale. *High* 2D 168
Weyhill. *Hants* 2B 24
Weymouth. *Dors* 5B 14
Weythel. *Powy* 5E 59
Whaddon. *Buck* 2G 51
Whaddon. *Cambs* 1D 52
Whaddon. *Glos* 4D 48
Whaddon. *Wilts* 4G 23
Whale. *Cumb* 2G 103
Whaley. *Derbs* 3C 86
Whaley Bridge. *Derbs* 2E 85
Whaley Thorns. *Derbs* 3C 86
Whalley. *Lanc* 1F 91
Whalton. *Nmbd* 1E 115
Wham. *N Yor* 3G 97
Whaplode. *Linc* 3C 76
Whaplode Drove. *Linc* 4C 76
Whaplode St Catherine. *Linc* 3C 76
Wharfe. *N Yor* 3G 97
Wharles. *Lanc* 1C 90
Wharley End. *Beds* 1H 51
Wharncliffe Side. *S Yor* 1G 85
Wharram-le-Street. *N Yor* 3C 100
Wharton. *Ches* 4A 84
Wharton. *Here* 5H 59
Whashton. *N Yor* 4E 105
Whasset. *Cumb* 1E 97
Whatcote. *Warw* 1A 50
Whateley. *Warw* 1G 61
Whatfield. *Suff* 1D 54
Whatley. *Som* 2G 13
(nr. Chard)
Whatley. *Som* 2C 22
(nr. Frome)
Whatlington. *E Sus* 4B 28
Whatmore. *Shrp* 3A 60
Whatstandwell. *Derbs* 5H 85
Whatton. *Notts* 2E 75
Whauphill. *Dum* 5B 110
Whaw. *N Yor* 4C 104
Wheatacre. *Norf* 1G 67
Wheatcroft. *Derbs* 5A 86
Wheathampstead. *Herts* 4B 52
Wheathill. *Shrp* 2A 60
Wheatley. *Devn* 3B 12
Wheatley. *Hants* 2F 25
Wheatley. *Oxon* 5D 50
Wheatley. *S Yor* 4F 93
Wheatley. *W Yor* 2A 92
Wheatley Hill. *Dur* 1A 106
Wheatley Lane. *Lanc* 1G 91
Wheatley Park. *S Yor* 4F 93
Wheaton Aston. *Staf* 4C 72
Wheatstone Park. *Staf* 5C 72
Wheddon Cross. *Som* 3C 20
Wheelerstreet. *Surr* 1A 26
Wheelock. *Ches* 5B 84
Wheelock Heath. *Ches* 5B 84
Wheelton. *Lanc* 2E 90
Wheldrake. *York* 5A 100
Whelford. *Glos* 2G 35
Whelpley Hill. *Buck* 5H 51
Whelpo. *Cumb* 1E 102
Whelston. *Flin* 3E 82
Whenby. *N Yor* 3A 100
Whepstead. *Suff* 5H 65
Wherstead. *Suff* 1E 55
Wherwell. *Hants* 2B 24
Wheston. *Derbs* 3F 85
Whetsted. *Kent* 1A 28
Whetstone. *G Lon* 1D 38
Whetstone. *Leics* 1C 62
Whicham. *Cumb* 1A 96
Whichford. *Warw* 2B 50
Whickham. *Tyne* 3F 115
Whiddon. *Devn* 2E 11
Whiddon Down. *Devn* 3G 11
Whigstreet. *Ang* 4D 145
Whilton. *Nptn* 4D 62
Whimble. *Devn* 2D 10
Whimple. *Devn* 3D 12
Whimpwell Green. *Norf* 3F 79
Whinburgh. *Norf* 5C 78
Whin Lane End. *Lanc* 5C 96
Whinnyfold. *Abers* 5H 161
Whinny Hill. *Stoc T* 3A 106
Whippingham. *IOW* 3D 16
Whipsnade. *Beds* 4A 52
Whipton. *Devn* 3C 12
Whirlow. *S Yor* 2H 85
Whisby. *Linc* 4G 87
Whissendine. *Rut* 4F 75
Whissonsett. *Norf* 3B 78
Whisterfield. *Ches* 3C 84
Whistley Green. *Wok* 4F 37
Whiston. *Mers* 1G 83
Whiston. *Nptn* 4F 63
Whiston. *S Yor* 1B 86
Whiston. *Staf* 1E 73
(nr. Cheadle)
Whiston. *Staf* 4C 72
(nr. Penkridge)
Whiston Cross. *Shrp* 5B 72
Whiston Eaves. *Staf* 1E 73
Whitacre Heath. *Warw* 1G 61
Whitbeck. *Cumb* 1A 96
Whitbourne. *Here* 5B 60
Whitburn. *Tyne* 3H 115
Whitburn. *W Lot* 3C 128
Whitburn Colliery. *Tyne* 3H 115
Whitby. *Ches* 3F 83
Whitby. *N Yor* 3F 107
Whitbyheath. *Ches* 3F 83
Whitchester. *Bord* 4D 130
Whitchurch. *Bath* 5B 34
Whitchurch. *Buck* 3G 51
Whitchurch. *Card* 4E 33
Whitchurch. *Devn* 5E 11
Whitchurch. *Hants* 2C 24
Whitchurch. *Here* 4A 48
Whitchurch. *Pemb* 2C 42
Whitchurch. *Shrp* 1H 71
Whitchurch Canonicorum. *Dors* 3G 13
Whitchurch Hill. *Oxon* 4E 37
Whitchurch-on-Thames. *Oxon* 4E 37
Whitcombe. *Dors* 4C 14
Whitcot. *Shrp* 1F 59
Whitcott Keysett. *Shrp* 2E 59
Whiteash Green. *Essx* 2A 54
Whitebog. *High* 2B 158
Whitebridge. *High* 2G 149
Whitebrook. *Mon* 5A 48
Whitecairns. *Abers* 2G 153
White Chapel. *Lanc* 5E 97
Whitechurch. *Pemb* 1F 43
White Colne. *Essx* 3B 54
White Coppice. *Lanc* 3E 90
White Corries. *High* 3G 141
Whitecraig. *E Lot* 2G 129
Whitecroft. *Glos* 5B 48
White Cross. *Corn* 4D 5
(nr. Mullion)
Whitecross. *Corn* 1D 6
(nr. Wadebridge)
Whitecross. *Falk* 2C 128
White End. *Worc* 2C 48
Whiteface. *High* 5E 164
Whitefaulds. *S Ayr* 4B 116
Whitefield. *Dors* 3E 15
Whitefield. *G Man* 4G 91
Whitefield. *Som* 4D 20
Whiteford. *Abers* 1E 152
Whitegate. *Ches* 4A 84
Whitehall. *Devn* 1E 13
Whitehall. *Hants* 1F 25
Whitehall. *Orkn* 5F 172
Whitehall. *W Sus* 3C 26
Whitehaven. *Cumb* 3A 102
Whitehaven. *Shrp* 3E 71
Whitehill. *Hants* 3F 25
Whitehill. *N Ayr* 4D 126
Whitehills. *Abers* 2D 160
Whitehills. *Ang* 3D 144
White Horse Common. *Norf* 3F 79
Whitehough. *Derbs* 2E 85
Whitehouse. *Abers* 2D 152
Whitehouse. *Arg* 3G 125
Whiteinch. *Glas* 3G 127
Whitekirk. *E Lot* 1B 130
White Kirkley. *Dur* 1D 104
White Lackington. *Dors* 3C 14
Whitelackington. *Som* 1G 13
White Ladies Aston. *Worc* 5D 60
White Lee. *W Yor* 2C 92
Whiteley. *Hants* 2D 16
Whiteley Bank. *IOW* 4D 16
Whiteley Village. *Surr* 4B 38
Whitemans Green. *W Sus* 3E 27
White Mill. *Carm* 3E 45
Whitemire. *Mor* 3D 159
Whitemoor. *Corn* 3D 6
Whitenap. *Hants* 4B 24
Whiteness. *Shet* 7F 173
White Notley. *Essx* 4A 54
Whiteoak Green. *Oxon* 4B 50
Whiteparish. *Wilts* 4H 23
White Pit. *Linc* 3C 88
Whiterashes. *Abers* 1F 153
White Rocks. *Here* 3H 47
White Roding. *Essx* 4F 53
Whiterow. *High* 4F 169
Whiterow. *Mor* 3E 159
Whiteshill. *Glos* 5D 48
Whiteside. *Nmbd* 3A 114
Whiteside. *W Lot* 3C 128
Whitesmith. *E Sus* 4G 27
Whitestaunton. *Som* 1F 13
Whitestone. *Abers* 4D 152
Whitestone. *Devn* 3B 12
White Stone. *Here* 1A 48
Whitestones. *Abers* 3F 161
Whitestreet Green. *Suff* 2C 54
Whitewall Corner. *N Yor* 2B 100
White Waltham. *Wind* 4G 37
Whiteway. *Glos* 4E 49
Whitewell. *Lanc* 5F 97
Whitewell Bottom. *Lanc* 2G 91
Whiteworks. *Devn* 5G 11
Whitewreath. *Mor* 3G 159
Whitfield. *D'dee* 5D 144
Whitfield. *Kent* 1H 29
Whitfield. *Nptn* 2E 50
Whitfield. *Nmbd* 4A 114
Whitfield. *S Glo* 2B 34
Whitford. *Devn* 3F 13
Whitford. *Flin* 3D 82
Whitgift. *E Yor* 2B 94
Whitgreave. *Staf* 3C 72
Whithorn. *Dum* 5B 110
Whiting Bay. *N Ayr* 3E 123
Whitington. *Norf* 1G 65
Whitkirk. *W Yor* 1D 92
Whitland. *Carm* 3G 43
Whitleigh. *Plym* 3A 8
Whitletts. *S Ayr* 2C 116
Whitley. *N Yor* 2F 93
Whitley. *Wilts* 5D 35
Whitley Bay. *Tyne* 2G 115
Whitley Chapel. *Nmbd* 4C 114
Whitley Heath. *Staf* 3C 72
Whitley Lower. *W Yor* 3C 92
Whitley Thorpe. *N Yor* 2F 93
Whitlock's End. *W Mid* 3F 61
Whitminster. *Glos* 5C 48
Whitmore. *Dors* 2F 15
Whitmore. *Staf* 1C 72
Whitnage. *Devn* 1D 12
Whitnash. *Warw* 4H 61
Whitney. *Here* 1F 47
Whitrigg. *Cumb* 4D 112
(nr. Kirkbride)
Whitrigg. *Cumb* 1D 102
(nr. Torpenhow)
Whitsbury. *Hants* 1G 15
Whitsome. *Bord* 4E 131
Whitson. *Newp* 3G 33
Whitstable. *Kent* 4F 41
Whitstone. *Corn* 3C 10
Whittingham. *Nmbd* 3E 121
Whittingslow. *Shrp* 2G 59
Whittington. *Derbs* 3B 86
Whittington. *Glos* 3F 49
Whittington. *Lanc* 2F 97
Whittington. *Shrp* 2F 71
Whittington. *Staf* 2C 60
(nr. Kinver)
Whittington. *Staf* 5F 73
(nr. Lichfield)
Whittington. *Warw* 1G 61
Whittington. *Worc* 5C 60
Whittington Barracks. *Staf* 5F 73
Whittlebury. *Nptn* 1E 51
Whittleford. *Warw* 1H 61
Whittle-le-Woods. *Lanc* 2D 90
Whittlesey. *Cambs* 1B 64
Whittlesford. *Cambs* 1E 53
Whittlestone Head. *Bkbn* 3F 91
Whitton. *N Lin* 2C 94
Whitton. *Nmbd* 4E 121
Whitton. *Powy* 4E 59
Whitton. *Bord* 2B 120
Whitton. *Shrp* 3H 59
Whitton. *Stoc T* 2A 106
Whittonditch. *Wilts* 4A 36
Whittonstall. *Nmbd* 4D 114
Whitway. *Hants* 1C 24
Whitwell. *Derbs* 3C 86
Whitwell. *Herts* 3B 52
Whitwell. *IOW* 5D 16
Whitwell. *N Yor* 5F 105
Whitwell. *Rut* 5G 75
Whitwell-on-the-Hill. *N Yor* 3B 100
Whitwick. *Leics* 4B 74
Whitwood. *W Yor* 2E 93
Whitworth. *Lanc* 3G 91
Whixall. *Shrp* 2H 71
Whixley. *N Yor* 4G 99
Whoberley. *W Mid* 3G 61
Whorlton. *Dur* 3E 105
Whorlton. *N Yor* 4B 106
Whygate. *Nmbd* 2A 114
Whyle. *Here* 4H 59
Whyteleafe. *Surr* 5E 39
Wibdon. *Glos* 2A 34
Wibtoft. *Warw* 2B 62
Wichenford. *Worc* 4B 60
Wichling. *Kent* 5D 40
Wick. *Bour* 3G 15
Wick. *High* 3F 169
Wick. *Som* 2F 21
(nr. Bridgwater)
Wick. *Som* 1G 21
(nr. Burnham-on-Sea)
Wick. *Som* 4H 21
(nr. Somerton)
Wick. *S Glo* 4C 34
Wick. *V Glam* 4C 32
Wick. *W Sus* 5B 26
Wick. *Wilts* 4G 23
Wick. *Worc* 1E 49

Wick Airport. *High* 3F **169**
Wicken. *Cambs* 3E **65**
Wicken. *Nptn* 2F **51**
Wicken Bonhunt. *Essx* 2E **53**
Wickenby. *Linc* 2H **87**
Wicken Green Village. *Norf* 2H **77**
Wickersley. *S Yor* 1B **86**
Wicker Street Green. *Suff* 1C **54**
Wickford. *Essx* 1B **40**
Wickham. *Hants* 1D **16**
Wickham. *W Ber* 4B **36**
Wickham Bishops. *Essx* 4B **54**
Wickhambreaux. *Kent* 5G **41**
Wickhambrook. *Suff* 5G **65**
Wickhamford. *Worc* 1F **49**
Wickham Green. *Suff* 4C **66**
Wickham Heath. *W Ber* 5C **36**
Wickham Market. *Suff* 5F **67**
Wickhampton. *Norf* 5G **79**
Wickham St Paul. *Essx* 2B **54**
Wickham Skeith. *Suff* 4C **66**
Wickham Street. *Suff* 4C **66**
Wick Hill. *Wok* 5F **37**
Wicklewood. *Norf* 5C **78**
Wickmere. *Norf* 2D **78**
Wick St Lawrence. *N Som* 5G **33**
Wickwar. *S Glo* 3C **34**
Widdington. *Essx* 2F **53**
Widdrington. *Nmbd* 5G **121**
Widdrington Station. *Nmbd* 5G **121**
Widecombe in the Moor. *Devn* 5H **11**
Widegates. *Corn* 3G **7**
Widemouth Bay. *Corn* 2C **10**
Wide Open. *Tyne* 2F **115**
Widewall. *Orkn* 8D **172**
Widford. *Essx* 5G **53**
Widford. *Herts* 4E **53**
Widham. *Wilts* 3F **35**
Widmer End. *Buck* 2G **37**
Widmerpool. *Notts* 3D **74**
Widnes. *Hal* 2H **83**
Widworthy. *Devn* 3F **13**
Wigan. *G Man* 4D **90**
Wigbeth. *Dors* 2F **15**
Wiggaton. *Devn* 3E **12**
Wiggenhall St Germans. *Norf* 4E **77**
Wiggenhall St Mary Magdalen. *Norf* 4E **77**
Wiggenhall St Mary the Virgin. *Norf* 4E **77**
Wiggenhall St Peter. *Norf* 4F **77**
Wiggens Green. *Essx* 1G **53**
Wigginton. *Herts* 4H **51**
Wigginton. *Oxon* 2B **50**
Wigginton. *Staf* 5G **73**
Wigginton. *York* 4H **99**
Wigglesworth. *N Yor* 4H **97**
Wiggonby. *Cumb* 4D **112**
Wiggonholt. *W Sus* 4B **26**
Wighill. *N Yor* 5G **99**
Wighton. *Norf* 1B **78**
Wightwick. *Staf* 1C **60**
Wigley. *Hants* 1B **16**
Wigmore. *Here* 4G **59**
Wigmore. *Medw* 4C **40**
Wigsley. *Notts* 3F **87**
Wigsthorpe. *Nptn* 2H **63**
Wigston. *Leics* 1D **62**
Wigtoft. *Linc* 2B **76**
Wigton. *Cumb* 5D **112**
Wigtown. *Dum* 4B **110**
Wigtwizzle. *S Yor* 1G **85**
Wike. *W Yor* 5F **99**
Wilbarston. *Nptn* 2F **63**
Wilberfoss. *E Yor* 4B **100**
Wilburton. *Cambs* 3D **65**
Wilby. *Norf* 2C **66**
Wilby. *Nptn* 4F **63**
Wilby. *Suff* 3E **67**
Wilcot. *Wilts* 5G **35**
Wilcott. *Shrp* 4F **71**
Wilcove. *Corn* 3A **8**
Wildboarclough. *Ches* 4D **85**
Wilden. *Beds* 5H **63**
Wilden. *Worc* 3C **60**
Wildern. *Hants* 1C **16**
Wilderspool. *Warr* 2A **84**
Wilde Street. *Suff* 3G **65**
Wildhern. *Hants* 1B **24**
Wildmanbridge. *S Lan* 4B **128**
Wildmoor. *Worc* 3D **60**
Wildsworth. *Linc* 1F **87**
Wildwood. *Staf* 3D **72**
Wilford. *Nott* 2C **74**
Wilkesley. *Ches* 1A **72**
Wilkhaven. *High* 5G **165**
Wilkieston. *W Lot* 3E **129**
Wilksby. *Linc* 4B **88**
Willand. *Devn* 1D **12**
Willaston. *Ches* . . . . . 5A **84** (nr. Crewe)
Willaston. *Ches* . . . . . 3F **83** (nr. Neston)
Willaston. *IOM* 4C **108**
Willen. *Mil* 1G **51**
Willenhall. *W Mid* . . . . . 3A **62** (nr. Coventry)
Willenhall. *W Mid* . . . . . 1D **60** (nr. Wolverhampton)
Willerby. *E Yor* 1D **94**
Willerby. *N Yor* 2E **101**
Willersey. *Glos* 2G **49**
Willersley. *Here* 1G **47**
Willesborough. *Kent* 1E **28**
Willesborough Lees. *Kent* 1E **29**
Willesden. *G Lon* 2D **38**
Willesley. *Wilts* 3D **34**
Willett. *Som* 3E **20**
Willey. *Shrp* 1A **60**
Willey. *Warw* 2B **62**
Willey Green. *Surr* 5A **38**
Williamscot. *Oxon* 1C **50**
Willian. *Herts* 2C **52**
Willingale. *Essx* 5F **53**
Willingdon. *E Sus* 5G **27**
Willingham. *Cambs* 3D **64**
Willingham by Stow. *Linc* 2F **87**
Willingham Green. *Cambs* 5F **65**
Willington. *Beds* 1B **52**
Willington. *Derbs* 3G **73**
Willington. *Dur* 1E **105**
Willington. *Tyne* 3G **115**
Willington. *Warw* 2A **50**
Willington Corner. *Ches* 4H **83**
Willisham Tye. *Suff* 5C **66**
Willitoft. *E Yor* 1H **93**
Williton. *Som* 2D **20**
Willoughbridge. *Staf* 1B **72**
Willoughby. *Linc* 3D **88**
Willoughby. *Warw* 4C **62**
Willoughby-on-the-Wolds. *Notts* 3D **74**
Willoughby Waterleys. *Leics* 1C **62**
Willoughton. *Linc* 1G **87**
Willow Green. *Worc* 5B **60**
Willows Green. *Essx* 4H **53**
Willsbridge. *S Glo* 4B **34**
Willslock. *Staf* 2E **73**
Willsworthy. *Devn* 4F **11**
Wilmcote. *Warw* 5F **61**
Wilmington. *Bath* 5B **34**
Wilmington. *Devn* 3F **13**
Wilmington. *E Sus* 5G **27**
Wilmington. *Kent* 3G **39**
Wilmslow. *Ches* 2C **84**
Wilnecote. *Staf* 5G **73**
Wilney Green. *Norf* 2C **66**
Wilpshire. *Lanc* 1E **91**
Wilsden. *W Yor* 1A **92**
Wilsford. *Linc* 1H **75**
Wilsford. *Wilts* . . . . . 3G **23** (nr. Amesbury)
Wilsford. *Wilts* . . . . . 1G **23** (nr. Devizes)
Wilsill. *N Yor* 3D **98**
Wilsley Green. *Kent* 2B **28**
Wilson. *Here* 3A **48**
Wilson. *Leics* 3B **74**
Wilsontown. *S Lan* 4C **128**
Wilstead. *Beds* 1A **52**
Wilsthorpe. *E Yor* 3F **101**
Wilsthorpe. *Linc* 4H **75**
Wilstone. *Herts* 4H **51**
Wilton. *Cumb* 3B **102**
Wilton. *N Yor* 1C **100**
Wilton. *Red C* 3C **106**
Wilton. *Bord* 3H **119**
Wilton. *Wilts* . . . . . 5A **36** (nr. Marlborough)
Wilton. *Wilts* . . . . . 3F **23** (nr. Salisbury)
Wimbish. *Essx* 2F **53**
Wimbish Green. *Essx* 2G **53**
Wimblebury. *Staf* 4E **73**
Wimbledon. *G Lon* 3D **38**
Wimblington. *Cambs* 1D **64**
Wimborne Minster. *Dors* 2F **15**
Wimborne St Giles. *Dors* 1F **15**
Wimbotsham. *Norf* 5F **77**
Wimpstone. *Warw* 1H **49**
Wincanton. *Som* 4C **22**
Winceby. *Linc* 4C **88**
Wincham. *Ches* 3A **84**
Winchburgh. *W Lot* 2D **129**
Winchcombe. *Glos* 3F **49**
Winchelsea. *E Sus* 4D **28**
Winchelsea Beach. *E Sus* 4D **28**
Winchester. *Hants* 4C **24**
Winchet Hill. *Kent* 1B **28**
Winchfield. *Hants* 1F **25**
Winchmore Hill. *Buck* 1A **38**
Winchmore Hill. *G Lon* 1E **39**
Wincle. *Ches* 4D **84**
Windermere. *Cumb* 5F **103**
Winderton. *Warw* 1B **50**
Windhill. *High* 4H **157**
Windle Hill. *Ches* 3F **83**
Windlesham. *Surr* 4A **38**
Windley. *Derbs* 1H **73**
Windmill. *Derbs* 3F **85**
Windmill Hill. *E Sus* 4H **27**
Windmill Hill. *Som* 1G **13**
Windrush. *Glos* 4G **49**
Windsor. *Wind* 3A **38**
Windsor Green. *Suff* 5A **66**
Windyedge. *Abers* 4G **153**
Windygates. *Fife* 3F **137**
Windyharbour. *Ches* 3C **84**
Windyknowe. *W Lot* 3C **128**
Wineham. *W Sus* 3D **26**
Winestead. *E Yor* 2G **95**
Winfarthing. *Norf* 2D **66**
Winford. *IOW* 4D **16**
Winford. *N Som* 5A **34**
Winforton. *Here* 1F **47**
Winfrith Newburgh. *Dors* 4D **14**
Wing. *Buck* 3G **51**
Wing. *Rut* 5F **75**
Wingate. *Dur* 1A **106**
Wingates. *G Man* 4E **91**
Wingates. *Nmbd* 5F **121**
Wingerworth. *Derbs* 4A **86**
Wingfield. *Beds* 3A **52**
Wingfield. *Suff* 3E **67**
Wingfield. *Wilts* 1D **22**
Wingfield Park. *Derbs* 5A **86**
Wingham. *Kent* 5G **41**
Wingmore. *Kent* 1F **29**
Wingrave. *Buck* 4G **51**
Winkburn. *Notts* 5E **86**
Winkfield. *Brac* 3A **38**
Winkfield Row. *Brac* 4G **37**
Winkhill. *Staf* 5E **85**
Winklebury. *Hants* 1E **24**
Winkleigh. *Devn* 2G **11**
Winksley. *N Yor* 2E **99**
Winkton. *Dors* 3G **15**
Winlaton. *Tyne* 3E **115**
Winlaton Mill. *Tyne* 3E **115**
Winless. *High* 3F **169**
Winmarleigh. *Lanc* 5D **96**
Winnal Common. *Here* 2H **47**
Winnard's Perch. *Corn* 2D **6**
Winnersh. *Wok* 4F **37**
Winnington. *Ches* 3A **84**
Winnington. *Staf* 2B **72**
Winnothdale. *Staf* 1E **73**
Winscales. *Cumb* 2B **102**
Winscombe. *N Som* 1H **21**
Winsford. *Ches* 4A **84**
Winsford. *Som* 3C **20**
Winsham. *Devn* 3F **19**
Winsham. *Som* 2G **13**
Winshill. *Staf* 3G **73**
Winsh-wen. *Swan* 3F **31**
Winskill. *Cumb* 1G **103**
Winslade. *Hants* 2E **25**
Winsley. *Wilts* 5C **34**
Winslow. *Buck* 3F **51**
Winson. *Glos* 5F **49**
Winson Green. *W Mid* 2E **61**
Winsor. *Hants* 1B **16**
Winster. *Cumb* 5F **103**
Winster. *Derbs* 4G **85**
Winston. *Dur* 3E **105**
Winston. *Suff* 4D **66**
Winstone. *Glos* 5E **49**
Winswell. *Devn* 1E **11**
Winterborne Clenston. *Dors* 2D **14**
Winterborne Herrington. *Dors* 4B **14**
Winterborne Houghton. *Dors* 2D **14**
Winterborne Kingston. *Dors* 3D **14**
Winterborne Monkton. *Dors* 4B **14**
Winterborne St Martin. *Dors* 4B **14**
Winterborne Stickland. *Dors* 2D **14**
Winterborne Whitechurch. *Dors* 2D **14**
Winterborne Zelston. *Dors* 3E **15**
Winterbourne. *S Glo* 3B **34**
Winterbourne. *W Ber* 4C **36**
Winterbourne Abbas. *Dors* 3B **14**
Winterbourne Bassett. *Wilts* 4G **35**
Winterbourne Dauntsey. *Wilts* 3G **23**
Winterbourne Earls. *Wilts* 3G **23**
Winterbourne Gunner. *Wilts* 3G **23**
Winterbourne Monkton. *Wilts* 4F **35**
Winterbourne Steepleton. *Dors* 4B **14**
Winterbourne Stoke. *Wilts* 2F **23**
Winterbrook. *Oxon* 3E **36**
Winterburn. *N Yor* 4B **98**
Winter Gardens. *Essx* 2B **40**
Winteringham. *N Lin* 2C **94**
Winterley. *Ches* 5B **84**
Wintersett. *W Yor* 3D **93**
Winterton. *N Lin* 3C **94**
Winterton-on-Sea. *Norf* 4G **79**
Winthorpe. *Linc* 4E **89**
Winthorpe. *Notts* 5F **87**
Winton. *Bour* 3F **15**
Winton. *Cumb* 3A **104**
Winton. *E Sus* 5G **27**
Wintringham. *N Yor* 2C **100**
Winwick. *Cambs* 2A **64**
Winwick. *Nptn* 3D **62**
Winwick. *Warr* 1A **84**
Wirksworth. *Derbs* 5G **85**
Wirswall. *Ches* 1H **71**
Wisbech. *Cambs* 4D **76**
Wisbech St Mary. *Cambs* 5D **76**
Wisborough Green. *W Sus* 3B **26**
Wiseton. *Notts* 2E **86**
Wishaw. *N Lan* 4B **128**
Wishaw. *Warw* 1F **61**
Wisley. *Surr* 5B **38**
Wispington. *Linc* 3B **88**
Wissenden. *Kent* 1D **28**
Wissett. *Suff* 3F **67**
Wistanstow. *Shrp* 2G **59**
Wistanswick. *Shrp* 3A **72**
Wistaston. *Ches* 5A **84**
Wiston. *Pemb* 3E **43**
Wiston. *S Lan* 1B **118**
Wiston. *W Sus* 4C **26**
Wistow. *Cambs* 2B **64**
Wistow. *N Yor* 1F **93**
Wiswell. *Lanc* 1F **91**
Witcham. *Cambs* 2D **64**
Witchampton. *Dors* 2E **15**
Witchford. *Cambs* 3E **65**
Witham. *Essx* 4B **54**
Witham Friary. *Som* 2C **22**
Witham on the Hill. *Linc* 4H **75**
Witham St Hughs. *Linc* 4F **87**
Withcall. *Linc* 2B **88**
Witherenden Hill. *E Sus* 3H **27**
Withergate. *Norf* 3E **79**
Witheridge. *Devn* 1B **12**
Witheridge Hill. *Oxon* 3E **37**
Witherley. *Leics* 1H **61**
Withermarsh Green. *Suff* 2D **54**
Withern. *Linc* 2D **88**
Withernsea. *E Yor* 2G **95**
Withernwick. *E Yor* 5F **101**
Withersdale Street. *Suff* 2E **67**
Withersfield. *Suff* 1G **53**
Witherslack. *Cumb* 1D **96**
Withiel. *Corn* 2D **6**
Withiel Florey. *Som* 3C **20**
Withington. *Glos* 4F **49**
Withington. *G Man* 1C **84**
Withington. *Here* 1A **48**
Withington. *Shrp* 4H **71**
Withington. *Staf* 2E **73**
Withington Green. *Ches* 3C **84**
Withington Marsh. *Here* 1A **48**
Withleigh. *Devn* 1C **12**
Withnell. *Lanc* 2E **91**
Withnell Fold. *Lanc* 2E **90**
Withybrook. *Warw* 2B **62**
Withycombe. *Som* 2D **20**
Withycombe Raleigh. *Devn* 4D **12**
Withyham. *E Sus* 2F **27**
Withypool. *Som* 3B **20**
Witley. *Surr* 1A **26**
Witnesham. *Suff* 5D **66**
Witney. *Oxon* 4B **50**
Wittering. *Pet* 5H **75**
Wittersham. *Kent* 3D **28**
Witton. *Norf* 5F **79**
Witton. *Worc* 4D **60**
Witton Bridge. *Norf* 2F **79**
Witton Gilbert. *Dur* 5F **115**
Witton-le-Wear. *Dur* 1E **105**
Witton Park. *Dur* 1E **105**
Wiveliscombe. *Som* 4D **20**
Wivelrod. *Hants* 3E **25**
Wivelsfield. *E Sus* 3E **27**
Wivelsfield Green. *E Sus* 4E **27**
Wivenhoe. *Essx* 3D **54**
Wiveton. *Norf* 1C **78**
Wix. *Essx* 3E **55**
Wixford. *Warw* 5E **61**
Wixhill. *Shrp* 3H **71**
Wixoe. *Suff* 1H **53**
Woburn. *Beds* 2H **51**
Woburn Sands. *Mil* 2H **51**
Woking. *Surr* 5B **38**
Wokingham. *Wok* 5G **37**
Wolborough. *Devn* 5B **12**
Woldingham. *Surr* 5E **39**
Wold Newton. *E Yor* 2E **101**
Wold Newton. *NE Lin* 1B **88**
Wolferlow. *Here* 4A **60**
Wolferton. *Norf* 3F **77**
Wolfhill. *Per* 5A **144**
Wolf's Castle. *Pemb* 2D **42**
Wolfsdale. *Pemb* 2D **42**
Wolgarston. *Staf* 4D **72**
Wollaston. *Nptn* 4G **63**
Wollaston. *Shrp* 4F **71**
Wollaston. *W Mid* 2C **60**
Wollaton. *Nott* 1C **74**
Wollerton. *Shrp* 2A **72**
Wollescote. *W Mid* 2D **60**
Wolseley Bridge. *Staf* 3E **73**
Wolsingham. *Dur* 1D **105**

Wolstanton—Wyatt's Green

Wolstanton. *Staf* .1C **72**
Wolston. *Warw* .3B **62**
Wolsty. *Cumb* .4C **112**
Wolterton. *Norf* .2D **78**
Wolvercote. *Oxon* .5C **50**
Wolverhampton. *W Mid* .1D **60**
Wolverhampton Airport. *Staf* .1C **60**
Wolverley. *Shrp* .2G **71**
Wolverley. *Worc* .3C **60**
Wolverton. *Hants* .1D **24**
Wolverton. *Mil* .1G **51**
Wolverton. *Warw* .4G **61**
Wolverton. *Wilts* .3C **22**
Wolverton Common. *Hants* .1D **24**
Wolvesnewton. *Mon* .2H **33**
Wolvey. *Warw* .2B **62**
Wolvey Heath. *Warw* .2B **62**
Wolviston. *Stoc T* .2B **106**
Womaston. *Powy* .4E **59**
Wombleton. *N Yor* .1A **100**
Wombourne. *Staf* .1C **60**
Wombwell. *S Yor* .4D **93**
Womenswold. *Kent* .5G **41**
Womersley. *N Yor* .3F **93**
Wonersh. *Surr* .1B **26**
Wonson. *Devn* .4G **11**
Wonston. *Dors* .2C **14**
Wonston. *Hants* .3C **24**
Wooburn. *Buck* .2A **38**
Wooburn Green. *Buck* .2A **38**
Wood. *Pemb* .2C **42**
Woodacott. *Devn* .2D **11**
Woodale. *N Yor* .2C **98**
Woodall. *S Yor* .2B **86**
Woodbank. *Ches* .3F **83**
Woodbastwick. *Norf* .4F **79**
Woodbeck. *Notts* .3E **87**
Woodborough. *Notts* .1D **74**
Woodborough. *Wilts* .1G **23**
Woodbridge. *Devn* .3E **13**
Woodbridge. *Dors* .1C **14**
Woodbridge. *Suff* .1F **55**
Wood Burcote. *Nptn* .1E **51**
Woodbury. *Devn* .4D **12**
Woodbury Salterton. *Devn* .4D **12**
Woodchester. *Glos* .5D **48**
Woodchurch. *Kent* .2D **28**
Woodchurch. *Mers* .2E **83**
Woodcock Heath. *Staf* .3E **73**
Woodcombe. *Som* .2C **20**
Woodcote. *Oxon* .3E **37**
Woodcote. *Telf* .4B **72**
Woodcote Green. *Worc* .3D **60**
Woodcott. *Hants* .1C **24**
Woodcroft. *Glos* .2A **34**
Woodcutts. *Dors* .1E **15**
Wood Dalling. *Norf* .3C **78**
Woodditton. *Cambs* .5F **65**
Woodeaton. *Oxon* .4D **50**
Wood Eaton. *Staf* .4C **72**
Wood End. *Beds* .4H **63**
Woodend. *Cumb* .5C **102**
Wood End. *Herts* .3D **52**
Woodend. *Nptn* .1E **50**
Woodend. *Staf* .3F **73**
Wood End. *Warw* .2G **61**
(nr. Bedworth)
Wood End. *Warw* .1G **61**
(nr. Dordon)
Wood End. *Warw* .3F **61**
(nr. Tanworth-in-Arden)
Woodend. *W Sus* .2G **17**
Wood Enderby. *Linc* .4B **88**
Woodend Green. *Essx* .3F **53**
Woodfalls. *Wilts* .4G **23**
Woodfield. *Oxon* .3D **50**
Woodfields. *Lanc* .1E **91**
Woodford. *Corn* .1C **10**
Woodford. *Devn* .3D **9**
Woodford. *Glos* .2B **34**
Woodford. *G Lon* .1E **39**
Woodford. *G Man* .2C **84**
Woodford. *Nptn* .3G **63**
Woodford. *Plym* .3B **8**
Woodford Green. *G Lon* .1F **39**
Woodford Halse. *Nptn* .5C **62**
Woodgate. *Norf* .4C **78**
Woodgate. *W Mid* .2D **61**
Woodgate. *W Sus* .5A **26**
Woodgate. *Worc* .4D **60**
Wood Green. *G Lon* .1D **39**
Woodgreen. *Hants* .1G **15**
Wood Hall. *E Yor* .1E **95**
Woodhall. *Inv* .2E **127**
Woodhall. *Linc* .4B **88**
Woodhall. *N Yor* .5C **104**
Woodhall Spa. *Linc* .4A **88**
Woodham. *Surr* .4B **38**
Woodham Ferrers. *Essx* .1B **40**
Woodham Mortimer. *Essx* .5B **54**
Woodham Walter. *Essx* .5B **54**
Woodhaven. *Fife* .1G **137**
Wood Hayes. *W Mid* .5D **72**
Woodhead. *Abers* .2G **161**
(nr. Fraserburgh)
Woodhead. *Abers* .5E **161**
(nr. Fyvie)
Woodhill. *N Som* .4H **33**
Woodhill. *Shrp* .2B **60**
Woodhorn. *Nmbd* .1G **115**
Woodhouse. *Leics* .4C **74**
Woodhouse. *S Yor* .2B **86**
Woodhouse. *W Yor* .1C **92**
(nr. Leeds)
Woodhouse. *W Yor* .2D **93**
(nr. Normanton)
Woodhouse Eaves. *Leics* .4C **74**
Woodhouses. *Ches* .3H **83**
Woodhouses. *G Man* .4H **91**
(nr. Failsworth)
Woodhouses. *G Man* .1B **84**
(nr. Sale)
Woodhouses. *Staf* .4F **73**
Woodhuish. *Devn* .3F **9**
Woodhurst. *Cambs* .3C **64**
Woodingdean. *Brig* .5E **27**
Woodland. *Devn* .2D **9**
Woodland. *Dur* .2D **104**
Woodland Head. *Devn* .3A **12**
Woodlands. *Abers* .4E **153**
Woodlands. *Dors* .2F **15**
Woodlands. *Hants* .1B **16**
Woodlands. *Kent* .4G **39**
Woodlands. *N Yor* .4F **99**
Woodlands. *S Yor* .4F **93**
Woodlands Park. *Wind* .4G **37**
Woodlands St Mary. *W Ber* .4B **36**
Woodlane. *Shrp* .3A **72**
Woodlane. *Staf* .3F **73**
Woodleigh. *Devn* .4D **8**
Woodlesford. *W Yor* .2D **92**
Woodley. *G Man* .1D **84**
Woodley. *Wok* .4F **37**
Woodmancote. *Glos* .3E **49**
(nr. Cheltenham)
Woodmancote. *Glos* .5F **49**
(nr. Cirencester)
Woodmancote. *W Sus* .2F **17**
(nr. Chichester)
Woodmancote. *W Sus* .4D **26**
(nr. Henfield)
Woodmancote. *Worc* .1E **49**
Woodmancott. *Hants* .2D **24**
Woodmansey. *E Yor* .1D **94**
Woodmansgreen. *W Sus* .4G **25**
Woodmansterne. *Surr* .5D **39**
Woodmanton. *Devn* .4D **12**
Woodmill. *Staf* .3F **73**
Woodminton. *Wilts* .4F **23**
Woodnesborough. *Kent* .5H **41**
Woodnewton. *Nptn* .1H **63**
Woodnook. *Linc* .2G **75**
Wood Norton. *Norf* .3C **78**
Woodplumpton. *Lanc* .1D **90**
Woodrising. *Norf* .5B **78**
Woodrow. *Cumb* .5D **112**
Woodrow. *Dors* .2C **14**
Wood Row. *W Yor* .2D **93**
Woods Eaves. *Here* .1F **47**
Woodseaves. *Shrp* .2A **72**
Woodseaves. *Staf* .3B **72**
Woodsend. *Wilts* .4H **35**
Woodsetts. *S Yor* .2C **86**
Woodsford. *Dors* .3C **14**
Wood's Green. *E Sus* .2H **27**
Woodshaw. *Wilts* .3F **35**
Woodside. *Aber* .3G **153**
Woodside. *Brac* .3A **38**
Woodside. *Cumb* .1B **102**
Woodside. *Derbs* .1A **74**
Woodside. *Dum* .2B **112**
Woodside. *Dur* .2E **105**
Woodside. *Fife* .3G **137**
Woodside. *Herts* .5C **52**
Woodside. *Per* .5B **144**
Wood Stanway. *Glos* .2F **49**
Woodstock. *Oxon* .4C **50**
Woodstock Slop. *Pemb* .2E **43**
Woodston. *Pet* .1A **64**
Wood Street Village. *Surr* .5A **38**
Woodthorpe. *Derbs* .3B **86**
Woodthorpe. *Leics* .4C **74**
Woodthorpe. *Linc* .2D **88**
Woodthorpe. *York* .5H **99**
Woodton. *Norf* .1E **67**
Woodtown. *Devn* .4E **19**
(nr. Bideford)
Woodtown. *Devn* .4E **19**
(nr. Littleham)
Woodvale. *Mers* .3B **90**
Woodville. *Derbs* .4H **73**
Woodwalton. *Cambs* .2B **64**
Woodyates. *Dors* .1F **15**
Woody Bay. *Devn* .2G **19**
Woofferton. *Shrp* .4H **59**
Wookey. *Som* .2A **22**
Wookey Hole. *Som* .2A **22**
Wool. *Dors* .4D **14**
Woolacombe. *Devn* .2E **19**
Woolage Green. *Kent* .1G **29**
Woolage Village. *Kent* .5G **41**
Woolaston. *Glos* .2A **34**
Woolavington. *Som* .2G **21**
Woolbeding. *W Sus* .4G **25**
Woolcotts. *Som* .3C **20**
Wooldale. *W Yor* .4B **92**
Wooler. *Nmbd* .2D **121**
Woolfardisworthy. *Devn* .4D **18**
(nr. Bideford)
Woolfardisworthy. *Devn* .2B **12**
(nr. Crediton)
Woolfords. *S Lan* .4D **128**
Woolgarston. *Dors* .4E **15**
Woolhampton. *W Ber* .5D **36**
Woolhope. *Here* .2B **48**
Woolland. *Dors* .2C **14**
Woollard. *Bath* .5B **34**
Woolley. *Bath* .5C **34**
Woolley. *Cambs* .3A **64**
Woolley. *Corn* .1C **10**
Woolley. *Derbs* .4A **86**
Woolley. *W Yor* .3D **92**
Woolley Green. *Wilts* .5D **34**
Woolmere Green. *Worc* .4D **60**
Woolmer Green. *Herts* .4C **52**
Woolminstone. *Som* .2H **13**
Woolpit. *Suff* .4B **66**
Woolridge. *Glos* .3D **48**
Woolscott. *Warw* .4B **62**
Woolsery. *Devn* .4D **18**
Woolsington. *Tyne* .3E **115**
Woolstaston. *Shrp* .1G **59**
Woolsthorpe. *Linc* .3G **75**
(nr. Colsterworth)
Woolsthorpe. *Linc* .2F **75**
(nr. Grantham)
Woolston. *Devn* .4D **8**
Woolston. *Shrp* .2G **59**
(nr. Church Stretton)
Woolston. *Shrp* .3F **71**
(nr. Oswestry)
Woolston. *Som* .4B 7
Woolston. *Sotn* .1C **16**
Woolston. *Warr* .1A **84**
Woolstone. *Glos* .2E **49**
Woolstone. *Oxon* .3A **36**
Woolston Green. *Devn* .2D **9**
Woolton. *Mers* .2G **83**
Woolton Hill. *Hants* .5C **36**
Woolverstone. *Suff* .2E **55**
Woolverton. *Som* .1C **22**
Woolwell. *Devn* .2B **8**
Woolwich. *G Lon* .3F **39**
Woonton. *Here* .5F **59**
(nr. Kington)
Woonton. *Here* .4H **59**
(nr. Leominster)
Wooperton. *Nmbd* .2E **121**
Woore. *Shrp* .1B **72**
Wooth. *Dors* .3H **13**
Wooton. *Shrp* .2B **60**
Wootton. *Beds* .1A **52**
Wootton. *Hants* .3H **15**
Wootton. *IOW* .3D **16**
Wootton. *Kent* .1G **29**
Wootton. *Nptn* .5E **63**
Wootton. *N Lin* .3D **94**
Wootton. *Oxon* .5C **50**
(nr. Abingdon)
Wootton. *Oxon* .4C **50**
(nr. Woodstock)
Wootton. *Shrp* .3G **59**
(nr. Ludlow)
Wootton. *Shrp* .3F **71**
(nr. Oswestry)
Wootton. *Staf* .3C **72**
(nr. Eccleshall)
Wootton. *Staf* .1F **73**
(nr. Ellastone)
Wootton Bassett. *Wilts* .3F **35**
Wootton Bridge. *IOW* .3D **16**
Wootton Common. *IOW* .3D **16**
Wootton Courtenay. *Som* .2C **20**
Wootton Fitzpaine. *Dors* .3G **13**
Wootton Rivers. *Wilts* .5G **35**
Woottons. *Staf* .2E **73**
Wootton St Lawrence. *Hants* .1D **24**
Wootton Wawen. *Warw* .4F **61**
Worcester. *Worc* .5C **60**
Worcester Park. *G Lon* .4D **38**
Wordsley. *W Mid* .2C **60**
Worfield. *Shrp* .1B **60**
Workhouse Green. *Suff* .2C **54**
Workington. *Cumb* .2A **102**
Worksop. *Notts* .3C **86**
Worlaby. *N Lin* .3D **94**
Worlds End. *Hants* .1E **17**
Worldsend. *Shrp* .1G **59**
World's End. *W Ber* .4C **36**
Worlds End. *W Mid* .2F **61**
World's End. *W Sus* .4E **27**
Worle. *N Som* .5G 3
Worleston. *Ches* .5A
Worley. *Glos* .2
Worlingham. *Suff*
Worlington. *Suff*
Worlingworth. *Suff*
Wormbridge. *Here*
Wormegay. *Norf* **85**
Wormelow Tump. *Here* 3F **145**
Wormhill. *Derbs* .2C **54**
Wormiehills. *Ang* .5E **51**
Wormingford. *Ess* .2F **49**
Worminghall. *B* .2A **22**
Wormington. .1F **137**
Worminster. .5B **62**
Wormit. *Fi* rw .5D **52**
Wormlei .2A **26**
Wormlr .5C **40**
Worm Kent .1H **47**
Wo y. Here .5A **38**
W esdon. Surr .1H **85**
rrall. S Yor .4D **92**
Worsbrough. S Yor .4F **91**
Worsley. G Man
Worstead. *Norf* .3F **79**
Worsthorne. *Lanc* .1G **91**
Worston. *Lanc* .5G **97**
Worth. *Kent* .5H **41**
Worth. *W Sus* .2E **27**
Wortham. *Suff* .3C **66**
Worthen. *Shrp* .5F **71**
Worthenbury. *Wrex* .1G **71**
Worthing. *Norf* .4B **78**
Worthing. *W Sus* .5C **26**
Worthington. *Leics* .3B **74**
Worth Matravers. *Dors* .5E **15**
Worting. *Hants* .1E **24**
Wortley. *Glos* .2C **34**
Wortley. *S Yor* .1H **85**
Wortley. *W Yor* .1C **92**
Worton. *N Yor* .5C **104**
Worton. *Wilts* .1E **23**
Wortwell. *Norf* .2E **67**
Wotherton. *Shrp* .5E **71**
Wothorpe. *Nptn* .5H **75**
Wotter. *Devn* .2B **8**
Wotton. *Glos* .4D **48**
Wotton. *Surr* .1C **26**
Wotton-under-Edge. *Glos* .2C **34**
Wotton Underwood. *Buck* .4E **51**
Wouldham. *Kent* .4B **40**
Wrabness. *Essx* .2E **55**
Wrafton. *Devn* .3E **19**
Wragby. *Linc* .3A **88**
Wragby. *W Yor* .3E **93**
Wramplingham. *Norf* .5D **78**
Wrangbrook. *W Yor* .3E **93**
Wrangle. *Linc* .5D **88**
Wrangle Lowgate. *Linc* .5D **88**
Wrangway. *Som* .1E **13**
Wrantage. *Som* .4G 2
Wrawby. *N Lin* .4D
Wraxall. *N Som* .4
Wraxall. *Som*
Wray. *Lanc*
Wraysbury. *Wind*
Wrayton. *Lanc*
Wrea Green. *Lanc*
Wreay. *Cumb*
Wreay. *Cumb*
Wrecclesham. S00
Wrecsam. *Wr* H **71**
Wrekenton. .1D **66**
Wrelton. *N* .2G **67**
Wrenbur .2D **92**
Wrenir .5G **71**
Wrer .1H **93**
Wr .4C **94**
Beds .1C **52**
.1B **66**
rf .1F **65**
orf .5F **83**
m. Wrex
nam Industrial Estate.
Wrex .1F **71**
.4A **12**
Wreyland. Devn .2A **60**
Wrickton. Shrp .3D **90**
Wrightlington Bar. Lanc .4F **53**
Wright's Green. Essx .1B **72**
Wrinehill. Staf .5H **33**
Wrington. N Som .5G **53**
Writtle. Essx .4A **72**
Wrockwardine. Telf .4H **93**
Wroot. N Lin .5H **39**
Wrotham. Kent .5H **39**
Wrotham Heath. Kent .3G **35**
Wroughton. Swin .4D **16**
Wroxall. IOW .3G **61**
Wroxall. Warw .5H **71**
Wroxeter. Shrp .4F **79**
Wroxham. Norf .1C **50**
Wroxton. Oxon .1F **73**
Wyaston. Derbs .1G **39**
Wyatt's Green. Essx

Wybers Wood. NE Lin 4F 95
Wyberton. Linc 1C 76
Wyboston. Beds 5A 64
Wybunbury. Ches 1A 72
Wychbold. Worc 4D 60
Wych Cross. E Sus 2F 27
Wychnor. Staf 4F 73
Wychnor Bridges. Staf 4F 73
Wyck. Hants 3F 25
Wyck Hill. Glos 3G 49
Wyck Rissington. Glos 3G 49
Wycliffe. Dur 3E 105
Wycombe Marsh. Buck 2G 37
Wyddial. Herts 2D 52
Wye. Kent 1E 29
Wyesham. Mon 4A 48
Wyfold Grange. Oxon 3E 37
Wyfordby. Leics 4E 75
Wyke. Devn 3B 12
Wyke. Dors 4C 22
Wyke. Shrp 5A 72
Wyke. Surr 5A 38
Wyke. W Yor 2B 92
Wyke Champflower. Som 3B 22
Wykeham. Linc 3B 76
Wykeham. N Yor 2C 100
            (nr. Malton)
Wykeham. N Yor 1D 100
            (nr. Scarborough)
Wyken. Shrp 1B 60
Wyken. W Mid 2A 62
Wyke Regis. Dors 5B 14
Wyke, The. Shrp 5B 72
Wykey. Shrp 3F 71
Wykin. Leics 1B 62
Wylam. Nmbd 3E 115
Wylde Green. W Mid 1F 61
Wylye. Wilts 3F 23
Wymering. Port 2E 17
Wymeswold. Leics 3D 74
Wymington. Beds 4G 63
Wymondham. Leics 4F 75
Wymondham. Norf 5D 78
Wyndham. B'end 2C 32
Wynford Eagle. Dors 3A 14
...re Piddle. Worc 1E 49

Wysall. Notts 3D 74
Wyson. Here 4H 59
Wythall. Worc 3E 61
Wytham. Oxon 5C 50
Wythenshawe. G Man 2C 84
Wythop Mill. Cumb 2C 102
Wyton. Cambs 3B 64
Wyton. E Yor 1E 95
Wyverstone. Suff 4C 66
Wyverstone Street. Suff 4C 66
Wyville. Linc 3F 75
Wyvis Lodge. High 1G 157

Y

Yaddlethorpe. N Lin 4B 94
Yafford. IOW 4C 16
Yafforth. N Yor 5A 106
Yalberton. Torb 3E 9
Yalding. Kent 5A 40
Yanley. N Som 5A 34
Yanwath. Cumb 2G 103
Yanworth. Glos 4F 49
Yapham. E Yor 4B 100
Yapton. W Sus 5A 26
Yarburgh. Linc 1C 88
Yarcombe. Devn 2F 13
Yarde. Som 3D 20
Yardley. W Mid 2F 61
Yardley Gobion. Nptn 1F 51
Yardley Hastings. Nptn 5F 63
Yardley Wood. W Mid 2F 61
Yardro. Powy 5E 58
Yarhampton. Worc 4B 60
Yarkhill. Here 1B 48
Yarlet. Staf 3D 72
Yarley. Som 2A 22
Yarlington. Som 4B 22
Yarm. Stoc T 3B 106
Yarmouth. IOW 4B 16
Yarnbrook. Wilts 1D 22
Yarnfield. Staf 2C 72
Yarnscombe. Devn 4F 19
Yarnton. Oxon 4C 50
Yarpole. Here 4G 59

Yarrow. Nmbd 1A 114
Yarrow. Bord 2F 119
Yarrow. Som 2G 21
Yarrow Feus. Bord 2F 119
Yarrow Ford. Bord 1G 119
Yarsop. Here 1H 47
Yarwell. Nptn 1H 63
Yate. S Glo 3C 34
Yateley. Hants 5G 37
Yatesbury. Wilts 4F 35
Yattendon. W Ber 4D 36
Yatton. Here 4G 59
              (nr. Leominster)
Yatton. Here 2E 48
              (nr. Ross-on-Wye)
Yatton. N Som 5H 33
Yatton Keynell. Wilts 4D 34
Yaverland. IOW 4E 16
Yawl. Devn 3G 13
Yaxham. Norf 4C 78
Yaxley. Cambs 1A 64
Yaxley. Suff 3D 66
Yazor. Here 1H 47
Y Bala. Gwyn 2B 70
Y Bont-Faen. V Glam 4C 32
Y Dref. Gwyn 2D 69
Y Drenewydd. Powy 1D 58
Yeading. G Lon 2C 38
Yeadon. W Yor 5E 98
Yealand Conyers. Lanc 2E 97
Yealand Redmayne. Lanc 2E 97
Yealmpton. Devn 3B 8
Yearby. Red C 2D 106
Yearngill. Cumb 5C 112
Yearsett. Here 5B 60
Yearsley. N Yor 2H 99
Yeaton. Shrp 4G 71
Yeaveley. Derbs 1F 73
Yeavering. Nmbd 1D 120
Yedingham. N Yor 2C 100
Yelden. Beds 4H 63
Yeldersley Hollies. Derbs ..1G 73
Yelford. Oxon 5B 50
Yelland. Devn 3E 19
Yelling. Cambs 4B 64
Yelsted. Kent 4C 40

Yelvertoft. Nptn 3C 62
Yelverton. Devn 2B 8
Yelverton. Norf 5E 79
Yenston. Som 4C 22
Yeoford. Devn 3A 12
Yeolmbridge. Corn 4D 10
Yeo Mill. Devn 4B 20
Yeovil. Som 1A 14
Yeovil Marsh. Som 1A 14
Yeovilton. Som 4A 22
Yerbeston. Pemb 4E 43
Yetlington. Nmbd 4E 121
Yetminster. Dors 1A 14
Yett. N Lan 4A 128
Yett. S Ayr 2D 116
Yettington. Devn 4D 12
Yetts o' Muckhart. Clac 3C 136
Y Fali. IOA 3B 80
Y Felinheli. Gwyn 4E 81
Y Fenni. Mon 4G 47
Y Ferwig. Cdgn 1B 44
Y Fflint. Flin 3E 83
Y Ffor. Gwyn 2C 68
Y Gelli Gandryll. Powy 1F 47
Yieldshields. S Lan 4B 128
Yiewsley. G Lon 2B 38
Yinstay. Orkn 6E 172
Ynysboeth. Rhon 2D 32
Ynysddu. Cphy 2E 33
Ynysforgan. Swan 3F 31
Ynyshir. Rhon 2D 32
Ynyslas. Cdgn 1F 57
Ynysmaerdy. Rhon 3D 32
Ynysmeudwy. Neat 5H 45
Ynystawe. Swan 5G 45
Ynyswen. Powy 4B 46
Ynys-wen. Rhon 2C 32
Ynys y Barri. V Glam 5E 32
Ynysybwl. Rhon 2D 32
Ynysymaerdy. Neat 3G 31
Yockenthwaite. N Yor 2B 98
Yockleton. Shrp 4G 71
Yokefleet. E Yor 2B 94
Yoker. Glas 3G 127
Yonder Bognie. Abers 4C 160
Yonderton. Abers 5G 161

York. York 4A 100
Yorkletts. Kent 4E 41
Yorkley. Glos 5B 48
Yorton. Shrp 3H 71
Yorton Heath. Shrp 3H 71
Youlgreave. Derbs 4G 85
Youlthorpe. E Yor 4B 100
Youlton. N Yor 3G 99
Young's End. Essx 4H 53
Young Wood. Linc 3A 88
Yoxall. Staf 4F 73
Yoxford. Suff 4F 67
Yr Hob. Flin 5F 83
Yr Rhws. V Glam 5D 32
Ysbyty Cynfyn. Cdgn 3G 57
Ysbyty Ifan. Cnwy 1H 69
Ysbyty Ystwyth. Cdgn 3G 57
Ysceifiog. Flin 3D 82
Yspitty. Carm 3E 31
Ystalyfera. Neat 5A 46
Ystrad. Rhon 2C 32
Ystrad Aeron. Cdgn 5E 57
Ystradfellte. Powy 4C 46
Ystradffin. Carm 1A 46
Ystradgynlais. Powy 4A 46
Ystradmeurig. Cdgn 4G 57
Ystrad Mynach. Cphy 2E 33
Ystradowen. Carm 4A 46
Ystradowen. V Glam 4D 32
Ystumtuen. Cdgn 3G 57
Ythanbank. Abers 5G 161
Ythanwells. Abers 5D 160
Y Trallwng. Powy 5E 70
Y Waun. Wrex 2E 71

Z

Zeal Monachorum. Devn 2H 11
Zeals. Wilts 3C 22
Zelah. Corn 3C 6
Zennor. Corn 3B 4
Zouch. Notts 3C 74